Bringing together substantial essays by leading scholars, this volume offers a comprehensive introduction to and analysis of the politics of the People's Republic of China from 1949 through the mid-1990s. The first four chapters are drawn from the *Cambridge History of China,* Volumes 14 and 15. The last two chapters were specifically commissioned to cover events through the mid-1990s.

The particular strength of the volume is the depth of expert knowledge provided for each extraordinary political era; each period is covered by a specialist on the events of that time. The volume should be equally useful to general readers with an interest in China and to students; as well, it should serve as a valuable reference for specialists.

THE POLITICS OF CHINA
SECOND EDITION

THE POLITICS OF CHINA

SECOND EDITION

The Eras of Mao and Deng

Edited by

RODERICK MACFARQUHAR

CAMBRIDGE
UNIVERSITY PRESS

To the memory of

JOHN KING FAIRBANK
(1907 – 1991)

PUBLISHED BY THE PRESS SYNDICATE OF THE UNIVERSITY OF CAMBRIDGE
The Pitt Building, Trumpington Street, Cambridge CB2 1RP, United Kingdom

CAMBRIDGE UNIVERSITY PRESS
The Edinburgh Building, Cambridge CB2 2RU, UK http: //www.cup.cam.ac.uk
40 West 20th Street, New York, NY 10011-4211, USA http: //www.cup.org
10 Stamford Road, Oakleigh, Melbourne 3166, Australia

First published 1993
Second edition 1997
Reprinted 1997, 1998

Printed in the United States of America

Typeset in Garamond

A catalogue record for this book is available from the British Library

Library of Congress Cataloguing-in-Publication Data is available

ISBN 0-521-58141-9 hardback
ISBN 0-521-588634 paperback

CONTENTS

PREFACE

The aim of this book is to provide a comprehensive account of the politics of the People's Republic of China from 1949 to the mid-1990s. The first four chapters, covering the years 1949–82, are drawn from Volumes 14 and 15 of the *Cambridge History of China* (*CHOC*). The fifth and sixth chapters were specially commissioned to extend the story of Chinese politics through the mid-1990s.

The chapters drawn from *CHOC* are part of an integrated schema that includes chapters on economics, education, culture, society, and foreign policy, but since "politics took command" of everything in Mao's China, these chapters on politics touch on those other topics as well.

Readers of *CHOC* will detect one important modification of the chapters that appeared there: The romanization of Chinese terms has been changed from the formerly almost universal Wade-Giles system to the *pinyin* one, the official system on the Chinese mainland. A desire for consistency throughout *CHOC* dictated the earlier decision, taken before *pinyin* became widespread; a recognition that today most books on and students of contemporary China use only *pinyin* made a change on republication seem sensible. A few hardy perennials of the old system remain; for instance, it seemed appropriate to continue to refer to the Nationalist Party by the familiar KMT and to accept the inconsistency of spelling it out as "Guomindang." Nancy Hearst, the librarian of Harvard's John King Fairbank Center for East Asian Research, painstakingly undertook the time-consuming tasks of ensuring the accuracy of the changeover and of adapting and expanding the bibliography from *CHOC* Volumes 14 and 15. She also collaborated with Zhu Hong and Li Zhuqing, who worked hard and fast to prepare the index.

This volume is dedicated to the memory of John King Fairbank, the organizing genius behind the six *CHOC* volumes on modern China. Sadly, he died shortly before the final one (15) appeared.

RLM

TABLES AND MAPS

TABLES

MAPS

ABBREVIATIONS

AF	Air Force
alt	alternate
APC	Agricultural Producers' Cooperative
APC	[chap. 5] armored personnel carrier
BSAF	Beijing Students' Autonomous Federation
CAC	Central Advisory Commission
CASS	Chinese Academy of Social Sciences
CC	Central Committee
CCP	Chinese Communist Party
CDIC	Central Discipline Investigation Commission
CITIC	China International Trust and Investment Corporation
CMC	Central Military Commission
CO	commanding officer
CPPCC	Chinese People's Political Consultative Conference
CPSU	Communist Party of the Soviet Union
CRG	Cultural Revolution Group
CUST	Chinese University of Science and Technology
f	female
FYP	Five-Year Plan
GLF	Great Leap Forward
GPCR	Great Proletarian Cultural Revolution
HQ	headquarters
KMT	(Kuomintang) Guomindang
MAC	Military Affairs Commission
MAT	Mutual Aid Teams
MR	Military Region
NCNA	New China News Agency
NKVD	*Narodnyi Komissariat Vnutrennikh Del*
NPC	National People's Congress

PAP	People's Armed Police Force
PKI	Communist Party of Indonesia
PLA	People's Liberation Army
PRC	People's Republic of China
PSC	Politburo Standing Committee
Rev Comm.	Revolutionary Committee
SC	Standing Committee
SEC	State Economic Commission
SEZ	Special Economic Zone
SPC	State Planning Commission
TVE	township and village enterprise
USSR	Union of Soviet Socialist Republics
VC	vice-chairman

INTRODUCTION

RODERICK MacFARQUHAR

On 1 October 1949, Mao Zedong proclaimed the foundation of the People's Republic of China from the Gate of Heavenly Peace (Tiananmen) in the heart of Beijing. The Chinese people had "stood up," Mao declared. A century of foreign aggression and civil war was coming to an end. Even those who rejected Marxism and feared the Chinese Communist Party (CCP) could welcome the prospect of peace, unity, and the chance to rebuild China. The CCP had seized the traditional "mandate of heaven."

Forty years later, Mao's eventual successor, Deng Xiaoping, presided over National Day celebrations in a very different atmosphere. The Chinese people had again stood up, in Tiananmen Square six months earlier, but this time in defiance of the Communist government and in search of democratic change. The movement had been put down by military force on 4 June 1989, but so fearful were the Beijing authorities of renewed trouble that the 1 October anniversary had to be marked under conditions of martial law. It was a dismal contrast to that confident day of hope and determination forty years earlier. In his final years Deng pressed forward with economic development to try to restore the CCP's lost mandate.

Chapter 1 describes how the CCP established its power in impressive fashion, rehabilitating and then developing the economy and appearing to transform society. By the mid-1950s, China was widely respected abroad for its relative success in tackling the problems of nation building and backwardness.

Then things went awry. The Anti-Rightist Campaign of 1957 ended Mao's chances of enlisting the wholehearted participation of the intellectual community in national development. In the subsequent Great Leap Forward (1958–60), described in Chapter 2, Mao turned to the peasantry to carry out the economic breakthrough he craved, but their herculean efforts were misdirected and led to the worst man-made famine in human history. The sense of crisis was exacerbated by the simultaneous rupture of the alliance with the Soviet Union.

The resilience of the CCP and the Chinese people facilitated an economic recovery by 1965. A new five-year plan was drawn up; the "four modernizations" – of agriculture, industry, science, and defense – were its goals. China seemed ready to resume its earlier rate of progress. Mao decided otherwise.

In May 1966, China was plunged into the Great Proletarian Cultural Revolution. Mao purged the CCP of many of its leaders, one-time comrades-in-arms, as he sought to rear a more revolutionary generation of successors from among the young. His appearances at hysteria-laden mass rallies in Tiananmen Square encouraged the student Red Guards to "bombard the headquarters" of party power up and down the country, subjecting officeholders to humiliation, often to torture, sometimes to execution. Outside Mao's immediate circle, the institutional life of the CCP withered away.

The Red Guard phase of the Cultural Revolution (1966–8), described in Chapter 3, was a watershed. It ended when Mao had to stop the internecine warfare and urban chaos it had spawned; 12 million young people were rusticated. The Red Guards had thought to inherit the earth; instead they ended up tilling it. But during their moment of power, they had demonstrated the force that society could bring to bear against the party-state and the capacity of educated youth for autonomous action.

The demise of the Red Guards did not signal the revival of the CCP. Instead, army generals, who had gladly restored order, effectively took over the CCP's functions. Defense Minister Lin Biao was formally designated Mao's successor. Even after Lin's death and disgrace less than three years later, described in Chapter 4, a return to regularized CCP rule was delayed by the desperate struggle for survival of the last true believers in Mao's entourage. In the end, it was a military leader who masterminded the coup against the Gang of Four within a month of the Chairman's death on 9 September 1976, foreclosing the possibility of Maoism after Mao.

When Deng Xiaoping took over the leadership of China in December 1978 after a brief interregnum, civilian rule was revived. Old comrades were rehabilitated; Party routines were restored. Disgraced twice during the Cultural Revolution, Deng wanted not merely to repair its damage, but also to set China upon a new course. His reform decade rekindled some of the hope generated by the 1949 victory. The dark night of the Cultural Revolution was over; class struggle was set aside. Production rose, people prospered. On 1 October 1984, Deng turned the thirty-fifth anniversary of the CCP's victory into a personal triumph. There seemed no reason, granted longevity, why he should not plan an even bigger celebration for the fortieth anniversary. Instead, his regime was brought to the verge of collapse, as described in Chapter 5. For a third time, the People's Liberation Army (PLA) saved the day.

Deng's reform program had compounded the earlier damage to the morale of the CCP and simultaneously weakened its authority over society. The rural communes were dissolved, and farm families were freed from CCP direction for the first time in thirty years; pre-Communist social practices reemerged. Private enterprise was permitted, foreign investment was solicited, and "To get rich is glorious" replaced "Serve the people" as the national watchword.

Deng's support for "practice as the sole criterion of truth" left no room for ideology. Deprived of its doctrinal compass, the CCP increasingly depended on economic performance to justify its right to rule. CCP cadres were told that their careers now depended more on technocratic know-how than on agitational skills. China was opened up to foreign ideas often diametrically opposed to Marxist-Leninist-Maoist dogmas and CCP methods.

Political relaxation permitted a questioning of the proletarian dictatorship. Intellectuals and students sought new models for the relationship between state and society, first in Eastern Europe and then in the West. Caught between his desire to emulate Western-style modernization and his insistence on preserving CCP rule, Deng alternated political relaxation with successive assaults on alien "spiritual pollution." The ultimate futility of this approach was shown in Tiananmen Square.

Mao had dealt a fateful blow to the legitimacy and authority of the CCP during the Cultural Revolution. Deng's reform program compounded the damage. The hypercult of Mao Thought during the Cultural Revolution debased ideology; in reaction, Deng effectively discarded this ultimate justification of CCP rule.

Simultaneously with these successive attacks on the key elements of the totalitarian state, the two leaders provided the opportunity for social action. Mao had sown the wind during the Cultural Revolution, and Deng reaped the whirlwind in Tiananmen Square. A quarter century of revolution from above had provided the opening for revolution from below. Its position undermined by Mao's earlier assaults and by Deng's own reforms, the CCP buckled. When the five-man Politburo Standing Committee split, only a reassertion of power by the octogenarians of the Long March generation saved the day.

China's pro-democracy movement was without precedent. Never before had a long-established Communist regime been endangered by massive peaceful protest. When similar demonstrations took place in Eastern Europe six months later, they were against puppet regimes from which Soviet support had been withdrawn, conditions that did not apply in China.

When the Soviet Communist Party collapsed after the abortive coup of 1991, there was a background of economic crisis, ethnic upheaval, and the emergence of elected alternatives to its leaders. In China in early 1989, inflation, corruption, and simmering unrest in Tibet did not add up to a comparable threat. Yet the regime could be sustained only with military force. As Communism collapsed in Eastern Europe and the Soviet Union during the following two years, Deng and his fellow gerontocrats congratulated themselves on having used the PLA to preserve the power it had won for them forty years before. Deng also took steps to reinvigorate his economic reform program, continuing even more vigorously to seek Party legitimacy through national prosperity. As the "paramount leader" faded from the political stage in the mid-1990s, the new successor, Jiang Zemin, whom Deng had chosen in the aftermath of the Tiananmen events, endeavored to solidify his personal position by promoting his followers and courting the military. But Jiang and his peers still faced the problem of transforming a short-term expedient into a long-term solution.

The dilemma of Deng and his heirs mirrors that of nineteenth-century Chinese statesmen: how to emulate the West while retaining a distinct identity. The maxim then was to maintain Chinese learning as the core and adopt Western knowledge for practical use; Deng's call, maintained by his successors, was to "build socialism with Chinese characteristics." Neither formulation was ultimately effective in enabling the Beijing government of the day to head off pressure for political change.

As heirs to twenty centuries of Confucian civilization, the last emperors at least had a conception of what China was. With the overthrow of the Confucian imperial system in 1912 and the denial of its intellectual, social, and moral values in the subsequent May Fourth Movement, that China was seemingly erased. Deng, far more than Mao, was a product of that era, and for much of his life he sought to build a new China as part of a prospective Marxist-Leninist world civilization. With the final collapse of that dream between 1989 and 1991, China was left with no past and no future.

But China, of course, persists, not as a notion in some leader's mind, let alone the blank page upon which Mao proposed to inscribe the characters of his utopian dreams, but as a rich palimpsest, layered by the genius of many generations. As China enters the twenty-first century and the Long Marchers are succeeded by lesser leaders, increasingly unable to control the momentum or direction of this vast nation's economic, social, and, eventually, political evolution, the Chinese people will finally have their own opportunity to reclaim their past and define their future.

CHAPTER 1

THE ESTABLISHMENT AND CONSOLIDATION OF THE NEW REGIME, 1949–57

FREDERICK C. TEIWES

AN OVERVIEW

When the People's Republic of China (PRC) was formally established on 1 October 1949 the nation's new leaders faced daunting problems. Society and polity were fragmented, public order and morale had decayed, a war-torn economy suffered from severe inflation and unemployment, and China's fundamental economic and military backwardness created monumental impediments to the elite's goals of national wealth and power. Yet by 1957 the leaders of the Chinese Communist Party (CCP) could look back on the period since 1949 with considerable satisfaction. A strong centralized state had been established after decades of disunity, China's national pride and international prestige had grown significantly as a result of fighting the world's greatest power to a stalemate in Korea, the country had taken major steps on the road to industrialization and achieved an impressive rate of economic growth, the living standards of its people had made noticeable if modest progress, and the nation's social system had been transformed according to Marxist precepts in relatively smooth fashion.

Moreover, all this had been accomplished with only limited divisions within the Party elite. Thus Chairman Mao Zedong could convincingly claim at the Eighth CCP Congress in September 1956 that "we . . . have gained a decisive victory in the socialist revolution [and] our Party is now more united, more consolidated than at any time in the past."[1] A year later, intervening events and persistent problems set the stage for considerably enhanced elite conflict as the CCP began to evolve the bold new developmental strategy of the Great Leap Forward (GLF); yet Mao reaffirmed that the socialist revolution had been achieved,[2] while his leading colleague Liu

1 "Opening address at the Eighth National Congress of the Communist Party of China" (15 September 1956), in *Eighth National Congress of the Communist Party of China*, 1.7.

2 In his "Talk at a meeting with Chinese students and trainees in Moscow" (17 November 1957), in *CB*, 891.26, Mao declared that the victory represented by the change of ownership systems in 1956 had not

Map 1. PRC: political (*pinyin* romanization)

S
R
HEILONGJIANG
Daqing
Harbin
Ulan Bator
OLIA
JILIN
Changchun
INNER MONGOLIA A.R.
Shenyang
Fushun
LIAONING
Anshan
NORTH KOREA
Hohhot
Beidaihe
BEIJING
Baotou
NINGXIA-HUI A.R.
TIANJIN
Luda
JAPAN
SOUTH KOREA
HEBEI
Yinchuan
Taiyuan
Shijiazhuang
Dazhai
Jinan
Qingdao
SHANXI
SHANDONG
Yan'an
Yellow R.
Luoyang
Kaifeng
Zhengzhou
Xian
SHAANXI
HENAN
JIANGSU
Hefei
Nanjing
SHANGHAI
ANHUI
HUBEI
Yangtze R.
Hangzhou
Wuhan
(Wuchang)
Lushan
ZHEJIANG
UAN
Nanchang
Okinawa
Wenzhou
Changsha
Shaoshan
JIANGXI
Zunyi
Jing-gangshan
HUNAN
Guiyang
Fuzhou
FUJIAN
Taipei
GUIZHOU
Ruijin
Xiamen
TAIWAN
GUANGXI-ZHUANG A.R.
GUANGDONG
West R.
Shantou
Guangzhou
Nanning
HONG KONG
VIETNAM
Hanoi
Haiphong
PHILIPPINES

Shaoqi, plausibly argued that Party unity remained firm.[3] As China began to move in uncertain directions, the official judgment of the PRC's first eight years as a period of achievement and cohesion was still fully credible.

What explains the achievements of this initial period? To a considerable degree, the unity of leadership sustained throughout 1949–57 was the bedrock upon which other successes were built. The extent of this unity was remarkable in view of not only the drastic purges and bitter conflicts that marked the history of the Communist Party of the Soviet Union, but also the factional cleavages that had afflicted the inner Party life of the CCP in the 1920s and 1930s. Only one major purge – that of Gao Gang and Rao Shushi in 1954–5 – affected the top elite; as we shall see, even this conflict had a relatively limited impact on Party cohesion. Even more significantly, nearly all the surviving Central Committee (CC) members chosen at the Seventh Party Congress in 1945 were reelected in 1956. In addition, elite stability was reflected in the largely undisturbed pecking order within the higher reaches of the regime. Although subtle shifts of rank and influence inevitably occurred, dramatic rises such as that of Deng Xiaoping who vaulted from the relatively low twenty-fifth position on the 1945 CC to Politburo status in 1955 and then to the Party's General Secretaryship in 1956, were rare indeed. And apart from the very small number actually dropped from the CC in this period, key figures who suffered losses of power and influence were generally restored to equal status after relatively short periods of penance.

Such leadership was an enormous political asset. With a strong elite commitment to maintaining both clearly defined power relations and the principle of Party unity, policy issues could be vigorously debated within official forums without danger to the regime. Since personal maneuvering for advantage was kept to a minimum under such circumstances – indeed, too blatant maneuvering would be counterproductive – relatively unfettered debate maximized the likelihood of balanced and flexible decisions. Once a decision was made, the commitment to unity as well as formal norms of Leninist discipline usually guaranteed prompt implementation by responsible leaders of the various hierarchies of the PRC. More broadly, the aura of authority and confidence generated by a united leadership served to impress ordinary officials and the populace and thus facilitate their enthusiasm for or acquiescence in Party programs.

The sources of leadership unity were varied. The victory of 1949 against

been conclusive but "genuine success in the socialist revolution" had been achieved as a result of political and ideological movements in 1957.

3 After various debates in 1957, Liu in December told visiting Indian Communists: "Our Party has guarded its unity at all times, there's been no split . . .; no one has gone his own way." Cited in MacFarquhar, *The origins of the Cultural Revolution*, 1.311.

considerable odds was obviously a crucial factor. This victory, which represented both the culmination of a protracted revolutionary struggle and an opportunity for national renewal, greatly enhanced the authority of the top leaders who had developed the Party's successful strategy. At a more prosaic level, revolutionary success provided the spoils of power that were widely shared within the elite. Individuals and groups from the many pre-1949 CCP civilian and military organizations, leaders whose revolutionary credentials were linked to particular episodes such as the Nanchang uprising of 1927, which marked the founding of the Red Army, or the December 9 movement of Beijing students against Japan in 1935, and various personal networks within the leadership, all benefited from the parceling out of positions and influence. Although the Long Marchers who were closest to Mao tended to predominate in the highest bodies overall, no major revolutionary group was discriminated against except those leaders who had challenged Mao before he achieved unquestioned preeminence, and even those figures received some symbolic positions and tangible power. Thus there were few groups with immediate grievances that threatened unity.

After 1949, moreover, shared ideological commitment to Marxism and a broad consensus on ambitious industrialization and social transformation further contributed to elite cohesion. Although ideological movements are notorious for splits and infighting – phenomena the CCP would experience in later years – and broad agreement on goals does not necessarily prevent bitter conflict over means and priorities, circumstances operated to inhibit such developments in the early and mid-1950s. To a substantial degree, this resulted from the mutually reinforcing interplay of Party unity and policy success throughout the period. Unity contributed to effective solutions to problems; success in solving problems further deepened leadership solidarity. Success also served to mask or diminish any latent conflict over goals. As long as rapid rates of economic growth were attained, any unpalatable by-products of modernization would hardly give cause for a fundamental challenge to existing policy. Another vitally important element was the existence of a model that specified not only goals but means as well: the experience of the Soviet Union in building socialism. A wide consensus existed on following the Soviet model, which served to focus policy debate on incremental modifications rather than on fundamental approaches, and thus lower the stakes of any conflict.

The high level of unity from 1949 to 1957 did not mean an absence of leadership cleavages but simply that they remained latent in comparison with later periods. One potential source of division was the diversity of revolutionary careers among the Party elite. Although unified by the larger struggle, at the same time participants in different revolutionary events and organizations developed their own personal networks and group identities. During the Cultural Revolution after 1965, such groupings would become critically important: For example, those who had engaged in "white area" or underground work under the leadership of Liu Shaoqi generally shared the fate of their leader during the troubled 1966–7 period. From 1949 to 1957, however, contrasting pre-1949 experiences normally did not disrupt the larger leadership cohesion. The one major attempt to use such differences for political gain, the Gao Gang–Rao Shushi affair, was ultimately a failure.

Another source of tension carried over from revolutionary days was the inevitable friction among various personalities at the apex of the CCP elite. A clear example was the prickly relationship between Mao and one of his leading generals, Peng Dehuai, which reportedly led Peng to complain in 1953 that "The Chairman doesn't like me [nor] does he hold me in esteem."[4] Such personal conflict would arguably contribute to Peng's dismissal as minister of defense in 1959, yet in the early years of the PRC it was basically submerged as Peng's talents were utilized in key military roles and on the supreme policy-making body, the Party Politburo.

Other cleavages arose from the circumstances of the early years themselves. Inevitably the large agenda of policy issues facing the new elite produced different views and thus conflict among various advocates. One recurring cause of conflict was the question of how quickly to push economic development and social transformation. On any given question some voices would be heard for pressing ahead to achieve the desired goals, whereas others could be raised in warning against disruption due to too rapid a pace. Yet differences among various approaches were relatively narrow; furthermore, the positions of top leaders were not rigidly linked to one or another tendency but shifted according to the issue and circumstances. As a result, leadership polarization did not occur as it did in later periods, when conflicting policy views were much more fundamental.

A related source of limited, nonpolarized conflict was the increasing identification of individual leaders with institutions and departments they headed as the new system took shape and became increasingly bureaucratized by the mid-1950s. Thus, for example, Premier Zhou Enlai undoubtedly had an interest in developing the roles and powers of the government apparatus as distinct from the Party organization, which was more the direct concern of Liu Shaoqi and Deng Xiaoping, whereas while army leaders such as Peng Dehuai had a natural concern with maximizing military resources. From 1949 to 1957, however, such conflicting bureaucratic

4 As quoted in a Red Guard publication, *Mass criticism and repudiation bulletin* (Guangzhou), 5 October 1967, trans. in URI, *The case of Peng Teh-huai 1959–1968*, 123.

interests were largely accommodated in the pursuit of larger goals, and direct institutional clashes such as that of Party and army during the Cultural Revolution were avoided. Despite an increasing tendency to approach issues from the perspectives of the departments they led, individual leaders still placed priority on the overall Party line and the consensus of the Politburo collective.

In sum, important cleavages and tensions existed within the CCP elite, including the Politburo, throughout the early and mid-1950s, but they did not seriously disrupt the predominantly consensual mode of leadership. Ultimately it was not the lack of tensions but the willingness of Mao and his colleagues to minimize the tensions that did exist that created the unusual unity of these early years. Such willingness, however, was inseparable from the circumstances examined in this chapter. When these circumstances no longer prevailed – when the Soviet model no longer commanded general agreement and official policies produced major disasters rather than a string of successes – latent cleavages became manifest and Party unity was eroded and then shattered. Throughout this drama the character of Mao Zedong's leadership was a central factor. We turn now to Mao's crucial role in sustaining the unity of 1949–57.

The role of Mao Zedong

Mao Zedong was clearly the unchallenged leader of the CCP throughout the 1949–57 period. Mao's preeminent position within the Party was already indisputable by the mid-1940s. Not only was Mao the subject of a major personality cult, but by 1943 his leading colleagues ceased voicing subtle doubts about his theoretical capabilities and in 1945 "the thought of Mao Zedong" was enshrined in the CCP's new constitution. Moreover, despite the emphasis of Party rules on collective leadership, Mao was granted formal powers to act unilaterally in certain instances.[5] The basis of Mao's burgeoning power was the success of Party strategies and policies after the onset of the Sino-Japanese War in 1937, which he had shaped more than any other leader; the conclusive success of these strategies and policies from 1945 to 1949 further bolstered his ultimate authority. Much as the victory of 1949 deepened Party unity generally, it also solidified Mao's authority. By virtue of that victory, Mao approximated the ideal charismatic leader whose exceptional abilities were acknowledged as the key to success, as well as the ideal

5 According to a recent inner Party report by Liao Kai-lung, "Historical experiences and our road of development" (25 October 1980), in *Issues & Studies*, November 1981, 92, in March 1943 a Politburo decision appointed a Secretariat of Mao, Liu Shaoqi, and Ren Bishi to handle day-to-day work, but granted Mao individually the power to make final decisions concerning matters before the Secretariat.

founder of a new dynasty, with all the implications of obedience that role carried in traditional culture.

Mao's authority was further enhanced by his major initiatives in the 1949–57 period, instances where his individual judgment clashed with that of key colleagues and/or broader elite opinion. The Chairman apparently took such initiatives on only three occasions during these years. The first, in October 1950, concerned China's response to the northward march of American forces in Korea. On that occasion Mao seemingly overrode reservations of the great majority of his associates concerning costs and dangers, secured their acquiescence, and ordered the involvement of Chinese troops in the war.[6] Although the costs of the PRC's Korean venture were indeed high, the benefits achieved in security and international peace were widely perceived as outweighing these costs and thus reinforced Mao's reputation for political wisdom. The second instance, which will be examined in more detail later, was the Chairman's initiative to speed up the pace of agricultural cooperativization in mid-1955 despite an official decision a few months earlier to temper the rate of growth. The resultant basic achievement of collectivization by the end of 1956, far in advance of the most optimistic projections, once again seemed to demonstrate Mao's insight.

The final initiative, Mao's efforts in the face of substantial reservations within the elite to promote intellectual criticism of the Party through the Hundred Flowers movement in 1956–57 (also analyzed later), was less successful. However, the damage to his prestige was minimized by his abrupt shift of position in mid-1957.

On balance, both the broader achievements of the initial period and the specific successes of Korea and collectivization left Mao's position at the end of 1957 as strong as ever despite the setback of the Hundred Flowers. The Chairman's strength was reflected in his moves, apparently dating from 1953, developed at the Eighth Party Congress, and reaffirmed in early 1958, to divide the leadership into two "fronts." Under these arrangements Mao would retreat to the "second front," where he could contemplate matters of theory and overall policy while divorced from daily operations. Such steps indicated not only great confidence that his ultimate authority was secure but considerable faith in his leading colleagues as well.

The fact of Mao's unchallenged authority was the linchpin of the entire edifice of elite stability. Apart from the decisive initiatives described previously, Mao served as the final arbiter of policy disputes when his associates were unable to reach a consensus. Under these circumstances, policy advocacy

6 In addition to Cultural Revolution sources, this version of the Korea decision is supported by the excerpts from the recollections of Peng Dehuai published in 1981. *Peng Dehuai zishu* (Peng Dehuai's own account), 257–8.

to a substantial degree was aimed at winning the Chairman's approval rather than functioning as a tool in the pursuit of supreme power, as in the Soviet Union after the deaths of Lenin and Stalin. With all groups within the leadership owing loyalty to Mao, any latent tensions among them were largely kept in check.

Although Mao's authority made leadership unity possible, it by no means guaranteed cohesion. Stalin had amply demonstrated how a supreme leader could consciously create disunity among his subordinates, and in later years Mao's erratic behavior would exacerbate existing elite tensions. In the 1949–57 period, however, Mao sought to enhance elite solidarity by generally adhering to official Party norms of collective leadership and democratic discussion and more broadly by emphasizing ability and achievement as criteria for leadership. Unlike Stalin, Mao did not set his colleagues at each other's throats; nor did he demand that they have close factional links to himself. Instead, the ranking members of the ruling elite were men of talent and major figures in the history of the CCP in their own right. Liu Shaoqi had a quite distinct career involving work in the so-called white areas behind enemy lines, while Zhou Enlai, the third-ranking figure and leading government administrator, had even opposed Mao in the early 1930s. Red Army leader Zhu De and economic specialist Chen Yun had been more closely associated with Mao but were still individuals of independent prestige, and only Deng Xiaoping of the inner core of the 1950s could be considered a member of Mao's long-standing personal faction. With his own power secure, Mao chose to utilize the considerable talents of such leaders and mold them into a cooperative team. Thus, in addition to there being no advantage in challenging the Chairman, there was little gain in exaggerating policy differences to outmaneuver potential rivals because of Mao's commitment to solidarity.

Closely linked to this commitment was Mao's willingness to observe, by and large, the formal rules of collective leadership. Although Mao obviously reserved the right to insist on his own way in matters of prime concern and collective leadership in fact did not mean simple majority rule,[7] his general practice in the early and mid-1950s was to arrive at policies through wide-ranging discussions where the opinions of all relevant officials were valued for the contributions they could make to informed decisions. Moreover, again with some lapses, Mao chose to observe the principle of minority rights,

7 Mao acknowledged this in 1962 when he defined his adherence to democratic centralism in the following terms: "[W]hen I say something, no matter whether it is correct or incorrect, *provided that everyone disagrees with me,* I will accede to their point of view because they are the majority" (emphasis added). "Talk at an enlarged central work conference" (30 January 1962), in Stuart Schram, ed., *Mao Tse-tung unrehearsed: Talks and letters: 1956–71*, 165.

whereby dissenters within the leadership could retain their views and even reiterate them at a future date without fear of punishment. This relatively democratic style served Mao well by encouraging debate on key issues, deepening elite commitment to the relatively open policy process generally, and thus reinforcing the overall sense of leadership solidarity.

Mao's contributions to effective decision making and Party unity were further enhanced by the nature of his main political concerns during the 1949–57 period. In these years Mao tended to limit his interventions largely to those areas he knew best – agriculture and revolution above all else. The Chairman clearly considered himself an expert on the peasantry after years of leading a rural-based revolution, and in the 1950s he continued to spend considerable amounts of time in the countryside. By "revolution" Mao meant overall strategies for extending CCP power and furthering the process of socialist transformation, concerns well suited to his experience in the pre-1949 period.

In addition, together with Zhou Enlai, Mao was the architect of China's foreign policy, as befitted someone who had dealt with major international actors during the anti-Japanese and civil wars. Finally, as the author of the CCP's basic policy on literature and the arts in 1942, Mao continued to take a keen if sometimes idiosyncratic interest in this sphere and the affairs of higher intellectuals generally. As a result, with the possible exception of the cultural sphere, in all these areas Mao possessed credentials his colleagues respected; his assertions of authority regarding them could not be regarded as arbitrary or ill-informed. Equally important was the fact that the Chairman generally restricted his role in areas he was not familiar with to the synthesis of and arbitration among the opinions of his more specialist colleagues. This was particularly the case in one of the most crucial policy areas of the period – economic construction. Thus both Mao's prestige and elite solidarity were reinforced by the hesitancy to impose his views in matters where, by his own admission, he lacked understanding. In contrast to later periods, Mao's *substantive* policy impact was relatively limited throughout 1949–57; his contribution to Party unity came from actively performing the role of ultimate arbiter while keeping dramatic personal initiatives to a minimum.

Finally, leadership unity was also bolstered by the fact that Mao's intellectual position in these years was on the whole orthodox and mainstream. In good Marxist fashion his notion of social change centered on the transformation of ownership patterns, and in good Stalinist manner he gave high priority to rapid industrialization. In most matters he shared with his colleagues a deep commitment to economic and technical advance, a keen awareness of objective limits to Party policies, and a determination to steer a course between "leftist" excesses and "rightist" timidity. Thus when debate did occur, generally Mao's relatively centrist position served to ameliorate conflict and build a consensus rather than polarize differences within the leadership. The Chairman's intellectual position, then, aided his pursuit of consensus politics. But both Mao's orientation and his consensual politics depended to a substantial degree on the existence of the Soviet experience of building socialism.

The Soviet model

In the 1949–57 period, broad agreement existed within the CCP leadership on adopting the Soviet model of socialism. This model provided patterns of state organization, an urban-oriented developmental strategy, modern military techniques, and policies and methods in a wide variety of specialized areas. As already suggested, given the consensus on following the Soviet path, policy debate was shifted from the fundamental to the incremental level. In contrast to the bitter disputes of Bolshevik politics in the 1920s due to basic differences over both the ultimate shape of and the means to achieve socialism, with an established model of socialism already in existence, Chinese policy debates by and large dealt with matters of nuance and degree.

The basic issues were these: Precisely what were the positive and negative features of the Soviet model? How should the CCP adapt the model to suit Chinese conditions? How fast should the Soviet path be followed? Although such questions did result in spirited debate, they were hardly the types of issues to split the Party. In addition, the presence of an existing and ostensibly successful socialist system in the Soviet Union served to bolster the confidence of the Chinese elite and society generally in official policies, since the broad outlines of both process and outcome were presumed to be known.

Various aspects of the Soviet model and Chinese adaptations will be analyzed in both this and later chapters. Here it suffices to say that CCP leaders never adopted a position of uncritical borrowing from the Soviet experience. The essence of Mao's program for revolution before 1949 had been the need to address Chinese realities, and he was not about to disown that principle during the stage of building socialism. Moreover, Mao's strong nationalism had led in the early 1940s to a clear declaration of independence from any Soviet control over CCP affairs, and this too militated against unthinking imitation.

Nevertheless, the willingness to alter the model varied considerably from sphere to sphere and over time. Where the Party had its own established competence, as in rural policy, distinctive Chinese approaches were common – although even in such areas the Soviet model remained relevant. In contrast, where the CCP was without experience, its creativity was limited. As Mao put it after the fact: "In the early stages of nationwide liberation we lacked the experience to administer the economy of the entire country. Therefore, during the First Five-Year Plan (FYP) we could only imitate the methods of the Soviet Union."[8] Yet CCP leaders gained confidence with time, and by 1956 they began to modify Soviet experience regarding the economy and other key areas. It would only be with the GLF of 1958, however, that a fundamental break with the Soviet model would take place.

Why was the Soviet model adopted so decisively by the Chinese leadership after 1949? To a certain extent this was a logical corollary of the decision to "lean to one side" in foreign policy. Whatever the possibilities might have been for a more balanced international posture had American diplomacy been less hostile to the CCP during the civil war, in 1949 the PRC found the Soviet Union the only available source of military and economic aid. Following the Soviet precedent was a least in part a price that had to be paid for securing that aid. More fundamental, however, was a long-term ideological orientation toward Soviet Russia. This not only involved a sense of being part of a common movement against international capitalism and imperialism but was also reflected in basic organizational principles and practices. Despite unique emphases and Mao's insistence on independence, in a fundamental sense the CCP had been following the Soviet model since its earliest days, when Leninist organizational principles and methods were infused into the fledgling Party by agents of the Communist International.

Moreover, even though Mao continued to insist on a degree of ideological distinctiveness in the immediate post-1949 period, there was still a sense in which the Soviet Union remained an authority on basic ideological questions. This was perhaps most graphically demonstrated by Mao's nocturnal visits to the residence of Soviet Ambassador Yudin to thrash out theoretical issues – sessions that may have contributed to doctrinal adjustments in the Chairman's *Selected works* when they appeared in 1951.[9] Given the acceptance of Soviet ideological authority in the broadest sense, Russian pronouncements on building socialism were sure to carry weight.

Although international factors and general ideological orientation undoubtedly made CCP leaders receptive to the Soviet model, the crucial factor was their deep commitment to socialist modernization. The men who led the CCP to victory in 1949 were not mere agrarian revolutionaries; they were both Marxists seeking a socialist future and modernizers striving to realize

8 "Reading notes on the Soviet Union's *Political economics*" (1960–62?), in *Miscellany of Mao Tse-tung Thought* (hereafter cited as *Miscellany*), 2.310.

9 Khrushchev reported Mao's visits to Yudin in *Khrushchev remembers*, 464–5; see also *Khrushchev remembers: The last testament*, 242.

the dream of a "rich and powerful" China. They were acutely aware of their own inexperience with developmental problems. As Mao declared in mid-1949: "We shall soon put aside some of the things we know well and be compelled to do things we don't know well."[10] Given both the desire for development and the fact that the Soviet Union was the only existing example of a state that both was socialist and had achieved rapid growth on a backward economic base, the decision to follow the Soviet path was all but inevitable.

The decision was further facilitated by the fact that as good Marxists the CCP leaders accepted the transition to urban-oriented developmental strategies as a natural consequence of revolutionary success. Although CCP leaders were proud of their revolutionary traditions and concerned about the corrupting tendencies of the cities, there is little to indicate that Mao or anyone else initially saw any fundamental contradictions between the revolutionary experience of Yan'an and the Soviet model. The predominant feeling, rather, was one of desirable progression to a higher stage. Mao had regarded guerrilla warfare never as an end in itself but rather as a necessary stage of struggle forced on the CCP by its relative weakness; when the time came for large-scale operations by massed troops, the more advanced military style was pressed enthusiastically.

Similarly, the whole rural phase of the revolution had been necessary but was always seen as a prelude to the capture of the cities. At the moment of victory, Party leaders were eager to get on with the task of nation building and showed little awareness that the imported Soviet strategies might clash with CCP traditions. And even when that awareness developed in the mid-1950s, they expected that any contradictions would be, in Mao's terms, "nonantagonistic" and thus safely handled by adjustments within the overall framework of the Soviet model.

In conclusion, a few general remarks about the Soviet model are in order. First, no single Soviet model in fact existed. Although the basic institutional and economic pattern to be followed was that of the Stalinist system as it developed after the mid-1930s, CCP leaders had a whole range of periods and practices in Soviet history to choose from. During agricultural cooperativization, for example, the CCP looked for guidelines more to the principles articulated by Stalin in 1927–9 during his debate with Bukharin than to Stalinist collectivization practice after 1929. Second, even where a strong desire to institute Soviet methods on a broad scale may have existed, lack of requisite technical resources could severely inhibit their adoption. Another consideration is that in altering specific Soviet practices, the CCP was not

10 Mao, *SW*, 4.422.

necessarily rejecting Soviet advice. Throughout the 1949–57 period, Soviet leaders and specialists considered their mistakes as lessons the Chinese could and should benefit from. In particular, the Russian's own criticisms of Stalinist practice after the dictator's death often influenced CCP thinking on the need to alter existing approaches.

Finally, it is important to emphasize that Soviet influence had a wide impact beyond the attitudes of top policy makers. Although key leaders were always, albeit in fluctuating degrees, aware of the need to adapt Soviet experiences to Chinese realities, ordinary officials and the general populace were often overwhelmed by the public emphasis on advanced Soviet experience. Propaganda treatment of the Soviet Union as a respected "elder brother" and such slogans as "The Soviet Union of today is our tomorrow" hardly encouraged critical emulation, with the result that mindless copying did occur in many fields. In still another sense, the positive image of the Soviet Union allowed elements of China's intelligentsia to pick up some less orthodox tendencies of Russian intellectuals despite the disapproval of both Soviet and Chinese officialdom. All in all, throughout the 1949–57 period Soviet influences affected both CCP policy and Chinese society in a variety of complex ways. In some senses the process was beyond the control of Party leaders, but more fundamentally it reflected their conscious choice. And when those leaders – or a dominant group of them – saw the need to break away from the Soviet path after 1957, it was well within their capabilities to do so, even though many Soviet influences inevitably remained.

CONSOLIDATION AND RECONSTRUCTION, 1949–52

In 1949, victory came with startling suddenness. The traditional northern capital, Beijing fell by negotiated surrender in January. The People's Liberation Army (PLA) crossed the Yangtze and quickly seized Shanghai in April and the central China urban complex of Wuhan in May. Thereafter the PLA met little sustained military resistance. It took the southern commercial center of Guangzhou in October shortly after the formal establishment of the PRC, and finally reached the southwest city of Chengdu in December. At the end of the year only Tibet and Taiwan were beyond reach of the new leadership in Beijing. The Tibetan situation would be rectified by 1951 through a combination of military action and negotiation with the local authorities, whereas the Taiwan question would remain a major item of unfinished national business over three decades later.

To a significant degree, the military victories of 1949 solved one of the major problems of the preceding forty years – the lack of national unity. This very fact was a substantial asset for CCP leaders as they grappled with still unresolved questions. The national unity that was necessary to restore China's greatness was a heartfelt goal for all patriotic Chinese. Mao expressed their sentiments in September 1949 by declaring, "Ours will no longer be a nation subject to insult and humiliation. We have stood up."[11]

But although the achievement of national unity considerably legitimized the new regime in the eyes of the educated elite, to secure the deeper political control required for both social transformation and modernization, it would have to confront the parochialism that had dominated Chinese society from time immemorial. Although the CCP had attained some success in broadening horizons in the North China villages that the Party controlled during the revolutionary period, in most rural areas the awareness and interests of the peasants were limited to events in their villages and nearby areas. Even in China's cities, the lives of ordinary people were bound by small social groups and involved little consciousness of developments at either the municipal or national level.

An integrated national political system would, therefore, require the state's penetration of society in a way that had never been attempted by previous regimes, and such penetration in turn would necessitate both the careful development of organizational resources and intense mass mobilization to jar various sections of society out of their narrow frames of reference. By reaching deep into society, the CCP could tap new sources for support. At the same time, it ran the risk of alienating affected groups. The new leaders also faced tasks arising from the more immediate legacy of a dozen years of large-scale warfare – the need to overcome continued resistance by elements that had long struggled against the CCP, to rehabilitate a severely damaged economy, and to restore orderly governmental operations. All of this would tax CCP resources and ingenuity. But at the same time, the situation created a substantial reservoir of backing from a war-weary populace longing for peace and order.

In the early days of the PRC, Mao and his colleagues spoke of a three-year period to restore China's production to prewar levels and establish the political control and organizational capacity needed before socialist construction and transformation could be undertaken in earnest. The projection proved remarkably close to the mark.

This recovery period inevitably saw conflicting emphases. On the one hand, the initial needs of economic revival and political acceptance argued for reassuring key groups in society and making tangible concessions to their interests. The policy of reassurance, however, was in tension with the imperative of establishing firm organizational control as a prelude to planned devel-

11 Mao, *SW*, 5.17.

opment. Although this contradiction was always present and the subject of debate within the leadership, a marked shift in emphasis occurred in late 1950. From that time, roughly corresponding with the Chinese entry into the Korean War, the CCP's social programs intensified, mass movements were launched, and the regime penetrated society in a much more thorough manner than initially. But in the first year or so of power, the stress was on reassurance in view of both the fragility of the situation and the limited resources the Party had at its disposal.

Initial problems and policies

The problems encountered in 1949 by the new leaders and the policies they designed for dealing with them varied enormously over the vast face of China. Differences in economic and cultural levels, agricultural patterns, local customs, and ethnic composition all required suitably varied responses. The crucial difference, however, was the degree of CCP presence in various areas before 1949. Although the gradations in this regard are quite complex, in broad terms three types of areas manifested fundamental differences. First were the "old liberated areas" of North China, the Northeast, and parts of the Northwest and East China containing about one-quarter of the nation's population, where the CCP had basically established its power in the countryside by 1947–8 and often much earlier. These were the areas where the revolution was essentially won; as Mao put it in 1950: "It was the victory of the agrarian reform [in the old liberated areas] that made possible our victory in overthrowing Chiang Kai-shek."[12] Here the CCP had created an organizational presence down to the grass roots, drawn substantial numbers of peasants into the Party, basically eliminated organized resistance, and made substantial progress in social reform programs that generated considerable mass support among the poorer sections of rural society. As Mao indicated, it was from this base that the CCP launched its classic strategy of the "countryside surrounding the cities" as the conclusive battles of the civil war were fought in 1947–8. By 1949 the main tasks in these areas were to extend political control and begin land reform in those pockets where the Party had not ruled, and to check up on the results of land reform and develop low-level forms of cooperative agriculture elsewhere. By mid-1950 land reform was declared complete in the old liberated areas, and in that year something like one-third peasant households in these areas had been organized into mutual aid teams (MAT), the first step on the road to collectivization.

In sharp contrast to the old liberated areas stood the "new liberated areas,"

12 Ibid., 33.

consisting of much of East and Central China, the overwhelming portion of the Northwest, and the vast expanse of territory south of the Yangtze. Here, apart from some scattered revolutionary bases left over from the rural revolution of the 1920s and 1930s (plus some underground Communists in the cities), the Party lacked organizational resources or mass support. Unlike the protracted revolutionary struggle in the north, victory in the new areas came by military conquest from without by what were to a substantial extent alien armies. Rather than the countryside surrounding the cities, the pattern was the opposite one of first seizing cities and then extending control outward to the rural areas.

A corollary of the absence of a CCP presence was the strength of anti-Communist groups even after basic military victory. In its most extreme form, continued armed resistance was offered by remnant Kuomintang (KMT; Guomindang) military units and the forces of secret societies, ethnic minorities, and other locally organized self-defense groups. Even in mid-1950 Mao spoke of more than 400,000 "bandits" scattered in remote regions of the new liberated areas that had not yet been wiped out, and PLA mopping-up actions continued against such forces, especially in the Northwest, as late as 1954. Most areas, however, were reported clear by mid-1951. Although such armed resistance obviously prolonged the process of establishing control, more significant was the political and social influence of local elites whose interest was in maintaining the status quo. To counter this influences, thorough land reform would be required, and it would have to start from scratch.

Finally, all the tasks that faced cities in the old liberated areas – establishing public order, restoring production, curbing inflation, and checking unemployment – also had to be dealt with in the urban centers of the new areas from a more precarious position, given the unsettled state of the surrounding countryside. Although the more advantageous rural conditions in the old liberated areas allowed cities there to achieve the goals of urban reconstruction considerably more quickly than those in the new areas, China's urban centers, containing some 50 million people, can be considered a separate category from both the old and new areas.

With the exception of a few small and medium-sized cities in North and Northeast China, the CCP had not held urban centers before late 1948, and its hold over those seized was often tenuous and short-lived. The vast majority of cities before 1949 were centers of anti-Communist power where CCP presence was limited to relatively weak underground forces, albeit much weaker in the south than the north. These forces could play only an auxiliary role in the takeover of the cities, and Party cadres from the liberated areas were often scornful of underground Communists who, in their eyes, had contributed so little to success. This attitude was further reflected in the new regimes established in the cities in which underground workers were given clearly secondary roles, whereas power gravitated to the outsiders whose careers had been made in the PLA and rural areas.

As the CCP moved into China's major cities, it held substantial assets, but it also suffered from major inadequacies. Ironically, in some senses the problems encountered in 1949 were exacerbated by the very rapidity of a final victory that considerably exceeded the expectations of Party leaders. At the start of the civil war in 1946, many top leaders such as Zhou Enlai anticipated a struggle of up to twenty years before the Communists could achieve ultimate success, and even in the spring of 1948, when the tide of battle in North China had turned in favor of the CCP, Mao predicted that another three years would be required for victory.[13] The sudden and vast expansion of the areas under Communist control left the Party acutely short of the personnel and skills needed for nationwide rule.

One solution was the rapid recruitment of new Party members as the CCP extended its geographical control; in the period from 1948 to the end of 1950, CCP membership increased from about 2.8 million to 5.8 million. Such a vast influx at a time of revolutionary struggle and then the multiplying demands of rule could not be carefully regulated. At the 1956 CCP Congress, Deng Xiaoping criticized the "undue speed [of Party growth during] the two years just before and after liberation [where] in certain areas [the CCP] grew practically without guidance and without plan."[14] Given such uncontrolled growth and the lack of systematic training, the predominantly peasant new Party members often lacked even rudimentary knowledge of Marxist ideology or basic skills of literacy. An additional problem was that most new recruits had entered the fold under circumstances where eventual success was clear. As a result, Party leaders could not be sure whether such individuals joined out of genuine commitment or out of opportunism. Thus although the rapid Party expansion around the time of takeover was undoubtedly necessary, it was only a partial answer at best to personnel and skill shortages.

Inadequacies of manpower, skills, and experience affected the countryside of the new liberated areas but were most sharply felt in the cities. We have already noted the Party leadership's acute sense of inexperience when it came to the modern sector. In terms of personnel, the CCP had at its disposal some 720,000 qualified individuals to serve as civilian cadres in government ad-

13 Zhou's views are reported in *The New York Times*, 25 September 1946. Mao's prediction is in Mao, *SW*, 4.225.

14 Teng Hsiao-p'ing, "Report on the revision of the constitution of the Communist Party of China" (16 September 1956), in *Eighth National Congress*, 1.215.

ministration where more than 2 million posts had been filled under the KMT.[15] But although the CCP's inadequacies and shortages were pronounced, it must be emphasized that the skills and experience the Communists brought with them from the rural base areas were considerable and relevant. Although the base areas were far less complex than the cities, the administration of more than 100 million people had obviously nurtured a whole range of governmental skills.

Similarly, despite the egalitarian ethos that marked the Yan'an years, the CCP was already developing specialized career lines with cadres versed in finance, commerce, and education, as well as agriculture and military affairs. In addition, the CCP's control of cities as early as 1945–6, however restricted, had provided direct experience in consolidating urban control, dealing with the bourgeoisie, and actually running urban enterprises. Indeed, when the major cities fell in 1949, the CCP possessed sufficient cadres trained in economic management to take immediate control of the 2,700 large enterprises that dominated the modern sector. The radical excesses of the Party's earliest urban experience, moreover, facilitated the development of a more moderate policy in 1947–8 that became the basis of programs fully articulated in 1949.

But perhaps the most valuable asset the Party possessed was the attitude of its leaders that the urban phase of the revolution was to be eagerly welcomed. When Mao declared in early 1949 that "[t]he period 'from the city to the village' and of the city leading the village has now begun,"[16] he expressed not only a willingness to give priority to urban affairs but also a recognition that urban modes were most progressive and the only path to modernization. This was reflected in many ways, such as the 1950 decision to emphasize the recruitment of workers into the Party, a measure that had the bonus of bringing the CCP more into line with Soviet orthodoxy. The overriding effects of the leadership's orientation were to ensure that urban problems were dealt with on their own terms and to discredit the "charming but useless" notion of "urbanizing the countryside [while] ruralizing the towns."[17] The key to CCP success in the base areas of North China had been the insistence on focusing on the actual problems of the villages, and the achievements of the initial period of urban rule would similarly flow from a preoccupation with the tasks at hand there.

These assets notwithstanding, the shortage of skills and personnel clearly

15 The CCP figure is given by An Tzu-wen, "Training the people's civil servants," *People's China*, 1 January 1953. The KMT figure is estimated by Yi-maw Kau, "Governmental bureaucracy and cadres in urban China under communist rule, 1949–1965," 237, on the basis of data from the 1948 statistical yearbook of the Republic of China.

16 Mao, *SW*, 4.363.

17 From a 1949 CCP pamphlet cited in Suzanne Pepper, *Civil war in China: The political struggle, 1945–1949*, 379.

left the Party unable to assume total operational control of the cities in 1949. In these circumstances, two strategies were adopted. One was to limit Party involvement to critical areas while allowing other segments of society to carry on as before; the second was to tap additional sources of personnel to ensure the orderly functioning of government and public utilities. One of the earliest acts of the occupying authorities was to call on existing personnel to remain at their posts. Only a small number of people with close ties to the KMT were detained; the great bulk of officials continued to work in the same jobs and at the same salaries as before. Communist cadres were dispatched to the various administrative organs and key economic enterprises to assume political control and gain an understanding of operations, but actual administration and management to a substantial extent remained in the hands of the "retained personnel" from KMT days.

A second major source of personnel was the recruitment of "new cadres" (not necessarily new Party members) from the ranks of students and other literate urban youth. These intellectual youths possessed skills lacked by many "old cadres" from the base areas who had accompanied the PLA to the cities. Although the inclusion of these additional groups was absolutely necessary, it led to considerable tensions within the hastily thrown together official class. Many old cadres considered themselves tested by years of revolutionary struggle and looked down upon new cadres and retained personnel as untrustworthy. In particular, they deeply resented the choice posts obtained by young intellectuals by virtue of their abilities and the fact that retained personnel continued to receive salaries while they received only daily necessities under the revolutionary supply system. New cadres and retained personnel, for their part, resented the domineering attitude of old cadres, who they felt received preferential treatment on the basis of past political services. In the short term, Party leaders coped with the resultant problems by urging the various groups to lay aside their grievances and strive for amicable relations. In the longer term, from 1951 on, measures included transferring old cadres lacking the necessary skills for urban work back to the countryside, stepping up political and professional training of new cadres while at the same time weeding out those who were judged unreliable, and ousting retained personnel from official positions as newly recruited cadres became available.

While expanding its personnel resources, the Party initially limited its scope of activities. Given that many functions were beyond the new government's immediate capabilities, various private groups were allowed or even encouraged to provide services to the public. For example, the government mobilized traditional benefit societies to provide relief for the needy, and in 1950 private and religious bodies still controlled nearly 40 percent of China's higher educational institutions. This approach flowed from a decision taken early on not merely to limit but actually to contract the scope of Party activities. Despite warnings from the highest CCP authorities not to import the methods of rural class struggle to the cities, in late 1948 and early 1949 many of the cadres entering the newly liberated cities still clung to leftist notions of mobilizing the downtrodden and sought to do so on a broad basis. They spread their limited resources thinly and in uncoordinated fashion throughout residential areas and small-scale enterprises. This practice was reversed by measures initiated by Liu Shaoqi in Tianjin in April and May 1949 and subsequently adopted in other urban centers. Liu centralized political organization and reallocated cadres to the modern economic sector, the educational sphere, and government administration while leaving the traditional sector to its own devices. The net effect was to enhance the CCP's capacity to shape the future course of events by giving it control of the institutions and forces that really mattered.

Liu's Tianjin interlude also enabled the Party to come to terms with the key economic problem that Mao had only shortly before singled out as the primary focus of urban work – the restoration of production, especially industrial production. Here again the enthusiasm of recently arrived cadres was proving an obstacle. Given both the Party's earlier official encouragement of workers' demands under KMT rule and the continuing labor unrest, such cadres backed the workers against management, with the result that many factories did not function, owing to industrial strife. This, Liu argued, was a leftist deviation preventing economic recovery. He instituted policies calling for labor discipline, managerial authority to limit wages and fire excess personnel, and "reasonable" settlements of disputes. The interests of workers regarding wages and conditions were far from ignored, but the emphasis was to restrict their demands and appeal to them to make short-term sacrifices in the interest of long-term gains.

These policies succeeded in restoring production; on a national basis, prewar peaks were achieved in many spheres by 1952. As a result, major inroads were made in alleviating serious urban unemployment. Moreover, the revival of industrial production, together with the opening of supply routes from the hinterland, helped bring under control the severe inflation that had discredited the KMT. These developments – together with such measures as removing money from circulation by taxes, bonds, and forced savings; curbing government expenditures; controlling key commodities through state trading companies; and severe punishment of speculation – succeeded in reducing the astronomical levels of KMT inflation to the manageable rate of about 15 percent by 1951.

Meanwhile, the CCP was able to combine economic recovery with an increasing capacity to control the private sector. Whereas capitalists saw Communist-controlled trade unions as a useful device for securing labor concessions, the unions, together with labor laws, provided the CCP with potent devices for enforcing its demands as well as modestly improving the lot of urban workers. In addition, the leading economic role of the large nationalized enterprises, state trading companies, and banks provided potent external controls over capitalist enterprises through loans, contracts to purchase products and supply raw materials, designated selling agents, and officially determined prices. As a result, the process of economic recovery not only secured broad public support for the CCP, but further added to the Party's capabilities for determining subsequent developments.

United front and democratic dictatorship

One of the keys to the CCP's initial success in consolidating control was its ability to maximize support and minimize fears. A number of factors worked in the Party's favor. As previously indicated, the very fact of unification resulted in the patriotic support of educated elites and broader public relief that peace had been restored. This also had a traditional aspect, since the PRC was widely accepted as a new dynasty that had the right to establish its own orthodoxy. Another favorable circumstance was the near-total discrediting of the KMT, especially among urban middle classes. The Communists were welcomed even by groups such as the industrial bourgeoisie that had good reason to fear their ultimate aims. The hopes and receptiveness of the population, in the cities at least, were not simply a product of circumstances; they reflected sustained CCP efforts to reassure key groups and the public as a whole. As we have seen, civil servants were kept at their posts and capitalists were assisted in reviving their enterprises. Meanwhile, the populace as a whole was impressed by the generally impeccable behavior of the occupying troops – in sharp contrast to the performance of KMT forces when they returned to the cities in 1945.

These and other measures, it must be stressed, were not improvisations. Rather, they reflected one of the characteristic features of Mao's strategy – the united front. To a significant degree, revolutionary success was built on the principle of gathering a wide collection of allies by setting relatively limited goals and defining enemies as narrowly as possible. It was this united front practice that was now applied to the postliberation situation.

The approach was reflected in the general program and institutional arrangements proclaimed at the founding of the PRC. A key element was the effort to seek the broadest base of legitimacy by linking the new regime to the past. In theory, the temporary supreme organ of state power pending the establishment of a system of people's congresses was designated as the Chinese People's Political Consultative Conference (CPPCC), a body that drew its lineage from the Political Consultative Conference convened by the KMT in early 1946 as a multiparty body ostensible, seeking to avoid civil war. Similarly, the united front itself was traced back to the founder of the KMT, Sun Yat-sen.

Into the united front and CPPCC were drawn the so-called democratic parties, the small middle-class and intelligentsia-based groups that had futilely attempted to become a third force during the struggle between the KMT and CCP. Not only did delegates from these parties vastly outnumber those formally assigned the CCP, but more significantly, eleven of the twenty-four ministers appointed in the new government were minor party representatives or unaffiliated "democratic personages." Although political power clearly rested in the hands of the CCP, these positions were not mere formalities. More broadly, the advice of prestigious non-Communist figures was genuinely sought throughout the early years of the PRC.

Equally significant was the moderate, conciliatory nature of the CCP blueprint for the future: the Common Program. The hallmark of this document was gradualism. Although longer-term objectives, particularly in the economic sphere, were included, the emphasis was on immediate tasks. In Zhou Enlai's words, the ultimate goals of socialism and communism were "not put . . . in writing for the time being [although] we do not deny [them]."[18] Mao even more strongly emphasized the gradual nature of the Party's program in mid-1950 when he declared, "The view . . . that it is possible to eliminate capitalism and realize socialism at an early date is wrong [and] does not tally with our national conditions."[19]

In addition to gradualism, the Common Program adopted the classic united front tactic of narrowly defining enemies as "imperialism, feudalism and bureaucratic capitalism." Policies for reasserting China's national rights and squeezing out Western enterprises were genuinely popular, although this patriotic appeal was somewhat undercut by the decision to align with the Soviet Union. "Bureaucratic capital" – the limited number of large enterprises that had been run by figures closely connected with the KMT and were now confiscated by the new state – was also a popular target, particularly among private capitalists (the "national bourgeoisie") who had suffered grievously from KMT favoritism toward well-connected firms. Finally, feudal forces were defined as landlords, who made up only 3 to 5 percent of the rural population. Not only were rich peasants excluded from the list of enemies, but the need to maintain the "rich peasant economy" became a key aspect of

18 *Selected works of Zhou Enlai*, 1.406. 19 Mao, *SW*, 5.30.

CCP rural policies. This approach further served, as Mao elaborated in early 1950, to "isolate the landlords, protect the middle peasants [and] set at rest the minds of the national bourgeoisie," which was closely tied up with the land problem.[20]

The united front was also enshrined at the level of Marxist theory. A "new democratic state" was established that was not an orthodox dictatorship of the proletariat but, instead, a "people's democratic dictatorship" in which the peasantry, petty bourgeoisie, and national bourgeoisie joined the working class as ruling classes. In adopting this concept, the CCP broke with current Soviet orthodoxy on state forms. Although Soviet theoreticians had also accepted the bourgeoisie as part of the state apparatus in the East European "people's democracies" before 1948, that stand had been reserved in conjunction with the split with Tito, and the Russians now refused to acknowledge Chinese claims. By persisting in their position until 1953–4, when CCP writers began to acknowledge the fundamental similarity of the proletarian and people's democratic dictatorships, Party leaders indicated not only the importance they attached to the united front tactic but a determination to insist on ideological as well as political independence where circumstances warranted.

Such assertions of independence notwithstanding, the Soviet influence in the general theoretical as well as specific policy sense was considerable. Various Soviet theoretical texts were widely studied in China and Lenin's New Economic Policy served as a reference for the gradualism of the new democratic economy. And in the larger political sense that state form was, of course, identical to that of the Soviet Union – the dictatorship was ultimately that of the Communist Party. For as the theory of the people's democratic dictatorship made clear, the classes making up the state were not an alliance of equals. The alliance was led by the working class – that is, its vanguard, the Party – and the other members were to be educated by the proletariat. In the case of the national bourgeoisie – a bone of contention with the Soviets – this education could be harsh indeed, since that class was described as vacillating and having an exploitative side. Initially the united front approach emphasized the role of the bourgeoisie and the vast majority of the population in building the new China, but the democratic dictatorship could always quickly redefine the political status of any segment of the "people."

Military and regional rule

The situation in 1949 guaranteed that in the first instance Communist rule would be military and decentralized. Since the newly liberated areas fell to the

20 Ibid., 24–5.

PLA and the task of eliminating bandit opposition remained, Military Control Commissions were initially established as the supreme local authority. These, however, were explicitly temporary. According to the Common Program, the duration of military control would be determined strictly according to local conditions, and it would give way to civilian authority as soon as this was feasible. Similarly, the great variations from area to area required decentralized administration because no uniform policy could apply to the whole nation. But this too was seen as transitional from the outset. For this function China was divided into six large regions (excluding Inner Mongolia and Tibet, which were administered separately). Reflecting the conditions of the period, four of these regions – the Central-South, East China, the Northwest, and the Southwest – were run by military-administrative committees, whereas North China and the Northeast were given people's governments to indicate the successful completion of the military tasks. These regional administrations, with some changes in nomenclature, remained in existence until 1954, but their powers were gradually transferred to the center as conditions allowed. Party regional bureaus and military regions existed on the same geographical bases, but these were too phased out in 1954–5.

The shift from military to civilian rule was remarkably smooth. Although the Military Control Commissions initially exercised wide powers over governmental and Party organs, their personnel were soon absorbed into the units they were sent to control. Within a matter of months the commission became a coordinating and supervisory body whose offices were largely empty of staff as administrative functions were increasingly undertaken directly by the new governments. By 1951, its functions were largely reduced to security and garrison matters as local governments now issued decrees alone. The fact that close relations had been built up between political and military figures during the prolonged revolutionary struggle undoubtedly goes far to explain the smoothness of the shift to civilian rule. But at least equally important was the clear distinction between civilian and military authority that Mao articulated in 1938: "Our principle is that the Party commands the gun, and the gun must never be allowed to command the Party."[21] This principle was reflected in appointments to the large regions; the key position of Party first secretary was held by political figures in every region except the Central-South, where Lin Biao, one of the PLA's most successful commanders and a long-standing favorite of Mao's, occupied the post. Moreover, the relatively limited degree of differentiation of political and military roles was to be significantly widened. The Common Program called for military modernization, including the formation of an air force and navy, and the Korean War provided the impetus for

21 Ibid., 2.224.

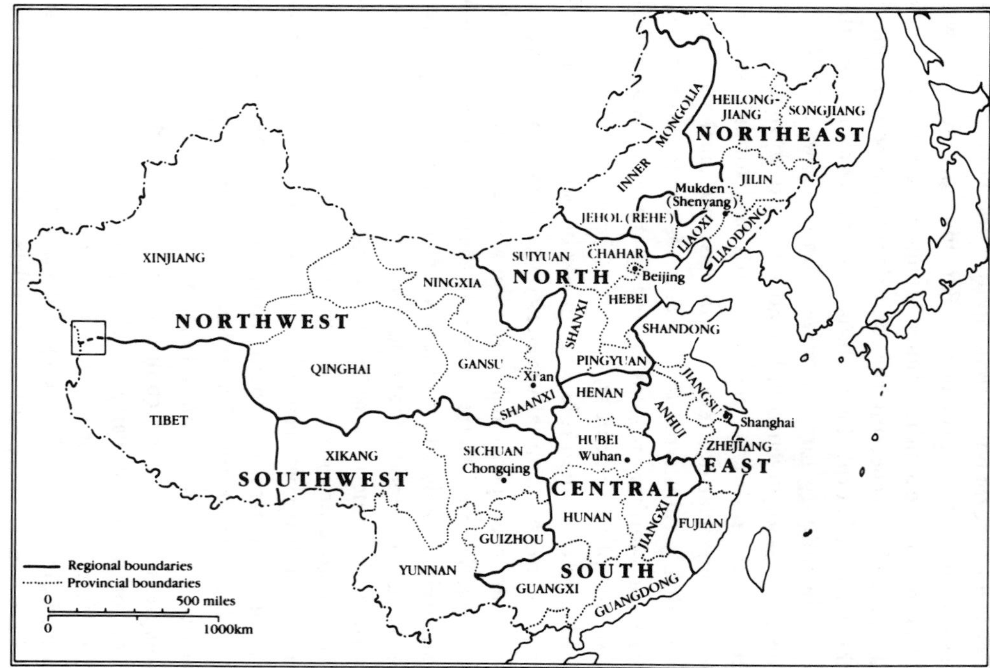

Map 2. Administrative regions, 1949–54 (Note: By the end of 1952, Chahar had been divided between Inner Mongolia, Shanxi and Hebei, and Pingyuan between Henan and Shandong. In 1954, when the administrative regions were abolished, Songjiang was incorporated into Heilongjiang, Liaodong and Liaoxi were combined to form Liaoning. Suiyuan was merged with Inner Mongolia, and Ningxia became part of Gansu. In 1955, Sikang was divided between Sichuan and Tibet, and Jehol was divided between Inner Mongolia, Liaoning and Hebei. Ningxia reappeared as the Ningxia-Hui Autonomous Region in 1958)

modernization in earnest with the help of substantial Soviet aid. Although many PLA commanders adopted civilian roles, the great bulk found ample career opportunities in an increasingly professionalized military.

Meanwhile, the powers of the regional administrations remained considerable over the 1949–52 period. This was not apparent in the strict legal sense, since they were placed directly under the Government Administrative Council or cabinet in Beijing, with no autonomous rights of their own. In fact, however, given that the fledgling governmental structure was finding its legs and had only rudimentary planning and statistical capabilities, much was necessarily left to the regions. In addition, given the vast differences in conditions and problems from area to area, central leaders remained uncertain as to exactly how much regional authority was required and allowed considerable local experimentation. The overall pattern was for the center to lay down policies in fairly general form and leave to the regions the issues of pace and means of implementation. For example, in mid-1950 the Beijing authorities passed an agrarian reform law but apparently did not establish any central monitoring body; the process of implementation was placed in the hands of land reform committees set up in each regional administration.

The powers of the regions were also reflected in the fact that initially some of the CCP's most powerful figures headed military-administrative committees and people's governments. Looking at the top elite broadly, some two-thirds of the Central Committee served outside Beijing in these years. One key sign of change was the gradual transfer of such leaders to the center as the period wore on. By 1952 the most powerful regional figures had assumed important duties in Beijing, even if they generally still continued to exercise their local powers on a concurrent basis. Moreover, as the capacities of the central bureaucracies increased and conditions in the regions became more uniform, specific powers were transferred to Beijing. Thus in March 1950 the Government Administrative Council enacted a decision unifying national financial and economic work, but in other cases, such as a November 1951 decision increasing the appointment powers of the regions, the continued need for decentralized administration was acknowledged.

Decentralized administration, of course, gave scope for the "localist" deviation of ignoring the spirit of central directives in order to further some parochial interest. Perhaps the clearest case of this in the 1949–52 period occurred with regard to land reform in the southern province of Guangdong. There local cadres carried out a milder and slower process of reform than elsewhere, resulting in higher-level criticism and eventually the displacement of key figures by new leaders sent in from the outside. But what is significant about this episode is that the main antagonists of the local cadres were less the central authorities in Beijing than the leaders of the Central-

South military-administrative committee in Wuhan. Indeed, there is little evidence to suggest regional resistance to central authority in these years, although the inevitable "errors" of the regions were criticized in Beijing. The variations that did occur were accepted by the central leaders as not only necessary but desirable under the circumstances. Basically, this meant that programs were initiated first in North and Northeast China, where conditions were more stable and organizational resources more plentiful, and extended south only as the situation allowed. The Northwest and Southwest in particular lagged in the implementation of programs, but unlike the Guangdong case this was accepted by Beijing as logical given the strong resistance of bandit forces in these regions.

The outstanding case of regional particularity was the Northeast. This had little to do with later distorted charges that Gao Gang had established an "independent kingdom" there (to be discussed later). Rather, it reflected the fact that the Northeast was the most advanced region and served as a bellwether for the rest of the country for a number of reasons. First, having benefited from industrialization under Japanese rule, the Northeast had the most developed economic base. It provided 34 percent of China's industrial output in 1949 and 52 percent in 1952. Second, by virtue of being the first region totally liberated, the Northeast could move more quickly toward comprehensive policies and was able to begin regional planning by 1950. And finally, proximity to the Soviet Union and Soviet holdings in the regional railroads and the port of Luta (Port Arthur–Dalian) combined to provide easy access to Soviet aid and influence. Thus the Northeast instituted Soviet methods of economic management, albeit with difficulty due to shortages of skilled personnel, and these methods were generally endorsed by the central leadership in Beijing for extension to China as a whole.

The model role of the Northeast, whereby policies were tested and refined there before being popularized on a nationwide basis, was not limited to the advanced industrial sector. In youth work the region in general and Harbin in particular were held up for emulation, and one of the critical mass movements of the period, the Three Antis Campaign focusing on urban corruption, was first carried out on a trial basis in the Northeast. The attitude of the central leadership toward the Northeast was summed up in an article recording impressions of the region by Song Qingling, Sun Yat-sen's widow and a leading united front figure in Peking. According to Song, China had a bright future and "our Northeast is leading the way."[22] Beijing encouraged the Northeast's trailblazing role while at the same time viewing the Northwest and Southwest as backward areas where far different policies were needed and proper.

22 *Renmin ribao* (People's daily, hereafter *RMRB*), 1 May 1951.

Land reform

The crucial task for the new liberated areas generally was land reform. To this task the CCP brought experience and personnel that were often lacking for the more complex conditions of the cities. The Party, after all, had been engaging in rural revolution for over two decades by the time the PLA crossed the Yangtze. In that time Party leaders had attempted a variety of approaches and refined a set of methods for peasant mobilization. Yet in some senses the job facing the Communists in the vast rural areas was even more difficult than that undertaken in the cities. For one thing, it was not totally clear even to top Party leaders just how applicable past experience was to the new situation. Mao called attention to the altered circumstances in early 1950: "[T]he agrarian reform in the north was carried out in wartime, with the atmosphere of war prevailing over that of agrarian reform, but now, with the fighting practically over, the agrarian reform stands out in sharp relief, and the shock to society will be particularly great!"[23]

Even more significant was the vastness of the territories now seized. Even if the CCP could have miraculously dispatched all its 4.5 million members in 1949 to these areas, the resultant cadre force would still have been inadequate for penetrating the widely dispersed peasant population. Moreover, the Communists came to the villages of the new liberated areas as outsiders with little knowledge of local conditions, carrying ideas based on quite different agricultural and ownership patterns, and often not even speaking the native dialect. Given both the sparseness of personnel and their alien status, the success of the CCP in completing land reform in areas occupied by over 90 percent of the rural population by fall 1952 is testimony to the relevance of its earlier experience and particularly to the determination of Party leaders.

The initial penetration of the countryside came in the form of PLA units that fanned out from the cities to the rural market towns and then to the villages. These troops, apart from bandit suppression, generally limited themselves to disarming the local population, carrying out security functions, and organizing village militias. In the wake of the PLA, small groups or somewhat larger work teams of cadres came to the village. Only a small proportion, perhaps 10 percent at most, were old cadres with experience in the northern agrarian struggle. The bulk was made up of students and other urban intellectuals, young rural intellectuals with family ties to landlords and rich peasants, urban unemployed, and, where available, local Communist underground workers. Extreme

23 Mao, *SW*, 5.24.

youth as well as questionable class backgrounds often characterized these political workers.

One of their earliest tasks was, with the aid of the PLA, to collect taxes to support the new regime. This undertaking was bound to create friction between cadres and peasants, as suggested by the fact that more than 3,000 cadres were killed in the first year after takeover trying to collect the grain tax. As it became apparent that the new policies were shifting the burden away from the poor to the rich, however, support was generated for the new order. Other measures undertaken by the cadres in this initial period included the organization of peasant associations, carrying out a program of rent and interest reduction, and conducting struggles against "despots" or "local bullies," in other words, the most oppressive elements of the old elite. None of these efforts went without a hitch. Despots were sometimes arbitrarily designated; peasants frequently returned rent money to landlords in secret; and by the fall of 1950 in many areas only about 20 percent of the hastily organized peasant associations were judged reliable. Indeed, in these later stages of land reform, programs often had to be repeated two or three times before success was achieved. The limitations of the entire effort were further revealed by surveys at the end of land reform showing that only 40 percent of the peasants in some areas belonged to peasant associations.

All these measures were preparatory for the main work of agrarian reform – the confiscation and redistribution of landlord land. In June 1950 the central authorities promulgated the agrarian reform law to guide this work. Reflecting Mao's views on the differences of the current situation from the wartime land reform of North China and the policy of maintaining the "rich peasant economy," the new law and Liu Shaoqi's report on it advanced an explicitly economic rationale for the program. Thus the view that land reform's main function was to relieve the poor was rejected, and "freeing the rural productive forces" and "paving the way for industrialization" were emphasized. Moreover, the law was sanguine about the ease with which landlord opposition could be overcome under peacetime conditions and insisted on political order as a prerequisite for implementation.

This analysis was, however, already being undercut by difficulties encountered in preparations for land reform in the villages of the new liberated areas. One factor was peasant uncertainty as to how far the CCP program would go, especially the concern that redistribution would affect the land of rich peasants and even middle peasants. More ominous from the CCP's perspective was the traditional power and influence of the landlords over the peasantry generally. Ordinary peasants were simply afraid to oppose the forces that had been dominant on the local scene for so long, because they had little confidence that Communist rule was irreversible. A particularly difficult problem was the blurring of class lines in the traditional village. The distinction between various better-off peasant strata and landlords was often clearer to work teams of outsiders than to local poor peasants. Also, social tensions were mitigated by traditional obligations of landlords toward peasants in hard times, as well as particularistic ties of family, local residence, and clan. All these links could be and were used by landlords to subvert the peasant associations, conceal land and other wealth, and maintain the existing power structure through secret societies and other devices.

As reports indicating the entrenched power of the existing rural social order came to the attention of responsible Party leaders in the late summer of 1950, policy began to be reconsidered. The shift to a more radical line came definitively in November and December, shortly after the Chinese intervention in Korea. Some official statements cited the Korean conflict as a justification, and certainly increased social tension and rumors of the return of the KMT were a factor. Nevertheless, the fundamental reason for the change was the great difficulties the relatively moderate program had already encountered.

As a result, the new land reform program of stepped-up implementation, an emphasis on class struggle, and mass mobilization even at the risk of some social disorder was in sharp contrast to the principles of the agrarian reform law. When Deng Zihui, a leading Central-South official who would soon become the CCP's top agricultural specialist, attacked peaceful land reform and asserted that politics must come before economics, he was in effect criticizing the official line of six months earlier. It is important to note that even so substantial a policy shift had little political fallout, as Liu Shaoqi and others who had articulated the earlier line retained their prominence. Undoubtedly this was partially due to the fact that the milder policy had been Mao's own, but it also reflected the willingness of all concerned to treat program changes as necessary adjustments in the light of new evidence rather than as issues for political advantage.

Under the new line, land reform proper was launched. The major steps were a class identification of all village inhabitants, followed by the confiscation and redistribution of landlord land and other productive property. A leading role in the process was played by work teams dispatched by county-level land reform committees, and one of their main functions was to purify the peasant associations and select activists from their midst for local leadership positions. This new leadership was predominantly drawn from the poor peasants, although official policy reserved one-third of the leading peasant association posts for middle peasants. In many areas, by virtue of their skills, middle peasants were able to dominate. In addition, the work teams sought to mobilize the entire village against the landlords through such devices as "speak bitterness" meetings and mass trials. These methods subjected the landlords to public humiliation, and the trials also resulted in the execution of members of this class on a significant scale, perhaps 1 to 2 million individuals.[24] Moreover, under the new guideline of "not correcting excesses prematurely," the aroused masses frequently engaged in unchecked outbreaks of violence and brutality against landlords that resulted in additional deaths. Although reports of peaceful land reform persisted throughout the movement, it appears that continued efforts to draw class lines and generate antagonism had a considerable effect.

As an economic reform program, land reform succeeded in redistributing about 43 percent of China's cultivated land to about 60 percent of the rural population. Poor peasants substantially increased their holdings, but middle peasants actually benefited most because of their stronger initial position. It remains debatable how much of a contribution land reform made to overall agricultural productivity. In any case, the main achievement of the movement was political. The old elite was stripped of its economic assets, some of its members were killed, and as a class it had been humiliated. The crucial fact was the old order proved powerless, and peasants could now confidently support the new system. The old village institutions of clan, temple, and secret society had been displaced by the new, which assumed their educational, mediatory and economic functions. And a new elite of village cadres from the ranks of poor and middle peasants whose horizons had been broadened by the class-oriented perspective of the CCP.

In achieving this rural revolution, the Party had used both coercive and persuasive methods. Constant propaganda on the evils of the old system and benefits of the new was undoubtedly a significant factor in winning the peasants to the CCP program, but the force used against the landlords was crucial in convincing the entire rural population where power lay. Yet as important as coercion were the tangible rewards Party policies provided for the poorer elements in the villages. A more equitable tax burden, reduced rents, and finally land – in addition to leading posts for the most active – did much to convince the peasant masses of the rightness of the Party's cause. By demonstrating its credibility during land reform as both a force to be feared and a provider of a better life, the CCP greatly enhanced its future persuasive capabilities among the peasants.

24 In the absence of official statistics it is impossible to know the numbers involved, but it appears clear that early 1950s estimates by anti-Communist sources of 14 to 15 million deaths are far too high. For a careful review of the evidence and a cautious estimate of 200,000 to 800,000 executions, see Benedict Stavis, *The politics of agricultural mechanization in China*, 25–30. A larger number is suggested by reports based on refugee interviews of a "policy to choose at least one landlord, and usually several, in virtually every village for public execution." A. Doak Barnett with Ezra Vogel, *Cadres, bureaucracy and political power in communist China*, 228.

Urban mass movements

Although land reform radically altered life in China's countryside, a series of urban mass movements left an indelible impact on the cities. The most important of these were the campaign to suppress counterrevolutionaries that was launched in February 1951 and lasted into 1953, and from fall 1951 to summer-fall 1952 the Three Antis Campaign against corrupt cadres, the Five Antis drive against the hitherto respected national bourgeoisie, and the thought reform campaign aimed at the intellectuals. All these movements were extremely intense and generated considerable tension and apprehension in society. As in the countryside, official violence was used on a substantial scale, particularly in the counterrevolutionaries campaign and to a far lesser degree in the Three and Five Antis campaigns.[25] In addition, intense psychological pressure was brought to bear by various measures, including forced confessions in small groups and mass trials attended by tens of thousand (and broadcast to millions). This not only fostered a climate of distrust that broke down established personal relationships, it also resulted in large numbers of suicides – possibly on the order of several hundred thousand.[26] These campaigns indicated to broad sections of society the full extent of the Party's aims for social transformation. As the emphasis shifted from reassurance to tightening control, many groups that had hitherto been left basically alone were now drawn into the vortex of directed struggle. By the end of 1952 the CCP had become, for the majority of China's urban population, a force to be reckoned with.

All these campaigns were launched after the Chinese entry into the Korean War in late 1950, and their intensity was undoubtedly linked to Korea. Party leaders saw a genuine need for vigilance, given not only the danger of American attack but also the possibility of KMT efforts to return to the mainland. In any case, KMT sabotage operations were real, and dissident elements were encouraged by the potential opportunities created by the Korean involvement. The general level of social tension was further raised by

25 Again, in the absence of precise official statistics, the number of executions cannot be known. But the primarily urban campaign against counterrevolutionaries may have resulted in as many as 500,000 to 800,000 deaths (see Stavis, *The politics of agricultural mechanization*, 29). The matter is obscure, since these figures are based on a 1957 reference by Mao to counterrevolutionaries who had been liquidated, but from the context it is impossible to tell whether the people in question were the targets of this particular campaign or a more general category including the victims of land reform and other movements.

26 The main sources of the scope of suicides are refugee accounts. Chow Ching-wen, *Ten years of storm: The true story of the communist regime in China*, 115, 133, estimates that more than 500,000 people committed suicide during the suppression of counterrevolutionaries and another 200,000 plus during the Three and Five Antis movements. Although these estimates may be exaggerated, it is clear from official sources that suicides were a significant phenomenon.

a campaign directed at all groups to "resist America and aid Korea" launched in late fall 1950. The shift in leadership attitudes at the time of the Korean intervention is indicated in Mao's comments on counter-revolutionaries. In late September 1950, shortly before the decision to intervene, Mao declared, "It is imperative that we do not kill even a single agent"; by the start of 1951 he argued that "we must firmly kill all those reactionary elements who deserve to be killed."[27]

But although the Korean War undoubtedly contributed to the change in attitude and probably made the various campaigns harsher than they would have been otherwise, in another sense Party leaders used the Korean situation to press ahead on tasks that would have been undertaken anyway. Measures to deal with counterrevolutionaries had been drafted before Korea, and the vacillating bourgeoisie and Western-oriented intellectuals had clearly been targeted for ideological transformation. Indeed, the most significant campaigns started in the fall of 1951, a year after the Korean involvement, and Mao subsequently indicated that internal considerations were primary by observing that only "after the completion of agrarian reform [were we] able to launch the 'Three Antis' and 'Five Antis' campaigns."[28]

The suppression of counterrevolutionaries movement was aimed at spies and others engaged in active resistance to the new regime. High on the list of those under attack were former members of the KMT and KMT-linked organizations, as well as secret society leaders. The definition of "counterrevolutionary," however, was extremely broad, and in implementing the campaign it appears that not only active opponents but also genuinely popular local figures who had the potential to become alternative leaders were affected. In the conduct of the movement, the CCP displayed a conscious effort to avoid Soviet methods of public security work. Although in many respects the drive was a classic police effort marked by midnight arrests, Mao's directives emphasized a uniquely Chinese approach. First, there was an effort to secure mass participation in the process of uncovering counterrevolutionaries and a sensitivity to the need to avoid offending public opinion by excesses; to this end non-Party personages were invited to participate on committees overseeing the movement. Even more important was Mao's insistence on Party committee authority over all public security work. In direct contrast to Stalinist practice, where the secret police were virtually an independent hierarchy capable of terrorizing the Party, Mao emphasized precise control over counterrevolutionary matters by higher-level Party organs.

27 "Comments on the work of suppressing and liquidating counterrevolutionaries" (1950–1), in *Miscellany,* 1.6.

28 "Summing-up speech at 6th expanded plenum of 7th CCP Central Committee" (September 1955), in *Miscellany,* 1.16.

The general public seemingly found the counterrevolutionaries campaign frightening but understandable, especially at a time of external threat. The tree interrelated campaigns of 1951–2, however, came as a rude awakening to groups who had up to then received mild and even supportive treatment from the CCP. The key targets of the Three Antis Campaign were urban cadres, especially those in financial and economic departments, who had become involved in corruption as a result of their dealings with the bourgeoisie. Although these individuals included some relatively high-ranking Communists (although no one of Central Committee or ministerial rank), the vast majority were either retained personnel or new cadres whose commitment to the Communist cause had always been suspect. The Five Antis Campaign was directed explicitly at lawbreaking capitalists, particularly large capitalists, who allegedly engaged in a whole range of economic crimes and defrauded the state and public, but its larger target was the national bourgeoisie as a class. And although thought reform focused on higher-level intellectuals who assertedly aided "American cultural imperialism," the more general objective was to weaken the influence of all intellectual currents that strayed from the CCP's version of Marxism-Leninism.

What was being attacked in the largest sense was a whole complex of urban non-Communist values that had hitherto been tolerated. Many cadres, taking their lead from official policy encouraging the bourgeoisie, had come to regard capitalists as progressive and capable members of society. Capitalists, for their part, hoped to continue both their business practices and well-to-do style of life. Finally, leading intellectuals valued independent thinking and resisted being pushed into a Marxist straitjacket.

The overall effect of the three movements was to bring these elements to heel. This had several aspects. Direct punishment of the most serious offenders plus the enormous psychological pressures brought to bear destroyed the self-confidence of the concerned groups. Moreover, these pressures undermined existing patterns of social relations; *quanxi* – that is, personal relations based on family, school, or workplace ties – could no longer guarantee protection against the demands of the state. Related to this was the success of the Party in discrediting these groups in the eyes of others who traditionally had had submissive attitudes toward them. Thus workers in small enterprises who had previously accepted the paternalism of their employers now began to adopt official class struggle attitudes.

Organizationally, the control of the bourgeoisie over their enterprises was weakened by both the establishment of new trade union organs and the purging of existing unions that had often been run by friends and relations of the capitalists. Of critical importance was the recruitment of a new elite for lower-level positions in economic enterprises and government. As retained personnel and tainted new cadres were weeded out, their positions and others opened up by economic expansion were filled by worker activists who had emerged in the course of the Three and Five Antis campaigns or earlier. To a substantial degree, the attack on retained personnel was made possible by the availability of workers trained for administrative tasks in the preceding year who were now promoted to more responsible posts, and the campaign itself generated large numbers of new cadres ostensibly loyal to the CCP program. Given the continuing need for the managerial and intellectual skills of existing groups, the change was not as dramatic as in the countryside, but China's cities as well as villages saw the emergence of new elite elements in these years.

Finally, the Three and Five Antis campaigns had an important economic impact. Apart from generating substantial funds for investment and development through fines and back taxes, the movements greatly enhanced state control over private enterprises through new loans and government contracts that capitalists found necessary in their financially weakened state. Moreover, these toughened external controls were now accompanied by internal controls. A key measure was that businesses with heavy fines to pay would meet their obligations by selling stock to the state and creating joint public-private enterprises – a process that resulted in sending state cadres to assume leading positions in the concerned firms. Together with the strengthened trade unions, the setting up of Party branches in many large and medium-sized enterprises, and especially the vast amounts of information gathered during the investigation of capitalists' "crimes," this now gave the authorities a much greater knowledge of the internal workings of the private economic sphere. As a result, CCP leaders had achieved a position where planned economic development was genuinely feasible.

SOCIALIST CONSTRUCTION AND TRANSFORMATION, 1953–6

On the basis of the substantially increased political control resulting from the various mass campaigns in rural and urban areas, the PRC entered a new phase of socialist construction and transformation in 1953. In that year, nationwide economic planning began. At first, due to China's primitive planning and statistical capabilities, the demands of the Korean War, and apparent delays in negotiations with the Soviet Union for economic aid, only annual plans were possible. But with the Korean War and Soviet aid negotiations both concluded in mid-1953, more comprehensive planning could be started. Finally, in mid-1955 a first FYP for the entire 1953–7 period was approved.

With planned construction went socialist transformation – the change from private to state and collective ownership in agriculture, handicrafts, and capitalist industry and commerce. A new emphasis on transformation came with the formulation of the "general line for the transition to socialism" in mid-1953 and its public announcement in October. In some respects this general line reflected continuity with the preceding period. First, its hallmark was gradualism; both industrialization and transformation would take place over a fairly long period of about fifteen years in a step-by-step manner. Also, the practice of the general line was still within the framework of the united front. The national bourgeoisie in particular would continue to play a vital role. The initial stage of transition would be "state capitalism," where the private sector was increasingly linked to the state sector, but capitalists would still retain about one-quarter of the profits from their enterprises. Given the nature of the CCP's united front policies, however, the process of transformation naturally contained threatening aspects for the bourgeoisie, albeit in muted form. As Liu Shaoqi put it in September 1954, "The idea that there is no longer class struggle in our country is completely wrong [but] the aim [of restricting capitalist exploitation] can be achieved by peaceful means."[29]

Despite its continuities, the general line meant a somewhat more radical policy, reflected in the concept of a transition to socialism rather than New Democracy. The politics of its adoption in 1953, furthermore, indicated differences within the leadership going back several years over precisely how much emphasis to place on reassuring key groups in society and how much on controlling and transforming them. Although Mao does not appear to have taken quite so individual an initiative as in the Korean War, agricultural cooperativization, and Hundred Flowers decisions, the Chairman now played a major role in shifting the emphasis more decisively to the side of transformation. At an important financial and economic work conference in summer 1953, Mao addressed a number of issues, including concessions to rich peasants and hesitations in developing socialized agriculture. But the sharpest issue, which became entangled in the Gao Gang affair (discussed later), was the new tax system introduced by Minister of Finance Bo Yibo in December 1952 that lightened the tax load on private capitalists. This, Mao declared, was based on "bourgeois ideas which are favorable to capitalism and harmful to socialism."[30]

The attack on Bo served to warn others of like views of the need to step up the process of change. This warning was effective without being disruptive, since the policy shift called for was relatively moderate, and the Chairman

29 *Collected works of Liu Shao-ch'i 1945–1957*, 292–3. 30 Mao, *SW*, 5.104.

emphasized the need to guard against left as well as right deviations. Moreover, the handling of Bo's case was an instance of limiting elite conflict in the interests of Party unity. At the conference Mao declared that Bo's error was not a mistake in line and appealed for unity. And although Bo stepped down as minister of finance, in little more than a year he was again appointed to one of the PRC's leading economic posts.

By 1953 the CCP had amassed substantial resources on the basis of which socialist construction and transformation could begin. In economic terms, 70 to 80 percent of heavy industry and 40 percent of light industry were state owned in late 1952. State trading agencies and cooperatives handled more than 50 percent of total business turnover, and government leverage over the remaining sectors had increased due to the development of joint firms and revamped trade unions. Organizationally, in addition to the large numbers of cadres and activists who had emerged from training programs and mass movements, the CCP had been strengthed as a result of a "Party rectification and Party building" movement begun in 1951 that would conclude in early 1954. This campaign for reform and recruitment weeded out about 10 percent of CCP members (some 580,000 individuals) who were either tainted by ties to enemy classes or simply lacked commitment to or understanding of Party programs, and at the same time in relatively cautious manner recruited about 1.28 million new members, to bring total membership to 6.5 million at the end of 1953.

In another organizational move, by late 1952 the CCP had expanded its network to cover most elements of the urban population and part of the peasantry as well. In addition to the impact made by the campaigns of 1951–2, the Party extended its control to the urban grass roots by developing residents' committees on a street-by-street basis, a process that was finally formalized in 1954. At the same time, the articulation of bureaucratic "units" (*danwei*) further enhanced the CCP's organizational sway in the cities. The *danwei* became a potent force for political control both by providing the framework for work, residence, and social intercourse for most employees in official organizations and by establishing regular political rituals involving all unit members in directed activities such as the study of documents and mutual criticism in small groups.

Moreover, "mass organizations" originally organized as national bodies in 1949 to educate and mobilize major population groups had taken on substantial proportions. By 1953, the New Democratic Youth League had grown to 9 million members, the trade unions numbered 12 million, and the women's federation at least formally enrolled 76 million. Although these and other mass organizations were often passive in their actual activities, they nevertheless represented an impressive framework for providing contact with Party policies and some sense of popular participation. Such organizational scope with "the great majority . . . belong[ing] to some organization," Mao noted in 1955, had never happened in thousands of years. But as a result, he claimed, it had changed the oft-lamented Chinese condition of "being like loose sand" into national unity.[31]

In focusing these resources on economic development, the CCP won genuine support from a people attracted by the promise of both improved living conditions and national glory. Within leadership circles there was unanimity that *planned* construction was the only acceptable method – not only ideologically preferred but more efficient than "chaotic" capitalist development. One important consequence of the emphasis on planning was that it created a critical link between economic objectives and social transformation. The projected change in ownership patterns not only expropriated suspect classes, it gave the state the direct control over economic resources without which planning would be ineffective. Thus, although arguments often raged over the precise nature of that link, there was fundamental consensus on socializing not only the modern sector but also agriculture, since, in the words of the Chairman of the State Planning Commission, Li Fuchun: "Socialism cannot be built on the basis of a small peasant economy; it must have a foundation of large scale industry and large scale collective farming."[32] Clearly there was no basic contradiction between economic and political objectives for CCP leaders as the first FYP unfolded.

Another consequence of the planning ethos was the push for regularization in all spheres of life. At the overall institutional level this was manifested in the 1953–4 elections for a National People's Congress and the adoption by that Congress when it met in September 1954 of a formal state constitution. Administratively, regularization meant centralization. As the State Planning Commission and new economic ministries were created in the latter half of 1952, various regional powers were reduced and others placed directly under central authority. Then, in 1954–5 the regional administrations and parallel Party and military bodies were abolished on the grounds of incompatibility with the needs of planned construction. Given the long buildup of increased central control, this explanation is convincing, although there are indications that the timing may have been influenced by the Gao Gang affair. More broadly, regularization affected a whole spate of efforts to codify administrative practice, organizational structures, and cadre recruitment, training, and wages. By 1955, new tables of organization appeared to standardize previ-

31 Ibid., 173–74.

32 "Report on the First Five-Year Plan for development of the national economy of the People's Republic of China in 1953–1957" (5–6 July 1955), in *Communist China 1955–1959: Policy documents with analysis*, 47.

ously diverse administrative demarcations, staff offices were created to coordinate the work of related bureaus, new record-keeping and accounting practices were introduced to provide a basis for comprehensive planning, cadre recruitment procedures completed the transition from ad hoc training classes and personal introductions to reliance on the regular school system and formalized assessments, and the previous uncoordinated mix of cash wages and supplies gave way to fixed, highly articulated salary scales for various categories of state employees. A particularly significant development was a series of military professionalization measures in 1955, including the introduction of insignia, ranks, and wage scales that significantly altered the informal and egalitarian traditions of the PLA. Clearly the new planned society contained elements at variance with the CCP's revolutionary history, but there is little evidence that in those days of high expectations Party leaders were particularly concerned about the discrepancies.

The start of planned economic construction also deepened the impact of the Soviet model; as Mao put it in early 1953: "There must be a great nationwide upsurge of learning from the Soviet Union to build our country."[33] The emulation of Soviet methods, study of Soviet theory, placing Soviet experts in key ministerial, enterprise, military, and scientific and educational advisory posts, dispatching Chinese students and specialists to Russia, and publication of large numbers of translated Soviet texts had been part of the Chinese scene since 1949–50 or earlier, but the arrival of even primitive central planning significantly enhanced the importance of these features. The crucial element, of course, was the Stalinist economic strategy of high rates of reinvestment, emphasis on capital-intensive high-technology projects, agriculture as a major source of funds for industrial growth, and priority investment in heavy industry. Although there were continual debates over the details of the plan and allocation of resouces within it, when the first FYP was belatedly formulated in 1955, it closely followed the Soviet model in principle. Also of great importance was Soviet financial and technical aid for the large-scale modern plants that were the core of the plan.

The great weight of the model and the assistance of the Soviet government, however, did not eliminate independent thinking in China. Some ministries discussed problems caused by too hastily adopting the Soviet model, and in areas where Chinese officials felt particularly competent they were known to reject Soviet advice. Nevertheless, the trend was the other way among many PRC administrators and specialists dealing with the modern sector. As Mao complained subsequently: " 'Dogmatism' took hold in

33 "Closing speech of the fourth session of the [C]PPCC" (7 February 1953), in K. Fan, ed., *Mao Tse-tung and Lin Piao: Post-revolutionary writings,* 102.

many fields: It didn't matter whether [a Soviet] article was correct or not, the Chinese listened all the same and respectfully obeyed."[34] In the 1953–5 period, however, there was little sign of effort from the top to correct this state of affairs.

The Gao Gang affair

Soon after socialist construction and transformation were launched, the CCP suffered its only major leadership purge of the 1949–57 period. The ousting of Gao Gang and Rao Shushi from key Party and state posts in early 1954, followed by their formal expulsion from the CCP a year later, marked not only the most serious high-level conflict of the period but one different in character from other instances of elite friction. The principals were among the most powerful in the regime: Gao was a Politburo member, head of the State Planning Commission, and the top Party, government, and military official of the Northeast region; Rao was director of the Central Committee's organization department, which controlled high-level appointments, a Planning Commission member, and the leading Party and government figure in East China. Seven lesser officials from the Northeast and East China were denounced with them, and Cultural Revolution sources linked about a dozen high-ranking central and local leaders to the affair with varying degrees of credibility.

The Gao–Rao affair has long been one of the most obscure chapters in CCP history. Contemporary sources were relatively limited in number and content, and the case received only minor attention during the Cultural Revolution. In the absence of extensive information, various analysts have advanced speculative interpretations emphasizing such factors as possible policy differences, regionalism, Gao's alleged ties to the Soviet Union, and Mao's health.[35] Although all these explanations have some relevance, none is adequate. Fortunately, new data have become available in the post-Mao period that allow a more detailed and accurate understanding of the political maneuvering that briefly threatened the Party's hardwon unity.[36]

34 "Talks at the Chengtu conference" (March 1958), in Schram, ed., *Mao unrehearsed*, 98.

35 The most comprehensive account of the Gao–Rao case is Frederick C. Teiwes, *Politics and purges in China: Rectification and the decline of Party norms 1950–1965*, ch. 5, which emphasizes Mao's deteriorating health as the key circumstantial factor influencing Gao Gang. Other interpretations include: Franz Schurmann, *Ideology and organization in communist China*, ch. 4 (on policy differences); John W. Lewis, *Chinese Communist Party leadership and the succession to Mao Tse-tung: An appraisal of tensions* (on regionalism); and Mineo Nakajima, "The Kao Kang affair and Sino-Soviet relations," *Review*, March 1977 (on the Soviet connection).

36 The major post-Mao sources relied on in the following interpretation are: Chen Shihui, "Guanyu fandui Gao Gang, Rao Shushi fandang yinmo huodong de wenti" (Questions concerning opposition to the anti-Party conspiratorial activities of Gao Gang and Rao Shushi); Zhengzhi xueyuan Zhonggong

The essence of the Gao–Rao affair was their attempt to oust Liu Shaoqi and Zhou Enlai from the number two and number three positions in the CCP. The primary target was Liu, who as the generally acknowledged successor to Mao, was the main obstacle to Gao's ambitions. Although there were maneuvers at formal Party meetings, Gao and Rao basically operated outside established bodies and conducted private negotiations with some of the regime's highest figures. As the 1955 official verdict on the case declared, their activities could fairly be described as "conspiratorial" and as an "unprincipled" effort to grasp enhanced personal power.

The immediate context for these activities, which were primarily carried out from June to December 1953, included both the process of centralization and regularization then underway and the debates surrounding the implementation of the new general line. The former consideration involved changes of institutional structure, and thus of personnel to staff new structures, to meet the needs of planned economic construction. In addition to a new state structure, consideration was being given to holding an Eighth Party Congress, which would require electing a new Party leadership. The possibilities for reallocation of power inherent in this situation were intensified by the end of the year when Mao, who wished to lighten his responsibilities, raised the question of dividing the leadership into two fronts, with others taking over some of his duties. The second matter, debates relating to the general line, meant that policy discussions were taking place in a potentially divisive political climate. Although the policy issues were in fact comparatively narrow, the opportunity was there for ambitious politicians to attempt to enlarge differences into questions of line.

If these circumstances opened up the possibility of conflict, the key factor in Gao Gang's bid for power was his assessment of Mao's attitude. Although Gao was reportedly reluctant to leave his regional power base,[37] when he arrived in Beijing in late 1952 he both assumed impressive new powers as head of the Planning Commission and resumed his close personal relationship

dangshi jiaoyanshi (Political academy CCP history teaching and research office), *Zhongguo gongchandang liushinian dashi jianjie* (Brief introduction to major events in the CCP's sixty years), 297–400, 405–9; *Deng Xiaoping wenxuan* (Selected works of Deng Xiaoping), 257–58; Liao Kai-lung, "Historical experiences," *Issues & Studies*, October 1981, 79; and discussions with Chinese officials and scholars.

37 The monopoly of regional power is the key to the official charge that Gao had set up an "independent kingdom" in the Northeast. Gao reportedly sought to place all power in the region in the hands of his close personal followers and deny real authority to other officials such as the second-ranking Party secretary, Lin Feng. This did not mean that the Northeast took an independent policy line from the center; in fact, the Northeast vigorously implemented central directives and was in turn repeatedly praised for its trailblazing efforts in carrying out new policies. The prompt implementation of central policy notwithstanding, Mao later cited Gao's exploitation of shortcomings in regional administration as one reason for subsequently abolishing the regions. Mao, *SW*, 5. 293–4. See Teiwes, *Politics and purges*, 184–91, for further analysis of the regionalism issue.

with Mao. Gao had been on friendly terms with the Chairman in Yan'an. Mao respected Gao as a founder of the Northwest revolutionary base area and felt he was a local cadre with a good grasp of grass-roots reality. The two also hit it off personally. After 1949, Mao was further impressed by Gao's achievements in the Northeast and considered him a capable leader who could strengthen the work of the CC. This favorable disposition toward Gao coincided with a certain dissatisfaction toward the work of Liu and Zhou – especially their advocacy of greater caution in both economic construction and the development of agricultural cooperatives than Mao desired. Mao expressed this dissatisfaction in several private talks with Gao in the first part of 1953. Whatever the Chairman's intentions, Gao took this as a sign of trust and an opportunity to move against Liu and Zhou.

Another factor apparently feeding Gao's ambitions was the initial outcome of the post-Stalin succession in the Soviet Union, where the relatively youthful Malenkov assumed the reins of leadership despite the claims of the more senior Molotov and Kaganovich. By analogy, Gao seemingly reasoned, he could supersede Liu and Zhou, who represented a slightly older generation of CCP leaders. By this point Gao had already gained the support of Rao Shushi, who became persuaded that Gao's rising status was a prelude to his supplanting Liu as successor. Rao did not want to back the wrong horse, despite his own historical links to Liu. In fact, historical connections enhanced Rao's receptiveness to Gao's blandishments, since Rao's deputy in the Central Committee organization department, An Ziwen, had much closer ties to Liu than he had. Rao apparently felt he was not in full control of his new post, and this facilitated his willingness to make common cause with Gao Gang against Liu Shaoqi.

Although the official verdict in both 1955 and the post-Mao period claimed that the Gao–Rao conspiracy lacked any policy content, this was not strictly the case. Gao and Rao did not present any comprehensive policy program of their own, but they did use the debates surrounding the new general line to attack the policies of others. The key instance was the attack on Bo Yibo's tax policies at the June–August 1953 finance and economic conference. Gao Gang initiated the attack by likening Bo's policies to Bukharin's peaceful transformation. Mao seemingly was impressed with Gao's theoretical sophistication and joined the criticism. The Chairman, however, was unwilling to press the case to the extremes implied by Gao and by the end of the conference concluded that there was no mistake in line and that it was imperative to safeguard Party unity. It is unclear, however, whether Mao at this stage realized the full implications of Gao's activities. By attacking Bo, much as was the case when Rao attacked An Ziwen at the subsequent September–October organization work conference, Gao was actually aiming at his patron, Liu Shaoqi. In any case, Mao seems to have contented himself with the appeal to unity and did not directly criticize Gao Gang.

Gao Gang also sought to bolster his position by cultivating good relations with the Soviet Union. As Party leader in the Northeast Gao naturally had close working relations with Soviet personnel, but these extended into gray areas. He apparently developed particularly close ties with Soviet consular personnel in the Northeast and with Kosygin, who was dispatched on business from Moscow. In discussions with these people, Gao pictured Liu and Zhou as anti-Soviet in contrast to himself. Subsequently, once he had already been defeated politically, revelations of these links were used to build opinion against Gao. But although his relations were regarded as abnormal, they were not seen as equivalent to working for the Soviet Union. Contrary to some Western interpretations, which saw Gao as Stalin's agent in the Northeast, Gao apparently was attempting to bank on Soviet support in any fluid situation that might arise during his bid for enhanced power. Given the economic, political, and ideological ties with the Soviet Union in this period, a favorable attitude on Moscow's part could be a political plus. But it was a dubious game given the strong commitment to national independence among CCP leaders – a commitment none felt stronger than Mao. In the event, Gao's cultivation of the Soviets did not play a minor part in his conspiratorial activities or his fall, but it was nevertheless part of the overall design.

More important than criticism of the performance of Liu, Zhou, and their allies or the pursuit of Soviet support was Gao's effort to win backing for his cause by promising posts in a new Gao regime to high-level leaders, and by fanning resentment on the part of leaders whose revolutionary careers had centered in the Red Army or rural base areas against specialists in white area work behind enemy lines, such as Liu and Zhou. The latter consideration seemingly had considerable force in the context of the forthcoming reallocation of posts. The opportunity was presented to Gao by a draft list for the new Politburo prepared by An Ziwen, supposedly without the knowledge of Liu Shaoqi, which shortchanged military leaders and gave disproportionate prominence to white area figures. The key distortion, from the point of view of military cadres, was that An's list included his white area colleague Bo Yibo's but not the great military leader Lin Biao. Although such cadres could accept Liu Shaoqi's position as number two, given his many contributions to the revolutionary cause, they were disgruntled at the prominence given to Peng Zhen and Bo at the expense of leading PLA figures.

Armed with this issue, Gao Gang headed south on summer holidays to recruit additional adherents to his cause. Already having secured East China through Rao Şhushi, as well as his own Northeast, he calculated he could win over all of the six large administrative regions except North China, where

Peng Zhen and Bo Yibo ruled. In his approaches Gao apparently claimed that he had Mao's blessing and this – together with the resentment generated by An's list paid dividends. Both Lin Biao of the Central-South and Peng Dehuai of the Northwest expressed agreement with Gao's views on reorganizing the Party and state and reallocating leading positions, although this apparently was the extent of their involvement. Gao was less successful in his dealings with two other key leaders, Deng Xiaoping and Chen Yun. Although Deng, the key figure in the Southwest, apparently found Gao's entreaties compelling enough to enter "formal negotiations" (*zhengshi tanpan*), he ultimately rejected them on the basis that Liu's role in the Party "was the outcome of historical development."[38] Chen Yun, the center's economic overlord who was offered a Party vice chairmanship upon Gao's return to Beijing seemingly was even less receptive than Deng.

The turning point came when Chen and Deng, apparently operating independently, brought Gao's actions to Mao's attention. Whatever the Chairman's intentions had been in his personal conversations with Gao at the start of the year, he now expressed anger at Gao's "underground activities." The culmination of the affair came at a December Politburo meeting when Mao proposed that he go on holiday and that, in accord with existing practice, Liu would take charge in his absence. Mao had been planning a holiday before Gao's maneuvers had been revealed to him for several reasons – poor health, a desire to reflect on the new state constitution, and depression over the death of one of his sons in Korea. But at the Politburo meeting he drew out Gao, who now proposed leadership by rotation rather than entrusting power to Liu and indicated his own desire to be Party vice chairman, general secretary, or premier. Mao then did what he had failed to do at the finance and economic conference – he criticized Gao sharply. This, together with carrying out his holiday plans and entrusting Liu with the organization of the February 1954 plenum, which would emphasize the theme of Party unity, effectively squashed the plans of Gao Gang and Rao Shushi.

Unity was indeed emphasized in the winding up of the affair. Mao apparently hoped Gao could be saved for important future duties, but Gao attempted suicide during the February plenum and eventually succeeded in August 1954. Lin Biao and Peng Dehuai were not punished for their complicity; instead, their assertions that they had been deceived by Gao into believing he had Mao's support was deemed sufficient explanation.[39] Moreover, the need to repair the damage to unity which had been created by An Ziwen's list

38 *Deng Xiaoping wenxuan*, 257.

39 Tensions continued to linger under the surface, however. A major reason for Liu Shaoqi's strong support of Mao against Peng Dehuai at Lushan in 1959 was Liu's bitterness over Peng's role in the Gao–Rao affair.

was recognized and Lin Biao, along with Deng Xiaoping, was raised to Politburo status in 1955.

Several lessons can be drawn from the Gao–Rao affair that at once indicate the importance and the fragility of Party unity. In political terms, Gao Gang could not expect to match the enormous strength of Liu and Zhou. These leaders could not be easily categorized as white area figures; their careers intertwined with crucial experiences throughout the entire history of the CCP, including armed struggle in base areas. Indeed, Liu and particularly Zhou had substantially broader contacts among PLA leaders than Gao Gang, who had played no role in the pre-1935 southern phase of the revolution. Yet this inherent weakness notwithstanding, Gao managed to win the support of four of China's six large administrative areas. Party unity started to fray at the possibility of the military being shortchanged in the new leadership structure. The commitment to Party unity on the part of Chen Yun and Deng Xiaoping, on the other hand, played a crucial role in derailing Gao's plans. These men valued the Party rules, which rejected secret factional activities of the type engaged in by Gao and Rao, and they feared the damage to the Party if those activities succeeded.

But undoubtedly the greatest lesson of the affair was the crucial role of Mao. The Chairman's private statements to Gao, whatever their intent, fueled Gao's ambitions and launched his activities. The claim that Mao supported his initiatives was enough to give pause to or gain support from those approached by Gao Gang. Finally, when Mao confronted Gao, the conspiracy collapsed with virtually no resistance. Mao emerged from the Gao Gang–Rao Shushi case as the crucial support of leadership stability. But the overall course of the affair also indicated his potential to threaten Party unity.

The constitutional and institutional pattern

In September 1954 the PRC replaced the temporary arrangements made in 1949 by adopting a state constitution. Strictly speaking, this was not a permanent constitution; it was designed to meet the needs of the period of transition to socialism. But given the long-term nature of that period, it was expected to last many years. Continuity with the past was explicitly asserted: "This constitution is based on the Common Program of the CPPCC of 1949, and this is an advance upon it."[40] In addition to the united front stance of the Common Program, there were some basic structural similarities with the institutional arrangements laid down in 1949 by the Organic law of the

40 "Constitution of the People's Republic of China" (20 September 1954), in Harold C. Hinton, ed., *The People's Republic of China, 1949–1979: A documentary survey*, 1.99.

Central People's Government. Those arrangements, however, had been comparatively skimpy, and the constitution laid out a much more articulated state structure. The major changes reflected the difference between the unsettled conditions of 1949 and the new period of planned development. The system of people's congresses promised in 1949, theoretically the highest organs of state power, was now formally established.

Of greater political significance, the shift from military to civilian rule that had taken place in the first few years was also formalized. Thus under the Organic Law, the military, in the form of the People's Revolutionary Military Council, had stood equal to the cabinet and directly under the Central People's Government Council. Now, however, a Ministry of Defense was established and placed under the new cabinet, the State Council, on a par with thirty-four other ministries and commissions.

Although Mao claimed in mid-1954 that the constitution was "based mainly on our own experience but has drawn upon what is good in the constitutions of the Soviet Union and the [East European] People's Democracies,"[41] in fact the document basically followed the pattern of the Stalin constitution of 1936. The basic structure consisted of "elected" congresses from the local to national levels, which theoretically appointed government administrative bodies at each level. These administrative organs were legally responsible to the congresses that appointed them and to higher-level administrative organs. In addition, an ostensibly independent judicial system of courts and people's procurators was set up.

All of this, as well as a similar list of citizens' rights and duties, was found in the 1936 Soviet document. Of the differences that did exist, some – such as the Chinese failure to guarantee the universal, equal, and direct suffrage by secret ballot of the Soviet electoral system – were attributed to the fact that conditions lagged behind those in Russia and, indeed, often reflected provisions of the earlier 1924 Soviet constitution. In a few major instances, however, Chinese leaders clearly rejected Soviet practice as unsuitable. For example, a few state bodies and offices had no Soviet counterpart. The most significant was the creation of a clearly separate and highly visible state chairman – in the event, Mao – rather than simply relying on top officials of the congress system (the Supreme Soviet in the USSR) to perform the functions of a head of state. In this CCP leaders were adopting imperial practice and, like the KMT before them, clearly felt that Chinese tradition required such an office.

Another area where the new constitution deliberately parted from Soviet precedent was in discarding the fiction that ethnic minority areas could

41 Mao, *SW*, 5.143.

secede. The PRC was declared a "unified multinational state" where "autonomous" minority regions were inalienable parts of the national territory. In the Soviet Union, the "right" to secede went back to the postrevolutionary civil war, when it was a useful weapon against White and foreign forces who temporarily held most minority areas. In addition, the fact that over the following decades minorities grew to half of the Soviet population undoubtedly made any withdrawal of the right unseemly as well as unnecessary. In China, the problem is intrinsically less threatening, since minorities make up only 6 percent of the population. But it is a key issue, nevertheless, since minority areas occupy 60 percent of national territory, including most strategic borderlands, contain extensive mineral and pastoral resources, and had been a major preoccupation of successive pre-Communist regimes.

Historically, the Han (ethnic Chinese) had explained their sphere of control outward from the North China plain by absorbing or pushing back the minority "barbarian" peoples that stood in their path. How to deal with these barbarians thus became an important question of imperial policy. The thrust of this policy was minimal control; it aimed at little more than nonaggression and securing a vague commitment of loyalty to the imperial court while interfering as little as possible in local ways of life. In contrast, the KMT regime, influenced by Western concepts of nationalism, followed a much more assimilationist approach denying minority autonomy, but the inherent weakness of that regime forced it to compromise or resulted in policies that alienated minorities without being able to impose domination.

When the CCP came to power, it had an incentive to avoid the counterproductive practices of the KMT, but its long-term goals required more than the minimal imperial policies. As in other matters, CCP leaders saw Soviet practice as the appropriate model. Although the right to secede was not taken over (indeed, it had been discarded as early as 1938, probably in response to the minority hostility that the Communists encountered on the Long March and the encouragement of independence movements by foreign powers), the basic Soviet institutional device of autonomous areas became the basis of Chinese policy. Administrative subdivisions from the provincial to autonomous village (*xiang*) level were given autonomous status, often using traditional minority nomenclature; native languages and cultures were developed in these autonomous areas; and minority figures were placed in official positions, although ultimate power remained with the normally Han Party leaders.

Although the autonomy principle has been a constant of the Soviet model, the content given it by the CCP reflected more the benign Soviet approach of the 1920s than the assimilationist approach of the Stalinist period after 1929. Thus the emphasis was on "nationalization" – a process that involved not only the adoption of national minority forms but also the recruitment of minority cadres, efforts to train Han cadres in local ways, and genuine cooperation with the "patriotic upper strata" – traditional leaders who had both local prestige and expertise and thus could guarantee smooth relations with the populace.

These policies were linked to others that sought gradually to deepen CCP control – the development of transport and communications links with Han areas, Han emigration to some but not all minority areas, modest efforts to improve economic conditions without disrupting local customs, the development of new administrative organs to replace traditional structures, political education emphasizing that minorities were part of the larger Chinese motherland, and social reforms in most nationality regions patterned on developments in Han areas but implemented more slowly in light of local conditions. Overall, CCP policies sought to draw the minorities gradually into the Chinese mainstream; they aimed at fundamental transformation but at a pace and in a manner sensitive to local customs and avoiding unnecessary disruption.

The CCP, using these policies, had considerable success in bringing the far-flung minority areas under central control and beginning the process of social transformation, but such efforts in areas traditionally hostile to the Han and possessing "backward" social structures inevitably produced tensions. Despite the relatively moderate approach, throughout the early 1950s reports surfaced of "Han chauvinism" as Han cadres alienated local populations by applying Chinese practices mechanically. During the relaxation begun in 1956 and extended during the Hundred Flowers movement in 1957 (see Chapter 5), official efforts to promote criticism of Party shortcomings led to a flood of attacks on Han cadre misbehavior and more fundamentally on the limitations of autonomy, and even resulted in separatist demands. The most extreme manifestation of minority alienation was a 1956 revolt in the Tibetan areas of Sichuan against the introduction of reforms. One consequence was the emigration to Tibet proper of a significant number of refugees who later became an important factor in the major 1959 Tibetan rebellion (see Chapter 2). Clearly, even the skillfully modulated policies of 1949–57 had not eliminated resistance to Chinese control; but on balance, the PRC had gained a much firmer foothold in minority areas than any previous regime.

As suggested by the minorities question, the actual institutional pattern in operation was more significant than the constitutional prescription, and here too there were similarities to but also major differences from Soviet practice. Basically, this was a system of parallel Party and state hierarchies, with the Party, unmentioned in the constitution, the ultimate locus of authority. In this the Chinese system was patterned more on the formal relationships in the Soviet Union than on actual Stalinist practice. For Stalin the Party, although theoretically supreme, was merely one of several hierarchies, including the virtually independent secret police, which he could personally manipulate to guarantee his dominance. In China, true to Leninist principles, Party leadership had a more concrete reality. Ultimate policy-making power rested with central Party bodies, especially the Politburo and Secretariat, and at local levels Party committees were more powerful than people's governments. Party control was also ensured by the wearing of dual hats: Leading Party secretaries also held key administrative posts, a practice at variance with the more distinct Soviet hierarchies even after Stalin. Indeed, as the institutional pattern for planned construction was taking hold in China, the Soviet Party was only gradually reasserting its dominance in post-Stalin Russia.

In another regard, however, institutional relationships were fundamentally influenced by the Soviet pattern. The Soviet-style command economy required a set of centralized administrative practices that enhanced the relative position of the state structure. Although there was no question of ultimate Party authority over policy, a vast number of administrative decisions related to economic management fell to the State Council and its subordinate bodies. The dominant administrative pattern was that of vertical rule – units in the modern sector were placed directly under central ministries, thus bypassing local Party committees. Mao accurately captured the situation when he declared, "The major powers grasped by the Central Committee consist only of revolution and agriculture. The rest are in the hands of the State Council."[42] At the central level, operational decisions increasingly flowed to the specialists required by the capital- and technology-intensive Soviet model, and these administrators exercised direct control over skilled personnel at each subordinate level. This bolstered not only the position of Premier Zhou Enlai but also those of such key economic officials as Chen Yun, Li Fuchun, Li Xiannian and Bo Yibo.

At the basic level in the modern sector, the industrial enterprise, this often left the Party organization in a fairly peripheral role. After an initial period of considerable confusion and variation in the roles of factory Party committees, by 1953 the trend was toward restricting their functions to education and propaganda, and the factory manager assumed control of overall operations. This situation, as we shall see, was changed by 1956, but in the early days of the first FYP, factory Party committees were often simply another functional organization within the enterprise. Overall the Party remained supreme, but throughout the 1953–7 period the state's powers frequently eclipsed those of specific Party organizations.

42 "Talks at the Nanning conference" (11–12 January 1958), in *Miscellany*, 1.84.

Another key part of the state apparatus, the "political and legal work system" of courts, procurators (public prosecutors), and police, was deeply influenced by the Soviet model, although it departed from Stalinist practice in crucial respects. As in the Soviet Union, not only were courts and procurators declared constitutionally independent, but by 1954 they had adopted Soviet-style administrative practices that granted a substantial degree of functional autonomy. As part of the overall emphasis on regularization and professionalization in the mid-1950s, these bodies, as well as the police who theoretically were an integral part of the government under the Ministry of Public Security, increasingly handled individual cases without interference from local Party committees or government councils. Ultimately, of course, political and legal departments were subject to CCP authority in the basic policies were laid down by central Party bodies and closely coordinated with the overall goals of the official line. Moreover, local Party committees maintained general oversight over this sensitive area, which sometimes led to friction with the departments as they attempted to assert the autonomy sanctioned by state policy.

The police were clearly the most important of the political and legal departments. Although there are huge gaps in hard information about the public security apparatus, it obviously played a crucial role from the founding of the PRC as an instrument of public order and control. In addition to ordinary police functions and its obscure role as a political police, the public security force administers a large penal system, including labor camps whose inmates undoubtedly number in the millions and provide significant economic resources for the state.[43] With such resources at its disposal, the police had required firm Party control. As already indicated, Mao, unlike Stalin, moved to ensure that the police did not operate as an independent coercive apparatus capable of destroying the integrity of Party and state organizations. In the 1955 campaign against counterrevolutionaries, as in the earlier 1951–3 effort, strict oversight by Party bodies was again imposed. Day-to-day control over the police was exerted by Minister of Public Security Luo Ruiqing, a Party official of high rank but below Politburo status. Luo reported directly to Mao and also to Peng Zhen, the Politburo member most heavily involved in political and legal work.[44] Although guidance of the

43 Although remarkably little firm data are available on the PRC's labor reform system, useful descriptions are found in A. Doak Barnett, *Communist China: The early years, 1949–55*, 60–7; and the firsthand account in Bao Ruo-wang (Jean Pasqualini) and Rudolph Chelminski, *Prisoner of Mao*. Both sources speculatively estimate a labor camp population in the millions, with Bao and Chelminski (p. 10n) suggesting a likely number well in excess of 10 million.

44 Foreign observers have speculated that Kang Sheng, a Politburo member heavily involved in security work in the 1930s and early 1940s, continued to control the police after 1949, but this was not the case. Kang was relieved of security duties after the Seventh Party Congress in 1945 and subsequently

public security apparatus undoubtedly provided individual figures with a potentially potent instrument for inner elite conflict, under the conditions of the 1950s it was a resource of strictly limited utility.

Although the Party and state hierarchies were clearly crucial, an important auxiliary role was played by the various mass organizations. These bodies were designed according to Lenin's concept of "transmission belts." Although transmission belts performed the role of representing the views of their members to leading Party authorities, their primary function in both Leninist and Stalinist practice was to act as purveyors of Party policies to the masses they represented. In the initial period after liberation there was a significant debate as to the relative weight of these two roles in the most significant mass organization, the All-China Federation of Trade Unions, but the issue was settled by the end of 1951 in favor of orthodox Soviet practice.

In this debate many in the trade unions, apparently led by Li Lisan, argued that unions had become too subservient to management in both privately owned and state-run enterprises and as a result had alienated the workers. These cadres held that the basic task of the unions was to uphold workers' interests, and to accomplish this aim some degree of operational autonomy was necessary. At the end of 1951 Party leaders intervened to denounce these views as "economism" and "denying Party leadership of the trade unions," and in a top-level reshuffle of union personnel in 1952, Li Lisan was replaced as trade union chief. Although Li's personal setback was limited – he retained his posts as minister of labor and Central Committee member – and was perhaps related to the fact that he had been one of Mao's main opponents in the early 1930s, the net effect of the affair was firmly to subordinate the union structure to Party leadership. This standard Soviet role also applied to all other mass organizations, and it became even more pronounced in the first FYP period, when virtually all bodies centered their activities on plan fulfillment.

Agricultural cooperativization

The successful completion of agricultural cooperativization by the end of 1956 was one of the most significant developments of the entire first FYP period in a number of senses. First, it was an enormous achievement of social and institutional transformation to bring the great bulk of the Chinese people under socialist forms of organization – a task fundamentally more

went on sick leave in 1949, allegedly out of pique that Rao Shushi was given the top regional post in East China. Kang reemerged after the Gao–Rao affair but concentrated on theoretical work. It was only in the Cultural Revolution that he again became involved with coercive instruments of rule. See Zhong Kan, *Kang Sheng pingzhuan* (Critical biography of Kang Sheng), 83, 96, 106–12, 114, 191, 284.

difficult than the socialization of the modern sector – and one that on this ground alone demands detailed examination. Second, although Soviet collectivization more than twenty years was relevant experience in a number of ways, CCP leaders developed their own approach and methods, which resulted in a far less disruptive process than had occurred in Russia. Moreover, as a policy issue, cooperativization was a hotly debated question within the leadership, although these debates did not fundamentally erode Party unity. Finally, the resolution of this issue came as a result of Mao's personal initiative in calling for a stepped-up pace of building agricultural cooperatives in mid-1955.

As Vice-Premier Chen Yi put it, Mao's intervention "settled the debate of the past three years."[45] Subsequently cooperativization was accomplished far more quickly than had been previously thought possible, although the pace also greatly exceeded Mao's expectations and the methods often violated his guidelines. In any case, the achievement of an almost totally socialized agricultural sector by late 1956 was widely seen as both a great success for the Party and a vindication of Mao personally. (For a more specifically economic analysis of this development, see *CHOC* 14, Chapter 3.)

Moves toward socialized agriculture had begun even before nationwide liberation with the development of mutual aid teams (MATs) – arrangements for pooling peasant labor – in the base areas of North China. Mutual aid was developed after 1949 in both old and new liberated areas, so that by the end of 1952 about 40 percent of all peasant households were in MATs. Meanwhile, experimental Agricultural Producers' Cooperatives (APCs) were established, but it was only in 1952–3 that they appeared in substantial numbers. From 1952 until Mao's intervention in 1955, the rate of cooperativization intensified and relaxed several times. As Table 1 demonstrates, in the winters of 1952–3 and 1954–5 sharp increases were registered in the number of cooperatives, but in each following spring the rate of growth was reduced and some cooperatives were disbanded. This pattern was clearly linked to the ongoing debate, but it also reflected the problems of disorganization and planning confusion, harsh cadre methods, and the alienation of better-off peasants that resulted from hasty implementation of the program. After Mao's intervention, in contrast, not only did the movement surge forward at a stepped-up tempo, but the following spring of 1956 saw the reorganization of the cooperatives into so-called higher-stage or fully collectivized bodies instead of a new period of consolidation.

Chinese policy contained several major modifications of the Soviet experience. First, cooperativization was designed as a gradual, stage-by-stage pro-

45 *RMRB*, 13 November 1955.

TABLE I

Agricultural cooperatives: Development and targets

	Existing APCs	1954–5 target	1956 target	1957–8 target
Fall 1952	3,644[a] (0.1%)[b]			
Spring 1953	5,800 reduced to 3,645 in Hebei province			
Mao 11/53	ca. 15,000 (0.2%)			700,000–1 million (ca. 15–22%) "by 1957"
Central Committee 12/53	14,900 (0.2%)	35,800 (ca. 0.5%) fall 1954		800,000 (ca. 18%) "by 1957"
Deng Zihui 7/54 (Head of CCP Rural Work Department)	ca. 114,000 (2%)	600,000 (ca. 12–13%) spring 1955	1.5 million (ca. 33%) "by 1956"	3 million (ca. 66%) "by 1957"
Central Committee 10/54	ca. 230,000 (4.7%)	600,000 (ca. 12–13%) spring 1955		
February–March 1955	670,000 reduced to 633,000 (14.2%)			
Central Committee Rural Work Department spring (May?) 1955	ca. 633,000 (14.2%)		1 million (ca. 22%) October	
June 1955	634,000 (14.2%)			
First FYP 7/30/55	650,000 (ca. 14.3%)			33% "by 1957"
Mao 7/31/55	650,000 (ca. 14.3%)		1.3 million (ca. 29%) October	50% spring 1958
Average 17–20 provinces 9/55	?		37.7% spring	60.3% 1957
Central Committee 10/55	1.277 million (32%)			70–80% in advanced areas, spring 1957; 70–80% overall, spring 1958
21 provinces 11/55	1.583 million (41.4%)	70–80% in advanced areas, end 1955	70–80% overall, end 1956	
Mao 12/55	1.905 million (63.3%) (4% hi APCs)[c]		70–80% end 1956	
Agricultural draft program 1/56	1.53 million (80.3%) (30.7% hi APCs)		85% "in 1956"	"hi APCs practically complete by 1958"
March 1956	1.088 million (88.9%) (54.9%; hi APCs)			
June 1956	994,000 (91.9%) (63.2% hi APCs)			
December 1956	756,000 (96.3%) (87.8% hi APCs)			

[a]Number of APCs; lower-stage APCs until December 1955, thereafter divided into lower- and higher-stage APCs as indicated. Number of APCs declines throughout 1956 owing to larger size of higher APCs.

[b](%) = peasant households in APCs.

[c]hi = higher stage.

Sources: Shi Jingtang et al., eds., *Zhongguo nongye hezuohua yundong shiliao* (Historical materials on China's agricultural cooperativization movement), 989–91; "Agricultural cooperativization in Communist China," *CB*, 373; Mao, *SW*, 5.139–40; and *Communist China 1955–1959*, 120.

cess, rather than the sudden and chaotic pattern of the Soviet Union. CCP policy envisioned a three-step process: first MATs, where labor was pooled but ownership rights over land and other productive factors were retained by individual peasants; then the lower stage APC, where productive property was now controlled by the collective but each peasant received a dividend according to his relative contribution of land, tools, and animals; and finally the higher-stage APC (or full collective), where the dividend was abolished and payment was strictly according to labor.

Another important difference was the policy of restricting rather than liquidating rich peasants. In contrast to the forced deportation and killing of Russian *kulaks,* Chinese rich peasants saw their economic position eroded by various means and were used as a target for political mobilization until the latter stages of the movement, when they were allowed into the APCs. Thus although the rich peasants were still objects of class struggle, their comparatively mild treatment limited the disorder and destruction of economic resources that marked the Soviet campaign.

A third feature, which also ameliorated the rural situation, was CCP avoidance of Stalin's single-minded stress on extracting agricultural surplus to support industrialization. China's first FYP also relied heavily on agriculture supporting industry, but CCP leaders realized that China's countryside had far less surplus to extract than Russia's. As a result, throughout the first FYP, official policy aimed at increasing agricultural production so that *both* the industrial development plans of the state would be met and peasant living standards would rise. Although it remains uncertain just how consistently this objective was realized, the Party concern for peasants' livelihood served to reduce resistance as well as build support. Finally, a more strictly economic and technical modification was the emergence by mid-1954 of a policy that in view of China's backward industrial base, collectivization should precede the mechanization of agriculture rather than be developed in tandem.

These substantial changes from the Soviet pattern did not mean total rejection of the Soviet experience, however. On the contrary, not only were various Soviet writings studied to bolster the official case for cooperatives, but the developed Soviet collective as laid down in the model *kolkhoz* (collective) rules of 1935 was the concrete form of higher-stage APC that the CCP basically adopted. In terms of process, moreover, the Soviet experience provided lessons and sources of support for all sides of the debate within the CCP. Those who argued against rapid expansion cited Stalin's warning against being "dizzy with success" when excesses threatened the Soviet program. But others, like Mao in July 1955, could argue that the Soviet experience showed it was possible to correct errors quickly and accomplish cooperativization according to a more optimistic schedule.

Some aspects of the crucial stage of the debate during the first seven months of 1955 are clear, including Mao's decisive role and the nature of the arguments, but the precise political contours are less certain.[46] As we have seen, there was undoubted consensus in early 1955 on the desirability of cooperativization for economic as well as social and political goals; promulgation of the first FYP in July reemphasized the importance of building APCs for planned economic growth. There was also the relatively recent agreement on collectivization before mechanization, although differences remained over precisely how far ahead of mechanization the socialization process should develop. Moreover, a shared awareness of the problems facing the CCP existed. Socially and politically, there was broad agreement that the continued existence of small peasant production engendered rural capitalism and thus threatened the consolidation of socialism. Economically, all participants believed that the failure of agricultural growth to keep pace with the planned rate of industrialization threatened the entire first FYP, since agricultural production substantially determined industrial growth rates.

Since there is little indication of any key policy maker advocating a substantial scaling down of industrial targets, how to increase farm production became a key concern. The central issue was the pace of setting up APCs. Throughout these months a cautious approach was advanced primarily by the Central Committee's Rural Work Department and its head, Deng Zihui, in conjunction with the Politburo's leading economic specialist, Chen Yun. This approach was initially endorsed not only by Liu Shaoqi but also by Mao himself. Deng emphasized the overambitious planning, cadre excesses, and disillusionment of the more productive peasants that had accompanied the rapid expansion of APCs in 1954 and early 1955. In this view, a careful consolidation of existing APCs and a modest rate of future growth aiming for a million cooperatives by fall 1956 was called for if peasant hostility was not seriously to damage agricultural production. In pursuing this policy, Deng ordered the dissolution of 20,000 newly established but badly organized APCs. Against this approach were those advocating a more expansionary policy on the grounds that APCs had a demonstrated capacity for increasing

46 The following account differs somewhat from interpretations which, drawing on Cutural Revolution sources, emphasize differences between Mao on the one hand and a whole array of central officials on the other. See, for example, Parris H. Chang, *Power and policy in China*, 9–17. "Agricultural cooperativization in communist China," *CB*, 373; Kenneth R. Walker, "Collectivisation in retrospect: The 'socialist high tide' of autumn 1955–spring 1956," *CQ*, 26 (1966); and particularly documents in the post-Mao internal publication, *Dangshi yanjiu*, 2.1 (1981), (Research on Party history), 28 February 1981, namely, Deng Zihui, "Zai quanguo disanci nongcun gongzuo huiyi shang de kaimu ci" (Inaugural speech at the third national rural work conference) (21 April 1955) 1981.1, 2–9; and Qiang Yuangan and Lin Bangguang, "Shilun yi jiu wu wu nian dangnei guanyu nongye hezuohua wenti de zhenglun" (A discussion of the debate within the Party in 1955 concerning the issue of agricultural cooperativization).

production, could more easily obtain the agricultural surplus for the state, and would also check tendencies to rural class polarization that seemed to be growing with agriculture still overwhelmingly private.

As indicated earlier, Mao initially supported Deng's policies. In March the Chairman proposed the slogan "halt, shrink, develop," which reflected the importance of consolidation before new advances. In mid-May, however, Mao shifted his position to one of dissatisfaction with the pace of cooperativization, and a sharp debate with Deng ensued. While Deng upheld the rural work department's target of 1 million APCs by October 1956, Mao warned against a passive approach and argued for a goal of 1.3 million.[47] In retrospect, it appears that Mao's initiative in the latter part of May, and not his 31 July speech on cooperativization normally cited by scholars,[48] was decisive in producing policy change. Not only were the number of APCs again expanding in June and July, but May also saw the decision to launch a new campaign against counterrevolutionaries – a major aim of which was to silence opposition to collectivization within society at large. Moreover, owing to conviction, conversion, or calculation, in the days before Mao's speech such leading officials as Minister of Agriculture Liao Luyan and Deng's erstwhile ally Chen Yun spoke out sharply in defense of collectivization.

Mao's intervention starting in May 1955 and culminating in his July speech was less significant as policy innovation than as a decisive political act. In policy terms, although doubling the number of APCs to be established over the next fourteen months was a significant intensification of the campaign, Mao's program was not overly radical. It called for careful preparations for new APCs, allowed peasants to withdraw or even dissolve unsatisfactory cooperatives, and warned against rashness as well as timidity in cooperativization. Moreover, even though Mao's targets substantially raised those earlier decided on by the rural work department, the rate of increase was less than that achieved in the year from early 1954 to early 1955, and the absolute numbers inolved were only slightly larger. Indeed, Mao's targets for 1956–7 were more conservative than the projection made by Deng Zihui in mid-1954.

But if the Chairman's program was not excessively radical, its political

47 Mao's target was laid down in his 31 July speech on cooperativization but was apparently argued during the May debate with Deng. See Mao, *SW,* 5.187; and Qiang Yuangan and Lin Bangguang, "Shilun dangnei zhenglun," 13.

48 Analysts writing without benefit of post-Mao information on the Chairman's May activities often stressed the suddenness and decisiveness of Mao's July speech because of its apparently more radical targets than those incorporated in the first FYP published the day before Mao spoke. See, for example, Stuart R. Schram, "Introduction: The Cultural Revolution in historical perspective," in Schram, ed., *Authority, participation and cultural change in China,* 39. Such analyses, however, overlook the fact that the first FYP target of one-third of all peasant households in APCs "by 1957" was not necessarily more conservative than Mao's target of 50 percent by *spring 1958,* since the winter season of 1957–8 would surely be a period of significant growth.

impact was. Mao ended the hesitation of the previous months by indicating that expansion was the only ideologically correct course. He began his July speech with a criticism of "some of our comrades [who are] tottering like a woman with bound feet,"[49] and throughout this period he applied the "right deviationist" label to Deng, who continued to express reservations. In the face of Mao's sharpened political definition of the issue, few officials held out; vigorous implementation of cooperativization unfolded.

Mao's success was undoubtedly due in the first instance to his unchallenged role as leader, but several other factors were working in his favor. One was the comparatively moderate nature of his program and the argumentation behind it. Although the political tone of the July speech was ultimately decisive, the marshaling of survey data and careful reasoning carried considerable weight. Also aiding Mao was the fact that his program at least came to grips with the serious problems facing the rural sector, although the more conservative approach held little promise of a breakthrough. Politically, the fact that Mao was not speaking alone but expressing the views of a significant segment of the elite gave his recommendations an important boost, as did the fact that even those opposed to rapid increases shared a belief in the desirability of APC's on both economic and social grounds. Although in later years objections would be voiced to using the "rightist" label against Deng Zihui, at the time the traditional mild approach to inner elite dissent also contributed to closing ranks behind Mao. Deng was required only to make a self-criticism and temporarily suffered a reduction in power, but he never lost his posts. Finally, as the campaign picked up steam, the overfulfillment of the Chaiman's targets seemed to discredit contrary views.

Indeed, the nearly complete establishment of fully collectivized APCs by the end of 1956 was due more to the zealous implementation of the campaign by the Party apparatus than to Mao's program. Cadres throughout rural China, reacting to the pressures created by Mao's speech and the campaign against counterrevolutionaries, concluded that it was "better to err to the left than the right." From the time of the July speech until the end of 1955, China went through a cycle of Mao and the Party center setting goals, the provinces outstripping those goals, the center revising its targets upward, and the provinces once again overfulfilling central targets. Even at the end of the year, Mao estimated it would take another three to four years basically to complete the higher-stage APCs. But in 1956 the localities yet again greatly outstripped his targets. In the process, however, the policy of advancing by stages that the Chairman had carefully advocated in 1955 was discarded. More than a quarter of all peasant families joined APCs without prior organi-

49 Mao, *SW*, 5.184.

zation into MATs, and a widespread tendency to skip the lower-stage APCs altogether appeared. Although Mao continued to warn against leftist excesses in the fall and winter of 1955 – 6, he was fundamentally elated by the rapid progress. This breakneck speed would cause serious problems of adjustment in 1956–7, but the basic organizational breakthrough had been achieved.

In comparative terms, Chinese cooperativization was accomplished in a considerably smoother manner than its Soviet counterpart, but outright revolts apart, nearly all forms of peasant resistance that had occurred in Russia – withdrawing from cooperatives, reducing levels of productive investment and activity, slaughtering livestock, spreading rumors – appeared in China, albeit to a lesser degree.

Various factors explain the easier passage. The conscious adaptation of Soviet practice in the direction of gradualism and reduced social tensions were, of course, of major significance. Also crucial was the disciplined Party apparatus in the countryside, an organizational force that had been far weaker or even nonexistent in the Soviet case. Strong Party committees at the county level were able to organized large numbers of work teams and guide fundamental change in villages. Particularly important was the CCP's presence in the villages themselves. Seventy percent of all *xiang* had Party branches by the start of 1955, and 90 percent had them by the end of the year.

The basis of this rural elite was the cadres who had emerged during land reform. Added to this base were new recruits drawn from activists during the cooperativization movement itself, a process that intensified and increasingly focused on poorer peasants in 1955, and demobilized soldiers who became available as the PLA stepped up modernization measures in 1954–5. Equally important were repeated training programs and indoctrination of this rural cadre force in socialist principles. Although there were pronounced tendencies for cadres to seek a life of independent farming at the end of land reform, such tendencies were checked by constant reinforcement that sought to relate all official tasks to the concept of socialist transformation. At no time did the rural leadership structure fall completely under the sway of small peasant production, as had happened in the Soviet Union in the 1920s.

Another major reason for the relative success of the Chinese program was the CCP's carefully constructed rural economic policies, which not only provided benefits for a majority of the peasants but also gave the peasantry as a whole little choice but to cooperate. Credit cooperatives, supply and marketing cooperatives, and the planned marketing of grain and other key commodities all increasingly restricted the private economic opportunities of rich peasants and channeled economic resources preferentially to the cooperative sector, thus increasing the attractiveness of joining the APCs.

Policies were explicitly framed with an eye to protecting the interests of the relatively well-off and productive middle peasants who before mid-1955 often had a dominant role in APCs. Beyond this, the basic propaganda appeal emphasizing better living standards and the general ability of official policies to at least avoid a decline in standards despite fair to poor harvest conditions in 1953 and 1954 gave the peasants some reason to expect tangible results from the APCs. When the "high tide" of cooperativization was launched in the context of a bumper harvest in mid-1955, the regime's economic credibility, which had been established during land reform, was still working for it.

The potent combination of administrative pressures, normative appeals, coercion, and tangible results that had achieved remarkable success in land reform and the initial period of cooperativization now came into play during the high tide. The situation differed markedly from the immediately preceding stage in that tangible benefits were now increasingly focused on the poorer peasants, to the detriment of better-off middle peasants. The cancellation of the land dividend in the higher-stage APCs represented a direct transfer of economic resources between the two groups, and given the numerical dominance of the poorer elements – estimated at 60 to 70 percent of the peasantry – a powerful interest group for the change was created. Normative appeals, which continued to be heavily laced with the promise of prosperity, as a result were especially potent for the poor, although even within this group, those who hesitated were with some frequency forcefully herded into APCs. Pressure often bordering on coercion was applied to the better-off middle peasants, and outright coercion in the form of arrests and mass struggle was used against counterrevolutionaries, including some rich peasants.

In all of this, the cadres continued to be a driving force that responded to a similar set of pressures. Increasingly drawn from the poor peasants by the recruiting measures of late 1955, village leaders were at once the prime target of educational efforts, the direct recipients of administrative pressures with coercive overtones, and the main beneficiaries of local transformation. The switch to higher-stage APCs not only benefited cadres as it did less well-off peasants, it also eased their administrative tasks because they no longer had to calculate the divisive land dividend. And it cemented their political dominance by weakening the middle peasants. With this key group highly motivated, the majority of peasants having reason to anticipate material gains, and disadvantaged groups under tight control but not threatened with liquidation, the momentum for rapid collectivization proved irresistible.

Transforming the modern sector and the first leap forward

By fall 1955 the mounting evidence of a breakthrough in cooperativization allowed Mao and his colleagues to turn some of their attention to the transformation of industry and commerce. The Three and Five Antis campaigns had been launched only after the basic success of land reform. Similarly, with the vast, difficult to control countryside now advancing rapidly toward socialism, Party leaders felt the time had come to use their great leverage in the modern sector. Earlier debates on the speed of the socialist transformation of industry and commerce had paralleled those over the rate of building APCs.

Some saw the need for pushing ahead in order to facilitate central planning, whereas others urged caution on the grounds that conditions were not yet ripe and that overly hasty socialization would disrupt production and overwhelm the state's nascent planning capabilities. In the fall of 1955, however, there was general agreement that socialization of the modern sector would have to keep pace with cooperativization. Although socialized industry and commerce were well in advance of cooperativization in mid-1955, first FYP goals were modest in calling for only "the greater part" of privately owned businesses to adopt some form of state capitalism by the end of the Five-Year-Plan period.

From the end of October 1955 to January 1956, however, Mao and other leaders met with prominent capitalists to impress upon them the need for a stepped-up pace of transformation while ostensibly soliciting their views. In these encounters Mao, as he had with agricultural cooperatives, warned against excessive rashness and even declared himself more cautious than Chen Yun, but the invited businessmen did not fail to pick up the essential message and quickly pledged support for an accelerated program. On the basis of these pledges, a new target of completing transformation into joint state-private enterprises by the end of 1957 was laid down.

What followed paralleled the overfulfillment of APC targets but in even more startling form. Chen Yun organized meetings of provincial leaders to press for the new target but was quickly overtaken by the actions of another Politburo member, Beijing mayor Peng Zhen. In December Peng set the end of 1956 as the target date for Beijing, and in January the actual transformation was completed in the first ten days of the month. Other cities did not want to appear laggard, and by the end of January the process had been basically completed in all major urban centers. Obviously such an extremely rapid transformation was superficial. Instead of the prescribed process of careful preparatory work that allowed the state to take operational control, it amounted to a formal declaration of a change in ownership without any change in personnel or internal organization. To avoid disrupting production, the State Council in early February ordered that existing operations be unchanged for six months following transformation. The actual work of taking inventories and economic reorganization was done gradually and was heavily dependent on the private capitalists whose skills were still required in a modern sector where the shortage of cadres remained acute.

Although the extension of rapid socialization from agriculture to industry and commerce was to be expected, a less predictable development occurred as Mao sought a "leap forward" in economic construction. In December Mao attacked "right conservative thinking" in a wide range of work: "The problem today . . . lies in agricultural production; industrial production; . . . handicraft production; the scale and speed of capital construction in industry, communications and transport; the coordination of commerce with other branches of the economy; the coordination of the work in science, culture, education and health. . . . In all these fields there is an underestimation of the situation, a shortcoming which must be criticized and corrected."[50] In late 1955 and early 1956 Mao apparently saw an opportunity to attack China's economic and cultural backwardness in much the same way as he had the socialist transformation. Despite continued warnings against "left adventurism" as well as "right conservatism," Mao's thought underwent a subtle shift in the direction of radicalism in the period between his July speech and the end of 1955.[51] This was particularly apparent in his commentary on a volume dealing with cooperativization, where he claimed that "a raging tidal wave [is] sweeping away all demons and monsters" and if "600 million 'paupers' . . . take their destiny into their own hands . . . they can overcome any difficulty on earth."[52]

Mao would soon retreat from this highly optimistic view in the face of mounting problems, but at the time there was little to indicate significant opposition within top leadership circles. Whether because of genuine enthusiasm over the advances in socialization or an unwillingness to challenge a determined Chairman, other leaders joined in the effort to push China's first leap forward.

In terms of concrete policies, in November 1955 Mao proposed a number of long-term measures to boost agricultural production that were expanded and approved in January as a twelve-year draft program for agricultural development over the 1956–67 period. This program laid down ambitious goals, including 100 to 140 percent increases in grain yields, something Mao had expressed doubts over as recently as the previous fall. To accomplish this, the mass mobilization of peasant labor and rural financial resources was assigned a central role. But the program also place a heavy emphasis on scientific and technical inputs and material incentives. In implementing the program, the same phenomena occurred as with regard to socialist transformation – lower-level units significantly increased the targets of the draft program and began to implement its measures in a blind, disruptive

50 Ibid., 5.240.

51 See the 1980 report of Liao, "Historical experiences," November 1981, 88, which traces the origins of Mao's leftist thinking to his late 1955 prefaces to *Socialist upsurge in China's countryside*.

52 Mao, *SW*, 5.244, 250.

manner. Similarly, spurred on by Mao's slogan demanding "more, faster, better, and more economical" results, officials at all levels raised short-term targets for both industrial and agricultural production in an effort to reach first FYP goals a year ahead of schedule. Various industrial ministries increased their 1956 targets by 25 percent or more; Zhou Enlai set a 9 percent growth in grain output as a minimum goal for the year; and some *xiang* leaders called for 40 percent increases in grain production. This too led to economic dislocations as the administrative system had again proved itself too responsive to pressures from above. These dislocations and the other problems arising from the high tide and leap forward soon forced their attention on the leadership, and dealing with them became a major feature of the period of adjustment that followed.

ADJUSTING THE NEW SOCIALIST SYSTEM, 1956–7

The new course that emerged in early 1956 was built on a basic reassessment of conditions in China. According to Mao in January, the high tide of socialist transformation had resulted in a "fundamental change in the political situation."[53] This view, which would be modified by the latter part of 1957, reflected the orthodox Marxist concern with the relations of production – that is, ownership. With the means of production now largely in the hands of the state or collective units, the victory of socialism over capitalism had been basically decided.

A number of related propositions flowed from this analysis. First, although class struggle was by no means eliminated, in the new situation where enemies of socialism no longer had significant economic means at their disposal, class conflict would markedly attenuate so that, as Mao would put it a year later: "The large scale, turbulent class struggles . . . characteristic of . . . revolution have in the main come to an end. . . ."[54] Second, this situation called for a fundamental shift in Party priorities to economic development. Mao outlined this new direction while promoting the leap forward in January: "The object of the socialist revolution [is] to set free the productive forces [and] wipe out China's economic, scientific and cultural backwardness within a few decades."[55] But the new priority was not simply a product of the economic push; later in the year, after the leap forward was discarded, the Eighth Party Congress identified economic backwardness as the heart of the "main contradiction."

53 "Speech to Supreme State Conference" (January 1956), in Helene Carrère d'Encausse and Stuart R. Schram, comps., *Marxism and Asia*, 292.

54 Mao, *SW*, 5.395.

55 "Speech to Supreme State Conference" (January 1956), 292–3.

A third proposition was that the broadest range of social forces could now be rallied behind the developmental effort in a new adaptation of the united front. Under the slogan of "mobilize all positive factors," the leadership sought not simply to win the backing of dubious sections of society but to encourage creative inputs by all groups, especially China's intellectuals, who had skills urgently required for modernization. Finally, the victory of socialism meant the establishment of a new system that inevitably had its shortcomings and conflicts – what Mao termed "contradictions among the people." In this view, tensions in society were predominantly manifestations of legitimate divergences of interest, and the task of the Party became one of mediating the claims of different economic sectors and social groups while performing the new institutions of socialism.

A key innovation in these circumstances was a new policy toward intellectuals. In 1955, steps were taken to win intellectual support through forums addressing their problems and awards for top scientists, but these measures were compromised by attacks on such figures as the literary theorist Hu Feng in the context of the campaign against counterrevolutionaries. In 1956, however, the approach to the intellectuals was pursued in a more relaxed political atmosphere influenced in part by the thaw in Soviet treatment of its intelligentsia begun in late 1955, but more fundamentally by the assumption of the weakening of class struggle after socialist transformation.

A major statement of the new policy was made by Zhou Enlai in January 1956 in the context of promoting the leap forward in the economy, and a further step came in a May speech by the head of the Central Committee's propaganda department, Lu Dingyi. Zhou advocated improved salaries and living conditions, the provision of better working conditions and resources, and more rapid promotions and easier admission into the CCP, and Lu explained Mao's new slogan "Let a hundred flowers bloom, let a hundred schools contend." According to Lu, free discussion and independent thinking were necessary to avoid academic stagnation, and the imposition of dogmatic restrictions on intellectual life was hostile to true Marxism-Leninism.

A further measure was an effort to bolster the status of the small democratic parties that had been drawn into the united front in 1949. Under the slogan of "long-term coexistence and mutual supervision," these parties of intellectuals, one-time KMT officials, and businessmen were urged to criticize the performance of the government and build up their own memberships and organizations. Despite the more relaxed atmosphere, all these measures were circumscribed by reassertions of the principle of Party leadership, calls for the continuing ideological remolding of intellectuals, and assertions that the handling of such dissidents as Hu Feng had been entirely correct. As a result, throughout 1956 most intellectuals responded cautiously, although there were enough sharp criticisms to cause a substantial number of cadres to adopt an obstructionist attitude despite efforts by the top leadership to push the new program.

Although the new policies toward intellectuals continued to mid-1957, the economic leap forward, together with the rapid pace of socialist transformation, created a set of problems necessitating institutional adjustments and policy reversals by late spring 1956. By this time central officials were becoming aware of the imbalances and planning chaos in the overall economy, plus peasant disillusion with both wasteful efforts to realize the draft agricultural program and the rigidities of the new APCs. Starting in April 1956 and continuing into the summer of 1957, measures to deal with these problems were undertaken under a program that became known as "opposing rash advance" – measures including insistence on realistic targets, emphasis on coordination in planning and quality in output, increasing the scope of peasants' private production within the APC framework, reestablishing a limited rural free market, reducing the size of APCs, and heavy criticism of coercive leadership methods by APC cadres. The major architects of this program were Zhou Enlai and Chen Yun, and broad support by the Party's leading economic officials quickly formed.

Mao was far from enthusiastic. Although he surely agreed with some aspects of the program, particularly those increasing material incentives for the peasants, and initially accepted the need to curb excesses, by mid-1956 he was clearly distressed by retrenchment measures that had ended the leap forward in production. Nevertheless, Mao did not attempt to challenge the new program but, instead, accepted the views of his colleagues in an area where, by his own admission, he lacked competence. In so doing the Chairman adhered to the consensual style he normally followed in the 1949–57 period, but he also harbored doubts and regrets that would play a key role in the launching of the GLF.

Adapting the Soviet model

As CCP leaders developed policies for the new situation, they began to examine the Soviet model in a more self-consciously critical manner. Previously Mao and his associates had made significant alterations in the Soviet pattern and called in a general way for adapting Soviet experiences to Chinese conditions, but they had not dwelled on Russian shortcomings or CCP innovations in public or internal statements. Indeed, as late as January 1956 Mao could still profess to believe that the CCP had merely elaborated on

Soviet achievements and "since the October Revolution there have been no new things of note."[56] By this time, however, a systematic review of the Soviet model was already underway that would soon lead to explicit and sharp criticisms of defects in the Russian system.

All this would develop within the context of strains in Sino-Soviet relations following the Twentieth Soviet Party Congress in February 1956, but such strains were not a fundamental cause of the reexamination of the model. In any case, throughout 1956 and most of 1957, the emphasis was still on learning from the Soviet Union, but in a highly selective fashion that rejected backward aspects of Soviet practice.

A growing realization that the Soviet Union had begun from a much higher industrial base than the PRC, yet had only achieved a pace of growth that seemed somewhat slow, apparently set the stage for the reevaluation of the model. This involved Politburo discussions with leading personnel from thirty-four central economic departments and led to one of Mao's most significant speeches, the April 1956 "Ten great relationships." As Mao later observed, this talk, which drew general conclusions based upon the previous months' discussions and thus represented more than Mao's personal view, "made a start in proposing our own line for construction [that] was similar to that of the Soviet Union in principle, but had our own content."[57] Although references to Soviet shortcomings covered a wide scope, in many areas such as agriculture Chinese practice had long been distinctive. Where Mao called for adjustments in existing practices, the changes suggested were modest and left the basic Soviet-style institutional structure and economic strategy in place.

A central question was the ratio of investment between heavy industry on the one had and light industry and agriculture on the other. Mao attacked Soviet overemphasis on heavy industry but reaffirmed its primary claim for investment funds, asking only that "the proportion for agriculture and light industry must be somewhat increased."[58] This was indeed done in June 1956, when the ration of heavy industry to light industry investment was marginally reduced from 8:1 to 7:1; and in September proposals for the second FYP slightly increased agricultural investment from 7 to 10 percent in comparison to the first FYP.

Another key concern of the "Ten great relationships" was economic administration: "We must not follow the example of the Soviet Union in concentrat-

56 "Zai Zhonggong zhongyang zhaokai de guanyu zhishi fenzi wenti huiyi shang de jianghua" (Speech at the conference on the question of intellectuals convened by the CCP Central Committee) (20 January 1956), in *Wansui* (1969), 33.

57 "Talks at the Chengtu conference" (March 1958), in Schram, ed., *Mao unrehearsed,* 101.

58 Mao, *SW,* 5.286.

ing everything in the hands of the central authorities, shackling the local authorities and denying them the right to independent action."[59] Here too Mao was cautious, calling for greater consultation with the localities, the enlargement of their powers "to some extent" within the framework of unified central leadership, and further investigation of the problem. What was envisioned here was a move away from vertical ministerial control to a form of "dual rule" where powers were shared between the ministries and regional authorities, but there was no clarity as to method.

The State Council subsequently held a series of meetings on how to curb excessive centralization, and the proposals for the second FYP assigned more construction projects to local authorities. Moreover, other approaches to combating overcentralization were advocated that emphasized indirect planning (norms for reference only) and the use of market mechanisms. Proposals in this regard were made by Chen Yun in September 1956 at the Eighth Party Congress, and in the following months experiments with methods of enhancing enterprise autonomy and selective purchasing on the market were carried out. In January 1957, however, the State Council decided that the basic pattern of planned allocation would continue for the year because of the complex administrative problems any change would require, and undoubtedly also because of the opposition of many economic planners. Similarly, despite intense debate in economic journals over methods of decentralization throughout 1957, until the fall of the year no major decision had been taken.

Throughout this debate on how to modify Soviet-style administration, it is important to note, contemporary Soviet developments were a contributing factor. The Soviet Union had undertaken decentralization measures of its own in mid-1955, and views of Soviet economists on the need to overcome the rigidities of central planning had made a significant impact on leading participants in the Chinese debates. Indeed, even in areas where the CCP was far less beholden to the Soviet model than in economic planning, Soviet reforms played an influential role. Thus Party leaders had initially adopted the Soviet machine tractor station as the method for spreading the mechanization of agriculture. These stations, which were separate entities contracting their services to APCs, had many inefficiencies and often worked at cross-purposes with the cooperatives. Criticism of their faults in the Soviet Union and Eastern Europe and Soviet experiments with placing tractors under the direct control of collectives were already underway in spring 1956 when Politburo member Kang Sheng represented the CCP at the East German Party Congress. The problem was discussed extensively at this Congress, and

59 Ibid., 292.

upon his return Kang conducted an investigation in China. This resulted in a critical report in November, experiments with alternatives in 1957, and finally the decision to place agricultural machinery directly in the hands of the APCs in 1958, the same year the machine tractor station was abolished in the Soviet Union.

Additional aspects of modifying the Soviet model are illustrated by another issue raised in the spring 1956 Politburo discussions – the system of factory management. In the early 1950s the Soviet system of "one-man management," which placed ultimate authority in the hands of the factory manager, had been widely introduced in the Northeast. This system had been recommended, but not ordered, for the entire country in early 1953. Beginning in 1954, criticisms of the system were increasingly aired but defenses were also published, and during 1954 – 6 it continued to be allowed as one variant of enterprise management pending a Politburo decision. One of the factors at work in this case was that the PRC simply lacked sufficient numbers of competent personnel to make one-man management work. The system not only never predominated in China as a whole but was only partially implemented even in the Northeast. In addition, there was significant resistance from Party cadres who objected to restrictions on their powers and resented the authority the system vested in managers from suspect class backgrounds.

Moreover, these cadres raised the potent charge that the system violated CCP traditions of Party control and collective decision making, that it was "only centralism and no democracy." Such arguments, in conjunction with the inadequate resources for one-man management and the increasing number of Party cadres who had been recruited and trained in industry in the preceding years, were crucial when the leadership decided on a new system upgrading the powers of the factory Party committee above those of the factory manager. In announcing this decision to the Eighth Party Congress, the Party official responsible for industry, Li Xuefeng, emphasized the importance of Party traditions. This change, however, was far from a rejection of Soviet industrial methods. Indeed, in the same period Soviet-style piecework wage systems were being extended throughout most of China.

Another area where CCP traditions became a central issue in adapting the Soviet model was modernizing the PLA. By 1956, Party leaders clearly felt that political traditions were being eroded by the Soviet-aided modernization effort and began a series of measures to check this trend. These included intensified political education for officers, a strengthening of the Party committee structure within the PLA, attacks on overspecialization and excessive emphasis on ranks and titles, increased PLA participation in production, salary cuts for higher-ranking officers, and an emphasis on democratic relations between officers and men. By such measures Party leaders sought, in the words of Tan Zheng, deputy director of the PLA's political department, to ensure that "no amount of modernization will change the fact that ours is a people's army."[60] This, however, in no way implied a downgrading of military modernization. Thus Tan criticized the "guerrilla" tendencies of those who refused to adjust to the needs of modern warfare; the need to assimilate Soviet military experiences, albeit in an undogmatic manner, continued to be emphasized; modernization measures continued unabated; and at the end of 1957 a program was unveiled for professionalizing all officers within five years. The basic aim of the 1956–7 adjustments was still to modernize, but within the context of PLA traditions. This would cause some strains within the officer corps, but Party and army leaders saw no inherent incompatibility in the effort.

Other policy shifts in 1956–7 represented modifications of the Soviet model. Particularly in 1957, there was increasing attention to small- and medium-scale industry, in contrast to the Soviet emphasis on large, capital-intensive plants. Similarly, in education, the expansion of elite specialized institutions that were the core of the Soviet approach slowed down, and a renewed emphasis on small community-run schools appeared (see *CHOC* 14, Chapter 4). Thus a second low-technology leg was gaining increased prominence, but it would become a major feature of Chinese developmental strategies only under the "walk on two legs" slogan of the Great Leap Forward. For the time being, such programs were clearly auxiliary and did not challenge the continued predominance of the modern, large-scale sector. Finally, the reexamination of the Soviet model meant a new receptiveness to alternative foreign sources of ideas, including not only Communist Yugoslavia but also the advanced capitalist states of the West. But there was, in fact, little of such eclectic borrowing, and the Soviet-style structures and strategy remained fundamentally in place until late 1957.

The Eighth Party Congress

When the Party Congress convened in September 1956 for the first time in eleven years, the occasion was marked by an outpouring of both self-congratulation and self-criticism. There was indeed much reason for congratulation over both the victory of 1949 and the success of socialist transformation in 1955–6. Moreover, the Party had grown during the period of transformation into a mammoth organization of 10.7 million members that now penetrated most aspects of social, economic, and political life. But Party leaders also

60 "Speech by Comrade T'an Cheng" (18 September 1956), in *Eighth National Congress,* 2.265.

recognized that many tasks remained and many faults existed within the new system, and the Congress was marked by a remarkably frank yet ultimately self-confident analysis of the problems facing the regime.

The main task, as affirmed by the political resolution of the Congress, was getting on with the job of economic development. The policy line for this task elaborated the "opposing rash advance" theme, although (perhaps with a view to Mao's sensibilities) right conservatism received pride of place in the official listing of deviations to be avoided. The proposals for the second FYP announced by Zhou Enlai reflected balance, moderation, and realism, but they still called for a slight increase in the rate of reinvestment compared with the first FYP. Overall, the program of the Congress was not one of retreat, but the emphasis was decidedly on *steady* advance.

In many ways the 1956 Party Congress was less of a personal triumph for Mao than its predecessor in 1945, which had put the seal on his leadership of the Party. On the surface, several developments diminished Mao's role: The reference to his thought as part of the CCP's guiding ideology was deleted from the new Party constitution, and the Congress placed heavy stress on collective leadership. In 1956, however, there were a number of factors operating against any outpourings of adulation, although fundamentally Mao's position remained unchallenged.[61] One consideration arose from external events – Khrushchev's denunciation of Stalin's "personality cult" at the Soviet Party Congress in February. Under these circumstances, any lavish praise of the Chinese leader would have been unseemly, and Mao later stated that he fully concurred in the decision to delete his thought from the constitution.

A second consideration, one that suggests both Mao's self-assurance and his confidence in his associates, was the need to arrange for an orderly succession. Mao's subsequent statements indicate that he took several concrete steps at the Eighth Congress for his eventual retirement to the second front – removed from operational decisions – so that his colleagues could gain sufficient prestige to ensure a smooth transition after his death and thus avoid the strife that marked Soviet politics after Stalin. The post of honorary Party Chairman was created for Mao's eventual retirement; Liu Shaoqi's status as heir apparent was bolstered by entrusting him with the presentation of the political report (a role Mao filled in 1945); and strong collective organs were established in the Politburo Standing Committee and an enlarged Party Secretariat. None of this meant Mao was abdicating real power. As he put it

61 This analysis (cf. Teiwes, *Politics and purges*, 226–30) differs from interpretations seeing "Mao in eclipse" at the Congress (e.g., Chang, *Power and policy*, 29ff.) and those emphasizing conflicts between Mao and other leaders (e.g., MacFarquhar, *Origins*, 1, part 2).

in early 1958, when proposing new measures for his retreat to the second front, "Whenever the nation is urgently in need . . . I will shoulder this leadership task once again."[62]

Linked to Mao's continued dominance was a much broader pattern of leadership stability. This stability was reflected not only in the reelection of virtually all CC members but in personnel arrangements at all levels. The new Politburo Standing Committee consisted of the same five men who had made up the old Secretariat, formerly the inner core of leadership, plus the rapidly promoted Deng Xiaoping. The size of the full Politburo was nearly doubled to take in all pre-Congress members plus most PLA marshals who were not already included and all vice-premiers except Deng Zihui, who apparently was made to pay for his views on cooperativization. Within this top body there were some alterations in the pecking order, but apart from the significant rise of Deng Xiaoping and the dropping of Zhang Wentian (an old opponent of Mao's in the 1930s) and Kang Sheng to alternate status, these were relatively minor.

Similarly, the more than doubled ranks of full Central Committee members included not only nearly all former full members but also all but three alternates, who were promoted en masse. In addition, over 100 new individuals were added to the new CC – roughly one-third as full members and the remainder as alternates – yet the background characteristics of the 170-person body were remarkably similar to the 1945 CC.

The new central bodies also reflected the PRC's emerging institutional pattern. The expansion of the Politburo and CC was essentially accomplished by coopting the key figures in the regime's various hierarchies. As a result, the broader elite tendency toward specialization was carried into the highest bodies, guaranteeing that the views and interests of each major sector would be represented. Particularly important at the Politburo level was the selection of three key officials responsible for the economy – Li Fuchun, chairman of the State Planning Commission, Finance Minister Li Xiannian, and the chairman of the State Economic Commission Bo Yibo (as an alternate) – who now joined Chen Yun on the vital policy-making organ. The appointments further demonstrated the centralized nature of the system under the first FYP, since nearly three times as many CC members served in Beijing as in the provinces. Finally, the composition of the new top elite also reflected the post-1949 shift to civilian rule and the central role of the Party in the system. Full-time civilian Party and government officials outnumbered PLA leaders by 2 to 1 on the Politburo and nearly 3 to 1 on the CC while the ratio

62 "Sixty points on working methods" (19 February 1958), in Jerome Ch'en ed., *Mao papers: Anthology and bibliography*, 75.

of full-time Party, government, and military leaders was something on the order of 6:5:4.

The institutional representation on the new CC was a manifestation of the substantial degree to which Chinese politics had become bureaucratized. Party leaders had long been critical of various bureaucratic practices – red tape, organizational proliferation, decisions made in offices without firsthand knowledge of actual conditions – and by the mid-1950s were increasingly aware of the constraints placed on their options by the ever more specialized administrative machine they had created. Despite measures to reassert control, including transfers of Party cadres to key ministerial posts, strengthening the role of Party committees within government agencies, and attacks on excessive professionalization, leaders at all levels found their perspectives increasingly dominated by the organizations in which they served. Even the top decision-making generalists were trapped; as Mao complained in early 1958: "The Politburo has become a voting machine, . . . you give it a perfect document and it has to be passed."[63] The qualms of Mao and others notwithstanding, in ways besides the composition of the new ruling bodies, the proceedings of the Eighth Party Congress represented a full flowering of bureaucratic politics.

With the period of revolutionary transformations ostensibly past and economic development the main task, the Congress heard a long series of speeches by leaders articulating their departments' opinions on how to accomplish the broader goal. Similarly, the need to adjust the institutions of the new socialist system generated proposals advancing the interests of specific organizations. In some cases a degree of restraint was required when decisions had already gone against the institution concerned, but even her bureaucratic interests were expressed. Thus Minister of Defense Peng Dehuai could not explicitly call for more resources, since the decision had been made to cut defense spending from 32 to 20 percent of budgetary expenditure in the second FYP, but he still emphasized the need to press ahead with military modernization and to strengthen defense.

Where policies were still undecided, however, appeals for organizational interests were often blatant. This was especially the case in speeches by provincial Party leaders who sought favorable consideration from the central authorities over resources and policy guidelines. For example, Shandong's Tan Qilong hoped that "the central Ministry of Water Conservancy . . . will give us support with regard to technology, investments, and similar problems," and also asked "the relevant central ministries when settling sowing plans . . . not to be too rigid [and] enable us to make a reasonable apportion-

63 "Talks at the Nanning conference" (11–12 January 1958), *Miscellany*, 1.80.

ment in accordance with . . . actual conditions of the area."[64] Given the relaxed political atmosphere and the specialized nature of the job at hand, the Eighth Congress was a fitting occasion for articulating the views and interests of a vast array of bureaucratic organizations.

Party rectification and the Hundred Flowers

The criticisms of shortcomings in the system that had marked not only the Eighth Congress but much official commentary since spring 1956 foreshadowed a more systematic effort to overcome faults through a Party rectification movement. Initially, this campaign was to be patterned on the great Yan'an rectification of 1942–4, an effort to combat by relatively persuasive means dangerous ideological and political tendencies within the Party so that it could more successfully pursue the struggle against the Japanese and KMT. Now, with new problems and opportunities arising in the socialist era, the Party would again be reformed in an even more low-key manner, like a "gentle breeze and mild rain," to make it a more effective force for economic construction.

A major target of the reform effort was "subjectivism," the backward ideological state where unfamiliarity with changing conditions caused Party officials to apply unsuited concepts and methods arbitrarily to current problems. A particularly significant manifestation criticized at this juncture was the dogmatic copying of foreign (Soviet) experiences, and the recommended cure was to raise the general level of Marxist-Leninist theory in the Party, develop knowledge of specialized fields, and carry out research into actual conditions.

Closely linked to subjectivism was the sin of "bureaucratism," the drifting away of officials from the masses and social reality and toward becoming a privileged elite. This was particularly dangerous because as a part of a ruling organization, Party members were in a position to seek their own advantage and ignore the interests of the people. Various forms of supervision were required to prevent such abuses.

The third main evil attacked was "sectarianism," the tendency of Party members to feel superior to non-Party people and discriminate against them in organizational life. This was a problem of critical importance regarding the skilled intellectuals, and the Hundred Flowers and mutual supervision policies were aimed at overcoming it.

Concrete steps indicating a Party reform movement began in mid-1956 with a program for the study of rectification documents, but at the Eighth

64 Cited in Roderick MacFarquhar, "Aspects of the CCP's Eighth Congress (first session)," paper presented to the University Seminar on Modern East Asia: China, Columbia University, 19 February 1969, 10, 13.

Congress rectification was still a relatively low-priority item despite frequent attacks on the three evils. External events – the Polish October and the abortive Hungarian revolt – forced a higher priority for rectification. Mao subsequently claimed that the danger of letting problems fester, revealed by Hungary and Poland, convinced him of the need to handle "contradictions among the people" correctly, and at a November 1956 CC plenary meeting the Chairman announced a mild rectification campaign for "next year."

The lessons of Eastern Europe, however, were ambiguous. On the one hand, restiveness of the population as a result of bureaucratic perversions – a situation manifested to a more limited degree in China by a significant number of industrial strikes in 1956 – argued for dealing with such deviations before matters got out of control and thus enhanced the significance of rectification. On the other hand, the situation in Eastern Europe exploded in large part because political controls had been eroded, and the official CCP analysis of these events cited "revisionism" – the challenge to orthodox Party rule – as the main danger. This position argued for caution regarding Party reform, and in January a decision for full-scale rectification was announced for 1958, not 1957.

Mao clearly contributed to this more cautious approach with warnings against an "antisocialist tide" that allegedly had appeared in the latter half of 1956, but it is equally clear that he did not want a total halt to reform efforts or a return to arbitrary methods of dealing with intellectuals. In winter 1956–7, however, many middle- to upper-echelon officials and ordinary cadres attempted to do just that as a decidedly more restrictive atmosphere emerged.

By February, Mao concluded that bold action was required if Party reform was not to be totally eroded, and he intervened with two major speeches. In them Mao reverted to the fundamentally confident view of 1956. Victory had been achieved, and the main task was attending to flaws in the system. The intellectuals were a basically loyal force that could make great contributions to economic and cultural development. Now the nation was united as never before, and shortcomings could be overcome in a nondisruptive fashion. The Chairman, however, when revealing that rectification was once again scheduled for 1957, also introduced some novel and unsettling ideas concerning reform methods. Not only would Marxism-Leninism not be stipulated as the guiding ideology for criticism, but intellectuals would be invited to play a key role in offering criticism of the Party. Thus the Hundred Flowers was converted from an encouragement of academic debate to a method of conducting rectification. Mao sought to reassure cadres that intellectuals' criticism would be helpful and that rectification would still be according to "gentle breeze and mild rain" methods. But the prospect of CCP members being directly criticized by bourgeois intellectuals was enough to send shudders of concern throughout the Party elite.

There was considerable resistance to Mao's innovative approach, although the precise contours of opposition remain unclear.[65] Mao himself claimed in April that 90 percent of "Party comrades" had a negative attitude toward the refurbished Hundred Flowers and added that "I have no mass base."[66] Indeed, there does appear to have been widespread opposition among lower- and middle-rank cadres charged with controlling intellectuals on a day-to-day basis. These officials, whose immediate powers and prerogatives were at stake, had a different perspective from the more removed top leadership. Fearing that the process would get out of hand, such cadres failed to encourage the "blooming and contending" of intellectuals, but instead indiscriminately attacked their critical opinions.

At higher levels, there is good reason to believe that some leaders in the Party propaganda apparatus responsible for both publicizing the Hundred Flowers and organizing many of the conferences of intellectuals where blooming and contending took place were less than enthusiastic about the new policy. Clearly the CC's newspaper, the *People's Daily,* was laggard in responding to Mao's initiative and was sharply criticized by the Chairman as a result. This apparent resistance can be explained in essentially similar terms to the opposition of lower-ranking cadres: As officials responsible for the daily management of intellectuals, they probably felt the dangers of the new approach outweighed any possible benefits.

Conflict within the Politburo itself over rectification remains uncertain, despite some scholarly analysis that sees Mao seriously at loggerheads with his colleagues.[67] Certainly it is likely that such a novel policy, which exposed the Party of the proletariat to rebukes by intellectuals from bourgeois backgrounds, caused debate within the highest circles. Some information claims opposition to Mao on this issue by Liu Shaoqi and Peng Zhen, but the total pattern of evidence is inconclusive. Peng in particular was a vigorous supporter of blooming and contending in his publicized statements, and Liu, although silent in public, nevertheless toured the provinces and advanced views consistent with Mao's to closed Party meetings. In any case, if reservations were expressed behind the closed doors of the Politburo, they did not sharply polarize the leadership. The combination of Mao's power and the

65 The following analysis and that for the subsequent section on the Anti-Rightist Campaign is drawn from Teiwes, *Politics and purges,* chs. 6–7. For contrasting interpretations, see the sources cited in note 67.

66 "Talk at the Hangchow conference of the Shanghai bureau" (April 1957), in *Miscellany,* 1.67.

67 Major analyses holding that both the rectification and subsequent Anti-Rightist campaigns were occasions for major dissension within the top leadership are: MacFarquhar, *Origins,* 1, parts 3 and 4; and Richard H. Solomon, *Mao's revolution and the Chinese political culture,* ch. 17. This interpretation is also adopted in Chapter 2 of this volume.

general leadership's commitment to free debate within Party councils but disciplined implementation outside undoubtedly were the crucial factors in dampening any divisions. Other factors were also at work – the broad consensus on the nature of the new situation; the fact that Mao had not over a long period consistently pushed radical rectification methods that might have crystallized opposition but instead had changed his position according to altered circumstances; and finally, the fact that the initial response of the intellectuals to Mao's invitation was restrained and thus did not pose a dramatic threat to Party rule.

The at first tepid response of the intellectuals was understandable, given the ideological remolding they had been subjected to since the thought reform campaign of 1951–2. Despite anxiety that relaxation would be followed by renewed pressure, they finally reacted to repeated official prodding and to the fact that throughout May 1957 those who were bold enough to speak out were not punished with an outpouring of countercriticism. In one sense, the intellectuals' criticism by and large was not threatening to Party rule. The bulk of it dealt with problems and conflicts directly related to their roles and functions. Moreover, in the overwhelming number of cases, the criticisms advanced were similar to strictures directed at subjectivism, bureaucratism, and sectarianism in the official media since 1956. Even proposals for institutional change, such as the idea of turning the CPPCC into an upper house of the National People's Congress, reflected ideas that had been advanced by the highest Party leaders.

In another sense, however, the attacks were deeply unsettling. This was due less to some suggestions that deviations might be somehow intrinsic to the system or even the few extreme sentiments calling for the Party's demise than to the cumulative vehemence of complaints concerning intellectuals' daily confrontations with Party authority and the depth of discontent they reflected. The strength of feeling was particularly apparent in the views and actions of students, who even took to the streets to articulate their grievances. By focusing on the shortcomings of Party cadres in the everyday affairs of their work units, intellectuals were in effect raising the issue of the Party's competence to guide China in the new peiod of socialist construction. Yet it must be emphasized that this did not amount to a rejection of the system. Even some of the most outspoken student critics still supported public ownership, hailed Mao as "the revolutionary leader who saved China," and expressed a loyal if ambivalent attitude toward the CCP: "We want Party leadership, but we are resolutely opposed to the Party alone making decisions."[68] The results of

68 From a Beijing student pamphlet translated in Dennis J. Doolin, *Communist China: The politics of student opposition*, 50, 55.

blooming and contending suggested continuing support for the broad outlines of the system and for the CCP program of building a new China, but at the same time a deep alienation among skilled groups from the concrete manifestations of Party rule. By mid-May the Party leadership was dismayed at what had unfolded. The extent of discontent among intellectuals who had been assigned such a key role in development, and especially among students who had been raised in the PRC, was deeply distressing. Moreover, cadre morale had suffered a severe jolt as a result of being required to endure the critical onslaught.

Why did the Hundred Flowers experiment fail? Essentially the failure was due to some fundamental misconceptions concerning the new situation in China. Assuming that the intellectuals essentially stood on the side of socialism and had no fundamental clashes of interest with the system, Mao concluded that they could make positive contributions even to so sensitive an affair as Party rectification. This did not take into account the facts that bourgeois intellectuals as a group had often been subjected severe pressure since the early days of the PRC, that their interests as they conceived them had often been grievously violated, and that their relations with Party cadres were marked by mutual mistrust. When Mao thrust the intellectuals into the forefront of rectification, he in effect asked them to perform an impossible task: to criticize boldly Party authorities they often feared and loathed, yet to do so in the spirit of a gentle breeze and mild rain.

Party cadres too were placed in an unprecedented position. In effect, they were being asked to redefine Party leadership in ways that were never precisely stipulated to take into account the views and talents of non-Party intellectuals. Moreover, they were themselves subject to the criticism by these individuals of suspect class origins and backward ideology, something that seemed most unjust. Given the underlying tensions between cadres and intellectuals, any effort that exacerbated those tensions, however unwittingly, was bound to get out of control. (For further discussion, see *CHOC* 14, Chapter 5.)

The Anti-Rightist Campaign

Although a direct counterattack was launched only in early June 1957, by mid-May top CCP leaders decided that unchecked blooming and contending was unacceptably weakening Party control over the intellectuals. Mao was in the forefront of this effort despite his earlier championing of the Hundred Flowers. Not only did the Chairman undertake the key initiatives that began the policy shift, but throughout the summer of 1957 Party policies toward "rightists," as the non-Party critics were dubbed, all bore his imprint. Mao, moreover, was not shy about reversing himself on a whole series of specific issues. For example, in April Mao hailed the non-Party Shanghai paper *Wenhui bao* for publicizing critical opinions. In July he bitterly attacked the same newspaper as a rightist organ. In February he proposed a review of counterrevolutionary cases, but in October he denounce the democratic Party leader Luo Longji for a similar proposal.

Whatever the reasons for so unscrupulous an about-face in these and other instances, the net effect was to remove any differences that may have existed between the Chairman and other leaders. With his illusions about the intellectuals shattered, Mao came down strongly on the side of firm Party control.

The counterattack on the critics took the form of an Anti-Rightist Campaign. This campaign was defensive in tone. It attempted to refute critical arguments advanced by intellectuals in the spring and restore Party dominance in the urban organizations where blooming and contending had been primarily conducted. Ironically, given the intellectuals' criticism of heavy-handed Party methods, organizational measures taken in conjunction with the Anti-Rightist Campaign – particularly the transfer of reliable Party cadres to leadership positions in educational and cultural units – resulted in a substantial increase in Party control compared with the situation before the Hundred Flowers. The main focus of the movement itself was initially on leading members of democratic parties who were singled out as the core of rightist groups. These individuals had quite accurately been disparaged by student critics as "cautious old men" for the moderate views they advanced in the spring, yet now they were charged with plotting the overthrow of the regime. They were subjected to violent press attacks and large-scale struggle meetings and forced into abject confessions; yet by late 1958–9 most were restored to posts in the democratic parties, indicating that the harshest accusations against them were not taken seriously.

Nevertheless, they served as useful symbols to set the tone for the campaign, which spread to rightists generally within intellectual organizations from mid-July. Although non-Party intellectuals were the key targets, Party intellectuals who had spoken out for their professional rather than their Party interests in the spring also suffered on a smaller scale. The total impact on China's intellectuals was devastating: Altogether some 550,000 were labeled rightists, the psychological pressures of struggle sessions resulted in a significant number of suicides, and reform through labor was apparently meted out on a large scale. In the post-Mao period the severity of the campaign has been regarded as a major mistake of "enlarging the scope of class struggle," with perhaps 98 percent of all rightist labels wrongly applied.[69] (For further discussion, see *CHOC* 14, Chapter 5.)

69 The 98 percent assessment, and also the 550,000 figure for rightists, appears in the 1980 report by Liao, "Historical experiences," October 1981, 80–1. The 1981 official *Resolution on certain questions in*

The harshness of the movement should not obscure the fact that the leadership's attitude toward intellectuals did not become totally negative in mid-1957. In an effort to avoid complete alienation, official guidelines for the campaign held that only a small number of intellectuals were rightists and advocated a lenient overall approach. This reflected a continuing belief that intellectuals had an important role to play in China's modernization despite their ideological backwardness.

Mao expressed the leadership's ambivalence in July by attacking intellectuals as unwilling to submit to the Party but, nevertheless, citing the need to win over individual "great intellectuals [who are] useful to us."[70] The Hundred Flowers fiasco had demonstrated that intellectuals could not be relied on politically, but it did not settle the issue of their role in economic and cultural development. As the Anti-Rightist Campaign unfolded in the summer of 1957, overall economic policy initially remained on the same moderate course as in 1956, an approach requiring a major role for professional expertise. Thus it was still quite possible that once Party control was reestablished, a policy of concessions to intellectuals short of a leading role in Party rectification could have been adopted. The severity of the Anti-Rightist Campaign, however, undoubtedly damaged the enthusiasm of intellectuals for the Party's developmental goals. The leadership, moreover, now had reason to doubt a strategy that placed wavering intellectuals in so central a role.

Other factors were also at work. The general attempt to deal with grievances in society by political relaxation had adverse social effects with important economic ramifications. Of particular significance was the situation in the countryside. The critical atmosphere toward APC abuses officially encouraged in 1956 led to what subsequently was called a "small typhoon" including substantial peasant withdrawals from the cooperatives in the winter of 1956–7. The Hundred Flowers led to further deterioration of the situation as disgruntled peasants, reportedly encouraged by press and radio reports of urban blooming and contending, challenged the rural cadre structure and increasingly engaged in such "spontaneous capitalist" activities as decentralizing APC responsibility to individual peasant households, demanding more money and grain from the state while selling less surplus to it, and speculative activities.

Particularly disturbing was the fact that some cadres participated in capitalist behavior and conspired with peasants to conceal or underestimate grain

the history of our Party since the founding of the People's Republic of China {27 June 1981}, NCNA, 30 June 1981, trans. in *FBIS Daily Report: China*, 1 July 1981, K1–38. more cautiously affirmed the correctness of counterattacking rightists but held that the scope of attack was too broad.

70 "Zai Shanghai shi gejie renshi huiyi shang de jianghua" (Speech at the conference of all circles in Shanghai municipality), (8 July 1957) in *Wansui* (1969), 121.

output. This, together with another poor crop whereby food output lagged behind the rate of population increase, resulted in a severe grain supply crisis. Party leaders responded with a summer 1957 decision to clamp down on the rural free market and launch a rural socialist education movement. This movement conducted propaganda on the claimed superiority of socialism among the peasants generally, arrested offending former landlords and rich peasants, carried out a limited purge of rural Party members who engaged in irregular practices, and as a result of bolstering the collective sector, restored overall cadre authority vis-à-vis the peasantry. Once again the combination of persuasive and coercive methods, together with a direct appeal to the interests of the new rural elite, was successful in achieving Party objectives.

Added to such social and political problems were related economic ones. The unsatisfactory performance of the agricultural sector was underlined by consecutive below-par years in 1956 and 1957. Not only had the new cooperative structure failed to provide a production spurt, but the subsequent emphasis on material incentives within the APC framework had also been unsuccessful. The lag in agriculture had its impact on industrial growth, and Zhou Enlai announced a 20 percent cut in capital construction in June 1957. Following the logic of the "Ten great relationships," the leadership modestly increased total state investment in agriculture in 1957, but this promised no breakthrough. With the Soviet economic strategy called into question, one possible alternative was to focus on gradually increasing agricultural output while accepting a reduced rate of overall growth. But since Party leaders viewed a high rate of growth as a key goal, such as alternative was an unlikely long-term strategy.

Thus by fall 1957 a number of pressures were converging for change in developmental strategy: perceived deficiencies of the Soviet model, the questionable reliability of the intellectuals, the socially disruptive consequences of political relaxation, and a sluggish economy. Moreover, the cautious marginal adjustments that had been made to the Soviet model – greater awareness of the key economic role of agriculture, moves toward administrative decentralization, and more emphasis on smaller-scale industrial projects and locally supported education – provided outlooks and programs that could be developed into a grander innovative strategy. Finally, Mao and some of his leadership colleagues could look back from the latter part of 1957 over the events of the preceding two years and draw some dubious but nevertheless influential conclusions.

On the positive side, Mao decided that although his initial view on the decisive victory of socialist transformation in 1956 had been premature, as success had been limited to the ownership front, the rectification and Anti-

Rightist campaigns had achieved that fundamental victory on the political and ideological fronts. Therefore, the Chinese people were ready as never before to carry out an economic and technical revolution. From a more negative perspective, Mao declared that the "opposing rash advance" policies had been a serious mistake that not only caused economic losses by dampening the enthusiasm of the masses but also encouraged the rightists to launch their political assault. The lesson to be drawn was that the leap forward approach of early 1956 must be pushed without reservation in order to sustain the ardor of the workers and peasants. These ideas began to become dominant during the plenary meeting of the Central Committee in September – October 1957, and by the end of the year China was well on the road to the Great Leap Forward.

Conclusions

Although major problems faced Party leaders in late 1957, the overall performance of the PRC since 1949 had been remarkably successful. Despite resentment of particular features of CCP rule, the regime had obtained far-reaching popular support as a result of achievements in securing social order, launching economic development, improving living conditions, and restoring national pride. At the same time it had accomplished a basic social and institutional transformation, so that by 1956 China had entered the socialist stage.

The reasons for these successes varied. As emphasized throughout this analysis, the Soviet model and leadership unity were critical factors, factors, that would be removed or weakened with the Great Leap Forward. In particular, with the model providing clear goals and unity producing strong commitment to official programs, conditions were optimal for utilizing to full advantage the disciplined Party apparatus that had played a central role in revolutionary victory. Although hardly immune to organizational and political shortcomings, the Party organization generally proved responsive to major initiatives and policies – sometimes overzealously so. In the 1949–57 period, with brief exception of the Hundred Flowers experiment, CCP programs reinforced the authority of this disciplined apparatus and thus enhanced the regime's capabilities for development and transformation.

Success was also due to CCP leaders' skillfully combining persuasive, coercive, and tangible appeals in securing compliance. Constant efforts to convince the populace of the Party's view persuaded many individuals and groups of the correctness of Communist policies and made even more people aware of acceptable modes of behavior. Coercion was used both to break the opposition of hostile groups and to impress the majority that the Party was a force that could not be resisted. And programs designed to further the tangible interests of key social groups – especially poorer peasants and the burgeoning cadre elite – provided crucial support for the CCP on the basis of perceived self-interest.

Another important factor was the applicability of strategies and methods that had served so well during the revolutionary period. The mass mobilization techniques developed in the rural base areas of North China proved adaptable to land reform and agricultural cooperativization throughout China after 1949. Also, notwithstanding the miscalculations of 1956–7, the united front tactic that had been effective against the Japanese and KMT generally succeeded in narrowing active resistance, neutralizing wavering elements, and maximizing support under conditions of CCP rule. Especially important was the fact that the pre-1949 realism and careful marshaling of resources largely prevailed between 1949 and 1957. Although the ambitious programs of this initial period often stretched organizational resources, they rarely overextended them to the point where official hierarchies could no longer effectively guide social and economic change. And when this did occur in early 1956, it was corrected in a matter of months.

Finally, the accomplishments of the first eight years were due in large measure to the absence of any perceived incompatibility among the goals pursued or methods used by the CCP. Social goals and economic objectives were regarded as mutually reinforcing. Agricultural cooperatives were the accepted solution to production problems as well as ideologically desirable, and socialization of the modern sector both eliminated capitalism and facilitated planned economic growth. Similarly, institutionalization and mass campaigns were both accepted as appropriate means for socialist ends. Campaigns were suited to major efforts at social transformation, and strong institutions were needed to guide planned development and manage a socialist society. Even where tensions were acknowledged, as between military modernization and PLA traditions, it was assumed that contradictions could be resolved without damage to any important goal. In later years, as Mao and other Party leaders increasingly realized that economic objectives had major social costs, that strong institutions could threaten some values while safeguarding others, and that the very content of socialism was uncertain, the potential for conflict grew and the relatively smooth advances of the formative period became increasingly difficult to sustain.

CHAPTER 2

THE GREAT LEAP FORWARD AND THE SPLIT IN THE YAN'AN LEADERSHIP 1958–65

KENNETH LIEBERTHAL

AN OVERVIEW

The year 1958 began with the Chinese Communist leaders optimistic about their ability to lead the country up the path of rapid economic development and social progress. To be sure, not all Politburo members agreed on the best methods to use to accomplish these great tasks, but overall confidence was high and the degree of underlying unity clearly sufficient to enable the Chinese Communist Party (CCP) to act in a consistent and decisive manner. Seven years later, deep fissures had rent this leadership to the point where Mao Zedong himself stood on the verge of launching a devastating attack against many of the colleagues with whom he had worked for more than three decades. That attack would, in turn, launch China into a decade so tumultuous that even in the early 1980s leaders in Beijing would look back to the eve of the 1958–65 era wistfully as the time when the Party's power, prestige, and unity had reached pinnacles. The eight years between 1958 and 1965 were a period of major transition in the Chinese revolution.

To be sure, not all had gone smoothly for the Chinese Communists after 1949. There had been significant disagreement among the leaders over the pace and contours of the development effort. During 1953, for example, Finance Minister Bo Yibo had come under sharp criticism for advocating tax policies that would, Mao felt, slow down the development of the public sector of the economy. In 1955, Mao openly disagreed with his colleagues over the pace of the proposed collectivization of agriculture and effectively overturned the program they had adopted. His efforts in 1957 to encourage non-Party intellectuals to criticize the Party had brought bitter disagreement at the highest levels. And throughout this period there were repeated efforts to rectify what were seen as unhealthy tendencies in the Party and government bureaucracies as the new system of political power became consolidated.

The key point about the 1949–57 period, however, is that the conflicts were handled in a way that managed to preserve basic unity among the elite and maintain the élan of the revolutionary movement. Similarly, although many citizens dissented bitterly from the CCP's policies of this period, the overall prestige of the Party and of the new system remained high. The Communists could rightly proclaim that their policies were making China stronger and wealthier, even if they were forced to "break some eggs" to make their national omelette. It was precisely this prestige that the CCP lost during the 1958–65 period, with virtually catastrophic consequences. It is ironic that this period proved on balance to be so destructive, for it began with the Great Leap Forward (GLF), a program based on almost utopian optimism about what the Party, with its methods of mass mobilization, could accomplish.

During the spring and summer of 1958 Mao and his colleagues pushed the Great Leap idea as an alternative to the development strategy that had been imported from the Soviet Union for the first Five-Year Plan (FYP) of 1953–7. Needing some way to overcome bottlenecks that appeared to preclude a simple repetition of the first FYP strategy, the Chinese leaders settled on an approach that utilized the mass mobilization skills they had honed to a fine edge during the Anti-Japanese War years in Yan'an. This new strategy (with its various component parts, including communization of the countryside), threw the country into a frenzy of production activity that lasted into 1959. Key elements in this strategy, however, ultimately made the production upsurge a prelude to economic disaster rather than to the anticipated time of plenty.

The Great Leap strategy entailed significant changes in the political situation. It stripped considerable power from the central government bureaucracy and transferred it in many cases to local Party cadres. It shunted technical specialists aside in production units and replaced them with political generalists good at firing up the enthusiasm of the workers. It raised the pervasiveness of political demands in all fields to a new level, as superhuman work motivated by political zeal was key to the successful implementation of this new developmental approach. And it introduced important new strains into Sino-Soviet relations, as it de facto decreased the authority of the many Soviet advisers in China and implicitly challenged the previously sacrosanct Soviet model.

Given the extent of these changes, serious problems naturally arose when the Great Leap began to falter. By the end of 1958 Mao and others were aware that extremism in the name of the Leap was already causing some damage, and they made appropriate modifications in targets and policies to keep the movement on track. But information about the actual results of state grain procurement in early 1959 revealed that the situation was worse than was previously thought, and during that spring Mao led the effort to bring greater rationality and efficiency to the program. The movement proved difficult to bring under control, however, as those who had inherited greater power during 1958 continued to resist any retreat from the policies of that year.

During the summer of 1959 this problem of bringing the GLF under control became entangled in elite politics in a very damaging way. Peng Dehuai, a leading military man who had long had a stormy relationship with Mao, returned from a trip to the Soviet Union and Eastern Europe in June and shortly thereafter made a biting critique of the "petty-bourgeois fanaticism" of the Great Leap at a major Party work conference convened at Lushan. The rationale for Peng's actions at Lushan remains uncertain, but Mao chose to interpret it as a direct attack on his personal leadership and responded sharply. Mao demanded that Peng and his supporters be removed from power, and he suggested that the Soviet Union had become involved in Peng's challenge. The immediate results were twofold: The purge of Peng swamped the efforts to rein in the Great Leap and produced a second upsurge in radical policies lasting into 1960, and relations between China and the Soviet Union became more strained.

Both these results bore bitter fruit in 1960. The Leap upsurge caused enormous further damage to the economy, to the extent that by late 1960 famine was stalking the land. Relations with Moscow continued to deteriorate to the point that in the summer of 1960 the Soviets suddenly withdrew all their assistance from China. Soviet aid was at that time still sufficiently crucial to a number of key industrial development projects that this action produced grave economic consequences in the People's Republic of China (PRC). It also distracted Beijing's attention from the economic disaster that was looming in the countryside, thus delaying timely measures to salvage the situation there.

By the end of 1960, therefore, the GLF had produced economic disaster in the hinterland, and during 1961 this fundamental economic malaise spread through the cities. Beijing now recognized the full gravity of the problem and drafted a series of programmatic documents to deal with the situation. During this year of crisis, there is every indication that Mao supported the far-reaching retreat from the GLF that his colleagues devised. Indeed, in June 1961 Mao made a self-criticism at a key Party meeting in Beijing,[1] and the Party as a whole adopted policies of retrenchment as official doctrine.

Once the crisis began to ease, however, tensions among the leaders rose as

1 Since not full text of this confession is available, it is unfortunately not possible to characterize it as either thorough or perfunctory.

Mao sought to regain his position as the person who defined the basic tasks of the moment. His power and image had eroded as a consequence of his serious misjudgments during the GLF, and his concern about a potential waning of his influence had increased. He had reached the conclusion that recent events in the Soviet Union had demonstrated that under improper leadership, a Communist state could actually degenerate into a highly exploitative system. Substantively, Mao concluded that the GLF had discredited the notion of making phenomenal economic progress by relying on mass mobilization, but he still firmly believed in the importance of mass mobilization for preventing the bureaucratic degeneration of the revolution that had occurred in the Soviet Union.

Those of Mao's colleagues in direct control of the CCP apparatus disagreed with this latter judgment. They were anxious to restore internal CCP discipline and to pursue a path of economic development that made appropriate use of specialists and technical expertise. Although they shared many of Mao's goals, therefore, they shied away from some of his methods. Given the distribution of executive power in the wake of the Great Leap, they probably would have carried the day – implementing Mao's basic agenda but modifying it in ways that made it compatible with their more bureaucratic approach – had Mao not found some key allies to boost his strength.

These allies were his wife, Jiang Qing; the man he had put in to replace Peng Dehuai, Lin Biao; and a key member of the security system, Kang Sheng, who joined forces with the Chairman and his former secretary, Chen Boda, to overthrow the system that had emerged in the wake of the GLF. The gradual formation of this coalition between 1962 and 1965 will be detailed further on. Each member had personal reasons for joining the coalition, and all agreed on the desirability of changing the succession so that Liu Shaoqi (or someone else like Liu) would not eventually take over full power from Mao. The period thus became tangled up with coalition politics and intrigues over the succession.

The specific issues in contention, of course, changed over the years. During the early part of 1962 there was a significant disagreement over the degree of recovery that had already taken place in the countryside. Mao felt that recovery had gone far enough to permit Beijing again to seize the initiative and reassert its authority. Liu Shaoqi, Deng Xiaoping, Chen Yun, and others disagreed, arguing that the Party must continue to implement emergency measures to salvage the situation. The question of rehabilitating those who in 1959 had warned about the dangers inherent in the Leap also arose then. Mao agreed that many of these "rightists" should now be rehabilitated, but he drew the line at bringing back Peng Dehuai, to the chagrin of many of his colleagues (but not of Lin Biao).

By the fall of 1962 Mao had carried the day on the issue of the degree of recovery from the GLF, and the question now shifted to the best means to restore the regime's power and prestige in the country. Mao advocated a policy of rebuilding the Party in the countryside using means that entailed extensive political mobilization of the peasantry. His colleagues subsequently tried to achieve rural Party rectification through internal bureaucratic means instead. In his frustration with the bureaucratic biases of other Politburo leaders, Mao adopted two measures to enhance the role of his brand of politics in the system.

Starting in 1963, the Chairman increasingly promoted the People's Liberation Army (PLA) as the model organization for Chinese to follow. The PLA had, under Lin Biao, acquitted itself well in technical military tasks, from progress toward building an atom bomb (the first Chinese atom bomb test took place in October 1964) to achieving an impressive series of victories in the border war with Indian forces in the fall of 1962. At the same time, Lin had promoted political work among the troops, centered on the study of Mao Zedong's thoughts as condensed and dogmatized in the *Quotations from Chairman Mao.* The PLA in Mao's eyes became an organization that had achieved the optimum synthesis of technique and politics, and Mao sought to expand its role in the political system. Lin Biao strongly encouraged this development – and the power of the Chairman on whom it depended.

Also beginning in 1963, Mao supervised the drafting of nine "letters" from the Central Committee (CC) of the CCP to the CC of the Communist Party of the Soviet Union (CPSU). These polemical documents spelled out Mao's contention that the Soviet Union had degenerated into a nonsocialist political system, a development Mao called going down the path of "revisionism." Mao used these letters to give wide publicity in China to the issue of revisionism and, essentially, to make his case (somewhat obliquely) against the policies of colleagues whom he opposed.

Between 1963 and 1965 Liu Shaoqi and the other Party leaders who later were to become the key initial targets of the Cultural Revolution carried out a very impressive program of economic recovery, bringing production in 1965 back up to the levels achieved on the eve of the GLF in almost every sector (and, of course, ahead of these levels in some sectors). As noted, these leaders appear to have tried to accommodate many of Mao's demands while channeling them so as to make them less disruptive to the bureaucratic system they had reconstructed. The available documentation suggests that these leaders were not oblivious of the dangers lurking in the machinations of Lin Biao, Jiang Qing, Kang Sheng, and their followers, but there appears little reason to believe that before 1965 they saw these dangers as threatening in a fundamental sense.

Liu Shaoqi, Deng Xiaoping, and their colleagues of like mind seem to have regarded the situation as difficult but not impossible to manage. They were ultimately proved disastrously wrong in this evaluation. They had tried to meet Mao partway and to limit as much as possible the leverage of his eventual coalition partners in the system. Thus, for example, the attempt to enhance the power of the army by establishing military-type political departments in the civilian governing organs starting in 1964 met strong resistance, as did Jiang Qing's repeated efforts to acquire authority over cultural policy. But as the middle of the decade approached, Mao himself saw this ongoing give-and-take less as the inevitable frictions of national politics and more in terms of a Manichean struggle of good against evil. This new perspective, of course, raised the stakes enormously, and an increasingly disturbed and restless Mao began to take the fateful steps that led to unleashing the Cultural Revolution in 1966.

This brief overview captures the highlights of a period in which four fundamental transitions took place: from a basically united leadership to one that was deeply divided; from a wholly legitimate CCP rule to one far less readily accepted; from a relatively disciplined and spirited CCP membership to one demoralized and uncertain; and from agreed-upon ways of handling intra-Party conflicts to disagreement over basic norms for resolving such tensions. In short, during 1958–65 the Chinese Communist movement lost some of its key political assets, both in terms of the organizational weapon it possessed in the Party and in terms of its reservoir of legitimacy among the population. These losses contributed to the deep divisions that led in turn to the Cultural Revolution. In greater detail, this story unfolded as follows.

ORIGINS OF THE GLF

Many forces contributed to the decision to adopt the policies collectively known as the GLF. Among these, the most fundamental were the problems produced by the first FYP, modeled after the Soviet Union's development strategy. These problems were political, social, and economic, with the economic issues at their heart.

The Soviet strategy developed by Stalin and adopted by the PRC demanded two conditions: that a planning mechanism channel resources overwhelmingly into the development of heavy industry, with the metallurgical industry receiving first priority; and that the rural areas be starved for funds and exploited as needed to provide resources to permit the growth of heavy industry in particular and of the urban sector in general. The Chinese copied their planning apparatus so successfully from the Soviets that during their respective first FYPs, the Chinese managed to devote nearly 48 percent of their public capital investment to industrial development, whereas the comparable Soviet figure was under 42 percent. The problem arose in the other part of the equation – the exploitation of the rural areas to support this urban industrial policy.

The Soviet Union had used agriculture during the first FYP both as a source of exports that would enable the government to import machinery and technology for industry and as a source of food for the rapidly expanding urban working force. Peasant deaths in the millions occurred either directly from Moscow's harsh imposition of the collective farm system or less directly from the resulting famine when the government maintained constant levels of agricultural procurement even as agricultural production fell more than 25 percent from 1929 to 1932–3. This approach assumed that there was a real surplus in agriculture and sought a way to make that surplus serve the goals of the political leadership.

The Chinese case differed in two fundamental respects from that of the Soviet Union. First and more important, per capita output in China in 1957 was only half that of the Soviet Union in 1928 in the production of grain (290 vs. 566 kg per person) and vegetable oils (1.7 vs. 3.0 kg per person). Thus, whereas the Soviets could debate how best to secure control over a consistent rural surplus, the Chinese had to develop a means first to create and enhance that surplus and then to gain control over its distribution. Second, whereas Soviet Party membership was more than 70 percent urban, the CCP was more than 70 percent rural in social composition. These differences in the social compositions of the two parties presumably made the CCP somewhat more reluctant to adopt a strategy premised on the misery of the countryside and the starvation of millions of country dwellers. Thus, in late 1957 China groped for a strategy that would enhance agricultural output while still permitting the rapid growth of capital-intensive heavy industry. The different elements of such a strategy, especially with regard to agriculture, were hotly debated at the Third Plenum of the Eighth CC in September and early October 1957.

The problem in agriculture was how to persuade the peasants to increase their output and marketings while Beijing devoted state investment to the heavy industrial sector. There was clear recognition among the leaders that the formula followed up to then would not solve the problem. Mao Zedong wanted to utilize political and organizational tools to boost peasant output. Chen Yun, the fifth-ranking member of the Party and the highest-ranking economic specialist, however, premised his recommended solution on the assumption that the peasants would respond only to increased material incentives and not to either coercion or ideological exhortation. Material incentives required not only that the peasants receive good prices for their products but also that they have consumer goods available to purchase with the money they earned. State investment would, therefore, have to shift somewhat in the direction of light industry in order to provide the consumer goods necessary to make this rural strategy work. The light industrial sector would also produce relatively quick turnover on capital with a substantial profit rate, thus providing over time an adequate capital pool for the speedy development of heavy industry.

In this balanced approach, therefore, Chen argued essentially that each sector could help the others and that the Chinese need not view trade-offs among sectors as a zero-sum game. He also pointed out the impossibility of feeding the large numbers of highly paid urban industrial workers if his advice were to be ignored (as, in fact, it was). In many ways, Chen Yun's policies in 1957 paralleled those of Nikolai Bukharin in the Soviet Union in 1927–8; and as Bukharin was brushed aside by Stalin, Chen was pushed from center stage by Mao.

Chen's policy recommendations, which amounted to the most comprehensive developmental alternative put forward in the China of the 1950s, were defeated in part by simple impatience. Chen himself readily admitted that his formula for balanced growth would not produce any developmental miracles in the next few years. But the explanation for Chen's defeat is in fact more complex. His strategy presumed that the Chinese government, as distinct from the CCP, would continue to play the central role in running the economy. The system established under the first FYP placed enormous power in the central government ministries. Although these were, like all bodies, under overall Party control, the greatest concentration of non-Communist experts was employed in the staffs of these ministries.

Ministerial work inevitably placed a premium on literacy, statistical skills, and the ability to deal in abstractions – all skills far more prevalent among the urban intelligentsia than among the peasant mass that had contributed so many stalwarts to the Party during the years in the wilderness. But the Hundred Flowers movement and the resulting Anti-Rightist Campaign in 1957 had largely discredited the urban intelligentsia and any development strategy that depended centrally on their contributions. Indeed, the harsh penalties exacted of the rightists in the wake of this campaign literally reduced the numbers of intellectuals outside of prison camps and thus changed the parameters of human capital that would inevitably shape the development strategy the government adopted.

The more radical, anti-intellectual atmosphere spread from the urban to the rural areas during the late summer and fall of 1957. In the countryside the Anti-Rightist Campaign was directed against those who had voiced doubts about the efficacy of the rapid cooperativization (essentially, collectivization) of agriculture that had swept China during the previous two years. Collectivization at China's low level of agricultural development and mechanization had itself been a policy signifying the primacy of human organizational factors in the country's economic growth. Thus, the Anti-Rightist Campaign in both urban and rural areas bolstered the position of those who believed that proper mobilization of the populace could accomplish tasks that the "bourgeois experts" dismissed as impossible. As such, the Anti-Rightist Campaign in the countryside facilitate the adoption of a policy of mass mobilization to build irrigation facilities during the winter of 1957–8. This policy proved highly successful, but it also highlighted several problems inherent in the rural organizational structure at that time.

First, a lack of appropriate organizational units to marshal people and resources hampered large-scale mobilization. Second, there was an absolute shortage of labor if the peasants were to put in millions of man-days at nonagricultural tasks such as dam building. Third, there was a continuing problem over establishing a good fit between basic-level government units and the economic units in the countryside. In 1956 the government had abolished the districts (*qu*) and amalgamated the administrative villages (*xiang*), but this had led to a series of escalating organizational problems that had not been resolved by the winter of 1957–8. The upshot of these issues was pressure in the countryside to devise a bigger unit that would be able to control large labor resources and also to fit neatly into the government administrative hierarchy.

The solution devised after some experimentation in early 1958 was the People's Commune (*renmin gongshe*), which itself then underwent major organizational changes between 1958 and 1962. The initial communes were huge, centralized units embracing several standard marketing areas.[2] They served both as the basic-level government organs and the key economic units. Their size permitted them to take control over not only agricultural production but also local industry, commerce, education, and the militia. Under commune direction, moreover, the organization of agricultural labor changed dramatically, with many peasants now assigned to specialized work teams that traveled from one village to another to perform particular tasks.

These initial communes proved too large to manage, and their attempt to base members' incomes on the total production of units that embraced tens of

2 The standard marketing area included the villages that traditionally marketed their goods at the same periodic market. These areas had social as well as economic identities, as marriages often took place between peasants of different villages within the same SMA. See G. William Skinner, "Marketing and social structure of rural China," *JAS* (November 1964, February 1965, and May 1965). A June 1961 CC decision had mandated that communes be reduced to the size of former *xiang* or amalgamated *xiang:* Fang Weizhong, ed., *Zhonghua renmin gongheguo jingji dashiji* (Record of major economic events in the PRC), 306.

thousands of peasants provided too few incentives for individual effort. Therefore, in a series of stages from 1959 to 1962, the effective level of collective organization became smaller. Within the communes, this evolution entailed the formation first of brigades and then of smaller units called "teams," with the income of individual peasants depending on the total output of these successively smaller units. Also, by 1962 the communes themselves had been reduced in size, with the total number of communes increasing from the original 25,000 to 75,000. By 1962 these changes made many communes conform roughly to the former standard marketing areas and made the most important economic unit within the commune, the team, coincide with either small villages themselves or with socially relatively cohesive neighborhoods within larger villages.

The shift from expertise toward mobilization in both urban and rural areas as of the conclusion of the Anti-Rightist Campaign meant that the apparatus best suited to mobilization efforts – the CCP – would assume a relatively greater role than it had under the Soviet-style strategy followed since 1953. This expansion in the span of control of the CCP would inevitably come at the cost of the government bureaucracy. Some administrative decentralization would strip power from central ministries. An important result of the discrimination against expertise would be the dismantling of the state statistical system, the bulwark of a development strategy that depended on expert calculation of possibilities and optimalities. And at the highest levels, the CCP apparatus directed by the Politburo and the Secretariat (headed by Deng Xiaoping) would play a far more important role, with the functions of the premier and the State Council reduced accordingly.

Two more sets of issues fed into the development of the Great Leap strategy. On a social level, the first FYP had adopted the Soviet approach to material and status differentials, with the result that Chinese urban society was becoming increasingly stratified by the mid-1950s. This stratification extended into the government bureaucracies, where the free supply system was replace by a complex system of civil service grades in 1955. Similar grading systems were applied to various sectors of industry, commerce, and the educational system. The natural results were increasing status consciousness among the Chinese and encouragement of the type of careerism that was good for economic growth but rubbed against Mao Zedong's revolutionary grain. A strategy that relied more on ideological and coercive than on economic and status incentives might upset this unwanted social spinoff of the first FYP.

Second, Mao's own position in the system would be affected by the type of economic development strategy pursued. The Chairman's personal political strengths lay in the areas of foreign policy (especially toward the great powers), rural policy, and issues of revolutionary change (essentially, defining how rapidly change could be carried out, given the prevailing mood and conditions in the country). Urban economics, and especially the technicalities of finance and planning, were subjects about which he knew very little. Thus, Mao complained bitterly at the Nanning Conference in January 1958 that the Finance Ministry had for several years been sending the Politburo position papers so technical and complex that he simply had to sign them without even reading them. This situation naturally limited Mao's role in the system, and he determined to change it by forcing through a strategy of development that shifted the action from the areas in which he lacked strength to those where he felt more confident.

On the most fundamental level, finally, the motivations producing the GLF strategy drew from very deep currents in the history of the Chinese Communist movement. Once before, when the revolution faced seemingly intractable odds, a creative set of military and political policies centered on mobilizing a wide range of forces had saved the day. The CCP had entered Yan'an as a bedraggled remnant of what it had been in the mid-1930s. By the end of World War II the CCP and its army had vastly increased in size, strength, and vigor, even though the intervening years had witnessed almost constant military challenges from the Guomindang or the Japanese. The CCP quite naturally tended in later years to idealize this time in the wilderness, seeing it as a period when the Party was truly close to the masses, when bureaucratism and social stratification did not tarnish revolutionary idealism, and when well-motivated leaders and their followers overcame seemingly insuperable odds to survive and eventually conquer. Given Mao's disgust with the sociopolitical results of the first FYP and the fundamental agricultural bottleneck that seemed to threaten the chances for the rapid industrial development that he craved, Mao and much of the rest of the top leadership seem to have harkened back to the Yan'an spirit (and methods) as the source of their hope. Mass mobilization, social leveling, attacks on bureaucratism, disdain for material obstacles – these approaches would again save the Chinese revolution for its founders.

Thus, a broad range of forces pushed the leadership, and Mao in particular, toward adoption of a Great Leap strategy in 1958. A developmental dilemma, combined with dissatisfaction over the social consequences of the Soviet model, produced the search for a mobilizational alternative to previous practice. Organizational tensions between the Party and state apparatuses and between basic-level governmental and economic units in the countryside added to the stresses. Finally, beginning at the Qingdao Conference in July 1957 and continuing through the following year, Mao began advocating a radically new approach toward making China strong and wealthy. This strategy, which was fleshed out during a series of meetings (at the Third Plenum in September–October, the Hangzhou and Nanning conferences in January 1958, and the Chengdu Conference in March), called for use of organizational and mobilizational techniques to bring about simultaneous rapid development of agriculture and industry. The logical next step, the GLF, was formally adopted at the Second Session of the Eighth Party Congress in May 1958. One of its most prominent features, the communization of agriculture, became official policy at the Beidaihe Conference in August of that year.

The GLF strategy

Briefly, the strategy of the GLF had four key elements:[3]

1. To make up for a lack of capital in both industry and agriculture by fully mobilizing underemployed labor power. This approach would be especially important in the rural sector, where mass mobilization would produce essentially self-financed development that would solve the agricultural stumbling block to rapid overall growth and would provide inputs (especially food) for urban industrial growth. This, in turn, would allow China to accomplish the simultaneous development of industry and agriculture.

2. To carry out "planning" by setting ambitious goals for China's leading economic sectors and in essence simply encouraging any type of innovation necessary to permit the other sectors to catch up with these key sectors. "Bottlenecks be damned" captures the spirit of this approach.

3. In industry, to rely on both modern and traditional methods to enhance output. Thus, for example, major steel complexes would receive substantial new investment at the same time that "backyard" steel would be smelted by any group capable of doing so. Overall, the traditional sectors were to feed inputs into the modern sector while taking virtually nothing back in return.

4. In all areas, to disregard technical norms (and the specialists who stressed them) in favor of, in the lexicon of the times, achieving "more, faster, better, and more economical results." In practice the "more and faster" overwhelmed the "better and more economical."

This seemingly know-nothing approach appeared to work for a while. To an extent, of course, the appearances were false – the virtual destruction of the statistical system combined with tremendous pressure on cadres down the line to produce astonishing results. The not too surprising consequence was that an enormous amount of false reporting seriously misled the leadership as to the actual state of affairs in the country. Two elements did combine to

3 The economic strategy of the GLF is analyzed in *CHOC*, 14, Chapter 8.

make 1958 a year of substantial real economic achievements, however, and thus to lend some credibility to the Great Leap strategy.

First, the 1958 weather was exceptionally good, with the result that agricultural performance was better, other things being equal, than would normally have been the case. The organizational confusion attendant on the rapid formation of communes undoubtedly decreased agricultural yields, but the underlying weather conditions were sufficiently favorable to give at least the appearance of abundance throughout most of that fateful year.

Second, in the industrial sector many of the major projects that had been begun during the first FYP began to come on stream during 1958, producing impressive growth in industrial output. Again, objective conditions made it possible for a leadership that wanted to believe in the efficacy of the radical Great Leap strategy to find some support for its faith.

These various factors produced a rising crescendo of support for the GLF, both within the CCP and among the general populace, through the early and middle months of 1958. Foreign observers were astonished at the fervor of the popular efforts to leap into Communism by performing shock-force work tasks. Groups of peasants put in incredibly long hours with virtually no rest and sustained this grueling pace for weeks on end. The leadership's claims for the efficacy of these efforts grew as the fervor built. In some areas, the newly formed communes began to do away with money as a medium of exchange, and by the fall the common assumption that the country's perennial food problem had been solved led to free supplies of food for many commune dwellers. In carrying out this mass mobilization strategy, the CCP cadres took over an increasing portion of the work from their government counterparts, and at the center the Party Secretariat under Deng Xiaoping assumed unprecedented power and authority. Had the GLF produced even a substantial portion of what was hoped, undoubtedly it would have further knit together the already impressive solidarity of the central leadership. But things did not turn out that way.

Politics of the GLF

The record makes clear that Liu Shaoqi, Deng Xiaoping, and most other leaders supported the GLF strategy wholeheartedly throughout 1958. Indeed, the only obvious civilian dissenters at the Politburo level that year were Premier Zhou Enlai and the top economic administrator, Chen Yun. Within the military, many army leaders did not like the new obligations to support the militia and to participate in civilian work that the GLF imposed on the PLA. Perhaps the most prominent among these military dissenters was Defense Minister Marshal Peng Dehuai.

Liu Shaoqi and Deng Xiaoping had much to gain from the GLF. Both worked primarily in Party affairs and, as noted earlier, the CCP apparatus as a whole greatly expanded its power under the Leap. Deng personally had played a prominent role in the Anti-Rightist Campaign in 1957, and going back to the 1930s he could be considered to have been a part of Mao Zedong's personal clique in the Party. The GLF was primarily a Maoist alternative to the Soviet development strategy, and Deng identified himself closely with the success of this effort. He played a key role in managing the GLF via his position as head of the CCP Secretariat.

Liu Shaoqi had greater personal independence from Mao, but Liu also had to consider the succession. In the mid-1950's Mao had proposed that he should step back to the "second line," and by the beginning of 1958 he indicated that he would relinquish his position as head of state and remove himself from much of the day-to-day work in the Party leadership. In that way he could both determine the line of succession and devote himself more fully to working on the future direction of the Chinese revolution. During 1958 Liu Shaoqi probably had the succession very much on his mind, and personal support for Mao's plans would have been important in his strategy for obtaining the Chairman's blessing as the next in line.[4] Not surprisingly, therefore, Liu gave the keynote address on the GLF to the Second Session of the Eighth Party Congress, the meeting that formally adopted a Great Leap strategy for China. And in fact Liu did replace Mao as head of state when Mao relinquished that position in April 1959. In addition, of course, insofar as the GLF set China on the path of rapid progress toward Communism, it would create an enviable situation for a successor to inherit. There is no indication that during 1958 Liu Shaoqi felt it would do anything other than this.

The concerns of the other three leaders mentioned earlier are easily understood. Chen Yun's opposition centered on strongly held views about the proper development strategy for China to pursue, views that differed fundamentally from the core elements of the leap. Zhou Enlai certainly must have resented having his own organization – the State Council – assume a diminished position in China's development strategy, and Zhou may very well in addition have believed in a strategy closer to that advocated by Chen Yun. Peng Dehuai had differed with Mao over many issues since the 1940s. Peng had taken charge of the Hundred Regiments campaign against the Japanese then and was subsequently sharply criticized by Mao for the conception and conduct of this offensive. Peng Dehuai had led the Chinese troops in Korea,

4 Liu had formally obtained this in 1945, but that probably was not sufficient to make him fully confident as of 1958–9.

and under his command Mao's son was lost when his plane was shot down. At the conclusion of the Korean War, relations between Mao and Peng worsened. For these personal reasons alone, Peng may well have opposed a strategy so closely identified with Mao as was the GLF.

But Peng's opposition had stronger grounds than personal animosity. Peng wanted a strong, modernized, professional military organization, and he believed the Soviet Union was the only possible source of the necessary weapons, equipment, technology, and aid. Peng sought good relations with Moscow and, not surprisingly, modeled the PLA after the Red Army. Given his view of the importance of Soviet military aid, he could do little else. Mao, however, disagreed on all these counts. He felt that military spending had to be curtailed and that the best way to accomplish this would be to have the PLA enhance its capacity to wage guerilla war (to defend against invasion and prolonged occupation of the country) while at the same time developing an indigenous nuclear weapons capability. The latter would discourage the type of nuclear blackmail to which the PRC might otherwise be susceptible. The nuclear component of this strategy certainly put a premium on Soviet cooperation, but the conventional side suggested that China should develop its own military manuals and materials rather than rely on the Soviet model.

As noted earlier, Mao conceived of the GLF as a way to break out of the Soviet economic development model's constraints, given China's very different factor endowments. On the military side too, Mao now sought to cast off the Soviet model, and he made this clear at a prolonged enlarged meeting of the Military Affairs Commission (MAC). It met directly after the Great leap strategy was adopted by the Second Session of the Eighth Party Congress in May and continued until July 1958. Khrushchev had been supportive of Mao's desire for nuclear aid (for reasons having more to do with Communist bloc affairs than with Sino-Soviet relations), but this switch in China's conventional military strategy increased the already rapidly growing strains in Sino-Soviet relations.[5] To add insult to injury from Peng's perspective, the guerrilla conception of the role of the PLA demanded that the army create closer working relationships with the civilian population, a task that cut into military training and put the army in charge of the development and management of an enormous militia force.

Finally, at just this time Mao moved Lin Biao, long a close supporter on one of China's finest military tacticians, into a position on the Politburo that gave Lin a higher CCP rank than Peng. The implications must have been clear – to both Lin and Peng. During 1958 these tensions paled beside the overall enthusiasm of the bulk of the leadership for the GLF strategy; but

5 On Sino-Soviet relations during this period, see *CHOC*, 14, Chapter II.

when the Great Leap began to encounter serious problems, they rose to the surface to cause great resentment and prevent a timely shift in tactics for management of the GLF itself, ultimately producing a political and economic disaster of the first magnitude.

Inspection trips by the leaders during the fall of 1958 indicated that problems were brewing. In some places, peasant stories of food shortages belied the official statistics that showed abundance almost everywhere. In other areas, the excellent crops were not harvested fully and on time because too many workers had been shifted into local industry or had left to join the large state-run factories in the cities. Indeed, urban population growth skyrocketed during 1958. At the same time, the performance of the steel sector made it clear that the original utopian goal of producing 30 million tons of steel in 1959 (1957 production had been 5.35 million tons!) could not be reached. Thus, by late 1958 Mao realized that adjustments were necessary, although he still felt the basic GLF strategy was sound.

Mao began to advocate these adjustments at the First Zhengzhou Conference in November and then followed this up at the Wuchang Central Work Conference and at the Sixth Plenum that followed it in November–December 1958. He called for the 1959 steel target to be reduced from 30 million to 20 million tons, and he suggested that the government publicize grain production statistics that were lower than the highest internal estimates of the time. Mao himself characterized his approach in this period as having combined the revolutionary fervor of the August Beidaihe Meeting with a practical spirit.[6] But soon the practical spirit – spurred on by alarming findings about the actual state procurement of grain at the end of 1958 – forced the Chairman to take stronger measures to rein in the increasingly obvious excesses of the GLF.

By the time the Chinese leadership gathered to map out strategy for 1959 at the Second Zhengzhou meeting in late February, Mao had decided that strong words were necessary to prevent the Leap from becoming a disaster. Focusing on problems in the rural communes, Mao declared himself in favor of "right opportunism." Essentially, he demanded that the level of communization be decreased, with more ownership rights being vested below the commune level itself. He called for a less cavalier attitude toward the interests of the basic-level cadres and peasants and threatened (for dramatic effect) to resign from the Party if appropriate reforms were not adopted. One senses here that Mao still fully believed in the correctness of the basic Great Leap strategy but that he worried that "leftist" errors among cadres carrying out the policy would produce a catastrophe that would do great harm both to

6 Mao, *Wansui* (1969), 258.

China and to the Chairman's own position. During this same period, Mao invited Chen Yun to assume an active role in devising appropriate industrial targets and implementing related measures to make the Great Leap more rational and effective.

Events of the following few months made it clear that Mao was having trouble bringing middle-level cadres to heel in rectifying the errors of 1958. Some of the early stalwarts of the Leap, such as Wu Zhipu in Henan and Li Jinquan in Sichuan, showed little inclination to pull back on their earlier positions now. Ke Qingshi, the First Party Secretary in Shanghai and one of the key supporters of the backyard steel production drive, was reluctant to admit the problems of this effort. And more generally, sentiment in favor of going all out seemed to remain strong at the provincial through commune levels of the Party apparatus.

It is not completely clear just why this should have been the case. It may have reflected in part the fact that these cadres had won increased power and influence as a result of the Great Leap strategy and yet had not worked at the basic levels, where they would feel more acutely the personal tensions the policy was creating. Also, the greater concentration of peasant cadres at the provincial through commune levels may partially explain this phenomenon, as the Great Leap had some of the atmosphere of a millenarian movement that would free the countryside from the chains of the cities and free the peasant cadres from the scrutiny of the urban-bred experts. In any case, all evidence suggests that Mao devoted much attention throughout the remainder of the spring of 1959 to reining in the excesses of the Great Leap in order to make his basic development strategy work.

The Tibetan revolt broke this concentration on development problems during the spring of 1959. This border region, whose society was so vastly different from the socialist community the Chinese sought to establish, had been smoldering for some time. Although a truce of sorts had been worked out that had kept things calm in Tibet through the promised postponement of significant reforms, news of the Great Leap that came in from elsewhere significantly raised tensions. There had been revolts by Tibetans living in Sichuan in 1956 and in Gansu and Qinghai provinces in 1958, with refugees from these areas living in Lhasa and contributing to the unease there. Some specific actions and missteps by Han soldiers and civilians in Tibet in early 1959 sparked an actual revolt in this tense atmosphere, and the Dalai Lama fled to India for safety.

The revolt evidently took the Chinese by surprise, and additional troops had to be sent in from outside the region to quell it. Although the main body of the revolt was put down with relative ease, the issue of how to handle the diplomatic and security fallout continued to trouble the leadership into the summer.[7] There is, however, no evidence suggesting that the leadership was divided over how to deal with this issue at the time.

THE LUSHAN CONFERENCE, JULY 1959

By July, when the top leadership gathered at the mountain resort of Lushan, the Tibetan revolt had been suppressed militarily, even if its diplomatic repercussions were just beginning. Mao and his colleagues now turned their attention back to reviewing the economic situation and mapping out a new strategy. Mao, at least, seems to have felt fairly well satisfied that his efforts at reining in the excesses of the Great Leap were achieving adequate results.

The Lushan Conference, however, lasted for almost the entire month of July and proved to be one of the most fateful in the history of the PRC. By the end of the meeting, Mao had launched a ferocious attack against Peng Dehuai, China's defense minister and one of the ten marshals in the PLA, and had set in motion the effort necessary to replace Peng with Marshal Lin Biao. While still indicating that consolidation rather than expansion of the Great Leap was the order of the day, Mao had also launched an Anti-Right Opportunist Campaign that swamped the consolidation effort and itself produced a "second leap," with disastrous consequences. An enormous amount of data have been made available on the Lushan Conference over the years, but key questions about personal motivations and individual strategies still remain unanswered.

Indeed, the problems of interpretation extend back to before the conference itself. Peng had traveled to several Warsaw Pact countries and returned to Beijing on 12 June 1959. He had met with Khrushchev on this trip and may well have voiced his general consternation at the commune program and its effects on, among other things, the army and Sino-Soviet relations. In any case, almost immediately after Peng's return to Beijing, Khrushchev suddenly canceled the agreement under which Moscow was providing Beijing with the nuclear aid so valued by Mao and launched a public attack on the commune idea, the first such public criticism of the Chinese effort by the Soviet leader.

When Mao unleashed his counterattack against Peng, he tried to suggest that Khrushchev and Peng had colluded in a strategy that had Khrushchev pressure the Chinese over the Great Leap at the same time that Peng attacked the policy privately at Lushan. To add further mystery to the situation, one of Peng's close collaborators in his activities at Lushan was Zhang Wentian, a

7 Peng Dehuai subsequently recollected that he had the Tibetan question very much in mind as the Lushan Conference of July got under way: *Peng Dehuai zishu* (Peng Dehuai's own account), 267.

vice-minister of foreign affairs who had long had close ties with the Soviet Union. MacFarquhar suggests, indeed, that it was Zhang who put Peng up to his critique of the GLF at Lushan.[8]

In any case, at Lushan itself Peng Dehuai first voiced some criticisms of the Great Leap during small group discussions that overall seemed in keeping with the types of remarks Mao himself had been making during the previous few months. The one exception lay in a comment to the effect that Mao may not have fully understood what was going on in his own home village, as it appeared that the people there had received far more state aid than Mao had realized (an explosive assertion, given Mao's implicit claim that *he* understood China's rural situation better than any other leader).

On 14 July Peng wrote a letter to Mao that summed up his feelings about the problems of the GLF. Peng may have decided to take this action as a result of what he perceived to be a disturbing and continuing air of unreality at Lushan, or he may have been incited by Zhang Wentian. Indeed, it is possible that Peng's object was to embarrass Mao and possibly to upset the succession to Liu Shaoqi that Mao had set in train. Under interrogation during the Cultural Revolution, Peng claimed that he had intended the letter as a heartfelt and respectful communication to the Chairman for the latter's eyes only.[9] Much to his surprise, however, the Chairman had the letter printed and circulated to all participants at Lushan and gave it the rather formal sounding title of Peng Dehuai's letter of opinion" (*Peng Dehuai de yijian shu*).

On 23 July Mao responded to the letter with a vengeance. Intervening comments by Zhang Wentian and probably by others at the meeting may have convinced the Chairman he had a snowballing problem on his hands that he had better deal with quickly and decisively. Alternatively, it is possible that Mao had essentially set up Peng once he had received the marshal's letter, using his actions as an excuse to replace Peng with his own favorite, Lin Biao. If the latter is true, the Khrushchev's open criticism of the communes in a speech in Eastern Europe on 18 July played right into Mao's hands.

In any case, Mao's counterattack on 23 July drew a sharp line between permissible criticism and Peng's "right opportunist" remarks. He claimed that Peng sought to attack the Chairman rather than simply give advice on how to run the GLF better. He asked sarcastically why Peng had not expressed his views at meetings earlier in the spring, since Peng by then had

8 Roderick MacFarquhar, *Origins of the Cultural Revolution*, 2. 204–6.

9 For Peng's recollections of Lushan while under interrogation and the only authorized version of the letter to be published in China, see *Peng Dehuai zishu*, 265–87.

already carried out the investigations that had led him to his negative conclusions. Mao reminded his audience that he himself had been sharply critical of the methods used in the GLF, but Peng had held his silence. Now, at a major meeting designed to set the tone for policy over the coming months leading up to the tenth anniversary of the victory of the revolution in October, Peng had chosen to launch an attack out of the blue, and evidently with substantial support from some quarters. The fact that Peng lived in the house next to Mao's in the Zhongnanhai compound in Beijing must have added to the Chairman's sense of chagrin and betrayal. Mao's conclusion was clear – Peng had so grossly violated permissible behavior that he and his "clique" would have to undergo rectification. Khrushchev's criticism of the commune movement opened Peng to the accusation that he had taken his criticisms to the Soviet leader to enlist his help before he had made them known to his fellow members of the Politburo.

Mao's biting presentation shocked his audience. Peng himself did not sleep for nights afterward, reportedly being caught totally unawares by Mao's response. Given that much of what Peng had to say had in fact been the type of language Mao himself had encouraged during the previous few months, others were evidently baffled by the vehemence of the Chairman's position. As noted, Mao did have a legitimate complaint about Peng's previous silence. Also, some of Peng's comments in the letter to Mao seemed in a subtle way to be direct and serious criticisms of the Chairman personally rather than simply of the policies the Chairman had encouraged (and about which Peng had remained largely silent). Yet Mao's reaction was so contrary to normal practice that there may well have been some additional considerations at stake.

First, Peng belonged to the group of marshals that in general had been disgruntled over the distribution of top posts after the Communist victory in 1949. During the several decades of struggle for power, most of the key CCP leaders had been in the base areas, but some had spent much of their time either running the underground networks in China's cities (as had Liu Shaoqi) or doing formal liaison work with the Guomindang (as had Zhou Enlai). After 1949, the latter groups took a disproportionate share of top posts. The shadowy Gao Gang affair in 1954–5, the only Politburo-level purge before the Lushan meeting, seems to have involved a challenge by some of the former base area leaders (principally to Zhou Enlai and Liu Shaoqi) for leading posts in the new regime. Peng Dehuai was allegedly involved in that affair, but the desire to limit the damage produced a decision to hold the resulting purge to the smallest possible number of people. Peng's actions at Lushan may, therefore, have been seen by Mao as his second attempt to position himself for higher office. The fact that Mao had recently moved Peng's rival, Lin Biao into a higher-ranking CCP post than Peng's suggests that the Chairman had, by contrast, in fact been looking for a way to ease Peng out of power. Peng's criticism at Lushan may have provided an opportunity for Mao, with circulation of Peng's letter as the first step in this maneuver.

Several months before Lushan, Liu Shaoqi had assumed the post that Mao relinquished as Chairman of the PRC. This reaffirmed Liu's claim to be the successor to Mao, and Liu's practice began for the first time to be given equal status with that of Mao in public displays. This transition may well have heightened the implicit contention over the succession issue and sparked Peng to undertake more serious action than he otherwise might have taken. It may also have increased Mao's own sensitivities to the succession dimension of the issue and made him see Peng's criticism more readily in terms of a bid to weaken Mao's power (and Mao's ability to designate his own successor).

Zhang Wentian also plays into this scenario. Zhang had become the General Secretary of the Party during the Long March but was later eased out by Mao in Yan'an. A highly educated and articulate man, Zhang had been demoted bit by bit since 1949. His close ties with the Soviet Union made him the natural choice for Beijing's first ambassador to Moscow, but when he returned from that post he languished as a vice-minister of foreign affairs. Perhaps more important, he was demoted from full to alternate member status on the Politburo at the Eighth Party Congress in 1956 (he was formally removed from the Politburo altogether in 1961). Zhang may well have viewed his rightful position as more exalted than the one to which he was being consigned, and with the tensions over the GLF and over the succession in 1959 he may have decided to act. His private conversations with Peng Dehuai at Lushan could have sharpened his sense of opportunity, and he may have manipulated the less sophisticated Peng into making the comments that the latter put forward. Through Peng, Zhang may have felt he could ally his personal ambitions with those of many of the old marshals. Also, Peng was held in close affection among many top leaders, and Zhang was not. In this scenario, then, Peng may have been more a stooge than a plotter, used by Zhang to create the atmosphere at Lushan that would justify Zhang's own eloquent critique of the GLF. Zhang delivered such a critique at length at the meeting on 20 July.[10]

Mao would probably have been highly sensitive to this type of maneuvering by Zhang, and this may have determined the framework in which the Chairman viewed Peng's criticism. This would also help explain the fact that

10 MacFarquhar presents the strongest case for the scenario involving Zhang Wentian as a principal instigator: MacFarquhar, *Origins*, 2. 204–6.

Mao waited nine days after receipt of Peng's letter before making a counterattack. Alternatively, of course, Mao may simply have wanted to circulate Peng's letter and allow enough time for any sympathizers to show themselves in subsequent discussions before the Chairman made his own strong views plain. Should Mao have accepted the "Zhang Wentian as instigator, Peng Dehuai as stooge" scenario, the Chairman could still have decided to counterattack by aiming primarily at Peng, for several reasons: his general desire to downgrade Peng and promote Lin Biao; his need for a more well-known scapegoat; or Peng's own discussions with Khrushchev, which may have made him the more vulnerable of the two.

One last possibility is that Peng's challenge was implicitly more dangerous to Mao than Zhang's. Unlike Zhang, Peng had close ties to a key constituency, the old marshals. Also, unlike Zhang's, Peng's position as minister of defense gave him unique access to information to understand the views of two key groups that Mao was anxious to keep firmly under his own aegis: China's peasants (whose views Peng learned via military mail and other sources, as almost all conscripts in the PLA were from the countryside); and the PLA itself. Thus Mao may have felt it was imperative to train his fire on Peng, even if Zhang was the key figure behind the criticisms at Lushan.

The confrontation at the Lushan conference was then played out during the Lushan Plenum (the Eighth Plenum of the Eighth Central Committee) in August and an Enlarged MAC meeting in September. During the latter, Peng formally lost his defense portfolio and was told to engage in study for several years. Zhang Wentian and two others (Huang Kecheng, chief of staff of the PLA, and Zhou Xiaozhou, first secretary of Mao's home province of Hunan) were similarly purged as members of a (seemingly misnamed)[11] "military clique."

The consequences of Lushan

As suggested previously, the long-term consequences of the Lushan Conference and the Peng Dehuai affair were profound. One of the most significant was that Mao seems at Lushan to have broken the unwritten rules that had governed debate among the top leadership to that point. Before Lushan, it was accepted that any leader could freely voice his opinions at a Party gathering, and debate could be heated. Nobody would be taken to task subsequently for what he said, as long as he formally accepted and acted in

11 Peng several years later still expressed befuddlement as to why the four of them were called a military clique. Aside from Peng's denial that any clique existed, two of the four were not connected with the military. But Peng recalled that his detractors had been absolutely adamant in giving them this label. See *Peng Dehuai zishu*, 278–9.

accord with the final decision reached. But Mao's actions at Lushan can be interpreted as having changed all that.

First, Mao labeled internal criticism by a top colleague "unprincipled factional activity." He then demanded that others choose between himself and his adversary and that the loser be punished. At a minimum, this stance would hinder future free discussion among Politburo members. Given the fact that it required almost all other top leaders to take a stance,[12] it undoubtedly sowed some personal bitterness that would later bear fruit. There is no evidence that any top-ranking leader voted against Mao after the Chairman had drawn the line at Lushan.

The Peng Dehuai affair also produced some personnel changes of both short- and long-term significance. The most immediate result was Lin Biao's promotion to minister of defense. Lin, as noted, was a long-time follower of Mao's, and his new position gave Mao perhaps more secure control over the PLA than had previously been the case. Lin, in turn, was determined to keep Peng from staging a political comeback that would threaten Lin's own power.[13] As will be seen later, this issue continued to fester in Chinese politics throughout the early 1960s.

Other personnel shifts took place in connection with Lushan. Luo Ruiqing yielded his position as minister of public security to become PLA chief of staff. A more obscure change elevated Hua Guofeng to a higher post in Hunan province than he had previously held. Hua's promotion may have stemmed from an act of loyalty to Mao during the Chairman's time of need at Lushan. If so, Hua's service probably consisted of supporting Mao's version of developments in his home village of Shaoshan against the charges of Peng Dehuai, backed up by Hua's superior, Hunan First Secretary Zhou Xiaozhou. Hua's willingness to undercut a long-time mentor in service to Mao stood him in good stead more than a decade later, when Mao again needed loyal subordinates to ferret out opposition in the wake of the Lin Biao affair.

Finally, as noted earlier, the dynamics of the Lushan meetings and the campaign against right opportunism that followed cut short the rectification and consolidation efforts Mao had set in motion during the previous half year. Opposition to opportunism swept the country during the fall of 1959, removing all those who had expressed doubts about the efficacy of the GLF policies during the previous months. Not surprisingly, this campaign effectively termi-

12 Some, like Deng Xiaoping and Chen Yun, were absent from Lushan for different reasons.

13 Peng in fact was designated to head the effort to develop a "third front" in Southwest China in 1965 in response to Mao's increasing sense of a security threat from the United States. But the Cultural Revolution cut short Peng's effort. Peng was summoned to Beijing, where he endured Red Guard criticism, beatings, and incarceration until his death in 1974.

nated the spring 1959 effort to rectify and consolidate the communes, and by early 1960 a new Great Leap was under way. Mao encouraged this development through, for example, his March 1960 endorsement of a new "constitution" for the Anshan Iron and Steel Works that replaced the previous management approach there (modeled after the steel workers at Magnitogorsk) with one that put primary emphasis on politics. In April, the National People's Congress (NPC) formally adopted the Chairman's twelve-year agricultural program (a prominent feature of the brief "little" leap in the first half of 1956), and at the same NPC Mao's close supporter, Tan Zhenlin, again endorsed the commune program. Indeed, these spring 1960 months witnessed an attempt to organize urban communes and a renewal of the effort to "send down" (*xiafang*) cadres. It is not clear what occurred – other than the attack by Peng Dehuai – that made Mao abandon his analysis of early 1959 in favor of renewed faith in a Great Leap strategy. The fact that during the first half of 1960 the leaders focused their attention primarily on Sino-Soviet relations permitted this leap strategy to mushroom to disastrous proportions.

The second Great Leap failed with a vengeance. According to figures released in 1981, agricultural output in 1960 was only 75.5 percent of that in 1958 (1961 output went down another 2.4 percent). Light industry uses primarily agricultural products as inputs, and thus light industrial shifts tend to lag one year behind those in agricultural output. In 1960, light industrial output decreased by 9.8 percent. It then declined by 21.6 percent in 1961 and by another 8.4 percent in 1962. The cumulative impact was to produce a serious goods famine to match the food shortages. Heavy industrial output also declined sharply, going down 46.6 percent in 1961 compared with 1960, and another 22.2 percent in 1962 over 1961.[14]

Overall, this renewed leap in late 1959 and 1960 produced the most devastating famine of the twentieth century in China (and probably in the world). The fundamental cause of this mass starvation was political, in that mistaken policies (such as insisting that the peasants leave land fallow in 1959 to avoid losses from not having enough storage facilities to handle the anticipated surplus) led inevitably to serious food shortfalls. These shortfalls were exacerbated enormously by the regime's blindness to the problem, to the extent that high agricultural procurement quotas continued to drain the countryside of available supplies into 1961. Bad weather and the mid-1960 withdrawal of Soviet technicians added to the difficulties, but neither of these latter two elements would have produced the more than 20 million "excess"

14 Figures from an article by Ma Hong in *RMRB*, 29 December 1981, 5, trans. in *FBIS*, 8 January 1982, 11–12. Ma Hong does not indicate how his percentages are calculated; presumably he used gross value of output each year.

deaths (deaths over and above the normal death rate) that occurred during 1959–61.[15]

The terrible consequences of the renewed Great Leap and the rancor over the purge of Peng Dehuai combined to unravel the political consensus that had held the Yan'an leadership together through its days in the wilderness and its first decade in power. This process of political deterioration developed through a range of issues, any one of which in itself might have been manageable. But taken together they set the stage for the final split of the Yan'an leadership: the Great Proletarian Cultual Revolution (GPCR). Six different strands were woven into this tapestry of political decay during the early 1960s.

First, Khrushchev's decision to try to bring a halt to the GLF and demonstrate to China the great importance of its Soviet connection by swiftly withdrawing Soviet advisors and aid at the height of the 1960 crisis had the unintended effort of shocking Mao into a fundamental reevaluation of the development of the Russian Revolution. To be sure, Mao had previously found much to fault in the evolution of the Soviet Union and the actions of its leaders, but the Chairman had not previously thought in terms of a fundamental degeneration of the Soviet system. Khrushchev's crude pressure tactics raised this possibility, and the thought was frightening. By implication, if the Soviet revolution could change from socialist to fascist (or social imperialist), then any socialist revolution was in theory reversible. Given Mao's very much weakened position in Beijing as a result of the Great Leap fiasco, he evidently began to fear that his life's work in China might have laid the basis ultimately not for the most just society in the world but, rather, for an extremely exploitative system.

Mao thus began to devote a large portion of his energy to dealing with the Soviet issue, and he brought Kang Sheng, who had training in Marxism-Leninism and understood Soviet affairs well, to center stage to help him wrestle with Sino-Soviet relations. When within several years Mao began to have very serious doubts about the course his own successors were following, he then used the struggle with "Soviet revisionism" to give publicity in China to what amounted in reality to a critique of the policies of his own colleagues. Relatedly, Kang Sheng had learned his approach to political infighting in the Soviet Union of the mid-1930s, and Kang's ascendancy in Beijing in the early 1960s therefore increased the tendency in the Forbidden City to wage struggles by Stalinist rather than more traditionally Maoist rules of the game.

15 From 1959 to 1961 the total size of China's population fell by 13.5 million. The number of excess deaths was, of course, far higher. State Statistical Bureau, comp., *Statistical yearbook of China, 1984*, 81. For a further discussion, see *CHOC*, 14, Chapter 8, notes 27 and 28.

Second, Mao's own prestige in the highest levels of the CCP suffered badly because of the GLF fiasco. Indeed, the Chairman made some form of self-criticism at a CCP Central Work Conference in Beijing in June 1961. As noted earlier, Mao had in any case planned to retreat to the second line in the Politburo as of 1959 so that he could devote more time to major issues and be less involved in daily administrative affairs. But once the disasters of 1960–1 became fully evident, Mao found himself pushed more effectively out of day-to-day affairs than he would have liked. At the same time, some of his previous key supporters, such as Deng Xiaoping, no longer paid him the deference he felt was his due (Lin Biao proved to be the notable exception). Thus, for example, Mao complained during the Cultural Revolution that Deng had not listened to him since 1959. Deng had, as noted earlier, previously been a key supporter of Mao's. But when it came time to pick up the pieces from the GLF catastrophe, Deng played a central role via his stewardship of the CCP Secretariat, and he did not fully agree with the Chairman over the proper remedies and the lessons to be drawn.

The third strand is precisely the fact that different leaders drew different conclusions from the utter failure of the GLF. Mao personally recognized, as his subsequent actions showed, that political mobilization cannot itself produce rapid economic growth, and thus the Chairman did not proclaim major production increases as a goal of the Cultural Revolution. But as the GPCR also illustrates, Mao retained his faith in the efficacy of political mobilization to produce changes in outlook, values, and the distribution of political power. Most of Mao's supporters against Peng Dehuai at Lushan, by contrast, concluded after their investigations of the situation in 1960–2 that large-scale political campaigns and the entire Yan'an style of "high tide" politics had become counterproductive in virtually every way. Thus, although Mao no longer saw political movements as the basis for economic growth, many of his colleagues wanted to eschew campaign politics altogether.

Fourth, the CCP itself had taken charge of running the GLF, and the CCP suffered in prestige and organizational competence as a result of the failure of this monumental effort. The demoralization of the lower ranks of the CCP became still more acute as the country slowly pulled out of the Great Leap because in the end the cadres who had supported the second Leap were now purged for their "leftism," while Mao's own responsibility was carefully shielded to protect his legitimacy. For example, Mao's June 1961 self-criticism was never circulated to lower levels of the Party. Given the enormous strains on basic-level CCP cadres during 1960–2, it is not surprising that many lost their sense of revolutionary élan, thus giving the CCP apparatus to an extent feet of clay. The question of how best to rectify the basic-level CCP organs caused additional dissension in the upper levels, as various leaders proposed their own somewhat different methods of dealing with this important issue.

A fifth problem concerned disagreement over just how quickly China was recovering from the depredations of the GLF. Different assessments naturally justified different measures for bringing about a more normal situation. Mao tended to be more optimistic than many of his colleagues as this issue was debated in 1962, and indeed the Chairman seems to have begun to suspect that the pessimists were trying to limit his own flexibility and room for maneuver in the system. As Mao became more concerned with revisionism, this set of issues assumed increasing importance for him.

Finally, whatever one's views about the speed of China's recovery, there was no doubt about the extraordinary extent of the damage that the GLF (and especially its second stage) had done. In other words, the events of 1959–61 essentially vindicated what Peng Dehuai had said and written at Lushan. To add insult to injury, Peng carried out fairly extensive rural investigations during 1962, and that August he summarized his findings and submitted an 80,000-character document to the Central Committee justifying his rehabilitation on the grounds that his principled criticism at Lushan had been correct. But Lin Biao could not tolerate Peng's rehabilitation, and Mao did not want it either. In addition, by 1962 Mao may already have been thinking about the need to rely increasingly on Lin and the PLA as his concerns about his other colleagues grew. Thus, Mao blocked Peng's rehabilitation – and in so doing did further damage to the norms that had governed relations among the leaders to that date.

AFTER THE LEAP: THE LIU-DENG PROGRAM

In sum, the failure of the GLF left a full menu of problems on the plates of the central leaders. These varied from interpersonal relations among the top people, to frayed institutional capabilities, to the relation of foreign to domestic policy. Basic political methods as well as immediate economic and other goals were at issue. All these concerns, moreover, interacted in a way that tended to heighten Mao's suspicions and make it more difficult to find agreed-upon solutions. In more detail, these issues arose as follows:

The leadership began to turn its attention to coping with the Great Leap disaster during a meeting at Beidaihe in July–August 1960. The termination of all Soviet aid to China that June forced Beijing to think in terms of a self-reliant development effort and to take stock of the deteriorating situation in the countryside. Several types of initiatives flowed out of Beidaihe and subsequent deliberations over the following few months, as the magnitude of the summer crop failure became evident. First, the second Great Leap was formally terminated, and the guiding policy now became one of "agriculture as the base, industry as the leading factor," with "readjustment, consolidation, filling out, and raising standards" replacing the previous formula of "more, faster, better, and more economical results." Mao had first put forward the "agriculture as the base" formula in 1959, but it was not implemented until the fall of 1960. It became official CCP policy at the Ninth Plenum in January 1961.

Second, the CCP center sought to increase its control over its badly damaged nationwide apparatus through the re-creation of six regional bodies. (The parallel regional government bodies that had existed in the early postliberation years were not established.) Relatedly, efforts were made to salvage the situation in the countryside through moving back toward a system that provided greater material incentives. The disastrous fall harvest drove home the magnitude of the problem to the extent that in November Zhou Enlai presided over the drafting of an emergency measure on rural policy, called the Twelve Articles of People's Communes. This stopgap document essentially permitted great decentralization within the communes. Indeed, in Byung-joon Ahn's words, with the implementation of the Twelve Articles, "the GLF simply collapsed."[16]

Taking the pressure off cadres to implement GLF policies did not, however, make clear where the CCP should go from there. The specific reasons for the failure of the Great Leap remained unclear, and the CCP had not yet devised appropriate responses to put the country back on a long-term path of development. Rather, during the spring of 1961, local leaders were in general given great leeway to implement whatever measures – even including, in many places, a de facto dissolution of the communes – they felt were necessary to alleviate the famine that was devastating China. On a policy level, two types of responses were adopted. The first, initiated by Lin Biao and focused on the military, stressed renewed study of politics as a way to boost morale and increase discipline. The second, led by Liu Shaoqi and Deng Xiaoping, produced a series of investigations that provided the material used for programmatic policy documents in major spheres of work.

In the military, in September 1960, Lin called for a program of concentrated study of Mao's works. Famine in the countryside had produced considerable demoralization among the soldiers, and Lin felt it important to revive political work to combat it. Since this effort was directed in general toward barely educated peasant recruits, it inevitably involved a simplification and dogmatization of Mao's Thought. The attempt to make Mao's Thought comprehensible to simple soldiers eventually produced the *Quotations from*

16 Byung-joon Ahn, *Chinese politics and the Cultural Revolution*, 47.

Chairman Mao Zedong, the "little red book," which would become the Bible of the Red Guards during the Cultural Revolution. During 1960–3, however, those responsible for work in urban China disparaged the idea that Lin's dogmatic exegesis of Mao's writing could serve any useful purpose outside the military.

Liu and Deng supervised the investigation and drafting process that culminated in a series of programmatic documents that are generally known by the number of articles in each. During 1961–2 the following major policy papers were produced: Sixty Articles on People's Communes; Seventy Articles on Industry; Fourteen Articles on Science; Thirty-five Articles on Handicraft Trades; Six Articles on Finance; Eight Articles on Literature and Art; Sixty Articles on Higher Education; and Forty Articles on Commercial Work. Although, of course, the specifics concerning the drafting process varied for each of these policy papers, all shared some elements. In each case a Party leader took charge of the drafting process. Thus, Mao oversaw the drafting of the Sixty Points, Bo Yibo supervised the Seventy Articles on Industry (after preliminary work under the aegis of Li Fuchun), Li Xiannian covered finance, Zhou Yang and Lu Dingyi managed literature and art, Peng Zhen handled education, and so forth.

In addition, three broad policy groups were established under the Secretariat to oversee and coordinate policy toward major issue areas: Li Fuchun and Chen Yun's group reviewed economic policies, Peng Zhen's took charge of cultural and educational affairs, and Deng Xiaoping's covered political and legal work. This mode of operation thus had Chen Yun, for example, make significant policy reports and pronouncements in the following areas in 1961: fertilizer production, foreign trade, urban population growth, agricultural policy, and coal production. In early 1962, as will be noted, Chen became centrally involved in the overall evaluation of China's conditions and the policies to be pursued in the future.[17]

In drafting the various program documents, the person in charge typically first ascertained the actual situation and problems through carrying out on-the-spot investigations, often including (where appropriate) visits to units or locales with which he had ties from the past. In addition, meetings were convened with the experts or practitioners involved so as to mobilize their

17 The precise institutional roles of various CCP and state organs in this process are not clear. The Secretariat under Deng Xiaoping seems to have assumed overall charge of the drafting of these documents. But key individuals involved, including Bo Yibo, Zhou Yang, Lu Dingyi (until 1962), and Chen Yun did not themselves serve on the Secretariat. Evidently the Secretariat tapped the resources of a range of organs, including the pertinent State Council staff offices, to develop the policies noted. The role of the State Council in this drafting process remains unclear. It did, of course, become involved in the implementation of these policies once they had been approved by the Politburo.

support and solicit their opinions. These documents went through a number of drafts, most of which reflected additional consultation both within the Party and among the non-Party experts. This presumption that experts could make valuable contributions conflicted sharply with the approach Lin Biao was taking at the very time in the military. To Lin, Mao's Thought contained both the answers and the source of any necessary inspiration. The division among top leaders in the wake of the GLF disaster thus went beyond personal political likes and dislikes and included fundamental aspects of policy process and political calculation.

The substance of the policies developed by the apparatus under Liu Shaoqi and Deng Xiaoping also struck at the heart of the assumptions that underlay the GLF. In fertilizer production, for example, Chen Yun called for construction of fourteen additional plants, each with a 50,000-ton-per-year capacity for production of synthetic ammonia. These plants would be large and modern, supplanting the inefficient small-scale chemical fertilizer production that had become so popular during the GLF. They would also require substantial imports of key components from abroad, moving China away from its previous policy of self-reliance. Bo Yibo's Seventy Articles on Industry placed renewed stress on the role of experts and on the use of material incentives – almost directly contradicting the Anshan Iron and Steel Constitution that Mao had promulgated the previous year. The Eight Articles on Literature and Art promised the reintroduction of traditional art forms and permitted a broader range of topics to be explored by artists. The Sixty Articles on Education stressed quality of education and undercut many of the locally run (*minban*) schools that had been opened as a part of the GLF strategy. And the Sixty Articles on People's Communes articulated a detailed set of regulations that fixed the team as the basic accounting unit, made provision for private plots, and in general tried to shift agricultural production toward a system that provided greater material incentives for peasant labor.

These policies overall marked a dramatic shift from the priorities of the GLF. They brought experts and expertise back to center stage, produced greater reliance on modern inputs to achieve growth, reimposed central bureaucratic controls over various spheres of activity, and appealed to the masses more on the basis of material self-interest than of ideological mobilization. There is no evidence that Mao Zedong objected to these trends during 1961. Indeed, Mao himself had actively participated in drafting the Sixty Articles on People's Communes and had called for serious investigations to be carried out at the Guangzhou meeting in March 1961. In June the Chairman had made a self-criticism at a central work conference in Beijing. But as these investigations and consultations yielded to policy programs, Mao evidently became increasingly disconcerted – and he was not alone.

The Seven Thousand Cadres Conference, January–February 1962

The situation erupted during 1962, when basic disagreement arose as to how quickly the country was recovering and, therefore, over what future goals and time frames should be. In January–February a Seven Thousand Cadres Work Conference convened to review methods of leadership and to sum up the situation. There was more agreement on the former than on the latter. Liu Shaoqi made the key report and several other speeches to this conference, and he called for greater use of democratic centralism and less personal command by key individuals. In addresses on 26 and 27 January, he blamed much of the recent trouble on the Party center and stressed the importance of avoiding the brutal purges and counterpurges that had racked the Party during the twists and turns of the previous few years. Liu specifically criticized the vehemence of the attack on right opportunism in the wake of the Lushan Conference, and he is reported to have called for the rehabilitation of Peng Dehuai, among other rightists. Mao's own talk to the conference on 30 January generally endorsed these themes, and Mao informed the cadres in the audience that he himself had made a self-criticism the previous June (he also warned them to be prepared to do the same). Thus, this conference in general helped to patch up the rather tattered decision-making apparatus within the Party.

But in other areas the conference failed to produce a consensus. In terms of what had caused the Great Leap disaster, Liu argued that wrong political decisions accounted for 70 percent, with the Soviet withdrawal of aid and the several years of bad weather accounting for the other 30 percent. Mao felt this stood the true situation on its head. Liu also felt that the economy still remained in a crisis and would take a long time to put back into shape. Mao argued, by contrast, that things had now largely returned to normal. Perhaps Mao meant his evaluation to apply only to the political and not the economic situation. Liu, in any case, appears to have harbored a far gloomier assessment of the general situation than Mao at this time. His more pessimistic evaluation would, in turn, provide a rationale for more far-reaching measures to salvage the situation.

Interestingly, Zhou Enlai supported Mao at this meeting and seems to have given an overall positive assessment of the GLF. On substantive issues later in 1962, by contrast, Zhou strongly backed Liu Shaoqi and Chen Yun. Thus, the premier's performance at the Seven Thousand Cadres Conference evidently reflected his operational practice of siding with Mao whenever there was an open clash more than his substantive agreement with the Chairman's position. Zhou is often compared by Chinese to a "willow branch," and his actions during the spring of 1962 reconfirm the appropriateness of a characterization that includes both strength and a graceful ability to bend with the wind. Not surprisingly, Mao also received strong verbal backing from Lin Biao at the conference.

Three other leaders were less clear in their positions. Deng Xiaoping reiterated the correctness of Mao Zedong's Thought but then supported Liu Shaoqi on substantive issues such as the rehabilitation of rightists. Chen Yun had been asked to present a report on the situation in finance and trade, but he demurred on the basis that he had not yet fully clarified the situation in that sphere. Perhaps, however, Peng Zhen's performance sums up most clearly the difficult and uncertain position in which Politburo members found themselves in January 1962.

Peng had ordered his subordinates in the Beijing municipal hierarchy to investigate the real causes of the GLF disaster and prepare a report for him. It is not clear whether he did this on his own or as an integral part of a broader leadership effort to determine the lessons that should be drawn from the GLF. In any case, the initial investigation started in late May 1961, and in November Peng issued a second order that all central directives between 1958 and 1961 should be reviewed as part of this effort. Deng Tuo, a Beijing Party secretary who had edited the *People's Daily* until 1957, assumed charge of this investigation. After convening a meeting at the Changguanlou in December 1961, Deng Tuo reported on the group's findings to Peng Zhen.

The report they made placed the blame for the disaster directly on the mobilizational politics of the GLF strategy. The center had approved and circulated too many false reports, had issued too many conflicting directives, and had virtually totally ignored economic reality in its calls for action by local cadres. In short, the GLF disaster must be laid largely at the doorstep of the Politburo. Given Mao's headstrong leadership of that body since 1958, there is little question that the Changguanlou report in fact amounted to a severe critique of the Chairman's own work.

Peng reportedly went to the Seven Thousand Cadres Conference in January 1962 prepared to spell out the case made in the Changguanlou report. When he grasped the tenor of the meeting, however, he hesitated and in fact did not criticize the Chairman's leadership at this major conference. Peng by then fully recognized the magnitude of the GLF catastrophe and certainly would not support that type of mobilizational effort again in the future. At the same time, he could not bring himself to confront Mao on the issue directly. This kind of lingering ambivalence meant, in turn, that even after the searing experiences of 1961, a current in support of GLF-type policies would remain strong within the Party throughout 1962 and thereafter.

Given the enormity of the problems engendered by the GLF, it is a tribute to Mao's inherent authority that he could still shape the outcome of conclaves such as the Seven Thousand Cadres Conference in 1962. This reflects the unique position that the Chairman had assumed within the Chinese Party after 1949. Unlike other Communist parties in power, the Chinese created distinctive roles for the First Secretary (or General Secretary) and the Chairman. The former role was an integral part of the organizational hierarchy of the Party. The latter position stood apart from and above that hierarchy. It was a position whose formal authority evolved somewhat during successive Party constitutions but whose real power derived from the stature of the incumbent, who was regarded as virtually a philosopher-king. In the eyes of his colleagues, Mao had conceptualized the Chinese revolution itself. Although people recognized that he could make serious mistakes and thus might try to vitiate his initiatives through bureaucratic devices, none had the courage (or gall) to question directly Mao's fundamental evaluation of the current situation and the priority tasks of the Party. There were, in short, no effective institutional curbs on Mao's power, and the Chairman used this advantage with great skill when he felt challenged or threatened.

Unfortunately, insufficient documentation is available from the Seven Thousand Cadres Conference to specify the dynamics of the discussions or the details of the final consensus at the meeting. It appears that on balance the conference left many issues only partly resolved. Indeed, the major issues with which it grappled continued to engender disagreement and tension among the leaders throughout the remaining years before the Cultural Revolution. These issues included the following. The rehabilitation of rightists: This meeting split the difference by agreeing that many should be brought back but that Peng Dehuai and some other leading rightists should remain under a cloud. An evaluation of the current situation: This conference did not reach an agreement that would hold for more than a month or two. Mao seems to have forced a reasonably optimistic perspective on the conference, but this was challenged almost immediately and subsequently remained a contentious issue. Party rectification: Although this conference made some progress toward accomplishing the vitally necessary task of reconstructing a disciplined and responsive Party apparatus, the issue of how best to carry out this task would continue to sow discord among the leaders. Thus, the January–February 1962 conference marked an uncertain transition from the desperation of 1961 to a more positive effort to shape events in 1962 and afterward. While the meeting reflected the fact that Beijing was again ready to begin to seize the initiative, it also revealed the fissures within the central leadership that the traumatic previous three years had produced.

These fissures cracked open a bit wider under the strain of a Ministry of Finance projection, made available to Chen Yun just after the Seven Thousand Cadres Conferences in February 1962, that the central government would face a budget deficit on 2 to 3 billion *yuan* that year under current plans and projections. Chen, always sensitive to the inflationary pressures budget deficits produced, prepared a wide-ranging report that cast the overall situation in gloomy terms and called for appropriate changes in plans. This included a significant scaling down of the production targets discussed during the previous month. Chen feared a deteriorating food situation and suggested emergency measures to increase marginally the supplies of fish and soybeans. He also argued that the poor agrarian situation demanded a revision of the recently adopted plans for recovery. This would entail designating 1962–5 as a period of recovery, where energies would remain focused on rural production, and growth in the metallurgical and machine-building industries would necessarily be held back.

With Mao in Wuhan, Liu Shaoqi had assumed charge of day-to-day affairs of the Politburo. He called the Xilou Conference, named for the building in Beijing in which it was convened on 21–3 February, to discuss Chen's views. The Xilou meeting strongly endorsed Chen's sober assessment, which in any case seems to have come close to the picture that Liu himself had painted at the recently concluded Seven Thousand Cadres Conference. In addition, at Xilou both Liu and Deng Xiaoping endorsed the various systems of "individual responsibility" in agriculture (a de facto partial decollectivization) that had been tried in hard-hit provinces such as Anhui. These endorsements reflected a belief that the agricultural situation still not "bottomed out" as of the time of the conference. Also, at Xilou Li Xiannian admitted the accuracy of Liu Shaoqi's criticism of recent state financial work.

The Xilou Conference decided to convene a meeting of Party core groups in the State Council to discuss this new assessment. They met on 26 February and, enthusiastically endorsing Chen's analysis, passed the issue to the Secretariat. Liu Shaoqi urged the Secretariat to circulate Chen's report as a CC document, with an attached comment by the Standing Committee of the Politburo. Since (unnamed) people objected to the tone of the proposed document, Liu, Deng, and Zhou traveled to Wuhan to report to Mao on its contents and background. Mao reportedly approved circulation of the document. After this, Chen had the Central Finance and Economics Small Group discuss the document and a related report on commercial work that also reflected Chen's views.

Following the Central Finance and Economics Small Group meeting, Zhou Enlai took charge of this key body. Reportedly, Chen had to pull back from day-to-day involvement due to illness, although he evidently remained an influential counselor behind the scenes.[18] The Ministry of Metallurgy

18 In 1966 Liu Shaoqi "confessed" that during 1962 he had been overly influenced by Chen's views. Chen also seems to have attended the Tenth Plenum in September 1962, even though no other public appearances by him were recorded before the Cultural Revolution.

refused to accept Chen's analysis and continued to hold out for a larger steel target – placed at 25 to 30 million tons by 1970 – as the core of the new Five-Year Plan. Chen stressed instead the need for a recovery period followed by balanced growth. In early summer 1962 Zhou Enlai brought together the secretaries of the six regional Party bureaus, along with members of the Politburo, to focus on Chen's ideas, which Zhou put forward as the correct framework for CCP planning. Ke Qingshi, the Maoist stalwart from Shanghai who had been a key force in the backyard steel furnace drive of 1958, objected to Zhou's position on the ground that the premier was characterizing the situation in terms far worse than those used at the Seven Thousand Cadres Conference. Zhou countered that the budget deficit that sparked this revision became known only after the conference had been adjourned. Zhou's speech was then circulated to a wider audience, evidently over Ke's strong objections.

Thus, two significantly different assessments of the situation emerged during the first half of 1962. Mao Zedong, supported at least by some provincial officials, by Lin Biao in the military and by people in the heavy-industry sector,[19] argued that the country was well on the way to recovery and thus that the time had come to begin to exercise some initiative in moving China farther along a socialist path. Mao thus opposed further decollectivization in agriculture and backtracking in other areas, such as culture. Mao's ruminations on the development of the Soviet revolution were spurring his concern over trends in China during these months, but overall he seems to have spent most of the time from February 1962 until the August Beidaihe Central Work Conference in partial seclusion in central China.

Liu Shaoqi, Deng Xiaoping, Chen Yun, and others, by contrast, had concluded by late February that the situation remained almost desperately bad and that a significant recovery period would be necessary before Beijing could again really assume the initiative. The grim rural situation demanded further concessions to peasant material interests in the form of official endorsement of speculative activities by the peasants and the type of decollectivization referred to as "going it alone" (*dan gan*). The general social demoralization demanded that the regime yield to popular tastes in cultural fare, permitting the staging of old operas and plays and the composition of other works that played down revolutionary politics in favor of traditional favorite themes and characters. The desperate economic situation also demanded that the regime woo former capitalists and the technical intelligen-

19 Mao's support almost certainly also came from others, such as Tan Zhenlin in agriculture, but the documentation to support this conclusion is lacking.

tsia into active efforts to revive the urban economy. Thus, whereas Mao felt the general situation permitted renewed efforts to move the country again toward his socialist ideals, many of his colleagues demurred. They thought the regime would have to retreat further and nurse its institutional capabilities back to health before a more active strategy would be feasible.

The Beidaihe Conference and the Tenth Plenum

The clash between these two approaches came at the August 1962 Beidaihe meeting.[20] Liu and his confreres came to this meeting having spent the preceding months actively pursuing the policy implications of Chen Yun's analysis of China's situation. Thus, for example, in February they convened a National Conference on Scientific and Technological Work in Guangzhou, and a month later they brought together a National Conference for the Creation of Dramas and Operas in the same city. Both meetings tried to mobilize support by yielding to the preferences of the groups of non-Party participants. As of early August, a related conference on short novels about the countryside was in session in Dalian. In the interim, Deng Xiaoping convened a meeting of the Secretariat to review the data on individual farming (*dan gan*), at which he pronounced his subsequently famous dictum "It does not matter whether a cat is black or white, so long as it catches mice." And, of course, the already recounted succession of events around Chen Yun's assessment was unfolding.

Mao Zedong approached this meeting in another frame of mind. He evidently felt increasingly isolated from the mainstream of decision making, even thought his signature continued to be sougt on CC documents before they were disseminated. Mao reportedly had ceased sitting in on Politburo meetings as of January 1958.[21] Originally, this had probably reflected his assumption of more independent decision-making authority at the start of the Great Leap; or it may have been part of a genuine effort to retire to the second line and give his colleagues more prestige. But over time it may well have taken on other significance for him, making him feel increasingly isolated and neglected by his colleagues. Mao clearly began in 1962 to search

20 This work conference began on 6 August and continued until the latter part of that month. These major summer central work conferences were more than simply business meetings. Although they were extremely important in policy formulation, in addition, they were social gatherings, with wives frequently in attendance, evening entertainment provided, and time allowed for side trips and diversions. Key leaders might miss significant parts of the conferences, presumably reading the stenographic record to keep posted on the deliberations. Thus, conferences often appeared to drag on for one to two months and may even, as here, have shifted location partway through. Since these conferences generally were not covered in the press at the time, it is often impossible to establish precise dates for their opening and closing.

21 *Yomiuri Shimbun*, 25 January 1981, trans. in *FBIS/PRC* Annex, 13 March 1981, 7.

for ways to reassert himself in the system, and one of the most interesting dimensions of the politics of the period 1962–5 is the putting together of the coalition that would enable the aging Party Chairman to break into a position of dominance in 1966.

This search coincided with the development of the independent political ambitions of three key individuals – Jiang Qing, Lin Biao, and Kang Sheng. Others hovered in the background, at times playing important roles. Chen Boda, always the Maoist loyalist, was willing to encourage any move that would enhance the role of his patron. Wang Dongxing, a former bodyguard of Mao's, became involved in the byzantine palace security dimension. Zhou Enlai played the political game cautiously, always keeping his lines open to both the Chairman and other members of the Politburo. At the crucial moment in 1966, however, Zhou put himself squarely on Mao's side, enabling the Chairman to complete the coalition necessary to launch the Cultural Revolution.

As Mao faced the Central Work Conference at Beidaihe in the late summer of 1962, however, he had yet to formulate fully either the challenge or his strategy. He was highly troubled by the events of the months since the Seven Thousand Cadres Conference, though, and he listened to the reports during the first days of the Beidaihe meeting with chagrin. Zhu De, one of the most respected of the old marshals, called for expansion of the individual responsibility system in agriculture and for other measures that put him solidly with Liu's and Deng's evaluation of the problems in the countryside. Chen Yun reiterated his position on the rural situation and tasks. Other Politburo members reported on major issue areas,[22] but unfortunately no information is available on either the timing or the substance of their remarks. The timing is important, because on 9 August, Mao addressed the meeting, employing such biting sarcasm that his talk probably seriously affected the tone of the entire proceedings.

Mao bitterly attacked the Ministry of Finance, whose budget deficit projection had provided the basis for Chen Yun's February report and all that had followed from it. He then stressed the fact that China still faced the need for class struggle, and it was obvious that he felt the continuing retreat from socialist policies simply exacerbated the dangers in this sphere. He attacked directly the adoption of an individual responsibility system in farming and called for a campaign of "socialist education" to rectify the Party apparatus in the rural areas. And he warned against the possibility of capitalist or even feudal restoration in the PRC. Jiang Qing subsequently revealed that she had

22 Chen Boda, only an alternate Politburo member at the time, reported on agriculture; Li Xiannian on commerce; Li Fuchun (possibly with Bo Yibo) on industry and planning; and Chen Yi on the international situation. Liu Shaoqi also addressed this meeting.

been working on the Chairman to sensitize him to the "degeneration" of the arts and culture since 1959, and her proddings had found a reflection in Mao's stress on the need for proletarian ideology in his address to the Beidaihe meeting.[23]

Mao thus succeeded in turning the agenda around so that at least in part it reflected his own priorities. His commanding presence was most easily brought to bear at these central conclaves, and he took full advantage of his political resources there. Liu Shaoqi evidently challenged the Chairman's priorities in at least some respects at this meeting, as Liu subsequently commented that he had "inclined to the right" at Beidaihe and had not begun to correct himself until the Tenth Plenum that convened on 24–27 September. What emerged was a patchwork compromise in an atmosphere of somewhat heightened political tension.

The Tenth Plenum revealed all the cleavages and contradictions that had boiled up at the Beidaihe meeting. Mao presided over this meeting, and his speech to the participants closely linked the degeneration of the Soviet Union to the fact that class struggle would still exist in China for decades to come. Mao was persuaded by Liu and others at this meeting, however, to make clear that the issue of class struggle should not be allowed to swamp other policy decisions coming out of the Tenth Plenum, as had happened after the Eighth Plenum at Lushan in 1959.[24]

Mao's general concern with class struggle reflected a more basic fear of his that the Chinese revolution was beginning to head down the path of revisionism. A cynic might note that revisionism to Mao seemed to be anything that he disliked, but dismissing the term on this level would in fact be misleading. Mao was very concerned to shepherd the revolution along collectivist and relatively egalitarian paths. He distrusted urban-based bureaucracies and China's intellectuals as a whole. Even though many of his concrete policy proposals had the effect of exploiting the countryside to develop urban-based industry, he nevertheless seems genuinely to have thought of himself as a representative of China's poor peasants. Although Mao believed in the efficacy of technological progress, he nevertheless distrusted the high culture and its carriers that were essential for nurturing technical development.

In the aftermath of the GLF tragedy, Mao could not argue as of 1962 that mass mobilization could restore the country's productive capacities. He therefore continued to yield to the entreaties that the Party make full use of

23 Roxane Witke, *Comrade Chiang Ch'ing*, 304–5. Witke places this speech on 6 August, whereas other documentary sources give the 9 August date used in the text.

24 *RMRB*, 15 January 1982, 5, trans. in *FBIS/PRC*, 25 January 1982, K-22. A partial text of Mao's speech is available in *Chinese law and government*, 1.4 (Winter 1968–9), 85–93.

material incentives and technical expertise to recoup the situation. But Mao also, as of the Tenth Plenum, decided to draw the line. He resolutely opposed decollectivization in agriculture and insisted that the communes remain intact (or be restored where they had been abandoned). He also recognized that current policies would increase the strength of the groups in society that he trusted least – the former landlords and rich peasants in the countryside, former capitalists, technical specialists, and intellectuals in the cities. He also feared that a period of normality would nurture tendencies toward sluggish bureaucratism among the many middle-level cadres that had shown themselves so prone to this evil in the past. Thus, Mao called for measures to bring political issues onto the agenda (but without disrupting normal work). He also strengthened the organs responsible for handling those who slip into counterrevolution – the Public Security Ministry and the CCP Control Commission.

The Tenth Plenum embraced Mao's overall analysis in theory but in its concrete provisions kept close to the methods that had been worked out during 1961–2 to bring about a recovery from the GLF. This compromise produced a communiqué that in some paragraphs echoed Mao's rhetoric and in others drove home the logic that Liu, Deng, and Chen had put forward. That this compromise was not put together easily is confirmed by reports that at this plenum Liu Shaoqi, Li Xiannian, Deng Zihui, and Xi Zhongxun made self-criticisms. A subtheme that continued to rankle at this meeting was the Peng Dehuai affair. As noted, Peng wrote and circulated an 80,000-character self-justifying report to provide a basis for his full rehabilitation. Mao demurred, agreeing only to assign Peng some low-level work in the future. The Chairman argued that only those who fully recognized their errors would be rehabilitated – evidently unwilling to admit that in Peng's case, the error was Mao's.

Much Chinese and Western historiography has portrayed 1963–5 as a time of two-line struggle between a Maoist camp, on the one hand, and a Liu–Deng headquarters, on the other. The real situation, though, was not so simple. The group that helped Mao launch the Cultural Revolution in 1966 consisted of diverse elements that had joined together for different reasons. Thus, one important desideratum of these years concerns how the various components of the Maoist coalition formed, and the impact each had on the politics of this era. The other key dimension is the evolution of Mao's own thinking as he came to grips both with his potential coalition partners and with the policies that Liu Shaoqi and his colleagues were implementing. The two key coalition groups were those headed by Lin Biao and Jiang Qing. After analyzing these, we turn to Mao's direct attempts to deal with the major policy initiatives of Liu and company during 1963–5.

THE RISE OF LIN BIAO

Lin Biao faced two tasks after he became minister of defense in September 1959. One was to consolidate his position in the PLA; the other was to solidify his relationship with Mao Zedong and help Mao to enhance his own power in the Chinese political system. Lin executed a complex strategy for accomplishing these related tasks, one that eventually put him in a key position to help Mao launch and sustain the Cultural Revolution.

Lin began his reform of the PLA by bringing back into prominence the Military Affairs Commission (MAC) of the Party. This body had existed nominally throughout the period of Peng Dehuai's stewardship, but in reality its role seems to have diminished with the increasing estrangement of Peng and Mao. Lin revived the MAC, appointing to its standing committee seven of China's ten marshals (leaving out Peng Dehuai and Zhu De, who allegedly supported Peng in 1959).

Little is known about the composition of the MAC, as the Chinese have never published a full list of its members or details on its staff.[25] Before 1976, though, all individuals identified as being MAC members were uniformed members of the military, with the sole exception of Mao Zedong, its chairman. The MAC is formally a Party body and is the command vehicle through which the Party exercises control over the professional military. Party leaders such as Zhou Enlai in fact addressed major meetings of the MAC. But the day-to-day leadership of this body generally resided in the Minister of Defense. And, given that Mao was the only civilian identified as a MAC member, it appears that this body's real purpose was to give the Chairman of the CCP[26] a special place in military decision making. Thus, the revival of the MAC should perhaps more accurately be viewed as a reassertion of Mao's close association with the uniformed military command.

Lin not only moved the MAC to center stage, he also made personnel changes to ensure his control over the Ministry of Defense. He quickly dropped three of the seven vice-ministers in office as of the time of his appointment and appointed six new vice-ministers of his own. Relatedly, he made virtually a clean sweep of the Chinese high command, recognizing the former seven departments into three and appointing to each people who appeared to be his supporters (including Luo Ruiqing, the head of the Public Security apparatus until the showdown at Lushan). These personnel changes

25 The most complete account of the MAC available in the secondary literature is in Harvey Nelsen, *The Chinese military system*.

26 The chairmen of the CCP have been ex officio chairmen of the MAC until Deng Xiaoping stopped this practice during Hua Guofeng's tenure in these positions.

in the ministry were probably linked to the revival of the MAC: The MAC formally makes all high-level appointments in the Ministry of Defense.

At about this time, Lin began, as noted, to stress the use of Mao Zedong Thought in the military. Many others in the PLA disagreed with this approach, but Lin made it a centerpiece of his reign as minister of defense. Lin's approach became official policy at the conclusion of the enlarged meeting of the MAC in September–October 1960. This occurred just as the fourth volume of Mao Zedong's *Selected Works* was being published. Whether or not the two were linked in planning and execution, there is little doubt that Lin's tack further endeared him to an increasingly beleaguered Chairman Mao.

Indeed, the fact that the propagation of the works of specific leaders was seen as an important political question is highlighted by the plans for publication of the *Selected Works of Liu Shaoqi* and a collection of essays by Chen Yun, both of which were being put together in 1962. Neither appeared, reportedly because Liu himself objected to the publication of his works, and Mao essentially pigeonholed the Chen volume.[27] The question of the relative treatment of Mao and Liu had become a sensitive political issue after Liu took over the chairmanship of the PRC from Mao in April 1959.

Lin Biao then took a series of initiatives to enhance the role of the PLA in CCP affairs. He quickly began to increase the number of Party members in the military, perhaps because that would give him a greater say in national CCP affairs. During 1963–5, moreover, he worked to expand the PLA's organizational responsibilities, blurring at some points the boundaries between Party and military. These years saw the heads of the various military districts become secretaries in five of the six regional Party bureaus that had been formed in the wake of the GLF. At the same time, at least half of the provincial Party first secretaries became political commissars in the military districts, putting them at least partially into the chain of command of the General Political Department of the PLA. This multiple officeholding in Party and Army could, in theory, have been used to increase Party control over the PLA, but experience indicates that the real effect was very much the opposite. These were essentially predatory moves by the PLA to increase its power vis-à-vis the Party. The PLA under Lin was also increasing its control over the civilian population. Mao in 1962 ordered the formation of a civilian militia under military control, and the implementation of this order enhanced the military's contacts with the civilian sector.

Given these activities by the army, Mao increasingly pointed to the PLA as the type of organization that could successfully integrate politics and

27 On Liu, see *RMRB*, 15 January 1982, trans. in *FBIS/PRC*, 25 January 1982, K 19–22. On Chen, see Deng Liqun, *Xiang Chen Yun tongzhi xuexi zuo jingji gongzuo* (Study how to do economic work from comrade Chen Yun), 8–9.

expertise – that could, in the terminology of the time, be both Red and expert. For during these same years Lin was bolstering the professional training and discipline in the ranks, and the military was heading the effort to develop China's atomic bomb. Also, in October 1962 the PLA acquitted itself well in the brief border war with India, thus adding to its prowess and prestige.

During 1963 the PLA generated several models of political rectitude, including a selfless soldier (Lei Feng) who had died in an accident and an outstanding military company, the Good Eighth Company of Nanjing Road. Following initiatives to have people emulate these military models, in December 1963 Mao issued a general call for people to "learn from the PLA," a startling slogan given that the Party was supposedly the fount of all wisdom. In the Chairman's eyes, the problems with the first FYP had essentially demonstrated the inadequacies of the government administration, and the Great Leap catastrophe had substantially discredited the CCP. Thus, Mao began to look toward the military as the type of organization that might achieve the balance of political virtue and technical/organizational expertise that he regarded as vital for the PRC.

Soon Mao went from hortatory campaigns to learn from the PLA to a far more direct approach to increasing the military's leverage within the government and Party. In 1964, at Mao's direction, government units – and subsequently some CCP organs also – began to form political departments within the units. These were modeled after the political system within the army, and a number of the people who staffed them either went through training courses run by the military for this purpose or were themselves recently demobilized army personnel. These departments never became solidly established – partly because of resistance in the government and Party, partly because they could not define clearly their role, and partly because there were constant skirmishes over who would be the personnel to staff them. But the whole exercise again reflected the increasingly aggressive posture of the PLA vis-à-vis the Party and government – and Mao's encouragement of this trend.

In May 1965 Lin Biao took the unusual measure of having all ranks in the PLA abolished. This initiative again made the military appear to be the most advanced politically, since it alone was acting to implement the egalitarian ideals of the revolution. From the point of view of political power, moreover, this measure may in some degree have strengthened Lin's hand within the PLA. It meant, essentially, that a former officer's power now derived solely from his actual operational assignment. He would no longer have rank that could itself convey certain rights and privileges. Given that Lin held the top operational position within the army, the independent power of the other eight marshals (Luo Ronghuan had died in 1963) and of the officer corps itself should have been weakened somewhat by this measure.

Also in 1965 the PLA took direct control over the Public Security forces. Luo Ruiqing, former minister of public security and a man with extremely strong ties in its apparatus, was at the time the chief of staff of the PLA. As we shall see later, Lin turned against Luo in December 1965 and by May 1966 had him purged and vilified. One effect of the purge was to leave Lin in a better position to marshal the resources of the public security apparatus – one of the most powerful organizations in the country – to support Mao and Lin himself. He appears to have used these resources well once the Cultural Revolution began.[28]

The conflict with Luo Ruiqing was broader than the issue of control over the public security forces, however. The year 1965 was a very bad one for China's foreign policy. Zhou Enlai had hoped to put together an Afro-Asian Conference that would take an anti-Soviet line in the spring, but this effort failed. The PRC also tried unsuccessfully to influence the outcome of the August–September Indo-Pakistani war, and the Soviet Union proved in the final analysis to be able to play a constructive mediating role in that conflict. And the PRC's careful cultivation of the Communist Party of Indonesia (PKI) ended in disaster when in September 1965 the PKI supported a coup attempt against the military that failed. All these missteps produced a growing feeling of isolation and seige in Beijing, just as the United States began to increase substantially its involvement in Vietnam, posing the possibility of a direct U.S. attack on southern China in the near future.

Within this troubling international context, Beijing's leaders debated options and strategy. Luo Ruiqing appears to have preferred an approach that would relieve some of the tension on China by seeking better relations with the Soviet Union – based on joint efforts to combat the United States in Vietnam. Luo recommended the Soviet strategy of the eve of World War II, a strategy of projecting conventional force to engage the enemy well outside of the country's boundaries. This strategy demanded, in turn, that China maximize the output of its military-related heavy industry, striving for efficient industrial production as a high priority goal. Given the logistical demands of this strategy, it also presumed that China's cities would serve as the key production bases for the effort and that Soviet help would be available to supplement the PRC's inadequate industrial base.

Lin Biao, by contrast, argued that Vietnam should basically fight the war itself, with indirect Chinese support but no direct intervention. He lauded the CCP's strategy against the Japanese, a strategy that required luring the

28 As will be noted, Kang Sheng played a significant role vis-à-vis the Public Security apparatus, too.

enemy deep into the country and then wearing him down through guerrilla war techniques. This in turn demanded the dispersal of industry, a policy of regional basic self-sufficiency, playing up the role of the militia and of unconventional forces rather than of the regular army and whipping up high political fervor among the population. It did not demand – and indeed it argued against – a strategy of rapprochement with the post-Khrushchev leadership of the Soviet Union. Lin laced his argument with quotations from Mao Zedong, and the strategy he advocated dovetailed neatly with a whole series of civilian, foreign policy, and military policy preferences of the Chairman's. Liu Shaoqi and Deng Xiaoping seem to have been opposed to many of these.

Thus, while building up his position in the military and enhancing the role of the PLA vis-à-vis the Party and government, Lin also carefully cultivated Mao and tried to support the Chairman's policy preferences in the system. In general terms, the Mao cult in the army redounded to the Chairman's overall political benefit. Indeed, starting in 1964, the book of Mao quotations that had been developed for use in the army was distributed among model youth to reward their accomplishments. On a more specific level also, as indicated by his wide-ranging strategic recommendations about Vietnam, Lin injected himself directly into the increasingly fractious relations that Mao had with Liu, Deng, and company. In some cases, his main purpose seems, indeed, to have been precisely to exacerbate tensions between Mao and his Politburo colleagues.

For example, at the September 1959 enlarged meeting of the MAC that formally stripped Peng Dehuai of his post as minister of defense, Lin's attack on Peng and his characterization of the latter's errors were far harsher than those of Mao. Lin, trying to solidify his own newly acquired position, argued that Peng was virtually irredeemable and the Mao Zedong Thought was the quintessence of Marxism-Leninism. Lin's position, finally accepted by Mao, helped to drive a wedge between the Chairman and the other members of the Politburo more sympathetic to Peng. At the Seven Thousand Cadres Conference in January–February 1962, Lin leaped to Mao's defense (and that of the GLF itself) when debate occurred over the causes of the difficulties in which China found itself. Lin not only strongly supported Mao and the Three Red Banners (the GLF, the People's Communes, and the general line), but he also called on all present to study Mao Zedong Thought. Although documentary evidence is lacking to spell out Lin's role in other meetings involving the Party elite, it seems that he had continued to try both to build up the Chairman and to exacerbate Mao's relations with other leaders. For example, in May 1966 Lin spoke darkly about the chances of a coup against Mao and the need for the Chairman to protect himself against such a threat.

These activities indicate that Lin Biao was an ambitious man who had developed a clear political strategy soon after taking office as defense minister in 1959. That strategy was to link his fortune with that of Mao, and the disastrous effects of the Great Leap then required that Lin use his resources to bolster Mao's position in the system, in addition to simply solidifying his own position in the Chairman's eyes. Taken together, Lin's initiatives show that he was more than simply a puppet of the Chairman. Rather, although his interests overlapped with those of Mao, he also seems to have worked hard to prevent any improvement in relations between Mao and his colleagues on the Politburo. By the very nature of the situation, what were probably Lin's most effective efforts in this endeavor would remain known only to the few prinicipal participants themselves.

Mao, it should be noted, never became fully a captive of Lin's initiatives. As noted elsewhere, for example, Mao perceived a major national security threat to China growing out of the potential escalation of the Vietnam War after the Gulf of Tonkin incident in 1964. In response, the Chairman undercut the original strategy for the third FYP and called instead for devotion of major investment resources to building a "third line" of industries in the remote hinterland of Southwest China. Mao created an informal State Planning Commission headed by Yu Qiuli to oversee this new strategy. The body consisted basically of the people who in the 1970s would become known as the "petroleum clique," and during the Cultural Revolution it essentially merged with and superseded the formal State Planning Commission. The plan advocated by this group was the same one Lin Biao espoused for dealing with Vietnam. But Mao assigned Peng Dehuai, Lin's nemesis, to take charge of the Sichuan-based headquarters for constructing the third line.

Culture: Jiang Qing

A second key component of the coalition that formed to launch the Cultural Revolution was Mao's wife, Jiang Qing, and the group she put together in the cultural sphere. Indeed, in February 1966 Lin Biao and Jiang Qing clearly linked up when Lin invited Jiang to stage a Forum on Literature and Art for Troops and made her the official cultural adviser to the military. This for the first time gave Jiang an official position that she could use as a base for pursuing her political goals.[29] But she obtained that help from Lin only because she had spent considerable effort over the preceding years building

29 Jiang had held a minor position in cultural affairs in the early 1950s.

up her own resources in the cultural realm and winning her husband to her point of view.

Jiang Qing had long held strong views about the directions in which cultural policy should move, and for an equally long time she had nursed hatreds against the Communist cultural establishment that kept her at arm's length. When Jiang Qing had gone to Yan'an and won Mao's heart, she replaced Mao's popular second wife, He Zizhen, who had suffered terribly as one of the very few women on the Long March. Mao's colleagues obtained the Chairman's agreement that he would keep Jiang Qing out of politics if they would not object to his having Jiang replace He in his bedroom.

Even in Yan'an Jiang Qing had advocated developing a new type of revolutionary cultural repertoire, and she had been active in the development of revolutionary plays during those years. A very bright, astute, and ambitious woman, she evidently felt acutely the ostracism imposed on her by the male-dominated cultural and propaganda apparatus. After 1949, Jiang remained very much in the background, owing in part to her continuing health problems and in part to the unwillingness of the cultural establishment to listen to her or give her an official place in the system. Jiang does, however, seem to some extent to have served the Chairman as an informal political confidante. For example, she flew to Lushan when Mao informed her that trouble had erupted at the Lushan conference in July 1959. On that occasion Mao asked her not to come, but he evidently did not forbid her to participate, and indeed he called her from the meeting to discuss with her his response to Peng's challenge.

The year 1959 seems to have been the start of a turning point in Jiang's health, and as her physical well-being became more assured, her energy for participating in politics and cultural affairs also grew. After the Lushan meeting, Jiang went to Shanghai to rest, and while there she had gone to a number of theaters. She was appalled at the content of the productions, finding that "old" themes and styles were very much in vogue and feeling that this should be rectified. Jiang gradually began to put together a faction of people who would help her carry out her plans to revolutionize Beijing Opera and other aspects of Chinese culture.

Mao, of course, was central to Jiang's efforts, and she herself claims that by 1962 she had convinced him that the cultural sphere needed attention. Indeed, Mao instructed her in the spring of 1962 to draft a policy statement for the CC on policy toward culture. Jiang's effort provided some of the background for Mao's call at the August 1962 Beidaihe meeting to promote "proletarian" culture. But Jiang's position paper did not become official policy until May 1966, when a considerably revised draft of it became one of the basic documents that led to the Cultural Revolution

Jiang Qing and Kang Sheng

Jiang found a natural conjoining of interests with two others with whom she had ties from prerevolutionary days: Kang Sheng and Ke Qingshi. Kang Sheng came from Jiang's home town of Zhucheng in Shandong province, and the two of them had known each other before Jiang went to Yan'an. Kang specialized in three areas of work: liaison with other Communist parties, public security, and higher education. What brought them all together was Kang's evidently fairly sophisticated training in Marxism-Leninism while he was learning the finer points of police work from the NKVD in the Soviet Union in the mid-1930s, and his ongoing involvement with the issues of revisionism and counterrevolution.

Kang had had major responsibility in public security affairs prior to the 1950s, and as a result took some of the blame when Khrushchev made his de-Stalinization speech to the Soviet Twentieth Party Congress. Kang was dropped from full membership in the Politburo in September 1956, at the same time that the Party dropped Mao Zedong Thought as part of the guiding ideology specified in the CCP constitution. As of the early 1960s, however, things were moving in a direction potentially favorable to Kang. With the Sino-Soviet dispute having reached a critical stage, Mao – who remained the dominant figure in handling the dispute on the Chinese side – needed a theorist with Kang's knowledge to help him draft the CCP CC's attacks on "Khrushchev revisionism." At the same time, Kang – probably through his long friendship with Jiang Qing – learned that Mao was planning to push for the proletarianization of Chinese culture. Kang could play a useful role in that effort, especially if he could link it to counterrevolutionary activities to justify his involvement.

Kang effected this linkage at the Tenth Plenum in September 1962, where he launched an attack on Xi Zhongxun for the latter's involvement in the production of a purportedly counterrevolutionary novel about Liu Zhidan, one of the early Communist guerrilla fighters in Shaanxi who had died in 1936. Claiming that the novel about Liu in fact vilified Mao, Kang argued that using novels for purposes of contemporary political criticism was a new invention. He thus established an intellectual link with Jiang Qing, who was trying to call Mao's attention to the political attacks against the Chairman that she had seen in the writings of intellectuals during the previous few years.

Kang subsequently served as a bridge between Jiang Qing and some of the radical intellectuals she brought to the fore in the early stage of the Cultural Revolution. Kang's work in higher education gave him entrée to major educational units, and he took advantage of this to cultivate key individuals. The most prominent among these turned out to be Guan Feng and Qi Benyu of the Research Institute of Philosophy of the Academy of Sciences, Nie Yuanzi of the Philosophy Department of Peking University, and several people at the Higher Party School.[30] Kang, like Lin Biao, was willing to foment trouble if need be to attain his purposes. For example, in the Higher Party School he attacked Yang Xianzhens's theory of "two combine into one" as an anti-Maoist negation of the Chairman's philosophical premise that "one divides into two." Through such theoretical skulduggery, Kang managed to purge Yang and to increase the influence of his followers in the Higher Party School. As of mid-1964, Kang also heavily and personally involved himself in Jiang Qing's efforts to revolutionize Beijing Opera.[31]

Ke Qingshi, Shanghai's mayor, was an old friend of Jiang Qing's. Ke had in 1958 been one of the most vociferous supporters of the GLF and especially of the backyard steel furnace campaign. He was made a full member of the Politburo in the spring of 1958, and Shanghai became a major beneficiary of the Leap strategy.[32] As noted earlier, even in mid-1962 Ke had continued to support a Maoist interpretation of the current situation as opposed to the more pessimistic views of Chen Yun and others. Ke, then, like Kang Sheng, Lin Biao, and Jiang Qing, had good reason to want to bolster Mao's standing.

In late 1962 Kang Sheng spoke with Ke about the need to have literature and art portray heroes drawn from the ranks of people who had emerged over the thirteen years since 1949, a line very much in tune with Jiang Qing's own thinking. Ke during the GLF had already sided with Shanghai's "worker-writers" against the professional authors.[33] In January 1963 Ke made just such an appeal in Shanghai, calling on the local intelligentsia to abandon old repertoires, adopt the class struggle of the Tenth Plenum, and stage new dramas with heroes drawn from the ranks of post-1949 workers, peasants, and soldiers. Mao soon chimed in with support, calling the Ministry of Culture a "ministry of emperors and princes, generals and ministers, gifted scholars and beauties."

Jiang Qing had been in touch with Ke in 1959 about cultural matters in Shanghai, and she remained in contact with him throughout the early 1960s (Ke died in 1965) on this issue. Through Ke, Jiang linked up with Zhang Chunqiao (who was in the cultural apparatus in Shanghai) and Yao Wenyuan, a Shanghai critic. Yao, in turn, had cultivated good ties among the newly developing "proletartian writers" – workers who had taken up the pen during the 1950s – in Shanghai.[34]

30 *Zhengming* (Hong Kong), 34 (August 1980), 45. 31 Ibid.

32 See Christopher Howe's contribution to Christoper Howe, ed., *Shanghai: Revolution and development in an Asian metropolis,* 173–9.

33 See Ragvald contribution to Howe, ed. *Shanghai,* 316.

34 See ibid., 309–23.

Thus, Jiang Qing during the early 1960s worked on her husband and began to put together her own coterie of advocates of a "revolutionization" of China's culture. The Ministries of Culture and Education and the Propaganda Department of the CCP, all manned by old opponents of Jiang's, paid her no heed and scoffed at her efforts. Clashes occurred at national meetings dealing with culture such as the June–July 1964 Festival of Beijing Opera on Contemporary Themes. Jiang had been developing her own model plays in Shanghai and through Mao kept up pressure to reform the cultural fare offered the Chinese people. Finally, in about June 1964 the Party Secretariat formed a Five-Man Group to coordinate efforts toward cultural reform. Peng Zhen, who conceivably was being considered by Mao as a potential replacement for Liu Shaoqi as the Party Chairman's successor, took charge of the group. Kang Sheng was the member, however, who most clearly was loyal to Mao and Jiang Qing, rather than to Liu Shaoqi or Deng Xiaoping.

To Jiang Qing, the Five-Man Group proved more a hindrance than a force for positive changes in cultural policy. The group generally followed the preferences of the Beijing cultural establishment (represented on the group by Lu Dingyi, the head of the Propaganda Department of the CCP). Jiang continued to seek other avenues for putting her priorities in the cultural and political spheres on the national agenda. The approach she adopted that eventually proved to have the greatest impact on national politics was to focus on the issue that Kang Sheng had raised at the Tenth Plenum in 1962 – that novels and plays could be used for political purposes. Jiang particularly pointed to the play *Hai Rui dismissed from office,* written by Wu Han. This play concerned the upright actions of a Ming official in the face of unfair attacks from his political enemies, and Jiang argued to Mao that the play in fact represented a veiled defense of Peng Dehuai. Chiang's specific accusation is plausible but probably wrong – Wu Han had begun work on a play about Hai Rui before the Lushan Conference, and he did so at the specific request of one of Mao's current secretaries, Hu Qiaomu.[35] Nonetheless, in the increasingly suspicion-charged atmosphere of 1965, Jiang persuaded Mao to have Yao Wenyuan write a critique of the play that raised the hidden political issues supposedly involved.

Yao's critique, published in November 1965, was important for three reasons. It cast the issue of cultural reform as a political rather than a purely academic matter, thus raising the possibility that the regime would again carry out a major political campaign against the intellectuals. It attacked a play written by a subordinate and close friend of Peng Zhen's, thus putting

35 For an early examination of this problem, see MacFarquhar, *Origins of the Cultural Revolution,* 2. 207–12.

Peng to the test as to whether he would protect Wu Han or side with Mao.[36] And it came from Shanghai (where Mao was then residing), symbolizing Mao's decision that the leaders in Beijing had moved so far away from his preferred positions that he would have to launch an attack on them that relied primarily on forces outside the central political apparatus. Jiang Qing's group provided important resources for this effort.

But Jiang's contacts as of 1965, other than Kang Sheng, were among radical intellectuals and people at lower levels of the system. Thus, when Jiang joined in the coalition to launch the Cultural Revolution, she brought in people unsympathetic to the bureaucratic values and practices that had developed since 1949. These were the people of ideas, not the people of organizational skills. Not surprisingly, therefore, they would prove themselves adept at manipulating ideas but disastrously inadequate at managing the economy.

The fact that Jiang's coalition included Kang Sheng proved important for the politics of the 1960s. Kang was ruthless and more than willing to destroy those who stood in his way. His movement toward the center of the political stage in and after 1962 permitted him to build on the bitterness of the Peng Dehuai affair, with its damage to previous norms of intra-Party struggle, and contribute to changing completely the way the Party leaders dealt with each other in political disputes. The radical intelligentsia in Jiang's entourage had never been schooled in these intra-Party norms, and thus easily joined in wholesale violations of previous practice. Zhang Chunqiao was the only one in this group as of the mid-1960s who had enjoyed an extensive career as a bureaucrat outside secret police work. Not surprisingly, Zhang also became the person in this group most sensitively attuned to the need to preserve order, build authority, and secure a bureaucratic base as the group acquired power.

Overall, Jiang Qing wanted to change Chinese culture and to avenge the many years of slights she had suffered at the hands of Lu Dingyi and other leaders of the cultural establishment. Her coalition included people who were willing to wage ruthless struggles in order to destroy the Party establishment. Lin Biao had a more careful bureaucratic game to play, one that would lead to his replacing Liu Shaoqi as Mao's successor. For this, he could utilize the destructive power of Jiang Qing (and her ability to cultivate Mao's worst instincts), and thus in February 1966, as noted previously, Lin cemented a

36 Actually, Peng would lose either way. If he protected Wu Han (as he subsequently tried to do), he made himself vulnerable by that act. If he attacked Wu Han, however, he would also have been weakened by the acknowledgement that he had permitted an anti-Maoist to achieve high position in his own Beijing municipal apparatus. Given the likely negative effect of this episode on Peng Zhen's career, one would like to know more about the real background to Yao Wenyuan's article.

coalition with Jiang by appointing her cultural adviser to the army. Jiang then used this position as a platform from which to make a wide-ranging attack against those who opposed her views on culture, whether related to the military or not.

RECTIFICATION

Let us now shift our focus from Mao's eventual coalition partners to the Chairman himself. As of 1962 Mao saw the revolution threatened by adverse forces at both the apex and the base of the political system. At the apex, his colleagues wanted to continue policies that Mao felt would simply strengthen the hands of the anti-Communist forces in the society. At the base, the Chairman recognized that the damage that the GLF had done to basic-level Party units, especially in the countryside, had been enormous. He determined, as Harry Harding has written,[37] to use rectification campaigns to remedy both problems. Rectification essentially allowed Mao to order the formation of a new hierarchy of temporary organs that would deal with the established institutions to remedy a problem. It was an ideal tool for Mao to use to enhance his leverage in the system.

Mao highlighted the need for Party rectification at the August 1962 Beidaihe meeting and at the CC's Tenth Plenum that September. There was little argument over the need for rectification, but subsequent events would prove that there could be significant disagreement over the tools to be used. Experiments in rural rectification were carried out in selected spots following the Tenth Plenum, and the results of these provided the basis for the initial programmatic document of the rural rectification effort, the Socialist Education Campaign.

Mao personally played a determining role in drafting this document at central work conferences in February and May 1963. The resulting Former Ten Points called into being "poor and lower middle peasants' associations" to serve as a vehicle for exercising supervision over the erring basic level cadres. The problem, it turned out, was that poor and lower middle peasants had also suffered badly during the GLF, and many of them by 1963 were either disillusioned or corrupt. As this became evident during the course of the year, new measures (the Later Ten Points) were drafted by Deng Xiaoping and Peng Zhen and promulgated in September 1963.

The Later Ten Points recognized the problems in the poor and lower middle peasants' associations and called for stricter recruitment criteria for them. More significantly, this document worked on the assumption that they

37 Harry Harding, *Organizing China*, 196.

were by nature unable to supervise adequately the commune and brigade committees. It therefore called for the formation of urban-based work teams to carry out this rectification campaign. It further asserted that these teams should first take care of problems at the provincial, prefectural, and county levels before dealing with the basic-level cadres. Since these higher-level organs were located in cities, the document initiated an urban Five Antis Campaign to rectify the higher levels and lay an appropriate groundwork for follow-up work at the basic levels.[38] The effect of these shifts was to leave the peasants' associations essentially without a significant task to perform. Rectification had been shifted to a purely internal Party matter. Mao, however, had seen mobilization of non-Party people as one of the benefits of the rectification process, and in June 1964 the Chairman indicated his concern that the implementation of the Socialist Education Campaign was not involving sufficient mobilization of the poor and lower middle peasants.

During the first part of 1964, high-level cadres went down to the basic levels to carry out investigations of the conditions there. This method of acquiring data harkened back to the work style of the Yan'an period and reflected the fact that the leaders knew they could not rely on the reporting that came up through normal channels. Thus, for example, Liu Shaoqi went to Henan province for eighteen days – the province that had been a pacesetter during the Great Leap and had ended in a parlous state at the conclusion of the movement. Liu's wife, Wang Guangmei, spent five months incognito at the Taoyuan Brigade near her native city of Tianjin.

The Lius' findings made them deeply pessimistic about the situation in the rural areas. They ascertained that corruption was widespread and that many basic-level cadres opposed the Party (as did a large percentage of the peasants). As they came back from these trips, they felt that counterrevolution had a grip on a large portion of rural China and that draconian measures would be necessary to rescue the situation. Mao may well have agreed with this diagnosis – but he subsequently disagreed strongly with the measures taken to effect a cure.

The Revised Later Ten Points were drafted in September 1964 and reflected Liu's approach to the rectification campaign. They called for large work teams to go to selected communes and virtually take over the communes and shake them to the foundations in order to put them into shape. A work team would stay in one locale for appproximately six months and would deal harshly with those cadres who were found to have become lax and corrupt. While in the communes, these work teams would also carry out a

38 This Five Antis Campaign should not be confused with the other campaign of the same name that peaked in early 1952. See Chapter 1.

new class categorization in the countryside – the first such effort since land reform at the beginning of the 1950s. The whole Socialist Education movement would, according to the calendar of the Revised Later Ten Points, take five to six years to carry out throughout the country.

Mao Zedong had three complaints about the implementation of the Revised Later Ten Points. First, they narrowed the target of attack from revisionism to corruption. Second, they imposed penalties that were too harsh on the cadres. And third, they involved the imposition of massive work teams on the communes rather than mobilizing the masses themselves to carry out the campaign. In short, the Socialist Education movement had been twisted around to the point where it no longer served as a vehicle for propagating Mao's ideas about revisionism but, rather, had become a relatively savage effort to reimpose discipline in the rural Party organs.

Mao's response to this set of trends was to seize the initiative with his own new program document for the Socialist Education movement. Issued in January 1965, Mao's Twenty-three Articles reoriented the campaign so that it would become a general educational effort on the evils of revisionism at all levels of the Party. In the rural areas, this meant that the work teams pulled back, and many of the former cadres who had been severely punished by them were now rehabilitated – and their replacements removed. This simply increased the divisions among cadre ranks in the countryside on the eve of the Cultural Revolution.

Mao's efforts to use rectification as a means of forcing his political agenda on the society, then, proved only partially successful. As in his attempt to bring his version of politics more directly to bear through the formation of political departments in government and Party organs starting in 1964, the ruling bureaucracies proved capable of protecting their right to handle their own organizational affairs themselves. The Revised Later Ten Points were harsh, but they were also an approach that kept the rectification problem within the Party and precluded large-scale use of non-Party bodies to rectify the CCP. But it was precisely Mao's growing concern about the directions of policy within the CCP – a concern nurtured by Jiang Qing, Kang Sheng, and Lin Biao (along with Chen Boda and others) – that made the Chairman increasingly determined to enhance his leverage over this core political organization.

A changing Mao

Mao personally did not share the sense of personal insult that haunted Jiang Qing, and there is no reason to believe that he felt comfortable with the notion of Lin Biao as his successor at any point before the late 1960s, if then.[39] It appears, in fact, that during 1963–5 Mao had been toying with the notion of building up Peng Zhen as the replacement for Liu as his successor. Thus, as suggested earlier, Mao gradually put into place a coalition of partners to launch the Cultural Revolution, but he fully shared the goals and perspectives of none of them. How, then did the Chairman himself arrive at the conclusion that it was necessary to launch a frontal assault on his colleagues in the Politburo?

Three elements appear crucial to understanding Mao's psychological evolution during the critical years of 1959–66: his changing understanding of the potential evolution of the Chinese revolution; his continuing concern with the problem of succession; and his related sense of impending death. All of these intertwined in a way that escalated his fear that his life's work had produced a political system that would, in the final analysis, turn away from his values and prove as exploitative as the one it had replaced.

Mao's concerns about the future of the revolution cannot be separated from his evolving analysis of the degeneration of the Soviet political system. To be sure, Mao had spent much of his career fighting Soviet influences in the CCP, and in both substance and style he was the least Soviet of the Chinese leaders. During the mid-1950s he had launched concerted efforts to move China away from the Soviet model of development, and starting in 1958 he had included the military and military doctrine in this effort. But whereas before 1959 Mao had felt that the Soviet leaders had often been overbearing and lacking in understanding of the Chinese situation, after 1959 he began to wrestle with the question of whether the Soviet revolution itself had not gone fundamentally astray and changed its nature.

Essentially, as the Soviet Union began to try to interfere in Chinese internal affairs, to declare that its own revolutionary era was over, and to seek a more stable accommodation with the United States, Mao began to wonder whether the victory of socialism in a country ensured that there could not be a resurgence of capitalism in that society. Many things contributed to this intellectual shift. Mao thought he saw Khrushchev attempt to establish leverage over the Chinese navy in 1958, and perceived another attempt by Khrushchev to interfere in Chinese affairs via cancellation of the nuclear sharing agreement and collusion with Peng Dehuai in 1959. In that year also, Mao saw Khrushchev's declaration that the Soviet Union had become a "state of the whole people" rather than a "dictatorship of the proletariat";[40]

39 Indeed, at the height of Mao's reliance on Lin during 1966, he is said to have written to Jiang expressing his distrust of Lin.

40 By calling the Soviet Union a state of the whole people, Khrushchev indicated that the exploiting classes had been destroyed and class struggle had ended in the Soviet Union. A dictatorship of the proletariat, by contrast, is the form of dictatorship used by a Communist Party in power to wage class struggle against the remnants of the exploiting classes.

his Camp David summit with the United States and the related effort to achieve peaceful coexistence with the West; Moscow's seeming neutrality in the 1959 border tensions between Beijing and New Delhi; and the Soviet withdrawal of advisers from China in mid-1960. These were but a few examples.

Growing out of this new concern, Mao began a period of study of Soviet political economy, and he concluded that even Stalin had made some fundamental errors in this central theoretical sphere. He instructed Chinese delegations to debate the Soviets on the issues on which there was disagreement, and the Soviet responses increased his concerns. Jiang Qing noted that the swift withdrawal of Soviet advisers in 1960 had "shaken" Mao,[41] and probably from that point on he determined that, at a minimum, Khrushchev himself must be ousted in order to put the Soviet system back on solid ground. The refusal of the Soviet leadership to remove Khrushchev simply increased Mao's anxiety.

Having waged struggles with Khrushchev at meetings since 1958, Mao in 1963 decided that it was time to make the polemics open. On this central ideological plane, his Politburo colleagues evidently could not deny him the lead. Thus, during 1963–4 Mao supervised the writing of nine polemics, each of which was given wide publicity in China. As noted previously, Mao enlisted Kang Sheng's talents in writing these pieces, at a time when Kang had already become involved in the struggle against revisionism in the cultural arena at home.

It appears in retrospect that Mao used the nine polemics as a device for giving publicity to his political thinking within China. These polemics raised all the issues on which Mao in fact disagreed with his colleagues on the Politburo, and they provided a vehicle for identifying the Chairman's political views with the anti-Soviet struggle then being waged. This linkage of Chinese nationalism with Mao's political critique of revisionism proved a potent mixture – so potent, in fact, that Mao subsequently had the Chinese media attack Liu Shaoqi during the Cultural Revolution simply as "China's Khrushchev."

But beyond the shrewd politics in this approach there lay a human tragedy. There is no reason to suspect that Mao himself did not believe what he was saying about the degeneration of the Soviet revolution. He evidently could see the same forces underway in China, where his colleagues now argued (as they had in 1956) that class struggle must be subsumed under the overriding importance of the struggle for production. Inevitably, if these trends were allowed to continue, the younger generation would grow up with

41 Witke, *Comrade Chiang Ch'ing*, 304.

a revisionist perspective. Undoubtedly, history would then prove to be as unkind to Mao as it had been to Stalin after his death. Mao was a man with a keen sense of China's history, who compared himself in 1965 with the country's greatest emperors. He could now see the possibility of being remembered as a man who had in fact led the country astray. Equally disconcerting, his legacy to China might be a political system that exploited his beloved countryside and colluded with imperialism. Thus, Mao's observations of the evolution of the Soviet revolution significantly raised the stakes for him as he saw the trends in China during the first half of the 1960s.[42]

Mao's changing role in the Chinese political process also contributed to his sense of urgency. As noted previously, the Chairman reportedly had stopped his regular attendance at Politburo meetings in January 1958.[43] After that, he still received reports on Politburo discussions, and he had to approve all documents issued in the name of the CC before they could be circulated as official documents.[44] The same stricture evidently did not, however, apply to the documents issued by the Party Secretariat headed by Deng Xiaoping, and the Secretariat assumed a major role in the policy process of the first half of the 1960s. Mao subsequently complained, as noted earlier, that Deng did not consult with him on policy matters after 1959. Although this complaint may well have been exaggerated for effect, the sense of grievance undoubtedly was there.

More fundamentally, when Mao had pulled back from regular participation in Politburo meetings, it in fact marked the beginning of a period in which he dominated the political system more than at any time previously. Mao at that point indicated also that he would like to give up his role as head of state so that he could concentrate on the larger issues of the development of the revolution. On both the Party and state sides, therefore, in 1958 Mao saw himself as moving to a somewhat more Olympian role, in firm control over the central directions of policy while at the same time moving into place successors in whom he would have confidence. The greater responsibilities acquired by Liu Shaoqi, Deng Xiaoping, and Lin Biao in 1958–9 reflect the implementation of this strategy.

But after the collapse of the GLF, Mao found that in 1962 he was not able

42 Parenthetically, the fact that the Soviet leadership did not change Moscow's position on the issues in dispute with China in the wake of Khrushchev's ouster in October 1964 confirmed to Mao that it was the system and not simply an individual that had degenerated. This also helps to explain the vehemence of Mao's opposition to Luo Ruiqing's suggestion in the spring of 1965, noted earlier, that China cooperate with the Soviet Union to oppose the escalating U.S. commitment in Vietnam.

43 After that date, Mao attended only those Politburo meetings that he wanted to address. Otherwise, he relied on reports of what had happened at the meetings.

44 Documents issued by the Politburo were said to be issued by the Central Committee, so this rule in fact enabled the Chairman to ride herd on all official documents set out by the Politburo.

to assume full control of the basic directions of policy again. Rather, Liu and Deng now appeared to restrict his access to the policy flow and to twist the meaning of his directives, such as those on rectification. Thus, although Mao had wanted to step back to the second line in 1958–9, he was dismayed as that changed its meaning in the wake of the GLF. He then began to test his proposed successors to determine whether they would support the general policies he believed to be central to the future of the revolution. The more he tested, the more they (with the exception of Lin Biao) demonstrated their inadequacy.

The heart of this growing disparity between Mao's priorities and those of his successors lay in the different lessons they drew from the GLF. Mao, as noted earlier, learned that mass mobilization is not the key to rapid economic development. But at the same time, he retained his faith in mass mobilization as an instrument of ideological renewal, social change, and rectification. Mass mobilization was not, however, a policy that could be carried out by central ministries in Beijing. Rather, by its very nature, it relied on the skills of CCP generalists, rather than technical specialists, and demanded tolerance of sufficient decentralization to permit the flexibility this strategy inevitably entailed. Thus mass mobilization was to an extent an inherently anti-intellectual and anti-bureaucratic approach, although it could be implemented without totally dismantling a centralized, specialist-dominated political system.

Liu Shaoqi and his colleagues concluded from the Great Leap that China had progressed beyond the point where mass mobilization was any longer a useful tool of policy. Given the parlous state of the country's economy and political institutions in 1962, they felt that strong measures must be taken to put control over the economy back in the hands of experts in the central ministries and commissions, and that related efforts must be made to rebuild disciplined Party and state organizations that would link the center to the basic levels. The high tide politics inherent in major political campaigns could only disrupt the effort they were making to salvage what they could from a bad situation. The campaign approach had served the CCP well in the days in Yan'an and the early 1950s, but it was no longer suited to the complex task of governing the country in the 1960s.

Mao tried to nudge the system back toward his own priorities through a series of measures. Some, like the use of rectification campaigns to bring mass mobilization back into the system, have already been detailed. Aside from these, the Chairman periodically indicated specific policy preferences in various fields that had the effect of attacking the urban orientation and technical premises of the Liu–Deng strategy. In culture, egged on by his wife and Kang Sheng, he demanded that writers and artists go to the grass roots in order to understand life through living with average people, especially in the countryside. In medicine, he leveled a series of blasts at the Ministry of Health and demanded that the best doctors of the country leave the cities and practice in the rural areas.[45] In education, he advocated a shorter curriculum, more concentration on applied studies rather than theory, and the integration of manual labor with the academic curriculum in a significant way. He also wanted school textbooks rewritten to take better account of local needs and conditions.[46] In all these areas, the Chairman's recommendations would have the effect of undercutting the control exercised by the authorities in the relevant ministries in Beijing.

Mao also objected to the economic centralization and specialization inherent in the program of forming specialized national companies to run major sectors of the economy. Calling these companies "trusts," Mao argued instead for greater regional self-sufficiency. As noted earlier, this approach also tied in neatly with Mao's preferred strategy for coping with the escalating threat from the United States in Vietnam in 1965.[47]

The results in virtually every area were largely the same. In each case, Liu Shaoqi and others accepted the general thrust of Mao's critique of current policy and took some measures to implement his ideas. But at the same time, these measures fell far short of the drastic restructuring of the system Mao had in mind. As a result, Mao increasingly saw his colleagues as running a bureaucratic leviathan that gobbled up his pressing demands and turned them into relatively innocuous reforms that did little to affect the basic functions and trends of the system.

Finally, Mao's concerns about these issues grew rapidly in 1964–5 because, as his available speeches and interviews indicate, he began to focus on his own mortality. Beginning in 1964, he made repeated references to "going to see Karl Marx" and the inevitable mortality of any man. He also revealed these concerns in startling fashion in an interview with André Malraux in early 1965. Although it is impossible to be precise about Mao's mental state at the time, it seems reasonable to conjecture, as Robert Lifton has, that the Chairman increasingly saw his physical life coming to a close and his fundamental identity as defined by the fate of the revolution he had fathered. In other words, Mao thought he could achieve immortality only through the continuation of his revolution along proper paths,[48] but what the Chairman saw as he looked around him was the subversion of that revolution through the revisionism of his chosen successors. The psychological and political

45 For details, see David Lampton, *The politics of medicine in China,* 129–92.
46 For details, see Peter Seybolt, ed., *Revolutionary education in China,* Introduction and 5–62.
47 On trusts, see Ahn, *Chinese politics and the Cultural Revolution,* 139–44.
48 Robert Lifton, *Revolutionary immortality.*

stakes for him thus became so high that he felt compelled eventually to launch a brutal frontal assault on the Party he had spent his life creating.

The split in the Yan'an leadership

This analysis has focused on the different components that came together to launch the Cultural Revolution in 1966. It has said relatively little about the targets of that major campaign. Much could be written about the policies and developments of 1962–5, a time of impressive economic recovery and policy initiatives in a range of areas related to the economy. But the economic side of this analysis belongs in another chapter, and on a political level it appears that the leaders tried to reestablish the system that had developed by late 1956: a system of clear division of responsibility, with a powerful Secretariat serving the needs of the Politburo, with extensive ministerial direction of the government and the use of wide-ranging State Council commissions to prevent the system from becoming too fractionated along functional lines, and so forth.[49]

It seems too that the leaders of this system did not see themselves as approaching a showdown with Mao. They continued to respect him and tried to accommodate what they must have felt were his somewhat misguided policy demands. But they were concerned overwhelmingly with putting the country back on its feet after the GLF and recapturing the initiative in their dealing with Chinese society. In this, as noted, they disagreed with Mao's more optimistic assessment of the situation as of 1962 – and probably thereafter. And they were almost certainly aware of the potential dangers of allowing Mao's future coalition partners to realize their ambitions. Thus, as noted, they tried to limit the PLA penetration of other organs and attempted to keep Jiang Qing out of power in the cultural arena. Unfortunately, too little data are available to specify what, if any, measures were taken against Kang Sheng's growing power.

Indeed, so much of our information on the period from the Great Leap to the Cultural Revolution comes from the polemical literature of 1966–76 (and the often almost equally biased material from after 1976) that it is important to bear in mind the issues that remain in doubt about the history of these eight years. The key unknowns or areas of significant doubt are the following:

First, what did the various members of the leadership who did not join the Cultural Revolution coalition think about the Chairman and his policy prefer-

49 As of 1965, the number of State Council ministries and major commissions stood at fifty-five, the same number as existed at the height of the first Five-Year Plan, before the streamlining of the government during the GLF.

ences during these years? The record presented during the Cultural Revolution is almost wholly negative, but it is also highly selective. For example, although the propaganda apparatus purportedly tried to play down Mao's preferences, in point of fact the official media of the day gave enormous prominence to the cult of Mao and the critique of revisionism. Also, even though a range of indicators suggests that throughout much of the later part of this period Mao was purposely elevating Peng Zhen, virtually every quotation from Peng made available during the Cultural Revolution had him disparaging Mao's health policies, Jiang Qing's attempts to reform opera, and the like. Indeed, on substantive issues it appears that the leaders around Liu always tried to meet Mao more than halfway (although they were understandably less tolerant of Jiang Qing and more wary of Kang Sheng[50] and Lin Biao). By about 1964 Mao may, therefore, have begun to distort reality quite seriously in his own mind, his suspicions fed by his wife and others who hoped to gain by a reordering of the leading organs. Although Liu and colleagues clearly did not fully share Mao's sense of priorities and methods, the Chairman's changing mental state and concerns about his mortality may have cause him to turn normal types of policy disagreements into a moral struggle between the forces of good and evil.

Second, one important dimension of this story – the role of the public security apparatus and of Mao's personal security forces – is unfortunately too well hidden from public view to be told. Both Kang Sheng and Luo Ruiqing, as noted, had been key figures in the public security system. When Luo left the Ministry of Public Security to move into the PLA in the wake of Lushan, he was replaced by Xie Fuzhi, who in turn rocketed to political power during the early part of the Cultural Revolution. Xie's meteoric rise in 1966–7 suggests that the Ministry of Public Security played a key part in the conflicts leading to the Cultural Revolution, but the details are not available. The former head of the CCP's General Office, Yang Shangkun, was formally purged in 1966, and he was said to have planted listening devices in Mao's private quarters. Once Yang was out of the way, Mao's personal security force (the 8341 Division, which also provided security for other ranking leaders), under the Chairman's long-time bodyguard Wang Dongxing, moved quickly to take over the former functions of the General Office. This same unit assumed charge of the detention of ranking leaders during the Cultural Revolution. But little concrete can be said about the role of Wang Dongxing and the entire security apparatus during the years before 1966.

Third, the role of Zhou Enlai remains somewhat obscure, even though the

50 For example, Wang Jiaxiang prevented Kang Sheng from gaining full access to the materials on the CCP's relations with other Communist Parties: *Gongren ribao* (Worker's daily), 4 February 1981, trans. in *FBIS/PRC*, 26 February 1981, L-9.

premier maintained a high profile throughout these years. Zhou's entire career suggested that he would lean toward Liu Shaoqi's preferences on policy issues during 1962–5, and yet in the summer of 1966 Zhou's support proved crucial to Mao's launching of the Cultural Revolution. Zhou's 1966 performance, in turn, raises questions about his real role during the previous years. Did he himself begin to think of replacing Liu Shaoqi as Mao's successor? If so, did he quietly contribute to the Chairman's distrust of his colleagues? Perhaps Zhou simply adhered to a rule that he would support Mao in any showdown, even though he might try to curtail some of the Chairman's policy thrusts with which he disagreed. Unfortunately, Zhou is such an important figure that the different hypotheses about him support considerably different interpretations of these crucial years – and the data necessary to discriminate among them are missing.

In sum, for all the years that have passed and the data that have become available, the period from the GLF to the Cultural Revolution remains at best partially understood and will be so for some time to come. Much more can be pieced together now that the "moderates" are having their chance to contribute to the literature, but these additions to the record leave uncomfortably large gaps. On the basis of what can be learned at this point, however, there is a clear answer to the question "What caused the split in the Yan'an leadership?" The answer is that it was a combination of three factors: different lessons drawn from the catastrophic consequences of the GLF; the tensions arising from the issue of the succession to Mao, which was constantly on the agenda after 1958; and the growing fears of an aging and possibly increasingly senile leader. Too much information is missing, though, to enable us to judge the relative weight and influence of each of these factors.

CHAPTER 3

THE CHINESE STATE IN CRISIS, 1966–9

HARRY HARDING

The Great Proletarian Cultural Revolution, which by official Chinese reckoning lasted from the beginning of 1966 to the death of Mao Zedong some ten years later, was one of the most extraordinary events of this century. The images of the Cultural Revolution remain vivid: the young Red Guards, in military uniform, filling the vast Tiananmen Square in Beijing, many weeping in rapture at the sight of their Great Helmsman standing atop the Gate of Heavenly Peace; veteran Communist officials, wearing dunce caps and placards defiling them as "monsters" and "freaks," herded in the backs of open-bed trucks, and driven through the streets of major cities by youth only one-third their age; the wall posters, often many sheets of newsprint in size, filled with vitriolic condemnations of the "revisionist" or "counterrevolutionary" acts of senior leaders. The little red book carried by the Red Guards – a plastic-bound volume containing selected quotations from Chairman Mao – remains a symbol of the revolt of the young against adult authority.

From a purely narrative perspective, the Cultural Revolution can best be understood as a tragedy, both for the individual who launched it and for the society that endured it. The movement was largely the result of the decisions of a single man, Mao Zedong. Mao's restless quest for revolutionary purity in a postrevolutionary age provided the motivation for the Cultural Revolution, his unique charismatic standing in the Chinese Communist movement gave him the resources to get it underway, and his populist faith in the value of mass mobilization lent the movement its form. Mao's breadth of vision and his ability to shape the destiny of 800 million Chinese are the elements of myth, producing a man who appears larger than life.

But, as in classical tragedy, these seemingly heroic elements were, in the end, fatally flawed. Mao's quest for revolutionary purity led him to exaggerate and misappraise the political and social problems confronting China in the mid-1960s. His personal authority gave him enough power to unleash potent social forces but not enough power to control them. And his confidence that the masses, once mobilized, would be the salvation of the country proved woefully misplaced as the mass movement degenerated into violence, factionalism, and chaos. The Cultural Revolution, which Mao hoped would be his most significant and most enduring contribution to China and to Marxism–Leninism, instead became the monumental error of his latter years.

Because of Mao's ability to move China, what was a tragedy for the man became simultaneously a tragedy for the nation. China's leaders now describe the Cultural Revolution as nothing less than a calamity for their country. Although the economic damage done by the Cultural Revolution was not as severe as that produced by the Great Leap Forward (GLF), and although the human costs were not as devastating as those of the Taiping Rebellion, the Japanese invasion, or the Communist revolution itself, the effects of the Cultural Revolution in terms of careers disrupted, spirits broken, and lives lost were ruinous indeed. The impact of the movement on Chinese politics and society may take decades finally to erase. What is more, these costs of the Cultural Revolution were largely the predictable consequences of Mao's perception that China was on the brink of the restoration of capitalism, and of his prescription that the mobilization of urban youth was the best way to prevent it.

From a different point of view, that of political analysis, the Cultural Revolution is equally intriguing. Political scientists have become accustomed to speaking of "crises" of political development, during which established political institutions are challenged and shaken by the pressures of economic transformation, intellectual ferment, political mobilization, and social change.[1] Unless effective reforms can be undertaken, political crises can produce violence and disorder, and even revolt and revolution. In this sense, the Cultural Revolution appears at first glance to have been similar to crises of political modernization experienced by many other developing countries in the twentieth century. The Chinese Communist Party (CCP) faced high levels of urban protest, rooted in widespread dissatisfaction with a variety of social, economic, and organizational policies. It proved unable either to suppress the dissent or to accommodate it effectively. The result of these circumstances, in China as elsewhere, was chaos and anarchy, until the military intervened to restore order and begin the reconstruction of political institutions.

What is unique about the Cultural Revolution, however, is that this political crisis was deliberately induced by the leader of the regime itself. It was Mao who called into question the legitimacy of the CCP. It was Mao who mobilized the social forces that would undermine his own government. And

1 Leonard Binder et al., *Crises and sequences in political development.*

it was Mao who provided the political and ideological vocabulary for protest and dissent. The man who had undertaken a revolution against China's old regime now sought to launch a revolt against the new political establishment that he himself had created.

But Mao's victory in his first revolution was not matched by comparable success in the second. Successful revolutions are, as Mao himself recognized, acts of construction as well as destruction: They build a new order even as they destroy an old one. Mao's first revolution was guided not only by a critique of the existing system but also by a relatively coherent image of a new economic and political order. Similarly, the first revolution not only mobilized mass discontent but also produced a disciplined revolutionary organization, the CCP, that could govern effectively after the seizure of power. Mao's second revolution, in contrast, had no clear guiding vision and produced no unified organization to implement a new set of programs and policies. It toppled the old regime but left only chaos and disorder in its place.

This chapter is a history and analysis of the first three and a half years of the Cultural Revolution, from its initial stirrings in late 1965 to the convocation of the Ninth National Congress of the CCP in April 1969. This is the period that some have described as the Red Guard phase of the Cultural Revolution and others as its manic stage. It is the period in which the political crisis induced by Mao was the deepest, the chaos the greatest, and the human costs the highest.

These three and a half years encompass several shorter periods, each of which is dealt with in turn in this chapter. First, there was the growing confrontation between Mao and the Party establishment from the fall of 1965 to the summer of the following year. During that period, Mao began to develop a power base with which to confront those leaders in the Party whom he regarded as revisionists. Using his political resources, Mao secured the dismissal or demotion of selected officials within the armed forces, the cultural establishment, the Beijing municipal government, and the Politburo itself. Then, at the Eleventh Plenum in August 1966, Mao obtained the formal endorsement of the Party's Central Committee (CC) for a criticism of revisionism on an even broader scale.

The second period, from the Eleventh Plenum through the end of 1966, was one in which Mao's assault on the Party establishment spread across the country, with the Red Guards now its major instrument. The outcome of this period was not, however, what Mao had intended. He had apparently hoped that the Red Guards would form a unified mass movement, that officials would accept criticism from these ad hoc organizations in a sincere and open manner, and that the Party would therefore emerge from the

Cultural Revolution with its orientation corrected and its authority intact. In fact, none of these developments occurred. The Red Guards split into competing organizations, with some attacking the Party establishment and others defending it. Party leaders at the provincial and municipal levels sought first to suppress the mass movement, then to coopt it, and finally to evade it. The escalation of conflict, both between competing Red Guard organizations and between the mass movement and the Party establishment, served not to strengthen the authority of the Party but to weaken it. By the end of 1966, the political institutions in many of China's most important cities were in total collapse.

During the third period, from January 1967 until mid-1968, Mao ordered that political power be seized from the discredited Party establishment. After a few weeks of uncertainty as to the procedures by which this would be done, Mao decided that political power would be shared, at the provincial and municipal levels, by coalitions of three forces: the mass organizations that had emerged during the Cultural Revolution, those cadres who were able to survive the movement, and the People's Liberation Army (PLA). The problem was that none of these groups was completely reliable. The mass organizations were prone to violence and anarchy, and the cadres and the PLA, particularly at the provincial and municipal levels, tended to work together to suppress the most obstreperous of the Red Guard activists. Unable completely to control the forces he had unleashed, Mao's only recourse was to play one against another. Once again, the result was near chaos, and Mao ultimately concluded that the only way to prevent collapse was to demobilize the Red Guards and allow the PLA to restore order.

This decision marked the beginning of the final stage under consideration in this chapter: the reconstruction of the Chinese political system. This process culminated with the Ninth Party Congress in April 1969, which elected a new CC, approved a new Politburo, and adopted a new Party constitution. Given the preeminent role of the Chinese military during this period, it should not be surprising that army officers occupied the plurality of the leadership positions filled at the Ninth Congress, or that Minister of Defense Lin Biao secured anointment as Mao's successor. But even the growing power of the military in civilian affairs was not sufficient to restore political stability. Power remained divided among the radical intellectuals who had mobilized the Red Guards, the veteran officials who had survived their assault, and the military who had finally suppressed them. As the next chapter in this volume will reveal, the legacy of the Red Guard stage of the Cultural Revolution was chronic instability that was ultimately to be removed only by the death of Mao Zedong, the purge of the radicals, and the emergence of Deng Xiaoping as China's preeminent leader.

TOWARD A CONFRONTATION

Sources of political conflict

Mao Zedong surveyed the political scene in China in the early 1960s with increasing dissatisfaction. On issue after issue, the Party had adopted policies that Mao regarded as unnecessary or unacceptable: a return to private farming in agriculture, the resurrection of material incentives in industry, a concentration on urban medicine in public health, the development of a two-track system in education, and the reappearance of traditional themes and styles in literature and the arts. Most of these policies had been advanced by their proponents as ways of restoring social cohesion and economic productivity after the Anti-Rightist Campaign and the GLF. In Mao's view, however, these measures were creating a degree of inequality, specialization, hierarchy, and dissent that was incompatible with his vision of a socialist society.[2]

Mao's dissatisfaction with Party policies was exacerbated by growing personal tensions between the Chairman and some of his chief lieutenants. There were, to begin with, an increasing number of incidents that Mao chose to regard as acts of *lèse-majesté.* Although Mao had supposedly withdrawn voluntarily from day-to-day leadership in late 1958, he increasingly resented the way in which some leaders, particularly the Party's secretary-general, Deng Xiaoping, failed to consult with him before making decisions on major issues. In October 1966, for example, Mao would complain that "Whenever we are at a meeting together, [Deng] sits far away from me. For six years, since 1959, he has not made a general report of work to me."[3] In March 1961, when he discovered that Deng had made some major decisions on agricultural reorganization without consulting him, Mao asked sarcastically, "Which Emperor decided these?"[4] Mao was irritated by the allegorical criticisms of his leadership that began to appear in Chinese literature and journalism in the early 1960s, and must have been even more angered that officials responsible for intellectual matters, including Peng Zhen and Lu Dingyi, were doing nothing to bring the offending writers to task.

In addition, Mao became increasingly frustrated by his inability to bend the bureaucracy to his will. Between 1962 and 1965 he tried, in five areas of long-standing personal interest, to alter the policies that the Party had

2 On the emerging conflict between Mao and his colleagues in the early 1960s, see Byung-joon Ahn, *Chinese politics and the Cultural Revolution: Dynamics of policy processes;* Harry Harding, *Organizing China: The problem of bureaucracy, 1949–1976*, ch. 7; Roderick MacFarquhar, *The origins of the Cultural Revolution. 2. The Great Leap Forward 1958–60;* and Chapter 2 of this volume.

3 Jerome Ch'en, ed., *Mao papers: Anthology and bibliography,* 40.

4 Parris H. Chang, *Power and policy in China* (rev. ed.), 131.

adopted in the immediate post-Leap period. Mao attempted to halt trends toward private farming in agriculture, proposed reform of the curriculum and examination system in higher education, criticized the concentration of public health facilities in urban areas, proposed the creation of peasant organizations to uncover corruption and inefficiency among rural Party and commune cadres, and denounced the reappearance of traditional themes and revisionist theories in intellectual affairs.

Although the Party establishment ultimately responded to each of these initiatives, it did so in a way that Mao justifiably believed to be half-hearted and unenthusiastic. In part, this was because many senior leaders continued to support the policies that had been adopted in the post-Leap period and were reluctant to alter them at Mao's behest. In part, too, the sluggishness in responding to Mao's wishes reflected the normal attempt of bureaucracies to act gradually and incrementally, preserving as much of existing routines as possible even while undertaking some of the new initiatives that Mao proposed. Moreover, Mao's intentions were often expressed in vague and ambiguous language, with the Chairman better able to criticize emphatically tendencies he disliked than to suggest concrete alternatives.

In any event, Mao's conclusion was that the sluggishness of the bureaucracy, the emergence of traditional and "bourgeois" ideas in intellectual life, and the emphasis on efficiency in national economic strategy together created the danger that revisionism – a fundamental departure from a genuinely socialist path of development – was emerging in China. At first, Mao voiced these concerns in a rather low-keyed manner. In 1962, for instance, he called on the Party to overcome revisionism, but said that this task should not "interfere with our [routine] work . . . or be placed in a very prominent position."[5] Equally important, Mao initially attempted to overcome revisionist tendencies in the Party through rather modest and traditional means: the launching of campaigns within the bureaucracy to study Marxist–Leninist doctrine and to emulate model leaders.

But as the ineffectiveness of these measures became apparent, Mao's warnings became more pointed. He ultimately concluded that revisionism was more widespread than he had anticipated and that the highest leaders of the Party, because of their reluctance to cope with the problem effectively, were possibly guilty of revisionist thinking themselves. At a work conference in September 1965, Mao asked his colleagues, "If revisionism appears in the Central Committee, what are you going to do? It is probable that it will appear, and this is a great danger."[6]

5 Stuart R. Schram, ed., *Chairman Mao talks to the people: Talks and letters, 1956–1971*, 193–5.
6 Ch'en, *Mao papers*, 102.

It was only gradually that these warnings about revisionism were transformed into a systematic theory justifying a Cultural Revolution. Significantly, in fact, the movement itself was launched before a full theoretical justification was provided for it. But two editorials published in 1967 have been identified by the Chinese as laying out in fullest form Mao's emerging theory of "continuing the revolution under the dictatorship of the proletariat."[7] Although these essays were not written by Mao himself, there is little reason to doubt that the ideas expressed in them reflected the Chairman's views.

Taken together, the editorials conclude that, in Mao's eyes, the greatest danger to a successful socialist revolution is not the threat of attack from abroad, but rather the restoration of capitalism at home. Mao believed that the experience of the Soviet Union after the death of Stalin proved that the restoration of capitalism could occur if "revisionists" usurped power within the ruling Communist Party. To prevent this, it would be necessary to wage continuing class struggle against those "Party persons in authority" who might attempt to follow the capitalist road. Indeed, this would be the major form of class struggle in socialist society after the nationalization of industry and the collectivization of agriculture. The method for waging this class struggle would be to "boldly arouse the masses from below" in a Cultural Revolution, in order to criticize not only revisionist power holders within the Party but also the selfish and liberal tendencies within their own minds. Because the problem of revisionism was thus rooted in human selfishness, it would be necessary to have a succession of Cultural Revolutions over many decades to preserve the purity of purpose of a socialist society.

Forging Mao's power base

By 1964, the basis began to be created for such an assault on the Party establishment. The elements of this power base were created initially in a piecemeal and seemingly uncoordinated manner. One element was produced by the impersonal operation of social and economic policy, which created disadvantaged and disenchanted groups in society, particularly among the urban young. A second, under the guidance of Mao's wife, Jiang Qing,

7 Editorial department of *Renmin ribao* and *Hongqi*, "A great historic document," 18 May 1967, in *PR*, 19 May 1967, 10–12; and editorial departments of *Renmin ribao*, *Hongqi*, and *Jiefangjun bao*, "Advance along the road opened up by the October socialist revolution," 6 November 1967, in *PR*, 10 November 1967, 9–11, 14–16. Recent accounts have revealed that the latter essay was drafted under the supervision of Chen Boda and Yao Wenyuan. See Sun Dunfan et al., eds., *Zhongguo gongchandang lishi jiangyi* (Teaching materials on the history of the Chinese Communist Party), 2.268. (Hereafter *Lishi jiangyi*.)

began to emerge in the intellectual and cultural spheres. A third was produced, within the army, by Minister of Defense Lin Biao. Between 1964 and 1966, these three elements were more systematically assembled into a political coalition that, under Mao's leadership, was powerful enough to conduct the Great Proletarian Cultural Revolution against even an entrenched Party apparatus.

The PLA

The most crucial element in Mao's power base, given its control of organized armed force in China, was the PLA under the leadership of Lin Biao.[8] After succeeding Peng Dehuai as minister of defense at the Lushan Plenum in 1959, Lin had devoted particular attention to reviving political work in the military apparatus – a policy intended both to ensure the loyalty of the armed forces to Maoist leadership and to bolster his own reputation in Mao's eyes. Lin rebuilt the Party branches at the basic levels of the PLA, resurrected the network of political departments that had deteriorated under Peng's stewardship, and tightened the control of the Party's Military Affairs Commission (MAC) over military matters. Lin intensified the army's program of political education, basing it in large part on a new compilation of quotations from Mao Zedong, a collection that would serve as the model for the little red book later used by the Red Guards.

At the same time, Lin sought to restore some of the military traditions of the revolutionary period. In the 1950s, the organizational and tactical principles of guerrilla warfare as practiced in the 1930s and 1940s had been set aside in favor of those characteristic of more regularized armed forces. A formal system of ranks and insignia had been instituted. The militia had been deemphasized, with Peng Dehuai proposing that it be supplanted by a more formal system of military reserves. Greater priority had been placed on hierarchy and discipline, as against the "military democracy" of earlier years. Soviet military doctrine, with its stress on positional warfare and modern ordnance, replaced the Maoist doctrine of mobile warfare using primitive weapons.

A reaction against the abandonment of the PLA's revolutionary heritage in favor of these "foreign doctrines" was apparent as early as the mid-1950s. Accordingly, some attempts to redress the balance were undertaken in the

8 On the PLA in the early 1960s, see John Gittings, "The Chinese army's role in the Cultural Revolution," *Pacific Affairs,* 39.3–4 (Fall–Winter 1966–7), 269–89; John Gittings, *The role of the Chinese army,* ch. 12; Ellis Joffe, "The Chinese army under Lin Piao: Prelude to political intervention," in John M. H. Lindbeck, ed., *China: Management of a revolutionary society,* 343–74; and Ellis Joffe, *Party and army: Professionalism and political control in the Chinese officer corps, 1949–1964.*

latter part of the decade, while Peng Dehuai still served as minister of defense. But the process of "rerevolutionization" accelerated under Lin Biao's leadership. New military manuals stressed such traditional concepts as joint command by political commissars and line officers, the importance of political work in maintaining the loyalty and morale of the troops, close ties between the army and civilian society, and egalitarian relations between officers and men. Military strategy once again emphasized the infantry (as opposed to specialized services), the militia (as opposed to the regular forces), and small-unit tactics (as opposed to maneuvers by larger, multiservice forces). Finally, in a step with enormous symbolic significance, military ranks were abolished in 1965, and officers removed the Soviet-style uniforms and insignia they had worn since the mid-1950s and returned to the unadorned olive-drab uniforms of the Yan'an years.

And yet, Lin Biao never allowed this policy framework to weaken the military prowess of the PLA. Even as he proclaimed that men were more important than weapons in ensuing military victory, Lin simultaneously sponsored the modernization of the air force and the development of China's nuclear capability. He said that political education should have the highest priority in military training, but he saw to it that the troops actually devoted more time to military exercises than to ideological study. Lin reassured the PLA's adherence to the principle of people's war, but the level of militia activity declined from the heights reached during the GLF, and rural militia units devoted more attention to agricultural production and internal security than to military affairs.

Thus, during the early 1960s, Lin presided not only over the revitalization of the political structure in the armed forces and the restoration of some traditional military concepts, but also over the successful border campaign against India in 1962 and the detonation of China's first atomic bomb two years later. These achievements indicated that the "redness" of the PLA did not come at the expense of its military expertise.

The successful performance of the PLA in the early 1960s contrasted with the widely perceived decay of the Party and state agencies during the same period. It is little wonder, therefore, that Mao came to see Lin Biao as a more effective organizational manager and a more loyal lieutenant than either Liu Shaoqi or Deng Xiaoping, and began to identify the PLA as a model for civilian bureaucracies to emulate. To that end, a nationwide campaign to "Learn from the PLA" was launched in February 1964. As part of that movement, the government bureaucracy was ordered to form political departments, modeled on those in the PLA, that would be responsible for the regular political education of civilian officials. Between 30 and 40 percent of the positions created in those new political departments were held by demobilized PLA cadres or by officers seconded from the armed forces.[9]

Lin Biao was hardly reluctant to see the army assume this new role. It is quite likely, in fact, that Lin suggested the formation of political departments in state agencies in the first place; and it is even possible that he proposed they be placed under the supervision of the General Political Department of the armed forces. If adopted, such a recommendation simultaneously would have dramatically increased the influence of the PLA in civilian affairs and would have made significant inroads into the traditional responsibilities of the Party organization. Although Liu Shaoqi accepted Mao's decision to establish political departments within government bureaus, he allgedly insisted that they be placed under the jurisdiction of the Party agencies responsible for economic work, rather than under the PLA's political apparatus.[10]

Even so, the initiation of the "Learn from the PLA" Campaign and the creation of the political departments in the government bureaucracy gave the PLA and Lin Biao more influence over civilian affairs than at any time since the early 1950s. In February 1966, the PLA held a conference on cultural matters that, although nominally dealing only with literature and art in the armed forces, had great impact on civilian cultural circles as well.[11] And in March 1966, Lin wrote a letter to a work conference on industrial and commercial affairs advocating that economic administrators be more active in the study of Maoism – a relatively innocuous message, but one that symbolized Lin's growing ability to speak out on matters concerning national economic policy.[12]

The radical intellectuals

The second element in the nascent Maoist coalition was a group of radical intellectuals who, by mid-1966, would come to serve as the doctrinal arbiters and mass mobilizers of the Cultural Revolution. The key person in assembling these leftist propagandists and writers was Mao's wife, Jiang Qing, who quickly realized that the emerging tensions between Mao and the Party establishment gave her an unusual opportunity to realize her own political ambitions.

Before traveling to Yan'an to join the Communist movement in 1937,

9 On the campaign to learn from the PLA, see Ahn, *Chinese politics*, ch. 6; John Gittings, "The 'Learn from the army' campaign," *CQ*, 18 (April–June 1964), 153–9; Harding, *Organizing China*, 217–23; and Ralph L. Powell, "Commissars in the economy: The 'Learn from the PLA' movement in China," *Asian Survey*, 5.3 (March 1965), 125–38.

10 Radio Peking, 16 December 1967, cited in John Gittings, "Army-Party relations in the light of the Cultural Revolution," in John Wilson Lewis, ed., *Party leadership and revolutionary power in China*, 395.

11 Kenneth Lieberthal, *A research guide to central Party and government meetings in China 1949–1975*, 238–9.

12 Michael Y. M. Kau, ed., *The Lin Piao affair: Power politics and military coup*, 321–2.

Jiang Qing had been a second-string actress and an active participant in Shanghai's artistic and political demimonde. Her liaison with Mao in 1938 seemed at first to offer this ambitious woman the chance to switch from the theater to politics. But, given Jiang Qing's rather checkered background, her marriage to the Chairman was bitterly opposed by many other senior Party leaders and may have been accepted only after she agreed to refrain from political activity for thirty years.[13] Ill health forced her to keep the bargain throughout the 1950s; but in the early 1960s, with her health if not her temperament somewhat improved, she undertook a new project: the reform of Chinese culture. This was a task for which her earlier theatrical career had given her some minimal credentials, and for which Mao's growing impatience with "revisionism" in culture provided substantial encouragement and support.

Jiang's initial efforts to reform traditional Beijing Opera encountered the disdain of established performers, the opposition of officials responsible for cultural affairs, and thus the neglect of the press.[14] Faced with these obstacles, Jiang turned to a group of young, relatively radical intellectuals in Beijing and Shanghai. Compared with more prestigious members of China's urban intelligentsia, these were younger men, lower in rank, less cosmopolitan in outlook, and more steeped in Marxist intellectual traditions. Many had taken, out of a combination of conviction and careerism, relatively radical positions on academic and cultural matters ever since the Anti-Rightist Campaign of 1957 and had been engaged in an ongoing debate with their more liberal seniors throughout the cultural relaxation of the early 1960s.[15]

Jiang Qing developed contacts with two main groups of these radical intellectuals: One was centered in the Institute of Philosophy and Social Science of the Chinese Academy of Sciences in Beijing (including Guan Feng, Qi Benyu, and Lin Jie), and another was centered in the Municipal Propaganda Department in Shanghai (including Zhang Chunqiao, the director of the bureau, and Yao Wenyuan). The former group, more academic in character, specialized in history and philosophy. The Shanghai group, in contrast, was more experienced in journalistic criticism and more knowledgeable about the creative arts. Jiang's entrée to these groups was facilitated, in the case of Beijing, by Chen Boda, who for years had served as Mao Zedong's

13 Ross Terrill, *The white-boned demon: A biography of Madame Mao Zedong,* 154.

14 On Jiang Qing's role in this period and her relationship with young, radical intellectuals, see Merle Goldman, *China's intellectuals: Advise and dissent,* ch. 3; and Roxane Witke, *Comrade Chiang Ch'ing,* 321–2.

15 The distinction between the Shanghai and Beijing groups is drawn from Goldman, *China's intellectuals,* ch. 3.

personal secretary and theoretician; and, in the case of Shanghai, by Ke Qingshi, the Party chief for the East China region, who, unlike many Party leaders, remained close to Mao even after the debacle of the GLF.

Between 1963 and 1966, Jiang Qing and her coterie of intellectuals focused principally on cultural and artistic matters, particularly on her interest in the reform of Beijing Opera and other performing arts. (In this undertaking another regional Party secretary, Tao Zhu of the Central-South region, also proved supportive of Jiang Qing.) Gradually, however, as the confrontation between Mao and the Party establishment grew more intense, the radical intellectuals began to turn to more overtly political themes, providing, as we shall see, both the criticism of Mao's rivals and the ideological rationale for the Cultural Revolution.

This second element in the Maoist coalition, to use Lowell Dittmer's apposite expression, played the role of "imperial favorites."[16] The radical intellectuals had narrow careers, rather dogmatic and idealistic political positions, and little political standing independent of their association, through Jiang Qing, with Mao. They had little stake in the established political order in China and perceived clearly that their own careers would be advanced more rapidly through opposition to the system than through patient accommodation. But their power would increase as Mao found that their loyalty to him, their skills at propaganda, and their mastery of radical doctrine made them useful tools in his assault on the Party establishment.

A mass base

The final element in the Maoist coalition, latent until the middle and latter parts of 1966, was a mass base, composed of those elements of urban Chinese society that regarded themselves as disadvantaged. Paradoxically, social tensions in Chinese cities had been substantially increased by two policies, adopted under Mao's prodding, that were supposed to create a more egalitarian society: the reemphasis on class background in educational recruitment and job assignment, and a program of part-time industrial employment for suburban peasants.

The most active in Mao's mass base were China's high school and college students. Their participation in the Red Guard movement of the Cultural Revolution can be explained in large part by the normal idealism of the young, which made them ready to share Mao's indignation at the elitism, inequality, and bureaucratic stagnation that seemed to be plaguing China in

16 Lowell Dittmer, "Bases of power in Chinese politics: A theory and an analysis of the fall of the 'Gang of Four,' " *World Politics*, 31.1 (October 1978), 42.

the mid-1960s. China's student population doubtless also welcomed the sense of importance and power provided by their involvement in Mao's campaign against revisionism.

In addition, the educational policies of the early 1960s had produced serious cleavages and grievances among China's students. While opportunities for primary and junior middle school education were expanding, enrollment at both senior middle schools and universities declined sharply from the levels attained during the GLF, as the state sought to retrench overextended budgets during a period of serious economic recession. There was a sharper differentiation between elite middle schools, whose graduates had a good chance to go to college, and lesser institutions, whose graduates had little prospect for higher education. By 1964–5, furthermore, in a program foreshadowing the mass rustification policies of later years, middle school students who had not been placed in universities or industrial enterprises were being sent, in large numbers, to frontier and rural areas.[17]

These declining opportunities for upward mobility – and the real danger of a permanent transfer to the countryside – focused student concern on the standards for advancement. Formally, three criteria were important in assigning students to elite middle schools, universities, and the most desirable jobs: class background, academic achievement, and political behavior. But the relative weight of the criteria was changing in the mid-1960s, with class background and political behavior becoming more important and academic achievement becoming less so. By the eve of the Cultural Revolution, the most fortunate students were thus those from cadre or military families. These students' academic records were not always superior, but they were increasingly benefiting from the new emphasis on class background as a criterion for enrollment in senior middle schools, universities, and the Communist Youth League. Next came students from worker and peasant families, whose good class background now offered some compensation for what was often mediocre classroom performance. At the bottom were students from bourgeois or intellectual families, who often enjoyed superior academic records but whose bad or middling class background was becoming an ever greater obstacle to advancement.[18]

Just as students were divided by the politics of the early 1960s, so too were urban workers. The economic policies of the 1950s had already produced

17 On educational policy in the early 1960s, see John Gardner, "Educated youth and urban–rural inequalities, 1958–66," in John Wilson Lewis, ed., *The city in communist China*, 235–86; and Donald J. Munro, "Egalitarian ideal and educational fact in communist China," in Lindbeck, *China*, 256–301.

18 This categorization of Chinese students is based on Hong Yung Lee, *The politics of the Chinese Cultural Revolution: A case study;* and Stanley Rosen, *Red Guard factionalism and the Cultural Revolution in Guangzhou (Canton).*

cleavages between permanent workers and apprentices, between skilled and unskilled laborers, and between workers at large state factories and employees of smaller collective enterprises. In each case, the former received substantially higher salaries and job benefits than did the latter.

These divisions, the result of the application of the Soviet model to China, were widened by the implementation of the "worker-peasant system" of industrial employment in 1964. Under this policy, industrial workers were hired from suburban communes on a temporary or part-time basis, as required by specific factories and enterprises. The system was officially justified as an effort to reduce the social and economic disparities between city and countryside by producing a class of people who were simultaneously workers and peasants. In practice, however, the principal appeal of the worker-peasant system was much less noble: Factories welcomed the opportunity to hire temporary contract workers who were paid lower wages, who were ineligible for the pensions or medical benefits that state enterprises were required to provide to permanent employees, and who could be fired for poor performance.[19]

The consequence of the worker-peasant system, therefore, was to exacerbate social tensions rather than to ameliorate them. This employment policy not only produced an underclass of dissatisfied workers, who received less remuneration and less job security for the same work than did permanent employees, but also raised the specter of downward mobility for many more. The tendency in many state enterprises was to reassign positions from the permanent payroll to the more flexible worker-peasant system. Thus, apprentices saw the opportunities for advancement drying up, and even permanent workers faced the danger that they would find themselves transferred to the countryside to become contract employees.

When the Cultural Revolution broke out in mid-1966 and when mass protest was officially encouraged, many of these collective resentments, as well as individual grievances, formed the emotional fuel for the Red Guard movement. As in any complex social movement, there was only a loose correlation between one's socioeconomic standing in the mid-1960s and one's political orientation during the Cultural Revolution. But a common pattern in the Red Guard movement was the anger against the Party establishment by students from bad or middling classes, who felt that their chances for upward mobility were steadily declining, and by those workers who occupied lower positions on the ladder of economic specialization.[20]

19 Lee, *Politics of the Cultural Revolution*, 129–39.

20 Marc J. Blecher and Gordon White, *Micropolitics in contemporary China: A technical unit during and after the Cultural Revolution*.

The emerging crisis

The issues and tensions just discussed came to a head between the fall of 1965 and the summer of 1966 as Chinese leaders engaged in heated controversies over Chinese military policy, strategy toward Vietnam, policy toward the literary community, and the rectification of the Party. These debates enabled Lin Biao and Jiang Qing, with Mao's backing, to push potential rivals aside, extend their control over China's military and cultural establishments, and thus strengthen Mao's political base. In the case of the PLA, a dispute over China's response to the escalating conflict in Vietnam provided the occasion for the purge of the chief of staff, Luo Ruiqing, who was potentially able to challenge Lin's control over the armed forces. In the cultural realm, an early skirmish over a historical drama that was allegedly critical of Mao led ultimately to the dismissal of the first Party secretary in Beijing, the reorganization of the Party's Propaganda Department, and the appointment of Chen Boda, Jiang Qing, and Kang Sheng – a longtime public security specialist with close ties to Mao – as leaders of the unfolding campaign against revisionism. Within a few months, Mao had broken decisively with Liu Shaoqi over the way to extend that campaign from the cultural community into the universities and the bureaucracy.

The spring of 1966 also witnessed the gradual melding of the three elements of Mao's political base – the army, the radical intellectuals, and the disenchanted youth – into a relatively coherent coalition that could spearhead the Cultural Revolution. A linkage between Jiang Qing and Lin Biao was forged at a forum on literature and art in the armed forces in February 1966, at which Jiang Qing, who had little connection with the PLA in the past, came to assume a leading role in the military's cultural activities. Within the next few months, the radical civilian and military leaders surrounding Mao Zedong began to mobilize support among disenchanted sectors in urban China. During June and July, the Cultural Revolution Group under Chen Boda, Jiang Qing, and Kang Sheng started to build connections with radical students and faculty in key universities in Beijing, and encouraged them to launch intense criticism of university, Party, and government leaders. By the end of July, the PLA had begun to provide supplies and logistical support to the leftist organizations that were springing up on major campuses.

Finally, in August 1966, the CC of the CCP held a rump session in Beijing. Attended by little more than half the members of the CC and packed with Red Guards, the plenum adopted a resolution authorizing the mobilization of China's urban population to criticize "those persons in authority who are taking the capitalist road." It was this decision that authorized what, by year's end, had become an all-out assault by Mao and his lieutenants against the Party establishment. With it, the Cultural Revolution entered its most chaotic and destructive period.

Luo Ruiqing

The military policies of Lin Biao had not gone unchallenged in the high command of the PLA. Lin's principal rival was the chief of staff, Luo Ruiqing, who came to question the appropriateness of Lin's military policies in 1964–5, as the escalation of American involvement in the war in Vietnam presented China with an unexpected threat on its southern borders.[21]

In retrospect, Luo Ruiqing's challenge to Lin Biao still appears somewhat surprising. Luo had been a political commissar throughout much of his pre-1949 career and had served as minister of public security (rather than a troop commander) during the 1950s. There was little reason, therefore, to suspect that Luo would have opposed the emphasis on ideological indoctrination and political loyalty that characterized Lin's service as minister of defense. What is more, Lin and Luo had had a close personal relationship during the Communist revolution. Luo had served under Lin in the First Corps of the Red Army in the early 1930s, and had been Lin's deputy at both the Red Army College and Kangda (the Resist-Japan Military and Political University in Yan'an). When Lin Biao became minister of defense in 1959, Luo was promoted to the position of chief of staff. If Luo's appointment was not at Lin's initiative, it was at least with his approval.

Lin Biao had, since the early 1950s, been a victim of chronic illness – variously described as a war wound, stomach difficulties, tuberculosis, or a combination – that periodically forced him to curtail his physical and political activities. The recurrence of these physical ailments in the early 1960s apparently created serious tensions between Lin and Luo Ruiqing. At a minimum, Luo may have wished, in light of Lin's illness, to be granted greater operational authority over the armed forces; or, alternatively, Luo may have hoped that Lin would resign as minister of defense in his favor. According to one dramatic account, Luo actually told Lin to his face that "a sick man should give his place to the worthy! Don't meddle! Don't block the way!"[22]

The growing participation of American forces in the Vietnam War – a step Chinese leaders had apparently not anticipated – also strained the relationship between the two men. Luo began to propose more intensive military

21 On the Luo Ruiqing affair, see Harry Harding and Melvin Gurtov, *The purge of Lo Jui-ch'ing: The politics of Chinese strategic planning;* and Michael Yahuda, "Kremlinology and the Chinese strategic debate, 1965–66," *CQ,* 49 (January–March 1972), 32–75.

22 Harding and Gurtov, *Lo Jui-ch'ing,* 10.

preparations, in case the United States should decide to carry the war to China. As Luo put it in May 1965:

It makes a world of difference whether or not one is prepared once a war breaks out. . . . Moreover, these preparations must be made for the most difficult and worst situations that may possibly arise. Preparations must be made not only against any small-scale warfare but also against any medium- or large-scale warfare that imperialism may launch. These preparations must envisage the use by the imperialists of nuclear weapons as well as of conventional weapons.

Moreover, Luo argued that if war did come to China, the PLA should be prepared to defend the country from prepared positions and then counterattack across China's borders to destroy the enemy "in its own lair."[23]

Luo's recommendations, which may have reflected the views of China's professional military planners, proved unacceptable to Lin Biao. For one thing, the strategy of linear defense that Luo proposed contradicted the principles of people's war, according to which the Chinese Army would attempt to lure an invader deep inside China so as to overextend his supply lines and destroy him piecemeal. What is more, Luo's insistence that, as he put it in September 1965, there were "a thousand and one things to do" before China was ready for war[24] implied that the PLA should reorder its priorities, at least temporarily, so as to place greater stress on military preparation. Of these two considerations, it was the second that was probably the more controversial. The PLA was playing an ever larger role in civilian society and was becoming a critically important part of Mao's power base in his emerging confrontation with the Party establishment. If adopted, Luo's proposals would have reversed this process: They would have drawn the army from political affairs, and thus largely removed it from the Maoist coalition.

The controversy between Lin Biao and Luo Ruiqing reached its climax in early September, when the two men published articles on the twentieth anniversary of the surrender of Japan at the end of World War II that contained very different implications for Chinese defense policy.[25] Luo argued that China "certainly must have sufficient plans and certainly must complete preparations" in case the United States attacked China. Lin, in contrast, implied that the Americans were unlikely to be so rash, and that even if they were, there would be ample time to mobilize "the vast ocean of several hundred million Chinese people in arms." This was to be Luo's last major public utterance, and by the end of November, he dropped from public view

23 [Luo Ruiqing] Lo Jui-ch'ing, "Commemorate the victory over German facscism! Carry the struggle against U.S. imperialism through to the end!" *PR*, 20 (14 May 1965), 7–15.

24 [Luo Ruiqing] Lo Jui-ch'ing, "The people defeated Japanese fascism and they can certainly defeat U.S. imperialism too," *CB*, 770 (14 September 1965), 1–12.

25 Lo, "The people defeated fascism"; Lin Piao, *Long live the victory of People's War.*

altogether. Lin Biao began assembling a bill of particulars against his colleague, which he presented to a CC conference in Shanghai on 8 December. The conference appointed a seven-man team, headed by Marshal Ye Jianying, to examine Lin's case against Luo.

The investigation soon took an inquisitorial turn. The team, accompanied by representatives from various branches of the military, engaged in what was later described as "face-to-face" struggle against Luo in March 1966. After Luo's self-criticism was rejected as inadequate, he tried unsuccessfully to commit suicide by leaping from the building in which he was confined. On 8 April, the investigation team concluded its work by recommending to the CC that Luo be dismissed from all his posts in the PLA, as well as from his duties as a vice-premier and a member of the Party Secretariat. That report, in turn, was approved by an enlarged meeting of the Politburo in early May. There is some reason to believe that Peng Zhen, a Politburo member serving concurrently as first Party secretary in Beijing, defended Luo during the course of the investigatory process, but his views were rejected.[26]

The Luo Ruiqing affair was important for two reasons. It provided persuasive evidence that Mao and Lin had the will and the ability to secure the dismissal of officials who disagreed with their policies and who challenged their personal standing. It also enabled the two to increase their control over two key elements in the coercive apparatus of China. The dismissal of Luo as chief of staff, and his replacement somewhat later by Yang Chengwu, gave Lin further influence over the main forces of the PLA. In addition, the purge of Luo was followed by the dismissal of some of his former lieutenants in the Ministry of Public Security, thus enabling Kang Sheng to strengthen his control over the state security apparatus.

Wu Han and Peng Zhen

At the same time as Luo Ruiqing was coming under serious attack, Mao turned his attention to the problem of dissent among the intellectuals.[27] He focused his fire on *Hai Rui dismissed from office* (*Hai Rui ba guan*), a play by Wu Han, an author and scholar who served concurrently as a deputy mayor of Beijing. The Chairman charged that this historical drama, which nominally depicted an upright Ming dynasty official unjustly dismissed by the emperor, Jiaqing, was actually an allegorical criticism of Mao's purge of Peng Dehuai at the Lushan Plenum in 1959. That Mao may well have encouraged Wu to

26 On the fate of Luo, see Ahn, *Chinese politics*, 203–4; and Lieberthal, *Research guide*, 248–9.

27 On the Wu Han affair, see Ahn, *Chinese politics*, 195–213; Goldman, *China's intellectuals*, ch. 5; Jack Gray and Patrick Cavendish, *Chinese communism in crisis: Maoism and the Cultural Revolution*, ch. 4; Lee, *Politics of the Cultural Revolution*, ch. 1; and James R. Pusey, *Wu Han: Attacking the present through the past*.

write the play in the first place did not affect the Chairman's judgment of the final product.

In dealing with Wu Han and *Hai Rui,* Mao took a two-pronged approach. Initially, he assigned the responsibility of criticizing Wu Han's play to a Five-Man Group on revolution in culture (*wenhua geming wuren xiaozu*), headed by Peng Zhen, which had been established in 1964. This put Peng in a difficult position, for, as first Party secretary of Beijing municipality, he was responsible for the actions of one of his own deputy mayors. Perhaps because of his personal connections with Wu Han, as well as his more general beliefs about the best way to handle policy toward intellectuals, Peng soon made clear what his approach would be: to focus on the historical issues raised by Wu Han's play rather than on its possible allegorical content, and to discuss those issues in an open way in which "everyone is equal before the truth."[28]

Aware of Peng's predilections on the case, Mao decided simultaneously to take a second tack. He asked Yao Wenyuan, one of the Shanghai intellectuals associated with Jiang Qing, to prepare his own criticism of Wu Han's play. Mao emphasized that Yao's article should address what he considered to be the crucial issue: that Wu Han had intended Hai Rui to be a historical analogue for Peng Dehuai. The extent of Mao's personal interest and involvement in this matter is suggested by his reviewing Yao's essay three times before agreeing that it was ready for publication.[29]

Yao's article – a harsh direct attack on Wu Han – was published in Shanghai in early November, before the Five-Man Group in Beijing had taken any formal action on the Wu Han case. Peng Zhen's reaction was one of outrage, not merely because his subordinate was being criticized so strongly, but also because he believed that publication of such an article, without the formal approval of the responsible Party organs, was a violation of the principles of inner-Party struggle. Together with Lu Dingyi, director of the Party Propaganda Department and a member of the Five-Man Group, Peng succeeded in blocking republication of Yao's essay in any central or Beijing municipal newspapers. It was only after the personal intervention of Zhou Enlai, apparently acting as Mao's behest, that the article appeared in newspapers with wider circulation – first in the *Jiefangjun bao* with a laudatory editorial note, and then in the *Renmin ribao* (People's Daily) with a skeptical introduction.

Even though he had lost the battle to suppress the publication of the Yao

28 "The Great Proletarian Cultural Revolution – a record of major events: September 1965 to December 1966," *JPRS*, 42, 349. *Translations on Communist China: Political and sociological information* (25 August 1967), 3.

29 Yao Wen-yuan, "On the new historical play *Dismissal of Hai Rui*," reprinted in *Jiefangjun bao,* 10 November 1965, trans. in *CB*, 783 (21 March 1966), 1–18.

Wenyuan essay, Peng still vigorously attempted to keep criticism of intellectuals on what he considered to be the proper course. With a working majority on the Five-Man Group (of whose members only Kang Sheng was a firm supporter of Mao's position), Peng continued to obstruct the publication of further articles by radical writers such as Qi Benyu that he considered to be excessively critical of Wu Han. He stuck to this position despite direct criticism from Mao toward the end of December, when the Chairman accused Peng of ignoring the possible analogy between Hai Rui and Peng Dehuai. Peng defended himself on the somewhat narrow grounds that there had been no personal contact between Peng and Wu, and that Wu Han was therefore innocent of any factionalist behavior. But Peng promised Mao that the Five-Man Group would reach a final decision on the issue within two months.

The Five-Man Group held at least two crucial meetings on the subject: the first on 2 January 1966 and the second on 4 February. Despite all the evidence that Mao would be dissatisfied with their report – evidence provided not only by Mao's conversations with Peng in December but also by warnings from Kang Sheng – the group decided to stick with the approach Peng Zhen had originally adopted. On 3 February, two deputy directors of the Propaganda Department, Yao Zhen and Xu Liqun, drafted a statement summarizing the views of the majority of the Five-Man Group.

This document, known as the "February Outline" (*eryue tigang*), acknowledged the problem of bourgeois tendencies in culture but emphasized the desirability of focusing on the academic issues involved.[30] Implicitly, the outline distinguished two different approaches to the problem of "people like Wu Han." The first approach would treat such problems as a political issue, would characterize dissenting views or unorthodox approaches as antisocialist or counterrevolutionary, and would use administrative means to suppress them. The second approach, in contrast, would treat such matters as serious academic issues that should be "reasoned out," under the principle of "seeking truth from facts."

The outline opted decisively for the second approach, declaring that the Party's policy toward intellectuals should continue to be guided by the principle of "letting one hundred schools of thought contend." The goal should be to overcome dissidence and unorthodoxy through superior academic work, not by "beating them [dissident intellectuals] politically." The process should be a lenient one, and critics should not "behave like scholar-tyrants who are always acting arbitrarily and trying to overwhelm people with their power." Above all, the outline proposed that the struggle against

30 "Outline report concerning the current academic discussion of the Group of Five in charge of the Cultural Revolution," in URI, *CCP documents of the Great Proletarian Cultural Revolution, 1966–1967*, 7–12.

bourgeois ideology be conducted "under leadership," "prudently," and over a "prolonged period of time."

The February Outline departed decisively in two significant ways from the views of Mao Zedong and the radicals around Jiang Qing. It pointedly avoided any conclusion as to whether Wu Han had intended *Hai Rui* as an indirect criticism of Mao's dismissal of Peng Dehuai, and thus evaded the responsibility that Mao had explicitly assigned it. What is more, the outline criticized the radical intellectuals exemplified by Yao Wenyuan as much as the allegedly revisionist scholars such as Wu Han. The Five-Man Group refrained from criticizing any radical writers by name. But it warned that some "revolutionary Leftists" were acting like "scholar-tyrants," and even called for the "rectification" of the incorrect ideas among the left.

The February Outline was discussed and approved by the Standing Committee of the Politburo, chaired by Liu Shaoqi, on 5 February. Peng Zhen and others then traveled to Wuhan to discuss the matter with Mao. As expected, Mao apparently objected to the harsh treatment of the radicals in the outline report and its failure to issue a decisive criticism of Wu Han. Nonetheless, Peng returned to Beijing claiming that Mao had approved the February Outline, and the document was circulated under the imprimatur of the CC on 12 February.

In the fall of 1965, Yao Wenyuan's direct criticism of Wu Han had stood in sharp counterpoint to the milder approach favored by Peng Zhen and the Party Propaganda Department. Now, in February 1966, the outline issued by the Five-Man Group would stand in contrast to another document prepared under the joint auspices of Lin Biao and Jiang Qing. The document was the summary of the meeting on literary and art work in the armed forces, held in Shanghai on 2–20 February 1966 that forged the political alliance between Jiang Qing and Lin Biao.[31] Like Yao Wenyuan's earlier article, the Forum Summary (known in Chinese as the February Summary, or *eryue jiyao*) was drawn up under Mao's personal supervision and was reportedly revised by Mao three times before it was circulated through inner-Party channels.

The Forum Summary took a position on intellectual problems that was diametrically opposed to that of the February Outline. It not only described China's cultural life as having been characterized by "sixteen years of sharp class struggle" between the revolutionary and revisionist perspectives, but also claimed that cultural affairs were now under the "dictatorship of a black anti-Party and anti-socialist line" – a sharp attack on the leadership provided by the Propaganda Department and the Five-Man Group. The Forum Sum-

31 "Summary of the forum on the work in literature and art in the armed forces with which Comrade Lin Piao entrusted Comrade Chiang Ch'ing," *PR*, 10.23 (2 June 1967), 10–16.

mary called for active mass criticism of these tendencies rather than the more lenient and scholarly kind of criticism envisioned by the February Outline.

The Forum Summary ignored the case of Wu Han and *Hai Rui* altogether. This was because the issue at this point was no longer Wu Han but, rather, the behavior of Peng Zhen, the Party Propaganda Department under Lu Dingyi, and the Five-Man Group they controlled. At a Central Work Conference at the end of March, Mao Zedong harshly attacked Peng Zhen, Wu Han, and the February Outline; and threatened to disband the Five-Man Group, the Beijing Municipal Party Committee, and the CC's Propaganda Department. As he said to Kang Sheng, using vivid imagery drawn from ancient Chinese mythology:

> The central Party Propaganda Department is the palace of the Prince of Hell. It is necessary to overthrow the palace of the Prince of Hell and liberate the Little Devil. . . . The local areas must produce several more [Monkey Kings] to vigorously create a disturbance at the palace of the King of Heaven. If P'eng Chen, the Peking Municipal Party Committee, and the central Propaganda Department again protect the bad people, then it will be necessary to dissolve the Peking Municipal Committee, and it will be necessary to dissolve the Five-Man Group. Last September, I asked some of the comrades what should be done if revisionism emerged in the central government. This is very possible.[32]

After the work conference, Peng Zhen apparently realized that further defiance of Mao would be useless. In a desperate attempt to preserve his own position, he encouraged the Beijing Party Committee to intensify its criticism of Wu Han, began an attack against Deng Tuo, another Beijing Party official who had written veiled criticisms of Mao's leadership, and even began to prepare his own self-criticism. In early April, according to one Red Guard account, Peng called a joint meeting of the Five-Man Group, the leadership of the Propaganda Department, and members of the Beijing Municipal Party Committee at his residence. With deep emotion, he acknowledged that he had made serious mistakes in his handling of the revolution in culture but insisted that the rest of his political record was exemplary. He pleaded for the support of his colleagues; "As the old saying goes, we depend on [our] parents' protection at home but depend on [our] friends' kind help outside. I am now looking forward to your help."[33]

But it was too late. At a meeting of the Party Secretariat between 9 and 12 April, Peng found himself the target of criticism not only by Kang Sheng and Chen Boda, but also by Deng Xiaoping and Zhou Enlai. The Secretariat decided to disband Peng Zhen's Five-Man Group and to propose to the Politburo the establishment of a new leading group for cultural reform that

32 *Miscellany of Mao Tse-tung Thought*, 2.382. 33 Ahn, *Chinese politics*, 207.

would be more sympathetic to Mao's concerns.[34] During many of these dramatic developments, Liu Shaoqi was away from Beijing on an ill-timed visit to Pakistan, Afghanistan, and Burma, and was thus unable to lead a defense of Peng Zhen and Lu Dingyi.

The May Politburo meeting

The final fates of the two principal targets thus far – Luo Ruiqing and Peng Zhen – were decided together at an enlarged meeting of the Politburo between 4 and 18 May. The highlight of the meeting was an impromptu speech by Lin Biao, much of the data for which, it was later charged, had been provided by Zhang Chunqiao.[35] In it, Lin linked the question of Luo Ruiqing with that of Peng Zhen and Lu Dingyi by accusing the three men of planning, in conspiracy with Yang Shangkun, the director of the Secretariat of the CC, a military coup against Mao and the radicals. "You may have smelled it – gunpowder," Lin told the Politburo melodramatically.

Lin supported these fantastic charges with a detailed discussion of the role of military force in acquiring political power. He emphasized the prevalence of military coups in both Chinese and contemporary world history, chronicling assassinations and usurpations in nearly every major dynasty and noting that there had been an "average of eleven coups per year" in the Third World since 1960. Although these facts were intended to make his case against Luo, Peng, Lu, and Yang more plausible, they also reflected Lin's fascination with the use of military force to pursue political goals. And he revealed that he had already put this historical lesson into practice: Acting under Mao's orders, Lin said, loyal troops had been sent into radio broadcasting stations, military installations, and public security offices in Beijing to prevent further attempts at "internal subversion and counterrevolutionary coups d'état."

Equally interesting was Lin's sycophantic portrait of Mao. Accusing Luo, Peng, Lu, and Yang of being "opposed to Chairman Mao and opposed to Mao Zedong Thought," Lin went on to extol Mao's genius, and to identify loyalty to Mao as a key criterion for holding Party or government office. "Chairman Mao has experienced much more than Marx, Engels, and Lenin. . . . He is unparalleled in the present world. . . . Chairman Mao's sayings, works, and revolutionary practice have shown that he is a great proletarian genius. . . . Every sentence of Chairman Mao's works is a truth; one single sentence of his surpasses ten thousand of ours. . . . Whoever is against him shall be punished by the entire Party and the whole country."

The enlarged meeting of the Politburo received, and approved, the report

34 Lieberthal, *Research guide,* 246–7; "Record of major events," 10–11.

35 Lieberthal, *Research guide,* 248–9; Kau, *Lin Piao,* 326–45; *RMRB,* 18 May 1978, in *FBIS Daily Report: China,* 24 May 1978, E2–11.

of the work group that had investigated Luo Ruiqing and instructed that it be circulated within the Party and the armed forces. It also issued a circular on 16 May, which Jiang Qing later claimed to have drafted, on problems in cultural affairs.[36] The 16 May Circular (*wuyiliu tongzhi*) revoked the February Outline, charging that it tried to "turn the movement to the Right" by obscuring the contemporary political issues that were being discussed within the intellectual community, and that it attempted to "direct the spearhead against the Left" by criticizing the emergence of "scholar-tyrants." The circular blamed Peng Zhen for the February Outline, dissolved the Group of Five, and established a new Cultural Revolution Group (*wenhua geming xiaozu*) (CRG) that would report directly to the Standing Committee of the Politburo (i.e., to Mao) rather than to the Party Secretariat (i.e., to Deng Xiaoping and Liu Shaoqi), as had its predecessor. Whereas a majority of the Five-Man Group had opposed Mao's views on the handling of the Cultural Revolution, the new Cultural Revolution Group was dominated by Mao's personal supporters and the radical intellectuals surrounding Jiang Qing. The group was headed by Chen Boda, with Kang Sheng as an adviser, and with Jiang Qing, Zhang Chunqiao, Yao Wenyuan, Qi Benyu, Wang Li, and Guan Feng as members.

Although the principal purpose of the new Cultural Revolution Group was to continue the criticism of bourgeois ideas in the cultural sphere, the 16 May Circular also warned that ranking Party and state officials might well suffer the same fate as Peng Zhen and Luo Ruiqing. It was necessary, the circular said, to eliminate the

> representatives of the bourgeoisie who have sneaked into the Party, the government, and the army. When conditions are ripe, they would seize power and turn the dictatorship of the proletariat into a dictatorship of the bourgeoisie. Some of them we have already seen through, others we have not. Some we still trust and are training as our successors. There are, for example, people of the Khrushchev brand still nestling in our midst.

In this way, the circular presented a major escalation of Mao's drive against revisionism: from a movement directed principally at intellectuals, to one aimed at the Party as a whole.

The May Politburo meeting set the stage for the reorganization of the Beijing Municipal Party Committee, the Party Propaganda Department, and the Party Secretariat, which was announced in early June. Peng Zhen was replaced as Beijing's first secretary by Li Xuefeng, then the first secretary of

36 "Circular of the Central Committee of Communist Party of China," in "Collection of documents concerning the Great Proletarian Cultural Revolution," *CB*, 852 (6 May 1968), 2–6. On Jiang Qing's role, see Witke, *Chiang Ch'ing*, 320.

the North China Bureau; Lu Dingyi was replaced as head of the Propaganda Department by Tao Zhu, previously first secretary of the Party's Central-South Bureau; and Yang Shangkun was replaced as staff director of the Party Secretariat by Wang Dongxing, a vice-minister of public security who concurrently commanded the elite guards unit in the capital.

The dismissals of men of such rank in late May and early June showed that Mao was determined to have his way on issues that were of importance to him, and that he was able to secure the replacement of officials who did not comply with his wishes. Moreover, each reorganization – of the General Staff Department of the PLA, of the group responsible for cultural reform, of the Beijing Municipal Party Committee, of the Party Propaganda Department, of the Party Secretariat – strengthened Mao's coalition and weakened those who would resist or oppose him. Rather than appeasing Mao, in other words, each purge simply made it easier for him to escalate his assault on revisionism in the Party.

The Fifty Days

By warning of "representatives of the bourgeoisie" who had "sneaked into the Party, the government, and the army," the 16 May Circular indicated that Mao wanted a thoroughgoing purge of revisionism throughout China, not just in the cultural sphere but throughout the bureaucracy. Still away from Beijing, in relative seclusion in Central China, Mao left the conduct of this effort in the hands of Liu Shaoqi, a man whom he would later say he already suspected of revisionism, and who other radicals would claim was one of the officials referred to indirectly in the 16 May Circular as "people of the Khrushchev brand" being trained as Mao's successors.

Whether or not Liu was fully aware of Mao's suspicions, he did face a serious dilemma in June 1966. On the one hand, if he were to have any hope of survival, he would have to show enthusiasm and efficiency in combating revisionism. On the other, he had to do so in a way that preserved central control over a rapid process of political mobilization, particularly on college campuses, and that protected what was left of his eroding political base. Liu's attempts to resolve this dilemma were reflected in his actions during a fifty-day period in June and early July 1966, during which, in Mao's absence from Beijing, he was principally responsible for the day-to-day affairs of the Party.

By this time, radical students and teachers, particularly in Beijing, were well aware of the debate over cultural reform and of Mao's views about the February Outline. In part, this was simply because younger professors who were members of the Party had access to the documents on the subject, such as the 16 May Circular, that were being circulated within the Party organization. But it was also because the leaders of the newly established CRG were sending representatives to major college and university campuses in Beijing to mobilize mass support.[37]

On 25 May, a group of radical professors and teaching assistants at Peking University (Beida) led by Nie Yuanzi, a teaching assistant in the philosophy department, wrote a large-character wall poster (*dazibao*) criticizing the university's leadership for having supported the liberal policies of the February Outline and for having prevented mass discussion of the political issues raised by the *Hai Rui* affair. According to accounts published well after the Cultural Revolution, Nie received direct encouragement from a "theoretical investigation group from the central authorities," led by Kang Sheng's wife, Cao Yiou, which had arrived at Beida under orders to "kindle the flames and spread the fire to upper levels."[38]

The university administration, not surprisingly, took prompt action to suppress this kind of dissent. In this they were supported by Zhou Enlai, who sent a second central work group to criticize Nie's wall poster the night it was displayed at Beida. But, having learned of the contents of the *dazibao,* Mao Zedong ordered that it be broadcast and published nationally, with favorable commentary, on 1 June. This decision, followed presently by the announcement that the entire Peking University leadership was being reorganized, served to legitimate spontaneous mass protest as part of the campaign against revisionist officials. So, too, did increasingly inflammatory editorials that began to appear in *Renmin ribao* after the newly reorganized central Propaganda Department had undertaken a restaffing of the central news media.

With this encouragement, wall posters written by students and faculty began to appear at university campuses and in middle schools throughout China. Most probably focused on educational issues – the admissions process, course examinations, and curricula were the questions of greatest concern – but some accused university leaders and higher-level officials of supporting revisionist policies. As at Beida, it is very likely that much of this explosion of dissent was encouraged and coordinated by the new CRG under Chen Boda, Jiang Qing, and Kang Sheng. In short order, the authority of university leaders on other campuses collapsed, and discipline among students and faculty quickly eroded.

It was this rapid process of political decay – the rise of dissent and the collapse of authority – that must have been of particular concern to Liu Shaoqi.[39] Operating without clear instructions from Mao, he decided on several mea-

37 Sun, *Lishi jiangyi,* 2.247.

38 The events at Beida are drawn from *HQ,* 19 (October 1980), 32–6.

39 On the fifty days, see Ahn, *Chinese politics,* ch. 9; Jean Daubier, *A history of the Chinese Cultural Revolution,* ch. 1; Lowell Dittmer, *Liu Shao-ch'i and the Chinese Cultural Revolution: The politics of mass criticism,* 78–94; and Harding, *Organizing China,* 225–9.

sures he hoped would simultaneously demonstrate his willingness to combat revisionism and bring the student movement under Party leadership. To begin with, he ordered the suspension of university enrollment for half a year to permit a thorough reconsideration and reform of the examination system and the university curriculum. At the same time, he organized a large number of work teams – perhaps 400 teams with more than 10,000 members in all – and dispatched them to universities and high schools and to bureaucratic agencies responsible for finance, trade, industry, and communications. Given the frequent use of work teams in past Party rectification campaigns, Liu doubtless considered his decision to be routine, appropriate, and noncontroversial.

What was ultimately Liu's undoing was less the principle of dispatching work teams than the instructions under which they operated. They apparently were told that large numbers of ordinary bureaucratic officials and university faculty were to be subject to criticism and possibly dismissal. In the Ministry of Finance, for example, 90 percent of the cadres reportedly were criticized; in the Ministry of Culture, work teams were authorized to dismiss two-thirds of the ministry's officials. In universities, large numbers of administrators and faculty came under attack, beginning a reign of terror that would last for a decade.

The work teams were also told to reestablish Party leadership over the student movement in the nation's major universities and high schools. A Politburo conference on 13 July, after reviewing the Cultural Revolution in Beijing's middle schools, concluded that the most important task on each campus was to "restore the leading role of the Party branch" and to "strengthen the work teams."[40] Putting the same point in somewhat blunter language, the first Party secretary of Anhui province announced that, "for units where the leadership is not in our hands, work teams must be sent immediately to win it back."[41]

The reassertion of Party leadership over the student movement implied the demobilization of the radical students and their faculty supporters. National policy was still to permit student demonstrations, rallies, and wall posters as long as they were confined to campus. But many local Party committees and work teams, in their zeal to impose control over the student movement, took a stricter approach. In some places, *dazibao* and rallies were banned altogether, and in others they were allowed only if permission had been obtained from the work team. Some radical students were expelled from the Communist Youth League, others were subjected to struggle meetings, and still others were sent to the countryside for a stint of labor reform. As a result of

40 Sun, *Lishi jiangyi,* 2.250. 41 Radio Hefei, 16 July 1966.

such stringent measures, the work teams were able to restore a modicum of normality to many universities.

But although some students were persuaded to cease political activity, the restrictions imposed by the work teams drove others into deeper opposition. Secret student organizations, some of which took on the name "Red Guards" (*hongweibing*), formed to resist the activities of the work teams, despite Liu Shaoqi's ruling that such organizations were "secret and [therefore] illegal."[42] Other student groups were organized at the behest of the work teams to provide them with support. The result, in other words, was not only the partial demobilization of the student movement but also the polarization of the remaining activists.

The work teams' suppression of the radicals soon became a matter of considerable controversy at the highest levels of the Party. In early July, the case of Kuai Dafu, one of the leading radical students at Qinghua University, who had been criticized by the work teams sent there, was the subject of a high-level Party meeting in Beijing. In that meeting, Liu Shaoqi attacked Kuai as a troublemaker, and Kang Sheng defended his right to criticize revisionism in the Party. It was by this time common knowledge that activists such as Kuai Dafu had direct connections with the central CRG advised by Kang Sheng, whereas the work teams with which Kuai had come into conflict had been dispatched on the order of Liu Shaoqi. What gave this particular case special poignancy was the fact that the leader of the work team sent to Qinghua was none other than Liu Shaoqi's wife, Wang Guangmei.[43] In this way, Liu's political future had become inextricably intertwined with the performance of the work teams.

As Mao Zedong saw it, the work teams repeated the same mistakes that Liu Shaoqi had committed during the rural Socialist Education Campaign earlier in the 1960s.[44] In that campaign, directed against corruption and "capitalist tendencies" among rural cadres, Liu's approach had been to dispatch large numbers of work teams to grass-roots Party organizations, restrict peasant participation in cadre rectification, criticize large numbers of commune officials, and downplay the responsibility of higher-level Party leaders. In Mao's eyes, Liu's conduct of the rectification of the universities and the urban bureaucracy in mid-1966 was guilty of similar errors. Once again, large numbers of lower-level officials were being attacked and mass involvement was being restricted, without any recognition that the ultimate cause of revisionism lay in the sympathetic attitudes of higher officials.

42 "Record of major events," 25. 43 Ahn, *Chinese politics*, 218.

44 On the Socialist Education Movement, see Ahn, *Chinese politics*, ch. 5; Richard Baum, *Prelude to revolution: Mao, the Party, and the peasant question, 1962–66;* and Harding, *Organizing China*, ch. 7.

The Eleventh Plenum

Thus, in mid-July, angered at Liu Shaoqi's conduct of the campaign against revisionism in the bureaucracy and his management of the radical student movement, Mao abruptly ended his stay in Hangzhou and headed for Beijing. On the way back to the capital, Mao stopped for a swim in the Yangtze River – an act intended to demonstrate that he had the physical vigor needed for the political battles ahead. Although Mao had been active behind the scenes in Hangzhou, this was his first public appearance in many months, and it received unprecedentedly syncophantic coverage in the Chinese media. The official report of the event carried by the New China News Agency began with the sentence "The water of the river seemed to be smiling that day" and went on to tell of a militiaman from the Hankou Thermal Power Plant who "became so excited when he saw Chairman Mao that he forgot he was in the water. Raising both hands, he shouted: 'Long live Chairman Mao! Long live Chairman Mao!' He leapt into the air, but soon sank into the river again. He gulped several mouthfuls, but the water tasted especially sweet." Thereafter, the president of the World Professional Marathon Swimming Federation invited Mao to take part in two forthcoming races, for the Chairman's speed, as reported by the New China News Agency dispatch, was nearly four times the world record.[45]

Upon his arrival at the capital, Mao called a meeting of regional Party secretaries and members of the CRG where he demanded the withdrawal of the work teams dispatched by Liu Shaoqi. "The work teams know nothing. Some work teams have even created trouble. . . . Work teams only hinder the movement. [Affairs in the schools] have to be dealt with by the forces in the schools themselves, not by the work teams, you, me, or the provincial committees."[46] The Beijing Municipal Party Committee immediately announced that work teams would be withdrawn from all universities and high schools in the city, and would be replaced by "Cultural Revolution small groups" to be elected by the teachers, students, and staff at each school.[47]

But Mao was not mollified by the Beijing Party Committee's quick capitulation. He began preparations for a CC plenum, the first since 1962, that would endorse the measures already undertaken and legitimate his vision of a revolution against revisionism in China. The session, which convened in early August, was probably attended only by about half of the full and alternate members of the CC – a reflection of both the depth of division within the Party and the haste with which the meeting had been called. The plenum was

45 "Quarterly chronicle and documentation," *CQ*, 28 (October–December 1966), 149–52.

46 Ch'en, *Mao papers*, 26–30. 47 Sun, *Lishi jiangyi*, 2.250.

packed, not only by Party officials who were not members of the CC but also by "representatives of revolutionary teachers and students from the institutions of higher learning in Peking."[48] In addition, Lin Biao apparently reinforced military control over key installations in the capital area – thus tightening the grip over the city that he had first announced at the enlarged Politburo meeting in May. Even so, Mao himself later admitted that he received the support of a bare majority of those attending the meeting.[49]

This rump session of the CC made decisions in three principal areas. On personnel matters, it agreed to the promotion of several of Mao's principal supporters and the demotion of those who had resisted him or who had misread his intentions over the past several months. The plenum endorsed the May Politburo decisions concerning the dismissals of Peng Zhen, Luo Ruiqing, Lu Dingyi, and Yang Shangkun, and dropped Peng and Lu from the Politburo. For his mishandling of the "Fifty Days" Campaign, Liu Shaoqi was stripped from his Party vice-chairmanship and demoted from the second to the eighth position in the Party hierarchy. Lin Biao succeeded Liu as second in command and was made sole Party vice-chairman, thus replacing Liu as Mao's heir apparent. Chen Boda and Kang Sheng, leaders of the new CRG, were promoted from alternate membership on the Politburo to full membership. And Minister of Public Security Xie Fuzhi, who came to form a rather close association with the CRG, was appointed an alternate member of the Politburo and named the member of the Party Secretariat responsible for all political and legal matters, the position formerly held by Peng Zhen.

Not all the new appointments to the Politburo were close associates of Lin Biao or Jiang Qing. Other personnel decisions made at the Eleventh Plenum seemed to reflect compromises that Mao, Lin Biao, and the Cultural Revolution Group made with the Party and military establishments. A number of veteran civilian and military officials, not closely associated with Jiang Qing, Chen Boda, or Lin Biao, were added to the Cultural Revolution Group. Four senior provincial leaders – Tao Zhu, the new director of the Propaganda Department; Li Xuefeng, the new first Party secretary in Beijing; and regional Party secretaries Song Renqiong and Liu Lantao – received appointments as Politburo members. And three more PLA marshals – Ye Jianying, Xu Xiangqian, and Nie Rongzhen – were also added to the Politburo, perhaps as a way of counterbalancing Lin Biao's growing political influence.

On policy matters, the formal political report given by Liu Shaoqi was overshadowed by the text of Lin's May talk on coups d'état and by a friendly letter sent by Mao to a group of Qinghua Middle School Red

48 Lieberthal, *Research guide*, 255–7. 49 *Miscellany of Mao Tse-tung Thought*, 2.457–8.

Guards in late July, both of which were circulated among the delegates to the plenum.[50] In reviewing the crucial issues of the early 1960s, the plenum's communiqué endorsed all the positions associated with Mao Zedong and indirectly criticized some of those taken by Liu Shaoqi. Mao's approach to the Socialist Education Campaign, as embodied in the Former Ten Points of May 1963 and the Twenty-three Articles of January 1965, was said to be the correct way of dealing with organizational problems in the countryside. The plenum cited with approval Mao's concern with promoting revolutionary successors and his theory that class struggle continues in socialist society. It also noted favorably his calls to learn from such model units and organizations as the Dazhai production brigade, the Daqing oil field, and the PLA.

Finally, the plenum adopted a Sixteen Point Decision on the Cultural Revolution (*wenge shiliu tiao*), laying out Mao's vision for the movement.[51] The principal goal was nothing less than to "change the mental outlook of the whole of society." It was to

> struggle against and overthrow those persons in authority who are taking the capitalist road, to criticize and repudiate the reactionary bourgeois academic "authorities" and the ideology of the bourgeoisie and all other exploiting classes, and to transform education, literature and art, and all other parts of the superstructure not in correspondence with the socialist economic base.

The principal mechanism was to be the mobilization of "the masses of the workers, peasants, soldiers, revolutionary intellectuals, and revolutionary cadres." Even though they could be expected to make mistakes, the Decision proclaimed, the key to success in the Cultural Revolution was "whether or not the Party leadership dares boldly to arouse the masses." It was improper either to resist the movement, or even to attempt to control it.

The Sixteen Points, reflecting serious differences within the CC, were highly ambiguous on the question of the degree of disorder that would be tolerated during the Cultural Revolution. On the one hand, the Decision acknowledged approvingly that there were likely to be "disturbances" in the course of the Cultural Revolution. It cited Mao's remarks in his 1927 report on the Hunan peasant movement that revolutions cannot be "so very refined, so gentle, so temperate, kind, courteous, restrained and magnanimous." It also set a sweeping goal for the movement: the "dissmiss[al] from their leading posts [of] all those in authority who are taking the capitalist road [so as to] make possible the recapture of the leadership for the proletarian revolu-

50 Sun, *Lishi jiangyi*, 2.251.

51 "Decision of the Central Committee of the Chinese Communist Party concerning the Great Proletarian Cultural Revolution," in "Collection of documents Concerning the Great Proletarian Cultural Revolution."

tionaries." And it prohibited any reprisals against students in high schools or universities who participated in the movement.

On the other hand, reportedly at the instigation of Zhou Enlai and Tao Zhu, the Decision contained several specific provisions that were clearly intended to moderate the conduct of the Cultural Revolution.[52] It emphasized the possibility of uniting "ninety-five per cent of the cadres" and prohibited the use of coercion or force. It largely exempted ordinary scientists, technicians, cadres, and Party and government agencies in the countryside from the full force of the movement. It insisted that the Cultural Revolution not be allowed to hamper economic production. And it stipulated that although "bourgeois academic 'authorities' " and revisionists in the Party should be criticized, they should not be attacked by name in the press without the approval of the cognizant Party committee.

Even so, the general tone of the Eleventh Plenum was significantly different from what these formal caveats might suggest. Even as the plenum was in session, Mao wrote his own *dazibao,* which he posted outside the CC's meeting room, in which he accused "some leading comrades" – the reference was clearly to Liu Shaoqi and Deng Xiaoping – of "adopting the reactionary stand of the bourgeoisie" by sending out work teams to college campuses and government offices during the Fifty Days.[53] And the plenum itself endorsed the decision to dismiss or demote three of the twenty-one members of its Politburo. Together, these two developments symbolized the broad significance of the Eleventh Plenum: to legitimate a broad attack on the Party establishment and the intellectual community, at the personal initiative of Mao Zedong, that would entail a high degree of mass mobilization and an intense degree of political struggle.

THE COLLAPSE OF AUTHORITY

The emergence of the Red Guards

The Eleventh Plenum endorsed Mao's vision of the Cultural Revolution as the "arousal of the masses" to criticize revisionist tendencies in "all . . . parts of the superstructure not in correspondence with the socialist economic base." In so doing, it brought together two themes that had been present in Mao's thinking since the early 1960s: first, that the Party establishment itself had been responsible for the emergence of revisionism in China since the GLF and, second, that the best way to combat revisionism was to

52 *RMRB,* 5 January 1986, in *FBIS Daily Report: China,* 24 January 1986, K12–22.
53 Ch'en, *Mao papers,* 117.

mobilize the ordinary citizenry of China – and especially China's young people – against it.

The Sixteen Point Decision of the Eleventh Plenum on the Cultural Revolution envisioned a mechanism for popular participation that survived for only a few weeks. The plan was to establish popularly elected Cultural Revolution committees (*wenhua geming weiyuanhui*) in grass-roots units from factories and communes to universities and government organs. These organizations were to be modeled after the Paris Commune of 1871 in that their members were to be selected through a system of general election and were to be subject to criticism and recall by their constituents at any time. They were, in short, to be broadly representative of the organization in which they were formed.

Significantly, however, the Cultural Revolution committees were not expected to replace the Party committees or the administrative structure. Instead, the Decision of the Eleventh Plenum described them somewhat ambivalently as a "bridge to keep our Party in close contact with the masses." On the one hand, the committees were supposed to be permanent organizations for criticizing revisionism and struggling against "old ideas, culture, customs, and habits." But on the other, the Decision specified that they were to remain "under the leadership of the Communist Party."

The problem, from a Maoist perspective, is that this conception of the Cultural Revolution committees had inherent flaws that stripped them of their effectiveness. To begin with, the stipulation that the committees accept Party leadership made it possible for the local Party committees to coopt or control them by ensuring that the masses "elected" committee members who were relatively conservative in outlook. And the provision that the committees be elected virtually ensured, in the universities at least, that they be divided in reflection of the increasingly polarized student body. In many cases, the Cultural Revolution committees were dominated by the children of high-level cadres, not only because children from cadre families had come to constitute the largest single group among university students, but also because higher-level Party committees were likely to favor their colleagues' children as leaders of the mass movement. What is more, the Cultural Revolution committees were preoccupied with the problems of their particular units rather than with the broader questions of national policy that the Maoists intended should be the more important focus of the Cultural Revolution.

But another model of popular participation was immediately available: that of the Red Guards. Just before the Eleventh Plenum approved the concept of Cultural Revolution committees, Mao Zedong wrote a letter to a group of Red Guards at the Qinghua Middle School in Beijing that tacitly endorsed that alternative form of organization. Although the Eleventh Plenum's Decision on the Cultural Revolution did not even mention the Red Guards by name, Red Guard representatives were present in the meeting room. Compared to the Cultural Revolution committees, the Red Guards must have appeared to be a way of lifting the Cultural Revolution out of an exclusive concern with the affairs of grass-roots units and toward the consideration of broader issues and criticism of higher-level leaders. Whereas the Cultural Revolution committees seemed likely to fall under the control of the Party apparatus, the Red Guards could more readily be manipulated by the Cultural Revolution Group.[54]

Thus, within a week after the close of the Eleventh Plenum, a series of massive Red Guard rallies began in Beijing. Although the Cultural Revolution committees were never repudiated, and even received sporadic attention in the press for the rest of the year, it was clear nevertheless that they had been eclipsed by the Red Guards. The eight rallies, organized with the logistical support of the PLA, brought together 13 million Red Guards from all over China in the three months between 18 August and 26 November 1966.[55] Films of the events present vivid images of these enraptured young middle school students: some chanting revolutionary slogans, tears streaming down their faces; others waving their copies of Mao's quotations at the distant deity reviewing them on the Gate of Heavenly Peace. The Red Guard organizations bore such martial names as the "Red Flag Battalion," the "Three Red Banners Group," and the "Thorough Revolution Corps." Many Red Guards wore military uniforms, and Mao himself put on a Red Guard armband, thus conveying the clear message that the Red Guards had the support of both Mao and the PLA. Directives issued by the CRG in the name of the CC gave the Red Guards the right to organize parades and demonstrations, use printing presses and publish newspapers, and post *dazibao* criticizing Party committees at all levels.

The Red Guard movement drew on many of the socioeconomic cleavages and grievances discussed earlier in this chapter, particularly the tension between class background and academic performance as criteria for success in China's educational system. Beyond this, the mobilization of Red Guards was facilitated by several other factors: a sense of excitement at being called upon by the leader of their country to become involved in national affairs; a sense of opportunity that one's future would be fundamentally affected by involvement in the Cultural Revolution; the suspension of classes and admissions examinations, which relieved millions of middle school and university students of academic responsibility; and, above all, the provision of free

54 On the interplay of these two models of organization, see Harding, *Organizing China*, ch. 8.
55 Sun, *Lishi jiangyi*, 2.254.

railway transportation to Red Guards seeking to travel around the country to "exchange revolutionary experiences." The Red Guard organizations drew not only on urban youth but also on the large numbers of young people who had been sent down to the countryside in the early 1960s and who now took advantage of the disorder of the time to return to the cities.

But the Red Guard movement did not, in the fall of 1966, achieve the goals that Mao had foreseen for it. To begin with, the Red Guards remained fascinated with what the Chairman must have regarded as secondary, even trivial, issues. Taking seriously the injunction of the Eleventh Plenum to combat the "four olds" – old ideas, old culture, old customs, and old habits – the Red Guards took to the streets looking for evidence of bourgeois culture. Young men and women wearing long hair were stopped on the streets and shorn on the spot. Women wearing tight slacks were subjected to the "ink bottle test": If a bottle of ink placed inside the waistband could not slip freely to the ground, the pants would be slashed to shreds. Shopkeepers were forced to take down signboards bearing traditional store names and to replace them with more revolutionary labels. Red Guards themselves often changed the names of streets, occasionally arguing among themselves over which new name would be the more progressive. One group of Red Guards proposed that the menaing of traffic signals be changed so that red, the color of revolution, would signify "go" rather than "stop."

Another Red Guard organization from a middle school in Beijing drew up a list of 100 examples for "smashing the old and establishing the new," which give some flavor of this aspect of the Cultural Revolution. They told "rascals and teddy boys" to "shave away your long hair" and "remove your rocket-shaped shoes." They insisted that people should stop drinking, desist from smoking, and give up the "bourgeois habits of keeping crickets, fish, cats, and dogs." Laundries, they said, should refuse to launder the clothing of "bourgeois families," and "bath houses must as a rule discontinue serving those bourgeois sons of bitches, and stop doing massage for them." This group of Red Guards also demanded that their own school change its name from the "No. 26 Middle School" to the "School of Mao Zedong's Doctrine."[56]

Some Red Guard activities were much less amusing. Teachers and school administrators were often regarded as principal representatives of the "bourgeois" class in China, and untold numbers were harrassed, beaten, or tortured at the hands of their own students – often to death. Homes of former industrialists or landlords were invaded and ransacked, in a search for "contraband materials" or hidden wealth. Art objects were confiscated, ornate furniture smashed or painted red, and walls covered with quotations from Mao

56 *SCMM*, 566 (6 March 1967), 12–20.

Zedong. Members of the pariah classes, such as landlords, were rounded up and forcibly deported from major cities. At Peking University alone, 100 homes of faculty and staff were searched, books and other personal effects seized, and 260 persons forced to work under "supervision" with placards around their necks listing their "crimes."[57] The descent into often mindless violence and brutality simply continued and intensified, albeit under less official auspices, the reign of terror against China's bourgeois classes, particularly intellectuals, that had begun under Party leadership during the Fifty Days earlier the same year.

From the outset, the Red Guard movement was plagued with serious factionalism, with the main issue under dispute being the identity of the principal targets of the Cultural Revolution. To a very large degree, the divisions among the students occurred along the fault lines created by the educational policies of the early 1960s.[58] Students from cadre or military families usually insisted that the Red Guard movement remain under Party leadership, and tried to moderate the criticism leveled at the Party establishment. Instead, they sought to direct the spearhead of the movement against a different set of targets: intellectuals, scholars, former industrialists and landlords, and signs of bourgeois culture in China's urban society.

Students from bourgeois backgrounds, in contrast, saw the Cultural Revolution as an opportunity to overcome the discrimination they had experienced in the early 1960s, when the growing emphasis on class background had put them at a disadvantage in university admissions, Yough League and Party recruitment, and job assignments. From their perspective, the Red Guard movement offered an unparalleled chance to demonstrate a degree of revolutionary conduct that would outweigh their undesirable family origins and a legitimate opportunity to vent their grievances against the Party establishment. Maoist sympathizers who had been suppressed and persecuted during the Fifty Days now saw the possibility of reversing the verdicts that had been imposed on them by the work teams. They argued that their resistance to the teams had been an act of rebellion against "incorrect" Party leadership – a right now guaranteed them by the Sixteen Points adopted at the Eleventh Plenum.

The divisions within the student movement have been captured in a number of detailed case studies of Red Guard organizations in Beijing and Guangzhou. One reveals that, in a sample of nearly 2,200 middle school

57 For descriptions of Red Guard violence, see Gordon A. Bennett and Ronald N. Montaperto, *Red Guard: The political biography of Dai Hsiao-ai;* Ken Ling, *The revenge of heaven: Journal of a young Chinese;* and *HQ,* 19 (October 1980), 32–6.

58 On cleavages within the Red Guard movement, see Lee, *Politics of the Cultural Revolution;* Rosen, *Red Guard factionalism;* and Anita Chan, "Images of China's social structure: The changing perspective of Canton students," *World Politics,* 34.3 (April 1982), 295–323.

students in Guangzhou, the overwhelming majority of students from cadre families (73 percent) joined organizations that defended the Party establishment, while a slightly smaller majority of students from intellectual backgrounds (61 percent) and a plurality of students from other bourgeois families (40 percent) joined rebel organizations. Analyzed somewhat differently, the same data show that the "loyalist" organizations drew the bulk of their membership (82 percent) from children from cadre and worker backgrounds, whereas the "rebel" organizations recruited their members principally from families of intellectuals (45 percent).[59]

From a Maoist perspective, this was an irony of the highest order in that the most radical students in a revolutionary campaign against reivsionism were representatives not of the proletariat, as the rhetoric of the day insisted, but rather of the bourgeoisie itself. From a less ideological point of view, however, the divisions within the student movement are much more understandable. Those who criticized the Party most vehemently were those who had gained the least from the Party's educational policies and whose families had been the principal victims of the Party's "class line," whereas those who supported the Party against attack were the children of Party officials and were those who had benefited the most from the prevailing system of Party recruitment, university admissions, and job assignments.

The reaction of the Party establishment

The failure of the Red Guard movement to follow the course that Mao had intended, and its descent into disorder, factionalism, and violence, can be attributed to a number of causes. In part, it was because the restraints on the mass movement contained in the Sixteen Points were not strong enough to counterbalance the inflammatory rhetoric of that same document, of the official Party press, and of the leaders of the Cultural Revolution Group. In part, it was because the Cultural Revolution was conducted in a way that significantly departed from the original vision embodied in the Eleventh Plenum in that the movement was implemented not by Cultural Revolution committees under Party leadership, but rather by Red Guard organizations that took as their right and obligation the rejection of Party authority. Perhaps most important, it was the result of a decision to mobilize millions of immature young people in a highly charged political atmosphere, to encourage them to engage in "revolutionary struggle" against vaguely defined targets, and to denounce as "suppression of the masses" any attempt to bring them under leadership or control.

59 Chan, "Images of China's social structure," 314, Table 2.

Another reason for the difficulties of the Red Guard movement can be found in the opposition of the Party establishment itself. Officials could only have been bewildered by the notion that their records were to be evaluated by loosely organized groups of high school and university students, wearing military uniforms and waving small red books of Mao's quotations. But it was clear that their jobs were at stake. The Eleventh Plenum Decision had spoken of dismissing Party people in authority taking the capitalist road. And, in a speech to the plenum, Lin Biao had discussed the same matter in even blunter terms. The Cultural Revolution, he said, would involve "an overall examination and overall readjustment of cadres" according to three political criteria: whether they "hold high the red banner of Mao Zedong Thought," whether they "engage in political and ideological work," and whether they are "enthusiastic about the revolution." Those who met the criteria were to be promoted or retained in office; those who did not were to be dismissed so as to "break the stalemate" between those who supported Mao's programs and those who opposed them.[60]

Even more alarming, it was rapidly becoming apparent that more than careers were involved. As already mentioned, an untold number of teachers and principals had by this time been beaten, tortured, and even murdered by their own students. And Party cadres were by no means exempt from similar forms of violence. In the first few months of the Red Guard movement alone, at least one Party official – the first secretary of Tianjin municipality – died as a result of a struggle meeting with radical students, and another – Pan Fusheng of Heilongjiang – was hospitalized after being denied food for four days.[61]

In some places, officials may have heeded the Party's injunctions to submit themselves freely to interrogation and criticism by the Red Guards. But the overall pattern was one in which officials tried to delay, divert, or disrupt the movement.[62] Initially, some attempted to ban the Red Guard organizations outright on the grounds that they had not been officially sanctioned by the Eleventh Plenum. Another tactic was to permit the formation of Red Guard organizations but then to place their activities under tight restrictions, similar to those imposed by the work teams during the Fifty Days, that prohibited them from holding parades or demonstrations, posting wall posters, or printing their own newspapers.

The convocation of the huge Red Guard rallies in Beijing, and the publica-

60 Kau, *Lin Piao,* 346–50. 61 Dittmer, *Liu Shao-ch'i,* 132.

62 On the response of Party officials to the Red Guard movement, see Parris H. Chang, "Provincial Party leaders' strategies for survival during the Cultural Revolution," in Robert A. Scalapino, ed., *Elites in the People's Republic of China,* 501–39; and Richard Baum, "Elite behavior under conditions of stress: the lesson of the 'Tang-ch'uan p'ai' in the Cultural Revolution," in Scalapino, *Elites,* 540–74.

tion of laudatory editorials in the central press, however, soon made it impossible to deny the legitimacy of the Red Guard organizations. Consequently, local officials began to employ a more subtle approach. Some tried to sacrifice a few subordinates (in an analogy with chess, the Chinese used the phrase "sacrificing the knights to save the king" to describe this tactic) as a way of demonstrating sincerity without placing themselves in jeopardy. Some staged "great debates" to discuss whether or not their Party committee had exercised truly "revolutionary" leadership but manipulated the meetings so as to ensure the correct outcome. Some sought to prevent Red Guards from posting wall posters by covering blank walls with quotations from Mao Zedong, in the confident belief that covering such sayings with *dazibao* would be tantamount to sacrilege. Still others tried to evade the Red Guards by moving their offices to local military compounds, which the radical students could not enter.

The principal tactic, however, was for provincial and local cadres to encourage the formation of conservative mass organizations to defend them against criticism by the radicals. Working through the Party organization and the Youth League within each university and middle school, it was possible to organize students who had a stake in maintaining the status quo and to portray more radical Red Guard groups as being members of bourgeois families seeking revenge on the Party. Working through the trade unions, the local leaders also organized more conservative workers into "Scarlet Guards" (*chiweidui*) to defend Party and government buildings against assaults by radical Red Guards. As a result of such maneuvers, the Red Guard movement, which had originally been based on college and middle school campuses, began to move outward into the ranks of the industrial work force.

This tactic was facilitated by a set of central regulations that, ironically, favored the Party establishment over the CRG. Central policy at first restricted membership in Red Guard organizations to students from what were called "five red" family backgrounds – workers, peasants, soldiers, cadres, or revolutionary martyrs – and prohibited students from bourgeois backgrounds from participating in the Red Guard movement. This not only limited the size of the student movement – only 15 to 35 percent of middle school and university students belonged to the original Red Guard organizations in the late summer and early fall of 1966[63] – but it also paradoxically restricted membership in the Red Guards to precisely those students who were more likely to defend the Party establishment.

Why did officials resist the Red Guard movement in all these ways? Part

63 Lee, *Politics of the Cultural Revolution*, 85.

of the answer lies in their desire for self-preservation in the face of a movement they must have regarded as anarchic and uncontrolled. But local and provincial officials must have also believed that they had support in Beijing, and that their best strategy would be to try to ride out the worst of the campaign and hope that it would soon be brought to an end. After all, neither Liu Shaoqi, Deng Xiaoping, nor Zhou Enlai had been dismissed from the Politburo by the Eleventh Plenum. Liu, to be sure, had been demoted in rank, but he remained president of the People's Republic. Deng and Zhou retained their positions as secretary general of the Party and prime minister of the State Council. And Tao Zhu, the former head of the Party's Central-South regional bureau, who had been named director of the Party Propaganda Department in early June, was also attempting to prevent the Red Guard movement from claiming too many victims. All these central leaders, in their speeches, actively supported efforts to restrict membership in the Red Guards to students from five red backgrounds, to maintain unity and discipline of Red Guard organizations, and to use the principle of majority rule to subordinate the radical minority to the more conservative majority.

The response of the Maoists

By the end of September, therefore, it was becoming clear to Mao, Lin, and the CRG that the Cultural Revolution was not proceeding as originally intended. There had been much criticism of the four olds but little criticism of leading officials. Only a few lower-level cadres had been forced to resign. The main trend was for the Party establishment to evade, subvert, and coopt the movement.

Accordingly, early October saw a substantial radicalization of the Cultural Revolution and the strengthening of the CRG at the expense of the Party establishment. This development was first reflected in a series of speeches and editorials, most of which were written by members of the CRG on the occasion of China's National Day on 1 October. These statements criticized Party cadres for their resistance to the Cultural Revolution, reiterated that the Red Guards had the right to rebel against the Party organization, and emphasized that the main target of the Cultural Revolution was revisionists in the Party and not, as conservative organizations had argued, the four olds. Perhaps most important, they announced that the restrictions on membership in Red Guard organizations would be overturned so that radical students from bad class backgrounds could legally join the mass movement.

Moreover, between 9 and 28 October a central work conference was held in Beijing to assess the Cultural Revolution's progress thus far, and to find ways of overcoming the obstacles it had encountered.[64] At first, Mao and Lin sought to gain the delegates' support for the Cultural Revolution by reassuring them about the movement's purposes. They promised that most cadres would be able to "pass the test" of the Cultural Revolution, if only they would welcome, instead of trying to evade, mass criticism. "If [cadres] have made mistakes," Mao said, "they can probably correct them! When they have corrected them, it will be all right, and they should be allowed to come back and go to work with a fresh spirit." Mao even submitted his own self-criticism, in which he acknowledged that the emergence of revisionist policies in the early 1960s was partly the result of his own choice to retire to a "second line" of leadership and relinquish responsibility for day-to-day decisions. What is more, Mao admitted, he had not anticipated the "big trouble" that was created by the mobilization of the Red Guards.[65]

But the delegates to the work conference were still not mollified. What was originally expected to be a three-day meeting stretched on to more than two weeks, and what was supposed to have been a conciliatory atmosphere gradually became more and more acrimonious.[66] Chen Boda gave a report charging that the struggle between the "proletarian" and "bourgeois" lines that had been evident in the early 1960s was now being reflected in the conduct of the Cultural Revolution. Mao Zedong and Lin Biao stopped giving reassurances to worried cadres and now vehemently attacked officials who tried to check or elude the movement. Mao complained that "only a very few people firmly place the word 'revolt' in front of other words. Most people put the word 'fear' in first place." Lin attributed the resistance of the Party to the obstruction of some central officials, and he named Liu Shaoqi and Deng Xiaoping as the probable culprits. Both men were compelled to submit self-criticisms to the conference.

The effect of these developments in October 1966 was greatly to reduce the influence of conservative mass organizations.[67] Late in the year, some loyalist organizations in Beijing did engage in a last stand, attacking radical Red Guard groups, criticizing Lin Biao, defending Liu Shaoqi, and insisting that the proper course was to "kick away the CRG to make revolution on our own." But their power was clearly on the wane. Some conservative organizations submitted self-criticisms, some were taken over by radical students, and others collapsed as their leaders were arrested by public security forces.

64 Lieberthal, *Research guide*, 259–62. The dates, which differ somewhat from those given by Lieberthal, are from Sun, *Lishi jiangyi*, 2.255.

65 Ch'en, *Mao papers*, 40–5; and Jerome Ch'en, ed., *Mao*, 91–7.

66 Sun, *Lishi jiangyi*, 2.255.

67 On events following the October work conference, see Daubier, *History of the Cultural Revolution*, ch. 3; Dittmer, *Liu Shao-ch'i*, ch. 5; Lee, *Politics of the Cultural Revolution*, 118–29. The escalation is also reflected in the central directives issued during the period, in "Collection of documents."

The CRG was also able in late 1966 to intensify the mass assault on the Party establishment. Easing restrictions on membership in mass organizations quickly increased the size of the radical factions. At the same time, the CRG strengthened its liaison with those organizations that it considered to be most sympathetic, and urged them to amalgamate into larger, more effective bodies. In November and December, Red Guards were allowed to enter factories and communes, and workers were authorized to form their own "revolutionary rebel" organizations, thus breaking the effective monopoly previously enjoyed by the Party establishment in organizing workers and peasants. Free transportation to Beijing was ended so as to encourage Red Guards to end their "revolutionary tourism" and return to their home cities and provinces to "make revolution" against local Party committees.

Most important of all, the CRG began to identify high-ranking officials for the mass organizations to attack and provided friendly Red Guards with information that could be used as the basis for their criticisms. Red Guard delegations were sent from Beijing to major provincial capitals with specific instructions as to which local officials should be put to the test. Radical Red Guard organizations were informed that Liu Shaoqi and Deng Xiaoping had opposed Mao Zedong and could be subjected to criticism. The CRG provided the Red Guards with copies of Liu's and Deng's self-criticisms at the October work conference, and wall posters attacking the two men began to appear in greater numbers in November and December. According to evidence presented at the trial of the "Gang of Four" in 1980–1, Zhang Chunqiao met with the Qinghua student radical Kuai Dafu at Zhongnanhai on 18 December and told him to discredit Liu and Deng publicly. "Make their very names stink," Zhang is alleged to have said. "Don't stop halfway."[68] And, toward the end of the year, Tao Zhu was dismissed from the directorship of the Propaganda Department, for attempting to shield provincial officials and central propaganda and cultural affairs cadres from criticism, and for allegedly seeking to strip control over the movement from the Cultural Revolution Group. Five other important central officials – Yang Shangkun, Luo Ruiqing, Lu Dingyi, Peng Zhen, and He Long – were forced to attend mass rallies in Beijing, where they were denounced and abused for hours on end.

The message of these developments was clear: No one in China, save Mao Zedong himself, was to be exempt from criticism, and the methods of criticism could be harsh indeed.

68 *A great trial in Chinese history: The trial of the Lin Biao and Jiang Qing counter-revolutionary cliques, Nov. 1980–Jan. 1981*, 35.

The collapse of provincial authority

The result of the escalation of the Cultural Revolution in the last three months of 1966 differed from one part of China to another. In more remote provinces, where the mobilization of radical students was difficult, provincial leaders remained well entrenched. But where mobilization did occur, the consequence was not the rectification of local officials, as Mao had hoped, but rather the nearly complete collapse of provincial authority.

Shanghai provides the best example of this latter process.[69] The inflammation of central rhetoric in October encouraged the formation of the first radical, citywide workers' organization, the "Workers' Headquarters," early the following month. This organization, composed primarily of such underprivileged workers as apprentices and temporary contract laborers, was apparently formed by some lower-level cadres (such as Wang Hongwen of the No. 17 State Cotton Mill, who would rise to national prominence later in the Cultural Revolution) with the assistance of radical students. The mayor of Shanghai, Cao Diqiu, had by some accounts been willing to comply, albeit reluctantly, with the central directives on the Cultural Revolution. But he resisted the formation of the Workers' Headquarters, on the grounds that the creation of independent workers' organizations had not yet been sanctioned by central directives, and that the formation of such groups would almost certainly interfere with production.

When the Workers' Headquarters approached Cao, seeking official recognition and material support, he therefore denied their request. Angered, the leaders of the Headquarters commandeered a train and left for Beijing to present their case to the central leadership. Cao ordered the train sidetracked at a suburban station outside Shanghai, where his representatives again tried to explain his position.

At first the central CRG supported Cao's stand. But when the workers still refused to return to their factories, the radical leaders in Beijing sent Zhang Chunqiao to negotiate with them. Zhang undercut Cao Diqiu by agreeing to recognize the Workers' Headquarters, on the condition that their Cultural Revolutionary activities not be permitted to interefere with their normal production assignments – a decision that Cao had no alternative but to endorse.

The city government's position was further weakened by the arrival, in Shanghai, of Nie Yuanzi, apparently with instructions to expose the head of the city's education department as a revisionist and to accuse Cao Diqiu of

69 Accounts of events in Shanghai in this period can be found in Neale Hunter, *Shanghai journal: An eyewitness account of the Cultural Revolution;* and Andrew G. Walder, *Chang Ch'un-ch'iao and Shanghai's January Revolution.*

shielding him. In the aftermath of her arrival, a group of radicals took over the local newspaper, the *Jiefang ribao,* demanding that it distribute copies of Nie's address. Several days later, the government capitulated.

The collapse of Cao's authority, however, was not primarily the result of these actions by radical workers and intellectuals. It was, instead, the result of a countermobilization, at least partly spontaneous, by more conservative Shanghai citizens. During the occupation of the *Jiefang ribao,* groups of Scarlet Guards and other supporters attempted to storm the building to retake it from the radicals. Postal workers refused to distribute copies of the tabloid containing Nie's speech. The Scarlet Guards issued demands that Cao repudiate his "capitulation" to the radicals, and that he not concede anything further to them.

Cao's response to this process of polarization was, according to the careful study by Andrew Walder, to "sign any and all demands that were made to his office" by either faction.[70] The result was a torrent of requests by disadvantaged sectors of society for economic benefits. Workers who had been transformed into temporary laborers, and contract workers who had been laid off, demanded reinstatement and back pay. Permanent workers lobbied for higher wages and for increases in benefits, and charged that the disruption of production by the radicals would cause a reduction in their own bonuses.

Fights and riots broke out between the conservative and radical factions, and after one in which eight conservatives were reportedly killed, the Scarlet Guards called a general strike. This, coupled with the strategy of the besieged municipal government – to meet the demands of all factions – led to the collapse of the Shanghai economy: runs on banks, hoarding of supplies, disruption of electricity and transportation. By the end of December, China's largest city was in chaos.

THE SEIZURE OF POWER

The "January Revolution"

The situation in Shanghai was, in extreme form, representative of what had happened in much of urban China by the end of 1966. Essentially, three processes were at work, which taken together caused the collapse of Party authority. First of all, there was the mobilization of large sectors of Chinese society, who were making ever greater demands on the Party bureaucracy. The process had begun as a deliberate attempt by the Maoists in Beijing to organize a force to criticize the Party. But once it began, the process fed on

70 Walder, *Chang Ch'un-ch'iao,* 36.

itself, with mobilization by the Maoists engendering a form of countermobilization – some spontaneous, some highly organized – in support of the Party establishment.

Accordingly, the process of mass mobilization produced a high degree of polarization in Chinese society, mirroring the intense factionalism that already existed at the highest levels of the Party leadership. In calling on the students (and later the workers) of China to criticize revisionism in the Party, Mao seems to have naively believed that they would act as a relatively unified force – that the "great union of the popular masses," of which he had spoken and written since the mid-1920s, would form in the course of the Cultural Revolution.[71] What happened was precisely the opposite. Mass mobilization aggravated deep cleavages within Chinese society, particularly those separating students of cadre fmailies from those with bourgeois backgrounds, and those separating skilled permanent workers from less skilled and temporary employees.

Third, mobilization and polarization were accompanied by the delegitimization of Party authority. By authorizing the Red Guards to rebel against revisionists in the Party, and by asserting that people should obey only those Party directives that corresponded with Mao Zedong Thought, the Maoists in effect stripped the Party of unconditional legitimacy without providing any alternative structure of authority in its place. At the same time, the delegitimation from above was reinforced by a withdrawal of legitimacy from below. As beleaguered Party organizations sought to cope with the explosion of popular demands by trying to please everyone, they ultimately pleased no one. The Shanghai experience vividly illustrates the authority crisis that occurs when a regime loses control over an escalating process of mobilization and countermobilization.

Mao's response to the collapse of authority was, in effect, to authorize radical groups to push aside the discredited (or recalcitrant) Party committees and constitute new organs of political power in their place. Once again, Shanghai was the frontrunner in this stage of the Cultural Revolution.[72] On 6 January 1967, a mass rally in Shanghai confirmed officially what had already occurred in fact: It dismissed Cao Diqiu and other municipal officials from their posts. On that same day, Zhang Chunqiao, as a representative of the CRG, returned to Shanghai from Beijing to establish a new municipal government to replace the overthrown Party committee. With his encouragement, and with the support of the CRG, constituent organizations of the radical

71 On this tendency in Mao's thinking, see Stuart R. Schram, "From the 'Great Union of the Popular Masses' to the 'Great Alliance,' " *CQ*, 49 (January–March 1972), 88–105.

72 On events in Shanghai, see Walder, *Chang Ch'un-ch'iao*, ch. 7. A similar seizure of power took place in Shanxi.

Workers' Headquarters issued demands for the restoration of social order and economic production: demands that the economic grievances of workers be shelved until a "later stage" of the Cultural Revolution, that workers remain at their posts, and that enterprise and bank funds be frozen. At the same time, rebel organizations, backed by units of the PLA, began taking over factories, docks, newspapers, and other economic enterprises. From these beginnings, it was only a short time before the ultimate step was taken: The radical organizations announced the formation of a new organ of political power in Shanghai that would assume the political and administrative functions of the old Party committee and municipal government.

In the latter part of the month, this sort of power seizure was authorized for all of China. On 22 January, a vitriolic editorial in *Renmin ribao* encouraged radical organizations throughout the country to rise up and take power away from the Party committees:

> Of all the important things, the possession of power is the most important. Such being the case, the revolutionary masses, with a deep hatred for the class enemy, make up their mind to unite, form a great alliance, [and] seize power! Seize power!! Seize power!!! All the Party power, political power, and financial power usurped by the counterrevolutionary revisionists and those diehards who persistently cling to the bourgeois reactionary line must be recaptured![73]

The following day, a formal CC directive repeated *Renmin ribao's* call for a mass seizure of power from "those in authority who are taking the cpitalist road." It described the Cultural Revolution not simply as a criticism of bourgeois and revisionist tendencies in China, as had the Decision of the Eleventh Plenum, but rather as "a great revolution in which one class overthrows another."[74]

The radicalization of the goals of the Cultural Revolution was accompanied by a radicalization of the composition of the CRG. In January and February 1967, all the representatives of the PLA and the regional and provincial Party organizations that had been appointed to the group the previous year were removed – along, of course, with Tao Zhu, who lost membership in the group when he was purged as director of the Propaganda Department in December. This meant that, once again, the CRG reflected solely the interests of the radical intellectuals associated with Jiang Qing, Kang Sheng, and Chen Boda. No longer was their viewpoint moderated by the more conservative outlooks of senior Party and army officials.

The CC's 23 January directive also initiated an escalation of the Cultural

73 *RMRB*, 22 January 1967, in *PR*, 10.5 (27 January 1967), 7–9.

74 "Decision of the CCP Central Committee, the State Council, the Military Commission of the Central Committee, and the Cultural Revolution Group under the Central Committee on resolute support for the revolutionary masses of the left," 23 January 1967, in "Collection of documents," 49–50.

Revolution along a second dimension. Through the latter half of 1966, the PLA had played a somewhat aloof and ambivalent role in the Cultural Revolution. In some ways, to be sure, it had been actively involved on the side of the Maoists: by providing a forum for Jiang Qing's assault on the prevailing line in literature and art; by providing, through the *Jiefangjun bao,* a mouthpiece for radical viewpoints in the spring of 1966; by securing Beijing during such crucial meetings as the May 1966 central work conference and the Eleventh Plenum, in August; and by providing logistical support for the Red Guards. In other ways, however, it had stood on the sidelines or even taken a hostile position. The Decision of the Eleventh Plenum had specifically exempted the army from the jurisdiction of the Cultural Revolution Group, and other directives had apparently ordered military units to take a posture of noninvolvement in the confrontation among mass organizations and between radical groups and the Party establishment. And in many areas, the PLA had served as an "air raid shelter," providing sanctuary for local and provincial Party officials and a force for suppressing radical organizations.

Until 23 January, then, the most active elements in the Maoist coalition had been the radical brain trust, as symbolized by the CRG, and the mass base, as typified by the radical Red Guard and revolutionary rebel organizations. Now, in light of the general stalemate that had occurred throughout the fall, and the collapse of authority that had begun to appear around the turn of the year, Mao decided to throw the army – the third element of his power base – more fully into the fray. The 23 January directive, citing a recent directive from the Chairman that "the PLA should support the broad masses of the Left," ordered that the armed forces drop any pretense of noninvolvement, stop serving as an "air raid shelter for the handful of Party power holders taking the capitalist road," give "active support . . . to the broad masses of revolutionary Leftists in their struggle to seize power," and "resolutely suppress" any "counterrevolutionaries or counterrevolutionary organizations" that offered resistance.

Once the decision had been taken to authorize the seizure of power, however, other equally important decisions remained. Who should seize power? Who should exercise it? Through what organizational forms? Perhaps the most pressing issue in this regard was whether or not the masses could really assume the role that had been assigned to them. The language of the 22 January *Renmin ribao* editorial and the CC's directive of the following day suggested a kind of Marxist jacquerie: a mass uprising to depose those who had usurped power and departed from correct policies. But the masses of China were deeply divided into competing interests and largely ignorant of the details of political administration, rather than a unified political force that could provide an effective alternate government.

Both these problems were reflected in the wave of power seizures across the country in late January. In some places, competing mass organizations each claimed to have seized power, and appealed to Beijing for support. In other places, Party officials used friendly mass organizations to stage what were later described as "sham" seizures of power. In still other localities, mass representatives entered Party or government offices, demanded the seals with which official documents were "chopped," and then walked out, in the belief that the capture of the symbols of power meant that power itself had somehow been seized. As Zhou Enlai himself put it, power was "surrendered" by the Party but was not effectively "retained" by the Red Guards.[75]

The extent of these difficulties was indicated by the fact that China's central news media acknowledged and endorsed only four of the thirteen power seizures that occurred across the country at the end of January. An important editorial published on 1 February in *Hongqi* (Red Flag), the Party's theoretical journal, tacitly admitted that the concept of a Marxist jacquerie was unworkable. Instead, the editorial stipulated that power should be seized not simply by a "great alliance" of mass organizations, but rather by a "three-in-one combination" (*sanjiehe*) of representatives of the "revolutionary masses," local military officers, and Party and government officials whose attitude was judged to be sufficiently "revolutionary." The presence of mass representatives would reflect the original populist ethos of the Cultural Revolution. But, as the editorial admitted, "it will not do to rely solely on the representatives of these revolutionary mass organizations." Without the other two components of the "three-in-one combination," "the proletarian revolutionaries will not be able to solve the problem of seizing and wielding power in their struggle . . . , nor can they consolidate power even if they seize it." Cadres were necessary because of their administrative experience and their knowledge of the details of policy and programs; military representatives, who became, as we will see, the most important part of the three-in-one combination, would be able to ensure discipline and suppress any opposition to the seizure of power.[76]

With this issue resolved, the second problem taken up by the Maoist center was the form that the new organs of power would assume. For a brief period, the Maoists flirted with the idea of reorganizing China around the principles of the Paris Commune: All officials would be drawn from the ranks of ordinary citizens, be chosen by general election, be paid the same salaries as ordinary workers, report regularly to their constituents, and be subject to recall at any time. These principles, which imply a form of government

75 Philip Bridgham, "Mao's Cultural Revolution: The struggle to seize power," *CQ*, 34 (April–June 1968), 7.

76 *HQ*, 3 (1 February 1967), in JPRS, 40,086, *Translations from Red Flag* (1 March 1967), 12–21.

completely different from that of classic bureaucracy, had been endorsed by Marx, Engels, and the pre-1917 Lenin as the form of political institutions that the dictatorship of the proletariat would introduce, replacing the bureaucracies that, in Lenin's words, were "peculiar to bourgeois society."[77]

The model of the Paris Commune had been fashionable among Chinese radicals in 1966, the ninety-fifth anniversary of the Commune's short existence. A long article in the February issue of *Hongqi,* well before the Eleventh Plenum, had recounted the history of the Commune and advocated that its principles be applied to China. The plenum itself, in authorizing the formation of Cultural Revolution committees, had provided that these new organizations embody the principles of the Commune, even though it simultaneously stipulated that the committees would supplement, and not supplant, the more bureaucratic Party and state organizations.[78]

With this as background, it was not surprising that radical Chinese would again turn to the model of the Paris Commune once the decision had been taken to seize power from the Party and state bureaucracies in January 1967. Implicitly echoing comments by Marx a century earlier that the proletariat could not simply take over the state machinery of the bourgeoisie but would have to create new forms of organization, the *Hongqi* editorial of 1 February argued that the revolutionary rebels of China could not merely seize power in the existing Party and government agencies, but would have to create completely new organizational forms. Although it provided no clear guidelines as to what these new forms should be, the editorial strongly implied that they should be patterned after the Paris Commune. In keeping with this suggestion, many of the new provincial and municipal governments formed in late January announced that, in line with the principles of the Commune, their officials would be selected through mass elections and would be subject to supervision and recall. Some, such as Shanghai and Harbin, actually proclaimed themselves to be "people's communes."

In the situation prevailing in early 1967, however, such a step was as unrealistic as had been the earlier call for a mass uprising to seize power. The situation in Shanghai, for example, in no way reflected the exercise of immediate democracy, Paris Commune style. In organizing the Commune, Zhang Chunqiao had ignored the principle of direct election, promising only that such elections might be held at some future point "when conditions become

77 Vladimir I. Lenin, "The state and revolution," in Henry M. Christman, ed., *Essential works of Lenin,* 290.

78 *HQ,* 4 (15 February 1966), in JPRS, 35,137, *Translations from Red Flag* (21 April 1966), 5–22; *Decision,* sec. 9. On the use of the Paris Commune as a model in this period, see John Bryan Starr, "Revolution in retrospect: The Paris Commune through Chinese eyes," *CQ,* 49 (January–March 1972), 106–25.

ripe." In fact, the formation of the Shanghai Commune immediately produced grumblings that Zhang had favored representatives of the Workers' Headquarters at the expense of other groups and that he was using the PLA to suppress opposition. Some people complained that he was ignoring the economic demands raised by workers in late December, and that he himself, as a former director of the municipal Propaganda Department and a current member of the central CRG was hardly an "ordinary citizen." As Andrew Walder has pointed out, "Despite the utopian images conjured up by the commune . . . , the Shanghai Commune was probably supported by less than one-fourth of Shanghai's politically active working population and relied heavily upon the PLA for its very survival."[79]

Realizing that talk of "people's communes" raised expectations of immediate democracy that could not possibly be realized in a highly mobilized and polarized setting, Mao Zedong called Zhang Chunqiao and Yao Wenyuan back to Beijing to persuade them to change the name of the Shanghai Commune. Mao's concern was that a faithful implementation of the Paris Commune model would produce a further collapse of political authority, the exclusion of cadres and military representatives from the three-in-one combination, an inability to restore order and suppress counterrevolutionaries, and problems in finding a role for a reconstituted CCP later on. All these tendencies the Chairman labeled "most reactionary."[80]

Thus on 19 February, the day after Mao's meetings with Zhang and Yao, the CC banned the use of the term "people's commune" at the national, provincial, or municipal levels.[81] (It retained its original meaning, of course, as the name of the largest level of joint economic and political administration in the countryside.) Instead, the CC resurrected a term from revolutionary days – "revolutionary committee" (*geming wenyuanhui*) – to describe the "revolutionary, responsible, and proletarian provisional power structures" formed as a result of the seizure of power. The historical reference was particularly apt, for the revolutionary committees of the 1940s had also been three-in-one combinations of mass representatives, Party cadres, and military personnel, formed as provincial governments in areas recently "liberated" by the Red Army. But the use of the term in 1967 also underlined a key point: Like their predecessors of the Yan'an years, the revolutionary committees of the Cultural Revolution were now regarded

79 Walder, *Chang Ch'un-ch'iao*, 61.

80 For the texts of Mao's remarks, see *Miscellany of Mao Tse-tung Thought*, 2.451–5; and JPRS, 49,826, *Translations on Communist China* (12 February 1970), 44–5.

81 "CCP Central Committee's notification on the question of propagandizing and reporting on the struggle to seize power," 19 February 1967, in "Collection of documents," 89; Ch'en, *Mao papers*, 136–7.

only as provisional governments, pending the organization of something more permanent. Already, it seemed, Mao was envisioning ways of reducing the high level of mass mobilization that the Cultural Revolution had produced.

The third issue at stake in early 1967 was the process by which these revolutionary committees would be formed. With the notion of general elections discarded and the Party apparatus in shambles, the only element of the three-in-one combination that was in a position to organize the revolutionary committees on a nationwide basis was the PLA. Thus, the procedure authorized by Beijing was that, after the overthrow of the local Party committees, the local military garrison (for cities) or military district command (for provinces) would form a "military control committee" (*junshi guanzhi weiyuanhui*), responsible for restoring order, maintaining production, and beginning the selection of the mass representatives, cadres, and military officers to serve on the revolutionary committee. In essence, the army became a national work team, with responsibility for deciding not only which cadres would survive the Cultural Revolution, but also which mass organizations deserved representation on the revolutionary committees.[82]

The overthrow of the Party committees in early 1967 has been described by the Chinese themselves as the "January Revolution" (*yiyue geming*) and has been described outside the country as tantamount to a military seizure of power. But neither the analogy of a mass revolution nor that of a military coup is an adequate way of understanding this period. It is true that the January Revolution involved a level of popular dissent, mass organization, and political protest unknown since 1949. But official rhetoric notwithstanding, the main purpose of the seizure of power in January was less to overthrow authority than to restore order. Granted, too, that the main beneficiary of the seizure of power was the PLA, as the country fell under military rule. But military intervention in Chinese politics in early 1967 occurred at the behest of civilian authorities in Beijing, not in defiance of them. If the events of January 1967 in China amounted to a revolution, in other words, it was a revolution from above; and if they resulted in military rule, then that outcome reflected the decision by one civilian faction to use military force to overthrow another, rather than a military coup against civilian authority.

The main participants in the three-in-one combination

The establishment of the three-in-one combination as the official framework for the creation of revolutionary committees defined the principal issue for

82 Harding, *Organizing China*, 253.

the next ten months. In how many administrative units and at what levels of government should power be seized? What balance should be struck among the three components of the three-in-one combination as each revolutionary committee was formed?

The principle of the three-in-one combination also illustrated quite clearly the main lines of cleavage in Chinese politics produced by the Cultural Revolution. At the provincial and municipal levels, cadres, mass organizations, and military units all competed for representation on the revolutionary committees. In Beijing, in turn, each component of the three-in-one combination had its sponsors at the highest levels of Party leadership: Zhou Enlai and other senior civilian leaders represented the interests of cadres; the CRG, under Jiang Qing, Chen Boda, and Kang Sheng, represented the interests of the radical mass organizations; and Lin Biao and his associates in the MAC of the Party sponsored the interests of the armed forces.

But it would be incorrect to imply that these three vertical networks were internally unified. Just as there was conflict within the mass movement among radical and conservative Red Guard organizations, so too were there cleavages inside the armed forces between those sympathetic to Lin Biao and those who opposed him, and divisions between those cadres who were willing to accommodate to the Cultural Revolution and those who chose to resist it. And, significantly, none of the three organizational networks, or their elite sponsors in Beijing, was able to secure or maintain the unqualified support of Mao Zedong.

An understanding of the events of the remainder of 1967 and the first half of 1968 can therefore be facilitated by a brief analysis of the interests and behavior of each of these three vertical networks in Cultural Revolutionary China, beginning with what remained of the Party and state bureaucracy. By the end of January 1967, it was clear that every government and Party official in China was subject to criticism, dismissal, and even physical assault by radical organizations. Some cadres had already fallen from power, including the early targets of the Cultural Revolution, such as Peng Zhen, Lu Dingyi, and Luo Ruiqing; and the victims of the radicalization of the Red Guard movement in late 1966 and the first power seizures in January 1967, such as Tao Zhu and Cao Diqiu. Still others, such as Liu Shaoqi and Deng Xiaoping, and Zhou Enlai and his vice-premiers, had come under heavy criticism but had not actually been dismissed. Elsewhere, the fate of the vast majority of cadres was still uncertain. Leaders at each level waited to see whether they could secure appointment to the revolutionary committees that were now being formed under military sponsorship, while their subordinates remained in office with their authority weakened but not completely eliminated.

The interest of the cadres, as symbolized by Zhou Enlai, was primarily to moderate the impact of the Cultural Revolution on the state and Party bureaucracy. Zhou's goals throughout the movement were, to the greatest degree possible (1) to exempt the most important agencies of the Party and government from the most disruptive Cultural Revolutionary activities, (2) to prevent mass organizations from seizing power without authorization from a higher level, (3) to limit the geographic scope of operation of any particular mass organization, and (4) to ensure the maintenance of normal production and administrative work.[83] In addition, Zhou sought to protect a number of high-level officials from Red Guard attack. In January, he reportedly invited between twenty and thirty cabinet ministers to take turns living in the guarded leadership compound in Zhongnanhai, and enabled the first Party secretaries from a number of regions, provinces, and major cities to move to Beijing, where they would be free from harassment or criticism by local Red Guards.[84]

Despite the common interests of cadres in limiting the scope of the Cultural Revolution, there were differences of outlook within the ranks of Chinese officialdom. Some cadres, particularly those of lower ranks, saw the Cultural Revolution as an opportunity for more rapid advancement or for revenge against colleagues with whom they had poor personal relations. In some provinces and municipalities, therefore, a pattern emerged by which lower-echelon officials joined with radical mass organizations in seizing power from their superiors. Important examples include Hua Guofeng, a secretary of the provincial Party committee in Hunan; Ji Dengkui, an alternate secretary in Henan; and, of course, Zhang Chunqiao of Shanghai – all of whom rose to positions of even greater prominence in their provinces as a direct result of the Cultural Revolution. This would be the basis for later controversy as those cadres who benefited from the Cultural Revolution in this way came into confrontation in the latter half of the 1970s with those who had been its principal victims.

The second main vertical network was that of the CRG and the radical mass organizations it mobilized, protected, and to some degree directed. The main interests of the CRG appear to have been to discredit as many cadres as possible, to give mass organizations the greatest scope and autonomy in their activities, and to maximize the participation of mass representatives on revolutionary committees. To this end, the CRG began, as early as August 1966 but on a wider scale late in 1967 and in 1968, to draw up lists of CC members, provincial Party and state leaders, and members of the National People's Congress and Chinese People's Political Consultative Conference

83 On Zhou Enlai's role in the Cultural Revolution, see Thomas W. Robinson, "Chou En-lai and the Cultural Revolution," in Thomas W. Robinson, ed., *The Cultural Revolution in China*, 165–312.

84 Sun, *Lishi jiangyi*, 2.260–1.

whom they considered to have been "capitulationists" during the revolutionary period or "revisionists" after 1949. By August 1968, for example, Kang Sheng had allegedly compiled a list of more than 100 members of the CC and 37 members of the Party's central disciplinary apparatus whom he wanted to see expelled from the Party.[85] In addition, the CRG used friendly Red Guard organizations to organize mass demonstrations and criticism against Party and government officials, to seize compromising materials from their homes, and to obtain useful information through detention and torture of suspected revisionists and, in some cases, members of their families, their servants, or their office staff.[86]

These activities brought the CRG into conflict with both of the other two vertical networks active in the Cultural Revolution. The CRG tried to expand the scope of political struggle to include virtually all officials at all levels of the bureaucracy, whereas the cadres obviously sought to narrow the targets of the Cultural Revolution to a smaller number. The CRG wished to grant radical mass organizations greater autonomy to seize power from Party committees and government agencies, whereas civilian officials such as Zhou Enlai attempted to place power seizures under the control of higher authorities and to restrict mass organizations to supervisory rather than administrative functions.

In addition, the CRG came into increasing conflict with the PLA over the military's role in the Cultural Revolution. In January 1967, when the seizure of power first got underway, Chen Boda contrasted the Cultural Revolution with the final stages of the revolution in China in the 1940s. Then, he said, the Red Army seized power, "exercised military control, and issued orders from top to bottom." During the Cultural Revolution, he said, it would be the masses, and not the military, "who take over."[87] The role that Mao granted to the PLA in overthrowing the Party establishment and organizing revolutionary committees was thus far greater than the CRG would have preferred. Even worse, the local military forces did not always appoint mass representatives to revolutionary committees in the numbers that the CRG wanted or from the mass organizations that it supported. The formation of revolutionary committees inevitably led, therefore, to attacks on local military headquarters by some dissatisfied Red Guard organizations, and thus to tensions between the PLA and the CRG in Beijing.

This leads to the third vertical network active in the Cultural Revolution: the PLA itself. The role of the army, as we have seen, escalated steadily throughout 1966 and 1967. Now, once the Cultural Revolution entered the

85 Ibid., 2.271. 86 *A Great trial*, passim.
87 *Huo-ch'e-t'ou*, 7 (February 1967), in *SCMP*, 3898 (14 March 1967), 4–7.

stage of the seizure of power, the military played an even greater part in Chinese politics. Its job was not only to help seize power from the Party establishment, as it was ordered to do on 23 January, but also to ensure thereafter that order was maintained. This second purpose was served by military occupation of key warehouses, banks, broadcasting stations, and factories; military supervision of spring planting; military management of civil aviation; and establishment of military control commissions in major administrative jurisdictions where power had been seized.[88] Altogether, 2 million officers and troops of the PLA participated in civilian affairs during the Cultural Revolution.[89]

In general, the military appears to have had a single major interest during the Cultural Revolution: to maintain order and stability, prevent the collapse of the Chinese social and political fabric, and thus avoid a situation in which China would be vulnerable to foreign invasion. In addition, some military officers had a related interest in maximizing their own influence on the new revolutionary committees, increasing the number of military representatives, and protecting the military against attacks by Red Guards.

Beyond these common interests, however, the divisions within the military during the Cultural Revolution appear to have been every bit as great as those within ranks of the cadres or among the country's mass organizations.[90] Some of the cleavages were structural, resulting largely from the division of the PLA into local and main forces. The main forces – including the navy, air force, and the elite elements of the ground forces – were better equipped and directly subordinated to central command. The local forces, in contrast, were composed of lightly equipped infantry forces, commanded by military districts (corresponding in virtually all cases to provinces) and military regions (comprising several neighboring provinces), and responsible for a wide range of civilian activities.

During the Cultural Revolution, it was the main forces that remained more faithful to central directives from Lin Biao, not only because they came directly under the command of a General Staff and a MAC that he had packed with his own supporters, but also because they were the main beneficiaries of the program of military modernization that Lin had undertaken in the early 1960s. In contrast, the local forces, whose commanders often had close ties

88 The escalation of military involvement can be traced through the central directives in "Collection of documents."

89 Edgar Snow, *The long resolution*, 103.

90 See Jürgen Domes, "The Cultural Revolution and the army," *Asian Survey*, 8.5 (May 1968), 349–63; Jürgen Domes, "The role of the military in the formation of revolutionary committees, 1967–68," *CQ*, 44 (October–December 1970), 112–45; Harvey W. Nelsen, "Military forces in the Cultural Revolution," *CQ*, 51 (July–September 1972), 444–74; and Harvey W. Nelsen, "Military bureaucracy in the Cultural Revolution," *Asian Survey*, 14.4 (April 1974), 372–95.

with local Party officials, often acted in conservative fashion as defenders of the provincial and municipal Party establishments. A study by Jürgen Domes, for example, has suggested that, of the twenty-nine military district commanders at the outset of the Cultural Revolution, only five gave the movement their backing, eight gave it nominal support only after they had brought local mass organizations under their control, and sixteen were unsupportive.[91]

A second set of cleavages within the military formed around personal factions. During the latter part of the Communist revolution, the Red Army had been divided into five great "field armies," each responsible for liberating a different part of the country. The personal associations established during this period formed the basis for factional networks of officers far after 1949. It was widely believed that Lin Biao, in seeking to consolidate his control over the PLA after his appointment as minister of national defense in 1959, had favored officers from the field army he had commanded (the Fourth) over officers from other factions.[92] After his purge, Lin was accused of having assembled derogatory materials about ranking officers from other field armies, particularly Nie Rongzhen, Xu Xiangqian, He Long, and Ye Jianying, who might have thwarted his attempt to establish exclusive personal control over the armed forces.[93]

As a final element in this assessment of the major participants in the three-in-one combination, it is important to underscore the tensions and conflicts that emerged from time to time between Mao and each of these three vertical networks. Mao's main differences were obviously with the Party and state cadres, for it was they whom he suspected of revisionism and against whom he directed the Cultural Revolution. On the other hand, Mao seems to have acknowledged the need for trained administrators to serve on the revolutionary committees. He claimed to hope that the cadres would be able to "pass the test" of the Cultural Revolution ("Who wants to knock you down? I don't," he told the central work conference in October 1966),[94] and he protected a few ranking civilian officials, particularly Zhou Enlai, from Red Guard criticism.

But Mao also had his differences with both Lin Biao and the CRG. Although Mao had selected Lin to head the Ministry of Defense in 1959 and chose him as his heir apparent at the Eleventh Plenum in 1966, the Chairman apparently questioned many of Lin's views on questions of history and

91 Domes, "Role of the military."

92 The *locus classicus* for an analysis of the importance of field armies in Chinese military politics is William W. Whitson with Chen-hsia Huang, *The Chinese high command: A history of communist military politics, 1927–71*. See also Chien Yu-shen, *China's fading revolution: Army dissent and military divisions, 1967–68;* and William L. Parish, "Factions in Chinese military politics," *CQ*, 56 (October–December 1973), 667–99.

93 *A great trial*, 82–9. 94 Ch'en, *Mao papers*, 45.

ideology. In a letter to Jiang Qing in early July 1966, he criticized Lin for overstating the importance of military coups and military power in the history of China and the history of developing countries, and for exaggerating Mao's own personality cult. "I have never believed that those several booklets of mine possessed so much magic," Mao wrote to his wife. "This is the first time in my life that I have involuntarily agreed with others on an issue of major significance."[95]

Much of Mao's criticism of Lin could simultaneously be read as a criticism of the CRG, for the encomiums to Mao Zedong Thought in mid-1966 and the sycophantic treatment of Mao in the Chinese press were as much its responsibility as that of the PLA. Some of Mao's statements in January about the Shanghai Commune suggest that Mao was concerned about anarchistic tendencies among the Cultural Revolution Group and about their desire to overthrow all of the country's cadres.[96] There is no evidence to suggest that Mao was ever willing to authorize the use of armed force by mass organizations, as Jiang Qing and her colleagues on the Cultural Revolution Group were sometimes prepared to do.

Mao had a variety of resources and strategies to employ against any of these three networks should they prove insubordinate or recalcitrant. The cadres were the most easily controlled, as they had the weakest power base at the time. As a general instrument, Mao could allow the central Cultural Revolution Group to intensify its criticism of Party and government officials, confident that this would be promptly reflected in the actions of radical mass organizations. More specifically, Mao could identify particular cadres for exclusion from revolutionary committees, for punishment, or for protection.

The PLA, in contrast, had much more power than civilian officials, for army officers controlled the organized armed force that now was essential to the stability of the regime. But the army could be controlled – in part by increasing the leeway given to radical mass organizations to criticize army officials and in part by disciplining errant officers through the military chain of command. Thus, commanders unsympathetic to the Cultural Revolution were removed or transferred in five military regions and six military districts in the spring of 1967, and about eight more district commanders met similar fates later that year. In extreme situations, as we shall see, Mao and Lin could dispatch main force units into provinces where local comanders had been particularly obdurate.

Mao also had a variety of mechanisms for controlling the mass organizations. He could tighten restrictions on radical mass activities, giving Red

95 *CLG*, 6.2 (Summer 1973), 96–9.

96 *Miscellany of Mao Tse-tung Thought*, 2.451–5; and JPRS, 49,826, *Translations on Communist China* (12 February 1970), 44–5.

Guard and revolutionary rebels less leeway to criticize civilian and military officials when their tendencies toward fragmentation and violence seemed to get out of hand. In addition, Mao and his representatives could label particular organizations as either "revolutionary" or "counterrevolutionary," depending on their subservience to central directives, and could give local military units the authority to suppress and disband mass organizations that had been deemed counterrevolutionary.

The shifting balance

Given these cleavages – within each vertical system, among the three organizational networks, and between each vertical system and Mao Zedong – the formation of revolutionary committees in 1967–8 was thus an exceedingly complicated task. In only a few places – Heilongjiang, Shanghai, Guizhou, and Shandong – were revolutionary committees formed smoothly in the first two months of 1967. Here the key was the existence of alternative leadership, usually from the pre–Cultural Revolution provincial or municipal Party establishment, which was able quickly to fill the collapse of authority that occurred in January. In other provinces, where the existing military and civilian leadership was divided and the mass organizations were deeply fragmented, the formation of revolutionary committees was a much more protracted process, involving continued conflict and competition.

The twenty months during which the revolutionary committees were selected, March 1967 to October 1968, were essentially a period of shifting balances among the three competing organizational networks in which each would periodically gain or lose power relative to the others. Throughout the period, Mao retained the ability to determine the balance of power among the three vertical networks, although his decisions were clearly made in response to the actions of the cadres, the military, and the mass organizations, and although he never controlled the situation completely. The dynamics of the period can best be understood by examining four key turning points: the "February Adverse Current" of February–March 1967: the Wuhan Incident of late July 1967, the purge of a so-called "516" Group of radicals in early September, and the dismissal of Chief of Staff Yang Chengwu and the disbanding of the Red Guards in the summer of 1968.

Each of these turning points is important both for its origins and for its consequences. Each episode emerged from the tensions within and among the three key vertical networks already discussed. Each reflected, from Mao Zedong's perspective, the unreliability of one or more of the three organizational systems: The February Adverse Current showed that senior Party leaders still resisted the Cultural Revolution and the Red Guard movement;

the Wuhan Incident demonstrated that high-ranking military commanders, particularly at the regional level, tended to side with conservative mass organizations against their radical opponents; and the 516 affair and the disbanding of the Red Guards in mid-1968 reflected the proclivities of the mass movement and, indeed, of the leaders of the Cultural Revolution Group itself, toward violence and disorder.

Together, the three episodes also produced a shift in the balance of power among the three organizational systems that dominated Chinese politics during this period. Although the three networks had begun, at least in theory, as equal participants in the three-in-one combination, by the end of 1967 it was evident that the PLA was well on its way to establishing predominance over both the civilian cadres and the mass organizations. The disbanding of the Red Guards in mid-1968, and the transfer of millions of young people to the countryside, removed these participants from the Chinese political stage altogether.

The February Adverse Current

The Decision on the Cultural Revolution adopted by the Eleventh Plenum in August 1966 had envisioned a mass movement that would be sweeping yet controlled. The emphasis on mass mobilization and mass criticism – particularly on the part of young people – promised to make life much more complex for the nation's Party and government officials. But significant limits were imposed in three areas. First, the cadre policy outlined in the Sixteen Points involved strict criticism but lenient treatment. The Eleventh Plenum had stipulated that most cadres were "good" or "relatively good," and had implied that they could remain at or return to their posts once they had made "serious self-criticism" and "accepted the criticism of the masses." Second, the movement was undertaken in the name of the Party and was to be conducted under the leadership of the CC, if not of the Party apparatus at lower levels. And third, Cultural Revolutionary activities within the PLA were to be insulated from those in the rest of society and placed under the leadership of the Party's MAC rather than that of the Cultural Revolution Group.

By the end of January 1967, however, it was abundantly clear that the Cultural Revolution was overstepping each of these boundaries. A number of ranking cadres, including Peng Zhen and Luo Ruiqing, had been "detained," without any warrant or other legal sanction, by radical mass organizations. Others were paraded through the streets of China's cities, with dunce caps on their heads and placards around their necks listing their "counterrevolutionary offenses." At least one member of the State Council, Minister of Coal

Industry Zhang Linzhi, had been beaten to death, and other high-ranking officials had been physically abused. Liu Shaoqi and Deng Xiaoping had come under virulent verbal attack.

The authorization to mass organizations to "seize power," and the creation of Shanghai Commune, suggested that even the principle of Party leadership was being abandoned, for, as Mao himself pointed out, there was no room for a vanguard Party within the structure of a Paris Commune. What is more, the turmoil of the Cultural Revolution now threatened to spread into the ranks of the armed forces, as the PLA was ordered to intervene in civilian politics in support of the left. And Lin Biao himself seemed eager to incite his followers within the armed forces to criticize, in Red Guard style, those senior marshals, such as Zhu De, He Long, and Ye Jianying, who might challenge Lin's control over the armed forces.[97]

To cope with these problems, the central authorities issued a series of directives and statements throughout the month of February that were intended to limit the chaos being produced by the Cultural Revolution. The attempts at political stabilization proceeded along four tracks. First, as we have already seen, the model of the Paris Commune, which promised direct democracy without Party leadership but would have delivered little but factionalism and disorder, was repudiated by Mao personally. It was replaced by the model of the revolutionary committee and the directives to the PLA to intervene in the Cultural Revolution to support the left – both of which measures were intended to provide an organizational framework for restoring order and discipline to the country. As part of the implementation of the three-in-one combination, the central media began a campaign to publicize Mao's policy of relative leniency toward cadres who had "committed errors" either before the onset, or during the early months, of the Cultural Revolution.

Second, Mao intervened to limit the use of force and violence by Red Guard organizations. Writing to Zhou Enlai on 1 February, Mao criticized the tendency to force cadres under criticism to "wear dunce caps, to paint their faces, and to parade them in the streets." Describing such actions as "a form of armed struggle," Mao declared that "we definitely must hold to struggle by reason, bring out the facts, emphasize rationality, and use persuasion. . . . Anyone involved in beating others should be dealt with in accordance with the law."[98] Similar injunctions against the use of force were contained in a directive issued by the MAC on 28 January, a document said to have been drafted under the sponsorship of such senior military officials as Ye Jianying, Xu Xiangqian, and Nie Rongzhen and then approved by Mao. The

97 "Collection of documents," 19–20, 21; *A Great trial,* 160, 164.

98 JPRS, 49,826, *Translations on Communist China* (12 February 1970), 22.

directive declared: "Arresting people at will without orders is not permitted; ransacking of homes and sealing of doors at will is not permitted. It is not permitted to carry out corporal punishment or disguised corporal punishment, such as making people wear tall caps and black placards, parading them in streets, forcing them to kneel, etc. Earnestly promote civil struggle, resolutely oppose struggle by brute force."[99]

Third, attempts were made to limit the impact of the Cultural Revolution on those state and military organizations that were crucial to the maintenance of economic production and political order. In February, outside mass organizations were ordered to leave all central party departments and those central state ministries and bureaus responsible for national defense, economic planning, foreign affairs, public security, finance and banking, and propaganda; power seizures in the armed forces were limited to such peripheral organizations as academies, schools, cultural organs, and hospitals; and all Cultural Revolution activities of any kind were "postponed" in seven crucial military regions.[100] In addition, the CC and the State Council issued a further directive attempting to preserve the confidentiality of all secret documents and files, including the personnel dossiers of Party and state cadres, which had been the source of much of the evidence used by mass organizations in their criticism of leading officials.[101]

Finally, central directives tried to narrow the scope of activity allowed to mass organizations, to the point that, if these directives had been implemented, the Red Guard movement would have been brought to an end. Mass organizations were told to stop traveling about the country to "exchange revolutionary experiences," and were ordered to return to their native cities and towns. Middle school students were told to return to school, resume classes, and "attend their lessons on the one hand and make revolution on the other." National alliances of Red Guard organizations, which had begun to form spontaneously (or with encouragement from the CRG) during the January Revolution and which potentially threatened to become so powerful that they could not be controlled, were described as "counterrevolutionary organizations" and were ordered to disband immediately. Disgruntled elements of the work force, notably contract workers, temporary laborers, and workers who had been transferred to jobs in border regions, were told that they should stay at their posts and that their demands would be dealt with at a later stage of the Cultural Revolution.[102]

Encouraged by these developments, a group of senior Party leaders from both the civilian and military spheres began to launch an attack on the whole

99 "Collection of documents," 54–5. See also Dittmer, *Liu Shao-ch'i,* 152–3.
100 "Collection of documents," 56, 61, 66, 71–2, 78–9, and 89. 101 Ibid., 84.
102 Ibid., 72, 82, 83, 85, 87–8.

concept of the Cultural Revolution.[103] These officials included Marshals Ye Jianying, Nie Rongzhen, and Xu Xiangqian, and Vice-Premiers Chen Yi, Li Fuchun, Li Xiannian, and Tan Zhenlin. They used the occasion of a series of meetings on "grasping revolution and promoting production" that were convened by Premier Zhou Enlai in mid-February to express their criticism of the Cultural Revolution. These veteran cadres apparently raised four principal issues: whether it was proper to separate the mass movement from the leadership of the Party; whether it was correct to attack so many senior officials; whether it was justified to produce disorder in the armed forces; and, on that basis, whether the Cultural Revolution should be continued or, as these officials clearly believed, be brought to a rapid end.

The most dramatic of these meetings occurred in Huairen Hall, inside the Zhongnanhai complex in Beijing, on an afternoon in mid-February. At this meeting, the contending groups were literally arrayed along two sides of a long table, with Zhou Enlai sitting at one end. To Zhou's left were Chen Boda, Kang Sheng, Xie Fuzhi, and other members of the Cultural Revolution Group; to the prime minister's right were the three marshalls, the five vice-premiers, and State Council officials Yu Qiuli and Gu Mu. The meeting soon turned into a shouting match between the two sides, with Tan Zhenlin, the vice-premier responsible for agricultural work, at one point rising from the table and declaring his intention to resign, only to be restrained by Chen Yi and Zhou Enlai.

An account of the proceedings – distorted, it was later charged – was soon relayed to Mao Zedong by members of the Cultural Revolution Group. Mao was furious at some of the opinions expressed at the meeting, which he considered to be a repudiation of his leadership. Aware of Mao's anger, the radicals soon described these meetings as a "February Adverse Current" (*eryue niliu*) and used them as evidence in their mounting campaign to purge all surviving senior cadres from office.

In some ways, therefore, the result of the meetings in Zhongnanhai was similar to that of the Lushan Conference of the summer of 1959, during the GLF. On both occasions, China was in the midst of a tumultuous mass movement launched by Mao Zedong. In both cases, the disruptive consequences of the campaign had already become apparent, and efforts were underway to limit them. But on both occasions, some senior officials not only criticized the excesses of the campaigns but also expressed some opposition to the movement as a whole. In both cases, Mao took the criticisms as a

103 This account of the February Adverse Current is based on *RMRB*, 26 February 1979, in *FBIS Daily Report: China*, 28 February 1979, E7–20; and the recollections of Nie Rongzhen, in *Xinhua ribao*, 21 and 22 October 1984, in *FBIS Daily Report: China*, 6 November 1984, K21–4. See also Lee, *Politics of the Cultural Revolution*, ch. 6; Daubier, *History of the Cultural Revolution*, ch. 5.

challenge to his personal leadership. As a result, not only did the two movements continue long after their adverse consequences had become clear, but some of the measures originally intended to remedy those consequences were canceled or postponed.

Thus, the February Advent Current had the effect of reradicalizing the Cultural Revolution by discrediting the attempts that had been made earlier that month to restore order. One manifestation of this development was the decision to move criticism of Liu Shaoqi and Deng Xiaoping from Red Guard wall posters and tabloids into the official Party press, albeit through the use of such epithets as "China's Khrushchev" and "The Number Two Party Person in Authority Taking the Capitalist Road." Given the fact that Liu and Deng served, respectively, as president of the Republic and the general secretary of the Party, this step removed any remaining doubts that all cadres throughout the country were legitimate targets of attack. In a related measure, the 16 May Circular of 1966, with its harsh attack on "representatives of the bourgeoisie" in the Party, government, and army, appeared in the public media on the first anniversary of its adoption.

Emboldened by these developments, radical mass organizations issued stronger and more frequent criticisms of a number of surviving civilian officials throughout the spring of 1967. A prominent target was Tan Zhenlin, who had been one of the most active participants in the February Adverse Current and whose outspokenness made him a favorite quarry of the radicals. At the climactic meeting at Huairen Hall, Tan had described Kuai Dafu, the Qinghua University radical who was then one of the darlings of the CRG, as a "counterrevolutionary clown." Tan allegedly sent several written reports to Mao and the CC urging an end to the Cultural Revolution, in one of which he called Jiang Qing a "latter-day Empress Wu Zetian." According to accounts sympathetic to the radicals, Tan had also attempted to reinstate Ministry of Agriculture officials who had been overthrown during the January Revolution.

Another goal of the radicals was the dismissal of Foreign Minister Chen Yi, who like Tan Zhenlin, made no attempt to hide his acerbic attitude toward the Cultural Revolution and the Red Guard movmeent. In one widely circulated although possibly apocryphal account, Chen Yi responded to an unpleasant encounter with one group of Red Guards by waving his own copy of the little red book, the *Quotations from Chairman Mao Zedong,* and saying: "Now it's my turn. Allow me to quote for you from Chairman Mao, page 320. Chairman Mao has said: 'Chen Yi is a good and faithful comrade.' " It was up to the Red Guards to discover that the Chinese edition of the *Quotations* had no such page.[104]

104 Daubier, *History of the Cultural Revolution,* 220.

But the ultimate target of many of the radical mass organizations, and possibly the CRG was Zhou Enlai, who was regarded by the radicals as the "backstage supporter" of the February Adverse Current and the protector of officials such as Tan and Chen. In Beijing, a number of wall posters were displayed that began as attacks on Tan and Chen but ended with criticisms of Zhou Enlai.

In this way, the February Adverse Current placed senior cadres in an increasingly vulnerable and passive position. To be sure, there were still periodic interventions by Mao, reasserting his conviction that 95 percent of China's cadres could be redeemed. Mao and Zhou also attempted to save some cadres from public criticism and physical assault, at least for a time. Zhou himself was protected by Mao, and Zhou worked to protect such officials as Liao Chengzhi, Chen Yi, Li Fuchun, and Li Xiannian. It was at this point that a number of provincial and municipal officials were brought to Beijing, so that their physical safety could be ensured.

But such measures did not protect everyone or prevent the progressive weakening of the political positions of veteran civilian officials. Liu Shaoqi and Deng Xiaoping were placed under house arrest sometime in the summer of 1967. The central CRG came to assume many of the powers of the Politburo and the State Council. And the radicals continued to use the February Adverse Current as evidence that senior cadres opposed the Cultural Revolution, the CRG, and Mao's leadership. Of the three vertical networks in the Cultural Revolution, the veteran officials were now in by far the weakest position.

The Wuhan Incident

Three of the most significant developments in China in mid-1967 were the serious divisions that emerged between radical and conservative mass organizations, between conservative and radical forces within the PLA itself, and between the CRG and the armed forces. The Wuhan Incident of 20 July (referred to in Chinese as the "7/20 Incident," the *qierling shijian,* after the date on which it occurred) provides the best example of the development and implications of these cleavages.[105]

When the PLA was ordered to supervise the formation of revolutionary committees at the provincial and municipal levels across the country, that task was assigned principally to the military regions and to the local and garrison forces under their command. Many regional commanders had close

105 This discussion of the Wuhan Incident is drawn from Chen Zaidao, "Wuhan 'qierling shijian' shimo" (The beginning and end of the "July 20th Incident" in Wuhan), *Gemingshi ziliao,* 2 (September 1981), 7–45; and Thomas W. Robinson, "The Wuhan Incident: Local strife and provincial rebellion during the Cultural Revolution," *CQ,* 47 (July–September 1971), 413–38.

personal associations with the Party officials in the provinces, which disposed them to side with the more conservative mass organizations to protect the Party establishment. Similarly, the PLA's proclivity for maintaining order and discipline placed it in conflict with more radical mass organizations that sought to overthrow all officials and disregarded economic production for the sake of making revolution.

During the month of February, therefore, many regional commanders, using as justification the restrictions on the Cultural Revolution that had recently been issued by the central authorities, began to clamp down on the most obstreperous radical organizations. In the Wuhan Military Region, this involved decisions by the commander, Chen Zaidao, first to dissociate himself from, and then to order the disbanding of, a coalition of radical organizations known as the "Workers' General Headquarters" on the grounds that they were persistently engaging in disruptive activities that endangered both social order and economic stability.

The criticism of the February Adverse Current gave radicals in both Beijing and the provinces the opportunity to protest the "suppression" of leftist mass organizations by the PLA. On 2 April, *Renmin ribao* published an editorial calling for "proper treatment of the Young Generals" (i.e., the Red Guards) that was based on information supplied by disgruntled radicals in the Wuhan and Chengdu military regions. The same week, the CC and the MAC published separate directives that greatly reduced the PLA's ability to suppress radical mass organizations.[106] The directives stripped the armed forces of the authority to declare any mass organization to be counterrevolutionary, to suppress those who criticized military leadership, or to make mass arrests. Henceforth, the power to classify mass organizations was to be made by Beijing alone, and those who had been labeled as counterrevolutionaries by regional military commanders were to be pardoned. The directives were reportedly the result of joint efforts by Lin Biao and members of the CRG, which suggests that, at this point at least, there was still a high degree of cooperation between these two elements of the Maoist coalition.

Because these directives greatly reduced the PLA's ability to restore order, they also significantly increased the degree of conflict between conservative and radical mass organizations. Radicals began to seize weapons from military armories and, in southern China, from shipments of munitions intended for North Vietnam. In some places, the PLA responded by supplying weapons to more conservative organizations. The incidence of armed struggle vastly increased, exacting a toll not only in human lives but also in economic production. In Wuhan, the principal consequence was that the radicals

106 "Collection of documents," 111–12, 115–16.

launched a series of protests and demonstrations calling for a reversal of the "adverse currents" in the city. These activities apprarently received Jiang Qing's personal endorsement.

Because the directives of early April had provided that only the central authorities would have the right to decide on the political orientation of competing mass organizations, Chen Zaidao requested a meeting with Zhou Enlai and the CRG to discuss the situation in Wuhan. According to Chen's own account, the meeting concluded that the behavior of the Wuhan Military Region had been basically correct, and that the radicals in the city should be told to stop attacking it. Unfortunately for Chen, word of this agreement leaked out in Wuhan before it had been officially announced in Beijing, thus leading Jiang Qing to charge that Chen was taking undue advantage of his success, and emboldening her to try to undo the agreement.

Meantime, the struggle among mass organizations in Wuhan intensified. In mid-May there came into existence a conservative umbrella organization known as the "Million Heroes," which took as its program the defense of the military region and the majority of veteran cadres. According to Chen Zaidao, the Million Heroes counted among their membership about 85 percent of the Party members in Wuhan and enjoyed at least the tacit support of most of the local armed forces. Chen claimed that the military region command officially took a neutral position between the competing mass organizations and called for unity between them. But it is likely that the true preferences of Chen and his subordinates were clear to all those involved.

Thus a second series of meetings was held, this time in Wuhan in mid-July, to try again to resolve the problems in the city. Participating in the meetings from Beijing were Zhou Enlai, two representatives of the central military command (Li Zuopeng and Yang Chengwu), two members of the Cultural Revolution Group (Wang Li and Xie Fuzhi), and, for some of the meetings, Mao himself. Both Mao and Zhou now criticized Chen for his disbanding of the Workers' General Headquarters in February and ordered that that organization be reinstated. But Mao apparently urged unity of the competing mass organizations and disclaimed any intention of "knocking down" Chen Zaidao.

Zhou then returned to Beijing, leaving Xie and Wang to convey the results of the meetings to all parties in Wuhan. Fairly or not, the two men presented Mao's and Zhou's instructions as a repudiation of the military region command, a criticism of the Million Heroes, and an endorsement of the city's radical mass organizations. Angered by this development, representatives of the Million Heroes stormed the hotel where Xie and Wang were staying, and then a group of soldiers from the local garrison seized Wang Li, detained him, and possibly beat him. Xie was spared only by his formal position as a vice-premier and minister of public security.

This insurgency was suppressed by dispatching Zhou back to Wuhan to secure Wang Li's release and by mobilizing substantial numbers of naval and airborne forces to seize control of Wuhan. Wang, Xie, and Chen Zaidao all flew off to Beijing, the first two to receive a hero's welcome, the latter to undergo criticism and interrogation.

As in the case of the February Adverse Current, the immediate results of the Wuhan Incident were remarkably limited. Like Tan Zhenlin, Chen Zaidao received much less punishment than one might have expected for his act of disloyalty – for what in Chen's case was portrayed by the radicals as an act of mutiny. He was dismissed as military region commander but was otherwise treated relatively leniently and was rehabilitated less than two years after the fall of Lin Biao. Chen himself has attributed this to the goodwill of Mao and Zhou Enlai, but one also wonders about the degree to which Lin Biao would have welcomed the complete humiliation of a regional commander, even a recalcitrant one, at the hands of the CRG.

The purge of the 516 Group

Although the Wuhan Incident had relatively slight effects on its principal participants, its broader consequences were devastating. Radicals, including members of the CRG, took the occasion to call for a further assault against conservatives and revisionists in both Beijing and the provinces. On 22 July, only two days after the Wuhan Incident, Jiang Qing introduced the slogan "Attack with words, defend with force" (*wengong wuwei*).[107] This was the first time a leader of her rank had endorsed the armed struggles that were sweeping the country, and her statement only complicated any efforts to restore order.

The targets of this upsurge of radicalism included foreign diplomats in China, the Ministry of Foreign Affairs, and Zhou Enlai. Diplomats from a number of countries were harassed, and the British legation was burned to the ground. A young diplomat named Yao Dengshan, who had formerly been stationed in Indonesia, engineered a power seizure in the Foreign Ministry, directed not only against Chen Yi but also, by implication, against Zhou Enlai, who had attempted to protect Chen.[108] Radical wall posters written during this period called for the downfall of the "old government," for the criticism of the "backstage boss of Chen Zaidao," and for dragging out

107 *SCMP, Supplement*, 198 (August 1967), 8.

108 On the struggles in the Ministry of Foreign Affairs during this period, see Melvin Gurtov, "The Foreign Ministry and foreign affairs in the Chinese Cultural Revolution," in Robinson, *Cultural Revolution*, 313–66.

"another Liu Shaoqi, one who has stood guarantee for the greatest number of people."[109] Zhou was apparently detained in his office for two and a half days by radical Red Guards, who wanted to drag him out for "struggle."

The most important target this time was not Zhou Enlai, however, but the PLA itself. An editorial in *Hongqi* in early August called on radicals to strike down the "handful of military leaders taking the capitalist road."[110] That there might be revisionists in the PLA was hardly an unprecedented notion: It had been contained in the 16 May Circular of 1966, as well as numerous editorials in the first half of 1967. But in the aftermath of the Wuhan Incident, such a slogan was explosive and had immediate consequences. Regional commanders, including some closely associated with Lin Biao, came under attack: Huang Yongsheng, commander of the Guangzhou Military Region and an ally of the defense minister, was described as the "Tan Zhenlin of Guangzhou" by radical Red Guards.[111] If not checked, such a formula threatened the ability of the armed forces to maintain any kind of order in China.

Mao, Zhou, and Lin all had common cause for opposing this escalation by the CRG: Lin because it threatened the unity and legitimacy of the armed forces; Zhou, because it threatened his control over foreign affairs and the State Council and brought his own political position under attack; and Mao, because it moved China even further away from the elusive goal of unity that he appeared to seek.

In late August, therefore, the Cultural Revolution Group was reorganized. Four of its most radical members – Wang Li, Mu Xin, Lin Jie, and Guan Feng – were dismissed, and a fifth, Qi Benyu, fell from power four months later. The Party's theoretical journal *Hongqi,* which, under the editorship of Chen Boda, had been the mouthpiece of the Cultural Revolution Group, was forced to suspend publication. This 516 Group (*wuyiliu bingtuan*) – named after the 16 May Circular of 1966 – was accused of using the February Adverse Current as a pretext for criticizing first Yu Qiuli, then Li Xiannian, Li Fuchun, and Chen Yi, all with the ultimate goal of overthrowing Zhou Enlai, himself. The radicals were assigned responsibility for the wall posters attacking Zhou Enlai in August.[112]

On 5 September, all four of the central authorities in China – the CC, the MAC, the State Council, and the CRG – issued a joint directive attempting

109 On the renewed surge of radicalism in this period, see Lee, *Politics of the Cultural Revolution,* ch. 8, and Daubier, *History of the Cultural Revolution,* ch. 8.

110 *HQ,* 12 (August 1967), 43–7.

111 Daubier, *History of the Cultural Revolution,* 207.

112 On the fall of the "516" Group, see *CB,* 844 (10 January 1968); and Barry Burton, "The Cultural Revolution's ultraleft conspiracy: The 'May 16 Group,' " *Asian Survey,* 11.11 (November 1971), 1029–53.

to end armed struggle in the country and to revive the tattered authority of the PLA. Red Guard organizations were forbidden to seize arms from the armed forces, and the army was forbidden to transfer arms to mass organizations without central authorization. The PLA was now allowed to use armed force, as a last resort, against mass organizations that resisted its attempts to restore order.[113]

That same day, in a rambling extemporaneous speech to a Red Guard rally in Beijing, Jiang Qing sought to distance herself and the survivors of the CRG from the four who had been dismissed. Without referring to them by name, she described the 516 Group as a small number of "extreme leftists" who had attempted to seize control of the mass movement. She repudiated the call to "drag out a handful from the PLA" as a "trap" set by these ultra-leftists to bring China into chaos. While still defending her own formulation "attack with words, defend with force," she now argued that the situation in China did not warrant the use of force in any circumstance. Despite doing her utmost to deny any personal responsibility for the 516 Group, Jiang Qing had in fact been forced into making a statement that amounted to self-criticism.[114]

The chaos of August and the 516 affair had important implications for the course of the Cultural Revolution. First, as we will see, it shifted the focus of the Cultural Revolution from the destruction of the old political order to the creation of a new one. In September, Mao Zedong revealed his "great strategic plan" for the rest of the Cultural Revolution, based on his travels across the country throughout the summer. In essence, this called for an end to disorder and the most rapid possible progress toward the formation of revolutionary committees in the twenty-two provincial-level units in which they had not yet been organized.

As that process got underway toward the end of 1967, it appeared that the events of the summer had also readjusted the balance between the radical mass organizations and the regional military commanders in favor of the latter. In the spring of 1968, as we shall see shortly, there was a final resurgence of radicalism, but it never reached the high water mark set in August 1967. When forced to choose between the mass movement and the PLA – between continued disorder and the only hope for political stability – Mao selected the latter. As a result, the military was now able to move relatively steadily toward institutionalizing its dominant position in the new provincial revolutionary committees.

The 516 affair also changed the pattern of alignment among the central leadership in Beijing. Of all the leading members of the CRG, the one most closely associated with the victims of the 516 purge, and thus the one most

113 *SCMP*, 4026 (22 September 1967), 1–2. 114 Ibid., 4069 (29 November 1967), 1–9.

seriously weakened by it, was Chen Boda. All five victims of the 516 affair had apparently served as deputy chief editors of *Hongqi* directly under Chen; all had been closely associated with Chen in the radical intellectual and journalistic establishment in Beijing in the early 1960s; and the closing of *Hongqi* could only be interpreted as a repudiation of Chen's editorial policies. Realizing that his position was weakening, Chen Boda now sought new sources of political support. He appears to have chosen Lin Biao. This was a marriage of political convenience that offered advantages to both parties. Chen could offer Lin the ideological and theoretical trappings that had been noticeably lacking in Lin's own public pronouncements. In turn, Lin could grant Chen the backing of the vertical network – the PLA – that now seemed certain to emerge from the Cultural Revolution in the strongest position. It is highly plausible that Chen Boda began to work more closely with Lin Biao in late 1967, offering the ghostwriting services he had earlier provided to Mao and the CRG.

The purge of Yang Chengwu and the suppression of the Red Guards

The 516 affair notwithstanding, there was one final resurgence of radical mass activity in the spring and early summer of 1968. This brief radical revival was made possible by a still mysterious leadership shuffle within the PLA: the dismissal, in March 1968, of Acting Chief of Staff Yang Chengwu, along with the political commissar of the air force and the commander of the Beijing Military Region.[115]

The purge of Yang Chengwu appears to have been a prototypical example of the cleavages produced by the Cultural Revolution: the divisions between radicals and conservatives in the provinces, the conflict betweeen Zhou Enlai and the CRG, and the tensions within the PLA among representatives of different field army factions. All of these conflicts seem to have played their part in Yang's sudden fall from grace.

Toward the end of 1967, Yang had been responsible for resolving a number of provincial disputes, just as he had accompanied Mao to Wuhan on a similar assignment in July. In both Shanxi and Hebei, Yang supported the conservative factions against their more radical opponents. In Shanxi, Yang refused to back the radical chairman of the provincial revolutionary committee against a challenge from more conservative military officers in the province; and in Hebei, Yang supported a coalition of conservative military units

115 Accounts of the dismissal of Yang Chengwu by participants in the event include those by Lin Biao, in Kau, *Lin Piao,* 488–50; by Nie Rongzhen, in *Xinhua ribao* (9 and 10 October 1984), in *FBIS Daily Report: China,* 5 November 1984, K18–21; and by Fu Chongbi, in *Beijing wanbao,* 12 April 1985, in ibid., 1 May 1985, K9–10. See also Harvey W. Nelsen, *The Chinese military system: An organizational study of the Chinese People's Liberation Army,* 97–101.

and mass organizations against a similar coalition of radicals that had been endorsed by Xie Fuzhi.

What is more, Yang Chengwu and Fu Chongbi, the commander of the Beijing Military Region, took Zhou Enlai's side in the premier's dispute with the CRG and radical mass organizations. It was apparently Yang and Fu who provided military protection for a number of civilian and military leaders close to Zhou. And after the dismissal of Qi Benyu, Yang encouraged Fu Chongbi to send a small force of soldiers to the offices of the CRG, nominally to arrest Qi's followers and to search through the files looking for evidence of wrongdoing. Whatever Yang's ultimate intentions, it was not unreasonable for the remaining members of the CRG, including Jiang Qing and Xie Fuzhi, to believe that Yang was looking for materials that might incriminate them.

Finally, Yang was also involved in internecine struggles within the armed forces. Although Yang had some historical ties to Lin Biao, he had served in the final years of the revolution in the Fifth Field Army, not the Fourth. Yang's relations with Lin's closest lieutenants, including Air Force Commander Wu Faxian, were quite strained, and Lin apparently came to doubt Yang's loyalty. At the same time, Lin could use the purge of Yang Chengwu as a way of attacking his own rivals Nie Rongzhen and Xu Xiangqian, who had served as Yang's superiors in the Fifth Field Army.

Yang Chengwu was therefore accused of having supported a second February Adverse Current, which, like the first, had as its intention the protection of conservative forces, particularly senior cadres, against attack by the radicals. The immediate effect of his dismissal was twofold. First, it enabled Lin Biao to strengthen his control over the Administrative Office of the Party's MAC, which exercised day-to-day control over the armed forces. Lin was now in a position to staff this crucial body with five people personally loyal to him: Wu Faxian, Huang Yongsheng, the commander of the Guangzhou Military Region who now replaced Yang Chengwu as chief of staff; Li Zuopeng, the political commissar of the navy; Qiu Huizuo, the head of military logistics; and Ye Qun, Lin's own wife.[116]

The second consequence of the Yang Chengwu affair was to legitimate a resurgence of activity by radical mass organizations in protest against their alleged underrepresentation on the new revolutionary committees. Violence was particularly widespread in Shanxi, Hebei, Shandong, and Guangdong. At Beijing's Qinghua University, rival factions barricaded themselves in campus buildings behind cement barricades and wire fences, and used catapults to launch chunks of brick and concrete against their adversaries.

116 Sun, *Lishi jiangyi*, 2.270–1.

In provinces such as Guangxi, where the revolutionary committee had not yet been formed, factional violence flared to even greater proportions. Competing organizations stole weapons from trains carrying military supplies to Vietnam and fought each other with machine guns, bazookas, and even antiaircraft weapons. The victims of the violence, often bound and trussed, floated down the Pearl River, to be discovered in the waters off Hong Kong.

It was the violence at Qinghua University that caused the final suppression of the mass movement and the demobilization of the Red Guards. Mao ordered troops from Unit 8341, the elite security force protecting central Party leaders, together with workers from a knitwear mill and a printing plant in Beijing, to enter Qinghua in late July. A few days later, on the night of 28 July, Mao met with student leaders from both Qinghua and Peking universities. Noting that Kuai Dafu had complained that a "black hand" had sent workers to the universities to suppress the Red Guards, Mao declared: "The black hand is still not captured. The black hand is nobody else but me." Mao complained that the Red Guards were engaged in factional armed struggle, instead of carrying out the Cultural Revolution in a principled way:

> In the first place, you are not struggling; in the second place, you are not criticizing; in the third place, you are not transforming. Yes, you are struggling, but it is armed struggle. The people are not happy. The workers are not happy. The peasants are not happy. Peking residents are not happy. The students in most of the schools are not happy. Most students in your school are also not happy. Even within the faction that supports you there are people who are unhappy. Can you unite the whole country this way?[117]

Unless the Red Guards could shape up, Mao warned, "we may resort to military control [of the schools], and ask Lin Piao to take command."

Shortly thereafter, just as Mao had threatened, "worker-peasant Mao Zedong Thought propaganda teams," supervised by military officers, began to enter China's major universities. On 5 August, Mao sent some mangoes, which he had received from a group of Pakistani visitors, to the propaganda team at Qinghua as a personal endorsement of their activities. Mao justified the suppression of the Red Guards by arguing that the leadership of the Cultural Revolution should be in the hands of the "working class" rather than students. In the middle of the month, Mao issued a directive declaring that "it is essential to bring into full play the leading role of the working class in the Great Cultural Revolution." A few weeks later he ordered that the "masses of the workers," in cooperation with "Liberation Army fighters," should take the lead in the "proletarian revolution in education."[118]

Toward the end of August, Yao Wenyuan, whose article on Hai Rui had

117 *Miscellany of Mao Tse-tung Thought*, 2.470. 118 Ch'en, *Mao papers*, 105.

launched the Cultural Revolution, now wrote another essay, which, in essence, brought the Red Guard stage of the movement to an abrupt end. Entitled "The working class must exercise leadership in everything," Yao's article was a scathing critique of the excesses of the mass movement, written by a man who had ridden to power on its back. The anarchism and factionalism of the Red Guard movement were ascribed to the "petty-bourgeois" outlook of its participants. "The facts show," Yao stated, "that under [the] circumstances it is impossible for the students and intellectuals by themselves alone to fulfill the task of struggle-criticism-transformation and a whole number of other tasks on the intellectual front; workers and People's Liberation Army fighters must take part, and it is essential to have strong leadership by the working class."[119] Under such leadership, the remaining mass organizations were disbanded and Red Guard newspapers and periodicals ceased publication.

By the end of the year, the demobilization of the Red Guard organizations had been accompanied by the physical removal of millions of youths from the cities to the countryside. In December, Mao issued yet another directive that deemed it "very necessary for educated young people to go to the countryside to be reeducated by the poor and lower-middle peasants. Cadres and other city people should be persuaded to send their sons and daughters who have finished junior or senior middle school, college, or university to the countryside." By the end of 1970, about 5.4 million youths had been transferred to rural areas, mostly in their home provinces, but often to remote border and frontier regions. Few had any hope that they would ever be able to return to their homes.[120]

THE RECONSTRUCTION OF THE POLITICAL SYSTEM

With the purge of the 516 Group in late August 1967 and the demobilization of the Red Guards the following spring, the emphasis of the Cultural Revolution shifted from the destruction of the old order to the creation of a new one – from what the Chinese called a period of "struggle and criticism" (*doupi*) to one of "criticism and transformation" (*pigai*). Reconstructing the political system involved two principal elements: the completion of the organization of revolutionary committees and the rehabilitation of the Party itself.

What is particularly noteworthy about this period is that the formal structure of China's "new" political order differed very little from that which

119 *PR*, 11.35 (30 August 1968), 3–6.
120 Thomas P. Bernstein, *Up to the mountains and down to the villages: The transfer of youth from urban to rural China*, 57–8.

existed on the eve of the Cultural Revolution.[121] The movement began with utopian rhetoric about "overthrowing" bureaucracy and establishing direct democracy along the lines of the Paris Commune. But when the work of political reconstruction actually got underway, the blueprint that was followed was much less visionary. Officials were "reeducated" in "May 7 cadre schools" (*wuqi ganxiao*) where, through physical labor and political study, they were supposed to cultivate a more selfless and efficient style of work. The revolutionary committees, and the bureaucracies they supervised, were supposed to be smaller, more capable, and more committed to Maoist values than their predecessors. And because they contained a small number of mass representatives, they were presumed to be more responsive to popular concerns. Still, the organizational policies of the period of reconstruction made it clear that government institutions would still be structured along bureaucratic lines, and that the CCP would remain a Leninist organization that would guide the work of the revolutionary committees.

What distinguished the new political system from its predecessor was less its structure than its staffing. Military officers played a much more important role, particularly at higher levels, than at any time since the early 1950s. Veteran civilian officials were pushed aside in favor of men and women who were less experienced, less educated, less cosmopolitan, and less qualified – although not necessarily any younger. Party recruitment was resumed and emphasized the absorption of large numbers of mass activists from the Red Guard movement. Moreover, Party and state organizations were plagued by serious factionalism as a result of the unresolved conflicts among the victims, activists, and bystanders of the Cultural Revolution.

Mao's "strategic plan"

In September 1967, Mao Zedong devised what was described as his "great strategic plan" for concluding the Cultural Revolution. While defending the disorder of the previous twenty months ("Don't be afraid of making trouble. The bigger the trouble we make, the better"), Mao acknowledged that this troublemaking had served its purpose and should now be brought expenditiously to an end. "The car will overturn if it is driven too fast," Mao warned. "It is therefore necessary to be cautious."[122]

The immediate task, as Mao saw it, was to complete the formation of China's twenty-nine provincial revolutionary committees. Up to then, the process had been agonizingly slow: Only six revolutionary committees had been established at the provincial level between January 1967 and the end of

121 For a description and evaluation of organizational changes wrought by the Cultural Revolution, see Harding, *Organizing China*, chs. 8 and 9, passim.

122 *CLG*, 2.1 (Spring 1969), 3–12.

July. "What we must principally accomplish now," Mao instructed, "is the great alliance and the three-in-one combination." This Mao hoped could be done by January 1968.

Mao appears to have believed that two guidelines would facilitate the formation of the remaining revolutionary committees. To begin with, Mao was now prepared to see the PLA dominate the process, in fact if not in name, and was therefore willing to testify to the army's authority and loyalty and to forgive its occasional failures. As he put it in late summer, "The army's prestige must be resolutely safeguarded. There can be no doubt whatsoever about that." In a rather magnanimous reference to the Wuhan Incident, Mao continued: "It was unavoidable that the army should have made mistakes in tackling for the first time the large scale fighting tasks of supporting the left, supporting industry and agriculture, and carrying out military control and military training. The chief danger at the moment is that some people want to beat down the PLA."[123] The importance Mao assigned to the army was reflected in his reluctance to see the PLA become a target of general criticism after the dismissal of Yang Chengwu the following spring.[124]

As a second guideline, Mao recognized that the formation of revolutionary committees could be accelerated if their mass representatives were drawn from a broad spectrum of mass organizations rather than solely from those that had been endorsed by local military commanders. This concept of inclusiveness was embodied in an instruction that the PLA should "support the left, but no particular faction," and in Mao's directive that "the working class has absolutely no reason to split into two hostile factional organizations."[125] The promulgation of Mao's ideal of national unity was accompanied in late 1967 by increasingly virulent press attacks against factionalism and anarchism, both of which were now described as manifestations of petty bourgeois ideology.

The completion of the formation of revolutionary committees occurred in two stages after Mao's tour of China in the summer of 1967. Between August 1967 and July 1968, committees were formed in eighteen provincial-level units. The last five, in such deeply divided provinces as Fujian and Guangxi, and in such sensitive border areas as Xinjiang and Tibet, were created after the final suppression of the Red Guard movement in July. In general, the committees were produced in a series of negotiated settlements, in which local military commanders and Beijing leaders sought to impose unity on competing mass organizations.

Because of Mao's stipulation that they should be broadly representative of

123 Nelsen, *Chinese military system*, 83.

124 Philip Bridgham, "Mao's Cultural Revolution: The struggle to consolidate power," *CQ*, 41 (January–March 1970), 5.

125 *Jiefangjun bao*, 28 January 1968, in *PR*, 11.5 (2 February 1968), 8–9; and Ch'en, *Mao papers*, 146.

a wide range of viewpoints, the revolutionary committees were generally large and unwieldy organs, composed of between 100 and 250 members each.[126] The standing committees of the revolutionary committees, however, was more manageable bodies, often smaller than the comparable Party and state leadership groups that had existed before the Cultural Revolution. The composition of the standing committees varied with the trends of the times, with more mass representatives appointed in more radical periods and fewer named in more moderate phases. Although mass representatives secured a reasonable number of places on the revoultionary committees formed during this period (61 of the 182 chairmen and vice-chairmen), effective power was concentrated in military hands. Of the twenty-three chairmen, twelve were troop commanders and five were professional commissars. Of the first vice-chairmen, fourteen were commanders and five were commissars. All the rest were Party officials; not one was a mass representative.[127]

Over the longer term, Mao also foresaw the reconstruction of the Party once the revolutionary committees had been established as provisional governments in all China's provinces. From the beginning, the Chairman had seen the Cultural Revoultion as a movement to purify the Party, not to destroy it. The purpose of the Cultural Revolution committees, as described in the Sixteen Points of the Eleventh Plenum, had been to serve as a bridge linking the Party to the masses, not to act as a replacement for the Party. Similarly, the purpose of the Red Guards had been to overthrow "capitalist roaders" in the Party but not the Party as an organization. Mao's principal objection to applying the model of the Paris Commune to China in early 1967, it will be recalled, was that there was no clear role for the Party in such a structure. "If everything were changed into a commune, then what about the Party? Where would we place the Party? . . . There must be a party somehow! There must be a nucleus, no matter what we call it. Be it called the Communist Party, or Social Democratic Party, or Kuomintang, or I-kuan-tao, there must be a party."[128] If the Party had been set aside by the Red Guards and the revolutionary committees, that was a temporary phenomenon, not an ultimate goal of the Cultural Revolution.

Now, in September 1967, Mao believed that the time had come to think about the reestablishment of the Party. "The party organization must be restored," Mao said, and "party congresses at all levels should be convened." Mao was optimistic that this could be accomplished relatively quickly: "I see

126 Frederick C. Teiwes, *Provincial leadership in China: The Cultural Revolution and its aftermath*, 27, 29.
127 These data are based upon those in Richard Baum, "China: year of the mangoes," *Asian Survey*, 9.1 (January 1969), 1–17.
128 *Miscellany of Mao Tse-tung Thought*, 2.453–4. The Yiguandao, in Communist historiography, was a reactionary secret society during the Nationalist period.

that it will be about this time next year [i.e., September 1968] that the Ninth Party Congress is convened."[129] Mao assigned the task of rebuilding the Party to Zhang Chunqiao and Yao Wenyuan, with Xie Fuzhi, who was responsible for political and legal affairs during the Cultural Revolution, also playing an active role. On 10 October, Yao presented a preliminary report that laid out some basic principles for Party reconstruction.[130] Yao's report envisioned a top-down process, which would begin with the convocation of a national Party Congress to select a new CC and to adopt a new Party constitution. The delegates to the Congress would be appointed by the central authorities after "negotiation" with the provinces. After the conclusion of the Party Congress, the rebuilding of the Party at lower levels could begin. New Party committees at each level would embody, according to Yao's report, no fewer than three three-in-one combinations: Each would be a combination of the old, the middle-aged, and the young; of workers, peasants, and soldiers; and of masses, army officers, and cadres.

On the basis of Yao's report, the CC issued, on 27 November, a "Notice on the opinions about convening the Ninth Party Congress" and then, on 2 December, a further document "On the opinions regarding the rectification, restoration, and reconstruction of the Party structure." These documents followed the outlines of Yao's report, with two important amendments. First, the "Notice" added a decision that had been implicit from the beginning of the Cultural Revolution: that Lin Biao was now to become Mao's successor. "A great many comrades suggest," the "Notice" declared, "that the Ninth Party Congress vigorously propagandize the fact that Vice-Chairman Lin is Chairman Mao's close comrade-in-arms and successor, and that this be written down into the Ninth Party Congress's reports and resolutions so as to further enhance Vice-Chairman Lin's high prestige."

Second, the CC documents announced the resumption of "Party life" at the basic levels. Provisional Party branches, often called "Party core groups," were formed within revolutionary committees to guide the rectification of the Party at the basic levels. Their task was to begin a "purification of the ranks" of Party members, expelling those who had been shown to be revisionist, and absorbing "fresh blood" from the activists of the Cultural Revolution.

The Twelfth Plenum

Although the reconstruction of the Party was thus anticipated in the fall of 1967, the process did not really get underway until the formation of the last

129 *CLG*, 2.1 (Spring 1969), 3–12.

130 On Yao's report and the two subsequent Party documents, see Lee, *Politics of the Cultural Revolution*, 296–301.

provincial-level revolutionary committees in September 1968. Once that crucial task had been accomplished, however, the surviving central leadership quickly convened the Twelfth Plenum of the CC, which was held in Beijing between 13 and 31 October.

Like the Eleventh Plenum, in August 1966, the Twelfth Plenum was a rump session of the Party's CC. Only fifty-six full members of the CC attended the meeting, representing a bare quorum of the surviving members of the body.[131] Furthermore, like its predecessor, the Twelfth Plenum was packed with people who were not CC members. But where the additional observers in 1966 had been the "revolutionary students and teachers" from the Red Guard movement, in 1968 the extra participants were members of the CRG, representatives of the provincial revolutionary committees, and "principal responsible comrades of the Chinese People's Liberation Army" – the officials, in other words, who were now the survivors and beneficiaries of the Cultural Revolution.[132]

The radicals entered the meeting with ambitious goals: to win endorsement of the events of the preceding two years and to complete the purge of the highest levels of the Party establishment. They were more successful in achieving the first objective than the second. The plenum's final communiqué praised the accomplishments of the Cultural Revolution, lauded Mao's theory of "continuing the revolution under the dictatorship of the proletariat," held that Mao's "important instructions" and Lin's "many speeches" given during the movement were "all correct," and described the CRG as having "played an important role in the struggle to carry out Chairman Mao's proletarian revolutionary line." It endorsed Mao's assessment that the Cultural Revolution was "absolutely necessary and most timely for consolidating the dictatorship of the proletariat, preventing capitalist restoration, and building socialism." It declared that "this momentous Cultural Revolution has won [a] great and decisive victory." And, with an eye to the future, the plenum adopted a new draft Party constitution and announced that the Ninth Party Congress would be held "at an appropriate time."[133]

In perhaps its most important decision, the plenum announced that Liu Shaoqi was being dismissed from all his government and Party positions, and

131 On the participants in the Twelfth Plenum, see Hu Yaobang, "Lilun gongzuo wuxu hui yinyan" in *Zhonggong shiyijie sanzhong quanhui yilai zhongyang shouyao jianghua ji wenjian xuanbian* (Introduction to theoretical work conference), in (Compilation of major central speeches and documents since the Third Plenum of the Eleventh Central Committee), 2.55; and Deng Xiaoping, "Remarks on successive drafts of the 'Resolution on certain questions in the history of our Party since the founding of the People's Republic of China,' " in *Selected works of Deng Xiaoping (1975–1982)*, 290.

132 For the communiqué of the Twelfth Plenum, see *PR*, 11.44 (1 November 1968), supplement, v–viii.

133 The text of the draft Party constitution is in Union Research Institute, *Documents of the Chinese Communist Party Central Committee, September 1956–April 1969*, 235–42.

was being expelled from the party "once and for all." The plenum's resolution on the subject – the first time Liu had been criticized by name in an official public document during the Cultural Revolution – disparaged Liu in inflammatory language. He was described as a "renegade, traitor, and scab hiding in the Party," as "a lackey of imperialism, modern revisionism, and the Guomindang reactionaries," and as having "committed innumerable counter-revolutionary crimes." And yet, the supporting documents circulated after the plenum (at least those available in the West) dealt principally with Liu's activities in 1925, 1927, and 1939, during the early stages of the revolution, and said little about his behavior after the establishment of the People's Republic.[134] This would suggest that the plenum was unable to agree on how to characterize Liu's post-1949 activities.

During the small group sessions surrounding the meeting of the CC, the CRG and Lin Biao launched a vigorous attack upon the February Adverse Current of 1967. Curiously, Mao's closing speech to the plenum took a more conciliatory view of that episode than he had in the past. The Chairman now described the infamous meeting in Huairen Hall as an occasion for members of the Politburo to exercise their right to express their opinions on critical political issues. Nonetheless, Mao did nothing to prevent the plenum's communiqué from denouncing the February Adverse Current as an attack on the "proletarian headquarters with Chairman Mao as its leader and Vice Chairman Lin as its deputy leader."

But despite their best efforts, the radicals were unable to secure the removal from the CC of any of the most active participants in the February Adverse Current, save for Tan Zhenlin, who had already been purged the previous year. Li Fuchun, Li Xiannian, Chen Yi, Ye Jianying, Xu Xiangqian, and Nie Rongzhen all remained on the CC. Above all, the CRG's proposal that Deng Xiaoping not only be removed from the CC but also be expelled from the Party altogether, along with Liu Shaoqi, was rejected after a personal intervention by Mao Zedong.[135]

Beyond these points, the Twelfth Plenum made few important policy decisions. It spoke vaguely of a "revolution in education" that would be undertaken under the leadership of the workers' propaganda teams but did not indicate what specific new programs would be adopted. Similarly, it described the Cultural Revolution as "promoting the emergence of a new leap in our socialist construction" but announced no new economic plans. The

134 The indictment of Liu Shaoqi, entitled "Report on the examination of the crimes of the renegade, traitor, and scab Liu Shao-ch'i," is in URI, *Documents of the Central Committee,* 243–50.

135 For these aspects of the Twelfth Plenum, see Sun, *Lishi jiangyi,* 2.274; and the recollections of Nie Rongzhen, in *Xinhua ribao,* 23 October 1984, in *FBIS Daily Report: China,* 7 November 1984, K20–1.

Cultural Revolution may have been intended to repudiate some of the economic and social policies of the early 1960s that Mao regarded as revisionist, but the plenum indicated that no new revolutionary policies had yet been established to replace them.

The Ninth Party Congress

The Ninth Party Congress, convened in April 1969, reflected many of these same trends. Much of the political report, delivered to the Congress by Lin Biao, was an attempt to justify the Cultural Revolution as a "new and great contribution to the theory and practice of Marxism-Leninism."[136] Lin praised both the army and the CRG for their achievements since 1966 and, in a veiled reference to surviving senior civilian cadres, again criticized the February Adverse Current (here described as an "adverse current lasting from the winter of 1966 through the spring of 1967") as a "frenzied counterattack" on the Cultural Revolution that was intended to "reverse the verdict on the bourgeois reactionary line."

On matters of domestic policy, Lin's political report – like the communiqué of the Twelfth Plenum – said virtually nothing. It simply noted that the economic situation was good – that there had been "good harvests," "a thriving situation in industrial production," a "flourishing market," and "stable prices" in the preceding years – and concluded that it was "certain that the great victory of the Great Proletarian Cultural Revolution will continue to bring about new leaps forward on the economic front." It also claimed that the seizure of power in "departments of culture, art, education, the press, health, etc." would end the domination of these sectors by "intellectuals" and "persons of power taking the capitalist road," but it did not indicate what new policies would result. The report also referred at some length to the expulsion of old members from the Party and the recruitment of new ones, but it did not provide any fresh clues as to the process by which this would occur.

The contribution of the Ninth Party Congress to China's political reconstruction, then, lay in the decisions it took about the new Party constitution and central Party leaders. Compared to the previous Party constitution, adopted by the Eighth Party Congress in 1956, the new document stressed

136 Lin Biao's report is in *PR*, 12.18 (30 April 1969), 16–35. The drafting of this report is subject to various interpretations. Zhou Enlai reported at the Tenth National Congress in 1973 that the first draft had been written by Lin Biao and Chen Boda but was "rejected by the Central Committee." See *The Tenth National Congress of the Communist Party of China (Documents)*, 5. More recently, Hu Yaobang has claimed that the report was written by Kang Sheng and Zhang Chunqiao. See Hu, "Lilun gongzuo wuxu hui yinyan," 57.

the guiding role of Mao Zedong Thought and the importance of continued class struggle – neither of which concepts had appeared in the earlier version.[137] In addition, opportunities for membership in the Party were now offered only to those who had the proper class background. The 1956 constitution had opened the doors of the Party to anyone who "works and does not exploit the labor of others" and who accepted the responsibilities of Party membership. The 1969 constitution, in contrast, restricted Party membership principally to those from worker, poor and lower-middle peasant, and military backgrounds.

The most important feature of the new constitution, however, was its brevity and lack of precision. Containing merely twelve articles, the new document was only about one-fifth as long as the 1956 constitution. The new constitution contained no reference to the rights of Party members. No attempt was made to specify in any detail the structure and powers of Party committees and various levels, the procedures for disciplining Party members, or the relation between the Party and the state – all of which had been important features of the earlier constitution. Eliminated from the Party structure were the Secretariat, which had supervised the central Party apparatus; the office of the general secretary, who had overseen day-to-day Party functions; and the entire network of control commissions, which had been responsible for inner-Party discipline. Thus, the organizational structure for the Party that emerged from the Ninth Party Congress was significantly more flexible, less institutionalized, and therefore more open to manipulation by elements of the top leadership, than had been the case before the Cultural Revolution.

The Ninth Party Congress also selected a new central leadership not only for post-Cultural Revolution China but, it appeared, for the post-Mao era as well. Lin Biao's position as sole vice-chairman and as "Comrade Mao Zedong's close comrade-in-arms and successor" was established as a formal provision of the new Party constitution. Only 54 of the 167 members of the previous CC were reelected at the Ninth Party Congress. Those who were removed from the Party elite at this point included a large number of provincial and regional Party leaders who had not been appointed to revolutionary committees, as well as important economic specialists, such as Bo Yibo and Yao Yilin, who had previously served in the State Council. After a protracted campaign by the radicals, most of the veteran civilian and military officials connected with the February Adverse Current lost their positions on the Politburo, although they retained their memberships in the CC. The

137 The 1969 Party constitution is in *PR*, 12.18 (30 April 1969), 36–9. The 1956 constitution is in URI, *Documents of the Central Committee*, 1–30.

most prominent victim of the Ninth Party Congress was Deng Xiaoping, who was dropped from the CC but who still was not criticized by name in the official Congress documents.

The delegates to the Congress, and the CC it elected, gave plain evidence of the effects of the Cultural Revolution on the Chinese political system. First, they illustrated the preeminence of the military. An analysis of the films of the Congress revealed that approximately two-thirds of the 1,500 delegates appeared in military uniforms. Of the CC, 45 percent were military representatives, compared with 19 percent of the CC elected at the Eighth Party Congress in 1956.[138] The rise of the military came at the expense of both civilian officials, who were the main targets of the Cultural Revolution, and mass representatives, who might have been expected to be its principal beneficiaries. Mass representation on the new central Party organs was minimal. To be sure, 19 percent of the CC members were "of the masses," but they tended to be older workers and peasants rather than the younger mass activists who had emerged during the Cultural Revolution. Greater representation of military officers also meant a decline in representation of civilian officials, particularly from the State Council, who fell to about a third of CC membership. Given the differences in education and career path between the PLA and those government leaders, this change in the composition of the CC was correlated with a decline in the level of education and amount of experience in foreign countries.

Second, and equally important, the Congress demonstrated the decentralization of power that had been produced during the Cultural Revolution. In 1956, about 38 percent of the CC held provincial offices, and the rest occupied positions in the central military, Party, and government agencies. In 1969, in contrast, fully two-thirds of the CC members were provincial representatives. This trend was not, however, so clearly reflected on the Politburo. Only three of the members of the Politburo on the eve of the Cultural Revolution could be classified as provincial or regional representatives. By comparison, two civilian officials with exclusively provincial responsibilities (Ji Dengkui and Li Xuefeng) and three local military commanders (Chen Xilian, Xu Shiyou, and Li Desheng) were elected to the Politburo at the Ninth Party Congress.

Third, the Ninth CC saw a shift of power to a more junior generation of leaders, although not to a younger one. Indeed, "inexperience without

138 For analyses of the composition of the Ninth Central Committee, and comparisons with its predecessor, see Gordon A. Bennett, *China's Eighth, Ninth, and Tenth Congresses, Constitutions, and Central Committees: An institutional overview and comparison;* and Robert A. Scalapino, "The transition in Chinese Party leadership: A comparison of the Eighth and Ninth Central Committees," in Scalapino, *Elites*, 67–148.

youth" is one way of characterizing the CC produced by the Ninth Party Congress. Of the 170 full members of the Committee, 136 (and 225 of the 279 full members and alternates) had not served on the CC before the Cultural Revolution. But, with an average age of about sixty, the Ninth CC was only slightly younger than the one it replaced and was substantially older than the Eighth CC had been at its election in 1956. Furthermore, the Ninth CC was of distinctly lower rank than its predecessor because of the influx of regional military leaders, second-echelon provincial officials, and mass representatives into CC membership.

In a final development, the Politburo approved by the CC illustrated the continued fragmentation of power at the highest levels in Beijing. The twenty-five full and alternate members of the Politburo included, in addition to Mao and Lin, five central military officials closely linked to Lin, six people associated with the CRG, three regional and provincial military commanders not closely tied to Lin, two senior civilian officials attacked during the Cultural Revolution, one other PLA marshal to counterbalance Lin Biao, three mid-level Party officials who had risen to power as a result of the Cultural Revolution, and three veteran Party leaders well past their prime. The composition on the Politburo thereby reflected the divisions among the victims, survivors, and beneficiaries of the Cultural Revolution; between the military and the civilian radicals who had come to power during the movement; between Lin Biao and his rivals in the central military leadership; and between the central military establishment and the regional commanders.

In short, despite the successful attempts to end the violence of the Red Guard movement and the preliminary efforts to begin the reconstruction of the Chinese political system, the Ninth Party Congress left the country with a volatile political situation. The outlines of post–Cultural Revolution policy were undecided; power was divided among groups with noticeably different interests; and the structure of the Party and state was vague and uninstitutionalized. Although he was the nominal successor to Mao Zedong, Lin Biao's power base was highly fragile. Over the next two years, Lin would attempt to strengthen it by perpetuating military dominance of civilian affairs and by putting forward a policy platform that he believed would have wide appeal. These efforts, however, ultimately led to Lin's physical demise, as well as his political downfall.

CONCLUSIONS

How can we fairly judge the origins and development, consequences, and significance of this first stage of the Great Proletarian Cultural Revolution in

China? The task is an unusually difficult one, bedeviled by the complexity of the events, the uncertain reliability of the information contained in the Red Guard press, and the lack of clear historical perspective on events that, as of this writing, took place less than twenty years ago.

The job of analysis is also entangled in the extreme and changing evaluations of the Cultural Revolution that have appeared in both China and the West since the Ninth Party Congress. During the late 1960s and early 1970s, the Chinese described the Red Guard movement as a creative and effective way, in Mao Zedong's words, "to arouse the broad masses to expose our dark aspect openly, in an all-round way, and from below." In the official interpretation of the day, the Cultural Revolution enabled the Chinese working classes to "smash revisionism, seize back that portion of power usurped by the bourgeoisie," and thereby "ensure that our country continues to advance in giant strides along the road of socialism."[139] As late as 1977, even after the purge of the Gang of Four, Chinese leaders continued to portray the Cultural Revolution in glowing terms. "Beyond any doubt," Hua Guofeng declared at the Eleventh Party Congress, "it will go down in the history of the proletariat as a momentous innovation which will shine with increasing splendor with the passage of time." Indeed, Hua promised that further Cultural Revoultions "will take place many times in the future" as a way of continuing the struggle against bourgeois and capitalist influences within the Party.[140]

Within two years, however, the official Chinese line had completely changed. In mid-1979, Ye Jianying described the Cultural Revolution as "an appalling catastrophe suffered by all our people." The interpretation that has prevailed more recently is that China was never in danger of a capitalist restoration, that Mao's diagnosis of China's political situation in 1966 "ran counter to reality," that the programs produced in the latter stages of the Cultural Revolution were impractical and utopian, and that the Red Guards were naive and impressionable youth led by "careerists, adventurists, opportunists, political degenerates, and the hooligan dregs of society."[141] An official resolution on Party history, adopted in 1981, condemned the Cultural Revolution as causing "the most severe setback and the heaviest losses suffered by the party, the state, and the people since the founding of the People's Republic."[142]

139 These quotations are drawn from Lin Biao's report to the Ninth Party Congress, in *PR*, 12.18 (30 April 1969), 21.

140 *The Eleventh National Congress of the Communist Party of China (Documents)*, 51–2.

141 *Beijing Review*, 5 October 1979, 15, 18, 19.

142 "Resolution on certain questions in the history of our party since the founding of the People's Republic of China," *FBIS Daily Report: China*, 1 July 1981, K14.

The reassessment of the Cultural Revolution in China has been fully replicated in the West. During the 1970s, the Cultural Revolution was described by many Americans as a worthy example of Mao's desire to preserve communitarian, egalitarian, and populist values in the course of economic development and of his conviction that "bureaucracy and modernization do not necessarily lead to an improved quality of life." The origins of the movement were said to lie in Mao's "noble vision" of a society in which "the division involving domination and subjection will be blurred, the leaders will be less distinguishable from the led . . . , and the led will take part more directly in the policy-making process." It was believed that the Cultural Revolution would devise socioeconomic programs that would prevent China from "ossifying in the morass of bureaucratism and statism."[143]

As the Chinese have become more critical of the Cultural Revolution, so too have Western observers. Mao's "fanaticism" has been compared to that of Hitler and Stalin, and the Cultural Revolution has been likened to the Inquisition and the Holocaust. The origins of the movement are traced not to a noble vision, but to a perverted perception of China's social and poitical problems in the mid-1960s. The decade from 1966 to 1976 is portrayed as a period of "chaos and destruction" that produced "one of the worst totalitarian regimes the ancient land had ever seen." By "destroy[ing] the intellectuals, wip[ing] out the universities, and . . . wreck[ing] what there was of China's economy, the Cultural Revolution set back China's modernization for at least a decade."[144]

These rapidly changing interpretations of the Cultural Revolution shoud raise doubts about our abilities to portray accurately and fairly the tumultuous events of the late 1960s. Nonetheless, what is now known about the Cultural Revolution suggests the following assessment of the origins and consequences of the movement.

Origins

The ultimate responsibility for the Cultural Revolution rests squarely with Mao's diagnosis of the problems confronting Chinese society in the early and mid-1960s. It cannot be denied that many of the shortcomings Mao identified were indeed rooted in observable reality. Local Party organizations, particularly in the countryside, had become seriously corrupt and ineffective. Higher-level administrative agencies, both state and Party, were overstaffed,

143 These quotations are drawn from Harry Harding, "Reappraising the Cultural Revolution," *The Wilson Quarterly*, 4.4 (Autumn 1980), 132–41.

144 These quotations are taken from Harry Harding, "From China, with disdain: New trends in the study of China," *Asian Survey*, 22.10 (October 1982), 934–58.

underskilled, and enmeshed in bureaucratic routine. The social and economic policies introduced in the aftermath of the GLF were reviving industrial and agricultural performance, but at the cost of growing inequality between skilled and unskilled workers, between communes blessed with fertile land and those to whom nature had been less kind, between bright students and their more mediocre classmates, and between urban dwellers and rural folk.

But Mao characterized these problems in extreme form. He chose to interpret the emergence of bureaucratism and inequality as signs that China was proceeding along a revisionist course, and to trace their origins to the presence of disguised "capitalists" and "bourgeois elements" at the highest levels of Party leadership. In so doing, Mao brought his lifelong concern with class struggle in China to its logical conclusion. For most of the first two-thirds of his life, Mao had waged revolution against those whom he considered to be the enemies of the Chinese people. For a short period in the mid-1950s, after the unexpectedly successful collectivization of agriculture and nationalization of industry, Mao briefly considered the notion that class struggle in his country might now basically be over. But it was difficult for him to hold to such a conclusion for long. By the time of the Anti-Rightist Campaign in late 1957, he had developed the view that the struggle between antagonistic classes continued to be the principal political contradiction in the socialist period, just as it had been in China's presocialist years. And if not by the Lushan Plenum of 1959, then certainly by the Tenth Plenum in January 1962, Mao had come to the conclusion that the focal point of this class struggle was inside the leadership of the Party itself.

Thus, contemporary Chinese leaders and intellectuals are correct in saying that Mao was accustomed to seek the "class origins" (*jieji genyuan*) of problems in Chinese society and to interpret differences of opinion inside the Party as evidence of class struggle. As one Chinese historian has concisely put it, "Mao thought that inequalities and shortcomings in society were a sign that class struggle had not been handled well."[145]

Mao was also strongly influenced by developments in the Soviet Union in the late 1950s and early 1960s. Confronted with evidence of Moscow's attempts to manipulate China's foreign policy and to control its economy, and concerned by signs of growing inequality and stagnation inside the Soviet Union, Mao reasoned that the great-power chauvinism and revisionism

145 Shao Huaze, "Guanyu 'wenhua da geming' de jige wenti" (On several questions concerning the "Great Cultural Revolution"), in Quanguo dangshi ziliao zhengji gongzuo huiyi he jinian Zhongguo gongchandang liushi zhounian xueshu taolun hui mishu chu (Secretariat of the National Work Conference on Party Historical Materials and the Academic Conference in Commemoration of the Sixtieth Anniversary of the Chinese Communist Party), ed., *Dangshi huiyi baogao ji* (Collected reports from the Conference on Party History), 252.

apparent in Soviet foreign and domestic policy could only reflect the degeneration of the leadership of the Communist Party of the Soviet Union (CPSU). Once having reached this conclusion, Mao logically inferred that the risk of a similar retrogression existed in China as well.

In his analysis of the Soviet Union, Mao stressed the consequences of the political succession from Stalin to Khrushchev. Although Mao had been quick to criticize Stalin's shortcomings, he was still persuaded that Stalin remained, on balance, a great Marxist revolutionary. Concerning Khrushchev, the Chairman reached the opposite conclusion. From the Twentieth Congress of the CPSU on, Mao appears to have become ever more persuaded that Stalin's successor was himself a revisionist, whose rise to power had made possible nothing less than the restoration of capitalism in the birthplace of the October Revolution. Given Mao's own advanced years in the mid-1960s, the lesson was poignant. As he said to Ho Chi Minh in June 1966, "We are both more than seventy, and will be called by Marx someday. Who our successors will be – Bernstein, Kautsky, or Khrushchev – we can't know. But there's still time to prepare."[146]

Mao's strategy for dealing with the emergence of revisionism in the course of succession is also of crucial importance in understanding the origins and outcomes of the Cultural Revolution. Mao's approach was to call on the country's university and middle school students to criticize capitalist tendencies in China, first on their own campuses and then at higher levels of the Party bureaucracy. Paradoxically, however, Mao's view of Chinese youth in the mid-1960s was tinged with large doses of skepticism. In 1965, he told Edgar Snow that since the young people of China had not yet personally experienced their own revolution, they might "make peace with imperialism, bring the remnants of the Chiang Kai-shek clique back to the mainland, and take a stand beside the small precentage of counter-revolutionaries still in the country."[147] But Mao seemed confident – unwarrantedly so, as later developments would prove – that relying on the youth would serve to temper them as well as to purify the Party. In this sense, the Cultural Revolution was to provide a revolutionary experience for an entire new generation of Chinese, even as it offered a means of testing the revolutionary commitment of an older generation of Party officials.

The strategy was characteristically Maoist in at least two regards. First, it embodied long-standing populist elements in his thinking: his conviction that even the vanguard Party needed to be rectified and reformed through criticism from the people it led, and his belief that the masses of China should be encouraged to become involved in even the highest affairs of state.

146 Shao, "Guanyu . . . jige wenti," 356. 147 Mao is quoted in Snow, *Long revolution*, 221–2.

In the fall of 1967, in evaluating the results of the Cultural Revolution, Mao would stress the degree to which this populist ideal had been realized: "The important feature of this excellent situation is the full mobilization of the masses. Never before in any mass movement have the masses been mobilized so broadly and deeply as in this one."[148]

Second, Mao's strategy for the Cultural Revolution reflected his tendency to rely on the unreliable in uncovering the darker side of Party leadership. For Mao deliberately to seek criticism of the Party from those very groups that lacked firm commitment to socialism was not unprecedented. In the mid-1950s, he had done so from intellectuals during the Hundred Flowers Campaign. During the Socialist Education Campaign of the early 1960s he had mobilized the peasantry to purify the rural Party organization, although he simultaneously acknowledged the existence of spontaneous capitalist tendencies even among the poorer peasants. And now, in the mid-1960s, he mobilized millions of students – at best naive and immature; at worst, in Mao's own words, ready to "negate the revolution" – to attack revisionism in the Party.[149]

Although this strategy was characteristic of Mao, it was still highly unorthodox for the Party. As Frederick Teiwes has demonstrated, the mobilization of students to criticize "Party persons in authority taking the capitalist road" ran counter to at least three major Party traditions: that Party leaders should not be penalized for their views on matters of policy, and should be allowed to retain their opinions even if they were in the minority; that Party rectification campaigns should result in mild sanctions rather than "merciless blows"; and that mass participation in Party rectification, if allowed at all, should be under the firm leadership either of the regular Party apparatus or ad hoc Party work teams.[150] What is more, by launching the Cultural Revolution through irregular procedures, in the face of reluctance or opposition from the greater part of the central Party leadership, Mao simultaneously violated a fourth norm as well: that of collective leadership and majority rule.

Only a leader with Mao's unique authority within the Chinese Communist movement could have successfully abandoned all these simultaneously. It is no exaggeration, therefore, to conclude that the principal responsibility for the Cultural Revolution – a movement that affected tens of millions of Chinese – rests with one man. Without a Mao, there could not have been a Cultural Revolution.

But if Mao was a necessary condition for the Cultural Revolution, he was

148 Stuart R. Schram, *The political thought of Mao Tse-tung*, rev. ed. 370.

149 Snow, *Long revolution*, 223.

150 Frederick C. Teiwes, *Leadership, legitimacy, and conflict in China: From a charismatic Mao to the politics of succession*, ch. 3.

not a sufficient one. To begin with, Mao had, as we have seen, crucial political resources in addition to personal legitimacy. These included, first, a sizable popular base. This mass support included both the sincere and the opportunistic, both the enthusiastic and the acquiescent. Some participated out of personal devotion to Mao, the man who had liberated their country from imperialism and warlordism. Others joined the Cultural Revolution for the same reason that so many supported reform in the 1980s: their concern that a Soviet model of development would take China down the road of ossification, inequality, and authoritarianism. Still others became Red Guards and revolutionary rebels because of specific grievances against particular cadres. As a former Red Guard has put it, Chinese used the Cultural Revolution to "get back at their superiors for everything from tiny insults to major abuse of policy."[151]

Over time, this mass base began to dissipate as many of those who participated in the Cultural Revolution became disillusioned with the violence and chaos it engendered. Nonetheless, Mao was able to mobilize enough mass support in late 1966 and early 1967 to shake the CCP to its very foundations. And for this, the Chinese people themselves must bear some accountability.

Mao also relied on political support within China's national leadership. As we have repeatedly emphasized in this chapter, Mao's resources included a group of ambitious political ideologues and organizers in both Beijing and Shanghai who could develop more systematically his rather inchoate observations about the dangers of revisionism in China, enhance Mao's personal charisma through the manipulation of the mass media, mobilize the disenchanted sectors of urban society, and, to a degree, direct the activities of the mass movement. At the same time, Mao enjoyed the support of important elements of the PLA, particularly Lin Biao and major figures in the high command, who provided political support to the Chairman in early 1966, gave logistical assistance to the Red Guard movement later that year, overthrew the Party establishment in early 1967, and then undertook the restoration of order between mid-1967 and mid-1969.

But responsibility must also be assigned to the rest of the Party establishment for not resisting Mao more vigorously. The official Chinese version of the Cultural Revolution now places great stress on the opposition to Mao, at both central and local levels, that emerged after January 1967. The February Adverse Current of 1967 is singled out for particular credit as an example of "unceasing struggle" carried out by the Party against the Cultural Revolution. But by this time the Cultural Revolution had already received the

151 Liang Heng and Judith Shapiro, *Son of the revolution*, 47.

formal endorsement of the Eleventh Plenum of the CC. The forces of mobilization, conflict, and chaos were already irreversible.

The Party establishment might have been able to stop the Cultural Revolution if, earlier, it had acted in a more unified way to oppose Mao rather than acceded to his decisions. Of particular importance was Zhou Enlai's assistance in securing the wider publication of Yao Wenyuan's article on Hai Rui in November 1965, his involvement in the criticism of Peng Zhen in April 1966, his defense of radical students such as Kuai Dafu in September and of the CRG as late as December 1966, and his failure to associate himself unambiguously with the February Adverse Current of February 1967. Of special interest is the revelation that Zhou was the author of one of the most vitriolic denunciations of bureaucracy to come out of the Cultural Revolution, a document previously attributed to Mao Zedong.[152] This suggests that Zhou may have genuinely believed that the danger of bureaucratic rigidification required drastic measures. Alternatively, Zhou may have supported Mao for reasons of personal loyalty or self-preservation. In either event, Deng Xiaoping later acknowledged that Zhou had done things during the Cultural Revolution for which he later had been "forgiven" by the Chinese people.[153]

But Zhou should not be singled out for blame. Ye Jianying and Yang Chengwu were involved in drafting the report justifying the purge of Luo Ruiqing.[154] Deng Xiaoping appears to have joined Zhou in the criticism of Peng Zhen in April 1966. And, more generally, the entire Politburo consented to the dismissal of Luo Ruiqing, the reshuffling of the Beijing municipal Party committee, and the purge of the Party Secretariat and Propaganda Department in May 1966, and to the adoption of the Sixteen Points on the Cultural Revolution at the Eleventh Plenum in August.

On the complexity of the Party leadership in the early stages of Mao's assault against it, the official resolution on Party history is silent. But Chinese historians have been more forthcoming. As one has put it, the Politburo may have adopted such measures as the 16 May Circular without believing in them, or even because it felt compelled to do so; but it endorsed Mao's decisions nonetheless, and must therefore "bear some responsibility" for the Cultural Revolution.[155]

152 *RMRB*, 29 August 1984, in *FBIS Daily Report: China*, 31 August 1984, K1–4.

153 Deng Xiaoping, "Answers to the Italian journalist Oriana Fallaci," in *Selected works of Deng Xiaoping*, 329–30.

154 Lieberthal, *Research guide*, 243, 249.

155 Jin Chunming, " 'Wenhua da geming' de shinian" (The decade of the "Great Cultural Revolution"), in Zhonggong dangshi yanjiuhui, (Research Society on the History of the Chinese Communist Party), ed., *Xuexi lishi jueyi zhuanji* (Special publication on studying the resolution on history), 159–60, and Shao, "Guanyu . . . jige wenti," 378.

In explaining the acquiescence of the Party establishment in the spring and summer of 1966, the Chinese have emphasized the importance of Mao's personal authority over the rest of his colleagues on the Politburo and the CC. This implies that Mao enjoyed charistmatic standing among the Party leadership, as well as among the Chinese masses. It further suggests that his ability to lead the CCP to victory against enormous odds in the late 1930s and 1940s had given him an air of infallibility that had been only slightly tarnished by the disaster of the GLF.

Recent Chinese accounts have also revealed that Mao was, in effect, presenting the Party with a choice between Lin Biao and Liu Shaoqi as his successor, and that many Party leaders initially agreed that Lin was the better man. In the words of Deng Liqun, a man who was Liu Shaoqi's secretary before the Cultural Revolution and who was responsible for propaganda work in the early 1980s, Mao's preference for Lin "could not be said to have been without support within the Party." This was because, compared to Liu Shaoqi, Lin was more loyal to Mao, appeared to have a deeper commitment to ideology, and certainly had a better understanding of military matters. At a time when China was faced with the escalation of American involvement in the Vietnam conflict and a deepening military confrontation with the Soviet Union, many senior Party leaders apparently were persuaded by the argument that "to run a country and a Party like ours well, it won't do only to know politics and not military matters."[156]

Just as Mao can be held accountable for the origins of the Cultural Revolution, so too must he bear much of the blame for its outcomes. Many of the most devastating consequences of the movement – particularly the violence, disorder, and loss of life – can be considered the predictable, if not inevitable, results of the strategy that Mao employed. In mobilizing the masses, Mao sanctioned the use of highly inflammatory rhetoric, casting the movement as nothing less than a Manichaean struggle between the forces of revolution and counterrevolution in China. He brought to the surface deep cleavages and grievances within Chinese society without creating any mechanisms for organizing or directing the social forces he unleashed. He seems to have envisioned a self-disciplined revolutionary movement, but he produced a divided and factionalized force over which he, the CRG, and even the army could exercise only limited control. He expected Party cadres to welcome and support mass criticism of their own leadership, and he reacted in disappointment and outrage when, not surprisingly, they attempted to suppress or manipulate the mass movement in order to preserve their own positions.

The flaw in Mao's strategy, in other words, was that he waged only half a

156 Deng Liqun, "Xuexi 'Guanyu jianguo yilai dangde ruogan lishi wenti de jueyi' de wenti he huida" (Questions and answers in studying the "Resolution on certain historical questions since the founding of the state").

revolution between 1966 and 1969. He failed to design a viable and enduring alternative political order to replace the one he sought to overthrow, or to transform the political resources he had mobilized from a destructive force into a constructive one. In this sense, the Cultural Revolution was the second unsuccessful Chinese revolution of the twentieth century. In 1911, Sun Yatsen had succeeded in overthrowing the Manchu dynasty; but he was unable to create effective republican institutions to replace the fallen monarchy, and China fell under military rule. In the late 1960s, Mao succeeded in seizing power from the Party establishment, but he was unable to design effective populist institutions to replace the Leninist Party-state. Once again, political power fell into the hands of the Chinese military.

In Mao's defense, perhaps the most that can be said is that at the height of the Cultural Revolution, he did try to moderate its destructive impact on the Party apparatus and on society as a whole. Mao attempted to prevent armed struggle and physical persecution, as is apparent in a number of central directives that he authorized forbidding beating, house raiding, looting, incarceration, and destruction of personal property.[157] He criticized the factionalism that had plagued the mass movement and called on revolutionary committees to include representatives of all competing mass organizations. Mao not only repeatedly emphasized that the majority of cadres were good, but he was also personally responsible for protecting a number of high-ranking officials, the most important of whom was Zhou Enlai, against attack.[158]

The problem was that these interventions were not completely successful in controlling the factionalism and violence of the Cultural Revolution. In the final analysis, the only way in which Mao could have regained control over the movement would have been to repudiate it completely. And this he refused to do. He never abandoned the concept of the Cultural Revolution, the theory behind it, or the strategy it reflected. Nor did Mao repudiate his own lieutenants who were responsible for much of the violence. To the end of his life, he continued to believe that the Cultural Revolution was a timely, necessary, and appropriate device for ensuring that China would follow a truly revolutionary course after his death.

Consequences

There is a certain all-or-nothing quality to the Cultural Revolution between 1966 and 1969. Important sectors of Chinese society were affected in a

157 See, in particular, the 6 June 1967 directive prohibiting "armed struggle, illegal arrest, looting, and sabotage," in *CCP documents of the Great Proletarian Cultural Revolution,* 463–4. Recent Chinese accounts attribute this directive to Mao personally. See Jin, " 'Wenhua da geming' de shinian," 164.

158 Witke, *Comrade Chiang Ch'ing,* 363.

thorough manner, whereas other equally important parts of the country were hardly touched at all. Similarly, some of the consequences of the Cultural Revolution have already proved ephemeral, whereas others will continue to affect China for decades to come.

The Cultural Revolution largely spared rural China and the 620 million people who lived there in the late 1960s. The exceptions were a relatively small number of communes close to large and medium-sized cities, especially those in suburban counties located within municipal boundaries. These suburban areas did experience some Cultural Revolutionary activities as peasants engaged in struggles for power at the commune and brigade levels and participated in mass protest in the neighboring cities. In his careful study of the Cultural Revolution in the Chinese countryside, Richard Baum has identified 231 places in which rural disorder was reported by the Chinese press between July 1966 and December 1968. Of these, 42 percent were in suburban counties, especially around Beijing, Shanghai, and Guangzhou; and another 22 percent were within 50 kilometers of large of medium-sized cities. Less than 15 percent, in contrast, were more than 100 kilometers away from an urban place. Baum's findings do not imply, of course, that only 231 communes were directly involved in the Cultural Revolution. But his data do suggest that the Red Guard stage of the Cultural Revolution did not have a deep impact far beyond the major cities of China. It was, instead, principally an urban movement.[159]

If the countryside was touched lightly, relatively few urban residents remained unaffected by the Cultural Revolution, since the movement was conducted in virtually every high school, factory, university, office, and shop in China. In an interview with Yugoslav journalists in 1980, Hu Yaobang estimated that 100 million people – roughly half the urban population and virtually all those of working age – were treated "unjustly" during the Anti-Rightist Campaign, the Cultural Revolution, and other Maoist movements. Allowing for a bit of exaggeration, we can regard Hu's figure as a reasonably accurate indication of the comprehensive impact of the Cultural Revolution on urban China.[160]

Economically, China suffered surprisingly little from the Red Guard phase of the Cultural Revolution. Grain production rose in both 1966 and 1967, fell substantially in 1968, but then regained 1966 levels in 1969. The poor performance registered in 1968 may have been partly related to the political

159 Richard Baum, "The Cultural Revolution in the countryside: Anatomy of a limited rebellion," in Robinson, *Cultural Revolution,* 367–476.

160 Tanjug, 21 June 1980, in *FBIS Daily Report: China,* 23 June 1980, L1. Some Western accounts mistakenly assign responsibility for these 100 million victims to the Cultural Revolution alone; see, for example, *Washington Post,* 8 June 1980.

turmoil of that year, but it also reflected the fact that the weather in 1968 was significantly worse than in 1967. Moreover, the rapid recovery of grain production the following year suggests that the Cultural Revolution had only limited and temporary effects on agricultural output.

A similar pattern was evident in industry. Industrial output fell some 13 percent in 1967 as a result of the disruption of the normal work of both factories and transportation lines. As a result, state revenues, state expenditures, and investment in state-owned enterprises also fell precipitously in 1967 and 1968. But the industrial economy quickly revived. Industrial output in 1969 once again exceeded the level of 1966, and state revenues, expenditure, and investment followed suit the following year.[161] By the beginning of 1971, according to Western estimates, industrial production had achieved full recovery, regaining the levels that would have been projected from the growth rates of the early 1960s.[162]

Thus the effects of this phase of the Cultural Revolution on the Chinese economy were limited in extent and duration; they were certainly far less severe than those of the GLF one decade earlier. But the consequences of the Cultural Revolution for cultural and educational affairs were much greater.[163] The Chinese stage and screen stopped presenting any work of art other than a handful of "revolutionary" films, operas, and ballets written under the sponsorship of Jiang Qing. The sale of traditional and foreign literature was halted, and libraries and museums were closed. Universities were shut down in the summer of 1966, and middle schools suspended instruction in the fall, so that their students could participate in the Cultural Revolution. Although middle school education was resumed the following spring, college classrooms remained dark for the next four years. It was only in the summer of 1970 that the first new class of university students was recruited, and even that process was limited to a fraction of China's institutions of higher learning.

From a strictly curricular perspective, the damage of the early phase of the Cultural Revolution to the Chinese educational system was only moderate. More detrimental were policies implemented after 1969 that politicized the curriculum, reduced the length of training, required lengthy doses of physical labor, and selected students on the basis of class background rather than

161 Data on industrial and agricultural output are drawn from Arthur G. Ashbrook, Jr., "China: Economic modernization and long-term performance," in U.S. Congress, [97th], Joint Economic Committee, *China under the Four Modernizations*, 1.104. Data on state revenues, expenditures, and investment are from *Beijing Review*, 19 March 1984, 27–8.

162 Robert Michael Field, Kathleen M. McGlynn, and William B. Abnett, "Political conflict and industrial growth in China: 1965–1977," in U.S. Congress, [95th], Joint Economic Committee, *Chinese economy post-Mao*, 1.239–83.

163 This discussion of the effects of the Cultural Revolution on the educational system draws upon Marianne Bastid, "Economic necessity and political ideals in educational reform during the Cultural Revolution," *CQ*, 42 (April–June 1970), 16–45.

academic promise. On the other hand, many cultural and educational institutions sustained serious physical damage. The collections of many libraries and museums were damaged, disrupted, or dispersed. Red Guards defaced or destroyed numerous historical sites, religious structures, and cultural artifacts. And the military, once it had been sent into the universities to restore order, requisitioned many campus buildings for its own use. Many of these effects were not fully remedied until well after the death of Mao Zedong in 1976.

The most serious impact of the Cultural Revolution on the cultural and educational spheres was on scholars, writers, and intellectuals. No precise figures are yet available on the persecution and harassment suffered by cultural circles between 1966 and 1969, but the trial of the Gang of Four in 1980–1 has provided some illustrative data. The indictment in that trial claimed that 2,600 people in literary and art circles, 142,000 cadres and teachers in units under the Ministry of Education, 53,000 scientists and technicians in research institutes, and 500 professors and associate professors in the medical colleges and institutes under the Ministry of Public Health were all "falsely charged and persecuted," and that an unspecified number of them died as a result.[164] Most suffered at the hands of relatively autonomous Red Guard organizations in their own units, but a minority were victimized by Jiang Qing personally. Concerned that damaging information about her career in Shanghai in the 1930s might be released by her opponents, Jiang Qing organized groups to search the homes of writers and artists in Shanghai to confiscate letters and photos relating to her past.

The persecution of intellectuals was fully matched by the maltreatment of Party and government leaders. The rate of political purge was extremely high. It reached 70–80 percent at the regional and provincial levels, where four of six regional Party first secretaries and twenty-three of twenty-nine provincial Party first secretaries fell victim to the Cultural Revolution. In the central organs of the Party, the purge rate was about 60–70 percent. Only 9 Politburo members out of 23, 4 secretariat members out of 13, and 54 CC members out of 167 survived the Cultural Revolution with their political positions intact. Only about half of the fifteen vice-premiers and forty-eight cabinet ministers remained on the State Council at the end of the movement.[165]

The rates of purge were not, of course, uniform throughout the bureaucracy.[166] Studies of the organizational impact of the Cultural Revolution have

164 *A great trial*, 182–3.

165 On the rates of purge, see Bennett, *China's Eighth, Ninth, and Tenth Congresses, Constitutions, and Central Committees;* Donald W. Klein and Lois B. Hager, "The Ninth Central Committee," *CQ*, 45 (January–March 1971), 37–56; Scalapino, "The transition in Chinese Party leadership"; and Teiwes, *Provincial leadership in China*.

166 Richard K. Diao, "The impact of the Cultural Revolution on China's economic elite," *CQ*, 42 (April–June 1970), 65–87.

suggested that the turnover was higher in some functional areas (especially agriculture, industry, planning, and culture and education) than in others (such as national defense, and finance and trade); that, predictably, the higher one's rank, the more likely one was to fall victim to the Cultural Revolution; and that, somewhat ironically, non-Party cadres suffered somewhat less from the Cultural Revolution than did officials who were Party members. All told, the level of purge can be estimated in a rough manner by reference to a Chinese claim that some 3 million cadres who had been labeled as revisionists, counterrevolutionaries, or "Party persons in authority taking the capitalist road" were rehabilitated in the late 1970s. This may have represented as much as 20 percent of a bureaucracy of 15 to 20 million officials.

The Cultural Revolution was not characterized by the great purge trials and mass executions of the Stalin period. Most victims of the Cultural Revolution survived the movement and secured their political rehabilitation after the death of Mao and the purge of the Gang of Four. But the experience for China's bureaucracy was still not pleasant. A large number – again perhaps as many as 3 million – were sent to May 7 cadre schools, usually in rural areas, to engage in physical labor, conduct intense ideological study, and forge "close ties" with neighboring peasants. Although some officials, especially those younger in years, found the experience to be rewarding in ways, the May 7 schools represented a true physical hardship for older cadres, especially those who remained in the schools, separated from their families, for a long period of time.

Other officials experienced fates worse than a stint in the May 7 cadre schools. Some were placed in isolation in their own work units, where they underwent severe psychological harassment aimed at inducing confessions of political malfeasance. An unknown number were beaten and tortured. Some were killed, some died in confinement, and others committed suicide. Liu Shaoqi was placed under house arrest in 1967, beaten by Red Guards later that year, and died in prison in 1969. He Long, a marshal in the Chinese armed forces, was hospitalized for the malnutrition he suffered while under house arrest and then died after glucose injections complicated his diabetic condition.[167] Other ranking officials known to have died during the Cultural Revolution include Peng Dehuai and Tao Zhu, both members of the Politburo; two Beijing municipal Party secretaries, Liu Ren and Deng Tuo; Wu Han, the author of *Hai Rui,* who was concurrently a deputy mayor of Beijing; Shanghai's Mayor Cao Diqiu and Deputy Mayor Jin Zhenghuan; and Vice-Minister of Public Security Xu Zirong. Luo Ruiqing, the former chief of staff, attempted suicide.

167 David Bonavia, *Verdict in Peking: The trial of the Gang of Four,* passim.

The children of leading officials also suffered political persecution and physical torture. Some, like Deng Xiaoping's daughter, joined their parents in internal exile. Others, like Deng's son, were crippled for life at the hands of Red Guards. An adopted daughter of Zhou Enlai's was allegedly tortured by Red Guards. And others were subject to intense criticism and abuse because they were the sons and daughters of their parents.

The total number of deaths attributable to the Cultural Revolution is not known with certainty. Of the 729,511 people named in the indictment of the Gang of Four as having been deliberately "framed and persecuted" by them and their associates, 34,800 are said to have been persecuted to death. These include nearly 3,000 people in Hebei, 14,000 in Yunnan, 16,000 in Inner Mongolia, and more than 1,000 in the PLA.[168] Fox Butterfield attributes to a well-informed Chinese the estimate that 400,000 people died during the Cultural Revolution.[169] Extrapolations based on deaths in particular provinces, such as Fujian and Guangdong, are somewhat higher, ranging between 700,000 and 850,000, but these figures are based on provinces that experienced higher than the average level of violence and disorder. It might not be unreasonable to estimate that approximately half a million Chinese, out of an urban population of around 135 million in 1967, died as a direct result of the Cultural Revolution.

Beyond the immediate effects just considered, the events of 1966–9 also had longer-term consequences. To begin with, the Red Guard years produced an explosive combination of a deeply fragmented leadership and weak political institutions. Leadership at the central and provincial levels was divided among veteran Party officials, regional and main force military commanders, mass representatives, and lower-level cadres who had risen to power as a result of the Cultural Revolution. The authority of the Party itself had been brought into serious question, but the institutions that had taken the place of the Party, the revolutionary committees, were described as only temporary organs of government. The Cultural Revolution had discredited the socioeconomic policies and organizational norms of the early 1960s, but the new leadership had not yet come to any consensus on what should replace them.

This fragmentation of power established the patterns that dominated Chinese politics for the next seven and a half years, until the death of Mao Zedong in September 1976. There was, first, a struggle between civilian and military leaders over the role of the armed forces in post–Cultural Revolution China. Lin Biao's unsuccessful effort to institutionalize military dominance of civilian poiltics was followed, after his death in the fall of 1971, by more effective attempts to disengage the PLA from civilian affairs. The events of

168 *A great trial*, 21. 169 Fox Butterfield, *China: Alive in the bitter sea*, 348.

the late 1960s also produced a struggle over the definition of post–Cultural Revolution programs, pitting more conservative officials, who sought to resurrect the policies of the early 1960s, against radical leaders, who wished to formulate a set of more egalitarian and populist programs in industry, agriculture, and intellectual life. And the fragmentation of power so evident in the Politburo selected at the Ninth Party Congress led ineluctably to a serious struggle to succeed Mao Zedong among the officials (like Deng Xiaoping) who had been victims of the Cultural Revolution, the ideologues and organizers (like Jiang Qing) who had led it, the military leaders (like Lin Biao) who had ended it, and the middle-level cadres (like Hua Guofeng) who had survived it. In short, the "manic phase" of the Cultural Revolution from 1966 to 1969 produced seven or eight years of lesser turmoil, resolved only by the purge of the Gang of Four in October 1976 and the emergence of Deng Xiaoping's reform program in December 1978.

The restoration of order in 1976, and the initiation of economic and political reform in 1978, did not, however, mark the final elimination of the effects of the Cultural Revolution. Two enduring consequences remained very much in evidence as China entered the mid-1980s. One was a deep-seated factionalism infecting almost every government agency, industrial and commercial enterprise, and Party committee. Factional conflict was created by the struggle for power at the height of the Cultural Revolution, was preserved by the insistence on broad consensus and representation in the formation of revolutionary committees, and was strengthened by the rehabilitation of large numbers of victims of the Cultural Revoultion during the mid-1970s. Such conflict seriously reduced the effectiveness of political institutions by making both policy decisions and personnel appointments captives of factional considerations.

Second, the events of the late 1960s created a serious crisis of confidence among the young people of China. For the more than 4 million high school and university students – many of them former Red Guards – who were relocated to the countryside in 1968 and 1969, the suspension of normal patterns of schooling meant a dramatic and often devastating change in their future prospects. Although almost all were able to return to their homes by the end of the 1970s, the fact that most were unable to complete their education meant that their career paths and life chances had changed for the worse. The fact that so calamitous an event was launched in the name of Marxism served to undermine their faith in ideology, and the inability of the Party to prevent the Cultural Revolution served to weaken their confidence in the existing political system.

The process of disillusionment occurred for different youth at different times. For some, the turning point was the restriction and eventual demobilization of the Red Guards after the January Revolution, a clear sign that those who had once been told that they were the leaders of the movement were now to be made its scapegoats. For others, the critical event was the discovery of the poverty of the Chinese countryside, whether during the exchange of revolutionary experiences in 1966–7 or during the rustification programs of later months. One former Red Guard, who experienced both of these awakenings, spoke for an entire generation when he vented his rage and frustration in an interview with American scholars after his escape to Hong Kong in 1967:

> Nothing can describe my anger at the way the situation had developed in March [1967]. Those sons of bitches (the PLA and the military training platoon in his middle school] had thrown us all out the window. . . . We had virtually succeeded in seizing power, in making a true revolution. Now the bastards had thrown it all away.
>
> [My time in the countryside] was another eye-opening experience. [The peasants] ceaselessly complained about their hard life. They said they had little food to eat, even in good crop years. . . . Times had been better, they felt, even under the Kuomintang, when a man could work, save some money, invest it, and improve himself. . . . They also preferred Liu Shao-ch'i to Mao because they identified Liu with the private plots which gave them the chance to put some savings [away] and move up the ladder. . . . I had thought that only capitalist roaders and counterrevolutionaries had such thoughts. But I had just heard them from the mouth of a revolutionary poor peasant who had worked for the Party for more than twenty years. . . . In ten short days, my world outlook had been challenged by the reality of peasant life and attitudes.[170]

The effects of that disillusionment also varied from individual to individual. For some young people, China's so-called Lost Generation, the consequences were political cynicism, a passivity and lack of initiative in work, and a growing materialism and acquisitiveness. This crisis of confidence among youth, coupled with the decline in the rule of law during the Cultural Revolution, is widely believed to have contributed to a rise in crime and antisocial activities in the late 1970s. For others, especially those who had received some college education before 1966, time in the countryside provided an opportunity for reading, reflection, and debate about the future of their country. Many of these former Red Guards later constituted a group of younger intellectuals who, in the late 1970s and early 1980s, helped to formulate the general principles and specific policies for the economic reforms of the post-Mao era.

As of the late 1980s, in fact, it appeared that, paradoxically, the chaos of the Cultural Revolution had been an important condition for the reforms of

170 Bennett and Montaperto, *Red Guard*, 214–17 and 222–4, passim.

the post-Mao era. The fact that so many senior cadres had suffered so greatly during the Cultural Revolution, and yet had survived it, helped create the leadership for economic and political liberalization once the movement had come to an end. The disillusionment of thousands of educated youth and intellectuals during the Red Guard movement stimulated many of the radical ideas that would later be translated into concrete reforms. And the devastating impact of the Cultural Revolution on the CCP, all in the name of preventing revisionism, weakened the Party's ability to resist a restructuring of the political and economic order that went far beyond that which Mao had found so objectionable in the Soviet Union. In short, had there been no Cultural Revolution, it is unlikely that reform in the post-Mao period would have gone as far or as fast.

But the long-term consequences of the Cultural Revolution remain uncertain. It is not yet clear whether the Cultural Revolution served as a precedent for, or immunization against, the recurrence of similar undertakings in the future. From the vantage point of the 1980s, of course, the inoculatory effects of the Cultural Revolution appeared to be greater. The damage done by the Red Guards, without any countervailing accomplishments, warns strongly against launching a similar "open door" rectification soon. Over time, however, it remains possible that memories will dim, and that the Cultural Revolution will appear more noble and salutary in retrospect than it does today. If so, the Cultural Revolution could still serve as a prototype for another struggle for political power in China or another attempt to purify the country of inequality, corruption, and elitism through mass mobilization. The issue is whether the post-Mao reforms will create sufficient political institutionalization, economic prosperity, social stability, and cultural modernization such that the Cultural Revolution will have little appeal even after the inoculatory effects have worn off.

CHAPTER 4

THE SUCCESSION TO MAO AND THE END OF MAOISM, 1969–82

RODERICK MACFARQUHAR

INTRODUCTION

The Great Proletarian Cultural Revolution was an attempt to shape the future of China. Its method was to change the nature of the Chinese people. It was to be a "great revolution that touches people to their very souls."[1] The masses were to liberate themselves by class struggle against the main target, "those within the Party who are in authority and are taking the capitalist road."[2] These so-called Soviet-style revisionists were alleged to be seeking to corrupt the masses by using old ideas to restore capitalism. By transforming the ideological realm – education, literature, the arts – and embracing Mao Zedong Thought, the Chinese people were to inoculate themselves against poisonous contagion.

Mao's objective was a China that was pure though poor, more egalitarian and less privileged, more collectivist but less bureaucratic, a society in which all worked as one, not so much because they were led by the Communist Party (CCP) as because an inner compass – Mao Zedong Thought – pointed them toward the magnetic pole of true communism.

The goal of the Cultural Revolution was to provide the right answer to the question, After Mao, what? But success would depend on the answer to an earlier question, After Mao, who? If alleged capitalist-roaders like head of state Liu Shaoqi survived the Chairman in positions of power, then China would "change its color." China must not only be guided by the correct line and policies, but had to "train and bring up millions of successors who will carry on the cause of proletarian revolution."[3] In the storm of the Cultural

The author is grateful to Thomas Bernstein, John Fairbank, Merle Goldman, Kenneth Lieberthal, and Michael Schoenhals for comments and suggestions on drafts of this chapter.

1 "Decision of the Central Committee of the Chinese Communist Party concerning the Great Proletarian Cultural Revolution," URI, *CCP documents of the Great Proletarian Cultural Revolution, 1966–1967*, 42.

2 Ibid., 45, 46.

3 "On Khrushchev's phoney communism and its historical lessons for the world," *The polemic on the general line of the international communist movement*, 477. This is the last and most important of the nine polemics

Revolution, new leaders were to emerge, steeled in struggle, "proletarian" in outlook, in whose hands the Maoist brand of socialism would one day burn fiercely.

In the interim, Mao had to cleanse the top ranks of the CCP and install a new successor whom he could trust implicitly to preserve his vision and hand it down. Hence the internecine struggle and purges described in Chapter 3. Mao's victory in that battle was heralded at the CCP's Ninth Congress in the spring of 1969, which rubber-stamped his personal choice as heir, Defense Minister Lin Biao. But this produced a new conundrum, After Mao, which? Was it the demoralized and decimated Party that would run China, or the army, a body with equally revolutionary credentials, which had emerged after three years of Cultural Revolution as the master of the country? This was an institutional issue of supreme importance, with momentous implications for hundreds of millions of Chinese. But for the most part it was fought out between small coteries of leaders, plotting in their residences, clashing at central meetings, with the liquidation of one clique or the other finally emerging as the only viable solution.

THE MILITARIZATION OF CHINESE POLITICS

The CCP's Ninth Congress in April 1969 was a triumph for Lin Biao individually and for the People's Liberation Army (PLA) institutionally. Defense Minister Lin's position as second only to Mao, first achieved at the Eleventh Plenum of the Central Committee (CC) in August 1966, was confirmed. The new Party constitution formally designated him Mao's successor, the first time a comrade-in-arms of the Chairman had achieved that distinction.[4] Lin's military colleagues, as Chapter 3 pointed out, were very

issued by the CCP against the revisionism of the CPSU in 1963–4. These documents are crucial for understanding Mao's concerns on the eve of the Cultural Revolution.

4 Indeed, the only time any Communist Party has ever taken such a step. Lin Biao's new status was attested to by the extravagant praise lavished on him by Zhou Enlai in his speech to the CCP's Ninth Congress; Zhou's address is included in a sixteen-page unpublished collection of speeches to the Congress, and has been translated and annotated for publication by Michael Schoenhals.

A Party historian has stated that when the presidium for the Ninth Congress was being appointed, Mao suggested that Lin should chair it and that he, Mao, should be vice-chairman, only to be interrupted by a loud shout of "Long live Chairman Mao" from Lin Biao.

The same historian has suggested that Mao indicated his preference for Lin Biao as his successor as early as 1956. It seems that when votes were cast for Party Chairman at the first plenum after the CCP's Eighth Congress in September that year, Mao was one vote short of unanimous approval. It was established that Mao had not voted for himself, nor for his number two, Liu Shaoqi, but for Lin Biao! See Tan Zongji, "Lin Biao fangeming jituan de jueqi jige fumie," (The sudden rise of the Lin Biao counterrevolutionary clique and its destruction), in *Jiaoxue cankao: quanguo dangxiao xitong Zhonggong dangshi xueshu taolun hui, xia* (Reference for teaching and study: national Party school system's academic conference on CCP history, vol. 2) (hereafter *Jiaoxue cankao, xia*), 40, 42. The author is grateful to Michael Schoenhals for sharing both these items with him.

prominent at the congress; PLA representation on the CC rose from 19 to 45 percent.[5] At the First Plenum of the new CC after the Congress, the number of active-service soldiers appointed to the Politburo rose dramatically.[6]

The rise of Lin Biao and the military was in some ways a logical culmination of the Chinese revolution and indeed conformed to a pattern familiar from Chinese history. Whenever political control broke down, often under the impact of economic disaster, uprisings took place. Force was met with force, and a process of militarization of the upper levels of the polity took place. Eventually some more able and ambitious rebel leader, sometimes a peasant, more often an aristocrat, would seize the chance to overthrow the dynasty by force, eliminating other aspirant rebel chiefs in the process. The generals who had backed the founding emperor in his struggle for power would assume powerful positions under the new dynasty.[7]

This process of replacement of one dynasty by another normally took many decades, a period of warfare disguised by the neat traditional assignment of a single year as the moment of passage of the mandate of heaven. This is particularly evident in the long-drawn-out decline and fall of the Qing dynasty and the subsequent struggle for power between aspirant successor regimes, culminating in the CCP victory in 1949.

During the decades that followed the defeat of the Qing by the British in the first Opium War (1839–42), the Manchus were beset by both foreign invaders and domestic rebels. The dynasty's initial response was to rearm on traditional lines, but this proved ineffective. Regional loyalists had to set up their own forces to supplement hapless imperial armies.[8] Finally, the dynasty embarked upon defense modernization, with sufficient success to ensure that the creator of the new army, Yuan Shikai, emerged as both the power broker who arranged the abdication of the last emperor in 1912 and the power holder who dominated early republican politics.[9] The era of the general as political leader had begun.

After the collapse of Yuan Shikai's ill-judged attempt to set up a new dynasty and the death of the would-be emperor himself shortly thereafter,

5 See Chapter 3. In view of the participation of virtually every older member of the CCP leadership in armed struggle at some point in his career, the calculation of military representation on the CC is often a question of definition. The "Quarterly Chronicle" of the *CQ* (39, [July–Sept. 1969], 145) estimated it at about 40 percent, Ying-mao Kau (*CLG* [Fall–Winter 1972–3], 8) at 38 percent. Domes, on the other hand, has estimated PLA representation as 40.3 percent at the Eighth Congress and 50 percent at the Ninth; see Jürgen Domes, *The internal politics of China, 1949–1972*, 210.

6 See Table 2.

7 For the Qin-Han transition, see *CHOC*, 1.110–27; for the Sui-Tang one, see *CHOC*, 3. 143–68; for the Yuan-Ming, see *CHOC*, 7.44–106.

8 See *CHOC*, 11, ch. 4, and Philip A Kuhn, *Rebellion and its enemies in late imperial China: Militarization and social structure, 1796–1864*.

9 See *CHOC*, 11.383–8, 529–34, and *CHOC*, 12, ch. 4.

TABLE 2
Politburo named after CCP's Ninth Congress, April 1969

(Leaders named to the Politburo after the two sessions of the Eight Congress in 1956 and 1958 appear in ordinary type; those added at the CC's Eleventh Plenum in 1966 appear in caps; those added after the Ninth Congress are in boldface.)

Standing committee: ranked	
Mao Zedong	Chairman
Lin Biao	Vice-chairman
Standing committee: unranked	
Chen Boda	Chair, CRG[a]
Zhou Enlai	Premier
Kang Sheng	Adviser, CRG
Full members: unranked	
Ye Qun	PLA
YE JIANYING	Marshal
Liu Bocheng	Marshal
Jiang Qing	Vice-chair, CRG
Zhu De	Marshal
Xu Shiyou	Gen.; CO Nanjing MR[a]; Chair, Jiangsu RevCom[a]
Chen Xilian	Gen.; CO Shenyang MR; Chair, Liaoning RevCom
Li Xiannian	Vice-premier
Li Zuopeng	Gen.; Navy Political Commissar
Wu Faxian	Gen.; Air Force CO
Zhang Chunqiao	Vice-chair, CRG; Chair, Shanghai RevCom
Qiu Huizuo	Gen.; Head, PLA Logistics
Yao Wenyuan	Member, CRG; Vice-chair, Shanghai RevCom
Huang Yongsheng	Gen.; PLA chief of staff
Dong Biwu	Vice-head of state
XIE FUZHI	Min. Public Security; Chair, Beijing RevCom
Alternates: unranked	
Ji Dengkui	Vice-chair, Henan RevCom
LI XUEFENG	Chair, Hebei RevCom
Li Desheng	Gen.; Chair, Anhui RevCom
Wang Dongxing	CO Central Bodyguard
Actual ranking[b]	
Mao Zedong	
Lin Biao	
Zhou Enlai	
Chen Boda	
Kang Sheng	
Jiang Qing	
Zhang Chunqiao	
Yao Wenyuan	

Note: (1) Of twenty-three members of the pre-GPCR Politburo, fourteen dropped. (2) Of sixteen new members since the GPCR started, ten = military. (3) Of twenty-five members of the new Politburo, twelve = military; of these, ten were on active service. This compares with seven out of twenty-six in the 1956–8 Politburo, of whom only two were on active service. Eighth CC: civil = 76.3%, PLA = 23.7%; ninth CC: civil = 52.5%, PLA = 47.5%. (4) Three men with provincial jobs in the pre-GPCR Politburo, eight in this one. Provincials in eighth CC = 37%; ninth CC = 58.6%.

[a] CRG = Cultural Revolution Group; MR = Military Region; RevCom = Revolutionary Committee.

[b] Derived from picture in *Zhongguo gongchandang dijiuci quanguo daibiao da hui* (*huace*) (Ninth Congress of the Chinese Communist Party [picture volume]).

China entered the warlord era (1916–28), during which none of Yuan's erstwhile subordinates and rivals proved sufficiently powerful to take over his role.[10] But as control of China's nominal government in Beijing passed from one warlord to another, it became clear to the revolutionaries who had conspired to overthrow the Qing dynasty and then been thrust aside by Yuan that without military power of their own, they would remain helpless or beholden to the unreliable favors of a warlord. It was then that Sun Yat-sen turned to Moscow, and in 1924 his military aide, Chiang Kai-shek, set up the Whampoa Military Academy with Soviet advisers, in order to train officers for a revolutionary army loyal to the KMT (Guomindang).[11]

Had Sun lived longer, perhaps the reshaped KMT would have emerged as a powerful political organization able to subordinate its army to its purposes. But his death in 1925 unleashed a struggle for the succession, which was soon won by Chiang Kai-shek because of his military power base. Although the KMT played an important role when Chiang set up the Nationalist government in 1928, the army remained the ultimate source of power within his regime.[12]

On Moscow's orders, the newborn CCP collaborated with the KMT, and Communist officers and cadres served in the Northern Expedition that enabled Chiang to triumph over the warlords. But when Chiang turned on the CCP in 1927, it became clear to Mao Zedong, as it had become clear to Sun before him, that without its own military force, there was no future for a political movement in China. Political power grew out of the barrel of a gun.[13] On Jinggangshan and in the Jiangxi Soviet, he and his colleagues created the forces and developed the strategy that brought victory in the civil war with the KMT two decades later.[14]

There was a fundamental difference between what the CCP later called the People's Liberation Army (PLA) and Chiang Kai-shek's forces. Mao insisted that the Party should command the gun and that the gun must never be allowed to command the Party.[15] The PLA was not to be just another warlord army, or even a military-dominated party-army amalgam on the KMT model, but a revolutionary force led by the CCP in the service of a cause delineated by it.

But it was never quite that simple. Theoretical princples of Party control may be hard to enforce in the heat of battle when life or death rests on the decision of the military commander.[16] Military subordination may be impoli-

10 See *CHOC*, 12, ch. 6. 11 See *CHOC*, 12.540.

12 See Lloyd E. Eastman, *The abortive revolution: China under Nationalist rule, 1927–1937*.

13 Mao, *SW*, 2.224. 14 See *CHOC*, 13, ch. 4. 15 Mao, *SW*, 2.224.

16 During the anti-Japanese war, Peng Dehuai launched the Hundred Regiments campaign in clear defiance of the principles laid down by Mao on avoiding major offensives that carried no certainty of

tic to insist on if, like Mao, you rely on the support of the generals for your rise to power.[17] Mao's personal political power did indeed grow out of the barrel of the gun; his way of ensuring political control of the army was to retain his chairmanship of the CC's Military Affairs Commission (MAC) from 1935 until his death more than four decades later.

Moreover, when political triumph has been engineered by generals can they be denied the fruits of power? Not with impunity. When Gao Gang made his bid to be recognized as Mao's successor in the mid-1950s, he sought and found support from generals who, he argued, had been short-changed in the post-Liberation distribution of posts.[18] Although Gao Gang lost out, the Party leadership got the message. Lin Biao, one of the military men who seems to have been attracted by Gao's arguments, was quickly raised to the Politburo, and after the CCP's Eighth Congress in 1956, seven of the PLA's ten marshals emerged as members of that body.[19]

The importance of the military within the polity was further demonstrated at the Lushan Conference in 1959, when then Defense Minister Peng Dehuai implicitly challenged Mao's handling of the Great Leap Forward (GLF). Peng's willingness to stick his neck out can be attributed to a number of factors, but its significance is that only the current head of the military establishment had the institutional base from which to initiate an attack that impugned the Chairman's competence and thus his authority. The extent to which Mao felt threatened and outraged by an assault from within what he had always considered his stronghold can be gauged from the bitterness of his rebuttal; only by portraying the issue as a choice between himself and the turbulent defense minister did he force the other marshals to accept Peng's dismissal.[20]

Ironically, Peng Dehuai's disgrace led to an increase in the PLA's status within the polity. Peng's replacement as defense minister by Lin Biao, Mao's

victory. In his memoirs, Peng admitted mistakes with respect to this campaign, including launching the offensive early without consulting the CC's MAC, but he cited a telegram from Mao as indicative of the Chairman's approval. In view of the shrill attacks made on Peng over this issue during the Cultural Revolution after the passage of a quarter of a century, it seems possible that this campaign may have been launched against Mao's wishes or at least against his better judgment, and that his approval had been forthcoming only to preserve a facade of unity. For Mao's views on strategy in the anti-Japanese war, see Mao, *SW*, 2.180–3, 227–32; for Peng Dehuai's version, see his *Memoirs of a Chinese Marshal*, 434–47.

17 See Raymond F. Wylie, *The emergence of Maoism: Mao Tse-tung, Ch'en Po-ta and the search for Chinese theory, 1935–1945*, 68–71.

18 See *CHOC*, 14.97–103.

19 The founder of the Ming dynasty, Zhu Yuanzhang, who came to power after long military campaigns, was careful to award noble titles to all his principal generals shortly after his proclamation as emperor; see *CHOC*, 7.105.

20 See *CHOC*, 14.311–22. The Kangxi emperor was not so fortunate; he had to fight an eight-year-long civil war to subdue the dynasty's three most powerful generals before consolidating the Qing regime in the late seventeenth century; Lawrence D. Kessler, *K'ang-hsi and the consolidation of Ch'ing rule, 1661–1684*, 74–90.

disciple from the early 1930s, gave the Chairman greater confidence in the military's loyalty to himself and his ideas. As Lin promoted the study of Mao Zedong Thought and issued the first edition of the "little red book" of Mao quotations to the armed forces, the PLA was designated the exemplar even to the CCP.[21]

Thus when Mao launched his assault on the Party leadership at the outset of the Cultural Revolution, he could be confident that the other major revolutionary institution would support him. Later, when the Red Guards found the overthrow of provincial leaders harder than expected, Mao was able to call on the PLA to support the left. When the triumphant Red Guards fell to internecine warfare and many cities of China were the scenes of armed clashes, it was a general – Chen Zaidao in Wuhan in the summer of 1967 – who blew the whistle. Although Chen himself was disciplined, ultra-leftist cadres were also purged, and a year later Mao authorized the rustication of the Red Guards. The mass base of the Central Cultural Revolution Group was dissolved. The way was clear for the triumph of Lin Biao and his generals at the Ninth Congress.[22]

For Mao the issue must have seemed stark, even though among his colleagues he dismissed Soviet attacks on China's "military bureaucractic dictatorship" as not worth refuting.[23] All his life he had insisted on the primacy of the Party over the army; after his death, the prospect was that the army would dominate the Party. The CCP might go the way of the KMT. Could he accept this?

THE FALL OF LIN BIAO

The CCP's Ninth Congress should have signaled a return to some semblance of normalcy: Mao's "proletarian revolutionary line" reigned unchallenged, his enemies had been defeated, a new leadership was in place, and civil strife had been suppressed. Mao had heralded a "great victory" as early as October 1968, and in his political report to the Congress, Lin Biao proclaimed: "The victory of the Great Proletarian Cultural Revolution is very great indeed."[24] When discussing the future, Lin Biao talked of "continuing the revolution in the realm of the superstructure,"[25] that is, building the new society for which the Cultural Revolution had been launched. For the victors, if not for the victims when they were finally able to rewrite the histories, the Cultural

21 See *CHOC*, 14.335–42. 22 See Chapter 3.

23 At the First Plenum of the Ninth CC; see Wang Nianyi, *1949–1989 nian de Zhongguo: da dongluan de niandai* (China from 1949 to 1989: decade of great upheaval), 395.

24 *CB*, 880 (9 May 1969), 37. 25 Ibid., 34.

Revolution was over. The year 1969 was meant to mark a new beginning after revolution, like the Liberation twenty years earlier.

But if this had been a "Congress of Victors," the calm it should have presaged was as short-lived as that after the CPSU's Seventeenth Congress in 1934 for which that appellation was coined. Insofar as the Cultural Revolution meant a struggle for power among the elite to determine who had the right to shape the future, it was far from over, and indeed was soon to take an even more dangerous turn. There were three arenas: the reconstruction of the Party, the rebuilding of the state structure, and foreign affairs. Underlying all three was the specter of Bonapartism conjured up by Lin Biao's rise to power.

The reconstruction of the Party

In the absence of any properly constituted lower-level Party committees, delegates to the Ninth Congress had supposedly been chosen either by "consultation" between revolutionary committees and local "rebel" groups[26] or simply by directive from the higher levels.[27] Because the PLA dominated the revolutionary committees,[28] it was hardly surprising that the military were so much in evidence at the Congress. With the Congress resulting in many promotions for PLA officers, it was even less surprising that the process of provincial party construction reflected the prevailing power realities.

Mao had begun to call for the reconstruction of the Party as early as October 1967 with his "fifty character policy" statement, directing that party organs should be formed from advanced elements of the proletariat. At the new CC's First Plenum after the Ninth Congress, he repeated his call to revive the Party. But although the declared hope of the leadership was to rebuild from the bottom up, and in 1970 the CC publicized the party construction experience of Peking University, Beijing No. 27 Rolling Stock Plant, and the No. 17 State Cotton Mill in Shanghai as models,[29] Party branches proved difficult to set up.

By late 1969, the major effort had been transferred upward to the counties and municipalities, but even at this level progress was slow. In the year between November 1969 and November 1970, only 45 of the nation's 2,185

26 These were the organizations of blue-collar workers, the Red Guard groups having been disbanded.

27 Teaching and Research Office for CCP History of the [PLA] Political Academy, ed., *Zhongguo gongchandang liushi nian dashi jianjie* (A summary of the principal events in the 60 years of the Chinese Communist Party), 559.

28 Of twenty-nine provincial revolutionary committees, twenty-one were headed by PLA officers; Domes, *The internal politics of China*, 205.

29 Hao Mengbi and Duan Haoran, eds., *Zhongguo gongchandang liushi nian, xia* (Sixty years of the Chinese Communist Party, part 2), 610.

counties had set up Party committees. Presumably recognizing the futility of proceeding on these lines, the central leadership authorized the prior formation of provincial-level committees. The first was formed in Mao's home province, Hunan, in December 1970, with one Hua Guofeng as its first secretary, and by mid-August 1971 all twenty-nine provincial-level units were similarly endowed, with the PLA well in evidence. The military had supplied twenty-two of the twenty-nine first secretaries and 62 percent of the cadres running the provincial secretariats.[30]

According to post–Cultural Revolution accounts, Party rebuilding resulted in the induction of many disruptive rebel elements and the exclusion of old officials. Although a prime focus of the continuing "purify the class ranks" campaign launched in May 1968 had been to exclude ultra-leftist elements, allegedly the net was cast far wider and the campaign was used against blameless cadres.[31] This in itself probably displeased Mao, who appears to have wanted to reeducate, rehabilitate, and reemploy experienced cadres as part of an effort to restore stability and unity. But the more pressing issue was the clear failure of Lin Biao and the PLA to accept his injunctions to help rebuild a civilian Party that would reestablish its control over army and nation.[32] Well before the formation of the last provincial Party committees, it must have been obvious that the PLA would dominate them as it dominated the provincial revolutionary committees. Moreover, Lin Biao was giving evidence of wanting to dominate the state structure at the center as well as in the provinces.

Rebuilding the state structure

On 8 March 1970, Mao gave his opinions on rebuilding the state structure. He advocated convening the Fourth National People's Congress, at which a revised state constitution would be agreed upon. The constitution would abolish the position of head of state. The following day the Politburo endorsed Mao's opinion, and on 16 March it formulated some principles regarding the NPC session and the constitution, which were submitted to the Chairman and endorsed by him. On 17 March, a central work conference met to flesh out what had been agreed on. But Lin Biao soon joined issue on the question of the office of head of state. On 11 April, he proposed in writing that Mao should resume the office of head of state, which he had ceded to the late Liu Shaoqi in 1959, otherwise "it would not be in accord with the psychology [*xinli zhuangtai*] of the people." The Chairman summarily re-

30 See Domes, *The internal politics of China*, 215.
31 Hao and Duan, *Zhongguo gongchandang liushi nian, xia*, 608–11.
32 Philip Bridgham, "The fall of Lin Piao," *CQ*, 55 (July–September 1973), 429–30.

jected this suggestion, telling the Politburo on 12 April: "I cannot do this job again; this suggestion is inappropriate." At a Politburo conference toward the end of the month, Mao used a historical analogy from the period of the Three Kingdoms in the third century A.D. when stating for the third time that he would not take on the state chairmanship and that the post should be abolished.

Yet Lin Biao persisted. Two of his military allies in the Politburo were on the constitution-drafting group: Wu Faxian, the air force head, and Li Zuopeng, the navy's chief commissar. In mid-May, Lin asked them to include a clause on the post of head of state, and despite a fourth disclaimer by Mao in mid-July that one should not create a post for the sake of a person, behind the scenes Lin Biao's wife, Ye Qun, kept promoting the idea with Lin's supporters. Ye asked Wu Faxian plaintively what Lin Biao would do if the state chairmanship were not reestablished, an indication of Lin's own interest in the post if Mao continued to decline it.[33]

Why would the Chairman's formally anointed successor in the Party press this issue in the teeth of Mao's opposition? Why would he want a ceremonial post with no more prestige than its occupant's status within the Party? Philip Bridgham has argued that Lin was dismayed that the new constitution would leave him junior in governmental status to Premier Zhou Enlai, in whose cabinet he was a vice-premier and minister of defense, and at the implication that the Chairman was now contemplating a joint leadership of Lin and Zhou to succeed him.[34] It can also be argued that Mao's tenure in the state chairmanship had conferred a certain aura on it, certainly a status senior to the premier's, and that Liu Shaoqi's tenure in the post before the Cultural Revolution had shown that it guaranteed considerable publicity, as well as exposure in the international arena.

The key to Lin Biao's behavior in this matter, however, is almost certainly a deep sense of insecurity, probably exacerbated by the relative isolation to which illness and temperament confined him.[35] He had emerged as Mao's principal colleague as early as 1966, but he still required the reassurance, never granted to Liu Shaoqi, of being named successor in the Party constitu-

33 Wang, *Da dongluan de niandai,* 392–4; Hao and Duan, *Zhongguo gongchandang liushi nian,* 613.

34 Bridgham, "The fall of Lin Piao," 432–3.

35 See Zhang Yunsheng, *Maojiawan jishi* (An on-the-spot report on Maojiawan), passim. Zhang was one of Lin Biao's secretaries from 19 August 1966 until 17 November 1970. Lin apparently feared light, wind, water, and cold and hated to sweat. He did not take baths and did not eat fruit. He insisted that his accommodation should be kept at a constant 21°C (about 70°F), with no greater variation than half a degree. (Ye Qun liked her room temperature to be 18°C!) But probably the most debilitating aspect of Lin's condition, as far as carrying out his duties was concerned, was his inability or refusal to read documents, with the result that his secretaries had to select and summarize from the mass of paper that reached his office as much as they could read to him in 30 minutes. Ibid., 8–12; Wang, *Da dongluan de niandai,* 373–5, 377.

tion. Now he sought the further reassurance of being named head of state. Personal psychology aside, this insecurity probably stemmed in part from an uneasy consciousness that the manner in which he had risen to power was illegitimate and was bitterly resented by survivors of the Cultural Revolution among his generation of leaders. Even this would have mattered little had he had total confidence in Mao's backing. He was surely unnerved by Mao's suggestion to him that since he (Lin) was also old, he, too, should have a successor, and that Zhang Chunqiao would be a good candidate;[36] and as the documents circulated after Lin's fall indicate, he seems to have viewed Mao as someone always ready to knife his closest associates in the back:

> Today he uses sweet words and honeyed talk to those whom he entices, and tomorrow puts them to death for fabricated crimes. . . . Looking back at the history of the past few decades, [do you see] anyone whom he had supported initially who has not finally been handed a political death sentence? . . . His former secretaries have either committed suicide or been arrested. His few close comrades-in-arms or trusted aides have also been sent to prison by him.[37]

Why, then, did Lin Biao defy Mao so blatantly? Possibly he felt that the Chairman might relent; possibly he wanted to use the issue as a litmus test of Mao's attitude toward himself. Or possibly, with his military colleagues grouped around him, he now felt strong enough to force Mao to concede; after all, Mao had been dependent upon the PLA for the success of the Red Guards, and later the generals' anxieties had helped compel Mao to suppress them. Could not the dominant role of generals within the Politburo be used to promote the defense minister's interests?

Moreover, Lin Biao had another important ally in his quest for status: Chen Boda, Mao's longtime ideological adviser and onetime political secretary.[38] Chen had headed the Central Cultural Revolution Group from its creation in the spring of 1966, a confirmation of his closeness to the Chairman, and he soon rose to the fourth position in the leadership under Mao, Lin, and Zhou Enlai, a ranking confirmed by pictures taken at the Ninth Congress. Yet, a year later, Chen, after years of loyal service to Mao, had chosen to support Lin Biao in defiance of the Chairman's repeatedly stated views.

One explanation is that the dissolution of the Cultural Revolution Group in late 1969 had deprived Chen of a starring role in the post–Ninth Congress constellation, and that he may have felt threatened by the campaign against

36 Ibid., 387–8.

37 Michael Y. M. Kau, *The Lin Piao affair: Power politics and military coup*, 87. These words were probably written by Lin Biao's son, but they clearly reflect the knowledge and experience of the older man.

38 For Mao's indebtedness to Chen Boda, see Wylie, *The emergence of Maoism*, passim.

ultra-leftism.[39] Equally, the crumbling of the original coalition that backed Mao at the outset of the Cultural Revolution under the impact of events of 1966–9 may have left Chen feeling isolated. The Shanghai leftists Zhang Chunqiao and Yao Wenyuan were linked through Jiang Qing (Madame Mao) to the Chairman; indeed, the youthful Yao seemed to have replaced Chen Boda as the favored bearer of Mao's message. Yet, at the outset of the Cultural Revolution, Zhang, Yao, and even Jiang Qing had been Chen's subordinates in the Cultural Revolution Group. In preparation for the Ninth Congress, Chen had originally been chosen as the principal drafter of Lin Biao's political report, with Zhang and Yao as his aides; but when Chen proved unable to produce a satisfactory draft in time, Zhang and Yao took over the task, under the supervision of Kang Sheng. Kang, Mao's longtime aide in the internal security field, also had close ties to his fellow provincial Jiang Qing, and Chen appears to have been jealous of Kang's connections.[40]

Lin Biao, on the other hand, had consolidated his position on a PLA base and no longer seemed to need the support of the leftists. Indeed, Lin and his followers and Jiang Qing and hers were increasingly divided into rival camps; and whereas Lin may have had long-term worries about the security of his role, he seems to have had excessive confidence that in the short run he could dominate Jiang's clique. Perhaps Chen Boda agreed and, looking to the future, thought his best prospect was to offer to perform for Lin Biao the same role he had previously performed for Mao.[41] The decision was to prove disastrous for Chen's career.

The struggle over the state chairmanship came to a head at the Ninth CC's Second Plenum, held at the ill-starred Lushan mountain resort from 23 August to 6 September 1970. Once again, Mao was locked in struggle with a defense minister, although this time he was not sure enough of his own strength or the minister's discipline to risk a direct confrontation at this stage.

On the eve of the plenum, 22 August, the Politburo Standing Committee, consisting of Mao, Lin Biao, Zhou Enlai, Chen Boda, and Kang Sheng, met to agree on the main themes of the plenum. Mao pointedly stressed the need

39 Bridgham, "The fall of Lin Piao," 432.

40 See Zhong Kan, *Kang Sheng pingzhuan* (A critical biography of Kang Sheng), 15–16, 146–7. For Chen Boda's jealousy of Kang Sheng, see Zhang, *Maojiawan jishi,* 190–2; for Chen's problems with the report for the Ninth Congress, see ibid., 210–11, and Wang, *Da dongluan de niandai* 387. According to the latter source, Chen Boda, miffed, continued working on his own draft, but it was the Zhang–Yao one that Mao, after several revisions, eventually approved. Lin Biao was apparently interested only in Mao's input and the final version of the report.

41 At his trial in the winter of 1980–1, Chen Boda said only that "after he learned of the power struggle between Lin Biao and Jiang Qing, he sympathized with Lin Biao"; see *A great trial in Chinese history,* 116. For the development of rival camps and the confidence of Lin's side, see Zhang, *Maojiawan jishi,* 382–9, and Wang, *Da dongluan de niandai,* 382–8.

for unity and the avoidance of factionalism, his habitual device when seeking to undercut opposition.[42] But Lin Biao and Chen Boda again proposed the retention of the state chairmanship and urged Mao to assume it. Mao refused once more but pointedly added that whoever wanted to take on the job should do so.[43]

The plenum was opened the next day by Zhou Enlai, who listed the agenda as the revision of the state constitution, the national economic plan, and war preparedness. Unexpectedly, and without clearing his remarks with Mao in advance,[44] Lin Biao intervened to express his conviction that it was extremely important for the new constitution to express Mao's role as the great leader, head of state (*guojia yuanshou*), and supreme commander, as well as the guiding role of Mao Zedong Thought as the national ideology. Implicitly, he was threatening the opponents of retaining the state chairmanship with accusations of being anti-Mao.[45]

As in the past, Lin was stressing Mao's transcendent genius and role in order to display his own devotion and thus achieve his own ends, a strategy that Mao appears to have been aware of and uncomfortable with even from the beginning of the Cultural Revolution.[46] But for most of the 255 CC members present who were not in the know, Lin Biao was giving the opening, keynote address on behalf of the central leadership, and they were hardly likely to express opposition. His wife, Ye Qun, sought to press home this advantage, urging Lin's PLA allies Wu Faxian, Li Zuopeng, and Qiu Huizuo, the chief of logistics, to speak up in support and to lobby CC members from their own arm of the services. Another PLA supporter, Chief of Staff Huang Yongsheng, was telephoned in Beijing and informed of Lin's demarche.[47] At a Politburo meeting held that evening to discuss the economic plan, Wu Faxian proposed revising the following day's arrangements so that the plenary session could listen to a tape recording of Lin's speech and discuss it. That night, without formal authorization, Chen Boda was busy drafting a clause on the state chairmanship for the constitution and collecting quotations on the theory of genius.[48]

42 See Mao's behavior at the 1959 Lushan Conference; see Roderick MacFarquhar, *The origins of the Cultural Revolution*, 2.220.

43 Hao and Duan, *Zhongguo gongchandang liushi nian*, 613–14.

44 Gao Gao and Yan Jiaqi, *"Wenhua da geming" shinian shi, 1966–1976* (A history of the ten years of the "Great Cultural Revolution," 1966–1976), 348.

45 Ibid., 614.

46 See Mao's letter of 8 July 1966 to Jiang Qing in *CLG*, 6.2 (Summer 1973), 96–9. Later that year, in a speech to the Military Academy devoted to the theme of raising the study of Mao's writings to a new stage, Lin Biao praised the Chairman as the "greatest talent of the present era" and urged everyone studying Marxism–Leninism to devote 99 percent of their effort to his works; see *I&S*, 8.6 (March 1972), 75–9.

47 Hao and Duan, *Zhongguo gongchandang liushi nian*, 614.

48 Teaching and Research Office for CCP History, *Zhongguo gongchandang lishi nian dashi jianjie*, 561–2.

It is not clear whether Mao attended the Politburo session on the evening of 23 August – presumably not – but Wu Faxian's proposal was accepted and the plenum listened to the Lin Biao tape the following morning. On the afternoon of 24 August, after agreeing on their plan of action, Chen Boda, Ye Qun, Wu Faxian, Li Zuopeng, and Qiu Huizuo divided up and spoke in favor of the Lin line at the sessions of the North China, Central-South, Southwest, and Northwest regional groups. They distributed a selection of quotations from Engels, Lenin, and Mao on the theory of genius to bolster Lin's position, and Chen Boda told the North China group that anyone opposing Mao's assumption of the state chairmanship was opposing the concept of Mao as a genius. Reports of their remarks were printed in the group bulletins and distributed. No one at the group meetings suggested Lin Biao for head of state.[49]

Mao, it was later claimed, was well aware that Lin's tactic was for the CC to agree that the new constitution should retain the state chairmanship and then to take the position himself if Mao persisted in refusing it.[50] If so, then Mao's remark at the Politburo Standing Committee meeting on the eve of the plenum was perhaps a provocation, designed to suggest to Lin that Mao's real objection was not to the post but to occupying it himself. Thus Lin and his supporters would be encouraged to promote the state chairmanship proposal and, given enough rope, would hang themselves.

Certainly Mao acted speedily when the speeches of Lin's supporters in the regional groups were brought to his attention by Jiang Qing and Zhang Chunqiao on 25 August, an action Mao later described as his wife's meritorious service against Lin. Jiang and Zhang, whose political base outside Shanghai had crumbled with the rustication of the Red Guards and the suppression of civil strife, presumably had no wish to see Lin Biao's already formidable power and status increased further. Indeed, by now, their own hopes of inheriting any portions of Mao's mantle clearly depended on the erosion of Lin Biao's position, and Zhang Chunqiao had earlier clashed with Wu Faxian on the Lin program in a group discussion.[51]

Mao must have realized that Lin's supporters were moving so fast that the plenum might be jockeyed into supporting the state chairmanship proposal if he did not declare himself. Even Wang Hongwen, a close follower of Zhang Chunqiao and the latter's deputy in Shanghai, was sufficiently enthused or

49 Hu Hua, ed., *Zhongguo shehuizhuyi geming he jianshe shi jiangyi* (Teaching materials on the history of China's socialist revolution and construction), 300; Teaching and Research Office for CCP History, *Zhongguo gongchandang liushi nian dashi jianjie*, 562; Gao and Yan, *"Wenhua da geming" shinian shi*, 348; Hao and Duan, *Zhongguo gongchandang liushi nian*, 614. For quotations from these speeches, see ibid., 614–15, n. 1; Wang, *Da dongluan de niandai*, 398–9.

50 Hao and Duan, *Zhongguo gongchandang liushi nian*, 615–16.

51 Ibid., 616; Wang, *Da dongluan de niandai*, 402.

naive to trumpet the praises of Lin Biao's keynote speech in the Shanghai caucus and was preparing to repeat the performance before the East China group.[52] In the key North China group, a man as close to Mao as Wang Dongxing was persuaded by Chen Boda's rhetoric. So, later on 25 August, Mao called the Politburo Standing Committee into session, an expanded meeting, presumably in order to allow the Chairman to pack it with additional supporters such as his wife and Zhang Chunqiao. was decided that discussion of Lin Biao's speech in the group sessions should cease forthwith, and the bulletin of the North China group with Chen Boda's offending remarks was recalled. Chen was ordered to make a self-criticism.[53]

Mao set the tone for a counterattack by circulating, on 31 August, "A few of my opinions," a document in which he exposed his erstwhile ideological adviser's "bourgeois idealism" and accused him of rumor-mongering and sophistry. Mao's broadside provided ammunition for the criticism of Chen, Wu Faxian, and Lin's other supporters in group sessions.[54] Only Chen Boda, however, was hounded out of office, perhaps because he could be credibly accused of being the fount of Lin's theoretical position. Probably more important, his disgrace did not threaten Lin directly, as the dismissal of one of his PLA allies would have done. Mao knew Lin Biao's power and, as he later admitted, he was not yet ready to confront him. He spoke privately to Lin but told other leaders that his deputy had to be protected.[55]

Even so, Lin Biao had got the real message. In a brief two and a half days,[56] Lin's attempt to obtain the state chairmanship had been defeated, an awesome reminder of Mao's power to manipulate the Party elite. Before leaving Lushan after the close of the plenum on 6 September, Lin summed up the lesson he had learned to Wu Faxian: "Doing things in the civilian manner didn't work; using armed force will work."[57]

Disagreement over foreign policy

The issues of Party building and the reconstruction of state institutions basically were about power. There also seems to have been one issue of policy dividing Mao and Lin, although it is given less attention in Chinese sources:

52 Gao and Yan, "*Wenhua da geming*" *shinian shi*, 349. After Mao's intervention, Wang hastily changed his speech of approval into a criticism of Chen Boda!

53 Teaching and Research Office for CCP History, *Zhongguo gongchandang lishi nian dashi jianjie*, 562.

54 Hao and Duan, *Zhongguo gongchandang liushi nian*, 616; a full text of Mao's remarks is in Wang, *Da dongluan de niandai*, 403–4.

55 Gao and Yan, "*Wenhua da geming*" *shinian shi*, 349–50.

56 That is, from 23 August through noon on 23 August; ibid., 349.

57 "*Gao wenti buxing, gao wuti xing;* see Hu, *Zhongguo shehuizhuyi geming he jianshe shi jiangyi*, 302.

the opening to America. This is dealt with in detail in *CHOC* 15,[58] and it will only be sketched here.

The origins of the startling turnabout in Sino-American relations that brought President Nixon to China in February 1972 are well known. The bloody reverse sustained by the Chinese in a frontier clash with Soviet troops on Zhenbao (Damansky) Island in the Ussuri River in March 1969 clearly aroused concern in Beijing that Moscow was going to escalate what had hitherto been a series of minor confrontations. There was subsequently a series of clashes on the northwestern frontier, a particularly serious one occurring in Xinjiang in August, and rumors began to emanate from Eastern European sources that the Russians were sounding out their allies about a "surgical strike" against Chinese nuclear weapons installations.

The immediate tension was somewhat defused by the brief meeting between Premier Kosygin and Premier Zhou Enlai at Beijing airport on 11 September, but the Chinese clearly continued to take the danger very seriously. In the aftermath of the Ussuri River clash, the Beijing press had already drawn an analogy with the Soviet invasion of Czechoslovakia in the summer of 1968, a move the Russians had subsequently justified with the "Brezhnev doctrine," which effectively allowed the Soviet Union to overthrow any Communist government of which it did not approve. The question for the Chinese leadership was how to achieve national security in these new circumstances.

It is conceivable that the clash on Zhenbao Island began with an ambush by the Chinese, and that this was intended by Lin Biao to provoke a frontier flare-up in order to impress upon delegates to the CCP's Ninth Congress the importance of the heroic PLA, and so justify the role it was assuming within the Party.[59] Whether or not this is correct, the lesson learned by Mao and Zhou Enlai from the clashes of 1969 was almost certainly the opposite: The Soviet Union was embarked on a far tougher line on the border,[60] and, however determined in border clashes, the PLA probably would be incapable of defending China effectively if the Soviet Union were to launch a major attack. Hence the receptivity of Beijing to the overtures of the Nixon administration. An opening to Washington could undermine the calculations of the Russians as to the impunity with which they could attack China. Indeed,

58 See *CHOC*, 15, Chapter 5.

59 A twenty-nine-year-old commander involved in the Zhenbao clash, Sun Yuguo, was introduced to the Ninth Congress by PLA Chief of Staff Huang Yongsheng, and was given an emotional welcome by Mao; see Mao's brief remarks in a collection of major speeches to the Ninth Congress available in the library of Harvard's Fairbank Center.

60 See, for instance, the estimate of a Chinese officer involved in the clashes as reported in Neville Maxwell, "The Chinese account of the 1969 fighting at Chenpao," *CQ*, 56 (October–December 1973), 734. See also *CHOC*, 15, ch. 3.

even before the forging of the Sino-American link, the Nixon administration had indicated that Moscow could not assume its benevolent neutrality in the event of Soviet aggression.[61] The original Sino-Soviet rift derived in large measure from Chinese anger at Soviet-American détente; Chinese denunciations of the revisionism of the CPSU leadership began after the Russians and the Americans had signed the partial test ban treaty; the Cultural Revolution had been launched in order to prevent the emergence of similar revisionism in China. It is hardly surprising, therefore, that the breakthrough in Sino-American relations would require a great deal of explanation for Chinese nurtured on a diet of ideological principle rather than realpolitik.[62]

Lin Biao may well have felt revulsion at what looked like an Asian equivalent of the Nazi–Soviet pact. He may have reasoned that if China really could not stand alone if threatened by both superpowers simultaneously, would it not be better to come to terms with a revisionist Soviet Union rather than an imperialist United States? Lin's position on this issue has never been fully clarified. He was later accused of "isolationism" and "great nation chauvinism,"[63] which suggests that he opposed any link-up with the United States or the Soviet Union[64] and argued that China was strong enough to protect itself. Mao told Nixon and other foreign visitors that Lin Biao had opposed contacts with America.[65]

If Mao were reporting accurately, it is easy to understand his motives. The PLA would loom larger than ever in a China isolated and menaced. And under conditions of national peril, the right of one of the great revolutionary marshals to inherit the mantle of Mao could not be disputed. The arts of peace and diplomacy, the province of Zhou Enlai, would seem less important.

Unfortunately for Lin, Mao felt he had to buy time with diplomacy, and on 7 October the New China News Agency (NCNA) announced that Sino-Soviet border negotiations were about to begin. Yet Mao remained suspicious of the Russians, and in mid-October the Politburo decided to heighten vigilance immediately. On 17 October 1969, apparently acting on Mao's somber analysis of the world situation, Lin issued his "Order No. 1," putting the PLA on emergency alert and ordering the evacuation of cities.

Lin was resting in Suzhou at the time, in a house once owned by Madame Chiang Kai-shek. According to the secretary who transmitted Lin's order to Chief of Staff Huang Yongsheng in Beijing, the defense minister's concern

61 Henry Kissinger, *White House years*, 184.

62 See, for instance, the documents circulated within the Kunming Military Region in *Chinese Communist internal politics and foreign policy*, 115–45.

63 Ibid., 132. 64 See *CHOC*, 15, ch. 3.

65 Kissinger, *White House Years*, 1061; *NYT*, 28 July 1972, quoted in Bridgham, "The fall of Lin Piao," 441–2. See also *CHOC* 15, ch. 5. Yet Lin Biao's secretary testifies that his late chief took virtually no interest in foreign affairs; Zhang, *Maojiawan jishi*, 329–33.

was that the Russians might be preparing a surprise attack when the PRC's guard was down because of the arrival of the Soviet negotiating mission. Mao was apparently sent a copy of the order for approval two hours before Huang was sent his copy and evidently did not countermand it. Later condemnation of Lin's order was probably at least partly due to contemporary concern about the sharp reactions to it by the Russians, the Americans, and the Taiwan regime; so obvious a preparation for war might have been used by the Russians as an excuse for further military action on the border. After Lin was disgraced, Mao was able to blame him for an action that was clearly sparked by himself.[66]

The border negotiations began on 20 October without mishap. Simultaneously, the Chinese and the Americans were initiating what Henry Kissinger later called an "intricate minuet"[67] as they cautiously probed through twenty years of hostility and suspicion. By the end of 1969, it was clear to the Americans that their signals, messages, and hints had borne fruit. Throughout 1970, as Lin Biao was campaigning to become head of state, Sino-American contacts grew. By 21 April 1971, when Zhou Enlai invited Kissinger to visit Beijing,[68] Lin's civilian route to more power had proved a dead end, and he was launched upon a more perilous course.

"Throwing stones, mixing in sand, and digging up the cornerstone"

Lin Biao's decision to seize power by force was almost certainly triggered by his political rebuff at the Lushan Plenum, but its timing was probably determined by the relentless campaign that Mao waged against his associates after that meeting. During the autumn and winter of 1970–1, it must have

66 Ibid., 316–23; *Zhonggong dangshi dashi nianbiao* (A chronological table of major events in the history of the Chinese Communist Party), 372. Zhang's account gives a sobering revelation of how hurriedly members of the Chinese leadership took steps that might have resulted in war.

The evacuation order probably had an additional advantage, if not motivation: to get senior cadres, potential threats to Lin Biao's power, out of Beijing. A number of marshals were dispersed along the Beijing–Guangzhou railway line: Chen Yi at Shijiazhuang, Nie Rongzhen at Handan, Xu Xiangqian at Kaifeng, Ye Jianying at Changsha, Liu Bocheng at Hankou, Zhu De and former chief planner Li Fuchun in Conghua county in greater Guangzhou. Some had probably lined up against Lin Biao at the recent Lushan plenum; all but Li were potential obstacles if he wanted to use military means to achieve power. For the dispersal process, see Nie Rongzhen, *Nie Rongzhen huiyi lu, xia* (The memoirs of Nie Rongzhen, part 3), 861–4. Ye Jianying was soon back in harness investigating Chen Boda; see the later discussion. The NCNA report on the Sino-Soviet negotiations is quoted in Kissinger, *White House years*, 186. See also *CHOC*, 15, ch. 3.

67 Kissinger, *White House years*, 187.

68 Ibid., 193, 684–703, 714. Kissinger speculates that an attempt by PRC fighter planes to intercept an American intelligence-gathering aircraft a hundred miles off the Chinese coast on 2 July, at a time when diplomatic relations were improving, may have been a reflection of an internal power struggle in Beijing; ibid., 697. In view of Lin Biao's close relationship with PLA Air Force Chief Wu Faxian, this seems a reasonable speculation.

become clear to the defense minister that if he did not act soon, he would be finished. Mao's actions seem almost provocative, as if he wanted to force Lin Biao to make a false move. If he did, he would court death.

The postplenum campaign against Chen Boda took a number of forms. First, there was the denigration of Chen himself, the gradual buildup of a campaign from November 1970 through April 1971 and beyond, which started from the premise that he was anti-Party and a sham Marxist. Simultaneously, senior cadres were told to study Marxism–Leninism and prescribed six books by Marx, Engels, and Lenin and five articles by Mao, the proclaimed objective being to enable them to distinguish materialism and idealism. In fact, Mao was hitting at Lin Biao, who had advocated shelving the study of the Marxist–Leninist classics and reducing the study of Mao's Thought to the recitation of quotations. Chen's crimes were investigated by Ye Jianying, who visited Fujian, Guangdong, and Guangxi to look into his activities, and were made the excuse for a rectification campaign clearly designed to wean cadres from loyalty to Lin.[69]

Mao later described his tactics against Lin Biao and his followers as "throwing stones, mixing in sand, and digging up the cornerstone."[70] "Throwing stones" meant sniping at Lin's allies. At Lushan, Zhou Enlai had privately told Wu Faxian, Li Zuopeng, and Qiu Huizuo that they should make self-criticism to the CC. The day after the plenum ended, at Jiujiang airport at the foot of Lushan, Lin Biao posed for a souvenir snapshot with them and Huang Yongsheng, and discussed tactics with them and his wife. It was agreed that Wu's position had to be restored, Lin and Huang had to be protected, and that in response to Zhou's order, false self-criticisms would be made.[71]

But when the written self-criticisms appeared on Mao's desk the following month, he scribbled dissatisfied comments all over them. When the MAC called a conference of 143 officers on 9 January 1971, and Lin's allies neither criticized Chen Boda nor self-criticized despite Mao's repeated strictures, the Chairman expressed his displeasure by ordering the proceedings of the conference to be ignored. Finally, on 29 April, at a central meeting called to discuss

69 The CC's first anti-Chen document, issued on 16 November 1970, already set out the main accusations against him: anti-Party, sham Marxist, careerist, and plotter. On 26 January 1971, the CC issued a collection of materials to document Chen's "crimes" throughout his career. Two CC notifications, on 21 February and 29 April, detailed how the movement to criticize Chen should be carried out. See Hao and Duan, *Zhongguo gongchandang liushi nian*, 617–18; Wang, *Da dongluan de niandai*, 406–9. For Ye's investigation, see *Yingsi lu: huainian Ye Jianying* (A record of contemplation: remembering Ye Jianying), 265, 294, 301–4.

70 "*Shuai shitou, shan shazi, wa qiangjiao*"; *CLG*, 5.3–4 (Fall–Winter 1972–3), 38; Hu, *Zhongguo shehuiyizhuyi he jianshe shi jiangyi*, 302.

71 Gao and Yan, "*Wenhua da geming*" *shinian shi*, 349–50. The photograph at Jiujiang is reproduced in Yao Ming-le, *The conspiracy and murder of Mao's heir*, 57.

progress in the anti–Chen Boda rectification campaign, Zhou Enlai accused Huang Yongsheng, Wu Faxian, Ye Qun, Li Zuopeng, and Qiu Huizuo of mistakes in political line and factionalism.[72]

"Mixing in sand" meant adding Mao loyalists to bodies otherwise dominated by Lin's people. Ji Dengkui, elected to alternate membership of the Politburo at the Ninth Congress, and a general, Zhang Caiqian, were appointed to the MAC's administrative group on 7 April 1971, to offset the power there of Huang Yongsheng and Wu Faxian. Mao had already taken other organizational measures to ensure his control of personnel and propaganda. On 6 November 1970, a new Central Organization and Propaganda Group, reporting directly to the Politburo, was set up to oversee the CC's Organization Department, the Central Party School, the *People's Daily,* the theoretical journal *Hongqi* (Red flag), the New China News Agency, the Central Broadcasting Bureau, the *Guangming Daily,* and a number of other organs. The group head was Kang Sheng, and its members were Jiang Qing, Zhang Chunqiao, Yao Wenyuan, Ji Dengkui, and a general, Li Desheng. Kang Sheng soon cried off because of illness and Li Desheng became first secretary of the new Anhui provincial Party committee in January 1971. Mao's wife and her Shanghai colleagues were left in charge, taking over what had once been Chen Boda's media empire,[73] thereby achieving a major national power base for the first time since the end of the Red Guard movement.[74]

"Digging up the cornerstone" meant reorganizing the Beijing Military Region. In an increasingly tense confrontation with his minister of defense, Mao had to be sure that the troops in charge of the capital were loyal to himself and not Lin Biao. On 16 December 1970, he called for a conference to explain why the Party committees of the North China region and the North China Military Region had allowed Chen Boda to become their backstage boss (*taishang huang*) when he had not been given the appropriate powers by the CC. Insofar as there may have been any justice in the accusation – and it is easier to picture the bookish Chen Boda as a surrogate for Lin Biao than as the *éminence grise* of a military unit – it probably only reflected the normal deference any sensible party official would pay to a member of the Politburo Standing Committee; it is hard to imagine so lofty an individual being quizzed about his credentials. No matter: For Mao, who himself disdained going through channels, any credible infraction of organizational discipline was grist to his mill.

Zhou Enlai called a North China conference on 22 December 1970, ostensi-

72 Hao and Duan, *Zhongguo gongchandang liushi nian,* 619–20, Hu, *Zhongguo shehuizhuyi geming he jianshe shi jiangyi,* 302; *CLG,* 5.3–4 (Fall–Winter 1972–3), 38.

73 *A great trial in Chinese history,* 226. 74 Hao and Duan, *Zhongguo gongchandang liushi nian,* 618.

bly to criticize Chen Boda's crimes and those of his imitators in the region. During the course of the month-long conference, the leadership of the Beijing Military Region was reorganized: Lin Biao's followers, the commander and the second political commissar, were reassigned, and the Thirty-eighth Army, thought to be loyal to the defense minister, transferred out.[75]

"571": Lin Biao's abortive coup

According to subsequent testimonies, Lin Biao authorized the preparation of plans for a possible coup during a visit to Suzhou with his wife and son in February 1971. The planning for the coup was to be conducted by a small band of relatively junior officers led by his son, Lin Liguo, from his base in the air force. The precipitating events were presumably Mao's rebuff to Lin Biao's allies' stand at the recent MAC meeting and the reorganization of the PLA in the capital. How was Lin to respond? He evidently opted for attack as the only method of defense.

Perhaps the most extraordinary aspect of Lin's bid for power, apart from its ineptitude, was his demonstrated weakness in his own bailiwick. Despite his position as minister of defense, he did not rely on his Politburo allies at the head of various arms of the PLA. According to the evidence brought out at the trial of Lin Biao's surviving supporters in 1980–1, whatever else they did, Huang Yongsheng, Wu Faxian, Li Zuopeng, and Qiu Huizuo were not involved in any plot to assassinate Mao.[76]

Lin Liguo's formal position in the air force, which he owed to his father's influence, was deputy director of the General Office – a key bureau through which all paper flowed – and concurrently deputy chief of operations. According to the evidence of his chief, Wu Faxian, at his trial in 1980, from 6 July 1970, "everything concerning the Air Force was to be reported to Lin Liguo and everything of the Air Force should be put at his disposal and command."[77]

Lin Liguo formed his group of conspirators (see Table 3), known as the "joint fleet," from an investigation team Wu Faxian had authorized him to set up. Most members were thus officers of the PLA Air Force. (AF). Lin

75 Ibid., 618; Hu, *Zhongguo shehuizhuyi geming he jianshe shi jiangyi*, 302; Ying-mao Kau, "Introduction: The case against Lin Piao," *CLG*, 5.3–4 (Fall–Winter 1972–3), 12.

76 See *A great trial in Chinese history*, 117–25. The following account of Lin Biao's plot has been put together from a number of sources, but virtually all are official or semiofficial versions, written by the victors or based on their evidence. In events so momentous as the demise of an heir apparent, there are many reasons why evidence should be doctored, and there can be no guarantee that if the CC's innermost archives are one day opened, another version will not emerge. It still seems worthwhile to spell out in detail the currently most believable version of the Lin Biao affair in order to depict the nature of Chinese politics of the time. Any revised version is likely only to underline the way in which the fate of China was settled by the ambitions and intrigues of a very small group of desperate leaders and their families.

77 Ibid., 93.

TABLE 3
Lin Biao's team: Allies and conspirators

Lin Biao[a]
Ye Qun[a]
Allies
Politburo members
Huang Yongsheng, PLA chief of staff[b]
Wu Faxian, PLA AF CO[b]
Li Zuopeng, PLA Navy, 1st political commissar[b]
Qiu Huizuo, director, PLA logistics dept.[b]
Others
Zheng Weishan, acting CO, Beijing MR?)
Conspirators
"Joint Fleet"
Lin Liguo, deputy director, PLA AF General Office[a]
Wang Weiguo, political commissar, PLA AF 4th Group, Nanjing
Chen Liyun, political commissar, PLA AF 5th Group, Zhejiang
Zhou Jianping, deputy CO, PLA AF Nanjing units
Jiang Tengjiao, former political commissar, PLA AF, Nanjing[b]
Zhou Yuchi, deputy director, general office PLA AF, Beijing[c]
Hu Ping, deputy chief of staff, PLA AF, Beijing
Guan Guanglie, political commissar, PLA unit 0190
Li Weixin, deputy director, PLA AF 4th Group political Dept.
Liu Beifeng, PLA AF HQ CCP office[a]
Lu Min, director, PLA AF Operations Dept., Beijing
Wang Fei, deputy chief of staff, PLA AF, Beijing
Yu Xinye, deputy section chief, PLA AF HQ, Beijing[c]

[a] Killed in an air crash in Mongolia.
[b] Tried in 1980–1.
[c] Committed suicide after the failure of 571.

Liguo's "command unit" was drawn, apart from himself, mainly from the Nanjing Military Region, which controlled East China.

In February 1971, Lin Liguo picked up Yu Xinye, a deputy section chief in the PLA AF HQ, in Hangzhou, summoned a deputy director of the PLA AF HQ's general office, Zhou Yuchi, from Beijing to Shanghai, where between 20 and 24 March he plotted with them and Li Weixin, a deputy director of the Political Department of the PLA's Fourth Group in Nanjing, on the basis of his father's orders.

The discussions of the conspirators indicate an assessment of the political situation by the Lin family that the moment to strike was almost nigh, and that delay in a time of stability could allow civilian leaders to strengthen their positions; Mao was engaged in his habitual playing off of factions, building up Zhang Chunqiao to offset the defense minister.[78] Yet a peaceful

78 Kau, *The Lin Piao affair*, 90–1.

transition to power seems not to have been ruled out even at this stage. A second possibility was that Lin would be thrown out. Again, surprisingly, in view of events at the Second Plenum and since, some conspirators felt this was unlikely in the next three years. But Lin Liguo at least knew the perils of such forecasts: "Nothing is predictable. The Chairman commands such high prestige that he need only utter one sentence to remove anybody he chooses." When Yu Xinye objected that Lin Biao had been Mao's personal choice, Lin Liguo reminded him dryly that Liu Shaoqi had been accorded the same honor.[79]

The third option for Lin Biao was to assume power "ahead of time." Two alternative scenarios were discussed: to get rid of his rivals, principally Zhang Chunqiao, and to get rid of Mao himself. The conspirators expressed no qualms about the latter act but were concerned as to how it could be presented to the nation without negative repercussions. Zhou Yuchi suggested that the blame for Mao's murder could be put on others, even Jiang Qing, but added that politically, Lin "would pay a very high price for resorting to this alternative." So the decision was taken to strive for Lin's peaceful transition to power, but to make preparations for a coup.[80]

Lin Liguo decided to code-name the plot "571," because the Chinese words for these numbers (*wuqiyi*) are a homonym for armed uprising (*wu* [*zhuang*] *qiyi*). Mao was referred to as "B-52." As initially discussed, the plot involved only arresting Zhang Chunqiao and Yao Wenyuan. The idea of assassinating Mao seems to have been devised by Yu Xinye late in the day,[81] perhaps in response to the Chairman's activities in southern China.

No actions of the Chairman could have been better calculated to have alarmed Lin Biao than the comments Mao made during his whistle-stop tour from mid-August to mid-September 1971. His principal visits were to Wuhan, Changsha, and Nanchang, and he met Party and PLA officials from Hubei, Henan, Hunan, Guangdong, Guangxi, Jiangsu, and Fujian.[82] Talking to them, he described the activities of Lin Biao's allies at the Second Plenum as a "two-line struggle," thus equating it with the cases of Liu Shaoqi, Peng Dehuai, Gao Gang, and other anathematized former leaders.

At first, refraining from blaming Lin Biao by name, Mao accused his henchmen of "planned, organized, and programmed" "surprise attacks and underground activities" at the Second Plenum. However, no one could have failed to realize his real target when he remarked: "A certain person was very anxious to become state chairman, to split the Party, and to seize power." When he finally mentioned Lin's name it was more in sorrow than in anger,

79 Ibid., 92. 80 Ibid., 92–3. 81 Ibid., 93–5.
82 Hao and Duan, *Zhongguo gongchandang liushi nian*, 621.

but the defense minister could not have been deceived: "This time, to protect Vice-Chairman Lin, no conclusions concerning individuals were reached. But, of course, he must take some of the responsibility. What should we do with these people?"[83]

Mao's likely answer to his own question could not have been in doubt in the Lin household. Equally interesting, however, was the clear indication in the Chairman's remarks of why he was pursuing his struggle against his anointed successor. At one point he criticized the practice of local Party committees taking their decisions to PLA Party committees for approval. At another, he modified his own earlier slogan that "the whole country should learn from the PLA" by adding on "the PLA should learn from the people of the whole nation."[84] It was the threat of military domination of the polity that moved Mao.

The Chairman must have known and intended that his remarks would soon reach Lin Biao. They were, in fact, reported to Navy Commissar Li Zuopeng, who informed Chief of Staff Huang Yongsheng and Logistics Director Qiu Huizuo on 6 September. Huang immediately telephoned Ye Qun, who was with her husband and son at the seaside resort Beidaihe. Two days later, Lin Biao issued Lin Liguo with what was allegedly his authorization to activate the plan for a coup: "Expect you to act according to the order transmitted by Comrades Liguo [Lin Liguo] and Yuchi [Zhou Yuchi]." The same day, Lin Liguo left for Beijing to make the final arrangements for Mao's assassination.[85]

From 8 to 11 September, Lin Liguo and members of his joint fleet discussed a number of methods for killing Mao as his special train journeyed north back to the capital: attacking the train with flame throwers, 40-mm rocket guns, or 100-mm antiaircraft guns; dynamiting a bridge the train had to cross; bombing the train from the air; or, less dramatic but perhaps surer, face-to-face assassination by pistol.[86]

All these plans were to prove fruitless. While the conspirators were learning about Mao's activities, the Chairman had got wind in Nanchang at the end of August that Lin Biao might be up to no good.[87] On his return journey, therefore, Mao made sudden departures and curtailed stopovers,

83 Kau, *The Lin Piao affair*, 57–61. 84 Ibid., 64.

85 *A great trial in Chinese history*, 96–97. According to a much later account based on an interview with Lin Biao's daughter, Lin Doudou; Huang telephoned on 5 September, but since she was not in Beidaihe when the call came through and the trial version tells of telephone logs, 6 September seems the more likely date for Huang's call; see "Lin Doudou who lives in the shadow of history," *Huaqiao ribao* (Overseas Chinese news), 15 June 1988, 3. However, one recent mainland history states that Lin Liguo was informed directly by one of the participants in Mao's meetings late on the night of 5 September; see Hao and Duan, *Zhongguo gongchandang liushi nian*, 621.

86 *A great trial in Chinese history*, 97.

87 Hao and Duan, *Zhongguo gongchandang liushi nian*, 622; "Lin Doudou who lives in the shadow of history."

leaving Shanghai far sooner than expected, heading back to Beijing on 11 September, passing through the places where his special train might have been intercepted before the plotters were ready.[88] On the afternoon of 12 September, he stopped the train at Fengtai station just outside Beijing and held a two-hour conference with senior military and civilian officials based in the capital, before pulling into the main station later that evening.[89] There is no indication that Mao's precipitate action was triggered by any knowledge of a specific plot, let alone its details. Possibly he had acted on an instinct for survival honed by long years of guerrilla warfare. Whatever the motives, his run for cover precipitated the crisis the Chinese now refer to as the "13 September Incident" (*jiuyisan shijian*).

The 13 September Incident

When Lin Liguo learned the Chairman had escaped death, he immediately put into high gear a plan to set up a rival regime in Guangdong, which Lin Biao and Ye Qun had been considering for some time; it had been prepared simultaneously with the assassination plot. It was agreed that Lin and Ye would fly south on 13 September, leaving Beidaihe at 8:00 A.M., and expect to rendezvous in Guangzhou with Lin's top military allies – Huang Yongsheng, Wu Faxian, Li Zuopeng, and Qiu Huizuo – and Lin Liguo's coconspirators. After completing arrangements in Beijing, Lin Liguo flew to Shanhaiguan, the airport for Beidaihe, in one of China's few British-built Tridents, secretly commandeered through his network of air force supporters, to supervise the evacuation of his parents.[90] He would perhaps have succeeded, but for the intervention of his sister, Lin Liheng.

Lin Liheng was better known by her nickname Doudou (Bean Curd) which her father had given her because of his fondness for that food. Doudou was very close to Lin Biao but was treated brutally by her mother Ye Qun, whom both she and her brother called "Director Ye!"[91] Driven to distraction, Doudou began to believe that Ye Qun could not possibly be her real mother, and the doctor who had delivered her in Yan'an had to be summoned to testify that Ye was.[92] On one occasion, Doudou had tried to

88 Gao and Yan, *"Wenhua da geming" shinian shi*, 379–80.

89 Hu Hua, *Zhongguo shehuizhuyi geming he jianshe shi jiangyi*, 309.

90 Gao and Yan, *"Wenhua da geming" shinian shi*, 381–3.

91 "Lin Doudou who lives in the shadow of history," *Huaqiao ribao*, 14 June 1988. According to one admittedly suspect source, Lin Doudou was born in 1941 in the Soviet Union. This would have been toward the end of Lin Biao's three-year period of hospitalization there; see Yao, *The conspiracy and murder of Mao's heir*, 130.

92 "Lin Doudou who lives in the shadow of history," *Huaqiao ribao*, 14 June 1988. It may have been this story that was the ultimate source for the assertions by Jaap van Ginneken that Doudou was the child of Lin Biao's first wife, Liu Ximing, and that Ye and Lin Biao were not married until 1960; van

commit suicide. Director Ye's reaction was "Let her die"; Doudou's father was not told.[93]

On 6 September, Lin Doudou had been summoned to Beidaihe from Beijing by her brother on the pretext that her father was ill. When she arrived, Lin Liguo had informed her of Mao's activities in southern China, indicated that Lin Biao's back was against the wall and candidly revealed the three options being considered: to kill Mao; to set up a rival government in Guangdong; or to flee to the Soviet Union. Doudou argued with her brother for two days, rejecting all three courses, suggesting that Lin Biao should simply retire from the political limelight like China's senior soldier, Zhu De.[94]

According to her account, Doudou's sole concern was her father's safety. She encouraged the servants to eavesdrop on Lin Biao, Ye Qun, and Lin Liguo to find out what they were up to; on 8 September, after her brother had left for Beijing, she got word to the detachment of PLA Unit 8341 – the guards regiment assigned to CCP leaders – stationed by her parents' house, to be sure to protect Lin Biao whatever happened.[95] Despite Doudou's agitated behavior, no one had the courage to intervene, especially because Ye Qun had been putting it about that her daughter was distraught because she was in love; indeed, she was on the verge of becoming formally engaged.[96]

The engagement celebrations took place on the afternoon of 12 September, beginning before Lin Liguo's return from Beijing. On his arrival, he told his sister he had come especially for the occasion, but aroused her suspicions by immediately hurrying off to confer with his parents. At about 10:20 P.M. Doudou went personally to alert the CO of Unit 8341. This time the commander telephoned Beijing.[97]

When the report reached Premier Zhou Enlai at about 10:30 P.M., he was chairing a meeting at the Great Hall of the People to discuss his government report to the Fourth NPC session. He immediately telephoned Wu Faxian and Li Zuopeng to check whether or not there was a Trident at Shanhaiguan airfield.

While all this was going on, Ye Qun had spent a quiet hour gossiping on

Ginnekan, Jaap, *The rise and fall of Lin Piao,* 263, 272. The date of Ye's marriage to Lin Biao is uncertain; see Klein and Clark, *A biographic dictionary of Chinese communism, 1921–1965,* 1. 567; but one resident of Yan'an in the mid-1940s has confirmed that they were married then (private communication). For a longer account of Doudou's unhappy position in the Lin–Ye household, see Zhang, *Maojiawan jishi,* 256–92, 429. Despite Zhang's critical account of Ye's activities, he asserts that working for her was slightly better than working for Jiang Qing; ibid., 429.

93 *Huaqiao ribao,* 15 June 1988. 94 Ibid. 95 Ibid., 15 and 16 June 1988.

96 Gao and Yan, *"Wenhua da geming" shinian shi,* 384.

97 Ibid., 384–5. Another account says that Doudou approached the guard commander at about 8:30 P.M.; see "Lin Doudou who lives in the shadow of history,"*Huaqiao ribao,* 16 June 1988. Wang, *Da dongluan de niandai,* 427–30, has an account of the events of 11 and 12 September as seen by Lin Liguo's fiancée, Zhang Ning.

the telephone with Madame Qiu Huizuo. Alerted via Lin Liguo's network to Zhou's inquiries, Ye decided to try to disarm suspicion. At 11:30 P.M. she telephoned the premier to tell him of the Lin family's interest in leaving Beidaihe to go to a hot-springs resort. In response to the premier's queries, she said they wanted to go by air rather than rail, but had not arranged a plane. Zhou warned that the weather was currently bad and that he would discuss the Lins' proposed air journey with Wu Faxian.[98]

Once Ye was off the line, Zhou again called Wu Faxian and Li Zuopeng, who, as senior naval officer, was in charge of the Shanhaiguan naval air base, and ordered that the Trident was not to be allowed to take off unless permission was jointly given by Zhou, Li, Huang Yongsheng, and Wu Faxian. In Beidaihe, Ye sprang into action. With Lin Liguo, she aroused Lin Biao, who had taken a sleeping pill, telling him that people were coming to arrest him. Papers were burned, and the family got into their car and left for the airport. The Unit 8341 guards were too timid to stop them. Fortunately for the fugitives, Li Zuopeng had distorted Zhou Enlai's instructions and had told the Shanhaiguan base authorities that the Trident could take off if just one of the four men named gave permission, which Li did. At 12:32 A.M., Lin Biao, with his wife and son, took off.[99]

Zhou had been informed at about midnight that the Lins had fled their compound. On hearing the news, Zhou ordered Wu Faxian to ground all aircraft in China, and then sent an aide to Wu's headquarters to keep an eye on him.[100] Zhou then drove to Mao's residence in the Zhongnanhai to brief him personally. When radar indicated the Trident would be crossing into Mongolian territory, Wu Faxian telephoned to ask whether the plane should be shot down. Zhou asked Mao for his orders. Mao is quoted as replying philosophically: "Rain has to fall, women have to marry, these things are immutable; let them go."[101] Zhou, not knowing the details of Lin's activities and wanting to prevent any threat to Mao's safety, got the Chairman to leave his residence and move to the Great Hall.

Only now did Mao order Zhou to summon senior officials there for a

98 Yu Nan, "Zhou zongli chuzhi '9.13' Lin Biao pantao shijian de yixie qingkuang" (Some of the circumstances regarding Premier Zhou's management of the 13 September incident when Lin Biao committed treachery and fled), *Dangshi yanjiu* (Research on Party history), 3 (1981), 59; Wang, *Da dongluan de niandai,* 431; Hao and Duan, *Zhongguo gongchandang liushi nian,* 622; Gao and Yan, *"Wenhua da geming" shinian shi,* 386; *Huaqiao ribao,* 16 June 1988. The latter account says that it was Zhou who telephoned Ye.

99 *Huaqiao ribao,* loc. cit., 16, 17 June 1988; Hao and Duan, *Zhongguo gongchandang liushi nian,* 622; *A great trial in Chinese history,* 99; Gao and Yan, *"Wenhua da geming" shinian shi,* 387–91. According to Wang, *Da dongluan de niandai,* 432, Mao's imprimatur had also to be obtained.

100 Yu, "Zhou zongli," 59. The Air Force CO failed to prevent some of Lin Liguo's collaborators from trying to escape by helicopter; *A great trial in Chinese history,* 99–100.

101 *"Tian yao xiayu, niang yao jiaren, dou shi meiyou fazi de shi; you tamen chu ba."* See Hao and Duan, *Zhongguo gongchandang liushi nian,* 623.

Politburo conference, the clearest indication of how China was ruled. The meeting convened after 3:00 A.M., but Mao did not attend, whether for security reasons or out of embarrassment at the defection of his personally chosen heir is uncertain. Zhou informed his Politburo colleagues of Mao's return to the capital the previous afternoon and of Lin Biao's flight. He warned them to be prepared for anything.[102] It was not until the afternoon of 14 September that Zhou learned from the PRC embassy in Ulan Bator that Lin Biao's Trident had crashed at approximately 2:30 A.M. on 13 September near Undur Khan in Mongolia, killing the eight men and one woman on board.[103]

A more recent, unofficial account throws doubt on this description of events by focusing on the main question it prompts: Why did the Lins not fly south as arranged? The new account suggests that the Lin family did not immediately abandon their original plan to set up a rival regime in Guangdong, a plan that, after all, they would have had to advance by only about eight hours. This version argues that the Trident was in the air for almost two hours, whereas the flying time to Undur Khan for such a plane should have been less than an hour. It claims that the Trident in fact first flew south for about ten minutes and then returned to Shanhaiguan, but found the air base closed, as Zhou Enlai had instructed. Why the Lins should have abandoned their southern strategy is not explained, but the implication of the story is that Zhou refused to let Lin land to force the latter to flee to the Soviet Union, thus putting himself beyond the pale as a national traitor.[104] Whatever the truth, the most dangerous threat to Mao's power and person since the Liberation was over. The specter of Bonapartism had been exorcised for the time being.

The impact of the fall of Lin Biao

The death of Lin Biao enabled Mao and Zhou Enlai to purge the Politburo of the central military leaders who had been his allies, if not his coconspirators.

102 Yu, "Zhou zongli," 59. This account was written partly to dispel rumors that Zhou had withheld the news of the flight from Mao until just before the plane was about to cross the frontier. A more hard-nosed view preferred by some scholars to explain Mao's apparent relaxed attitude toward Lin Biao's escape is the the PLA Air Force's night-fighter capability was too limited to permit it to bring down the fleeing plane.

103 Ibid.

104 See *Huaqiao ribao,* 17 June 1988. An alternative explanation could be that the Trident did not fly a straight course toward Mongolia but zigzagged to avoid interception. Another version retailed by a former public security official to a China scholar was that Premier Zhou managed to talk the pilot into flying back into Chinese air space, but that the latter was then shot down by Lin Liguo, who took over the controls. Lin proved unable to handle the plane and it crashed. An even more sensational, supposedly "insider" account of the demise of Lin Biao, discounted by many scholars as fabricated, alleges that he was killed on Mao's orders in a rocket attack when driving home after a banquet at the Chairman's villa outside Beijing on 12 September. See Yao, *The conspiracy and murder of Mao's heir,* ch. 16.

On the morning of 24 September, Zhou Enlai summoned PLA Chief of Staff Huang Yongsheng, PLA AF head Wu Faxian, PLA Navy Political Commissar Li Zuopeng, and PLA Logistics Director Qiu Huizuo to the Great Hall to tell them that they were dismissed and had to make thorough self-examinations. Each left under arrest, and each would eventually stand trial. The survivors among Lin Liguo's group of young turks in the PLA AF were also swept away.

But although the PLA had lost its most powerful figures in the civilian leadership and its high-profile role had been diminished, it was far from the end of PLA institutional dominance within the civilian polity. A major military presence in Party and government remained. Ye Jianying, one of China's ten marshals and a longtime ally of Zhou Enlai, took charge of a revamped MAC, directed the investigation into Lin Biao's activities within the major military units,[105] and played an increasingly important political role. His loyalty to Mao and the premier could be assumed, but he was nevertheless a representative of the military establishment.[106] Wang Dongxing, the CO of the central bodyguard, PLA Unit 8341, was even more committed to the Chairman and was a public security official rather than part of the military mainstream,[107] but he was certainly not a civilian cadre. These men, in contrast to Lin Biao, would faithfully support Mao in his continuing efforts to recivilianize the polity.

The continuing power of PLA cadres in the provinces was symbolized by the continuing presence within the Politburo of three generals with top provincial responsibilities: Xu Shiyou, chairman of the Jiangsu Revolutionary Committee and CO of the Nanjing Military Region; Chen Xilian, chairman of the Liaoning Revolutionary Committee and CO of the Shenyang Military Region; and alternate member Li Desheng, chairman of the Anhui Revolutionary Committee and CO of the Anhui Military District. All of them had kept on the right side of Mao during the Cultural Revolution.

What is less easy to assess is the impact of Lin's fall on Mao. Liu Shaoqi had been axed in the heat of the Cultural Revolution, at a time when Mao

105 Hao and Duan, *Zhongguo gongchandang liushi nian*, 624; *Yingsi lu*, 305–8, 346. For the dismissal of Lin's senior military allies, see Yu, "Zhou zongli," 59.

106 Among Mao's remarks during his southern tour in the summer of 1971 is an admonition on 28 August to respect Ye Jianying because of his firmness in crisis, as demonstrated by his loyalty to the future Chairman during the latter's struggle with Zhang Guotao in 1935. This comment, which occurs in what appears to be an unexpurgated manuscript version of Mao's remarks available in Harvard's Fairbank Center Library, illustrates both the importance of Ye to Mao in his dealings with the military at this time, as well as how the Chairman never forgot a favor or a slight. I am grateful to Michael Schoenhals for bringing this remark to my attention.

107 Wang Dongxing is not listed among the senior officers named "Wang" whose biographies are given in volumes 1 and 2 of the official, *Zhongguo renmin jiefangjun jiangshuai minglu* (The names and records of marshals and generals of the Chinese People's Liberation Army).

had generated enough momentum to gain widespread support for the need to change leaders. Even Liu's former secretary, Deng Liqun, later admitted that in 1966 he had felt it was probably right that Mao's successor should be someone able to handle military as well as Party affairs, and he testified that this was a common opinion within the CCP.[108] Lin Biao was an authentic revolutionary hero and unquestionably a longtime Mao loyalist. The Chairman's assessment that Lin was a better bet than Liu may have been resented by the latter's followers in the Party machine, but it was probably accepted unquestioningly within the broader political world.

Now the "best pupil" had not merely been found wanting but, as Zhou Enlai would reveal at the CCP's Tenth Congress in 1973,[109] had even attempted to assassinate the Chairman himself. How could Mao have been so wrong for so long? His letter to Jiang Qing in 1966 expressing concern about Lin Biao's activities was quickly circulated within the Party,[110] but it underlined rather than explained away Mao's failure to prevent this dangerous man from emerging as his officially anointed successor. Was the Chairman unable to detect traitors and sham Marxists among men who had been close to him for decades?

Perhaps equally damaging was the revelation of how the top ranks of the CCP were riddled with treachery and intrigue worthy of the palace politics of the old imperial Chinese court, with plenty of obvious equivalents for the traditional panoply of empresses and eunuchs, officials and generals. Was this the purified politics the Cultural Revolution should have produced? While the turbulence and purges of the early years of the Cultural Revolution

108 See Deng Liqun, "Xuexi 'Guanyu jianguo yilai dangde ruogan lishi wenti de jueyi' de wenti he huida" (Questions and answers in studying the 'Resolution on certain historical questions since the founding of the state'), in *Dangshi huiyi baogao ji* (Collection of reports to the Party history conference), 153. Confirmation that Deng Liqun was not exceptional in this regard is in Tan Zongji, "Lin Biao fangeming jituan de jueqi jiqi fumie," 42, 43. According to this latter source, when Liu Shaoqi was criticized at the Eleventh Plenum and a new number two had to be found from the PSC, Deng Xiaoping was ruled out because he, too, was under fire; Chen Yun, because he was rightist; Zhu De, because he was too old; and Zhou Enlai, because Mao was not satisfied with him and Zhou himself had often said that he was not able to assume command (*wo zhege ren shi buneng guashuaide*). That left only Lin Biao; ibid., 42.

109 *The Tenth National Congress of the Communist Party of China (Documents)*, 5–6.

110 Hao and Duan, *Zhongguo gongchandang liushi nian*, 625–6; also see n. 43. This letter was so convenient for Mao to be able to circulate after the death of Lin Biao that post–Cultural Revolution Party historians seem to have questioned its authenticity. In response, one senior historian recounted the following episode: Lin Biao had been most agitated when he had learned about Mao's letter in 1966, so much so that Mao decided not to have it circulated and indeed ordered it burned. When the burning ceremony took place, the leftist propagandist Qi Benyu protested to Zhou Enlai that Mao's words were too precious to be destroyed in this way; the premier reassured him that he had ordered Tao Zhu, then director of propaganda, to make a copy! It was copies of this copy that had to be circulated after Lin's death, thus presumably giving rise to doubts about its authenticity. See Tan Zongji's account, "Lin Biao fangeming jituan." This fascinating anecdote, which tells as much about Zhou Enlai as about Lin Biao, was first noticed by Michael Schoenhals.

probably disillusioned most of Mao's closest colleagues, the fall of Lin Biao almost certainly spread that disillusionment among a far wider group[111] and would be a source of political malaise when Mao's successors tried to rebuild after his death.

THE RISE AND FALL OF THE GANG OF FOUR

The succession problem

For the moment, Mao's main problem was to reconstruct the top leadership and, in particular, to select a credible successor. He had destroyed the very procedures by which he had hoped to spare China the succession struggles experienced by other totalitarian states, notably the Soviet Union after the death of Stalin. His "two fronts" system had been devised in the 1950s to give his colleagues experience and exposure in the front line while he monitored them from the second line. Liu's takeover from Mao of the post of head of state had been part of that process, but it did not outlast Liu himself. Similarly, the "best pupil" model could not outlast Lin Biao.[112] How was the Chairman to solve the problem of "After Mao, who?" and the even more crucial question "After Mao, what?"

Three groups began to emerge in the Politburo in the wake of Lin: radicals, survivors, and beneficiaries of the Cultural Revolution. The radicals were the rump of the original ultra-leftist coalition that had formed around Mao to launch the Cultural Revolution. By 1967, the interests of Lin Biao and the Cultural Revolution Group had already begun to diverge sharply, but they remained on the same side in important ways. With the disappearance of Lin Biao and his allies, the former coalition was reduced to Kang Sheng, Jiang Qing, Zhang Chunqiao, Yao Wenyuan, and Xie Fuzhi, who had not originally been a member of the core group but had made himself extremely useful to it as the Cultural Revolution got underway from his vantage point as minister of public security. Kang Sheng, however, appears to have played an increasingly nominal role owing to failing health, and Xie died in 1972, leaving a rump of Jiang, Zhang, and Yao.

The survivors were those senior officials who had collaborated with Mao, even though they almost certainly opposed the main thrust of the Cultural Revolution: Premier Zhou Enlai, Vice-Premier Li Xiannian, acting head of

111 Hao and Duan, *Zhongguo gongchandang liushi nian,* 624. This argument has also been made to the author by Chinese friends who experienced this disillusionment at that time.

112 For a longer discussion of the problem of succession under Mao and Deng Xiaoping, see Roderick MacFarquhar, "Passing the baton in Beijing," *New York Review of Books,* 35.2 (18 February 1988), 21–2.

state Dong Biwu, and three old marshals: Zhu De, Liu Bocheng, and Ye Jianying. Of these, only Zhou, Li, and Ye were active politically; the other three had survived in the Politburo because their loyalty to Mao could be relied upon under almost any circumstances. Indeed, Liu Bocheng's continued membership was essentially a courtesy to a great revolutionary warrior, who was apparently mentally competent but physically blind and politically inert.

After the shock of the Lin Biao affair, Mao seems to have felt it expedient to reinforce his ties to this group by agreeing to rehabilitate a number of senior officials whose fall could credibly be blamed on Lin Biao. Those early critics of the Cultural Revolution known as the "February adverse current" were restored to grace if not to their old offices. When one of them, former Foreign Minister Chen Yi, died in January 1972, Mao unexpectedly attended the memorial ceremony and gave a high appraisal of the old marshal.[113]

One rehabilitation would profoundly affect China's history: that of "the number two Party person in authority taking the capitalist road," former CCP General Secretary Deng Xiaoping. Deng and some of his family were in Jiangsi province, where they had been moved from Beijing as a result of Lin Biao's evacuation order in October 1969. Deng worked a half day as a fitter in a country tractor plant. When Lin Biao fell, he wrote twice to Mao, in November 1971 and August 1972, asking to be allowed to work once more for the Party and nation. After receiving the second letter, Mao made approving comments on Deng's revolutionary record, although it was not until March 1973 that the formalities for his return to Beijing were completed.[114] The reasons for Deng's second coming and its results will be explored later in the chapter.

The beneficiaries of the Cultural Revolution were those officials who had risen as a result of the purge of their seniors, as well as through their own ability to manipulate the turbulent politics of the late 1960s and early 1970s.

113 Hao and Duan, *Zhongguo gongchandang liushi nian,* 624. For a description of Mao's last-minute decision to attend the Chen Yi memorial ceremony on 10 January 1972, at which he told Prince Sihanouk of Cambodia that Chen had supported him, whereas Lin Biao had opposed him, see the series of eleven articles by Zhang Yufeng, "Anecdotes of Mao Zedong and Zhou Enlai in their later years," in *GMRB,* 26 December 1988–6 January 1989, translated in *FBIS Daily Report: China,* 27 January 1989, 16–19, and 31 January 1989, 30–7. This was the last such ceremony that Mao was able to attend.

114 See Gao and Yan, *"Wenhua da geming" shinian shi,* 528–30; Hao and Duan, *Zhongguo gongchandang liushi nian,* 624. For a more detailed account of Deng's sojourn in Jiangxi, see Qiu Zhizhuo, "Deng Xiaoping zai 1969–1972" (Deng Xiaoping in 1969–1972), *Xinhua wenzhai* (New China digest), 112 (April 1988), 133–55. A copy of Deng's letter of 3 August 1972 is available in the library of Harvard's Fairbank Center. In it, he expresses his support for the Cultural Revolution, without whose "incomparably immense monster-revealing mirror" (*wubi juda de zhaoyaojing*) men like Lin Biao and Chen Boda would not have been exposed. The letter, which Michael Schoenhals drew to my attention, is a combination of flattery, self-abasement, and an account of Deng's own opinions about and experience of Lin and Chen.

In the immediate aftermath of the fall of Lin Biao, these were principally military figures: Xu Shiyou, Chen Xilian, Li Desheng, and Wang Dongxing; but they also included a civilian cadre, Ji Dengkui, who was involved in the post-Lin cleanup and would achieve increasing prominence.[115]

The problem for Mao now was that there was no obvious successor among the three groups likely to preserve the gains of the Cultural Revolution. Zhou Enlai was, without question, the highest-ranking official under Mao. If the Chairman had considered him an appropriate successor, he could have appointed him long since, to widespread approval. But Mao was not prepared to entrust his ultra-leftist program to any of the survivors. Anyway, Zhou could not be assumed to outlive Mao, for in May 1972, in the course of a regular checkup, he was found to have cancer at an early stage.[116]

The rump of the old Cultural Revolution Group was the obvious place for Mao to look for a like-minded successor. The Chairman must have been aware, however, that the PLA was unlikely to accept as supreme leader anyone who had done so much to stir up violence, bloodshed, and disorder as Jiang Qing or Zhang Chunqiao. Nor, apparently, did any beneficiary of the Cultural Revolution yet have the stature to attract broad-based support and the Chairman's endorsement.

In these difficult circumstances, Mao took an extraordinary step. He catapulted a junior radical into the very apex of the leadership. Wang Hongwen, aged only thirty-six at the time of Lin Biao's demise, had risen during Shanghai's January Revolution from a humble position as a Shanghai factory security chief to a workers' leader in support of Zhang Chunqiao and Yao Wenyuan. By this time he was the effective boss of China's most populous city and leftist stronghold, as well as political commissar of its PLA garrison.[117] In the autumn of 1972, Wang was transferred to Beijing, appearing in public there for the first time in October at the celebration of the fiftieth birthday of Prince Sihanouk in the Great Hall of the People, to the bewilder-

115 For Ji's role in the post-Lin cleanup, see *Huaqiao ribao,* 18 June 1988. For an explanation of Ji's promotion under Mao's aegis, see Wang Lingshu, "Ji Dengkui on Mao Zedong," *Liaowang* (Observer), overseas edition, 6–13 February 1989, translated in *FBIS, Daily Report: China,* 14 February 1989, 22–6.

116 For the claim that the cancer was discovered in May, see Gao and Yan, *"Wenhua de geming" shinian shi,* 474. *Bujin de sinian* (Inexhaustible memories), 583, provides the information that the cancer was in its early stages and tells how Mao ordered a special group to be set up to supervise Zhou's treatment. Curiously, *Zhou zongli shengping dashiji* (Major events in the life of Premier Zhou), 494, only gives the year, though it provides a month-by-month chronology.

117 For Wang Hongwen's life, see Ting Wang, *Wang Hongwen, Zhang Chunqiao pingzhuan* (Biographies of Wang Hongwen and Zhang Chunqiao), 49–134. See also Gao and Yan, *"Wenhua da geming" shinian shi,* 442–8. Neale Hunter, *Shanghai journal: An eyewitness account of the Cultural Revolution,* and Andrew G. Walder, *Chang Ch'un-ch'iao and Shanghai's January Revolution,* which cover the period of Wang Hongwen's emergence, but with little mention of Wang himself.

ment of junior Chinese officials.[118] At Mao's direction, Wang was effectively inducted into the Politburo in May 1973, along with two beneficiaries of the Cultural Revolution: Hua Guofeng, the Hunan first secretary, who seems to have distinguished himself in the post–Lin Biao investigations,[119] and Wu De, the Beijing first secretary.[120]

The rise of Wang Hongwen was clearly designed to provide a more acceptable image for the radical faction. Wang, at thirty-seven, was good-looking and personable, and symbolized two constituencies critically important in the Cultural Revolution: youth and the workers. Through Wang, the radicals may have hoped to rekindle the youthful enthusiasm that had been dampened by the disbanding of the Red Guards. Wang's proletarian credentials could also be expected to attract the support of the urban workers. And whatever Wang's role in Shanghai, no general could blame him for the nationwide urban anarchy in 1967 and 1968.

After the CCP's Tenth Party Congress in August 1973, Wang was thrust into the Party's number three position and was named a vice-chairman and member of the Politburo Standing Committee.[121] The fourth member of what would later be known as the Gang of Four was now in place, outranked only by Mao and Zhou Enlai. With only six years' experience of revolutionary struggle and politics, he was expected to keep up with and contend against men like the premier, who had survived six decades of revolutions, civil wars, foreign invasion, and Party infighting. It was a grossly unequal contest, another Maoist gamble that would fail.

Zhou Enlai's anti-leftist offensive

When Wang Hongwen arrived in Beijing, his radical colleagues, Jiang Qing, Zhang Chunqiao, and Yao Wenyuan, were on the defensive. They had benefited from the fall of Lin Biao and his military clique, which removed a major obstacle to their inheriting Mao's mantle, but Lin Biao's actions had tarnished the leftist cause. Some of the dishonor he had in-

118 The present author witnessed officials' inability to explain what Wang Hongwen was doing in Beijing, shaking hands with the assembled VIPs along with elders and betters like Zhou Enlai, Li Xiannian, and Foreign Minister Ji Pengfei. Curiously, a banquet given for Prince Sihanouk was made the occasion for another equally amazing first appearance in Beijing: the return of Deng Xiaoping to public life on 12 April 1973; see John Gardner, *Chinese politics and the succession to Mao,* 62.

119 See Ting Wang, *Chairman Hua: Leader of the Chinese Communists,* 77–80

120 Hao and Duan, *Zhongguo gongchandang liushi nian,* 628.

121 The consternation in China at Wang's meteoric rise can be guessed at when one remembers the disbelief with which American politicians and press reacted during the 1988 presidential campaign to then Vice-President Bush's choice of an unknown forty-one-year-old senator, Dan Quayle, as his running mate, a position that, unlike Wang's, conferred only potential power.

curred inevitably rubbed off on his erstwhile allies from the Cultural Revolution Group.

Zhou Enlai took advantage of the radicals' disarray in the wake of the 13 September Incident to renew his year-old campaign to stabilize administration and encourage production. In December 1971, he lectured officials of the State Planning Commission (SPC) on the need to restore order and responsibility to an anarchic industrial management system. Intimidated by leftist threats, plant directors were afraid to maintain discipline. The guidelines produce by the SPC as a result of Zhou's prodding were vetoed by Zhang Chunqiao and thus could not be distributed as formal documents. It was claimed that they nonetheless had a salutary effect on industrial production, although the figures do not bear this out.[122]

In agriculture, Zhou ordered that the egalitarianism of the Dazhai brigade should be imitated only when local circumstances permitted.[123] One such manifestation of egalitarianism had been a tendency to shift the accounting unit from production team to production brigade. During the grim famine years after the GLF when incentives for the peasants were vital to stimulate production, the Party had made the production team into the unit for accounting. The team was the smallest, lowest-level organization in the three-tier setup of the rural communes, and accounting at the team level meant that income was distributed within the most cohesive and homogeneous rural collective entity. When the right to act as the accounting unit was ceded by a group of teams to the production brigade, of which they were part, it entailed redistributing income from richer to poorer teams. This aroused great resentment. The radicals had encouraged a movement toward brigade accounting starting in 1968, but this had already been checked in 1970, before Zhou Enlai's counterattack.[124] Another indicator of rural radicalism was the tolerance accorded peasants' private plots. Here, too, leftism seemed to be on the retreat as early as 1970, well before the fall of Lin Biao.[125] Nor do grain

122 Hao and Duan, *Zhongguo gongchandang liushi nian*, 626; *Guanyu jianguo yilai dangde ruogan lishi wenti de jueyi zhushi ben (xiuding)* (hereafter *Zhushi ben*) (Revised annotated edition of the Resolution on certain questions in the history of our party since the founding of the People's Republic), 414–16. According to the PRC State Statistical Bureau, *Zhongguo tongji nianjian, 1981* (Chinese statistical yearbook, 1981), 233, steel production figures for these years were as follows (m. = million): 1969 – 13.3 m. tons; 1970 – 17.7 m. tons; 1971 – 21.3 m. tons; 1972 – 23.3 m. tons; 1973 – 25.2 m. tons; i.e., bigger increases in the years up to and including Lin Biao's fall than thereafter. See also Yan Fangming and Wang Yaping, "Qishi niandai chuqi woguo jingji jianshe de maojin ji qi tiaozheng," (The blind advance in our national economic construction in the early 1970s and its correction), *Dangshi yanjiu*, 5 (1985), 55–60. For an analysis of the relative lightness of the effect of the Cultural Revolution on industry after the anarchy of 1967–8, see *CHOC*, 15, Chapter 6.

123 *Zhushi ben*, 416.

124 See David Zweig, *Agrarian radicalism in China, 1968–1981*, 57–60 and ch. 5; also Zweig, "Strategies of policy implementation: policy 'winds' and brigade accounting in rural China, 1966–1978," *World Politics*, 37.2 (January 1985), 267–93.

125 Zweig, *Agrarian radicalism in China*, 57–60 and ch. 6.

output figures suggest a general boost in agricultural production after 13 September 1971.[126]

Nevertheless, 1972 could be called Zhou Enlai's year. There was relaxation in the cultural sphere. With the premier's encouragement, a call for a restoration of educational standards and scientific research was published by a leading academic, albeit not in the *People's Daily*, which was controlled by the radicals, and not without a counterattack by Zhang Chunqiao and Yao Wenyuan.[127] At a major conference of more than 300 senior central and provincial officials held in Beijing from 20 May to late June 1972, Zhou deepened the attack on Lin Biao and won a ringing personal endorsement from the Chairman.[128] Yet the premier was unable to liquidate the leftist positions because, in the last analysis, the radicals were still backed by Mao. By December 1972, the Chairman had decided that the antileftist tide had gone too far. In response to the urgings of Zhang and Yao, he decreed that Lin Biao had not been an ultra-leftist after all, but an ultra-rightist![129] The radicals resumed their offensive.

The Tenth Party Congress

Wang Hongwen, Zhang Chunqiao, and Yao Wenyuan were put in charge of preparing the three main documents for the Tenth Party Congress, held in Beijing from 24 to 28 August 1973, striking proof that they had recaptured the ideological high ground. The documents were the political report, which was delivered by Zhou Enlai; the report on the revision of the Party constitution, delivered by Wang; and the draft new constitution.[130]

126 The grain output figures are as follows: 1969 – 210.9 m. tons; 1970 – 239.9 m. tons; 1971 – 250.1 m. tons; 1972 – 240.4 m. tons; 1973 – 264.9 m. tons; see State Statistical Bureau, *Zhongguo tongji nianjian, 1983*, 158.

127 That 1972 was the year of Zhou Enlai is the assessment of Laszlo Ladany, *The Communist Party of China and Marxism, 1921–1985: A self-portrait*, 355–6, who deals with the issues to be covered. Zhou took the opportunity to try to rebut decisively an allegation that he had betrayed the CCP in 1932, which had apparently been discreetly encouraged by Kang Sheng and Jiang Qing in 1967. But although he circulated a brief statement from Mao that exonerated him, the Gang of Four continued to use the charge against him almost until his death; see "Guanyu Guomindang zaoyao wumie de dengzai suowei 'Wu Hao Qishi' wenti de wenjian" (Document on the problem of the Guomindang maliciously concocting and publishing the so-called 'Wu Hao notice'), *Dangshi yanjiu*, I, (1980), 8; 'Wu Hao' was one of Zhou Enlai's aliases at that time. See Hao and Duan, *Zhongguo gongchandang liushi nian*, 626–7, for a discussion of the article on educational reform by Zhou Peiyuan; and Merle Goldman, *China's intellectuals: Advise and dissent*, 162–6, for a general discussion of the attempt to revive science. For Zhou's inability to control the *People's Daily*, see Jin Chunming, " 'Wenhua da geming' de shinian" (The decade of the Great Cultural Revolution), 203–4.

128 Hao and Duan, *Zhongguo gongchandang liushi nian*, 625–6.

129 For a discussion of this politically necessary but ideologically bizarre redefinition, see a series of ten articles by Wang Ruoshui entitled "Cong pi 'zuo' daoxiang fanyou de yici geren jingli" (The experience of one individual of the reversal from criticizing 'leftism' to opposing rightism), in *Huaqiao ribao*, 12–21 March 1989.

130 Hao and Duan, *Zhongguo gongchandang liushi nian*, 628.

Not surprisingly, the reports and the constitution reflected the line of the Ninth Congress, despite the dramatic developments within the Chinese leadership since then. In Wang Hongwen's words, "Practice over the past four years and more has fully proved that both the political line and organizational line of the Ninth Congress are correct."[131] Naturally, Lin Biao's name was excised from the new constitution, but the radicals would not have wanted to discard a document that reflected the ideals and achievements of the first three years of the Cultural Revolution. Instead they reaffirmed the concept of the Cultural Revolution, inserting into the general program of the new constitution the words: "Revolutions like this will have to be carried out many times in the future."[132] There is no way of knowing if they attempted to make Zhou Enlai say something similar, but no such assertion appears in his report.[133]

Other additions to the constitution reflected other major concerns of the radicals: criticizing revisionism; going against the tide; the need to train revolutionary successors; the inviolability of Party leadership over other institutions, most importantly the PLA; the impermissibility of suppressing criticism.[134]

The new central leadership of the CCP, chosen at the postcongress CC plenum, reflected the resurgence of the radicals. The Politburo Standing Committee was greatly enlarged, nine members compared with five in 1969. Of those nine, Mao, Wang Hongwen, Kang Sheng, and Zhang Chunqiao could be regarded as strong supporters of the goals of the Cultural Revolution; Zhu De (age eighty-six) and Dong Biwu (age eighty-seven) were grand old men with little remaining political clout, whose presence might have comforted a few nostalgic senior officials, but who (if consulted) would almost certainly back Mao; Li Desheng, a dark-horse entrant soon to become CO of the Shenyang Military Region, had shown himself sensitive to radical demands during the early years of the Cultural Revolution and could be counted as an opportunistic supporter of the radicals. This left only Zhou Enlai and Ye Jianying as effective voices of moderation.

New entrants to the Politburo like Hua Guofeng, Wu De, and Chen Yonggui (the peasant Stakhanovite who headed the party committee of the Dazhai Brigade) were nearly all beneficiaries of the Cultural Revolution who could presumably be expected to support its goals. Senior cadres like Li Jingquan and Tan Zhenlin, whom Zhou had managed to get rehabilitated

131 *The Tenth National Congress of the Communist Party of China (Documents)*, 42. Zhou Enlai used virtually the same words; ibid., 9–10.

132 Ibid., 45.

133 William A. Joseph has argued that Zhou's report contains subtle hints that Lin Biao really was a leftist not a rightist; see his *The critique of ultra-leftism in China, 1958–1981*, 138–9. If so, then Zhou presumably modified the draft after Wang and Zhang submitted it to him.

134 *The Tenth National Congress (Documents)*, 47, 48, 50, 52, 55.

TABLE 4
Leadership changes, April 1969–August 1973

(Names in boldface are of new entrants into the Politburo; names in capital letters represent promotions within the Politburo as of the Ninth Congress. At both congresses, only the chairman and vice-chairmen were ranked; the rest were given in order of the number of strokes in the characters of their surnames. The order of the post–Ninth Congress Politburo has been juggled to make it easier to note the changes between 1969 and 1973.)

Ninth Congress		Tenth Congress	
Mao Zedong	PSC	Mao Zedong	PSC
Lin Biao	PSC		
Zhou Enlai	PSC	Zhou Enlai	PSC VC
Chen Boda	PSC		
		Wang Hongwen	PSC VC
Kang Sheng	PSC	Kang Sheng	PSC VC
Ye Jianying		YE JIANYING	PSC VC
Li Desheng	(alt)	LI DESHENG	PSC VC
Zhu De		ZHU DE	PSC VC
Zhang Chunqiao		ZHANG CHUNQIAO	PSC
Dong Biwu		DONG BIWU	PSC
Jiang Qing (f)		Jiang Qing (f)	
Ye Qun (f)			
Liu Bocheng		Liu Bocheng	
Xu Shiyou		Xu Shiyou	
Chen Xilian		Chen Xilian	
Li Xiannian		Li Xiannian	
Li Zuopeng			
Wu Faxian			
Qiu Huizuo			
Yao Wenyuan		Yao Wenyuan	
Huang Yongsheng			
Xie Fuzhi			
Ji Dengkui	(alt)	JI DENGKUI	
Li Xuefeng	(alt)		
Wang Dongxing	(alt)	WANG DONGXING	
		Wei Guoqing	
		Hua Guofeng	
		Wu De	
		Chen Yonggui	
		Wu Guixian	(alt)
		Su Zhenhua	(alt)
		Ni Zhifu	(alt)
		Saifudin	(alt)

Notes: PSC = Politburo Standing Committee; VC = vice-chairman; alt = alternate member; (f) = female.

during the antileftist interlude, made it onto the CC but failed to return to the Politburo.

In the aftermath of their success, the radicals dipped their brushes in vitriol as they prepared to denounce their most formidable opponent: Premier Zhou Enlai himself.

"Pi Lin, pi Kong"

On 18 January 1974, with Mao's approval, the party center circulated a document prepared under the direction of Jiang Qing entitled "The doctrines of Lin Biao, Confucius and Mencius."[135] According to one account, the original authorization for this bizarre-seeming linkage was a comment by Mao to a Qinghua University study group in August 1973 that Lin and Confucius could be criticized together.[136] But the Qinghua inquiry itself must have been sparked by Mao's remark in March 1973 at a central work conference called to criticize Lin Biao that it was also necessary to criticize Confucius. Mao reinforced his message in a couple of poems written in May and August criticizing China's senior intellectual, Guo Moruo, for praising the Confucians and reviling their principal tormentor, China's First Emperor, Qin Shihuangdi.[137] It was not inapposite that Mao himself was often seen by his countrymen as a founding emperor similar to Qin Shihuangdi,[138] a ruler excoriated as a tyrant by generations of Chinese historians.

By August, Mao's words must have been widely known among the political cognoscenti. That month, the *People's Daily,* controlled by the radicals, carried an article by a Guangzhou professor that laid out some of the major themes of the subsequent campaign, including the one most relevant to current politics. The Confucian *Analects* were quoted as saying: "Revive states that have been extinguished, restore families whose line of succession has been broken and call to office those who have retired to obscurity." This was an oblique but unmistakable critique of Zhou's rehabilitation of senior cadres, particularly clear to those who knew that this passage referred to the actions of Zhou's namesake, the great statesman of the twelfth century B.C. the Duke of Zhou.[139]

While this article was being debated up and down China, Jiang Qing got Qinghua to form a group to provide the intellectual ammunition for a full-scale and credible official campaign.[140] The group was led by Chi Qun,

135 "Lin Biao yu Kong-Meng zhidao"; see Hu, *Zhongguo shehuizhuyi geming he jianshe shi jiangyi,* 316.

136 Yue Daiyun and Carolyn Wakeman, *To the storm: The odyssey of a revolutionary Chinese woman,* 323.

137 Teaching and Research Office for CCP History, *Zhongguo gongchandang liushi nian dashi jianjie,* 568. Mao pursued his comparison of Confucius and Qin Shihuangdi in conversation with a doubtless mystified visiting Egyptian leader; ibid. I have been unable to trace the poems referred to in this source. Mao was accustomed to using Guo Moruo's poems as a foil for his own; see, for instance, *Chinese Literature,* 4 (1976), 43–4, 48–50. But there is no indication in *Moruo shici xuan* (Selected poems of Moruo) of any recent poems of Guo's to which Mao might have been replying.

138 Union Research Institute, *The case of Peng Teh-huai,* 36.

139 "Quarterly chronicle and documentation," *CQ,* 57 (January–March 1974), 207–10. The fact that the remarks by Zhou Enlai on foreign affairs, a field he had made very much his own, were criticized by the Politburo in November 1973 at Mao's suggestion, of course encouraged the Gang of Four to believe their moment was coming; Wang, *Da dongluan de niandai,* 417.

140 Yue and Wakeman, *To the storm,* 323. The key role of Qinghua in the launching of the *Pi Lin, pi Kong* campaign, and Jiang Qing's links with that institution, suggests that she may have prompted its original submission to Mao.

formerly head of the propaganda section of the political department of the central guards, PLA Unit 8341, but by this time the chairman of the Qinghua University Revolutionary Committee, with responsibility also for educational reform at the capital's other major institution of higher education, Peking University. His second-in-command was Xie Jingyi, also originally from PLA Unit 8341, a woman who was very close to Mao and Jiang Qing, possibly serving as the latter's secretary before moving to Qinghua to become Chi Qun's deputy chairman.[141]

In autumn 1973, these two recruited twelve scholars (a number later increased to thirty-two) from Qinghua and Peking universities to do the research and writing needed to link Lin Biao and Confucius and, presumably, to pinpoint the historical analogies that could be used for more urgent current purposes. This ideological hit team was designated the Beida-Qinghua Two Schools Big Criticism Group, and known as *Liang Xiao* (Two Schools) for short. Its members were moved into special accommodation, given special food, and taken on fact-finding missions, often in the company of Jiang Qing.[142] They became the core of a network of followers that the Gang established up and down the country.[143] The document circulated on 18 January 1974 was *Liang Xiao*'s first major product.

This marked the formal start of the official campaign to "Criticize Lin Biao, criticize Confucius" (*pi Lin, pi Kong*), masterminded by Jiang Qing and Wang Hongwen, and foreshadowed by the 1974 New Year's Day joint editorial in the *People's Daily, Hongqi,* and the *Liberation Army News.*[144] This might have seemed like an amplification of the ongoing drive to weed out supporters of Lin Biao in the Party and the PLA. Indeed, it was later alleged that a "Book-reading Group" (*dushu ban*) headed by Wang Hongwen attempted to gain control in military units. But its real purpose, formulated by Kang Sheng, was to undermine Zhou Enlai, as had been clear from the first salvo the previous August.[145]

On 24 January, allegedly without permission but probably with Mao's consent, Jiang Qing held a *pi Lin, pi Kong* rally for the Beijing garrison; the

141 Ibid., 303. For a transcript of discussions between Jiang Qing and these two, see Wang, *Da dongluan de niandai*, 479–89.

142 Yue and Wakeman, *To the storm*, 323–6. Yue Daiyun's knowledge of this group is extensive because her husband, Tang Yijie, was one of the twelve scholars.

143 Jin, "*Wenhua da geming*," 194.

144 Gao and Yan, "*Wenhua da geming*" *shinian shi*, 495.

145 Hu, *Zhongguo shehuizhuyi geming he jianshe shi jiangyi*, 316. See *Yingsi lu*, 295–6, for the allegation about the reason for the *dushu ban;* Michael Schoenhals has brought to my attention a reference to these study groups in *Zhonggong zhongyang dangxiao nianjian, 1984*, 4, which suggests that they had less ambitious aims. For Kang Sheng's role, see Zhong, *Kang Sheng pingzhuan*, 310–11. Merle Goldman argues that Zhou Enlai was able partly to diffuse the campaign, in *China's intellectuals*, 166–76. A leading member of the *Liang Xiao* group has since claimed that at no time were articles authored or supervised by him aimed consciously at Zhou.

following day she held a similar one for central Party and government cadres, at which she, Yao Wenyuan, Chi Qun, and Xie Jingyi made speeches.[146] Thereafter, she and her team traveled far and wide, penetrating even high-security military establishments, making speeches, or "lighting fires," as their activities were later described.[147] The campaign flooded the media and dominated the political activities of units in town and country.[148]

The unjustified restoration of old families was one theme. It was emphasized that there was an ongoing battle between those who wanted to go forward and those whose desire was to turn back the wheel of history.[149] Another was the contrast between the Confucians and the Legalist scholar-statesmen who worked for Qin Shihuangdi.[150] It was the Legalists who had convinced the Qin dynasty of a ruler's need to impose stern discipline and harsh punishments, an analogy perhaps intended to elevate class struggle over rehabilitation. The misdeeds of the Duke of Zhou figured largely in speeches and articles.[151]

Whatever the psychological impact of this historical onslaught on the living Zhou, the premier was increasingly incapacitated by his cancer, having to cut engagements, and finally to agree to surgery.[152] He left his office in the Zhongnanhai complex on 1 June 1974 and moved into the Capital Hospital, which became his base for the remaining eighteen months of his life.[153] He left the hospital only occasionally, mainly to make sorties for important political purposes.[154] But if the radicals had cause to rejoice that a foe whom they had so far failed to topple was weakening, their satisfaction was short-lived. The terminal illness of Zhou Enlai posed Mao a major political problem, and he solved it in a manner repugnant to his radical followers.

The return of Deng Xiaoping

Mao had to find someone to take Zhou Enlai's place, to oversee the day-to-day running of the country. Although the Chairman evidently considered it

146 Goldman, *China's intellectuals*, 166–76; Hao and Duan, *Zhongguo gongchandang liushi nian*, 634; Wang, *Da dongluan de niandai*, 489–94.

147 Yue and Wakeman, *To the storm*, 324–7; Gao and Yan, *"Wenhua da geming" shinian shi*, 496–7; Hao and Duan, *Zhongguo gongchandang liushi nian*, 634.

148 "Quarterly chronicle," *CQ*, 58 (April–May 1974), 407; ibid., 59 (July–September 1974), 627–30.

149 Ibid., 58 (April–May 1974), 407–8.

150 Ibid., 408.

151 Teaching and Research Office for CCP History, *Zhongguo gongchandang liushi nian dashi jianjie*, 569.

152 Zhou always insisted on getting Mao's permission before submitting to surgery; see *Bujin de sinian*, 583. For his letter to Mao reporting in detail on his condition and asking permission for his third operation in March 1975, see *Zhou Enlai shuxin xuanji* (Zhou Enlai's selected letters), 633–5.

153 *Zhou zongli shengping dashiji*, 504; *Huainian Zhou Enlai* (Longing for Zhou Enlai), 585–6.

154 Zhou also made at least one sortie for sentimental reasons when in September 1975 he paid his last visit to his barber of twenty years in the Beijing Hotel; see Percy Jucheng Fang and Lucy Guinong J. Fang, *Zhou Enlai: A profile*, 184.

nationally therapeutic and probably also personally exhilarating to encourage upheaval, he was well aware of the need for a stabilizing force to prevent total chaos. During the early years of the Cultural Revolution, and on earlier occasions like the GLF, too, Zhou had played that role. Although he could still rise to (or rather, for) the occasion – most notably, leaving the hospital to deliver the report on the work of the government at the first session of the Fourth NPC on 13 January 1975 – it was no longer possible for him to work the long hours needed to supervise every major national concern.

Unfortunately for Mao, Wang Hongwen turned out not to have the political skills that the Chairman presumably thought he had detected in the young man when he was operating in Shanghai.[155] More important: Despite his senior ranking, Wang had proved to be little more than a cat's-paw in the hands of Jiang Qing and Zhang Chunqiao,[156] thus destroying his credibility as an independent new force. Although post-Cultural Revolution historians have axes to grind, there seems little reason to doubt their evidence that during the *Pi Lin, pi Kong* campaign, Wang Hongwen had collaborated so closely with Jiang and Zhang as to force Mao to realize he was not a viable replacement for Zhou. By the time Mao started warning Wang against allying with Jiang, it was already too late.[157]

Quite apart from her activities on Mao's behalf earlier in the Cultural Revolution, Jiang Qing was barred from power by the prejudices built into the political culture by two millennia of Chinese male historiography. Mao recognized that, as a woman, Jiang Qing was a political liability. Female rulers were traditionally denounced by male historians for their disruption of the Confucian patrilinear succession system and for their alleged misdeeds. From 1974, Jiang Qing tried belatedly to revise the negative historical images of the Empress Lü of Han and Empress Wu of Tang,[158] who were, along with the Empress Dowager of the late Qing, the historians' main bêtes noires.

What is less easy to understand about this period is Mao's periodic dissociation from Jiang Qing and her Shanghai followers while they remained so important to the promotion and preservation of his Cultural Revolution goals. Marital conflict is a possible explanation. According to Terrill's ac-

155 Wang Hongwen's most spectacular failure, his inability to restore order to strife-torn Hangzhou in 1975, was still to come; see Gardner, *Chinese politics and the succession to Mao*, 74.

156 Jin, "*Wenhua da geming*," 187.

157 Hao and Duan, *Zhongguo gongchandang liushi nian*, 638.

158 Gao and Yan, "*Wenhua da geming*" *shinian shi*, 513–17. For Kang Sheng's role in this campaign, see Zhong, *Kang Sheng pingzhuan*, 315. See also Roxane Witke, *Comrade Chiang Ch'ing*, 464–66, 473; Ross Terrill, *The white-boned demon: A biography of Madame Mao Zedong*, 308–11; History Writing Group of the CCP Kwangtung Provincial Committee, "The ghost of Empress Lü and Chiang Ch'ing's empress dream," *Chinese Studies in history*, 12.1 (Fall 1978), 37–54; Yuan Ssu, "Bankruptcy of Empress Lü's dream," *Chinese Studies in History*, 12.2 (Winter 1978–9), 66–73.

count, in 1975 Jiang Qing moved out of the Zhongnanhai compound, where China's leaders lived, and took up residence in the Diaoyutai guest house complex. This source implies that political difficulties may have been the cause rather than the result of the rift.[159] Mao certainly chose to give that impression, telling her on 21 March 1974: "It's better not to see each other. You have not carried out what I've been telling you for many years; what's the good of seeing each other anymore. You have books by Marx and Lenin and you have my books; you stubbornly refused to study them." It was at a Politburo meeting in July 1974 that the Chairman first criticized his wife's political actions in front of their colleagues, and referred to her and her allies as a "Gang of Four." Jiang Qing, he told people, represented "only herself," had "wild ambitions," wanting "to become chairman of the Communist Party."[160] But a story widespread in Chinese political circles is that Jiang Qing moved because she was outraged by Mao's liaison with a young railway car attendant whom he had introduced into his household.[161] Yet another version is that Jiang Qing, whatever her views of Mao's amours, had in fact moved out of his house long before the Cultural Revolution. What does seem certain is that politically Mao and Jiang Qing still needed each other, and it is significant that whatever his strictures, he usually maintained that her errors were corrigible,[162] lending some credence to one Chinese view that Mao's attacks on the Gang of Four were part of an elaborate smoke screen designed to disarm their foes by implying he had deserted their cause. If so, then his principal dupe was Deng Xiaoping.

On 4 October 1974, no longer able to ignore the implications of Zhou Enlai's illness, Mao proposed that Deng Xiaoping should take the premier's place in charge of the government with the title of first vice-premier. One of Mao's two principal victims at the onset of the Cultural Revolution was to return to run China. The meteoric rise of Wang Hongwen had been extraordinary enough, but this was an even more astonishing appointment. Yet it had been clear since the end of the previous year that Deng's star was again in the ascendant and why. The issue was the PLA's role in the polity.

Mao had told a Politburo conference on 12 December 1973 that he wanted the COs of the military regions reshuffled, clearly to deprive them of their long-standing PLA commands and connections and their recently acquired Party and government posts. He complained that the Politburo did not deal with politics and that the MAC did not deal with military affairs, a not very subtle hint to the military to get out of politics. To lessen the anxiety of the

159 Terrill, *The white-boned demon.*

160 Ibid., 324–5; Witke, *Comrade Chiang Ch'ing,* 476; Hao and Duan, *Zhongguo gongchandang liushi nian,* 637–80

161 Terrill recounts this story in *The white-boned demon,* 317.

162 Jin, "*Wenhua da geming,*" 210.

generals at the implications of these proposals, Mao did two things: He suggested that Deng Xiaoping should enter the MAC and take on the job of chief of staff, and he criticized himself for being taken in by Lin Biao's denunciation and harsh treatment of the PLA's revolutionary heroes. Whether this explanation deceived the generals as to the ultimate responsibility for the mistreatment of their colleagues is doubtful, but it was at least an apology, coupled with a plea to let bygones be bygones.

Mao got his way: The MAC promulgated the reshuffle of eight COS of military regions, and on the same day the CC authorized Deng's return to a major political role in the MAC and a place on the Politburo. The elements of the bargain were clear. In return for giving up political power, the generals were promised that it would be put into the responsible hands of a trusted old comrade. Deng later commented approvingly, perhaps even wonderingly, that all eight COs reported for duty at their new posts within ten days.[163] To the disgust of the Gang, Deng was chosen to lead the Chinese delegation to a special session of the United Nations in April 1974 and deliver a speech introducing Mao's theory of the three worlds to a global audience.

The Gang of Four could at least console themselves that by rehabilitating Deng, Mao had weakened their strongest potential opponents, the military. But when in October Mao revealed his intention of putting Deng in charge of the country, the Gang of Four were spurred into furious activity to try to deflect the Chairman from his purpose. Wang Hongwen flew secretly to see him in Changsha on 18 October.[164] Through Wang and other emissaries, the Gang alleged that Zhou was shamming illness and secretly plotting in the hospital with Deng, and the atmosphere in the capital had the flavor of the 1970 Lushan Conference. Mao rejected their protests, praising Deng's ability. When Zhou, disregarding his illness, flew with Wang Hongwen to Changsha on 23 December, the Chairman reaffirmed his commitment to Deng, and proposed to implement his earlier suggestion that Deng be made a vice-chairman of the MAC and PLA chief of staff. Political balance was preserved by the appointment of Zhang Chunqiao as director of the PLA's General Political Department and second-ranking vice-premier. At a CC plenum in Beijing from 8 to 10 January 1975, presided over by the ever vigilant Zhou Enlai, these appointments were formally agreed upon, along with the even more striking decision that Deng should return to the

163 *Zhonggong dangshi dashi nianbiao*, 386; "Quarterly chronicle and documentation," *CQ*, 58 (April–May 1974), 410; for an analysis of the regional reshuffle, see ibid., 57 (January–March 1974), 206–7; for Deng's comment, see *Selected works of Deng Xiaoping (1975–1982)*, 97.

164 For a description of Wang Hongwen's visit to Mao, see Zhou Ming, *Lishi zai zheli chensi* (History is reflected here), 2.196–203.

Politburo Standing Committee as a vice-chairman of the Party.[165] The stage was set for the last great campaign of Mao's career.

Deng Xiaoping's year in charge

Deng Xiaoping has not revealed his thoughts on assuming day-to-day control of both Party and government in January 1975.[166] Did he believe that the Chairman had turned his back on the Cultural Revolution and had licensed him to revive the more rational policies that had been pursued on its eve?

There were some encouraging signs: the rehabilitation if not reinstatement of men like himself; Zhou Enlai's speech to the Fourth NPC promoting, with Mao's support, long-term economic planning and what later became known as the "four modernizations" – of agriculture, industry, defense, and science and technology;[167] most important, there was Mao's call for stability and unity and his criticism of the factional activities of the Gang of Four. Mao also seemed to wish to turn back the clock to more permissive policies in the cultural sphere, advocating the restoration to office of former officials like Zhou Yang, and telling Deng Xiaoping that a hundred flowers should bloom again in all branches of the arts. Encouraged, perhaps led on, by the Chairman, Deng Xiaoping and his principal supporters, Ye Jianying and Li Xiannian, criticized the Gang at Politburo meetings in May and June for their allegations that an eleventh "line struggle" was in progress and that the new leadership was guilty of pragmatism. Ever a weather vane, Wang Hongwen made a self-criticism, thereafter retiring to Shanghai for a few months, but his three comrades remained stubbornly silent.[168]

165 Hao and Duan, *Zhongguo gongchandang liushi nian*, 637–9; Gao and Yan, "*Wenhua da geming*" *shinian shi*, 530–7. Recent mainland historians are coy about how Zhang Chunqiao's appointment was brought about, presumably because they wish to avoid clouding their image of Mao playing a strongly positive role in the restoration of Deng at this time. An alternative or an additional explanation for Mao's recall of Deng, still current in China, is that he wanted to use him to displace Zhou Enlai. According to this scenario, Mao worried that Zhou might outlast him; the premier had cancer, but the Chairman allegedly had a serious stroke in late 1972, which could have convinced him that he might still die first. Mao's preference for Deng may have been partly because he considered him a less formidable opponent for the Gang of Four; it might also have had to do with his close earlier relation with him – Deng had remained loyal to Mao when the latter's back was up against the wall; for the Mao-Deng relationship, see MacFarquhar, *Origins*, 1.140–5.

166 Hao and Duan, *Zhongguo gongchandang liushi nian*, 639–40.

167 When Zhou had first called for the four modernizations in 1964, he had not cited Mao in his support; see Gardner, *Chinese politics and the succession to Mao*, 67.

168 Hao and Duan, *Zhongguo gongchandang liushi nian*, 645–7; Fang Weizhong, ed., *Zhonghua renmin gongheguo jingji dashiji* (*1949–1980*) (A record of the major economic events of the PRC [1949–1980]), 544–5; Jin, "*Wenhua da geming*," 212. A struggle over the political line was, of course, the most serious type of intra-Party dispute: the Lin Biao affair had been numbered the tenth such struggle, the Liu Shaoqi purge the ninth.

Deng energetically tackled pressing problems:[169] first, the military issue, which was a prime motive for Mao to recall him to office. Of Deng's eight speeches made in 1975 republished in his *Selected works,* three dealt with military affairs. Less than three weeks after he had formally assumed his military offices, Deng was attacking the bloated size and budget of the PLA, its inefficiency and lack of discipline, and the factionalism endemic among its officer corps. He stressed the need for PLA obedience to Party policies. In a later speech, he added conceit and inertia to his list of PLA faults.[170]

A more urgent problem was labor unrest, most notably the strikes and sabotage by railway workers at Xuzhou, Nanjing, Nanchang, and elsewhere, apparently resulting from leftist rabble-rousing during the *Pi Lin, pi Kong* campaign. Communications had been disrupted on four major trunk lines, causing massive economic dislocation. Deng restored order by a mixture of threats and conciliation, and the reinstatement of central control.[171] Wang Hongwen had been unable to settle leftist-fomented strife in Hangzhou. Deng simply sent in the PLA and arrested the troublemakers.[172]

In search of solutions to deep-seated, longer-term problems relating to the economy, Deng called conferences and launched a number of initiatives. Three major policy documents were produced: "Some problems in accelerating industrial development" on 18 August, prepared by the State Planning Commission: "Outline report on the work of the Academy of Sciences" on 26 September, prepared by Hu Yaobang, Hu Qiaomu, and others;[173] and "On the general program of work for the whole Party and nation" in mid-October, written by Deng Liqun.[174]

The industry document dealt with the roots of a wave of strikes that broke out in the middle of the year in Central and South China in response to leftist agitation for a more egalitarian wage system.[175] The document talked of "a handful of bad people sabotaging the work under the banner of 'rebellion' and 'going against the tide' "; of management being "in chaos"; of low productivity, low quality, expensive maintenance, high costs, and frequent

169 For a summary of Deng Xiaoping's activities from January through October 1975, at which point he was no longer able to exercise effective power, see Hao and Duan, *Zhongguo gongchandang liushi nian,* 640–1.

170 *Selected works of Deng Xiaoping* (*1975–1982*), 11–13, 27–42.

171 Jürgen Domes, *The government and the politics of the PRC: A time of transition,* 127; Fang, ed., *Zhonghua renmin gongheguo jingji dashiji* (*1949–1980*), 541–3. The trunk lines were: Tianjin–Pukou; Beijing–Guangzhou; the Longhai (Lianyungang–Tianshui) line, a major east–west artery linking coastal Jiangsu with Gansu in the northwest; and the Zhe-Gan line joining Hangzhou and Nanchang.

172 Gardner, *Chinese politics and the succession to Mao,* 74.

173 For an analysis of these two documents, see Kenneth Lieberthal, *Central documents and Politburo politics in China,* 33–49.

174 Fang, ed., *Zhonghua renmin gongheguo jingji dashiji* (*1949–1980*), 550–5; translations exist in Chi Hsin, *The case of the Gang of Four,* 203–86.

175 Domes, *The government and politics of the PRC,* 128.

breakdowns; and of the particularly serious problems in the raw materials, fuel, and power industries.[176] In his comments when the document was presented to the State Council, Deng stressed the need to support agriculture, introduce foreign technology, strengthen industrial research, bring order to management, put "quality first," enforce rules and regulations, and restore material incentives.[177] A month later, in the discussions of the report on the Academy of Sciences, Deng pressed for better training, higher educational standards, more expert leadership, and more time to be spent on science (and by implication, less on politics).[178]

But it was the document formulating a general program for Party and nation that struck at the leftists most broadly, copiously quoting from early Mao writings to drive home the point that revolution could not be stressed to the detriment of production: "It is purely nonsense to say that a certain place of work or unit is carrying out revolution very well when production is fouled up. The view that once revolution is grasped, production will increase naturally and without spending any effort is believed only by those who indulge in fairy tales."[179] No wonder Jiang Qing denounced these documents as "three great weeds" and characterized this one as a "political manifesto for the restoration of capitalism."[180]

Jiang Qing joined battle with Deng also on the issue of agriculture. At the First National Conference on Learning from Dazhai [brigade] in Agriculture, which brought together 3,700 delegates from 15 September to 19 October, she called for a return to the commune ideal of the height of the Great Leap Forward in 1958, with an emphasis on egalitarianism and class struggle. Deng, on the other hand, looked back to the early 1960s, and the various incentives used then to encourage peasant initiative.[181]

In another bizarre example of invoking historical or literary texts for contemporary political purposes, Jiang Qing used her Dazhai speech to get at Deng Xiaoping by excoriating the hero of a famous old novel, the *Shuihu zhuan* (Water margin). She asserted that "this book must be read carefully to see the features of this renegade. . . . That man Song Jiang had many double-dealing tricks![182] . . . Song Jiang made a figurehead of Chao Gai; aren't there people just now who are trying to make a figurehead of the

176 Chi, *The case of the Gang of Four,* 246, 247, 257.

177 Selected works of *Deng Xiaoping,* 43–6; Fang, ed., *Zhonghua renmin gongheguo jingji dashiji* (1949–1980), 550–2.

178 Chi, *The case of the Gang of Four,* 287–95. 179 Ibid., 227.

180 Teaching and Research Office for CCP History, *Zhongguo gongchandang liushi nian dashi jianjie,* 576.

181 Domes, *The government and politics of the PRC,* 129–30; Fang, ed., *Zhonghua renmin gongheguo jingji dashiji* (1949–1980), 552–3.

182 History Writing Group, "The ghost of Empress Lü," 55.

Chairman? I think there are some."[183] Typically, the *Shuihu zhuan* analogy was not her idea but stemmed from criticism by Mao of Song Jiang's capitulationism or revisionism, a theme immediately pounced on by the Gang's sophisticated polemicist, Yao Wenyuan.[184]

Mao's behavior throughout Deng Xiaoping's year in power was contradictory.[185] He backed Deng's measures and defended them from attacks by the Gang of Four, but he simultaneously propounded his own leftist views and allowed Zhang Chunqiao and Yao Wenyuan to publicize theirs. He bemoaned wage differentials, payment according to work, and commodity exchange; in those respects, he said, the PRC did not differ much from pre-1949 China; only the system of ownership had changed. Encouraged by Mao's statements, Zhang Chunqiao and Yao Wenyuan published in the *People's Daily* a set of thirty-three quotations from Marx, Engels, and Lenin on the theory of proletarian dictatorship, carefully choosing comments that lent credence to their own position.[186] With the Chairman's permission, Zhang and Yao both wrote major theoretical exegeses to justify their own views and his: on the overriding importance of class struggle and the proletarian dictatorship; on the danger of commodity exchange undermining the socialist planned economy; on the worrying emergence of new bourgeois elements encouraged by material incentives; on the urgency of pressing forward to higher stages of collective ownership and then to state ownership; and on the continuing danger of China turning revisionist.[187]

Mao's ambivalence may have reflected indecision, a genuine conflict between head and heart. It may also have been a manifestation of his increasing infirmity. From early 1974 until August 1975, when he had an operation to remove one of two cataracts in his eyes, he was unable to read; with his confidential secretary terminally ill in hospital, Mao was forced to depend on his young female companion, Zhang Yufeng, to read official documents and newspapers to him. By the end of 1975, Parkinson's disease was rendering him literally speechless, even in some of his meetings with foreign VIPs, able to communicate only by writing or by grunts comprehensible only to his attendants. According to Zhang:

> Having trouble speaking, he could only utter some mumbled words and phrases. Having worked around him for a long time, I could manage to understand what he

183 Teaching and Research Office for CCP History, *Zhongguo gongchandang liushi nian dashi jianjie,* 574.

184 Ibid., 573–4. For a detailed discussion of the *Shuihu zhuan* affair, see Goldman, *China's intellectuals,* 201–13.

185 Hao and Duan, *Zhongguo gongchandang liushi nian,* 648.

186 Ibid., 644–45.

187 Yao Wen-yuan, "On the social basis of the Lin Piao anti-Party clique," and Chang Ch'un-ch'iao, "On exercising all-round dictatorship over the bourgeoisie," are translated in Raymond Lotta, *And Mao makes 5: Mao Tse-tung's last great battle,* 196–220.

said. Whenever the Chairman talked with other leading comrades, I had to be present to repeat his words. But when his speech and pronunciation became extremely unclear, all I could do was to lipread or guess from his expression. When his speech was at its worst, he could only write down his thoughts with a pen. Later, the Chairman had a great difficulty getting about. He could not walk on his own; he could not even move a step without help.[188]

Mao's leftist nephew, Mao Yuanxin, seems to have been transferred from the Northeast in late September 1975 to act as the Chairman's liaison officer with the Politburo. He, too, weighed in against Deng. Iago-like, Mao Yuanxin slanted his reports and poured doubts about Deng's loyalty to the Cultural Revolution into the Chairman's ear. He found a sympathetic listener.[189]

All these factors may have helped shape Mao's attitude. But in the light of Mao's long acquaintance with Deng, it seems unlikely that, in 1973, the Chairman was so naive as to think that the onetime number two capitalist-roader had changed his spots. The more likely hypothesis is that Mao's elevation of Deng Xiaoping was a tactic designed partly to hoodwink the military in order to deal more effectively with the problem "After Mao, which?" and partly to buy time while he sought a solution to the problem "After Mao, who?" The views he expressed during 1975 give no indication that he had changed his long-cherished ideas on the correct answer to "After Mao, what?"

The death of Zhou and the fall of Deng

Even before the death of Zhou Enlai on 8 January 1976, there was a rising tide of criticism of Deng Xiaoping's policies. Probably the Gang of Four realized that the Chairman's tolerance of Deng was wearing thin and decided to move in for the kill. As at the start of the Cultural Revolution, the initial battleground was the intellectual sphere.

A Qinghua University Party official, perhaps instigated by Deng's supporters, had written twice to Mao, complaining of the ideas and lifestyle of the Gang's loyal followers there, Chi Qun and Xie Jingyi. Mao took this as an attack on the Cultural Revolution, and his reply in support of Chi and Xie was publicized by them on 3 November as the opening salvo of a campaign to "repulse the right deviationist wind to reverse the verdicts."[190] They also

188 Zhang, "Anecdotes of Mao Zedong and Zhou Enlai in their later years." Ross Terrill in *Mao*, 395–7, 400–1, 411–13, 417–18, traces the Chairman's deteriorating health as manifested at his meetings with successive foreign visitors through the summer of 1976.

189 Hu, *Zhongguo shehuizhuyi geming he jianshe shi jiangyi*, 326; Hao and Duan, *Zhongguo gongchandang liushi nian*, 648–49. One report suggests that Mao Yuanxin was only with his uncle until November 1975, but other indications are that he remained in Beijing at the Chairman's side until his death.

190 "*Fanji youqing fan'an feng*"; see Hao and Duan, *Zhongguo gongchandang liushi nian*, 649.

seized their chance to attack the minister of education, Zhou Rongxin, who at Deng's request had been pressing for a restoration of educational standards.[191] At stake for Mao and the Gang of Four was one of the surviving legacies of the Cultural Revolution, or "new socialist things," an egalitarian education system emphasizing simpler and more practical courses that would be more easily accessible to worker-peasant-soldier entrants to universities.[192]

Toward the end of November, at Mao's orders, the Politburo called a notification conference, at which Hua Guofeng read out a summary of a speech by the Chairman, thereafter circulated to senior Party officials in the provinces. The burden of the Mao text and subsequent supportive central documents was that from July through September, political rumors had been rife, attempts had been made to split the top leadership, and attacks had been made on the Cultural Revolution in an effort to reverse its verdicts.[193] Effectively Mao had withdrawn his mandate from Deng and reshaped the current campaign into a drive to "criticize Deng and repulse the right-deviationist wind to reverse the verdicts."

It was at this point that Zhou Enlai died, precipitating a political crisis that would reverberate through China during the rest of the year. Zhou had been relatively inactive for months, but while he still lived, he symbolized rationality and restraint, a guarantee that however chaotic the country became, somewhere, someone was attempting to restore order and to protect people from the worst effects of the Cultural Revolution. Deng Xiaoping, who had been a worker-student with him in Paris in the early 1920s, probably summed up the general attitude to Zhou in an interview four years later:

> Premier Zhou was a man who worked hard and uncomplainingly all his life. He worked 12 hours a day, and sometimes 16 hours or more, throughout his life. . . . Fortunately he survived during the "Cultural Revolution" when we were knocked down. He was in an extremely difficult position then, and he said and did many things that he would have wished not to. But the people forgave him because, had he not done and said those things, he himself would not have been able to survive and play the neutralising role he did, which reduced losses. He succeeded in protecting quite a number of people.[194]

191 Gardner, *Chinese politics and the succession to Mao,* 75–6. For a detailed analysis of educational developments during the Cultural Revolution, see *CHOC,* 15, Chapter 7.

192 Other new socialist things included Jiang Qing's revolutionary operas; the rural "barefoot doctor" or paramedic system; the May 7 cadre schools where officials spent months, sometimes years, performing manual labor; emulation of the collectivism of Dazhai brigade. See "Nothing is hard in this world if you dare to scale the heights," *RMRB, HQ, JFJB* Joint editorial, 1 January 1976, translated in "Quarterly chronicle and documentation," *CQ,* 66 (June 1976), 412.

193 Hao and Duan, *Zhongguo gongchandang liushi nian,* 649.

194 "Answers to the Italian journalist Oriana Fallaci," in *Selected works of Deng Xiaoping (1975–1982),* 329–30. For a suggestion that at the outset of the Cultural Revolution, Zhou Enlai took a positive view of it, see Zhou, *Lishi zai zheli chensi,* 1. 57–8.

Zhou held the office of premier until the day he died. Now the choice of his successor could no longer be put off. Deng was the obvious candidate. His selection would have signaled a continuing willingness to retain a moderating figure at the helm. Despite the mounting tide of leftist criticism of his restorationist policies, Deng had not yet suffered any public humiliation, and was allowed to give the memorial address at Zhou Enlai's funeral.[195]

But Mao must have calculated that to allow Deng to inherit Zhou's mantle would make him virtually immovable, certainly after his own death. Deng had to be struck down now or he would eventually remove those who sincerely sought to preserve the Maoist vision and the achievements of the Cultural Revolution. The same argument militated against the succession of other leading survivors like Ye Jianying and Li Xiannian.

The likeliest radical candidate for the premiership was the most capable member of the Gang of Four, the second-ranking vice-premier under Deng Xiaoping, Zhang Chunqiao. But Mao had almost certainly decided long since that a radical would not be a viable successor to Zhou. Far from being able to preserve Maoism, a radical premier would precipitate a backlash that would remove both person and program.

So Mao had to choose a beneficiary of the Cultural Revolution, presumably on the shrewd assumption that such a person would be sufficiently indebted to Mao and committed to the Cultural Revolution to try to tread the same path. A beneficiary might also want to preserve a radical element in the leadership to balance any threat to his own position from the old guard. Thus the pure Maoist torch would be kept alight within the Politburo, even if not at its very apex.

Mao chose Hua Guofeng, for reasons that are still not known; perhaps the Chairman simply made another mistake in selecting an appropriate heir. Hua's work as an official in Mao's home province had brought him early to the Chairman's favorable attention.[196] It has also been suggested that Hua played a key role in the post–Lin Biao cleanup, but so did Ji Dengkui, another potential candidate as successor. Hua's position as minister of public security, assumed at the Fourth NPC a year earlier, gave him a power base that Mao may have thought an untested successor would need. On 21 and 28 January, he conveyed to the Politburo that Hua should be made acting premier and take over from Deng the control of the Party's daily work.[197]

195 Deng's speech is in "Quarterly chronicle and documentation," *CQ*, 66 (June 1976), 420–4.

196 See Michel Oksenberg and Sai-cheung Yeung, "Hua Kuo-feng's pre–Cultural Revolution Hunan years, 1949–1966: The making of a political generalist," *CQ*, 69 (March 1977), 29–34.

197 Why "acting?" Conceivably for protocol reasons: Hua could not formally be named premier until so appointed by the NPC; but when he did obtain the full title in April, it was not as a result of some constitutional process. Possibly Mao, conscious of the error he had made in elevating an untried Wang Hongwen to a top slot, put Hua on probation to minimize the damage if he proved equally

Mao also ordered that Deng's ally, Ye Jianying, be replaced as head of the MAC by a military beneficiary of the Cultural Revolution, Chen Xilian, presumably to prevent Hua being outflanked.[198] The covert campaign against Deng was stepped up.

The Gang of Four's strategy

The Gang of Four were furious at the elevation of Hua Guofeng, especially Zhang Chunqiao, who had apparently long coveted the premiership.[199] This led them to commit a major strategic error that probably cost them whatever slim hope they might have had of retaining power after Mao's death. Instead of collaborating with potential allies, they went all out for power.

The political complexion of the Politburo at this time was not unfavorable to the Gang. (See Table 5.) The survivors from among the pre-Cultural Revolution old guard were on the defensive and weak in active members. With Deng and Ye Jianying neutralized on the sidelines, Wang Hongwen and Zhang Chunqiao could have worked with Hua Guofeng to dominate the Party from their vantage point within the Politburo Standing Committee. Hua would presumably have welcomed such support at this critical time, especially since it would have come with Mao's blessing. The Gang's natural allies were beneficiaries like Hua. They were relatively young and active; and, as Mao probably sensed, because of the manner in which they had risen to power, they would be suspected by and suspicious of the survivors. Moreover, the beneficiaries included key military and political figures who could be important allies in any showdown: Chen Xilian, the commander of the Beijing Military Region; Wang Dongxing, the commander of the leaders' guards, PLA Unit 8341; Wu De, the party boss of the capital.[200]

But without Mao in firm daily control, the Gang brooked no compromise, instead allowing their naturally combative attitudes free rein. Accustomed

incompetent. Or possibly he wished to diminish opposition from among his old comrades by implying that Deng had not been permanently displaced but only temporarily set aside. The latter hypothesis might also serve to explain why Mao, in his attacks on Deng, was careful to say that the latter's sins were contradictions among the people and could be resolved; see Hao and Duan, *Zhongguo gongchandang liushi nian,* 650.

198 Fang, ed., *Zhonghua renmin gongheguo jingji dashiji* (1949–1980), 559. According to this account, Chen Xilian was to replace Ye Jianying while the latter was sick, but since no other account I have seen (e.g., Hao and Duan, *Zhongguo gongchandang liushi nian,* 649; Gao and Yan, *"Wenhua da geming" shinian shi,* 575) mentions this as a motive, one must assume that this was a political illness brought on by anger at Mao's decision about Hua. Certainly Ye had been well enough to attend Zhou's memorial service on 15 January.

199 For Zhang Chunqiao's reactions to his personal setback, see Gao and Yan, *"Wenhua da geming" shinian shi,* 575–6.

200 The suitability of these men as allies of the radicals is underlined by the fact that Deng Xiaoping insisted on their removal when he returned to power after the death of Mao. These three, together with Ji Dengkui, were nicknamed the "little gang of four."

TABLE 5

The political complexion of the Politburo after the death of Zhou Enlai

(Names in boldface are of members of the Standing Committee; those in capitals are of full members, others are of alternate members. A name in parentheses means the person probably was politically dormant owing to age or illness.[a])

Radicals	Beneficiaries	Survivors
Mao Zedong	**Hua Guofeng**	**Deng Xiaoping**
Wang Hongwen		**Ye Jianying**
Zhang Chunqiao		**(Zhu De)**
JIANG QING	LI DESHENG[b]	LI XIANNIAN
YAO WENYUAN	CHEN XILIAN	(LIU BOCHENG)
	JI DENGKUI	XU SHIYOU
	WANG DONGXING	WEI GUOQING
	WU DE	
	CHEN YONGGUI	
	Wu Guixian	Su Zhenhua
	Ni Zhifu	Saifudin

[a] Kang Sheng and Dong Biwu died in 1975.
[b] For reasons that are not clear, Li Desheng "asked to be relieved of" his vice-chairmanship of the CCP and membership of the PSC when Deng Xiaoping took over the running of the country in January 1975; see *Zhonggong dangshi dashi nianbiao,* 391. Li had been a commander in the Second Field Army led by Liu Bocheng and Deng Xiaoping during the Civil War. In 1982, he wrote the preface to one of the many accounts of their military exploits: see Yang Guoyu, et al., eds., *Liu Deng da jun zhengzhanji* (A record of the great military campaigns of Liu [Bocheng] and Deng [Xiaoping]), 1.1–4.

until recently to acting as the Chairman's gatekeeper and representative,[201] Jiang Qing was not about to play second fiddle to a political upstart. As early as the Dazhai conference the previous autumn, she had begun sniping at the timidity with which the rising Hua Guofeng, whom she described as a "nice gentleman of Malenkov's ilk," sought to pursue their shared goals.[202] Now, instead of reassessing their position in the wake of Hua's appointment, the Gang stepped up their campaign against him,[203] thus ensuring he would eventually have to turn to the survivors for support. Yet the reality of interdependence was about to be dramatically demonstrated.

Not content with pursuing Deng and undermining Hua, the Gang recklessly flouted what they must have known was popular sentiment about Zhou Enlai. When the premier died, no announcement was made that he would be cremated or where and when the ceremony would take place. But the news got out, and an estimated 1 million people lined the route from Tiananmen Square to the Babaoshan Cemetery, many clutching white paper chrysanthemums to symbolize their mourning. At one point, the crowd surged forward and stopped the cortege to demand that Zhou be buried, which would be in

201 Jin, "*Wenhua da geming,*" 191–2. 202 Domes, *The government and politics of the PRC,* 130.
203 Gao and Yan, "*Wenhua da geming*" *shinian shi,* 576–7.

accordance with the Chinese custom; only after Zhou's widow, Deng Yingchao, got out of her car and assured the crowd that cremation had been the premier's wish was the cortege allowed to continue.[204] In the weeks that followed there was evidence from all around the country of the popularity of Zhou and the unpopularity of his enemies.[205]

The Gang's reaction was not to lie low for a time, but rather to confront Zhou's memory. Their control of the media enabled them to restrict the public airing of grief and to sanction blatant attacks on his policies, although he was not denounced by name.[206] They finally overstepped the mark on 25 March, when the *Wenhui bao,* a major Shanghai newspaper controlled by them, printed a front-page article in which Zhou Enlai was unmistakably referred to as a "capitalist-roader." In Nanjing, there were strong student-led protests against the Gang, which were not covered by the media. But the news reached Beijing and other cities because students, using tar, wrote slogans on the outside of railway carriages.[207] This "Nanjing incident" was the prelude to a far more dramatic demonstration of support for Zhou and Deng and hatred for the Gang of Four in the heart of the capital, right in front of the large portrait of Mao on the Gate of Heavenly Peace, the Tiananmen.

The Tiananmen incident, 1976

It was the time of the traditional Qing Ming Festival when ancestors were remembered and their graves swept. In an effort to stamp out "superstition" years earlier, the CCP had attempted to transform this festival into a time for remembering revolutionary heroes. Now the people of Beijing seized this opportunity to commemorate one of the greatest of all the CCP's heroes and to express their views on the current political situation.

Pupils of Beijing's Cow Lane Primary School placed the first wreath by the Heroes' Monument in the center of Tiananmen Square on 19 March. Four days later, a man from Anhui province laid another one, with a dedication to Zhou Enlai's memory. Both were swiftly removed by the police. The head of the capital's public security bureau muttered darkly about a "serious class struggle at the back of the wreaths." At dawn on 25 March, a middle school left its wreath, and shortly thereafter some workers left their memorial board beside it. On 30 March, the first group of soldiers left theirs. These tributes were not removed, and they had a galvanizing effect on the city's population.[208]

204 Roger Garside, *Coming alive!: China after Mao,* 8–9.

205 Gao and Yan, "*Wenhua da geming*" *shinian shi,* 582–6. 206 Ibid., 581–2.

207 Ibid., 586–97; Hao and Duan, *Zhongguo gongchandang liushi nian,* 652; Garside, *Coming alive!* 110–14.

208 Gao and Yan, "*Wenhua da geming*" *shinian shi,* 598–9.

From 30 March on, the laying of wreaths at the monument escalated rapidly, in defiance of the orders of the city authorities. Column after column, dozens of units, thousands of people, marched to the square to place their wreaths, declaim their tributes, and read those of others. On the festival day, 4 April, a Sunday holiday, an estimated 2 million people visited the square.

The bottom part of the Heroes' Monument was buried in wreaths. Surrounding it, an army of wreaths mounted on stands marched outward toward the sides of the square. A typical wreath was homemade of paper flowers, usually in mourning white, with a picture of Zhou Enlai in its center, and two ribbons of white silk hanging from it, inscribed with a memorial tribute. Many had eulogies or poems pinned to them; other poems were pasted on the monument. It was these tributes that became the focus of attention of the crowds, packed tight but eager to find out to what degree others shared their feelings.[209]

Some eulogies simply commemorated the premier:

> He left no inheritance, he had no children, he has no grave, he left no remains. His ashes were scattered over the mountains and rivers of our land. It seems he left us nothing, but he will live forever in our hearts. The whole land is his, he has hundreds of millions of children and grandchildren and all China's soil is his tomb. So he left us everything. He will live in our hearts for all time. Who is he? Who is he? He is our Premier![210]

Such sentiments were widely shared, but it was the attacks on the Gang of Four that were most keenly read. Some were hidden behind veils of allusion. Others were totally transparent:

> You must be mad
> To want to be an empress!
> Here's a mirror to look at yourself
> And see what you really are.
> You've got together a little gang
> To stir up trouble all the time,
> Hoodwinking the people, capering about.
> But your days are numbered. . . .
> Whoever dares oppose our Premier

209 Garside, *Coming alive!* 115–36. Garside, a Chinese-speaking British foreign service officer who had been posted back to the British embassy in Beijing in January 1976, gives an elegiac eyewitness account of these events. The fullest and most vivid Chinese account is probably that in Gao and Yan, "*Wenhua da geming*" *shinian shi,* 598–637; the estimate of the numbers in the square on 4 April is in this source, 611. The present author was in Beijing from 1 to 4 April, but this account relies heavily on these two sources.

210 Quoted in Garside, *Coming alive!* 117.

Is like a mad dog barking at the sun –
Wake up to reality![211]

In the face of this verbal onslaught, the Gang of Four temporarily woke up to reality. They collaborated with the beneficiaries in the Politburo to take strong action. The Politburo had already met on 1 April to agree that the Nanjing incident had been splittist and supportive of Deng Xiaoping. On the basis of that negative assessment, the Beijing police had begun to take action in Tiananmen Square on 2 and 3 April, trying to inhibit the mourners, removing some wreaths.[212]

On the evening of 4 April, as the Qing Ming Festival drew to a close, the Politburo met again to assess the situation in Tiananmen Square. Prominent members of the old guard – Zhu De, Ye Jianying, Li Xiannian, and the general Xu Shiyou, who had supported them – were not present;[213] Deng Xiaoping could not have been there either. The beneficiaries and the Gang of Four appeared to be in total command. Hua Guofeng blamed provocateurs for what was happening in Tiananmen Square and opined that some poems were vicious direct attacks on the Chairman and many others in the central leadership. Another beneficiary, the Beijing Party first secretary, Wu De, detected coordinated activity and attributed it directly to preparations made by Deng during 1974–5. He said, "The nature of [the activity] is clear. It's a counterrevolutionary incident."[214] Jiang Qing asked if the safety of the central leadership was guaranteed and why their opponents had not been arrested.[215]

The basis for continued collaboration between the Gang of Four and the beneficiaries became clear during the meeting. Both groups felt threatened. What they stood for was being rejected. If Hua were correct in asserting that Mao personally was a target of some of the mourning verses, then even the ultimate basis of their shared power was being questioned.[216] If that could happen while the Chairman was still alive, what about when his backing was only posthumous? At the very least, this massive and unprecedented upsurge of support for Zhou meant that the Chinese people now rejected Mao as the unique and godlike guide to their future. There was an alternate path, and

211 Xiao Lan, *The Tiananmen poems,* 29–30. This set of English translations comprises only a small fraction of the poems and eulogies pasted up in the square at this time. See, for instance, *Geming shichao* (A transcript of revolutionary poems), in two volumes, republished later as Tong Huaizhou, ed., *Tiananmen shiwen ji* (Poems from the Gate of Heavenly Peace).

212 Hao and Duan, *Zhongguo gongchandang liushi nian,* 652.

213 Ibid.

214 Hu, *Zhongguo shehuizhuyi geming he jianshe shi jiangyi,* 331.

215 Gao and Yan, *"Wenhua da geming" shinian shi,* 619.

216 One clear dig at Mao and his "feudal-style" cult came in a reference to the emperor Qin Shihuangdi, to whom the Chairman was often implicitly compared: "China is no longer the China of the past, And the people are no longer wrapped in utter ignorance, Gone for good is Qin Shi Huang's feudal society." Quoted in Garside, *Coming alive!,* 127.

they preferred it. They rejected, too, Mao's choice of successor. The implication of their homage to Zhou was that they wanted Deng Xiaoping back as his rightful heir. Everyone at the Politburo meeting that night knew that his return would spell disaster for them.

It was thus necessary to act swiftly and firmly. Mao Yuanxin relayed the conclusions of the meeting to his uncle, and when the Chairman sent back his agreement, the police were ordered into action. By 4:00 A.M. on 5 April, the square had been totally cleared of wreaths and writings; people who stayed late to read the verses or stand guard over the memorials were arrested.[217] By about 5:00 A.M., Wang Hongwen was instructing the police on how to behave when day came.[218]

News of the authorities' action spread rapidly, and people began converging on the square from all over the city, this time as individuals rather than in groups. But one group, ten middle school students, did turn up just after 6:00 A.M. to lay their tribute, only to find their way barred by soldiers and workers' militia who surrounded the monument, explaining that it had to be cleaned.[219] A foreign eyewitness who arrived at 8:00 A.M. reported that already there were 10,000 people in the square. Facing the Great Hall of the People on the west side of the square, they shouted, "Give back our wreaths! Give back our comrades-in-arms!"[220] Ordered to disperse but given no explanation for the removal of the wreaths, the crowd lost its temper. A police van was overturned and its occupants forced to apologize for alleging that the crowd was being led astray by "class enemies." A radical and presumably rehearsed Qinghua student who had the temerity to criticize wreath laying on behalf of the "biggest capitalist-roader in the Party" was roughed up and forced to retreat. By the early afternoon, several police vehicles had been burned, and a police command post had been stormed and set on fire.[221]

At 6:30 P.M., Wu De broadcast an appeal through the square's loudspeaker system, calling on people to disperse.[222] Most did, all but a few hundred, according to Chinese accounts.[223] Then, at 9:35 P.M., the square was suddenly flooded with light. Martial music was played over the loudspeakers. Members of the militia, the public security forces, and the Beijing garrison troops, who had been assembled in the Forbidden City behind the

217 Hu, *Zhongguo shehuizhuyi geming he jianshe shi jiangyi*, 331.

218 Gao and Yan, *"Wenhua da geming" shinian shi*, 621. 219 Ibid.

220 *"Huan wo huaquan, huan wo zhanyou"*; *Zhonggong dangshi dashi nianbiao*, 401; Garside, *Coming alive!* 129.

221 Garside, *Coming alive!* 129–39.

222 The text is Gao and Yan, *"Wenhua da geming" shinian shi*, 629–30.

223 Ibid, 633; Hao and Duan, *Zhongguo gongchandang liushi nian*, 653, specifies 388 arrests. Garside, *Coming alive!* 132, says that 4,000 remained in the square after Wu De's speech, but this was on the basis of estimates rather than police records.

Tiananmen, appeared on the square, armed with sticks, and began beating people. By 9:45 P.M., the carnage was over and the wounded members of the "masses" were taken away for interrogation.[224]

Meeting that evening, the Politburo concluded that this "incident" had been a "counterrevolutionary riot." On 7 April, informed of the events by Mao Yuanxin, the Chairman ordered the publication of the *People's Daily*'s version of what had happened together with the text of Wu De's appeal. Deng was to be relieved of all his posts, but allowed to retain his Party membership in case he reformed; what else might have befallen him is unclear, for on the same day he is said to have been spirited away to safety in the south by the PLA, where his allies on the Politburo, Xu Shiyou and Wei Guoqing, controlled the local armed forces.[225]

In perhaps his most important decision on 7 April, Mao ordered that Hua Guofeng should be immediately elevated to the premiership and first deputy chairmanship of the CCP.[226] Either the situation was too dangerous to delay longer or Hua had met whatever test Mao had set him; at any rate, the Chairman had made his final choice of successor. Three weeks later, on the evening of 30 April, after the new first deputy chairman reported to him on the state of the country, Mao used the legitimating words that Hua would later brandish as a talisman: "With you in charge, I'm at ease."[227] In fact, Hua was to prove no more viable than any of his three predecessors. But Mao would never know.

The death of Mao

For superstitious or tradition-minded Chinese, which probably meant the majority of the nation, the year 1976 was replete with omens of disaster. The death of Zhou in January was followed in July by the death at eighty-nine of the grand old soldier of the revolution, Zhu De, the general whose loyalty to Mao during the early years in the wilderness had ensured military subservience to the Party. Three weeks later, a massive earthquake hit the area of the North China coal-mining city of Tangshan, killing more than 242,000 people and leaving more than 164,000 seriously injured.[228]

Throughout the country there was unrest, sparked on the one hand by

224 Hao and Duan, *Zhongguo gongchandang liushi nian,* 653; Gao and Yan, *"Wenhua da geming" shinian shi,* 634–5. Garside cites contemporary noncommunist reports of 100 killed; *Coming alive!* 132.

225 Domes, *The government and politics of the PRC,* 132. I am unaware of any Chinese source that has admitted that this was how Deng's safety was preserved, and many Chinese analysts believe he remained in the capital.

226 Hao and Duan, *Zhongguo gongchandang liushi nian,* 653.

227 *"Ni ban shi, wo fangxin"*; Gao and Yan, *"Wenhua da geming" shinian shi,* 699.

228 Fang, ed., *Zhonghua renmin gongheguo jingji dashiji (1949–1980)*, 568.

leftist agitation against Deng Xiaoping and on the other by popular anger over the way he had been purged. There were stoppages again on the railways. Steel production was 1.23 million tons below target in the first five months of 1976. The production of chemical fertilizer, cotton yarn, and other key industrial goods fell precipitously, causing a drop of 2 billion yuan in national financial receipts. Targets for the annual plan had to be scaled back.[229]

At this time of natural disaster, political turmoil, and economic disruption, it became clear to the elite that Mao's life was drawing to a close.[230] With Deng down but not yet out, it would clearly have been sensible for the Gang of Four to solidify the alliance forged with the Politburo beneficiaries during the Tiananmen riot in order to be sure of weathering the critical weeks ahead. But they threw away their last opportunity by attacking Hua Guofeng at a national planning conference in July. They had evidently decided to confront the beneficiaries by military force if necessary, and in August, as the Chairman's life was ebbing away, they began to put the Shanghai militia, which they had been building up since 1967, into a state of readiness.[231]

The generals, too, were preparing. As the senior marshal by virtue of his place on the Politburo, Ye Jianying was lobbied by General Wang Zhen to move against the Gang of Four. Ye's fellow marshal Nie Rongzhen and General Yang Chengwu also had frequent strategy sessions with him. Ye was having consultations with members of the Politburo, presumably including Hua Guofeng and other beneficiaries whom the Gang had spurned. He also traveled to his native Guangdong, where he reportedly found Deng Xiaoping in a combative mood:

> Either we accept the fate of being slaughtered and let the Party and the country degenerate, let the country which was founded with the heart and soul of our proletarian revolutionaries of the old generation be destroyed by those four people, and let history retrogress one hundred years, or we should struggle against them as long as there is still any life in our body. If we win, everything can be solved. If we lose, we can take to the mountains as long as we live or we can find a shield in other countries, to wait for another opportunity. At present, we can use at least the strength of the Canton Military Region, the Fuchou Military Region, and the

229 Ibid., 567. For reports of pro-Deng poular unrest, see Gao and Yan, *"Wenhua da geming" shinian shi*, 641–59; for an analysis of leftist agitation, see ibid., 662–76.

230 For an account of Mao's parlous condition at the time of the annual Spring Festival, see Zhang, "Anecdotes of Mao Zedong and Zhou Enlai in their later years."

231 Hao and Duan, *Zhongguo gongchandang liushi nian*, 654–5; Gao and Yan, *"Wenhua da geming" shinian shi*, 678–9. In early September, Jiang Qing was revisiting the Dazhai brigade when an urgent message came from Beijing saying that the Chairman was sinking fast. She allegedly went on playing poker with her guards and medical attendants for some time before leaving for the capital; Ibid., 691.

Nanking Military Region to fight against them. Any procrastination and we will risk losing this, our only capital.[232]

But Ye wanted to wait. He indicated to Wang Zhen that he did not think it appropriate to move before Mao's death;[233] he justified procrastinating with the phrase "Spare the rat to save the dishes" (*tou shu ji qi*),[234] implying that he did not want to humiliate Mao by arresting his wife as a counterrevolutionary while he was still alive. When Mao died at ten minutes past midnight on 9 September, Ye Jianying was ready to act.[235]

The arrest of the Gang of Four

The strategic mistake of the Gang of Four had been to fail to make common cause with the beneficiaries. Their tactical error was for all of them to remain in Beijing after Mao's death. Lin Biao's plan to set up a rival CC in Guangdong, Deng's – indeed, the whole history of the Chinese revolution – should have taught them the critical importance of relocating to a secure base area when faced with potentially superior force. They ignored those lessons.

Jiang Qing and her colleagues were clearly affected by hubris. They had risen to power rapidly and easily by virtue of Mao's support, and they had exercised that power in an imperious manner with his acquiescence. All of them had luxuriated in a degree of privilege that the CCP had launched a revolution to eliminate but that, as Milovan Djilas has pointed out, is an inevitable companion of bureaucratic dictatorship.[236] In an earlier century, they would have been a court cabal, presuming upon their closeness to the emperor, insufficiently acquainted with the realities of power outside his penumbra.

Unlike most such cabals, the Gang of Four had a considerable regional power base in Shanghai to which they could have temporarily retreated. Instead, they apparently assumed that the combination of their relationship to Mao, membership in the Politburo Standing Committee, and control of

232 Quoted in Garside, *Coming alive!* 140–1; the source of the quotation is unclear. Garside does not explore the implications of Deng's remark about finding "a shield in other countries."

233 Xue Yesheng, ed., *Ye Jianying guanghui de yisheng* (Ye Jianying's glorious life), 342–3. Formally, Ye and Nie were ex-marshals, as military ranks had been abolished under Lin Biao before the Cultural Revolution.

234 Wang Nianyi, " 'Wenhua da geming' cuowu fazhan mailuo" (Analysis of the development of the errors of the 'Great Cultural Revolution,') *Dangshi tongxun* (Party history newsletter), October 1986.

235 At some point during Mao's last days (hours?) of life, all members of the Politburo were brought in one by one to pay their final farewell; see Fan Shuo, "The tempestuous October – a chronicle of the complete collapse of the 'Gang of Four,' " *Yangcheng wanbao,* 10 February 1989, translated in *FBIS Daily Report: China,* 14 February 1989, 17.

236 Milovan Djilas, *The New Class: An analysis of the communist system,* 42–7. Terrill devotes much space to a discussion of Jiang Qing's privileged lifestyle, and to a comparison of her and outstanding Chinese empresses; see Terrill, *The white-boned demon,* esp. 317–23.

the media had equipped them to take power in the capital, and they bent all their efforts to that goal. At the predawn Politburo meeting just after Mao's death, Jiang Qing appeared to be more interested in securing the immediate expulsion of Deng Xiaoping from the CCP than in settling the funeral arrangements.[237]

The Gang seem to have had a three-pronged plan of action: to assert their right to Mao's ideological mantle; to attempt to gain control of the Central Party apparatus; and to prepare for armed confrontation. Under Yao Wenyuan's direction, the main media organs were soon trumpeting the importance of Mao's alleged deathbed injunction (*linzhong zhufu*): "Act according to the principles laid down" (*An jiding fangzhen ban*). Not to do so would be to "betray Marxism, socialism, and the great theory of continuing the revolution under the dictatorship of the proletariat."[238] Clearly the objective was to head off any attempt either to reverse the current campaign against Deng Xiaoping or, even more threatening, to disavow the Cultural Revolution.

By creating an appropriate ideological climate through the press, the Gang could sway lower-ranking cadres' judgment of the balance of forces in the capital.[239] But this was not tantamount to taking over the reins of power. Shortly after Mao's death, the Gang attempted to assert a right of leadership over provincial organs. Wang Hongwen set up his own "duty office" in the Zhongnanhai, sending a message to provincial committees in the name of the CC's General Office ordering all major problems to be referred to himself.[240] From 12 September, the Gang promoted a write-in campaign to pressure the Politburo to appoint Jiang Qing chairman in Mao's place.[241] Pictures published on the occasion of the obsequies for the late Chairman were designed to accustom the public to the idea of Jiang Qing emerging as his successor.[242]

237 Xue, ed., *Ye Jianying guanghui de yisheng*, 342.

238 Hao and Duan, *Zhongguo gongchandang liushi nian*, 656. According to post-Cultural Revolution accounts, Mao actually said to Hua Guofeng on 30 April 1976, "Act according to past principles" (*Zhao guoqu fangzhen ban*); see Gao and Yan, *"Wenhua da geming" shinian shi*, 699. One analysis of the difference between the formulations argues that the Gang of Four's version suggests obedience to specific policies that they had been promoting on Mao's behalf or that they might claim to have documentary proof of in the Chairman's papers, whereas the Hua Guofeng version advocates no more than a vague continuity. See Gardner, *Chinese politics and the succession to Mao*, 111–13.

239 Provincial papers immediately began repeating Mao's alleged deathbed injunction; see Hu, *Zhongguo shehuizhuyi geming he jianshe shi jiangyi*, 335.

240 Whether in doing this Wang exceeded his authority as a member of the Politburo Standing Committee as afterward alleged must remain uncertain. Two years earlier, Wang had apparently attempted to insert Shanghai cadres in central CCP and government organs, though with what success is unclear; see Zhong, *Kang Sheng pingzhuan*, 316.

241 Ibid., 334–35; *Zhonggong dangshi dashi nianbiao*, 403.

242 Ladany, *The Communist Party of China and Marxism, 1921–1985*, 385. For an eyewitness account of the memorial service on 18 September, see Garside, *Coming alive!* 147–49. In late September, a mimeographed copy of Mao's purported last wishes reached Hong Kong; according to it, Mao had asked a group of leaders in June to help Jiang Qing in "hoisting the Red Flag" after he was dead. See Ting, *Chairman Hua*, 112.

The Gang pressed for a swift decision. On 19 September, Jiang Qing demanded that the Politburo Standing Committee – at this point consisting of Hua Guofeng, Wang Hongwen, Ye Jianying, and Zhang Chunqiao – hold an emergency conference and that she and Mao Yuanxin should attend, but Ye should not. At the meeting, Jiang proposed the Mao Yuanxin should be entrusted with sorting through his uncle's papers, presumably with a view to his discovering, or at least "discovering," a last will favoring her takeover. The vote went in favor of keeping the Chairman's papers locked up in the CC's General Office.[243]

On 29 September, at another Politburo conference, Jiang Qing and Zhang Chunqiao tried to force the issue of her future role. They rejected a proposal from Ye Jianying and Li Xiannian that Mao Yuanxin should return to his job in Liaoning province, countering with a suggestion that he should be entrusted with preparing the political report for the next CC plenum.[244] The Gang were outvoted, however: Mao Yuanxin was ordered back to Liaoning, and the leadership question was shelved.[245]

The Gang's third measure was to prepare for confrontation. The militia in Shanghai, perhaps 100,000 strong, was issued with weapons and arms, and warned to be ready for a fight. Secret contacts were established with Ding Sheng, the CO of the Nanjing Military Region. Wang Hongwen and the others breathed fire in speeches before friendly audiences.[246]

Mao Yuanxin caused a momentary panic on 2 October when he ordered an armored division to move to Beijing, but a telephone call to Ye Jianying from the Military Region headquarters elicited an immediate countermanding order.[247] Despite, or perhaps because of, the vicissitudes of the Cultural Revolution, the military chain-of-command loyalty was firmly in place, and the Gang and their adherents were not part of it.

Post–Cultural Revolution historians may well have exaggerated the extent to which the Gang were bent on a military coup. Even in their wildest fantasies, they could not have believed that their Shanghai militia could prevail over the likely opposition of most of the PLA. Shanghai could perhaps be a last-ditch stronghold, but not a Yan'an-style springboard for victory. Indeed, by remaining in Beijing, Jiang Qing and her colleagues gave every impression of having deluded themselves into thinking that even after Mao, it would be politics as usual. The struggle would go on, but under Cultural Revolution rules that had always brought the Gang out on top. But their

243 Jin, "*Wenhua da geming,*" 214–15. Another version has Jiang Qing and Mao Yuanxin bullying Mao's secretary into handing over some documents, which were only returned after Hua Guofeng's intervention; see Ting, *Chairman Hua,* 111.

244 Jin, "*Wenhua da geming,*" 214–15. 245 Xue, ed., *Ye Jianying guanghui de yisheng,* 345.

246 Hao and Duan, *Zhongguo gongchandang liushi nian,* 655–66; Jin, "*Wenhua da geming,*" 214–15.

247 Gao and Yan, "*Wenhua da geming*" *shinian shi,* 699.

patron was dead, and they were up against men who had fought long years to win China, and had made a revolution by disregarding the rules and taking swift and ruthless action when need be.

Sooner or later, such action was inevitable, for the reasons Deng Xiaoping had given. Ye Jianying apparently felt that Hua Guofeng had to play a key role because of his positions as the CCP's first deputy chairman and premier. Ye found Hua indecisive. Hua had originally wanted to convene a CC plenum to settle the leadership dispute with the Gang of Four, but after the Politburo confrontation on 29 September, and after Ye had promised him the support of the old comrades if he stood up and fought, Hua became convinced that the time for formal procedures was long past.[248]

An ideologically uncompromising article in the *Guangming ribao* on 4 October, following provocative speeches by Jiang Qing and Wang Hongwen, finally triggered the coup against the Gang, according to one account.[249] There were worrying indications that the Gang were planning some sort of action, for their followers were told to expect good news by 9 October. Alarmed, Ye Jianying went into hiding in the capital. Then, on 5 October, Hua Guofeng, Ye Jianying, and Li Xiannian held a Politburo conference at the PLA General Staff HQ in the Western Hills outside Beijing, to which the Gang were not invited. It was unanimously agreed that Jiang Qing, Wang Hongwen, Zhang Chunqiao, Yao Wenyuan, Mao Yuanxin, and their principal supporters had to be seized. Wang Dongxing and PLA Unit 8341 were ordered to carry out this decision. They did so on 6 October. When Jiang Qing was arrested at her residence, her servant spat on her. The Cultural Revolution was over.[250]

248 Xue, ed., *Ye Jianying guanghui de yisheng,* 344–5.

249 This article was prepared by two members of the *Liang Xiao* group, apparently at the urging of the editors of the *GMRB*. According to one of the authors, the article was dashed off with no prior consultation with members of the Gang of Four. Nevertheless, it was sufficiently disquieting for Politburo member Chen Xilian to return immediately to Beijing from Tangshan to consult with Ye Jianying.

250 There is some disagreement as to the precise manner and moment of the arrest of the Gang of Four. According to Fan, "The tempestuous October," 21, a meeting of the Politburo Standing Committee was called (presumably by Hua Guofeng) to discuss the final proofs of the fifth volume of Mao's *Selected works* and to study the proposals for the Mao mausoleum to be built in Tiananmen Square. In addition to Wang Hongwen and Zhang Chunqiao, who would come to the 8:00 P.M. meeting in the Huairentang in the Zhongnanhai complex as of right, Yao Wenyuan was also invited under the pretext that as the nation's leading propagandist, he would be the obvious person to carry out any last-minute revisions or polishing for the Mao volume. When each arrived, Hua Guofeng read out an agreed statement: "The central authorities maintain that you have committed unforgivable crimes, and have made a decision on investigating your case. You are prohibited from having access to the outside world during the investigation." Thereupon, Wang Dongxing's personnel escorted the prisoners away. Simultaneously, Jiang Qing and Mao Yuanxin were being arrested in their residences elsewhere in the Zhongnanhai. See also Wang, *Da dongluan de niandai,* 607–9; Xue, ed., *Ye Jianying guanghui de yisheng,* 345–6; *Yingsi lu,* 74–5. According to Gao and Yan, "*Wenhua da geming" shinian shi,* 700–3, however, the Gang of Four were all arrested in their residences in the Diaoyutai in the early hours of 6 October.

INTERREGNUM

In the immediate aftermath of the death of Mao and the purge of the Gang of Four, the urgent national need was for calm and stability. The Party, the PLA, and the people had to be reassured that the era of upheaval was over and that the country was under firm but moderate leadership. A somewhat contradictory image of change combined with continuity had to be conveyed.

A priority was to settle the question that had rent the leadership since the outset of the Cultural Revolution: "After Mao, who?" The leading survivors, Ye Jianying and Li Xiannian, presumably decided that this was no time for renewed struggle within the rump of the Politburo, already reduced by death and defeat to sixteen of the twenty-five appointed at the Tenth Congress only three years earlier. Whatever his merits, Hua Guofeng wore the mantle of legitimacy and had the rights of occupancy. He had been the Chairman's choice, he was in place, and he had led the beneficiaries into the anti-Gang camp. On 7 October, his assumption of Mao's posts as chairman of both the Party and its MAC was announced. Because he retained the premiership, Hua was now formally the heir of both Mao and Zhou Enlai. By combining the roles of both men, he seemed to have been placed in an impregnable position. He would discover that position conferred prestige and privilege, but power had deeper roots.

Simultaneously with agreeing on a new leader, the Politburo had to neutralize the country's one radical bastion. Fortunately Shanghai turned out to be a paper tiger. Deprived of their national leaders, the Gang's deputies there vacillated, allowed themselves to be lured to Beijing by transparent stratagems, and finally collapsed without fulfilling any of their threats of a fight to the finish. In the event, there was a week of light armed resistance. The Politburo dispatched two of their alternative members, Su Zhenhua, and Ni Zhifu, to take control; Xu Shiyou temporarily reassumed his old command of the Nanjing Military Region, displacing the unreliable Ding Sheng, to provide the politicians with any necessary military backup.[251] With Shanghai reclaimed, it was now up to Hua Guofeng to provide the country with leadership.

Hua Guofeng's dilemma

From the outset, Hua Guofeng's leadership was hamstrung by an insoluble dilemma, symbolized by the contradictory heritages of Mao and Zhou that he

251 Gao and Yan, *"Wenhua da geming," shinian shi*, 703–8; Hao and Duan, *Zhongguo gongchandang liushi nian*, 657; *Zhonggong dangshi dashi nianbiao*, 405. Domes's account suggests greater bloodshed – *The government and politics of the PRC*, 138.

had been bequeathed. On the one hand, there was no doubt that Mao wanted the goals and gains of the Cultural Revolution to be maintained. To disavow the Cultural Revolution would be to undermine the position of the man who had chosen him as his successor, and indeed to negate the whole period whose upheavals had permitted Hua to rise from relative obscurity to his current eminence. Hua's only claim to legitimacy was Mao's blessing, and he moved swiftly to ensure that only he had control of Mao's legacy. On 8 October, it was announced that a fifth volume of the late Chairman's selected works would be published under the editorial control of Hua Guofeng. A simultaneous decision was to erect a mausoleum for Mao in Tiananmen Square, in defiance of a twenty-seven-year-old rule agreed to by the Chairman and his colleagues not to emulate the Soviet pattern of honoring leaders by erecting tombs and renaming cities and streets.[252] Hua had no doubt of Mao's continuing significance for himself; he, and presumably his fellow beneficiaries, wanted to try to ensure that Mao's continuing significance for the country would be set in marble.

Hua's personal amulet was Mao's now oft-echoed sentence "With you in charge, I'm at ease." But it was necessary to coin a slogan that would convey in the ideological realm the symbolism enshrined in the mausoleum: The Chairman is forever with us. Appropriately, Hua approved a formula proposed by Wang Dongxing that seemed to set Mao Zedong Thought in concrete: "Whatever policy Chairman Mao decided upon, we shall resolutely defend; whatever directives Chairman Mao issued, we shall steadfastly obey." Their aim was to head off questioning of the actions of the later Mao, which had helped to bring them and other members of what came to be known as the "whatever faction" to power.[253] Moreover, the preservation of the Mao cult provided a basis and a justification for the burgeoning cult of Hua Guofeng himself, badly needed if this unknown successor was to establish a position among Party and people.[254]

But the attempt of Hua and the whatever faction to don Mao's protective mantle had already been challenged by Deng Xiaoping's protectors in the south. In a letter to Hua, Xu Shiyou and Wei Guoqing queried the advisability

252 *Zhonggong dangshi dashi nianbiao*, 405.

253 First divulged in a joint editorial of *RMRB*, *HQ*, and the *Jiefangjun bao* on 7 February 1977; *Zhonggong dangshi dashi nianbiao*, 406–7; Hao and Duan, *Zhongguo gongchandang liushi nian*, 670.

254 Ibid. Books and pamphlets about Hua were churned out by the presses. According to Stuart R. Schram, writing in 1984, the card index in the library of Peking University contained approximately 300 entries of books and pamphlets contributing to the Hua cult, a small fraction, in his judgment, of those published around the country; Stuart R. Schram, " 'Economics in command?' Ideology and policy since the Third Plenum, 1978–84," *CQ*, 99 (September 1984), 417, n. 1. A favorite publicity photograph of Hua at this time was of him with Mao, supposedly at the moment when the late Chairman had uttered the magic words of benediction. Some observers claimed to detect that Hua changed his hairstyle to make him resemble Mao.

of hushing up Mao's shortcomings, which were known to all; indicated that Mao's blessing of Hua as successor was insufficient legitimation and that it had to be confirmed by a CC plenum; and hinted broadly of a challenge to Hua at such a plenum if Mao's incorrect verdict on Deng were not reversed.[255]

Hua fought back. At the central work conference held from 10 to 22 March to discuss progress on the anti-Gang campaign, he reaffirmed the "two whatevers," repeated formulas from the Cultural Revolution, maintained that the Tiananmen incident was counterrevolutionary, and asserted that the campaign against Deng and the right-opportunist wind to reverse the verdicts had been correct. He even denounced the Gang of Four as extreme rightists (the tactic *they* had used in the aftermath of the Lin Biao affair) in an effort to defend the continuation of leftist policies.

Hua came under fire from Party veterans, notably Chen Yun, who had been a member of the Politburo Standing Committee and its predecessor for more than two decades up to the Cultural Revolution. Chen and another critic, Wang Zhen, focused on the linked questions of the assessment of the Tiananmen incident and the need for a second rehabilitation of Deng Xiaoping, which they claimed was universally demanded. Hua must have wondered if this was the support of veteran cadres that Ye Jianying had promised him in return for taking a lead against the Gang of Four. At any rate, he rejected the demands of Chen and Wang and even refused to allow their speeches to be printed in the conference record.[256]

There is no suggestion in Chinese accounts of this work conference that Ye Jianying or Li Xiannian joined in their old comrades' criticisms of Hua's position. Almost certainly their feelings must have been mixed. Formally, it would have been unusual for a member of the Politburo Standing Committee like Ye to criticize another member of that select body in front of a large gathering of more junior Party officials. More importantly, Ye and Li owed a certain loyalty to Hua, who was now in a sense their creation as well as Mao's. And while Ye and Li had doubtless supported everything Deng had tried to do during 1975, they must have been ambivalent about him returning in 1977. With Deng absent, they dominated the political picture as elder statesmen guiding Hua; with Deng back, they would at the very least have to cede part of that role to him. And what would be Deng's attitude toward them? Would he not feel that they, like Zhou, had done and said things they regretted in order to survive the Cultural Revolution? And if so, would he forgive the living as well as the dead?

255 Domes, *The government and politics of the PRC*, 146–7.

256 Hao and Duan, *Zhongguo gongchandang liushi nian*, 670–1; *Zhonggong dangshi dashi nianbiao*, 407–8. The gist of Chen Yun's speech is to be found in *Chen Yun wenxuan (1956–1985)* (Selected works of Chen Yun [1956–85]), 207.

Yet Ye and Li would have appreciated the strength of sentiment within the Party and PLA and realized that with Mao gone it would be difficult to hold the line against Deng's return. They must have known, too, that Deng was more likely than Hua to be able to engineer the post-Cultural Revolution turnaround that most desired. Political confusion, factional battles, and indiscipline encouraged by years of leftist agitation were once again damaging the economy. There were widespread reports of strikes, sabotage, and renewed disruption of rail traffic. The 1976 plan results, affected in part by the Tangshan earthquake, had been considerably below target, and the estimated losses over the last three years of the Cultural Revolution, 1974–6, were 28 million tons of steel, 100 billion yuan in value of industrial production, and 40 billion yuan in state revenues.[257] Hua Guofeng had called for a return to "great order," but Deng was more likely to bring it about.

After the work conference, Ye and Li must have advised Hua that to resist the Deng tide could be politically disastrous for him. The most that could be done was to obtain a guarantee from Deng that he would let bygones be bygones. On 10 April, Deng wrote to the CC condemning the two whatevers, and proposed instead the use of "genuine Mao Zedong Thought taken as an integral whole." He was subsequently visited by two "leading comrades" of the CC's General Office, one presumably its director, Wang Dongxing, seeking to negotiate a deal before the beneficiaries, now the whatever faction, agreed to his return. Deng, to judge from his own account, was not in a mood for compromise, pointing out that if the two whatevers were correct, there could be no justification for his rehabilitation or reversing the verdict on the Tiananmen incident. Even Mao himself had never claimed that whatever he said was correct, nor had Marx or Lenin.[258]

Deng's letter has never been released, so it is uncertain whether in it or an earlier communication he indicated, as rumored, his willingness to support Hua Guofeng's continued leadership of the Party.[259] Some such undertaking seems likely, or there would have been no reason for the whatever faction to agree to his return. If it were given, that could be why the letter was not included in Deng's *Selected works:* It would have contrasted sharply with Hua Guofeng's eventual fate.

257 Fang, ed., *Zhonghua renmin gongheguo jingji dashiji (1949–1980)*, 573–4; Domes, *The government and politics of the PRC*, 140–2.

258 *Selected works of Deng Xiaoping (1975–1982)*, 51–2; Hao and Duan, *Zhongguo gongchandang liushi nian*, 671.

259 Garside, *Coming alive!* 174. For Deng's expression of support in conversation with Hua Guofeng, see the manuscript minutes of Hua's visit to Deng and Liu Bocheng in a hospital on 26 October 1976, available in Harvard's Fairbank Center Library. I am grateful to Michael Schoenhals for drawing my attention to this source.

Whatever the understanding, it enabled Deng Xiaoping to attend the Tenth CC's Third Plenum from 16 to 21 July and be reinstated in all his offices: Party vice-chairman and member of the Politburo Standing Committee; vice-chairman of the MAC; vice-premier; and PLA chief of staff. Hua Guofeng had his positions formally endorsed, and stubbornly maintained his support for the two whatevers and the Cultural Revolution. The available text of Deng's speech indicates that he repeated his advocacy of an integrated view of Mao Zedong Thought, but was discreet enough not to attack the two whatevers frontally at this time; he had to prepare the ground before his next attack. Instead, he promoted an old slogan of Mao's that was to become the essence of Deng Xiaoping's post-Mao policies: "Seek truth from facts."[260]

On the basis of the compromise cemented at the plenum, the CCP was able to hold its Eleventh Congress in August. On this occasion, it was Hua's turn to be discreet, not reasserting the two whatevers or repeating his estimation of the Tiananmen incident as counterrevolutionary. But he clearly felt unable to criticize Mao or disavow the Cultural Revolution without undermining his own position. Instead, he opened with a long and effusive eulogy of the late Chairman, went on to reaffirm the necessity for and success of the Cultural Revolution, the correctness of the line of the Tenth Congress (at which he entered the Politburo), and the need to persist with class struggle and continue the revolution under the proletarian dictatorship; and he observed chillingly that "Political revolutions in the nature of the Cultural Revolution will take place many times in the future."[261]

Deng Xiaoping emerged at the Congress as the CCP's third-ranking leader, after Hua and Ye Jianying (who reported on the new Party constitution). Deng's brief closing speech was the only other address to be accorded publicity. He referred to Hua as "our wise leader" but did not emulate his wisdom by praising the Cultural Revolution. He avoided controversy by calling for a return to honesty and hard work, modesty and prudence, plain living and hard struggle, and, of course, seeking truth from facts. But he, too, had to compromise and express support for the current line to "grasp the key link of class struggle" and "continue the revolution under the dictatorship of the proletariat," dogmas of the Eleventh Congress later condemned by Chinese Party historians.[262] No wonder Deng chose not to include this

260 The slogan *shishi qiushi* dates back to the Han period; *Selected works of Deng Xiaoping*, 55–60; *Zhonggong dangshi dashi nianbiao*, 409–10.

261 *The Eleventh National Congress of the Communist Party of China (Documents)*, 52.

262 Ibid., 191–5; Hao and Duan, *Zhongguo gongchandang liushi nian*, 674. One report has it that Deng was originally scheduled to deliver a speech on seeking truth from facts, written by Hu Qiaomu, but that when Deng was assigned the closing address, Nie Rongzhen gave the Hu text, which was later published in *Red Flag*, though no longer described as a Congress speech; I am indebted to Michael Schoenhals for this information.

speech in his *Selected works,* despite the importance for him and the CCP of the occasion on which it was given.

Out of this Congress there emerged a leadership that was purged of the left but that did not particularly favor the left's victims. One third of the CC elected at the Tenth Congress disappeared, which included more than 75 percent of its representatives from mass organizations, presumably for leftist sympathies. Another category of probable leftists, the more recent entrants into the Party, also suffered heavily, being reduced by more than 70 percent.

The Politburo was also a compromise, but weighted in favor of survivors and beneficiaries of the Cultural Revolution, with only six of twenty-six members drawn from the ranks of the victims. One man who would later help spearhead Deng's reform program secured a toehold as an alternate member: Zhao Ziyang. In the new five-man Politburo Standing Committee, Deng was the only one who would later emerge as a strong critic of Hua and the whatever faction. Hua was now buttressed by his key supporter in that grouping, Wang Dongxing, who was presumably being recognized both for his service against the Gang and for the power he wielded as head of PLA Unit 8341. Ye Jianying was joined by his joint guarantor of Hua's position, Li Xiannian.[263]

Hua's "great leap"

Insofar as Hua Guofeng had a vision of "After Mao, what?" it seems to have been an unlikely combination of mid-1960s radicalism and mid-1950s economics. Certainly, the more generally acceptable part of Hua's dual heritage was Zhou Enlai's commitment of China to the four modernizations. Here was a goal around which all except the most rabid leftists could unite. And surely Hua visualized a successful development program as providing the answer to the many who were asking themselves what right he had to be at the top. An unexceptionable but also unexceptional bureaucratic career in the provinces before the Cultural Revolution; junior enough not to have been in the first group of provincial officials to be targeted by the Red Guards; the luck still to be around when the tide turned and experienced cadres were once again in demand; senior enough to be transferred to the capital when the Lin Biao affair left large gaps in the leadership; competent enough and leftist enough to have been acceptable to Mao when Wang Hongwen failed him – no one could blame Hua for being lucky, but was his record justification enough for him to try to lead China after Mao and Zhou when his elders and betters were

263 *The Eleventh National Congress of the Communist Party of China (Documents)*, 227–36. For a more detailed breakdown of the composition of the new CC and Politburo, see Domes, *The government and politics of the PRC*, 150–1.

available? Probably not, in many people's eyes, and hence Hua's need to prove himself.

Unfortunately for Hua, his need to deliver the goods outstripped China's ability to produce them. At the first session of the new (Fifth) NPC in February–March 1978, Premier Hua unveiled his grandiose version of the original Ten-Year Plan (1976–85) foreshadowed by Zhou in his last NPC speech in 1975. The plan target for steel output in 1985 was 60 million tons (1977: 23.7 m. tons), for oil, 350 million tons (1977: 93.6 m. tons). For the remaining eight years, Hua called for the construction of 120 major projects, 14 major heavy industrial bases, and capital investment equivalent to that expended in the previous twenty-eight years. The plan failed to take account of the lessons of the 1960s and the economic damage of the 1970s.[264] As is explained in *CHOC* 15, Chapter 6, the plan could not have reflected any careful thought or accurate data: The oil fields on which expanded production would supposedly be based were a pipe dream; the foreign exchange costs would have been enormous, because what came to be known as Hua's "great leap outward" placed heavy reliance on machinery imports. Instead of picking up Zhou's torch, Hua had mimicked Mao's grandiose visions. Instead of covering himself with glory, he had pointed China toward another economic disaster. This, too, would be used against him.

The Third Plenum

The manner in which Deng Xiaoping turned the tables on Hua and the whatever faction is an illustration of the mysterious nature of power in the PRC. Hua was supreme leader in all branches of Party and state, Deng was not. The whatever faction was in power; Deng's supporters were not. Yet, in the relatively short period between the Third Plenum of the Tenth CC, in July 1977, and the Third Plenum of the Eleventh CC, in December 1978, those power relations had been turned around. The method appears to have been mobilization of elite opinion through the press.

On 11 May 1978, the *Guangming ribao* published a pseudonymous article entitled "Practice is the sole criterion for testing truth," which became a second rallying cry for the Deng forces. The author of the article, Hu Fuming, was then vice-chairman of the Philosophy Department of Nanjing University and a Party member. He later claimed he had submitted the article for publication in the autumn of 1977 in opposition to the two whatevers entirely on his own initiative, because he felt that without rebutting that doctrine there was no hope of Deng's returning to power.[265] Self-generated it may have

264 Fang, ed., *Zhonghua renmin gongheguo jingji dashiji*, (1949–1980), 595–6.

265 See Stuart R. Schram's report of his interview with Hu in his " 'Economics in command?' " 417–19.

been, but the article that appeared had undergone considerable revision and strengthening on the basis of the ideas of two theoreticians working at the Central Party School under Hu Yaobang.[266] It struck at the roots of Cultural Revolution doctrine, which, whether expressed by Lin Biao, Jiang Qing, or Hua Guofeng, held that Mao's writings and statements were eternal verities that should not be tampered with, whatever the circumstances.

To the annoyance of Hua Guofeng and Wang Dongxing, the article was quickly republished in the *People's Daily* and the *Liberation Army News* and was the spark that lit a prairie fire of nationwide debate.[267] Deng Xiaoping himself joined in the fray in a speech to a PLA political work conference in June, when he reasserted the need to "seek truth from facts."[268] Astutely, he used quotations from Mao's works to prove that this principle did not mean rejecting him but, on the contrary, represented a return to the best traditions and practice of the Chairman himself,[269] and concluded with a rhetorical flourish:

> Comrades, let's think it over: Isn't it true that seeking truth from facts, proceeding from reality and integrating theory with practice form the fundamental principle of Mao Zedong Thought? Is this fundamental principle outdated? Will it ever become outdated? How can we be true to Marxism-Leninism and Mao Zedong Thought if we are against seeking truth from facts, proceeding from reality and integrating theory with practice? Where would that lead us? Obviously, only to idealism and metaphysics, and thus to the failure of our work and of our revolution.[270]

At this stage the battle was far from won. Earlier at this PLA conference, Hua Guofeng and Ye Jianying had both spoken, but neither had saluted Deng's banner of truth.[271] Yet on 24 June, the *Liberation Army News* published an article supporting Deng, immediately republished in the *People's Daily,* which had been prepared under the direction of Luo Ruiqing.[272] Luo had been dismissed as chief of staff on the eve of the Cultural Revolution but

266 For instance, Hu Fuming's original title had been "Practice is a criterion of truth," which was then revised to read "Practice is the criterion of all truths" before finally appearing as "Practice is the sole criterion of truth." The genesis of this article has been minutely investigated by Michael Schoenhals, who presented a seminar paper on the subject at Harvard's Fairbank Center on 3 February 1989.

267 Hao and Duan, *Zhongguo gongchandang liushi nian,* 680–3; Domes, *The government and politics of China,* 187. On hearing of the negative reaction of leading politicians, Hu Fuming, according to Schoenhals, got so worried that he dissociated himself from the article (which was noted in internal bulletins) on the grounds that it had been changed beyond recognition. A follow-up article, by one of Hu Yaobang's two acolytes, was published in the *Liberation Army News* as a result of the intervention of Luo Ruiqing; this was Luo's last major political act before his death in August 1978.

268 *Selected works of Deng Xiaoping,* 127–32. Hu Jiwei, the editor of *RMRB,* had been reprimanded by his former chief at the paper, Wu Lengxi, for republishing the article, and Hu Qiaomu rebuked Hu Yaobang for the activities of his subordinates. Deng's intervention was thus a crucial development and was given big play by Hu Jiwei in *RMRB;* Schoenhals seminar.

269 Schram, " 'Economics in command?' " 419. 270 *Selected works of Deng Xiaoping,* 132.

271 Domes, *The government and politics of the PRC,* 156.

272 Hao and Duan, *Zhongguo gongchandang liushi nian,* 682. Michael Schoenhals tells me that the *Liberation Army News* article was the first to criticize the two whatevers.

had rejoined the CC at the Eleventh Congress; if his authorship were widely known within the elite, it would doubtless have influenced a lot of senior officers to throw their weight to Deng's side. Certainly, from this point on the debate heated up, and by mid-September, when Deng returned to the attack on the two whatevers in a speech in the Northeast,[273] something he had eschewed in Hua's and Ye's presence in June, conferences in ten provinces had supported his position.[274] Perhaps as dispiriting for the whatever faction, that quintessential survivor, Li Xiannian, had hinted that he was prepared to abandon Hua and back the new line. By November, leading officials in all provinces and military regions had thrown their weight on Deng's side. It was at this point that a central work conference, originally proposed by Deng two months earlier, convened in Beijing on 10 November.[275]

The principal elements on the agenda were how to reinvigorate agriculture and settling the 1980 economic plan. But Chen Yun again took a lead in quickly transforming the meeting into a full-scale debate on the errors of the Cultural Revolution. He wanted retrospective justice to be done to Bo Yibo, whose revolutionary record had been besmirched, and posthumous justice done to Tao Zhu, who had fallen at the end of 1966, and Peng Dehuai, who had been dismissed in 1959 and then been publicly denounced during the late 1960s. Kang Sheng's grave errors should be acknowledged. But Chen's most provocative proposal for the whatever faction was his insistence that the positive nature of the Tiananmen incident be affirmed.[276]

Chen Yun's speech triggered a wave of supporting speeches, notably from Tan Zhenlin, demanding that a whole series of incidents during the Cultural Revolution should be reassessed.[277] Hua Guofeng had evidently anticipated this onslaught, or moved very quickly to accommodate himself to it. On 15 November, it was announced that the Beijing Party committee had reassesed the Tiananmen incident as "completely revolutionary," and the following day that Hua himself had written an inscription for the first officially approved anthology of Tiananmen poems. Similar reassessments of similar incidents in Nanjing, Hangzhou, and Zhengzhou had been announced earlier.[278] With that position conceded, it was less surprising that the whatever faction were also prepared to accept the rehabilitation of a large number of victims of the Cultural Revolution, most of whose fates were not directly attributable to themselves.

273 *Selected works of Deng Xiaoping*, 141. 274 Domes, *The government and politics of the PRC*, 157.

275 Hao and Duan, *Zhongguo gongchandang liushi nian*, 682–3, 686–7. Deng was touring in Southeast Asia and missed the opening of the conference.

276 *Chen Yun wenxuan (1956–1985)*, 208–10.

277 Hao and Duan, *Zhongguo gongchandang liushi nian*, 689.

278 Garside, *Coming alive!* 200–201; the text of the Beijing Party announcement is in "Quarterly chronicle and documentation," *CQ*, 77 (March 1979), 659.

A far more dangerous setback for Hua Guofeng and the whatever faction was the entry of a group of victims into the Politburo at the CC's Third Plenum, held 18–22 December to formalize the results of the work conference, large enough to tip the balance of the leadership in Deng's favor. Chen Yun was restored to his old position as a CCP vice-chairman and a member of the Politburo Standing Committee, and made first secretary of a new body, the Discipline Inspection Commission, which set out to purify the Party ranks of Cultural Revolution leftists.[279] Three other Deng supporters, Hu Yaobang, Wang Zhen, Deng Yingchao, Zhou Enlai's widow, joined the Politburo. In addition, nine senior victims were made full CC members. At a Politburo meeting summoned on 25 December, an embryo central secretariat was re-created, with Hu Yaobang at its head; Wang Dongxing was simultaneously sacked from his leadership of the CC General Office, which had functioned as a secretariat during the Cultural Revolution.[280] Wang and other members of the whatever faction maintained their positions on the Politburo, but the writing was now on the wall for them.

Their predicament was underlined by the decisive swing away from leftism, even of their variety, that the conference and plenum represented. The two whatevers were rejected. Class struggle was no longer to be the "key link"; the four modernizations were to take precedence. The theory of "continuing the revolution under the proletarian dictatorship" was abandoned. Deng indicated in his speech to the plenum that the time had not yet come for an overall appraisal of the Cultural Revolution and Mao himself.[281] But the policies adopted by the plenum represented a radical turn from the previous decade.

First and foremost, the Third Plenum took the first steps away from agricultural collectivization so strongly maintained by Hua Guofeng. As already indicated, where rural socialism was concerned, Hua differed only in pace and not in goal from the Gang of Four. Even after the latter had been purged, he pressed forward with policies for greater egalitarianism, such as promoting brigade accounting and curbing private plots and rural fairs. By mid-1978, reflecting Hua's weakening position, those policies were beginning to be attacked.[282] The Third Plenum rejected Hua's program and the

279 Deng Xiaoping made clear in his speech to the plenum that the kind of people whom he detested were those who had engaged in "beating, smashing and looting, who have been obsessed by factionalist ideas, who have sold their souls by framing innocent comrades, or who disregard the Party's vital interests. Nor can we lightly trust persons who sail with the wind, curry favour with those in power and ignore the Party's principles"; *Selected works of Deng Xiaoping*, 160.

280 For a full summary of the results of the work conference and the Third Plenum, as well as some of the events leading up to them, see Materials Group of the Party History Teaching and Research Office of the CCP Central Party School, *Zhongguo gongchandang lici zhongyao huiyi ji, xia* (Collection of various important conferences of the CCP), 274–80.

281 *Selected works of Deng Xiaoping*, 160–1.

282 Domes, *The government and politics of the PRC*, 163–4.

Dazhai model. To unleash the "socialist enthusiasm" of the peasantry, the plenum returned to the policies of the early 1960s and established a framework that proved to be only the beginning of a radical restructuring of rural China:

The right of ownership by the people's communes, production brigades and production teams and their power of decision must be protected effectively by the laws of the state; it is not permitted to commandeer the manpower, funds, products and material of any production team; the economic organizations at various levels of the people's commune must conscientiously implement the socialist principle of "to each according to his work," work out payment in accordance with the amount and quality of work done, and overcome equalitarianism; small plots of land for private use by commune members, their domestic side-occupations, and village fairs are necessary adjuncts of the socialist economy, and must not be interfered with; the people's communes must resolutely implement the system of three levels of ownership with the production team as the basic accounting unit, and this should remain unchanged.[283]

Not even in the industrial sphere was Hua's program endorsed. His Ten-year Plan went conspicuously unmentioned. Instead, Chen Yun's influence was again clearly visible in the plenum's call for more balanced and steadier growth, rather than the massive investment in heavy industry preferred by Hua.[284] When he addressed the annual session of the NPC in June, he had to announce that rather than press ahead at the hectic speed he had espoused a year earlier, reassessment by the State Council since the Third Plenum had led to a decision to dedicate the years 1979–81 to "readjusting, restructuring, consolidating and improving" the economy.[285]

Democracy Wall

The defeat of Hua and the whatever faction at the Third Plenum was mainly the product of successful mobilization by Deng Xiaoping and his supporters of the "silent majority" of cadres and officers who had always opposed the Cultural Revolution. But the work conference and plenum took place against a backdrop of vigorous public support in the capital for Deng's line that could not but have influenced a leadership with vivid memories of the impact of the Tiananmen incident.

That incident had demonstrated the degree to which national discipline, so strikingly instilled in the early 1950s, had been weakened by the Cultural Revolution. "To rebel is justified," Mao had proclaimed, and on 5 April 1976, thousands in the capital had rebelled against the political leadership

283 Quoted in "Quarterly chronicle and documentation," *CQ*, 77 (March 1979), 170.
284 Ibid., 169. 285 Ibid., *CQ*, 79 (September 1979), 647.

and the economic and social program that the Chairman was attempting to set in place for after his demise. The strikes, slowdowns, and simple hooliganism taking place in various parts of China in the mid-1970s underlined that it was not simply the politically aware inhabitants of the capital who understood that the authority of the CCP had been gravely undermined.

The death of Mao, and the gradual reemergence of leaders who wished to disavow the whole Cultural Revolution, triggered a new outburst of public activity in the capital designed to help that process along. The Tiananmen incident had been Act 1 in the popular struggle to rehabilitate Deng and what he stood for. The entr'acte had been the replacement of Mayor Wu De, heavily responsible for the repression of the Tiananmen protesters, in October 1978 after eighteen months of veiled attacks in the press and open attacks in posters.[286] Democracy Wall was supposed to be Act 2. But this time the curtain was rung down early, and by Deng himself.

A week after the beginning of the central work conference, the first posters went up on a stretch of wall along the Chang'an dajie, the wide avenue that passes the Tiananmen, not far from the square.[287] The very first, put up by a mechanic, criticized Mao by name for supporting the Gang of Four and dismissing Deng Xiaoping. Another early one called Deng "the living Zhou Enlai" and denounced the authorities' handling of the Tiananmen incident. A third attacked a "small group of highly place people," clearly the whatever faction, for preventing a reassessment of the alleged counterrevolutionary nature of the incident.

These themes of support for Deng, antagonism toward the whatever faction, and criticism of Mao characterized many of the posters. They must have given Deng and his supporters at the work conference a feeling of satisfaction that at this critical juncture they could claim popular backing. But the poster writers did not stop there. Soon they were putting out pamphlets, papers, and magazines and setting up discussion groups such as the Human Rights Alliance and the Enlightenment Society. Within a week of the first poster's going up, people at Democracy Wall were no longer content simply to read each other's posters, but were actively debating issues, and even with foreigners. On 26 November, the American syndicated columnist Robert Novak was given questions to ask Deng Xiaoping when he interviewed him the following day. When, on the evening of the 27th, Novak's colleague John

286 Garside, *Coming alive!* 194–96.

287 This following brief summary of Democracy Wall is based principally on the eyewitness reports of Garside, *Coming alive!* 212–98, and Canadian journalist John Fraser's *The Chinese: Portrait of a people,* 203–71, and the analysis and poems contained in David S. G. Goodman, *Beijing street voices: The poetry and politics of China's democracy movement.* Both Garside and Fraser made many contacts with participants in the "democracy movement."

Fraser, the Toronto *Globe and Mail*'s Beijing correspondent, relayed to a mass audience the fact that Deng had told Novak that Democracy Wall was a good thing, "pandemonium broke out"; but Fraser's excited auditors sobered up when they heard that Deng, in a foretaste of things to come, had said that not all the things written up at the wall were correct.[288]

Democracy Wall was a more profound phenomenon than the Tiananmen incident. The latter was a brief burst of anger against Mao and the Gang of Four; most of the poems mourned Zhou Enlai or excoriated Jiang Qing. At Democracy Wall, on the other hand, young Chinese, mainly blue collar with a junior high or high school education,[289] explored a wide range of political and social problems and, though often displaying a considerable degree of naiveté, were clearly enthused with the possibility of China embracing the "fifth modernization," democracy:

> The 5th National People's Congress opens red flowers,
> Drawing up the people's new constitution.
> Eight hundred million people joyously sing together,
> Of one heart to establish a new nation.
>
> The fresh blood of the revolutionary martyrs is sprinkled,
> In exchange for today's new constitution.
> Protect democracy, protect people's rights,
> Advance the Four Modernizations.[290]

As his interview with Novak illustrated, Deng Xiaoping's first reactions to the democracy movement were broadly positive. The day before that interview, Deng had told a leading Japanese politician: "The writing of big-character posters is permitted by our constitution. We have no right to negate or criticize the masses for promoting democracy. . . . The masses should be allowed to vent their grievances!"[291] Unfortunately for the movement, Deng Xiaoping quickly perceived contradictions between democracy and the four modernizations and, whatever his earliest reactions, soon found Democracy Wall more of an embarrassment than an advantage in his current political struggles.

The contradiction was that widespread political debate could get out of hand and undermine the stability and unity that he proclaimed as vital for China's economic advance. He surely remembered that it was when young people went on the rampage in the early Cultural Revolution that China's

288 Fraser, *The Chinese,* 245.

289 This is the analysis of a Chinese participant quoted by Goodman, *Beijing street voices,* 141. This person, who was arrested in May 1979, blamed the "arrogance" of the intellectuals for their lack of participation.

290 From Li Hong Kuan, "Ode to the constitution," quoted in Goodman, *Beijing street voices,* 70.

291 Quoted in Garside, *Coming alive!* 247–8.

cities were thrown into chaos and the Chinese economy suffered its worst setbacks of that decade. The embarrassment was that the silent majority of old cadres and senior PLA officers upon whose support he relied in his struggle with the whatever faction were not happy at a new threat to their authority and position. They had not welcomed the overthrow of the Gang of Four just to allow some new form of Cultural Revolution to spring up.

Nothing could be done for fear of adverse publicity before Deng's visit to the United States from 28 January to 4 February. But despite that overseas triumph, Deng's position thereafter may have been weakened temporarily as a result of the inability of the PLA to teach Vietnam a convincing military lesson during the border war from mid-February to mid-March, a cause that was close to Deng's heart. One report suggests that as late as mid-March, Deng was telling senior colleagues that suppressing the democracy movement would have unfavorable results: "Counter-revolution can be suppressed, sabotage can be restricted, but to walk back down the old road of suppressing differing opinion and not listening to criticism will make the trust and support of the masses disappear."[292] But he agreed to abide by majority opinion, and at the end of March he proclaimed that the four modernizations demanded that the country adhere to the "four cardinal principles": the socialist road; the dictatorship of the proletariat; the leadership of the CCP; and Marxism–Leninism and Mao Zedong Thought.[293] In justifying the introduction of criteria highly reminiscent of Mao's action at the outset of the Anti-Rightist Campaign in 1957, Deng said that

> certain bad elements have raised sundry demands that cannot be met at present or are altogether unreasonable. They have provoked or tricked some of the masses into raiding Party and government organizations, occupying offices, holding sit-down and hunger strikes and obstructing traffic, thereby seriously disrupting production, other work and public order. Moreover, they have raised such sensational slogans as "Oppose hunger" and "Give us human rights," inciting people to hold demonstrations and deliberately trying to get foreigners to give worldwide publicity to their words and deeds. There is a so-called China Human Rights Group which has gone so far as to put up big-character posters requesting the President of the United States to "show concern" for human rights in China. Can we permit such an open call for intervention in China's internal affairs?[294]

Wei Jingsheng, the editor of the journal *Exploration* and a prominent figure in the democracy movement, condemned Deng for laying aside "the mask of protector of democracy." Three days later the Beijing authorities issued regulations to curb the democracy movement, and the following day Wei was arrested. At his trial in October 1979, he was given a fifteen-year jail term.[295]

292 Quote in ibid., 256. 293 *Selected works of Deng Xiaoping,* 172. 294 Ibid., 181.
295 Garside, *Coming alive!* 256–7, 262.

On the basis of a CC Plenum decision in February 1980, at the 1980 NPC session, the clause in the state constitution guaranteeing citizens free speech and the right of assembly was shorn of the commitment so dear to Mao: the right to engage in great debate and to put up big-character posters.[296] For the moment, the democracy movement had been shut down.

The fall of Hua Guofeng

The Third Plenum is rightly appraised by Chinese Party historians as a major turning point in post-1949 history. Had Hua Guofeng been adept or swift enough, he might have made common cause with the old cadres against Deng on the issue of the democracy movement. Perhaps it was concern that this could happen that led Deng to move so fast. But in fact, Hua and the whatever faction were too mired in the Cultural Revolution for such an alliance to have had more than temporary success.

In the event, Hua watched helplessly as an anti-whatever coalition was inexorably built up within the top leadership. At the CC's Fourth Plenum from 25 to 28 September 1979, Zhao Ziyang was promoted to full membership of the Politburo. The rehabilitated Peng Zhen, the former Beijing first secretary who, after Deng and Liu Shaoqi, had been the most senior victim at the start of the Cultural Revolution, returned to the Politburo. Eleven other prominent old cadres were readmitted to the CC.

A bigger breakthrough for Deng occurred at the Fifth Plenum from 23 to 29 February 1980, when Hua's supporters in the whatever faction – Wang Dongxing, Ji Dengkui, Wu De, and Chen Xilian (the "little gang of four") – were relieved of all their Party and state posts. Chen Yonggui, the model peasant leader from Dazhai, who was regarded as incompetent rather than malevolent, was simply allowed to drop out of Politburo activities. Hu Yaobang and Zhao Ziyang were elevated to the Politburo Standing Committee. Hu, a Deng loyalist who had been leader of the Youth League in the 1950s, was made the CCP general secretary, a job that had been vacant since Deng was removed from it early in the Cultural Revolution. The newly reconstituted secretariat was staffed almost exclusively with Deng's supporters. Finally, it was agreed that all the charges against the Cultural Revolution's number one capitalist roader, Liu Shaoqi, were false and that he should be rehabilitated.[297]

Deng's next step was to eradicate the influence of the whatever faction from the State Council. Vice-premiers Chen Xilian and Ji Dengkui were removed in April 1980 as a consequence of the decisions at the Fifth Plenum,

296 *Zhonghua renmin gongheguo diwujie quanguo renmin daibiao dahui disanci huiyi wenjian* (Documents of the third session of the fifth NPC of the PRC), 169.

297 Materials Group, *Zhongguo gongchandang lici zhongyao huiyi ji, xia*, 281–9.

but ousting Hua Guofeng from the premiership proved more difficult. Deng advocated separating the functions of Party and government, and proposed that in addition to Hua, a number of other old cadres including himself would resign as vice-premiers, thus also permitting the rejuvenation of the State Council. Although Deng's desire to eliminate overlapping of the two institutions was genuine, this device could have deceived nobody, least of all Hua. Hua may well have tried to use his chairmanship of the MAC to seek succor from the PLA; a brief report of his speech to a PLA political work conference in May 1980 suggested that he might have hoped to forge bonds of loyalty on the basis of shared Maoist values.[298] But even if PLA generals were beginning to get restive about some of Deng's policies, it was highly unlikely that they would select Hua as their champion.

After a Politburo conference in August (and a postponement of the annual NPC session until the very end of the month), the top leadership agreed that Hua should be replaced as premier by Zhao Ziyang. Deng, Li Xiannian, Chen Yun, and three other senior cadres duly resigned as vice-premiers, and Chen Yonggui was also relieved of that duty.[299] Three new vice-premiers were appointed, including Foreign Minister Huang Hua, leaving the State Council purged of all beneficiaries of the Cultural Revolution and comprising only survivors and victims.[300]

The stage was now set for the shredding of Hua's reputation and his eviction from his remaining posts. At a Politburo meeting in November–December, at the request of a large number of high-ranking cadres, Hua's record was submitted to pitiless scrutiny. He was accorded merit for helping to get rid of the Gang of Four but was censured for serious erros and failure to correct himself on a number of issues of principle. Even the mistakes he had apparently corrected were brought up again.

He had persisted with the slogans of the Cultural Revolution; he had not taken the initiative in repairing the damage caused by it. Here he was again being attacked for pursuing the anti-Deng campaign after the Cultural Revolution and refusing to reverse verdicts on the Tiananmen incident. He was held responsible for rushing a decision to create the Mao mausoleum and to publish the fifth volume of the Chairman's works, both of which had presumably been agreed to by Ye Jianying and Li Xiannian. He was also

298 Hua stressed moral values alongside material incentives; see "Quarterly chronicle and documentation," *CQ*, 83 (September 1980), 615.

299 The announcement of the resignations of Deng and the five other senior cadres was made separately from that of Chen Yonggui, and in slightly different terminology, to indicate that Chen was going in disgrace rather than in honorable retirement; see *Zhonghua renmin gongheguo diwujie quanguo renmin daibiao dahui disanci huiyi wenjian*, 175–6.

300 Domes, *The government and politics of the PRC*, 173–5; Hao and Duan, *Zhongguo gongchandang liushi nian*, 705–9.

blamed for hindering the rehabilitation of victims of the Cultural Revolution. He had been "pragmatic" [*sic*] in his attitude toward the Mao problem and hence his support for the two whatevers. He was held largely responsible for the blind advance and the resulting serious losses to the economy in the previous two years.[301] In sum, the meeting agreed that Hua "lacks the political and organizational ability to be the chairman of the Party. That he should never have been appointed chairman of the Military Commission, everybody knows."[302]

Totally humiliated, Hua asked to be relieved of all his posts, but in the interests of protocol and perhaps of saving Ye Jianying's face,[303] he was not accorded the merciful release of a coup de grace. He would not be removed from the chairmanship of the Party or the MAC until a formal decision could be made by the CC's Sixth Plenum. But although he would thus retain his titles until the end of June 1981, at which point he would be demoted to a vice-chairmanship of the Party, his jobs were immediately taken over: the party chairmanship by Hu Yaobang, and the MAC chairmanship by Deng himself – the person everyone knew should have been appointed chairman of the MAC!

In the end, because of delays in holding the CCP's Twelfth Congress,[304] Hua remained a titular member of the Chinese top leadership for perhaps eighteen months longer than had been intended. But in September 1982, Hua Guofeng was reduced to membership of the CC. His erstwhile collaborator Wang Dongxing scraped into the bottom place among the CC alternates. The Hua interregnum had formally ended.

DENG XIAOPING'S PROGRAM

After Mao, who?

At the time of the Third Plenum in December 1978, it became clear that Hua Guofeng, however imposing his titles, was only a stopgap heir and that Mao's

301 Hao and Duan, *Zhongguo gongchandang liushi nian*, 709–10; *Zhonggong dangshi nianbiao*, 438–9; Materials Group, *Zhongguo gongchandang lici zhongyao huiyi ji*, 290–1.

302 Quoted in Domes, *The government and politics of the PRC*, 176.

303 As was already argued, Ye bore a certain responsibility for Hua's retention of the leadership after the purge of the Gang of Four in 1976 and for persuading him to readmit Deng to the leadership in 1977. When the Sixth Plenum did meet in June 1981, Ye Jianying was absent, apparently ill, but sent a letter agreeing to the personnel changes and the criticisms of Hua Guofeng. That an official Party account thought it necessary to publish extracts from this letter suggests concern lest his absence be misinterpreted. See Materials Group, *Zhongguo gongchandang lici zhongyao huiyi ji*, 293.

304 Domes points out that the Fifth Plenum in February 1980 had decided to call the CCP's Twelfth Congress ahead of time, i.e., before the Eleventh Congress's five-year term expired in 1982. He suggests that the hoped-for date was early in 1981, but that disagreement over the assessment of Mao and administrative reforms forced a delay, so that the Eleventh Congress ran its full term; see *The government and politics of the PRC*, 183.

real successor would be Deng Xiaoping. Ironically, Deng's eventual triumph was due in large part to Mao's own actions. If Mao had not recalled Deng to office as Zhou sickened, Deng could not have emerged as the obvious man to run China in absence of the premier. If Mao had not purged him again after Zhou's death, Deng would not have become the symbol of a new political order to replace that of the Cultural Revolution. Certainly, the triumvirate of Hua Guofeng, Ye Jianying, and Li Xiannian would have been in a stronger position to keep the angry victims of the Cultural Revolution at bay.

What is striking about Deng's ascendancy was the way in which, from the very start, he shunned titular confirmation of his power. He insisted on ranking himself below Ye Jianying in the list of CCP vice-chairmen long after Ye's role as post-Mao power broker had ended.[305] At no time was there any suggestion that Deng contemplated taking over the Party chairmanship, the general secretaryship, or the premiership. Instead, he quickly gathered around him the men he wished to succeed him, giving them posts and responsibilities so that they could gain experience and respect. This was the successor-training operation that Mao had talked about but never really implemented.

A principal reason for Deng's self-denial was his determination to avoid appearing to covet a Mao-like role. Indeed, the chairmanship was dropped from the Party constitution at the Twelfth Congress in order to prevent anyone from attempting to assume Mao's mantle. Another preventive measure was the Party's long-expected reappraisal of Mao. The object was to demystify his godlike image by coolly assessing his achievements and his errors, especially during the Cultural Revolution. The CCP was better placed to be courageous than the CPSU had been with Stalin. When Mao's faults came to be listed, Deng, a victim, had no reason to fear the question reportedly shouted at Khrushchev, an accomplice, when he made his secret speech denouncing Stalin in 1956: "And where were you, comrade, when all this was going on?"

Nevertheless, Deng also had more reason to be cautious than Khruschchev had a quarter of a century earlier. However intemperate the Chinese may have considered the latter's secret speech, Khrushchev always knew that the CPSU had the untarnished image of Lenin on which to fall back. For the CCP, Mao was both Lenin and Stalin, and if an assessment were not carefully handled, both images might be damaged, with incalculable effect on the Party's legitimacy.

305 In his letter to the Sixth Plenum (n. 304), Ye suggested that the order of the top three members of the Politburo Standing Committee should be Hu Yaobang, Deng Xiaoping, and Ye Jianying, thus reversing the standings of himself and Deng. This was perhaps politeness, perhaps realism in the wake of the fall of Ye's protégé Hua, but Deng ensured that Ye retained his senior ranking.

Moreover, even among those who deplored the Cultural Revolution, there were many who wanted Mao protected and some of his actions upheld as correct. PLA generals in particular did not want excessive condemnation either of the man who led them to victory or of their role in the Cultural Revolution. One device was to blame as much as possible on Lin Biao and the Gang of Four, and from 20 November 1980 to 25 January 1981, the regime staged a Nuremberg-style trial of the surviving leaders of the Cultural Revolution.

The trial did publicize considerable evidence of their misdeeds. The claim was made that almost 730,000 people had been framed and persecuted and that nearly 35,000 of them had been "persecuted to death." Most of the accused meekly admitted their guilt and cooperated with the court. Zhang Chunqiao, on the other hand, chose to remain silent throughout the proceedings, and Jiang Qing defended herself forcefully, repeatedly insisting that she had only done what Chairman Mao had told her.[306]

The trial was an effective means of allowing victims to see that their persecutors had been humiliated and punished and of enabling some even to denounce them in public. But Jiang Qing's testimony served to underline that the ultimate guilt was Mao's and that the Party would have to find some means of coming to terms with that fact while steering clear of a root-and-branch condemnation that would be too damaging even for the survivors. Early indications that Mao would be accused of "crimes" during the Cultural Revolution did not materialize. Some PLA behavior in that period was assessed positively. Deng made sure that armchair historians would not undermine his important constituency in the PLA.[307]

Thus, in his earliest comments to the drafters of what eventually emerged as the "Resolution on certain questions in the history of our Party since the founding of the PRC," Deng insisted that the first and most essential point to be covered was

> affirmation of the historical role of Comrade Mao Zedong and explanation of the necessity to uphold and develop Mao Zedong Thought. . . . We must hold high the banner of Mao Zedong Thought not only today but in the future. . . . The first [point] is the most important, the most fundamental, the most crucial.[308]

Three months later, when he found the latest draft inadequate on this issue, he called it "no good" and demanded rewriting. The tone of the draft

306 *A great trial in Chinese history,* 102–3; the figures for the numbers of victims are on 20–1. A good analysis of the trial, with extracts, is contained in David Bonavia, *Verdict in Peking: The trial of the Gang of Four.* The full official text of the proceedings is in Research Office of the Supreme People's Court, ed., *Zhonghua renmin gongheguo zuigao renmin fayuan tebie fating shenpan Lin Biao, Jiang Qing fangeming jituan an zhufan jishi* (A record of the trial by the Special Tribunal of the PRC's Supreme People's Court of the principal criminals of the Lin Biao and Jiang Qing revolutionary cliques); Jiang Qing's appearances are covered on 117–21, 194–9, 227–41, 296–302, 341–7, 399–414.

307 Domes, *The government and politics of the PRC,* 180–2.

308 *Selected works of Deng Xiaoping,* 276, 278.

was "too depressing"; criticizing Mao's personal mistakes alone would not solve problems.[309] In a later comment, he underlined how politically sensitive the issue was. Without an appropriate evaluation of Mao's merits and faults, "the old workers will not feel satisfied, nor will the poor and lower-middle peasants of the period of land reform, nor the many cadres who have close ties with them." He hinted at potential PLA dissatisfaction.[310]

After more than a year of discussions among thousands of officials and historians, the Resolution was adopted by the Sixth Plenum in time for the sixtieth anniversary of the founding of the CCP, on 1 July 1981. It placed the blame for the Cultural Revolution squarely on Mao: "The 'cultural revolution,' which lasted from May 1966 to October 1976, was responsible for the most severe setback and the heaviest losses suffered by the Party, the state and the people since the founding of the People's Republic. It was initiated and led by Comrade Mao Zedong."[311] After an analysis of all the crimes and errors of the period, the Resolution supplied the balance that Deng had insisted on. It described Mao's leftist error in the Cultural Revolution as, after all, "the error of a proletarian revolutionary." In his later years, Mao had confused right and wrong and mistakenly believed that his leftist theories were Marxist. "Herein lies his tragedy."[312] Even during the Cultural Revolution, he could be praised for protecting some cadres, fighting Lin Biao, exposing Jiang Qing, and pursuing a successful foreign policy.[313] The Resolution concluded that although it was true that Mao had made "gross mistakes" during the Cultural Revolution, "if we judge his activities as a whole, his contributions to the Chinese revolution far outweigh his mistakes."[314]

The Resolution achieved the balance Deng had wanted while also explaining why Mao had gone wrong. As his prestige had increased, he had become arrogant and put himself above the CC. His colleagues failed to take preventive action, and collective leadership was undermined. Intra-Party democracy was not institutionalized; relevant laws lacked authority. The Stalinist model of leadership had had its impact, as had centuries of Chinese "feudal autocracy."[315] The assessment of Mao sounded right, but Deng's Resolution suc-

309 Ibid., 282, 283.

310 He did this by referring to PLA soldiers' approval when they read what he had said about Mao in an interview with a foreign journalist, i.e., PLA troops were keenly concerned with what was said publicly about Mao.

311 *Resolution on CPC history (1949–81)*, 32.

312 The description of Mao as a tragic hero was a repetition of the formula the CCP had suggested for Stalin in the aftermath of Khrushchev's secret speech in 1956. The concept was, in fact, a breakthrough. Hitherto, in both the Soviet Union and the PRC, there had been a Manichean insistence on the simple juxtaposition of good and evil, black and white, with no allowance made for shades of gray. If one committed an error, one either purged oneself of it totally or was condemned as a reactionary or a counterrevolutionary. The model of the flawed leader had implications for politics and literature.

313 *Resolution on CPC history (1949–81)*, 41–2.

314 Ibid., 56.

315 Ibid., 48–9.

ceeded no better than Khrushchev's secret speech in explaining how democracy could be institutionalized or laws respected under a system of proletarian dictatorship and CCP rule.

If Deng would not reject the system he had helped create, he personally would attempt to learn the negative lessons of Mao's leadership. Yet his rejection of Mao's titles and cult failed to deal with tendencies deep in the "feudal" political culture. Deng had taught Hua that position did not confer power or authority. Now he himself had to come to terms with the corollary: Power and authority could not be wished away simply by refusing titles; the imperial tradition could not be exorcised by Party resolution. No matter how loudly he protested that he participated in only one or two key decisions a year, he was regarded by both supporters and opponents as the court of last resort.

Partly this was a matter of generations. In sharp contrast to post-Stalin Russia, in which only survivors and beneficiaries remained, in post-Mao China many of the leader's victims, who were also fellow Long Marchers, were still alive.[316] They could return to power untarnished by his errors and garlanded still with their revolutionary achievements. It was impossible for men like Hu Yaobang and Zhao Ziyang, whom Deng picked out as his successors to match the legitimacy he could claim as of right.

Partly it was a question of relationships, *guanxi*. Deng had a network of friends, colleagues, and contacts in both the Party and the army who could be vital to the successful promotion of a policy. Hu Yaobang and, to a lesser extent, Zhao Ziyang had their networks, too, but they were not comparable in power and prestige as allies for governing China.

Partly it was a question of emergent factionalism. In the initial post-Mao era, all the returning victims could agree on the urgent tasks of removing the beneficiaries of the Cultural Revolution and liquidating the policies of that era. As that task neared completion, the original coalition began to split over where to go next. Deng did not always see eye to eye with Chen Yun or Peng Zhen, to name the two most prestigious returned victims besides Deng himself. Had Deng been able to retire and take with him his whole revolutionary cohort, leaving Hu and Zhao to cope with their own generation, the succession process would have been easier to manage. But since Deng's old comrades-in-arms evinced no desire to leave the stage, Deng had to stay on to prevent them from using *their* superior credentials to derail his protégés.

Partly it was a question of talent. Deng Xiaoping was clearly an exceptional leader even among an extraordinary array of revolutionary veterans.

316 Had Bukharin been allowed to survive, he would have been only sixty-four on Stalin's death. Deng was seventy-four at the time of the Third Plenum.

Neither Hu Yaobang nor Zhao Ziyang was able to prove himself an equally outstanding successor.

Partly it was a reflection of an only partially solved question: Which would dominate, Party or PLA?

After Mao, which?

When the Politburo summed up Hua's shortcomings in late 1980, it was far more contemptuous about his right to be chairman of the MAC than about his right to lead the CCP. Yet in a state where the Party commanded the gun, any leader whom the Party chose should automatically have received the respect of the generals. Clearly that was never accorded to Hua. He became MAC chairman in 1976 presumably because the obvious available candidate, Marshal Ye Jianying, insisted on it and stood by Hua to lend him authority. When Deng returned as vice-chairman of the MAC and chief of staff of the PLA in mid-1977, the generals probably took little further account of Hua. When Deng effectively took over the chairmanship in late 1980, their world seemed correctly ordered again.

Deng may have felt he had no option but to assume this one of Mao's titles, but his action caused as many problems as it solved. It confirmed to the PLA generals that they had a right to be commanded only by the person with supreme authority in the country; that they had a direct line to the top, without interruption by layers of bureaucracy; that although the minister of defense was responsible to the premier, who in turn was responsible to the Party, none of this mattered, because all important issues would be thrashed out in the MAC. It thus confirmed what everyone knew – that the PLA was an institution apart – just when the generals needed to be brought back into line.

Deng's objective was to restore PLA discipline and end its unwillingness to obey orders or to implement Party policies laid down by the CC. As we have seen, he had brought up these problems in 1975, but he now admitted that they had not been solved then.[317] He may well have thought that only he could bring the PLA to heel. Given the difficulties even he experienced, perhaps he was right. The problems were both political and institutional.

The rehabilitation of Liu Shaoqi in May 1980 was one major political issue. That action had undermined a major justification for the Cultural Revolution and was thus a direct repudiation of Mao, whose reputation the generals had consistently wanted to safeguard. Ye Jianying, and even Xu Shiyou, Deng's protector in 1976, evinced disapproval by failing to show up

317 *Selected works of Deng Xiaoping*, 29–30, 97–8.

for the memorial meeting at which this symbolically important act took place.[318] The generals were also angry at two successive rounds of severe military budget cuts in late 1980 and early 1981; it may have been partly in retaliation for these that the PLA initiated a drive for ideological discipline. But probably the more important reason was the generals' desire to counter the more relaxed political atmosphere that Deng and the reformers were trying to encourage but that had produced many attacks on military privilege. An army writer, Bai Hua, was made the exemplary target to stand for all critical intellectuals.

In the face of evident PLA anger, Deng must have decided to excise from the Resolution on Party history any criticisms of the role of the PLA in the Cultural Revolution. But even this failed to appease the generals, for on the eve of the CCP's Twelfth Congress, in September 1982, an article in the *Liberation Army News* attacked "some responsible comrades in cultural fields" for supporting bourgeois liberal points of view. Deng's reaction to this gross breach of military and political discipline was swift. Immediately after the Congress, the director of the PLA's General Political Department, Wei Guoqing (another Deng protector in 1976), and the head of the navy were both dismissed.[319]

Deng evidently realized the institutional problem in the relationship between the PLA and the CCP, but his efforts to remedy it failed. In the new state constitution promulgated at the Fifth Session of the Fifth NPC in late 1982, an important institutional innovation was included: the creation of a Central Military Commission, responsible to the NPC, to direct the PLA. According to the explanation given by Peng Zhen in his speech to the NPC, "The leadership by the Chinese Communist Party over the armed forces will not change with the establishment of the state Central Military Commission. The Party's leading role in the life of the state, which is explicitly affirmed in the Preamble, naturally includes its leadership over the armed forces."[320] What Peng Zhen conspicuously failed to mention was that the preamble made no mention of the Party's MAC as the instrument of that leadership. What then was to be the relationship of the MAC to the new body?

An article in a Party journal gave a strong hint of what was in the wind. It detailed the history of the Central Military Commission, showing how at some times it had been a Party organ and at other times a state organ. Both types of military commission had been legitimate. Referring to the creation of the new state body, the writer affirmed that the MAC would continue to

318 Domes, *The government and politics of the PRC*, 171–2. Domes argues that in the case of Xu, personal pique at not being made defense minister or chief of staff may have been another motive for his action on this occasion.

319 Ibid., 178–82, 185. 320 *Fifth session of the Fifth National People's Congress*, 94.

exist as a Party organ. Yet the implication was that the time had come to sever the direct CCP–PLA link and make the PLA simply a part of the state structure, as in most other countries. The history of the PLA showed that this had been normal practice from time to time and therefore nothing to be feared.[321] For double reassurance, Deng Xiaoping legitimated the new body at the NPC by taking on its chairmanship in addition to his chairmanship of the MAC.

If Deng's objective was to prepare the ground for the abolition of the MAC, he did not achieve it. The new commission raised the profile of the PLA in the state structure by subordinating it no longer to a mere State Council ministry but to an NPC commission, but no general seems to have been ready to accept it as a substitute for the MAC. Instead, just when Deng and his colleagues were urging a general retrenchment of the bureaucracy, the country was saddled with two identical military commissions, both led by Deng Xiaoping and Yang Shangkun (as executive vice-chairman).

Even when Deng would finally manage to resign from the Politburo at the CCP's Thirteenth Congress in 1987, taking all his old comrades with him, he still could not retire from his MAC chairmanship. The CCP constitution stipulated that the MAC chairman had to be a member of the Politburo Standing Committee, so Deng endorsed a constitutional revision that permitted him to stay on.[322] He installed the new CCP general secretary, Zhao Ziyang, as first vice-chairman of the MAC, which suggested that the MAC would be preserved and that the NPC equivalent had been set up in vain.

The recent history of the MAC has confirmed the tenacity with which the PLA has maintained its institutional position within the CCP over the years. Under Deng's leadership, civilian control of the PLA would be gradually reinstated, especially after he engineered the exodus of virtually all remaining generals from the Politburo and sharply reduced PLA representation in the CC during the major central meetings held in September 1985. But the MAC issue illustrated that civilian control was still on the PLA's terms: that it must be asserted through the MAC, and the MAC must be headed by Deng as long as possible. Perhaps when the PLA is further denuded of revolutionary generals and colonels by retirements and deaths, and the Long March is history not memory, the post-Deng generation of CCP leaders will be able to assert its primacy over the military and assign to it a more conventional role in the state system. Until then it can be assumed that the PLA, the agent of victory during the revolution and the repository of power during the Cultural

321 Yan Jingtang, "Zhongyang junwei yange gaikuang" (Survey of the evolution of the Central Military Commission), in Zhu Chengjia, ed., *Zhonggong dangshi yanjiu lunwen xuan, xia* (Selection of research papers on the history of the CCP), 3. 567–87.

322 *Documents of the Thirteenth National Congress of the Communist Party of China* (1987), 85.

Revolution,[323] will remain a major factor in the polity. As the above account has indicated, how its political influence will be utilized will depend on the CCP's program and policies.

After Mao, what?

The conservatism of the PLA generals was a factor that Deng Xiaoping had to take into account in his drive to revitalize China. For Deng's reform program challenged not merely the ultra-leftist Maoism of the Cultural Revolution, but also what might be called the "Sinified Stalinist" line pursued by Mao and his colleagues when copying the Soviet model in the 1950s. Moreover, the reforms relaxed central control and allowed more freedom of thought and action, a permissiveness unlikely to commend itself to the ultimate guardians of law and order in the wake of the upheavals of the Cultural Revolution.

The economic reforms and their impact are covered in detail in *CHOC* 15, Chapter 6.[324] Deng turned back the clock, dismantling the commune system set up during the GLF in 1958, returning control over production to the farm family for the first time since land reform in the early 1950s. The regime might claim that no ideological change had taken place because the land was formally still owned by the collective; it was only contracted back to the peasantry. Peasants might worry that their newly granted freedom to plan their own cropping patterns, hire labor to assist them, and sell part of the harvest in rural free markets[325] would suddenly be snatched back in yet another 180-degree policy shift. But in fact, private farming had been reinstated, even in cases where the peasants were reluctant to forfeit the security of the collective.[326]

This second liberation of the peasantry, bolstered by higher procurement prices, had a massive impact on production and on rural incomes, as *CHOC* 15, Chapter 6 shows. The political implications were also of enormous significance. A majority of the 800 million peasants had been given a major

323 During the discussions of the resolution on Party history, Deng got quite angry at the suggestion that the Ninth Congress should be declared illegitimate or that the Party should be considered to have ceased to exist during the Cultural Revolution. Perhaps it was partly because he realized that to say that would constitute a formal admission that the PLA had been the only functioning revolutionary organization during that turbulent decade, that it had survived whereas the CCP had not, and that it had run most of the country while the CCP had not; *Selected works of Deng Xiaoping*, 290–1.

324 See the following discussion. For details about the various forms of rural reform in the early stages, see also Kathleen Hartford, "Socialist agriculture is dead; long live socialist agriculture!: Organizational transformations in rural China," in Elizabeth J. Perry and Christine Wong, eds., *The political economy of reform in post-Mao China*, 31–61.

325 See Terry Sicular, "Rural marketing and exchange in the wake of recent reforms," in Perry and Wong, eds., *The political economy of reform in post-Mao China*, 83–109.

326 Hartford suggests that not all peasants welcomed the destruction of the commune system; ibid., 138–9.

stake in the reform program, and they trembled when conservative ideological winds blew coldly from Beijing. But even Chinese neoconservatives like Chen Yun had welcomed the short-lived experiments with agricultural responsibility systems in the early 1960s, and it eventually became clear that no Beijing politician would challenge the rural new deal, unless either its economic justification declined drastically or its impact on rural and regional equity became so negative as to carry grave dangers of renewed class struggle.

Rural cadres were initially unhappy about their new tasks and diminished control.[327] But as they began to use their political skills and connections to preserve their status and increase their incomes by assuming brokering roles, the cadres realized that the new deal could benefit them too.[328] From a long-term perspective, the initial distrust of aging cadres was less important than the implications of the reforms for the CCP. Dynamic rich peasants (often former cadres) were held up as models, and their recruitment to the Party was mandated. In some cases this aroused envy.[329] But provided that the recruitment policy was maintained, the prospect was the transformation of a poor peasant party into a rich peasant one, with considerable implications for class attitudes and ideological predilections. The "serve the people" ethos of the CCP was bound to be adulterated by the new slogan "To get rich is glorious." This, in turn, would almost certainly ensure that the CCP would continue to eschew class struggle and focus on economic development as its prime goal.

The complexities of industrial restructuring and market reform posed far greater problems for Deng Xiaoping and his colleagues, as Dwight Perkins shows in *CHOC* 15, Chapter 6. There was no single step, like decollectivization, capable of generating an economic breakthrough that could not be gainsaid. On the contrary, many people stood to lose by urban reform: bureaucrats who forfeited power as greater independence was ceded to managers of state enterprises; managers of state enterprises who envied the even greater freedom accorded collective and private companies; workers in state enterprises who feared harder work and job insecurity in the search for efficiency, and who envied the rising incomes of workers in the nonstate sector and peasants in the countryside; and every urban dweller, including intellectuals and students, who was hurt by the higher prices accompanying the reforms.

The reform program also implied a fundamental if dimly perceived threat to the legitimacy of the CCP. Party cadres were told to "seek truth from facts"

327 See Richard J. Latham, "The implications of rural reforms for grass-roots cadres," in ibid., 57–73.

328 This comment is based on the author's own observations and conversations in China, along with those of others.

329 For a discussion, see Elizabeth J. Perry, "Social ferment: grumbling amidst growth," in John S. Major, ed., *China briefing, 1985*, 39–41, 45–6.

and told that "practice is the sole criterion of truth." They were instructed to acquire knowledge that would equip them for the new era. The long-standing tension within the CCP between the demand for "redness" (political fervor) and the demand for "expertise" (professional skills), which formerly had been resolved in favor of the *yang* of redness, now seemed to have been settled in favor of the *yin* of expertise.

This was a potential blow to the roughly 50 percent of Party cadres who had been recruited during the Cultural Revolution, for their strengths were presumably in the field of political agitation. But it also placed a question mark over the role of the Party itself. The claim of the CCP to its vanguard role, like that of the CPSU and other parties, was rooted in its ideology. The premise was that its mastery of the ever correct ideology of Marxism–Leninism–Mao Zedong Thought enabled it to understand the present and plan for the future with a sureness inaccessible to non-Marxists. But if correctness was now to be found in practice or facts, what was the function of ideology?

Ideology had already been greatly devalued by the hyperbole of the Cultural Revolution and the attribution of almost supernatural powers to Mao Zedong Thought.[330] The new emphasis on practice was a very grave blow. Deng Xiaoping's declaration that Marxism–Leninism–Mao Zedong Thought was one of four cardinal principles that could not be questioned did little to soften it.[331] CCP rule, although itself one of the four cardinal principles, now appeared to be justifiable only by competence and success, shaky foundations in view of the problems facing post-Mao China. At risk was the deep-rooted attachment in the Chinese political culture to the concept of an elite bureaucracy sanctioned simply by its commitment to and mastery of a totalist ideology that claimed to explain the world and man's place in it.

The increasing irrelevance of the Party was underlined by reformers' attempts to separate its functions from those of the government.[332] The declared aim was to free Party cadres to concentrate on overall questions of principle and line. Local government functionaries and managers who were not all CCP members were to be granted greater leeway to get on with their jobs regardless of ideological considerations.

But in a state in which virtually all top government officials were senior Party members and participated in the discussions of the Politburo or the CC, it was not clear what should be the role of the "pure" Party official. Of

330 See George Urban, ed., *The miracles of Chairman Mao: A compendium of devotional literature*, 1966–70, 1–27.

331 See "Uphold the four cardinal principles," *Selected works of Deng Xiaoping*, 172–4, 179–81. The other three were the socialist road, the dictatorship of the proletariat, and the leadership of the CCP.

332 "On the reform of the system of Party and state leadership," ibid., 303.

course, he had to run the Party machine, but its role, too, was unclear in an era when class struggle and movement politics had given way to economic development.[333] During his tenure as CCP general secretary, Hu Yaobang ignored the separation of roles, seeming to want to assert a right as China's top leader to make pronouncements on all spheres of national life. He made a number of overseas trips as if he were head of state or government.[334]

The Party's powers were further restricted by the provision in its new constitution passed at the Twelfth Congress in 1982 that "the Party must conduct its activities within the limits permitted by the Constitution and the laws of the state." As Hu Yaobang explained this "most important principle" in his report, it was now formally "impermissible for any Party organization or member, from the Central Committee down to the grass roots, to act in contravention of the Constitution and laws."[335] A constitutional provision by itself was hardly a guarantee. But the emphasis on legality after the Third Plenum, in reaction to the anarchy of the Cultural Revolution when the elite had suffered most, together with the passage of various legal codes for the first time, at least signified an understanding that the unbridled power of the Party ultimately threatened everyone.[336]

Such formal restrictions on the Party were accompanied by concrete attempts to diminish "bureaucratism," whose harmful manifestations included

> standing high above the masses; abusing power; divorcing oneself from reality and the masses; spending a lot of time and effort to put up an impressive front; indulging in empty talk; sticking to a rigid way of thinking; being hidebound by convention; overstaffing administrative organs; being dilatory, inefficient, and irresponsible; failing to keep one's word; circulating documents endlessly without solving problems; shifting responsibility to others; and even assuming the airs of a mandarin, reprimanding other people at every turn, vindictively attacking others, suppressing democracy, deceiving superiors and subordinates, being arbitrary and despotic, practising favouritism, offering bribes, participating in corrupt practices in violation of the law.

333 The dilemma may be loosely compared to that of party officials in the Western European democracies. During periods of opposition, the life of the party qua party looms large, for it is the instrument of agitation with which class war is waged in the country at large in order to oust the government of the day. If the strategy is successful and party leaders become government ministers in their turn, the role of the party greatly diminishes as its leaders occupy themselves with running the country and ensuring its economic prosperity. Purely party officials from then on take a subordinate role and rarely interfere with government policy, but are expected, rather, to ensure the loyalty of the party rank and file to whatever the government does.

334 There was perhaps some justification for this during Hu's brief period as CCP chairman, after the Sixth Plenum of the Eleventh CC in June 1981, but none after the Twelfth Congress in September 1982 when the chairmanship was abolished and the newly supreme post of general secretary became his only job. I use the term "formal" because, of course, ultimate power rested with Deng Xiaoping, whatever his nominal title.

335 *The Twelfth National Congress of the CPC*, 49.

336 For a discussion of some of the issues involved in the new emphasis on legality in the PRC, see R. Randle Edwards, Louis Henkin, Andrew J. Nathan, *Human rights in contemporary China*.

According to Deng, such practices had reached "intolerable dimensions both in our domestic affairs and in our contacts with other countries."[337]

Attacks on bureaucratism were nothing new within the CCP, dating back at least to the Rectification Campaign in Yan'an in the early 1940s. The Cultural Revolution itself could in part be explained as Mao's final and most devastating attempt to destroy bureaucratism in order to unleash the pure revolutionary fervor of the masses. Deng's methods were less devastating, but he, too, wished to unleash the masses, though to create wealth rather than make revolution. Here again, Party cadres were being pushed to one side.

Despite these limits on the authority of the Party, the average peasant, worker, manager, or intellectual continued to behave circumspectly in the presence of its officials. Habits of obedience and memories of suffering inhibited any attempt to test the new permissiveness too far. The bureaucracy might be on the defensive, but it was still enormously powerful.

That may be the historians' final verdict on the Cultural Revolution. By the CCP's Twelfth Congress, in 1982, the erosion of the Party's authority as a result of the Cultural Revolution, the subsequent moves to restrain arbitrary use of power, the decline in the force of ideology, the unleashing of the peasant and the attempt to free up the urban economy all carried the potential for a role for society vis-à-vis the state possibly greater than at any previous time when China was united under a strong central government. Mao had always stressed that out of bad things came good things. Those burgeoning social forces would finally challenge the bonds of state authority in the Tiananmen demonstrations of 1989.

337 "On the reform of the system of Party and state leadership," *Selected works of Deng Xiaoping*, 310.

CHAPTER 5

THE ROAD TO TIANANMEN: CHINESE POLITICS IN THE 1980s

RICHARD BAUM

INTRODUCTION

By the time the Twelfth Party Congress met in September 1982, China's new leaders had done much to overcome the post-Mao crisis of confidence. They had repudiated Mao's Cultural Revolution, renounced his economic theories, and reinstated his purged opponents. But acknowledging past mistakes was one thing; charting a viable course for the future was quite another. Although members of the reform coalition forged by Deng Xiaoping could agree among themselves, in principle, on the need for economic reform and opening up to the outside world, they differed over just how far and how fast to move toward revamping the basic ideology and institutions of Chinese socialism. Most important, they differed over precisely how much "bourgeois liberalization," if any, could be countenanced in a society that continued to call itself Marxist–Leninist.

Sometimes, disagreement took the form of arcane academic debates over such issues as the special characteristics of China's "spiritual civilization" or the relevance to China of such foreign concepts as "universal humanism" and "alienation." As often as not, academic debates served to mask highly contentious policy disputes – for example, over the tolerable limits of free market activity and private accumulation of wealth, the severity of the problem of "spiritual pollution" posed by the influx of Western cultural influences, and the proper boundaries of free expression for artists, writers, and other creative intellectuals whose contributions were deemed essential to the success of China's modernization drive.

Just beneath the surface of these debates lay the potent issue of stability

Research for this chapter was completed in the autumn of 1990 at the Sinology Institute, University of Leiden. I would like to express my deep appreciation to the director, staff, and students of the Institute for giving so unselfishly of their time and energy during my term as a visiting scholar. Special thanks are due to Tony Saich and Geor Hintzen for their valuable insights and comments on earlier drafts of this chapter.

versus chaos. Throughout the decade, China's top leaders repeatedly tempered their expressed desire for modernization and reform with a deep concern for maintaining political order and discipline. Wanting to enjoy the fruits of modernity without the destabilizing effects of spontaneous, uncontrolled social mobilization, they tended to follow each new round of reform with an attempt to retain or regain control. Letting go (*fang*) with one hand, they instinctively tightened up (*shou*) with the other.

As early as the spring of 1979, with the closure of the Xidan democracy wall and the concurrent issuance of Deng Xiaoping's inviolable "four cardinal principles" – adherence to the socialist road, the people's democratic dictatorship, Communist Party leadership, and Marxism–Leninism–Mao Zedong Thought – this ambivalent pattern of relaxation and control, *fang* and *shou,* began to display recurrent, periodic fluctuations and phase changes. The result was a distinctive *fang–shou cycle,* characterized by an initial increase in the scope of economic or political reform (in the form, e.g., of price deregulation or intellectual liberalization), followed by a rapid release of pent-up social demand (e.g., panic buying or student demonstrations); the resulting "disorder" would set off a backlash among party traditionalists, who would then move to reassert control. A conservative retrenchment would follow, marked by an ideological assault on "liberal" tendencies and an attempt to halt (or even to reverse) the initial reform. The ensuing freeze would serve, in turn, to exacerbate existing internal contradictions and stresses, leading to the generation of renewed pressures for relaxation and reform – and so on.[1]

Three complete repetitions of the multiphase *fang–shou* cycle occurred in the 1980s. Although the cycles were broadly recursive, over time there occurred a discernible intensification of their underlying antinomies as each new swing of the pendulum served to amplify existing socioeconomic tensions and evoke more intense political reactions. As the amplitude of the oscillations increased, so too did the polarization of forces; as a result, what began as a series of nonantagonistic debates over the ends and means, scope and magnitude, consequences and limits of reform escalated steadily from the realm of philosophic discourse to become, by the spring of 1989, an acute struggle for survival among mutually antagonistic political forces.

1 For variations on the theme of *fang–shou* cycles in post-Mao China, see Tang Tsou, "Political change and reform: The middle course," in Tang Tsou, ed., *The cultural revolution and post-Mao reforms: A historical perspective,* 219–58; also Thomas B. Gold, "Party-state versus society in China," in Joyce K. Kallgren, ed., *Building a nation-state: China at forty years,* 125–52; also Harry Harding, *China's second revolution: Reform after Mao,* Chapter 4; and Lowell Dittmer, "Patterns of elite strife and succession in Chinese politics," *China Quarterly* (hereafter, *CQ*) 123 (September 1990), 405–30. The *locus classicus* for analysis of cyclical phenomena in modern Chinese politics remains G. William Skinner and Edwin A. Winckler, "Compliance succession in rural communist China: A cyclical theory," in Amitai Etzioni, ed., *Complex organizations: A sociological reader* (second edition).

Throughout all the polarizing vicissitudes of the 1980s, one figure loomed larger than all others: "senior leader" Deng Xiaoping. Deng personally embodied all the complex antinomies of *fang* and *shou.* He believed that China could have both market competition *and* a monistic political order; socioeconomic modernity *and* a "socialist spiritual civilization"; a vigorous, creative intelligentsia *and* a high degree of ideological conformity. As the decade wore on, however, and as these goals began to oscillate rather than to converge, Deng found it increasingly difficult to steer a middle course between *fang* and *shou.* He (and China) began to swerve, first one way and then the other, as he searched in vain for a viable, coherent center.

For the better part of a decade, Deng, who turned eighty in 1984, tried to reform China's inefficient command economy, create a rationalized governmental structure, and effect an orderly political succession. Twice he supported a major overhaul of China's patriarchal leadership system; in both cases, the ensuing polarization of forces compelled him to abort the project. Twice he tried to leave the political stage, designating pragmatic, reform-oriented heirs apparent to succeed him; both times his choices were eventually rejected, as first Hu Yaobang and then Zhao Ziyang ran afoul of Party conservatives. Twice he backed wide-ranging structural reforms in China's urban economy; both times a rising tide of inflation, corruption, and resultant social unrest forced him to retreat.

With the middle ground of orderly, institutionalized reform becoming more elusive, Deng was increasingly forced to rely upon his personal prestige and authority to preserve a semblance of political stability and unity. Unable to create a viable structure of authority that combined both *fang* and *shou,* and unable to locate a successor acceptable to all major factions, he was unable to retire from active leadership. Consequently, his personal authority became more, rather than less, critical to the coherence, indeed the very survival, of the regime. Yet the more he intervened in the decision process *ex cathedra,* the more elusive became his quest for a rationalized political order. Therein, perhaps, lay the supreme paradox of Deng's political stewardship: In his quest to lead China out of the "feudal autocracy" of the Maoist era toward modernity and rule by law, Deng increasingly resorted to highly personalized instruments of control – instruments that were the very antithesis of the system he sought to create.[2]

With fundamental institutional reform blocked, Deng was forced to improvise as he went along, introducing a series of ad hoc, piecemeal measures designed to promote the objective of orderly change. In the early 1980s, for

2 This theme is explored in Stuart R. Schram, "China after the 13th congress," *CQ* 114 (June 1988), 177–97.

example, when old guard Party leaders proved reluctant to retire, Deng gave them their very own Central Advisory Commission (CAC) to help ease them into inactivity. Yet many still refused to leave the stage voluntarily, and Deng could not (or would not) force them off. Consequently, the temporary became permanent: The CAC became a virtual shadow cabinet, parallel and powerful. Still active in the late 1980s, this "sitting committee," as it was popularly (and derisively) known, played a key role in fashioning the June 1989 military crackdown at Tiananmen Square.

In similar fashion, as part of his campaign to modernize and professionalize China's outmoded Maoist military establishment, Deng tried to move the People's Liberation Army (PLA) out from under CCP control (as had been the traditional practice), placing it directly under the jurisdiction of the central government. But since outright abolition of the Party's powerful Military Affairs Commission (MAC) would have alienated China's conservative old guard, Deng improvised once again. He created a parallel governmental MAC alongside the existing CCP organ, which was allowed to remain wholly intact. He then proceeded to staff the new body with exactly the same Party veterans who controlled the existing MAC, thereby ensuring the redundancy – and virtual impotence – of the new government commission. When PLA troops were called to Beijing to put down student protests in May–June 1989, it was the Party's MAC that gave the orders.

When China's urban consumers balked at the prospect of reform-induced commodity price hikes in the late 1980s, Deng once again offered an expedient compromise: He slowed down the decontrol of prices and granted city dwellers a series of temporary food and housing subsidies to help ease the pain of transition to market-regulated pricing. Shortly thereafter, a combination of consumer panic buying and conservative criticism forced the government to halt price decontrol altogether; as a result, the temporary once again became semipermanent as China limped along with a semireformed, two-tier price structure that retained many of the worst irrationalities of the old system while perpetuating the costly transitional subsidies of the new one. More than one observer likened the government's indecisive, start-and-stop approach to price reform to an attempt to leap across the Grand Canyon serially in several jumps.

In each of the preceding examples, an *ad hoc* policy improvisation, originally intended to serve as a bridge or stepping stone to fundamental structural reform, was frozen in place due to a conservative backlash, becoming in the process an impediment to further systemic change. Cumulatively, the effect was to exacerbate existing structural tensions and stresses rather than to resolve them.[3]

3 The paradoxical consequences of partial reform are discussed in David Zweig, "Dilemmas of partial reform," in Bruce Reynolds, ed., *Chinese economic policy*, 13–40; Susan Shirk, *The political logic of economic*

Notwithstanding the increasing turbulence and frequent policy improvisations of the 1980s, for a brief period in late 1987 and 1988 it appeared that a viable developmental formula might, after all, be found. Under Zhao Ziyang, a new path for China's political development was sketched out, one that was neither totalitarian nor democratic, but that contained the first ideological and institutional sprouts of emergent social pluralism. This was the "new authoritarianism" (*xin quanwei zhuyi*), a hybrid system that purported to combine the economic vitality of *fang* with the centralized political authority of *shou*. The proposed system was characterized by continued one-party tutelage and a "consultative" structure of limited political participation, on the one hand, and a state-induced shift toward market regulation of the economy and the recognition of diverse, pluralistic societal aspirations and interests, on the other.[4]

Unhappily for China, the new formula was never adequately tested. Mounting consumer unrest over surging inflation, made worse by rumors of impending price decontrol and rendered politically volatile by deepening public resentment over flagrant official profiteering, triggered a wave of urban consumer panic in the summer of 1988. CCP conservatives, afraid of incipient political instability, instinctively reacted by halting price deregulation, freezing structural reform, and reasserting centralized control over the economy.

By the spring of 1989, reform-related stresses had reached critical levels. With the economy and society stalled midway between plan and market, between bureaucrats and entrepreneurs, between *shou* and *fang,* China continued to suffer from the worst distortions of the old system without enjoying the anticipated benefits of the new. It was truly a "crisis of incomplete reform."[5] Following the unexpected death of Hu Yaobang in mid-April, the political center began to crumble as a student-led, inflation-bred, corruption-fed protest movement in Beijing brought the Chinese capital to the very brink of governmental paralysis. Faced with a mounting urban revolt against a government whose authority was being openly challenged by its citizens, in early June a group of elderly, semiretired Party conservatives, supported now by a clearly exasperated Deng Xiaoping, reentered the political arena with a vengeance and played their trump card, the PLA.

reform; and Richard Baum, "The perils of partial reform," in Richard Baum, ed., *Reform and reaction in post-Mao China: The road to Tiananmen,* 1–17.

4 The concept of "new authoritarianism" is discussed in *Jiushi niandai* (hereafter, *JSND*), April 1989, 82–4. See also Mark Petracca and Mong Xiong, "The concept of Chinese neo-authoritarianism: An exploration and democratic critique," *Asian Survey* (hereafter, *AS*) 30.11 (November 1990), 1099–1117; Ma Shu Yun, "The rise and fall of neo-authoritarianism in China," *China Information* (hereafter, *CI*) 5.3 (Winter 1990–1), 1–19; and "The debate on the new authoritarianism," *Chinese Sociology and Anthropology* 23.2 (Winter 1990–1), passim. For further analysis, see the subsections "Political reform: Toward 'neoauthoritarianism' and "Zhao's neoauthoritarian counteroffensive."

5 The term is borrowed from Lowell Dittmer, "China in 1989: The crisis of incomplete reform," *AS* 30.1 (January 1990).

The bloody crackdown and repression that followed put an end, at least temporarily, to the developmental dynamism of the 1980s. With the massacre of several hundred – perhaps more than a thousand – civilians in the streets of Beijing, Deng Xiaoping appeared on the verge of losing his biggest gamble: that modernization and socioeconomic reform could be achieved without undermining the country's political stability. Under the cumulative stresses engendered by a decade of reform-induced sociopolitical mobilization, Deng's carefully crafted coalition came unglued. Zhao Ziyang was dismissed and placed under house arrest for aiding and abetting a "counter-revolutionary rebellion"; a number of his more liberal supporters were sacked, arrested, or driven into exile; and a new wave of repression, recrimination, and regimentation spread throughout China. Though energetic efforts were made by Party leaders to keep up the appearance of political unity and consensus, the subsequent rigidity and paralysis of government policy bespoke the existence of deep, painful political wounds that mere words of self-assurance could not assuage. This chapter seeks to describe and analyze how – and why – the reform decade ended so disastrously for China, belying the greatly elevated hopes and aspirations of the early 1980s.

FIRST CYCLE: LIBERALIZATION AND RESTRAINT

The Twelfth Party Congress

There were few, if any, signs of the debilitating trauma to come when the Twelfth CCP Congress met in September 1982. In his opening address to the Congress, Deng Xiaoping struck a moderate note, declaring that the Party's principal domestic task for the remainder of the decade was "to intensify socialist modernization . . . [with] economic construction at the core." In line with this objective, Deng carefully balanced his call for the further deepening of reform with an injunction to build a new "spiritual civilization" to ensure that China's modernization would maintain its socialist orientation.[6]

On the political side, the Twelfth Congress emphasized the twin tasks of rejuvenating the Party's leadership and creating a more highly institutionalized, collectively responsible structure of command and control. A formidable obstacle to the realization of the former objective was the absence of any regular mechanism of retirement for superannuated Party cadres. Historically, there had been two principal avenues of exit from political life in the

6 The text of Deng's speech is translated in BBC, *Summary of World Broadcasts/Far East* (hereafter, *SWB/FE*) 7120 (2 September, 1982). For analysis of the Twelfth Party Congress, see Lowell Dittmer, "The 12th congress of the Chinese Communist Party," *CQ* 93 (March 1983), 108–24; and *Issues and Studies* (hereafter, *I&S*) 18.11 (November 1982), 14–62.

People's Republic of China (PRC): death (or disability) and purgation.[7] In an effort to create a more appealing third alternative, the Twelfth Party Congress created the CAC, one of Deng's previously mentioned "temporary" innovations, to serve as a way station en route to full retirement for senior Party leaders with more than forty years of service to the revolution. Members of this council of elders would be entitled to retain their full salaries, ranks, and perks, and would continue to be regularly consulted by Party leaders on matters of importance; but they would cease serving on the Party's regular decision-making bodies, thus making room for younger, more vigorous, and technically proficient cadres.

On the eve of the Twelfth Congress it had been widely speculated that with the creation of the CAC, a substantial number of eligible Party veterans would choose to retire from active duty.[8] In the event, such expectations proved overly optimistic, as at least fourteen top-level veterans, most notably Politburo Standing Committee members Ye Jianying (eighty-six), Chen Yun (seventy-seven), and Li Xiannian (seventy-three), chose not to exercise the retirement option.[9] Through an adroit parliamentary maneuver, Deng Xiaoping (seventy-seven) managed to finesse the question of his own retirement: As newly elected chairman of the CAC, he was constitutionally mandated to serve, *ex officio,* as a voting member of the Politburo's Standing Committee.

Defending his own decision not to retire, Chen Yun argued that "there aren't many young cadres qualified to take over leadership posts. . . . Some [of us] still have to stay on the front line." Chen's Standing Committee colleague, Ye Jianying, was even more blunt in his refusal to step down: "I'll [continue to] perform my duties with all my energy . . . and stop only when I die" (which he finally did in 1986).[10]

7 See Michel Oksenberg, "The exit pattern from Chinese politics and its implications," *CQ* 67 (September 1976), 501–18.

8 See, for example, the statement by vice-premier Wan Li in *SWB/FE* 7109 (20 August 1982).

9 Other veteran Politburo members who declined to retire at the Twelfth Congress included Nie Rongzhen (eighty-three), Xu Xiangqian (eighty-three), Deng Yingchao (eighty-one), Peng Zhen (eighty), Ulanfu (seventy-seven), Wang Zhen (seventy-four), Song Renqiong (seventy-three), Liao Chengzhi (seventy-three), and Yang Dezhi (seventy-two). In preliminary discussions of the proposal to establish the CAC prior to the Twelfth Congress, it had been the stated intent of the commission's designers (including Deng Xiaoping, who first proposed the idea in an August 1980 address on leadership reform) to make the CAC independent of, and coequal with, the CC in power and authority. A third leading party body, the newly established Central Discipline Inspection Commission (CDIC), had also been slated to enjoy coequal status with the CC and the CAC. The idea of three-way parity was rejected at the Twelfth Congress, however, and the two new party commissions were given a reduced role in policymaking – a fact that may have contributed to the last-minute decision of several elderly Politburo members to put off their retirement. Over time, the CAC gained de facto veto power over important Politburo decisions, making it in effect a shadow CC (see the subsections "Combatting bourgeois liberalism," "Toward reform and renewal: The Thirteenth Party Congress," "Reenter the gerontocrats," and "Waging moral warfare: Gorbachev, the media, and the hunger strike."

10 *Renmin ribao* (hereafter, *RMRB*), 7 September 1982.

As an added retirement sweetener for recalcitrant veteran cadres, the new Party constitution, ratified by the Twelfth Congress, stipulated that all members of the CAC were entitled to attend plenary meetings of the Central Committee (CC) in a nonvoting capacity; at the same time, the several vice-chairmen of the CAC were granted the statutory right on nonvoting participation in plenary sessions of the Politburo.[11] Such provisions apparently helped take the sting out of retirement, as a group of sixty-five CC members over the age of seventy (including fourteen alternates) relinquished their seats and accepted appointment to the new commission. In addition to these 65 voluntary retirees, another group of 131 incumbent members and alternates of the Eleventh CC (elected in 1977) failed to gain reelection to the Twelfth CC. The majority of the unseated cadres were erstwhile "leftists" and "whateverists" who had risen to prominence during the Cultural Revolution or the Hua Guofeng interregnum, and who were now being systematically weeded out by Deng's followers.

Despite the obvious reluctance of some of China's most senior leaders to leave the political stage, in the end a rather substantial turnover in Party leadership did take place below the level of the Politburo. Fully 60 percent of the 341 CC members and alternates elected by the Twelfth Congress were newcomers. The average age of these first-timers was fifty-eight; the youngest new member was thirty-eight; many had received a college education. While applauding this overall rejuvenation of the Party's leadership, official Chinese accounts of the proceedings of the Twelfth Congress conveniently ignored the fact that on average, the twenty-five members of the new Politburo were actually *older,* at seventy-two, than their predecessors.[12]

If cadre retirement proved a difficult hurdle, so too did the task of institutionalizing the Party's command structure. During the late Maoist period, the CCP had come under the putative influence of "feudal autocracy" and the "cult of personality," leading to an "over-concentration of power" in the hands of Mao and a small group of his lieutenants.[13] To help remedy this problem and to strengthen the norm of collective leadership, the Twelfth Congress formally abolished the posts of CC chairman and vice-chairmen, supplanting them with a revitalized Central Party Secretariat, an organ that had been abolished during the Cultural Revolution. Under the revised party *nomenklatura* that governed high-level personnel appointments and ranks, the general secretary of the Central Secretariat nominally became the top-ranking

11 See "Constitution of the Communist Party of China," *Beijing Review* (hereafter, *BR*) 25.38 (20 September 1982), 14–16.

12 The six-member Politburo Standing Committee (Deng, Hu Yaobang, Ye Jianying, Zhao Ziyang, Li Xiannian, and Chen Yun) was older still, averaging seventy-four years – just one year younger than the average age of the retirees on the CAC.

13 See the earlier discussion by Roderick MacFarquhar.

party leader, though his autonomy was constrained by a new constitutional provision that held that "no party member, whatever his position, is allowed to stand above the law or . . . make decisions on major issues on his own."[14]

Unlike the Politburo, which continued to be dominated by elderly revolutionaries of the first (i.e., Long March) generation, the Central Secretariat, under the direction of newly elected general secretary Hu Yaobang (sixty-seven), was staffed with a number of younger, better-educated cadres, including members of both the second (anti–Japanese war) and third (civil war) generations of Party leaders. The average age of the twelve full and alternate members of the new Secretariat was sixty-three, almost a full decade younger than their Politburo counterparts.[15]

BUILDING "SOCIALIST SPIRITUAL CIVILIZATION"

A final programmatic theme raised at the Twelfth Party Congress was the call to create a "socialist spiritual civilization" that would offer CCP members effective moral protection against the corrosive effects of "bourgeois liberalization" and other unwanted by-products of China's structural reform and opening to the outside world. In his address to the Congress, General Secretary Hu Yaobang asserted that the successful construction of a socialist material civilization in China ultimately depended on the prior attainment of a high level of spiritual civilization. In postulating such a causal relationship between spirit and matter, Hu tacitly reversed the priorities established at the time of the Third Plenum in December 1978, when the development of society's productive forces had been elevated to the position of summum bonum.

The reason for the reversal was clear: A wind of bourgeois liberalization had blown across China since the Third Plenum. In such a situation, Hu Yaobang asserted, "capitalist forces and other forces hostile to our socialist cause will seek to corrupt us and harm our country." Confronted with such a challenge, he continued, "it will not be possible to prevent in all cases the degeneration of some members of our society and party or block the emergence of a few exploiting and hostile elements." To minimize the effects of

14 See "Constitution of the Communist Party." It was reported at the time that the main reason Party leaders favored a general secretary over a chairman was that the former, as part of a collective leading body, would merely be first among equals, thus reducing the likelihood of the emergence of a potentially overbearing dictator. For analysis of the Party constitution, see Tony Saich, "The People's Republic of China," in W. B. Simons and S. White, eds., *The party statutes of the communist world*, 83–113.

15 On generational change in China's leadership in the early 1980s, see Hong Yung Lee, "China's 12th central committee," *AS* 23.6 (June 1983), 673–91; also William de B. Mills, "Generational change in China," *Problems of Communism* (hereafter, *POC*) 32.6 (November–December 1983), 16–35.

such degeneration, CCP members were called upon to hold firmly to the Party's established ideals, moral values, and organizational discipline.[16]

In raising the specter of renewed disturbances by capitalist forces, Hu Yaobang was ostensibly bowing to the demands of Party traditionalists rather than expressing his own deeply felt convictions.[17] Consequently, he hedged his warnings against the dangers of ideological degeneration, couching them in relatively restrained, nonmilitant language. While acceding to the traditionalists' claim that class struggle "still exists," for example, he added two significant caveats: It existed only "within certain limits," and it no longer constituted the "principal contradiction."[18] Finally, in announcing the leadership's intention to launch a comprehensive three-year Party consolidation and rectification drive in the latter half of 1983, Hu Yaobang went out of his way to stress that Maoist-style methods of mass mobilization and struggle would not be employed in the new campaign.[19]

In sum, the Twelfth Congress took an ambivalent stance on China's most pressing developmental issues, seeking thereby to minimize conflict among contending leadership factions and constituencies. While pragmatically stressing the need to further deepen the process of economic reform and opening up to the outside world, Party spokesmen simultaneously intensified their warnings of spiritual degeneration; by the same token, while declaring class struggle in the main to be over, they held out the clear possibility (made explicit in the new CCP constitution) that class struggle could become even sharper in the future. Although the Twelfth Congress thus split the difference on a number of troublesome issues of ideological and political orientation, the resulting compromises left considerable room for future discord.

Constitutional reform: Strengthening socialist legality

In the aftermath of the Twelfth Congress, political attention was focused on the newly revised PRC state constitution, approved by the National People's Congress (NPC) on 4 December. Two years in the making, the new constitution reflected a clear rejection of the ultra-left political philosophy of the Cultural Revolution and a reversion to a more routinized form of "socialist

16 Hu Yaobang's speech is translated in *SWB/FE* 7125 (8 September 1982).

17 Party leaders in China are frequently called upon publicly to express consensual positions that may differ from their own personal views. This is a major feature of Party discipline under "democratic centralism"; for this reason, it is sometimes difficult to sort out what is personal and discretionary from what is consensual and obligatory in the formal speeches and reports of Party leaders.

18 The idea that class struggle continues to exist "within certain limits" was first officially formulated in the CCP's 1981 *Resolution on CPC history, (1949–81)*.

19 *SWB/FE* 7125 (8 September 1982). No details were given in Hu's speech concerning the forthcoming Party consolidation movement.

legality," closely akin to the system originally imported from the Soviet Union in 1954.[20]

Echoing a theme raised at the Twelfth Congress, the new constitution emphasized the creation of orderly, accountable, legally regulated governmental institutions and procedures. Toward this end, the legislative functions and powers of the NPC and its Standing Committee (SC) were augmented; tenure in office for government leaders was limited to two consecutive five-year terms; and new prohibitions were added against certain officials serving concurrently in more than one leadership post. Such measures were ostensibly intended to create a "clear division of power" and to ensure a "strict system of responsibility in implementing laws."[21]

The 1982 constitution sought to strike a careful balance between civil liberties and civic duties. Although a number of new citizens' rights and safeguards were incorporated into the document, including the right to personal dignity, sanctity of the home, and protection against deliberate frame-up, false accusation, and libel, the practical effects of this constitutional innovation were sharply reduced by a series of explicit caveats and qualifiers. For example, the right of citizens to enjoy "freedom and privacy of correspondence" was subject to the proviso, "except in cases involving state security or criminal investigation." Equally limiting was a clause that held that "The exercise by citizens . . . of their freedoms and rights may not infringe upon the interests of the state, of society, and of the collective, or upon the lawful freedoms and rights of other citizens."[22] Finally, the 1982 constitution reaffirmed the Party's four cardinal principles, though it did so in watered-down language that appeared to give virtually equal emphasis to the importance of strengthening China's socialist democracy and legal system.[23]

On the whole, China's new constitution represented a careful attempt to balance the inherently conflicting imperatives of *fang* and *shou*. Relatively tolerant and permissive compared to previous charters, the document re-

20 The text of the 1982 state constitution appears in *BR* 25.52 (27 December 1982), 10–18. For analysis, see Tony Saich, "The fourth constitution of the People's Republic of China," *Review of Socialist Law* 9.2 (1983), 113–24; and Richard Baum, "Modernization and legal reform in post-Mao China: The rebirth of socialist legality," *Studies in Comparative Communism* (hereafter, *SICC*) 19.2 (Summer 1986), 69–103.

21 See Peng Zhen, "Report on the draft of a revised constitution of the PRC," *BR* 25.50 (13 December 1982), 9–20.

22 Similar language had been invoked by China's top leaders in the spring of 1979, when the government closed down the democracy wall and arrested human rights activist Wei Jingsheng. See the earlier discussion by MacFarquhar.

23 The relevant passage (in the preamble to the constitution) stated that "Under the leadership of the CCP and the guidance of Marxism–Leninism–Mao Zedong Thought, the Chinese people will . . . continue to adhere to the people's democratic dictatorship and follow the socialist road, steadily improve socialist institutions, develop socialist democracy, improve the socialist legal system, and work hard . . . to turn China into a socialist country with a high level of culture and democracy."

flected a clear break from the political philosophy of the Cultural Revolution. At the same time, however, it fell far short of institutionalizing the pluralistic rule of law, resembling instead a rationalized variant of neoclassical Leninist rule *by* law.[24]

From socialist legality to socialist humanism

After almost two years of relative quiescence brought on by the spring 1981 conservative literary attack against PLA writer Bai Hua,[25] China's critical intellectuals became markedly bolder in the months following the constitutional reform of December 1982. In the early winter of 1982–3, a vigorous academic debate unfolded in Beijing on the question of the contemporary relevance of such concepts as "alienation" (*yihua*) and "humanism" (*rendao zhuyi*) in socialist society. Among the more prominent participants in this debate were Wang Ruoshui, deputy editor-in-chief of the *People's Daily*, and Ru Xin, vice-president of the Chinese Academy of Social Sciences (CASS).[26]

The debate began to heat up in mid-January 1983 with the publication of Wang Ruoshui's controversial essay "In defense of humanism." In this essay Wang noted that certain "well-meaning comrades" in the party disapproved of humanist values, regarding them as anti-Marxist heresy. "They set Marxism and humanism in total opposition to one another," he wrote; hence they are unable to see any universal relevance in the idea of "human worth." Rejecting this view on the grounds that it erroneously equated the concept of human worth with *bourgeois* humanism, Wang proposed an entirely different type of humanism:

Socialist humanism implies resolutely abandoning the "total dictatorship" and merciless struggle of the ten years of chaos, abandoning the deification of one individ-

24 Following Jowitt's typology of the stages of development of postrevolutionary Leninist regimes, H. C. Kuan has characterized China's 1982 constitution as "inclusionary" in nature, reflecting the Party's desire to coopt the active support of intellectuals and other relevant social forces. See his "New departures in China's constitution," *SICC* 17.1 (Spring 1984), 53–68. On the distinction between rule *of* law and rule *by* law, see Jerome A. Cohen, *The criminal process in the People's Republic of China, 1949–63: An introduction*, 5ff.

25 Bai Hua's controversial screenplay, *Ku Lian* (*Bitter Love*), was attacked by conservatives for being too negative and pessimistic about China's recent past, in particular about the damage inflicted by CCP policies during the Great Leap Forward and the Cultural Revolution. The Bai Hua affair is discussed in Tsou, "Political change and reform," 227–31; see also Richard Kraus, "Bai Hua: The political authority of a writer," in Carol Lee Hamrin and Timothy Cheek, eds., *China's establishment intellectuals*, 201–11.

26 Along with a handful of other liberal critics of dogmatic Marxism, Wang and Ru had begun writing essays on the relationship between socialism and humanism as early as 1980. See David A. Kelly, "The emergence of humanism: Wang Ruoshui and the critique of socialist alienation," in Merle Goldman with Timothy Cheek and Carol Lee Hamrin, eds., *China's intellectuals and the state: In search of a new relationship*, 159–82. For further analysis of the origins and development of the debate over socialist humanism, see Stuart Schram, " 'Economics in command?': Ideology and policy since the Third Plenum, 1978–84," *CQ* 99 (September 1984), 433ff.

ual . . . , upholding the equality of all before truth and the law, and seeing that the personal freedoms and human dignity of citizens are not infringed upon. . . . Why should this sort of socialist humanism be treated as a strange, alien, or evil thing?[27]

Academic advocacy of humanist values reached a high water mark in the spring of 1983. In March, at a Beijing symposium marking the centenary of Karl Marx's death, a leading Communist literary cadre and one-time guardian of Maoist intellectual orthodoxy, Zhou Yang, presented a paper pointedly upholding the contemporary relevance and utility of socialist humanism. Defending the controversial notion that alienation could arise under socialism, Zhou suggested that China's previous lack of democracy and sound legal norms had given rise to a situation wherein the people's servants had become their masters. This, he said, was a relevant example of political alienation. Economic alienation also existed, averred Zhou, because of China's critical "lack of understanding and experience" of socialist construction. As a result, he charged, "we did many stupid things" and "ate our own bitter fruit." Arguing that economic and political alienation existed objectively, he concluded that it was "pointless" for people to be alarmed by such terms.[28]

Adding another strong critical voice to the flourishing debate on socialist humanism and alienation, senior party theoretician Su Shaozhi, in a paper delivered at the Beijing centenary symposium on Marxism, affirmed that a "crisis of Marxism" existed. Calling the crisis "our punishment for having treated Marxism in a dogmatic fashion," Su argued that the bitter legacy of Cultural Revolution dogmatism had led "some people" to deny completely the contemporary relevance of Marxism. While carefully avoiding personal concurrence in such negative assessments, Su concluded that "only by creatively developing Marxism can we truly uphold [it]."[29]

For a brief period in the spring of 1983, even the conservative wing of the CCP appeared to accept the propriety (if not the validity) of such arguments. At a meeting on "Marx and Man" held in early April, for example, Deng Liqun, head of the CC's propaganda department and a leading Party traditionalist, grudgingly conceded that the debate on socialist humanism and alienation contained "many good points" and would contribute to the vigorous development of the Party's "double hundred" policy toward intellectuals.[30]

27 Wang Ruoshui, "Wei rendaozhuyi bianhu" (In defense of humanism), *Wenhui bao* (hereafter, *WHB*) (Shanghai), 17 January 1983. A partial translation appears in *Inside China Mainland* (hereafter, *ICM*), June 1983, Supplement 7–8.

28 Zhou Yang, "Inquiry into some theoretical problems of Marxism," *RMRB*, 16 March 1983.

29 Su Shaozhi, "Develop Marxism under contemporary conditions," *Selected Studies on Marxism* 2 (February 1983), 1–39. See also Schram, " 'Economics in command?'. . . ," 434–7.

30 *RMRB*, 12 April 1983. The term "double hundred" refers to the policy "Let a hundred flowers bloom, let a hundred schools of thought contend," first enunciated by Mao in 1956. Schram, " 'Economics in

After more than three months of free-flowing blooming and contending, official tolerance for the ongoing debate over socialist norms and values began to diminish noticeably. Social critics like Wang Ruoshui and Su Shaozhi had come uncomfortably, if only elliptically, close to denying the Party's doctrinal and political legitimacy, and such defenders of the faith as Deng Liqun were finding it increasingly difficult to refrain from calling them to account. By the end of May, the humanism–alienation debate was no longer being reported, benignly or otherwise, in the Party media; and by early June a new term had been coined to describe the heterodox ideas ostensibly being propagated by Wang, Su, and other members of the humanist school: "spiritual pollution" (*jingshen wuran.*)[31]

Straws in the wind: The Sixth NPC

The first significant public hint of a shift in the prevailing political wind was contained in Zhao Ziyang's "Report on the work of the government," delivered in early June to the opening session of the Sixth NPC. While defending the Party's established policies of economic reform, opening up to the outside world, and intellectual blooming and contending, Zhao added a fresh warning against the growing tendency of bourgeois liberalism in the ideological and cultural spheres. Examples were said to include writers and artists who "disregard the social consequences of their work" and who "view their work as a means to grab fame and fortune." Such behavior, said Zhao, was symptomatic of "decadent ideology" and was "incompatible with the policy of serving the people and socialism."[32] Although no concrete measures were called for beyond a general exhortation to criticize such trends, Zhao's remarks proved worrisome to China's oft-burned critical intellectuals.

Also of concern to careful readers of Zhao's report was the premier's use of strong language on the subject of law and order. Speaking of shortcomings in public security work, Zhao noted that a rising tide of serious crime, including a wave of violent offenses such as hijacking, murder, robbery, rape, and larceny, had begun to pose a definite problem in China. At the same time, he acknowledged a pronounced upsurge in the incidence of nonviolent economic

command?' " notes that Deng Liqun's remarks were published under a provocative headline supplied not by Deng himself but by the liberal-leaning editors of *People's Daily,* Hu Jiwei and Wang Ruoshui. The headline read, "To discuss humanism and the theory of human nature is an excellent thing." Hu and Wang were later criticized by Deng Liqun and "transferred" from their jobs for promoting "spiritual pollution." See the subsection "Combatting humanism and 'spiritual pollution.' "

31 The term was first used by Deng Liqun in a 4 June 1983 speech to the Central Party School in Beijing. See *Zhengming* (hereafter, *ZM*) 76 (1 February 1984), 6–11.

32 Zhao Ziyang, "Report on the work of the government," *BR* 26.25 (4 July 1983), XVIII–XIX.

crime and corruption on the part of government cadres who "seek personal gain by abusing [their] position and power." Attributing the breakdown in social order to the "intolerable political and ideological apathy" allegedly displayed by certain public security and law enforcement personnel, Zhao Ziyang stressed that it was necessary to "suppress counterrevolutionary activities" and "deal powerful blows" to criminals in all spheres.[33]

In the wake of the premier's call for enhanced law and order, a draconian crackdown on crime was launched in the summer of 1983. Marked by the suspension of certain constitutional and statutory rights of criminal defendants, the campaign witnessed a flurry of mass trials, hasty verdicts, truncated appeals, and summary executions.[34] Although not necessarily unpopular with China's increasingly crime-weary citizens, the anticrime campaign gave further impetus to the ideological chill that was beginning to envelop China. More important, it gave Party traditionalists a potent issue, law and order, and a viable pretext, the need to combat crime at its putative source, for launching a new offensive against ideological corrosion.

The offensive took shape at the end of the summer. Beginning in mid-September, there was a pronounced increase in the stridency of articles published in certain bellweather journals. The editors of *Red Flag* (*Hongqi*), for example, now pointedly criticized "some people in cultural circles" who had been "taken in" by "the allure of abstract humanity and humanism" to the point where "social and class nature have been abandoned." Calling this an erroneous viewpoint that reflected a "serious antagonistic struggle in the political sphere," the article stressed that since class struggle still existed, it was necessary to strengthen the organs of people's democratic dictatorship in order to combat harmful views.[35] In a subsequent article, *Red Flag*'s editors went even further, claiming a presumptive link between the influence of bourgeois mentality, on the one hand, and the severity of China's recent crime wave, on the other:

Although our country has already abolished the system of exploitation and established a socialist society, . . . all kinds of elements hostile to the socialist system and to the people still exist. *Various kinds of crime are bound to occur where the influence of*

33 Ibid., XX–XXI.

34 A resolution adopted by the NPC Standing Committee in early September served to suspend a number of statutory provisions governing the handling of criminal cases – including provisions setting time limits for the delivery of indictments, the issuance of subpeonas, and the right to appeal convictions. The stated purpose of the suspension was to "promptly punish criminals who seriously jeopardize social order" (*Xinhua* [hereafter, *XH*], 2 September 1983). According to various sources, between 6,000 and 10,000 convicted lawbreakers were executed in the second half of 1983. See *Far Eastern Economic Review* (hereafter, *FEER*), 10 November 1983 and 16 February 1984; also Amnesty International, *China: Violations of human rights*, 54–5. For a collection of media reports concerning implementation of the 1983 anticrime campaign, see *ICM*, October 1983.

35 *Hongqi* (hereafter, *HQ*) 18 (16 September 1983).

bourgeois extreme individualism . . . is still present. We must see that these serious offenders are detestable in the extreme. . . . If we let them get away with [their] crimes . . . and fail to suppress them, *if we speak of "mercy" and "humanism," it will be a grave dereliction of our duty . . . to the cause of socialism.*[36]

Combatting humanism and "spiritual pollution"

Under mounting pressure from Party traditionalists, the uneasy ideological compromise crafted by Party leaders a year earlier now began to show signs of stress. The fault lines in Deng Xiaoping's coalition were clearly evident at the Second Plenum of the Twelfth Party Congress, held on 11–12 October 1983. In his speech to the plenum, Deng steered a middle course between the increasingly polarized factions of his reform coalition. First, he addressed the principal concerns of the Party's moderate-to-liberal wing, led by Hu Yaobang and Zhao Ziyang. Speaking of the need to continue combatting remnant leftist influences from the Cultural Revolution, he noted that "three kinds of people" (*sanzhong ren*) were continuing to undermine Party unity and discipline from the left: those who rose to power in the Cultural Revolution on the coattails of the Lin Biao and Jiang Qing cliques; those who engaged in factional activities, rumor mongering, and various other forms of "subversive" partisan behavior; and those guilty of "looting, smashing, and grabbing" during China's ten years of chaos. Such people, said Deng, should be firmly disciplined, including expulsion from the Party where necessary. To accomplish this task, he said, the forthcoming Party consolidation movement would concentrate on exposing and rectifying the "three kinds of people."[37]

After thus addressing the main concerns of his centrist and liberal constituencies, Deng shifted his focus almost 180 degrees to launch a sharp, three-pronged attack on abstract humanism, the theory of socialist alienation, and spiritual pollution. Sardonically observing that a considerable number of Party theorists preferred to indulge in abstract contemplation of human nature rather than attempting to understand and resolve concrete problems encountered by real people, Deng tersely dismissed abstract humanism as "un-Marxist; it leads youth astray." On the related issue of the possibility of

36 *HQ* 17 (1 September 1983) (emphasis added). As early as 1982, Party conservatives had begun to attribute China's rising crime rate to an influx of corrosive foreign ideas under the open door policy. One internal (*neibu*) Chinese publication thus stated that "since [initiating] the policy of opening to the outside world, encroachments by bourgeois ideology from abroad [and] infiltration by hostile foreign influences [have] directly or indirectly [contributed to] criminal activities in society. This is the objective reason [why the situation of public security] has not taken a basic turn for the better." (*Look* Monthly, September 1983, trans. in *ICM*, October 1983, 7).

37 An unofficial transcript of Deng's address appears in *I&S* 20.4 (April 1984), 99–111.

alienation occurring under socialism, Deng sharply rebutted the viewpoint advanced by Zhou Yang and others in the spring of 1983:

> A number of comrades . . . say that alienation exists in socialist society . . . in the spheres of economics, politics, and ideology. . . . Such talk cannot help people gain a correct understanding . . . of the many problems which have appeared in socialist society. . . . In fact, this can only lead people to criticize, mistrust, and negate socialism, to lose confidence in the future of socialism and communism. . . .[38]

Turning to questions of political orientation, Deng noted that a number of unhealthy ideas had recently become fashionable among party theoreticians, including "the abstract concept of democracy," advocacy of "free speech for counterrevolutionaries," and "doubts about the four cardinal principles."[39] Such ideas "run counter to Marxist common sense," said Deng; in addition, they discredit the Party's proletarian character and engender doubts about the future of socialism, thereby sowing confusion among Party members. Displaying contempt for writers and artists who "dwell eagerly on the gloomy and the pessimistic," Deng called on Party workers in literature and the arts to eulogize the CCP's revolutionary history, the four cardinal principles, and the heroic achievements of the Chinese people under socialism.[40]

Continuing in this vein, Deng next decried a growing attitude of "doing anything for money" among writers and performing artists, many of whom "run around everywhere, . . . indiscriminately giving performances . . . using low and vulgar form and content to turn an easy profit." Such people are guilty of "pandering to the low tastes of a section of their audiences," Deng continued; they "commercialize spiritual productions" and thus "occupy an unworthy place in the world of art." Pointedly labeling such phenomena "spiritual pollution," Deng called for a vigorous ideological struggle to "resolutely overcome weakness, laxity, and liberal attitudes."[41]

Although the effects of spiritual pollution were said to have seriously affected only a minority of Party theoreticians and ideological workers, Deng warned of dire consequences if firm steps were not taken to combat the problem. "Don't imagine," he warned, "that a little spiritual pollution doesn't amount to very much and is not worth making a fuss over. . . . If we do not immediately . . . curb these phenomena, . . . the consequences could be extremely serious."[42]

Having thus addressed the principal concerns of his coalition's liberal and conservative wings, Deng instructed his comrades to avoid going to extremes to rectify ideological problems of the right or the left. In the forthcoming

38 Ibid.

39 Some liberal intellectuals, including *People's Daily* deputy editor Wang Ruoshui, among others, had openly expressed doubts about Deng's four principles as early as 1979.

40 *I&S*, 20.4 (April 1984). 41 Ibid. 42 Ibid.

Party consolidation movement, he urged, comrades must at all times "seek truth from facts" (*shishi qiushi*) and resist the temptation to employ the "crude and extreme" methods adopted in the past, characterized by "cruel struggle and merciless attacks." It was essential, he concluded, to adopt a kindly attitude toward comrades who had committed mistakes, resisting the temptation to "take every bush and tree for an enemy."[43]

At the conclusion of its brief two-day plenum, the CC adopted twin resolutions on Party consolidation and rectification. Responding to Deng Xiaoping's injunction to avoid crude and extreme methods, the resolutions hewed closely to the ideological midline, denouncing with equal vigor the three kinds of people on the left and spiritual polluters on the right.[44] Under the guidance of the CCP's newly created Central Discipline Inspection Commission (CDIC), headed by Chen Yun and Bo Yibo, the consolidation drive was to be carried out in two stages over a period of three years. Although no specific targets or quotas were announced, diplomatic sources in Beijing reported that some 3 million Party members, principally young leftists who had been recruited during the ten years of chaos, were initially targeted for rectification.[45]

Whatever Deng Xiaoping's original intent, the 1983 Party consolidation movement quickly veered off the tracks and out of control. No sooner had the Second Plenum ended than a barrage of newspaper articles appeared, canonizing the four cardinal principles, condemning spiritual pollution, and vigorously denouncing abstract humanism and the theory of socialist alienation.[46] By early November, a number of leading CCP traditionalists, including Deng Liqun, Wang Zhen, Peng Zhen, and Chen Yun, had weighed in on the dangers of liberal ideological corrosion, explicitly invoking Deng Xiaoping's remarks at the Second Plenum to support their arguments.[47]

43 Ibid.

44 The text of the resolution on Party consolidation appears in *XH* (Chinese and English), 12 October 1983.

45 *Asiaweek* 43 (28 October 1983), 13; *ICM*, February 1985, 20–1. Thomas Gold has argued that Deng Xiaoping's denunciation of spiritual pollution at the Second Plenum was a "tactical feint" designed to gain conservative support for his real objective, which was said to be to rid the Party of residual ultra-leftists. (Gold, " 'Just in Time!' China battles spiritual pollution on the eve of 1984," *AS* 24.9 [September 1984], 952.) After earlier sharing Gold's view, I am now inclined to believe (in light of Deng Xiaoping's subsequent behavior in 1986 and 1989, to be examined later) that Deng was being entirely candid in his denunciations of rightist dangers at the Second Plenum but that he wished to avoid giving leftists an excuse to reverse his hard-won economic reforms. For other views on this controversy, see Schram, " 'Economics in command?' . . ."; Tony Saich, "Party consolidation and spiritual pollution in the People's Republic of China," *Communist Affairs* 3.3 (July 1984), 283–9; and Colin Mackerras, " 'Party consolidation' and the attack of spiritual pollution," *Australian Journal of Chinese Affairs* (hereafter, *AJCA*) 11 (January 1984), 178.

46 See, for example, *RMRB*, 20, 23, 25, 31 October and 2 November 1983.

47 Chen Yun was somewhat enigmatic in his early response to the problem of spiritual pollution. At a CC meeting in May 1983, for example, Chen reportedly displayed considerable restraint in criticizing

Deng Liqun (no relation to Deng Xiaoping) was the conservatives' primary hatchet man. According to reports subsequently circulated in Hong Kong, Deng Liqun's leading role in the early attack on spiritual pollution was motivated by two main considerations: his own strong traditionalist values and an equally strong desire to undermine the growing prestige of Hu Yaobang. Deng's antipathy to Hu was said to stem from envy kindled when he (Deng) was passed over for the post of CCP general secretary prior to the Twelfth Party Congress in 1982. Armed with the potent issue of spiritual pollution, an issue on which Hu Yaobang was believed to be vulnerable, Deng Liqun now set out to undermine his rival.[48]

In the ensuing storm, a wide variety of social phenomena were singled out as manifestations of spiritual pollution. These included, inter alia, the "worship of individualism"; the proliferation of pornographic films and videotapes; the attitude of "looking to make money in everything"; the revival of "clan feuds" and "superstitious practices" in rural areas; and even the wearing of Western-style hairdos and high-heeled shoes by female college students.[49] In some areas, vigilantes reportedly harassed people whose hair was unusually long or who wore flared trousers. In other places, factory workers were organized to search for "yellow" (pornographic) audiotapes and books. And in the city of Lanzhou, provincial police headquarters reportedly organized local gendarmes to "read good books and sing revolutionary songs" as an antidote to such putative evils as "wearing mustaches and whiskers, singing unhealthy songs, being undisciplined, and not keeping one's mind on work."[50]

In addition to denouncing various social manifestations of spiritual pollu-

intellectuals who had strayed from the path of socialism and patriotism, arguing that "we must not [overreact]; we must not drag in too many people on account of some small matters." He also conceded that the much-criticized PLA writer Bai Hua was a "genius," and he recommended that his CC comrades should "see and welcome" Bai's banned screenplay, "Bitter Love." Chen's speech is unofficially reported in *ICM,* March 1984, 15–16.

48 Although the "sibling rivalry" theory of Deng's antagonism toward Hu Yaobang is based largely on circumstance, it nevertheless squares nicely with a number of known facts. For one thing, Deng Liqun and Hu Yaobang were among Deng Xiaoping's strongest supporters and closest confidants in the later years of the Maoist era. Hu had been Deng Xiaoping's pre–Cultural Revolution bridge partner and protégé, and Deng Liqun, who once served as personal secretary to Mao Zedong's one-time heir apparent, Liu Shaoqi, played a key role in defending Deng Xiaoping at a critical juncture in 1975 when the latter was under attack by the Gang of Four for having put forward the controversial idea of "taking the three directives as the key link" (*ZM* 78 [1 April 1984]). Whatever the truth of the sibling rivalry theory, it is clear that from the outset of the spiritual pollution campaign in 1983 until Hu Yaobang was finally ousted from power in January 1987, Deng Liqun wasted no opportunity to embarrass Hu and erode his base of support. For a detailed account of the growing rivalry between Deng and Hu, see *ZM* 76 (1 February 1984).

49 See, e.g., *RMRB,* 29 October and 5 November 1983; *Jingji ribao* (hereafter, *JJRB*), 1 November 1983; *Hubei people's broadcasting station,* 20 October 1983; and *Heilongjiang people's broadcasting station,* 2 November 1983.

50 See *RMRB,* 16 and 17 November 1983; *Foreign Broadcast Information Service* – China, *Daily Report* (hereafter, *FBIS*), 3 November 1983, Q2, T7; Gold, " 'Just in time!'. . . ," 956–8.

tion, China's cultural watchdogs attacked a number of alleged high-level purveyors of ideological corrosion. Wang Ruoshui and Zhou Yang were singled out for particularly strong criticism, as was Hu Jiwei, Wang Ruoshui's boss and chief editor of the *People's Daily,* who had been a key supporter of Hu Yaobang.[51]

At an enlarged Politburo conference held in November, Hu Yaobang and Zhao Ziyang fought back, claiming that the spiritual pollution campaign had gone too far and that ultra-leftists had taken advantage of the ideological cover provided by the campaign to sabotage the "correct line" of the Eleventh CC's Third Plenum, negating economic reform (particularly in rural areas) and opposing China's opening to the outside world. Calling the attack on spiritual pollution a "false show of force," Hu and Zhao argued that the main focus on Party consolidation and rectification should be the elimination of the three kinds of people.[52]

A short while later, at a meeting of the Central Party Secretariat, Hu and Zhao were reportedly assailed by an unidentified speaker (said to be Deng Liqun) who "shouted at the top of his voice that 'spiritual pollution threatens the life of the party.' " At that point, Zhao Ziyang played his trump card. Noting that "Japanese capitalists are postponing agreements with us . . . because they are frightened by the . . . movement to eliminate spiritual pollution," Zhao threatened to resign: "If things go on like this," he warned, "I shall be Prime Minister no longer."[53]

In the end, fearing disruption of his hard-won economic reform and open-door policies, Deng Xiaoping intervened on the side of Hu and Zhao to bring the campaign to a halt.[54] The two reform leaders did not emerge entirely unscathed, however; in return for securing the conservatives' agreement to end the campaign, Hu Yaobang was reportedly pressured into accepting the dismissal, technically labeled a "reassignment," of Wang Ruoshui and Hu

51 *ZM* 78, (1 April 1984). The attack on Zhou Yang was spearheaded by veteran party theoretician Hu Qiaomu, another member of Deng Liqun's anti–spiritual pollution coalition. Hu Qiaomu's lengthy critique of the abstract humanism-alienation school appears in *RMRB*, 27 January 1984. Under pressure from Hu Qiaomu and others, Zhou Yang made a series of self-criticisms in October and November 1983 in which he retracted many of his earlier statements on the subject of humanism and socialist alienation and accepted blame for spreading spiritual pollution in the cultural arena (*RMRB*, 11 November 1983; *BR* 26.50 [12 December 1983], 11–12; *XH*, 11 October 1983, reported in *ICM*, December 1983, 4–5). At around the same time, Hu Jiwei reportedly got into trouble because, among other reasons, he had tried to suppress publication of Wang Zhen's 23 October speech attacking Wang Ruoshui's theory of humanism (*Qishi niandai* [hereafter, *QSND*] 12 [December 1983], 57–8).

52 *ZM* 76 (1 February 1984), 6–11, in *FBIS*, 7 February 1984, W1–11.

53 *ZM* 78 (1 April 1984), in *FBIS*, 6 April 1984, W1–8.

54 In has been reported that Deng Xiaoping's son, Deng Pufang, warned his father that if the campaign was pursued too vigorously, it could undermine the reform program and thus erode Deng's own prestige. See Ian Wilson and You Ji, "Leadership by 'lines': China's unresolved succession," *POC* 39.1 (January–February 1990), 34.

Jiwei, his two top supporters at the *People's Daily.*[55] With the deal thus done, by early December the spiritual pollution storm began to abate; by the turn of the new year, 1984, all that remained were a few occasional squalls and a number of embittered feelings.[56]

Although Deng Liqun managed to secure the reassignment of two leading liberal media critics, he clearly emerged from the clash over spiritual pollution as the big loser. Not only did his own preferred policies fail to carry the day, but beginning in December 1983, he was placed in the unenviable position of having publicly to defend policies with which he strongly disagreed. In a series of press statements and interviews with visiting foreigners, the veteran propagandist now spoke approvingly (if reservedly) about economic reform and opening up to the outside world and less stridently about the dangers of ideological degeneration. Perforce, his antagonism toward Hu Yaobang remained undiminished by the experience.[57]

SECOND CYCLE: LIBERALIZATION AND REBUFFS

In the wake of the spiritual pollution campaign, China's reformers found themselves faced with a new set of problems on the economic policy front. Though the conservative ideological offensive was nipped in the bud, it had struck a raw nerve in many parts of the country where economic reform had at best brought only mixed blessings. In some rural districts, for example, village officials, resentful of the newfound prosperity of local entrepreneurs, had taken advantage of the antipollution drive to restrict the free-market activities of peasants and impose a variety of discriminatory taxes and fees on newly affluent "specialized households."[58] In China's less developed interior provinces, renewed opposition to Deng Xiaoping's preferential coastal development strategy (a key element of his open policy) also began to crystalize in this period. Throughout the country, those localities, groups, and individuals most highly disadvantaged by reform, or simply afflicted with envy of others more successful than themselves, a condition known in China as "red-eye disease" (*hongyanbing*), took advantage of the antipollution campaign to disparage the high costs and adverse side effects of reform. The result was a revival of leftism, which was especially pronounced in the rural hinterland.

55 *FBIS*, 14 November 1983, K1; *ICM*, December 1983, 2.

56 One early tipoff that Hu Yaobang and Zhao Ziyang were winning their confrontation with Deng Liqun came when both the general secretary and the premier wore Western-style suits and ties on their separate trips to Japan and America in late November and early January, respectively.

57 Deng Liqun's retreat is documented in Schram, " 'Economics in command?' . . . ," 453ff.; see also Gold, " 'Just in time!'. . . ," 961–2.

58 On the increasing incidence of such phenomena in the 1980s, see Jean Oi, *State and peasant in contemporary China*.

Confronting a potentially serious economic backlash, leaders of the reform coalition, most prominently Deng Xiaoping himself, now evinced renewed concern over the leftist challenge.[59] With Deng's support, Hu Yaobang began to speak out more forcefully on the need to reaffirm and strengthen economic reforms. At the end of February 1984, Hu instructed the editorial department of the *People's Daily* to draft for publication a series of hard-hitting commentaries favorable to renewed reform. After the articles were drafted, supporters of Deng Liqun reportedly tried to have them quashed, without success.[60]

Throughout the late winter and spring of 1984, editorials in official newspapers reinforced the impression that the Hu–Zhao group had regained the initiative. Five main themes were stressed: (1) the principal danger at the present time is leftism; (2) market reforms and responsibility systems in rural areas must be further expanded and perfected; (3) a key objective of economic reform is to "enable people to get rich"; (4) intellectuals are a precious national asset to be nurtured and cherished; and (5) the open policy and coastal development strategy are long-term policies to be further enriched and extended.[61]

The Party's shifting stance was fully revealed in a *People's Daily* editorial on 1 April. Based on a talk by Hu Yaobang, the article stated unequivocally that leftism, rather than bourgeois liberalism, was the principal source of ideological "weakness and laxity" at the present time.[62] Reviewing past damage inflicted on China by ultra-leftist ideas, the editorial called for the complete elimination of Cultural Revolution influences, which were said to have "penetrated very deeply."

The anti-leftist trend was quickly incorporated into the CCP's ongoing consolidation–rectification campaign, which entered its second phase in

59 See, the series of important editorials in *RMRB*, 20 February, 15 March, 1 April, and 23 April 1984.

60 One of the articles in question contained a sardonic echo of the ultra-leftist Cultural Revolution slogan "Boldly smash the old and create the new." According to reports out of Hong Kong, it was language such as this, now being used by Hu Yaobang's supporters to promote economic reform, that aroused the ire of Hu Qiaomu, Deng Liqun, and other traditionalists in the Party's central propaganda department. See *ZM* 78 (1 April 1984).

61 A major expansion of the open policy was announced in April, when fourteen coastal cities, including Shanghai, Tianjin, and Guangzhou, were added to the four existing special economic zones as preferred locations for foreign investment and technology transfer. See *China Daily* (hereafter, *CD*), 13 April 1984.

62 Deng Xiaoping himself had issued some of the strongest earlier warnings against liberal-induced ideological weakness and laxity; see his address to the Second Plenum of October 1983. Now Hu Yaobang clearly reversed the direction of the main threat. It is presumed that he did so with Deng Xiaoping's approval, since in a 1984 interview with foreign journalists Hu indicated that although he and Zhao Ziyang handled routine matters by themselves, on "important matters in foreign and domestic affairs" Deng Xiaoping alone decided things. See *Mingbao* (hereafter, *MB*), 6 December 1984, in *ICM*, March 1985, 2.

March 1984.[63] Throughout the spring, two themes dominated media discussions of Party rectification: admonitions to stamp out leftist "factionalism" and exhortations to promote young, technically competent members of the "third echelon" (*disan tidui*) to positions of responsibility in the Party and government.[64]

It was hardly coincidental that the Party consolidation drive should now focus on the search for talented younger leaders: Many of the harshest attacks on spiritual pollution in the fall of 1983 had come from veteran cadres who were at or near, and in some cases well beyond, the age of retirement, including such Politburo holdouts as Chen Yun, Peng Zhen, and Wang Zhen. Nor was it entirely coincidental that the man placed in charge of the Party's third-echelon executive head hunt, veteran CCP organizer and Mao biographer Li Rui, should use a literary review of Chen Yun's *Selected works* as the vehicle for launching the new youth movement.[65] Whatever the ironic intent behind Li's choice of venues, the media now published a number of articles praising the talents of younger intellectuals, technocrats, and other well-educated third-echelon leaders who had made outstanding executive contributions, some of whom, it was duly noted, had received advanced training in the West. At the same time, veteran Party bureaucrats were

63 The consolidation movement was carried out from top to bottom in two distinct stages, with each stage consisting of two (or more) phases. In the initial stage, Party committees and leading offices at the central, provincial, major municipal, and autonomous regional levels studied relevant documents and directives for three months (phase one) and then engaged in "examining and comparing" standards of organizational and individual behavior (phase two). Reportedly, some 960,000 Party cadres underwent examination during the latter phase of stage one. In stage two, which began in the winter of 1984–5, the movement was extended to some 13.5 million cadres in Party organs at the county, ordinary municipal, and local levels (including enterprises, research institutes, schools, and universities). In this second stage, the main tasks were to "unify thought" (*tongyi sixiang*), "correct work style" (*zhengdun zuofeng*), "strengthen discipline" (*jiaqiang jilu*), and "clean up organization" (*qingli zuzhi*). The ultimate phase involved the reregistration of Party members and the expulsion of those found guilty of serious attitudinal and behavioral impurities. Although some 3 million Party members had originally been slated for organizational discipline, official sources subsequently indicated that only about 30,000 to 40,000 people were expelled from the Party in the first two and a half years of the movement; of these, roughly 25 percent belonged to the ultra-leftist three kinds of people. The remainder had committed various non–Cultural Revolution–related offenses, most notably corruption, speculation, and profiteering. There was a marked increase in the frequency of expulsions beginning in mid-1985, following exposure of a rash of recent economic crimes. According to official statistics released in 1988, a total of 150,000 Party members were expelled for corruption between 1983 and 1987; if the earlier figures were correct, then the vast majority of these expulsions must have occurred after the middle of 1985. Sources on the Party rectification–consolidation movement include *FBIS*, 13 October 1983, K2–7; *SWB/FE* 7685 (3 July 1984), 7859 (26 January 1985), and 7868 (6 February 1985); *I&S* 20.8 (August 1984); *Liaowang* (hereafter, *LW*) 3 (14 January 1985); *ICM*, April 1985; and *BR* 28.10 (11 March 1985); *XH*, 11 August 1988; *Xue lilun*, April 1989.

64 On the changing emphasis of the consolidation campaign in this period, see *RMRB*, 15 and 20 April 1984. In August, the vice-chairman of the Party's CDIC, Bo Yibo (the man primarily responsible for supervising the Party's consolidation drive), argued that the elimination of leftist influences was an "essential prerequisite" for opening China to the outside world and for successfully adopting new technologies. See *SWB/FE* 7733 (28 August 1984).

65 See *RMRB*, 23 March 1984; Schram, " 'Economics in command?'. . . ," 450.

chastised for obstructing the proper employment, promotion, and utilization of younger talent.[66]

Addressing the issue of generational change (and resistance thereto), Hu Yaobang pointed out, in an interview with Hong Kong journalists, that despite a concerted effort to encourage veteran cadres to retire, well over two-thirds of the members of the CCP's CC were over the age of sixty. "If a crisis exists," Hu averred, "this is it." Flatly declaring that it was a "natural law" for old cadres to retire, he vowed to fill the CC with younger people the following year.[67]

Speeding up the reforms: Economics takes command

In line with the revised goals of Party consolidation, the mass media in the summer of 1984 stressed the need to further develop and expand economic reforms and the open policy. In June, "Central document no. 1" was published, granting expanded rights of private economic activity and extended land-use contracts to individual peasant households.[68] In early July, it was announced that urban economic reform would commence in the autumn of the year, centering on the restructuring of state-owned enterprises, with a view toward increasing the operational autonomy, managerial responsibility, and profit incentives of state firms.[69] Also in early July, Beijing's newest architectural monument, the glitzy chrome-and-glass Great Wall Hotel, opened for business, a joint Sino-American venture that neatly symbolized Deng Xiaoping's commitment to modernization and the open door.

Throughout this period of accelerated reform and relaxation, the mass media played up China's efforts to attract and protect foreign investment; to refine and enforce China's newly enacted commercial laws and procedures; to encourage individual and collective entrepreneurship; to discourage "eating out of a common pot"; and to "smash the iron rice bowl" of guaranteed

66 The pointed references to Western training were intended as a slap at the spiritual pollutionists, who had been highly critical of Western influences. See, e.g., *RMRB*, 30 March 1984; also *Guangming ribao* (hereafter, *GMRB*), 16 March and 6 April 1984; *RMRB*, 25 March and 12–16 April 1984.

67 Hu's interview, which was conducted on 19 October 1984, is serialized in *MB*, 5, 6, and 8 December 1984; a translation appears in *ICM*, March 1985, 1–2. The quoted passages from the general secretary's statement were very similar to statements made by Deng Xiaoping at a meeting of the CAC, also held in October 1984 (*BR* 28.9 [4 March 1985], 15). In Hu Yaobang's interview, he provided several examples of third echelon cadres who had recently been elevated to responsible positions in the central Party and government apparatus. Among the newly promoted leaders singled out for special attention were Hu Qili, secretary of the Central Party Secretariat; Wang Zhaoguo, director of the CCP General Office; Hu Jintao, head of the Communist Youth League; Tian Jiyun, vice-premier of the State Council; and Li Peng, also a vice-premier.

68 *RMRB*, 12 June and 3 July 1984. For analysis, see Kenneth Lieberthal, "The political implications of document no. 1, 1984," *CQ* 101 (March 1985), 109–13.

69 *BR* 27.29 (16 July 1984), 9–10.

lifetime employment. Occasionally, the examples selected for favorable publicity in the official media raised some eyebrows. Under the headline "Prosperous girls attract husbands," for example, a major metropolitan newspaper approvingly recounted the story of a group of peasant spinsters from a poor village near Shanghai who suddenly become objects of intense matrimonial interest on the part of young men from a nearby factory after the women struck it rich as a result of adopting the new household responsibility system in agriculture.[70] Other articles sounded the praises of all manner of private enterprise, from short-order cooks and free-lance photographers to young girls who hired themselves out as personal maids and nannies;[71] still other articles celebrated the achievements of such "trail-blazing" reformers as the director of a collectively owned shirt factory in Zhejiang who had introduced variable piece rates, individualized bonuses, and other "common pot"–smashing productivity incentives among workers in his plant.[72] In the face of unbridled official enthusiasm for such innovations, the occasional voices of ideological dismay or uncertainty that were raised in the media were generally drowned out by a chorus of entrepreneurial affirmation.[73]

Also reflective of China's new mood of permissiveness was the reappearance, with official approval, of high-fashion Western clothing, including short, slitted skirts for women,[74] and the proliferation of certain risqué art forms that less than a year earlier would have stood condemned as spiritual pollution. *Beijing Review,* for example, ran on its inside back cover photos of two seminude female sculptures,[75] and the new international lounge of the Beijing Airport featured a wall-length mural depicting bare-breasted ethnic minority women frolicking in their native habitat. In the high tide of socio-economic experimentation and openness that swept through China in the summer of 1984, such things were possible.

Urban reform and the economic boom of 1984–5

Although restrictions on private entrepreneurship were greatly relaxed in the summer of 1984, reform in state-owned enterprises lagged noticeably.[76] The

70 *WHB* (Shanghai), cited in *BR* 27.29 (16 July 1984), 30. 71 *BR* 27.33 (13 August 1984), 31.

72 *BR* 27.29 (16 July 1984), 19–23. To motivate his workers, the factory director in question reportedly composed a song to reflect the pride of the factory's work force: "Work hard, hard, hard; we are the glorious shirtmakers! With good workmanship and novel designs, we dedicate our youth to making life beautiful."

73 Although it was periodically acknowledged that "some people" entertained doubts about the introduction of certain liberal economic innovations that ostensibly "eliminated the superiority of socialism" or "slid back from socialism to capitalism," such reservations were generally dismissed as misplaced or ill-informed. (See, e.g., ibid., 21.)

74 *BR* 27.33 (13 August 1984), 32. 75 *BR* 27.30 (23 July 1984).

76 Thomas Bernstein notes that although media reports of managerial innovation proliferated in this period, large numbers of state enterprises, indeed whole industrial sectors, appeared to be almost

growing disparity between the dynamic private and collective economy and the static public sector was addressed in the CC's long-awaited "Decision on reform of the economic structure," promulgated in late October. Among the many reforms called for in the new CC decision were a reduction in the scope of mandatory central planning for state enterprises (with a concurrent increase in flexible guidance planning); the introduction of a tax-on-profit system of microeconomic incentives (to replace the previous system of profit remittances); and an expansion of enterprise autonomy in such areas as supply and marketing, product mix, hiring and firing of staff, and allocation of retained profits. Also included was a call for the coupling of a gradual reform of China's irrational pricing system with the phasing out of costly and inefficient state subsidies in such areas as urban housing, energy supply, grain, and transportation. Such steps were deemed essential to the overall success of the reform program.[77]

The CC decision, which was loosely patterned after the Hungarian prototype of "market socialism," envisioned a mixed economy that would incorporate elements of both central planning and market regulation.[78] The state would continue to own the bulk of large and medium-sized enterprises and would continue to regulate the production and pricing of a number of strategic commodities; but the market mechanism would now be permitted to play an increasingly important (albeit supplemental) role in the pricing and allocation of nonstrategic goods and services, as well as in the allocation and remuneration of labor.[79] China's new "socialist commodity economy" would, in other words, permit the "bird" of protocapitalist market forces to fly with considerably more freedom than before within the newly enlarged "birdcage" of central planning.[80]

Bold and innovative in at least some of its implications, the urban reform program was slow to get off the mark after the CC plenum. Lack of elite consensus over, for instance, the proper sequences, priorities, and pacing of reform led to chronic delays in implementation. Substantial resistance was also encountered among workers and staff in many state enterprises, who

entirely unaffected by such innovation. (Bernstein, "China in 1984: The year of Hong Kong," *AS* 25.1 [January 1985], 38.)

77 "Decision of the central committee of the CPC on reform of the economic structure," *BR* 27.44 (29 October 1984), III–XVI.

78 For analysis of the Hungarian influence on China's reforms, see Nina P. Halpern, "Learning from abroad: Chinese views of the East European economic experience, January 1977–June 1981," *Modern China* 1 (January 1985), 77–109.

79 For further analysis, see Christine Wong, "The second phase of economic reform in China," *Current History* 84.503 (September 1985), 260–63.

80 The birdcage analogy was first used by Chen Yun in the early 1980s. See David Bachman, "Differing visions of China's post-Mao economy: The ideas of Chen Yun, Deng Xiaoping, and Zhao Ziyang," *AS* 26.3 (March 1986), 297.

were reluctant to give up the security of their iron rice bowl and common pot. For all these reasons, by the winter of 1984–5 the plan still had not been put into effect in most urban areas.[81]

Even in the absence of widespread implementation, the 1984 reform decision exerted a strong psychological impact on urban residents throughout the country. Fearing that imminent decontrol of prices and the reduction of state subsidies would lead to a runup of retail prices on vital consumer goods and services, nervous urbanites in many areas, including Shanghai, Beijing, and Guangzhou, rushed to withdraw money from the bank to stock up on essential commodities. With demand sharply up and retail inventories depleted, production units saw a golden opportunity to raise prices; with demand and prices both rising, output and profits increased, putting more money into circulation, which led to an even greater upsurge in consumer demand, which led to still further retail shortages. The result was the beginning of an inflationary spiral in which the *fear* of rising prices was mother to the *fact* – a classic self-fulfilling prophecy under capitalism.[82]

Coincidental with the mounting economic insecurity of late 1984, there occurred a sudden, sharp spurt in urban private business activity. For various reasons, including official government encouragement and the demonstration effect of private entrepreneurs who had grown prosperous without suffering adverse political consequences, large numbers of urbanites now embarked on the road of private business.[83]

Alongside the burgeoning army of petit-bourgeois *getihu* (individual households engaged in small-scale domestic trade), a wholly new category of upscale, quasi-private urban entrepreneurs now began to appear. These were the so-called *gaogan zidi,* children and other blood relatives of high-level cadres whose family connections gave them excellent financial and commercial contacts throughout the Party and state bureaucracies. Such people were strategically positioned to take full advantage of the government's liberalized commercial policies and credit controls, enabling them to set up new trading companies, secure business loans, and establish supply and marketing net-

81 On the implementation of the 1984 enterprise reforms and their implications for factory management, see Yves Chevrier, "Micropolitics and the factory director responsibility system, 1984–1987," in Deborah Davis and Ezra F. Vogel, eds., *Chinese society on the eve of Tiananmen,* 109–33.

82 The earliest account of this inflationary surge that I have come across appears in *Zhongguo zhichun* (China Spring), December 1984, in *ICM,* March 1985, 4–7.

83 The number of urban private businesses reportedly doubled in the last half of 1984 and then doubled again in 1985. Prominent among the groups drawn into private business in this period were unemployed youths, former Red Guards, ex-prisoners, laid-off workers from other enterprises, disabled people, moonlighting state employees, pensioners seeking to supplement their incomes, and others. See Thomas Gold, "Urban private business and China's reforms," in Baum, ed., *Reform and reaction . . . ,* 90–2.

works.[84] Within a matter of months, China's overprivileged *gaogan zidi* began to wheel and deal on a scale not seen since before the revolution.[85]

As a result of the confluence of these various reform-related developments, China's economy began to overheat seriously in the fall and winter of 1984–5.[86] The money supply increased by almost 40 percent in the last quarter of 1984 (compared with the corresponding quarter of the previous year), and industrial wages and bonuses rose 19 percent. Bank loans were also up a steep 29 percent, while foreign exchange reserves plummeted, the result of a wave of big-ticket foreign imports. With the rate of inflation approaching double digits in some Chinese cities for the first time since the early 1950s, consumer unrest now became a cause for concern. The potential gravity of the problem was conveyed in a comment made by a Chinese housewife to a visiting journalist early in 1985: "My mother says that ten years ago China was in chaos, but Mao kept prices stable. She says now China is stable, but prices are in chaos."[87]

The seriousness of such concerns was acknowledged by Zhao Ziyang in his report to the third session of the Sixth NPC in March 1985. Noting that the "temporary difficulties" of an overheated, unbalanced economy could not be ignored, Zhao admitted that a major source of difficulty lay in the fact that "we lack experience in restructuring an entire economy." Notwithstanding such inexperience, Zhao announced the government's intention to stay the course with respect to the main components of structural reform.[88]

As it turned out, inflation, a runaway money supply, and an upsurge in unregulated business activity were only the tip of a rather ominous economic iceberg. Just beneath the surface, another, potentially even more debilitating, side effect of China's hybrid structural reforms was beginning to make itself felt: an epidemic of brazen, high-stakes economic profiteering and corruption, much of it committed by *gaogan zidi*.

84 The appearance of a group of cadre-connected, quasi-private entrepreneurs, though new to the PRC, was by no means unprecedented in China. In late imperial and republican times, entrepreneurial success was often a function of one's personal or family ties to officialdom. See Albert Feuerwerker, *China's early industrialization: Sheng Hsuan-huai (1844–1916) and mandarin enterprise*. On the recrudescence of this phenomenon in the 1980s, see Dorothy Solinger, "Urban entrepreneurs and the state: The merger of state and society" (unpublished paper presented at the conference "State and society in China: The consequences of reform," Claremont-McKenna College, 16–17 February 1990).

85 The phenomenon of high-level cadres, their relatives, and their friends setting up trading companies was quite widespread. In February 1985, CDIC vice-chairman Bo Yibo claimed that in one province alone, Liaoning, more than 900 *gaogan*-affiliated companies were established between the summer of 1984 and the spring of 1985. See *I&S* 21.4 (April 1985), 1.

86 The following discussion draws on Richard Baum, "China in 1985: The greening of the revolution," *AS* 26.1 (January 1986), 31–53.

87 *Los Angeles Times* (hereafter, *LAT*), 4 February 1985.

88 Zhao's address appears in *BR* 28.16 (22 April 1985), III–XV.

Crime and corruption: The Achilles heel of reform

Due to their bloated administrative bureaucracies, chronic shortages of consumer goods, and informal networks of "back-door" clientelist ties, Leninist systems tend to spawn a relatively high degree of corruption.[89] In China, although economic crime and corruption were hardly unknown during the Maoist era, their severity was limited by the relatively small financial rewards and relatively high social and political costs involved.[90] Now, however, in the more permissive, "to-get-rich-is-glorious" environment of postreform China, the cost–benefit calculus changed dramatically; now there was a manifold increase in both the *incentives* to engage in corruption (in the form of substantially greater economic payoffs and diminished ethical constraints) and the *opportunities* to do so (presented by the rapid proliferation of deregulated, contract-based commercial exchanges). With the stakes thus raised and the transaction costs lowered, corruption and economic crime began to flourish.

One important new source of corruption in the postreform era was the hybrid nature of China's partially restructured economy. Writing in December 1984, a dissident Chinese intellectual foresaw with uncanny accuracy how a series of emerging gaps – in productivity, in pricing, and in performance – between the new market-regulated sectors of the economy and the old centrally planned sectors would inevitably give rise to a plethora of illicit commercial transactions. With scattered islands of free-market autonomy floating in a sea of socialist planning, the clear result, he predicted, would be a tremendous upsurge in economic malfeasance and back-doorism:

> Some of the reforms will have the effect of loosening the constraints on [smaller, nonstrategic] enterprises, leaving their management in the hands of workers and staff. The products of these enterprises will be regulated by the market mechanism. However, major enterprises such as . . . those dealing with steel, oil and electricity will still fall under the centrally planned economy. It can be predicted that the pace of their development will fall behind that of the [market-regulated] enterprises. . . . Hence, energy resources and certain raw materials which were already in short supply before [the advent of reform] will tend to be in even shorter supply afterwards. When there is not enough to go around, the [market-regulated] enterprises will use all kinds of methods (including bribery) to get hold of energy resources and raw materi-

89 On the generic sources of clientelism and corruption in Leninist systems, see Kenneth Jowitt, "Soviet neotraditionalism: The political corruption of a Leninist regime," *Soviet Studies* 35.3 (July 1983), 275–97.

90 Under Mao, the Party's egalitarian, antibourgeois ethos made it extremely risky for anyone to engage in the conspicuous pursuit or consumption of wealth. What corruption did exist tended to be localized, unorganized, and limited in magnitude; much of it involved cadres extorting donations of various kinds, including sexual favors, from members of their work units. For a comparison of pre- and postreform patterns of corruption in China, see Connie Squires Meaney, "Market reform and disintegrative corruption in urban China," in Baum, ed., *Reform and reaction* . . . , 124–43.

als destined for large enterprises under the state plan. The income of the staff and workers in the large enterprises which are subject to guidance planning will not be as high as those working in [market-regulated] enterprises. It will be difficult to avoid a situation wherein certain staff members receive a "secondary salary" distributed in private by the [market-regulated] enterprises, in order to bribe the units to open wide their "back doors." This kind of unhealthy practice will increase and, if it does not attract notice, will become ever more prevalent. . . . Economic crime will increase by leaps and bounds.[91]

In other words (to use Chen Yun's birdcage analogy), once the bird of market-driven economic activity was permitted freer flight, it would readily exploit and enlarge back doors in its socialist cage, thereby undermining the structural integrity of the entire system.[92]

In addition to structurally induced corruption, economic crime of a different sort began to flourish in China's special economic zones and open coastal cities in the winter and spring of 1984–5. In these enclaves of commercial laissez-faire, a wave of speculation, smuggling, profiteering, and currency manipulation by *gaogan zidi* and other quasi-private entrepreneurs resulted in a series of major financial losses to the state. In one widely publicized scandal, military cadres and their offspring in the duty-free port of Hainan Island were arrested after having floated hard-currency bank loans and credits in the amount of US$1.25 billion for the purpose of importing 89,000 Toyota automobiles, 2.9 million television sets, 252,000 videocassette recorders, and 122,000 motorcycles, all destined for resale, at a high profit, on the domestic market. As a result of this and other unauthorized transactions, China's foreign exchange reserves plummeted by more than one-third, almost US$6 billion, in the first six months of 1985.[93]

Responding to such developments, the Party's chief rectification overseer, CDIC vice-chairman Bo Yibo, sounded a series of stern warnings in the spring and summer of 1985 against Party members and cadres engaging in improper commercial activities. Among the common practices cited were establishment and operation of dummy companies (*pibao gongsi;* lit., "briefcase companies") for private profit; black market buying and selling of foreign exchange certificates; unauthorized sale of lottery tickets and "bonus

91 *Zhongguo zhichun,* December 1984, in *ICM,* March 1985, 4–7.

92 For analysis of the design flaws inherent in the CC's October 1984 blueprint for a hybrid "socialist commodity economy," see Jan Prybyla, "Why China's economic reforms fail," *AS* 29.11 (November 1989), 1017–32.

93 Despite the subsequent arrest of the principal figures involved in the Hainan import scandal, it is not at all clear that any serious criminal acts were involved. The loans, foreign exchange transfers, import licenses, and commodity resale arrangements were all, strictly speaking, legal, though they were clearly not proper. This case illustrates how loopholes in reform laws and policies enabled unscrupulous profiteers (often *gaogan zidi*) to manipulate the system to their advantage. The Hainan scandal is documented in *JSND* 4 (1985) and *XH,* 31 July 1985. A collection of press reports on the upsurge in cadre corruption and economic crime in this period appears in *ICM,* June 1985, 10–17.

coupons"; distribution of money and goods under false pretexts; squandering of public funds on lavish feasts and gift giving; and the practice of nepotism and cronyism in personnel appointments and promotions. Bo Yibo attributed the rising incidence of such practices to a general decline in "Party spirit" (*dang jingshen*) among CCP members, many of whom allegedly "put money above everything else" and "seek personal gain by taking advantage of their authority."[94]

"What merits our grave concern," said Bo Yibo in October, "is that the principle of commodity exchange has permeated the political life of some party organs." Noting that indiscipline had become "very serious" in some Party organizations, he argued that a substantial number of CCP members and cadres were unqualified for membership. Calling such people "black sheep who have the appearance of party members," Bo stated that their behavior had infuriated the people, who "demand strongly that the party . . . and the people's courts take resolute action to punish" the offenders.[95]

Bo's demand for people's courts to play a stronger role in punishing corrupt Party members and *gaogan zidi* represented a major shift away from the CCP's traditional emphasis on punishment via internal Party discipline. Indeed, Bo Yibo's reference to mounting public fury over the lack of legal accountability of Party members proved highly sensitive within the Party.[96] Although a certain number of aberrant municipal, county, and provincial-level cadres and relatives of cadres were subsequently brought to trial and sentenced to prison terms for economic crimes, generally amid great fanfare, such cases generally involved extraordinarily blatant or heinous offenses. The vast majority of ordinary cases of cadre corruption, and cases involving people very high up in the leadership hierarchy, continued to be dealt with behind closed doors.[97]

94 Bo Yibo's various anticorruption commentaries appear in *SWB/FE* 7897 (12 March 1985), 7942 (4 May 1985), 7993 (3 July 1985), and 8085 (18 October 1985).

95 Ibid.

96 Beginning in 1984–5, the issue of corrupt *gaogan zidi* became a significant factor in factional politics within the Party. For example, Hu Yaobang reportedly raised the ire of several senior Party leaders, including Hu Qiaomu and Peng Zhen, by suggesting that their children should be investigated for corruption. During the Tiananmen demonstrations in May 1989, there were frequent references in wall posters and parade banners to Deng Xiaoping's son, Deng Pufang, who was widely reported to have enriched himself through a series of lucrative commercial transactions. Also in May 1989, Zhao Ziyang reportedly ran afoul of senior Party leaders when, in an attempt to shore up the Party's sagging public image, he volunteered to turn his own sons over to a special tribunal for criminal investigation. Zhao never had the chance to follow through with his offer; he was removed from power within a week.

97 The highest-level *gaogan zidi* to be judicially punished in this period was the daughter of Ye Fei, former commander of the Chinese navy. In 1986 she was sentenced to seventeen years in prison for her role in the Hainan import scandal. Other relatives of high-level cadres, including the offspring of Peng Zhen and Hu Qiaomu, were reportedly investigated for corruption in this period but were spared criminal prosecution because of their ostensible "inexperience." On the protection of the children of

Responding to strong calls for action to eliminate the spreading cancer of economic crime and corruption, the CDIC in 1985 shifted the main focus of its second-stage rectification drive. The first stage had stressed rooting out remnant Maoists, whateverists, and other assorted three kinds of people. Now, several months into the second stage (which had begun in the winter of 1984–5), the emphasis shifted to the elimination of a series of "new unhealthy tendencies" – tendencies that sprang not from remnant Cultural Revolution ultra-leftism, but from economic indiscipline, opportunism, and the pervasive "get rich quick" mentality that had begun to infect the country, and the Party, since the introduction of economic reform. With that shift, the sensitive directional indicators of the *fang–shou* cycle began to oscillate once more, moving back toward the reaffirmation of traditional, conservative values.

The battle over Marxism and capitalism

As it had in the past, the conservative ideological revival of early 1985 brought with it renewed expressions of concern for preserving the doctrinal integrity of Marxism. During the heyday of entrepreneurial liberalism in the fall of 1984, the position of orthodox Marxism had ostensibly been attenuated, among other things, by Deng Xiaoping's widely quoted statement to the effect that "a little capitalism isn't necessarily harmful."[98] By autumn's end, a mini-storm had erupted over the issue of whether (and how) Marxism could be creatively enriched to prevent it from becoming totally anachronistic and irrelevant to China's current needs.

The controversy began when the *People's Daily* declared, in a front-page commentary published on 7 December, that "since Marx has already been dead for 101 years . . . some of his assumptions are not necessarily appropriate." Calling the worship of individual words and sentences from Marxist texts "childish ignorance," the commentary said it was unrealistic to expect the works of Marx and Lenin, written in the nineteenth century, to "solve today's problems." A few days later, a Chinese government official went a bit further, asserting that "most people today don't care whether something is capitalist or socialist. They just want their lives to improve. The details are a matter for the theoreticians."[99] At this point a leading Party theoretician, Su

high-level cadres, see Stanley Rosen, "China in 1986: A year of consolidation," *AS* 27.1 (January 1987), 36–7. On the issue of intra-Party resistance to legal accountability for CCP members, see James D. Seymour, "Cadre accountability to the law," *AJCA* 21 (January 1989), 1–27.

98 Deng's statement was reportedly made at a meeting of the CAC in October 1984. See *New York Times* (hereafter, *NYT*), 13 January 1985.

99 Quoted in *NYT*, 17 December 1984.

Shaozhi, entered the fray and proclaimed bluntly: "There are no Marxist quotations for what we are doing now."[100] Reacting to such developments, a few foreign journalists were moved to speculate that Marxism had virtually been abandoned in China.[101]

In the event, such obituaries proved wishful thinking. In a rare editorial retraction, the *People's Daily* informed its readers that a mistake had been made in a key sentence of its 7 December commentary, and that the sentence in question should have stated that Marxist–Leninist works could not "solve *all of* today's problems."[102] In discussing the source of the "error," Chinese officials informed a group of foreign journalists that the original commentary had been flawed because it did "not sufficiently stress the continuing importance of Marxist principles."[103]

Mounting conservative pressures soon caused Deng Xiaoping to back away somewhat from his October assessment of the harmlessness of "a little capitalism." In a 1985 New Year's message to the Chinese people, Deng continued to defend his tolerance of a small amount of private enterprise on the grounds that without it, China would not be able "to catch up with the level of the developed countries within fifty years." But he now tempered such positive assessments with a candid acknowledgment that "some old comrades . . . can't bear [the idea that] after they fought all their lives for socialism, for communism, suddenly capitalism is coming back." In an attempt to mollify these old comrades, Deng ruled out the possibility of a wholesale departure from socialism, insisting that the "basic things will still be state-owned" in the twenty-first century.[104]

Deng's reassurance failed to stem the swelling ideological backlash, which was now being fueled by fresh reports of corruption, black marketeering, smuggling, and economic mismanagement. Such reports prompted Party conservatives to issue new allegations of moral degeneration.[105] Ever sensitive to such criticism, Deng continued to give ground. Speaking at a national science conference in March, he acknowledged that "some people are worried that China will turn capitalist. . . . We cannot say that they are worried for nothing."[106]

100 Quoted in ibid.

101 For example, soon after the 7 December *RMRB* commentary, the Associated Press sent out an "urgent" dispatch from Beijing under the headline "China abandons Marx." See also "Did Marx fall, or was he pushed?" *The Economist*, 15 December 1984.

102 *RMRB*, 8 December 1984 (emphasis added).

103 *NYT*, 11 December 1984. Reportedly, the offending sentence in the original commentary had been drawn directly from a talk given by Hu Yaobang at the end of November. See *ICM*, January 1985, 1–3.

104 *RMRB*, 1 January 1985.

105 See, e.g., *BR* 28.7 (13 February 1985), 4; *NYT*, 23 February and 31 March 1985.

106 *BR* 28.11 (18 March 1985), 15–16.

The attack on bourgeois liberalism

With the second stage of Party consolidation now focusing on the rectification of cadres afflicted with spiritual disorders of the get-rich-quick variety, conservatives soon broadened their ideological offensive. One of their principal targets was bourgeois liberalism in the mass media.

As on previous occasions, the lead role in the new offensive was played by Deng Liqun. Deng had reportedly been irritated by some recent liberal comments on the subject of press freedom made by Hu Yaobang and two of his key supporters, Hu Qili and Hu Jiwei.[107] At a meeting of the Party's Central Secretariat in early February, Deng Liqun reportedly pressed Hu Yaobang to reaffirm the party's traditional norms concerning obedience of the mass media to the line, principles, and policies of the CCP. Bowing to pressure (some of it presumably applied by Deng Xiaoping), Hu Yaobang conceded that the proper role of the official media was to serve as "mouthpiece of the party," though he hastened to add that the media should also faithfully reflect the views of the people.[108] At the same meeting, Hu gave even more ground to Deng Liqun and the conservatives, calling on the mass media to stop being so "gloomy" in their coverage of China's domestic situation. In general, he said, "newspapers should devote eighty percent of their space to achievements and the positive side, and only twenty percent to shortcomings and criticism." Continuing his tactical retreat, Hu conceded that a recent proliferation of unauthorized liberal tabloids (*xiaobao*) in several Chinese cities represented a harmful tendency that should be "boycotted and opposed."[109]

Deng Liqun's hard-line literary policies resulted in renewed political pressure being brought to bear on China's critical intellectuals. In March 1985, a

107 In December 1984, at the Fourth Congress of the Chinese Writers' Association, Hu Qili had stressed that "literary creation must be free" and that journalists and writers must not be subject to political litmus tests or discrimination (*NYT,* 31 December 1984). At the same meeting, Hu Yaobang said that people should no longer talk about eliminating spiritual pollution and combating bourgeois liberalization. See *Baixing* (hereafter, *BX*) 138 (16 February 1987), 4. Hu Jiwei, who had been "reassigned" to work at the Educational and Cultural Committee of the NPC following his ouster from *RMRB* in late 1983, made a similar plea for creative freedom at a meeting of journalists and scholars held in Shanghai early in 1985. See *ZM* 91 (1 May 1985) in *ICM,* July 1985, 1–10.

108 *SWB/FE* 7927 (17 April 1985); see also *ZM* 91 (1 May 1985). As mentioned earlier, it was not unusual in China for the losers in a policy dispute to display their fidelity to the Party line by articulating the policy of the winners.

109 Ibid. At this point in Hu's talk, Deng Liqun reportedly interrupted the general secretary with a sharp dig at Hu's liberal supporters in the official media, pointing out that some of the tabloids in question had actually been set up, financed, and run by the Party's own newspapers. Presumably, Deng had in mind such underground journals as *Yecao* (Weeds), published in Guangzhou, which had run two articles highly critical of him, calling him, among other things, a "sycophantic yes-man" who was out to "curry favor with Deng Xiaoping" (*Yecao,* February 1984, in *ICM,* October 1984, 9).

serialized essay written by investigative journalist Liu Binyan, entitled "A second kind of loyalty," was banned from publication, as was the tabloid that had featured it.[110] In this controversial essay, Liu disparaged the type of loyalty displayed by "obedient tools" of the Party who always agreed with their superiors and compulsively glorified the Party's line and policies. In place of such mindless obeisance, Liu proposed a higher standard of fealty: individual moral conscience and the courage to follow it. Among Party traditionalists, this theme did not prove popular. Nor did the ideas of writer Wang Ruowang, who, like Liu Binyan, had repeatedly asserted the primacy of the demands of individual conscience over the mandates of the state. Wang's works, too, were now banned from publication.[111]

Guerrilla warfare between Deng Liqun and Hu Yaobang continued for several months. In mid-April 1985, Deng (with the help of his patron, Hu Qiaomu) succeeded in embarrassing Hu Yaobang by arranging to have the full text of the general secretary's February remarks concerning restrictions on press freedom published in the *People's Daily* – without Hu's prior approval, while the general secretary was away on a visit to Australia and New Zealand.[112] Seeking to even the score, upon his return to China, Hu Yaobang gave a lengthy (and at times seemingly indiscreet) interview to a friendly Hong Kong journalist, Lu Keng. Responding to the interviewer's query about his adversarial relationship with Deng Liqun, Hu obliquely damned Deng with faint praise, noting that Deng was a man of great talent who should not be held solely responsible for all the shortcomings and mistakes in the Party's ideological work.[113]

Not to be outdone, Deng Liqun launched a broadside of his own, zeroing in once again on liberals in the mass media and their supporters in the Party hierarchy. In one statement, he noted with deep alarm that "some people" in the Party and the media treat as outmoded ideas such hallowed CCP traditions as plain living, sacrifice, and hard struggle. In another statement, he observed ruefully that under the onslaught of monetary transactions, China's "spiritual pillar" had been seriously eroded, to the point where "it has now become inadvisable to advocate . . . communist morality."[114] Deng's tactics apparently had a certain effect, for at the end of spring, third-echelon liberal Hu Qili, who only a few months earlier had championed total creative freedom for writers and artists, spoke out on the need to "criticise, educate

110 *I&S* 23.5 (May 1987), 48–56. The first installment of "A second kind of loyalty" (*Di'erzhong zhongcheng*) appeared in the March 1985 issue of *Kaituo* (Opening Up). The issue was withdrawn from circulation, and subsequent installments were banned by the Beijing authorities.

111 See Kyna Rubin, "Keeper of the flame: Wang Ruowang as moral critic of the state," in Goldman et al., *China's intellectuals and the state . . . ,*" 249.

112 *BX*, 1 June 1985, in *SWB/FE* 7970 (6 June 1985).

113 Ibid.; see also *ICM*, August 1985, 5–8.

114 *SWB/FE* 7973 (10 June 1985).

and help" those misguided Party members who, "having lost their socialist and communist convictions and ideals, have even advocated Western 'democracy' and 'freedom' and advertised the bourgeoisie's liberal thinking."[115]

Notwithstanding Deng Liqun's heavy-handedness and Hu Qili's apparently softening spine, Hu Yaobang was able to enjoy the last laugh, at least for the moment: Early in the summer, without comment or explanation, Deng Liqun was removed from his position as director of the CC's propaganda department; named to replace him was Hu ally Zhu Houze, a strong advocate of creative freedom for artists and writers.[116]

The struggle over SEZs and the open policy

Central to the bubbling furor over bourgeois liberalism was mounting conservative disillusionment with the free-wheeling economic and social environment of China's fourteen open coastal cities and five special economic zones (SEZs), in particular the thriving South China township of Shenzhen, near the Hong Kong border. Shenzhen's close proximity to, and increasingly intimate financial and social contacts with, the largest capitalist entrepot in East Asia made it an especially tempting target for those who had serious questions about the nature and implications of China's wide-ranging reforms.

At the beginning of 1985, the Chinese press had been filled with favorable publicity concerning Shenzhen's "remarkable progress" as a model development zone.[117] But in early spring, new concerns were voiced over a rising tide of illicit commercial activities, including foreign exchange laundering, fraudulent bank loans, excessive wage and bonus payments to workers and managers, smuggling, gambling, prostitution, and pornography.[118] As spring turned to summer, the attack grew sharper. Party theoretician Hu Qiaomu, speaking during a tour of the Xiamen SEZ in late June, warned against giving preferential treatment to foreigners in the SEZs. Citing the disastrous experience of the Qing dynasty in granting economic concessions to foreign powers in the late nineteenth century, Hu cautioned against giving up Chinese rights to outside interests, and he insisted that "foreign investment enterprises are not concessions; their inordinate demands cannot be given tacit consent."[119] Later in the summer, the irrepressible Deng Liqun

115 *SWB/FE* 8005 (17 July 1985).

116 Kyodo News Service (Tokyo), 12 July 1985. At the time, it was widely rumored (though never confirmed) that Deng Liqun's dismissal was related to his excessive criticism of Deng Xiaoping's open policy.

117 See, e.g., the five-part series "Reports from Shenzhen," in *BR* 27.47 (26 November 1984) through 28.6 (11 February 1985).

118 See, e.g., *FBIS*, 15 and 16 April and 15 July 1985; also *BR* 28.39 (30 September 1985), 5.

119 *SWB/FE* 7986 (25 June 1985).

joined the chorus, stating that all patriotic Chinese should "oppose the trend of worshipping things foreign and fawning on foreigners."[120]

The critics may have hoped to derail China's economic reforms by attacking them at their weakest link. Other major elements of the reform program, most notably the rural agricultural responsibility system, were less susceptible to challenge because of their visible contribution to the nation's economic growth and to the rising family incomes of the majority of China's 800 million rural dwellers. But the open policy was vulnerable to criticism on the highly sensitive issues of national autonomy and bourgeois corrosion. By pointing out the twin dangers of selling out the nation's sovereignty to foreigners and breathing too closely the toxic fumes of capitalism, conservatives could hope to cast sinister shadows on the propriety of the Zhao–Hu reform program.

Confronted with mounting economic difficulties and a rising conservative backlash, reformers began to give additional ground. Backing away from his earlier defense of the economic freedom and autonomy of the SEZs, Deng Xiaoping in early July declared that the SEZs were merely "an experiment" whose correctness "remains to be seen."[121] Concurrently, the Chinese government announced that ten of the fourteen coastal cities opened to foreign investors in the spring of 1984 would slow down the signing of new contracts with foreigners.[122]

But if Deng Xiaoping was willing to retreat a bit on the SEZs and open cities, he was clearly not prepared to backtrack on the general principles of his open policy. In October 1984 he had argued that the open policy was needed to overcome 300 years of impoverishment, backwardness, and ignorance caused by China's self-imposed isolation from the outside world.[123] Six months later, in the face of mounting furor over the spread of bourgeois corrosion along China's exposed eastern seaboard, Deng dug in his heels: "To open to the world is a fundamental policy for China," he asserted. "If there is to be any change in the policy, it will be that China's doors will be opened even wider."[124] Although the scope and limitations of the SEZ and open city experiments were thus negotiable, the open policy itself was not.

Reform of the PLA

In the midst of the swirling ideological currents of 1984–5, an important series of structural reforms was carried out affecting China's military establishment. Long considered a bastion of traditional Maoist thinking, the military

120 *XH*, 30 August 1985. For analysis of the Shenzhen experience, see *ZM* 94 (1 August 1985).
121 *FBIS*, 15 July 1985. 122 *NYT*, 4 August 1985. 123 *NYT*, 21 February 1985.
124 Quoted in *BR* 28.13 (1 April 1985), 15.

high command had, since the late 1970s, stubbornly resisted implementing the Third Plenum's reform agenda. Each time reformers had attempted to make inroads, military pressure had forced them to back off.[125] Frustrated by such intransigence, Deng Xiaoping had on at least one occasion referred to members of the PLA's senior officer corps as "undisciplined, arrogant, extravagant, and lazy";[126] and in a 1981 commentary on ideological problems within the army, Deng claimed that continued ultra-leftist factionalism had done great harm to the army's prestige and credibility.[127]

Following initiation of the Party rectification campaign in the late fall of 1983, the PLA was periodically criticized in the mass media for leftist tendencies.[128] When the rectification drive entered its second stage in the early winter of 1984–5, pressures on the PLA began to increase noticeably. Reformers now brought two main weapons to bear on the army: retirement and reorganization. In late December it was announced that forty senior general staff officers had opted to retire – the largest top-level group retirement in PLA history. In an interview that accompanied the announcement, Deng Xiaoping said that he "hoped to see more open-minded people in the army." Most of the retiring officers were over the age of sixty; several had served as section chiefs, equivalent to the rank of lieutenant general and above.[129]

This pruning of the general staff was followed, in early January 1985, by an announcement of substantial cutbacks in military budgets and manpower. PLA Chief of Staff Yang Dezhi, a Deng Xiaoping ally, explained the cuts as being vital to the success of the nation's overall modernizaton drive. In order to reduce military outlays and pave the way for the much-needed technological upgrading of the armed forces, Yang argued, it was necessary to streamline the PLA and reduce noncombatant personnel.[130]

In a bold reorganization measure, several hundred thousand PLA security troops were demobilized and reassigned to a state security force known as the "People's Armed Police." In a related move, the PLA Railway Corps, long

125 See Richard D. Nethercut, "Deng and the gun: Party–military relations in the People's Republic of China," *AS* 22.8 (August 1982), 691–704. For a somewhat different interpretation, which sees Deng as having asserted effective control over the army by the late 1970s, see Ellis Joffe, "Party and military in China: Professionalism in command?" *POC*, 32.5 (September–October 1983), 56–63.

126 Quoted in *NYT*, 6 March 1985.

127 Deng Xiaoping, "On opposing wrong ideological trends" (27 March 1981), in *Selected works of Deng Xiaoping (1975–1982)*.

128 See, e.g., *RMRB*, 30 April, 20 May, and 9 October 1984; *Jiefangjun bao* (hereafter, *JFJB*), 8 and 18 May 1984. The antileftist criticisms followed the exposure of serious corruption in a PLA tank division under the command of leftist general Li Desheng. See Alastair I. Johnston, "Party rectification in the People's Liberation Army, 1983–87," *CQ* 112 (December 1987), 611 (n. 57).

129 *JFJB*, 22 December 1984; *NYT*, 30 December 1984 and 20 April 1985; Johnston, "Party rectification."

130 *CD*, 3 January 1985. China's military budget for 1984 was estimated at RMB 18 billion *yuan* (US$6.4 billion), down from 22 billion in 1979, the year of the Sino-Vietnamese border war. See *NYT*, 3 January 1985.

known for its loyalty to Maoist ideas, was placed under civilian jurisdiction. Finally, thousands of factories engaged in defense production were turned over to the manufacture of nonmilitary consumer goods such as motorcycles and electronic appliances.[131]

Predictably, many aging veterans of the PLA's earliest guerrilla struggles, who now staffed the upper reaches of the military hierarchy, were unmoved by the logic of such reforms. In their speeches, they now began to refer defensively to the importance of giving "careful consideration" to any changes that might undermine the nation's military preparedness. Ignoring such precautionary pleas, the reformers pushed on, with Deng Xiaoping's clear blessing. In a highly symbolic gesture laced with deep political overtones, it was announced that the streamlined PLA would soon be outfitted with new uniforms, complete with insignias of rank, which had been abolished at Mao Zedong's behest in 1965, on the eve of the Cultural Revolution.[132]

Shortly after the 1985 Lunar New Year, a number of additional military reorganization measures were introduced. In early March, it was announced that 47,000 officers, approximately 10 percent of the entire officer corps, would be retired before the end of 1986, with 20,000 to 30,000 additional officers slated for retirement by 1990. In disclosing this decision, the official *Xinhua* News Agency said that the officers to be demobilized had joined the PLA during the anti-Japanese and civil wars of the 1930s and 1940s. Most were said to have attained junior rank up to regimental level – the equivalent of major – or lower. To help mollify the new retirees, a program of improved military pensions and welfare benefits, including new housing, was instituted.[133]

In April, while on a visit to New Zealand, Hu Yaobang announced that within the next year the Chinese army would be subject to conventional force reductions totaling 1 million men, approximately 25 percent of the current troop level. The money saved was to be earmarked for the technological modernization of China's antiquated weapons systems and for upgrading the professional qualifications of the officer corps.[134]

In May, Hu Yaobang was asked by a Hong Kong journalist whether disgruntled military critics of reform, including controversial Northeast regional commander General Li Desheng (whom the interviewer characterized as "a nail that can't be pulled out"), might use troops under their command to resist further military cutbacks, including their own forced retirement. Hu responded that such a thing would be "absolutely impossible" and could "never occur in our party." Responding to a question about whether General

131 *NYT*, 20 April 1985. 132 Ibid.; *FBIS*, 14 January 1985.
133 *XH*, 5 March 1985; *NYT*, 6 March 1985.
134 *Reuters* (Wellington), 19 April 1985; *NYT*, 20 April 1985.

Li Desheng was untouchable, Hu answered cryptically: "Outsiders *think* he cannot be removed."[135]

In early June, the other shoe dropped. At a meeting of the Party's MAC, chaired by Deng Xiaoping, it was decided to "readjust" the regional command structure of the PLA, consolidating the eleven existing military regions into seven and pensioning off several superannuated regional commanders, including the "untouchable" general, Li Desheng. The *Xinhua* News Agency dispatch that announced the shakeup pointedly noted that younger, better-educated, and professionally more competent officers had been selected to succeed the retiring commanders. By the end of summer, the readjustment had resulted in a full 50 percent reduction in the number of senior officers in the seven newly consolidated regional commands and a 24 percent cut in the number of ranking officers at the PLA general staff headquarters and its political and logistics departments.[136]

The influence of the PLA was further reduced by a series of top-level CCP leadership changes carried out at the end of summer 1985. At the Twelfth CC's Fourth Plenum, held in mid-September, six veteran military leaders, including the redoubtable Li Desheng, retired from the Politburo, leaving only a token contingent of military figures to sit on the Party's highest decision-making body. To all intents and purposes, it seemed that the reformers had succeeded in bringing the PLA to heel.[137]

The third echelon arrives

The retirement of the six Politburo military veterans represented only a small fraction of a much larger turnover in party leadership that took place in September 1985. After three years of alternately persuading, cajoling, and demanding that elderly cadres step down in favor of younger blood, Deng

135 *BX*, 1 June 1985, in *SWB/FE* 7970 (6 June 1985). Verbal indiscretions such as this one reportedly brought rebukes from several of Hu Yaobang's senior colleagues. When Hu was dismissed from office in January 1987, one of the reasons given was his penchant for talking out of school, without CC authorization. See "The 'resignation' of Hu Yaobang."

136 *XH*, 11 June and 27 October 1985; *NYT*, 11 and 23 June 1985; *XH*, 27 October 1985; *LAT*, 28 October 1985. Many of the regional commanders and field officers who survived the readjustment had strong career ties to Deng Xiaoping through their common service in the PLA's Second Field Army. See Li Kwok Sing, "Deng Xiaoping and the 2nd field army," *China Review* (Hong Kong), January 1990, 40–1.

137 In addition to Li Desheng (sixty-nine), the other five military retirees were Marshals Ye Jianying (eighty-nine), Nie Rongzhen (eighty-six), and Xu Xiangqian (eighty-six) and Generals Wang Zhen (seventy-seven), Song Renqiong (seventy-six), and Wei Guoqing (seventy-two). To help ease the pain of retirement, all were appointed to the CAC. Among the handful of military leaders who remained on the Politburo were longtime Deng Xiaoping associates Yang Shangkun (seventy-eight) and Yang Dezhi (seventy-five). For a slightly different interpretation of these events, see *I&S* 21.12 (December 1985), 76–92.

Xiaoping's youth movement finally reached fruition.[138] Altogether, sixty-four full and alternate members of the CC announced their retirement at the Fourth Plenum. With three exceptions, all were over the age of sixty-seven, including forty-four septuagenarians and seven octogenarians. Also included were one member of the Politburo Standing Committee (PSC) (Ye Jianying), nine ordinary Politburo members, and twenty-six military men.[139] Seven superannuated Politburo members failed to retire at the September plenum: Deng Xiaoping, Chen Yun, Li Xiannian, Peng Zhen, Yang Shangkun, Hu Qiaomu, and Yang Dezhi.

Ye Jianying's resignation from the Politburo SC reduced that body's membership from six to five, creating a virtual deadlock between the committee's first-echelon traditionalists (Chen Yun and Li Xiannian) and its second-echelon liberals (Hu Yaobang and Zhao Ziyang) – with Deng Xiaoping as the crucial swing vote.[140]

To replace the retiring CC members, a special "national party conference" was convened on 18 September, immediately following adjournment of the Fourth Plenum.[141] Of the sixty-four new CC members and alternates selected at this conference, the overwhelming majority belonged to the third echelon. Seventy-six percent were college educated; their average age was just over fifty.[142]

138 In his October 1984 speech to recent retirees on the CAC, Deng had noted that "It is not easy to ask older comrades to give up their posts. But we must; and we must stay this course. If the old do not vacate their posts, . . . how can our cause thrive?" (*BR* 28.9 [4 March 1985], 15).

139 In addition to the aforementioned six military leaders, the civilian Politburo retirees were Deng Yingchao (eighty-four), Ulanfu (seventy-nine), and Zhang Tingfa (sixty-eight). It was widely rumored that among the many inducements offered to elderly Politburo members to ease their retirement was the appointment of their offspring or other relatives to high-level administrative or commercial positions. See *I&S* 21.12 (December 1985), 25, 67.

140 At the time of the Fourth Plenum, it was widely rumored that the conservative group had wanted to promote old comrade Peng Zhen to the SC to replace Ye Jianying, whereas Deng and Hu Yaobang had preferred to add third-echelon newcomer Hu Qili. According to these reports, neither side would budge, so no one was selected (see ibid., 23–4). According to reports widely circulated in Beijing in late 1985, Peng's prestige and popularity among the people of Beijing had been badly damaged by his involvement in a plan to raze a large residential neighborhood near the Great Hall of the People to build an expensive new municipal government complex.

141 The convening of a special Party conference represented another of Deng Xiaoping's many ad hoc improvisations. The Party's constitution stipulates that the CC is elected by the National Party Congress, but the Thirteenth Congress was not scheduled to meet for another two years. Not wanting to wait, Deng resorted to creative institution making. When asked why the business of replacing old leaders couldn't be put off until the Thirteenth Congress, Party spokesman Zhu Muzhi said, "We cannot wait two years. . . . By then some comrades' state of health might have changed. . . . It is better to make gradual changes now" (*WHB*, 19 September 1985).

142 *XH*, 22 September 1985. The movement to promote educated young people to leadership roles was also reflected in Party recruitment figures in the mid-1980s. From 1984 to 1987, the proportion of party members with at least a senior high school education rose from 17.8 to 28.5 percent; in the same period, almost a million college graduates were added to the Party roster. See Stanley Rosen, "The Chinese communist party and Chinese society: Popular attitudes toward party membership and the party's image," *AJCA* 24 (July 1990), tables 1 and 3 and passim.

At the Fifth Plenum of the Twelfth CC, held immediately following the national work conference, six newcomers were named to the Politburo, including two men tabbed by informed sources as likely successors to Premier Zhao and General-Secretary Hu, respectively. The first, Vice-Premier Li Peng (fifty-seven), was a Soviet-trained, Russian-speaking engineer with experience both in the electric power industry and as deputy finance minister. He was the adopted son of outgoing Politburo member Deng Yingchao and the late Premier Zhou Enlai. The second major Politburo newcomer, Central Secretariat member Hu Qili, (fifty-six), was a protégé of Hu Yaobang, under whose leadership he had previously toiled as a cadre in the Party's youth league.[143]

For all the third echelon's highly acclaimed advances, Party traditionalists nevertheless managed to avoid a clean sweep in the leadership changes of September 1985. In addition to the carryover of certain members of the Politburo old guard, conservatives won two other skirmishes: First, despite reported opposition from the Party's liberal wing, Deng Liqun was permitted to retain his seat on the Central Secretariat; second, the PLA high command refused to ratify Deng Xiaoping's choice of Hu Yaobang to succeed him as chairman of the Party's MAC.[144]

Reflecting the mixed outcome of the September 1985 Party meetings, Deng Xiaoping's closing address contained a strong, measured appeal to all factions to close ranks in pursuit of the twin objectives of reform and socialist spiritual civilization. Calling on "old comrades" to overcome dogmatic tendencies and "new comrades" to resist the temptations of bourgeois liberalization, which he now ominously equated with "taking the capitalist road," China's senior leader sought once more to chart a middle course between the Scylla of ultra-leftism and the Charybdis of spiritual pollution.[145]

Social contradictions intensify

For a variety of reasons, Deng's middle course became progressively harder to steer. Despite the senior leader's periodic pleas for unity and stability, a series

143 Other new faces in the Politburo included vice-premier Tian Jiyun (fifty-six), a reform economist; former CCP organization department director Qiao Shi (sixty-one), who had reputedly had ties to Peng Zhen; and foreign minister Wu Xueqian (sixty-four). A sixth newcomer, vice-premier Yao Yilin (sixty-eight), a centrist with strong ties to Chen Yun, was promoted from alternate to full Politburo status. Members of the third echelon also gained five seats on the Party's Central Secretariat. In addition to Politburo appointees Li, Tian, and Qiao, the other newcomers were Wang Zhaoguo (forty-four), director of the Party's General Office, and Hao Jianxiu (fifty), a former cotton mill worker who had served briefly as a textile minister (and who was the only female promoted to a top Party post at the September Party meeting).

144 On military opposition to Hu Yaobang, see *ZM* 110 (1 December 1986), 6–8.

145 The complete text of Deng's address appears in *Dangde jiaoyu* (Party Education) (Tianjin) 5 (October 1985), 17–21; a partial translation, erroneously dated, appears in *ICM*, November 1985, 18.

of reform-related stresses now began seriously to pull apart the social fabric of urban China. Three emergent social trends contributed to this overall effect, comingling and ultimately synergizing to produce the beginnings of a serious urban crisis. The first was an incipient intellectual renaissance, partly inspired by China's rapidly expanding cultural contacts with the outside world and facilitated by the July 1985 ouster of Deng Liqun from his post as Party propaganda chief. Under the stewardship of Deng's successor, Hu Yaobang associate Zhu Houze, and a newly appointed minister of culture, the renowned writer Wang Meng, Chinese art and literature entered a new golden age of creative expression in the summer of 1985. The new era, which was to last for approximately sixteen months, witnessed a strong revival of pre–spiritual pollution campaign-era philosophical debates – for example, over socialist alienation, humanism, and the relevance of Marxist economic theory.[146] The period also witnessed a proliferation of new academic and professional societies; an outpouring of innovative theatrical, cinematic, artistic and literary works;[147] the birth of liberal newspapers such as the Shanghai *World Economic Herald* (*Shijie jingji daobao;*[148] and a resurgence of hard-hitting social commentary by such respected essayist-critics as Liu Binyan, Su Shaozhi, Wang Ruowang, and Fang Lizhi. Indeed, in many respects, it appeared that an incipient "civil society" might be emerging in China, one in which the opinions and attitudes of the creative and critical intelligentsia would play a significantly expanded role.[149]

The second major trend to emerge in 1985 was an increase in social mobilization among various newly articulate urban social groups and strata. With the fabric of daily life increasingly strained by the contradictions of partial reform, by frequent policy oscillations in the *fang–shou* cycle, by mounting inflation, economic corruption, and by a host of perceived inequi-

146 In mid-1985, Wang Ruoshui published a refutation of criticisms leveled earlier by Hu Qiaomu against his theory of alienation under socialism. Ma Ding (pseud.) and Liu Zaifu were two other liberal scholars who figured prominently in the 1985–8 revival of earlier themes. An article by Ma, questioning the contemporary relevance of Marxist economic theory, appeared in *Gongren ribao* (Workers' Daily; hereafter, *GRRB*), 2 November 1985, and is analyzed in *ZM* 103 (1 May 1986). Liu's defense of a humanist approach to socialism appears in *ZM* 104 (1 June 1986), trans. in *FBIS*, 12 June 1986, W6–13.

147 The impact of the 1985–6 literary and artistic renaissance is discussed in Bei Dao, "Terugblik van een balling," in *Het Collectieve Geheugen: Over Literatuur En Geschiedenis*, 77ff.

148 On the role played by the *World Economic Herald* and other liberal media in the reform debates in this period, see Kate Wright, "The political fortunes of Shanghai's 'World economic herald,' " *AJCA* 23 (January 1990), 121–32; and Seth Faison, "The changing role of the Chinese media," in Tony Saich, ed., *The Chinese people's movement: Perspectives on spring* 1989, 144–62.

149 For analysis of the main intellectual currents of this period, see David A. Kelly, "The Chinese student movement of December 1986 and its intellectual antecedents," *AJCA* 17 (January 1987), 127–42. On the emergence of an incipient civil society in China, see Gold, "Party-state versus society." Key speeches and writings of Liu Binyan, Fang Lizhi, Wang Ruowang, and Su Shaozhi from this period are translated in *Chinese Law and Government* (hereafter, *CLG*) 21.2 (Summer 1988).

ties in the social distribution of the costs and benefits of reform, frustration, alienation, and envy began to mount. For the first time since the reforms were introduced in the winter of 1978–9, Chinese cities now began to witness significant social unrest.[150]

On the surface, the various urban disturbances that broke out in 1985 seemed random, spontaneous, and almost wholly unrelated. In May, a riot occurred at a Beijing soccer match, touched off when the local club was upset by a team of Hong Kong Chinese. Shortly thereafter, a group of 300 former Beijing residents who had been "sent down" (*xiaxiang*) to rural areas in Shanxi province in the last years of the Maoist era held a sit-in at the headquarters of the Beijing municipal government, demanding the right to return to their homes in the Chinese capital. In late May, a new round of price decontrols in Beijing triggered a wave of vocal complaints and letters to newspapers from nervous, angry consumers.[151]

Chinese students, too, grew more restive in 1985. Their unhappiness reportedly stemmed from multiple sources, including poor food and unhealthy dormitory conditions, low monthly stipends (averaging around RMB 22 yuan), rising living costs, and flagrant profiteering by *gaogan zidi*.[152] Toward the end of the summer, students began to show signs of social activism. On 18 September, the fifty-fourth anniversary of Japan's invasion of Manchuria, 1,000 college students in Beijing took to the streets to protest Japanese Prime Minister Nakasone's visit to a Shinto shrine honoring the militarists responsible for Japan's World War II invasion of China. One hundred demonstrators were arrested in what was reported to be the largest Chinese student protest in over a decade.[153] In November, a fresh wave of student disturbances occurred, this time openly protesting the recent Japa-

150 On the relationship between economic reform and the social mobilization of urban discontent in this period, see Nina P. Halpern, "Economic reform, social mobilization, and democratization in post-Mao China," in Baum, ed., *Reform and reaction. . . .*," 38–59. On the dysfunctional social effects of partial reform, see Zweig, "Dilemmas of partial reform"; James T. Myers, "China: Modernization and 'unhealthy tendencies,' " *Comparative Politics* 21.2 (January 1989), 193–214; and James C. Hsiung, "Mainland China's paradox of partial reform: A postmortem on Tienanmen," *I&S* 26.6 (June 1990), 29–43.

151 See *ZM* 93 (1 July 1985); also *LW* 4 (21 January 1985).

152 For analysis of the sources of student unrest, see *Chaoliu yuekan* (Hong Kong) 1 (March 1987), 45–54; *Zhongbao* (hereafter, *ZB*), 31 December 1985; and *ICM*, February 1986, 4–6. The history of student protest in China is traced in Jeffrey N. Wasserstrom, "Student protests and the Chinese tradition, 1919–1989" in Saich, ed., *The Chinese people's movement* . . ., 3–24.

153 A collection of student posters from the 18 September demonstrations at Tiananmen Square is translated in *ICM*, January 1987, 3–6. Some of these posters alluded to mounting student resentment over a "new economic invasion" from Japan and called for a boycott of Japanese products; others criticized university authorities for trying to intimidate students by threatening to withhold job assignments after graduation; still others took a dim view of all authority, calling on the masses to rise up against "bureaucrats [who] make up rules and regulations whenever they please . . . [telling] us we can't march, . . . can't go to Tiananmen Square because they tell us not to."

nese "economic invasion." China's top leaders were reported to be "deeply concerned" about the latent antigovernment, antireform overtones of the new demonstrations.[154]

On the occasion of Sino-African Friendship Day in the autumn of 1985, several hundred Chinese students at Tianjin University blockaded the school's canteen, shouting insults at African students gathered there concerning their alleged social and sexual misconduct.[155] In an unrelated incident, in late December 1,500 students at the Beijing Agricultural University occupied campus dormitories and staged a march in protest over the continued presence of PLA personnel on campus. At around the same time, 100 Uighur students demonstrated in Beijing in a protest against continuing Chinese nuclear weapons tests in Lop Nor, Xinjiang.[156]

In the relatively permissive urban climate of 1985–6, students (and others) could give vent to their frustrations and anxieties more openly than at any time since the winter of 1978–9. In one extraordinary incident, the angry father of a student arrested during the 18 September anti-Japanese demonstrations in Beijing staged a successful jailbreak, freeing his son from police custody.[157]

Despite bringing enhanced freedom of expression, China's increasingly permissive urban milieu was a distinctly mixed blessing. Although it contained the embryo of an emergent civil society, marked by incipient socioeconomic pluralism and the first stirrings of autonomous behavior on the part of newly emerging social forces, it also served to amplify all the various social cleavages and contradictions engendered in the process of incomplete reform. The result was a situation that was both highly stressful and increasingly volatile.

154 On November 16, a Reuters dispatch, citing the Hong Kong journal *Zhengming,* reported that a CC directive had referred to recent student protests as potentially posing "the gravest challenge since the downfall of the 'gang of four.' " This tends to support Suzanne Pepper's assertion that the predominant cause of campus unrest in 1985 was student resentment of the negative consequences of the reforms, including China's opening to the outside world. See Suzanne Pepper, "Deng Xiaoping's political and economic reforms and the Chinese student protests," *Universities field staff international reports* 30 (1986).

155 Sporadic anti-African demonstrations continued for many months. In one incident, in late May 1986, 18 African students were beseiged by 500 Chinese students at a dance, resulting in several injuries; two weeks later, a group of 200 African students demonstrated in Beijing against campus discrimination. A similar demonstration was held in January 1988, when 300 African students marched from the Beijing Language Institute to African embassies demanding protection. See *I&S* 25:2 (February 1989), 9–11. The largest and most violent of the campus-based racial disturbances took place in Nanjing in December 1988 (see "The gathering storm: Winter 1988–9").

156 *ZB,* 28 December 1985; *ICM,* February 1986.

157 The father, a high-ranking military officer, surrounded the Beijing public security bureau with troops, demanding that the authorities release his son, whom he claimed had been unlawfully arrested. When Deng Xiaoping capitulated to the angry officer, refusing to halt the jailbreak, students throughout Beijing reportedly began to feel emboldened, as they now perceived themselves to be safe from arbitrary arrest. See *ZM* 111 (1 January 1987), trans. in *FBIS,* 5 January 1987, K9–10. The incident is recounted in Benedict Stavis, *China's political reforms: An interim report,* 91.

As early as mid-1985, public opinion polls began registering a slight downturn in popular enthusiasm for reform. In one eleven-city, sixteen-county survey taken in February, over 80 percent of the 2,400 urban respondents queried reported a rise in their standard of living since the advent of reform; by July of the same year, however, a follow-up survey revealed that the proportion had declined to 70 percent, with a threefold increase (from 4.3 to almost 14 percent) in the number of people who indicated that their living standard had actually declined overall. Not surprisingly, those who experienced a decline in living standards were notably less enthusiastic about reform than those who felt themselves to be doing well. By early 1986, public enthusiasm for economic reform had further diminished. Now only 29 percent of urban residents surveyed felt that the reforms provided equal opportunity for all; by November of the same year, almost 75 percent of the people queried expressed dissatisfaction with rising inflation.[158]

Young people were especially sensitive to the complex, mounting pressures and stresses of reform. Surveys in 1986 revealed a youth culture that was becoming significantly more cynical, materialistic, and hedonistic – and considerably less idealistic – than that of preceding generations.[159] For many urbanites, young and old alike, perceptions of unequal opportunity fueled a mounting sense of resentment. As revealed in various opinion surveys of this period, urban residents were becoming more and more convinced that the costs and benefits of reform had been inequitably distributed. For example, pollsters frequently encountered the view that whereas *getihu* (individual entrepreneurs) could pass rising costs on to consumers, and whereas government cadres could use their authority and/or commercial contacts to buy and sell goods and materials acquired in the state sector for a handsome profit, ordinary people (including industrial workers, lower-level administrative staff, students, housewives, and intellectuals, *inter alia*) had no such options or opportunities available to them.[160] Partly reflecting the prevalence of such views, there were increasing reports of reform-related labor disturbances in

158 These and other related survey research data are analyzed in Bruce Reynolds, ed., *Reform in China: Challenges and choices*, 59–63 and passim. On the nature and functions of survey research in the reform period, see Stanley Rosen, "The rise (and fall) of public opinion in post-Mao China," in Baum, ed., *Reform and reaction . . .*, 60–83.

159 See Stanley Rosen, "Youth and students in China before and after Tiananmen," in Winston Yang and Marcia Wagner, eds., *Tiananmen: China's struggle for democracy.*

160 Ibid. Disaffection with the inequitable effects of reform also began to rise in the countryside in this period. Most rural complaints appeared to center on the proliferation of illegal businesses, cadre corruption, discrimination against private households, and envy of "ten thousand yuan households." See *LW* 45 (11 November 1985); *ZB*, 18 December 1985; and *ICM*, February 1986, 7–13. For further analysis, see Jean C. Oi, "Partial market reform and corruption in rural china," in Baum, ed., *Reform and Reaction . . .*, 143–61.

the summer of 1986, including strikes, work slowdowns, and even occasional riots.[161]

The rising sense of popular malaise was also affected by the third major social trend of the mid-1980s – a new urban crime wave. After dropping sharply toward the end of 1983, the nation's crime rate began to creep up again in 1984. By 1985, crime and corruption were said to be increasing almost geometrically.[162] In response to the rising tide of lawlessness, 1 million new public security personnel were recruited in 1985;[163] the following year a nationwide crackdown on crime was initiated, with a reversion to earlier techniques of mass trials, heavy sentences, perfunctory appeals, and, in the most severe cases, immediate executions.[164] As before, the objective was to intimidate and deter potential lawbreakers through a demonstration effect of harsh and immediate punishment.[165]

Although these three emerging urban trends of 1985–6 – creative freedom for intellectuals, social mobilization of urban unrest, and rising crime – were not formally interconnected, they tended to cross over and mutually reinforce each other. With rising freedom of expression accompanied by rising crime rates, and higher food prices comingling with higher social frustrations, the resulting social chemistry was becoming volatile and more than a little worrisome to China's leaders.

Political reform redivivus: The summer of 1986

In part because of the perceived worsening of urban unrest and in part because of the growing political influence of the newly empowered third echelon, pressures for political reform began to increase again in the winter of 1985–6. In January, CASS published in its official journal a lengthy critique of China's system of government administration. Reporting on a National Conference on Administrative Reform, held in November 1985, the journal

161 *FEER,* 16 October 1986, 69–70.

162 See, e.g., *ZM* 94 (August 1985); *Faxue* (Legal Studies) (Shanghai) 11 (November 1985) and 2 (February 1986); *XH,* 19 December 1985; *ICM,* November 1985, 25. See also Lawrence R. Sullivan, "Assault on the reforms: Conservative criticism of political and economic liberalization in China, 1985–86," *CQ* 114 (June 1988), 209–12.

163 *LW* 33 (19 August 1985). Many of these new police recruits were ex-servicemen demobilized in the army reorganization of 1984–5.

164 It was widely rumored (but never officially confirmed) that the new crackdown had been precipitated by two incidents that occurred in the summer of 1986: the rape of a high-level Party official's daughter in Beijing and the armed robbery of a high cadre on the road from Beijing to the seaside resort of Beidaihe, near Tianjin.

165 In an unusual exception to the normal rule of exempting *gaogan zidi* from severe legal punishment, it was reported that a distant relative of president Li Xiannian was executed in 1986. Li was said to have become furious with Hu Yaobang when the Party Secretariat refused to intervene with the courts to prevent the execution.

claimed that all earlier efforts to rationalize China's administrative structure had failed because they lacked a systemic viewpoint and paid inadequate attention to political reform as an essential prerequisite for successful economic reform. In order to remedy these failings, CASS analysts argued that it was necessary to do two main things: (1) completely separate the Party from economic decision making and administration and (2) institute a civil service system for the recruitment, promotion, and dismissal of cadres.[166]

The CASS recommendations were favorably received (indeed, had originally been solicited) by technocratic cadres of the third echelon, whose political visibility had begun to increase noticeably following the Party conference of September 1985. Supported by Zhao Ziyang and Hu Yaobang, the third echelon's elevated status was reinforced in January 1986, when the CCP's ongoing rectification/anticorruption drive underwent yet another modification in orientation and leadership: A new "leading group" was now set up under third-echelon cadres Qiao Shi and Wang Zhaoguo for the purpose of monitoring improvements in the Party's work style. Henceforth, elderly CDIC watchdogs such as Chen Yun and Bo Yibo would have to share the rectification spotlight with these technocratic newcomers.[167]

The overall divergence in outlook between the revolutionary cadres of the first two echelons and the technocrats of the third echelon was striking. In analyzing the problems of economic crime and corruption, for example, younger leaders tended to stress the systemic, structural sources of aberrant behavior, arguing that institutional reform was a prerequisite for improved Party discipline and work style; by contrast, old guard conservatives tended to stress the moral and spiritual sources of behavioral malfeasance, arguing that it was individuals, not institutions, that required remolding.

By the spring of 1986, the technocrats had gained Deng Xiaoping's sympathetic ear. At a meeting of provincial governors in April, Deng repeated his August 1980 diagnosis of China's ossified and overbureaucratized leadership system.[168] At another April meeting, Deng pointed to the inseparability of economic and political reform, posing the rhetorical question, "What good is it to decentralize power [to enterprise managers] . . . if it is always being taken back again [by Party committees]?" Two months later, at a Party meeting on 20 June, Deng suggested that much of the official racketeering

166 *Shehui kexue* (Social Sciences; hereafter, *SHKX*) 1 (1986), in *ICM*, July 1986, 15–20.

167 The new leading group was set up at a meeting attended by 8,000 Party cadres. Significantly, neither Deng Xiaoping, Chen Yun, nor Li Xiannian was present. Although it did not replace the conservative-dominated CDIC, the new body was given a broad mandate to make recommendations on a variety of issues affecting Party organization, discipline, and spirit. See *XH*, 10–11 January 1986; *FEER*, 23 and 30 January 1986; and Rosen, "China in 1986 . . .," 37.

168 See *WHB* (Hong Kong), July 21–2, 1986; also *ICM*, September 1986, 4–5. For analysis of Deng's 1980 proposals, see Schram, " 'Economics in command'? . . ."

recently uncovered in China was not merely coincidental or occasional but was the product of flaws in the basic system. Without taking action to reform the political system, he argued, it would be impossible to root out unhealthy tendencies in the Party.[169]

With Deng Xiaoping now ostensibly on board the political reform bandwagon, the mass media soon fell into line. Taking their lead (and much of their language) from Deng's 1980 treatise on leadership reform, the media now began to publish frequent articles criticizing such "feudal vestiges" as patriarchal authority, bureaucratic work styles, corrupt personal networks based on kinship, special cadre privileges, and a host of other "serious abuses in the political system."[170] Increasingly, newspapers and journals treated political reform as an essential guarantee against future abuses of power and an essential prerequisite for successful economic reform.[171]

In June, CASS political scientist Yan Jiaqi published a broad critique of the Chinese political system. In Yan's analysis (which closely paralleled Deng's 1980 report), the Chinese polity suffered from four main defects, all of which were traceable to the "overconcentration of power":

> (1) We have never defined the scope of functions, powers, and responsibilities of party organizations, as distinct from governmental organizations. . . . Party organizations at all levels have, in practice, taken on matters which should have been handled by [executive] organs of state power. . . . (2) Not only does the party function in place of executive agencies, but the system of people's congresses has never functioned effectively. . . . (3) Powers are overcentralized, so that the initiative of local authorities cannot be brought fully into play. . . . (4) We have never defined the scope of functions, powers, and responsibilities of governmental bodies as distinct from those of economic enterprises and social institutions. [Hence,] enterprises and institutions became, in effect, subsidiary bodies of executive agencies. . . .[172]

Although Yan Jiaqi did not directly address the sensitive issue of political democratization, a handful of other liberal scholars did, albeit gingerly. This was uncharted territory, insofar as advocacy of anything other than "socialist democracy" (i.e., democracy under Party leadership) could be construed as contravening the four cardinal principles. Those writers who did broach the

169 *ICM*, September 1986, 4–5.; see also Rosen, "China in 1986 . . .," 38. At the same meeting, Deng suggested that China's ruling Communist Party should be "subject to restrictions."

170 A useful collection of newspaper articles, essays, and documents pertaining to proposals for political reform in this period appears in *CLG* 20.1 (Spring 1987).

171 Many of the leading theoretical articles on political reform were now authored by CASS scholars. Among the most active reform theorists in this period were Yan Jiaqi, director of the CASS Institute of Political Science; Su Shaozhi, director of the CASS Institute of Marxism–Leninism–Mao Zedong Thought; and Li Honglin, director of the Fujia, provincial Social Science Academy. Party leaders active in the political reform movement included Hu Qili, Tian Jiyun, Wang Zhaoguo, Zhu Houze, and Yan Mingfu, director of the CC's United Front Work Department.

172 Yan's critique is translated in *CLG* 20.1 (Spring 1987).

subject of democracy generally limited themselves to attacking safe, preapproved targets, such as (conveniently unnamed) "some feudal patriarchs," who purportedly "never consult with subordinates" and "always arbitrarily impose their will on others." Such people, wrote social scientist Li Honglin in June, "tremble with fear whenever they hear the word 'democracy.' " They treat democracy as a "weapon used by subordinates and the masses against higher-ups and cadres, a force to weaken and shatter stability and unity, even something tantamount to anarchy." Worse yet, wrote Li, they "take any expression of different opinions as a sign of rebellion, and put any convenient political label upon those who voice them."[173]

The issue of the detrimental effects of political labeling and intimidation was taken up by vice-premier Wan Li in an address to a national conference on "soft sciences" in late July. Arguing that such "feudal practices" had caused great damage in the past, Wan proposed the adoption of legislation to protect people engaged in policy-oriented research from the threat of political pressure, intimidation, or recrimination.[174]

With few exceptions, the great majority of voices urging leadership reform within the Chinese political establishment in the spring and summer of 1986 were moderate, technocratic, and nonprovocative – that is, they advocated such things as enhanced administrative rationalization, freedom of expression, and legislative supervision within the existing framework of the Leninist "Party leadership" model, rather than proposing any radical innovations such as limited government, separation of powers, or multiparty competition. A few theoretical articles did speak approvingly of such devices as checks and balances (*zhi heng*), but only insofar as these might be applied *within* the CCP, not *between* the party and other institutions. Similarly, the American doctrine of three separate, coequal branches of government, although occasionally praised, for example, for having "prevented the restoration of feudal dictatorship" in the West,[175] was generally rejected as inappropriate for a socialist country such as China, since the doctrine had allegedly been invented "to protect the secure rule of the bourgeoisie."[176]

As reform expectations heightened in the summer of 1986, a flurry of organizational activity took place. In July, a conference on reform of the political structure was held at the Central Party School in Beijing. Attended by several hundred younger cadres from various party organs who had been

173 *Shijie jingji daobao* (hereafter, SJJJDB), 2 June 1986, trans. in *CLG* 20.1 (Spring 1987).

174 *XH*, 14 August 1986; *I&S* 22.9 (September 1986), 4–7. Wan's speech also offered a strong rationale for the political insulation of social science think tanks, which had already begun to appear in China by this time. See Rosen, "China in 1986 . . .," 39–40.

175 *Faxue yanjiu* (Legal Studies) 10 (October 1986), trans. in *CLG* 20:1 (Spring 1987), 74–77.

176 *SHKX* 4 (1986), in *ICM*, November 1986, 1–4.

sent by their senior leaders, the conference was addressed by the Party's liberal propaganda chief, Zhu Houze. According to those in attendance, Zhu urged the young cadres to study, clarify, and absorb relevant Western, non-Marxist political ideas and institutions. Later, Deng Liqun would allege that "it was this conference that started a new upsurge in liberalism."[177]

Responding to Zhu Houze's call, a few reform theorists began to speak with bolder voices in the late summer of 1986. Yan Jiaqi, for example, now suggested that China should seriously study parliamentary forms of government, and Su Shaozhi recommended the introduction of political pluralism and multiparty competition.[178] Also in this period, Liu Binyan, Fang Lizhi, Wang Ruowang, and Yu Haocheng all began to intensify their ongoing criticisms of the Party's prevailing ideological ethos, characterized by blind obedience to authority, monistic interests, "forbidden zones," and intolerance toward creative intellectuals.[179]

Toward the end of the summer, the SC of the Politburo established a five-person "central discussion group for reform of the political structure." Made up of a cross section of leading Party reformers and traditionalists but pointedly excluding Hu Yaobang, the five-person group was instructed by Deng Xiaoping to "clarify the content of political restructuring, and work out the details."[180]

The question of "guiding principles"

Against this background of renewed organizational activity, party leaders gathered in August for their annual midsummer retreat at the seaside resort of Beidaihe, near Tianjin. The main topic on the agenda was how to understand the party's "guiding principles" in an age of societal transformation. Whereas Politburo reformers wanted to push ahead with new definitions and ideological orientation, conservatives balked at anything that might undermine the four cardinal principles, preferring instead to stress the struggle against bourgeois liberalization. In the estimation of people like Chen Yun, Li Xiannian, and Peng Zhen, pushing political reform too rapidly could easily undermine social stability; they remained largely unmoved by the

177 Feng Shengbao, "Preparations for the blueprint on political restructuring presented by Zhao Ziyang at the Thirteenth Party Congress" (unpublished paper presented to the Harvard University East Asia Colloquium, July 1990), 2.

178 *ZM* 108 (1 October 1986), 21, in *FBIS*, 19 September 1986, K20; *Dagong bao* (hereafter, *DGB*), 17 September 1986, in *FBIS*, 29 September 1986, K16.

179 For analysis of these developments, See Kelly, "The Chinese student movement . . .," 135–38; and Stavis, *China's political reforms . . .*, 51–9.

180 Feng, "Preparations for the blueprint . . . ." The five members of the group were Zhao Ziyang, Hu Qili, Tian Jiyun, Bo Yibo, and Peng Chong.

argument that political reform was an essential precondition for successful economic reform.[181]

With the two main factions deeply divided, no new ideological ground could be broken at the Beidaihe meeting. When the Twelfth CC's Sixth Plenum met in late September, China's leaders publicly papered over their differences, passing a highly ambivalent, middle-of-the-road resolution on "building a socialist society with an advanced culture and ideology." It was a convoluted document, filled with lofty and frequently self-contradictory moral generalities. For example, while exalting the four cardinal principles and condemning bourgeois liberalization, the resolution also stressed the importance of promoting intellectual freedom, democracy, socialist humanism, and learning from advanced capitalist countries.[182] Thus deadlocked, the Sixth Plenum postponed serious consideration of political reform for another year, until the Thirteenth Party Congress, scheduled to be held in 1987.

Despite the superficial blandness of the CC's resolution on guiding principles, a tense drama took place behind the scenes at the Sixth Plenum. Originally, Deng Xiaoping had decided not to raise the divisive issue of bourgeois liberalization at the plenum, for fear of alienating the Party's pro-reform wing. In the course of the meeting, however, he changed his mind; during debate over the Party's guiding principles, he delivered a strong condemnation of bourgeois liberalization. In his remarks, Deng alleged that the trend toward bourgeois liberalization, if allowed to continue, would "lead our present policies onto the capitalist road." He reminded reformers that it was not just a few diehard conservatives who opposed bourgeois liberalization: "I am the one," he admonished, "who has talked about it most often and most insistently."[183]

The reason for Deng's sudden intervention ostensibly lay in the fact that Hu Yaobang had failed to publicize adequately Deng's serious misgivings about liberalization. "Apparently my remarks had no effect," said Deng. "I understand they were never disseminated. . . . I haven't changed my mind about opposing spiritual pollution. . . . The struggle against bourgeois liberalization will last for at least twenty years."[184]

181 On the Beidaihe meeting, see *WHB* (Hong Kong), 8 August 1986, in *SWB/FE* 8335 (12 August 1986).

182 The text of the resolution appears in *BR* 29.40 (6 October 1986), I–VIII.

183 The text of Deng's address is in *BR* 30.26 (29 June 1987), 14; a slightly different version appears in *CLG* 21.1 (Spring 1988), 22–3.

184 *BR* 30.26, ibid.; *I&S* 23.6 (June 1987), 17–18. It is the context of Deng's remarks that strongly suggests his extreme personal displeasure with Hu Yaobang. Deng's reference to "not chang[ing] my mind about opposing spiritual pollution" appears to be a pointed reference to Hu Yaobang's December 1984 injunction to "no longer talk about spiritual pollution" (see footnote 107). Ironically, Deng's complaint about Hu Yaobang's lack of attention to his views was strongly reminiscent of Mao Zedong's famous 1965 complaint about Deng Xiaoping, in which the late chairman observed that Deng treated him "like an ancestral spirit at a funeral."

With the CC increasingly paralyzed by factional divisions, with political reform shelved for another year, and with Deng Xiaoping growing visibly impatient with Party liberals, the momentum of the reformers, built up over a period of several months, was now partially lost. Although activities of the Standing Committee's five-person group on reform of the political structure continued apace, the prevailing atmosphere in Beijing began to change.[185] The optimism of summer now gave way to a growing pessimism as rumors began to spread that liberal ideas and values were about to be targeted for criticism once again.[186] The evidence was fragmentary but palpable: A second young cadres' conference on reform of the political structure, scheduled to be held at the Beijing Central Party School in early November, now had its venue changed suddenly, as the school's top officials, conservative generals Li Desheng and Wang Zhen, refused permission for the convocation to be held on school grounds; in similar fashion, the Chinese Air Force now withdrew its sponsorship from a reform-oriented journal, *Lilun xinxi bao;* shortly thereafter, a nationwide academic conference on political reform, scheduled to be held in Shanghai in late November, was abruptly canceled a few days before its scheduled opening, with no explanation offered.[187]

In midautumn, Party conservatives mounted an ideological counterattack against liberalism. The point man for the assault this time was Peng Zhen. In November, Peng indirectly criticized one of the key economic tenets of the reformers: the idea that it was perfectly acceptable for some people to get rich before others. Under socialism, he admonished, "people [should] get rich together."[188] Addressing a session of the NPC's SC toward the end of November, Peng turned his attention to politics, noting sarcastically that "Some people cherish bourgeois democracy. To these people, it seems that even the moon in the capitalist world is brighter than the sun in our society."[189] In a pointed rejoinder to liberals who had complained about the undemocratic nature of Party discipline, Peng gave the following definition of intra-Party democracy:

> We follow whatever ideas are correct. If there is no unanimity of views [after discussion], then the minority submits to the majority, the individual submits to the organization, the lower level submits to the higher level, and the entire country

185 Feng, "Preparations for the blueprint . . . ." The reform group's major activity in this period was to sponsor a series of academic panels and symposia on various aspects of political reform in preparation for drafting a comprehensive reform plan to be introduced at the Thirteenth Party Congress.

186 Some newspapers began to react apprehensively to this change in the political climate. On 1 November, for example, *GMRB* ran an editorial arguing that it should not be a cause for alarm that some people in China no longer saw Communism as the ultimate goal. See *SWB/FE* 8407 (4 November 1986).

187 Feng, "Preparations for the blueprint . . . ," 2–4.

188 *RMRB*, 15 January 1987; transl. in *FBIS*, 16 January 1987, K14.

189 Quoted in *I&S* 23.6 (June 1987), 17.

submits to the central government. . . . This is the essential content of our system of collective democracy.[190]

Thus did Party conservatives sharpen their polemical swords. With ideological battle lines drawn, the battle itself was not long in coming.

Fang Lizhi and the students

During the student demonstrations of autumn 1985, astrophysicist Fang Lizhi had made a series of controversial speeches on Chinese college campuses, including Peking University (Beida) and Zhejiang University. One of Fang's main themes had been to challenge Chinese students boldly to "break all barriers" that served to impede intellectual awareness and creativity. At Beida he had urged young people to take their future into their own hands, speaking passionately about the continued prevalence of corruption and patronage within the Party organization. Unlike most establishment critics, however, Fang Lizhi named names. He cited, for example, the case of Beijing Vice-Mayor Zhang Baifa, who had recently traveled to the United States as a member of an academic delegation attending a seminar on high-energy physics. "What was he doing there?" asked Fang. "This kind of free-loading is corrupt. . . . I don't care if it is Zhang Baifa, I'm going to stand here and say it."[191]

Almost a year after delivering these remarks, Fang Lizhi went on another multicampus speaking tour. By all accounts, his November 1986 talks were even more provocative than the earlier ones. Speaking at Shanghai's Jiaotong University on 6 November, Fang elaborated on the theme of breaking barriers. He now urged students to challenge authority and to demand democratic rights and freedoms, rather than waiting for them to be bestowed from above by the party:

I really feel that now we should not be afraid of anybody. Some people do not dare to challenge our leaders; but I have found that if you challenge them, they dare not do anything against you. . . . For instance, last year I criticized Zhang Baifa by name. . . . Later he began to find fault with me. But he can no longer pick on anyone now. (Laughter from the audience) In August, I criticized Hu Qiaomu by name at a press conference, and he did not do anything against me. (Laughter from the audience) . . . This year I criticized leaders of the Politburo. (Laughter) . . . I insist on expressing my own opinion. . . .

The core problem is: If China's reforms depend completely on the moves of our

190 *XH*, 26 November 1986. Peng's definition of collective democracy was virtually identical to the classical Leninist concept of democratic centralism; as such, it differed substantially from the concept of socialist democracy widely advocated by reform leaders since 1978.

191 Fang's speech appears in *ICM*, December 1986, 8–10.

> top leaders, China will not become a developed nation. . . . Democracy granted by leaders is not true democracy. (Applause) What is the meaning of democracy? Democracy means that each human being has his own rights and that human beings, each exercising his own rights, form our society. Therefore, rights are in the hands of every citizen. They are not given by top leaders of the nation.[192]

Fang Lizhi reiterated these themes on other college campuses in the Shanghai area. On 18 November, at Tongji University, he delivered perhaps his most controversial statement: "I am here to tell you that the socialist movement, from Marx and Lenin to Stalin and Mao Zedong, has been a failure. . . . I think that complete Westernization is the only way to modernize." Everywhere Fang went, students were reportedly moved by his words; he rapidly became a campus hero.[193]

Party leaders, including many who supported political reform, were not so enthralled by Fang's rhetoric. On 30 November, Vice-Premier Wan Li paid a visit to Fang's home campus, the Chinese University of Science and Technology (CUST) in Hefei, where he delivered a thinly veiled warning, reminding Fang (who was vice-president of CUST) that university leaders had an obligation to implement the line, principles, and policies of the Party.[194] In an impromptu debate with Fang, the vice-premier failed to make any headway, either with the astrophysicist or with an informal audience of students. At one point, a visibly frustrated Wan Li reportedly said to Fang, "I have already granted you enough freedom and democracy." Thereupon Fang shot back "What do you mean, 'enough democracy'? It was the people who made you vice premier. It's not up to any single person to hand out democracy."[195]

Perhaps coincidentally, and perhaps not, when Chinese students began demonstrating in early December, the arc of political contagion paralleled rather closely (though not precisely) the itinerary of Fang's various lecture tours. Beginning at CUST in Hefei, protest spread to Jiaotong and Tongji in Shanghai before moving north to Beida. All along the arc of contagion, Chinese students began to break barriers.

Breaking barriers: December 1986

The movement began on 5 December, when several hundred students at CUST assembled to protest their exclusion both from the process of selecting the head of their local student union and from nominating candidates for the

192 Fang's speech appears in *I&S* 23.4 (April 1987), 124–42.
193 Stavis (*China's political reforms . . .*, 92–5) gives a vivid account of these events.
194 *XH*, 3 December 1986, in *FBIS*, 23 December 1986, K18–19.
195 *South China Morning Post*, 12 January 1987; *ZM* 111 (1 January 1987).

provincial people's congress.[196] Four days later, on the symbolic occasion of the fifty-first anniversary of the anti-Japanese student movement of 9 December 1935, some 2,000 to 3,000 CUST students marched through the streets of Hefei, criticizing the government, *inter alia,* for reneging on its promise of expanded electoral democracy. Embarrassed by the protest, authorities gave in to students' demands, postponing the provincial people's congress election. Smaller demonstrations also occurred on 9 December at a handful of college campuses in other cities, including Wuhan and Xian.[197]

When word of the success of the Hefei students reached other campuses, it served as a catalyst, amplifying local protest and creating a contagion effect. On 10 December, posters calling for democracy appeared at Jiaotong and Beida, among other universities. Small demonstrations also broke out on college campuses in Shandong, Shenzhen, and Kunming.

At Jiaotong and Beida, university authorities gave orders to remove posters; students at Jiaotong planned a march to protest the removal order. When Shanghai Mayor Jiang Zemin visited the campus on 18 December to try to cool down the students, pleading for unity and stability, he was heckled and repeatedly interrupted. At one point, a student provocatively asked Jiang Zemin whether he had been elected mayor by the citizens of Shanghai. Momentarily taken aback, the mayor asked for the student's name and department. Offended by this crude attempt at intimidation, a number of students in attendance leaped verbally to their classmate's defense.[198]

News of the Jiaotong confrontation spread quickly, and students at nearby Tongji and Fudan universities took to the streets on 19 December, angrily denouncing bureaucratism and demanding liberty and democracy. Congregating at Shanghai's People's Square, several thousand students demanded a meeting with the mayor. After a delay of several hours, during which time the movement began to dissipate, students marched to city hall, singing the *Internationale* en route. Eventually, Jiang Zemin sent a vice-mayor to meet

196 Just days earlier, China's election law had been amended to make selection procedures for people's congress candidates more democratic; among other things, the new law specifies that more candidates must be nominated than the number of seats to be filled (*XH,* 15 November 1986); the text of the new election law appears in *FBIS,* 8 December 1986. The day before the protest, on 4 December, Fang Lizhi reportedly told his students, "Democracy is not granted from the top down; it is won by individuals" (*BR* 29.8 [23 February 1987], 17–18).

197 According to eyewitnesses in these cities, the complaints of the demonstrators varied greatly and lacked coherent focus. Some students clamored for electoral democracy; others complained about the poor quality of campus food and living conditions (including the presence of rats in the dormitories); still others protested against inflation, corruption, rising tuition fees, and the elimination of automatic student aid. For analysis of the 1986 student demonstrations see Stavis, *China's political reforms . . . ,* 96–104; Julia Kwong, "The 1986 student demonstrations in China: A democratic movement?" *AS* 28.9 (September 1988), 970–85; Lowell Dittmer, "Reform, succession and the resurgence of Mainland China's old guard," *I&S* 24.1 (January 1988), 96–113; and *ICM,* January 1987, 2–6, and March 1987, 27–28.

198 *South China Morning Post,* 24 December 1986; Stavis, *China's political reforms . . . ,* 97.

with student representatives. The students presented four demands: (1) they wanted Mayor Jiang to address them personally; (2) they wanted their demonstration to be treated as legal and patriotic; (3) they wanted assurances against future recriminations; and (4) they wanted newspapers to carry fair and accurate reports of the demonstration.[199]

The vice-mayor tried to convince the students to return to their campuses, offering buses to escort them. Undaunted, hundreds of protesters remained at city hall. At around 5:45 A.M. the next morning, police marched in and forceably removed the students, putting them in buses to be driven back to their campuses. A handful of students who refused to leave were detained briefly; a few were roughed up; one reportedly suffered a broken leg. Over the next few days, the protests of People's Square grew larger, now involving more than 10,000 people, including substantial numbers of nonstudents. According to eyewitnesses, the level of emotional excitement now surpassed anything seen in China since the Cultural Revolution.

In Nanjing, Tianjin, and Beijing, thousands of students demonstrated during the week of 22–26 December, some in support of the Shanghai students and some merely in response to the heightened excitement of the times. Altogether, tens of thousands of people, students and nonstudents alike, in seventeen cities, representing more than 150 colleges and universities (out of a total of around 1,000), participated in demonstrations in the last half of December 1986.[200]

The official media, which had previously ignored the demonstrations altogether, now sought to cool things down by publishing commentaries urging moderation and restraint. On 22 December, *Xinhua* publicized a statement by Tianjin's pro-reform mayor, Li Ruihuan, in which the mayor exhorted people in his city not to be unduly alarmed by the disturbances. "There is nothing extraordinary about such incidents," he said; "there is no reason for us to lose our composure." At the same time, the mayor cautioned students against being led astray by people who claimed that China's future lay in "complete Westernization." Such notions were entirely inappropriate, said Li Ruihuan, and must be resolutely opposed.[201] A few days later, the *People's Daily* ran an editorial urging Chinese students to have patience, arguing that

199 These demands, as well as several other aspects of the December 1986 student movement, are of particular interest because of their striking similarity to events that transpired some twenty-eight months later, at the height of the 1989 Tiananmen Square demonstrations. See "Mourning becomes electric" and "The aftermath of 26 April: Public resentment deepens."

200 Estimates of total participation vary widely, from a low of around 20,000 (roughly 2 percent of China's total college population), as reported in the official *RMRB* (31 December 1986), to a high of over 75,000, representing a compilation of various foreign media estimates. The largest individual demonstrations were in Shanghai and Beijing, where some crowds (including both demonstrators and spectators) were estimated to have been as large as 30,000.

201 *XH*, 23 December 1986, in *ICM*, April 1987, 3–4.

democratization was a lengthy process that could not be realized overnight.[202] Meanwhile, municipal authorities in Beijing employed more direct, straightforward means of discouraging protest: On 26 December, they enacted new regulations restricting the issuance of parade permits; this was followed by the arrest of a handful of demonstrators on charges ranging from disturbing the peace to incitement to riot.

Despite the occasional arrests and sporadic use of intimidation tactics by public security forces, the local authorities generally refrained from using excessive force to quell student protests. In the absence of inflammatory government behavior, popular passions began to subside, and the movement lost momentum; by early January 1987, a combination of winter weather and the natural dissipation of student energies served to dampen the protesters' fervor. Before returning to their classes, however, Beijing students engaged in one final act of symbolic political defiance: On 5 January they publicly burned copies of the *Beijing Daily,* official organ of the municipal government, which the students claimed had presented a grossly distorted view of their movement.

The empire strikes back

Throughout most of December, China's party leaders outwardly maintained their composure. Inwardly, however, many of them began to bridle.[203] Beijing's Mayor Chen Xitong and municipal Party chief Li Ximing were said to be particularly angry over the burning of the *Beijing Daily.* On 28 December, Party conservatives spoke out: Bo Yibo, Hu Qiaomu, and Deng Liqun all issued statements denouncing bourgeois democracy, which they said would destabilize the country and retard modernization. Two days later, Wang Zhen issued a similar statement, going so far as to suggest the possibility of using military force to put an end to student demonstrations.[204]

Now Deng Xiaoping entered the fray. On 30 December, in a meeting with Wan Li, Hu Qili, Li Peng, and the deputy state counselor for education, He Dongchang, Deng delivered a talk "On the problem of the present student disturbances." In his remarks, Deng leveled what was by far his most vitriolic attack to date against liberalism. Placing the blame for escalating stu-

202 *RMRB,* 25 December 1986.

203 Shanghai mayor Jiang Zemin, at a meeting of municipal cadres, roundly denounced the students of Jiaotong University for opposing the Party. Afterwards, he reportedly ordered that "not one word" of his remarks should be repeated outside of the meeting (*ZM* 111 [1 January 1987], in *ICM,* March 1987, 24–6).

204 *SWB/FE* 8464 (13 January 1987); *ZB,* February 1987, 26. Wang Zhen was reportedly criticized for his provocative remarks; subsequently he was demoted from his post as president of the Central Party School. See Feng, "Preparations for the blueprint . . . ," 8.

dent "turmoil" (*dongluan*) squarely on the shoulders of "leaders in [various] places who failed to take a firm attitude . . . toward bourgeois liberalization," Deng asserted that this was "not just a matter of one or two places, or one or two years' duration"; rather, it was a question of "failing to take a clear stand . . . over a period of several years."[205]

Lashing out at members of the liberal intelligentsia, whom he blamed for instigating the students, Deng named names and demanded punishment: "I have seen statements by Fang Lizhi," he said. "They are absolutely unlike anything a party member ought to say. What point is there in allowing him to remain in the party?" Of Wang Ruowang, Deng said: "[He] is a cunning rascal. I said a long time ago that we ought to expel him. Why haven't we done it?" Next, Deng denounced bourgeois democracy: "When we speak of democracy, we must not mean bourgeois democracy. We cannot set up such gimmicks as the division of powers between three branches of government. This causes great trouble." Alluding to the way dissidents were handled during the short-lived democracy movement of 1978–9, Deng said that "We cannot allow people who turn right and wrong around . . . to do as they please. Didn't we arrest Wei Jingsheng? . . . We arrested him and haven't let him go, yet China's image has not suffered the slightest damage." Praising the Polish government's handling of the Solidarity crisis in 1981, Deng said that the Polish leaders had showed "cool and level-headed judgment. Their attitude was firm. . . . They resorted to martial law to bring the situation under control." For Deng, the lesson to be drawn was clear: "This proves," he said, "that you cannot succeed without recourse to methods of dictatorship."[206]

Arguing that it was generally advisable to "arrest as few as possible," Deng nevertheless asserted that a show of force was an indispensable tactic in dealing with unruly demonstrators. In a passage that ominously foreshadowed certain events of May and June 1989, Deng raised the question of how to deal with people who are determined to provoke a confrontation:

> [I]f they want to create a bloody incident, what can we do about it? . . . We do all we can to avoid bloodshed. If not even a single person dies, that is the best way. It is even preferable to allow our own people to be injured.[207] But the most important

205 The main points of Deng's talk were later incorporated into the text of "Central document No. 1, 1987," promulgated on 6 January 1987. The text of this document, along with other related documents, appears in *CLG* 21.1 (Spring 1988), 18–21.

206 Ibid.

207 In a somewhat more strident translation of this same passage, the *South China Morning Post* of 12 January 1987, quotes Deng as saying: "We can afford to shed some blood. Just try as much as possible not to kill anyone." An official Chinese government translation of the same passage reads: "We should . . . do our best to avoid shedding blood, even if it means some of our own people get hurt" (*BR* 30.26 [29 June 1987], 15–16).

thing is to grasp the object of struggle. . . . If we do not take appropriate steps and measures, we will be unable to control this type of incident; if we pull back, we will encounter even more trouble later on. . . . Don't worry that foreigners will say we have ruined our reputation. . . . We must show foreigners that the political situation in China is stable. . . .[208]

Such was senior leader Deng Xiaoping's prescription for dealing with the fire next time; for the moment, however, the students were quiescent, and the crisis went into remission.

The "resignation " of Hu Yaobang

The student demonstrations of December 1986 were the leading edge of a widening pattern of social unrest that began to affect urban China in the mid-1980s. Although demands for greater democracy comprised the broadest common denominator of student protest, such demands tended to be vague and unfocused, often masking a wide variety of underlying social stresses, grievances, and tensions. Some of these were preexisting, and others were reform-induced; all were subject to intensification in the swirling vortex of heightened expectations, loosened behavioral constraints, and accelerated social mobilization that characterized China in the mid-1980s.

If the students themselves were somewhat diffuse and unfocused in their demands and objectives, China's rebounding conservatives were not. They knew exactly what they wanted: the removal of Hu Yaobang. This was nothing new, of course; Chen Yun, Hu Qiaomu, and Deng Liqun (among others) had been visibly unhappy with Hu at least since 1982–3. Now, however, the conservatives had a powerful new weapon at their disposal, the wrath of Deng Xiaoping, and they used it with maximum effect. On 27 December, a delegation of seven conservative leaders visited Deng to request Hu Yaobang's dismissal, raising numerous allegations of misconduct.[209] Deng reportedly temporized: Having only recently expressed confidence in Hu's leadership to a group of foreign visitors, he could hardly fire the general secretary at this juncture without having it reflecting badly upon his own judgment.[210]

Meanwhile, the conservative backlash against the December "turmoil" was intensifying. On 6 January, following the public burning of copies of the *Beijing Daily,* the Politburo promulgated "Central document no. 1, 1987."

208 *CLG* 21.1 (Spring 1988).

209 *BX* 141 (1 April 1987), 3. The seven were Peng Zhen, Hu Qiaomu, Wang Zhen, Deng Liqun, Bo Yibo, Yang Shangkun, and Yu Qiuli.

210 On this point, see Parris Chang, "From Mao to Hua to Hu to Chao: Changes in the CCP leadership and its rule of the game, *I&S* 25.1 (January 1989), 66.

It called on leading cadres in all organizations and at all levels to take an "unwavering stand" on the "front lines of the battle" to quell student unrest. Those who violated the Party's injunction against supporting student turmoil would be dealt with "in accordance with Party rules and regulations"; where circumstances were serious, severe punishments would be meted out.[211] Three days later, it was unofficially reported that Fang Lizhi, Liu Binyan, and Wang Ruowang had been ordered expelled from the CCP.[212]

In the aftermath of the *Beijing Daily* incident, Deng Xiaoping made up his mind: Hu Yaobang had to go.[213] On 16 January, at an enlarged meeting of the Politburo, Hu was relieved of his duties as general secretary after reportedly having thrice rejected Deng Xiaoping's request that he resign. More than twenty people spoke out against Hu at the meeting, including some of his erstwhile supporters.[214]

The next day, the Politburo promulgated "Central document no. 3, 1987," cataloguing Hu's alleged misdeeds. Six separate charges were set out in the document: (1) Hu Yaobang had for several years resisted the Party's "entirely correct" efforts to combat spiritual pollution and bourgeois liberalization in the ideological sphere, thus contributing to an upsurge in liberal demands for "total Westernization," culminating in the student turmoil of December 1986;[215] (2) he had failed to provide correct leadership in the Party rectification–consolidation campaign, virtually ignoring the four cardinal principles and "only opposing the 'Left' " while "never opposing the Right"; (3) in economic work, he had overemphasized the need to stimulate and satisfy consumer demand, leading to undue acceleration in the rate of planned economic growth, making it impossible to adequately "lay the ideological groundwork" for rapid growth, and thus causing the economy to go "out of control"; (4) in political work, he frequently violated legal procedures and "repeatedly spoke out about government legislative work in a way that was not serious"; (5) in foreign affairs, he "said many things he should

211 The document appears in *ICM*, April 1987, 1–2.

212 Kyodo (Tokyo), 9 January 1987; *SWB/FE* 8462 (10 January 1987). The separate decisions to expel the three liberals were offically reported in *XH*, 14 January 1987; *XH*, 19 January 1987; and *RMRB*, 24 January 1987.

213 It has been reported that Deng ultimately decided to sack Hu Yaobang because Chen Yun persuaded him that Hu's leadership style risked splitting the Party and provoking the formation of autonomous labor unions (and strikes) among urban workers – a sort of Chinese Gdansk. See Wilson and Ji, "Leadership by 'lines' . . .," 34.

214 *SWB/FE* 8467 (16 January 1987).

215 The document makes an explicit reference to the late U.S. Secretary of State John Foster Dulles, who once said that "the policy of the American government is to encourage liberalization in the Soviet Union and the countries of Eastern Europe." Apparently, Hu Yaobang was being judged guilty by association for having (unwittingly) advanced the aims of U.S. imperialism. Similar allegations, to the effect that China's liberal reformers were promoting Western schemes for the "peaceful evolution" of bourgeois democracy, later provided a significant part of the government's rationale for cracking down on student demonstrators in the spring of 1989.

not have said"; and (6) he often disobeyed Party resolutions and frequently took the initiative in expressing his own ideas "without authorization from the Central Committee."[216]

Central document no. 3 also contained a summary of Hu Yaobang's self-criticism. In it, he apologized for overstepping the bounds of his authority as general secretary, acknowledging that because he had occupied a leading position, his errors had caused "very grave damage" to the Party, the nation, and the people. He also acknowledged that his errors "were not isolated mistakes but a whole series of major errors involving political principles"; at the same time, however, he carefully avoided conceding the substance of the most damaging charges against him, that is, that his ideological laxity had fostered spiritual pollution and bourgeois liberalization, thereby bringing on student turmoil.[217] Despite Hu's failure to confess to specifics, those present at his self-criticism "expressed satisfaction" with his "feelings and attitude"; consequently, he was not expelled from the Party and was even permitted to retain his seat on the Politburo.[218]

Toward the end of Central document no. 3, a short passage was devoted to the question of how to avoid future recurrences of reckless behavior by Party leaders. Though it received scant attention at the time, this passage subsequently provided the rationale for allowing retired Party elders to override younger leaders in time of crisis: "The comrades who took part in the session all felt that, for the long term peace and order of our country, it would be a good idea if, while such older generation revolutionaries as Deng Xiaoping, Chen Yun, and Li Xiannian are still in good health, a system might be devised to control and supervise the leaders at the highest levels in Party and government."[219] Such a system was put in place later in the year, at the Thirteenth Party Congress; it was actively invoked during the next round of student "turmoils" in May–June 1989.

Combatting bourgeois liberalism

Despite the vehemence of the Party leadership's denunciation of bourgeois liberalization, the ensuing propaganda drive was considerably milder than its

216 The text of "Central document no. 3" appears in *ICM*, May 1987, 1–3. Of the six charges raised against Hu, the first two were the most serious, and the last three were quite vague and skeletal. The document was said to be based on a report delivered by Bo Yibo summarizing the proceedings of a top-level leadership meeting held in Beijing from 10 to 15 January.

217 Ibid., 2–3.

218 Peng Zhen would subsequently boast (obliquely) that he and his old comrades played an instrumental role in ousting Hu (*DGB* [Hong Kong], 9 April 1987). Hu later expressed his regret for having capitulated to conservative pressures to engage in self-criticism.

219 *ICM*, May 1987, 3.

predecessor, the anti–spiritual pollution campaign of 1983. The reason was clear: Negative backlash from the earlier campaign had threatened to scare off foreign investors and undermine Deng's reform program. To avoid repetition, the 1987 campaign was narrowly circumscribed from the outset. It was not to be a mass movement but was to be confined within the ranks of the Party apparatus; expulsions from the Party were to be relatively few, as were removals from office. Indeed, aside from Hu Yaobang, the only other top Party official actually sacked in the aftermath of the December 1986 student demonstrations was Zhu Houze.[220] Although there followed a clear tightening of press censorship and a blacklisting of certain liberal magazines and journalists in the late winter and spring of 1987, no large-scale police crackdown was launched against people who had supported the student demonstrations;[221] only a handful of alleged troublemakers, most of them nonstudents, were reportedly jailed for instigating the December turmoil.[222] Finally, the new campaign was care-

220 Zhu, who retained his Party membership, was replaced as Party propaganda chief by Wang Renzhi, the former deputy editor-in-chief of *Red Flag*. Among prominent liberal critics, only Fang Lizhi, Wang Ruowang, and Liu Binyan were expelled from the Party in the immediate aftermath of the student disturbances, although five other liberal intellectuals, including Su Shaozhi and reform economist Yu Guangyuan, were pressured to resign from the CCP during the summer of 1987. They were reportedly spared loss of Party membership through the personal intervention of retired PLA marshal Nie Rongzhen, who was a patron of one of the five targeted intellectuals, Song Changjiang. See *ICM*, December 1987, 34; and *China News Analysis* (Hong Kong) (hereafter, *CNA*) 1342 (1 September 1987), 4. In addition to CUST vice-president Fang Lizhi, a number of other leading academic administrators, including Fang's boss, CUST president Guan Weiyan, and the president and vice-president of the Chinese Academy of Sciences, Lu Jiaxi and Yan Dongsheng, were dismissed from their jobs early in 1987. Even after being expelled from the Party, Fang Lizhi and Liu Binyan were permitted to attend professional meetings in China; Liu, Wang Ruowang, Su Shaozhi, and others were later granted permission to travel abroad.

221 "Central document no. 4, 1987," released in March, called for removing people with persistent bourgeois liberal tendencies from leading posts on newspapers and periodicals. The document also said that "we have decided to suppress further publication of those newspapers and periodicals that have commited political mistakes or which contain material not on a high level." See *SWB/FE* 8512 (10 March 1987); *BX* 140 (16 March 1987); and *ICM*, May 1987, 3–5, 10. Most of the periodicals affected by this decision were smaller, lesser-known journals, such as the *Society News* (Shanghai), the *Special Economic Zone Workers' News* (Shenzhen), the *Youth Forum* (Hebei), and the *Science, Technology and Financial Report* (Anhui). The more notorious *World Economic Herald* of Shanghai was criticized but not shut down in this period. Among the liberal editors and journalists suspended from their posts in the winter and spring of 1987 were Liu Zaifu of *Literary Criticism* and Liu Xinwu of *People's Literature*, both of whom had actively participated in the 1986 critical debates on Marxist theory. Although political scientist Yan Jiaqi and his wife Gao Gao had their book, *A history of the decade of the Cultural Revolution*, banned from publication in 1986, this was apparently not directly related to their activities in support of bourgeois liberalization. Other prominent intellectuals criticized or blacklisted in this period included Wang Ruoshui, Hu Jiwei, Su Shaozhi, Yu Guangyuan, Li Honglin, Wu Zuguang, Wen Yuankai, Zhang Xianyang, Xu Liangying, Guo Luoji, and Ge Yang. For documentation, see *BX* 140, (16 March 1987); *JSND* 4 and 5 (1987); and Kelly, "The Chinese student movement . . . ."

222 In late January, a student at Tianjin University was arrested on a charge of having supplied classified information to a French journalist during the December student demonstrations (a charge strikingly similar to one leveled against Wei Jingsheng in 1979). In March, two nonstudents wre convicted of inciting riots on college campuses and were sentenced to prison terms of three and five years, respectively (*ICM*, May 1987, 30); and in May there was a report that another individual arrested

fully prevented from spilling over into an attack on economic reform and the open policy, both of which were consistently upheld, by reformers and conservatives alike, as entirely "necessary and correct."[223]

In a move intended to ensure a modicum of leadership continuity in the reform process, the Politburo unanimously selected Zhao Ziyang as acting general secretary of the CCP to replace Hu Yaobang.[224] One of Zhao's first acts in his new role was to reassure the country and the outside world that "China will not launch a political movement to oppose bourgeois liberalization. . . . The current work of opposing bourgeois liberalization will be strictly limited within the CCP and will be mainly carried out in the political and ideological fields. Nothing of the sort will be conducted in rural areas, while in enterprises and institutions the task will be handled in the form of study and self-education."[225]

Even Deng Liqun showed new and rather uncharacteristic restraint. In a February article aimed at a youthful audience, the erstwhile firebrand gently admonished China's young people to consider the harmful impact of recent student disturbances; he questioned the appropriateness of letting young people "do their own thing" and advocated stepping up political and ideological study in schools and universities.[226] But his tone was now schoolmasterly rather than strident, didactic rather than dogmatic. He could afford to be avuncular: He had won; Hu Yaobang was gone.

Notwithstanding Deng Liqun's patronizing tone, Chinese students and educators soon found themselves subject to tightened security measures, strengthened political loyalty tests, and intensified ideological indoctrination. Vice-Premier Li Peng set the tone for these changes in a February speech to a national educational work conference. While urging educators to

during the December disturbances had been sent to prison for three years (Stavis, *China's political reforms . . .*, 123). There may well have been other criminal convictions, but they were not documented at the time.

223 The danger that the campaign against bourgeois liberalization might be used as a pretext by opponents of economic reform and the open policy to sabotage Deng's reform program was explicitly acknowledged in "Central document no. 4, 1987" (see ftn. 221), which "strictly prohibited" such pretexts and proscribed such devious tactics as "using the Left to criticize the Right." In calling for stricter controls to be exercised over the press, publishing companies, and various artistic media, document no. 4 added the important caveat that "no general housecleaning will be carried out," further stipulating that there should be "no sudden switching from Right to Left, no requiring permission for everything, and no interfering with the normal development of literature and art."

224 *BR* 30.4 (26 January 1987), 5. The "acting" designation was removed later in the year when Zhao's selection as general secretary was formally ratified at the Thirteenth Party Congress.

225 *BR* 30.5–6 (9 February 1987), 6–7. China's leaders were obviously concerned in this period about calming popular fears, both domestic and foreign, of a new ideological witch hunt. Thus, the same issue of *Beijing Review* that carried Zhao's reassuring message about "no political movement" also carried, on its inside front cover, a full-page color photo of a relaxed and smiling Deng Xiaoping, casually attired in Western-style sweater and open-necked sport shirt, playing bridge.

226 *Zhongguo qingnian bao*, 12 February 1987, in *ICM*, May 1987, 13–14.

"do our best to win the understanding and support of students," Li announced that all schools and universities in China would soon undergo a tightening of control in order to enforce rigorously the rules and regulations.[227] Changes in the focus of the educational curriculum were also called for, centering on the need to readjust the content of liberal arts courses in order to promote the goal of "graduating young people with high ideals, moral character, culture, and discipline." Finally, the vice-premier announced that henceforth political character and "attitude toward the four cardinal principles and bourgeois liberalization" would be taken into consideration as major qualifications for students taking high school and college entrance examinations.[228]

Also, in February 1987, in a proposal designed to enable China's conservative "old comrades" to gain a modicum of added control over the actions of their successors, Bo Yibo called for a revival of the previously discarded "three-in-one" (*san jiehe*) leadership formula, combining "old, middle-aged, and young" leaders. Bo's call was echoed a month later by Vice-Premier Yao Yilin in a press conference with foreign journalists.[229]

With Hu Yaobang in disgrace, with liberalism in ill repute, and with elderly conservatives once again balking at the prospect of total retirement, Zhao Ziyang found himself operating on a rather short leash. Although he remained an important symbol of reform continuity and moderation, Zhao was forced to accommodate to the Party's prevailing antiliberal mood. His political report to the NPC in late March thus reflected a delicate balance between continued strong support for "total overall reform" of the economy and an equally firm denunciation of bourgeois liberalization. Blaming the December student demonstrations on "ideological confusion" sown as a result of the "erroneous trend" of bourgeois liberalization, Zhao now dutifully repeated Deng Xiaoping's warning of the previous December: "If bourgeois liberalization were allowed to spread unchecked . . . it would plunge our country into turmoil and make it impossible for us to proceed with our normal construction and reform programs."[230] Arguing that China must resolutely adhere to the four cardinal principles, Zhao flatly rejected the notions of "total Westernization" and "Americanized bourgeois liberal democracy," which were said to have exerted a "pernicious influence" on China's socialist modernization.[231] Trying his best to bridge the deep chasm that

227 Li Peng's address appears in *XH*, 16 February 1987; trans. in *ICM*, April 1987, 5–6.

228 Ibid., 6. See also *XH*, 2 February 1987.

229 *DGB*, 14 February and 29 March 1987. Yao Yilin was widely regarded as a protégé of Chen Yun.

230 Zhao's report appears in *BR* 30.16 (20 April 1987), III–XX.

231 A similar theme had been stressed by president Li Xiannian in a meeting with Japanese politicians on 3 March. On that occasion Li had said that it was "wishful thinking" for foreigners to expect China to go in for a market economy, capitalism, and total Westernization (*RMRB*, 4 March 1987).

separated rival wings of the party, Zhao argued that there was no necessary antagonism between the four cardinal principles and the policies of structural reform and opening up to the outside world. "They are not mutually exclusive," he asserted; "they complement and penetrate each other, forming an integral whole."[232] It was an assertion Zhao would later have intensely personal reason to reconsider.

Zhao Ziyang's ideological bow to Party conservatives was apparently part of a bargain struck early in the spring: In exchange for Zhao's denunciation of bourgeois liberalism and support for the four cardinal principles, the conservatives would halt their antireform, antiretirement backlash. The deal was brokered by Deng Xiaoping, who was said to be growing increasingly concerned, as in November 1983, over the excessive zeal displayed by conservatives in combatting liberalism.[233]

Whether or not the deal was struck in precisely these terms, a trade-off was very much in evidence in the spring of 1987, as condemnations of bourgeois liberalization subsided in intensity while talk of leadership rejuvenation and political structure reform correspondingly increased, with Deng's own voice now added to the pro-reform chorus.[234] Signalling the new *modus vivendi,* Peng Zhen gave a rare interview to foreign journalists in April, in which he indicated that he and several other old comrades, pointedly excluding Deng Xiaoping, would announce their retirement at the Thirteenth Party Congress.[235] Reform of China's political and administrative structures would resume, Peng predicted, but only within the framework of the four cardinal principles; in the reform process, emphasis would be placed on enhancing the administrative autonomy of urban enterprises and rural villages and increasing the supervisory functions of people's congresses at all levels. It was a formula that strongly suggested moderation and compromise, if not long-term political viability.

Having gained some measure of policy leverage, Zhao Ziyang reportedly

232 *BR* 30.16 (20 April 1987), XVI.

233 Ian Wilson and You Ji suggest that Deng decided to modulate the anti-bourgeois liberalization campaign at the urging of his son, Deng Pufang ("Leadership by 'lines' . . . ," 34–35). See also Stuart R. Schram, "China after the 13th congress," *CQ* 114 (June 1988), 180; and Tony Saich, "The thirteenth congress of the Chinese Communist Party: An agenda for reform?" *Journal of Communist Studies* 4.2 (June 1988), 205.

234 In mid-March, Deng told the visiting governor-general of Canada that "at the Thirteenth Congress this year we shall discuss plans for reform of the political system." At around the same time, a new volume of Deng's collected writings was issued. Entitled *Fundamental issues in present-day China,* the book contained several of the senior leader's pre-December 1986 statements stressing the necessity of political reform. See *BR* 30.20 (18 May 1987), 14–17.

235 As for Deng Xiaoping, Peng said that "We should keep just him on the Standing Committee as an old timer, and let all the rest be relatively young." See *DGB,* 9 April 1987; and *BR* 30.17 (27 April 1987), 14–15. In the event, it was Yang Shangkun, not Deng Xiaoping, who remained on the new Politburo as the lone old-timer after the Thirteenth Congress, though he was not elevated to the SC.

resisted pressure from Party conservatives to discipline severely political reformers such as Yan Jiaqi and Su Shaozhi. On the recommendation of his political secretary, Bao Tong, who claimed that Deng Liqun had fabricated evidence against Yan Jiaqi, Zhao now exonerated Yan of the charge of bourgeois liberalism.[236]

Meanwhile, Zhao and his five-person group (which by this time had been expanded to nineteen members) now resumed work on their blueprint for reform of the political structure. In March 1987, the group transmitted a letter to Deng Xiaoping outlining some "initial thoughts" on the problem of reform. After a few days, Deng returned the letter with the annotation, "the design is good."[237] In May, the first working draft of a plan was submitted for Deng's approval. The core of the plan was a proposal to separate Party and government, one of Deng's principal reform recommendations of August 1980. However, Zhao and his colleagues apparently went further toward circumscribing and balancing Party power than Deng had intended, for now the senior leader balked at Zhao's draft, pointing out sharply that the bourgeois system of checks and balances was "still being dished up in new form." The political structure reform group thereupon went back to the drawing board.[238] At least four more drafts were prepared between May and September, some of which were disseminated for debate and discussion. The final version, draft number seven, was approved at the Seventh Plenum of the Twelfth CC, which met in mid-October on the eve of the Thirteenth Party Congress.[239]

Throughout the summer, there was a great deal of speculation about the upcoming Thirteenth Congress. In June, Deng had confounded party old-timers, who wished to retain a share of power at the top, by announcing his intention to retire.[240] In August, at the annual leaders' meeting at Beidaihe, there were reports that Deng had agreed, after intense lobbying by Chen Yun and others, to approve the promotion of two second-echelon conservatives, Song Ping and Yao Yilin, to the Politburo and its SC, respectively, in order to compensate partially for the retirement of elderly veterans.[241] Later in the summer, the name of Deng Liqun was also floated as a conservative choice for a Politburo seat.

236 *WHB* (Shanghai), 8 August 1989; Wilson and Ji, "Leadership by 'lines' . . . ," 35, n. 17.

237 Quoted in Michel Oksenberg, "China's 13th Party congress," *POC* 36.6 (November–December 1987), 15–16.

238 Feng, "Preparations for the blueprint . . . ," 7. Aside from the five original members of the political structure reform group, three other individuals who played a prominent role in shaping the draft reform proposals in this period were Zhao's political secretary, Bao Tong, who was also vice-minister of the State Commission on Economic Restructuring; political scientist Yan Jiaqi; and long-time reform advocate Liao Gailong, who was responsible for coordinating the theoretical recommendations made by the group's various study panels (ibid.).

239 Oksenberg, "China's 13th . . . ," 15–16. 240 *DGB*, 4 June 1987.

241 *I&S* 23.12 (December 1987), 96.

In late August, *Xinhua* revealed that the guiding document for political reform at the Thirteenth Congress would be Deng Xiaoping's recently rereleased 1980 essay "On the reform of the system of Party and state leadership."[242] Also at the end of August, Hu Qili indicated that "at least seven" members of the Politburo would resign at the Congress; Deng Xiaoping was not among them.[243] At around the same time, it was revealed that Vice-Premier Li Peng would soon be named to succeed Zhao Ziyang as premier, enabling Zhao to concentrate on his Party leadership duties.[244]

THIRD CYCLE: LIBERALIZATION AND REPRESSION

Toward reform and renewal: The Thirteenth Party Congress

The Thirteenth Party Congress met from 25 October to 1 November. As expected, two items dominated the agenda: leadership changes and Zhao Ziyang's reform blueprint. In both of these areas, the Congress appeared to represent a victory for the reformers.[245]

Fully half of the members of the old Politburo, ten out of twenty, announced their retirement at the Congress. Heading the list, unexpectedly, was Deng Xiaoping himself; the others were Chen Yun, Li Xiannian, Peng Zhen, Hu Qiaomu, Wang Zhen, Xi Zhongxun, Yu Qiuli, Yang Dezhi, and Fang Yi.[246] Among the Party's top leaders, only four Politburo members remained from the twenty elected at the Twelfth Party Congress in 1982: Yang Shangkun, Wan Li, Zhao Ziyang, and – somewhat surprisingly – Hu Yaobang, who easily gained reelection despite his recent disgrace. Yang Shangkun, at eighty, was by far the oldest member of the new Politburo; no one else was above the age of seventy-three.[247]

The new Politburo Standing Committee, headed by general secretary (no longer "acting") Zhao Ziyang, included Hu Qili, Li Peng, Qiao Shi, and

242 *XH*, 28 August 1987, in *SWB/FE* 8661 (1 September 1987).

243 *SWB/FE* 8676 (18 September 1987). The seven named included six elderly veterans (Chen Yun, Li Xiannian, Hu Qiaomu, Peng Zhen, Xi Zhongxun, and Fang Yi), as well as one relative newcomer to the Politburo, Ni Zhifu.

244 *SWB/FE* 8684 (28 September 1987).

245 The Thirteenth Congress is analyzed in Schram, "China after the 13th congress"; Saich, "The thirteenth congress . . . ."; Oksenberg, "China's 13th . . . ."; and *I&S* 23.12 (December 1987), 12–99.

246 Although both Peng Zhen and Hu Qili had previously indicated that Deng Xiaoping would not step down at the Thirteenth Congress, Deng's last-minute decision to retire was rumored to be part of a quid pro quo arranged at the insistence of Chen Yun, who reportedly refused to resign from the Standing Committee unless Deng joined him. See Saich, "The thirteenth congress . . . ," 204.

247 Yang, a longtime Deng Xiaoping associate, was reportedly retained as the result of an agreement between Deng and Chen Yun that would permit both leaders to retire while still giving China's old-timers one set of eyes and ears on the Politburo.

Yao Yilin. Politburo newcomers included CCP Organization Department Director Song Ping (seventy), Shanghai Mayor Jiang Zemin (sixty-one), Beijing municipal Party secretary Li Ximing (sixty-one), Tianjin Mayor Li Ruihuan (fifty-three), and State Commissioner for Economic Restructuring Li Tieying (fifty-one). Former alternate Qin Jiwei (seventy-two) was now elevated to full Politburo membership, thereby becoming the lone career military figure on the new ruling body.[248] Arguably the most significant of all the Politburo selections, however, was the one that wasn't made – that is, Deng Liqun.

Most of the personnel changes made at the Thirteenth Congress had been agreed to in advance by Party leaders. Deng Liqun's nonselection came as a surprise, however. His exclusion was the result of new election procedures introduced at the Thirteenth Congress, reportedly at Zhao Ziyang's behest. To ensure a modicum of democratic competition, the new rules required that there be ten more nominees for the CC than the actual number of seats to be filled; the ten candidates receiving the least support in the first round of voting (which was to be conducted by secret ballot) would be dropped and would have their names added to a list of nominees for alternate CC membership. A second ballot would then be taken, and the sixteen lowest vote getters in this latter round would be dropped altogether.[249]

When this system was used for the first time at the Thirteenth Congress, the candidate who reportedly received the lowest number of votes in the first round of balloting was none other than Deng Liqun. Deng's electoral rebuff was doubly embarrassing insofar as the seventy-two-year-old firebrand had previously been tabbed by Party leaders (reportedly after some heavy arm twisting by Chen Yun) to replace the retiring Hu Qiaomu on the Politburo. After having been flatly rejected for CC election on the first ballot, however, Deng Liqun apparently chose to avoid the possibility of further humiliation; he now withdrew his name from the second ballot, thereby forfeiting his eligibility for selection to the Politburo.[250] In the wake of this rebuff, Chen Yun reportedly lobbied hard to have Deng Liqun's name added to the ballot for election to the SC of the CAC. Once again Deng failed to gain peer acceptance, however, as he reportedly received less than half of the votes cast by members of the CAC. Utterly rejected, Deng's humiliation at the Thirteenth Party Congress must have come as sweet revenge for Hu Yaobang,

248 As a result of these changes, the average age of Politburo members declined from seventy to sixty-four.

249 This procedure is described in Oksenberg, "China's 13th . . . ."; see also Wilson and Ji, "Leadership by 'lines' . . . ," 36.

250 Schram, "China after the 13th . . . ," 184; Oksenberg, "China's 13th . . . ," 16. Since the Politburo was a subcommittee of the CC, Politburo members had to be selected from among CC members.

who, despite his recent fall from grace, received sufficient delegate support to be handily reelected to both the CC and its Politburo.[251]

As a result of revamped selection procedures adopted at the Thirteenth Congress, the new CC was considerably smaller, younger, and better-educated than its predecessor. Its size was reduced from 385 full and alternate members to 285, a drop of more than 25 percent. Forty-two percent of the CC members and alternates were first-timers, and more than 70 percent were college trained; fifty-seven members were employed in high-technology fields. Only 20 percent of the members were over the age of sixty-one; almost half were fifty-five years of age or younger. Significantly, although military representation on the new Politburo remained low, the picture was somewhat more ambiguous on the full CC, where almost 20 percent of the members were PLA officers.[252]

Even more ambiguous was the relationship between the Party and the army. Prior to the Thirteenth Congress, Deng Xiaoping had made it clear that he wanted to resign from his post as chairman of the Party's powerful MAC, and that he wished to have Zhao Ziyang installed as his successor. PLA leaders were apparently unmoved by Deng's appeal, for they refused to agree to Zhao's selection; consequently, Deng was forced to retain the MAC chairmanship, the only Party post he did not relinquish at the Congress.[253] In deference to Deng's wishes, senior military leaders did consent to name Zhao as first vice-chairman of the MAC; at the same time, however, they insisted on installing Yang Shangkun as "permanent" vice-chairman and Yang's younger half-brother, Yang Baibing, as chief of the PLA's general political department. Through such arrangements, China's conservative senior military leaders hoped to ensure against the possibility of a "hostile takeover" of the MAC in the event of Deng Xiaoping's early death or disability.[254]

Yet another important safeguard against a possible hostile takeover was put into place at the Thirteenth Congress, though it went unreported for almost two years. In response to the expressed concerns of certain old comrades, voiced at the time of Hu Yaobang's ouster, over possible future recurrences of reckless Party leadership, it was now stipulated that henceforth the PSC would consult with Deng Xiaoping on all important political matters, and with Chen Yun on all important economic matters, before making any major

251 Hu Yaobang's long-disgraced predecessor, Hua Guofeng, also received strong delegate support in the CC elections at the Thirteenth Congress.

252 *I&S* 23.12 (December 1987), 95ff.

253 Deng also retained his concurrent chairmanship of the governmental MAC.

254 In this respect, as with regard to his continued presence on the Party Politburo, Yang Shangkun's designated role on the MAC was to represent the interests of CAC old-timers.

decisions. In this way, China's outgoing elder statesmen would retain effective veto power over vital policy initiatives even after retiring from office. The irony of such an arrangement was considerable: In order to help effect a smooth transition to a more highly developed structure of formal, institutionalized political power, China's leaders were opening a back door to the reassertion of informal, highly personalized authority. It was, of course, precisely this arrangement that enabled China's old guard to reassert its policy-making prerogatives during the Tiananmen crisis of April–June 1989.[255]

Structural reform in the primary stage of socialism

If leadership change was one of the big stories of the Thirteenth Congress, a potentially even bigger story was the unveiling of Zhao Ziyang's long-awaited blueprint for structural reform. There were a number of significant doctrinal departures in Zhao's report to the Congress. These included a new basic Party line, identified as "one center and two basic points," and a novel, neo-Marxist ideological rationale for undertaking bold economic experiments, the theory of the "primary stage of socialism" (*shehuizhuyi de chuji jieduan*).[256]

"One center and two basic points"

As spelled out in Zhao's report, economic development was henceforth to be considered the "central task" of the present era, to be pursued by grasping simultaneously two "basic points": adherence to the four cardinal principles and persistence in the policy of reform and opening up to the outside world. What made this rather stylized formulation noteworthy was its explicit subordination of the four cardinal principles to the strategic requirements of economic development. "Whatever is conducive to the growth [of the productive forces]," said Zhao, "is in keeping with the fundamental interests of the people and is therefore needed by socialism and allowed to exist." Conversely,

255 The existence of such an arrangement, which had been anticipated by "Central document No. 1, 1987," was first confirmed in November 1987 in a speech by Zhao Ziyang to a plenary session of the CC. In the speech, Zhao said: "Comrade Xiaoping still has the power to convene our standing committees whenever he feels that it is necessary. When we have any major problems it is still to him that we should turn to seek instruction" (*ZM* 122 [December 1987], in *ICM*, January 1988, 9). The arrangement was publicly revealed in Zhao Ziyang's fateful meeting with Mikhail Gorbachev on 16 May 1989 (see the section "Waging Moral Warfare: Gorbachev, the Media, and the Hunger Strike"). Additional details concerning the arrangement were subsequently published in *ZM* 121 (1 November 1990).

256 Zhao's report appears in *BR* 30.45 (9–15 November 1987), I–XXVII.

Zhao continued, "whatever is detrimental to this growth goes against scientific socialism and is therefore not allowed to exist."[257]

"The primary stage of socialism"

If Zhao's "whatever works" ethos did not explicitly give Chinese reformers *carte blanche* to try out anything they thought might spur economic growth and call it "socialism," then it certainly came very close. In support of this pragmatic ethos, Zhao invoked China's developmental backwardness. Harking back to the New Democratic era of the early 1950s, Zhao stated that "because our socialism has emerged from the womb of a semi-colonial, semi-feudal society, with the productive forces lagging far behind those of the developed capitalist countries, we are destined to go through a very long primary stage." In this stage, said Zhao, China must use whatever means are available to catch up with the advanced capitalist countries. It would be "naive and utopian," he argued, to believe that China could skip over this primary stage and proceed directly to mature socialism; indeed, such a utopian belief comprised "the major cognitive root of Leftist mistakes."[258]

In the realm of economic strategy, Zhao's report went well beyond the party's cautious October 1984 "bigger birdcage" reform proposals, calling now for substantially stepped-up use of the free-market mechanism and for rapid expansion of the collective and privately owned sectors of the economy.[259] Under the slogan "The state regulates the market; the market guides the enterprise," Zhao urged the creation of private markets for "essential factors . . . such as funds, labor services, technology, information, and real estate." In another break from Marxist tradition, Zhao further indicated that "in the future, buyers of bonds will earn interest, and shareholders dividends; enterprise managers will receive additional income to compensate for bearing risks." New price reforms were also called for, to be introduced gradually and in conjunction with rising incomes, "so that actual living standards do not decline." The report further recommended the introduction of "new types of institutions for commodity circulation, foreign trade and banking, as well as

257 Ibid., XXVI. After the Congress, Zhao Ziyang combined the two whatevers of this formulation into one single, complex whatever, thereby avoiding invidious comparison with the two whatevers promulgated by former Party Chairman Hua Guofeng. See *CNA* 1354 (15 February 1988), 4.

258 *BR* 30.45 (9–16 November 1987), III–IV. The term "primary stage of socialism" was first used in the CCP's 1981 *Resolution on CPC history (1949–1981)*, 74. Su Shaozhi is widely credited with having popularized the term in 1986. Stuart Schram ("China after the 13th . . .," 177–8) states that the term's immediate antecedent, "undeveloped socialism" (*bufada de shehuizhuyi*), was first coined in 1979; however, the present author recalls hearing the latter term used in discussions with faculty members from the Beida department of politics and law as early as September 1978.

259 In an interview on 29 October, Zhao predicted that within two or three years only 30 percent of China's economy would be subject to central planning (*The Guardian*, 30 October 1987, cited in Saich, "The thirteenth congress . . .," 205).

networks of [autonomous] agencies to provide technology, information, and service." In an attempt to preempt conservative criticism that such radical economic innovations smacked strongly of capitalism, Zhao tersely asserted that the measures called for in his report "are not peculiar to capitalism."[260]

Political reform: Toward "neoauthoritarianism"

Turning next to the realm of politics, Zhao called political reform an "urgent matter," noting that the CC "believes it is high time to put reform of the political structure on the agenda for the whole party." Otherwise, he asserted, economic reform would be doomed to failure. Henceforth, the two were to be considered inseparable.

Zhao's specific proposals for political reform were more skeletal than substantive. Reiterating a basic theme initially raised in August 1980 by Deng Xiaoping and subsequently elaborated in 1986 by Yan Jiaqi, *inter alia,* Zhao argued that China's feudal heritage had created severe problems of overconcentrated power, bureaucratism, and feudalization of the political structure. To remedy these defects, Zhao called for reform in seven broad areas: (1) separating Party and government; (2) delegating state power and authority to lower levels; (3) reforming government bureaucracy; (4) reforming the personnel (cadre) system; (5) establishing a system of political dialogue and consultation between the Party and the people; (6) enhancing the supervisory roles of representative assemblies and mass organizations; and (7) strengthening the socialist legal system.[261]

Although few concrete measures for implementing reforms in these seven areas were elaborated in Zhao's report, some potentially far-reaching structural changes were suggested. For example, in proposing the gradual elimination of "party groups" (*dangzu*) in governmental organs at all levels, Zhao clearly sought to neutralize a major obstacle blocking the reformers' key goal of separating Party from government. In similar fashion, Zhao's recommendation that those CCP organs responsible for enforcing Party discipline (the CDICs) should no longer exercise exclusive jurisdiction over breaches of law by Party members represented a major departure from existing policy, insofar as it clearly implied that henceforth Party members ought not to be routinely shielded from criminal prosecution for their misdeeds.[262]

New also was Zhao Ziyang's call for a major overhaul of China's Leninist–

260 *BR* 30.45 (9–16 November 1987), XI–XIV. Despite the overall progressive thrust of his report, Zhao did make some notable compromises with Party conservatives. For example, he backed away from advocating rapid price reform, and he upheld the vital importance of grain production, two major concerns of Chen Yun since 1985 (ibid., IX).

261 Ibid., XV–XXI. 262 Ibid., XVI.

Stalinist personnel system, the *nomenklatura,* and its replacement by a civil service system of impersonal, professionalized cadre recruitment and evaluation. Although campaigns to eliminate excessive bureaucratism had been frequent occurrences in China under both Mao and Deng, never before had a top Chinese leader called for such broad, sweeping civil service reform. If implemented, Zhao's proposal could have spelled the end of the CCP's traditional monopoly of control over the government's personnel staffing and review procedures.[263]

In a section of his report detailing suggestions for improving the quality of "mutual consultation and dialogue" between the government and the people, Zhao made yet another noteworthy departure from China's established political tradition. He implicitly rejected the conventional notion of "unified public opinion" under socialism, arguing that the government should be concerned with listening to and reflecting the divergent opinions and interests of its citizens. "Different groups of people may have different interests and views," he said; "they too need opportunities and channels for the exchange of ideas."[264]

In each of these respects, Zhao Ziyang's report broke significant new ground, albeit only in preliminary fashion and only on paper. Painfully short on programmatic details, the report nonetheless offered some tantalizing glimpses into the political philosophy and strategy of Deng Xiaoping's newly designated successor. Perhaps most important, the report revealed Zhao to be an advocate not of Western-style liberalism but of Chinese "neoauthoritarianism," a doctrine that stressed the need for strong, centralized technocratic leadership throughout the "primary stage of socialism." Insofar as modernization and structural reform were inherently turbulent and stressful processes, Zhao argued, there were inevitably "many factors making for instability." For this reason, he averred, the transition to democracy had to be undertaken "step by step in an orderly way." Explicitly rejecting bourgeois democracy – with its separation of powers, multiparty competition, and freedom of political expression – as unsuited to China's current conditions, Zhao invoked the memory of Cultural Revolution chaos (and, by implicit extension, the more recent memory of student turmoil) to bolster his argument for limiting popular political participation and free expression. "We shall never again," he warned, "allow the kind of 'great democracy' that undermines state law and social stability." In lieu of competitive political

263 See John P. Burns, "Chinese civil service reform: The 13th party congress proposals," *CQ* 120 (December 1989), 739–70.

264 *BR* 30.45 (9–16 November), XIX. Zhao had made a similar appeal on the eve of the Thirteenth Congress, arguing that "Socialist society is not a monolith. . . . [S]pecial interests should not be overlooked. Conflicting interests should be reconciled." See *BR* 30.50 (14–20 December 1987), 16.

parties and elections, Zhao proposed to further refine and perfect the Party's existing institutions and mechanisms of "democratic consultation and mutual supervision."[265]

Although Zhao's composite vision for China's political development thus had a decidedly illiberal edge to it, it represented a significant break with the past. Falling far short of being a blueprint for bourgeois democratization, it nonetheless offered the first broad, tentative sketches of an emergent nontotalitarian Chinese political future, one that contained at least the seeds, if not yet the sprouts, of incipient pluralism. Viewed in this light, that is, as a transitional neoauthoritarian manifesto, Zhao Ziyang's report to the Thirteenth Party Congress was a most important – if not an obviously revolutionary – document.[266]

Consolidating the gains

In the aftermath of the October 1987 Party Congress, Zhao moved to consolidate his political gains. He first moved to reassert control over the Party's propaganda apparatus. Commenting that he "never read" the CC's principal ideological organ, *Red Flag* (*Hongqi*), Zhao indicated his intention to disband the journal, which had long been a thorn in the side of Party reformers.[267] Alarmed, a group of old-timers from the CAC, led by Bo Yibo, along with the Party's propaganda chief, Wang Renzhi, reportedly requested that the journal be placed on probation rather than shut down. Undeterred, Zhao initiated a shakeup in the Party's propaganda apparatus. In December 1987, *Red Flag*'s editor and deputy editor were quietly retired, as was the conservative deputy director of the CC propaganda department. A month later, propaganda chief Wang Renzhi was also squeezed out. In May 1988, it was officially announced that *Red Flag* would cease publication, to be replaced by a new journal with a significantly altered title: *Seeking Truth* (*Qiushi*).[268]

Meanwhile, it was decided that the traditional ceremonial portraits of Marx, Engels, Lenin, and Stalin would no longer grace Tiananmen Square

265 *BR* 30.45 (9–15 November 1987), VI, XV.

266 For elaboration of the concept of neoauthoritarianism, see note 4 and the sections "Political Reform: Toward 'Neoauthoritarianism' and "Zhao's Neoauthoritarian Counteroffensive."

267 The editors of *Red Flag* had been critical of Hu Yaobang and Zhao Ziyang's reform policies at the time of the 1983 anti–spiritual pollution campaign. Hu had reciprocated their dislike, claiming at one point that he found the magazine "boring." See *WHB* (Hong Kong), 24 December 1987; *CNA* 1351 (1 January 1988), 4.

268 These developments are documented in *I&S* 24.2 (February 1988), 1; *WHB* (Hong Kong), 28 April 1988; *RMRB*, 2 May 1988, 3; *CNA* 1360 (15 May 1988), 4; *Qiushi* (hereafter, *QS*) 1 (1 July 1988), 1, in JPRS Report: China (hereafter, JPRS) CAR-88-043 (4 August 1988). The new journal was placed under the jurisdiction of the Central Party School, rather than the CC's propaganda department, as before, thereby implicitly downgrading its status. For further analysis see Lowell Dittmer, "China in 1988: The dilemma of continuing reform," *AS* 29.1 (January 1989), 13–15.

after the PRC's fortieth anniversary celebration of October 1989. As if for emphasis, two oversized statues of Mao Zedong were quietly hauled away from the Beida campus in the dark of night, following at least one unsuccessful attempt at on-the-spot demolition.

With the Party's pragmatic reform wing seemingly in control, a mood of elation spread among China's intellectuals. In November 1987, a symposium was convened in Beijing to discuss the outcome of the Thirteenth Party Congress. At the meeting, a number of prominent Chinese political scientists expressed their deep satisfaction with the results of the Congress:

> [Zhao Ziyang's] report directly or indirectly contains all the proposals we have advocated.[269]

> The theory [of] the primary stage of socialism is a great breakthrough. . . . Stepping off the path is not running away from the road; differing with those at the top is not rebellion; esteeming things foreign is not toadying to alien ways.[270]

> This session of the party congress produced great results. . . . [It] went far beyond what was expected. . . . For the first time [it] elevated reform to the position of a major societal activity under socialism.[271]

> The most wonderful accomplishment of this session . . . was holding elections in which the number of candidates exceeded the number of positions.[272]

Not everyone shared the enthusiasm of these reform-oriented political scientists, however; indeed, some liberal critics of the regime were openly skeptical. Fang Lizhi, for example, reminded a Hong Kong interviewer that although Zhao Ziyang's report "was very moving to listen to," in his own time "Mao Zedong made speeches that were even better to listen to than this one. It's not enough just to read the speeches. . . . You also have to keep your eye on the concrete indicators."[273]

Signs of stress: The economy overheats

Not long after the Thirteenth Congress adjourned, the concrete indicators began to go sour. As during the previous reform-induced growth spurt of 1984–5, it was China's overheated, unbalanced economy that produced the early warning signs. Freed from some but not all of its traditional central planning constraints, the Chinese economy began to lurch out of control toward the end of 1987. The main problems were familiar enough: spiraling

269 Tan Jian (research department chairman, CASS Institute of Political Science), in *WHB* (Hong Kong), 7–8 November 1987; trans. in *ICM*, January 1988, 2.

270 Yu Haocheng (vice-chairman, Chinese Political Science Association), in ibid.

271 Gao Fang (professor of international politics, Beida), in ibid.

272 Ma Peiwen (chairman, Chinese Political Science Association), in ibid.

273 *BX* 155 (1 November 1987).

wage–price inflation, a runaway money supply, surging consumer demand, overinvestment in capital construction, rampant commercial speculation, and official profiteering. In a rather gloomy 1988 New Year's economic message, the government broke the bad news:

> Inflation has become a problem. . . . People worry that unless price rises are checked, the benefit from the reform will be cancelled out. . . . Price rises point to economic instability, resulting mainly from excessive demand. Inordinate investment in capital construction, consumption outstripping production, and excessive money supply have remained uncorrected for a number of years. . . .
>
> Many enterprises have failed to comply with the state's rule that enterprises should spend 60 percent of their operating funds on production . . . and have instead spent most of the money on welfare and bonuses, resulting in a further expansion of consumption funds.
>
> Taking advantage of relaxed controls, some enterprises raised prices without authorization. Some . . . joined lawless retailers in speculation to disrupt the market and harm the consumers' interests.[274]

With many enterprises granting unauthorized wage and bonus increases to workers, large quantities of money were pumped into an already overheated economy. As consumer demand rose, output and prices also soared for certain luxury goods, such as automatic washing machines, color TVs, stereo sets, and refrigerators. By contrast, output of vital capital goods for the national economy remained relatively static.[275]

Government statistics confirmed the worsening situation of economic imbalance. In the winter of 1987–8, the money supply grew at twice the rate of economic output. Food prices on urban markets, which had increased more than 10 percent in 1987, continued their upward march: In the first quarter of 1988, prices for nonstaple foods rose by 24.2 percent, and fresh vegetable prices soared 48.7 percent. To deal with surging demand (and surging prices), the government reintroduced rationing for pork, eggs, and sugar.[276]

For the first time since the reforms began, there was a real drop in the purchasing power of substantial numbers of urban wage earners. In a 1987 survey of more than 2,300 residents in thirty-three Chinese cities, more than two-thirds indicated that their real income was falling. Rising prices were

274 *BR* 31.1 (4–10 January 1989), 4.

275 In Guangzhou municipality, it was reported that the purchasing power of urban residents rose 55.4 percent in the first quarter of 1988 compared to the same quarter in 1987. The highest spending growth was in the areas of appliance purchases and "treating friends to meals" (*Nanfang ribao,* 3 May 1988, in *ICM*, July 1988, 21). In the electronics industry, over 70 percent of total national output in the early winter of 1987–88 was accounted for by luxury goods such as television sets, radios, and stereos (*ICM*, January 1988, 26).

276 *WHB* (Hong Kong), 5 June 1988; *BR* 31.1 (4–10 January 1988), 4. The problem of rising prices is discussed in *XH*, 12, 14 January and 1 February 1988, in *ICM*, March 1988, 12–18; see also *JSND*, March 1988, 44–6.

the number one source of worry for more than 70 percent of those sampled.[277] Reflecting such concerns, early in 1988 *Xinhua* reported that a married couple, each earning an average wage of 70–80 yuan per month, "cannot afford to raise a child in [Beijing]." Throughout the winter and early spring of 1988, a swelling flow of letters to the editors of China's major newspapers testified to the painful effects of inflation.

Searching for a viable economic strategy: The Seventh NPC

Against this background of declining urban economic health, the Seventh NPC convened in late March. The meeting was dominated by reformers of various stripes. The Party's conservative wing, dealt a major blow at the Thirteenth Congress, was little in evidence, save for some largely ceremonial appointments and functions. Indeed, the demographic composition of the NPC suggested the extent of the third echelon's dramatic ascent to political maturity: More than 70 percent of the almost 3,000 delegates were first-timers; the average age of all delegates was only fifty-two; 56 percent had received postsecondary education. Generational change was equally striking on the NPC Standing Committee, where 64 percent of the 135 ordinary members had been elected for the first time. Only at the very top of the NPC hierarchy was there substantial leadership continuity, as eleven of the nineteen previous SC vice-chairmen were reelected. At the apex of the organization stood the newly elected NPC SC chairman, Wan Li. The choice of Wan, an ally of Zhao Ziyang, to replace the retiring Peng Zhen augured the likely development of a more open and democratic NPC work style.[278]

The delegates to the Seventh NPC did, in fact, display a considerably stronger inclination toward independence, spontaneity, and critical scrutiny of the government than their predecessors. In a secret ballot to elect a successor to retiring PRC President Li Xiannian, Deng Xiaoping's hand-picked candidate, Yang Shangkun, received an unprecedented 124 "no" votes and an additional 34 abstentions. In the contest for vice-president, there were even more nay-sayers, as the party leadership's choice, conservative Wang Zhen, received 212 negative votes and 77 abstentions – more than 10 percent of the total ballots cast.[279]

277 *BR* 31.17 (12–18 September 1988), 29; *WHB* (Hong Kong), 4 September 1988; also John P. Burns, "China's governance: Political reform in a turbulent environment," *CQ* 119 (September 1989), 489.

278 For useful accounts of the NPC proceedings, see *CNA* 1360 (15 May 1988), 1–10; *FEER*, 21 April 1988, 12–13; and Dittmer, "China in 1988 . . .," 16–18.

279 The most frequent dissenting votes at the NPC were reportedly cast by delegates from Hong Kong, Macao, and China's coastal cities and provinces. One noncandidate for office, Hu Yaobang, received twenty-six write-in votes for the PRC presidency and twenty-three more for the vice-presidency. Aside from Wang Zhen, the only other leaders to draw more than a 10 percent negative vote at the

In addition to showing signs of incipient independence in the election of state leaders, NPC delegates engaged in a good deal of lively debate on government policies. Delegates held numerous small-group meetings, where they openly protested various social ills such as inflation, low pay for teachers, inequitable distribution of benefits from the coastal development strategy, and the forcible imposition of central policies in minority nationality areas such as Tibet.[280]

Although the Seventh NPC thus displayed a new degree of openness and a new diversity of opinions, arguably its most critical function was to serve as a sounding board for the government's emerging strategy for the next stage of economic reform. Generally speaking, two competing approaches were advocated by policymakers: speed and caution. Zhao Ziyang favored the former; newly installed premier Li Peng preferred the latter.[281]

On the eve of the NPC, Zhao had outlined a bold, optimistic plan for further structural reform. At the Second Plenum of the Thirteenth CC meeting in mid-March, he spelled out his three main concerns: to further emancipate thinking, to deepen reform, and to stabilize the economy. Central to Zhao's plan was the further extension of decentralized responsibility systems in state-owned industrial enterprises, breaking once and for all the industrial workers' iron rice bowl and eliminating the common pot of collective benefits for enterprise cadres and staff personnel. Zhao also stressed the need gradually to enlarge the scope of price reforms and to expand further the coastal development strategy in order to give preferential incentives to export-oriented areas and enterprises that could succeed in attracting foreign investment and technology.[282]

The priorities outlined in Zhao's plan stood in subtle, if marked, contrast to Li Peng's priorities, adumbrated earlier in the year. Where Zhao stressed emancipating the mind, Li stressed cultivating socialist ethics; where Zhao called for a deepening of reforms to be followed by efforts to stabilize the economy, Li called for stability first, then – and only then – deepened re-

Seventh NPC were SC candidate Chen Muhua, a female, who had unsuccessfully sought a Politburo seat at the Thirteenth Party Congress, and an eighty-nine-year-old man whom some delegates thought was too old to serve in an official capacity (*CNA* 1360 [15 May 1988], 3–4).

280 An opinion poll conducted among several hundred NPC delegates at the conclusion of the March 1988 NPC meeting revealed that a large number of people's deputies took seriously the notions of democratic "supervision" and "consultation" which had been the catchwords of Zhao Ziyang's neoauthoritarian proposals for democratic reform at the Thirteenth Party Congress. See Shi Tianjian, "Role culture and political liberalism among deputies to the seventh National People's Congress, 1988" (paper presented at the annual meeting of the Association for Asian Studies, Washington, D.C., March 1989).

281 Li had been named acting premier by the NPC SC shortly after the Thirteenth Party Congress; his appointment was formally confirmed at the Seventh NPC.

282 Zhao's report to the Second Plenum is summarized in *BR* 31.13 (28 March–3 April 1988), 5–6. For Zhao's views on coastal development, see *BR* 31.5 (1–7 February 1988), 5.

form. The word order was crucial, since the term "stabilize the economy" had become a euphemism for limiting the scope and pace of basic structural reforms.[283]

Li Peng's government work report to the Seventh NPC represented an effort to downplay differences within the leadership. It was a consensus-seeking document designed to minimize conflict and contention. Once again, however, Li's primary emphasis was on stabilization rather than emancipation, caution rather than boldness. Addressing himself to some of the key concerns of Party conservatives, Li stressed the need to increase grain production while simultaneously developing the country's basic industries and infrastructure – issues that were of perennial concern to central planners in command economies. On price reform, by contrast, the premier's report remained largely silent.[284]

In terms of new legislation, the most significant action taken at the Seventh NPC was final approval of a long-delayed law on enterprise reform. The new law, which had been bottled up for two years by the outgoing NPC SC chairman, Peng Zhen, had as its key provisions the separation of ownership from management (allowing state-owned enterprises greater autonomy, vis-à-vis their parent bodies, over management, contracts, and leasing arrangements) and the director responsibility system (giving enterprise managers legal authority to hire and fire workers, plan production, and allocate retained profits, free from interference by local Party secretaries). With the enterprise reform law enacted, the PRC's long-dormant bankruptcy law, approved in December 1986 but never implemented for lack of enterprise reform legislation, was now scheduled to take effect in three months. The bankruptcy law provided both a legal basis and a procedural framework for shutting down chronically unprofitable state-owned enterprises.[285]

Toward urban socioeconomic meltdown: The crisis of 1988

In the months following adjournment of the Seventh NPC, China's urban malaise, which had been deepening quietly throughout the winter, took a turn for the worse. As on previous occasions, students were the bellweather.

283 Li's priorities are outlined in *BR* 31.2 (11–17 January 1988), 5.

284 Li's report appears in *BR* 31.17 (25 April–1 May 1988), 18–43; for an analysis, see *I&S* 24.6 (June 1988), 12–18.

285 The Seventh NPC also enacted constitutional amendments guaranteeing the legal status of private enterprises and delegating additional powers over rural land contracting to local governments. The latter amendment, which established a legal basis for long-term leasing and transfer of use rights, gave Chinese farmers greater control over land-use decisions, thus encouraging them to invest in land improvement. Finally, the NPC approved creation of a new province-level administrative unit, Hainan Island, which was granted the autonomous commercial status of a special economic zone (SEZ).

In early April, students at Beida began to demonstrate again, first on campus and then moving to Tiananmen Square; the targets this time were rising living costs, meager student stipends, and an inadequate government education budget. Significantly, their protest coincided with the twelfth anniversary of the "April 5th incident" at Tiananmen Square.[286] In the first six months of 1988, seventy-seven colleges and universities in twenty-five cities were involved in direct or indirect protest demonstrations; in response, the central government decided to set up public security headquarters on many university campuses.[287]

Another focal point of rising urban discontent was the government's plan to privatize housing and to decontrol rents for urban dwellers, moves that would have the effect of forcing families to pay a larger share of their household income for rent at a time when food prices were already rising at an alarming rate. Fearful of a consumer backlash, government officials in many areas began to provide temporary cost-of-living subsidies to renters, in the form of redeemable "housing certificates," to offset the costs of decontrol. Like so many other stopgap measures of the 1980s, however, the housing subsidies, once they were in place, tended to become permanent.[288]

As inflation worries deepened, labor problems also began to increase. Following enactment of the enterprise reform law, managers of state enterprises became seriously concerned, in most cases for the first time, with the need to increase profits and cut production costs. Given enhanced authority over enterprise operations, factories now began to reduce wages and lay off redundant workers;[289] first to go were recently hired contract workers, who lacked lifetime job security.[290] In the spring and early summer of 1988, 400,000 workers were laid off from 700 factories in Shenyang;[291] by August, Chinese

286 *FEER*, 21 April 1988, 13; *I&S* 24.7 (July 1988), 9–11. Initially, Beida administrators pleaded unsuccessfully with the students to halt their demonstrations; the protest ended peacefully after student petitions were delivered by an NPC delegate to the presidium of the NPC and to the CPPCC.

287 *WHB* (Hong Kong), reported in *FEER*, 3 November 1988, 23; also *ICM*, January 1989, 15–16.

288 On the impact (real and anticipated) of housing reform, see *BR* 31.46 (14–20 November 1988), 14–18; *CNA* 1358 (15 April 1988), 1–9; and *FEER*, 26 May 1988, 72–3. For analysis, see Tony Saich, "Urban Society in China" (paper presented to the international colloquium on China, Saarbrucken, 3–7 July 1990), 4–12.

289 There were, at this time, reportedly between 20 and 30 million redundant or nonessential workers in state-owned Chinese factories. See *WHB* (Hong Kong), 4 July 1988; and *CNA* 1370 (15 October 1988), 1.

290 State-owned enterprises had started hiring new workers on fixed-term contracts in 1986 as a means of breaking the iron rice bowl and thereby strengthening productivity incentives. However, by 1988 only about 4 percent of the work force in state-owned enterprises were employed under such contracts. The figure rose to 10 percent by 1989 (Saich, "Urban society . . .," 16).

291 *SWB/FE* 0234 (19 August 1988). Tens of thousands of contract workers were also laid off in industrial reorganization drives in Hunan, Hubei, Shandong, and Shanghai, among other places (*ICM*, December 1988, 28–9).

officials had almost doubled their previous estimate of the 1988 urban unemployment rate – from 2 to 3.5 percent, representing over 4 million people. At around the same time, many enterprises were reported to be unable (or unwilling) to pay taxes. According to government estimates, fully 50 percent of all state and collectively owned enterprises failed to pay their due taxes in the first half of 1988; among private entrepreneurs the figure was even higher, officially put at 80 percent.[292] Enterprise failures were also up sharply, particularly in small towns and villages, with the majority of affected firms being collective and cooperatively owned ventures.[293]

With rural and small-town unemployment up, labor migration increased, as did urban vagrancy; in Beijing alone, almost half a million *youmin* (drifters) lived an illegal, and for the most part squalid, existence; for the first time since 1949, beggary was now widely observed in many Chinese cities.[294]

With the threat of layoffs and/or bankruptcy now looming over chronically unprofitable firms (which reportedly accounted for almost 20 percent of China's 6,000 largest state-owned enterprises), there was a rise in the incidence of labor unrest; in all, forty-nine industrial work stoppages were recorded in the first half of 1988.[295] Given the magnitude of the economic dislocations, however, the number of strikes was quite low; the most commonly cited reason was that Party control of the trade unions made organized protest difficult at best.[296]

The nation's crime rate also registered a sharp increase in 1988. After going up 21 percent in 1987, "serious crime" rose by 34.8 percent in the first

292 *RMRB*, 20 August 1988.

293 *JJRB*, 6 January 1988, 2, in *ICM*, April 1988, 14. Despite enactment of a bankruptcy law, in the absence of a national system of unemployment benefits or adequate job retraining programs there was a clear reluctance on the part of government officials to force closure of state-owned enterprises. Consequently, in the first two years of the law's operation, only a handful of state enterprises formally declared bankruptcy. However, a number of chronically unprofitable firms were either consolidated or sold off to collective and individual buyers. See Dorothy Solinger, "Capitalist measures with Chinese characteristics," *POC* 38.1 (January–February 1989), 22–3.

294 *BR* 31.35 (29 August–4 September 1988), 29; *GRRB*, 5 June 1988; *Fazhi ribao* (Legal System Daily), 5 August 1988; *LW* 32 (8 August 1988), 12–13; *CNA* 1371 (1 November 1988), 2; Saich, "Urban society . . .," 20–3.

295 See *LW* 36 (5 September 1988), 18–19, in *FBIS*, 14 September 1988, 36; *CNA* 1359 (1 May 1988), 1–8; and *ICM*, December 1988, 28–33; and *South China Morning Post*, 3 September 1988, in *FBIS*, 6 September 1988.

296 Saich, "Urban society . . .," 16–17. Andrew Walder notes that even during the massive Tiananmen protests of spring 1989, worker self-organization was extremely limited, and was more an effect of the upheaval than a cause. See Andrew G. Walder, "The political sociology of the Beijing upheaval of 1989," *POC* 38.5 (September–October 1989), 35. Walder further suggests that the economic problems posed by inflation were not serious enough, in isolation from other factors, to lead to significant political unrest among industrial workers. See his "Urban industrial workers" (paper presented to the conference "State and society in China: The consequences of reform," Claremont-McKenna College, 16–17 February 1990), 8.

half of 1988.[297] Profiteering and corruption by Party members and cadres were said to be particularly rampant.[298] With official misconduct reportedly at an all-time high, one Communist-sponsored newspaper acknowledged a precipitous decline in public confidence in the integrity of the Communist Party:

> The decay of party discipline, bribery and corruption, covering up for friends and relatives, deceiving and taking advantage of good cadres and party members, open violations of the law . . . being covered up through "special connections" of various kinds . . . – all these types of flagrant misconduct have produced such harmful social results and led to such a deterioration of the party's image that the damage done is inestimable.[299]

It may or may not have helped the Party's tarnished image when it was revealed, in the summer of 1988, that between 1983 and 1987 the CCP had expelled more than 150,000 members, mostly for corruption, with an additional 500,000 members receiving lesser punishment for assorted varieties of malfeasance.[300] Notwithstanding this internal housecleaning, the *People's Daily* in May 1988 conceded that official corruption still had not been punished severely enough. Many in China would have agreed, since only 97 of the more than 650,000 party members disciplined from 1983 to 1987 – a miniscule 0.01 percent of the total – were cadres at or above the provincial level. Those near the top clearly remained substantially immune from punishment.[301]

The CCP, which once had prided itself on the integrity, spirit, and devotion of its members, now suffered greatly diminished popular prestige. In one nationwide survey involving more than 600,000 Chinese workers, taken after three years of party rectification, only 7 percent of the respondents believed that there had been a "clear change for the better" in Party spirit. Among more than twenty occupations rank-ordered according to public image by 1,700 respondents in a 1988 survey, basic-level cadres, government cadres, and Party cadres all ranked in the bottom third, a notch below railroad workers and a notch above tax collectors. In a 1988 survey involving 2,000 educated rural youths in Gansu province, only 6.1 percent of the young people expressed any interest in joining the Party.[302]

297 According to Chinese government statistics, over 2 million people were prosecuted for various criminal offenses in China from 1983 to 1987, with the majority of these being economic crimes (*I&S* 24.6 [June 1988], 30).

298 In 1986, the Supreme People's Court handled over 77,000 serious cases of economic crime; the majority of these cases involved cadres. Between 1982 and 1986, more than 27 percent of the 11,000 people investigated for committing economic crimes in Beijing municipality were Party members (*FEER*, 16 June 1988, 22).

299 *DGB*, 12 April 1988, in *ICM*, June 1988, 1.

300 *XH*, 11 August 1988, in *FBIS*, 11 August 1988, 18. Another 25,000 were expelled in 1988.

301 The data are presented in Rosen, "The Chinese Communist Party . . .," 83.

302 Survey data cited in ibid., 21, 49, 53.

Students were among the most pessimistic of all groups surveyed about the CCP. After the 1986 student demonstrations, 92 percent of graduate students and 62 percent of undergraduates interviewed in a survey commissioned by the Beijing municipal Party committee saw the root causes of student unrest to be corrupt Party work style and/or lack of democracy. Fewer than 10 percent of the undergraduates surveyed said they were "very confident" that Party members' work styles would improve within the next few years.[303]

With public confidence in the Party, the government, and the economy sagging badly in the late spring and summer of 1988, a significant rise in anomic crimes of violence was recorded. In May, 130 people were injured in a soccer riot in Sichuan; most of the rioters were youths, half were peasants, and many were unemployed.[304] According to Chinese legal sources, cases of first-degree murder, assault with injury, gang violence, armed robbery, and even dynamiting had all dramatically increased. In one province, almost 300 enterprise managers were physically assaulted in the first six months of 1988 – mostly for reasons of personal revenge. Organized gangs operating along roads, highways, and railway lines in several areas reportedly hijacked dozens of buses and trains, robbing passengers and stealing cargo.[305]

The rising incidence of lawlessness triggered a backlash of social protest. In December 1987, more than 1,000 students from Beijing's University of International Business and Trade marched in protest over the murder of a student in a campus store; six months later, in what was said to be the most serious threat to public order since the student disturbances of December 1986, 2,000 Beida students gathered in Tiananmen Square in early June 1988 to demand action from the government following the murder of a

303 Ibid., 28–9. As public cynicism mounted, open defiance of Party authority also increased. In a widely publicized incident that occurred in the town of Shekou, near the Hong Kong border, a meeting of young workers organized in January 1988 by the local branch of the Communist Youth League was addressed by three veteran Party propaganda cadres. When one of the cadres finished his talk (in which he praised the virtues and successes of the Party's current line and policies), a young worker stood up and told the propagandist to "stop delivering empty sermons and speak about substantial questions." Referring to the propagandist's criticism of people who think only about "reaping profits" and "driving foreign cars," the young worker asked, "What's wrong with that? . . . What is illegal about making money in modern China?" When one of the cadres pointedly asked the young man for his name, members of the audience rallied around the worker, subjecting the cadre to verbal abuse for his intimidation tactics. Such open disrespect for the Party and its cadres had been virtually unknown in China before the "opening up" of the 1980s. This particular incident, known as the "Shekou storm," was talked about in newspaper editorials and letters-to-the-editor columns for months afterward. See *CNA* 1374 (15 December 1988), 2–4; and *FEER*, 27 October 1988, 41.

304 Agence France Presse (Hong Kong), 30 May 1988.

305 *ICM*, November 1988, 4; *WHB* (Hong Kong), 13 September 1988, 14; *CNA* 1371 (1 November 1988), 2–3. In some areas, things got so bad that foreign researchers were issued travel advisories by their work units warning them to avoid traveling on interior roads and highways because of the increasing threat of banditry.

student by a gang of local hoodlums. Some of the protesters put up posters criticizing the Party and government leaders; others called for mass demonstrations against corruption and in support of human rights.[306] In July, the governor of Guangdong province, Ye Xuanping, strongly condemned a rising tide of juvenile crime after vandals defiled the memorial stele of his father, Ye Jianying, at a cemetery for revolutionary heroes.[307]

In this situation of mounting social anxiety and unrest, a television documentary broadcast in China in the summer of 1988 provided a focal point for questioning the nation's fundamental goals and values. The documentary, "Heshang" ("River Elegy"), used the slow-moving, heavily silted waters of the Yellow River – long known as "China's Sorrow" – as a metaphor for the unbroken cultural continuity and conservatism of Chinese civilization. The image of a stagnant, meandering Yellow River, unwashed by the dynamic, vibrant blue waters of the oceanic littoral, neatly symbolized the traditional isolationism and xenophobia of the Middle Kingdom. Painting a grim picture of the enervating long-term effects of China's insular traditions and atavistic values, the authors of "River Elegy" were openly and severely critical of the dogmatic chauvinism inherent in classical Confucianism and revolutionary Maoism alike; by the same token, they were lavish in their praise of modern Western institutions and values.[308]

The six-part documentary was initially aired over Beijing's Central Television Station in mid-June, with several other provinces and municipalities rebroadcasting the series in quick succession. The Beijing telecast evoked a storm of excitement, as the station reportedly received more than 1,000 letters requesting that the series be rerun. It was even reported that a number of PLA generals and their wives took videotape copies of "River Elegy" to Beidaihe for summer vacation viewing.

Within the Party apparatus, the response was less enthusiastic; Wang Zhen was said to be livid. An informal discussion meeting was held at the Beijing Central Television Station, at which a number of speakers criticized the series for being anti-Party and antisocialist and for ostensibly advocating "total Westernization." Others defended the series as forthright and honest. After initially wavering, the Party's central propaganda department issued a

306 *I&S* 24.1 (January 1988), 162; *RMRB*, 8 June 1988; *SWB/FE* 0172 (8 June 1988); *FEER*, 16 June 1988, 18, and 21 July 1988, 19–21. Six people were subsequently arrested and tried for the murder of the Beida student.

307 *DGB* (Hong Kong), 6 August 1988. For additional documentation on social unrest in 1987–8, see Burns, "China's governance . . . "; and Lowell Dittmer, "China in 1988," 12–28.

308 Accounts of the "River Elegy" controversy appear in *FEER*, 1 September 1988, 40–3; *ICM*, January 1989, 1–10; and JPRS CAR-89-004 (11 January 1989), 6. See also Woei Lien Chong, "Present worries of Chinese democrats: Notes on Fang Lizhi, Liu Binyan, and the film 'River elegy,' " *CI* 3.4 (Spring 1989), 1–20.

notification that no further showings of "River Elegy" would be permitted, either at home or abroad.[309]

Conflict at the summit: Beidaihe, summer 1988

As China's urban malaise worsened in the first half of 1988, a debate raged among reform-oriented economists and their high-level political patrons in Beijing. At issue was whether to place primary stress on enterprise reform, price decontrol, or privatization of the economy.[310] Although Zhao Ziyang had been an early advocate of price reform, the inflationary spiral of 1984–5 had apparently convinced him of the need to give priority to enterprise reform. Deng Xiaoping, on the other hand, was a belated convert to the camp of the price reformers, apparently becoming convinced in the spring of 1988 that China could withstand the anticipated transitional shock of a "big bang" in price deregulation. Dragging a reportedly reluctant Zhao Ziyang along with him, Deng claimed at the end of May that "We now have the requirements to risk comprehensive wage and price reforms."[311] At a June Politburo meeting, Deng pushed through a proposal for accelerated deregulation of prices, and Zhao Ziyang dutifully instructed the CC's economic reform think tank to prepare plans for a multiyear program of wage and price reforms.[312] At around the same time, retail prices in urban markets were deregulated for four types of nonstaple foods: meat, sugar, eggs, and vegetables. In July, cigarettes and alcoholic beverages were added to the list of deregulated commodities. With each new step toward deregulation, real or only rumored, consumer anxiety mounted and retail demand surged as heightened fears of inflation fueled the beginning of a new urban spending spree.[313]

Against this background of renewed market volatility, China's Party lead-

309 *JSND* 11 (November 1988), 62–3, in *I&S* 25.6 (June 1989), 29–30. It was subsequently reported that Hu Qili, the Politburo Standing Committee member in charge of ideological work, had solicited various opinions about "River Elegy" before deciding to ban it, delaying his decision just long enough to permit the complete series to be shown (*ICM*, January 1989, 2).

310 The enterprise reform school was led by Beida economics professor Li Yining, an advisor to Zhao Ziyang. The price reform school was led by CASS economist Wu Jinglian. A leading figure in the privatization school was Chen Yizi, former director of the State Council's Institute for Reform of the Economic Structure, a pro-Zhao Ziyang think tank. On the economic debates of 1988, see Robert C. Hsu, "Economics and economists in post-Mao China," *AS* 28.12 (December 1988), 1225–8; and Gang Zou, "Debates on China's economic situation and reform strategies" (paper presented to the annual meeting of the Association for Asian Studies, Washington, D.C., March 1989).

311 *DGB* (Hong Kong), 26 July 1988, in *ICM*, September 1988, 26.

312 Zhao reportedly asked for three different plans to be studied, with three different timetables for price reform: three years, five years, and eight years. He subsequently combined elements of the three- and five-year plans into a four-year "preliminary price rationalization program." See *WHB* (Hong Kong), 30 July and 1 August 1988; and *DGB*, 26 July 1988, in *ICM*, September 1988, 26–8.

313 Ibid.; also *I&S* 24.9 (September 1988), 1–4; *FEER*, 26 May and 4 August 1988.

ers congregated at Beidaihe for their annual summer meeting. Discussions began on 20 July amid unconfirmed rumors of intense top-level disagreement over economic strategy. Rumors of conflict between Zhao Ziyang, who favored radical decentralization of economic authority and rapid structural reform of state-owned enterprises, and Li Peng, who favored a more cautious policy of gradual, balanced reform, slow growth, and centralized economic authority, became so thick that several top Party leaders, including Hu Qili, Qiao Shi, and Zhao Ziyang himself, went out of their way to deny them in meetings with foreign visitors.

Persisting reports of elite conflict were matched by new rumors of imminent, sweeping price decontrol. Fueled by reports out of Beidaihe that Deng Xiaoping remained committed to price reform, a fresh wave of panic buying broke out in several cities at the end of July as nervous consumers rushed to stockpile everything from blankets and sewing machines to color TV sets and refrigerators. In Harbin municipality, the city's largest department store sold over RMB 1.1 million yuan worth of electrical appliances in the month of July, 200 times its monthly average. To pay for these purchases, consumers drew down their savings. In one three-day period, from 25 to 27 July, Harbin's residents withdrew more than RMB 12 million yuan from local banks.[314] A similar run occurred in Guangzhou, where panicky consumers emptied their bank accounts to buy whatever they could in anticipation of imminent price hikes. To stem the outpouring of savings, China's banks announced substantial hikes in interest rates on long-term deposits; but even at the new rates of 10 to 13 percent, bank interest was considerably lower than the current rate of inflation, which unofficially exceeded 20 percent in midsummer.[315]

Sensitive to the new signals of alarm emanating from the urban economy, Deng began to back away from his previous support for a big push in price reform. According to reports out of Hong Kong, the unprecedented urban buying spree and bank run of late July and early August served to convince China's senior leader of the need to tighten the nation's money supply and delay further price deregulation.[316]

314 *FEER*, 22 and 29 September 1988.

315 A number of Chinese media reports about rising consumer complaints in this period are translated in *ICM*, October 1988, 11–14, and November 1988, 14–20.

316 According to these reports, Deng personally decided to abort price reform after reading two reports from Zhao's think tank on China's foreign debt and the reform experience in Eastern Europe, respectively (see Wilson and Ji, "Leadership by 'lines' . . . ," 35). True or not, there were certainly a number of alarming economic signals available to Deng at the time. For example, in the first half of 1988, total supply had grown by 17.2 percent while aggregate demand grew by 31.4 percent; also, by midyear 1988, urban subsidies were 59 percent higher than the corresponding figure for the previous year, and bonuses for urban staff and workers had registered a 36 percent increase in the same period.

With Deng suddenly changing his mind, Zhao Ziyang was left holding the bag of responsibility for China's mounting economic instability. Pressed by senior Party conservatives to clarify the nature and extent of his confidence in Zhao's economic leadership, Deng Xiaoping now distanced himself from the general secretary, visibly backing off from his previous unequivocal endorsement of Zhao. "I won't vouch for anyone," he said; "if the situation continues to deteriorate, let the general secretary be held responsible." Shaken by Deng's withdrawal of support, Zhao reportedly fought back, challenging the rationale for the conservatives' emphasis on slow growth and economic stability. Taking aim squarely at Li Peng, he challenged the premier: "You always stress tightening money [supplies]," he said. "Who will be responsible if production declines?" To this Li Peng responded, "There is nothing wrong with slowing down development. It is time to pour cold water on an overheated economy." With Deng now standing aloof, Zhao reportedly threatened to resign: "All of you say that I have failed to do my work well. You come and do it. I don't want to do it any more."[317]

Lost amid all the commotion and recrimination over price deregulation was a rather dramatic irony: The consumer panic that served to precipitate Deng's sudden decision to reverse his position on price reform was initially sparked by rumors emanating directly from top Party leaders themselves. By all accounts, the 1988 Beidaihe meetings were unusually well-publicized, being punctuated periodically by media interviews, policy briefings, and receptions for foreign visitors. Such unprecedented elite openness and accessibility – reflections of a new Chinese commitment to *glasnost* – provided much of the grist for the PRC's hyperexcitable rumor mill. In this respect it was the Party's own top leadership, including Deng Xiaoping himself, who arguably bear much of the responsibility for precipitating the consumer panic of 1988.[318]

Zhao descends; Li Peng rises

Having at least indirectly started the panic, Party leaders now moved to end it. After weeks of discord, the Politburo in mid-August passed favorably on a "tentative plan for price and wage reforms." The plan represented a tactical victory for Li Peng's "economic stabilization" line insofar as it effectively

317 *ZM* 131 (1 September 1988); *I&S* 24.10 (October 1988), 1. The 1988 Beidaihe debates are chronicled in *JSND* 9 (September 1989), 16–19; *ICM*, September 1988, 24–9; and Dittmer, "China in 1988 . . . ," 21–2.

318 On the spate of media rumors that circulated during the 1988 Beidaihe meetings, see *DGB* (Hong Kong), 14 August 1988, in *ICM*, October 1988, 26–7. The fact that Party leaders were responsible for stimulating the rumor mill suggests the intriguing possibility that perhaps the pro-"stability" faction deliberately planted some of the wilder and more unsettling rumors precisely in order to trigger an adverse public reaction to proposed price reforms.

delayed implementation of new price reforms while vaguely upholding, at least in principle, the ultimate goal of further decontrol.[319]

Having lost the policy initiative to Li Peng, and having lost Deng's personal endorsement as well, Zhao quickly fell from grace. In an interview with a foreign visitor in early September, the general secretary acknowledged that he no longer played a major role in economic policymaking. Asked how much time he spent each day handling his various duties, he responded: "I do not directly deal with economic affairs but concentrate my efforts on research and investigation so that I can discuss major policy issues with my colleagues at party meetings." With Zhao's economic star deeply descending, Li Peng's correspondingly rose. Primary responsibility for economic policymaking now shifted from the Party CC, where Zhao was in charge, to the State Council, where Premier Li and his top economic adviser, Vice-Premier Yao Yilin, were able to dominate discussions of economic strategy.[320]

With Li Peng seizing the initiative, a joint work conference of the Politburo and the State Council was held in mid-September; there Zhao came under heavy fire for his economic policies and was forced to make a self-criticism in which he acknowledged partial responsibility for China's economic difficulties. A week later, the Third Plenum of the Thirteenth CC was convened. Once again Zhao faced criticism; reportedly it was only the intervention of Deng Xiaoping that saved him from being dismissed.[321] The major action taken at the plenum was a decision to freeze consumer prices for two years. This and other related measures to tighten up the economy were said to be necessary to reduce total social demand, curb excessive capital construction, and check runaway inflation.[322]

Throughout the autumn of 1988, Li Peng and Yao Yilin moved further away from Zhao's accelerated reform agenda, back toward restabilization and a partial recentralization of economic decision making. What had initially been presented as a temporary respite from economic overheating thus took

319 It was subsequently reported that the CAC had been instrumental in securing Li Peng's victory at Beidaihe, backing the premier in his policy confrontation with Zhao Ziyang. See Wilson and Ji, "Leadership by 'lines' . . . ," 37.

320 *FEER*, 22 September 1988, 70–1. Despite having lost confidence in Zhao's economic policies, Deng did not completely abandon his former protégé, as he had Zhao's predecessor, Hu Yaobang. In political and diplomatic affairs Zhao continued to be highly visible, presiding over important Party meetings, attending to public ceremonies, and meeting foreign heads of state. On one occasion, Deng obliquely defended Zhao's economic thinking, venturing the opinion that China's inflation was due primarily not to price reform but to lax economic management. See *I&S* 24.9 (September 1988), 4. Still, the damage was done, and Zhao Ziyang would never recover his lost stature.

321 *Jingbao* (Hong Kong) [hereafter, *JB*] 11 (November 1988), 20–3, trans. in JPRS CAR-89-007 (19 January 1989), 10–11.

322 *RMRB*, 27 September and 1 October 1988; *CNA* 1370 (15 October 1988), 4. Despite Zhao's evident fall from grace, he presented the political report to the Third Plenum. The text appears in *BR* 31.46 (14–20 November 1988), I–VIII.

on the characteristic of a more long-range readjustment, one that favored a reduction of market controls and a reassertion of at least some of the prerogatives of central planning.[323] In early December, price controls were reimposed in Beijing on thirty-six categories of previously decontrolled goods, from beef and eggs to shoes, towels, television sets, and washing machines; fines of up to 10,000 yuan were to be levied against violators.

When local and provincial leaders balked at giving back some of their recently gained economic autonomy, Deng Xiaoping pointedly reminded them of their dependent status: "Since we can delegate power, we can also take it back any time we like."[324] In the event, however, Deng's boast proved at least partially hollow. Long after the Third Plenum had adjourned, provincial and local governments continued to issue their own laws and regulations, collect their own taxes, and provide their own incentive packages to lure business and investment away from other regions, all in defiance of central authority and all further contributing to China's emerging macroeconomic incoherence. In the view of an increasing number of observers, inside and outside China alike, Beijing had, by the autumn of 1988, lost the ability to regulate and control a considerable amount of provincial and local-level economic activity.[325]

As part of the attempt to bring China's runaway economy back under control, a new get-tough policy toward cadre-centered speculation and profiteering was initiated in the fall of 1988. Put in charge of the anticorruption drive was Politburo SC member Qiao Shi.[326] Targeted for special attention in the new campaign was the phenomenon of "bureaucratic racketeering" (*guandao*), the practice of high-level cadres and *gaogan zidi* using their official connections to bestow commercial favors on private trading companies with which they (or their family members) were affiliated. In his report to the Third Plenum, Zhao Ziyang had made a special plea to attack this problem:

323 Li Peng and Yao Yilin were also reportedly cool toward Zhao Ziyang's coastal development strategy, though they did not immediately act to reverse existing policy in this area. Zhao continued to speak out on behalf of the coastal strategy throughout the autumn of 1988.

324 *WHB* (Hong Kong), 11 October 1988, 1; *CNA* 1371 (1 November 1988), 4.

325 *FEER*, 27 October 1988, 38–42, and 8 December 1988, 60–1; *NYT*, 11 December 1988. On the causes, consequences, and political implications of diminishing central control over fiscal levers and resource allocations, see Barry Naughton, "The decline of central control over investment in post-Mao China," in David M. Lampton, ed., *Policy implementation in post-Mao China*, 51–80; Susan L. Shirk, " 'Playing to the provinces': Deng Xiaoping's political strategy of economic reform," *SICC* 23.3/4 (Autumn–Winter 1990), 227–58; Christine Wong, "Central–local relations in an era of fiscal decline" (paper presented at the annual convention of the Association for Asian Studies, New Orleans, April 1991); and Barry Naughton, "Macroeconomic Obstacles to reform in China" (paper presented at the Southern California China Colloquium, UCLA, November 1990).

326 Qiao, a specialist in Party organization and security affairs, was reportedly the swing vote in the five-man Politburo SC: Zhao Ziyang and Hu Qili formed the SC's liberal wing, whereas Li Peng and Yao Yilin took a more conservative line. Qiao Shi's views on the need to tighten Party discipline and combat profiteering are presented in *RMRB*, 29 October 1988, trans. in *ICM*, February 1989, 2–3.

"It is necessary to . . . severely punish 'bureaucratic racketeers.' All [private] companies . . . must sever their links with party and government organizations. . . . Otherwise, their licenses will be revoked."[327] To help put teeth into this exhortation, the State Council in October issued new regulations stipulating that retired cadres above the county level were forbidden either to set up or to accept employment in commercial enterprises.

More than 360,000 trading companies had been set up in China between 1986 and 1988; although the majority of these were small in size and modest in scale (e.g., the so-called briefcase companies), a few had vast dimensions and resources, including the "Big Four Companies," CITIC, Kang Hua, Everbright, and China Economic Development Corporation.[328] Among the senior staff of these giant corporations were many former ministers, vice-mayors, and Party secretaries; although nominally private, these companies all enjoyed high-level official patronage. As China's officially approved "windows to the world," they also enjoyed quasi-monopolistic access to foreign customers, markets, and hard currency reserves.[329]

It was this system of official patronage and protected market access that gave rise to the epidemic of *guandao* that beset China in the late 1980s. As observed in the Party's new theoretical journal, *Seeking Truth, guandao* was an "ulcer" growing out of the "sick system" of official corruption:

> With the deepening of reforms, we have been trying to separate the party from the government, the functions of the government from those of the enterprise, and administrative power from managerial power. Those who use their official posts to obtain profits for their own ends . . . lose no time in taking advantage of the transition between the old and new systems. They truly feel that if they miss the opportunity while they still have power, it will be too late. To transform power into currency is the card trick [performed by] *guandao*.
>
> If our old system breeds and covers up the corruption of some officials, the emergence of *guandao* is the ulcer that grows out of this sick system. Unless *guandao* is eliminated, there will not be any peace in China. . . .
>
> . . . What is peddled in the *guandao* is the party spirit of the members of the communist party and the conscience of society's public servants. If such commerce is not abolished, what will depreciate is not only the [money] in the hands of ordinary people, but their confidence in and support of the ruling party and government.[330]

Although the new antiracketeering drive was nominally directed at all firms engaged in speculation, profiteering, and currency manipulation, it

327 *BR* 31.46 (14–20 November 1988), II.

328 Kang Hua reportedly had more than 170 subsidiaries.

329 See *FEER*, 3 November 1988, 23–5, and 17 November 1988, 90–2. On the high-level patronage networks that served to protect and nurture private companies, see Solinger, "Urban entrepreneurs and the state . . . ."

330 *QS* 8 (16 October 1988), 46–7, in JPRS CAR-89-001 (3 January 1989), 41–2. For additional media accounts of the effects of *guandao*, see *ICM*, February 1989, 3–6.

was generally the smaller, less well-connected companies that bore the brunt of the government's get-tough policy. Only one of the major trading corporations, Kang Hua, was directly affected by the crackdown of autumn 1988; the vast majority of firms that got caught were much smaller in scale.[331] Despite an announcement by the CDIC in November that 330,000 Party cadres had been charged with racketeering-related crimes since 1983, there was a widespread popular perception that the really big fish had, as usual, been allowed to slip away.[332] The evident selectivity of the Party's antiracketeering drive was to become a major focus of public anger when China's unhappy students took to the streets once again in the spring of 1989.

Zhao's neoauthoritarian counteroffensive

In the autumn of 1988–9, Zhao Ziyang's supporters, seeking to restore their champion's badly tarnished image and to reverse his slip from power, began openly to promote the theory of neoauthoritarianism. Spearheaded by economist Chen Yizi and other leading members of various reform-oriented think tanks, and backed behind the scenes by key Zhao Ziyang political advisers Bao Tong and Yan Jiaqi, the neoauthoritarians raised a number of general proposals. Arguing that market forces alone could provide the dynamism necessary to reform the Chinese economy successfully, they proposed a wholesale dismantling of the bureaucratic apparatus of the command economy and a privatization of state-owned industrial and commercial property. This put them squarely at odds with the more cautious and conservative stability faction of Li Peng and Yao Yilin, who continued to assert the need for unified political and economic command under the people's democratic dictatorship. The conservatives' gradual, incremental approach to reform was doomed to failure, averred the neoauthoritarians, because the persistence of powerful bureaucratic vested interests served to block fundamental structural change. To overcome this obstacle and to get China started down the road toward genuine market reform, a clear separation between politics and economics was necessary. To effect such a clean break with China's Maoist–Stalinist past, strong political leadership, à la Mikhail Gorbachev, was necessary. This was precisely the role the neoauthoritarians sought to carve out for their

331 Because Deng Xiaoping's son, Deng Pufang, had close connections with Kang Hua, this case was closely watched as a possible bellwether of government intentions with respect to cleaning up racketeering among the *gaogan zidi*. Although Deng Pufang subsequently severed his connection with Kang Hua, he was never punished.

332 In those cases where criminal charges had been brought against party cadres, trials were frequently postponed or delayed indefinitely. Aware of this problem, the Supreme People's Court issued a notice on 3 November requiring all courts to enforce the law vis-à-vis cadre profiteers "in the strictest possible fashion" and to "bring all [pending] cases to trial." See *ICM*, January 1989, 29–30.

patron, Zhao Ziyang. For the sake of reform, they argued, "there must be sufficient authoritative power to remove the obstacles formed by forces such as the vested interests in the old system." This, in turn, "requires a strong centralization of power in the political sphere. . . . What neoauthoritarianism emphasizes is not the political *system* but a [political] *leader.*"[333]

Throughout the late fall and winter of 1988–9, reform-oriented journals such as the *Guangming ribao* and the *World Economic Herald* published a number of articles promoting neoauthoritarian theories and concepts. The common denominator of these articles was the call for strong political leadership to effect a withdrawal of the instruments of proletarian dictatorship from the economic sphere.[334] In their new emphasis on the need for a powerful central leader to effect needed structural reforms, the neoauthoritarians began to diverge markedly from their liberal-democratic counterparts, including Fang Lizhi, Yu Haocheng, Su Shaozhi, and Liu Binyan, who, throughout this period, continued to stress the urgent necessity of democratic political reforms. And although both groups shared a deep concern over the implications of Zhao Ziyang's recent loss of stature vis-à-vis Li Peng, the evident political Bonapartism of the neoauthoritarians put them increasingly at odds with China's liberal democrats.[335]

The gathering storm: Winter 1988–9

In the face of the neoauthoritarians' attempt to reverse Zhao Ziyang's political decline, Party conservatives in the autumn of 1988 stepped up their campaign to oust the general secretary. In November, Chen Yun issued the first of "eight opinions" on the subject of Zhao Ziyang's leadership. Chen was particularly unhappy about the general secretary's lack of firmness in dealing with bourgeois ideology. Complaining, among other things, that under Zhao "almost all proletarian ideological bridgeheads have been occupied by bourgeois ideologies," Chen asserted that "it is time for us to counterattack."[336]

Chen's concerns could hardly have been assuaged when, the following month, at a conference of reform-oriented intellectuals jointly sponsored by

333 Wu Jiaxiang, cited in Ma, "The rise and fall of neo-authoritarianism . . . ," 13–14 (emphasis added). Chinese proponents of neoauthoritarianism frequently cited Samuel P. Huntington's influential 1965 book, *Political order in changing societies,* as a key source for their ideas on the need for strong political leadership during the early stages of modernization.

334 See Petracca and Xiong, "The concept of Chinese neo-authoritarianism . . . ," 1106–11; and Ma, "The rise and fall of neo-authoritarianism . . . ," 8–13.

335 The growing fissure between neoauthoritarians and democrats was later reflected in the emergence of strategic disputes among various student groups and leaders during the Tiananmen demonstrations, particularly in the critical period of escalating conflict from 13 May to 30 May, 1989. See footnote 372.

336 *JB* 1 (January 1989), 29; *I&S* 25.6 (June 1989), 30.

the CCP propaganda department and CASS to commemorate the tenth anniversary of the historic Third Plenum of the Eleventh CC, Su Shaozhi gave a bold speech attacking the campaigns against spiritual pollution and bourgeois liberalization. With several members of the SC of the Politburo in attendance, Su called for a reevaluation of two prominent victims of the earlier campaigns, Wang Ruoshui and Yu Guangyuan. Although he did not actually name those responsible for persecuting Wang and Yu, Su tacitly pointed the finger of accusation at Hu Qiaomu as the individual most responsible for "appropriating Marxist theory" as his "private preserve."[337]

Visibly disturbed by the tone and content of Su's remarks, the Party's top propaganda officials, Hu Qili and Wang Renzhi (who, ironically, had helped organize the decennial conference), now sought to prevent publication of his speech; their efforts were foiled when Su's talk was printed on 26 December in the unofficial Shanghai newspaper *World Economic Herald,* whose publisher, Qin Benli, was an outspoken proponent of accelerated structural reform. Two days later, a leading government-run newspaper ran the first of two editorials that contended, among other things, that "there is a need courageously to draw lessons" from "modern democratic forms" that "have developed under Western capitalism."[338]

In late December 1988 and early January 1989, a new series of racially motivated campus disturbances revealed the existence of intensified urban stresses and tensions. The incidents, which involved clashes between Chinese and African students at various college campuses, seemed to be more a product of China's increasingly strained socioeconomic conditions than of the country's shifting intellectual or ideological currents. On Christmas Eve 1988, a riot broke out at Hehai University in Nanjing when a group of male African students reportedly brought Chinese women to their dormitory, refusing to register them in accordance with school regulations. The Africans were accosted by a crowd of Chinese youths who hurled sexual epithets and other verbal abuse at them. In the ensuing melee, two Africans and eleven university employees were injured. For several days thereafter, the situation in Nanjing remained tense as armed security troops were called in to maintain order among the more than 5,000 Chinese students who took part in anti-African demonstrations. On 31 December, Chinese security police, using clubs, forcibly dispersed a group of over 100 African

337 Although both Wang Ruoshui and Yu Guangyuan had been invited to attend the decennial reform conference, the two men boycotted the proceedings to protest the blacklisting of several of their colleagues, including Yan Jiaqi, who had been barred from participating. The proceedings of the conference are discussed in *JB* 137 (1988), 40–2, in JPRS-CAR-89-018 (1 March 1989), 12–16.

338 *GMRB,* 29 and 31 December 1988. These events are analyzed in Lowell Dittmer, "The Tiananmen massacre," *POC* 38.5 (September–October 1989), 4; see also Wright, "The political fortunes of . . . ," and Faison, "The changing role . . . ," 149.

students who had barricaded themselves in a guest house in suburban Nanjing.[339]

The next day, New Year's Day 1989, a similar incident occurred at the Beijing Language Institute, hundreds of miles to the north. There an African student who had allegedly abused a Chinese woman was the object of an angry protest by several hundred Chinese students who put up wall posters and demanded punishment for the African. Two weeks later, African students at Zhejiang Agricultural University went on strike to protest against Chinese officials who charged that the Africans were carriers of the deadly AIDS virus.[340].

Although these incidents clearly involved elements of racism, there were other, nonracial undercurrents and overtones as well. The anti-African protests served to rekindle many of the chauvinistic, anti-foreign sentiments that had previously risen to the surface during the 1985 and 1986 campus demonstrations; such sentiments tended to be symptomatic of the intensified, reform-induced social tensions and emotional stresses that characterized urban China in the middle and late 1980s. From this perspective, it did not matter so much that the targets of student hostility in the winter of 1988–9 were Africans rather than Japanese (or even corrupt Chinese officials); what mattered was that many Chinese, and not just students, were feeling threatened by forces not subject to their control; stressed and confused, they lashed out at convenient, culturally preordained targets.[341]

In this situation of rising social volatility, the renewed activism of China's liberal intellectuals further stirred things up. In early December, on the occasion of the tenth anniversary of the opening of the Xidan democracy wall, a former activist in China's short-lived democracy movement of 1978–9, Ren Wanding, publicly released a four-page letter addressed to the United Nations Commission on Human Rights, Amnesty International, and the Hong Kong Commission for Human Rights requesting inquiries into the condition of democracy activists imprisoned since the spring of 1979.[342]

On 6 January 1989, Ren Wanding's request for an investigation into the condition of China's political prisoners was carried a step further by Fang Lizhi. In an open letter to Deng Xiaoping, copies of which were made

339 Even before this particular incident, Hehai University had a rather long history of racial tensions. See *I&S* 25.2 (February 1989), 9–11; and *ICM*, February 1989, 29.

340 *I&S* 25.2, (February 1989).

341 For a slightly different interpretation of the anti-African riots of 1988, one that stresses elite manipulation of latent chauvinistic feelings among Chinese students, see Edward Friedman, "Permanent technological revolution and China's tortuous path to democratizing Leninism," in Baum, ed., *Reform and reaction* . . . , 162–82.

342 Ren himself had been arrested in April 1979 but was released in 1983. See *FEER*, 15 December 1989, 38–9.

available to the foreign press, Fang called for the release of *all* political prisoners in China, specifically mentioning Wei Jingsheng. Fang argued that 4 May 1989, the seventieth anniversary of China's historic May Fourth Incident, would provide a suitable symbolic occasion for such a general amnesty. In mid-February, two young Chinese writers, Bei Dao and Chen Jun, collected the signatures of thirty-three Chinese scholars and writers supporting Fang Lizhi's open letter and calling for an acceleration of political structure reform. A similar "letter of opinion," signed in early March by forty-two scholars and scientists, was sent to CCP leaders and to the SC of the NPC.[343]

Reenter the gerontocrats

As political pressure from liberal intellectuals increased, so did political counterpressure from conservative Party elders. After Chen Yun had delivered the first of his eight opinions about Zhao Ziyang's leadership, Bo Yibo circulated a "letter of appeal" protesting the December decennial conference at which Su Shaozhi had launched his attack on the anti–spiritual pollution and bourgeois liberalization campaigns. Bo charged that a number of "middle-aged intellectuals" were whipping up public opinion, undermining the four cardinal principles, and encouraging bourgeois liberalism, and he characterized the tenth anniversary conference as an "attack on the party CC." Several old-timers from the CAC, including Bo, Chen Yun, Li Xiannian, and Wang Zhen, now began pressuring Deng Xiaoping to sack Zhao Ziyang for his "failure to do public opinion, ideological and theoretical work properly." At one point during this process, Li Xiannian reportedly flew to Shanghai to consult secretly with Deng about possible scenarios for Zhao's resignation.[344] According to one such scenario, Zhao would be required to make a self-criticism for his errors and resign at the CC's Fourth Plenum, scheduled for March 1989. Deng is said to have refused, arguing that (1) one of his closest deputies (Hu Yaobang) had already been deposed and (2) there was no one suitable to replace Zhao. China's senior leader then decided that the question of whether to replace Zhao would be put off at least until summer, after Deng's anticipated summit meeting with Mikhail Gorbachev.[345]

343 *JB*, 10 April 1989, 22–3; *I&S* 25.3 (March 1989), 1, 4–6; *ZM*, 1 March 1989, 6–9. These events are analyzed in Chong, "Present worries . . . ," 2–4; and Dittmer, "The Tiananmen massacre," 4–5.

344 *I&S* 25.3 (March 1989), 4–7; *ZM* 138 (1 April 1989), 6–9; Dittmer, "The Tiananmen massacre."

345 *ZM* 138 (1 April 1989); *South China Morning Post*, 22 March 1989; *I&S* 25.6 (June 1989), 20. Although the conservatives were unable to secure Zhao's ouster, they did manage to prevent him from exercising leadership over the Party's MAC, where Yang Shangkun, though nominally ranking below Zhao, remained the principal decision maker. Zhao reportedly had access to Yang's decisions only after they were made. See Wilson and Ji, "Leadership by 'lines' . . . ," 38.

Under pressure, and in danger of losing the last remaining shred of Deng Xiaoping's confidence, Zhao now temporized. Though he refused to bow to hard-line conservative demands either to submit his resignation or undergo self-criticism, he nonetheless began to take a firmer stance toward liberal intellectuals. Together with Hu Qili, Zhao summoned *World Economic Herald* publisher Qin Benli to Beijing, where the journalist was reprimanded for publishing Su Shaozhi's incendiary decennial speech; thereafter, Qin Benli agreed to accept a six-month moratorium on publishing materials submitted by any of the thirty-three signatories to the petition demanding amnesty for Wei Jingsheng.[346] At around the same time, in a seminar for Party cadres, Zhao Ziyang explained that the improvement of ideological and political work within the Party was an "urgent concern" that would occupy 50 percent of the Party's attention in the near future.

Despite such evident backpedaling, Zhao managed to retain at least some freedom of maneuver. He did not, for example, move to have Su Shaozhi expelled from the Party,[347] nor did he agree to transmit around the country Chen Yun's eight opinions of November-December 1988, as Chen had insisted. And finally, in response to Bo Yibo's criticism, Zhao defended China's critical intellectuals by saying, "Intellectuals have their own understanding of problems. What is there to be surprised at?"[348]

In late February, Fang Lizhi inadvertently reentered the political arena. Newly elected U.S. President George Bush, paying a brief get-reacquainted visit to China in conjunction with his attendance at a state funeral for the deceased Japanese Emperor Hirohito, issued an invitation to Fang to attend a presidential banquet at Beijing's Great Wall Sheraton Hotel. Intended as a sign of strong American support for human rights in China, President Bush's gesture provoked an equally strong response from Chinese leaders: On the night of the banquet, 26 February, Fang's car was obstructed by Chinese police and prevented from reaching the hotel. Having missed the banquet, Fang later gave a press conference at which he sardonically quipped that the incident revealed the weakness of a Chinese leadership that "had to go to all this trouble" just to prevent one scholar from attending a banquet.[349]

Deng Xiaoping reportedly was not amused. Even Zhao Ziyang reacted with dismay, pointedly warning President Bush that any American meddling

346 *ZM* 137 (1 March 1989), 6–9. The Party's central propaganda department issued an order for the *People's Daily* not to publish any articles written by Yan Jiaqi (who had signed the petition of the thirty-three) without prior approval from the CC (*I&S* 25.3 [March 1989], 7).

347 Instead, Su was reportedly advised by his boss, CASS president Hu Sheng, to go abroad for a while.

348 *I&S* 25.3 (March 1989), 5; *ZM*, 1 March 1989, 6–9; Dittmer, "The Tiananmen massacre," 5.

349 *Washington Post,* 28 February 1989; Chong, "Present worries . . . ," 3. Two other prominent critical intellectuals, Su Shaozhi and playwright Wu Zuguang, had also been invited to the presidential banquet; neither one was prevented by the authorities from attending.

in China's internal politics could undermine the country's stability and thereby play into the hands of opponents of reform. A week after the Fang Lizhi incident, Zhao gave a speech at an enlarged Politburo meeting in which he attacked foreign critics of China's Tibetan policy.[350]

In this situation of mounting political tension, Hu Yaobang suddenly reentered the political arena. Returning to Beijing in early April from a sojourn in southern China, Hu registered to speak at an enlarged Politburo meeting convened to discuss problems in education. At the 8 April meeting, Hu delivered a passionate appeal for greater Party support of education. During the meeting, shortly after completing his remarks, the former general secretary collapsed, suffering from a massive heart attack. A week later, on 15 April, Hu Yaobang died of a myocardial infarction.

Mourning becomes electric

Even before Hu Yaobang died, rumors began circulating in Beijing to the effect that he had suffered his fatal heart attack while engaged in a heated debate with arch-nemesis Bo Yibo.[351] Whether true or not, the rumors added to the already powerful sense of frustration and alienation shared by many Chinese students, providing the catalytic spark that reignited the long-smoldering fuse of campus unrest.

One day after Hu's death, on 16 April, several hundred students from various Beijing universities marched to Tiananmen Square to place memorial wreaths at the foot of the Revolutionary Heroes' Monument.[352] Over the next several days, the ranks of the mourners swelled to tens of thousands. The first pro-democracy rallies also took place in this period, accompanied by demonstrations in front of the government's official Zhongnanhai residential com-

350 *The Economist* (London), 4 March 1989, 67; Chong, "Present worries . . . ," 3; *Asiaweek,* 7 July 1989, 26–31. Since October 1987 there had been recurrent episodes of political unrest in Tibet. Chinese troops had been used to quell protests on at least three occasions. In the late winter of 1989, following the death of the Panchen Lama (Tibet's pro-Chinese religious leader), the situation worsened; a series of pro-independence demonstrations occurred from mid-February to early March, leading to the imposition of martial law on 7 March. Thereafter, there were reports that a number of Tibetan protesters were killed by Chinese troops. See *I&S* 25.4 (April 1989), 8–11.

351 *JB,* 10 May 1989, 2–6. A number of other rumors were also spread about the circumstances of Hu's fatal heart attack. See *CLG* 23.1 (Spring 1990), 56–7.

352 There is a rich symbolic tradition of politicized displays of mourning at the Heroes' Monument. The "Tiananmen incident" of April 1976 began as a mourning display in honor of the late premier Zhou Enlai; the democracy movement of winter 1978–9 similarly involved a strong mourning theme. Noting this connection, Lucian Pye has written that "Funeral rituals provide one of the few opportunities Chinese have for publicly displaying emotion. . . . In Chinese culture, public grieving can legitimize the expression of sentiments that are only vaguely related to any sense of personal loss." See Lucian W. Pye, "Tiananmen and Chinese political culture: The escalation of confrontation from moralizing to revenge," *AS* 30.4 (April 1990), 331–47.

pound, west of Tiananmen. At this stage, the movement was composed almost entirely of university students.[353]

On 18 April, the first autonomous student organization was set up at Beida. Not coincidentally, the first set of student demands, addressed to the NPC Standing Committee, appeared the following day. Among the seven points raised by the students, the most important were those calling for a "correct evaluation" of the merits and demerits of Hu Yaobang; rehabilitation of all people wrongly persecuted in the campaigns against spiritual pollution and bourgeois liberalization; publication of the salaries and income sources of all top Party and government leaders and their offspring; new legislation promoting freedom of the press and public expression; and substantially increased stipends, salaries, and budgets for students, teachers, and educational programs.[354]

On the night of 18–19 April, student demonstrators, numbering more than 10,000, repeatedly attempted to gain entry into Zhongnanhai, demanding to see Premier Li Peng. The students eventually clashed with soldiers guarding the compound, and several students were injured in a police charge. When the official police report failed to mention student casualties, and referred to demonstration leaders as "troublemakers" who had incited students to injure police officers, the students were handed a potent new weapon: martyrdom. It was a weapon they would use against the government with great effect in succeeding weeks.

Over the weekend of 21–2 April, crowds of people began arriving at Tiananmen for the official memorial service for Hu Yaobang. In anticipation of possible disorder, 2,000 uniformed soldiers and riot police were mobilized

353 There are numerous discrepancies in the various available accounts of the student movement of 1989, particularly with respect to such things as crowd sizes and specific dates of unofficial events (e.g., the founding of the Beijing Students' Autonomous Federation). In reconstructing the events and political dynamics of this period, I have sought wherever possible to reconcile conflicting accounts. In doing so, I have found the following sources particularly useful: Ruth Cremerius, Doris Fischer, and Peter Schier, eds., *Studentenprotest und repression in China, April–Juni 1989: analyse, chronologie, dokumente;* (1990); Stefan R. Landsberger, "The 1989 student demonstrations in Beijing: A chronology of events," *CI* 4.1 (Summer 1989), 37–56; Yi Mu and Mark V. Thompson, *Crisis at Tiananmen: Reform and reality in modern China;* "CND interview with Gao Xin," *China News Digest* (global edition; hereafter, *CND*), 7–8 April 1991; Tony Saich, "The rise and fall of the Beijing people's movement," *AJCA* 24 (July 1990), 181–208; Dittmer, "The Tiananmen massacre"; Walder, "The political sociology . . . ."; Andrew J. Nathan, "Chinese democracy in 1989: Continuity and change," all in *POC* 38.5 (September–October 1989), 17–29; Pye, "Tiananmen and . . . ."; Corinna-Barbara Francis, "The progress of protest in China," *AS* 29.9 (September 1989), 898–915; Frank Niming, "Learning how to protest," in Saich, ed., "The Chinese people's movement . . . ," 83–105; and two special issues of *CLG*, edited by James Tong, 23.1 (Spring 1990) and 23.2 (Summer 1990).

354 *CLG* 23.2 (Summer 1990), 17–18. With the exception of the relatively new demands for making public the incomes of top leaders and their children (a product of rising popular anger over *guandao*) and for "reversing verdicts" on bourgeois liberalization, the demands were virtually identical to those raised in previous student demonstrations in 1985 and 1986.

for duty in and around the Square.[355] Despite official warnings to clear the Square, in the early morning hours of 22 April 100,000 people gathered quietly for the funeral ceremony. At 10:00 A.M. the service began inside the Great Hall, accompanied by the broadcast of somber music throughout the Square. Although Zhao Ziyang in his eulogy praised Hu Yaobang as "a great Marxist," the general tone of the service was reserved and low-key. When Party and government leaders left the Hall at the conclusion of the service around 11:30 A.M., students chanted, "Dialogue, dialogue, we demand dialogue" and "Li Peng, come out!" After having reportedly been told that the government would grant their request for an audience with high-level officials, the students waited for a government spokesman to appear; by 1:30 P.M., when no government official had shown up, student leaders conducted a ceremonial remonstrance on the steps of the Great Hall, presenting their scrolled-up demands on hands and knees in the exaggerated, ritually stylized manner of an imperial petition. Believing they had been fooled by government leaders, students angrily surged forward toward the Great Hall, only to be pushed back by police; a few students were reportedly hit with police batons; many students broke down in tears. The drama of the moment was powerful; the feelings were intense.[356]

Responding to the escalating threat of student protest and martyrdom, the Politburo on 22 April held an urgent meeting at which it was decided (1) to terminate the official period of mourning for Hu Yaobang; (2) not to capitulate to student pressures to soften the original verdict on Hu; and (3) to reaffirm the correctness of the 1987 campaign against bourgeois liberalism.[357] The next day, Zhao Ziyang left for a scheduled week-long visit to Pyongyang, North Korea. With Zhao out of the country, Li Peng convened an emergency session of the remaining members of the Politburo Standing Committee (Li, Qiao Shi, Yao Yilin, and Hu Qili), plus Yang Shangkun, who served as Deng Xiaoping's personal emissary. At the meeting, the student protest was described, for the first time, as "turmoil" (*dongluan*), the same term Deng had used to characterize the student demonstrations of December 1986.

On 25 April, Li Peng and Yang Shangkun briefed Deng Xiaoping on the Standing Committee meeting and on the developing student protest situa-

355 It was also reported that up to 20,000 troops from the PLA's 38th army, stationed in Baoding, north of Beijing, received orders to move to the capital.

356 These events are chronicled in *CLG* 23.2 (Summer 1990), 22–3. Chinese officials later claimed that no government spokesman had agreed to meet with students on the afternoon of 22 April – indeed, that none had even been asked to do so – and that protest leaders had invented the promise to whip up feelings of martyrdom and betrayal among the students. Although evidence on this point is inconclusive, such a scenario is not entirely implausible.

357 Reportedly, Wan Li disapproved of the Politburo's decision.

tion. Deng's response, which included a sharp jab at Zhao Ziyang's memorial characterization of Hu Yaobang as "a great Marxist," was subsequently circulated among party cadres:

> Some people want to build up [Hu Yaobang] as "a great Marxist." . . . Even when I die they will not call me a great Marxist. Who do they think that turtle egg Yaobang was? . . . Hu Yaobang was irresolute and made concessions in combatting bourgeois liberalism. The drive against spiritual pollution lasted only a little over twenty days. If we had vigorously launched the drive, the ideological field would not have been . . . so tumultuous [as it is today]. . . . Some people crave nothing short of national chaos. . . . We must take a clear-cut stand and forceful measures to oppose and stop the turmoil. Don't be afraid of students, because we still have several million troops.[358]

Claiming that the demonstrations had been organized and led by troublemakers with ulterior motives who were engaged in a plot to overthrow China's socialist system, Deng once again warned (as he had done in December 1986) of the dangers of a Polish-style uprising: "Events in Poland prove that making concessions provides no solutions. The greater the concessions made by the government, the greater the opposition forces became."

Deng might well have been concerned, for a new and potentially troublesome element was now being added to the equation of student protest: working-class involvement. On 20 April, a newly formed (and somewhat obscure) "Beijing Workers' Federation" issued a public manifesto blaming "dictatorial bureaucrats" for social ills ranging from soaring inflation and a sharp drop in urban living standards to "expropriating the minimal income of the people for their own use." The manifesto further exhorted the citizens of Beijing, specifically including police and firemen, to "stand on the side of the people and justice" and not become "tools of the people's enemies." "We the working class of Beijing," the manifesto concluded, "support the just struggle of the college students across the nation!"[359]

Between 22 and 25 April, students in several Chinese cities, organizing themselves into autonomous unions, launched protests of various types. In Shanghai, Tianjin, Nanjing, and Wuhan, as well as in Beijing, citywide boycotts of classes were initiated. In Beijing, a Students' Autonomous Federation (BSAF) was established on 26 April at a meeting attended by 2,000 students from ten universities.

358 *JB*, 10 May 1989, 22–6; Pye, "Tiananmen and . . . ," 337.

359 *CLG* 23.2 (Summer 1990), 31. It is not clear how many workers were actually represented by this organization, though as a rule, Beijing's working class did not join the student-led movement in large numbers until after the government's failed attempt to impose martial law on 20 May. See Niming, "Learning how to protest . . . ," 84–6.

For the most part, student protest in this period was relatively calm and orderly. In a few places, however, most notably the cities of Changsha and Xi'an, peaceful demonstration degenerated into anomic vandalism and rioting as nonstudent elements, including unemployed workers, drifters, and juvenile gang members, took advantage of student protest to stir up trouble, resulting in declarations of martial law in both cities.[360]

Faced with a seemingly contagious situation of expanding student protest, mounting worker unrest, and escalating anomic violence on the part of urban marginals, party leaders now toughened their stance. Basing themselves on Deng Xiaoping's uncompromising statement of 25 April, they drafted a hard-line editorial for publication in the *People's Daily.* The editorial, published on 26 April, appeared under the page-one headline "It is necessary to take a clear-cut stand to oppose turmoil." The editorial echoed Deng's allegations about the unpatriotic motives of student leaders, claiming that the students demonstrations constituted an "act of hooliganism" that had been "incited by a very small number of people with evil motives."[361] On the same day, Shanghai Party Secretary Jiang Zemin announced the Party's decision to "reorganize" the Shanghai *World Economic Herald* and fire its editor, Qin Benli.[362]

The aftermath of 26 April: Public resentment deepens

If the *People's Daily* allegations were calculated to have a sobering, intimidating effect on student demonstrators and their nonstudent sympathizers, the calculation apparently backfired. As soon as the editorial was published, the BSAF seized the moral initiative, calling for immediate "patriotic" mass marches on Tiananmen in support of "socialist order" and in opposition to "bureaucracy, corruption, and special privilege."

The counterproductivity of the government's approach became evident almost immediately. On 27 April, the day following publication of the *People's Daily* editorial, the number of protesters marching to Tiananmen

360 For a survey of provincial reactions to the Tiananmen demonstrations, see the special section in *AJCA* 24 (July 1990), 181–314.

361 The editorial had reportedly been assigned to Hu Qili to draft. When Hu attempted to soften the thrust of the commentary by describing the students' actions as "demonstrations," Deng reportedly crossed out the milder phrase and inserted the word "turmoil." See John H. Maier, "Tiananmen 1989: The view from Shanghai," *CI* 5.1 (Summer 1990), 5. Although Zhao Ziyang was out of the country on 26 April, and although he subsequently disavowed the hard line taken in the 26 April editorial, it was subsequently alleged (by Yang Shangkun) that Zhao had cabled his "complete support" of the editorial's contents from North Korea. See *CLG* 23.1 (Spring 1990), 80.

362 Two days earlier, the *Herald* had published a plea for a postmortem reevaluation of Hu Yaobang's contributions; at the time of his firing, Qin Benli was preparing to publish a "full account" of Hu's 1987 dismissal. See *FEER,* 11 May 1989, 12.

Square from Beijing's university quarter doubled over the previous day's total, involving up to 100,000 people; it was said to be the largest spontaneous demonstration to occur in the PRC since 1949. For the first time, large numbers of nonstudents marched alongside students; in addition, more than half a million Beijing residents lined the streets of the demonstration route, offering encouragement, food, and drink to the protesters. Arriving at Tiananmen to the accompaniment of approving crowds, the demonstrators broke through police lines positioned to obstruct their entrance to the Square; the police backed off without serious incident. Cognizant of government warnings concerning the possible use of the military to quell disorder, student organizers dispatched squads of monitors to maintain order and discipline within the ranks of the demonstrators.

After years of mounting socioeconomic stress, the cumulative pressures of a decade of uneven and incomplete reform now began to break through the restraining bonds of Party and government authority. Energized by the government's ineffectual attempt to intimidate them into submission, the students seized the initiative. Occupying the moral high ground, they made effective use of the weapons of irony, shame, and martyrdom. During their marches, for example, they regularly chanted orthodox socialist slogans, sang the *Internationale,* and carried ironic banners urging citizens to support the party's "correct" leadership. By the end of April, such devices had become part and parcel of the students' attempt to reverse the roles of hero and villain in the unfolding drama at Tiananmen, and thereby to shame and humiliate Party and government hard-liners in the eyes of the citizenry.[363]

Popular opposition to the government's heavy-handed tactics spread rapidly: A public opinion poll conducted by the psychology department of Beijing Normal University at the end of April indicated that a majority of inflation-averse, corruption-weary citizens in the nation's capital now supported the students.[364] Concerned over their tarnished image and reduced credibility, Party and government leaders sought ways to disarm a perilous situation. Their preferred responses varied considerably. For Beijing Party Secretary Li Ximing, the optimal solution was to get even tougher. He repeatedly threatened students with harsh reprisals and warned of the serious "unforeseen consequences" of a failure to terminate student demonstrations. At a high-level strategy session on 28 April, a group of younger, more reform-oriented Party leaders (including Zhao Ziyang's associates Bao Tong

363 This point is emphasized by Pye, "Tiananmen and . . . ," 339–40. The students' tactics were quite clever insofar as it would have been extremely awkward for the authorities to arrest students demonstrating peacefully while singing the *Internationale* and chanting pro-socialist slogans.

364 This and other opinion surveys concerning public attitudes toward the student movement in April–May 1989 are reproduced in *CI* 4.1 (Summer 1989), 94–124.

and Yan Mingfu) opposed Li Ximing's views, counseling against a government crackdown.

In a two-pronged attempt to deflect mounting public criticism and drive a wedge between different groups of Beijing students (i.e., divide and rule), government leaders now agreed to hold televised talks with representatives of the "official" student unions in Beijing but not with the Autonomous Federation. Having been refused the right to participate, the BSAF's newly elected president, Wu'er Kaixi, angrily withdrew from the proceedings. When the meeting was held on 29 April, State Council spokesman Yuan Mu pointed out that the target of the 26 April *People's Daily* editorial had not been the broad masses of patriotic student demonstrators, but rather a small group of "behind-the-scenes conspirators."[365] At the same meeting, State Education Commission spokesman He Dongchang reiterated the government's refusal to recognize the legality of the BSAF. Three days later, BSAF leaders delivered a twenty-four-hour ultimatum demanding government approval of their conditions for dialogue. The ultimatum was rejected by the government on 3 May. The following day, protest demonstrations reached a peak, as a crowd estimated at 150,000 people filled Tiananmen Square to mark the seventieth anniversary of the May Fourth movement.[366]

Returning from North Korea at the end of April, Zhao Ziyang traveled hurriedly to Beidaihe to confer with Deng Xiaoping and to convey his misgivings about the government's choice of tactics in dealing with rebellious students. Apparently taken by surprise by the strength of the popular backlash to the 26 April editorial, Deng agreed to allow Zhao to try a softer approach with the students, telling the general secretary: "The most important thing is to stabilize the situation. . . . [Once] the situation is stabilized, you may carry out your plans; if they prove feasible [you may] disregard what I said [before]."[367]

In line with Deng's instructions, on 4 May Zhao Ziyang outlined a more conciliatory government response in remarks delivered to representatives of the Asian Development Bank, meeting in Beijing. Claiming that most of the protesters "are in no way opposed to our basic system; they only demand that we correct malpractices in our work," the general secretary declared that "the reasonable demands of the students must be met through democratic and

365 *FEER*, 11 May 1989, 11–12.

366 Similar (though smaller) demonstrations occurred on 4 May in Shanghai, Changsha, Nanjing, Wuhan, Xi'an, Changchun, and Dalian. In Harbin and Shenyang, campus gates were locked to prevent students from marching. Altogether, demonstrations were reported in twenty cities, involving upward of 1 million people. According to official accounts, by the end of May, over 2.8 million students from 600 Chinese institutions of higher education in eighty cities joined demonstrations in support of the Beijing students (statistics cited in Rosen, "Chinese youth," 20).

367 *MB*, 26 May 1989; *South China Morning Post*, 29 May 1989.

legal means." "We must remain calm," he said, "we must employ reason and restraint."[368]

Zhao's conciliatory tone had the paradoxical effect of undermining the cohesion of the popular movement in a way that the government's previous hard line had failed to accomplish. For one thing, it prompted radical elements among the movement's leadership, whose sense of moral indignation was strong to begin with, to adopt an even more intransigent posture vis-à-vis the government; for another, in revealing the existence of a clear split among top Party leaders, Zhao's talk emboldened many previously inert social forces, including factory workers and journalists, to join in the movement to press for their own particular demands and interests, thereby both enlarging and diffusing the arena of protest. As a result, the movement's previous unity of purpose and outlook became increasingly strained.[369]

With students and nonstudents alike pursuing a plurality of diverse, often shifting agendas, some of which were rather murky, it became increasingly difficult to formulate a coherent strategy within the movement, and more difficult still for concerned Party leaders like Zhao Ziyang to respond effectively. With both government and students internally divided between hard- and soft-liners, the net result was a standoff, marked by immobility and stalemate.

Under these circumstances, the enthusiasm of many students began to ebb, and in the second week of May the number of demonstrators at the Square began to dwindle noticeably. Faced with the prospect of an imminent loss of critical mass, student leaders were hard pressed to sustain the momentum of their movement. At this critical juncture, a golden opportunity presented itself: the approaching visit of Soviet leader Mikhail Gorbachev, scheduled for 15–18 May. As the date of Gorbachev's arrival approached, the eyes of the entire world would focus on Beijing. It was "manna from Moscow," a situation made to order for the students and their increasingly media-conscious leaders.

Waging moral warfare: Gorbachev, the media, and the hunger strike

On 13 May, with scores of international journalists and television cameras converging on Beijing to record the Sino-Soviet summit, protest leaders dramatically escalated their confrontation with Chinese authorities. Declar-

368 *RMRB*, 5 May 1989; *ZM* 140 (1 June 1989), 6–10.

369 These effects are discussed in Saich, "The rise and fall . . . ," 190–3. In early May, core student demands centered on (a) retraction of the 26 April editorial (with apologies), (b) reevaluation of Hu Yaobang, and (c) government recognition of the BSAF. In addition to these core concerns, however, various groups of new participants raised other demands, including *inter alia,* demands for a reevaluation of bourgeois liberalization (raised by a group of nonstudent intellectuals), for publishing the salaries and benefits of top Party and government leaders and their offspring (raised by the newly organized Autonomous Workers' Federation, among others), and for enhanced freedom of the press (raised by a group of 500 journalists employed in Party-controlled newspapers).

ing their moral abhorrence of a government that callously labeled the patriotic actions of its loyal citizens as "turmoil," several hundred students began a sit-in and hunger strike in Tiananmen Square.[370] With the government unable to take strong countermeasures because of the presence of Gorbachev and the global mass media, the ranks of the hunger strikers soon swelled to over 3,000; large crowds of sympathetic onlookers also began to flock to the Square, forcing the Chinese authorities to reroute Gorbachev's motorcade and change the venue of the Soviet leader's scheduled press conference.

Originally conceived as a limited, symbolic protest, the hunger strike was so stunningly successful in generating favorable publicity for the student cause that movement leaders soon decided to fast "to the bitter end," or until the government capitulated to the movement's demands.[371] With an important foreign head of state in the Chinese capital, with a plethora of international television crews on hand to record the proceedings, and with public sympathy increasingly swinging over to their side, the students felt relatively safe from the threat of a government crackdown. The safer they felt, the more audacious and intransigent some of them became.[372]

By this time, the striking students and their supporters, now including people of all ages and from all walks of life, had taken effective control of Tiananmen and its immediate environs. Using sophisticated broadcasting equipment hooked up to loudspeakers in the Square, strike leaders could counteract government propaganda broadcasts and spread their own messages among the milling throngs. Mimeograph machines poured out a steady stream of handbills, policy statements, and other printed materials. Posters now went up in the Square (some written in English to attract foreign media attention) calling for the resignations of Li Peng and Deng Xiaoping. Unflattering cartoon caricatures of Chinese leaders were also in evidence.

In the face of polarizing attitudes on both sides, Zhao Ziyang persisted in trying to bring about a peaceful resolution. On 15 May he (along with Hu

370 Two early declarations of the hunger strikers appear in *CLG* 23.2 (Summer 1990), 50–3.

371 At this point, there were only two core demands: (a) the government must enter into a dialogue "on the basis of equality" with a Dialogue Delegation (*duihua daibiaotuan*) made up of student representatives from various universities in Beijing; and (b) the government must "stop its name calling" and confirm the patriotic nature of the democracy movement (ibid., 52–3; Francis, "The progress of protest . . . ," 912).

372 On the eve of Gorbachev's visit, student leaders in the Square reportedly rejected overtures from Zhao Ziyang designed to bring about a settlement, contemptuously referring to Zhao's emissaries as "neoauthoritarians." In one of the more dramatic student manifestos of this period, a group of hunger strikers waxed eloquent about their chosen path of martyrdom: "Fathers and mothers! Don't grieve because we are hungry. Uncles and aunts! Don't mourn when we bid life good-bye. Our sole desire is that everyone live a better life. . . . Farewell, fellow students, take care! Remember, though we may be dead, our loyal hearts remain among the living. Farewell, sweethearts, take care! We hate to leave you but we must. . . . Our pledge, written at the cost of our lives, will surely illuminate the skies of our Republic" (*CLG* 23.2 (Summer 1990), 52).

Qili) agreed to meet the demands of several hundred petitioning journalists to allow the mass media to report on the student demonstrations objectively, free from official censorship. The next day, at a meeting of the PSC, Zhao proposed among other things, to retract the 26 April editorial, publish the incomes and emoluments of top Party and government leaders, and set up an organization under the auspices of the NPC to investigate allegations of *guandao* among high officials and their offspring. The proposal was voted down by four to one; even Hu Qili, Zhao's erstwhile strongest supporter on the SC, now voted against him.[373]

The primary reason for Zhao's increasing isolation among his peers was clear: Deng Xiaoping had already made up his mind to get tough with the students. The growing popular support and self-assurance of the protest movement had confirmed the senior leader's presumption that further government concessions would bring not peace but the escalation of demands, leading to ultimate chaos, Gdansk-style. Under these circumstances, the hunger strike proved the last straw. On 16 May, Yang Shangkun, relaying Deng's views, instructed an enlarged meeting of the party's MAC to make preparations for assembling troops to impose military control in Beijing.[374]

Deng's loss of confidence in Zhao, and Zhao's consequent loss of influence over decisions affecting the handling of the student movement, were signaled to the world during a televised meeting between Zhao and Mikhail Gorbachev on 16 May. In this meeting, Zhao confirmed the existence of the secret protocol enacted at the Thirteenth Party Congress giving Deng Xiaoping the final say on all "important" policy matters. The next day Zhao, clearly on the defensive in his struggle against the gerontocrats of the CAC, who, by this time, had begun regularly to attend and speak out at all important leadership meetings, made one last attempt to bring about a peaceful resolution of the crisis. Sending a message to the hunger strikers in the Square (via Yan Mingfu) on behalf of the CC and the State Council, he formally acknowledged the "patriotic spirit" of the student movement and promised no reprisals if the students would terminate their strike. Although a clear majority of the young strikers reportedly favored accepting Zhao's offer, acceptance was blocked by a minority coalition of hard-line Beijing students and students from out of town.[375]

373 *FEER*, 1 June 1989, 12–18. Later, Yang Shangkun would allege that not all of Zhao Ziyang's proposals had been rejected outright by the SC and that everyone "agreed" with at least two of his earlier suggestions, i.e., that problems should be solved "on the basis of democracy and law" and that a "check-up" should be made of all private business companies (*CLG* 23.1 (Spring 1990), 72).

374 *ZM* 140 (1 June 1989), 6–10. Unofficial accounts of these events, given by Yang Shangkun and Li Peng, appear in *CLG* 23.1 (Spring 1990), 69–87.

375 The hard-line Beijing student faction was reportedly led by Chai Ling, who later gained notoriety by her harrowing escape from China in the aftermath of the 3 June crackdown. See Woei Lien Chong,

Later that same day, 17 May, Zhao attended an expanded meeting of the PSC, held in Deng Xiaoping's home. At the meeting, which was attended by Yang Shangkun and several old comrades, including Chen Yun, Li Xiannian, Peng Zhen, and Wang Zhen, Zhao once again appealed for a retraction of the 26 April editorial. Deng refused, arguing that "We cannot retreat. One retreat will lead to another"; and he added, "Comrade Ziyang, your speech to the Asian Development Bank officials on 4 May became a turning point, because after that the students created more serious disturbances." Deng next proposed to implement martial law. The old comrades present agreed, saying that things had "gone far enough." Zhao strongly objected, informing Deng and the SC that he could no longer serve as general secretary. His resignation was rejected out of hand, whereupon the SC approved Deng's proposal to implement martial law at the conclusion of Gorbachev's visit. Acknowledging defeat, Zhao sought to wash his hands of responsibility for the consequences that might follow: "Let comrade Xiaoping make the final decision," he said.[376]

Although senior leaders had thus decided by 17 May to crack down on the student movement, there was considerable anxiety among the leadership (shared by conservatives and moderates alike) that some of the hunger strikers, weakened by exhaustion and lack of nourishment, might die in front of the world's television cameras, providing the student movement with instant martyrs and thereby setting off a massive antigovernment reaction.[377] Under these circumstances, the authorities made a number of hastily improvised last-ditch efforts to coax the students into calling off their strike and peacefully evacuating the Square.

At 5:00 A.M. on 18 May, members of the Politburo's Standing Committee paid a highly publicized "comfort visit" to a group of hospitalized hunger strikers. In the televised film footage of this visit, Zhao Ziyang, Li Peng, Qiao Shi, and Hu Qili (Yao Yilin was not present) displayed visible concern for the health and well-being of the frail, weakened youngsters, shaking hands with them and stopping to chat at their bedsides. The dominant image

"Petitioners, Popperians, and hunger strikers," in Saich, ed., *The Chinese people's movement . . .*, 115, 121. According to eyewitness accounts, Yan Mingfu worked hard in this period to convince student leaders that they should narrow their demands to two: retraction of the 26 April editorial and governmental recognition of the BSAF. Yan's efforts to achieve a compromise settlement were reportedly rejected by Deng Xiaoping, as well as by Chai Ling, however, and one participant subsequently noted that "There was no majority opinion in Tiananmen Square at that time. Everybody had his own ideas. Even if Deng had accepted those two points, it was still useless." See "CND interview with Gao Xin."

376 These events are described in *CLG* 23.1 (Spring 1990), 69–72; *FEER*, 8 June 1989, 14–18; and *MB*, 30 May 1989.

377 By this time, approximately 2,500 hunger strikers had reportedly been treated for dehydration and heat exhaustion at local hospitals and makeshift health stations around the Square.

conveyed by the TV cameras was one of benevolent paternalism.[378] A second government initiative came later the same day in the form of a televised address by state counselor Li Tieying. Again adopting a paternalistic stance, Li sought to reassure the striking students. "Your country loves you," he said; and he implored the protesters to end their hunger strike: "Come back, students; come back!"[379]

By far the most important official initiative was a televised meeting on 18 May between Party and government officials, including Li Peng, Li Tieying, Chen Xitong, and Yan Mingfu, and leaders of the student hunger strike, represented by Wu'er Kaixi and Wang Dan, among others.[380] Wu'er, who had been rushed from the hospital to attend the meeting, was clothed in pajamas and bathrobe; looking pale and weak, he had an intravenous feeding device attached to his nose. At this remarkable meeting, Li Peng began by calmly striking a concerned, paternalistic posture; shortly thereafter, things began to deteriorate:

Li Peng: Today we will discuss one issue: How to relieve the hunger strikers of their present plight. The party and government are most concerned about the health of the students. You are all young, the oldest among you is only twenty-two or twenty-three, younger than my youngest child. None of my children are engaged in *guandao*. . . .

Wu'er Kaixi: Excuse me for interrupting you, premier Li, but time is running short. We are sitting here comfortably while students outside are suffering from hunger. You just said that we should discuss only one issue. [Wu'er points his index finger at Premier Li] But the truth is, it was not you who invited us to talk, but we, all of us on Tiananmen Square, who invited you to talk. So we should be the ones to name the issues to be discussed. . . .

Wang Dan: . . .For the students to leave the Square and call off the hunger strike, our conditions must be met in full. . . . First, a positive affirmation of the current

378 The hospital visit is described in *SWB/FE* 0462 (20 May 1989). During the visit, Zhao Ziyang told one student: "The goal of the party and government is identical with that of the students; there is no fundamental conflict of interests. A variety of methods can be adopted to exchange views and resolve problems; don't adopt the method of a hunger strike. . . . You should look after your health." Talking with another bedridden student, Hu Qili counseled patience, saying that "Some problems cannot be solved immediately." When the student indicated that the Party needed to reestablish its credibility in order to restore people's confidence, Hu Qili responded, "We fully agree with you." The student continued: "If you want to have prestige, I think that those who practice *guandao* and those high-ranking officials involved should start taking action against their own sons."

379 Although some observers are inclined to regard the government's show of concern for the welfare of the hunger strikers at this point as a cynical charade designed to mask the fact that a decision to impose martial law had already been taken, I am inclined to believe that many (if not most) Chinese leaders were quite sincere in their attempt to engineer an eleventh-hour settlement of the hunger strike, albeit for their own reasons, which ranged from genuine concern for the students' welfare to fear of massive rebellion in the event of deaths among the hunger strikers.

380 A formal transcript of the meeting appears in *CLG* 23.2 (Summer 1990), 46–54. However, certain impromptu remarks and gestures made during and at the conclusion of the meeting are not included in this transcript.

student movement as a democratic and patriotic movement, not a "turmoil." Second, a dialogue to be held as soon as possible. . . .

Yan Mingfu: . . . We are very worried about how events will continue to develop. The only influence you can now exert is to decide to evacuate all hunger strikers. . . . The major issue concerning people now is the lives of the young hunger strikers; we must treasure their lives and take responsibility for them. . . .

Li Peng: . . . Neither the government nor the party Central Committee has ever said that the students are causing a turmoil.[381] We have consistently acknowledged your patriotic fervor. . . . However, events are not developing in conformity with your good intentions. . . . The fact is, social disorder has occurred in Beijing and is spreading to the whole country. The current situation . . . is out of control. . . . Anarchy has reigned in Beijing for the past several days. I have absolutely no intention of putting the blame on [individual student leaders], but the anarchy I have just described is a reality. The government of the People's Republic of China . . . cannot disregard such phenomena. . . .

Wu'er Kaixi: . . . I want to repeat what I have just said: We don't want to be bogged down in discussions. Give an immediate response to our conditions, because the students in the Square are starving. If this is overruled, and we remain bogged down on this one question, then we will conclude that the government is not at all sincere in solving this problem. Then there will be no need for us representatives to stay here any longer.

Wang Dan: If premier Li thinks that turmoil will ensue that will cause a bad impact on society, then I can declare on behalf of all the students that the government will be entirely to blame. . . .

At the conclusion of this remarkable confrontation, Wu'er Kaixi collapsed on the floor in a faint.[382] As the meeting adjourned, Li Peng rose and extended his hand toward the students in a gesture of apparent conciliation. When his outstretched hand was brushed aside, the premier was heard to remark: "You've gone too far." Visibly angered and struggling to maintain his composure, Li walked stiffly out of the room.

With Gorbachev departing from China on 18 May, and with the students refusing to terminate their hunger strike, the situation moved quickly toward a confrontation.[383] In the early morning hours of 19 May, Zhao Ziyang made one last attempt to head off a declaration of martial law. At a Politburo

381 Strictly speaking, Li's point was correct, since it had been Deng Xiaoping and individual members of the PSC and the CAC who had used the term "turmoil"; though the term also appeared in the 26 April editorial, it had never been incorporated into official Party documents or directives.

382 Wu'er subsequently developed something of a reputation for "strategic fainting," a behavior he exhibited on more than one occasion in public appearances. See Joseph F. Kahn, "Better fed than red," *Esquire,* September 1990, 186–97.

383 By this time, facing a near-certain government crackdown, a substantial majority of fasting students favored evacuation from the Square. However, because the hunger strikers had previously agreed to abide by the rule of "decision by consensus," this meant that a small, vocal minority could, and did, block a settlement of the strike. A similar situation of an intransigent minority overruling a large majority later prevented the occupation of Tiananmen Square from ending peacefully on 30 May, following construction of the Goddess of Democracy.

meeting, he offered to take full responsibility for the student protest and volunteered to turn his own sons over to a special tribunal that would be charged with investigating high-level *guandao.* His offer was refused, and an argument reportedly ensued between Zhao and Deng Xiaoping, during the course of which Zhao once again offered to resign. As before, Zhao's resignation was rejected, on the grounds that it would reveal a deep split within the leadership and would thus encourage the students to continue their strike.

At this point, Zhao left the meeting, ordered a car, and asked to be driven to Tiananmen Square; he was accompanied by a visibly nervous Li Peng. Arriving at the Square around the crack of dawn, Zhao addressed the student strikers through a hand-held amplifier. "We've come too late," he said, his voice heavy with emotion. "I'm sorry. You should criticize us and blame us. It is reasonable that you should do so." This was to be Zhao's last public act as general secretary. Thereafter, he returned home and refused all requests to see visitors, claiming illness. Within several hours of Zhao's visit to the Square, the first contingents of PLA troops began arriving at the outskirts of Beijing. Soldiers were also moved into position to take over radio, television, and newspaper facilities throughout the capital.

Martial law: The crackdown that failed

At midnight on Friday, 19 May, Li Peng told a nationally televised meeting of several thousand Party leaders, military officers, and Beijing municipal officials that a declaration of martial law had been approved for certain parts of Beijing, to take effect at 10:00 A.M. the next morning. Four members of the PSC and president Yang Shangkun were on stage during Li Peng's address; conspicuous by his absence was Zhao Ziyang.[384]

By midday, 20 May, an estimated quarter of a million troops had taken up positions in and around Beijing. When military units moved into the city in truck convoys from the suburbs, huge crowds of Beijing citizens poured into the streets, erecting roadblocks and surrounding the military vehicles, preventing them from moving. Unarmed and apparently unprepared for such overwhelming popular resistance on the part of the Beijing *shimin* (urban residents), the soldiers were engulfed in a virtual sea of nay-saying humanity. The leadership's worst fears of a catalytic fusion of hitherto fragmented, atomized pockets of urban alienation and discontent into a single, coherent rebellion now began to come true.[385]

384 A few days later, Yang would allege that Zhao's nonattendance at the meeting of 19 May gave the students a feeling of hope that they had a high-level supporter, thus encouraging them to "stir up greater trouble" (*MB*, 29 May 1989).

385 Some army units reportedly failed to respond to orders issued by the martial law command to enter the city: see footnote 394. Eyewitnesses variously estimate the total number of *shimin* who took part in the 20 May effort to stop the PLA from entering the city at between 1 and 2 million.

The scene, though intensely emotional, was generally nonviolent. No shots were fired, and relatively few physical scuffles took place. Indignant residents, offended by the government's attempts to impose martial law, lectured soldiers about the peaceful, patriotic aims of the movement. A number of soldiers were seen flashing the "V for Victory" sign to the crowds that surrounded their vehicles; a few held hand-written placards attesting to their support for human rights and democracy; most simply appeared bored or bewildered as they awaited further instructions from their equally bewildered officers.

Because nothing like this had ever happened in the PRC, neither the students nor the *shimin* knew quite what to make of the situation or how to react. For almost two days, reports of government ultimatums and rumors of an imminent military crackdown circulated in Beijing and other cities, creating a tense, anxious situation. A near-total government blackout on news concerning conditions in Beijing, imposed following the martial law declaration, made it difficult to obtain accurate information.[386]

Notwithstanding the paucity of reliable news, the wave of unsubstantiated rumors, or the palpably heightened anxieties of the urban populace, on 21 May approximately 1 million Beijing residents demonstrated against the imposition of martial law.[387] The same day, the hunger strikers at Tiananmen Square terminated their nine-day fast in order to join forces with other urban groups and strata in the rapidly burgeoning movement of popular resistance.

Movement leaders now made active preparations to deal with a possible military assault on the Square. Makeshift roadblocks, set up on 19–20 May to prevent the entry of army vehicles into the city, were now hardened and reinforced; checkpoints were established by students along key thoroughfares, with coded identification required to pass in or out. "Flying Tiger" squads, composed of affluent young urban *getihu* on motorcycles, recruited their members to ride picket along the outer perimeter and to serve as messengers. Gifts of money, supplies, and equipment began to pour into Tiananmen from various places, including Hong Kong and Taiwan, as a

386 Despite the news blackout, urban residents along China's eastern seaboard were able to keep abreast of at least some of the latest developments in Beijing through Voice of America (VOA) short-wave radio transmissions, television satellite dishes, and telephone/telegraph contacts, inter alia. In Nanjing, for example, on 20–1 May young people with portable stereo "boom boxes," perched high in the branches of trees in the town square, played recorded tapes of hourly VOA news summaries for the benefit of large crowds of attentive listeners below. On 21–2 May, tourists in Shanghai were able to view the latest developments in and around Tiananmen Square from the comfort of their hotel rooms via a mysteriously unbroken satellite television link. On at least two occasions during that period, rumors swept through Shanghai that martial law troops were about to enter the city. Municipal authorities promptly denied the rumors and effectively calmed popular fears. On the effects of the 20 May martial law declaration on protest demonstrations in other Chinese cities, see *AJCA* 24 (July 1990), 226–7, 239–40, 251–2, 268–9, 287–8.

387 An equally massive demonstration took place in Hong Kong on 21 May, with approximately 1 million people parading in support of the Chinese students.

semipermanent encampment was erected in the Square.[388] By this time the student movement had become, in effect, a state within a state, complete with its own communications center, security apparatus, housing, and sanitation departments.

As the first tense days under martial law passed with no sign of a government reaction, the ranks of the demonstrators continued to swell. Now whole factories and government work units openly displayed their solidarity with the students; banner-waving contingents representing CCP organs and youth groups, government ministries, official media agencies, CASS research institutes, university departments, factories, labor unions, hotels, and even public security agencies and law courts marched together in open support of what had become, by this time, an extremely broad-based urban coalition.[389]

While popular support for the movement swelled, opposition to the government's hard-line tactics increased among a number of respected active and retired leaders of the Chinese army and government. On 21 May, the only two living PLA field marshals, Nie Rongzhen and Xu Xiangqian, were seen on national television praising the patriotism of the student movement; the following day, it was reported that seven senior PLA generals had drafted a letter to Deng Xiaoping protesting the imposition of martial law and affirming the view that the PLA "belongs to the people" and "should under no circumstances fire on the people." The letter was reportedly signed by 100 senior army officers.[390]

On the government side, a petition was circulated among members of the NPC Standing Committee on 22 May (reportedly at the initiative of Hu Jiwei, with logistical support from the Stone Computer Company) calling for a special session of the NPC SC to be convened for the express purpose of repealing martial law.[391] On the same day, NPC SC Chairman Wan Li, on a visit to the United States and Canada, criticized the decision to invoke martial law and declared his intention to "firmly protect the patriotic enthusi-

388 Financial support for the students in this period was also provided by the Stone Computer Company, a quasi-private enterprise whose president, Wan Runnan, reportedly donated US$25,000 in cash plus a great deal of electronic broadcasting equipment to the antigovernment forces.

389 Significantly, the one major occupational group not represented in the demonstrations in substantial numbers was the peasantry. By and large, China's peasants, particularly those living in the fertile valleys and deltas near the urban centers along China's eastern seaboard, had done quite well under Deng Xiaoping's agricultural and marketing reforms; consequently, most appeared relatively indifferent to the events unfolding in Beijing.

390 *FBIS*, 22 May 1989, 16. The letter's drafters were said to have included former defense minister Zhang Aiping, former PLA chief of staff Yang Dezhi, former naval commander Ye Fei, and generals Xiao Ke and Chen Zaidao.

391 Approximately 40 of the SC's 135 members reportedly signed the petition, well short of the majority needed to call a special session (*SWB/FE* 0466 [25 May 1989]). At the end of June, following the military crackdown at Tiananmen, several SC members who had signed the 22 May petition were subtly reprimanded by being excluded from receiving invitations to attend the next meeting of the committee.

asm of the young people in China." The next day, he cut short his visit to North America and returned to China, citing health problems as the reason.

Meanwhile, in Beijing, orders were passed down to martial law troops on 22 May to withdraw to the city limits. The orders were generally carried out calmly and without incident.[392] Following the army's withdrawal, the students and their supporters were effectively in control of the heart of Beijing. To all outward appearances, "the people" had won.[393]

Circling the wagons: Deng prepares his response

Behind the scenes, things appeared quite differently. Shortly after ordering the imposition of martial law, Deng Xiaoping reportedly flew to Wuhan to line up the support of PLA regional forces. By 26 May, commanders of all seven military regions had publicly declared their support, with the Beijing regional commander the last, and apparently the most reluctant, to do so.[394] Meanwhile, on 22 May, the PSC, minus Zhao Ziyang, convened an enlarged meeting of the Politburo. At the meeting, Yang Shangkun, Li Peng, and Qiao Shi all gave reports reaffirming their support for the decision to impose martial law and criticizing Zhao Ziyang's handling of the situation between 29 April and 19 May. Of the various reports, Qiao Shi's was the most foreboding. "At present," said the Party's top security expert, "we will on the one hand use troops as a deterrent, and on the other find [a suitable] occasion to clear the Square. . . . The reason we have procrastinated [until now] is that we . . . are trying to avoid bloodshed. But it won't do to [have the situation] drag on like this."[395]

Two days later, on 24 May, at yet another enlarged session of the Politburo, Zhao Ziyang's dismissal from the Politburo Standing Committee was approved; the reason given was Zhao's post facto withdrawal of support

392 There were at least two exceptions: on 23 May, at Liuliqiao and in the southwestern Beijing suburb of Fengtai, violence erupted when security forces assaulted citizens who had erected street barricades. Unofficial sources put the total number of people injured at forty.

393 Just before the troops were withdrawn, PSC security expert Qiao Shi had argued against such a move, warning that a troop pullback would have the effect of making the students "think they had won" the struggle (*CLG* 23.1 (Spring 1990), 77).

394 The reluctant deputy commander of the Beijing military region, General Yan Tongmao, was relieved of his duties shortly after the crackdown of 3–4 June. His boss, General Zhou Yibing, was subsequently transferred to another post. It was rumored at the time that General Zhou had a daughter among the student demonstrators at Tiananmen Square. Also disciplined for insubordination in this period was the commander of China's elite 38th army, General Xu Qinxian, who reportedly feigned illness to avoid ordering his troops to enforce martial law in Beijing. General Xu was arrested on 24 or 25 May and was subsequently court-martialed. See *FEER*, 8 June 1989, 16; 21 September 1989, 19–20; and 1 February 1990, 22.

395 In their remarks of 22 May, both Yang Shangkun and Li Peng were rather mild and circumspect in their criticism of Zhao Ziyang's behavior, accusing him of "making mistakes" but avoiding the inflammatory rhetoric used to attack Hu Yaobang in 1987.

for the 26 April *People's Daily* editorial, an act that, according to Deng Xiaoping, had sown confusion within the party and split the party leadership into "two headquarters."[396]

With the general secretary now officially in disgrace, Yang Shangkun stepped up his criticism of Zhao's behavior at an emergency meeting of the Party's MAC, also held on 24 May.[397] In affirming the opinion of "chairman Deng"[398] that Zhao's actions following his return from North Korea had served to split the Party into two competing headquarters, Yang now compared the behavior of the Zhao-inspired Beijing students with the anarchistic behavior of China's Gang of Four–inspired Red Guards during the Cultural Revolution.[399] This was a serious charge, one that could, if upheld, result in Zhao's expulsion from the Party, or worse.

At the conclusion of his 24 May remarks to the MAC, Yang Shangkun spoke ominously about preparations for future military action:

> We can no longer retreat, but must launch an offensive. I want to tell you about this today so that you can prepare yourselves mentally. In particular, the army must be consolidated; this is of vital importance. . . . If any troops do not obey orders, I will punish those responsible according to military law.[400]

Also on 24 May, Wan Li, whose return from Canada had been widely expected to provide a strong boost for the students in Tiananmen Square, was whisked into seclusion by Party officials as soon as his plane touched down in Shanghai. When he emerged three days later, it was to announce his support for martial law, though he continued to describe the student movement as "patriotic." Taking a considerably darker view of things, Chen Yun, in a televised address on 26 May, indirectly implicated Zhao Ziyang in the conspiratorial activities of a "treacherous anti-party clique." The same day, six of Zhao's supporters, including Hu Qili, defense minister Qin Jiwei, and political reform adviser Bao Tong, were singled out for criticism by CAC conservatives at a leadership meeting.

Meanwhile, in Tiananmen Square, there was a noticeable attrition in the ranks of the encamped students. Although massive public demonstrations continued to be held almost daily, dwindling numbers of students living and sleeping on the Square bespoke the growing exhaustion of the student movement. On 27 May, exactly one week after the declaration of martial law,

396 At this meeting, Hu Qili was said to have defended Zhao and opposed the martial law declaration of Li Peng.

397 Throughout the unfolding crisis of May–June 1989, Yang apparently functioned as Deng Xiaoping's alter ego, publicly articulating the private opinions of China's senior leader.

398 At the time, Deng's only remaining official posts were as chairman of the two MACs.

399 *CLG* 23.1 (Spring 1990), 80–1.

400 Ibid., 86–7.

student leaders Wu'er Kaixi and Wang Dan proposed to end the occupation of the Square on 30 May with one final, massive demonstration and triumphal procession. As before, however, a minority coalition composed of out-of-towners and radical Beijing students, led by Chai Ling, objected to the evacuation proposal, blocking its adoption and binding the students to remain in the Square until 20 June, the date of the next scheduled meeting of the NPC SC.

At dusk on 29 May, with fewer than 10,000 protesters remaining in Tiananmen Square, a group of students from Beijing's Central Arts Academy began to construct a bamboo scaffolding in the northern quadrant of the Square, directly opposite the portrait of Mao Zedong that hangs atop the entrance to the Forbidden City. With the scaffolding completed, the students next assembled, from prefabricated sections brought to the Square on bicycle carts, a thirty-foot-high statue of a woman grasping a torch in her upstretched arms. Variously known as the "Goddess of Democracy" (*minzhu nushen*), the "Spirit of Democracy" (*minzhu jingshen*), and the "Goddess of Liberty" (*ziyou nushen*), the statue was completed in the early morning hours of 30 May.

Construction of the statue, like Mikhail Gorbachev's visit to Beijing two weeks earlier, served to inject new life and energy into the dwindling student movement. As many as 300,000 spectators flocked to Tiananmen Square on 30–31 May to see the white plaster-and-styrene Goddess standing eyeball to eyeball with Mao Zedong, torch defiantly raised. Whether or not mockery had been the conscious intent of the art students, it surely was the effect, as dozens of television cameras expertly framed the ironic, silent confrontation between Goddess and Chairman. The students, their flagging spirits revived, announced their determination to continue occupying the Square.

Two days earlier, on 28 May, student leaders had been informally warned that they would be subject to arrest as "agents" of Zhao Ziyang. Even as the Goddess was being assembled in the Square on the night of 29 May, the detentions began. Students were not the immediate targets; their allies, the radicalized *shimin,* were. First to be arrested were three members of the newly formed Beijing Autonomous Workers' Federation; later the same day, eleven members of the Flying Tigers motorcycle squad were jailed. The crackdown had begun.[401]

401 It is not particularly surprising that nonstudents should be the first to be arrested. China's political tradition confers an unusual degree of paternalistic tolerance upon students, rendering them relatively immune from harsh punishment; such latitude is not granted to other occupational groups, however, and especially not to workers. See, e.g., Robin Munro, "Who died in Beijing, and why?" *The Nation,* 11 June 1990.

Clubs are trump: The June debacle

It is tempting to pinpoint the appearance of the Goddess of Democracy on 30 May as the final straw, or trigger, that brought the full, militarized wrath of Deng Xiaoping and the old comrades of the CAC down upon the heads of the audacious, libertarian students of Beijing and their newfound allies, the angry *shimin* of urban China. More likely, however, the decisive catalysts of the debacle that followed were, first, the rapid rise of a militant, autonomous workers' movement that was proclaiming its solidarity with the students in opposition to the regime, bringing ever closer to reality Deng's recurrent Polish nightmare;[402] and second, the progressive defection of substantial numbers of Party, government, and army leaders to the side of the students during the second half of May, lending critical weight and legitimacy to the antiregime fervor that was sweeping through the country's major urban centers. In short, China's leaders in early June acted to preempt what they viewed, not without reason, as a rapidly deteriorating and deeply threatening situation.[403]

Many things remain unclear about just what happened and why in the first week of June 1989. Two things are clear, however. First, a substantial number of Beijing *shimin* died in the course of a brutal assault by fully armed, heavily armored units of the PLA in central Beijing on the evening of 3–4 June and in subsequent mopping-up operations: Best available estimates place the total number of dead at between 600 and 1,200, including at least 39 students and "several dozen" soldiers, with an additional 6,000 to 10,000 civilians and soldiers injured. Second, there was no massacre of students in Tiananmen Square.[404]

The military crackdown was presaged, shortly after midnight on the morning of 3 June, by a puzzlingly ineffectual foray into Beijing by a column of several thousand unarmed and ostensibly ill-seasoned young PLA soldiers

402 By 1 June, autonomous workers' organizations had sprung up in most of China's major cities. In Beijing, membership in the Workers' Autonomous Federation increased rapidly following the 29 May arrest of three Federation members.

403 According to an internal Party investigation conducted after the crackdown of 3–4 June, more than 10,000 cadres from central-level Party and government departments took part in the May demonstrations (*FBIS*, 10 November 1989, 46–9). Unofficial estimates place the figure much higher – by several orders of magnitude. In light of events that subsequently unfolded in Eastern and Central Europe in the latter part of 1989, particularly in Romania, Chinese leaders' fears of being swept away in a burgeoning, out-of-control antigovernment rebellion may not have been so far off the mark as was originally supposed by many outside observers.

404 In the following discussion, I have relied on Munro, "Who died in Beijing . . . ?"; "CND interview with Gao Xin"; Mu and Thompson, *Crisis at Tiananmen . . . .;* and *Massacre in Beijing: China's struggle for democracy.* Other useful sources on the events of June 1989 include Amnesty International, *China: The massacre of June 1989 and its aftermath;* Michael Fathers and Andrew Higgins, *Tiananmen: The rape of Peking;* and Scott Simmie and Bob Nixon, *Tiananmen Square: An eyewitness account of the Chinese people's passionate quest for democracy.*

who had been sent jogging, double-time, sans officers, toward Tiananmen Square from the eastern suburbs of the city. After running for nearly two hours, the exhausted soldiers had their route blocked by a large crowd of people near the Beijing Hotel, east of the Square, at around 3:00 A.M. The hapless soldiers were surrounded and sternly lectured on the subject of civil-military amity by the irate *shimin,* who had been roused from their beds by reports of advancing troops. The soldiers, unarmed, weary, leaderless, and confused, were easily immobilized. Once again, as on 20 May, it seemed as though the people had won a major victory.[405]

This time, the victory was short-lived. On the afternoon of 3 June, thousands of PLA troops, unarmed but in battle dress, were disgorged from underground tunnels leading into the Great Hall of the People. Sent to clear Tiananmen Square, the troops were immediately surrounded by masses of *shimin* behind the Great Hall and prevented from reaching their destination. Though tempers were short and incidents of violence flared episodically, student monitors enforced discipline among the crowds, preventing any serious conflagration.

Such was not the case in other areas of Beijing. At around 2:00 P.M. in the afternoon, west of the Square on Chang'an dajie near Liubukou, loudspeakers blared out a directive from the martial law command headquarters, ordering the crowds to disperse immediately. Shortly thereafter, hundreds of soldiers and armed security forces rushed into the streets, firing tear gas shells and clubbing those unfortunate enough to get in their way. Similar incidents were reported from other areas of the city throughout the afternoon.

At 6:30 P.M., the Beijing municipal government and martial law headquarters issued an emergency notice warning Beijing residents not to go out onto the streets or into the Square; violaters would be "responsible for their own fate." The message was broadcast repeatedly from 7:00 to 9:00 P.M. on government radio and television stations. At 10:00 P.M., troops massed on the outskirts of Beijing received their orders to proceed immediately to Tiananmen and to clear the Square by 6:00 A.M. the following day, 4 June.

The first known shooting of civilians occurred at around 10:30 P.M. on Chang'an Boulevard near Muxidi, a few miles west of Tiananmen, where a column of advancing troops, armed with assault rifles and machine guns and

405 There is considerable controversy over the purpose of this curious foray. Some observers believe it was a deliberate provocation by the government, akin to throwing a lighted match into a gas tank, designed to precipitate a violent attack on the unarmed soldiers, which could then be used as a pretext for launching a violent crackdown on the students. Others have argued that the unarmed soldiers were to have been reunited with their weapons, which were being transported separately into the city on at least three unmarked buses, at Tiananmen Square. However, the buses (like the soldiers themselves) were intercepted and immobilized by crowds of *shimin* before they could reach the scheduled rendezvous point.

accompanied by tanks and armored personnel carriers (APCs), met a wall of nonviolent but unyielding *shimin*. Under orders to reach Tiananmen Square or face military discipline, which under the circumstances meant the strong likelihood of a firing squad, the soldiers first discharged their rifles into the air, hoping to frighten the crowds into dispersing. When the people did not yield, the soldiers gradually lowered their sights; eventually they began to fire into the crowd. At first paralyzed by dismay and disbelief, the crowd soon broke up. Many fled in panic; others stayed behind to care for the dead and wounded. Bullets flew in random, stray patterns, felling fleeing protesters and innocent bystanders alike.

Most of the killing took place between 10:30 P.M. and 2:30 A.M., as the scene at Muxidi was replayed, with minor variations, at other locations throughout the city. With armored PLA units continuing their relentless advance toward the Square, enraged *shimin* now began to fight back, using whatever materials were at hand, including rocks, bottles, Molotov cocktails, and an assortment of homemade knives and clubs. Jamming iron construction rods into the treads of army APCs, they succeeded in disabling a number of vehicles, several of which they then set afire; when the frightened APC crews tried to escape, some were set upon by the angry crowds and savagely beaten; a few were immolated, hanged, or even disemboweled; but a substantial number were escorted to safety by student monitors.

Although the Chinese government would subsequently charge "counter-revolutionary conspirators," "hooligans," and "rioters" with instigating the carnage of 3–4 June through acts of unprovoked violence against martial law forces, it was reasonably clear that such acts, which did in fact occur, were largely a consequence, rather than a cause, of the army's brutal assault on the *shimin* of Beijing. Even the government's vaunted "smoking gun," a crudely edited videotape showing civilians savagely attacking and torching army vehicles, turns out to have been recorded several hours *after* the initial slaughter of civilians had commenced at Muxidi.[406]

The "Tiananmen massacre"

As the PLA pincer movement approached Tiananmen after midnight, the mood among students in the Square became increasingly tense. All around, tracer bullets could be seen cutting a path through the night sky, and staccato bursts of machine gun fire could be heard from all directions. But in

406 It has been suggested, but never proved, that on the morning after the assault on Tiananmen Square, the government deliberately allowed a number of army vehicles to stall or break down in the immediate vicinity of strategically placed video cameras precisely in order to precipitate, and then record, violent acts by enraged citizens.

Tiananmen Square itself, where an estimated 3,000 to 5,000 students now sat huddled close together on the three tiers and steps of the Heroes' Monument, no shots were fired.

Beginning around 1:30 A.M., an "emergency notice" was broadcast repeatedly over government loudspeakers around the Square, reporting that a "serious counterrevolutionary rebellion" had broken out and that "ruffians" were "savagely attacking" PLA units, setting military vehicles afire, kidnapping soldiers, and seizing army weapons. After having previously acted with "great restraint," the PLA would now have to "resolutely counterattack the counterrevolutionary rebellion," the notice proclaimed.

Moving in from three directions, soldiers sealed off the Square between 2:00 and 3:00 A.M. Almost all nonstudents, including the vast majority of journalists, had left the Square by this time.[407] The students who remained at the Heroes' Monument reportedly had in their possession at least two rifles and one machine gun, which was manned by a team of "pickets" (*jiuchadui*) and pointed in the general direction of PLA troops arrayed in front of the Great Hall of the People. According to one eyewitness account, the soldiers facing the students shouted, "We will not attack unless we are attacked first"(*ren bufan wo, wo bufan ren*).[408]

At this point a dispute arose between Chai Ling, who was in favor of allowing those students who wished to remain in the Square "to the end" to do so, and another group of strike leaders who wished to persuade the remaining few thousand students to evacuate peacefully before it was too late. The Chai Ling group, which controlled access to the loudspeaker system mounted high up on the Heroes' Monument, announced its intention to lead the students in singing a final, defiant rendition of the *Internationale* as the final moment of truth approached.

After considerable heated debate, the pro-evacuation group, led by Beijing Normal University lecturers Liu Xiaobo and Gao Xin, social scientist Zhou Duo, and the well-known Taiwanese pop singer Hou Dejian, managed to take control of the machine gun at the base of the Heroes' Monument, which they proceeded to dismantle, thereby averting a potentially disastrous clash with the troops opposite. Their attempt to persuade the students to leave the Square suffered a setback, however, when the Chai Ling–controlled loudspeaker system suddenly went dead.

Some time after 3:00 A.M., Chai Ling left Tiananmen Square. At 4:00 A.M., all lights in the Square suddenly went out; for the few thousand

407 The withdrawal of foreign journalists in the early morning hours of 4 June helps to explain the dearth of reliable eyewitness reports describing the unfolding of subsequent events, including the army's recapture of Tiananmen Square and the students' eleventh-hour evacuation.

408 "CND interview with Gao Xin."

students who remained huddled around the base of the Heroes' Monument, the moment of truth was seemingly at hand. According to eyewitness observers, a curious calm now descended upon the Heroes' Monument: It was the eye of the hurricane.

Meanwhile, the four pro-evacuation leaders, Liu Xiaobo, Gao Xin, Zhou Dou, and Hou Dejian, redoubled their efforts to avoid an imminent holocaust by negotiating a last-minute student withdrawal from the Square. Descending from the Heroes' Monument and hitching a ride with a passing ambulance, Zhou and Hou sought out the local commander of the PLA forces in Tiananmen Square. After some initial confusion, they managed to locate a PLA regimental commissar, who listened to their evacuation proposal. A few minutes later, the local commander arrived and approved the plan, which called for the students to file out of the Square toward the southeast. The students were promised safe conduct and a period of grace in which to leave.

At around 4:30 A.M. the lights in the Square went back on, and a sea of troops poured out of the Great Hall of the People. After taking up positions on the east side of the Square, the troops proceeded to shoot out the student loudspeakers atop the Heroes' Monument.[409] At this point, a representative of the Beijing Autonomous Workers' Federation urged the students to evacuate the Square immediately, before a bloodbath took place; his advice was seconded by Hou Dejian, who had hurriedly rejoined the students after completing his negotiations. Hou's pleas were countered, however, by another speaker who urged the students to "stand firm." After a brief period of uncertainty, punctuated by the sound of tank engines coming to life at the northern edge of the Square, a voice vote was taken; someone then announced that a "democratic decision" had been made to leave the Square.

The evacuation, which was calm and orderly, began shortly before 5:00 A.M. and lasted approximately half an hour. By 5:30 A.M., only a small handful of people remained at the Monument; by the time the first line of bayonet-wielding soldiers climbed the steps to reclaim the Monument a few minutes later, most of these stragglers had also left.[410] As dawn broke on

409 It was apparently these bursts of gunfire, seen ricocheting off the top of the Monument, that triggered the subsequent rumors, spread by the mass media in Hong Kong and elsewhere, that soldiers had cold-bloodedly massacred rows of students sitting quietly at the base of the Monument. Wu'er Kaixi, who had himself left the Square shortly after midnight, would later claim that 200 students were killed in this early morning assault.

410 One eyewitness to these final moments at the Heroes' Monument was the Chinese scholar Yu Shuo, who later recounted her experience: "As I was talking to an [army] officer I suddenly realized that I was the last person left at the Monument. As I walked down the terrace . . . I saw that a soldier was about to pierce a bed with his bayonet. I saw two feet sticking out from it. . . . I rushed forward and dragged the feet. A boy fell down from the bed; he was not completely awake yet. He was the last student to leave the Square" (quoted in Munro, "Who died . . . ?"). An account by Gao Xin differs only marginally, on the question of who was the last to leave the Monument: "Chen Zheng might be the last one to leave. She and a friend from Hong Kong refused to leave, sat on a step of the

Sunday, 4 June, Chinese tanks at the northern end of Tiananmen Square crushed the Goddess of Democracy.

After the storm

Sporadic, often apparently random shootings of civilians, including innocent bystanders and apartment dwellers, by martial law troops continued at various points around Beijing for several days after 4 June.[411] Although there were frequent rumors in this period of an impending civil war involving allegedly rebellious armored units of the PLA, no organized military mutiny occurred; there were, however, numerous reported cases of intra-PLA dissension and failure to carry out orders.[412]

On 6 June, Beijing Mayor Chen Xitong publicly congratulated the martial law forces on winning "initial victory" in the struggle to quell counterrevolutionary rebellion; at the same time, he cautioned that final victory would require a "long and complicated struggle."[413] On the same day, Fang Lizhi and his wife, Li Shuxian, whose names were about to be placed on a government arrest warrant, sought and received sanctuary inside the U.S. Embassy in Beijing. Also on 6 June, antigovernment demonstrations broke out in at least a dozen Chinese cities. The most serious incidents took place in Chengdu, where rioting by angry crowds led to a declaration of martial law, culminating in the shooting of scores of *shimin,* and in Shanghai, where antigovernment workers set fire to a train that had hurtled into a crowd of protesters, killing six and wounding at least six others.[414]

The arrests began on 6 June; among the first group of pro-democracy activists to be detained by security forces were Ren Wanding and Liu Xiaobo. On 11 June, arrest warrants were issued for a number of student leaders, prominent Chinese intellectuals, and other outspoken supporters of human rights who stood accused of instigating or supporting the counterrevolutionary

Monument to the People's Heroes, and kept crying. A soldier stood on a higher step, ordered them to leave immediately, cursing and threatening. I ran to them and pushed them away" ("CND interview with Gao Xin").

411 On 7 June, the foreign diplomatic residential compound at Jianguomen, east of Tiananmen Square, was fired on by Chinese troops in an apparent attempt at intimidation.

412 See June Teufel Dreyer, "The People's Liberation Army and the power struggle of 1989," *POC* 38.5 (September–October 1989), 41–8.

413 On 6 June, State Council spokesman Yuan Mu held a press conference at which he presented the government's initial version of the events of 3–4 June. The text appears in *SWB/FE* 0476 (7 June 1989).

414 It was subsequently reported that between 30 and 300 people had been killed, and more than 1,000 others injured (including security forces), in the Chengdu violence, which continued for three days after 4 June. See Amnesty International, *China: The massacre . . . ,* 58–67; and Karl Hutterer, "Eyewitness: The Chengdu massacre," *China Update* 1 (August 1989), 4–5. On the violence in Shanghai, see Maier, "Tiananmen 1989 . . . ."

rebellion. Among the names appearing on government "most wanted" lists in this period were Fang Lizhi, Li Shuxian, Wu'er Kaixi, Wang Dan, Chai Ling, Bao Tong, Yu Haocheng, Yan Jiaqi, and Wan Runnan; arrest warrants were also issued for the outspoken coauthor and director of "River Elegy," Su Xiaokang, as well as for such inveterate human rights activists as economist Chen Ziming and newspaper editor Wang Juntao, both of whom had played prominent roles in earlier democratic protest movements.

On 7 June, China's highest prosecuting authority, the Supreme People's Procuratorate, issued an "emergency notice" to public security bureaus around the country, advising them not to be "hamstrung by details" in the detention and prosecution of hooligans and rebels. Over the next several days, large-scale detentions of suspected counterrevolutionaries were carried out in Beijing and elsewhere. Within two weeks, the number of officially reported arrests throughout the country reached 1,600, with unofficial estimates being many times higher.[415]

415 The official figures generally included only people formally charged with committing rebellion-related crimes; unofficial figures, compiled by foreign human rights groups, tended to include along with those formally arrested a much larger number of people, generally reckoned in the tens of thousands, who were picked up and detained for questioning (often for twenty-four or forty-eight hours) before being released.

According to official sources, at least forty fugitive student leaders and dissident intellectuals managed to escape from China in the first several weeks after the 4 June crackdown (*RMRB*, 7 July 1989). Escapees included Wu'er Kaixi, Chai Ling, Yan Jiaqi, Gao Gao, Wan Runnan, and Su Xiaokang. In the weeks that followed, a number of other dissidents were arrested in China, including Bao Tong (who was accused of leaking information from Politburo meetings to the students in the Square), Yu Haocheng, Wang Dan, Chen Ziming, and Wang Juntao. Singer Hou Dejian, after spending ten weeks hiding out in the Australian embassy, returned to his Beijing residence in August 1989. After initially corroborating the government's claim that no students had been massacred in Tiananmen Square on 4 June, Hou later declared himself in opposition to the regime. At the end of May 1990, he, along with two of the others who had helped negotiate the 4 June evacuation of Tiananmen Square, Zhou Duo and Gao Xin, announced their intention to hold a press conference on the first anniversary of the Tiananmen crackdown in order to read an open letter to Chinese leaders demanding the release of all political prisoners, including the fourth member of their Tiananmen negotiating team, Liu Xiaobo. When the three dissidents were detained by security police before they could hold their press conference, Hou Dejian, a celebrity whose international fame made it difficult for the government to crack down on him with impunity, negotiated his second evacuation agreement with the authorities: In exchange for a government pledge not to arrest him or his two collaborators, Hou agreed to accept deportation to his native Taiwan. He was escorted out of the country toward the end of June, at around the same time that Chinese authorities were permitting Fang Lizhi and Li Shuxian to leave the U.S. embassy in Beijing for exile in England.

In the winter of 1991, at the height of the Persian Gulf crisis, thirty-one Chinese intellectuals, jailed in the aftermath of the Tiananmen crackdown, were tried, convicted, and sentenced to prison terms of varying lengths for assorted "counterrevolutionary crimes." Eighteen other dissidents had all formal charges against them dropped, and an additional forty-five were released from detention in lieu of formal charges being filed. Among the thirty-one convicted dissidents, some, including Liu Xiaobo, were credited for time already served and were released from custody after reportedly showing "sincere repentance" for their actions; Wang Dan, whose alleged crimes included "counterrevolutionary propaganda and incitement," reportedly showed repentance at his trial and was sentenced to four years in prison; Ren Wanding, remaining unrepentant throughout, was sentenced to seven years; Chen Ziming and Wang Juntao, who were defiant in protesting their innocence, were

As a deterrent to would-be counterrevolutionaries, in the last two weeks of June at least thirty-five people in five different cities, mostly workers, unemployed youths, and members of the urban "floating population," were hastily tried, sentenced, and publicly executed for various acts of violence committed during the uprising of early June. Contrary to widespread rumors, no students or intellectuals were among those sentenced to death for their role in the June disturbances.[416]

While the public security apparatus mobilized for a crackdown on "ruffians," "thugs," and other assorted counterrevolutionaries, Party and government leaders turned their attention to the delicate task of fashioning an intraelite consensus in support of the 3–4 June crackdown. With the leadership deeply divided by the events of the previous two months, this proved no mean feat.

Damage control: The center tightens its grip

First came the self-congratulations; then came the denials. On 6 June, the government officially complimented the martial law forces for their bravery, restraint, and self-discipline in the face of counterrevolutionary rebellion. A day later, the political commissar of the PLA's 27th army appeared on Chinese television to assert that not a single student had been killed by troops during the operation to clear Tiananmen Square.[417] Seeking to shift the focus of attention from the PLA's bloody assault on the *shimin* of Beijing to acts of violence committed against the army by "ruffians" and "rioters," he described in detail a series of antimilitary atrocities. This was to become the pattern for government self-justification in the weeks and months that followed, that is, that the PLA's use of deadly force on 3–4 June was a "defen-

given the harshest sentences of all, thirteen years each, on charges of sedition. According to reports circulating in Beijing, the defense attorneys who represented Chen and Wang at their trials were subjected to considerable governmental harassment following the conclusion of the courtroom proceedings. See *CND,* 4 April 1991. For accounts of the trials of the Beijing democracy activists, see *NYT,* 27 January and 13 February 1991; Associated Press, 12 February 1991; and *CND,* 10 and 25 March 1991.

416 Among those executed were three young workers accused of setting fire to the Shanghai train that had plowed into a crowd of demonstrators on 6 June. By September 1990, Amnesty International had recorded the names of more than fifty people sentenced to death for crimes allegedly committed in connection with protests against the military crackdown of 3–4 June. See Amnesty International, *China: The massacre . . . ,* 54–8.

417 The distinction here was a rather fine one. Although the 27th army had been responsible for much of the bloodshed that occurred in the western part of Beijing, between Muxidi and Tiananmen Square, on the night of 3–4 June, neither it nor any other main force units of the PLA had actually gunned down students in the Square. There were some early reports of Chinese tanks crushing students in sleeping bags and tents on the Square, but these reports have generally been discounted due to lack of reliable eyewitness corroboration.

sive" reaction forced upon the martial law forces by the violent provocations of counterrevolutionary conspirators.[418]

On 8 June, Premier Li Peng, accompanied by a somber and restrained Wan Li, appeared on television to reaffirm the government's gratitude to the martial law forces for their heroic role in restoring order in Beijing.[419] The next day, 9 June, Deng Xiaoping appeared publicly for the first time in several weeks. In a televised meeting attended by virtually the entire Chinese civilian and military high commands, minus only Zhao Ziyang and Hu Qili, Deng effusively praised the martial law forces for their bravery in nipping a counterrevolutionary rebellion in the bud. Reflecting on the sources of China's crisis, Deng defended his reform policies and argued that the rebellion had been the inevitable result of Party leaders permitting the global climate of bourgeois liberalization to spread unchecked within China:

> In recent days I have pondered these points. . . . Is there anything wrong with the basic concept of reform and openness? No. Without reform and openness how could we have what we have today? . . . [Nor is] there anything wrong with the four cardinal principles. If there is anything amiss, it's that these principles haven't been thoroughly implemented; they haven't been used as the basic concept to educate the people, educate the students, and educate all the cadres and party members. The crux of the current incident is basically a confrontation between the four cardinal principles and bourgeois liberalization.[420]

Toward the end of June, Party leaders convened an enlarged CC plenum. Attended by almost 200 old-timers of the CAC, the Fourth Plenum formally removed Zhao Ziyang and Hu Qili from the Politburo and the Central Secretariat.[421] Zhao stood accused of a series of "grave errors and mistakes," including "splitting the Party," and was stripped of all formal Party posts (though he was not expelled); his request to address the plenum in his own defense was turned down.[422] Hu Qili, in turn, was reprimanded for having supported the wrong side at the critical moment but was spared further

418 The most detailed governmental account of the origins and development of the Tiananmen crisis was contained in a 30 June speech by mayor Chen Xitong to the NPC SC. The text of Chen's speech appears in *CQ* 120 (December 1989), 919–46.

419 The appearance of Wan Li, who did not speak, alongside Li Peng on this occasion was clearly designed to demonstrate to the Chinese people (and more particularly to restive Party, government, and army cadres throughout the country) that the top leadership had closed ranks, and that even those leaders who had previously sympathized with the student protests had now gone over to the side of the hard-liners.

420 Deng's speech is translated in *BR* 32.28 (10–16 July 1989), 14–17. See also *FEER*, 10 August 1989, 13.

421 The communiqué of the fourth plenum appears in *CQ* 119 (September 1989), 729–31; for analysis, see David L. Shambaugh, "The fourth and fifth plenary sessions of the 13th CCP central committee," *CQ* 120 (December 1989), 852–62.

422 At an earlier meeting of the Politburo, on 14 June, Zhao had steadfastly refused to acknowledge his culpability: "First, I did not make a mistake; second I still hold that the starting point of the student movement was good. They were patriotic" (*BX* 203 [1 November 1989], 19–22).

disciplinary action. Two other erstwhile Zhao loyalists, Yan Mingfu and Rui Xingwen, were also dismissed from the Party's Central Secretariat.[423]

After securing the dismissal of Zhao and his key allies, the Fourth Plenum turned to the business of selecting a new general secretary, an exercise that should have been largely pro forma, insofar as Deng Xiaoping had already made known his personal choice for the post: Shanghai party secretary (and former mayor) Jiang Zemin. Despite having the advantage of Deng's support, however, Jiang barely managed to muster a majority of votes in the CC.[424] To round out the new party leadership group, two other newcomers were promoted from the ranks of the Politburo to join Jiang Zemin on the revamped SC: the veteran economic planner and Party organization department head, Song Ping, and the reformist ex-mayor of Tianjin, Li Ruihuan.[425]

At a meeting of the NPC Standing Committee, held at the end of June, Hu Jiwei's 22 May petition drive, urging an emergency meeting of the SC for the purpose of reversing Li Peng's martial law declaration, was severely criticized, and Hu himself was accused of complicity in a plot to further the aims of the "turmoil creators," including the aim of securing Li Peng's dismissal. In his defense, Hu insisted that the petition drive had been wholly "reasonable and legal," and he denied that his real motive had been to oust Li Peng. Hu's arguments were dismissed as "flawed" and "lacking justification."[426] On 3 July, premier Li sent the NPC Standing Committee a draft law on demonstrations, stipulating, among other things, that henceforth protesters would not be allowed to question the leadership of the CCP or undermine the nation's unity or stability in any way.

423 Other key Zhaoists removed from Party posts at the Fourth Plenum included Zhao's political adviser, Bao Tong (who had already been arrested); An Zhiwen, vice-minister of the State Commission for Reform of the Economic Structure; Wen Jiabao, head of the CC General Office; and Du Runsheng, director of the Rural Policy Research Center. On 23 June, the pro-Zhao director and the chief editor of *RMRB* were removed from their posts, ostensibly for "reasons of health." Soon afterward, minister of culture Wang Meng was also forced to resign.

424 As early as 31 May, Deng had indicated that Jiang Zemin would be the "core" (*hexin*) of the new Party leadership (*I&S* 26.3 [March 1990], 13). Evidently, Chen Yun had initially recommended Yao Yilin to replace Zhao Ziyang as general secretary, whereas Peng Zhen had favored Qiao Shi (Li Peng had reportedly been tainted as a result of his role in declaring, and later enforcing, martial law). Jiang Zemin, a compromise candidate, had been nominated by Li Xiannian. Deng's expression of support for Jiang was ostensibly based on four primary criteria: First, Jiang occupied a centrist position on the reform spectrum, i.e., he was committed both to economic reform and to the four cardinal principles; second, he was an outsider who was not beholden to Chen Yun or any other factional interests; third, he had taken a firm stand against bourgeois liberalism in the Shanghai media; and fourth, he had succeeded in defusing student protest in Shanghai without recourse to martial law or organized violence (*I&S* 25.7 [July 1989], 1–4). For analysis of Jiang Zemin's role in handling student protest in Shanghai, see Maier "Tiananmen 1989 . . . ," 3–6, and passim.

425 Li Peng, Qiao Shi, and Yao Yilin all remained on the new SC, thus raising its total membership from five to six. To replace the three dismissed members of the Central Secretariat (Zhao, Yan, and Rui), Li Ruihuan and Party General Office director Ding Guang'en were added to that body.

426 *RMRB*, 11 July 1989; *CQ* 120 (December 1989), 894–5.

In the aftermath of the Fourth Plenum, China's elderly hard-liners sought to consolidate their gains. Calling Zhao Ziyang the " 'root of evil' . . who intended to reach his required goals through turmoil," Li Xiannian urged a new rectification drive to eliminate remnant pockets of Zhaoist influence within the Party. Wang Zhen charged Zhao with "surrendering to the bourgeoisie." Along similar lines, Peng Zhen accused Zhao of "working with hostile forces at home and abroad to overthrow the CCP and disrupt the socialist system." Official media sources now began to hold the former general secretary personally responsible for a wide variety of societal ills, including hyperinflation, social instability, and rampant official profiteering.[427]

In the face of strong conservative pressures to prosecute Zhao Ziyang, spearheaded by Chen Yun and supported by Li Peng and Yao Yilin, Deng Xiaoping refused to be drawn into an anti-Zhao vendetta. Counseling caution and restraint in the handling of Zhao's case, China's senior leader once again revealed his underlying concern for carefully counterbalancing *fang* and *shou*. "Let us not get tangled up in who is responsible for what right now," he said on 16 June; "Let those questions be raised two or three years from now."[428] Deng prevailed, and no formal charges were filed against Zhao; however, for the next several months the former general secretary remained confined to quarters, living in relative comfort at Hu Yaobang's former residence in Fuqiang Lane, Beijing.[429]

Although Deng's personal intervention enabled Zhao to avoid criminal prosecution, CAC old comrades nonetheless went forward with their attempt to root out remnant Zhaoists within the Party apparatus. At the end of June 1989, the CDIC, under Peng Zhen protégé Qiao Shi, launched a new rectification drive, in the course of which all Party members in Beijing and other cities were required to undergo investigation and reregistration in connection with their attitudes and behavior during the six weeks of turmoil. Notwithstanding its intended gravity, however, the new campaign was muted from the outset by a virtual conspiracy of silence on the part of leading cadres and work unit heads, many of whom withheld from investigation teams the names of people in their units who had taken part in the April–May demonstrations. Frustrated by this evident lack of cadre enthusiasm for the new rectification campaign, Party conservatives in mid-July created a special investigatory body to facilitate the work of "ferreting out the guilty ones." As before, however, the severity of the Party's internal probe continued to be

427 *WHB*, 24 July 1989; *FEER*, 10 August 1989, 13; *SWB/FE* 0518 (26 July 1989). For a summary of the charges against Zhao in this period, see *CQ* 120 (September 1989), 900–1.

428 *WHB*, 28 June 1989.

429 In the spring of 1990, Deng reportedly gave the go-ahead for Zhao eventually to begin resuming some administrative responsibilities after first undergoing an extensive period of "investigation and research," *South China Morning Post*, 24 and 25 July 1990.

effectively softened by a combination of passive resistance and pro forma compliance on the part of large numbers of unit leaders.[430]

Disarming urban anger: The new anticorruption drive

Even as Party and government leaders circled their wagons in defense of the June crackdown, they came under intense pressure to confront the underlying problems that had given rise to the massive urban protests of April and May. As early as 6 June, State Council spokesman Yuan Mu acknowledged the need to (re-)open a dialogue between government and citizens on a wide range of socioeconomic and political issues. "Once the whole situation is stabilized," he said, "the government will give much thought to proposals and suggestions raised by the people of various circles, including the students, on punishing official profiteering, uprooting corruption, and promoting democracy, and will earnestly accept suggestions from various quarters."[431] In a similar vein, Deng Xiaoping, in a speech on 16 June, explicitly linked the restoration of public confidence in the Party and government with the continuation of reforms and with the need to deal forthrightly with the problem of official corruption:

> We must perform certain acts to inspire satisfaction among the people. There are two aspects to this: one is to pursue the reform and openness policies more aggressively, and the other is to catch and punish those who engage in corruption. . . . If we fail to catch and punish corrupt people, particularly those inside the party, we run the risk of failure.[432]

In line with Deng's objective of regaining public confidence, the Party belatedly launched a high-profile antiracketeering drive in the summer of 1989. On 10 July, the *People's Daily* announced the expulsion of hundreds of corrupt Party members; two weeks later the Politburo decreed that all *gaogan zidi* would henceforth be banned from engaging in private business and that top Party officials would no longer have access to imported cars and private supplies of food. At the same time, the Politburo ordered the breakup of the notorious Kang Hua Development Corporation.[433] A month later, the Chi-

430 See, e.g., *JB*, 10 November 1989, in *FBIS*, 14 November 1989; and *BX*, 16 December 1989, in ibid., 19 December 1989; also Daniel Southerland, National Public Radio, *Weekend Edition*, 10 March 1990. Interestingly, some of the ostensibly toughest-talking Party leaders turned out to be among those most effective in shielding their subordinates from harm.

431 *SWB/FE* 0476 (7 June 1989).

432 *ICM*, September 1989, 3–5. Deng also recommended setting a public example by severely punishing one or two dozen high-level cadre profiteers.

433 As noted earlier, the name of Deng Pufang had frequently been linked to the activities, and enormous profits, of Kang Hua. In addition to his links with Kang Hua, the younger Deng was reported to be deeply involved in the activities of the Huaxia Publishing Company, a subsidiary of the China Welfare Fund for the Handicapped (Deng Pufang, director) that in 1988 had been fined

nese Auditing Administration imposed fines amounting to more than RMB 50 million yuan ($US 12.8 million) on five of China's largest quasi-private corporations: Kang Hua, CITIC, Everbright, China Economic Development Corporation, and China Rural Trust and Development Corporation. In September, the governor of Hainan province, Liang Xiang, was dismissed from his post on assorted charges of economic malfeasance, making him the highest-ranking official to be netted in the new anticorruption drive.[434]

The unquiet summer of 1989: "Neijin, Waisong"

By midsummer, a situation of uneasy calm, characterized as "*neijin, waisong*" ("internal tension, external tranquility"), had blanketed the nation's capital. Through an extraordinary assertion of personal authority and Party discipline, with strong backing from the so-called Yang family generals within the PLA, Deng Xiaoping had managed to weather the immediate crisis and stanch the flow of high-level Party and military defections that threatened to topple China's Communist regime.[435] Yet the government's visible success in restoring public order was achieved at considerable cost. Whether measured in terms of the severe loss of popular legitimacy in urban China, the further erosion of central authority over the provinces, the emergence of deep schisms within the PLA, the paralysis of economic decision making, or the diplomatic isolation and economic sanctions imposed upon China by foreign governments, investors, and lending agencies, the costs were staggering.[436]

Despite the initiation of high-profile campaigns to "emulate Lei Feng"[437] and to improve the public image of the PLA (e.g., by having soldiers clear garbage from sidewalks, give haircuts to civilians, and help old folks to cross

RMB 150,000 yuan for publishing erotic books. On the reputedly shady economic dealings of Deng and other *gaogan zidi,* see "The politics of prerogatives in China: The case of the *Taizidang* (Princes' party)" (unpublished manuscript, n.a., n.d., 1990).

434 By April 1991, 72,000 CCP members had reportedly been expelled, and an additional 256,000 subjected to lesser forms of discipline, in the post-Tiananmen crackdown on official corruption and bourgeois liberalism. No breakdown of these statistics, e.g., by type of offense, was given, however. See *CND,* 18 April 1991. On implementation of the 1989 anticorruption campaign, see Michael D. Swaine, "China faces the 1990s: A system in crisis," *POC* 39.3 (May–June 1990), 20–35.

435 It has been widely reported that Yang Shangkun threw his full weight, and the weight of his extended PLA "family" (including his half-brother, general Yang Baibing, and at least two other relatives reputed to be high in the command structure of the 27th army group), behind Deng's new centrist coalition, headed by Jiang Zemin, in exchange for a dominant voice in China's revamped post-Tiananmen military command structure. See *South China Morning Post,* 25 July 1990.

436 These negative effects are examined in Tony Saich, "The reform decade in China: The limits to revolution from above," in Marta Dassù and Tony Saich, eds., *The reform decade in China: From hope to dismay.* See also Swaine, "China faces the 1990s . . . ."; and Hsiung, "Mainland China's paradox . . . ."

437 Lei Feng was a young PLA recruit who died an accidental death in 1962. The "spirit of Lei Feng," characterized by unquestioning loyalty, self-sacrifice, and ceaseless devotion to duty, has recurrently been invoked by Chinese leaders in periods of severe ideological stress or flagging military morale.

streets), the PLA's prestige and morale reportedly fell to an all-time low. According to a high-level PLA source, over 100 senior military officers had "breached discipline in a serious manner" during the struggle to crush the student-led rebellion in early June; an additional 1,400 PLA soldiers had "shed their weapons and run away" during the crackdown.[438]

Isolated sniper attacks against martial law troops reportedly continued throughout the summer of 1989. In late July a Chinese newspaper revealed an attempt by a Beijing resident to kill martial law troops by offering them a bucket of drinking water laced with poison.[439] In a highly unusual display of intraelite dissidence, the commander of the Twenty-Seventh Army, who was believed to have given the initial order for troops to open fire on civilians near Muxidi on the night of 3 June, was audibly hissed by an audience composed primarily of civilian cadres when he rose to address a propaganda conference in Beijing in August; obviously flustered, he angrily denied that his troops had slaughtered innocent civilians.

Deep divisions were also at play within the PLA. According to one oft-repeated (but subsequently discounted) rumor that swept through China in the summer of 1989, Yang Shangkun, in an attempted putsch, had placed four high-level PLA officials, including Defense Minister Qin Jiwei and three regional commanders, Beijing's Zhou Yibing, Guangzhou's Zhang Wannian, and Nanjing's Xiang Shouzhi, under house arrest. Although the rumor proved false, it nonetheless pointed up the existence of a serious schism within the military between forces supporting the June crackdown (reportedly led by the Yang family generals) and those opposing it (including Qin Jiwei and a number of military region and district commanders).[440]

Continuing student unrest was another prime source of concern to Party and government leaders throughout the summer of 1989. In an attempt to deal with the problem of student rebelliousness at its putative source, the government on 21 July announced a decision to cut back on new college

438 These figures were revealed by the PLA's chief political commissar, Yang Baibing. The 111 officers charged with "breach of discipline" included 21 officers at or above the rank of divisional commander, 36 regimental or battalion commanders, and 54 company-level commanders (*South China Morning Post*, 28 December 1989). Subsequently, it was reported that between 1,500 and 3,000 army officers were required to undergo loyalty checks as a result of their questionable behavior during and after the June uprising (*The Observer* [London], 18 February 1990). On the role of the military during the May–June crisis and its aftermath, see Harlan Jencks, "Party authority and military power: Communist China's continuing crisis," *I&S* 26.7 (July 1990), 11–39; Dreyer, "The People's Liberation Army . . . ," 42–5; Wilson and Ji, "Leadership by 'lines' . . . ," 38–43; and Swaine, "China faces the 1990s . . . ," 26–7, 32–4.

439 *JJRB*, 31 July 1989.

440 A wholesale reshuffle of PLA regional commanders took place in the spring of 1990, in the course of which six of the seven regional commanders and five of their seven chief political commissars were transferred or retired. Evidently, the "Yang-family generals" were the prime beneficiaries of the reshuffle. See *FEER*, 14 June 1990, 32; also Jencks, "Party authority and military power . . . ," 25–6.

enrollments in the humanities and social sciences for 1989–90 by a total of 30,000 students; two days later, several hundred Beida students spontaneously marched through the campus late at night to protest both the cutbacks and the crackdown; as they marched, they sang, with more than a slight hint of irony and sarcasm, the lyrics to a well-known revolutionary song: "Without the communist party, there would be no new China." When the song was finished, the students began to chant, with gleeful double entendre, the lyrics to an animated television commercial for a pesticide spray: "We are the mighty pests! We are the mighty pests! Oh, oh, here come the dreaded pest-killers; let's bug out of here!" Three weeks later, in mid-August, the tolerant, reform-minded president of Beida, Ding Shisun, was dismissed; concurrently, it was announced that the entire 1989 Beida freshman class, whose numbers had been cut back from 2,000 to only 800, would be required to undergo a year of military training before being permitted to attend regular classes.

In mid-August, Beijing Mayor Chen Xitong disclosed that previously announced plans to hold a military parade in Beijing on 1 October, the fortieth anniversary of the founding of the PRC, had officially been scrapped. At the same time, it was announced that Tiananmen Square, closed to the public since 4 June, would soon be reopened to selected tour groups "in an organized manner." Although the government now routinely asserted that everything was back to business as usual in the nation's capital, the continued presence of large numbers of uniformed, fully armed martial law troops in the heart of Beijing bespoke a different condition: *neijin, waisong.* As if to underscore that condition, at summer's end the authorities in Beijing intervened at the eleventh hour to cancel a performance of Verdi's *Requium,* which was to have been presented on the Beida campus to commemorate the passing of 100 days since Tiananmen. In lieu of the canceled performance, Beida students held a candlelight vigil on school grounds. Though liberalization had given way to catastrophic repression in yet another revolution of the *fang–shou* cycle, the students' flickering candles appeared to bespeak a tremendous confidence that eventually there would be another round of letting go.

Epilogue: The end of an era?

In the aftermath of the Tiananmen crisis, the longer-term consequences of China's national trauma could only be guessed at. But when the PRC marked its fortieth anniversary on 1 October 1989, there were few congratulations and fewer smiles. Though legions of gaily outfitted dancers and a lavish display of fireworks brightened the appearance of Tiananmen Square, the mood in the nation's capital was anything but festive.

It was a far cry from 1 October 1949, when Mao Zedong had ascended the rostrum at Tiananmen to the sound of thunderous cheers, proclaiming triumphantly, "The Chinese people have stood up!" On that earlier occasion, there had been genuine popular elation and high hopes for China's future. Now, forty years later, the capital was under martial law, hope seemed strangely out of place, and elation was wholly absent as the nation's shoulders sagged visibly under the weight of the Tiananmen tragedy.

All great revolutions inspire millennarian visions; few ultimately deliver the goods. So it was with Mao's original revolution, which exhausted itself in the course of two grandiose, and ultimately hugely destructive, experiments in human social engineering: the Great Leap Forward and the Great Proletarian Cultural Revolution. Now, it seemed, Deng Xiaoping's "second Chinese revolution" had also reached a point of near-exhaustion, running out of fresh ideas and of people to implement them.

As the 1980s gave way to the 1990s, a cascading wave of bourgeois liberalization swept over the Soviet Union, Eastern Europe, and Central Europe, causing Communist regimes throughout the region to concede power. In Moscow, the original Bolshevik Party of V. I. Lenin formally accepted the principle of political pluralism, thereby relinquishing its seventy-two-year monopoly on power; in Warsaw, a rebellious union organizer was elected president; in Prague, a dissident playwright assumed the mantle of leadership; in Bucharest, the Communist army refused an order to fire upon its own people, and the dictator who gave the order was executed. Reacting to these events, a group of old comrades in Beijing, circling their wagons ever tighter, demanded renewed allegiance to the four cardinal principles and proposed, yet again, the name of their irrepressible paladin, Deng Liqun, for promotion to the CC Politburo. Under such circumstances, many Chinese citizens hunkered down for the long haul, taking what comfort they could from actuarial tables that suggested that the crusty old comrades of the CAC could not, despite their rumored periodic blood transfusions and Qigong breathing exercises, live forever.

CHAPTER 6

REACTION, RESURGENCE, AND SUCCESSION: CHINESE POLITICS SINCE TIANANMEN

JOSEPH FEWSMITH

Tiananmen shook the Chinese Communist Party (CCP) to its core. The charge leveled against former general secretary Zhao Ziyang was that "[a]t the critical juncture involving the life and death of the Party and state, he made the mistake of supporting turmoil and splitting the Party, and he bears unshirkable responsibility for the formation and development of the turmoil. The nature and consequences of his mistakes are very serious."[1] The issues the Party faced, however, ran far deeper than even this charge suggested. Tiananmen threw open a whole series of questions that had been simmering just below the surface for years.

The most fundamental of these was the nature of reform itself. Tiananmen, many Party leaders believed, was the inevitable denouement of the reform program that Zhao led and symbolized; more important, the content of that reform program was inextricably intertwined with Zhao's patron, senior leader Deng Xiaoping. The question raised by Tiananmen, then, was the nature of Deng's leadership and thus whether or not the Party should continue reform as Deng had defined it. Many believed it should not.

The question of the content of reform, or, in Chinese jargon, the political line,[2] was related to a number of state–society issues: the relations between

1 "Zhongguo gongchandang di shisanju Zhongyang weiyuanhui di sice quanti huiyi gongbao" (Communiqué of the Fourth Plenary Session of the Thirteenth Central Committee of the CCP), in *Shisanda yilai zhongyao wenxian xuanbian, zhong* (Important documents since the Thirteenth Party Congress, vol. 2; hereafter, *Shisanda yilai,* 2), 544.

2 In the reform period, different conceptions of the scope, pace, and goal of reform grew up around Chen Yun, on the one hand, and Deng Xiaoping, on the other. Although Chen never challenged Deng's "core" status directly, he and his colleagues did develop a systematic critique of Deng's approach to reform. This critique was used in an effort to limit reform. The conservative critique of reform became the basis for criticizing a whole series of policies, and implicitly Deng's leadership, in the post-Tiananmen period. It thus seems appropriate to refer to this struggle as a "line" struggle, even though it remained implicit. For a discussion of the conflict between Chen and Deng, see Joseph Fewsmith, *Dilemmas of reform in China.* For a contrary interpretation, see Frederick C. Teiwes, "The paradoxical post-Mao transition: From obeying the leader to 'normal politics,' " *China Journal,* 34 (July 1995), 55–94.

the central government and the localities; the rapidly changing social structure of Chinese society, including the emergence of a middle class; the growing independence of the intellectual elite; the rising expectations of society; and the very real fears of many people that reform might hurt rather than help their interests. In other words, reform had generated a range of profound social changes, and the question that had racked the Party for years was how it should respond to these changes. How should it channel, suppress, or incorporate the demands that increasingly emanated from this changing society?

Another broad area of questions generated by Tiananmen revolved around China's relations with the outside world. Deng Xiaoping himself raised this issue in his 9 June 1989 address to martial law troops. Deng declared the Tiananmen incident "the inevitable result of the domestic microclimate and the international macroclimate."[3] This sense that domestic upheavals were influenced (if not instigated) by outside forces raised the issue of readjusting China's relations with the outside world, particularly the United States. This issue has continued to intrude on Chinese domestic politics throughout the post-Tiananmen period as first East Europe and then the Soviet Union rejected communism, as relations with the United States have remained generally strained, and as closer ties with East Asia have suggested alternative development models.

In the seven years between Tiananmen and Deng's fading from the political scene, Chinese politics were driven by deep divisions among the elite, uncertainty about how to respond to the changing forces of society, a rapidly changing international environment, and finally, the emergence of a new generation to take the place of the founders of the People's Republic of China (PRC). In June 1989 a shaken and divided Party leadership tried to begin the process of reconstituting itself while sorting out how its domestic and foreign policies should or should not be changed. Looming over these initial efforts was the shadow of former general secretary Zhao Ziyang, who quickly became a foil for critics of reform.

THE QUESTION OF ZHAO

The question of how to deal with Zhao Ziyang was inevitably linked with the question of Deng Xiaoping's leadership, not just because Zhao's selection first as premier and then as general secretary now seemed to reflect poorly on Deng Xiaoping's judgment, but because Zhao had been implementing a

3 Deng Xiaoping, "Zai jiejian shoudu xieyan budui junyishang ganbu shi de jianghua" (Talk on receiving martial law cadres at the army level and above in the capital), in *Deng Xiaoping wenxuan* (Selected works of Deng Xiaoping), 3.302.

political-cum-economic line long supported by Deng.[4] Deng clearly recognized that dismissing a second successor (following former general secretary Hu Yaobang's ouster in January 1987) would raise doubts about his own judgment, and he was determined to salvage as much advantage as he could by denying the fruits of victory to the winners.

Four days before the crackdown and more than three weeks before the Party's Central Committee would meet to confirm changes in the leadership, Deng Xiaoping met with Premier Li Peng and Politburo Standing Committee (PSC) member Yao Yilin to tell them that Jiang Zemin, then CCP secretary of Shanghai, would be plucked from relative obscurity to become the "core" of the third generation of CPC leadership.[5] In explaining his decision, Deng almost contemptuously told Li and Yao, "The people see reality. If we put up a front so that people feel that it is an ossified leadership, a conservative leadership, or if the people believe that it is a mediocre leadership that cannot reflect the future of China, then there will be constant trouble and there will never be a peaceful day." He also tried to forestall an all-out attack on Zhao's policies (and himself) by declaring that "the political report of the Thirteenth Party Congress was passed by the representatives of the Party to the congress; not even one character must be changed."[6]

When Deng met with leaders of martial law troops on 9 June, he declared that the line of "one center and two basic points" (economic development was the center, and reform and opening to the outside world on the one hand and opposition to "bourgeois liberalization" on the other were the two basic points), which had been adopted at the Thirteenth Party Congress in 1987, was correct and that reform and opening up must be pursued even more vigorously.[7] Moreover, a week before the Fourth Plenum convened, Deng urged the Party to avoid destructive ideological struggles: "If at this time we open up some sort of discussion on ideology, such as a discussion regarding

4 One can draw distinctions between Zhao and Deng, but the similarities predominate. Overall, Zhao appears to have been closer to Deng on more issues than was Hu Yaobang. Although Zhao was more open-minded in his response to the Tiananmen demonstrations than Deng, Zhao was hardly a liberal. It was, after all, Zhao who sponsored discussions on the "new authoritarianism." The Thirteenth Party Congress, which clearly bears Zhao's imprint, was strongly supported by Deng. On economic issues, Deng was in some sense the more radical, or at least the more impatient, as suggested by his 1988 advocacy of rapid price reform. Certainly in the eyes of Zhao's and Deng's critics, the similarities were far greater than the differences.

5 In his 31 May talk to Li Peng and Yao Yilin, Deng defined three "generations" of leadership: the first was led by Mao Zedong, the second by himself, and the third by Jiang Zemin. See Deng Xiaoping, "Zucheng yige shixing gaige de you xiwang de lingdao jiti" (Organizing a reformist, hopeful leadership collective), in *Deng Xiaoping wenxuan,* 3.298–9.

6 Ibid., 296–301.

7 Deng, "Zai jiejian shoudu xieyan budui junyishang ganbu shi de jianghua," 3.302–8. Of course, Deng coupled his declaration of reform and opening up with the need to uphold the four cardinal principles and to increase ideological and political education.

markets and planning, then not only would bringing up this sort of issue be disadvantageous to stability but it would cause us to miss an opportunity."[8]

The Fourth Plenary Session of the Thirteenth Central Committee, which convened on 23–4 June 1989 following a three-day enlarged Politburo meeting, confirmed Deng's decision to name Jiang Zemin as general secretary and added him, veteran planner Song Ping, and Tianjin mayor Li Ruihuan to the PSC. Li Ruihuan and Ding Guan'gen, Deng's bridge partner, were added to the Secretariat in partial replacement of Zhao associates Hu Qili, Rui Xingwen, and Yan Mingfu, who were removed. On the critical question of Zhao, however, the plenum could not come to a final resolution. Having judged Zhao's actions harshly, the conclave nevertheless could only declare that the party would "continue to investigate his problem."[9]

The plenum's failure to conclude Zhao's case reflected the depth of division within the Party. Obviously, some within the Party wanted to pursue the issue of Zhao's guilt, perhaps even to the point of criminal prosecution, a course that would have had profound implications for Deng Xiaoping and the continuation of reform. For instance, Yuan Mu, the hard-line spokesman for the State Council and protégé of Premier Li Peng, stated that Zhao's case would be handled "in accordance with the criterion based on law," suggesting the possibility of legal prosecution.[10] Some Party elders were blunter. PRC president Li Xiannian allegedly called Zhao the "root cause of the riots and rebellion," while Party elder Peng Zhen accused Zhao of "attempting to topple the Communist Party and wreaking havoc with the socialist system in coordination with hostile powers at home and abroad."[11]

In fact, during the campaign against "bourgeois liberalization" that was unleashed following Tiananmen, it was impossible to separate criticism of Zhao Ziyang from issues of ideology and Party line, and there is every indication that hard liners within the Party wished to press such issues with an eye to curtailing Deng's authority and returning the Party to the more limited notion of reform that had prevailed in the late 1970s and early 1980s. In his 1989 National Day (1 October) address, Jiang Zemin asserted that there were two types of reform: one that upheld the four cardinal principles and another that was based on "bourgeois liberalization." The question, Jiang said, was whether the socialist orientation would be up-

8 Deng Xiaoping, "Disandai lingdao jiti de dangwu zhi ji" (Urgent tasks of the third generation leadership collective), in *Deng Xiaoping wenxuan*, 3.312.

9 "Zhongguo gongchandang di shisanju Zhongyang weiyuanhui di sice quanti huiyi gongbao," 2.543–6.

10 Xinhua, trans. in *FBIS Daily Report: China* (hereafter, *FBIS-Chi*), 12 July 1989, 25.

11 [Zeng Bin] Tseng Pin, "Party struggle exposed by senior statesmen themselves; meanwhile, the new leading group is trying hard to build new image," *JB*, 145 (10 August 1989), trans. in *FBIS-Chi*, 10 August 1989, 14. See also *WHB* (Hong Kong), 24 July 1989.

held.[12] In posing the question in this way, Jiang raised the issue that would dominate Chinese politics for much of the next two years: What was socialist and what was capitalist?

By the same reasoning, if Zhao had advocated a reform that was based on "bourgeois liberalization" and hence was capitalist in nature, then Zhao's mistake would not have been a simple error of implementation (one hand firm and the other lax, as Deng put it) but an error of line. Although the Party, in the interest of putting ideological battles behind it at the beginning of the reform era, had ceased to describe intra-Party conflicts as "line struggles," the notion of political line and hence of line struggle remained very much a part of Party life at the elite level. For instance, in a talk to a national meeting of organization department heads, Song Ping implicitly criticized Zhao for making line errors. For Song, Tiananmen was the inevitable outcome of a trend of bourgeois liberalization that extended back to Democracy Wall in 1978, had never been effectively opposed, and had resulted in such "absurd theories" (*miaolun*) as the "criterion of productive forces." The theory of productive forces, a phrase used (frequently by critics) to describe the view that anything that improves the economy is *ipso facto* socialist, was voiced prominently in an article by Zhao Ziyang that appeared in the *People's Daily* (*Renmin ribao*) in February 1988,[13] but Song's reference was clearly to Deng Xiaoping as well. It was, after all, Deng who had always asserted that "it doesn't matter what color the cat, the one that catches the mouse is a good cat."[14] This trend of bourgeois liberalization, Song asserted, went against the Marxist political line set by the Third Plenum in 1978, and Tiananmen was the "bitter fruit of violating this [Marxist] *line*."[15]

12 Jiang Zemin, "Zai qingzhu Zhonghua renmin gongheguo chengli sishi zhounian dahuishang de jianghua" (Talk celebrating the fortieth anniversary of the establishment of the PRC), in *Shisanda yilai,* 2.618. Deng had opened the way for this line of analysis in his 31 May talk with Li Peng and Yao Yilin. In that talk, Deng said that the "center of their [in reference to Zhao Ziyang and others] so-called 'reform' is capitalization. The reform I talk about is different." See "Zucheng yige shixing gaige de you xiwang de lingdao jiti," 3.297.

13 Zhao Ziyang, "Further emancipate the mind and further liberate the productive forces," *RMRB,* 8 February 1988, trans. in *FBIS-Chi,* 8 February 1988, 12–14.

14 In the aftermath of Deng's trip to the South in early 1992, a propaganda book put out to hype Deng's thought was unabashed in its touting of Deng's "criterion of productive forces." See Yu Xiguang and Li Langdong, eds., *Dachao xinqi: Deng Xiaoping nanxun qianqian houhou* (A great tide rising: Before and after Deng Xiaoping's southern sojourn).

15 Song Ping, "Zai quanguo zuzhi buzhang huiyi shang de jianghua" (Talk to a national meeting of organization department heads), in *Shisanda yilai,* 2.568–9, 574 (emphasis added). Contrast Song's emphasis on political loyalty with Li Ruihuan's statement that "[i]n assessing a leading cadre, his accomplishments in government are primary." See *Nanfang ribao,* 28 October 1989, trans. in *FBIS-Chi,* 6 November 1989, 22. See also Chen Yun's "six points," conveyed to the Central Advisory Commission in November 1991. The third point reads, "Marxists must admit that there are line struggles within the party, which is part of normal party life, and it is necessary to actively launch inner-Party criticism and self-criticism." [Luo Bing] Lo Ping and [Li Zejing] Li Tzu-ching, "Chen Yun raises six points of view to criticize Deng Xiaoping," *ZM,* 171 (1 January 1992), 18–19, trans. in *FBIS-Chi,* 3 January 1992, 22–3.

DENG'S STRATEGY

In the wake of the Tiananmen debacle and confronted by an outpouring of ideological vitriol from hard liners presenting themselves as true Marxists who had been attacked and suppressed by Zhao and his allies, Deng's strategy could only be the relatively passive one of emphasizing stability, promoting economic development, and relaxing the ideological atmosphere. In a talk with leaders on the eve of the Fourth Plenum, Deng urged that the Party not dissipate its energies in ideological disputes and called for "doing some things to satisfy the people."[16] In response, the State Council in July passed a resolution on resolving problems the people were concerned about, on restricting the activities of leading cadres' families, and on reorganizing suspect companies.[17] Similarly, Li Ruihuan, the former carpenter whom Deng had put in charge of ideology, made an effort to relax the ideological atmosphere in the summer by calling for a campaign against pornography.[18] It was a clever ploy that left conservatives nonplussed. After all, pornography was associated with Western influences, but it hardly raised the central ideological issues that conservatives wished to pursue. In September, Li asked in a sharply worded interview with the PRC-owned Hong Kong paper *Dagong bao,* "Why do we always have to go to excess?" Berating conservative ideologues, Li said, "We must not use dogmatic and rigid methods to criticize bourgeois liberalization."[19]

Deng also harped on the issue of stability (eventually coining the phrase "Stability overrides everything" [*wending yadao yiqie*])[20] and emphasized the continuity of reform and opening up. Deng had successfully employed similar tactics in 1987 after he had unceremoniously dumped General Secretary Hu Yaobang. In 1989, however, the situation was vastly different. First, the depth of Party division created by Tiananmen was far greater than at the time of Hu Yaobang's ouster. Second, Deng's prestige within the Party was also greatly diminished by Tiananmen and the disgrace of Zhao. Chen Yun had summed up the feelings of many conservatives when he had accused Deng of

16 Deng, "Disandai lingdao jiti de dangwu zhi ji."

17 "Zhonggong Zhongyang, Guowuyuan guanyu jinqi zuo jijian qunzhong guanxin de shi de jueding" (Decision of the CCP Central Committee and State Council regarding doing a few things of concern to the masses in the present period), in *Shisanda yilai,* 2.555–7.

18 The campaign started on 11 July 1989, when the Press and Publications Administration issued a circular on rectifying the cultural market. Over the summer, Li spoke on the issue of pornography many times. See, for instance, Beijing television service, 24 August 1989, trans. in *FBIS-Chi,* 25 August 1989, 15–16.

19 "Li Ruihuan meets with Hong Kong journalists," *DGB,* 20 September 1989, trans. in *FBIS-Chi,* 20 September 1989, 10–12.

20 Deng apparently first used this phrase in his 31 October 1989 talk with Richard Nixon. See Deng Xiaoping, "Jiesu yanjun de ZhongMei guanxi yao you Meiguo caiqu zhudong" (Resolving the serious situation in Sino-U.S. relations requires that the U.S. take the initiative), in *Deng Xiaoping wenxuan,* 3.331.

being rightist in his economic policies and leftist in his use of the military.[21] Deng could no longer dominate China's policy agenda.

Finally, the international situation made Deng's task much more difficult. On the one hand, China's relations with the West, particularly the United States, were strained badly by China's crackdown and the subsequent imposition of sanctions. Deng's room for maneuvering was extremely limited. On the other hand, the unraveling of communism in Eastern Europe made the threat of "peaceful evolution" very real to China's leaders and added weight to conservatives' contention that China should assert ideological leadership on issues of international socialism. Deng rejected such urgings, successfully arguing that China's leaders should "coolly observe, keep our feet steady, and react soberly." Whatever happened in the world, Deng said, China should concentrate on economic development.[22]

THE CONSERVATIVE CHALLENGE

As Deng and Li Ruihuan tried to cool the ideological atmosphere and refocus the Party's attention on reform and opening up, conservatives were determined to press their advantage. With the suppression of the protest movement in Beijing and elsewhere and the ouster of Zhao Ziyang, conservatives seized the opportunity to criticize Zhao's economic leadership and impose their own interpretation of economic reform. This effort began with the editing of Deng Xiaoping's remarks. In Deng's 9 June talk, he was quoted as referring to the "integration of planned economy and market regulation."[23] This expression restored the preferred usage of conservatives, which they had been able to impose during the 1981–2 retreat from more market-oriented reforms.[24] As later revealed, Deng had originally called for the integration of the "planned economy and the market economy," thus putting the two economic types on the same plane. Before his remarks were published in the *People's Daily,* however, conservatives had edited them to fit their agenda.[25]

In November 1989, Chen Yun's economic thought was restored as orthodoxy by the Fifth Plenary Session of the Thirteenth Central Committee. The "CCP Central Committee decision on furthering improvement and rectification and deepening reform" (frequently referred to as "the thirty-nine points") that was adopted by the plenum laid out a systematic, albeit im-

21 Richard Baum, *Burying Mao: Chinese politics in the age of Deng Xiaoping,* 319.

22 Deng Xiaoping, "Gaige kaifang zhengce wending, Zhongguo dayou xiwang" (If China's policy of reform and opening up remains stable, there is great hope for China), in *Deng Xiaoping wenxuan,* 3.321.

23 Deng, "Zai jiejian shoudu xieyan budui junyishang ganbu shi de jianghua," 306.

24 Fewsmith, *Dilemmas of reform in China,* ch. 3.

25 Baum, *Burying Mao,* 294.

plicit, critique of Zhao's management of the economy. That decision, like much commentary in the months after Tiananmen, intimated the implicit line struggle that had existed within the Party by suggesting that the economy had begun to go awry in 1984 – when the decision on the reform of the economic structure was adopted. Since that time, the Fifth Plenum decision declared, economic policy had ignored China's "national strength" (*guoli* – a famous Chen Yun thesis), allowing aggregate demand to "far, far" exceed aggregate supply, had upset the balance between industry and agriculture, had ignored basic industries, and had dispersed financial resources too widely, thus eroding the state's ability to exercise macroeconomic control. These problems, the decision declared, constituted a "mortal wound" (*zhimingshang*) to the economy.[26]

In his speech to the plenum, Jiang Zemin declared that the "greatest lesson" to be derived from the PRC's economic past was that the country must not "depart from its national conditions, exceed its national strength, be anxious for success, or have great ups and downs."[27] These were all well-known theses of Chen Yun, so Jiang's endorsement of Chen Yun's thought over Deng's line of reform and opening up was apparent.

Just as Party conservatives rejected Deng's economic line, they spurned efforts to reduce ideological tensions. As suggested above, their rejection of Deng's efforts to reduce tensions was based not only on the depth of division within the Party but also on the collapse of socialism in East Europe.[28]

On 15 December, Wang Renzhi, head of the Propaganda Department, launched a blistering attack on bourgeois liberalization in a talk to a Party-building class. In direct opposition to Deng's theses that economic development would promote social stability and that ideological debates should be put off, or better, not taken up, Wang argued that stability could be built only on the basis of Marxist ideology. Only in this way, Wang argued, could economic work be carried out without deviating from the socialist orientation. Wang, in effect, reinterpreted Deng's slogan "Stability overrides everything," a phrase coined to relax ideological tension, as a clarion call for making ideological struggle the basis of future stability. Lest anyone think that the time had come to relax the campaign against bourgeois liberaliza-

26 "Zhonggong Zhongyang guanyu jinyibu zhili zhengdun he shenhua gaige de jueding (zheyao)" (CCP Central Committee decision on furthering improvement and rectification and deepening reform [outline]), in *Shisanda yilai,* 2.680–708. All these charges were part of the conservative critique of reform that had been ongoing at least since 1984.

27 Jiang Zemin, "Zai dang de shisanju wuzhong quanhui shang de jianghua" (Talk to the Fifth Plenary Session of the Thirteenth CCP Central Committee), in *Shisanda yilai,* 2.711.

28 Some within the Party argued that the implementation of reform in East Europe had led to the collapse of communism there, while others argued that communism collapsed because the planned economy had continued to prevail in those countries. Wu Jinglian, *Jihua jingji haishi shichang jingji* (Planned economy or market economy), 41.

tion, Wang declared, "We have only just started" to clarify ideological errors and "The logic of struggle is cruel and merciless."[29]

Wang's speech was followed by a full-page article in the *People's Daily* praising the notorious "Zhuozhuo meeting" of 1987. At that meeting, conservative Party leaders, concerned that Zhao and others would blunt the campaign against bourgeois liberalization that unfolded in the wake of Hu Yaobang's ouster, tried to breathe new fire into the movement. It was after that meeting, and perhaps because of it, that Deng authorized Zhao's famous 13 May 1987 speech closing off the campaign against bourgeois liberalization and preparing the political atmosphere for the Thirteenth Party Congress in the fall. Now, in the wake of Zhao's ouster, conservative writer Chen Daixi, under the pseudonym "Yi Ren," accused Zhao of using "all kinds of dirty tricks with the most malicious motives" to suppress the Zhuozhuo meeting.[30] Obviously, Chen, as well as other conservative writers at the time, were aware that Deng had fully supported the stoppage of the 1987 campaign and they were determined to prevent him from doing so again.

REINFORCING STATE PLANNING

The strength of the conservative wing of the Party in the winter of 1989–90 was indicated not only by the directness of the challenge to Deng's ideological authority but also by a major effort to restore at least a significant measure of state planning to the economy. For years, conservatives had complained that reform had directed investment into small-scale, less efficient industries (mostly township and village enterprises – TVEs) that competed with large and medium-sized state-owned industries for scarce energy, transportation, and raw materials. As a result, basic energy and material sectors were drained of investment capital while transportation and energy supplies were always strained by the demand. Moreover, reform strategy had led to a regional bias as TVEs along the east coast grew and developed while industry and living standards in the interior lagged behind.

A major effort to strengthen the "pillars" of the economy, as the large and medium-sized state-owned industries were called, came in late 1989 when Li Peng announced that a State Council Production Commission (*guowuyuan shengchan weiyuanhui*) was being established to "promptly resolve major prob-

29 Wang Renzhi, "Guanyu fandui zechan jieji ziyouhua" (On opposing bourgeois liberalization), *RMRB*, 22 February 1990. See also the harsh speech Wang delivered to *Qiushi* staffers in August, "Lilun gongzuo mianlin de xin qingquang he dangqian de zhuyao renwu" (The new situation confronting theoretical work and the primary task at the moment), *Xuexi, yanjiu, cankao,* 11 (1990), 8–17.

30 Yi Ren, "Zhuozhuo huiyi de qianqian houhou" (Before and after the Zhuozhuo meeting), *RMRB,* 14 February 1990.

lems regarding production."[31] The new commission, which was headed by Ye Qing, a specialist in the coal industry, incorporated offices that had once belonged to the State Economic Commission (SEC).[32] Instead of resurrecting the SEC, which had often acted as an advocate of industry interests and had often clashed with the more conservative State Planning Commission (SPC), the new State Council Production Commission was clearly intended to be subordinate to the SPC. The idea behind the establishment of the State Production Commission was apparently to coordinate more effectively the functions of planning and plan implementation through a newly established "double-guarantee" system to be administered by the Production Commission, which would, in turn, be overseen by the SPC. The double-guarantee system was intended, on the one hand, to guarantee the supply of the necessary raw materials and funds to important state-owned enterprises and, on the other hand, to guarantee enterprises' delivery of profits, taxes, and output to the state.[33] The double-guarantee system was initially imposed on 50 major enterprises in Northeast China and then extended to cover 234 of China's largest enterprises.

The establishment of the Production Commission and the implementation of the double-guarantee system was a clear victory for the conservative wing of the Party and especially for Li Peng, who would have a chance to try out his policies for strengthening socialist management. The victory for Li Peng was underscored by the appointment of Zou Jiahua, Li's close colleague of many years, as head of the SPC in December 1989 (replacing the conservative planner Yao Yilin).

RENEWED DEBATE OVER THE DIRECTION OF THE ECONOMY

In the weeks and months after Tiananmen, there was virtually no debate over the course of the economy, at least in the major newspapers. In fact, most economic commentaries carried by the *People's Daily* and *Guangming ribao* in those early months were written by unknown reporters or economists. It was only after the Party's Fifth Plenum in November 1989 that the *People's Daily* began running serious economic views again: a number of well-known economists, including Ma Hong, Zhang Zhuoyuan, Li Chengrui, and Wang Jiye, all argued, in measured, academic terms, the case for the Fifth Plenum's call

31 *Hong Kong Standard,* 18 December 1989; and *JJDB,* 50 (18 December 1989), trans. in *FBIS-Chi,* 20 December 1989, 22–3.

32 *JJDB,* 50 (18 December 1989), trans. in *FBIS-Chi,* 20 December 1989, 22–3.

33 *Jinrong shibao,* 30 January 1990, trans. in *FBIS-Chi,* 14 February 1990, 24–5.

for continuing retrenchment.[34] At the same time, more liberal economists began to suggest that the policy of reform and readjustment had already achieved the major goal of controlling inflation and was beginning to hurt economic development by excessively reducing demand. The emergence of this debate over retrenchment policies marked the first time in nearly half a year that a tone of rational discussion had entered the press.

This trend continued the following spring with Li Peng's address to the National People's Congress (NPC) in March 1990. Although Li was uncompromising on the need to continue "improvement and rectification," the name given to the retrenchment policies adopted in the fall of 1988, he called for finding a means of successfully "integrating" planning and market regulation.[35] This talk inaugurated a public discussion on the topic – the third such discussion in the history of the PRC. The previous two rounds of discussion, however, had taken place in the wake of economic difficulties in 1959 and 1979 and had been intended to justify an expansion of market forces. In contrast, this new discussion was intended to justify integration on the basis of planning. But at least an opening for rational discourse on the economy had been created.

Even as Li Peng was seeking to define and defend a policy that would recentralize the economy and reimpose a significant degree of planning, economic trends were revealing just how wrong conservative views of the economy were. As Naughton has argued, China's economy in 1989 was far healthier than the conservatives' declaration of profound economic crisis would allow.[36] The harsh restrictions on credit and investment were so successful in reducing demand that by September 1989 consumer prices were actually falling – though China's planners, calculating inflation on a year-to-year rather than month-to-month basis, were unaware of this dramatic turnaround.[37] Even calculating on a year-to-year basis, inflation in the first half of 1990 was only 3.2 percent, making it apparent to everyone that the urgency that had generated the retrenchment policies had passed. Meanwhile, the profitability of large state firms – the very sector conservative policies had

34 See Ma Hong, "Have a correct understanding of the economic situation, continue to do a good job in economic improvement and rectification," *RMRB*, 17 November 1989, trans. in *FBIS-Chi*, 5 December 1989, 37–9; Zhang Zhuoyuan, "Promoting economic rectification by deepening reform," *RMRB*, 27 November 1989, trans. in *FBIS-Chi*, 7 December 1989, 28–31; Li Chengrui, "Some thoughts on sustained, steady, and coordinated development," *RMRB*, 20 November 1989, trans. in *FBIS-Chi*, 12 December 1989, 32–4; and Wang Jiye, "Several questions on achieving overall balance and restructuring," *RMRB*, 8 December 1989, trans. in *FBIS-Chi*, 19 January 1990, 30–3.

35 Li Peng, "Wei woguo zhengzhi jingji he shehui de jinyibu wending fazhan er fendou" (Struggle to take another step for the stable development of China's politics, economics, and society), in *Shisanda yilai*, 2.948–94.

36 Barry Naughton, *Growing out of the plan: Chinese economic reform, 1978–1983*, 275.

37 Ibid., 281, 347 n. 2.

been designed to shore up – was collapsing. In 1990, profits of in-budget state firms fell 57 percent.[38] At the same time, inventory stocks shot up, enterprise losses jumped 89 percent over the same period the previous year, and the retail sales of commodities fell 1.9 percent.[39] The difficulties in the state-owned sector would force the government to pump an additional 270 billion yuan of loans into that sector in 1990 on top of the 126 billion yuan of loans issued in the fourth quarter of 1989.[40]

The combination of subsiding inflationary fears and stagnating industrial production brought renewed calls to revive reform, although it is surprising how slowly such calls were heeded given the debacle produced by conservative control of the economy. In May and June of 1990 some leaders solicited input from economists by questioning whether China's economy had come out of the economic trough.[41] This request stirred a new round of economic debate, and in the summer the Economic Situation Group of the Chinese Academy of Social Sciences (CASS), headed by Liu Guoguang, proposed that the "weight" of reform be increased.[42] This proposal by no means rejected the austerity program adopted in 1988 (indeed, Liu had been one of the authors of that program), but it did emphasize that improvement and rectification were intended to bring about an atmosphere conducive to a market-oriented reform rather than a reinstitution of the planned economy.

CENTER–PROVINCIAL CONFLICT OVER THE EIGHTH FIVE-YEAR PLAN

One of the conservatives' biggest complaints about Zhao's management of the economy was that the strategy of decentralization pursued in the 1980s was leading to Beijing's loss of economic, and perhaps political, control over the provinces. Conservative instincts were to recentralize by exercising more direct control over the economy. This was the route mapped out by the draft of the Eighth Five-Year Plan as it neared completion in the summer of 1990. As Zou Jiahua, vice-premier and head of the SPC (the organization with primary responsibility for drafting the plan), put it, "The integration of central planning and market regulation is a basic principle" of economic

38 Ibid., 284–5.

39 [He Dexu] Ho Te-hsu, "China has crossed the nadir of the valley but is still climbing up from the trough: Liu Guoguang talks about the current economic situation in China," *JJDB*, 38–9 (1 October 1990), 12–13, trans. in *FBIS-Chi*, 12 October 1990, 27–30.

40 Wu, *Jihua jingji haishi shichang jingji*, 12–13.

41 Ibid., 14. Wu does not specify which leaders raised this issue.

42 Ibid., 25; "Promote stability through reform, achieve development through this stability: Basic concepts of development and reform based on 'seeking progress through stability' in the 1990s," *JJYJ*, 7 (20 July 1990), 3–19.

policy making, but "the two do not have equal status. Central planning is of primary importance. Market regulation is supplementary."[43]

The difference between this concept of planning and the provincial interest in continuing existing patterns of reform came to a head at the September 1990 Economic Work Conference. Two issues were central to the conflict. One was an evaluation of reform. Whereas Li Peng insisted that reform had led to various "dislocations" in the economy, the provinces insisted that reform be affirmed and written into the Eighth Five-Year Plan. The other issue concerned the financial interests of the provinces. The central government wanted to replace the local financial contract system, under which the provinces were responsible only for delivering a specified sum to Beijing, with a "dual tax system" that would designate clearly which taxes would go to the central government and which to the localities. Led by Ye Xuanping, governor of Guangdong, Zhu Rongji, CCP secretary and mayor of Shanghai, and Zhao Zhihao, governor of Shandong, the provinces virtually rebelled against the authority of the central government.[44]

The September work conference is often taken as a symbol of the growing independence of the provinces, and to a certain extent it was. Over the years, reform had allowed the provinces to accumulate considerable resources, primarily in the form of extrabudgetary revenues, which freed them from dependence on the central government. Provincial authorities went to elaborate lengths to nurture – and conceal – such funds, and they would not willingly yield their economic interests.

There was, however, another important aspect of this provincial "rebellion," namely that the central government was itself divided, with some political leaders and organizations sympathizing with the provinces. The most important of these was none other than Deng Xiaoping, who feared that the conservative agenda being pushed by Li Peng would negate the contributions of reform (and therefore of Deng Xiaoping) and would lead to lower growth rates. Throughout the 1980s, Deng had emerged as the champion of higher growth rates, not only because the economic achievements of China would reflect favorably on his own leadership and place in history but also because he believed that as the economy developed, political and social conflicts would be more easily resolved, thus reducing the possibility that major conflicts could lead to another cultural revolution.[45] Thus, on the eve of the Economic Work Conference, Deng sent Yang Shangkun to talk to such

43 *JJDB*, 5 November 1990, as cited in Willy Lam, *China after Deng Xiaoping*, 56.

44 Baum, *Burying Mao*, 326–8.

45 A third reason to support higher growth rates was that a greater percentage of the growth would necessarily occur outside the scope of the plan and thus limit the capacity of such conservative bureaucratic organs as the SPC to control and restrict reform.

provincial leaders as Zhu Rongji and Ye Xuanping, letting them know that they had Deng's support in their opposition to Li Peng.[46]

SINO-U.S. RELATIONS

A significant part of reformers' efforts to regain the initiative in 1990 lay in their improving Sino-U.S. relations. In his speech to martial law troops on 9 June, Deng Xiaoping laid the foundation for the campaign against "peaceful evolution" when he declared that the 4 June "storm" had been an inevitable product of the "international macroclimate" and the domestic "microclimate."[47] A week later, Deng was more explicit, saying that "[t]he entire imperialist Western world plans to make all socialist countries discard the socialist road and then bring them under the control of international monopoly capital and onto the capitalist road," and that if China did not uphold socialism, it would be turned into an appendage of the capitalist countries.[48] Moreover, in his October 1989 talk with former president Richard Nixon, Deng charged that the "United States was too deeply involved" in the student movement.[49]

Conservative leaders, deeply suspicious of the United States, were, on the basis of Deng's comments, able to whip up a campaign against "peaceful evolution." Such conservatives charged that the United States, having failed to contain and overthrow socialism in the 1950s and 1960s, had pinned its hope on the third or fourth generation of Chinese, who might be susceptible to Western influences and thus bring about change from within. These officials argued in the summer of 1989 that China should reorient its foreign policy away from the West to build stronger ties with the remaining socialist states and the Third World.[50]

Although these advocates did not carry the day, their views certainly influenced China's top leadership. In Jiang Zemin's 1 October 1989 speech marking the fortieth anniversary of the founding of the PRC, which was accorded the sort of press treatment reserved for only the most authoritative addresses, the Party general secretary charged that "international reactionary forces have never given up their fundamental stance of enmity toward and [desire to] overthrow the socialist system."[51]

Although conservatives were never able to bring about a fundamental

46 Gao Xin and He Pin, *Zhu Rongji zhuan* (Biography of Zhu Rongji), 212.
47 Deng, "Zai jiejian shoudu xieyan budui junyishang ganbu shi de jianghua," 302.
48 Deng, "Disandai lingdao jiti de dangwu zhi ji," 310.
49 Deng, "Jiesu yanjun de ZhongMei guanxi yao you Meiguo caiqu zhudong," 331.
50 Harry Harding, *The fragile relationship: The United States and China since 1972*, 236.
51 Jiang, "Zai qingzhu Zhonghua renmin gongheguo chengli sishi zhounian dahui shang de jianghua," 631.

reorientation of Chinese foreign policy, they certainly were able to constrain the Chinese government's capacity to take initiatives that might have improved relations. Thus, as Deng told Nixon, "The United States can take a few initiatives; China cannot take the initiative."[52]

The United States responded to Deng's advice by sending Deputy Secretary of State Lawrence Eagleburger and National Security Adviser Brent Scowcroft to Beijing in December 1989. The timing of the trip, it turned out, was not good. The collapse of socialism in East Europe was provoking new debate in Beijing and bringing about an upswing in conservative influence. Thus, China was able to make only minor concessions in return for the visit. It was not until June 1990 that Fang Lizhi, the Chinese astrophysicist who had taken refuge in the U.S. Embassy in Beijing after the 4 June crackdown, was finally permitted to leave the country. Fang's release came too late to be viewed as much of a concession by many in the U.S. Congress and the press, but it did begin to ease the tensions in Sino-U.S. relations. In late 1990, ties improved again with Chinese Foreign Minister Qian Qichen's visit to the United States, which culminated in a meeting with President Bush. After the meeting, Qian declared that the visit would "help open vast vistas for bilateral relations."[53]

DENG'S MOVE TO REVIVE REFORM

By late 1990, Deng seemed visibly distraught by China's situation and his own inability to reassert his leadership. Whereas the communiqué adopted by the party's Seventh Plenum in December 1990 "highly evaluated" China's "tremendous achievements" in reform and opening up, it nevertheless went on to stress the "integration of the planned economy with market *regulation*" and to repeat such staples of Chen Yun's economic thought as calling for "sustained, stable and coordinated" economic development and "acting according to one's capability" (*liangli erxing*).[54]

Such limited endorsement of Deng's views apparently left the patriarch frustrated. "Nobody is listening to me now," Deng allegedly complained. "If such a state of affairs continues, I have no choice but to go to Shanghai to issue my articles there."[55] So saying, Deng traveled to the east coast metropo-

52 Deng, "Jiesu yanjun de ZhongMei guanxi yao you Meiguo caiqu zhudong," 332.

53 Beijing radio, 1 December 1990, trans. in *FBIS-Chi,* 3 December 1990, 6–7.

54 "Zhongguo gongchandang di shisanju Zhongyang weiyuanhui di qice quanti huiyi gongbao" (Communiqué of the Seventh Plenary Session of the Thirteenth CCP Central Committee), in *Shisanda yilai,* 2.1420–6, emphasis added. The phrase *liangli erxing* was used widely in the 1980–1 period as Chen Yun's influence increased and as various retrenchment measures were adopted.

55 Cited in [Liu Bi] Liu Pi, "Deng Xiaoping launches 'northern expedition' to emancipate mind; Beijing, Shanghai, and other provinces and municipalities 'respond' by opening wider to the outside world," *JB,* 166 (10 May 1991), trans. in *FBIS-Chi,* 6 May 1991, 26–9.

lis and proceeded to give a number of talks intended to rekindle reform. In his talks, Deng declared that market and planning were both economic "methods" (rather than distinguishing characteristics of capitalism and socialism, respectively) and argued that whatever promoted the socialist economy was socialist. The Hong Kong press quickly dubbed Deng's comments his "new cat thesis" (because of the idea that anything that promotes production is socialist) after his famous aphorism from the 1960s that the color of the cat does not matter.

The gist of Deng's talks in Shanghai was summarized in four commentaries carried in the Shanghai Party paper, *Jiefang ribao* (*Liberation Daily*), under the pen name "Huangfu Ping." Their writing and publication were overseen by Deng's daughter Deng Nan and Shanghai Party secretary Zhu Rongji.[56] Using language not heard since the heyday of reform in the late 1980s, the commentaries excoriated "ossified thinking" and repeatedly called for a new wave of "emancipating the mind." For instance, one article declared that China would "miss a good opportunity" if it got bogged down in worrying about whether something was capitalist or socialist,[57] while another quoted Deng as saying that capitalist society was "very bold in discovering and using talented people" and urging the promotion of a large number of "sensible persons."[58]

RESPONSE FROM THE PROVINCES

It did not take long for several of China's provincial leaders to respond to Deng's initiative. On 11 March 1990, Guangdong's Party secretary Lin Ruo, who had close ties to Zhao Ziyang, published an article in the Guangdong Party paper *Nanfang ribao* (*Southern Daily*) and a shorter, somewhat watered-down version in the *People's Daily.* Lin pointedly attributed the rapid growth that Guangdong had enjoyed over the previous decade to the implementation of market-oriented policies. Similarly, Tan Shaowen, the Party secretary of Tianjin, declared that "it was because of the reform and opening up that we conducted that we withstood the severe tests of the changes in the international situation, the political storms in the country, and numerous difficul-

56 Huangfu Ping is homophonous with the characters for "Commentary from Shanghai." The four commentaries were published on 15 February, 2 March, 22 March, and 12 April 1991. The writers of Huangfu Ping articles were Zhou Ruijin, Ling He, and Shi Zhihong. See [Wei Yongzheng] Wei Yung-cheng, "Reveal the mystery of Huangfu Ping." According to Gao Xin and He Pin, the galleys of each article were personally approved by Deng's daughter, Deng Nan. See *Zhu Rongji zhuan,* 218.

57 Huangfu Ping, "The consciousness of expanding opening needs to be strengthened," *Jiefang ribao,* 22 March 1991, trans. in *FBIS-Chi,* 1 April 1991, 39–41.

58 Huangfu Ping, "Reform and opening require a large number of cadres with both morals and talents," *Jiefang ribao,* 12 April 1991, trans. in *FBIS-Chi,* 17 April 1991, 61–3.

ties." In good Dengist fashion, Tan argued that "[e]conomic stability is the foundation of political and social stability."[59]

At the same time, Hebei governor Cheng Weigao sharply criticized planners in Beijing who had recentralized authority over the economy and demanded that central policies regarding enterprise autonomy be enforced and the Enterprise Law (passed in 1988 but never really put into effect) be implemented.[60] Jiangxi governor Wu Guanzheng likewise called on his colleagues to "emancipate the mind" and "increase the weight of reform."[61]

Most surprising of all was the call from Beijing mayor Chen Xitong to "emancipate the mind." One of the most conservative of China's high officials and a hard liner who actively encouraged the use of force in suppressing the 1989 protest movement, Chen was nevertheless a close follower of Deng and responded to his call. Criticizing "ossified thinking," Chen gave explicit support to Deng's "new cat thesis."[62] In contrast, Beijing Party secretary Li Ximing, who would be ousted for his conspicuous resistance to Deng's policies following the patriarch's 1992 trip to Shenzhen, avoided the use of similar reformist rhetoric.

CAMPAIGN TO PROMOTE SCIENCE AND TECHNOLOGY

Even as Deng traveled to Shanghai to launch his "Northern Expedition," the dramatic outcome of the Gulf War was forcing the Chinese leadership to reassess the impact of science and technology – and by implication that of ideology – in the contemporary world. This reassessment, which apparently began as early as March 1991,[63] reached its peak in May when Deng Xiaoping's office wrote and forwarded to the *People's Daily* an article reviving many of the themes associated with the discussions on the new technological revolution that had been used by Zhao Ziyang and others in the 1983–4 period to turn back the campaign against "spiritual pollution."[64] That the Gulf War had a direct impact on this campaign was evident from Jiang

59 Tan Shaowen, "Emancipate the mind, seek truth from facts, be united as one, and do solid work," *Tianjin ribao,* 17 April 1991, trans. in *FBIS-Chi,* 18 June 1991, 62–8. Tan's speech was given to the municipal party's Fifth Plenary Session in January but not publicized until after the fourth Huangfu Ping commentary.

60 Cheng Weigao, "Further emancipate the mind and renew the concept, and accelerate the pace of reform and development," *Hebei ribao,* 18 April 1991, trans. in *FBIS-Chi,* 7 June 1991, 60–8.

61 "Increase weight of reform, promote economic development: Speech delivered by Wu Guanzheng at the provincial structural reform work conference," *Jiangxi ribao,* 4 May 1991, trans. in *FBIS-Chi,* 12 June 1991, 45–9.

62 *Banyuetan,* 25 March 1991. See also Chen's call for emancipating the mind at a meeting of the Beijing municipal government, *Beijing ribao,* 8 March 1991.

63 In an internal address, Li Peng elevated science and technology to first place in the four modernizations (up from their normal third-place listing). *WHB* (Hong Kong), 10 March 1991.

64 *XH,* 2 May 1991, trans. in *FBIS-Chi,* 3 May 1991, 23–6.

Zemin's statement that the performance of high-tech weapons in that war had prompted him to stress the importance of science and technology.[65]

ENTRY OF ZHU RONGJI INTO THE LEADERSHIP

One major success for Deng in the spring of 1991 was the elevation of Zhu Rongji to the position of vice-premier during the annual session of the NPC – though his promotion was balanced by the simultaneous selection of the conservative Zou Jiahua as a vice-premier.[66] Zhu has elicited intense interest from domestic and foreign observers alike because he is unique in Chinese politics. Named a rightist in 1957, Zhu has nevertheless risen to the inner circles of power; moreover, he has firm ideas on economic reform and the personality to push them against strong opposition. That Deng would reach out to such a person suggests his need and determination to counterbalance the conservative bureaucrats who had come to dominate the top of the system in the wake of Tiananmen.

Like Li Ruihuan in Tianjin, Zhu seems to have drawn Deng's interest by his skillful handling of the 1989 demonstrations in Shanghai. Despite pressure, Zhu rejected calls to declare martial law in the city, opting instead for organizing worker pickets to restore order. After the violent suppression of protesters in Beijing, Zhu became famous for his remark that "the facts will eventually be made clear."[67] But Zhu was no liberal. When a train accident led an inflamed crowd to beat the driver and set fire to the train, Zhu oversaw the arrest, conviction, and execution of three people within eight days.[68]

When Zhu first came to Beijing as vice-premier, Li Peng apparently declined to assign him a portfolio. Three months later, under pressure from Deng, Li finally allowed Zhu to take over the State Council Production Commission, the name of which was changed to State Council Production Office (*guowuyuan shengchan bangongshi*), which had failed in its initial task to oversee the double-guarantee system and had instead contributed to a ballooning of triangular debts among enterprises.[69] Zhu was also assigned the task of clearing up triangular debts, a job that had clearly not been completed by Zou Jiahua, Li Peng's old protégé, who had been given the

65 This acknowledgment, however, did not stop Jiang from saying in his Party Day speech that men, not weapons, were the most important thing in war.

66 After the NPC meeting, there were five vice-premiers: Yao Yilin, Tian Jiyun, Wu Xueqian, Zou Jiahua, and Zhu Rongji. Yao was a member of PSC, and Tian and Wu were members of the Politburo. Zou was a full member of the Central Committee, but Zhu was only an alternate member. It was highly unusual for an alternate member of the Central Committee to be promoted to vice-premier.

67 Ibid., 170. 68 Ibid., 173–8.

69 Triangular debts were debts that accrued between suppliers, producers, and buyers as enterprises, subject to mandatory plans, sent materials or finished products to others, but received little or no payment in return.

task in 1990.[70] Putting Zhu in charge of the State Council Production Office and clearing up triangular debts marked an obvious policy failure for Li Peng, Zou Jiahua, and Ye Qing, and it gave Zhu a chance to develop a bureaucratic apparatus.

Zhu quickly recruited his former associates from the old SEC, including former vice-chairmen Zhang Yanning and Zhao Weichen, who were made deputy directors of the new Production Office. The roles of Zhu and the Production Office were further enhanced in May 1993 when the office was expanded and reorganized as the State Economic and Trade Commission. The new office had a bureaucratic standing equivalent to that of the SPC, and effectively hollowed out the latter organization by taking over day-to-day management of the economy, leaving the SPC to deal with the macroeconomy.[71] Moreover, Zhu was successful, at least temporarily, in reducing the problem of triangular debts. In June 1991, such inter-enterprise debts had amounted to some 300 billion yuan; about two-thirds of that was cleared by the end of 1992.[72] Zhu's successes would eventually enable him to enter the PSC at the Fourteenth Party Congress in late 1992.

CONSERVATIVE RESPONSE

Deng's offensive from the fall of 1990 through the spring of 1991 would prove to be a trial run for his efforts of the following year, but in 1991 he came up short. He had indeed used provincial officials to undermine the draft of the Eighth Five-Year Plan and then to publicize and promote his own thought, and he had laid the basis for a later breakthrough by promoting Zhu Rongji and giving him an institutional base from which to rival Li Peng. But conservative opposition remained fierce. Despite Li Ruihuan's formal position as head of the Ideological Leading Small Group, conservatives had since 1989 dominated the top reaches of the Propaganda and Organization Departments as well as economic policy making.[73] They would not give up without a fight.

70 The Leading Group for the Resolution of Triangular Debt was established in March 1990 with Zou Jiahua in charge. At that time, triangular debt amounted to more than 100 billion yuan (up from 32 billion yuan in 1988). Despite a State Council circular setting a four-month deadline for the clearing of such debt and despite state expenditures of about 160 billion yuan to clear such debt, by the end of 1990 enterprise indebtedness was nearing 150 billion yuan. *CD*, 6 July 1991.

71 Gao and He, *Zhu rongji zhuan*, 242–56.

72 *XH*, 25 December 1992, trans. in *FBIS-Chi*, 28 December 1992, 36–9.

73 Defiance of Li Ruihuan's leadership of ideological work was evident not only from the speeches of such leaders as Wang Renzhi and Song Ping and from Gao Di's management of the *People's Daily* but also from such specific statements as Wang Renzhi's December 1989 comment that the campaign against pornography, championed by Li, "certainly cannot replace opposing bourgeois liberalization." See *RMRB*, 23 December 1989.

This opposition was led by the father–son combination of Chen Yun and Chen Yuan, the deputy governor of the People's Bank of China. Even as Deng carried his message to Shanghai, Chen Yun was quoted in the *People's Daily* as saying, "As leading cadres, we must pay attention to exchanging views with others, especially those who hold views opposite from our own" – a remark that implicitly criticized Deng for his failure to consult his colleagues.[74] At almost the same time, in December 1990, Chen Yuan presented a paper excoriating the decline in central authority that had resulted from a decade and more of devolving economic power. Chen called for a "new centralization" to deal with the emergence of "feudal lords" and the "disintegration of macrocontrol."[75] Then, in May 1991, Chen Yun presented Shanghai leaders with a rhymed couplet that enjoined them to "not simply follow what superiors or books say" but to "act only according to reality."[76]

If Chen in his reminders to Deng was gentle, almost obscure, others were willing to be much more direct. A sharp attack on the Huangfu Ping commentaries, and hence on Deng, came in the form of a Commentator article in the conservative journal *Dangdai sichao* (*Contemporary Trends*), which was excerpted shortly thereafter in the *People's Daily.* Reviving themes raised by Song Ping and Wang Renzhi the previous year, the commentary warned that those in favor of "bourgeois liberalization" remained "resolute" and that "we must be soberly aware that the liberalized trend of thought and political influence, which was once a major trend, will not disappear because we have won a victory in quelling the rebellion, but will again stubbornly manifest itself in a new form, spar with us, and attack us."[77]

A TROUGH IN THE ROAD TO REFORM

With the publication of the *People's Daily*'s excerpt of the article from *Dangdai sichao* and other attacks on the themes raised by the Huangfu Ping commentaries, reformers fell quiet. Four explanations for this sudden setback seem possible.

The first is that in the spring of 1991 Deng simply lacked the political strength to reinstate his vision of reform. Such an explanation assumes not only that Deng failed to win over (or intimidate) his opponents, but also that

74 *RMRB,* 18 January 1991.

75 Chen Yuan, "Wo guo jingji de shenceng wenti he xuanze (gangyao)" (China's deep-seated economic problems and choices [outline]), *JJYJ,* 4 (April 1991), 18–9. Joseph Fewsmith, "Neoconservatism and the end of the Dengist era," *AS,* 35.7 (July 1995), 635–51. On Chen Yuan, see He Pin and Gao Xin, *Zhonggong "taizi dang"* ("Princelings" of the CCP), 97–124.

76 *XH,* 15 May 1991, trans. in *FBIS-Chi,* 17 May 1991, 22.

77 "Why must we unremittingly oppose bourgeois liberalization?" *RMRB,* 24 April 1991, 5, trans. in *FBIS-Chi,* 26 April 1991, 18–21.

he failed to win the support of the "silent majority" of Party elders who seem to move to one side or the other in periods of political conflict, thereby shifting the political center of gravity. Second, and more plausibly, one can assume that Deng, faced with opposition and uncertainty, yielded once again, as he had apparently done several times over the preceding two years, biding his time until a more opportune moment arose to renew his assault. This explanation assumes that Deng possessed the power necessary to prevail (which he would demonstrate a year later), but that he believed the cost in terms of Party unity outweighed the importance of prevailing at that time. Third, the situation in the Soviet Union, namely Gorbachev's turn to the right, which culminated in cracking down on the Baltic republics in January 1991, may have bolstered conservatives in Beijing, who were likely to have seen such a shift as a sign that the Soviet Union, too, was finally backing away from radical reform.[78] Fourth, the swift U.S. victory in the Gulf War, which apparently caught China off guard, may very well have renewed fears in Beijing that the world was becoming unipolar and that the United States would apply new pressures on China. Such a concern would most likely have reinforced the tendency among Party leaders to hunker down, assess the situation, and avoid divisive conflicts.

In the event, with the publication of Jiang Zemin's speech on the seventieth anniversary of the CCP on 1 July 1991, it became clear that reform was, once again, on hold. Jiang's speech linked domestic class struggle to international class struggle, emphasizing that "the ideological area is an important arena for the struggle between peaceful evolution and anti-peaceful evolution."[79] Despite bows in a reformist direction, Jiang's speech clearly reflected conservative control over the overall ideological and policy agenda. More important, any reformist sentiments conveyed by Jiang's speech were soon played down as the Party responded to renewed liberalization in the Soviet Union by circling the wagons even more tightly.

In late July 1991, the Soviet Communist Party (CPSU) surrendered its monopoly on political power and moved its ideological stance toward democratic socialism. This shift caused obvious anxieties in China and prompted conservatives to take an even harder line. In particular, a 16 August Commen-

78 It should be noted that by mid-April to late April, just as the *People's Daily* was reprinting the *Dangdai sichao* article, Gorbachev was once again turning toward radical reform – which also scared conservatives into taking a harder line. Though it seems inconsistent, it can be argued that Chinese conservatives reacted to both a tightening up and a political relaxation in the Soviet Union by calling for heightening ideological orthodoxy in China. They would see in the former confirmation of the need to prevent reform from getting out of control and in the latter a hostile foreign environment that would necessitate a reassertion of socialist values at home.

79 Jiang Zemin, "Zai qingzhu Zhongguo gongchandang chengli qishi zhounian dahuishang de jianghua" (Talk celebrating the seventieth anniversary of the founding of the CCP), in *Shisanda yila,* 3.1627–60. The quotes are from 1647, 1640, 1646, 1639, and 1638, respectively.

tator article in the *People's Daily* put an even more conservative spin on Jiang's CCP anniversary speech, calling for building a "great wall of steel against peaceful evolution" in order to protect the country from "hostile forces" at home and abroad. If such hostile forces won, the Commentator article warned, it would be a "retrogression of history and a catastrophe for the people."[80]

THE SOVIET COUP

Given the reaction of Chinese hard liners to what they regarded as the downward spiral of events in the Soviet Union, it is no wonder that they could barely contain their glee when they heard the news of the conservative coup d'état launched on 19 August. China's ambassador congratulated the perpetrators of the coup, and conservative elder Wang Zhen, then in Xinjiang, called on China's party leaders "never to deviate" from Marxism–Leninism–Mao Zedong Thought and to "fight to the death" for communism. Jiang Zemin reportedly hailed the coup in a speech to a Politburo meeting, and the gist of his remarks were disseminated in a secret document entitled "The victory of the Soviet people is a victory for the Chinese people."[81] Apparently a variety of meetings of leftists were called to consider their response.

The ebullient mood did not last long. When the coup collapsed after only three days, Chinese leaders were despondent. Even Deng worried that if Yeltsin banished the CPSU, China would be the only major state practicing socialism. "Then what shall we do?" he reportedly asked.[82]

What the abortive coup in the Soviet Union did was to pose in the starkest possible terms the fundamental question of the period: Should the CCP try to preserve its own rule by emphasizing ideology and socialist values, or should it try to win popular support and strengthen the nation through continued economic reform? Leftists in the Party clearly wanted to take the former route. Chen Yun, in a scarcely veiled attack on newly promoted Vice-Premier Zhu Rongji, reputedly warned against allowing a "Yeltsin-like figure" to emerge in China.[83]

80 "Build up a great wall of steel against peaceful evolution," *RMRB* Commentator, 16 August 1991, trans. in *FBIS-Chi,* 19 August 1991, 27–8.

81 Xinjiang television, 24 August 1991, trans. in *FBIS-Chi,* 27 August 1991, 28–9; *RMRB,* 29 August 1991. While in Xinjiang, Wang gave a number of fiery speeches. See, for instance, Xinjiang television, 21 August 1991, trans. in *FBIS-Chi,* 22 August 1991, 20. The *People's Daily* account of Wang's trip deleted most of Wang's harshest language, including his vow to "fight to the death." On Jiang Zemin's reaction, see James Miles, *The legacy of Tiananmen: China in disarray,* 71.

82 *South China Morning Post,* 26 August 1991.

83 Ibid., 4 September 1991; Baum, *Burying Mao,* 333. Note *WHB*'s reference to Yeltsin as a "dangerous" person in its examination of the abortive coup. See *WHB* (Hong Kong), 23 August 1991, trans. in *FBIS-Chi,* 27 August 1991, 8–9.

If Deng was initially despondent over events in the Soviet Union, he did not stay that way for long. Reacting quickly to conservatives' efforts to assert themselves following the Soviet coup, Deng intervened to insist on speeding up reform and opening up. As a PRC-affiliated Hong Kong magazine later put it, "Deng played a crucial role in preventing China from incorrectly summing up the experiences of the Soviet coup and in rendering the 'leftist' forces in the party unable to use the opportunity to expand their influence."[84]

Internationally, Deng reiterated his call for caution, saying that China should "tackle calmly, observe coolly, and pay good attention to our own national affairs."[85] Domestically, he inaugurated a determined campaign to reassert his own leadership and to put his understanding of reform back in the center. That campaign would last from the time of the abortive Soviet coup until the convening of the Fourteenth Party Congress in October 1992.

The first public sign that political winds were shifting came on 1 September when the Xinhua News Service transmitted the text of an editorial to be run the following day by the *People's Daily.* The editorial contained some of the most reformist language to be used since the previous spring, and did so in a more authoritative context. However, the first sentence contradicted and effectively negated the rest of the editorial. It read, "While carrying out reform and opening up to the outside world, we must ask ourselves whether we are practicing socialism or capitalism, and we must uphold the socialist orientation." Seven hours after this editorial was transmitted, Xinhua released a new version in which the first sentence was changed dramatically to read, "While carrying out reform and opening up to the outside world, we must firmly adhere to the socialist course and uphold the dominant role of public ownership."[86] The critical question of whether a reform was "socialist" or "capitalist" had been cut.

It turned out that the second version was actually the editorial as originally approved, but before transmission Gao Di, director of the *People's Daily,*[87]

84 Sun Hong, "Anecdotes about Deng Xiaoping's political career and family life," *JB,* 11 (5 November 1993), 26–31, trans. in *FBIS-Chi,* 18 November 1993, 34–9.

85 [He Yuan] Ho Yuen, "CCP's 'five adherences' and 'five oppositions' to prevent peaceful evolution," *MB,* 29 August 1991, trans. in *FBIS-Chi,* 29 August 1991, 23–5.

86 Both statements were released by Xinhua on 1 September 1991, the first at 0723 GMT and the second at 1456 GMT. See *FBIS-Chi,* 2 September 1991.

87 In the early 1980s, the editor in chief was the highest-ranking official of the *People's Daily.* In the wake of the 1983 campaign against spiritual pollution, a separate post of director was created to allow Hu Jiwei, criticized during that campaign, to take up a "second line" position. Nevertheless, as director, Hu was able to exercise considerable influence over the paper, as evidenced by the replacement of Hu by the open-minded Qin Chuan as editor in chief. Thus, well before Tiananmen the director had become the effective head of the *People's Daily,* although the distinction between director and editor in chief continued. After the Tiananmen crackdown, Gao Di was named director (replacing Qian Liren), and Shao Huazi became editor in chief (replacing Tan Wenrui). In December 1992, Shao replaced Gao as director, and Fan Jingyi became editor in chief.

rewrote the first sentence to insert the conservative's pet thesis. This change was spotted, and at Deng's behest Li Ruihuan ordered that the offending sentence be removed. Thus, the editorial that appeared in the *People's Daily* on 2 September differed from what listeners had heard on the radio the evening before. Deng angrily declared that the "*People's Daily* wants to comprehensively criticize Deng Xiaoping."[88]

This incident not only underscores the deadly serious nature of "documentary politics" in the PRC, it also makes clear that reformers were responding quickly to evolving events in the Soviet Union by restoring the push that had stalled the previous spring.[89] Just how difficult that task would be was indicated by an article by former Organization Department head Chen Yeping that appeared in the *People's Daily* on 1 September. Taking the unusual step of criticizing former general secretary Zhao Ziyang by name (attacks by name having generally died out more than a year earlier), Chen accused him of advocating "productivity as the criterion for selecting cadres" – essentially what the Huangfu Ping commentaries had called for the previous spring – and claimed that his "erroneous viewpoint still has some effect in the cadre work of some regions and departments."[90]

Reformers responded almost immediately. In late September, Deng instructed Jiang Zemin and Yang Shangkun to persevere in reform and opening up,[91] and Yang subsequently gave a ringing endorsement of reform on the eightieth anniversary of the 1911 Revolution. Reform was, he said, a part of the historical effort to revive and develop China that had begun with Sun Yat-sen.[92] More important in terms of the immediate political debate, Yang declared unequivocally that "*all* other work must be subordinate to and serve" economic construction and that the party must not allow its "attention to be diverted or turned away" from economic construction.[93]

Despite such clear signals from Deng and his supporters, conservatives

88 Gao and He, *Zhu Rongji zhuan,* 231–2.

89 Guoguang Wu, "Documentary politics: Hypotheses, process, and case studies," in Carol Lee Hamrin and Suisheng Zhao, eds., *Decision-making in Deng's China: Perspectives from insiders,* 24–38.

90 Chen Yeping, "Have both political integrity, ability, stress political ability: On criteria for selecting cadres," *RMRB,* 1 September 1991, trans. in *FBIS-Chi,* 6 September 1991, 26–31.

91 Cited in Baum, *Burying Mao,* 334.

92 In its stress on patriotism and the assessment that economic development was the common goal of all Chinese, communist or not, Yang's speech echoed the 1986 Third Plenum resolution on building socialist civilization. That resolution played down the importance of communist ideology in favor of a "common ideal" to which all patriotic Chinese could subscribe. See "Resolution of the Central Committee of the Communist Party of China on the guiding principles for building a socialist society with advanced culture and ideology," *XH,* 28 September 1986, trans. in *FBIS-Chi,* 29 September 1986, K2–13.

93 Yang Shangkun, "Zai Xinghai geming bashi zhounian dahui shang de jianghua" (Speech at the meeting to commemorate the eightieth anniversary of the Xinghai Revolution), in *Shisanda yilai,* 3.1713–19. Emphasis added.

continued to resist. During his November visit to Shanghai, Li Peng could not resist telling Zhu Rongji, who had overseen the compilation of the Huangfu Ping articles, that "[t]he influence of the 'Huangfu Ping' articles was terrible. It caused the unified thinking that the center had expended a great deal of effort to bring about to become chaotic again."[94]

On 23 October, the *People's Daily* published a hard-hitting article by the leftist ideologue Deng Liqun, which declared that class struggle was more acute than at any time since the founding of the PRC. An editor's note said that "the harsh reality of struggle has made clear to us that pragmatism can make a breach for peaceful evolution."[95] The term "pragmatism" seemed a clear allusion to the policies of Deng Xiaoping.

At the meeting of the Central Advisory Commission (CAC) convened on 29 November, party elder Bo Yibo conveyed six points raised by Chen Yun that stressed strengthening party organization, the threat of peaceful evolution posed by the United States, and the danger posed by overzealous efforts to speed up economic development.[96]

In late November, Deng Xiaoping urged the leadership to improve relations with the United States by not raising the issue of peaceful evolution so frequently and by compromising with the United States on human rights issues. On hearing Deng's suggestion, Party elder Wang Zhen apparently flew into a rage, declaring that Deng's policies were leading the country down the road to capitalism.[97] At the time, as Wang Zhen's outburst showed, the Party remained deeply divided over the danger posed by "peaceful evolution." In September, Propaganda Department head Wang Renzhi and others had organized an "anti-peaceful evolution" study group at the Central Party School which warned that peaceful evolution could be boosted by "pragmatists" in the leadership. Conservatives participating in the group denounced Li Ruihuan as "a person who wants to be Gorbachev" and called Qiao Shi a "fence sitter."[98]

DENG'S "SOUTHERN TOUR"

On 19 January, almost eight years to the day since Deng's first visit to Shenzhen inaugurated a new push in opening China to the outside world, Deng once again set foot in the Special Economic Zone (SEZ). Accompanied by Yang Shangkun and other officials, Deng spent the next several days

94 Quoted in Gao and He, *Zhu Rongji zhuan*, 232.

95 [Jing Wen] Ching Wen, "Abnormal atmosphere in *Renmin ribao*," *JB*, 178 (5 May 1992), 46–7, trans. in *FBIS-Chi*, 18 May 1992, 22.

96 [Luo] and Li, "Chen Yun raises six points of view to criticize Deng Xiaoping."

97 *South China Morning Post*, 1 January 1992, 2 January 1992; Baum, *Burying Mao*, 336.

98 *Dangdai* 14 (15 May 1992), 21–2, trans. in *FBIS-Chi*, 21 May 1992, 18–20.

touring Shenzhen and then the Zhuhai SEZ, talking about the importance of reform and blasting his opponents as he went.

Perhaps the most critical point in his talks was his contention that without the ten years of reform and opening up, the CCP would not have survived an upheaval such as the Party had faced in the spring of 1989. This judgment was Deng's response to his opponents' contention that reform had led to the Tiananmen incident and would lead to the downfall of the CCP, just as it had to that of the CPSU and the various Communist parties of East Europe.

In order to defend his vision of reform against his critics' arguments, Deng reiterated the theoretically unsophisticated but ultimately effective argument that he had put forth in Shanghai the previous year, namely that planning and markets, far from being distinguishing characteristics of socialism and capitalism, were simply economic "methods" possessed by both types of systems. Moreover, Deng hit back directly at the numerous derogatory criticisms of the so-called criterion of productive forces made over the previous two years. In the baldest statement of that thesis since Zhao Ziyang had championed it on the front page of the *People's Daily* four years before, Deng declared that socialism could be defined in terms of the three "advantages": whether or not something was advantageous to the development of socialist productive forces, advantageous to increasing the comprehensive strength of a socialist nation, and advantageous to raising the people's standard of living.[99]

Deng blasted his cautious colleagues with one of Mao's most famous metaphors. He urged them not to act like "women with bound feet"; reform had to be bolder and the pace of development faster. "For a large, developing country like ours," Deng said, "the economic growth rate must be a bit faster; it cannot always be calm and steady." Underscoring his implicit but pointed criticism of Chen Yun's thought, Deng declared, "We must pay attention to the steady and coordinated development of the economy, but being steady and coordinated is relative, not absolute." He then called on Guangdong to catch up to the "four small dragons" (South Korea, Taiwan, Singapore, and Hong Kong) in twenty years.[100]

The most eye-catching passages in Deng's talks, however, were his blunt criticisms of the "Left." In sharp contrast to the constant criticism of bourgeois liberalization and peaceful evolution over the preceding two years, Deng pointed out that the main danger to the Party lay on the "Left." "The Right can bury socialism, the 'Left' can also bury socialism," declared the patriarch.[101] Not mincing words, Deng directly criticized a number of conser-

99 Deng Xiaoping, "Zai Wuchang, Shenzhen, Zhuhai dengdi de tanhua yaodian" (Essential points from talks in Wuchang, Shenzhen, Zhuhai, and Shanghai), in *Deng Xiaoping wenxuan,* 3.372.

100 Ibid., 3.377. 101 Ibid., 3.370–83.

vative leaders, though in the version later circulated in the Party and included in Deng's *Selected Works* these remarks were deleted.

THE STRUGGLE FOR DOMINANCE

Initially, the PRC media did not report Deng's trip and the CCP did not relay his comments internally. The obvious resistance to publicizing the trip and the subsequent process of yielding partially while continuing to resist reflect the ambiguity of authority relations at the highest level of the CCP in the early 1990s. To use Deng's evocative terminology, Deng, like Mao before him, had been the "core" of the Party since the Third Plenary Session of the Eleventh Central Committee in December 1978. The term "core" reflects a series of formal and informal power arrangements through which the supreme leader maintains and wields power; it evokes the image of a spider at the center of a web.[102]

Deng began to shed his formal authority by stepping down from the PSC at the Thirteenth Party Congress in September 1987 and then yielding leadership over the party's Central Military Commission (CMC) to Jiang Zemin in September 1989. Deng, however, seems to have been unwilling to shed all vestiges of formal authority and rule solely through informal politics. Thus, the Thirteenth Party Congress passed a secret resolution to refer all major decisions to Deng Xiaoping as the "helmsman" of the Party.[103] The authority conferred by this resolution, however, appears to have been ambiguous; "helmsman" was not a formal position and it was not clear whether Deng's wishes still had to be obeyed in the same way as before his retirement. With the Tiananmen incident, Deng's prestige within the Party plummeted, weakening his ability to exercise informal authority. The conservatives' strategy in the three years following that incident appears to have been one of hamstringing Deng's capacity to exercise authority but not to challenge directly his "core" position. The intention was to turn Deng into the titular leader of the Party, much as Liu Shaoqi and Deng himself might have hoped to do to Mao in the early 1960s.

As the struggle for dominance in the spring of 1992 would show, Deng had (or had regained) enough authority to force nominal compliance with his wishes but not enough to subdue opposition immediately. Unlike in the spring of 1991, when Deng had backed off a decisive confrontation with his

102 Tang Tsou, "Chinese politics at the top: Factionalism or informal politics? Balance-of-power politics or a game to win all?" *China Journal*, 34 (July 1995), 95–156.

103 Beijing television, 16 May 1989, trans. in *FBIS-Chi*, 16 May 1989, 28; *RMRB*, 17 May 1989, trans. in *FBIS-Chi*, 17 May 1989, 16.

opponents, in 1992, with the Fourteenth Party Congress looming on the horizon, Deng was determined to raise the stakes to the level of a contest for party leadership. In such a contest, the advantages of being "core," ambiguous as they were, would eventually secure victory for Deng – but his opponents would not yield without staunch resistance.

A turning point in this struggle for dominance – the first of several – came when a Politburo meeting on 12 February 1992, under obvious pressure from Deng, decided to relay the content of Deng's talks orally to cadres at and above the ministerial, provincial, and army ranks.[104] This limited dissemination of Deng's views reflected a pattern that would hold throughout most of the spring, namely yielding to direct pressure from Deng (thereby sidestepping direct confrontation) but doing so only as little as possible (in the hope that Deng would yield to resistance).

In the face of this passive resistance, Dengist forces used local media to step up the pressure on Beijing's still silent official media. Finally, the *People's Daily* began to yield to the pressure. On 22 February, it published an authoritative editorial, presumably reflecting the Politburo meeting ten days earlier, that called for strengthening reform. In contrast to the emphasis on slow and steady economic growth that had dominated press coverage in recent months, the *People's Daily* now declared that "the fundamental point for upholding socialism is developing the economy as fast as possible."[105] Two days later, a second editorial urged people to "be more daring in carrying out reform" and cited Deng's dictum "Practice is the sole criterion of truth."[106]

Despite the publication of the two editorials, Beijing's media remained silent about Deng's trip to the South, an indication of the deep opposition within the Party to Deng and his views. Indeed, Deng's opponents took active measures to resist his new offensive. Deng Liqun made his own trip to the South, visiting the cities of Wuhan and Xining, where he declared, "There is the core of economic work but also another core of fighting peaceful evolution and waging class struggle. And sometimes, the campaign against peaceful evolution is more important."[107] Chen Yun himself presided over a meeting of the CAC held in Beijing on 17 February at which he declared that

104 Suisheng Zhao, "Deng Xiaoping's southern tour: Elite politics in post-Tiananmen China," *AS* 33.8 (August 1993), 751.

105 "Adhere better to taking economic construction as the center," *RMRB* editorial, 22 February 1992, trans. in *FBIS-Chi,* 24 February 1992, 40–1. The editorial made clear its criticism of "leftists" within the Party by pointing out the "catastrophes" caused in the past by "taking class struggle as the key link."

106 "Be more daring in carrying out reform," *RMRB* editorial, 24 February 1992, trans. in *FBIS-Chi,* 24 February 1992, 41–2.

107 *South China Morning Post,* 11 May 1992.

the only way for the CCP to avoid a CPSU-style collapse was to emphasize communist ideology and strengthen Party building. Thirty-five senior leaders at the meeting drafted a strong letter to Deng demanding that communist ideology continue to be propagated and that the Party strongly maintain its opposition to peaceful evolution.[108]

It was not until 1 March that Deng's remarks were officially disseminated within the Party in the form of Central Document No. 2, but even this action did not squelch opposition. Not only did the propaganda system limit circulation of the document,[109] Party elder Song Renqiong declared that he could not detect any leftist tendencies, while Gao Di, the director of the *People's Daily,* declared defiantly, "We have already published two or three comments, and that is enough for the moment. No more articles will be published."[110]

In the midst of this acrimonious dispute, an enlarged meeting of the Politburo was convened on 10–12 March. Yang Shangkun, Deng's close associate and permanent vice-chairman of the CMC, led the charge by demanding that the body endorse Deng's view of economic work at the center. Jiang Zemin offered a self-criticism for his laxity in promoting reform and opening up and echoed Yang's views.[111] Politburo member and NPC chairman Wan Li also strongly endorsed Deng's views, and PSC member Qiao Shi argued pointedly that the leadership of the Party remained hindered by leftist ideology, which interfered with the effective implementation of the Party's principles and policies. In opposition, PSC member Yao Yilin argued that Deng's comments on guarding against leftism referred to the economic field; there were no indications of leftism in other fields. Yao's comments were echoed by Song Ping, also a member of the PSC.[112]

The outcome favored Deng. The communiqué issued by the Politburo meeting endorsed the "necessity" of upholding the "one center" of economic development and called on the Party to "accelerate the pace of reform and opening to the outside world." Moreover, it affirmed Deng's thesis that the main danger the Party faced was leftism.[113] Accordingly, China's central media finally publicized Deng's trip. On 31 March, the *People's Daily* reprinted a long, detailed account of Deng's activities in Shenzhen entitled,

108 Zhao, "Deng Xiaoping's southern tour," 754.

109 *MB,* 7 March 1992, trans. in *FBIS-Chi,* 9 March 1992, 26–7.

110 [Ling Xuejun] Ling Hsueh-chun, "Wang Zhen and Li Xiannian set themselves up against Deng," *ZM,* 175 (1 May 1992), 14–15, trans. in *FBIS-Chi,* 12 May 1992, 26; and [Jing] Ching, "Abnormal atmosphere in *Renmin ribao,*" 21.

111 *XH,* 11 March 1992; Baum, *Burying Mao,* 347.

112 [Ren Huiwen] Jen Hui-wen, "Political bureau argues over 'preventing leftism,' " *Xinbao,* 14 April 1992, 6, trans. in *FBIS-Chi,* 17 April 1992, 28–9.

113 Zhao, "Deng Xiaoping's southern tour," 752.

"East wind brings spring all around: On-the-spot report on Comrade Deng Xiaoping in Shenzhen."[114]

Despite this important endorsement, the meeting nevertheless decided to delete a reference to guarding against leftism from the draft of Li Peng's Government Work Report to the upcoming session of the NPC on the grounds that it would be inappropriate to include any reference to differences of opinion in a government (as opposed to party) work report.[115] A fusillade of criticism from the floor, clearly abetted by NPC chairman Wan Li, forced the premier to add a warning to his report that the main danger lay on the left – as well as to make 149 other major and minor changes.

The enormous stakes involved and Deng's willingness to use any and all methods to carry the day were clearly revealed at the NPC meeting when Yang Baibing, vice-chairman of the CMC, declared that the People's Liberation Army (PLA) would "escort and protect" (*baojia huhang*) reform.[116] Over the ensuing months, four delegations of senior PLA officers visited the Shenzhen SEZ to demonstrate their support for reform and opening up, and the army newspaper, the *Liberation Army Daily,* repeatedly ran articles in support of reform.[117] The effort to professionalize and depoliticize the military, which had suffered badly from the use of the military to crush the 1989 movement, was again thwarted. It became clear that military backing was the ultimate support for Deng's rule, and trying to secure that support would soon become central to Jiang Zemin in his quest to become "core" of the Party in reality as well as in name.

THE CONTINUING DEBATE

The March 1992 Politburo meeting and the subsequent NPC session marked important, if not unambiguous, victories for Deng. The battle over

114 *RMRB,* 31 March 1992, trans. in *FBIS-Chi,* 1 April 1992 (supplement), 7–15. The article had originally appeared in the *Shenzhen tequ bao* (Shenzhen special economic zone daily) on 26 March. By reprinting the article, the *People's Daily* demonstrated its desire to stay at arm's length from the content.

115 [Ren] Jen, "Political bureau argues over 'preventing leftism.'"

116 *XH,* 23 March 1992. Note that the *JFJB* editorial hailing the close of the NPC prominently played the theme of "protecting and escorting" reform. See "Make fresh contributions on 'protecting and escorting' reform, opening up, and economic development: Warmly congratulating conclusion of the Fifth Sessions of the Seventh National People's Congress and Seventh Chinese People's Political Consultative Conference," *JFJB,* 4 April 1992, trans. in *FBIS-Chi,* 21 April 1992, 36–7.

117 The first group of PLA leaders visited Shenzhen in late February, the fourth group in early June. See *WHB* (Hong Kong), 16 April 1992, 2, trans. in *FBIS-Chi,* 16 April 1992, 38; *XH,* 19 May 1992, trans. in *FBIS-Chi,* 21 May 1992, 31–2; *Xinwanbao,* 11 June 1992, 2, trans. in *FBIS-Chi,* 16 June 1992, 32–3. On *JFJB*'s support for reform, see, for instance, Shi Bonian and Liu Fang, "Unswervingly implement the party's basic line," *JFJB,* 18 March 1992, trans. in *FBIS-Chi,* 15 April 1992, 44–7; He Yijun, Jiang Bin, and Wang Jianwei, "Speed up pace of reform, opening up," *JFJB,* 25 March 1992, trans. in *FBIS-Chi,* 22 April 1992, 30–3; and Lan Zhongping, "Why do we say that special economic zones are socialist rather than capitalist in nature?" *JFJB,* trans. in *FBIS-Chi,* 11 June 1992, 25–6.

reform continued. On 8 April members of the CAC held a meeting to draft a letter to the Central Committee, which was subsequently forwarded on the 14th. The letter warned against the tendency to "completely negate" the theories of Marxism–Leninism–Mao Zedong Thought and declared, in direct opposition to Deng's comments in Shenzhen, that "the biggest danger is the 'rightist' tendency and bourgeois liberalization in the last 10 years."[118]

Shortly thereafter, on 14 April, the *People's Daily* ran a long article by Li Peng confidant Yuan Mu, head of the State Council Research Office, which did to Deng what Deng had previously done to Mao, namely reinterpret the leader's thought by insisting that it be viewed "comprehensively." For instance, while endorsing Deng's view about the importance of guarding against the Left, Yuan went on to stress the need to maintain "vigilance against bourgeois liberalization" in order to prevent the sort of "evolution" experienced by East Europe and the Soviet Union.[119]

In response, Deng's supporters rallied. On 6 April, Qiao Shi derided "some leading comrades" who only feigned compliance with the line of reform and opening up. Such people, Qiao urged, should step down from power.[120] Similarly, during his 16–22 April tour of Shanxi Province, Qiao touted Dengist themes, calling for an "ideological leap" in people's awareness of the need for reform.[121] On 13 April, Gong Yuzhi, former deputy head of the Propaganda Department and a longtime supporter of Deng, gave a talk called "Emancipating thought, emancipating productive forces" at the Central Party School. This talk marked an important signal to intellectuals and opened the way to harsher attacks on leftism.[122]

In late April, Vice-Premier Tian Jiyun went to the Central Party School, where he lambasted leftists for having "basically repudiated all the most fundamental and substantial elements that we have upheld since reform and opening up." In a barb apparently directed at General Secretary Jiang Zemin, Tian declared, "To do away with 'leftist' influence, one must particularly guard against those who bend with the wind, the political acrobats who

118 [Yue Shan] Yueh Shan, "Central Advisory Commission submits letter to CCP Central Committee opposing 'rightist' tendency," *ZM*, 175 (1 May 1992), 13–14, trans. in *FBIS-Chi*, 30 April 1992, 15–16.

119 Yuan Mu, "Firmly, accurately, and comprehensively implement the party's basic line: Preface to 'Guidance for studying the government work report to the fifth session of the Seventh NPC,' " *RMRB*, 14 April 1992, trans. in *FBIS-Chi*, 16 April 1992, 20–3.

120 Lin Wu, "Deng's faction unmasks face of 'ultraleftists,' " *ZM*, 175 (1 May 1992), 17–18, trans. in *FBIS-Chi*, 12 May 1992, 27–8.

121 *XH*, 22 April 1992, trans. in *FBIS-Chi*, 23 April 1992, 11–12.

122 Gong Yuzhi, "Emancipate our minds, liberate productive forces: Studying Comrade Deng Xiaoping's important talks," *WHB* (Shanghai), 15 April 1992, trans. in *FBIS-Chi*, 20 April 1992, 25–8. See also *Dangdai*, 14 (15 May 1992), 21–2, trans. in *FBIS-Chi*, 21 May 1992, 18–20.

readily vacillate in attitude." Using a parody rare in Chinese politics, Tian told his listeners that leftists should go to a "special leftist zone" in which there would be total state planning, supplies would be rationed, and people could line up for food and other consumer items.[123] Soon pirated copies of Tian's talk were being sold on the streets of Beijing.

Deng's demonstration that he would not back off this time, underscored by the mobilization of the army on his behalf, stirred Chen Yun to make some concessions. Appearing in Shanghai on the eve of Labor Day, the Party elder encouraged leaders there to "emancipate their minds" and "take bold steps." Chen, who had opposed the establishment of SEZs in 1978–9 and especially opposed the establishment of one in Shanghai, was now quoted as saying, "I very much favor the development and opening of Pudong!"[124] Apparently Chen also said, "Shanghai should sum up experiences of its own and should not mechanically follow the example of Shenzhen," but this was not reported by the media.[125]

Despite Chen's partial concession in Shanghai, Deng Xiaoping obviously remained frustrated by the lack of meaningful response from the leadership. On 22 May, Deng showed up at Capital Iron and Steel (usually referred to as Shougang) and listened to Zhou Guanwu, the longtime leader of the model enterprise and allegedly Deng's personal friend, report on the enterprise's reform experience. Deng complained that many leaders were "merely going through the motions" of supporting reform and that they were in danger of losing their jobs.[126] Just as important, Deng signaled his strong support for Zhu Rongji, whom he had sponsored to become vice-premier in March 1991. Zhu, Deng said, is "quite capable" in economics.[127]

Deng's criticism of China's leadership finally stirred Jiang Zemin to action. On 9 June, the general secretary followed in the wake of Qiao Shi and Tian Jiyun and gave a major speech at the Central Party School. Jiang finally openly endorsed the view that the "primary focus must be guarding against the 'Left.' " Quoting liberally from Deng's talks in Shenzhen, Jiang now

123 *South China Morning Post,* 7 May 1992; "Summary of Tian Jiyun's speech before Party school," *BX,* 266 (16 June 1992), 4–5, trans. in *FBIS-Chi,* 18 June 1992, 16–18; Baum, *Burying Mao,* 353.

124 *XH,* 1 May 1992, trans. in *FBIS-Chi,* 1 May 1992, 18–19.

125 [Ren Huiwen] Jen Hui-wen, "There is something behind Chen Yun's declaration of his position," *Xinbao,* 12 May 1992, trans. in *FBIS-Chi,* 13 May 1992, 21–2. According to Baum, Chen's supporters later accused Shanghai city officials of distorting Chen's comments. See *Burying Mao,* 449 n. 63.

126 Deng's comments were reported by Hong Kong media in May but were not publicized by PRC media until early July when Shanghai's *Jiefang ribao* finally broke the long silence. *MB,* 28 May 1992, trans. in *FBIS-Chi,* 28 May 1992, 15; *South China Morning Post,* 28 May 1992; and Agence France Presse, 7 July 1992. The following month, Deng followed up his trip to Shougang with a trip to the Northeast. See *South China Morning Post,* 24 June 1992.

127 [Yan Shenzun] Yen Shen-tsun, "Deng Xiaoping's talk during his inspection of Shoudu Iron and Steel Complex," *Guangjiaojing,* 238 (16 July 1992), 6–7, trans. in *FBIS-Chi,* 17 July 1992, 7–8.

argued that reform was like "steering a boat against the current. We will be driven back if we do not forge ahead."[128]

Reform was given new momentum in late May with the circulation of Document No. 4, "The CPC Central Committee's opinions on expediting reform, opening wider to the outside world, and working to raise the economy to a new level in a better and quicker way." The document, apparently drafted under the auspices of Zhu Rongji, marked a major new stage in China's policy of opening to the outside by declaring that five major inland cities along the Yangtze and nine border trade cities would be opened and that the thirty capitals of China's provinces and regions and municipalities would enjoy the same preferential treatment and policies as the SEZs. Moreover, the document stated formally what Deng had said in January, namely that Guangdong was to catch up with the four small dragons in twenty years.[129]

The more open political atmosphere of the spring encouraged long-silenced liberal intellectuals once again to raise their voices in protest against leftism. A collection of essays by such famous intellectuals as former minister of culture Wang Meng, former editor in chief of the *People's Daily* Hu Jiwei, and former editor of the *Science and Technology Daily* Sun Changjiang created a storm when it was published under the title *Historical trends.*[130] The book's sharp criticism of leftism quickly brought the wrath of the Propaganda Department, which banned the book.[131] Shortly after the book's publication, Yuan Hongbing, the law lecturer from Beijing University who had edited the book, presided over a gathering of more than 100 well-known intellectuals in Beijing. Such people as Wang Ruoshui, the former deputy editor of the *People's Daily,* and Wu Zuguang, the famous playwright who had been expelled from the Party in 1987, addressed the forum.[132] In the months that followed, other books denouncing leftism came off the press.[133]

The renewed activities of such liberal intellectuals was certainly grist for the leftists' mill. Shortly after the forum in Beijing, Deng Liqun launched a

128 *XH,* 14 June 1992, trans. in *FBIS-Chi,* 15 June 1992, 23–6. Jiang's speech was the occasion of the *People's Daily*'s first authoritative comment on reform since February. See "New stage of China's reform and opening to the outside world," *RMRB* editorial, 9 June 1992, trans. in *FBIS-Chi,* 9 June 1992, 17–18.

129 [Xia Yu] Hsia Yu, "Beijing's intense popular interest in CPC Document No. 4," *DGB,* 12 June 1992, trans. in *FBIS-Chi,* 12 June 1992, 17–18; "The CCP issues Document No. 4, fully expounding expansion of opening up," *DGB,* 18 June 1992, trans. in *FBIS-Chi,* 18 June 1992, 19–20.

130 Yuan Hongbing, *Lishi chaoliu* (Historical trends).

131 [Lu Mingsheng] Lu Ming-sheng, "Inside story of how *Historical trends* was banned," *ZM,* 177 (1 July 1992), 33–4, trans. in *FBIS-Chi,* 7 July 1992, 19–21.

132 *MB,* 15 June 1992, trans. in *FBIS-Chi,* 15 June 1992, 26–7.

133 See Zhao Shilin, ed., *Fang "zuo" beiwanglu* (Memorandum on opposing "leftism"); Wen Jin, ed., *Zhongguo "zuo" huo* (China's "leftist" peril); and Yuan Yongsong and Wang Junwei, eds., *Zuoqing ershinian, 1957–1976* (Twenty years of leftism, 1957–1976).

new attack. In an internal speech at the Office for the Research of Party History, Deng called for "extra vigilance over the recent rise in rightist tendencies."[134]

Many intellectuals had taken heart from Deng Xiaoping's trip to the South and his harsh denunciations of the Left. They hoped that at last the patriarch would deal a fatal blow to such leftist leaders as Deng Liqun, Wang Renzhi, and Gao Di. Deng's calculus, however, remained different from that of the intellectuals. His goals were twofold. First, he wanted to reassert his dominance in the Party. His southern tour, his harsh rhetoric, and his willingness to use the military in an intra-Party struggle demonstrated his determination, while the Fourteenth Party Congress's enshrinement of Deng's thought would signal his success. Second, however, Deng sought a path that might ensure stability after his passing, and the terrible intra-Party struggles that Tiananmen and the ensuing changes in the international environment had set off demonstrated just how precarious that goal was. In 1988 Deng had endorsed the concept of neoauthoritarianism – the idea that the authority of the state could be used to build a strong economy and stable society à la the authoritarian regimes on China's periphery. During his trip to the South, Deng praised the example of Singapore. And during his visit to Shougang, he signaled that he had found his tool for building such a society: Zhu Rongji.

Thus, the Fourteenth Party Congress that convened in October 1992 sought to do two seemingly contradictory things: establish clear dominance over Chen Yun and deny the fruits of victory to the "bourgeois liberals" within the Party.

THE FOURTEENTH PARTY CONGRESS

Deng's efforts over the preceding year and more, starting with his early 1991 trip to Shanghai and building momentum following the abortive coup in the Soviet Union and with his trip to Shenzhen, finally culminated in October 1992 with the adoption by the Fourteenth Party Congress of the most liberal economic document in CCP history. Whereas a year earlier Deng Liqun had been calling reform and opening up the source of peaceful evolution,[135] the Fourteenth Party Congress report declared that "the most clear-cut characteristic of the new historical period is reform and opening up" and that the "new revolution" inaugurated by Deng was "aimed at

134 *South China Morning Post,* 24 June 1992. See also Meng Lin, "Deng Liqun reaffirms disapproval of phrase 'Deng Xiaoping thought,' " *JB,* 180 (5 July 1992), 42, trans. in *FBIS-Chi,* 6 July 1992, 28–9.

135 Baum, *Burying Mao,* 334.

fundamentally changing the economic structure rather than patching it up." Underlining the profound changes called for by Deng's revolution, the political report endorsed the creation of a "socialist *market* economic system" as the goal of reform, thereby advancing a major step beyond the 1984 thesis of building a "socialist planned commodity economy" – which had itself been controversial.[136]

Moreover, the political report endorsed the important theses of Deng Xiaoping's southern tour, including his statement that planning and market were merely economic "means" for regulating the economy, his proposition that the 1978 Third Plenum line should be pursued for a hundred years, and – most important – his assertion that it was necessary "mainly to guard against 'leftist' tendencies within the Party, particularly among the leading cadres."[137]

The Fourteenth Party Congress was certainly a personal victory for Deng. Whereas his policies had been under nearly constant attack since 1989 and Chen Yun's economic thought had been repeatedly written into speeches and policy documents, the Fourteenth Party Congress lauded Deng for his "tremendous political courage in opening up new paths in socialist construction and a tremendous theoretical courage in opening up a new realm in Marxism." No other plenum or congress report in the reform era had been so personal or so laudatory. Rhetorically at least, Deng's status became comparable to, if not higher than, that of Mao.

Personnel changes at the Fourteenth Party Congress supported the policies Deng favored to some extent. Conservative leaders Yao Yilin and Song Ping were removed from the PSC, and Zhu Rongji, Liu Huaqing, a senior military modernizer who was also promoted to the position of vice-chairman of the CMC, and Hu Jintao, a fifty-one-year-old former China Youth League cadre and former Party secretary of Tibet, were added. The conservative Li Ximing, targeted by Deng during his southern tour, was removed from the Politburo and subsequently replaced as Beijing Party secretary by Chen Xitong, who had responded loyally to Deng's "emancipate the mind" campaign in 1991, despite his hard-line stance during the 1989 protest movement. Overall, the number of full Politburo members was increased to twenty from fourteen as a number of provincial and younger leaders joined the august body while several elders retired (Yang Shangkun, Wan Li, Qin Jiwei, Wu Xueqian, and Yang Rudai).[138] Moreover, the CAC, of which Chen

136 "Political report" to the Fourteenth Party Congress, Beijing television, trans. in *FBIS-Chi,* 13 October 1992, 23–43. Quotes taken from pages 25 and 24, respectively. Emphasis added.

137 Ibid., 29.

138 Joseph Fewsmith, "Reform, resistance, and the politics of succession," in William A. Joseph, ed., *China briefing, 1994,* 8–11.

Yun was the head and which had long served as a bastion of conservative opposition to Deng, was abolished.

While these changes reflected a major change in China's top-level policy-making body, Deng stopped short of a fundamental overhaul. In particular, Deng was determined to prevent supporters of former general secretary Zhao Ziyang from moving into the highest positions. Thus, Vice-Premier Tian Jiyun, a protégé of Zhao who had pushed Deng's themes with such devastating effectiveness the previous spring, was denied a PSC seat. Moreover, such Zhao associates as Hu Qili and Yan Mingfu, partially rehabilitated in June 1991, did not rejoin the Politburo and Secretariat, respectively, as some had hoped and expected.[139]

Most important, the changes stopped short of affecting the so-called Jiang–Li structure at the top of the system. Many had expected Zhu Rongji or Tian Jiyun to be elevated to the second slot, in line to succeed Li Peng as premier at the NPC meeting the following spring. Perhaps such predictions cum hopes were unrealistic. In restructuring the leadership, Deng carefully maintained a balance between reformers and conservatives. As the well-known writer Bai Hua put it, "It was as though he {Deng} were afraid that once the leftists had been wiped out, the {factional} balance would be upset and another wave of 'bourgeois liberalization' would set in."[140] The point of such balancing was to shore up the authority of Deng's third choice to succeed him, Jiang Zemin, though, as we shall see, it remains less than clear that Jiang remains committed to upholding Deng's legacy.

Deng did at least two things that bolstered Jiang. First and foremost, on the eve of the Fourteenth Party Congress, Deng decided to oust Yang Baibing, who had led the PLA to "escort reform" the previous spring, as vice-chairman of the powerful CMC. In so doing, Deng undercut the authority of his longtime confidant and supporter, Yang Shangkun, who is Yang Baibing's elder half-brother. Deng took this step in part because much of the professional military establishment (as opposed to the political commissars) resented Yang Baibing for his lack of professional military experience and because his rise was widely believed to be attributable to the influence of his older sibling. In addition, Yang Baibing stirred resentment in the military by promoting his own loyalists, and he undercut Jiang Zemin by conferring major promotions himself instead of deferring to Jiang as head of the CMC.

139 Former PSC member Hu Qili, purged for his support of Zhao during the 1989 demonstrations, was appointed vice-minister of the Ministry of the Machine-Building and Electronics Industry. Yan Mingfu, former member of the Secretariat and head of the party's United Front Work Department, was appointed a vice-minister of civil affairs. A third Zhao associate, Rui Xingwen, was named vice-minister of the SPC at the same time. *XH,* 1 June 1993, trans. in *FBIS-Chi,* 4 June 1991, 30.

140 Quoted in Lam, *China after Deng Xiaoping,* 171.

Following Yang's ouster, some three hundred high-level officers were retired or rotated. While many of these changes can be attributed to normal rotation, it seems clear that several protégés of the Yang brothers were removed from critical positions.

To replace the Yangs, Deng turned to the elderly (seventy-seven in 1992) Liu Huaqing, who was given a PSC seat and named vice-chairman of the CMC, and Zhang Zhen (seventy-nine in 1992), who was named second vice-chairman of the CMC. The surprise elevation of Liu and Zhang certainly underscored a renewed professionalism in the PLA (Liu is one of the leading modernizers in the PLA, particularly of the navy, which he led for many years, and Zhang was commandant of the National Defense University), but their promotion also highlighted the impossibility of turning over the leadership of the military to a younger generation, even as the age of the country's civilian leaders continued to fall.

In addition to shoring up Jiang's authority by shaking up the military hierarchy, Deng limited his purge of leftists. Although Li Ximing was removed from the Politburo and from his position as secretary of the Beijing Municipal CCP Committee and Gao Di was removed as director of the *People's Daily,* many leftists remained in influential positions.

BACK TO THE MIDDLE

The effort to strike a new balance was apparent in the aftermath of the Fourteenth Party Congress. Whereas Deng's new reform push had dominated Chinese politics since his trip to Shenzhen at the beginning of the year, shortly after the congress closed China's leaders began to warn liberal intellectuals not to go too far. In late November Jiang Zemin warned cadres to exercise caution in criticizing Marxism–Leninism–Mao Zedong Thought, saying that their viewpoints represented "the most updated reflection of class struggle inside society and inside the party in a certain realm." As the political atmosphere became more conservative, Yao Yilin, who had stepped down from the PSC at the Fourteenth Party Congress, sharply criticized economic czar Zhu Rongji first at a State Council meeting and then at a conference for Politburo members and state councilors. Yao argued that capital investment had exceeded the plan by too much (38 percent), that bank credits had likewise greatly exceeded the plan (120 percent), and that debt chains and stockpiles were again building up. Zhu reportedly defended himself by arguing that although there were problems with the economy, it was not "overheated."[141] Nevertheless, both Jiang Zemin and Li Peng

141 [Zheng Delin] Cheng Te-lin, "Yao Yilin launches attack against Zhu Rongji, Tian Jiyun," *JB,* 1 (5 January 1993), 44–5, trans. in *FBIS-Chi,* 22 January 1993, 46–7; [Ren Huiwen] Jen Hui-wen,

warned at the year-end National Planning Conference and National Economic Conference against the "overheated economy."[142]

This renewed attack on rapid economic growth prompted the patriarch to intervene again. For the third year in a row, Deng reappeared in Shanghai to encourage high growth and reform. This time, Deng was quoted as saying, "I hope you will not lose the current opportunities. Opportunities for great development are rare in China."[143] Immediately China's media began to explain why China's economy was not overheated, despite the opinion of many economists that it was.

Deng's intervention and the subsequent media campaign were apparently intended not only to keep up reform momentum in general but also specifically to influence the NPC meeting scheduled for March. In early March the Second Plenary Session of the Fourteenth Central Committee met to consider policy before the NPC and endorsed Deng's view that "at present and throughout the 1990s, the favorable domestic and international opportunities should be grasped to speed up the pace of reform, opening up, and the modernization drive." On the basis of this optimistic assessment, the plenum endorsed an upward revision of the annual growth target set by the Eighth Five-Year Plan (1991–5) from 6 percent to 8–9 percent.[144]

Following this plenum resolution, Li Peng and his drafting team had to go back to work on the text of the Government Work Report, much as Li had been forced to revise the text of the previous year's work report. According to the PRC-owned Hong Kong paper *Wenweibao,* the work report was revised to reflect "more positively, more comprehensively, and more accurately" the guiding principles of the Fourteenth Party Congress – an admission of just how far the initial draft had deviated from Deng's policies. The revised version of the work report highlighted the essence of Deng's talk in Shanghai, namely that it was necessary to "grasp the opportunity, because there will not be many big opportunities for China."[145]

THE EIGHTH NATIONAL PEOPLE'S CONGRESS

The first session of the Eighth NPC, which convened in March 1993, marked both a passing of generations and a change of political strategy. In

"Deng Xiaoping urges conservatives not to make a fuss," *Xinbao,* 1 January 1993, trans. in *FBIS-Chi,* 4 January 1993, 43–4; and [Chen Jianbing] Chen Chien-ping, "Zhu Rongji urges paying attention to negative effects of reform," *WHB* (Hong Kong), 13 January 1993, trans. in *FBIS-Chi,* 15 January 1993, 27–8.

142 *XH,* 27 December 1992, trans. in *FBIS-Chi,* 28 December 1992, 34–6.

143 Central television, 22 January 1993, trans. in *FBIS-Chi,* 22 January 1993, 20–1.

144 *XH,* 7 March 1993, in *FBIS-Chi,* 8 March 1993, 13–14.

145 "Major revisions to the government work report," *WHB* (Hong Kong), 16 March 1993, trans. in *FBIS-Chi,* 16 March 1993, 23–4.

the opening session, longtime Deng loyalist Wan Li, who had perhaps done more than anyone else to shepherd and nurture the early rural reforms, declared that the session would take "Comrade Deng Xiaoping's theory on building socialism with Chinese characteristics" as its guide and would "vigorously push ahead reform, opening up, and the modernization drive." Having said this, Wan turned the gavel over to his successor, Qiao Shi, and embraced him before leaving the hall.[146]

The appointment of Qiao Shi as head of the NPC not only upgraded the legislative body – in the reform era it had not previously been headed by a PSC member – but also marked the abandonment of Deng's long-term strategy of separating party and government. At least since his famous 1980 speech "On the reform of the Party and state leadership system," Deng had championed the separation of Party and state as a way of making state administration more efficient and the Party less intrusive.[147] This effort had culminated in Zhao Ziyang's proposal at the Thirteenth Party Congress to establish a civil service system and to remove Party groups (*dangzu*) from government organs. Apparently taking account of both the collapse of the Soviet Union, which Chinese analysts attributed in part to efforts to separate Party and state, and of similar but more limited efforts in China, Deng finally abandoned his former reform strategy and decided that only by having top Party leaders manage leading government posts could the Party's leadership be guaranteed.

The NPC also formally appointed Jiang Zemin as president of the PRC, replacing Yang Shangkun and making Jiang the first person to hold concurrently the top three posts in the Party, military, and state apparatus since the ill-starred Hua Guofeng – to whom Jiang has frequently been compared.[148] The NPC also reappointed Li Peng as premier, but 210 votes were cast against him, 120 delegates abstained, and 1 vote was cast for Zhao Ziyang. The concurrent session of the Chinese People's Political Consultative Conference (CPPCC) named fourth-ranking PSC member Li Ruihuan as its head. Thus, the top four members of the Politburo held all the leading positions in the government as well.[149]

The most important outcome of the NPC session, however, was the diminution of the authority of the SPC. The SPC, frequently referred to as the

146 *XH*, 14 March 1993, in *FBIS-Chi*, 15 March 1993, 19.

147 Deng Xiaoping, "Dang he guojia lingdao zhidu de gaige" (On the reform of the Party and state leadership system), in *Deng Xiaoping wenxuan (1975–1982)*, 280–302.

148 Hua Guofeng was Party chairman from the time of Mao's death in 1976 to 1980, when he was replaced by Hu Yaobang. The position of Party chairman was subsequently abolished (by the Party constitution of 1982), making the position of general secretary the top post in the Party.

149 Joseph Fewsmith, "Notes on the first session of the Eighth National People's Congress," *Journal of Contemporary China*, 3 (Summer 1993), 81–6.

"little State Council," had traditionally been the nerve center of China's planned economy. In the Dengist period, it had always been headed by loyal supporters of Chen Yun and was a bastion of conservative economic thought. When Zou Jiahua, a longtime protégé of Li Peng, was appointed to head the SPC in 1989 and subsequently was made a vice-premier in 1991, this trend was confirmed.

In March 1993, however, Chen Jinhua, a former vice-mayor of Shanghai (in the late 1970s and early 1980s) and general manager of the China Petrochemical Corporation (1983–90), was appointed to replace Zou Jiahua as head of the SPC. Although a member of the Central Committee, Chen was neither a member of the Politburo, much less its Standing Committee (as Yao Yilin had been), nor a vice-premier (as Zou Jiahua had been). This diminution in the status of the SPC would presage the emergence of the State Economic and Trade Commission, established in May 1993, as China's most authoritative economic policy-making body and made its head, Vice-Premier Zhu Rongji, even more powerful.

Zhu's role as economic czar was unexpectedly reinforced when Li Peng suffered a heart attack on or about 25 April. Li, Zhu's primary rival for control over the economy, disappeared from public sight for two months before he emerged for two brief appearances in mid-June and then disappeared for another two months. Although there seems little doubt that the premier was seriously ill in at least the early part of this period, his problems appear to have been political as well. After all, no one had done more on the economic front than Li Peng to shore up the old planned economy and to oppose Deng's new push for reform – as his need to revise his work reports to the NPC in 1992 and 1993 showed.

ZHU RONGJI AND THE ECONOMY

Zhu's control over economic management was greatly enhanced in June 1993. Jiang Zemin presided over a "Central Financial and Banking Work Conference" at which Zhu presented a sixteen-point proposal aimed at restoring economic order and reducing inflationary pressures. Zhu's proposals were sharply opposed by Li Guixian, a longtime protégé of Li Peng and head of the People's Bank of China. The showdown resulted in Li's ouster and Zhu's installation as concurrent head of the central bank.[150]

With Zou Jiahua demoted from leadership of the SPC and with Li Peng sidelined, Zhu Rongji's control over China's economy became nearly total.

150 [Ren Huiwen] Jen Hui-wen, "Different views within the CCP on the banking crisis," *Xinbao,* 9 July 1993, trans. in *FBIS-Chi,* 12 July 1993, 41–2.

Zhu was named to head a newly established leading group for reform of the financial, taxation, and banking structures, a position he added to his already powerful posting as deputy head of the Central Finance and Economics Leading Group.[151] Moreover, Zhu quickly brought in a number of his trusted aides to help him manage the economy. For instance, Dai Xianglong, president of the Shanghai-based Bank of Communications, and Zhu Xiaohua, vice-president of the Shanghai Branch of the Bank of China, were named vice-governors of the People's Bank of China, and a number of economists associated with market-oriented economist Wu Jinglian, who had been a prominent adviser to Zhao Ziyang, were brought in as advisers.[152]

The sixteen-point plan that Zhu had presented at the June meeting and was subsequently issued as a Central Committee circular (Document No. 6) marked the inauguration of a new round of austerity and the beginning of a long, new effort to combine reform of the economy with a redefinition of the relations between Beijing and the provinces.

Zhu has often been referred to as "China's Gorbachev" by the Western press (and by his domestic enemies as well), but there is little in his economic thinking, much less political position, to suggest that he either desires or can play such a role in China. Indeed, Zhu has engaged in considerable jousting with China's reform-minded economists.[153] Zhu's approach to economic reform and political control appears modeled after that of Park Chung-hee or Lee Kuan Yew, favoring strong state control combined with a marketized economy. On the one hand, he favors strong actions to move the economy away from the old planned economy, while on the other hand, he is inclined to use the "visible hand" to try to guide this process from the top. Unlike many of the reformers associated with Zhao Ziyang, who were willing to devolve much decision-making authority to lower levels, Zhu clearly believes that too much authority (and too many fiscal resources) have slipped out of Beijing's control. Drawing heavily on the experiences of the East Asian developmental state, this approach is often referred to as "neoauthoritarian."

151 Jiang Zemin was the head of this group, though there is little indication that he involved himself in the details of economic management. Li Peng was the other deputy head of the group.

152 Wang Qishan, then vice-president (and now president) of the Construction Bank of China and son-in-law of Yao Yilin, was also named a vice-governor of the People's Bank of China, perhaps in an effort to allay conservative opposition. Chen Yun's son, Chen Yuan, was the fourth vice-governor of the bank. On Wu Jinglian's economic thought, see Fewsmith, *Dilemmas of reform in China*, 161–6.

153 For instance, in October 1993, a number of liberal economists voiced concerns that Zhu's austerity program would lead to a retreat from reform. See *Zhongguo xinwen she*, 25 October 1993, trans. in *FBIS-Chi*, 29 October 1993, 38–9. In turn, Zhu has criticized some Chinese textbooks that "blindly worship" Western laissez-faire economics. See *Zhongguo tongxun she*, 2 December 1994, trans. in *FBIS-Chi*, 2 December 1994, 24–5. On Zhu's willingness to use administrative measures alongside market forces, see his speech, "Should the government intervene in the market and regulate prices in a socialist market economy?" *Jiage lilun yu shijian*, 10 (October 1993), 1–5, trans. in *FBIS-Chi*, 10 January 1995.

This approach was reflected in Zhu's campaign against speculation and inflation in the summer and fall of 1993. As control over the money supply was loosened in 1992 in response to Deng's call for faster economic growth, speculation and corruption mushroomed. The real estate market took off, and by the end of 1992 there were more than 12,000 real estate companies, a 2.4-fold increase over the year before.[154] At the same time, local areas continued to open up "developmental zones" in the hope of attracting foreign capital and to take advantage of loopholes in the financial regulations. By the end of 1992, there were said to be some 8,000 development zones.[155]

These speculative markets quickly drew large sums of money from the hinterland, exacerbating the problem of IOUs being given to peasants for the grain they grew. According to one report, at least Rmb 57 billion had been diverted through interbank loans to the coastal areas, where it was used to speculate in real estate and the stock market. The result was a "bubble economy" that could "vanish without warning."[156] In an effort to curb such speculative activity and bring the economy under control, Zhu ordered banks to recall loans that had not been issued according to regulations and mandated a 20 percent cut in government spending.[157]

THE THIRD PLENUM

The Third Plenary Session of the Fourteenth Central Committee, which was convened in Beijing on 11–14 November 1993, took up the task of translating the Fourteenth Party Congress's goal of building a "socialist market economy" into a concrete program of reform. The crux of the plenum decision lay in its promises, on the one hand, to reform the macroeconomic system by building the financial, tax, and monetary systems necessary to manage the economy through economic means, and, on the other hand, to reform the microeconomy by building "socialist modern enterprises." This proposed reform of China's enterprise system was apparently the hottest area of contention in the discussions leading up to the Third Plenum because it involved the issue of ownership, and ownership reform was inextricably bound up with both ideological issues and vested interests.

154 *XH*, 21 May 1993, trans. in *FBIS-Chi*, 21 May 1993, 28–9. See also Zhu Jianhong and Jiang Yaping, "Development and standardization are necessary: Perspective of real estate business," *RMRB*, 11 May 1993, trans. in *FBIS-Chi*, 24 May 1993, 56–7.

155 Xiang Jingquan, "Review and prospects of China's economic development," *GMRB*, trans. in *FBIS-Chi*, 19 March 1993, 48–50.

156 "Central authorities urge banks to draw bank loans and stop promoting the bubble economy," *DGB*, 1 July 1993, trans. in *FBIS-Chi*, 1 July 1993, 31–2.

157 [Chen Jianbing] Chen Chien-ping, "The CCP Central Committee announces 16 measures," *WHB* (Hong Kong), 3 July 1993, trans. in *FBIS-Chi*, 7 July 1993, 12–13.

Nevertheless, the Third Plenum decision specified that the property rights of socialist modern enterprises should be clarified and that enterprises would be entitled to manage their assets independently, would be responsible for profits and losses, and would maintain and increase the net worth of the enterprises.[158]

What was not specified by the decision was how property rights would be allocated and how state interests were to be protected. The decision was not intended to take the state out of the business of owning enterprises; after all, it specified that the "public ownership system" would remain the "foundation of the socialist market economy." But the decision moved further in the direction of ownership reform than had seemed possible only a year before – or even in the heyday of reform in the late 1980s. In an internal speech on the eve of the plenum, Jiang Zemin went so far as to declare that the dominance of the public ownership system meant only that public ownership had to remain dominant in national terms; individual localities and industries need not be subject to this requirement.[159] Perhaps the most important aspect of the plenum decision on enterprise reform was the promise that all enterprises, "especially" the state-owned sector, would compete equally and "without discrimination" on the market.[160] In other words, state-owned enterprises were to be "pushed onto the market" – a dramatic difference in official policy from the period following Tiananmen during which discrimination between types of ownership was taken as distinguishing socialist reform from bourgeois liberalization.

In order to implement this decision, the Third Plenum called for a major reform of the banking system and an overhaul of the tax system. The People's Bank of China was, at long last, to be turned into a genuine central bank that would "implement monetary policies independently."[161] Guo Shuqing, a close adviser to Zhu Rongji and head of the Comprehensive Section of the State Commission for Economic Restructuring, declared that the People's Bank should be as independent as the Federal Reserve or Bundesbank.[162] At the same time, "policy banks" would be set up to deal with enterprises and economic sectors as well as capital construction projects that were important to the state and/or in the red. In this way, the problems of deficit enterprises could be separated out from the overall management of the economy.

158 "Decision of the CCP Central Committee on some issues concerning the establishment of a socialist market economic structure" (hereafter, "Establishment of a socialist market structure"), *RMRB*, 17 November 1993, trans. in *FBIS-Chi*, 17 November 1993, 23.

159 [Ji Wenge] Chi Wei-ke, "Three new moves on the eve of the Third Plenary Session of the CPC Central Committee; Deng makes new comments on macrocontrol," *JB*, 12 (5 December 1993), 30–4, trans. in *FBIS-Chi*, 8 December 1993, 18–22.

160 "Establishment of a socialist market structure," 25.

161 Ibid., 28.

162 *South China Sunday Morning Post*, 14 November 1993.

REFORMING THE TAX SYSTEM

For both economic and political reasons, the Third Plenum also endorsed a major change in China's tax system. Economically it made sense to implement a uniform tax rate across all forms of enterprises; it would, after all, provide a financial underpinning to the nondiscrimination between state-owned and other enterprises called for by the plenum decision. But it was the political logic that was more compelling. Central government revenues as a proportion of GNP and as a proportion of all government revenues had fallen steadily throughout the reform period. The share of total state revenues in GNP had fallen monotonously from 31.2 percent in 1978 to 16.2 percent in 1993, and Beijing's portion of overall state revenues had fallen from 57 percent in 1981 to 33 percent in 1993.[163] Moreover, due largely to the mismanagement of the economy by conservatives in the 1989–90 period, state-owned enterprises could no longer serve as financial supports for the central budget. Long the milch cows of the central government, such enterprises, after subtracting their losses, repayments to banks, and retained profits, contributed no profit to the state budget after 1990.[164] New sources of revenue had to be found.

The basic reason for the decrease of central revenues with respect to overall government revenues was that in order to stimulate local "enthusiasm" for production at the beginning of the reform era, China had adopted a fiscal system popularly known as "eating in separate kitchens" (*fenzao chifan*), the essence of which was to stimulate local interest in developing the economy and collecting taxes by giving localities a fiscal interest. Later, the country adopted the fiscal contracting responsibility system, which basically allowed localities (and some industrial sectors) to pay either a set amount or a certain percentage of revenue to the center (and keep the rest).

These fiscal arrangements had in many ways achieved exactly what they were supposed to do – arouse the enthusiasm of the localities for promoting economic development. Indeed, much of the economic success China has enjoyed in the reform period has come about precisely because fiscal arrangements gave local governments a stake in developing their local economies. As Jean Oi put it, economic development in China came about because China "got the taxes wrong."[165]

Although China's tax system was critical for providing incentives for economic development, it also had a number of side effects that were less

163 Jae Ho Chung, "Central–provincial relations," in Lo Chi Kin, Suzanne Pepper, and Tsui Kai Yuen, eds., *China review, 1995*, 3.7.

164 Naughton, *Growing out of the plan*, 286.

165 Jean Oi, *Rural China takes off: Incentives for industrialization.*

benevolent. In particular, the system allowed localities to develop large sources of "extrabudgetary" revenues – revenues that did not have to be passed on to the central government – which local governments could allocate to develop, and protect, local industry. Extrabudgetary revenues increased very quickly over the course of reform, from a mere Rmb 34.7 billion in 1978 to 385 billion in 1992. Put another way, extrabudgetary funds rose from only 31 percent of budgetary revenues in 1978 to 98 percent in 1992. It was the amassing of this pot of extrabudgetary revenue that allowed China's localities to ride out the austere economic policies imposed during the period of "improvement and rectification." Despite central policies that were manifestly opposed to the TVE sector, most localities were able to protect their local industries and in many areas these industries continued to grow rapidly despite central proscriptions.[166]

The fiscal contracting system that had been so generous to local government led to Beijing's relative decline in revenue. Conservatives had long railed against the loss of central power implied by these figures; indeed, a major goal of the "improvement and rectification" policy was to reverse these trends. Nevertheless, in December 1990 the Seventh Plenum, in part to alleviate the tense central–provincial relationship, which had been reflected in the Economic Work Conference the previous September, promised to leave the tax structure unchanged during the course of the Eighth Five-Year Plan (1991–5).

The continuing erosion of the central government's fiscal position – including annual budget deficits, inflationary pressures, and growing tax evasion (estimated to be around 100 billion yuan in the early 1990s) – caused the issue of tax reform to be revisited. Perhaps more important, as he demonstrated repeatedly, Zhu Rongji was as much a statist as he was a marketeer. Zhu's objective, as reflected in the Third Plenum decision and other measures, was to use the power of the state to rationalize and marketize the economic system.

Thus, the Third Plenum declared that the fiscal contracting system would be replaced by the tax-sharing system (*fenshuizhi*). Under the new system, the consolidated commercial–industrial tax would be divided into a business tax (which would be retained by the localities) and a product circulation tax (which would be shared between the localities and the central government). At the same time, other shared taxes, including a value-added tax, were to be imposed. Under the new system, and consistent with the government's goal of "pushing state-owned enterprises onto the market," all enterprises would be taxed at the same 33 percent rate.[167]

166 Ibid. 167 Chung, "Central–provincial relations," 3.9–12.

The goal of this tax system was to raise the proportion of budgetary revenues in the national income from the current 16 percent to 25 percent in the short run and 35 percent over the longer term, and to raise the central share of budget revenues from the present 33 percent to 50 percent in the short run and more than 65 percent in the long run.[168]

This effort to recentralize fiscal control was predictably resisted by the provinces. Before the plenum, Zhu Rongji made forays to sixteen provinces and municipalities in an effort to strong-arm them into compliance. In some cases his discussions were extremely acrimonious. Jiangsu provincial Party secretary Shen Daren was a particularly outspoken critic of the tax reform, and Zhu Rongji apparently chose to make an example of him by having him removed from office. But other provincial officials, particularly from coastal provinces, were equally opposed, believing the tax reform to be a scheme to "rob from the rich to aid the poor." Officials from Guangdong and Fujian were critical of the reform, as were, for different reasons, leaders of Yunnan and Guizhou.[169] At the 1994 meeting of the NPC, nearly one-quarter of the delegates either voted against or abstained during the vote on the new budgetary law.[170]

The other major change that came out of the Third Plenum was the decision to end the use of foreign exchange certificates and to unify foreign exchange rates in a bid to move toward free convertibility of the renminbi. Under the new system, export firms are supposed to sell all of their foreign exchange earnings to thirteen banks and then purchase whatever amount of foreign currency they need with renminbi. Like the other measures adopted at the Third Plenum, this change appeared to be an effort to boost central authority even as it moved China more fully toward a market economy.[171]

TOWARD SUCCESSION

By late 1994, at least two things had begun to impinge on China's political situation. First and foremost, after many ups and downs and a constant stream of rumors, it finally seemed certain that Deng's physical ability to oversee affairs of state had finally given out. In particular, around December 1994 to January 1995, Deng apparently hung between life and death. His daughter, who goes by the name Xiao Rong, declared in an unusual interview with *The New York Times* in January 1995 that her father's health was

168 Ibid., 3.12.
169 Guizhou and Yunnan were opposed because the tax reform would take much of the revenues those provinces earned from their production of cigarettes and liquor. See ibid., 3.14.
170 Ibid., 3.15. 171 Ibid., 3.24.

declining "day by day."[172] Indeed, by the time of the interview, Deng had not appeared in public since the previous January, and the release of a photograph of a very old looking Deng sitting and enjoying the fireworks on National Day (1 October) 1993 underscored the fact that it would not be long before the patriarch finally "went to join the Premier" (as Deng had once put it).[173] Even reports that Deng's health had remarkably improved in the summer of 1995 could not dispell the impression that he no longer controlled political developments.

Second, Zhu Rongji's bold effort to move China firmly onto the path of a market economy had clearly stalled. Inflationary pressures remained strong throughout 1994, and hopes of pushing state-owned enterprises onto the market were checked by the very real fear of social disorder that a large number of unemployed workers might bring about.

Under these circumstances, Jiang Zemin began to adopt a more cautious course of economic reform while moving vigorously to prove that he was the successor in fact as well as in name. As already noted, Jiang was successful at the time of the Fourteenth Party Congress in gaining Deng's support against the Yang brothers. Another round of military rotations was launched in 1993–4 that resulted in the movement of nearly a thousand additional officers.[174] At the same time, Jiang made obvious efforts to cultivate the support of the army and to promote his own followers. In June 1993, he personally promoted nineteen senior officers to the rank of general, and he also moved a number of trusted officers into sensitive positions, although not always successfully. In particular, Jiang replaced Yang Dezhong, the head of the sensitive Central Guard Bureau, with You Kexi, a military associate from Shanghai. He also appointed as head of the People's Armed Police Force (PAP) Ba Zhongtan, who had served as head of the Shanghai garrison, but Ba was subsequently forced to step down after a PAP security guard killed NPC vice-chairman Li Peiyao.[175]

In the fall of 1994, as Deng's health declined, Jiang dropped economic issues from the agenda of the forthcoming Fourth Plenum in order to concentrate on Party-building issues. As a result, the "Decision of the Central Committee of the Communist Party of China concerning some major issues

172 *The New York Times*, 13 January 1995. Xiao Rong later claimed that she had been misquoted. See Jean Philippe Beja, "The year of the dog: In the shadow of the ailing patriarch," in Lo, Pepper, and Tsui, eds., *China review, 1995*, 1.8–10.

173 Deng reportedly spoke to some leaders about the upcoming Fourth Plenum on 9 October 1994. See *ZM*, 205 (1 November 1994), 6–8, trans. in *FBIS-Chi*, 4 November 1994, 15–17.

174 Lam, *China after Deng Xiaoping*, 213–16.

175 On the appointments of You and Ba, see R. N. Schiele, "Jiang's men move out of the shadows," *Eastern Express*, 27 December 1994, in *FBIS-Chi*, 27 December 1994, 27–9. On Ba's dismissal, see Tony Walker, "Security chief's sacking seen as rebuff for Jiang," *Financial Times*, 27 February 1996, 6.

on strengthening Party building," adopted by the plenum in October, stressed strengthening "democratic centralism," which emphasizes the subordination of lower levels to higher levels, the part to the whole, and everything to the party center.[176]

The plenum proved to be an important victory for Jiang Zemin. The *People's Daily* noted that "the second-generation central leading collective has been successfully relieved by its third-generation central leading collective" – a point reiterated by Li Peng during his November trip to Korea and again by Jiang Zemin a few days later during his trip to Malaysia.[177] Not only did the "Decision" reaffirm Jiang's position as the "core" of the leadership, it also promoted three of his protégés to the center. Huang Ju, mayor of Shanghai, was promoted to the Politburo, while Wu Bangguo, Party secretary of Shanghai and a member of the Politburo, and Jiang Chunyun, Party secretary of Shandong province, were added to the Party Secretariat.

The promotion of Wu Bangguo and Jiang Chunyun served not only to shore up Jiang Zemin's personal support at the center but also to diminish the authority of Zhu Rongji, a potential rival. With the reforms Zhu had spearheaded at the 1993 Third Plenum slowed, Jiang now began parceling out bits of Zhu's portfolio. Wu Bangguo was named deputy head of the Central Finance and Economic Leading Group (replacing Li Peng) and thus would share leadership of that critical body with Zhu, under the general supervision of Jiang, who remained head of the group. More important, Wu was placed in charge of the reform of state-owned enterprises, which was designated as the focus of economic reform in 1995. At the same time, Jiang Chunyun was given the task of overseeing agriculture, another task for which Zhu Rongji had previously been responsible.

Year-end economic meetings made it evident that Jiang intended to steer a slow, steady course, preferring to shore up inefficient state-owned enterprises rather than push them onto the market as Zhu had tried to do the year before. Jiang Zemin and other conservative leaders were afraid that biting the bullet, as Zhu had urged the year before, would erode the authority of the Party and government and undermine what remained of socialist ideology. As Premier Li Peng put it, "Without solid state-owned enterprises, there will be no socialist China."[178] Hence, reform in 1995 concentrated on the selection of a hundred state-owned enterprises for pilot projects in the creation of a modern "corporate" form – as if China has not carried out hundreds

176 "Decision of the Central Committee of the Communist Party of China concerning some major issues on strengthening Party building," *XH*, 6 October 1994, in *FBIS-Chi*, 6 October 1994, 13–22.

177 [Xu Simin] Hsu Szu-min, "On the political situation in post-Deng China," *JB*, 210 (5 January 1994), 26–9, trans. in *FBIS-Chi*, 30 January 1994, 13–17.

178 "Forward: Explosive economic growth raises warning signal," *JSND*, 10 (1 October 1993), 58–9, trans. in *FBIS-Chi*, 11 January 1994, 49–50.

of pilot projects over the past decade and more. At the same time, leaders vowed to control inflation, though they promised not to repeat the "hard landing" of the 1988–91 austerity program.

Even as Jiang tried to reinforce his personal strength through the strategic promotion of protégés, to rein in centrifugal tendencies by reemphasizing democratic centralism, and to steer a course of "stability and unity" by curbing inflation and slowing the pace of economic reform, he also made a dramatic bid to win public support by finally swatting some tigers in the ongoing campaign against corruption. Public anger at Party corruption had fed the 1989 protest movement as well as the subsequent "Mao craze" that surfaced in late 1989 and the early 1990s, but corruption had been difficult to tackle because of the political clout protecting some of the worst offenders. Hu Yaobang discovered this in 1986 when his hard-hitting campaign against corruption aroused the anger of Party elders and contributed to his own downfall the following January.

The Party had launched a campaign against corruption in the immediate aftermath of Tiananmen, but that had faded away like its predecessors. Finally, in the summer of 1993, amid evidence that corruption was spreading uncontrollably, the Party launched another campaign. For the first year, this campaign seemed to go pretty much as its predecessors had – catching many flies but few tigers.[179] In the winter of 1994–5, however, the campaign shifted into high gear. The first major casualty was Yan Jianhong, the wife of former Guizhou provincial Party secretary Liu Zhengwei, who was executed in January for taking advantage of her connections in order to embezzle and misappropriate millions of yuan.[180]

Then in February 1995, Zhou Beifang was arrested. Zhou, the head of Shougang (Capital Iron and Steel) International in Hong Kong, is the son of Zhou Guanwu, who was then not only head of the model enterprise Shougang but was well connected to such senior leaders as Wan Li, Peng Zhen, and Deng Xiaoping himself. The following day, the elder Zhou retired as head of Shougang. In addition, Deng Xiaoping's son, Deng Zhifang, who was a manager with Shougang International, was apparently detained and questioned with regard to the case, though no charges were filed against him.[181]

179 The slow pace of the campaign against corruption in 1993 might be attributable to Deng Xiaoping's apparent statement during an inspection trip around Beijing on 31 October that year that the campaign should not be allowed to undermine the "reform enthusiasm" of cadres and citizens. See *South China Morning Post,* 30 November 1993. This comment makes it all the clearer that Jiang Zemin's stepping up of the campaign in late 1994 really was intended to distance himself from his erstwhile patron – as his actions against protégés of Deng would strongly suggest.

180 "Crimes behind the power: Analyzing the serious crimes committed by Yan Jianhong," *RMRB,* 14 January 1995, trans. in *FBIS-Chi,* 24 January 1995, 29–31.

181 Zhang Weiguo, "Chen Xitong an yu quanli douzheng" (The Chen Xitong case and the struggle for power), *Beijing zhi chun,* 30 (November 1995), 30–2.

At the same time, an ongoing investigation into corruption in Beijing Municipality apparently resulted in the detention of some sixty cadres in the city, including the secretaries of Party chief Chen Xitong and Mayor Li Qiyan. Then in early April, Vice-Mayor Wang Baosen, who had been implicated by the investigation, committed suicide. The upheaval in the city came to a climax in late April when CCP secretary Chen Xitong, a member of the Politburo and ally of Deng Xiaoping, was removed from office and subsequently placed under investigation. At the Party's Fifth Plenary Session in September 1995, Chen was officially removed as a member of the Politburo – the highest-ranking official accused of corruption in PRC history.[182]

With the removal of Chen Xitong, it seemed apparent that the effort to strengthen "democratic centralism," the campaign against corruption, and the power struggle among the leadership had come together. In a single stroke, Jiang Zemin moved against one of the most entrenched local leaders in the country, made a bid for popular support in the campaign against corruption, and acted against powerful people who might oppose him in the future, including the Deng family and Party elder Wan Li (Wan was a longtime supporter of Shougang and, as a former vice-mayor of Beijing, had close ties to the city's leadership).

In the fall of 1995, Jiang Zemin made another move to establish himself as the real leader of China. At the Fifth Plenary Session of the Fourteenth Central Committee in October, Jiang gave a major speech outlining twelve critical relationships that the Party and government must deal with in the coming years. Overall, it was a speech that called for development and marketization on the one hand and for stability and enhancing state capabilities on the other. The speech was obviously intended to present Jiang as a thoughtful leader, cognizant of the difficulties facing China and reasonable in his approach to problems. It was, in short, an agenda-setting speech intended to lay the foundation for Jiang Zemin's leadership.[183]

But even as Jiang has moved to shore up his position as the core of the leadership, others have staked out rival issues and bases of power. The leader who seems to have the greatest likelihood of challenging Jiang for power, or at least restraining Jiang's core status, is Qiao Shi. When Qiao took over as head of the NPC in March 1993, he was stripped of his other positions as head of the powerful Central Political and Legal Commission and as head of the Central Party School. But Qiao appears to continue to have much influence in the security apparatus that he built his career in. Ren Jianxin, who

182 "Communiqué of the Fifth Plenary Session of the Fourteenth Central Committee of the CCP," *XH*, 28 September 1995, in *FBIS-Chi*, 28 September 1995, 15–17.

183 Jiang Zemin, "Correctly handle some major relationships in the socialist modernization drive," *XH*, 8 October 1995, trans. in *FBIS-Chi*, 10 October 1995, 29–36.

replaced Qiao as head of the Legal Affairs Leading Group, had been promoted by Qiao, and Wei Jianxing, who became head of the Comprehensive Group on Social Order and subsequently replaced Chen Xitong as Beijing Party secretary, likewise appears to have strong ties to Qiao.[184] Meanwhile, Qiao has turned the NPC into a real base of support, much as Peng Zhen, who headed that body from 1981 to 1988, had used it as a base from which to oppose reform.

Qiao, who was Jiang Zemin's superior in the Shanghai underground during the revolution, has frequently challenged Jiang by being out in front of him on reform issues. As noted earlier, he beat the drums for Deng's reform campaign in the spring of 1992 long before Jiang Zemin came out in support of it. Stressing institution building and the rule of law, Qiao declared in his inaugural speech to the NPC, "Democracy must be institutionalized and codified into laws so that this system and its laws will not change with a change in leadership, nor with changes in their viewpoints and attention."[185] In January 1995, even as Jiang Zemin was stressing democratic centralism and the role of the core, Qiao chose to stress political reform and democratization.[186] At the same time that Qiao has stepped up the pace of legislation and incorporated greater expertise into its formulation, he has also given greater weight to provincial initiative and to the speed of economic reform than have Jiang Zemin and Li Peng.[187]

Aiding Qiao in this effort has been Tian Jiyun, the Politburo member whose withering criticism of leftism in April 1992 may have cost him a seat on the PSC. During the March 1995 session of the NPC, Tian listened sympathetically to Guangdong delegates, who complained that China's rulers were not allowing the NPC to function as the "highest administrative organ" as called for by the constitution. The day after this raucous meeting, 36 percent of NPC delegates either abstained or voted against Jiang Chunyun, Jiang Zemin's handpicked nominee as vice-premier. Never had China's legislature registered such a large protest.[188]

TOWARD THE POST-DENG ERA

Tiananmen marked an upheaval along three interrelated fault lines: between conservatives and reformers within the Party leadership, between the Party–

184 Gao Xin and He Pin, "Tightrope act of Wei Jianxing," *Dangdai*, 23 (15 February 1993), 42–5, trans. in *FBIS-Chi*, 24 February 1993, 24–6.

185 *XH*, 31 March 1993, trans. in *FBIS-Chi*, 1 April 1993, 23.

186 *XH*, 5 January 1995, trans. in *FBIS-Chi*, 6 January 1995, 11–13.

187 See, for instance, *XH*, 13 October 1994, trans. in *FBIS-Chi*, 20 October 1994, 35–7.

188 *South China Morning Post*, 17 March 1995.

state on the one hand and the emerging forces of society on the other, and between China and the outside world, particularly the United States. Whereas Deng continued to insist that reform and opening up could continue as before (indeed, "even faster"), conservatives viewed the course of reform as championed by Deng as the source of the trouble in 1989. In their view, reform had to be redefined (or, more accurately, returned to its pre-1984 meaning), the development of relations with the outside world slowed down, and domestic controls tightened through a renewed emphasis on ideology and the "dictatorship of the proletariat." It took a full three years for Deng to emerge triumphant in this implicit "struggle between two lines."

This struggle between the conservative wing of the party, led by Chen Yun, and the reform wing, led by Deng Xiaoping, was a continuation and intensification of what had gone on between them for most of the decade preceding Tiananmen. But if that struggle was pursued with deadly earnestness, it was nevertheless fated to fade into history not only with the deaths of Chen Yun (in April 1995) and, inevitably, of Deng but also with the impossibility of restoring anything that resembled the old planned economy. So even as the struggle between the titans of the older generation played itself out, a new contest for the soul of China began to emerge more clearly.

The contours of a new political dynamic are now being shaped by generational change on the one hand and the emergence of a dynamic, diverse, and assertive society on the other. China's economic dynamism has been long apparent. In 1995, China's GDP reached 5.77 trillion yuan (about $660 billion at the official exchange rate and about $1.6 billion when calculated according to purchasing price parity), an increase of 10.2 percent over the GDP for 1994, which was, in turn, 11.8 percent above that for 1993. As China's economy has expanded rapidly, it has also diversified and become increasingly internationalized. In 1992, China's rural industrial sector for the first time accounted for more than 50 percent of China's industrial production, and, as noted earlier, China's provinces have developed unprecedented fiscal autonomy. In 1995, China's total imports and exports topped $280 billion, and in the same year China employed over $38 billion in foreign investment.[189]

Because of the various ways in which collective and private businesses are intertwined, it is difficult to estimate the size of China's private sector or interpret its significance. By the early 1990s, official statistics revealed 120,000 private enterprises with more than 2 million workers. That is in

189 State Statistical Bureau, "Intensify reform, accelerate structural adjustments, promote healthy development of the national economy: Economic situation in 1995 and outlook for 1996," *RMRB*, 1 March 1996, trans. in *FBIS-Chi*, 4 April 1996, 32–8; and *Zhongguo xinwen she*, 23 January 1996, trans. in *FBIS-Chi*, 24 January 1996, 40.

addition to the 23 million individual households (*getihu*) throughout the country.[190] The nonstate sector (which contains but is not limited to the private economy) was given a major boost by Document No. 4 of 1992, which permitted Party units and cadres to operate businesses. Bo Xicheng, the son of Party elder Bo Yibo, aroused popular interest when he left his position as head of the Beijing Tourism Bureau to start a hotel management company. His "plunge into the sea" (*xia hai*) of commerce led the way for a tidal wave of cadre offspring (usually referred to as "princelings") to join the nonstate economy. Of course, given their links with state-owned enterprises, government ministries, and high-level leaders, these princelings helped bring about an amalgam of public and private concerns (perhaps not unlike the "crony capitalism" of Indonesia and the Philippines) – as well as an unprecedented wave of corruption.

This entrepreneurial sector seems destined to play an increasingly important role in China's society and politics. Even before the latest group of nonstate enterprises was established, market-oriented businesses were finding allies at the state as well as the local level. An important example of this came in 1989 when central planners seemed determined to trim back the TVE sector. The interests of China's TVEs were defended not only by the localities that had an economic, social, and political interest in the livelihood of their residents but also by some state bureaucracies. For instance, the Ministry of Agriculture emerged as a leading advocate for the TVEs, and one of its newspapers, the *Township and Village Enterprise News* (*Xiangzhen qiye bao*), repeatedly emphasized the importance of TVEs for the rural as well as national economies. Other bureaucracies, such as the Ministry of Personnel and Labor, likewise voiced support for TVEs. The ensuing alliance of central bureaucracies and local governments goes a long way to explain why the plans of conservative leaders were blunted and then reversed.[191]

Increasingly the link between the entrepreneurial economy and the state at various levels appears to be more organized. For instance, in late 1993 the All-China Federation of Industry and Commerce was transformed into the China Non-Governmental Chamber of Commerce, whose charter was to "provide guidance" for the nonstate sector. It seems likely that that and other organizations will defend their constituents' interests as well as channel and curtail their activities. This trend suggests that China could evolve into a corporatist system.[192]

190 Susan Young, *Private business and economic reform in China.*

191 Dali Yang, *Catastrophe and reform in China,* ch. 9.

192 China's traditional organic conception of the state–society relationship resonates with many strains of corporatist thought, and certain forms of corporatist organization were implemented in the Nationalist period. See Joseph Fewsmith, *Party, state, and local elites in republican China.* On contemporary

As the economy has grown more complex and less statist, China's intellectuals have similarly become more independent of the regime and more critical in their thinking. Whereas Chinese intellectuals in the communist era have generally expressed dissent both cautiously and through personal links with like-minded party officials (and have paid dearly even for such limited expressions of opinion), they have in recent years increasingly moved, like much of the economy, out of the state orbit.[193] The obvious failures of CCP rule, the collapse of communist rule in East Europe and the dismemberment of the Soviet Union, and the crushing of expression at Tiananmen have all contributed to the declining persuasiveness, indeed the bankruptcy, of Marxist thought. The ensuing ideological vacuum has set off a search for meaning unprecedented since the May Fourth era, leading some intellectuals to return to traditional thought, others to look to the West, and still others to explore Eastern models.

Moreover, this search for ideological meaning has taken place at a time when the role of intellectuals in Chinese society has been undergoing a profound change. The commercialization of Chinese society, on the one hand, and the bureaucratization of the Chinese state, on the other, have left Chinese intellectuals far less able to play their traditional role of social conscience. To the dismay of some, Chinese intellectuals are themselves jumping into the sea of commerce, taking up unfamiliar jobs as writers for popular ("middlebrow") literature and soap operas.[194] Whether these trends will ultimately force the Chinese state to be more responsive to an articulate population or simply contribute to the marginalization of intellectuals in Chinese politics remains to be seen.

At the same time, China's ruling elite is no longer composed of the battle-hardened, mostly ill-educated cadres who fought the revolution and have ruled the country for nearly half a century. Their successors are generally technocrats and bureaucrats, people who might look for practical solutions and be more inclined to usher in a politics of compromise than their more ideologically driven elders.[195]

The political history of Chinese politics since Tiananmen and the economic, social, and intellectual trends outlined in this chapter suggest an enormously fluid situation that could evolve in a number of directions in the post-Deng era.

It should be apparent just how deeply Tiananmen traumatized the Party, setting off the most serious intra-Party struggle for control of ideology and

trends in a corporatist direction, see Jonathan Unger and Anita Chan, "China, corporatism, and the East Asian model," *AJCA*, 33 (January 1995), 29–53.

193 Merle Goldman, *Sowing the seeds of democracy in China*. 194 Jianying Zha, *China pop*.

195 Hong-yung Lee, *From revolutionary cadres to party technocrats in socialist China*.

policy since the Dengist coalition came to power in 1978. These struggles were, of course, continuations of positions that had been well staked out in the years before Tiananmen, and thus had contributed to the making of that tragedy, but the recriminations set off by Tiananmen and the subsequent collapse of communism in East Europe substantially increased tensions within the Party and weakened Deng Xiaoping's core position. Although such tensions eased with Deng's victory at the Fourteenth Party Congress and with the passing of several conservative leaders (CPPCC deputy secretary Wang Renzhong in March 1992, former president and CPPCC chairman Li Xiannian in June 1992, former Mao secretary Hu Qiaomu in September 1992, and Chen Yun in April 1995), the obvious debates within the Party among such leaders as Jiang Zemin, Zhu Rongji, and Qiao Shi make it apparent that neither leadership nor policy agenda has yet been established.

Indeed, the generation that is taking over leadership in China is characterized by its lack of revolutionary legitimacy, its technocratic training, its relatively narrow career paths, its bureaucratic route to power, and its general weakness, both individually and collectively.

The greatest handicap this generation faces in its efforts to establish its leadership and build the sort of institutions that China will need as it moves into the twenty-first century is its lack of revolutionary legitimacy. Although the role of the revolutionary elders remains palpable, their grip is weakening and political leadership, for better or for worse, will fall to the first nonrevolutionary generation of leaders in the history of the PRC. If they can establish their authority, they may be less ideological and less conflictual than their elders, but establishing their authority will not be easy. They lack legitimacy not only in the eyes of society, but in the eyes of their colleagues. There is, in short, no particular reason why leaders of similar age and experience, not to mention those who are older, will defer to people like Jiang Zemin and Li Peng.[196] Moreover, the new generation of leaders cannot count on institutional authority to bolster their leadership. Thus, they will pay a price for the most unfortunate legacy of the Mao and Deng eras, namely the failure to build sound and credible institutions.

This generation is also typified by its technical and bureaucratic backgrounds. Much of this successor generation has been trained as engineers. Jiang Zemin spent most of his career in electrical engineering, and Li Peng built his in the hydroelectric power industry, climbing the ladder of specialized bureaucratic systems step by step.

196 The unnamed son of "one of China's most famous military leaders" was quoted in *The New York Times* on 15 December 1995 as saying that if Jiang Zemin did not stand up for Chinese sovereignty, he "could be changed. It would not be a big thing. We have a collective leadership."

These career paths underscore other major differences between this successor generation and its revolutionary elders. People of Deng Xiaoping's generation were largely political generalists. There were very few who did not participate in a whole range of military, political, organizational, and ideological affairs. The revolutionary elders were also supremely self-confident people. They had engaged in one of history's great revolutionary struggles, "overturning heaven and earth" in their quest to create a new order. Both Mao and Deng had the confidence to launch bold experiments, believing that whatever happened they would be able to maintain control.

In contrast, the leaders of the third generation are products of that new order. They have risen, usually slowly and step by step, through a system that allows little imagination and creativity and demands great obedience to and respect for higher-ups and elders. They give little indication of being bold and innovative people.

These generational characteristics, combined with the divisions within the leadership outlined earler, as well as the problems the Party faces as an institution, its relations with the military, its loss of legitimacy, and the tense relations between the central government and the localities make it possible, as some predict, that the Party will collapse.[197] Indeed, there are plenty of smoldering conflicts in society that could burst into view and challenge the Party's hold on power. Public anger at official corruption appears to be rising once again, peasant anger at local officials has repeatedly boiled over into major and minor confrontations, closing of bankrupt state-owned enterprises could result in large-scale worker layoffs, and the growth of crime and drug-related gangs could all challenge the social and political order. Given the tensions within the Party and the passing of the generation that made the revolution, it is certainly possible that a repetition of the sort of social movement that took place in 1989 could irrevocably divide the Party and bring about its collapse.

However, many of these same developments could, if handled skillfully, facilitate a relatively smooth transition to the post-Deng era. As already suggested, China's nonstate economy has gained a degree of representation either through state agencies that support the interests of nonstate enterprises or through new associations that are set up at least in part to control these new social forces. One can imagine that such organizations could work with more reform-minded people within the regime to establish a more institutionalized, law-based order. With the growth of market forces, the state might

197 See the following articles by Roderick MacFarquhar in *The New York Review of Books*: "The end of the Chinese revolution" (20 July 1989), 8–10; "The anatomy of collapse" (26 September 1991), 5–9; and "Deng's last campaign" (17 December 1992), 22–8. See also the pessimistic portrait of contemporary China in Miles, *The legacy of Tiananmen*.

have no choice but to adapt to the new reality and evolve along the lines of China's neighbors by becoming a "developmental state."[198]

Although current socioeconomic trends may engender a more open, law-based society, it is also possible that current developments could well drive the political system in a more authoritarian direction. Indeed, the very success of reform threatens not only to overwhelm the old planned economy but also to drown the state-owned sector in the process, thereby arousing a counterreaction to defend the state-owned sector at all costs. Traditionally, the defense of the state-owned economy has fallen to conservatives, who have argued in Marxist–Leninist terms about the importance of public ownership and the superiority of planning. In recent years, however, a new breed of neoconservatives has emerged on the scene to argue the same case in different terms. Instead of stressing public ownership in ideological terms, neoconservatives argue in practical terms that state-owned industries support the state and that the state can exercise macroeconomic control only if it can control the "heights of the economy." In short, the state-owned economy is a matter of political control, not of realizing communism. Traditional conservatives were true believers; neoconservatives are pragmatists, albeit authoritarian ones.[199]

Similarly, the decentralization that has been the *sine qua non* of reform has come under attack from neoauthoritarians and neoconservatives alike. Both believe that the economic and political autonomy of the localities threatens the state's ability to exercise macroeconomic and political control over the nation and thus impairs the formulation and implementation of national policy. Decentralization has been accompanied by growing regional inequalities as the areas along China's "gold coast" have begun to take part in the East Asian miracle while hinterland areas remain very much a part of the Third World.

Perhaps of greatest popular salience is the number of peasants who migrate from the rural areas to the cities, which has now reached some 20 million a year. The spectacular growth of rural incomes that typified the early part of reform began to slow in the mid-1980s. As the terms of trade began to tilt increasingly in favor of the cities and as the impediments to migration began to disappear, an increasing number of peasants began seeking work, temporary or permanent, in the cities. In recent years, this flood of migrant workers has begun to overwhelm urban resources and to accelerate urban crime. The result has been intense urban hostility toward

198 This is the scenario projected by William Overholt in his *The rise of China: How economic reform is creating a new superpower.*

199 Fewsmith, "Neoconservatism and the end of the Dengist era."

these newcomers, and demands that national and local authorities take measures to stem the tide.[200]

Urban resentment of the influx of peasants from the countryside was one of the central issues explored (and exploited) in 1994's surprise best-seller, *Looking at China through the third eye.* The book argues that rural reforms have threatened the future stability of China by releasing peasants from their existence of semistarvation and bondage to the commune and by raising their expectations. Once the peasants filled their bellies, the book contends, they continuously raised new demands – and have begun leaving the land in order to fulfill their hopes. The result has been an immense floating population, which has led to urban crime and constitutes a "living volcano" threatening the stability of Chinese society and state.[201]

Neoconservatives, such as the author of *The third eye,* argue that reform is now careening out of control, with the result that social dissolution and class conflict have emerged and are likely to culminate in a social explosion.[202] In order to arrest such trends, neoconservatives call for a restoration of central authority, frequently invoking the need for a unifying ideology. Indeed, Jiang Zemin himself recognized such a need when he commented that while the first generation of communist leaders (led by Mao) created the theory of revolutionary socialism and the second generation (led by Deng) developed the theory of building socialism with Chinese characteristics, the third generation (of which Jiang is supposedly the core) has not yet put its ideological stamp on Chinese politics.[203] Indeed, one can read Jiang's speech to the 1995 Fifth Plenum, discussed earlier, as a bid to define such a vision.

THE LEGACY OF DENG XIAOPING

It is beyond question that Deng Xiaoping has done more than any other figure in modern Chinese history to realize the century-old dream of attaining wealth and power. With the not insignificant exceptions of a short war with Vietnam in 1979 and the Tiananmen crackdown in 1989, the eighteen years during which Deng has presided over China's affairs has marked the longest stretch of domestic and foreign tranquillity in China's modern history. When Deng came to power in 1978, per capita peasant income was a

200 Dorothy Solinger, "China's urban transients in the transition from socialism and the collapse of the communist 'urban public goods regime,' " *Comparative Politics* (January 1995), 127–46; and idem, "China's transients and the state: A form of civil society?" *Politics and Society,* 21.1 (March 1993), 91–122.

201 Luo yi ning ge er, *Disanzhi yanjing kan Zhongguo* (Looking at China through the third eye; hereafter, *The third eye*), 28, 60–3. Joseph Fewsmith, "Review of *Looking at China through the third eye,*" *Journal of Contemporary China,* 7 (Fall 1994), 100–4.

202 *The third eye,* 178. 203 *Hong Kong Standard,* 8 April 1995.

mere 132 yuan ($66 at the then-prevailing exchange rate), and fully one-quarter of China's rural population had a per capita income of less than 50 yuan. The urban population fared better, with an average per capita income of 383 yuan, but workers' salaries had actually been falling – by some 19 percent – since the beginning of the Cultural Revolution. In 1995 rural income had risen to 1,578 yuan, and urban income to 3,893 yuan.[204]

The statistics, of course, tell only part of the story, and in many ways the less significant part of the story. The transformation of Chinese society over those eighteen years has been no less startling – and far more benevolent – than the changes in Chinese society over which Mao Zedong presided. Politically, the beginning of the Dengist era was marked by the slogans "Seek truth from facts" and "Practice is the sole criterion of truth." It was nothing less than an effort to save the Party and the country from the man who had done more than any other to lead the Party to victory only to convulse it and the nation it ruled in turmoil.

Deng sought to "refunctionalize" the ideology of the Party by moving away from the radical, dysfunctional ideology of Mao and to ensure party control by upholding the four cardinal principles.[205] In contrast to the Cultural Revolution's struggle between two lines, Deng sought to carve out a middle course by struggling against both fronts (Left and Right).[206] But as many have pointed out, steering a middle course has been difficult; reform has unleashed many forces that threaten to overturn the institutions that freed them.[207]

As this chapter and Richard Baum's contribution (Chapter 5) show, the conflicts generated in the reform period have been both within the Party and between the Party–state and society; moreover, these different axes of conflict have interacted as different elements within the Party have adopted different stances vis-à-vis the pressures emanating from society.

Deng's greatest failing, as many have pointed out, has been his unwillingness or inability to address these pressures and conflicts adequately. This has been a failure not only to incorporate new demands into the system but, even more important, to address fundamental flaws in China's political system, flaws that are not limited to post-1949 politics. The central problem that Chinese politics must deal with is the assumption that political power is unified, monistic, and indivisible.[208] Instead of political conflicts being

204 *Zhongguo tongji zheyao, 1995,* 51; and State Statistical Bureau, "Intensify reform."

205 The term "refunctionalize" is from Peter Ludz, *Changing party elites in East Germany.*

206 Tang Tsou, "Political change and reform: The middle course," in Tang Tsou, ed., *The cultural revolution and post-Mao reforms: A historical perspective,* 219–58.

207 Gordon White, *Riding the tiger: The politics of economic reform in post-Mao China.*

208 Tang Tsou, "The Tiananmen tragedy," in Brantly Womack, ed., *Contemporary Chinese politics in historical perspective,* 265–327.

resolved through bargaining and compromise, they become part of a game to "win all."[209] In an earlier period, this underlying dynamic led to the split in the CCP leadership and ultimately to the Cultural Revolution. In the early reform period, Deng appeared to begin to address this political problematic by deemphasizing the role of ideology; what was or was not "socialist" would be decided not through polemics but rather through practice. This strategy reflected Deng's own impatience with ideological disputation, resonated with a long-suffering society's desire to return to normal patterns of life, and served to build a broad coalition within a Party shattered by a decade of turmoil.

Deng's understanding of the flaws within the Party and his apparent desire to address them, as reflected in his landmark 1980 speech, "On the reform of the Party and state leadership system," were ultimately submerged by the constraints of the political system itself as Deng fell back on long-standing patterns of political behavior to rule China.[210] Differences of opinion within the Party were not reconciled through a politics of compromise but rather became tectonic forces whose shifts would slowly undermine the Party's surface calm. Fault lines within the Party clearly deepened following the 1984 adoption of the "Decision on the reform of the economic structure" as Deng moved decisively away from the limited notion of economic reform championed by Chen Yun in the early years of reform. The constant barrage of conservative criticism that accompanied Zhao Ziyang's largely successful effort to transform China's economic system reflected the clashing of these subterranean forces, forces that would shift violently in the spring of 1989 and result in the deep fissures within the Party that are chronicled in this chapter.

Deng emerged victorious in this his final struggle, but it is evident from his struggle to regain ascendancy that the rules of political conflict remain largely unchanged in China. Thus, it is evident that Deng has not bequeathed a fundamentally transformed political system – either with regard to intra-Party conflict or between the Party–state and society – to go along with the transformed economic system that he has wrought. Thus, the question that remains as we assess Deng's legacy is whether he has created conditions that will allow the next generation of leaders to tackle the problems of China's political system that he himself did not resolve. From the vantage point of the present it appears that he has not. Deng accomplished many things in his eighteen years at the top of the political system; alas, institution building was not one of them.

209 The most elegant presentation of this thesis is Tsou, "Chinese politics at the top."

210 Lucian W. Pye, "An introductory profile: Deng Xiaoping and China's political culture," *CQ*, 135 (September 1993), 413–43.

APPENDIXES: LEADERS AND MEETINGS

APPENDIX 1
Party leadership, 1945–65

Seventh Congress[a] Yan'an 23 April–11 June 1945			Eighth Congress[g] Beijing 15–27 Sept. 1956
	Politburo	*Full members*	
MAO ZEDONG[b]	*Secretariat*	*Standing Committee*	**MAO ZEDONG**[b]
Zhu De			**Liu Shaoqi**[c]
Liu Shaoqi			**Zhou Enlai**[c]
Zhou Enlai			**Zhu De**[c]
Ren Bishi[d]			**Chen Yun**[c]
			Lin Biao[c,h]
Chen Yun[d]		*General Secretary*	Deng Xiaoping
Kang Sheng			
Gao Gang[e]			Lin Boqu[j]
Peng Zhen			Dong Biwu
Dong Biwu			Peng Zhen
Lin Boqu			Luo Ronghuan[k]
Zhang Wentian			Chen Yi
Peng Dehuai			Li Fuchun
Lin Biao[f]			Peng Dehuai
Deng Xiaoping[f]			Liu Bocheng
			He Long
			Li Xiannian
			Ke Qingshi[i]
			Li Jingquan[i]
			Tan Zhenlin[i]
			Alternate members
			Ulanfu
			Zhang Wentian
			Lu Dingyi
			Chen Boda
			Kang Sheng
			Bo Yibo

[a] Chosen at the Seventh CC's First Plenum after the CCP's Seventh Congress and added it to at its Fifth Plenum after the CCP National Conference in 1955.
[b] CC chairman; boldface capitalization indicates the party leader.
[c] CC vice-chairmen are noted in boldface.
[d] Ren Bishi died in 1950; Chen Yun took his place in the Secretariat.
[e] Gao Gang's purge and suicide were announced at the 1955 National Conference.
[f] Entered the Polititburo at the Seventh CC's Fifth Plenum.
[g] Chosen at the Eight CC's First Plenum after the CCP's Eighth Congress in 1956 and added to it at the Eighth CC's Fifth Plenum after the end of the second session of the Eighth Congress in 1958.
[h] Lin Biao was promoted to the PSC at the Eighth CC's Fifth Plenum.
[i] Entered the Politburo at the Eighth CC's Fifth Plenum; Ke Qingshi died in 1965.
[j] Died in 1960.
[k] Died in 1963.

APPENDIX 2
Party leadership, 1965–73[a]

Eve of Cultural Revolution, 1965	11th Plenum, 8th CC 1–12 Aug. 1966	Ninth Congress, 1–24 Apr. 1969
	Politburo Standing Committee	
MAO ZEDONG[b]	**MAO ZEDONG**[b]	**MAO ZEDONG**[b]
Liu Shaoqi[c]	**Lin Biao**[c]	**Lin Biao**[c,g]
Zhou Enlai[c]	Zhou Enlai	Zhou Enlai
Zhu De[c]	Tao Zhu	Chen Boda[h]
Chen Yun[c]	Chen Boda	Kang Sheng
Lin Biao[c]	Deng Xiaoping	
Deng Xiaoping[d]	Kang Sheng	
	Liu Shaoqi	
	Zhu De	
	Li Fuchun	
	Chen Yun	
	Full members[e]	
Dong Biwu	Dong Biwu	Ye Qun[g]
Peng Zhen	Chen Yi	Ye Jianying
Chen Yi	Liu Bocheng	Liu Bocheng
Li Fuchun	He Long	Jiang Qing
Peng Dehuai[f]	Li Xiannian	Zhu De
Liu Bocheng	Li Jingquan	Xu Shiyou
He Long	Tan Zhenlin	Chen Xilian
Li Xiannian	Xu Xiangqian	Li Xiannian
Li Jingquan	Nie Rongzhen	Li Zuopeng[g]
Tan Zhenlin	Ye Jianying	Wu Faxian[g]
		Zhang Chunqiao
		Qiu Huizuo[g]
		Yao Wenyuan
		Huang Yongsheng[g]
		Dong Biwu
		Xie Fuzhi[i]
	Alternate members[e]	
Ulanfu	Ulanfu	Ji Dengkui
Zhang Wentian[f]	Bo Yibo	Li Xuefeng
Lu Dingyi	Li Xuefeng	Li Desheng
Chen Boda	Song Renqiong	Wang Dongxing
Kang Sheng	Xie Fuzhi	
Bo Yibo		

[a] The precise date on which a leader lost his post during the early period of the Cultural Revolution is not easy to establish.

[b] CC chairman; boldface capitalization indicates the party leader.

[c] CC vice-chairmen are noted in boldface.

[d] General Secretary.

[e] Mao and Lin Biao apart, full and alternate members of the post–Ninth Congress Politburo were listed by the number of strokes in the characters of their names and are so listed here, except for the PSC, whose ranking is easy to pinpoint.

[f] Criticized at Eighth CC's Eighth Plenum; inactive thereafter.

[g] Lin Biao and Ye Qun died in a plane crash on 13 September 1971 while fleeing the country; Li, Wu, Qiu, and Huang were arrested on 24 September 1971.

[h] Disgraced at Tenth CC's Second Plenum.

[i] Died in 1972.

APPENDIX 3
Party leadership, 1973–87

Tenth Congress 24–28 Aug. 1973	Eleventh Congress 12–18 Aug. 1977	Twelfth Congress 1–11 Sep. 1982
	Politburo *Standing Committee*	
MAO ZEDONG[a,o]	**HUA GUOFENG**[a,l]	**HU YAOBANG**[b]
Zhou Enlai[c,o]	**Ye Jianying**[c]	Ye Jianying[q]
Wang Hongwen[c,d]	**Deng Xiaoping**[c]	Deng Xiaoping
Kang Sheng[c,p]	**Li Xiannian**[c]	Zhao Ziyang
Ye Jianying[c]	**Wang Dongxing**[c,k]	Li Xiannian
Li Desheng[c,f]	**Chen Yun**[c,b]	Chen Yun
Zhu De[e,o]		
Zhang Chunqiao[e,d]		
Dong Biwu[e,p]		
Deng Xiaoping[f,c]		
	Full members[e]	
Wei Guoqing	Wei Guoqing	Wan Li
Liu Bocheng	Ulanfu	Xi Zhongxun
Jiang Qing[d]	Fang Yi	Wang Zhen[q]
Xu Shiyou	Liu Bocheng	Wei Guoqing[q]
Hua Guofeng	Xu Shiyou	Ulanhu[n,q]
Ji Dengkui	Ji Dengkui[k]	Fang Yi
Wu De	Su Zhenhua	Deng Yingchao[q]
Wang Dongxing	Li Desheng	Li Desheng[q]
Chen Yonggui	Wu De[k]	Yang Shangkun
Chen Xilian	Yu Qiuli	Yang Dezhi
Li Xiannian	Zhang Tingfa	Yu Qiuli
Yao Wenyuan[d]	Chen Yonggui	Song Renqiong[q]
	Chen Xilian[k]	Zhang Tingfa[q]
	Geng Biao	Hu Qiaomu
	Nie Rongzhen	Nie Rongzhen[q]
	Ni Zhifu	Ni Zhifu
	Xu Xiangqian	Xu Xiangqian[q]
	Peng Chong	Peng Zhen
	Deng Yingchao[b]	Liao Chengzhi[r]
	Hu Yaobang[b,j,l]	Tian Jiyun[s]
	Wang Zhen[b]	Qiao Shi[s]
	Peng Zhen[i]	Li Peng[s]
		Wu Xueqian[s]
		Hu Qili[s]
	Alternate members[g]	
Wu Guixian	Chen Muhua	Yao Yilin[t]
Su Zhenhua	Zhao Ziyang[i,j,m]	Qin Jiwei
Ni Zhifu	Saifudin	Chen Muhua
Saifudin		

[a] CC chairman; boldface capitalization indicates the CCP leader. Mao Zedong died on 9 September 1976, and Hua Guofeng became chairman on 7 October 1976. He was replaced by Hu Yaobang at the Sixth Plenum (27–29 June 1981) of the Eleventh CC.
[b] General Secretary; boldface capitalization indicates CCP leader. This congress abolished the chairmanship in favor of the post of general secretary.
[c] CC vice-chairmen are indicated in boldface.
[d] The Gang of Four was arrested on 6 October 1976.
[e] These members were listed in stroke order.
[f] Deng Xiaoping was reappointed to the Politburo in December 1973 and to the PSC as a vice-chairman at the Tenth CC's Second Plenum (8–10 January 1975), on the latter occasion apparently in

Notes to Appendix 3 (*cont.*)

place of Li Desheng, who reverted to full Politburo member.
[g] Alternate members were listed in stroke order except at the Twelfth Congress, when they were listed in order of the number of votes received.
[h] Appointed at the Eleventh CC's Third Plenum (18–22 December 1978).
[i] Appointed full member at the Eleventh CC's Fourth Plenum (25–28 September 1979).
[j] Appointed member of the SC at the Eleventh CC's Fifth Plenum (23–29 February 1980).
[k] Dismissed at the Eleventh CC's Fifth Plenum.
[l] Hu Yaobang replaced Hua Guofeng as chairman at the Eleventh CC's Sixth Plenum (27–29 June 1981). Hua was reduced to vice-chairman.
[m] Appointed a vice-chairman at the Eleventh CC's Sixth Plenum.
[n] Romanization was changed between congresses.
[o] Died in 1976.
[p] Died in 1975.
[q] Resigned at the Twelfth CC's Fourth Plenum.
[r] Died in 1983.
[s] Appointed at the Twelfth CC's Fifth Plenum.
[t] Promoted to full membership at the Twelfth CC's Fifth Plenum.

APPENDIX 4
Party leadership, 1987–92

Thirteenth Congress 25 Oct.–1 Nov. 1987	Fourteenth Congress 12–18 Oct. 1992
Politburo	
Standing Committee	
Zhao Ziyang[a,b]	**Jiang Zemin**[a]
Li Peng	Li Peng
Qiao Shi	Qiao Shi
Hu Qili[b]	Li Ruihuan
Yao Yilin	Zhu Rongji
	Liu Huaqing
	Hu Jintao
Full members[f]	
Wan Li	Ding Guang'en
Tian Jiyun	Tian Jiyun
Jiang Zemin[c,d]	Li Tieying
Li Ruihuan[c]	Yang Baibing
Yang Rudai	Wu Bangguo
Yang Shangkun	Zou Jiahua
Wu Xueqian	Chen Xitong
Song Ping[c]	Jiang Chunyun
Hu Yaobang[e]	Qian Qichen
Qin Jiwei	Wei Jianxing
	Xie Fei
	Tan Shaowen[g]
Alternate members[f]	
Ding Guang'en	Wang Hanbin
	Wen Jiabao

[a] General Secretary; bold capitalization indicates CCP leader.
[b] Dismissed at Thirteenth CC's Fourth Plenum, 23–24 June, 1989.
[c] Promoted to PSC at Thirteenth CC's Fourth Plenum.
[d] Made General Secretary at Thirteenth CC's Fourth Plenum.
[e] Died 15 April 1989.
[f] Full and alternate members were listed in stroke order.
[g] Died 3 February 1993.

APPENDIX 5
State leaders, 1949–75[a]

1949 PRC Central People's Goverment Council	1954 PRC	1959 PRC	1965 PRC
	Head of State		
MAO ZEDONG[b]	**MAO ZEDONG**[b]	**LIU SHAOQI**[b]	**LIU SHAOQI**[b,e]
	Vice Heads of State		
ZHU DE[b]	**ZHU DE**[b]	Song Qingling	Song Qingling[e]
Song Qingling		**DONG BIWU**[b]	**DONG BIWU**[b,e]
Zhang Lan			
LIU SHAOQI[b]			
Li Jishen			
GAO GANG[b]			
	Chairman NPC		
	LIU SHAOQI[b]	**ZHU DE**[b]	**ZHU DE**[b]
Government Administration Council		*State Council*	
	Premier		
ZHOU ENLAI[b]	**ZHOU ENLAI**[b]	**ZHOU ENLAI**[b]	**ZHOU ENLAI**[b]
	Vice-Premiers		
DONG BIWU[b]	**CHEN YUN**[b]	**CHEN YUN**[b]	**LIN BIAO**[b]
Guo Moruo	Lin Biao	**LIN BIAO**[b]	**CHEN YUN**[b]
CHEN YUN[b]	**PENG DEHUAI**[b]	**PENG DEHUAI**[b]	**DENG XIAOPING**[b]
Huang Yanpei	Deng Xiaoping	**DENG XIAOPING**[b]	**HE LONG**[b]
Deng Xiaoping[d]	Deng Zihui	Deng Zihui	**CHEN YI**[b]
	He Long	**HE LONG**[b]	**KE QINGSHI**[b]
	Chen Yi	**CHEN YI**[b]	**Ulanfu**[c]
	Ulanfu	**Ulanfu**[c]	**LI FUCHUN**[b]
	Li Fuchun	**LI FUCHUN**[b]	**LI XIANNIAN**[b]
	Li Xiannian	**LI XIANNIAN**[b]	**TAN ZHENLIN**[b]
	Nie Rongzhen	Nie Rongzhen	Nie Rongzhen
	Bo Yibo	**Bo Yibo**[c]	**Bo Yibo**[c]
		TAN ZHENLIN[c]	**Lu Dingyi**[c]
		Lu Dingyi[c]	Luo Ruiqing
		Luo Ruiqing	Tao Zhu
		Xi Zhongxun	Xie Fuzhi

[a] The Central People's Government Council was appointed at the first session of the Chinese People's Political Consultative Conference (CPPCC), which met 21–30 September 1949. The CPPCC appointed Zhou Enlai premier of the Government Administration Council on 1 October 1949 and appointed the vice-premiers on 19 October 1949. The 1954, 1959, and 1965 appointments were made at the end of the first sessions of the first (15–28 September 1954), second (18–28 April 1959), and third (20 December 1964–4 January 1965) NPCs, respectively.

[b] Names in boldface capital letters indicate members of the Politburo at the time of appointment.

[c] Names in boldface indicate alternate members of the Politburo at the time of appointment.

[d] Appointed in 1952.

[e] These offices effectively disappeared early in the Cultural Revolution. Liu Shaoqi died in November 1969.

APPENDIX 6
State leaders, 1975–93[a]

1975	1978	1983	1988
	Head of State[d]		
		LI XIANNIAN[b]	**YANG SHANGKUN**[b]
	Vice Heads of State[d]		
		ULANHU[b]	Wang Zhen[n]
	Chairman, NPC[d]		
ZHU DE[b]	**YE JIANYING**[b]	**PENG ZHEN**[b]	**WAN LI**[b]
	State Council		
	Premier		
ZHOU ENLAI[b,e]	**HUA GUOFENG**[b,f]	**ZHAO ZIYANG**[b]	**LI PENG**[b]
	Vice-Premiers		
DENG XIAOPING[b]	**DENG XIAOPING**[b,i]	**WAN LI**[b]	**YAO YILIN**[b]
ZHANG CHUNQIAO[b,h]	**LI XIANNIAN**[b,i]	**YAO YILIN**[b]	**TIAN JIYUN**[b]
LI XIANNIAN[b,g]	**XU XIANGQIAN**[b,i]	**LI PENG**[b]	**WU XUEQIAN**[b]
CHEN XILIAN[b]	**JI DENGKUI**[b,k]	**TIAN JIYUN**[b]	Zou Jiahua[m]
JI DENGKUI[b]	**YU QIULI**[b]		Zhu Rongji[m]
HUA GUOFENG[b,e]	**CHEN XILIAN**[b,k]		
CHEN YONGGUI[b]	**GENG BIAO**[b]		
Wu Guixian[c]	**CHEN YONGGUI**[b,i]		
Wang Zhen	**FANG YI**[b]		
Yu Qiuli	**WANG ZHEN**[b,i]		
Gu Mu	Gu Mu		
Sun Jian	Kang Shien		
	Chen Muhua[c]		
	Wang Renzhong[l]		
	CHEN YUN[b,i,l]		
	Bo Yibo[l]		
	Yao Yilin[l]		
	Ji Pengfei[l]		
	Zhao Ziyang[c,f,l]		
	Wan Li[l]		
	Yang Jingren[l]		
	Zhang Aiping[l]		
	Huang Hua[l]		

[a] These appointments were made at the end of the first sessions of the Fourth (13–17 January 1975), Fifth (26 February–5 March 1978), Sixth (6–21 June 1983), and Seventh (25 March–13 April 1988) NPCs, respectively. Dismissals and additional appointments made between these sessions are annotated.

[b] Names in boldface capital letters indicate members of the Politburo at the time of appointment.

[c] Names in boldface indicate alternate members of the Politburo at the time of appointment.

[d] The posts of head of state and vice head of state were abolished in both new state constitutions promulgated at the first sessions of the Fourth and Fifth NPCs, in line with the views expressed by Mao Zedong in 1970. The chairman of the NPC acted as head of state.

[e] Zhou Enlai died on 8 January 1976, and Hua Guofeng became acting premier on 3 February. On 8 April, the *People's Daily* published the decision that he would no longer be "acting," but now would be premier in his own right.

[f] Hua Guofeng was replaced by Zhao Ziyang as premier at the third session (30 August–10 September 1980) of the Fifth NPC.

[g] Li Xiannian was the only vice-premier appointed in 1965 to serve throughout the GPCR; the precise dates of formal dismissal of the others are difficult to establish.

(*Notes continued*)

Notes to Appendix 6 (*cont.*)

[h] Arrested on 6 October 1976.
[i] Resigned in September 1980.
[k] Dismissed in April 1980.
[l] Wang Renzhong was appointed in December 1978; Chen Yun, Bo Yibo, and Yao Yilin in July 1979; Ji Pengfei in September 1979; Zhao Ziyang and Wan Li in April 1980; and Yang Jingren, Zhang Aiping, and Huang Hua in September 1980.
[m] Appointed at the Seventh NPC's Fourth session, April 1991.
[n] Died 12 March 1993.

APPENDIX 7
State leaders, 1993[a]

1993
Head of State
JIANG ZEMIN[b]
Vice Head of State
Rong Yiren
Chairman, NPC[b]
QIAO SHI
State Council
Premier
LI PENG[b]
Vice-Premiers
ZHU RONGJI[b]
Zou Jiahua[c]
Qian Qichen[c]
Li Lanqing

[a] These appointments were made at the Eighth NPC in March 1993.
[b] Names in boldface capital letters indicate members of the PSC at the time of appointment.
[c] Names in boldface indicate members of the Politburo at the time of appointment.

APPENDIX 8
High-level formal[a] Party meetings, 1945–92

CCP Seventh National Congress, Yan'an	23 Apr.–11 June 1945
1st Plenum, 7th CC, Yan'an[b]	19 June 1945
2nd Plenum, 7th CC, Xibaipo (Hebei)	5–13 Mar. 1949
3rd Plenum, 7th CC, Beijing	6–9 June 1950
4th Plenum, 7th CC, Beijing	6–10 Feb. 1954
CCP National Conference, Beijing	21–31 Mar. 1955
5th Plenum, 7th CC, Beijing	4 Apr. 1955
6th Plenum, 7th CC, Beijing	4–11 Oct. 1955
7th Plenum, 7th CC, Beijing	22 Aug., 8, 13 Sep. 1956
CCP Eighth National Congress, Beijing	15–27 Sep. 1956
1st Plenum, 8th CC, Beijing[b]	28 Sep. 1956
2nd Plenum, 8th CC, Beijing	10–15 Nov. 1956
3rd Plenum, 8th CC, Beijing	20 Sep.–9 Oct. 1957
4th Plenum, 8th CC, Beijing	3 May 1958
CCP Eighth National Congress, 2nd sess., Beijing	5–23 May 1958
5th Plenum, 8th CC, Beijing	25 May 1958
6th Plenum, 8th CC, Wuchang	28 Nov.–10 Dec. 1958
7th Plenum, 8th CC, Shanghai	2–5 Apr. 1959
8th Plenum, 8th CC, Lushan	2–16 Aug. 1959
9th Plenum, 8th CC, Beijing	14–18 Jan. 1961
10th Plenum, 8th CC, Beijing	24–27 Sep. 1962
11th Plenum, 8th CC, Beijing	1–12 Aug. 1966
12th Plenum, 8th CC, Beijing	13–31 Oct. 1968
CCP Ninth National Congress, Beijing	1–24 Apr. 1969
1st Plenum, 9th CC, Beijing[b]	28 Apr. 1969
2nd Plenum, 9th CC, Lushan	23 Aug.–6 Sep. 1970
CCP Tenth National Congress, Beijing	24–28 Aug. 1973
1st Plenum, 10th CC, Beijing[b,c]	30 Aug. 1973
2nd Plenum, 10th CC, Beijing	8–10 Jan. 1975
3rd Plenum, 10th CC, Beijing	16–21 July 1977
CCP Eleventh National Congress, Beijing	12–18 Aug. 1977
1st Plenum, 11th CC, Beijing[b]	19 Aug. 1977
2nd Plenum, 11th CC, Beijing	18–23 Feb. 1978
3rd Plenum, 11th CC, Beijing	18–22 Dec. 1978
4th Plenum, 11th CC, Beijing	25–28 Sep. 1979
5th Plenum, 11th CC, Beijing	23–29 Feb. 1980
6th Plenum, 11th CC, Beijing	27–29 June 1981
7th Plenum, 11th CC, Beijing	6 Aug. 1982
CCP Twelfth National Congress, Beijing	1–11 Sep. 1982
1st Plenum, 12th CC, Beijing[b]	12–13 Sep. 1982
2nd Plenum, 12th CC, Beijing	11–12 Oct. 1983
3rd Plenum, 12th CC, Beijing	20 Oct. 1984
4th Plenum, 12th CC, Beijing	16 Sep. 1985
CCP National Conference, Beijing	18–23 Sep. 1985
5th Plenum, 12th CC, Beijing	24 Sep. 1985

(*Continued*)

APPENDIX 8 (*cont.*)

6th Plenum, 12th CC, Beijing	28 Sep. 1986
7th Plenum, 12th CC, Beijing	20 Oct. 1987
CCP Thirteenth National Congress, Beijing	25 Oct.–1 Nov. 1987
1st Plenum, 13th CC, Beijing[b]	2 Nov. 1987
2nd Plenum, 13th CC, Beijing	15–19 Mar. 1988
3rd Plenum, 13th CC, Beijing	26–30 Sep. 1988
4th Plenum, 13th CC, Beijing	23–24 June 1989
5th Plenum, 13th CC, Beijing	6–9 Nov. 1989
6th Plenum, 13th CC, Beijing	9–12 Mar. 1990
7th Plenum, 13th CC, Beijing	25–30 Dec. 1990
8th Plenum, 13th CC, Beijing	25–29 Nov. 1991
9th Plenum, 13th CC, Beijing	5–9 Oct. 1992
CCP Fourteenth National Congress, Beijing	12–18 Oct. 1992
1st Plenum, 14th CC, Beijing[b]	19 Oct. 1992

[a] "Formal" is used to distinguish these meetings from other important high-level meetings, such as Politburo or central work conferences, which often preceded CC plenums.
[b] First Plenums are usually held immediately after national congresses for the purpose of voting formally in the new Politburo and other central organs.
[c] One source gives 31 August, but most others give 30 August.

REFERENCES

"Adhere better to taking economic construction as the center." *RMRB* editorial, 22 February 1992, trans. in *FBIS Daily Report: China*, 24 February 1992, 40–1.

Agence France Presse. Press service.

"Agricultural cooperativization in communist China." *CB*, 373 (20 January 1956), 1–31.

Ahn, Byung-joon. *Chinese politics and the Cultural Revolution: Dynamics of policy processes.* Seattle, Wash. and London: University of Washington Press, 1976.

AJCA. Australian Journal of Chinese Affairs.

Amnesty International. *China: The massacre of June 1989 and its aftermath.* London: 1990.

Amnesty International. *China: Violations of human rights.* London: 1984.

[An Ziwen] An Tzu-wen. "Training the people's civil servants." *PC*, 1 January 1953, 8–11.

AS. Asian Survey.

Ashbrook, Arthur G., Jr. "China: Economic modernization and long-term performance," in U.S. Congress [97th], Joint Economic Committee, *China under the Four Modernizations*, 1.99–118.

Asian Survey: A monthly review of contemporary Asian affairs. Monthly. Berkeley: Institute of East Asian Studies, University of California Press, 1961–. Cited as *AS*.

Asiaweek. Weekly. Hong Kong: Asiaweek Ltd., 1975–.

Associated Press. News service.

Australian Journal of Chinese Affairs, The. Semiannual. Canberra: Contemporary China Centre, Australian National University, 1979–. Cited as *AJCA*.

Bachman, David. "Differing visions of China's post-Mao economy: The ideas of Chen Yun, Deng Xiaoping, and Zhao Ziyang." *AS*, 26.3 (March 1986), 292–321.

[*Baixing*] Pai-hsing. Monthly. Hong Kong: 1981–. Cited as *BX*.

Bao Ruo-wang (Jean Pasqualini) and Chelminski, Rudolph. *Prisoner of Mao.* New York: Coward, McCann, 1973.

Barnett, A. Doak. *Communist China: The early years, 1949–55.* New York: Praeger, 1964.

Barnett, A. Doak, with Ezra Vogel. *Cadres, bureaucracy and political power in communist China.* New York: Columbia University Press, 1967.

Bastid, Marianne. "Economic necessity and political ideals in educational reform during the Cultural Revolution." *CQ,* 42 (April–June 1970), 16–45.

Baum, Richard. *Burying Mao: Chinese politics in the age of Deng Xiaoping.* Princeton, N.J.: Princeton University Press, 1994.

Baum, Richard. "China: Year of the mangoes." *AS,* 9.1 (January 1969), 1–17.

Baum, Richard. "China in 1985: The greening of the revolution." *AS,* 26.1 (January 1986), 30–53.

Baum, Richard. "The Cultural Revolution in the countryside: Anatomy of a limited rebellion," in Thomas W. Robinson, ed., *The Cultural Revolution in China,* 367–476.

Baum, Richard. "Elite behavior under conditions of stress: The lesson of the 'Tang-ch'üan p'ai' in the Cultural Revolution," in Robert A. Scalapino, ed., *Elites in the People's Republic of China,* 540–74.

Baum, Richard. "Modernization and legal reform in post-Mao China: The rebirth of socialist legality." *SICC,* 19.2 (Summer 1986), 69–103.

Baum, Richard. "The perils of partial reform," in Richard Baum, ed., *Reform and reaction,* 1–17.

Baum, Richard. *Prelude to revolution: Mao, the Party, and the peasant question, 1962–66.* New York: Columbia University Press, 1975.

Baum, Richard, ed. *Reform and reaction in post-Mao China: The road to Tiananmen.* New York and London: Routledge, Chapman and Hall, 1991.

"Be more daring in carying out reform." *RMRB* editorial, 24 February 1992, trans. in *FBIS Daily Report: China*, 24 February 1992, 41–2.

Bei Dao. "Terugblik van een balling," in *Het Collective Geheugen: Over Literatuur En Geschiedenis,* 77–84.

Beijing Review. Cited as *BR.* See *Peking Review.*

Beijing wanbao (Beijing Evening News). Daily. Beijing.

Beja, Jean Philippe. "The year of the dog: In the shadow of the ailing patriarch," in Lo Chi Kin, Suzanne Pepper, and Tsui Kai Yuen, eds., *China review, 1995,* ch. 1.

Bennett, Gordon A. *China's Eighth, Ninth, and Tenth Congresses, Constitutions, and Central Committees: An institutional overview and comparison.* Occasional Paper, no. 1. Austin: Center for Asian Studies, University of Texas, 1978.

Bennett, Gordon A., and Montaperto, Ronald N. *Red Guard: The political biography of Dai Hsiao-ai.* New York: Anchor Books, 1972; Garden City, N.Y.: Doubleday, 1971.

Bernstein, Thomas P. "China in 1984: The year of Hong Kong." *AS,* 25.1 (January 1985), 33–50.

Bernstein, Thomas P. *Up to the mountains and down to the villages: The transfer of youth from urban to rural China.* New Haven, Conn.: Yale University Press, 1977.

Binder, Leonard et al., contribs. *Crises and sequences in political development.* Studies in Political Development, no. 7. Princeton, N.J.: Princeton University Press, 1971.

Blecher, Marc J., and White, Gordon. *Micropolitics in contemporary China: A technical unit during and after the Cultural Revolution.* White Plains, N.Y.: M. E. Sharpe, 1979.

Bonavia, David. *Verdict in Peking: The trial of the Gang of Four.* New York: Putnam; London: Burnett Books, 1984.

BR. Beijing Review.

Bridgham, Philip. "The fall of Lin Piao." *CQ,* 55 (July–September 1973), 427–49.

Bridgham, Philip. "Mao's Cultural Revolution: The struggle to seize power." *CQ,* 34 (April–June 1968), 6–37.

Bridgham, Philip. "Mao's Cultural Revolution: The struggle to consolidate power." *CQ,* 41 (January–March 1970), 1–25.

British Broadcasting Corporation. *Summary of world broadcasts. Part 3: The far east.* Caversham Park, Reading: British Broadcasting Corporation, 1939–. Cited as *SWB/FE.*

"Build up a great wall of steel against peaceful evolution." *RMRB* Commentator, 16 August 1991, trans. in *FBIS Daily Report: China,* 19 August 1991, 27–8.

Bujin de sinian (Inexhaustible memories). Beijing: Zhongyang wenxian, 1987.

Burns, John P. "China's governance: Political reform in a turbulent environment." *CQ,* 119 (September 1989), 481–518.

Burns, John P. "Chinese civil service reform: The thirteenth party congress proposals. *CQ,* 120 (December 1989), 739–70.

Burton, Barry. "The Cultural Revolution's ultraleft conspiracy: The 'May 16 Group.' " *AS,* 11.11 (November 1971), 1029–53.

Butterfield, Fox. *China: Alive in the bitter sea.* New York: Bantam Books, 1983; New York: Times Books, 1982.

BX. Baixing.

Cambridge History of China, The (*CHOC*). Vol. 1. *The Ch'in and Han empires, 221 B.C.–A.D. 220,* ed. Denis Twitchett and Michael Loewe (1986). Vol. 3. *Sui and T'ang China, 589–906, Part 1,* ed. Denis Twitchett (1979). Vol. 7. *The Ming Dynasty, 1368–1644, Part 1,* ed. Frederick W. Mote and Denis Twitchett (1988). Vol. 10. *Late Ch'ing 1800–1911, Part 1,* ed. John K. Fairbank (1978). Vol. 11. *Late Ch'ing 1800–1911, Part 2,* ed. John K. Fairbank and Kwang-Ching Liu (1980). Vol. 12. *Republican China 1912–1949, Part 1,* ed. John K. Fairbank (1983). Vol. 13. *Republican China 1912–1949, Part 2,* ed. John K. Fairbank and Albert Feuerwerker (1986). Vol. 14. *The People's Republic, Part 1: The emergence of revolutionary China 1949–1965,* ed. Roderick MacFarquhar and John K. Fairbank (1987). Vol. 15. *The People's Republic, Part 2: Revolutions within the Chinese revolution 1966–1982,* ed. Roderick MacFarquhar and John K. Fairbank (1991). Cambridge: Cambridge University Press.

Carrère d'Encausse, Hélène, and Schram, Stuart Reynolds, comps. *Marxism and Asia: An introduction with readings.* London: Allen Lane, Penguin Press, 1969.

CB. See U.S. Consulate General, *Current Background.*

CCP. *Resolution on CPC history (1949–81).* Beijing: FLP, 1981.

CCP CC Documentary Research Office. Zhonggong zhongyang wenxian yanjiushi.

CCP CC Party History Research Office. Zhonggong zhongyang dangshi yanjiushi.

"CCP Central Committee's notification of the question of propagandizing and reporting on the struggle to seize power," 19 February 1967, in "Collection of documents."

CCP. Chinese Communist Party. Zhongguo gongchandang.

CCP documents of the Great Proletarian Cultural Revolution, 1966–1967. See Union Research Institute.

"The CCP issues Document No. 4, fully expounding expansion of opening up." *DGB*, 18 June 1992, trans. in *FBIS Daily Report: China*, 18 June 1992, 19–20.

CD. China Daily.

"Central authorities urge banks to draw bank loans and stop promoting the bubble economy." *DGB*, 1 July 1993, trans. in *FBIS Daily Report: China*, 1 July 1993, 31–2.

Chan, Anita. "Images of China's social structure: The changing perspectives of Canton students." *World Politics*, 34.3 (April 1982), 295–323.

Chang, Parris H. "From Mao to Hua to Hu to Chao: Changes in the CCP leadership and its rule of the game." *I&S*, 25.1 (January 1989), 56–72.

Chang, Parris H. *Power and policy in China.* University Park: Pennsylvania State University Press, 1978 [1975].

Chang, Parris H. "Provincial Party leaders' strategies for survival during the Cultural Revolution," in Robert A. Scalapino, ed., *Elites in the People's Republic of China,* 501–39.

Chaoliu yuekan. Monthly. Hong Kong: 1987–.

Ch'en, Jerome, ed. *Mao.* Englewood Cliffs, N.J.: Prentice-Hall, 1969.

Ch'en, Jerome, ed. *Mao papers: Anthology and bibliography.* London: Oxford University Press, 1970.

[Chen Jianbing] Chen Chien-ping. "The CCP Central Committee announces 16 measures." *WHB* (Hong Kong), 3 July 1993, trans. in *FBIS Daily Report: China*, 7 July 1993, 12–13.

[Chen Jianbing] Chen Chien-ping. "Zhu Rongji urges paying attention to negative effects of reform." *WHB* (Hong Kong), 13 January 1993, trans. in *FBIS Daily Report: China*, 15 January 1993, 27–8.

Chen Shihui. "Guanyu fandui Gao Gang, Rao Shushi fandang yinmo huodong de wenti" (Questions concerning opposition to the anti-Party conspiratorial activities of Gao Gang and Rao Shushi). In *Jiaoxue cankao, xia.* N.P.: Zhonggong Anhui shengwei dangxiao, December 1980.

Chen Yeping. "Have both political integrity, ability, stress political ability: On criteria for selecting cadres." *RMRB*, 1 September 1991, trans. in *FBIS Daily Report: China*, 6 September 1991, 26–31.

Chen Yuan. "Wo guo jingji de shenceng wenti he xuanze (gangyao)" (China's deep-seated economic problems and choices [outline]). *JJYJ*, 4 (April 1991), 18–26.

[Chen Yun]. *Chen Yun wenxuan (1956–1985)* (Selected works of Chen Yun). Beijing: Renmin, 1986.

Chen Zaidao. "Wuhan 'qierling shijian' shimo" (The beginning and end of the "July 20th incident" in Wuhan). *Gemingshi ziliao,* 2 (September 1981), 7–45.

Cheng Weigao. "Further emancipate the mind and renew the concept, and accelerate the pace of reform and development." *Hebei ribao*, 18 April 1991, trans. in *FBIS Daily Report: China*, 7 June 1991, 60–8.

Chevrier, Yves. "Micropolitics and the factory director responsibility system, 1984–1987," in Deborah Davis and Ezra F. Vogel, eds., *Chinese society on the eve of Tiananmen*, 109–33.

Chi Hsin. *The case of the Gang of Four.* Hong Kong: Cosmos Books, 1977.

Chien Yu-shen. *China's fading revolution: Army dissent and military divisions, 1967–68.* Hong Kong: Centre of Contemporary Chinese Studies, 1969.

China Daily. Beijing: 1981–. [Printed and distributed in Beijing, Hong Kong, New York, et al.] Cited as *CD.*

China Information. Quarterly. Leiden: Documentation and Research Center for Contemporary China, 1986–. Cited as *CI.*

China News Analysis. Fortnightly. Hong Kong: 1953–82; 1984–. [1953–82 issues published by Fr. Ladany.] Cited as *CNA.*

China News Digest (Global News). Daily. Internet Electronic Edition: CND-INFO. LIBRARY. UTA. EDU. Cited as *CND.*

China Quarterly, The. Quarterly. London: Congress for Cultural Freedom (Paris), 1960–8; Contemporary China Institute, School of Oriental and African Studies, 1968–. Cited as *CQ.*

China Review. Monthly. Hong Kong. 1988–90.

China Update. Irregular. Cambridge, Mass.: China Scholars Coordinating Committee, Fairbank Center, Harvard University, 1989–90.

Chinese communist internal politics and foreign policy: Reviews on Reference materials concerning education. Taipei: Institute of International Relations, 1974.

Chinese Law and Government: A journal of translations. Quarterly. Armonk, N.Y.: M. E. Sharpe, 1968–. Cited as *CLG.*

Chinese Literature. Monthly. Beijing: FLP, 1951–.

Chinese Sociology and Anthropology: A journal of translations. Quarterly. Armonk, N.Y.: M. E. Sharpe, 1968–.

Chinese statistical yearbook. See *Zhongguo tongji nianjian.*

Chinese Studies in History: A journal of translations. Quarterly. Armonk, N.Y.: M. E. Sharpe, 1967–. [Formerly *Chinese Studies in History and Philosophy.*]

CHOC. Cambridge history of China, The.

Chong, Woei Lien. "Petitioners, Popperians, and hunger strikers," in Tony Saich, ed., *The Chinese people's movement*, 106–25.

Chong, Woei Lien. "Present worries of Chinese democrats: Notes on Fang Lizhi, Liu Binyan, and the film 'River Elegy.' " *CI*, 3.4 (Spring 1989), 1–20.

Chow Ching-wen. *Ten years of storm: The true story of the communist regime in China.* Westport, Conn.: Greenwood Press, 1960.

Christman, Henry M. *See* Lenin, Vladimir Il'ich.

Chung, Jae Ho. "Central–provincial relations," in Lo Chi Kan, Pepper, Suzanne, and Tsui Kai Yuen, eds., *China review, 1995*, ch. 3.

CI. China Information.

"Circular of [the] Central Committee of [the] CCP [on the Cultural Revolution]," 16 May 1966, in "Collection of documents concerning the Great Proletarian Cultural Revolution."

CLG. Chinese Law and Government.

CNA. China News Analysis.

CND. China News Digest.

"CND Interview with Gao Xin." *CND,* 7–8 April 1991.

Cohen, Jerome A. *The criminal process in the People's Republic of China, 1949–63: An introduction.* Cambridge, Mass.: Harvard University Press, 1968.

"Collection of documents concerning the Great Proletarian Cultural Revolution." *CB,* 852 (6 May 1968).

"Communiqué of the Fifth Plenary Session of the Fourteenth Central Committee of the CCP." *XH,* in *FBIS Daily Report: China*, 28 September 1995, 15–17.

Communist Affairs: Documents and analyses. Quarterly. Guilford, Surrey: Butterworth Scientific, 1982–.

Communist China 1955–1959: Policy documents with analysis. With a foreword by Robert R. Bowie and John K. Fairbank. Cambridge, Mass.: Harvard University Press, 1965.

Comparative Politics. Quarterly. New York: Political Science Program, City University of New York, 1968–.

"Constitution of the Communist Party of China." *BR,* 25.38 (20 September 1982), 14–16.

CQ. China Quarterly, The.

Cremerius, Ruth, Fischer, Doris, and Schier, Peter, eds. *Studentenprotest und repression in China, April–Juni 1989: Analyse, chronologie, dokumente.* Hamburg: Institut für Asienkunde, 1990.

"Crimes behind the power: Analyzing the serious crimes committed by Yan Jianhong." *RMRB*, 14 January 1995, trans. in *FBIS Daily Report: China*, 24 January 1995, 29–31.

Current Background. See U.S. Consulate General.

Current History. 9/year (monthly except June, July, and August). Philadelphia: Current History, Inc., 1914–.

Dagong bao ("L'Impartial"). Hong Kong. Cited as *DGB.*

Dangde jiaoyu (Party education). Tianjin.

Dangshi huiyi baogao ji (Collected reports from the Conference on Party History). Quanguo dangshi ziliao zhengji gongzuo huiyi he jinian Zhongguo gongchandang liushi zhounian xueshu taolun hui mishu chu (Secretariat of the National Work Conference on Collecting Party Historical Materials and the Academic Conference in Commemoration of the Sixtieth Anniversary of the Chinese Communist Party), eds. Beijing: Zhonggong zhongyang dangxiao, 1982.

Dangshi tongxun (Party history newsletter). Bimonthly 1980–4; Monthly 1984–8; Biweekly 1989–. Title changed to *Zhonggong dangshi tongxun.* Beijing.

Dangshi yanjiu (Research on Party history). Beijing: Zhonggong zhongyang dangxiao, 1980–. Also see *Zhonggong dangshi yanjiu.*

Dassu, Marta, and Saich, Tony, eds. *The reform decade in China: From hope to dismay.* London: Kegan, Paul International, 1990.

Daubier, Jean. *A history of the Chinese Cultural Revolution.* Trans. Richard Seaver. Preface by Han Suyin. New York: Vintage Books, 1974.

Davis, Deborah, and Vogel, Ezra F., eds. *Chinese society on the eve of Tiananmen.* Cambridge, Mass.: Council on East Asian Studies, Harvard University, 1990.

"The debate on the neo-authoritarianism." *Chinese Sociology and Anthropology,* 23.2 (Winter 1990–1), 3–93.

"Decision of the CCP Central Committee . . . on resolute support for the revolutionary masses of the left," 23 January 1967, in "Collection of documents concerning the Great Proletarian Cultural Revolution."

"Decision of the CCP Central Committee on some issues concerning the establishment of a socialist market economic structure." *RMRB*, 17 November 1993, trans. in *FBIS Daily Report: China*, 17 November 1993, 22–35.

"Decision of the Central Committee of the Chinese Communist Party concerning the Great Proletarian Cultural Revolution," in "Collection of documents concerning the Great Proletarian Cultural Revolution."

"Decision of the Central Committee of the Communist Party of China concerning some major issues on strengthening Party building." *XH*, 6 October 1994, in *FBIS Daily Report: China*, 6 October 1994, 13–22.

"Decision of the Central Committee of the Communist Party of China on reform of the economic structure," 20 October 1984. *BR,* 27.44 (29 October 1984), I–XVI.

Deng Liqun. *Xiang Chen Yun tongzhi xuexi zuo jingji gongzuo* (Study how to do economic work from Comrade Chen Yun). Beijing: Zhonggong zhongyang dangxiao, 1981.

Deng Liqun. "Xuexi 'Guanyu jianguo yilai dangde ruogan lishi wenti de jueyi' de wenti he huida" (Questions and answers in studying the "Resolution on certain historical questions since the founding of the state"), in *Dangshi huiyi baogao ji,* 74–174.

Deng Xiaoping. "Answers to the Italian journalist Oriana Fallaci," in *Selected works of Deng Xiaoping* (*1975–1982*), 326–34.

Deng Xiaoping. "Dang he guojia lingdao zhidu de gaige" (On the reform of the Party and state leadership system), in *Deng Xiaoping wenxuan (1975–1982)*, 280–302.

[Deng Xiaoping]. *Deng Xiaoping wenxuan 1975–1982.* (Selected works of Deng Xiaoping). Beijing: Renmin, 1983.

Deng Xiaoping. *Deng Xiaoping wenxuan* (Selected works of Deng Xiaoping), vol. 3. Beijing: Renmin, 1993.

Deng Xiaoping. "Disandai lingdao jiti de dangwu zhi ji" (Urgent tasks of the third generation leadership collective), in *Deng Xiaoping wenxuan*, 3.309–14.

Deng Xiaoping. *Fundamental issues in present-day China.* Beijing: FLP, 1987.

Deng Xiaoping. "On opposing wrong ideological tendencies" (27 March 1981), in *Selected works of Deng Xiaoping* (*1975–1982*), 356–9.

Deng Xiaoping. "Gaige kaifang zhengce wending, Zhongguo dayou xiwang" (If China's policy of reform and opening up remains stable, there is great hope for China), in *Deng Xiaoping wenxuan*, 3.315 – 21.

Deng Xiaoping. "Jiesu yanjun de ZhongMei guanxi yao you Meiguo caiqu zhudong" (Resolving the serious situation in Sino-U.S. relations requires that the U.S. take the initiative), in *Deng Xiaoping wenxuan*, 3.330–3.

Deng Xiaoping. "On the reform of the system of Party and state leadership," in *Selected works of Deng Xiaoping (1975–1982)*, 302–25.

[Deng Xiaoping] Teng Hsiao-ping. "Report on the revision of the constitution of the Communist Party of China" (16 September 1956). *Eighth National Congress of the Communist Party of China*. I: 169–228. Beijing: FLP, 1956.

[Deng Xiaoping]. *Selected works of Deng Xiaoping (1975–1982)*. Beijing: FLP, 1984.

Deng Xiaoping. "Uphold the four cardinal principles," in *Selected works of Deng Xiaoping (1975–1982)*, 166–91.

Deng Xiaoping. "Zai jiejian shoudu xieyan budui junyishang ganbu shi de jianghua" (Talk on receiving martial law cadres at the army level and above in the capital), in *Deng Xiaoping wenxuan*, 3.302–8.

Deng Xiaoping. "Zai Wuchang, Shenzhen, Zhuhai dengdi de tanhua yaodian" (Essential points from talks in Wuchang, Shenzhen, Zhuhai, and Shanghai), in *Deng Xiaoping wenxuan*, 3.370–83.

Deng Xiaoping. "Zucheng yige shixing gaige de you xiwang de lingdao jiti" (Organizing a reformist, hopeful leadership collective), in *Deng Xiaoping wenxuan*, 3.296–301.

"Deng Xiaoping's visit to special zones shows China is more open." *WHB* (Hong Kong), editorial, 28 January 1992, trans. in *FBIS Daily Report: China*, 28 January 1992, 23–4.

Deng Zihui. "Zai quanguo disanci nongcun gongzuo huiyi shang de kaimu ci" (Inaugural speech at the third national rural work conference). *Dangshi yanjiu* 2.1, 1981, 2–9.

DGB. *Dagong bao*.

Diao, Richard K. "The impact of the Cultural Revolution on China's economic elite." *CQ*, 42 (April–June 1970), 65–87.

"Did Marx fall, or was he pushed?" *The Economist*, 15 December 1984.

Dittmer, Lowell. "Bases of power in Chinese politics: A theory and an analysis of the fall of the 'Gang of Four.' " *World Politics*, 31.1 (October 1978), 26–60.

Dittmer, Lowell. "China in 1988: The continuing dilemma of socialist reform." *AS*, 29.1 (January 1989), 12–28.

Dittmer, Lowell. "China in 1989: The crisis of incomplete reform." *AS*, 30.1 (January 1990), 25–41.

Dittmer, Lowell. *Liu Shao-ch'i and the Chinese Cultural Revolution: The politics of mass criticism*. Berkeley: University of California Press, 1974.

Dittmer, Lowell. "Patterns of elite strife and succession in Chinese politics." *CQ*, 123 (September 1990), 405–30.

Dittmer, Lowell. "Reform, succession and the resurgence of mainland China's old guard." *I&S*, 24.1 (January 1988), 96–113.

Dittmer, Lowell. "The Tiananmen massacre." *POC*, 38.5 (September–October 1989), 2–15.

Dittmer, Lowell. "The 12th congress of the Chinese Communist Party." *CQ*, 93 (March 1983), 108–24.

Djilas, Milovan. *The new class: An analysis of the communist system.* New York: Praeger, 1957.

Documents of the Chinese Communist Party Central Committee, September 1956–April 1969. See Union Research Institute.

Documents of the Thirteenth National Congress of the Communist Party of China (1987). Beijing: FLP, 1987.

Domes, Jürgen. "The Cultural Revolution and the army." *AS*, 8.5 (May 1968), 349–63.

Domes, Jürgen. *The government and politics of the PRC: A time of transition.* Boulder, Colo.: Westview Press, 1985.

Domes, Jürgen. *The internal politics of China, 1949–1972.* Trans. Rudiger Machetzki. New York: Praeger; London: C. Hurst, 1973.

Domes, Jürgen. "The role of the military in the formation of revolutionary committees, 1967–68." *CQ*, 44 (October–December 1970), 112–45.

Doolin, Dennis J., trans. *Communist China: The politics of student opposition.* Stanford, Calif.: Hoover Institution, 1964.

Dreyer, June Teufel. "The People's Liberation Army and the power struggle of 1989." *POC*, 38.5 (September–October 1989), 41–8.

"East wind brings spring all around: On-the-spot report on Comrade Deng Xiaoping in Shenzhen." *RMRB*, 31 March 1992, trans. in *FBIS Daily Report: China*, 1 April 1992 (supplement), 7–15.

Eastman, Lloyd E. *The abortive revolution: China under Nationalist rule, 1927–1937.* Cambridge, Mass.: Harvard University Press, 1974.

Economist, The. Weekly. London: Economist Newspaper Ltd., 1843–.

Edwards, R. Randle, Henkin, Louis, and Nathan, Andrew J. *Human rights in contemporary China.* New York: Columbia University Press, 1986.

Eighth National Congress of the Communist Party of China. Vol. I: *Documents.* Vol. II: *Speeches.* Beijing: FLP, 1956.

Eleventh National Congress of the Communist Party of China (documents). Beijing: FLP, 1977.

Esquire. Monthly. Chicago: Esquire, Inc., 1933–.

Etzioni, Amitai, ed. *Complex organizations: A sociological reader.* New York: Holt, Rinehart and Winston, 1969 [1961].

Faison, Seth. "The changing role of the Chinese media," in Tony Saich, ed., *The Chinese people's movement*, 145–63.

Fan, K., ed. *Mao Tse-tung and Lin Piao: Post-revolutionary writings.* Garden City, N.Y.: Anchor Books, 1972.

Fan Shuo. "The tempestuous October: A chronicle of the complete collapse of the 'Gang of Four.' " *Yangcheng wanbao*, 10 February 1989, trans. in *FBIS Daily Report: China*, 14 February 1989, 16–22.

Fang, Percy Jucheng, and Fang, Lucy Guinong J. *Zhou Enlai: A profile.* Beijing: FLP, 1986.

Fang Weizhong, ed. *Zhonghua renmin gongheguo jingji dashiji (1949–1980)* (A record of the major economic events of the PRC [1949–1980]). Beijing: Zhongguo shehui kexue, 1984.

Far Eastern Economic Review. Weekly. Hong Kong: Far Eastern Economic Review Ltd., 1946–. Cited as *FEER.*

Fathers, Michael, and Higgins, Andrew. *Tiananmen: The rape of Peking.* London: Doubleday, 1989.

Faxue. Shanghai: Shanghai faxue hui, 1957–.

Faxue yanjiu (Legal Studies). Bimonthly. Beijing: Zhongguo shehui kexue, 1979–.

FBIS. Foreign Broadcast Information Service.

FEER. Far Eastern Economic Review.

Feng Shengbao. "Preparations for the blueprint on political restructuring presented by Zhao Ziyang at the Thirteenth Party Congress." Unpublished paper presented to the Harvard University East Asia Colloquium, July 1990.

Feuerwerker, Albert. *China's early industrialization: Sheng Hsuan-huai (1844–1916) and mandarin enterprise.* Cambridge, Mass.: Harvard University Press, 1958.

Fewsmith, Joseph. *Dilemmas of reform in China: Political conflict and economic debate.* Armonk, N.Y.: M. E. Sharpe, 1994.

Fewsmith, Joseph. "Neoconservatism and the end of the Dengist era." *AS,* 35.7 (July 1995), 635–51.

Fewsmith, Joseph. "Notes on the first session of the Eighth National People's Congress." *Journal of Contemporary China,* 3 (Summer 1993), 81–6.

Fewsmith, Joseph. *Party, state, and local elites in Republican China.* Honolulu: University of Hawaii Press, 1985.

Fewsmith, Joseph. "Reform, resistance, and the politics of succession," in William A. Joseph, ed., *China briefing, 1994,* 7–34.

Fewsmith, Joseph. "Review of *Looking at China through the third eye.*" *Journal of Contemporary China,* 7 (Fall 1994), 100–4.

Field, Robert Michael, McGlynn, Kathleen M., and Abnett, William B. "Political conflict and industrial growth in China: 1965–1977," in U.S. Congress [95th], Joint Economic Committee, *The Chinese economy post-Mao,* 1.239–83.

Fifth session of the Fifth National People's Congress (main documents). Beijing: FLP, 1983.

Foreign Broadcast Information Service. Washington, D.C.: U.S. Department of Commerce, 1941–. Cited as *FBIS.* The *Daily Report* of this agency has appeared in sections designated for specific regions, but the names of these regions have been changed from time to time in a manner that makes it difficult to construct a precise genealogy. These designations have been used at various times: Asia and Pacific, China, Communist China, East Asia, Eastern Europe, Far East, People's Republic of China, USSR, USSR and Eastern Europe. *FBIS* is discussed in *CHOC,* 14.557 et passim.

Foreign Languages Press. Cited as FLP.

"Forward: Explosive economic growth raises warning signal." *JSND,* 10 (1 October 1993), 58–9, trans. in *FBIS Daily Report: China,* 11 January 1994, 49–50.

Francis, Corinna-Barbara. "The progress of protest in China." *AS,* 29.9 (September 1989), 898–915.

Fraser, John. *The Chinese: Portrait of a people.* London: Fontana/Collins, 1982; New York: Summit Books, 1980.

Friedman, Edward. "Permanent technological revolution and China's tortuous path to democratizing Leninism," in Richard Baum, ed., *Reform and reaction,* 162–82.

Gang Zou. "Debates on China's economic situation and reform strategies." Paper presented to the annual meeting of the Association for Asian Studies, Washington, D.C., March 1989.

Gao Gao and Yan Jiaqi. *"Wenhua da geming" shinian shi, 1966–1976* (A history of the ten years of the "Great Cultural Revolution," 1966–1976). Tianjin: Renmin, 1986.

Gao Xin and He Pin. "Tightrope act of Wei Jianxing." *Dangdai*, 23 (15 February 1993), 42–5, trans. in *FBIS Daily Report: China*, 24 February 1993, 24–6.

Gao Xin and He Pin. *Zhu Rongji zhuan* (Biography of Zhu Rongji). Hong Kong: Xinxinwen, 1993.

Gardner, John. *Chinese politics and the succession to Mao.* London: Macmillan, 1982.

Gardner, John. "Educated youth and urban–rural inequalities, 1958–66," in John Wilson Lewis, ed., *The city in communist China,* 235–86.

Garside, Roger. *Coming alive! China after Mao.* New York: McGraw-Hill; London: Andre Deutsch, 1981.

Geming shichao (A transcript of revolutionary poems). 2 vols. Beijing: Dier waiyu xueyuan, 1977.

Gemingshi ziliao (Reference materials of revolutionary history). Quarterly. Shanghai: 1979–. Formerly *Dangshi ziliao* (Reference materials of Party history).

Gittings, John. "Army–Party relations in the light of the Cultural Revolution," in John Wilson Lewis, ed., *Party leadership and revolutionary power in China,* 373–403.

Gittings, John. "The Chinese army's role in the Cultural Revolution." *Pacific Affairs,* 39.3–4 (Fall–Winter 1966–7), 269–89.

Gittings, John. "The 'Learn from the army' campaign." *CQ,* 18 (April–June 1964), 153–9.

Gittings, John. *The role of the Chinese army.* London and New York: Oxford University Press, 1967.

GMRB. Guangming ribao.

Gold, Thomas B. " 'Just in time!' China battles spiritual pollution on the eve of 1984." *AS,* 24.9 (September 1984), 947–74.

Gold, Thomas B. "Party–state versus society in China," in Joyce K. Kallgren, ed., *Building a nation-state,* 125–52.

Gold, Thomas B. "Urban private business and China's reforms," in Richard Baum, ed., *Reform and reaction,* 84–103.

Goldman, Merle. *China's intellectuals: Advise and dissent.* Cambridge, Mass.: Harvard University Press, 1981.

Goldman, Merle. *Sowing the seeds of democracy in China.* Cambridge, Mass.: Harvard University Press, 1994.

Goldman, Merle, with Cheek, Timothy, and Hamrin, Carol Lee, eds. *China's intellectuals and the state: In search of a new relationship.* Cambridge, Mass.: Council on East Asian Studies, Harvard University, 1987.

Gong Yuzhi. "Emancipate our minds, liberate productive forces: Studying Comrade Deng Xiaoping's important talks." *WHB* (Shanghai), 15 April 1992, trans. in *FBIS Daily Report: China*, 20 April 1992, 25–8.

Gongren ribao (Workers' daily). Beijing: 15 July 1949 (suspended 1 April 1967, resumed 6 October 1978–). Cited as *GRRB*.

Goodman, David S. G. *Beijing street voices: The poetry and politics of China's democracy movement*. London and Boston: Marion Boyars, 1981.

Gray, Jack, and Cavendish, Patrick. *Chinese communism in crisis: Maoism and the Cultural Revolution*. New York: Praeger, 1968.

"The Great Proletarian Cultural Revolution: A record of major events – September 1965 to December 1966." JPRS, 42,349 *Translations on Communist China: Political and Sociological Information*, 25 August 1967.

A great trial in Chinese history: The trial of the Lin Biao and Jiang Qing counter-revolutionary cliques, Nov. 1980–Jan. 1981. Beijing: New World Press, 1981.

GRRB. *Gongren ribao*.

Guangming ribao (Enlightenment daily). Beijing: 1949–. Cited as *GMRB*.

"Guanyu Guomindang zaoyao wumie de dengzai suowei 'Wu Hao Qishi' wenti de wenjian" (Document on the problems of the Guomindang maliciously concocting and publishing the so-called 'Wu Hao notice'). *Dangshi yanjiu* 1.1 (1980), 8.

⟨⟨Guanyu jianguo yilai dangde ruogan lishi wenti de jueyi⟩⟩ zhushi ben (xiuding). (Revised annotated edition of the Resolution on certain questions in the history of our party since the founding of the People's Republic). Beijing: Renmin, 1985.

Guo Moruo. *Moruo shici xuan* (Selected poems of [Guo] Moruo). Beijing: Renmin wenxue, 1977.

Guo Moruo. "On seeing 'The monkey subdues the demon.' " *Chinese Literature*, 4 (1976), 44.

Guo Moruo. "Three poems." *Chinese Literature*, 1 (1972), 50–2.

Gurtov, Melvin. "The foreign ministry and foreign affairs in the Chinese Cultural Revolution," in Thomas W. Robinson, ed., *The Cultural Revolution in China*, 313–66.

Halpern, Nina P. "Economic reform, social mobilization, and democratization in post-Mao China," in Richard Baum, ed., *Reform and reaction*, 38–59.

Halpern, Nina P. "Learning from abroad: Chinese views of the East European economic experience, January 1977–June 1981." *Modern China*, 1 (1985), 77–109.

Hamrin, Carol Lee. *China and the challenge of the future: Changing political patterns*. Boulder, Colo.: Westview Press, 1990.

Hamrin, Carol Lee, and Cheek, Timothy, eds. *China's establishment intellectuals*. Armonk, N.Y.: M. E. Sharpe, 1986.

Hamrin, Carol Lee, and Suisheng Zhao, eds. *Decision-making in Deng's China: Perspectives from insiders*. Armonk, N.Y.: M. E. Sharpe, 1995.

Hao Mengbi, and Duan Haoran, eds. *Zhongguo gongchandang liushi nian, xia* (Sixty years of the Chinese Communist Party, part 2). Beijing: Jiefangjun, 1984.

Harding, Harry. *China's second revolution: Reform after Mao*. Washington, D.C.: Brookings Institution, 1987.

Harding, Harry. *The fragile relationship: The United States and China since 1972*. Washington, D.C.: Brookings Institution, 1992.

Harding, Harry. "From China, with disdain: New trends in the study of China." *AS*, 22.10 (October 1982), 934–58.

Harding, Harry. *Organizing China: The problem of bureaucracy, 1949–1976*. Stanford, Calif.: Stanford University Press, 1981.

Harding, Harry. "Reappraising the Cultural Revolution." *The Wilson Quarterly*, 4.4 (Autumn 1980), 132–41.

Harding, Harry, and Gurtov, Melvin. *The purge of Lo Jui-ch'ing: The politics of Chinese strategic planning*. Santa Monica, Calif.: The RAND Corporation, R-548-PR, February 1971.

Hartford, Kathleen. "Socialist agriculture is dead; long live socialist agriculture! Organizational transformations in rural China," in Elizabeth J. Perry and Christine Wong, eds., *The political economy of reform in post-Mao China*, 31–61.

[He Dexu] Ho Te-hsu. "China has crossed the nadir of the valley but is still climbing up from the trough: Liu Guoguang talks about the current economic situation in China." *JJDB*, 38–9 (1 October 1990), 12–13, trans. in *FBIS Daily Report: China*, 12 October 1990, 27–30.

He Pin and Gao Xin. *Zhonggong "taizi dang"* ("Princelings" of the CCP). Hong Kong: Shibao, 1992.

He Yijun, Jiang Bin, and Wang Jianwei. "Speed up pace of reform, opening up." *JFJB*, 25 March 1992, trans. in *FBIS Daily Report: China*, 22 April 1992, 30–3.

[He Yuan] Ho Yuen. "CCP's 'five adherences' and 'five oppositions' to prevent peaceful evolution." *MB*, 29 August 1991, trans. in *FBIS Daily Report: China*, 29 August 1991, 23–5.

Het Collectieve Geheugen: Over Literatuur En Geschiedenis. Amsterdam: DeBalie/Novib, 1990.

Hinton, Harold C., ed. *The People's Republic of China, 1949–1979: A documentary survey*. 5 vols. Wilmington, Del.: Scholarly Resources, Inc., 1980.

History Writing Group of the CCP Kwangtung Provincial Committee. "The ghost of Empress Lü and Chiang Ch'ing's empress dream." *Chinese Studies in History*, 12.1 (Fall 1978), 37–54.

Hongqi (Red flag). Beijing: 1958–88. Cited as *HQ*.

Howe, Christopher, ed. *Shanghai: Revolution and development in an Asian metropolis*. Cambridge: Cambridge University Press, 1981.

HQ. Hongqi.

Hsiung, James C. "Mainland China's paradox of partial reform: A postmortem on Tienanmen." *I&S*, 26.6 (June 1990), 29–43.

Hsu, Robert C. "Economics and economists in post-Mao China." *AS*, 28.12 (December 1988), 1211–28.

Hu Hua. *Zhongguo shehuizhuyi geming he jianshe shi jiangyi* (Teaching materials on the history of China's socialist revolution and construction). Beijing: Zhongguo renmin daxue, 1985.

Hu Yaobang. "Lilun gongzuo wuxu hui yinyan" (Introduction to theoretical work conference), in *Zhonggong shiyijie sanzhong quanhui yilai zhongyang shouyao jianghua ji wenjian xuanbian,* 2. 48–63.

Huainian Zhou Enlai (Longing for Zhou Enlai). Beijing: Renmin, 1986.

Huaqiao ribao (China daily news). New York: 1940–89.

Huangfu Ping. "The consciousness of expanding opening needs to be strengthened." *Jiefang ribao*, 22 March 1991, trans. in *FBIS Daily Report: China*, 1 April 1991, 39–41.

Huangfu Ping. "Reform and opening require a large number of cadres with both morals and talents." *Jiefang ribao*, 12 April 1991, trans. in *FBIS Daily Report: China*, 17 April 1991, 61–3.

Hunter, Neale. *Shanghai journal: An eyewitness account of the Cultural Revolution.* New York: Praeger, 1969; Boston: Beacon Press, 1971.

Huntington, Samuel. *Political order in changing societies.* New Haven, Conn.: Yale University Press, 1968.

Hutterer, Karl. "Eyewitness: The Chengdu massacre." *China Update,* 1 (August 1989), 4–5.

IS. Issues & Studies.

ICM. Inside China Mainland.

"Increase weight of reform, promote economic development: Speech delivered by Wu Guanzheng at the provincial structural reform work conference." *Jiangxi ribao*, 4 May 1991, trans. in *FBIS Daily Report: China*, 12 June 1991, 45–9.

Inside China Mainland. Monthly. Taipei: Institute of Current China Studies, 1979–. Cited as *ICM.*

Issues & Studies. Monthly. Taipei: Institute of International Relations, 1964–. Cited as *IS.*

JB. Jingbao.

Jencks, Harlan. "Party authority and military power: Communist China's continuing crisis." *IS,* 26.7 (July 1990), 11–39.

JFJB. Jiefangjun bao.

[Ji Weige] Chi Wei-ke. "Three new moves on the eve of the Third Plenary Session of the CCP Central Committee; Deng makes new comments on macrocontrol." *JB*, 12 (5 December 1993), 30–4, trans. in *FBIS Daily Report: China*, 8 December 1993, 18–22.

Jiang Zemin. "Correctly handle some major relationships in the socialist modernization drive." XH, 8 October 1995, trans. in *FBIS Daily Report: China*, 10 October 1995, 29–36.

Jiang Zemin. "Zai dang de shisanju wuzhong quanhui shang de jianghua" (Talk to the Fifth Plenary Session of the Thirteenth CCP Central Committee), in *Shisanda yilai*, 2.709–20.

Jiang Zemin. "Zai qingzhu Zhongguo gongchandang chengli qishi zhounian dahuishang de jianghua" (Talk celebrating the seventieth anniversary of the founding of the CCP), in *Shisanda yilai*, 3.1627–60.

Jiang Zemin. "Zai qingzhu Zhonghua renmin gongheguo chengli sishi zhounian dahuishang de jianghua" (Talk celebrating the fortieth anniversary of the establishment of the PRC), in *Shisanda yilai*, 2.609–35.

Jiaoxue cankao: Quanguo dangxiao xitong Zhonggong dangshi xueshu taolun hui, shang xia (Reference for teaching and study: National Party school system's academic conference on CCP history, vols. 1 and 2). N.P.: Zhonggong Anhui shengwei dangxiao, December 1980. Cited as *Jiaoxue cankao, xia.*

Jiefangjun bao (Liberation Army news). 1956–. Cited as *JFJB.*

Jin Chunming. " 'Wenhua da geming' de shinian" (The decade of the "Great Cultural Revolution"), in Zhonggong dangshi yanjiu hui, ed., *Xuexi lishi jueyi zhuanji,* 144–69.

[Jing Wen] Ching Wen. "Abnormal atmosphere in *Renmin ribao.*" *JB*, 178 (5 May 1992), 46–7, trans. in *FBIS Daily Report: China*, 18 May 1992, 22.

Jingbao [Ching Pao]. Monthly. Hong Kong. 1977–. Cited as *JB.*

Jingji daobao (Economic reporter), Weekly, Hong Kong: 1947–. Cited as *JJDB.*

Jingji ribao (Economic daily). Beijing: 1955–. Cited as *JJRB.*

Jingji yanjiu (Economic studies). Bimonthly, 1995–7; monthly, 1958–66, 1978–. Beijing. Cited as *JJYJ.*

Jiushi niandai (The nineties). Monthly. Hong Kong: 1984–. From 1970 to 1983, titled *Qishi niandai* (The seventies). Cited as *JSND.*

JJDB. *Jingji daobao.*

JJRB. *Jingji ribao.*

JJYJ. *Jingji yanjiu.*

Joffe, Ellis. "The Chinese army under Lin Piao: Prelude to political intervention," in John M. H. Lindbeck, ed., *China: Management of a revolutionary society,* 343–74.

Joffe, Ellis. *Party and army: Professionalism and political control in the Chinese officer corps, 1949–1964*. Cambridge, Mass.: East Asian Research Center, Harvard University, 1965.

Joffe, Ellis. "Party and military in China: Professionalism in command?" *POC,* 32.5 (September–October 1983), 48–63.

Johnston, Alastair I. "Party rectification in the People's Liberation Army, 1983–87." *CQ,* 112 (December 1987), 591–630.

Joint Economic Committee. *See* United States Congress.

Joint Publications Research Service (JPRS). Washington, D.C.: U.S. Government. Various series. See Peter Berton and Eugene Wu, *Contemporary China: A research guide.* Stanford, Calif.: Stanford University Press, 1967, 409–30, and M. Oksenberg summary in *CHOC,* 14.557–8. Includes regional, worldwide, and topical translations and reports. Published periodically. The following items are cited in footnotes:

Joint Publications Research Service. *China Area Report (CAR).* 1987–.

Joint Publications Research Service. *Miscellany of Mao Tse-tung Thought. See* [Mao Zedong] Mao Tse-tung. *Miscellany . . .*

Joint Publications Research Service. *Translations on communist China: Political and sociological information.* 1962–8.

Joseph, William A. *The critique of ultra-leftism in China, 1958–1981*. Stanford, Calif.: Stanford University Press, 1984.

Joseph, William A., ed. *China Briefing, 1994*. Boulder, Colo.: Westview Press, 1994.

Journal of Asian Studies. Quarterly (irregular). Ann Arbor: Association for Asian Studies, University of Michigan, 1941–. Cited as *JAS*.

Journal of Communist Studies. Quarterly. London: Frank Cass, 1985–.

Jowitt, Kenneth. "Soviet neotraditionalism: The political corruption of a Leninist regime." *Soviet Studies*, 35.3 (July 1983), 275–97.

JPRS. *See* Joint Publications Research Service.

JSND. *Jiushi niandai*.

Kahn, Joseph F. "Better fed than red." *Esquire*, September 1990, 186–97.

Kallgren, Joyce K., ed. *Building a nation-state: China at forty years*. China Research Monograph, no. 37. Berkeley: Institute of East Asian Studies, University of California, 1990.

Kau, Michael Y. M. [Ying-mao], ed. *The Lin Piao affair: Power politics and military coup*. White Plains, N.Y.: International Arts and Sciences Press, 1975.

Kau, Yi-maw (Ying-mao). "Governmental bureaucracy and cadres in urban China under communist rule, 1949–1965." Ph.D. dissertation, Cornell University, 1968.

Kau, Ying-mao. "The case against Lin Piao." *CLG*, 5.3–4 (Fall–Winter 1972–73), 3–30.

Kelly, David A. "The Chinese student movement of December 1986 and its intellectual antecedents." *AJCA*, 17 (January 1987), 127–42.

Kelly, David A. "The emergence of humanism: Wang Ruoshui and the critique of socialist alienation," in Merle Goldman with Timothy Cheek and Carol Lee Hamrin, eds., *China's intellectuals and the state*, 159–82.

Kessler, Lawrence D. *K'ang-hsi and the consolidation of Ch'ing rule, 1661–1684*. Chicago: University of Chicago Press, 1976.

Khrushchev remembers: The last testament. Trans. and ed. Strobe Talbott, with detailed commentary and notes by Edward Crankshaw. Boston: Little, Brown, 1974; New York: Bantam, 1976.

Kissinger, Henry. *White House years*. Boston: Little, Brown, 1979.

Klein, Donald W., and Clark, Anne B. *Biographic dictionary of Chinese communism, 1921–1965*. 2 vols. Cambridge, Mass.: Harvard University Press, 1971.

Klein, Donald W., and Hager, Lois B. "The Ninth Central Committee." *CQ*, 45 (January–March 1971), 37–56.

Kraus, Richard. "Bai Hua: The political authority of a writer," in Carol Lee Hamrin and Timothy Cheek, eds., *China's establishment intellectuals*, 201–11.

Kuan, H. C. "New departures in China's constitution." *SICC*, 17.1 (Spring 1984), 53–68.

Kuhn, Philip A. *Rebellion and its enemies in late imperial China: Militarization and social structure, 1796–1864*. Cambridge, Mass.: Harvard University Press, 1980 [1970].

Kwong, Julia. "The 1986 student demonstrations in China: A democratic movement?" *AS,* 28.9 (September 1988), 970–85.

Kyodo. News service.

Ladany, Laszlo. *The Communist Party of China and Marxism, 1921–1985: A self-portrait.* Stanford, Calif.: Hoover Institution Press. 1988.

Lam, Willy Wo-lap. *China after Deng Xiaoping.* New York: Wiley, 1995.

Lampton, David M. *The politics of medicine in China: The policy process, 1949–1977.* Boulder, Colo.: Westview Press, 1977.

Lampton, David M., ed. *Policy implementation in post-Mao China.* Berkeley: University of California Press, 1987 [1985].

Lan Zhongping. "Why do we say that special economic zones are socialist rather than capitalist in nature?" *JFJB*, 22 May 1992, trans. in *FBIS Daily Report: China*, 11 June 1992, 25–6.

Landsberger, Stefan R. "The 1989 student demonstrations in Beijing: A chronology of events." *CI,* 4.1 (Summer 1989), 37–63.

LAT. Los Angeles Times.

Latham, Richard J. "The implications of rural reforms for grass-roots cadres," in Elizabeth J. Perry and Christine Wong, eds., *The political economy of reform in post-Mao China, 157–73.*

Lee, Hong Yong. "China's 12th Central Committee." *AS,* 23.6 (June 1983), 673–91.

Lee, Hong-yung. *From revolutionary cadres to party technocrats in socialist China.* Berkeley: University of California Press, 1991.

Lee, Hong Yung. *The politics of the Chinese Cultural Revolution: A case study.* Berkeley: University of California Press, 1978.

Lenin, Vladimir I. "The state and revolution," in Henry M. Christman, ed., *Essential works of Lenin.* New York: Bantam Books, 1966, 271–364.

Lewis, John Wilson. *Chinese Communist Party leadership and the succession to Mao Tse-tung: An appraisal of tensions.* Washington, D.C.: Policy Research Study, U.S. Department of State, January 1964.

Lewis, John Wilson, ed. *The city in communist China.* Stanford, Calif.: Stanford University Press, 1971.

Lewis, John Wilson, ed. *Party leadership and revolutionary power in China.* Cambridge: Cambridge University Press, 1970.

Li Chengrui. "Some thoughts on sustained, steady, and coordinated development." *RMRB*, 20 November 1989, trans. in *FBIS Daily Report: China*, 12 December 1989, 32–4.

Li Hong Kuan. "Ode to the constitution," in David S. G. Goodman, *Beijing street voices: The poetry and politics of China's democracy movement,* 70.

Li Kwok Sing. "Deng Xiaoping and the 2nd field army." *China Review,* 3.1 (January 1990), 40–2.

Li Peng. "Wei woguo zhengzhi jingji he shehui de jinyibu wending fazhan er fendou" (Struggle to take another step for the stable development of China's politics, economics, and society), in *Shisanda yilai,* 2.948–94.

"Li Ruihuan meets with Hong Kong journalists." *DGB*, 20 September 1989, trans. in *FBIS Daily Report: China*, 20 September 1989, 10–12.

Liang Heng and Shapiro, Judith. *Son of the revolution*. New York: Knopf, 1983; New York: Vintage, 1984.

[Liao Gailong] Liao Kai-lung. "Historical experiences and our road of development (October 25, 1980)." *I&S*, 17.10 (October 1981), 65–94; 17.11 (November 1981), 81–110.

Liaowang (Outlook weekly). Weekly. Beijing: 1981–. Cited as *LW*.

Liberation Army News. See *Jiefangjun bao*.

Lieberthal, Kenneth. "The political implications of document no. 1, 1984." *CQ*, 101 (March 1985), 109–13.

Lieberthal, Kenneth. *A research guide to central Party and government meetings in China 1949–1975*. Foreword by Michel Oksenberg. Michigan Papers in Chinese Studies, Special Number. White Plains, N.Y.: International Arts and Sciences Press, 1976.

Lieberthal, Kenneth, with the assistance of James Tong and Sai-cheung Yeung. *Central documents and Politburo politics in China*. Ann Arbor: Center for Chinese Studies, University of Michigan, 1978.

Lieberthal, Kenneth, and Dickson, Bruce J. *A research guide to central Party and government meetings in China 1949–1986*. Armonk, N.Y.: M. E. Sharpe, 1989.

Lifton, Robert Jay. *Revolutionary immortality: Mao Tse-tung and the Chinese Cultural Revolution*. New York: Vintage, 1968.

[Lin Biao] Lin Piao. "Long live the victory of People's War!" *PR*, 8.36 (3 September 1965), 9–30. Also Beijing: FLP, 1965.

"Lin Doudou who lives in the shadow of history." *Huaqiao ribao*, 14–16 June 1988.

Lin Wu. "Deng's faction unmasks face of 'ultraleftists.' " *ZM*, 175 (1 May 1992), 17–18, trans. in *FBIS Daily Report: China*, 12 May 1992, 27–8.

Lindbeck, John M. H., ed. *China: Management of a revolutionary society*. Seattle: University of Washington Press, 1971.

Ling, Ken. *The revenge of heaven: Journal of a young Chinese*. Trans. Miriam London and Lee Ta-ling. New York: Putnam, 1972.

[Ling Xuejun] Ling Hsueh-chun. "Wang Zhen and Li Xiannian set themselves up against Deng." *ZM*, 175 (1 May 1992), 14–15, trans. in *FBIS Daily Report: China*, 12 May 1992, 26.

Lishi jiangyi. See Sun Dunfan et al., eds. *Zhongguo gongchandang lishi jiangyi*.

[Liu Bi] Liu Pi. "Deng Xiaoping launches 'northern expedition' to emancipate mind; Beijing, Shanghai, and other provinces and municipalities 'respond' by opening wider to the outside world." *JB*, 166 (10 May 1991), 24–7, trans. in *FBIS Daily Report: China*, 6 May 1991, 26–9.

Liu Binyan. "Di'erzhong zhongcheng." *Kaituo*, March 1985.

[Liu Shaoqi]. *Collected works of Liu Shao-ch'i, 1945–1957*. Hong Kong: URI, 1969.

Lo Chi Kin, Suzanne Pepper, and Tsui Kai Yuen, eds., *China review, 1995*. Hong Kong: Chinese University Press, 1995.

Los Angeles Times. Daily. Los Angeles: Times Mirror Co., 4 December 1881–. Cited as *LAT*.

Lotta, Raymond, ed. *And Mao makes 5: Mao Tse-tung's last great battle.* Chicago: Banner Press, 1978.

[Lu Minsheng] Lu Ming-sheng. "Inside story of how *Historical trends* was banned." *ZM*, 177 (July 1, 1992), 33–4, trans. in *FBIS Daily Report: China*, 7 July 1992, 19–21.

Ludz, Peter. *Changing party elites in East Germany*. Cambridge, Mass.: MIT Press, 1972.

[Luo Bing] Lo Ping and [Li Zejing] Li Tzu-ching. "Chen Yun raises six points of view to criticize Deng Xiaoping." *ZM*, 171 (1 January 1992), 18–19, trans. in *FBIS Daily Report: China*, 3 January 1992, 22–3.

[Luo Ruiqing] Lo Jui-ching. "Commemorate the victory over German fascism! Carry the struggle against U.S. imperialism through to the end!" *HQ*, 5 (1965), in *PR*, 8.20 (14 May 1965), 7–15.

[Luo Ruiqing] Lo Jui-ching. "The people defeated Japanese fascism and they can certainly defeat U.S. imperialism too." NCNA, 4 September 1965, in *CB*, 770 (14 September 1965), 1–12.

Luo yi ning ge er [pseud.]. *Disanzhi yanjing kan Zhongguo* (Looking at China through the third eye). Taiyuan: Shanxi chubanshe, 1994.

LW. *Liaowang*.

Ma Hong. "Have a correct understanding of the economic situation, continue to do a good job in economic improvement and rectification." *RMRB*, 17 November 1989, trans. in *FBIS Daily Report: China*, 5 December 1989, 37–9.

Ma Shu Yun. "The rise and fall of neo-authoritarianism in China." *CI*, 5.3 (Winter 1990–1), 1–18.

MacFarquhar, Roderick. "The anatomy of collapse." *The New York Review of Books*, 38.9 (26 September 1991), 5–9.

MacFarquhar, Roderick. "Aspects of the CCP's Eighth Congress (first session)." University Seminar on Modern East Asia: China, Columbia University, 19 February 1969.

MacFarquhar, Roderick. "Deng's last campaign." *The New York Review of Books*, 39.12 (17 December 1992), 22–8.

MacFarquhar, Roderick. "The end of the Chinese revolution." *The New York Review of Books*, 36.7 (20 July 1989), 8–10.

MacFarquhar, Roderick. *The origins of the Cultural Revolution, 1: Contradictions among the people 1956–1957*. London: Oxford University Press; New York: Columbia University Press, 1974.

MacFarquhar, Roderick. *The origins of the Cultural Revolution, 2: The Great Leap Forward 1958–1960*. London: Oxford University Press; New York: Columbia University Press, 1983.

MacFarquhar, Roderick. "Passing the baton in Beijing." *The New York Review of Books*, 35.2 (18 February 1988), 21–2.

Mackerras, Colin. " 'Party consolidation' and the attack of 'spiritual pollution.' " *AJCA*, 11 (January 1984), 175–85.

Maier, John H. "Tian'anmen 1989: The view from Shanghai." *CI*, 5.1 (Summer 1990), 1–13.

Major, John S., ed. *China briefing, 1985*. Boulder, Colo.: Westview Press, 1987 [1986].

"Major revisions to the government work report." *WHB* (Hong Kong), 16 March 1993, trans. in *FBIS Daily Report: China*, 16 March 1993, 23–4.

"Make fresh contributions on 'protecting and escorting' reform, opening up, and economic development: Warmly congratulating conclusion of the Fifth Sessions of the Seventh National People's Congress and Seventh Chinese People's Political Consultative Conference." *JFJB*, 4 April 1992, trans. in *FBIS Daily Report: China*, 21 April 1992, 36–7.

Mao. *SW*. *See* [Mao Zedong] Mao Tse-tung. *Selected Works of Mao Tse-tung*.

[Mao Zedong] Mao Tse-tung. *Miscellany of Mao Tse-tung Thought (1949–1968)*. 2 vols. Arlington, Va.: JPRS, Nos. 61269–1 and –2, 20 February 1974. [Trans. of materials from *Mao Zedong sixiang wansui*.]

[Mao Zedong] Mao Tse-tung. "Opening address at the Eighth National Congress of the Communist Party of China" (15 September 1956). *Eighth National Congress of the Communist Party of China*. 1. 5–11.

[Mao Zedong]. *Selected works of Mao Tse-tung* [English trans.]. Beijing: FLP, vols. 1–3, 1965; vol. 4, 1961; vol. 5, 1977. Cited as Mao. *SW*. For the Chinese ed., *see* Mao Zedong, *Xuanji*.

Mao Zedong. *Xuanji* (Selected works). Beijing: Renmin, vols. 1–4, 1960; vol. 5, 1977.

Mao Zedong. "Zai Shanghai shi gejie renshi huiyi shang de jianghua" (Speech at the Conference of All Circles in Shanghai Municipality) (8 July 1957). *Wansui* (1969), 109–21.

Mao Zedong. "Zai Zhonggong zhongyang zhaokai de guanyu zhishi fenzi wenti huiyi shang de jianghua." (Speech at the conference on the question of intellectuals convened by the CCP Central Committee) (20 January 1956). *Wansui* (1969), 28–34.

Mao Zedong sixiang wansui (Long live Mao Zedong Thought). N.p.: n.p., 1969. Cited as *Wansui* (1969).

Massacre in Beijing: China's struggle for democracy. New York: Warner Books, 1989.

Materials Group of the Party History Teaching and Research Office of the CCP Central Party School. See *Zhongguo gongchandang lici zhongyao huiyi ji*.

Maxwell, Neville. "The Chinese account of the 1969 fighting at Chenpao." *CQ*, 56 (October–December, 1973), 730–9.

MB. *Mingbao*.

Meaney, Connie Squires. "Market reform and disintegrative corruption in urban China," in Richard Baum, ed., *Reform and reaction*, 124–42.

Meng Lin. "Deng Liqun reaffirms disapproval of phrase 'Deng Xiaoping thought.' " *JB*, 180 (5 July 1992), 42, trans. in *FBIS Daily Report: China*, 6 July 1992, 28–9.

Miles, James. *The legacy of Tiananmen: China in disarray* (Ann Arbor: University of Michigan Press, 1996).

Mills, William deB. "Generational change in China." *POC*, 32.6 (November–December 1983), 16–35.

Mingbao. Monthly. Hong Kong: 1968–. Cited as *MB*.

Miscellany of Mao Tse-tung Thought. See Mao Zedong.

Modern China: An international quarterly of history and social science. Quarterly. Newbury Park, Calif.: Sage, 1975–.

Munro, Donald J. "Egalitarian ideal and educational fact in communist China," in John M. H. Lindbeck, ed., *China: Management of a revolutionary society,* 256–301.

Munro, Robin. "Who died in Beijing, and why?" *The Nation,* 11 June 1990, 811–22.

Myers, James T. "China: Modernization and 'unhealthy tendencies.' " *Comparative Politics,* 21.2 (January 1989), 193–214.

Nakajima, Mineo. "The Kao Kang affair and Sino-Soviet relations." *Review.* Tokyo: Japanese Institute of International Affairs, March 1977.

Nathan, Andrew J. "Chinese democracy in 1989: Continuity and change." *POC,* 38.5 (September–October 1989), 16–29.

Nation, The. Weekly. New York: Nation Enterprises, 1865–.

Naughton, Barry. "The decline of central control over investment in post-Mao China," in David Lampton, ed., *Policy implementation in post-Mao China.*

Naughton, Barry. *Growing out of the plan: Chinese economic reform, 1978–1983.* Cambridge: Cambridge University Press, 1995.

Naughton, Barry. "Macroeconomic obstacles to reform in China." Paper presented at the Southern California China Colloquium, UCLA, November 1990.

NCNA. New China News Agency.

Nelsen, Harvey W. "Military forces in the Cultural Revolution." *CQ,* 51 (July–September 1972), 444–74.

Nelsen, Harvey W. *The Chinese military system: An organizational study of the Chinese People's Liberation Army.* Boulder, Colo.: Westview Press, 1981 [1977].

Nelsen, Harvey W. "Military bureaucracy in the Cultural Revolution." *AS,* 14.4 (April 1974), 372–95.

Nethercut, Richard D. "Deng and the gun: Party–military relations in the People's Republic of China." *AS,* 22.8 (August 1982), 691–704.

New China News Agency. (*Xinhua she*). Cited as NCNA. See *Xinhua tongxun she.*

"New stage of China's reform and opening to the outside world." *RMRB* editorial, 9 June 1992, trans. in *FBIS Daily Report: China*, 9 June 1992, 17–18.

New York Review of Books, The. 21/yr. New York: NYRB, 1963–.

New York Times, The. Daily. New York: 13 September 1857–. Cited as *NYT.*

[Nie Rongzhen] *Nie Rongzhen huiyi lu* (Memoirs of Nie Rongzhen). 3 vols. Beijing: Jiefangjun, 1983, 1984.

Niming, Frank. "Learning how to protest," in Tony Saich, ed., *The Chinese people's movement,* 83–105.

NMRB. *Nongmin ribao.*

Nongmin ribao. Daily. Beijing.

"Nothing is hard in this world if you dare to scale the heights." *RMRB, HQ, JFJB* joint editorial, 1 January 1976. Trans. in "Quarterly chronicle and documentation." *CQ,* 66 (June 1976), 411–16.

NYT. New York Times.

Observer, The. Daily. London. 1791–.

Oi, Jean C. "Partial market reform and corruption in rural China," in Richard Baum, ed., *Reform and reaction*, 143–61.

Oi, Jean. *Rural China takes off: Incentives for industrialization*. Berkeley: University of California Press, forthcoming.

Oi, Jean C. *State and peasant in contemporary China: The political economy of village government*. Berkeley: University of California Press, 1989.

Oksenberg, Michel. "China's 13th Party congress." *POC*, 36.6 (November–December 1987), 1–17.

Oksenberg, Michel. "The exit pattern from Chinese politics and its implications." *CQ*, 67 (September 1976), 501–18.

Oksenberg, Michel, and Yeung Sai-cheung. "Hua Kuo-feng's pre–Cultural Revolution Hunan years, 1949–1966: The making of a political generalist." *CQ*, 69 (March 1977), 3–53.

Overholt, William. *The rise of China: How economic reform is creating a new superpower*. New York: W. W. Norton, 1993.

Pacific Affairs: An international review of Asia and the Pacific. Quarterly. Vancouver, B.C.: 1926–. Vols. 1–33 published by the Institute of Pacific Relations. Vols. 34 to the present published by the University of British Columbia, Vancouver.

Parish, William L. "Factions in Chinese military politics." *CQ*, 56 (October–December 1973), 667–99.

Peking Review. Beijing: 1958–. Cited as *PR*. (From January 1979, *Beijing Review*.)

Peng Dehuai. *Memoirs of a Chinese marshal: The autobiographical notes of Peng Dehuai (1898–1974)*. Trans. Zheng Longpu; English text edited by Sara Grimes. Beijing: FLP, 1984.

Peng Dehuai. *Peng Dehuai zishu* (Peng Dehuai's own account). Beijing: Renmin, 1981. Translated as *Memoirs of a Chinese marshal*. Beijing: FLP, 1984.

Peng Zhen. "Report on the draft of a revised constitution of the PRC." *BR*, 25.50 (13 December 1982), 9–20.

People's China. Semimonthly. Beijing: 1950–7. Cited as *PC*.

People's Daily. See *Renmin ribao*.

Pepper, Suzanne. *Civil war in China: The political struggle, 1945–1949*. Berkeley: University of California Press, 1978.

Pepper, Suzanne. "Deng Xiaoping's political and economic reforms and the Chinese student protests." *Universities Field Staff International Reports*, 30 (1986).

Perry, Elizabeth J. "Social ferment: Grumbling amidst growth," in John S. Major, ed., *China briefing, 1985*, 39–52.

Perry, Elizabeth J., and Wong, Christine, eds. *The political economy of reform in post-Mao China*. Cambridge, Mass.: Council on East Asian Studies, Harvard University, 1985.

Petracca, Mark, and Xiong, Mong. "The concept of Chinese neo-authoritarianism: An exploration and democratic critique." *AS*, 30.11 (November 1990), 1099–117.

POC. *Problems of Communism*.

Polemic on the general line of the international communist movement, The. Beijing: FLP, 1965.

"Political report" to the Fourteenth Party Congress. Beijing television, trans. in *FBIS Daily Report: China*, 13 October 1992, 23–43.

"The politics of prerogatives in China: The case of the *Taizidang* (Princes' party)." Unpublished manuscript, 1990.

Powell, Ralph I. "Commissars in the economy: The 'Learn from the PLA' movement in China." *AS*, 5.3 (March 1965), 125–38.

PR. Peking Review.

Problems of communism. Bimonthly. United States Information Agency. Washington, D.C.: U.S. Government Printing Office, 1952–1992. Cited as *POC.*

"Promote stability through reform, achieve development through this stability: Basic concepts of development and reform based on 'seeking progress through stability' in the 1990s." *JJYJ*, 7 (20 July 1990), 3–19.

Prybyla, Jan. "Why China's economic reforms fail." *AS*, 29.11 (November 1989), 1017–32.

Pusey, James R. *Wu Han: Attacking the present through the past.* Cambridge, Mass.: East Asian Research Center, Harvard University, 1969.

Pye, Lucian W. "An introductory profile: Deng Xiaoping and China's political culture." *CQ*, 135 (September 1993), 413–43.

Pye, Lucian W. "Tiananmen and Chinese political culture: The escalation of confrontation from moralizing to revenge." *AS*, 30.4 (April 1990), 331–47.

Qiang Yuangan and Lin Bangguang. "Shilun yi jiu wu wu nian dangnei guanyu nongye hezuohua wenti de zhenglun" (A discussion of the debate within the Party in 1955 concerning the issue of agricultural cooperativization). *Dangshi yanjiu* 2.1 (1981), 10–17.

Qishi niandai (The seventies). Monthly. Hong Kong: 1970–1983. Cited as *QSND.* In 1984, title changed to *Jiushi niandai* (The nineties). Cited as *JSND.*

QS. Qiushi.

Qiushi (Seeking Truth). 24/yr. Beijing: July 1988–. Cited as *QS.*

Qiu Zhizhuo. "Deng Xiaoping zai 1969–1972" (Deng Xiaoping in 1969–1972). *Xinhua wenzhai,* 4 (April 1988), 133–55.

QSND. Qishi niandai.

Quanguo dangshi ziliao. . . . See *Dangshi huiyi baogao ji.*

"Quarterly chronicle and documentation." *CQ* in each issue.

Red Flag. See *Hongqi.*

[Ren Huiwen] Jen Hui-wen. "Deng Xiaoping urges conservatives not to make a fuss." *Xinbao*, 1 January 1993, trans. in *FBIS Daily Report: China*, 4 January 1993, 43–4.

[Ren Huiwen] Jen Hui-wen. "Different views within the CCP on the banking crisis." *Xinbao*, 9 July 1993, trans. in *FBIS Daily Report: China*, 12 July 1993, 41–2.

[Ren Huiwen] Jen Hui-wen. "Political Bureau argues over 'preventing leftism.'" *Xinbao*, 14 April 1992, trans. in *FBIS Daily Report: China*, 17 April 1992, 28–9.

[Ren Huiwen] Jen Hui-wen. "There is something behind Chen Yun's declaration of his position." *Xinbao*, 12 May 1992. Trans. in *FBIS Daily Report: China*, 13 May 1992, 21–2.

Renmin ribao (People's Daily). Beijing: 1949–. Cited as *RMRB*.

"Reports from Shenzhen." *BR,* 27.47–28.6 (26 November 1984–11 February 1985).

Research Office of the Supreme People's Court. See *Zhonghua renmin gongheguo. . . .*

"Resolution of the Central Committee of the Communist Party of China on the guiding principles for building a socialist society with advanced culture and ideology." XH, 28 September 1986, trans. in *FBIS Daily Report: China,* 29 September 1986, K2–13.

Resolution on certain questions in the history of our Party since the founding of the People's Republic of China [27 June 1981]. NCNA, 30 June 1981; *FBIS Daily Report: China,* 1 July 1981, K1–38; published as *Resolution on CPC History (1949–1981).* Beijing: FLP, 1981.

Reuters. News service.

Review of Socialist Law. Quarterly. Leiden: 1975–.

Reynolds, Bruce, ed. *Chinese economic policy.* New York: Paragon House, 1989.

Reynolds, Bruce I., ed. and intro. *Reform in China: Challenges and choices.* Chinese Economic System Reform Research Institute, Beijing. Armonk, N.Y.: M. E. Sharpe, 1987.

RMRB. Renmin ribao.

Robinson, Thomas W. "Chou En-lai and the Cultural Revolution," in Thomas W. Robinson, ed., *The Cultural Revolution in China,* 165–312.

Robinson, Thomas W. "The Wuhan Incident: Local strife and provincial rebellion during the Cultural Revolution." *CQ,* 47 (July–September 1971), 413–38.

Robinson, Thomas W., ed. *The Cultural Revolution in China.* Berkeley: University of California Press, 1971.

Rosen, Stanley. "China in 1986: A year of consolidation." *AS,* 27.1 (January 1987), 35–55.

Rosen, Stanley. "The Chinese Communist Party and Chinese society: Popular attitudes toward Party membership and the Party's image." *AJCA,* 24 (July 1990), 51–92.

Rosen, Stanley. *Red Guard factionalism and the Cultural Revolution in Guangzhou (Canton).* Boulder, Colo.: Westview Press, 1982.

Rosen, Stanley. "The rise (and fall) of public opinion in post-Mao China," in Richard Baum, ed., *Reform and reaction,* 60–83.

Rosen, Stanley. "Youth and students in China before and after Tiananmen," in Winston Yang and Marcia Wagner, eds., *Tiananmen: China's struggle for democracy,* 203–27.

Rubin, Kyna. "Keeper of the flame: Wang Ruowang as moral critic of the state," in Merle Goldman with Timothy Cheek and Carol Lee Hamrin, eds., *China's intellectuals and the state,* 233–50.

Saich, Tony. "The fourth constitution of the People's Republic of China." *Review of Socialist Law,* 9.2 (1983), 113–24.

Saich, Tony. "Party consolidation and spiritual pollution in the People's Republic of China." *Communist Affairs,* 3.3 (July 1984).

Saich, Tony. "The People's Republic of China," in W. B. Simons and S. White, eds., *The party statutes of the communist world,* 83–113.

Saich, Tony. "The reform decade in China: The limits to revolution from above," in Marta Dassu and Tony Saich, eds., *The reform decade in China,* 10–73.

Saich, Tony. "The rise and fall of the Beijing people's movement." *AJCA,* 24 (July 1990), 181–208.

Saich, Tony. "The thirteenth congress of the Chinese Communist Party: An agenda for reform?" *Journal of Communist Studies,* 4.2 (June 1988).

Saich, Tony. "Urban society in China." Paper presented to the International Colloquium on China, Saarbrucken, 1990.

Saich, Tony, ed. *The Chinese people's movement: Perspectives on spring 1989.* Armonk, N.Y.: M. E. Sharpe, 1990.

Scalapino, Robert A. "The transition in Chinese Party leadership: A comparison of the Eighth and Ninth Central Committees," in Robert A. Scalapino, ed., *Elites in the People's Republic of China,* 67–148.

Scalapino, Robert A., ed. *Elites in the People's Republic of China.* Seattle: University of Washington Press, 1972.

Schiele, R.N. "Jiang's men move out of the shadows." *Eastern Express*, 27 December 1994.

Schram, Stuart. "China after the 13th congress." *CQ,* 114 (June 1988), 177–97.

Schram, Stuart [R.]. " 'Economics in command?' Ideology and policy since the Third Plenum, 1978–1984." *CQ,* 99 (September 1984), 417–61.

Schram, Stuart R. "From the 'Great Union of the Popular Masses' to the 'Great Alliance.' " *CQ,* 49 (January–March 1972), 88–105.

Schram, Stuart R. *The political thought of Mao Tse-tung.* New York: Praeger, 1969 [1963].

Schram, Stuart R., ed. *Authority, participation and cultural change in China.* Cambridge: Cambridge University Press, 1973.

Schram, Stuart R., ed. *Chairman Mao talks to the people. See* Schram, Stuart R., ed., *Mao Tse-tung unrehearsed.*

Schram, Stuart R., ed. *Mao Tse-tung unrehearsed: Talks and letters, 1956–71.* Middlesex, Eng.: Penguin Books, 1974. Published in the United States as *Chairman Mao talks to the people: Talks and letters, 1956–1971.* New York: Pantheon, 1975.

Schurmann, Franz H. *Ideology and organization in communist China.* Berkeley and Los Angeles: University of California Press, 1968 [1966].

SCMM. See U.S. Consulate General (Hong Kong). *Selections from China Mainland Magazines.*

SCMP. See U.S. Consulate General (Hong Kong). *Survey from China Mainland Press.*

Selected Studies on Marxism. Irregular. Beijing: Institute of Marxism-Leninism and Mao Zedong Thought, 1981–.

Seybolt, Peter J., ed. *Revolutionary education in China: Documents and commentary.* White Plains, N.Y.: International Arts and Sciences Press, 1973.

Seymour, James D. "Cadre accountability to the law." *AJCA,* 21 (January 1989), 1–27.

Shambaugh, David L. "The fourth and fifth plenary sessions of the 13th CCP Central Committee." *CQ,* 120 (December 1989), 852–62.

Shao Huaze. "Guanyu 'wenhua da geming' de jige wenti" (On several questions concerning the "Great Cultural Revolution"), in *Dangshi huiyi baogao ji*, 337–92.

Shehui kexue. Cited as *SHKX*.

Shi Bonian and Liu Fang. "Unswervingly implement the Party's basic line." *JFJB*, 18 March 1992, trans. in *FBIS Daily Report: China*, 15 April 1992, 44–7.

Shi Jingtang et al., eds. *Zhongguo nongye hezuohua yundong shiliao* (Historical materials on China's cooperatization movement). Beijing: Sanlian shudian, 1957.

Shi Tianjian. "Role culture and political liberalism among deputies to the seventh National People's Congress, 1988." Paper presented to annual meeting of AAS, Washington, D.C., 1989.

Shijie jingji daobao (World economic herald). Weekly. Shanghai: 1980–9. Cited as *SJJJDB*.

Shirk, Susan L. "Playing to the provinces: Deng Xiaoping's political strategy of economic reform." *SICC*, 23.3/4 (Autumn–Winter 1990), 227–58.

Shirk, Susan. *The political logic of economic reform*. Berkeley: University of California Press, 1993.

Shisanda yilai zhongyao wenxian xuanbian, zhong, xia (Important documents since the Thirteenth Party Congress, vols. 2 and 3). Beijing: Renmin, 1991. Cited as *Shisanda yilai*, 2 and 3.

SHKX. *Shehui kexue*.

SICC. *Studies in Comparative Communism*.

Sicular, Terry. "Rural marketing and exchange in the wake of recent reforms," in Elizabeth J. Perry and Christine Wong, eds., *The political economy of reform in post-Mao China*, 83–109.

Simmie, Scott, and Nixon, Bob. *Tiananmen Square: An eyewitness account of the Chinese people's passionate quest for democracy*. Seattle: University of Washington Press, 1989.

Simons, W. B., and White, S., eds. *The party statutes of the communist world*. The Hague: Martinus Nijhoff, 1984.

SJJJDB. *Shijie jingji daobao*.

Skinner, G. William. "Marketing and social structure in rural China." *JAS*, Part I, 24.1 (November 1964), 3–43; Part II, 24.2 (February 1965), 195–228; Part III, 24.3 (May 1965), 363–99.

Skinner, G. William, and Winckler, Edwin A. "Compliance succession in rural communist China: A cyclical theory," in Amitai Etzioni, ed., *Complex organizations*, 410–38.

Snow, Edgar. *The long revolution*. New York: Vintage Books; London: Hutchinson, 1973.

Socialist Upsurge in China's Countryside. Beijing: FLP, 1957.

Solinger, Dorothy. "Capitalist measures with Chinese characteristics." *POC*, 38.1 (January–February 1989), 19–33.

Solinger, Dorothy. "China's transients and the state: A form of civil society?" *Politics and society*, 21.1 (March 1993), 91–122.

Solinger, Dorothy. "China's urban transients in the transition from socialism and the collapse of the communist 'urban public goods regime.' " *Comparative Politics*, 27.2 (January 1995), 127–46.

Solinger, Dorothy. "Urban entrepreneurs and the state: The merger of state and society." Unpublished paper presented at the Conference on State and Society in China, Claremont-McKenna College, 16–17 February 1990.

Solomon, Richard. *Mao's revolution and the Chinese political culture.* Berkeley: University of California Press, 1971.

Song Ping. "Zai quanguo zuzhi buzhang huiyi shang de jianghua" (Talk to a national meeting of organization department heads). In *Shisanda yilai*, 2.566–77.

South China Morning Post. Daily. Hong Kong. 1903–.

Soviet Studies. Quarterly. Glasgow: University of Glasgow, 1949–.

Starr, John Bryan. "Revolution in retrospect: The Paris Commune through Chinese eyes." *CQ*, 49 (January–March 1972), 106–25.

State Statistical Bureau. See *Zhongguo tongji nianjian.*

State Statistical Bureau. "Intensify reform, accelerate structural adjustments, promote healthy development of the national economy: Economic situation in 1995 and outlook for 1996." *RMRB*, 1 March 1996, trans. in *FBIS Daily Report: China*, 4 April 1996, 32–8.

State Statistical Bureau. *Statistical yearbook of China, 1984.* Hong Kong: Economic Information & Agency, 1984.

Stavis, Benedict. *China's political reforms: An interim report.* New York: Praeger, 1988.

Stavis, Benedict. *The politics of agricultural mechanization in China.* Ithaca, N.Y.: Cornell University Press, 1978.

Studies in Comparative Communism. Quarterly. Los Angeles: School of International Relations, University of Southern California, 1968–. Cited as *SICC.*

Su Shaozhi. "Develop Marxism under contemporary conditions." *Selected Studies on Marxism*, 2 (February 1983), 1–39.

Sullivan, Lawrence R. "Assault on the reforms: Conservative criticism of political and economic liberalization in China, 1985–86." *CQ*, 114 (June 1988), 198–22.

"Summary of the Forum on the Work in Literature and Art in the Armed Forces with which Comrade Lin Piao entrusted Comrade Chiang Ch'ing." *PR*, 10.23 (2 June 1967), 10–16.

"Summary of Tian Jiyun's speech before Party school." *BX*, 266 (16 June 1992), 4–5, trans. in *FBIS Daily Report: China*, 18 June 1992, 16–18.

Summary of World Broadcasts. Daily and weekly reports. Caversham Park, Reading: British Broadcasting Corporation, Monitoring Service, 1939–. Cited as *SWB/FE.*

Sun Dunfan et al., eds. *Zhongguo gongchandang lishi jiangyi* (Teaching materials on the history of the Chinese Communist Party). 2 vols. Jinan: Shandong renmin, 1983. Cited as *Lishi jiangyi.*

Sun Hong. "Anecdotes about Deng Xiaoping's political career and family life." *JB*, 11 (5 November 1993), 26–31, trans. in *FBIS Daily Report: China*, 18 November 1993, 34–9.

Swaine, Michael D. "China faces the 1990s: A system in crisis." *POC*, 39.3 (May–June 1990), 20–35.

SWB/FE. Summary of World Broadcasts/Far East.

Tan Shaowen. "Emancipate the mind, seek truth from facts, be united as one, and do solid work." *Tianjin ribao*, 17 April 1991, trans. in *FBIS Daily Report: China*, 18 June 1991, 62–8.

[Tan Zheng] T'an Cheng. "Speech by Comrade T'an Cheng" (18 September 1956). *Eighth National Congress of the Communist Party of China*. 2. 259–78.

Tan Zongji. "Lin Biao fangeming jituan de jueqi jiqi fumie" (The sudden rise of the Lin Biao counterrevolutionary clique and its destruction), in *Jiaoxue cankao, xia*, 38–57.

Tanjug. Press service. Yugoslavia.

Teaching and Research Office for CCP History of the [PLA] Political Academy. See *Zhongguo gongchandang liushi nian dashi jianjie.*

Teiwes, Frederick C. *Leadership, legitimacy and conflict in China: From a charismatic Mao to the politics of succession.* Armonk, N.Y.: M. E. Sharpe, 1984.

Teiwes, Frederick C. "The paradoxical post-Mao transition: From obeying the leader to 'normal politics.' " *China Journal*, 34 (July 1995), 55–94.

Teiwes, Frederick C. *Politics and purges in China: Rectification and the decline of Party norms 1950–65*. White Plains, N.Y.: M. E. Sharpe, 1979.

Teiwes, Frederick C. *Provincial leadership in China: The Cultural Revolution and its aftermath.* Ithaca, N.Y.: China–Japan Program, Cornell University, 1974.

The Tenth National Congress of the Communist Party of China (documents). Beijing: FLP, 1973.

Terrill, Ross. *Mao: A biography.* New York: Harper Colophon Books, 1981.

Terrill, Ross. *The white-boned demon: A biography of Madame Mao Zedong.* New York: William Morrow, 1984.

[Ting] Ding Wang. *Wang Hongwen, Zhang Chunqiao pingzhuan* (Biographies of Wang Hongwen and Zhang Chunqiao). Hong Kong: Mingbao yuekan, 1977.

Ting Wang. *Chairman Hua: Leader of the Chinese communists.* Montreal: McGill–Queen's University Press, 1980.

Tong Huaizhou [pseud.], ed. *Tiananmen shiwen ji* (Poems from the Gate of Heavenly Peace). Beijing: Renmin wenxue, 1978.

Tong, James, ed. *Chinese Law and Government,* 23.1 (Spring 1990) and 23.2 (Summer 1990).

Tsou, Tang. "Chinese politics at the top: Factionalism or informal politics? Balance-of-power politics or a game to win all?" *China Journal*, 34 (July 1995), 95–156.

Tsou, Tang. "Political change and reform: The middle course," in Tang Tsou, ed., *The Cultural Revolution and post-Mao reforms,* 219–58.

Tsou, Tang, ed. *The Cultural Revolution and post-Mao reforms: A historical perspective.* Chicago: University of Chicago Press, 1986.

Tsou, Tang. "The Tiananmen tragedy." In Brantly Womack, ed., *Contemporary Chinese politics in historical perspective*, 265–327.

Twelfth National Congress of the CPC (September 1982). Beijing: FLP, 1982.

Unger, Jonathan, and Chan, Anita. "China, corporatism, and the East Asian model." *AJCA*, 33 (January 1995), 29–53.

Union Research Institute [URI]. *The case of Peng Teh-huai, 1959–1968*. Hong Kong: URI, 1968.

Union Research Institute [URI]. *CCP documents of the Great Proletarian Cultural Revolution, 1966–1967*. Hong Kong: URI, 1968.

Union Research Institute [URI]. *Documents of the Chinese Communist Party Central Committee, September 1956–April 1969*. Hong Kong: URI, 1971.

United States Congress [95th]. Joint Economic Committee. *The Chinese economy post-Mao*. Vol. 1: *Policy and performance*. Washington, D.C.: U.S. Government Printing Office, 1978.

United States Congress [97th]. Joint Economic Committee. *China under the four modernizations*. 2 vols. Washington, D.C.: U.S. Government Printing Office, 1982.

Universities Fieldstaff International Reports.

Urban, George, ed. and intro. *The miracles of Chairman Mao: A compendium of devotional literature, 1966–1970*. London: Tom Stacey, 1971.

URI. Union Research Institute. Hong Kong.

U.S. Consulate General. Hong Kong. *Current Background*. Weekly (approx.). 1950–77. Cited as *CB*.

U.S. Consulate General. Hong Kong. *Extracts from China Mainland Magazines*. 1955–60. Cited as *ECMM*. Title changed to *Selections from China Mainland Magazines*, 1960–77.

U.S. Consulate General. Hong Kong. *Selections from China Mainland Magazines*. 1960–77. Cited as *SCMM*. Formerly *Extracts from China Mainland Magazines*.

U.S. Consulate General. Hong Kong. *Survey of China Mainland Press*. Daily (approx.). 1950–77. Cited as *SCMP*.

U.S. Consulate General. Hong Kong. *Survey of China Mainland Press, Supplement*. 1960–73.

van Ginneken, Jaap. *The rise and fall of Lin Piao*. Harmondsworth: Penguin Books, 1976.

Walder, Andrew G. *Chang Ch'un-ch'iao and Shanghai's January Revolution*. Ann Arbor: Center for Chinese Studies, University of Michigan, 1978.

Walder, Andrew G. "The political sociology of the Beijing upheaval of 1989." *POC*, 38.5 (September–October 1989), 30–40.

Walder, Andrew G. "Urban Industrial Workers." Paper presented to the Conference on State and Society in China, Claremont-McKenna College, 16–17 February 1990.

Walker, Kenneth R. "Collectivisation in retrospect: The 'Socialist high tide' of autumn 1955–spring 1956." *CQ*, 26 (April–June 1966), 1–43.

Walker, Tony. "Security chief's sacking seen as rebuff for Jiang." *Financial Times*, 27 February, 1996, 6.

Wang Lingshu. "Ji Dengkui on Mao Zedong." *LW*, overseas edition, 6–13 February 1989, trans. in *FBIS Daily Report: China*, 14 February 1989, 22–26.

Wang Jiye. "Several questions on achieving overall balance and restructuring." *RMRB*, 8 December 1989, trans. in *FBIS Daily Report: China*, 19 January 1990, 30–3.

Wang Nianyi. *1949–1989 nian de Zhongguo: Da dongluan de niandai* (China from 1949–1989: A decade of great upheaval). Zhengzhou: Henan renmin, 1988.

Wang Nianyi. " 'Wenhua dageming' cuowu fazhan mai luo" (Analysis of the development of the errors of the "Great Cultural Revolution"). *Dangshi tongxun,* October 1986.

Wang Renzhi. "Guanyu fandui zechan jieji ziyouhua" (On opposing bourgeois liberalization). *RMRB*, 22 February 1990.

Wang Renzhi. "Lilun gongzuo mianlin de xin qingkuang he dangqian de zhuyao renwu" (The new situation confronting theoretical work and the primary task at the moment). *Xuexi, yanjiu, cankao,* 11 (1990), 8–17.

Wang Ruoshui. "Cong pi 'zuo' daoxiang fanyou de yici geren jingli" (The experience of one individual of the reversal from criticizing "leftism" to opposing rightism). *Huaqiao ribao,* 12–21 March 1989.

Wang Ruoshui. "In defense of humanism." *WHB,* 17 January 1983, 4.

Wansui (1969). See *Mao Zedong sixiang wansui.*

Washington Post, The. Daily. Washington, D.C.: The Washington Post Co., 1877–.

Wasserstrom, Jeffrey N. "Student protests and the Chinese tradition," in Tony Saich, ed., *The Chinese people's movement,* 3–24.

[Wei Yongzheng] Wei Yung-cheng. "Reveal the mystery of Huangfu Ping." *DGB*, 7 October 1992, and 8 October 1992, trans. in *FBIS Daily Report: China*, 16 October 1992, 18–21.

Wen Jin, ed. *Zhongguo "zuo" huo* (China's 'leftist' peril). [Beijing]: Chaohua, 1993.

[*Wenhui bao*] *Wen-hui Pao* (Wenhui daily). Shanghai: 1938–. Cited as *WHB*.

WHB. *Wenhui bao.*

White, Gordon. *Riding the tiger: The politics of economic reform in post-Mao China.* Stanford, Calif.: Stanford University Press, 1993.

Whitson, William W., with Huang Chen-hsia. *The Chinese high command: A history of communist military politics, 1927–71.* New York: Praeger, 1973.

"Why must we unremittingly oppose bourgeois liberalization?" *RMRB*, 24 April 1991, trans. in *FBIS Daily Report: China,* 26 April 1991, 18–21.

Wilson, Ian, and Ji, You. "Leadership by 'lines': China's unresolved succession." *POC,* 39.1 (January–February 1990), 28–44.

Wilson Quarterly. 5/yr. Washington, D.C.: Woodrow Wilson International Center for Scholars, 1976–.

Witke, Roxane. *Comrade Chiang Ch'ing.* Boston: Little, Brown, 1977.

Womack, Brantly, ed. *Contemporary Chinese politics in historical perspective.* Cambridge: Cambridge University Press, 1991.

Wong, Christine. "Central–local relations in an era of fiscal decline." Paper presented at the annual convention of the Association for Asian Studies, New Orleans, April 1991.

Wong, Christine. "The second phase of economic reform in China." *Current History,* 84.503 (September 1985), 260–3.

World Economic Herald. See *Shijie jingji daobao.*

World Politics: A quarterly journal of international relations. Quarterly. Princeton, N.J.: Center of International Studies, Princeton University Press, 1948–.

Wright, Kate. "The political fortunes of Shanghai's 'World Economic Herald.' " *AJCA*, 23 (January 1990), 121–32.

Wu, Guoguang. "Documentary politics: Hypotheses, process, and case studies," in Carol Lee Hamrin and Suisheng Zhao, eds., *Decision-making in Deng's China: Perspectives from insiders*, 24–38.

Wu Jinglian. *Jihua jingji haishi shichang jingji* (Planned economy or market economy). Beijiing: Zhongguo jingji chubanshe, 1993.

Wylie, Raymond F. *The emergence of Maoism: Mao Tse-tung, Ch'en Po-ta and the search for Chinese theory, 1935–1945*. Stanford, Calif.: Stanford University Press, 1980.

XH. *Xinhua {tongxun she}*.

[Xia Yu] Hsia Yu. "Beijing's intense popular interest in CPC Document No. 4." *DGB*, 12 June 1992, trans. in *FBIS Daily Report: China*, 12 June 1992, 17–18.

Xiang Jingquan. "Review and prospects of China's economic development." *GMRB*, 23 February 1993, trans. in *FBIS Daily Report: China*, 19 March 1993, 48–50.

Xiao Lan, ed. *The Tiananmen poems*. Beijing: FLP, 1979.

Xinhua {tongxun she} (New China News Agency). Cited as *XH*.

Xinhua wenzhai (New China digest). Monthly. Beijing: 1981–.

[Xu Simin] Hsu Szu-min. "On the political situation in post-Deng China." *JB*, 210 (5 January 1994), 26–9, trans. in *FBIS Daily Report: China*, 30 January 1994, 13–17.

Xue lilun. Monthly. Harbin: 1981?–.

Xue Yesheng, ed. *Ye Jianying guanghui de yisheng* (Ye Jianying's glorious life). Beijing: Jiefangjun, 1987.

Yahuda, Michael. "Kremlinology and the Chinese strategic debate, 1965–66." *CQ*, 49 (January–March 1972), 32–75.

Yan Fangming and Wang Yaping. "Qishi niandai chuqi woguo jingji jianshe de maojin ji qi tiaozheng" (The blind advance in our national economic construction in the early 1970s and its correction). *Dangshi yanjiu*, 5 (1985), 55–60.

Yan Jingtang. "Zhongyang junwei yange gaikuang" (Survey of the evolution of the Central Military Commission), in Zhu Chengjia, ed. *Zhonggong dangshi yanjiu lunwen xuan, xia*, 567–87.

[Yan Shenzun] Yen Shen-tsun. "Deng Xiaoping's talk during his inspection of Shoudu Iron and Steel Complex." *Guangjiaojing*, 238 (16 July 1992), 6–7, trans. in *FBIS Daily Report: China*, 17 July 1992, 7–8.

Yang, Dali. *Catastrophe and reform in China*. Stanford, Calif.: Stanford University Press, 1996.

Yang, Winston, and Wagner, Marcia, eds. *Tiananmen: China's struggle for democracy*. Baltimore: University of Maryland School of Law, 1990.

Yang Guoyu et al., eds. *Liu Deng da jun zhengzhanji* (A record of the great military campaigns of Liu [Bocheng] and Deng [Xiaoping]). 3 vols. Kunming: Yunnan renmin, 1984.

Yang Shangkun. "Zai Xinghai geming bashi zhounian dahui shang de jianghua"

(Speech at the meeting to commemorate the eightieth anniversary of the Xinghai revolution), in *Shisanda yilai*, 3.1713–19.

Yangcheng wanbao (Yangcheng evening news). Daily. Guangzhou: 1957–1966; 1980–.

Yao Ming-le. *The conspiracy and death of Lin Biao*. Trans. with an introduction by Stanley Karnow. New York: Knopf, 1983. Published in Britain as *The Conspiracy and murder of Mao's heir*. London: Collins, 1983.

[Yao Wenyuan] Yao Wen-yuan. "On the new historical play *Dismissal of Hai Jui*," Shanghai, *WHB*, 10 November 1965. Reprinted in *RMRB*, 30 November 1965; *CB*, 783 (21 March 1966), 1–18.

[Yao Wenyuan] Yao Wen-yuan. *On the social basis of the Lin Piao anti-Party clique*. Beijing: FLP, 1975. Also in Raymond Lotta, ed., *And Mao makes 5*, 196–208.

Yi Mu and Thompson, Mark V. *Crisis at Tiananmen: Reform and reality in modern China*. San Francisco: China Books and Periodicals, 1989.

Yi Ren. "Zhuozhuo huiyi de qianqian houhou" (Before and after the Zhuozhuo meeting). *RMRB*, 14 February 1990.

"Yingsi lu" bianji xiaozu. *Yingsi lu: huainian Ye Jianying* (A record of contemplation: remembering Ye Jianying). Beijing: Renmin, 1987. Cited as *Yingsi lu*.

Yomiuri Shinbun. Daily. Tokyo.

Young, Susan. *Private business and economic reform in China*. Armonk, N.Y.: M. E. Sharpe, 1995.

Yu Nan. "Zhou Zongli chuzhi '9.13' Lin Biao pantao shijian de yixie qingkuang" (Some of the circumstances regarding Premier Zhou's management of the 13 September incident when Lin Biao committed treachery and fled). *Dangshi yanjiu*, 3 (1981), 59.

Yu Xiguang and Li Langdong, eds. *Dachao xinqi: Deng Xiaoping nanxun qianqian houhou* (A great tide rising: Before and after Deng Xiaoping's southern sojourn). Beijing: Xinhua shudian, 1992.

Yuan Hongbing. *Lishi chaoliu* (Historical trends). Beijing: Chinese People's University Press, 1992.

Yuan Mu. "Firmly, accurately, and comprehensively implement the party's basic line: Preface to 'Guidance for studying the government work report to the Fifth Session of the Seventh NPC.' " *RMRB*, 14 April 1992, trans. in *FBIS Daily Report: China*, 16 April 1992, 20–3.

Yuan Ssu. "Bankruptcy of Empress Lü's dream." *Chinese Studies in History*, 12.2 (Winter 1978–9), 66–73.

Yuan Yongsong and Wang Junwei, eds. *Zuoqing ershinian, 1957–1976* (Twenty years of leftism, 1957–1976). Beijing: Nongcun duwu chubanshe, 1993.

Yue Daiyun and Wakeman, Carolyn. *To the storm: The odyssey of a revolutionary Chinese woman*. Berkeley: University of California Press, 1985.

[Yue Shan] Yueh Shan. "Central Advisory Commission submits letter to CCP Central Committee opposing 'rightist' tendency." *ZM*, 175 (1 May 1992), 13–14, trans. in *FBIS Daily Report: China*, 30 April 1992, 15–16.

ZB. *Zhongbao*.

[Zeng Bin] Tseng Pin. "Party struggle exposed by senior statesmen themselves; meanwhile, the new leading group is trying hard to build new image." *JB*, 145 (10 August 1989), trans. in *FBIS Daily Report: China*, 10 August 1989, 14.

Zha, Jianying. *China pop*. New York: The New Press, 1995.

[Zhang Chunqiao] Chang Ch'un-ch'iao. "On exercising all-round dictatorship over the bourgeoisie," in Raymond Lotta, ed., *And Mao makes 5*, 209–20.

Zhang Weiguo. "Chen Xitong an yu quanli douzheng" (The Chen Xitong case and the struggle for power). *Beijing zhi chun*, 30 (November 1995), 30–2.

Zhang Yufeng. "Anecdotes of Mao Zedong and Zhou Enlai in their later years." *GMRB*, 26 December 1988--6 January 1989, trans. in *FBIS Daily Report: China*, 27 January 1989, 16–19 and 31 January 1989, 30–37.

Zhang Yunsheng. *Maojiawan jishi: Lin Biao mishu huiyi lu* (An on-the-spot report on Maojiawan: The memoirs of Lin Biao's secretary). Beijing: Chunqiu, 1988.

Zhang Zhuoyuan. "Promoting economic rectification by deepening reform." *RMRB*, 27 November 1989, trans. in *FBIS Daily Report: China*, 7 December 1989, 28–31.

Zhao Shilin, ed. *Fang "zuo" beiwanglu* (Memorandum on opposing "leftism"). Taiyuan: Shuhai chubanshe, 1992.

Zhao, Suisheng. "Deng Xiaoping's southern tour: Elite politics in post-Tiananmen China." *AS*, 33.8 (August 1993), 739–56.

Zhao Ziyang. "Further emancipate the mind and further liberate the productive forces." *RMRB*, 8 February 1988, trans. in *FBIS Daily Report: China*, 8 February 1988, 12–14.

Zhao Ziyang. "Report on the work of the government." *BR*, 26.25 (4 July 1983), XVIII–XIX.

[Zheng Delin] Cheng Delin. "Yao Yilin launches attack against Zhu Rongji, Tian Jiyun." *JB* 1 (5 January 1993), 44–5, trans. in *FBIS Daily Report: China*, 22 January 1993, 46–7.

Zhengming (Contention). Monthly. Hong Kong: 1977–. Cited as *ZM*.

Zhong Kan. *Kang Sheng pingzhuan* (A critical biography of Kang Sheng). Beijing: Hongqi, 1982.

Zhongbao. Daily. New York: 1982–7.

Zhonggong dangshi dashi nianbiao (A chronological table of major events in the history of the Chinese Communist Party). Zhonggong zhongyang dangshi yanjiushi, ed. Beijing: Renmin, 1987.

Zhonggong dangshi yanjiu (Research into the history of the CCP). Bimonthly. Beijing: Zhonggong zhongyang dangxiao, 1988. Replaced *Dangshi yanjiu*.

Zhonggong dangshi yanjiu hui (Research Society on the History of the Chinese Communist Party), ed. *Xuexi lishi jueyi zhuanji* (Special publication on studying the resolution on history). Beijing: Zhonggong zhongyang dangxiao, 1982.

Zhonggong shiyijie sanzhong quanhui yilai zhongyang shouyao jianghua ji wenjian xuanbian (Compilation of major central speeches and documents since the Third Plenum of the Eleventh Central Committee). 2 vols. Taipei: Chung-Kung yen-chiu tsa-chih-she, 1983.

Zhonggong zhongyang dangxiao nianjian, 1984 (CCP Central Party School Yearbook, 1984). Beijing: Zhonggong zhongyang dangxiao, 1985.

"Zhonggong Zhongyang guanyu jinyibu zhili zhengdun he shenhua gaige de jueding (zheyao)" (CCP Central Committee decision on furthering improvement and rectification and deepening reform [outline]), in *Shisanda yilai*, 2.680–708.

"Zhonggong Zhongyang, Guowuyuan guanyu jinqi zuo jijian qunzhong guanxin de shi de jueding" (Decision of the CCP Central Committee and State Council regarding doing a few things of concern to the masses in the present period), in *Shisanda yilai*, 2.555–7.

Zhongguo gongchandang. Chinese Communist Party.

Zhongguo gongchandang di jiuci quanguo daibiao da hui (Huace) (Ninth Congress of the Chinese Communist Party [pictorial volume]). Hong Kong: Sanlian shudian, 1969.

"Zhongguo gongchandang di shisanju Zhongyang weiyuanhui diqice quanti huiyi gongbao" (Communiqué of the Seventh Plenary Session of the Thirteenth CCP Cental Committee), in *Shisanda yilai*, 2.1420–6.

"Zhongguo gongchandang di shisanju Zhongyang weiyuanhui disice quanti huiyi gongbao" (Communiqué of the Fourth Plenary Session of the Thirteenth Central Committee of the CCP), in *Shisanda yilai*, 2.543–6.

Zhongguo gongchandang lici zhongyao huiyi ji (Collection of various important conferences of the CCP). Zhonggong zhongyang dangxiao dangshi jiaoyanshi ziliao zu, ed. Shanghai: Renmin, vol. 1, 1982; vol. 2, 1983.

Zhongguo gongchandang liushinian dashi jianjie (A summary of the principal events in the 60 years of the Chinese Communist Party). Zhengzhi xueyuan Zhonggong dangshi jiaoyanshi. Cited as Teaching and Research Office for CCP History of the [PLA] Political Academy, *Zhongguo gongchandang. . . .* Beijing: Guofang daxue, 1985.

Zhongguo qingnian bao (China youth news). 3/week. Beijing.

Zhongguo renmin jiefangjun jiangshuai minglu (The names and records of marshals and generals of the Chinese People's Liberation Army). Xinghuo liaoyuan bianjibu (A single spark can start a prairie fire editorial department). Beijing: Jiefangjun. Vol. 1, 1986; vol. 2, 1987; vol. 3, 1987.

Zhongguo tongji nianjian, 1981 (Statistical yearbook of China, 1981). Zhonghua renmin gongheguo guojia tongji ju, ed. Beijing: Zhongguo tongji nianjian, 1982.

Zhongguo tongji nianjian, 1983 (Statistical yearbook of China, 1983). Zhonghua renmin gongheguo guojia tongji ju, ed. Beijing: Zhongguo tongji nianjian, 1983.

Zhongguo tongji zheyao, 1995 (Essential Chinese statistics, 1995). Beijing: Zhongguo tongji chubanshe, 1995.

Zhongguo zhichun (China spring). Monthly. New York: 1982–.

Zhonghua renmin gongheguo diwujie quanguo renmin daibiao dahui disanci huiyi wenjian (Documents of the third session of the 5th NPC of the PRC). Beijing: Renmin, 1980.

Zhonghua renmin fayuan tebie fating shenpan Lin Biao Jiang Qing fangeming jituan an zhufen jishi (A record of the trial by the Special Tribunal of the PRC's Supreme People's Court of the principal criminals of the Lin Biao and Jiang Qing counter-revolutionary cliques). Zui gao renmin fayuan yanjiushi (Research Office, Supreme People's Court), ed. Beijing: Falu, 1982.

Zhou Enlai. See *Zhou zongli. . . .*

[Zhou Enlai]. *Selected works of Zhou Enlai.* Vol. 1. Beijing: FLP, 1981.

Zhou Enlai shuxin xuanji (Zhou Enlai's selected letters). Beijing: Zhongyang wenxian, 1988.

Zhou Ming, ed. *Lishi zai zheli chensi: 1966–1976 nian jishi* (History is reflected here: a record of the years 1966–1976). Vols. 1–3, Beijing: Huaxia, 1986; vols. 4–6, Taiyuan: Beiyue, 1989.

Zhou Yang. "Inquiry into some theoretical problems of Marxism." *RMRB,* 16 March 1983, 4–5.

Zhou zongli shengping dashiji (Major events in the life of Premier Zhou). Chengdu: Sichuan renmin, 1986.

Zhu Chengjia, ed. *Zhonggong dangshi yanjiu lunwen xuan, xia* (Selection of research papers on the history of the CCP, vol. 3). Changsha: Hunan renmin, 1984.

Zhu Jianhong and Jiang Yaping. "Development and standardization are necessary: Perspective of real estate business." *RMRB*, 11 May 1993, trans. in *FBIS Daily Report: China*, 24 May 1993, 56–7.

Zhu Rongji. "Should the government intervene in the market and regulate prices in a socialist market economy?" *Jiage lilun yu shijian*, 10 (October 1993), 1–5, trans. in *FBIS Daily Report: China*, 10 January 1995, 68–72

Zhushi ben. See *Guanyu jianguo yilai . . .*

ZM. Zhengming.

Zweig, David. *Agrarian radicalism in China, 1968–1981.* Cambridge, Mass.: Harvard University Press, 1989.

Zweig, David. "Dilemmas of partial reform," in Bruce Reynolds, ed., *Chinese economic policy,* 13–40.

Zweig, David. "Strategies of policy implementation: Policy 'winds' and brigade accounting in rural China, 1966–1978." *World Politics,* 37.2 (January 1985), 26–93.

INDEX

THE BEST TEST PREPARATION FOR THE

ADVANCED PLACEMENT EXAMINATION

EUROPEAN HISTORY

with CD-ROM for both
Windows & Macintosh
REA's Interactive AP European History TEST*ware*®

Miles W. Campbell, Ph.D.
Professor and Chair, Department of History
New Mexico State University
University Park, New Mexico

Niles R. Holt, Ph.D.
Professor of History
Illinois State University
Normal, Illinois

William T. Walker, Ph.D.
Associate Professor and Chair, Department of Humanities
Philadelphia College of Pharmacy and Science
Philadelphia, Pennsylvania

Research & Education Association
61 Ethel Road West • Piscataway, New Jersey 08854

The Best Test Preparation for the
ADVANCED PLACEMENT EXAMINATION
IN EUROPEAN HISTORY
with CD-ROM for both Windows & Macintosh
REA's Interactive AP European History TEST*ware*®

Printed in the United States of America

Library of Congress Control Number 00-132018

International Standard Book Number 0-87891-330-0

Research & Education Association
61 Ethel Road West
Piscataway, New Jersey 08854

REA supports the effort to conserve and protect environmental resources by printing on recycled papers.

C-II-1-B

CONTENTS

ABOUT RESEARCH & EDUCATION ASSOCIATION

Research & Education Association (REA) is an organization of educators, scientists, and engineers specializing in various academic fields. Founded in 1959 with the purpose of disseminating the most recently developed scientific information to groups in industry, government, high schools, and universities, REA has since become a successful and highly respected publisher of study aids, test preps, handbooks, and reference works.

REA's Test Preparation series includes study guides for all academic levels in almost all disciplines. Research & Education Association publishes test preps for students who have not yet completed high school, as well as high school students preparing to enter college. Students from countries around the world seeking to attend college in the United States will find the assistance they need in REA's publications. For college students seeking advanced degrees, REA publishes test preps for many major graduate school admission examinations in a wide variety of disciplines, including engineering, law, and medicine. Students at every level, in every field, with every ambition can find what they are looking for among REA's publications.

While most test preparation books present practice tests that bear little resemblance to the actual exams, REA's series presents tests that accurately depict the official exams in both degree of difficulty and types of questions. REA's practice tests are always based upon the most recently administered exams, and include every type of question that can be expected on the actual exams.

REA's publications and educational materials are highly regarded and continually receive an unprecedented amount of praise from professionals, instructors, librarians, parents, and students. Our authors are as diverse as the subject matter represented in the books we publish. They are well-known in their respective disciplines and serve on the faculties of prestigious high schools, colleges, and universities throughout the United States and Canada.

ACKNOWLEDGMENTS

In addition to our authors, we would like to thank Dr. Max Fogiel, President, for his overall guidance, which brought this book to completion; Larry B. Kling, Quality Control Manager of Books in Print, for his supervision of revisions; John Paul Cording, Manager of Educational Software Publishing, for coordinating development of REA's exclusive TEST*ware*® software; Omar J. Musni, Editorial Assistant, for coordinating revisions; and Marty Perzan for typesetting the manuscript.

ABOUT OUR BOOK AND TEST*ware*®

This book and the accompanying software (AP European History TEST*ware*®) provide an accurate and complete representation of the Advanced Placement Examination in European History. The six practice tests and the review section are based on the most recently administered AP European History Exams. Each test includes every type of question that can be expected to appear on the actual exam. Following each exam is an answer key complete with detailed explanations. The explanations discuss both the correct and incorrect responses and are designed to clarify the material for the student.

Tests 4, 5, and 6 of this book are also on CD-ROM as part of our special interactive AP European History TEST*ware*®. By taking these exams on the computer you will have the additional study features and benefits of enforced timed conditions, individual diagnostic analysis of which subjects need extra study, and instant scoring. For your convenience, our interactive AP European History TEST*ware*® has been provided for you in both Windows and Macintosh formats. Many features are included that you will find helpful as you prepare for the AP European History Test. For instructions on how to install and use our software, please refer to the appendix at the back of this book.

ABOUT THE TEST

The Advanced Placement program is designed to allow high school students to pursue college-level studies while attending high school. The three-hour exam is usually administered to high school students who have completed a year's study in a college-level European history course. The results are then used for determining course credit and/or placement level in college.

The AP European History course is designed to present college-level history studies. Students are expected to leave the course with college-level writing skills, knowledge of historical events and concepts, and an ability to interpret historical documents. The course is intended for students who possess strong backgrounds in history and writing.

The exam is divided into two sections:

1. **Multiple-choice:** This section consists of 80 multiple-choice questions designed to measure the student's ability to understand and analyze European history from the Renaissance to the recent past. This section tests factual knowledge, scope of preparation, and knowledge-based analytical skills. The student has 55 minutes to complete this section of the exam, which counts for fifty percent of the final grade.

2. **Free-response:** This section is composed of three essay questions designed to measure the student's ability to write coherent, intelligent, well-organized essays on historical topics. The essays require the student to demonstrate mastery of historical interpretation and the ability to express views and knowledge in writing.

They may relate documents to different areas, analyze common themes of different time periods, or compare individual and group experiences which reflect socioeconomic, racial, gender, and ethnic differences. Part A consists of a mandatory 15-minute reading period, followed by 45 minutes in which the student must answer a document-based question (DBQ). In Part B the student must answer two essay topics out of the six that are given. The student has 30 minutes to write each of the essays. In determining the score for the free-response section, the DBQ is weighted 45 percent while the two thematic essays are weighted 55 percent. The entire free-response section counts for one-half of the final grade.

These topics are broken down as follows:

Political and Diplomatic History	35-45%
Social and Economic History	30-40%
Intellectual and Cultural History	20-30%

The basic chronology of the exam runs from the high Renaissance to the present. The time periods are covered as follows: 50% from 1450 to 1789, 50% from 1789-1996. Major late medieval events bearing upon post-1450 events may also be included.

ABOUT THE REVIEW SECTION

This book begins with a comprehensive review of European history designed to give the student an idea of what type of information can be found on the exam. The review discusses the following historical time periods and events in depth:

1450 to 1648: The Renaissance, Reformation, and the Wars of Religion
Martin Luther; the European Wars of Religion; the Thirty Years' War; the Age of Exploration; the Scientific Revolution; the Peace of Westphalia

1648 to 1789: Bourbon, Baroque, and the Enlightenment
The Peace of Westphalia; Mercantilism; Beginnings of Modern Science and the Enlightenment; Bourbon France; the Hapsburgs; the Hohenzollerns; the English Civil War; the Restoration; Peter the Great and Russia; the Papacy; the Ottoman Turkish Empire in Europe; Baroque and Rococo

1789 to 1848: Revolution and the New European Order
The French Revolution; the Era of Napoleon; the Congress of Vienna; the Industrial Revolution; the Impact of Thought Systems on the European World; the Concert of Europe; the Revolutions of 1848

1848 to 1914: Realism and Materialism
The Failure of the Revolutions; Realpolitik and Nationalism; the Crimean War; Capitalism and the New Left; Karl Marx; the Second French Republic and the Second Empire; Imperial Russia; the Balkan States and the End of the Ottoman

Empire; the New Imperialism; the Age of Bismarck; Darwin, Wagner, and Freud; the Coming of the Great War

1914 to 1935: World War I and Europe in Crisis
The Russian Revolutions of 1917; the Paris Peace Conference 1919 – 1920; Weimar Politics; Benito Mussolini and Italian Fascism; Soviet Russia; the Death of Lenin and the Rise of Josef Stalin; the Rise of Adolf Hitler and Nazism; the League of Nations

1935 to 1996: World War II to the Demise of Communism
Including: The Great Democracies; the Cold War; Loss of European Overseas Empires; Spreading Communism; Russian-American Relations; Nuclear Weapons and the Arms Race; Changes Under Yeltsin; the Balkan Crisis; the Persian Gulf War; the Arab-Israeli Peace Movement; the European Community; NATO's Changing Role; Cultural and Social Developments Since World War II

In addition to studying the review presented in this book, test-takers should acquaint themselves with current issues affecting European society, thereby gaining the necessary perspective on modern European events.

SCORING THE EXAM

The multiple-choice section of the exam is scored by crediting each correct answer with one point and deducting one-fourth of a point for each incorrect answer. Unanswered questions receive neither a credit nor a deduction. The free-response essays are graded by over 200 instructors and professors who gather together each June for a week of non-stop AP essay grading. Each essay booklet is read and scored by several graders. Each grader provides a score for the individual essays. The score for the DBQ is a number on a scale from 0 to 15, 0 being the lowest and 15 the highest. Each topic-based essay receives a score from 0 to 9. These scores are covered up so that the next grader does not see them. When the essays have been graded completely, the scores are averaged, one score for each essay, so that the free-response section is comprised of three scores.

The total weight of the free-response section is 50 percent of the total score. The multiple-choice section also comprises 50 percent of the total score. Each year the overall grades fluctuate because the grading scale depends upon the performance of students in past AP administrations. The following method of scoring and the corresponding chart will give you an **approximation** of your score. It does not indicate the exact score you would get on the actual AP European History exam, but rather the score you achieved on the sample tests in this book.

SCORING THE MULTIPLE-CHOICE SECTION

For the multiple-choice section, use this formula to calculate your raw score:

_____ – (_____ x 1/4) = _____ (round to the nearest whole number)

number right	number wrong	raw score

SCORING THE FREE-RESPONSE SECTION

For the free-response section, use this formula to calculate your raw score:

_____ + _____ + _____ = _____ (round to the nearest whole number)

DBQ essay	essay #1	essay #2	raw score

You may want to give your essays three different grades, such as a 13, a 10, and an 8, and then calculate your score three ways: as if you did well, average, and poorly. This will give you a safe estimate of how you will do on the actual exam. Try to be objective about grading your own essays. If possible, have a friend, teacher, or parent grade them for you. Make sure your essays follow all of the AP requirements before you assess the score.

THE COMPOSITE SCORE

To obtain your composite score, use the following method:

1.13 x __________ = _____ (weighted multiple-choice score—**do not round**)

multiple-choice raw score

2.73 x __________ = _____ (weighted free-response score—**do not round**)

free-response raw score

Now, add the two weighted sections together and round to the nearest whole number. The result is your total composite score. Compare your score with this table to approximate your grade:

AP Grade	Composite Score Range
5	114-180
4	91-113
3	74-90
2	49-73
1	0-48

These overall scores are interpreted as follows: 5-extremely well qualified; 4-well qualified; 3-qualified, 2-possibly qualified; and 1-no recommendation. Most colleges will grant students who earn a 3 or above either college credit or advanced placement. Check with your school guidance office about specific school requirements.

AP EUROPEAN HISTORY STUDY SCHEDULE WITH BOOK AND SOFTWARE

The following is a suggested six-week study schedule for the AP European History Exam. You may condense or expand this schedule depending on how soon you will be taking the actual exam. Set aside time each week, and work straight through the activity without rushing. In this way, you will be sure to complete an adequate amount of studying, and be confident and prepared on the day of the actual exam.

Week	Activity
1	Acquaint yourself with the AP European History Exam by reading the Introduction. Take AP European History Diagnostic Software Exam I. This is the same as Test 4 in your book, but it is highly recommended that you take the exam first on computer for maximum study benefits. After the computer scores your exam, read through all the detailed explanations carefully (not just those for your incorrect answers). Make a note of any sections that are difficult for you, or any questions that are still unclear after reading the explanations. Review the specific field of difficulty in the AP European History course review included with this book, or by using the appropriate textbooks and notes.
2 and 3	Study the review material included in this book. Do not study too much at any one time. Pace yourself, so that you can better comprehend what you are reading. Remember that cramming is not an effective means of study.
4	Take AP European History Diagnostic Software Exams II and III. Follow the same procedures you did in week 1 when you took Diagnostic Software Exam I.
5 and 6	Take Tests 1, 2, and 3. Read through all the detailed explanations carefully (not just those for your incorrect answers). Continue reviewing any material that is causing you difficulty. Compare your progress between the exams. Note any sections where you were able to improve your score, and sections where your score remained the same or declined. Use any time remaining for extra study in areas that require added attention. Use sources of information, such as textbooks, notes, or course materials to review those areas that need clarification.

AP EUROPEAN HISTORY

◆

COURSE REVIEW

1 THE RENAISSANCE, REFORMATION AND THE WARS OF RELIGION (1450-1648)

THE LATE MIDDLE AGES

The Middle Ages ("medieval" is the French word) were chronologically between the classical world of Greece and Rome and the modern world. The papacy and monarchs, after exercising much power and influence in the high Middle Ages, were in eclipse after 1300. During the late Middle Ages (1300 – 1500) all of Europe suffered from the Black Death. While England and France engaged in destructive warfare in Northern Europe, in Italy the Renaissance had begun.

THE CHURCH AND CRITICISMS

The church was a hierarchical or pyramidal organization, with the believers at the base. These believers were ministered to by priests, who in turn were supervised by bishops . All were under the leadership of the pope. Monks, nuns, and friars existed outside the pyramid but were usually governed by the pope as well.

In the late Middle Ages, numerous criticisms were directed against individuals and church practices, but not the idea of the church itself or Christian beliefs.

Corruption was widespread, with numerous decisions within the church's bureaucracy being influenced by money, friendship, or politics. Simony – the purchase of church positions, such as a bishopric, rather than appointment to the positions based upon merit – was commonplace.

Pluralism also existed. A man could hold more than one office in the church even though he would not be able to do both jobs at once. He might hire an assistant to do one of the jobs for him or it might be left undone. As he could not be both places, he was also open to the criticism of absenteeism.

These criticisms, and others, such as those concerning extravagance, excessive wealth, political involvement, and sexual improprieties, were part of the hostility to the clergy called anticlericalism. Those who criticized were often attacked by the church as heretics

John Wycliff (1320 – 1384), an English friar, criticized the vices of the clergy, taxes collected by the pope, transubstantiation, and the authority of the pope. As he believed the church should follow only the Scriptures, he began translating the Bible from Latin into English. Wycliff's ideas were used by the peasants in the revolt of 1381, and his followers, Lollards, survived well into the fifteenth century.

John Huss (1369 – 1415), a Czech priest with criticisms similar to Wycliff's, produced a national following in Bohemia which rejected the authority of the pope. Huss was burned at the stake at the Council of Constance.

Lay Piety

In the Rhine Valley of Germany, mystics , such as Meister Eckhart (1260 – 1327) and Thomas à Kempis (1379 – 1471), sought direct knowledge of God through the realm of inner feelings, not observance of church rituals.

Gerard Groote (1340 – 1384) began a semi-monastic life for laymen in the Low Countries. The Brethren of the Common Life ran schools and led lives guided by the Christian principles of humility, tolerance, and love, all unconcerned with the roles of the institutional church.

POPES

The papacy, recognized as the leader of the western church since at least the thirteenth century, encountered a series of problems in the late Middle Ages which reduced the prestige of popes and interfered with their ability to deal with the problems underlying the criticisms.

Babylonian Captivity

In 1305, after a confrontation with the king of France, a new pope, Clement V was elected. He was a Frenchman and never went to Rome, settling instead in Avignon, near the French kingdom. While not held captive by the French kings, the popes in Avignon were seen as subservient to them. Also, the atmosphere was one of luxury, and the popes concentrated on money and bureaucratic matters, not spiritual leadership. Popes resided in Avignon from 1309 to 1377.

Great Schism

In 1377 Pope Gregory XI returned to Rome, ending the Babylonian Captivity, but dying soon afterward. Disputes over the election of his successor led to the election of two popes, one of whom stayed in Rome (Urban VI).The other, (Clement VII), returned to Avignon. The monarchs chose different sides (England and Germany for Rome; France, Scotland, Aragon, Castile, Portugal, and Italian city-states for Avignon), while neither pope prosecuted any reforms of the church. The existence of two popes lasted until 1417.

Conciliar Movement

An effort was initiated to have the church ruled, not by the pope, but by everyone in the church, such as bishops, cardinals, theologians, and abbots, as well as laymen. The idea gained impetus from the existence of two popes and the abuses they were not correcting. Marsiglio of Padua (1270 – 1342), author of *The Defender of the Peace*, argued that the church was subordinate to the state and that the church should be governed by a general council.

Efforts after 1409 by councils at Pisa (1409) and Constance (1414 – 8) united the church under one pope (Martin V) but failed to effect any reform of abuses, as all such efforts ended in struggles between the pope and councils over power in the church. Martin and his successors rejected the conciliar movement.

Renaissance Popes

After 1447, a series of popes encouraged and supported much artistic work in Rome. While their personal lives were often criticized for sexual laxness, these popes took more interest in political, military, and artistic activities than in church reform. Sixtus IV (1471 – 84) started the painting of the Sistine Chapel which his nephew, Julius II (1503 – 13), whom Sixtus had promoted within the church, finished with the employment of Michelangelo to paint the ceiling. Julius also successfully asserted his control over the Papal States in central Italy. These popes did not cause the Reformation, but they failed to do anything which might have averted it.

THE HUNDRED YEARS' WAR

The governments of Europe partially broke down in the late Middle Ages, as violence within and war without dominated the scene. Towards the end of the period monarchs began to reassert their power and control. The major struggle, between England and France, was the Hundred Years' War (1337 – 1453).

The English king was the vassal of the French king for the duchy of Aquitaine, and the French king wanted control of the duchy; this was the event that started the fighting. The English king, Edward III, had a claim to the French throne through his mother, a princess of France.

Additionally, French nobles sought opportunities to gain power at the expense of the French king. England also exported its wool to Flanders, which was coming under control of the king of France. Finally, kings and nobles shared the values of chivalry which portrayed war as a glorious and uplifting adventure.

The war was fought in France, though the Scots (with French encouragement) invaded northern England. A few major battles occurred — Crecy (1346), Poitiers (1356), Agincourt (1415) — which the English won due to the chivalrous excesses of the French. The fighting consisted largely of sieges and raids. Eventually, the war became one of attrition; the French slowly wore down the English. The technological changes during the war included the use of English longbows and the increasingly expensive plate armor of knights.

Joan of Arc (1412 – 1431), an illiterate peasant girl who said she heard voices of saints, rallied the French army for several victories. Due to Joan's victories, Charles VII was crowned king at Rheims, the traditional location for enthronement. Joan was later captured by the Burgundians, allies of England, and sold to the English who tried her for heresy (witchcraft). She was burned at the stake at Rouen.

Results of the Hundred Years' War

England lost all of its Continental possessions, except Calais. French farmland was devastated, with England and France both expending great sums of money. Population, especially in France, declined.

Both countries suffered internal disruption as soldiers plundered and local officials left to fight the war. Trade everywhere was disrupted and England's wool trade to the Low Countries slumped badly. To cover these financial burdens, heavy taxation was inflicted on the peasants.

In England, the need for money led kings to summon parliaments more often, which gave nobility and merchants more power. No taxes could be levied without parliamentary approval. Parliamentary procedures and institutions changed, giving nobles more control over government (impeachments). Representative government gained a tradition which enabled it to survive under later challenges.

A series of factional struggles led to the deposition of Richard II in 1399. After the Hundred Years' War ended the nobility continued fighting each other in the War of the Roses (1450 – 1485), choosing sides as Lancastrians and Yorkists.

In France, noble factions contended for power with the king, who refused to deal with noble assemblies. The king faced various problems, while holding certain advantages. First of all, the Duchy of Burgundy was virtually independent. Secondly, there was no national assembly to confront, but only a series of provincial bodies. Thirdly, the monarch had the right to levy a tax on salt, the gabelle, and a national tax, the taille, which exempted nobles and clergy. Lastly, a royal standing army existed so that reliance on nobles became unnecessary.

In both countries the war led to the growth of nationalism, the feeling of unity among the subjects of a country. Kings in both countries used propaganda to rally popular support. Hatred of the enemy united people, and military accomplishments fed national pride.

Literature also came to express nationalism, as it was written in the language of the people, instead of in Latin. Geoffrey Chaucer (1340 – 1400) portrayed a wide spectrum of English life in the Cantebury Tales, while Francois Villon (1431 – 1463), in his Grand Testament, emphasized the ordinary life of the French with humor and emotion.

THE HOLY ROMAN EMPIRE

After prolonged struggles with the papacy in the 13th century, the Holy Roman Emperor had little power in either Germany or Italy. After 1272, the empire was usually ruled by a member of the Hapsburg family, which had turned its interest to creating possessions in Austria and Hungary. The Ottoman Turks, following the conquest of Constantinople in 1453, continually pressed on the borders of the Empire.

In 1356 the Golden Bull was issued. This constitution of the empire gave the right of naming the emperor to seven German electors, but gave the pope no role.

The Swiss cantons gradually obtained independence, helped by stories such as that of William Tell.

In Italy, city-states, or communes, dominated by wealthy merchants, continued their efforts to obtain independence from the emperor.

In many cities, the governments became stronger and were dominated by despots (Milan had the Visconti and later the Sforza; Florence came under the control of the Medici) or oligarchies (Venice was ruled by the Council of Ten). Other smaller city-states disappeared as continual wars led to larger territories dominated by one large city.

THE NEW MONARCHS

After 1450, monarchs turned to strengthening their power internally, a process producing the "New Monarchy." However, several difficulties hindered their efforts.

The general economic stagnation of the late Middle Ages combined with the increasing expense of mercenary armies to force monarchs to seek new taxes, something traditionally requiring the consent of the nobles.

Additionally, nobles, long the chief problem for kings, faced declining incomes and rising desires to control the government of their king. If not fighting external foes, they engaged in civil war at home with their fellow nobles.

Unfortunately for the monarchs, many weak, incompetent or insane kings hindered their efforts.

Opposition to Monarchian Power

Nobles claimed various levels of independence under feudal rules or traditions. Forming an assembly provided some sort of a meeting forum for nobles. Furthermore, the core of royal armies consisted of nobles; monarchs were solaced only by the appearance of mercenary armies of pike which reduced royal reliance on noble knights. Many of the higher clergy of the church were noble born.

Additionally, some towns had obtained independence during times of trouble. Church and clergy saw the pope as their leader.

Help for France's Monarchy

The defeat of the English in the Hundred Years' war removed the external threat. The defeat of the duchy of Burgundy in 1477 removed a major military power holding part of eastern France. Trade was expanded, fostered by the merchant Jacques Coeur (1395 – 1456). Louis XI (1461 – 1483) demonstrated ruthlessness in dealing with his nobility as individuals and collectively in the Estates General.

Help for England's Monarchy

Many nobles died in the War of the Roses. Nobles were controlled by a royal court, the Star Chamber. Standard governmental procedures of law and taxation were developed.

Help for Spain's Monarchy

The marriage of Isabella of Castile (1474 – 1504) and Ferdinand of Aragon (1478 – 1516) created a united Spain. Navarre was conquered in 1512. Moslems were defeated at Granada in 1492.

Additionally, sheep farming was encouraged through a government organization, the Mesta. An alliance with a group of cities and towns, the Hermandad, was formed in opposition of the nobility. Finally, reform and control of the church was enacted through the Inquisition.

THE BLACK DEATH AND SOCIAL PROBLEMS

The bubonic plague ("Black Death") is a disease affecting the lymph glands, which causes death quickly. Existing conditions in Europe encouraged the quick spread of disease. There was no urban sanitation, and streets were filled with refuse, excrement and dead animals. Houses were made of wood, clay and mud with straw roofs. Living conditions were overcrowded, with families often sleeping in one room or one bed. Poor nutrition was rampant, due to population pressures on food supplies. There was also a general lack of personal cleanliness.

Carried by fleas on black rats, the plague was brought from Asia by merchants and arrived in Europe in 1347. The plague affected all of Europe by 1350 and killed perhaps 25 to 40 percent of the population, with cities suffering more than the countryside.

Consequences

Some of the best clergy died because they attempted to help the sick; the church was left to the less competent or sincere. With fewer people, the economy declined. Additionally, Jews were killed due to a belief that they poisoned wells of Christians.

A general pessimism pervaded the survivors. Flagellants whipped and scourged themselves in penance for sins which they believed caused the plague. Literature and art reflected this attitude, including such examples as the Dance of Death, which depicted dancing skeletons among the living.

Population

By 1300, Europe's population had reached the limit of available food resources and famines became common. A series of consequences manifested after the decline of population after 1350.

Wages became higher as the remaining workers could obtain better wages or move; governments often responded with laws trying to set wage levels, such as England's Statute of Laborers (1351). Serfdom ended in many places. Guilds were established which limited membership, and cities limited citizenship in efforts to obtain or protect monopolies. The Hanseatic League of German cities controlled the Baltic trade in the 14th and early 15th centuries. Finally, sheep farming increased and, as sheep needed fewer workers, the necessary enclosures of open fields in England eliminated peasants and their villages.

Peasant Revolts

Records do not reveal major peasant revolts prior to the 13th century. New conditions following the Plague led to increased revolutionary activity.

Taxation was increased due to the Hundred Years' War. Higher wages were desired after the Black Death. Rising expectations were frustrated after a period of relative prosperity. Hostility to aristocrats increased, as expressed in the words of a priest, John Ball, one of the leaders of the English Peasants' Revolt: "When Adam delved and Eve span / Who was then the gentleman?"

A number of subsequent revolts ensued. In England, the largest of these, the Peasants' Revolt of 1381, involved perhaps 100,000 people. France experienced the *Jacquerie* in 1358. Poor workers revolted in Florence in 1378.

The Low Countries, Germany, Sicily, Spain, and at other times in England and France all experienced similar occurences.

THE RENAISSANCE

The Renaissance occurred mainly in Italy between the years 1300 and 1600. New learning and changes in styles of art were two of the most pronounced characteristics of the Renaissance. The Renaissance contrasts with the Middle Ages in that the Renaissance was secular, not religious. Also, the individual, not the group, was emphasized during the Renaissance. The Renaissance occurred in urban, not rural, areas.

Italian city-states, such as Venice, Milan, Padua, Pisa, and especially Florence were the home to most Renaissance developments, which were limited to the rich elite.

Jacob Burckhardt, in *The Civilization of the Renaissance in Italy* (1860), popularized the study of the period and argued that it was a strong contrast with the Middle Ages. Subsequent historians have often found more continuity with the Middle Ages in terms of the society and its traditions. Whether the term applies to a cultural event or merely a time period is still debated.

Definitions

Renaissance – French for 'rebirth'; the word describes the reawakening, rebirth, of interest in the heritage of the classical past.

Classical past – Greece and Rome in the years between 500 B.C. and 400 A.D. Humanist scholars were most interested in Rome from 200 B.C. to 180 A.D.

Humanism – The reading and understanding of writings and ideals of the classical past. Rhetoric was the initial area of study, which soon widened to include poetry, history, politics, and philosophy. Civic humanism was the use of humanism in the political life of Italian city-states. Christian humanism focused on early Church writings instead of secular authors.

Individualism – Behavior or theory which emphasizes each person and is contrasted with corporate or community behavior; or, theory in which the group is emphasized at the expense of the individual. Renaissance individualism sought great accomplishments and looked for heroes of history.

Virtu – The essence of being a person through the showing of human abilities. This ability could be displayed in speech, art, politics, warfare, or elsewhere by seizing the opportunities available. For many, the pursuit of virtu was amoral.

Florentine or Platonic Academy – located in a country house and supported by the Medici, the leading Florentine political family, a group of scholars who initially studied the works of Plato, the ancient Greek. The leading members were Marsilio Ficino (1433 – 1499) and Pico della Mirandola (1463 – 1494).

Causes

While no cause can be clearly identified as the source of the Renaissance, several categories have been suggested by historians.

The first explanation is for economic reasons. Northern Italy was very wealthy as a result of serving as intermediary between the silk- and spice-producing East and the consuming West of England, France and Germany. Also, Italian merchants had built great wealth in the cloth industry and had often turned to international banking. This wealth gave people leisure to pursue new ideas, and money to support the artists and scholars who produced the new works.

Political interactions may have also contributed to the sweeping changes. Struggles between the papacy, the Holy Roman Empire, and merchants during the Middle Ages had resulted in the independence of many small city-states in northern Italy. This fragmentation meant no single authority had the power to stop or redirect new developments. The governments of the city-states, often in the hands of one man, competed by supporting artists and scholars.

Historical influences were also at hand. Northern Italian cities were often built on the ruins of ancient Roman ones, and the citizens knew of their heritage.

Finally, an influx of new ideas occurred. The appearance of men fleeing the falling Byzantine Empire brought new ideas, including the study of Greek, to Italy. Also, during the numerous wars between the Italian city-states, contestants sought justifications for their claims in the actions of the past, even back to the classical past. Finally, the study of Roman law during disputes between the popes and the Holy Roman Emperors led to study of other Roman writers.

LITERATURE, ART, AND SCHOLARSHIP

Literature

Humanists, as both orators and poets, were inspired by and imitated works of the classical past. The literature was more secular and covered more subjects than that of the Middle Ages.

Dante (1265 – 1321) was a Florentine writer who spent much of his life in exile after being on the losing side in political struggles in Florence. His *Divine Comedy*, describing a journey through hell, purgatory, and heaven, shows that reason can only take people so far and then God's grace and revelation must be used. Dealing with many other issues and with much symbolism, this work is the pinnacle of medieval poetry.

Petrarch (1304 – 1374), who wrote in both Latin and Italian, encouraged the study of ancient Rome, collected and preserved much work of ancient writers, and produced much work in the classical literary style. He is best known for his sonnets, including many expressing his love for a married woman named Laura, and is considered the father of humanism.

Boccaccio (1313 – 1375) wrote *The Decameron*, a collection of short stories in Italian, which meant to amuse, not edify, the reader.

Castiglione (1478 – 1529) authored *The Book of the Courtier* which specified the qualities necessary for a gentleman – including the development of both intellectual and physical qualities – and leading an active, non-contemplative life. Abilities in conversation, sports, arms, dance, music, Latin and Greek, he advised, should be combined with an agreeable personal demeanor. The book was translated into many languages and greatly influenced Western ideas about correct education and behavior.

Art

Artists also broke with the medieval past, in both technique and content.

Medieval painting, which usually depicted religious topics and was used for religious purposes, was idealized. Its main purpose was to portray the essence or idea of the topic. Renaissance art sometimes used religious topics, but often dealt with secular themes or portraits of individuals. Oil paints, chiaroscuro, and linear perspectives all combined to produce works of energy in three dimensions.

Medieval sculpture was dominated by works of religious significance. The idealized forms of individuals, such as saints, were often used in the education of the faithful who could not easily deal with concepts. By copying classical models and using free standing pieces, Renaissance sculptors produced works celebrating the individualistic and non-religious spirit of the day.

Medieval architecture included the use of pointed arches, flying buttresses, and fan vaulting to obtain great heights, while permitting light to flood the interior of the building, usually a church or cathedral. The result gave a 'feeling' for God rather than the approach through reach. The busy details, filling every niche, and the absence of symmetry also typify medieval work.

Renaissance architects openly copied classical, especially Roman, forms, such as the rounded arch and squared angles, when constructing town and country houses for the rich and urban buildings for cities.

Several artists became associated with the new style or art.

Giotto (1266 – 1336) painted religious scenes using light and shadow, a technique called chiaroscuro, to create an illusion of depth and greater realism. He is considered the father of Renaissance painting.

Donatello (1386 – 1466), the father of Renaissance sculpture, produced, in his *David*, the first statue cast in bronze since classical times.

Masaccio (1401 – 1428) emphasized naturalism in *Expulsion of Adam and Eve* by showing real human figures, in the nude, with three-dimensions, expressing emotion.

Leonardo da Vinci (1452 – 1519) produced numerous works, including *The Last Supper* and *Mona Lisa*, as well as many mechanical designs, though few were ever constructed.

Raphael (1483 – 1520), a master of Renaissance grace and style, theory and technique, represented these skills in The School of Athens.

Michelangelo (1475 – 1564), a universal man, produced masterpieces in architecture, sculpture (*David*), and painting (the Sistine Chapel ceiling). His work was a bridge to new, non-Renaissance style called Mannerism.

Scholars

Scholars sought to know what is good and to practice it, as did men in the Middle Ages. However, Renaissance people sought more practical results and did not judge things by religious standards. Manuscript collections enabled scholars to study the primary sources they used and to reject all traditions which had been built up since classical times. Also, scholars participated in the lives of their cities as active politicians.

Leonardo Bruni (1370 – 1444), civic humanist, served as chancellor of Florence, where he used his rhetorical skills to rouse the citizens against external enemies. He also wrote a history of his city and was the first to use the term humanism.

Lorenzo Valla (1407 – 1457), authored *Elegances of the Latin Language*, the standard text in Latin philology, and also exposed as a forgery, the Donation of Constantine, which had purported to give the papacy control of vast lands in Italy, as a forgery.

Machiavelli (1469 – 1527), wrote *The Prince*, which analyzed politics from the standpoint of reason, rather than faith or tradition. His work, amoral in tone, describes how a political leader could obtain and hold power by acting only in his own self interest.

THE RENAISSANCE OUTSIDE ITALY

The Renaissance in the rest of western Europe was less classical in its emphasis, as well as more influenced by religion, particularly that of Christian humanism.

In the Low Countries, artists still produced works on religious themes but the attention to detail in the paintings of Jan van Eyck (1385 – 1440) typifies Renaissance ideas. Later artists include the nearly surreal Pieter Brueghel (1520 – 1569) and Rembrandt van Rijn (1606 – 1669).

In Mainz, Germany, around 1450, the invention of printing with movable type, traditionally attributed to Johann Gutenberg, enabled new ideas to be spread throughout Europe more easily. Albrecht Durer (1471 – 1528) gave realism and individuality to the art of the woodcut.

Many Italian artists and scholars were hired in France. The Loire Valley chateaux of the 16th century and Rabelais' (1494 – 1553) Gargantua and Pantagruel reflect Renaissance tastes.

Interests in the past and new developments did not appear in England until the 16th century. Drama, culminating in the age of Shakespeare, is the most pronounced accomplishment of the Renaissance spirit in England.

In Spain, money from the American conquests supported much building, such as the Escorial, a palace and monastery, and art, such as that by El Greco (1541 – 1614), who is often considered to work in the style of Mannerism.

CHRISTIAN HUMANISM

Theme

Much of the Renaissance outside of Italy focused on religious matters through the study of writings of the early Christian church, rather thanthrough those of the secular authors of Rome and Greece.

Elements

Although they used the techniques of the Italian humanists in the analysis of ancient writings, language and style, Christian humanists were more interested in providing guidance on personal behavior.

The work on Christian sources, done between 1450 and 1530, emphasized education and the power of the human intellect to bring about institutional change and moral improvement. The many tracts and guides of Christian humanists were directed at reforming the church, but led many into criticisms of the church, which resulted in the Reformation. Additionally, the discovery that traditional Christian texts had different versions proved unsettling to many believers.

Though many Christian humanists were not clergymen, most early reformers of the church during the Reformation had been trained as Christian humanists.

Christian Humanism, with its emphasis on toleration and education, disappeared due to the increasing passions of the Reformation after 1530.

Biographies

Desiderius Erasmus (1466 – 1536), a Dutchman and the most notable figure of the Christian humanist movement, made new translations of the Greek and Latin versions of the New Testament in order to have 'purer' editions. His book *In Praise of Folly* satirizes the ambitions of the world, most especially those of the clergy. A man known throughout the intellectual circles of Europe, he emphasized the virtues of tolerance, restraint, and education at the time the church was fragmenting during the Reformation. Erasmus led a life of simple piety, practicing the Christian virtues, which led to complaints that he had no role for the institutional church. His criticisms of the church and clergy, though meant to lead to reforms, gave ammunition to those wishing to attack the church and, therefore, it is said "Erasmus laid the egg that Luther hatched."

Thomas More (1478 – 1536), an English laywer, politician, and humanist, wrote *Utopia* (a Greek word for 'nowhere'). Mixing civic humanism with religious ideals, the book describes a perfect society, located on an imaginary island, in which war, poverty, religious intolerance, and other problems of the early 16th century do not exist. *Utopia* sought to show how people might live if they followed the social and political ideals of Christianity. Also, in a break with medieval thought, More portrayed government as very active in the economic life of the society, education, and public health. Though a critic of the church and clergy of his day, More was executed by Henry VIII, king of England, for refusing to countenance Henry's break with the pope in religious matters.

Jacques Lefevre d'Etables (1454 – 1536), the leading French humanist, produced five versions of the Psalms, his *Quincuplex Psalterism*, which challenged the belief in the tradition of a single, authoritative Bible. Also, his work on St. Paul anticipated that of Luther.

Francesco Ximenes de Cisneros (1436 – 1517), leader of the Spanish church as Grand Inquisitor, founded a university and produced the *Complutensian Polyglot Bible*, which had Hebrew, Greek, and Latin versions of the Bible in parallel columns. He also reformed the Spanish clergy and church so that most criticisms of the later reformers during the Reformation did not apply to Spain.

THE REFORMATION

The Reformation destroyed Western Europe's religious unity, andinvolved new ideas about the relationships among God, the individual, and society. Its course was greatly influenced by politics, and led, in most areas, to the subjection of the church to the political rulers.

Earlier threats to the unity of the church had been made by the works of John Wycliff and John Huss. The abuses of church practices and positions upset many people. Likewise, Christian humanists had been criticizing the abuses.

Personal piety and mysticism, which were alternative approaches to Christianity and did not require the apparatus of the institutional church and the clergy, had been appearing in the late Middle Ages.

MARTIN LUTHER (1483 – 1546) AND THE BEGINNINGS

Martin Luther was a miner's son from Saxony in central Germany. At the urgings of his father, he studied for a career in law. He underwent a religious experience while traveling, which led him to become an Augustinian friar. Later, he became a professor at the university in Wittenberg, Saxony.

Religious Problems

Luther, to his personal distress, could not reconcile the problem of the sinfulness of the individual and the justice of God. How could a sinful person attain the righteousness necessary to obtain salvation? During his studies of the Bible, especially of Romans 1:17, Luther came to believe that personal efforts – good works such as a Christian life and attention to the sacraments of the church – could not 'earn' the sinner salvation but that belief and faith were the only way to obtain grace. "Justification by faith alone" was the road to salvation, Luther believed by 1515.

Indulgences

Indulgences, which had originated in connection with the Crusades, involved the cancellation of the penalty given by the church to a confessed sinner. Indulgences had long been a means of raising money for church activities. In 1517, the pope was building the new cathedral of St. Peter in Rome. Also, Albrecht, Archbishop of Mainz, had purchased three church positions (simony and pluralism) by borrowing money from the banking family, the Fuggers. A Dominican friar, John Tetzel, was authorized to preach and sell indulgences, with the proceeds going to build the cathedral and repay the loan. The popular belief was that "As soon as a coin in the coffer rings, the soul from purgatory springs," and Tetzel had much business. On October 31, 1517, Luther, with his belief that no such control or influence could be had over salvation, nailed 95 theses, or statements, about indulgences to the door of the Wittenberg church and challenged the practice of selling indulgences. At this time he was seeking to reform the church, not divide it.

Luther's Relations with the Pope and Governments

In 1519 Luther debated various criticisms of the church and was driven to say that only the Bible, not religious traditions or papal statements, could determine correct religious practices and beliefs. In 1521 Pope Leo X excommunicated Luther for his beliefs.

In 1521 Luther appeared in the city of Worms before a meeting (Diet) of the important figures of the Holy Roman Empire, including the Emperor, Charles V. He was again condemned. At the Diet of Worms Luther made his famous statement about his writings and the basis for them: "Here I stand. I can do no other." After this, Luther could not go back; the break with the pope was permanent.

Frederick III of Saxony, the ruler of the territory in which Luther resided, protected Luther in Wartburg Castle for a year. Frederick never accepted Luther's beliefs but protected him because Luther was his subject. The weak political control of the Holy Roman Emperor contributed to Luther's success in avoiding the penalties of the pope and the Emperor.

Luther's Writings

An Address to the Christian Nobility of the German Nation (1520) argued that nobles, as well as clergy, were the leaders of the church and should undertake to reform it.

The *Babylonian Captivity* (1520) attacked the traditional seven sacraments, replacing them with only two.

The *Freedom of the Christian Man* (1520) explains Luther's views on faith, good works, the nature of God, and the supremacy of political authority over believers.

Against the Murderous, Thieving Hordes of the Peasants (1524), written in response to the Peasants' Revolt, stated Luther's belief that political leaders, not all people, should control both church and society.

By 1534 Luther translated the Bible into German, making it accessible to many more people as well as greatly influencing the development of the German language. Also, his composition, "A Mighty Fortress is Our God," was the most popular hymn of the 16th century. The printing press enabled Luther's works to be distributed quickly throughout Germany.

Subsequent Developments of Lutheranism

Economic burdens being increased on the peasants by their lords, combined with Luther's words that a Christian is subject to no one, led the peasants of Germany to revolt in 1524. The ensuing noble repression, supported by Luther, resulted in the deaths of 70,000 to 100,000 peasants.

At a meeting of the Holy Roman Empire's leading figures in 1529, a group of rulers, influenced by Luther's teachings "protested" the decision of the majority – hence the term "Protestant." Protestant originally meant Lutheran but eventually was applied to all Western Christians who did not maintain allegiance to the pope.

After a failure of Protestant and Catholic representatives to find a mutually acceptable statement of faith, the Augsburg Confession of 1530 was written as a comprehensive statement of Lutheran beliefs.

Led by Philip Melanchthon (1497 – 1560), the "Educator of Germany," Lutherans undertook much educational reform, including schools for girls.

Denmark became Lutheran in 1523 and Sweden in 1527.

Lutheran rulers, to protect themselves against the efforts of Charles V, the Holy Roman Emperor, to re-establish Catholicism in Germany, formed a defensive alliance at Schmalkald, the Schmalkaldic League, in 1531.

Wherever Lutheranism was adopted, church lands were often seized by the ruler. This made a return to Catholicism more difficult, as the lands would need to be restored to the church.

After warfare in the 1540's, which Charles V won but was unable to follow up because his treatment of defeated political rulers in Germany offended the nobility of the Empire, the Peace of Augsburg (1555) established the permanent religious division of Germany into Lutheran and Catholic churches. The statement "cuius regio, eius religio" ("whose region, his religion") meant that the religion of any area would be that of the ruling political authority.

OTHER REFORMERS

Martin Luther was not so much the father as the elder brother of the Reformation, because many other reformers were criticizing the church by the early 1520's.

Ulrich Zwingli (1484 – 1531) introduced reforming ideas in Zurich in Switzerland. He rejected clerical celibacy, the worship of saints, fasting, transubstantiation, and purgatory. Rejecting ritual and ceremony, Zwingli stripped churchs of decorations, such as statues. In 1523 the governing council of the city accepted his beliefs. Zurich became a center for Protestantism and its spread throughout Switzerland.

Zwingli, believing in the union of church and state, established in Zurich a system which required church attendance by all citizens and regulated many aspects of personal behavior – all enforced by courts and a group of informers.

Efforts to reconcile the views of Zwingli and Luther, chiefly over the issue of the Eucharist, failed during a meeting in Marburg Castle in 1529.

Switzerland, divided into many cantons, also divided into Protestant and Catholic camps. A series of civil wars, during which Zwingli was captured and executed, led to a treaty in which each canton was permitted to determine its own religion.

Anabaptists

Anabaptist (derived from a Greek word meaning to baptize again) is a name applied to people who rejected the validity of child baptism and believed that such children had to be rebaptized when they became adults.

As the Bible became available, through translation into the languages of the people, many people adopted interpretations contrary to those of Luther, Zwingli, and the Catholics.

Anabaptists sought to return to the practices of the early Christian church, which was a voluntary association of believers with no connection to the state. Perhaps the first Anabaptists appeared in Zurich in 1525 under the leadership of Conrad Grebel (1498 – 1526), and were called Swiss Brethren.

In 1534, a group of Anabaptists, called Melchiorites, led by Jan Matthys, gained political control of the city of Munster in Germany and forced other Protestants and Catholics to convert or leave. Most of the Anabaptists were workers and peasants, who followed Old Testament practices, including polygamy, and abolished private property. Combined armies of Protestants and Catholics captured the city and executed the leaders in 1535. Thereafter, Anabaptism and Munster became stock words of other Protestants and Catholics about the dangers of letting reforming ideas influence workers and peasants.

Subsequently, Anabaptists adopted pacifism and avoided involvement with the state whenever possible. Today, the Mennonites, founded by Menno Simons (1496 – 1561), and the Amish are the descendents of the Anabaptists.

John Calvin

John Calvin (1509 – 1564), a Frenchman, arrived in Geneva, a Swiss city-state which had adopted an anti-Catholic position, in 1536 but failed in his first efforts to further the reforms. Upon his return in 1540, Geneva became the center of the Reformation. Calvin's Institutes of the Christian Religion (1536), a strictly logical analysis of Christianity, had a universal, not local or national, appeal.

Calvin brought knowledge of organizing a city from his stay in Strasbourg, which was being led by the reformer Martin Bucer (1491 – 1551). Calvin differed from Luther, as Calvin emphasized the doctrine of predestination (God knew who would obtain salvation before those people were born) and believed that church and state should be united.

As in Zurich, church and city combined to enforce Christian behavior, and Calvinism came to be seen as having a stern morality. Like Zwingli, Calvin rejected most aspects of the medieval church's practices and sought a simple, unadorned church. Followers of Calvinism became the most militant and uncompromising of all Protestants.

Geneva became the home to Protestant exiles from England, Scotland, and France, who later returned to their countries with Calvinist ideas.

Calvinism ultimately triumphed as the majority religion in Scotland, under the leadership of John Knox (1505 – 1572), and the United Provinces of the Netherlands. Puritans in England and New England also accepted Calvinism.

REFORM IN ENGLAND

England underwent reforms in a pattern differing from the rest of Europe. Personal and political decisions by the rulers determined much of the course of the Reformation there.

The Break with the Pope

Henry VIII (1509 – 1547) married Katherine of Aragon, the widow of his older brother. By 1526 Henry became convinced that his inability to produce a legitimate son to inherit his throne was because he had violated God's commandments (Leviticus 18:16, 20:21) by marrying his brother's widow.

Soon, Henry fell in love with Anne Boleyn and decided to annul his marriage to Katherine in order to marry Anne. The pope, Clement VII, the authority necessary to issue such an annulment was, after 1527, under the political control of Charles V, Katherine's nephew. Efforts to secure the annulment, directed by Cardinal Wolsey (1474 – 1530) ended in failure and Wolsey's disgrace. Thomas Cranmer (1489 – 1556), named archbishop in 1533, dissolved Henry's marriage, which permitted him to marry Anne Boleyn in January 1533.

Henry used Parliament to threaten the pope and eventually to legislate the break with Rome by law. The Act of Annates (1532) prevented payments of money to the pope. The Act of Restraint of Appeals (1533) forbade appeals to be taken to Rome, which stopped Katherine from appealing her divorce to the pope. The Act of Supremacy (1534) declared Henry, not the pope, as the head of the English church. Subsequent acts enabled Henry to dissolve the monasteries and to seize their land, which represented perhaps 25% of the land of England.

In 1536, Thomas More was executed for rejecting Henry's leadership of the English church.

Protestant beliefs and practices made little headway during Henry's reign as he accepted transubstantiation, enforced celibacy among the clergy and otherwise made the English church conform to most medieval practices.

Protestantism

Under Henry VIII's son, Edward VI (1547 – 1553), a child of ten at his accession, the English church adopted Calvinism. Clergy were allowed to marry, communion by the laity expanded, and images were removed from churches. Doctrine included justification by faith, the denial of transubstantiation, and only two sacraments.

Catholicism

Under Mary (1553 – 1558), Henry VIII's daughter and half-sister of Edward VI, Catholicism was restored and England reunited with the pope. Over 300 people were executed, including bishops and Archbishop Cranmer, for refusing to abandon their Protestant beliefs. Numerous Protestants fled to the Continent where they learned of more advanced Protestant beliefs, including Calvinism at Geneva.

Anglicanism

Under Elizabeth (1558 – 1603), who was Henry VIII's daughter and half-sister to Edward and Mary, the church in England adopted Protestant beliefs again. The Elizabethan Settlement required outward conformity to the official church, but rarely inquired about inward beliefs.

Some practices of the church, including ritual, resembled the Catholic practices. Catholicism remained, especially among the gentry, but could not be practiced openly.

Some reformers wanted to purify (hence "Puritans") the church of its remaining Catholic aspects. The resulting church, Protestant in doctrine and practice but retaining most of the physical possessions, such as buildings, and many powers, such as church courts, of the medieval church, was called Anglican.

REFORM ELSEWHERE IN EUROPE

The Parliament in Ireland established a Protestant church much like the one in England. The landlords and people near Dublin were the only ones who followed their monarchs into Protestantism, as the mass of the Irish people were left untouched by the Reformation. The Catholic church and its priests became the religious, and eventually, the national, leaders of the Irish people.

John Knox (1505 – 72), upon his return from the Continent, led the Reformation in Scotland. Parliament, dominated by nobles, established Protestantism in 1560. The resulting church was Calvinist in doctrine.

France, near Geneva and Germany, experienced efforts at establishing Protestantism, but the kings of France had control of the church there and gave no encouragement to reformers. Calvinists, known in France as Huguenots, were especially common among the nobility and, after 1562, a series of civil wars involving religious differences resulted.

The church in Spain, controlled by the monarchy, allowed no Protestantism to take root. Similarly Italian political authorities rejected Protestantism.

THE COUNTER REFORMATION

The Counter Reformation brought changes to the portion of the Western church which retained its allegiance to the pope. Some historians see this as a reform of the Catholic church, similar to what Protestants were doing, while other see it as a result of the criticisms of Protestants.

Efforts to reform the church were given new impetus by Luther's activities. These included new religious orders such as Capuchins (1528), Theatines (1534) and Ursulines (1535), as well as mystics such as Teresa of Vaila (1515 – 1582).

Ignatius of Loyola (1491 – 1556), a former soldier, founded the Society of Jesus in 1540 to lead the attack on Protestantism. Jesuits, trained pursuant to ideas found in Ignatius' *Spiritual Exercises*, had dedication and determination and became the leaders in the Counter Reformation. In addition to serving in Europe, by the 1540's Jesuits, including Francies Xavier (1506 – 1552), traveled to Japan as missionaries.

Popes resisted reforming efforts because of fears as to what a council of church leaders might do to papal powers. The Sack of Rome in 1527, when soldiers of the Holy Roman Emperor captured and looted Rome, was seen by many as a judgment of God against the lives of the Renaissance popes. In 1534, Paul III became pope and attacked abuses while reasserting papal leadership.

Convened by Paul III and firmly under papal control, the Council of Trent met in three sessions from 1545 to 1563. It settled many aspects of doctrine including transubstantiation, the seven sacraments, the efficacy of good works for salvation, and the role of saints and priests. It also approved the "Index of Forbidden Books."

Other reforms came into effect. The sale of church offices was curtailed. New seminaries for more and better trained clergy were created. The revitalized Catholic church, the papacy, and the Jesuits set out to reunite Western Christianity.

Individuals who adopted other views but who had less impact on large groups of people included Thomas Muntzer (d. 1525), Caspar Schwenckfeld (d. 1561), Michael Servetus (d. 1553), and Lelio Sozzini (d. 1562).

DOCTRINES

The Reformation produced much thought and writing about the beliefs of Christianity. Most of the major divisions of the Western church took differing positions on these matters of doctrine. Some thinkers, such as Martin Bucer, a reformer in Strasbourg, believed many things, such as the ring in the marriage ceremony, were "things indifferent" – Christians could differ in their beliefs on such issues – but with the increasing rigidity of various churches, such views did not dominate.

The role of the Bible was emphasized by Protestants, while Catholics included the traditions developed by the church during the Middle Ages, as well as papal pronouncements.

Catholics retained the medieval view about the special nature and role of clergy while Protestants emphasized the 'priesthood of all believers,' which meant all individuals were equal before God. Protestants sought a clergy that preached.

Church governance varied widely. Catholics retained the medieval hierarchy of believers, priests, bishops, and pope. Anglicans rejected the authority of the pope and substituted the monarch as the Supreme Governor of the church. Lutherans rejected the authority of the pope but kept bishops. Most Calvinists governed their church by ministers and a group of elders, a system called Presbyterianism. Anabaptists rejected most forms of church governance in favor of congregational democracy.

Most Protestants denied the efficacy of some or all of the sacraments of the medieval church. The issue which most divided the various churches came to be the one called by various names: the Eucharist, the mass, the Lord's supper, the communion.

According to the belief of Transubstantiation, the bread and wine retain their outward appearances but the substances are transformed into the body and blood of Christ; this was a Catholic doctrine.

According to the belief in Consubstantiation, nothing of the bread and wine is changed but the believer realizes the presence of Christ in the bread and wine ("a piece of iron thrust into the fire does not change its composition but still has a differing quality"); this was a Lutheran doctrine.

Other views included ones that the event was a symbolic one, utilizing the community of believers. It served as a memorial to the actions of Christ, or was a thanksgiving for God's grant of salvation.

The means of obtaining salvation differed. Catholics believed in living the life according to Christian beliefs and participating in the practices of the church – good words. Lutherans accepted the notion of Justification by faith – salvation cannot be earned and a good life is the fruit of faith. Calvinists believed in Predestination – that salvation is known only to God but a good life can be some proof of predestined salvation; this was a Calvinist doctrine.

Relation of the church to the state also differed. Catholics and Calvinists believed the church should control and absorb the state; when God is seen as ruling the society, this is a theocracy. Lutheran and Anglican belief held that the state controls the church. Anabaptists held that the church ignores the state.

RESULTS

By 1560, attitudes were hardening and political rulers understood the benefits and disadvantages of religion, be it Catholic or Protestant. The map of Europe and its religions did not change much after 1560.

Political rulers, be they monarchs or city councils, gained power over and at the expense of the church. The state thereafter could operate as an autonomous unit.

Religious enthusiasm was rekindled. While most of the reforms came from the political and religious leadership of the societies involved, the general populus eventually gained enthusiasm – an enthusiasm lacking in religious belief since far back into the Middle Ages.

All aspects of Western Christianity undertook to remedy the abuses which had contributed to the Reformation. Simony, pluralism, immoral or badly educated clergy were all attacked and, by the 17th century, considerably remedied.

Protestantism, by emphasizing the individual believer's direct contact with God, rather than through the intermediary of the church, contributed to the growth of individualism.

Thinkers have attempted to connect religious change with economic developments, especially the appearance of capitalism. Karl Marx, a nineteenth-century philosopher and social theorist, believed that capitalism, which emphasized hard work, thrift, and the use of reason rather than tradition, led to the development of Protestantism, a type of Christianity he thought especially attractive to the middle class who were also the capitalists.

Max Weber, a later 19th-century sociologist, reversed the argument and believed that Protestantism, especially Calvinism, with its emphasis on predestination, led to great attention being paid to the successes and failures of this world as possible signs of future salvation. Such attention, and the attendant hard work, furthered the capitalist spirit.

Most writers today accept neither view but believe Protestantism and capitalism are related; however too many other factors are involved to make the connection clear or easy.

THE WARS OF RELIGION

The period from approximately 1560 to 1648 witnessed continuing warfare, primarily between Protestants and Catholics. Though religion was not the only reason for the wars – occasionally Catholics and Protestants were allies – religion was the dominant cause of the bloodshed. In the latter half of the 16th century, the fighting was along the Atlantic seaboard between Calvinists and Catholics; after 1600, the warfare spread to Germany where Calvinists, Lutherans, and Catholics fought.

Warfare and the Effects of Gunpowder

Cannons became effective; therefore, elaborate and expensive fortifications of cities were required. Long sieges became necessary to capture a city.

The infantry, organized in squares of three thousand men and armed with pikes and muskets, made the cavalry charge obsolete.

Greater discipline and control of armies were required to sustain a siege or train the infantry. An army once trained would not be disbanded, due to the expense of retraining. The order of command and modern ranks appeared, as did uniforms.

The better discipline permitted commanders to attempt more actions on the battlefield, so more soldiers were necessary. Armies grew from the 40,000 of the Spanish army of 1600, to 400,000 in the French army at the end of the 17th century.

War and Destruction

Devastation of the enemy's lands became the rule. Armies, mostly made up of mercenaries, lived by pillage when not paid and often were not effectively under the control of the ruler employing them. Peasants, after such devastation and torture to reveal their valuables, left farming and turned to banditry.

THE CATHOLIC CRUSADE

The territories of Charles V, the Holy Roman Emperor, were divided in 1556 between Ferdinand, Charles' brother, and Philip II (1556-98), Charles' son. Ferdinand received Austria, Hungary, Bohemia and the title of Holy Roman Emperor. Philip received Spain, Milan, Naples, the Netherlands, and the New World. Both parts of the Hapsburg family cooperated in international matters.

Philip was a man of severe personal habits, deeply religious, and a hard worker. Solemn (it is said he only laughed once in his life, when the report of the St. Bartholomew's Day massacre reached him) and reclusive (he built the Escorial outside Madrid as a palace, monastery and eventual tomb), he devoted his life and the wealth of Spain to making Europe Catholic. It was Philip, not the pope, who led the Catholic attack on Protestants. The pope and the Jesuits, however, did participate in Philip's efforts.

Sources of the Power of Philip II

The gold and silver of the New World flowed into Spain, especially following the opening of the silver mines at Potesi in Peru.

Spain dominated the Mediterranean following a series of wars led by Philip's half-brother, Don John, against Moslem (largely Turkish) forces. Don John secured the Mediterranean for Christian merchants with a naval victory over the Turks at Lepanto off the coast of Greece in 1571.

Portugal was annexed by Spain in 1580 following the death of the king without a clear successor. This gave Philip the only other large navy of the day as well as Portuguese territories around the globe.

Nature of the Struggle

Calvinism was spreading in England, France, the Netherlands, and Germany. Calvinists supported each other, often disregarding their countries' borders.

England was ruled by two queens, Mary (1553–58), who married Philip II, and then Elizabeth (1558–1603), while three successive kings of France from 1559 to 1589 were influenced by their mother, Catherine de' Medici. Women rulers were a novelty in European politics.

Monarchs attempted to strengthen their control and the unity of their countries, a process which nobles often resisted.

CIVIL WAR IN FRANCE

Francis I (1515 – 47) obtained control of the French church when he signed the Concordat of Bologna with the pope, and therefore had no incentive to encourage Protestantism.

With the signing of the Treaty of Cateau-Cambresis in 1559, the struggles of the Hapsburgs and Valois ended, leaving the French with no fear of outside invasion for a while.

John Calvin was a Frenchman and Geneva was near France, so Calvinist ideas spread in France, especially among the nobility. French Calvinists were sometimes called Huguenots.

Three noble families, – Bourbon, Chatillon, and Guise – sought more power and attempted to dominate the monarchs after 1559. Partly due to politics, the Bourbons and Chatillons became Calvinists.

When Henry II (1547 – 59) died as a result of injuries sustained in a tournament, he was succeeded, in succession, by his three sons (Francis II, 1559 – 60, Charles IX 1560 – 74, Henry III 1571 – 89), each influenced by their mother, Catherine de' Medici (1519 – 89), and often controlled by one of the noble families. Though the monarch was always Catholic until 1589, each king was willing to work with Calvinists or Catholics if it would give him more power and independence.

The Wars

A total of nine civil wars occurred from 1562 to 1589. The wars became more brutal as killing of civilians supplanted military action.

The St. Bartholomew's Day Massacre on August 24, 1572, was planned by Catherine de' Medici and resulted in the deaths of 20,000 Huguenots. The pope had a medal struck commemorating the event and the king of Spain, Philip II, laughed when told of the massacre.

As a result of St. Bartholomew's Day and other killings, Protestants throughout Europe feared for their future.

Several important figures were assassinated by their religious opponents, including two kings (Henry III and Henry IV). The two leading members of the Guise family were killed at the instigation of the king, Henry III, in 1588.

Spain intervened with troops to support the Catholics in 1590.

Henry of Navarre (1589 – 1610)

A Calvinist and member of the Bourbon family, Henry of Navarre became king in 1589 when Henry III was assassinated. Personally popular, Henry began to unite France but was unable to conquer or control Paris, center of Catholic strength. In 1593 he converted to Catholicism saying "Paris is worth a mass." In this respect, he was a politique, more interested in political unity than religious uniformity.

In 1589 Henry issued the Edict of Nantes which permitted Huguenots to worship publicly, to have access to the universities and to public office, and to maintain fortified towns in France to protect themselves. The Edict was not a recognition of the advantages of religious tolerance so much as it was a truce in the religious wars.

THE REVOLT OF THE NETHERLANDS

The Netherlands was a group of seventeen provinces clustered around the mouth of the Rhine and ruled by the king of Spain. Each province had a tradition of some independence and each elected a stadholder, a man who provided military leadership when necessary. The stadholder often was an important noble and often became the most important politician in the province.

Since the Middle Ages the Netherlands had included many cities dominated by wealthy merchants. By 1560 the cities housed many Calvinists, including some who had fled from France.

Philip II, king of Spain, sought to impose on Netherland inhabitants a more centralized government, as well as a stronger Catholic church closely following the decrees of the Council of Trent. Philip's efforts provoked resistance by some nobles, led by William of Orange (1533 – 84), called "the Silent" because he discussed his political plans with very few people. An agreement and pledge to resist, called the Compromise of 1564 and signed by people throughout the provinces, led to rebellion.

Philip sent the Duke of Alva (1508 – 1583) with 20,000 soldiers to suppress the rebellion. Alva established the Council of Troubles (called the Council of Blood by its opponents) which executed several thousand Calvinists as heretics. Alva also imposed new taxes, including a sales tax of 10%. Most significantly, the Inquisition was established.

The resistance to Alva included groups of sailors, called Sea Beggars, and the opening of the dykes to frustrate the marches of the Spanish armies. In 1576 the unpaid Spanish sacked Antwerp, an event called the Spanish Fury, which destroyed Antwerp's commercial supremacy in the Netherlands.

The Calvinist northern provinces and the Catholic southern provinces united in 1576 in the Pacification of Ghent, but were unable to cooperate. They broke apart into two religious groups: the Calvinist Union of Utrecht (approximately modern day Netherlands) and the Catholic Union of Arras (approximately modern day Belgium).

International attention was attracted when a son of Catherine de' Medici attempted to become the leader of the revolt and when the English sent troops and money to support the rebels after 1585.

The Spanish were driven out of the northern Netherlands in the 1590's, and the war ended in 1609, though official independence was not recognized by Spain until 1648. Thereafter, the independent northern provinces, dominated by the province of Holland, were called the United Provinces and the southern provinces, ruled by the king of Spain, the Spanish Netherlands.

ENGLAND AND SPAIN

Mary (1553 – 58)

The daughter of Henry VIII and Katherine of Aragon, Mary sought to make England Catholic. She executed many Protestants, earning her the name "Bloody Mary" from her opponents.

To escape persecution, many of the English went into exile on the Continent where, settling in Frankfurt, Geneva, and elsewhere, they learned more radical Protestant ideas.

Cardinal Pole (1500 – 58) was one of Mary's advisers and symbolized the subordination of England to the pope.

Mary married Philip II, king of Spain, and organized her foreign policy around Spanish interests. They had no children.

Elizabeth (1558 – 1603)

A Protestant, though one of unknown beliefs, Elizabeth achieved a religious settlement between 1559 and 1563 which left England with a church governed by bishops and practicing Catholic rituals, but maintaining a Calvinist doctrine. This was seen as a via media – a middle way between extremes – by its supporters, or an impossible compromise of Protestantism and Catholicism by its opponents.

Puritans sought to purify the English church of the remnants of its medieval heritage and, though suppressed by Elizabeth's government, were not condemned to death.

Catholics, who sought to return the English church to an allegiance to the pope, participated in several rebellions and plots.

Mary, Queen of Scots, had fled to England from Scotland, in 1568, after alienating the nobles there. It was she, in Catholic eyes, who was the legitimate queen of England. Several plots and rebellions to put Mary on the throne led to her execution in 1587.

Elizabeth was formally excommunicated by the pope in 1570. A politique interested in the advancing English nation, Elizabeth did not "make windows into men's souls".

In 1588, as part of his crusade and to stop England from supporting the rebels in the Netherlands, Philip II sent the Armada, a fleet of over 125 ships, to convey troops from the Netherlands to England as part of a plan to make England Catholic. The Armada was defeated by a combination of superior English naval tactics and a wind which made it impossible for the Spanish to accomplish their goal.

Peace between Spain and England was signed in 1604. England remained Protestant and an opponent of Spain as long as Spain remained a world power.

THE THIRTY YEARS' WAR

Calvinism was spreading throughout Germany. The Peace of Augsburg, which settled the disputes between Lutherans and Catholics in 1555, had no provision for Calvinists. Lutherans gained more territories through conversions and often took control of previous church states – a violation of the Peace Augsburg. A Protestant alliance under the leadership of the Calvinist ruler of the Palatinate opposed a Catholic League led by the ruler of Bavaria.

The Bohemian Period (1618 – 25)

The Bohemians rejected a Hapsburg as their king in favor of the Calvinist ruler of Palatinate, Frederick. They threw two Hapsburg officials out a window – the "defenestration of Prague."

Frederick's army was defeated at White Mountain in 1620, Bohemia was made Catholic, and the Spanish occupied Frederick's Palatinate.

The Danish Period (1625 – 29)

The army of Ferdinand, the Holy Roman Emperor, invaded northern Germany, raising fear amongst Protestants for their religion and local rulers for their political rights. Christian IV (1588 – 1648), king of Denmark, led an army into Germany in defense of Protestants but was easily defeated. After defeating Christian, the Holy Roman Emperor sought to recover all church lands secularized since 1552 and establish a strong Hapsburg presence in northern Germany.

The Swedish Period (1629 – 35)

Gustavus Adolphus (1611 – 32), king of Sweden, who was monetarily supported by France and the United Provinces, that wanted the Hapsburgs defeated, invaded

Germany in defense of Protestantism. Sweden stopped the Hapsburg cause in the battle of Breitenfeld in 1630, but Gustavus Adolphus was killed at the battle of Lutzen in 1632.

The Swedish-French Period (1635 – 48)

France, guided by Cardinal Richelieu (1585 – 1642), supplied troops in Germany, as the war became part of a bigger war between France and Spain.

Treaty of Westphalia (1648)

The presence of ambassadors from all of the belligerents, as well as many other countries made settlement of nearly all disputes possible. Only the French-Spanish war continued, ending in 1659.

The principles of the Peace of Augsburg were reasserted, but with Calvinists included. The pope's rejection of the treaty was ignored.

The independence of the United Provinces from the king of Spain, and the Swiss Confederacy from the Holy Roman Empire, was recognized. Individual German states, numbering over three hundred, obtained nearly complete independence from the Holy Roman Empire.

Miscellaneous

Not all issues were ones of Protestants versus Catholics. The Lutheran ruler of Saxony joined the Catholics in the attack on Frederick, at White Mountain, and the leading general for the Holy Roman Emperor, Ferdinand, was Albrecht of Wallenstein, a Protestant.

The war brought great destruction to Germany, leading to a decline in population of perhaps one-third, or more, in some areas. Germany remained divided and without a strong government until the 19th century.

Results

After 1648, warfare, though often containing religious elements, would not be executed primarily for religious goals.

The Catholic crusade to reunite Europe failed, largely due to the efforts of the Calvinists. The religious distribution of Europe has not changed significantly since 1648.

Nobles, resisting the increasing power of the state, usually dominated the struggle. France, then Germany, fell apart due to the wars. France was reunited in the seventeenth century; Germany was not.

In most political entities, politiques, such as Elizabeth I of England and Henry IV of France, who sought more to keep the state united than to insure that a single religion dominated, came to control politics.

The branches of the Hapsburg family, the Austrian and the Spanish, continued to to cooperate in international affairs. Spain, though a formidable military power until 1648, began a decline which ended its role as a great power of Europe.

THE GROWTH OF THE STATE AND THE AGE OF EXPLORATION

In the 17th century the political systems of the countries of Europe began dividing into two types, absolutist and constitutionalist. While no country typified either type and all countries had part of both, the countries can be divided in their focus. England, the United Provinces, and Sweden moved towards constitutionalism, while France was adopting absolutist ideas.

Overseas exploration, begun in the 15th century, expanded, as the wealth of the New World flowing to Spain became apparent to the rest of Europe. Governments supported such activity in order to gain wealth, as well as topreempt other countries.

Definitions

Constitutionalism meant rules, often unwritten, defining and limiting government. Seeking to enhance the liberty of the individual as well to advance the individual as a person were goals; in this manner constitutionalism shaded over into Liberalism. Constitutional regimes usually had some means of group decision making, such as a parliament, but a constitutional government need not be a democracy and usually was not. Consent of the governed provided the basis for the legitimacy of the regime, its acceptance by its subject.

Absolutism emphasized the role of the state and its fulfillment of some specific purpose, such as nationalism, religion, or the glory of the monarch. The usual form of government of an absolutist regime was, in the seventeenth century, kingship, which gained its legitimacy from the notion of divine right or the traditional assumption of power.

Nobles and bourgeoisie, depending on the country, provided the chief opposition to the increasing power of the state. In constitutionalist states, they often obtained control of the state, while in absolutist states they became servants of the state.

POLITICAL THOUGHT

The collapse of governments during the wars of religion, and the subjection of one religious group to the government of another, stimulated thought about the nature of politics and political allegiances. The increasing power of the monarchs raised questions about the nature and extent of that power.

Both Protestants and Catholics developed theories of resistance to a government. Luther and Calvin had disapproved of revolt or rebellion against government. John Knox's *Blast of the Trumpet Against the Terrible Regiment of Women* (1558) approved rebellion against a heretical ruler. His text was directed against Mary, Queen of Scotland.

In France, Huguenot writers, stimulated by the St. Bartholomew Day's Massacre, developed the idea of a covenant (contract) between people and God and between subjects and monarch. If the monarch ceased to observe the covenant, the purpose of which was to honor God, the representatives of the people (usually the nobles or others in an assembly of some sort) could resist the monarch.

Catholic writers, such as Robert Bellarmine, saw the monarch as being given authority, especially religious authority, by God. With the pope as God's deputy on earth, the pope could dispose of a monarch who put people's souls in jeopardy by wrong beliefs.

Jean Bodin (1530 – 96), in response to the chaos of France during the civil wars, developed the theory of sovereignty. He believed that in each country one power or institution must be strong enough to make everyone else obey; otherwise chaos results from the conflicts of institutions or groups of equal power. Bodin provided the theoretical basis for absolutist states.

Resistance to the power of monarchs was based upon claims to protect local customs, "traditional liberties" and "the ancient constitution." Nobles and towns appealed to the medieval past, when sovereignty had been shared by kings, nobles, and other institutions.

The struggles in the seventeenth century produced varying results. At the extremes, an absolutist country was ruled by a monarch from whom all power followed, while a constitutional country would limit government power and have a means of determining the will of the people, or at least some of them.

The French king dispensed with all representative institutions, dominated the nobility, and ruled directly. The nobles controlled the English government through the representative institution of Parliament. In Germany, various components of the Holy Roman Empire defeated the Emperor and governed themselves independently of him.

ENGLAND

Problems Facing English Monarchs

The English church was a compromise of Catholic practices and Protestant beliefs and was criticized by both groups. The monarchs, after 1620, gave leadership of the church to men with Arminian beliefs.

Arminius (1560 – 1609), a Dutch theologian, had changed Calvinist beliefs so as to modify, slightly, the emphasis on predestination. English Arminians also sought to emphasize the role of ritual in church services and to enjoy the "beauty of holiness," which their opponents took to be too Catholic. William Laud (1573 – 1645), Archbishop of Canterbury, accelerated the growth of Arminianism.

Opponents to this shift in belief were called Puritans, a term that covered a wide range of beliefs and people. To escape the church in England, many Puritans began moving to the New World, especially Massachusetts. Both James I and Charles I made decisions which, to Puritans, favored Catholics too much.

In financial matters, inflation and Elizabeth's wars left the government short of money. Contemporaries blamed the shortage on the extravagance of the courts of James I and Charles I. James I sold titles of nobility in an effort to raise money but this annoyed the nobles with older titles, as well as debased the entire idea underlying nobility.

The monarchs lacked any substantial source of income and had to obtain the consent of a Parliament to levy a tax. The monarchs would face numerous concerns in dealing with a parliamentary body.

First of all, a Parliament only met when the monarch summoned it. Though Parliaments had existed since the Middle Ages, there were long periods of time between Parliamentary meetings. Parliaments consisted of nobles and gentry with a few merchants and lawyers. The men in a Parliament usually wanted the government to remedy grievances as part of the agreement to a tax. In 1621, for the first time since the Middle Ages, the power to impeach governmental servants was used by a Parliament to eliminate men who had offended its members.

The Counties

The forty English counties had a tradition of much local independence. The major landowners – the nobles and the gentry – controlled the counties and resented central government interference.

James I (1603 – 25)

James ended the war with Spain and avoided any other entanglements, despite the problem that the Thirty Years' War in Germany involved his son-in-law, who was the ruler of the Palatinate and a Protestant hero. The Earl of Somerset and then the Duke of Buckingham served as favorites for the king, doing much of the work of government and dealing with suitors for royal actions.

Charles I (1625 – 49)

Henrietta Maria, a sister of the king of France and a Catholic, became his queen.

Charles stumbled into wars with both Spain and France during the late 1620's.

A series of efforts to raise money for the wars led to confrontations with his opponents in Parliaments. A "forced loan" was collected from taxpayers with the promise it would be repaid when a tax was voted by a Parliament. Soldiers were billeted in subjects' houses during the wars. People were imprisoned for resisting these royal actions.

In 1626, the Duke of Buckingham was nearly impeached because of his monopoly of royal offices and his exclusion of others from power. In 1628, Parliament passed the Petition of Right, which declared illegal the royal actions in connection with the loans and billeting.

Charles ruled without calling a Parliament during the 1630's. A policy of "thorough" – strict efficiency and much central government activity – was followed. Money was raised by discovering old forms of taxation. A medieval law which required all landowners with a certain amount of wealth to become knights was used to fine those who had not been knighted. All counties were forced to pay money to outfit ships – "ship money" – which had previously been the obligation only of coastal counties.

Breakdown

Charles, with the help of the Archbishop Laud, attempted to impose English rituals and the English prayer book on the Scottish church. The Scots revolted and invaded northern England with an army.

To pay for his own army Charles called the Short Parliament, but was not willing to remedy any grievances or to changehis policies. In response, the Parliament did not vote any taxes. Charles called another Parliament, the Long Parliament, which attacked his ministers, challenged his religious policies, and refused to trust him with money.

Archbishop Laud and the Earl of Strafford, the two architects of "thorough," were driven from power. The courts of Star Chamber and High Commission, which had been used to prosecute Charles' opponents, were abolished. When the Irish revolted, Parliament would not let Charles raise an army to suppress them, as it was feared he would use the army against his English opponents. John Pym (1584 – 1643) emerged as a leader of the king's opponents in Parliament.

Civil War

In August, 1642, Charles abandoned all hope of negotiating with his opponents and, instead, declared war against them. Charles' supporters were called royalists or Cavaliers. His opponents were called Parliamentarians or Roundheads, due to the London apprentices amongst them who wore their hair cut short.

Historians differ on whether to call this struggle the Puritan Revolution, the English Civil Wars, or the Great Rebellion. The issues which precipitated the war were concerning religious differences and how much authority Charles should have in the government.

Charles was defeated. His opponents had allied with the Scots who still had an army in England. Additionally, the New Model Army, with its general Oliver Cromwell (1599 – 1658), was superior to Charles' army.

With the collapse of government, new religious and political groups, such as Levellers, Quakers, and Ranters, appeared.

Following the defeat of Charles, his opponents attempted to negotiate a settlement with him but, with that failing, he was executed on January 30, 1649, and England became a republic for the next eleven years.

The search for a settlement continued until 1689, when the nobles, gentry, and merchants, acting through Parliament, controlled the government and the monarchy.

FRANCE

Problems Facing the French Monarchs

The regions of France long had a large measure of independence, and local parliaments could refuse to enforce royal laws. The centralization of all government proceeded by replacing local authorities with intendants, civil servants who reported to the king.

The Huguenots, as a result of the Edict of Nantes, had separate rights and powers. They were, in effect, a state within the state. All efforts to unify France under one religion (Catholicism) faced both internal resistance from the Huguenots and the difficulty of dealing with Protestant powers abroad.

By 1650, France had been ruled by only one competent adult monarch since 1559. Louis XIII came to the throne at age 9 and Louis XIV at the age of 5. The mothers of both kings, Maria de' Medici and Anne of Austria, governed until the boys were of age. Both queens relied on chief ministers to help govern: Cardinal Richelieu (1585 – 1642) and Cardinal Mazarin (1602 – 61).

Henry IV (1589 – 1610)

Henry relied on the duke of Sully (1560 – 1641), the first of a series of strong ministers in the seventeenth century. Sully and Henry increased the involvement of the state in the economy, acting on a theory known as mercantilism.

Monopolies on the production of gunpowder and salt were developed. Only the government could operate mines. A canal was begun to connect the Mediterranean to the Atlantic.

Louis XIII (1610 – 43)

Cardinal Richelieu, first used by Louis' mother, became the real power in France. Foreign policy was difficult because of the problems of religion.

Due to the weakness of France after the wars of religion, Maria de' Medici concluded a treaty with Spain in 1611. In order to keep the Hapsburgs from gaining ascendancy in Germany, Richelieu supplied troops and money to Gustavus Adolphus, a Lutheran, after 1631.

The unique status of the Huguenots was reduced through warfare and the Peace of Alais (1629) when their separate armed cities were eliminated.

The nobility was reduced in power through constant attention to the laws and the mprisonment of offenders.

Breakdown

Cardinal Mazarin governed because Louis XIV (1643 – 1715) was a minor. During the Fronde, from 1649 to 1652, the nobility controlled Paris, drove Louis XIV and Mazarin from the city, and attempted to run the government. Noble ineffectiveness, the memories of the chaos of the wars of religion, and the overall anarchy convinced most people that a strong king was preferable to a warring nobility. The lack of impact of the movement was symbolized by the name of the Fronde, which meant a slingshot used by children to shoot rocks at carriages, but which caused no real damage.

Absolutism

By 1652, the French people were willing to accept, and the French monarchy had developed the tools, to implement a strong, centralized government. Louis XIV personally saw the need to increase royal power and his own glory, and dedicated his life to these goals. He steadily pursued a policy of "one king, one law, one faith."

OTHER CONSTITUTIONAL STATES

United Provinces

The seven provinces sent representatives to an Estates General, which was dominated by the richest provinces, Holland and Zealand, and which had few powers. Each province elected a stadholder, and a military leader. Usually, all of the provinces elected the same man, the head of the house of Orange.

Calvinism divided when Arminius proposed a theology that reduced the emphasis on predestination. Though the stricter Calvinism prevailed, Arminians had full political and economic rights after 1632, and Catholics and Jews were also tolerated, though with fewer rights.

The merchants dominating the Estates General supported the laxer Arminianism and wanted peace, while the house of Orange adopted the stricter Calvinism and sought a more aggressive foreign policy. In 1619, Jan van Oldenbarenveldt (1547 – 1619), representing the merchants, lost a struggle over the issue of renewing war with Spain to Maurice of Nassau, the head of the house of Orange. Until 1650, Maurice, and then William II, dominated, and the Dutch supported anti-Hapsburg forces in the Thirty Years' War. The merchants regained power, and Jan de Witt (1625 – 72) set about returning power to the provinces in 1653.

The 17th century witnessed tremendous growth in the wealth and economic power of the Dutch. The Bank of Amsterdam, founded in 1609, provided safe and stable control of money, which encouraged investments in many kinds of activities. Amsterdam became the financial center of Europe. The Dutch also developed the largest fleet in Europe devoted to trade, rather than warfare, and became the dominant trading country.

Sweden

Gustavus Adolphus (1611 – 32) reorganized the government, giving the nobles a dominant role in both the army and the bureaucracy. The central government was divided into five departments, each with a noble at its head. The very capable Axel Oxenstierna (1583 – 1654) dominated this government.

The Riksdag, an assembly of nobles, clergy, townsmen, and peasants, nominally had the highest legislative authority, The real power, however, lay with the nobles and the monarch.

From 1611 to 1650, noble power and wealth greatly increased. In 1650 Queen Christina, who wanted to abdicate and become a Catholic (which eventually she did in 1654), used the power of the Riksdag to coerce the nobles into accepting her designated successor.

As a result of Gustavus Adolphus' military actions, the Baltic became a Swedish lake and Sweden became a world power. Swedish economic power resulted fromdominating the copper mines, the only ones in Europe.

In both the United Provinces and Sweden, the government was dominated by rich and powerful groups who used representative institutions to limit the power of the state and produce non-absolutist regimes.

EXPLORATIONS AND CONQUESTS

Motives

Gold and silver were early and continuing reasons for explorations. Still further, the thrill of exploration explains the actions of many. Spices and other aspects of trade quickly became important, especially in Portuguese trade to the East Indies.

Religion proved to be a particularly strong motivation. To engage in missionary work, Jesuits, including Francis Xavier, appeared in India, Japan, and other areas by 1550. English unhappy with their church moved to North America in the 17th century.

Results

The wealth, especially the gold and silver of Mexico and Peru, enabled Spain to embark on its military activities. European inflation, which existed prior to the discoveries, was further fueled by the influx of gold and silver.

Disease killed perhaps 25 million, or eighty percent, of the Indians of the Americas. Syphilis appeared in Europe for the first time.

Many foods, such as potatoes and tomatoes, were introduced to Europe.

Europeans began transporting slaves from Africa to the Americas.

A large number of English settled in North America and a smaller number of Spaniards in Central and South America. Other areas were dotted by only a few Europeans.

Early Explorations

Portugal. Prince Henry the Navigator (1394 – 1460) supported exploration of the African coastline, largely in order to seek gold. Bartholomew Dias (1450 – 1500) rounded the southern tip of Africa in 1487. Vasco de Gama (1460 – 1524) reached India in 1498 and, after some fighting, soon established trading ports at Goa and Calicut. Albuquerque (1435 – 1515) helped establish an empire in the Spice Islands after 1510.

Spain. Christopher Columbus (1446 – 1506), seeking a new route to the (East) Indies, discovered the Americas in 1492. Ferdinand Magellan (1480 – 1521) started a voyage which first circumnavigated the globe in 1521 – 22. Conquests of the Aztecs by Hernando Cortes (1485 – 1547), and the Incas by Francisco Pizarro (1470 – 1541), enabled the Spanish to send much gold and silver back to Spain. Thus began the process of subjugating the American Indians.

In 1494, Spain and Portugal, with the treaty of Tordesillas, divided amongst themselves portions of the world they had newly discovered.

Other Countries. In the 1490's the Cabots, John (1450 – 98) and Sebastian (1474 – 1557), explored North America and, after 1570, various Englishmen, including Francis Drake (1545 – 96), fought the Spanish around the world. The English, discovering a route to Russia through the White Sea, commenced trading there. Jacques Cartier (1491 – 1557) explored parts of North America for France in 1534.

Early 17th-Century Explorations and Settlements

Governments took an increasing interest in settlements, seeking to control both them and trading ports from European capitals.

England's Virginia Company settled Jamestown in the Chesapeake Bay in 1607. Soon tobacco became a major export crop. Catholics were allowed to settle in Maryland after 1632. The Pilgrims arrived in Massachusetts in 1620. Other settlers of the Massachusetts Bay, chartered by the king in 1629, soon arrived. Between 1630 and 1650, over 20,000 people, unhappy with religious developments in England, emigrated to Massachusetts.

Various West Indies Islands were also settled.

Following Samuel de Champlain's (1567 – 1635) first efforts in 1603, the French explored the St. Lawrence River. Trade, especially for furs, was the goal. The Company of the Hundred Associates, founded in 1627, undertook the development of Canada. The West Indies attracted groups of investors, such as the Company of St. Christopher, which was organized in 1626.

The Dutch sent Henry Hudson (d. 1611) to explore North America in 1609, soon establishing settlements at New Amsterdam and in the Hudson River valley. The Dutch founded trading centers in the East Indies, the West Indies, and southern Africa. Swedes settled on the Delaware River in North America in 1638.

SCIENCE, LEARNING AND SOCIETY

The scientific revolution of the 16th and 17th centuries replaced religion as the explanation for the occurrences of the physical world. In contrast to religious articles of faith, the approach of science relied on experiment and mathematics. Learning, including the arts, moved away from Renaissance models to emphasize the emotions and individual variations.

While the family as an institution remained unchanged, much of society was transformed through population growth, inflation, and new patterns of landholding, trade, and industry.

THE SCIENTIFIC REVOLUTION

Astronomy, and to a lesser degree physics, first produced the new ways of thought called the scientific revolution.

The ideas of the ancient Greek, Aristotle (384 – 22 B.C.), provided the system of explanations. Aristotle believed that the motionless earth occupied the center of the universe, and that the sun, planets, and stars revolved around it in circular orbits determined by crystalline spheres. Aristotle's system was further refined by Ptolemy, a second-century astronomer, to make it correspond to the observed movements of the stars and planets.

Accepting both the Aristotelian idea that the circle is the closest to the perfect figure and, also, the Renaissance belief in simple explanations, Nicolaus Copernicus (1473-1543) suggested that the sun was at the center of the universe and that the earth and planets revolved around it in circular orbits. His *On the Revolutions of the Heavenly Spheres* was published in 1543, the year of his death. Copernicus' ideas that the universe was immense removed people from occupying the center of the universe, to inhabiting a small planet in a vast system. It also eliminated distinctions between the earth and the heavens.

Copernicus' views were not immediately accepted because they contradicted the words of the Bible. Although he posited circular orbits for the planets, his predictions of their locations were not accurate.

A Danish nobleman, Tycho Brahe (1546-1601) built the best observatory of his time, for which he collected extensive data on the location of the stars and planets. Brahe did not totally accept Copernicus' views, as he believed that the earth still occupied the center of the universe and that the other planets revolved around the sun, which, in turn, revolved around the earth.

Brahe's discovery of a new star in 1572, and the appearance of a comet in 1577, shattered beliefs in an unchanging sky and crystalline spheres.

Johannes Kepler's (1571 – 1630) reworking of Copernicus' theory and Brahe's observations produced the idea that the planets move around the sun in elliptical, not circular, orbits. The three new laws of Kepler accurately predicted the movements of the planets and were based on mathematical relationships.

Galileo (1564 – 1642) discovered four moons of Jupiter using a new invention of the time, the telescope. He also conducted other experiments in physics whichrelated to the relationship of movement of objects and the mathematics necessary to describe the movement, such as that of the pendulum. A propagandist for science, Galileo defended his discoveries and mocked his opponents. The Catholic Church in Italy, where Galileo lived and worked, forced him to recant his views, which demonstrated the conflict of the older religious views and the new scientific approach.

Scientific Methodologies

The author of *Advancement of Learning* (1605) and an advocate of experimental approaches to knowledge, Francis Bacon (1561 – 1626) formalized empiricism, an approach using inductive reasoning. An Englishman, Bacon himself did few experiments but believed empiricism would produce useful, rather than purely theoretical, knowledge.

Beginning from basic principles, Rene Descartes (1596 – 1650) believed scientific laws could be found by deductive reasoning. Formulating analytic geometry, Descartes knew that geometry and algebra were related and that equations could describe figures. Later developments merged inductive experimentalism, with deductivemathematical rationalism, to produce today's epistemology method, used to obtain and verify knowledge.

Connections with the Rest of Society

During the Renaissance, many universities established the study of mathematics and physics. All of the great scientists involved in the changes in astronomy studied at universities.

The demands of explorers, especially those at sea, for more accurate measurements of the stars, increased attention on the details of the heavenly movements.

Warfare, particularly the developing use of artillery, required and permitted explanations involving precise measurements.

Initially, Protestant areas were more hostile than Catholic ones to the new learning. After Galileo, however, Catholic authorities led in trying to suppress the new ideas.

Consequences

The new approaches of the scientific method spread to inquiries far beyond astronomy and physics. Many sought new explanations as well as order and uniformity in all aspects of the physical world and society.

William Harvey (1578 – 1657) demonstrated the circulation of blood and the role of the human heart. Thomas Hobbes (1558 – 1679), an English writer on political theory, studied society. Using a few basic premises, he described politics in *Leviathan* (1651).

Blaise Pascal (1623 – 62), a French mathematician and scientist, developed several new ideas, including the basis for calculus. He worried, however, about the increasing reliance on science, which he believed could not explain the truly important things in life; those which can only be perceived by faith. Human beings, who had been at the center of the universe and the central link in the Great Chain of Being, became merely creatures in an unintelligibly vast universe.

Scientists slowly replaced the clergy as the people able to explain the happenings of the physical world. However, few of the discoveries – except for the aids to explorers – had any consequences on the lives of Europeans.

LITERATURE AND THE ARTS

Literature

Cervantes (1547 – 1616), a Spaniard, was a former soldier and slave concerned with the problems of religious idealism. *Don Quixote* (1605) satirized chivalric romances, describing a worldly-wise, skeptical peasant (Sancho Panzo), and a mentally unstable religious idealist (Don Quixote).

William Shakespeare (1564-1616) mixed country, court, and Renaissance ideas of the English in the 1600s, to produce tragedies, comedies, histories and sonnets. In addition to the timelessness of his themes, Shakespeare had a gift for skillfully portraying the psychological aspects of his characters. The unique manner in which he utilized the English language permanently altered its future use.

Influenced by the Renaissance while travelling in Italy, the Englishman, John Milton (1608 – 1674), had developed strong Puritan religious beliefs. *Paradise Lost* studied the motives of those who reject God. Milton took an active part in the troubles in England from 1640 to 1660, as secretary to a committee of Parliament.

Michel de Montaigne (1533 – 92), a Frenchman, became obsessed with death and the problems it raised. The inventor of the essay form, he adopted skepticism, embracing the doubt that true knowledge can be obtained, before turning to a belief in the value of individual self-study.

The Arts

Rejecting the balance and calm of Renaissance arts, Mannerists, who dominated painting and sculpture in the latter part of the sixteenth century, emphasized dramatic and emotional qualities. El Greco (1541 – 1614), a Greek who lived in Spain, took Mannerist qualities to the extreme.

17th century artists attempted to involve the viewer by emphasizing passion and mystery, as well as drama. Baroque, which emphasized grandeur, was connected with the Counter Reformation and monarchies, and was found primarily in Catholic countries.

The works of Bernini (1598 – 1680), such as his *David*, capture the appeal to emotion, the sense of tension in the object, and the subjects' human energy. Rubens (1577 – 1640), painting both religious and secular themes, conveyed the strength and majesty of his subjects.

In music, Monteverdi (1647 – 1643), using many new instruments, such as strings and woodwinds, wrote *Orfeo* (1607). He is known as the creator of the opera and the orchestra. Later in the 17th century, architecture, especially that of palaces, displayed the forces of power through the adoption of baroque forms.

SOCIETY

Hierarchy

A system whereby people, usually as members of groups, are ranked from highest to lowest in terms of power, wealth, or status, became the dominant view in the Europe of the 16th and 17th centuries.

Two major hierarchies existed: the countryside and the cities. Rural hierarchy consisted of landlords, peasants, and landless laborers. Urban hierarchy was comprised of merchants, artisans, and laborers. Clergy, lawyers, teachers, and civil servants fit somewhat awkwardly in both hierarchies.

New and expanding groups relied on education or wealth to open doors to older groups. People seeking to join the aristocracy often sought education as a means of acquiring noble status and behavior. Wealth permitted an artisan to become a merchant or, after a generation or two, a rich peasant to become a noble. The advantages of being in a higher group, besides the status, could include separate taxes and exemption from some taxes.

Social mobility – the changing from one group to another – was not accepted in the writings of the day, but did occur, though it was very hard to measure.

Demography

Exact numbers concerning population are not possible, as complete censuses do not exist. Following the Black Death and its repeated appearances in the fourteenth century, the population remained stagnant. Population began growing again in the sixteenth century and continued its upward climb until about 1650, when it levelled off for another century. The population of Europe nearly doubled between 1500 and 1650.

The population (very approximate) of some European countries in 1650 can be estimated at the following levels:

England	5.5 million
France	18.0 million
Holy Roman Empire	11.0 million
Italian peninsula	12.0 million
Spain	5.2 million
Sweden	1.5 million
United Provinces	1.5 million

Cities grew much faster than the population as a whole, as people migrated from the countryside. London grew from 50,000 in 1500 to 200,000 in 1650. Cities contained perhaps 10 to 20 percent of the total population of Europe.

The Family

The majority of households consisted of the nuclear family. A baby had a twenty-five percent chance of surviving to the age of one, a fifty percent chance of surviving to the age of twenty and a ten percent chance of reaching sixty. The average age of marriage was approximately 27 for men and 25 for women, though the nobility married younger. Few people married early enough or lived long enough to see their grandchildren.

The theory of family relationships, as expressed in sermons and writings, was one of patriarchy, with the father and husband responsible for, and in command, of the rest of the family. The reality of family relationships was more complex and, due to lack of sources, is not clear to historians.

Romantic love did exist, especially after marriage, but historians disagree as to whether it was the dominant element in forming marriages. Women, particularly in urban areas, shared in the work of their artisan and merchant husbands but rarely operated a business on their own.

The family was stable, as divorce was very rare.

Witchcraft

Witch-hunting, though found in the late Middle Ages, occurred primarily in the 16th and 17th centuries. Belief in witches was found among all parts of society - the educated, the religious, and the poor.

Historians and anthropologists provide many explanations as to why people believed in witches, and to why witch-hunting occurred when and where it did. Perhaps people needed a reason when things went badly. Another explanation is that the increased concern with religion, as a result of the Reformation, focused more attention on the role of the devil in life.

A charge of witchcraft could punish the aberrant, the nonconformist. Repression of sexuality could result in the projection of fears and hopes onto women, who then had to be punished. Though exact numbers are not possible, we know that thousands of witches were executed, with numbers varying from place to place.

Food and Diet

Bread was the staff of life - the chief item in the diet of the laboring classes. Vegetables included only peas and beans, as the vegetables from the Americas were not widely used by 1650. Meat and eggs were saved for special occasions except among the richer elements of society. Beverages included beer and wine, as milk was considered unhealthy except for the young.

Nobles and the bourgeoisie ate lots of rich meats, fish, cheeses and sweets, but consumed few vegetables or fruit. The English ate better than the rest of Europe, with the peoples of the Mediterranean areas being the worst-off. Local famines were still common, as governments lacked the ability to move food from one area of surplus to another of dearth.

The Economy

Inflation, sometimes called the price revolution, began around 1500 and continued until about the middle of the seventeenth century. Foodstuffs rose in price tenfold. The rise in population was the primary cause of the inflation, as there were more mouths to feed than food available. Another possible cause was the flow of silver from the Americas, which increased the amount of money available to buy things.

Farmers sought to increase output as the price of food rose. Land that had been idle since the Black Death of 1348 was brought under cultivation. In England, enclosures produced larger, more efficient farms, but resulted in fewer people living on the land. In Eastern Europe, landlords turned their lands into large wheat exporting operations and began the process of converting the peasants and laborers into serfs

Trade and industry grew, with the rest of the world as well as within Europe. Certain areas began to specialize: for example, the lands south and east of the Baltic produced wheat for northwestern Europe. The Dutch fleet dominated European trade.

The textile industry, the chief industry of Europe since the Middle Ages, underwent change. Regional specialization occurred on a larger scale. The putting-out system appeared, whereby the industry moved out of the cities into the countryside, and the process of production was divided into steps, with different workers doing each step.

Mercantilism

The conscious pursuit by governments of policies designed to increase national wealth, especially that of gold, became common in the seventeenth century. The chief aim was to obtain a favorable balance of international payments. Governments sought to create industries in order to avoid importing items.

2 BOURBON, BAROQUE, AND THE ENLIGHTENMENT (1648-1789)

HISTORICAL SETTING

The Thirty Years' War (1618 – 1648) had just ended, leaving a devastated Germany and Central Europe of some four hundred semi-autonomous states, referred to as "The Empire" (i.e., the Holy Roman Empire of the Middle Ages).

The Bourbon dynasty emerged stronger than the Hapsburgs, who had dominated Europe for a century and a half.

Peace of Westphalia (1648)

The principle that "the religion of the Prince is the religion of the realm" was extended to permit the Reformed faith (Calvinism) in Germany as well as Catholic and Lutheran Churches.

Dutch and Swiss republics were granted formal recognition as independent powers. Additionally, Sweden, Prussia, and France gained new territory.

Treaty of the Pyrenees (1659)

The war between France and Spain continued for eleven more years until Spain finally ceded to France part of the Spanish Netherlands and territory in northern Spain. A marriage was arranged between Louis XIV, Bourbon king of France, and Maria Theresa, daughter of the Hapsburg king of Spain, Philip IV.

War of Devolution (First Dutch War), 1667 – 68

After the death of his father-in-law, Philip IV, Louis XIV claimed the Spanish Netherlands (Belgium) in the name of his wife. The Law of Devolution granted inheritance to the heirs of a first marriage precedent to those of a second marriage. This law applied in private relationships to property rights, but Louis XIV applied it to political sovereignty.

France invaded the Spanish Netherlands with 50,000 troops in 1667 without a declaration of war. As a defensive measure, England, Holland, and Sweden formed the Triple Alliance.

Treaty of Aix-la-Chapelle (1668)

France received twelve fortified towns on the border of the Spanish Netherlands, but gave up Franche-Comté (Burgundy). Furthermore, the question of sovereignty over the Spanish Netherlands was deferred.

Second Dutch War (1672 – 78)

Louis XIV sought revenge for Dutch opposition to French annexation of the Spanish Netherlands. As a Catholic king, he also opposed Dutch Calvinism and republicanism.

France disputed the Triple Alliance by signing separate treaties with England (Charles II: Treaty of Dover, 1670) and with Sweden (1672).

In 1672, France invaded southern Holland with 100,000 troops. WILLIAM III of Orange became head of state. The Dutch opened the dikes to flood the land, saving Holland and the city of Amsterdam from the French.

At the war's end, the Peace of Nijmegan (1678 – 79) granted Holland all of its lost territory, while Spain and France exchanged more than a dozen territories.

Invasion of the Spanish Netherlands (1683)

France occupied Luxemburg and Trier and seized Lorraine while signing a twenty-year truce with The Empire.

The League of Augsburg was formed in 1686 to counteract the French and restore the balance of power. Members includedThe Empire, Holland, Spain, Sweden, the Palatinate, Saxony, Bavaria, and Savoy.

War of the League of Augsburg (1688 – 97)

The Glorious Revolution of 1688 brought William III of Orange and his wife, Mary, to the throne of England.

The War of the League of Augsburg opened the long period of Anglo-French rivalry which continued until the defeat of Napoleon in 1815. France fought against the two leading naval powers of the day, Holland and England, and in three theaters of war--the Rhine, in the Low Countries, and in Italy.

Known in North America as King William's War (1689 – 97), English and French colonials clashed along the New York and New England frontiers.

Treaty of Ryswick (1697)

France, England, and Holland agreed to restore captured territories. Fortresses in the Spanish Netherlands were to be garrisoned with Dutch troops as a buffer zone between France and Holland. Additionally, French sovereignty over Alsace and Strasbourg was acknowledged as permanent.

War of the Spanish Succession (1701 – 13)

Charles II, the last of the Hapsburg kings of Spain, died childless on November 1, 1700.

The king's will named Philip of Anjou, the grandson of Louis XIV and Maria Theresa, to be king of Spain. In 1698 King Charles had named Emperor Leopold's grandson, the seven-year-old Electoral Prince Joseph Ferdinand of Bavaria, as his sole heir. The boy died a few months later and in October 1700, and the king signed the new will in favor of Philip.

The Second Partition Treaty, however, signed by England, Holland, and France in May 1700, agreed that the son (later, Emperor Charles VI) of the Austrian Hapsburg Emperor Leopold would become king of Spain and Philip of Anjou would be compensated with Italian territories. (Both the mother and first wife of Leopold were daughters of Spanish kings.)

Issues involved in the War of the Spanish Succession concerned the future of the Spanish Empire. Additional primary causes concerned the possible separation of Austrian Hapsburg lands from Spain as well as the question of French/Bourbon strength in Spain.

In a sense, Charles II made war almost inevitable. Louis XIV had to fight for his grandson's claims against those of his enemy and Leopold had to do the same.

The Grand Alliance

William III, king of England, and Stadholder, of Holland, did not want to see the Spanish Netherlands fall into French control. England also faced Spanish and French competition in the New World. A merger of the Spanish and French thrones would result in a coalition of Spain and France against England and Holland in the Americas.

In response, England, Holland, The Empire, and Prussia formed the Grand Alliance in September 1701.

War

France and Spain were stronger on land. England and Holland controlled the sea.

The Battle of Blenheim, August 13, 1704, was a brilliant victory for England and the Duke of Marlborough, and one of the key battles of the war. It began a series of military reverses that prevented French domination of Europe.

At the great Battle of Ramillies, May 23, 1706, Marlborough shattered the French army in four hours and held onto the Netherlands.

In September 1709, the bloody Battle of Malplaquet had a contrasting result when the Allies lost 24,000 men and the French lost 12,000.

The allies invaded Spain and replaced Philip with Charles. The French and Spanish, however, rallied and drove the allies from both countries, restoring the Spanish throne to the Bourbons.

The war was known as Queen Anne's War (1702 – 13) in North America. England was faced for the first time with an alliance of its two great rival empires, Spain and France. Though the results there were inconclusive, English colonials were more reliable in fighting than Spanish and French.

Treaty of Utrecht (1713)

This was the most important European treaty since the Peace of Westphalia in 1648.

The Spanish Empire was partitioned and a Bourbon remained on the throne of Spain. Philip V (Philip of Anjou) retained Spain and the Spanish Empire in America. He explicitly renounced his claims to the French throne. The Hapsburg Empire in Central Europe acquired the Spanish Netherlands (Austrian Netherlands thereafter) and territories in Italy.

England took Gibraltar, Minorca, Newfoundland, Hudson's Bay, and Nova Scotia. France retained Alsace and the city of Strasbourg.

As a result, the Hapsburgs became a counterbalance to French power in western Europe, but no longer occupied the Spanish throne.

War of the Austrian Succession (1740 – 48)

Charles VI died in 1740 and his daughter ,23-year-old Maria Theresa (reigned 1740 – 80), inherited the Austrian Hapsburg Empire. Frederick the Great, age 28, (reigned 1740 – 86) had just inherited the Prussian throne from his father, Frederick William I. In 1840 Frederick suddenly invaded the Hapsburg territory of Silesia, and England joined Austria against Prussia, Bavaria, France, and Spain.

Frederick's brilliant military tactics won many victories. His long night marches, sudden flank attacks, and surprise actions contrasted with the usual siege warfare of the time.

The war was known in North America as King George's War (1744 – 48). Colonial militia from Massachusetts captured Louisburg, the fortified French naval base on Cape Breton Island commanding the entrance to the St. Lawrence River and Valley. Louisburg was returned to France after the war in exchange for Madras in India, which the French had captured.

The Treaty of Aix-la-Chapelle (1748), ended the war and Prussia emerged as one of the Great Powers. By retaining Silesia, Prussia doubled its population.

The Seven Years' War (1756 – 63)

Britain and France renewed hostilities as the French and Indian War (1754 – 63) began at the entrance to the Ohio Valley. At stake was control of the North American continent.

In Europe, Austria sought to regain Silesia with its important textile industry and rich deposits of coal and iron. Maria Theresa persuaded Louis XV to overlook their traditional Bourbon-Hapsburg enmity and aid Austria in a war with Prussia.

Russia, under Czarina Elizabeth (reigned 1741 – 62), joined the alliance. She disliked Frederick the Great intensely and feared Prussian competition in Poland. Great Britain provided Prussia with funds but few troops. Prussia was then faced with fighting almost alone against three major powers of Europe: Austria, France, and Russia. Their combined population was fifteen times that of Prussia.

The Seven Years' War was the hardest fought war in the eighteenth century. In six years Prussia won eight brilliant victories and lost eight others. Berlin was twice captured and partially burned by Russian troops. Still Prussia prevailed. In the process Prussia emerged as one of the Great Powers of Europe and established the reputation of having the best soldiers on the Continent.

William Pitt the Elder led the British to victory. The Royal Navy defeated both the French Atlantic and Mediterranean squadrons in 1759. Britain's trade prospered while French overseas trade dropped to one-sixth its pre-war level. The British captured French posts near Calcutta and Madras in India, and defeated the French in Quebec and Montreal.

In 1762 Elizabeth of Russia died and her successor, Czar Peter III, was a great admirer of Frederick the Great. Though he occupied the Russian throne only from January to July, he took Russia out of the war at a historically decisive moment.

By the Treaty of Hubertsburg (1763) Austria recognized Prussian retention of Silesia.

Treaty of Paris (1763)

France lost all possessions in North America to Britain. (In 1762 France had ceded to Spain all French claims west of the Mississippi River and New Orleans.) France retained fishing rights off the coast of Newfoundland and Martinique and Guadeloupe, sugar islands in the West Indies. Spain ceded the Floridas to Britain in exchange for the return of Cuba.

The American War for Independence as a European War, 1775 – 83

France entered the French-American Alliance of 1778 in an effort to regain lost prestige in Europe and to weaken her British adversary. In 1779 Spain joined France in the war, hoping to recover Gibraltar and the Floridas.

French troops strengthened Washington's forces. The leadership of French field officers such as Lafayette aided in strategic planning. Admiral DeGrasse's French fleet prevented the evacuation of Lord Cornwallis from Yorktown in the final decisive battle of the war in 1781. Rochambeau's and Lafayette's French troops aided Washington at Yorktown.

Treaty of Paris (1783)

Britain recognized the independence of the United States of America, and retroceded the Floridas to Spain.

Britain left France no territorial gains by signing a separate and territorially generous treaty with the United States.

ECONOMIC DEVELOPMENTS

Traditional Economic Conditions

Poverty was the norm during the Middle Ages. Infant mortality rate was 50% and sometimes half the surviving children died before reaching adulthood. As late as 1700, the overall life expectancy was 30 years of age.

Subsistence farming was the dominant occupation historically and famine was a regular part of life. One-third of the population of Finland, for example, died in the famine of 1696 – 97. France, one of the richer agricultural lands, experienced eleven general famines in the 17th century and sixteen in the 18th century.

Contagious diseases decimated towns and villages: smallpox, measles, diptheria, typhoid, scarlet fever, bubonic plague, and typhus.

Political and economic freedoms associated with the Protestant Reformation and biblical work ethic gradually began to change the economy of Europe as innovation, hard work, frugality, and entrepreneurship became the norm.

Social Institutions Necessary for Commerce and a Prosperous Economy

A prosperous economy needs a moral system as a base for reliance on a complex system of expectations and contracts. This was found both in traditional Catholic morality and in the Protestant Reformation of the 16th century. A modern economy could not function without confidence in people living up to their agreements with a sense of individual responsibility towards the following: 1) Credit; 2) Representations as to quality; 3) Promises to deliver products or to buy them when produced; 4) Agreements to share profits; 5) Honoring a bank check or bill of exchange; 6) Obligations of contracts – written or verbal.

The legal system in society reinforced individual morality with the recognition of legal enforcement of contracts and property claims--bills of exchange and banking (checks); insurance and payment of claims; recognition of property rights; and avoidance of confiscatory taxation.

Innovations in business arrangements abounded. Joint stock companies enabled enterprises to accumulate capital from many investors. Double entry bookkeeping provided a check on clerical accuracy, enabling managers to detect errors. Banknotes were used as a medium of exchange. The divided European political structure enabled merchants and businessmen to compete as they sought to locate themselves in places with a favorable business climate.

Mercantilism

There were several basic assumptions of mercantilism: 1) Wealth is measured in terms of commodities, especially gold and silver, rather than in terms of productivity and income-producing investments; 2) Economic activities should increase the power of the national government in the direction of state controls; 3) Since a favorable balance of trade was important, a nation should purchase as little as possible from nations regarded as enemies. The concept of the mutual advantage of trade was not widely accepted; and 4) Colonies existed for the benefit of the mother country, not for any mutual benefit that would be gained by economic development.

The philosophy of mercantilism had mixed results in the economy of Europe. On the one hand, the state encouraged economic growth and expansion. On the other, it tended to stifle entrepreneurship, competition, and innovation through monopolies, trade restrictions, and state regulation of commerce.

As a generalization, taxes were low enough not to discourage economic expansion since the expectations of the government from domestic society were small. There were relatively few administrative officials in a day when communication and transportation was slow. Compare France, one of the most bureaucratic states of Europe in the 18th century, with France in the 20th century. Then, 12,000 civil servants meant one bureaucrat for every 1,250 people. Today it is one for every 70 people.

The wars of the 17th and 18th centuries involved dynastic disputes, balance-of-power struggles, and mercantilistic competition for trade, raw materials, and colonies. Though economics was involved, it was not as important a factor as the more traditional power politics of international competition. It would have been less of a factor without some of the philosophical assumptions of mercantilism.

In the 19th century, more thought was directed toward encouraging economic initiative by average citizens to benefit temselves and by extention the entire country. Adam Smith's *The Wealth of Nations*, published in 1776, led the way to a more laissez-faire approach. Smith wrote at the beginning of the American War for Independence:

"To prohibit a great people ... from making all that they can of every part of their own produce, or from employing their stock and industry in the way that they judge most advantageous to themselves, is a manifest violation of the most sacred rights of mankind."

It was the Dutch and the English who led the way toward the concept of productivity as a measure of national wealth. As a result, Holland became one of the most productive countries in the world in the 17th century, and England in the 18th and 19th centuries. There was always a certain ambivalence, however, in the English attitude as laws like the Navigation Acts indicated. Such restrictive laws were passed in the early Industrial Revolution.

In France, Jean Baptiste Colbert (1619 – 1683), economic adviser to Louis XIV, used the government to encourage economic productivity and aided in the prosperity of France. But his dictatorial regulations were also counter-productive. For example, he forbade the emigration of skilled French workers and specified in detail methods of production. He also believed that foreign trade was a fixed quantity rather than one that grew with demand and lower prices. France, as most states, had high protective tariffs.

The lowering of interest rates also stimulated investment and productivity. Here England led the way: 1600: 10%; 1625: 8%; 1651: 6%; 1715: 5%; 1757: 3%.

Growth of Trade

Expansion of Europe's overseas trade resulted from the discovery of an all-water route to Asia around Africa as well as the discovery of the Western Hemisphere which provided an area of settlement and trade. The need for spices for food -preservation, and the desire for luxury goods from the Far East and the Near East, served as incentive.

Population growth expanded domestic markets far in excess of overseas trade. European population at the beginning of the seventeenth century was 70 million. By the end of the eighteenth century it had doubled. Productivity and economic growth increased even faster during the same period.

Innovative scientific and technological discoveries and inventions stimulated trade. Likewise, three-masted trading vessels lowered the costs of transportation and made possible trading over greater distances. Canal and road building also stimulated trade and productivity.

Capitalist systems of banking, insurance, and investment made possible the accumulation of capital essential for discovery and economic growth.

Urbanization was both a cause and a result of economic growth. Urbanization requires and creates a network of market relationships. Towns with prosperous tradeincreased in population while towns which did not prosper in trade quickly stagnated. Additionally, urbanization provided the opportunity and market for commercial services such as banking, insurance, warehousing, and commodity trading, as well as medicine, law, government, and churches.

Agricultural Changes

Feudal/manorial changes began in Europe, especially in England, and were replaced by absentee landlords and by commercial farms. Urbanization, increased population, and improvements in trade stimulated the demand for agricultural products.

The design of farm implements was improved. All-metal plows came into use in England as well as horse-drawn cultivators. Drainage and reclamation of swamp land was expanded. Experiments with crops, seeds, machines, breeds of animals, and fertilizers were systematically attempted.

Improvements In Transportation

The construction of canals and roads was of fundamental importance (Railroads were not developed until the 1830's).

The canal lock was invented in Italy in the 17th century soon after Holland began building canals.

The major rivers of France were linked by canals during the 17th century. England's coastal shipping made canals less pressing and so it was not until the 18th century that canals were built there.

All-weather roads were constructed after the mid-18th century when John Macadam (1756–1836) discovered that a gravelled and raised road-bed could carry vehicles year round.

Industrial Technology

Thomas Necomen in 1706 invented an inefficient steam engine as a pump. James Watt, between 1765 and 1769, improved the design so that the expansive power of hot steam could drive a piston. Later, Watt translated the motion of the piston into rotary motion.

The steam engine became one of the most significant inventions in human history. It was no longer necessary to locate factories on mountain streams where water wheels were used to supply power. Its portability meant that both steamboats and railroad engines could be built to transport goods across continents. Ocean-going vessels were no longer dependent on winds to power them.

At the same time, textile machines revolutionized that industry.

John Kay introduced the flying shuttle in 1733. James Hargreave invented the spinning jenny in 1770. Richard Arkwright perfected the spinning frame in 1769. Samuel Crompton introduced the spinning mule in 1779. Edward Cartwright invented the power loom in 1785.

Factors In Sustained Economic Growth

Innovation was a key elemet – by extension of trade and discovery of new resources; by lowering costs of production; by introducing new products and new ways of doing things; in organizing production and marketing methods; and in overcoming resistance to innovation.

The development of free enterprise stimulated new ideas. This was made possible where the state was not excessively involved in the economy. In England, the Puritan Revolution of the 1640's challenged the royal right to grant monopolies and trade privileges. The English common law afterwards adopted the principle of free enterprise open to all. With free enterprise came the responsibility of risk-taking with the possibilities of losses as well as profits.

Free movement of populations provided necessary labor resources. People "voted with their feet" and found their way to new jobs. Many moved to England from Europe. The population of England in 1700 was about 5.5 million and only 6 million by 1750. The economic growth during the last half of the century increased the population of England to 9 million by 1800, a fifty percent growth in a half century. Because of the Industrial Revolution of the 19th century, this figure doubled to 18 million by 1850.

BEGINNINGS OF MODERN SCIENCE AND THE AGE OF THE ENLIGHTENMENT

Scientific Revolution

Modern science had its origins in the 16th and 17th century "Scientific Revolution". "The Enlightenment" was an eighteenth century movement.

Nicholas Copernicus (1473 – 1543) discovered that the earth is but one of many planets revolving around the sun and turning on its own axis to make day and night. He demonstrated that the Greek mathematician, Ptolemy, was mistaken in his idea that the earth was a stationery planet in the center of the universe.

Tycho Brahe (1546 – 1601), a Danish nobleman, built an expensive observatory and systematically pursued Copernicus' theories.

Johann Kepler (1571 – 1630), the first great Protestant scientist and assistant to Brahe, discovered that the orbits of the planets are ellipses which complete their orbits in equal times. He explained the speed of the planets in their orbits and found that the planets do not move with the sun as focal point.

Galileo Galilei (1564 – 1642) was Professor of Physics and Military Engineering at the University of Padua. He was the first to use the telescope as a scientific instrument and built a powerful telescope himself. His discoveries and use of the telescope were a great aid in the voyages of discovery and had a direct effect on navigation. He provided artillery with a means of surveying distant targets for more accurate marksmanship. Galileo's discoveries in mechanics had far-reaching significance. He proved that all falling bodies descend with equal velocity, regardless of weight. He found that a long pendulum swing takes the same time as the short one, so that some force increases the speed of each swing by equal amounts in equal times.

Francis Bacon (1561 – 1626), Lord Chancellor of England, specified inductive method for scientific experimentation. Inductive observation, the development of hypotheses, experimentation, and organization were to be the keys to scientific inquiry.

Rene Descartes (1596 – 1650) wrote his *Discourse on Method* to build on the scientific method by using deductive analysis on scientific discoveries. He wrote that science must begin with clear and incontrovertible facts and then subdivide each problem into as many parts as necessary, following a step-by-step logical sequence in solving complex problems. Descartes was particularly a leader in mathematics and philosophy.

Scientific Societies

Scientific societies were organized in many European countries in the 17th century. Italy began the first scientific societies in Naples, Rome, and Florence. The Royal Observatory was established at Greenwich in 1675 and the Royal Society in 1662; private donations and entrance fees from members financed the society. The French

Academie des Sciences was founded in 1666. King Frederick I of Brandenburg-Prussia chartered the Berlin Academy of Sciences in 1700. Finally, Peter the Great founded the St. Petersburg Academy of Sciences in 1725.

Sir Isaac Newton (1642 – 1747) taught mathematics at Cambridge, was Master of the Royal Mint in London, and for twenty-five years was the President of the Royal Society. Most of his work was done in astronomy, the dominant science of the seventeenth century. He worked with magnification, prisms, and refraction. He used lenses with different curvature and different kinds of glass. Newton's greatest contribution, however, was in discovering his principle of universal gravitation, which he explained in *Philosophiae Naturalis Principia Mathematica*, published in 1687. He claimed to "subject the phenomena of nature to the laws of mathematics" and saw order and design throughout the entire cosmos.

Science and religion were not in conflict in the seventeenth and eighteenth centuries. Scientists universally believed they were studying and analyzing God's creation, not an autonomous phenomena known as "Nature." There was no attempt, as in the nineteenth and twentieth centuries, to secularize science. "Natural law," they believed, was created by God for man's use. A tension between the natural and the supernatural simply did not exist in their world view. The question of the extent of the Creator's involvement directly or indirectly in his Creation was an issue of the eighteenth century but there was universal agreement among scientists and philosophers as to the supernatural origin of the universe.

The Age of the Enlightenment

For the first time in human history, the 18th century saw the appearance of a secular world view to capture the imagination of many intellectuals. In the past some kind of a religious perspective had always been central to western civilization. This was true of the ancient Egyptians, Hebrews, Persians, Greeks, and Romans. It was also true of medieval Catholic Christendom and of the 16th century Protestant Reformation. By contrast, the 18th century philosophers, who declared themselves "enlightened," thought that "light" came from man's ability to reason. They rejected the idea that light must come from God, either through the Church (the Catholic position) or the Scriptures (the Protestant position). The Enlightenment opened the door to a secularized anthropocentric universe instead of the traditional theocentric view.

The philosophical starting point for the Enlightenment was the belief in the autonomy of man's intellect apart from God. The most basic assumption was faith in reason rather than faith in revelation. The "Enlightened" claimed for themselves, however, a rationality they were unwilling to concede to their opponents.

The Enlightenment believed in the existence of God as a rational explanation of the universe and its form, but that "god" was a deistic Creator who created the universe and then was no longer involved in its mechanistic operation. The mechanistic operation was governed by "natural law." Enlightenment philosophers are sometimes characterized as being either basically rationalists or basically empiricists.

Rationalists

Rationalists stressed deductive reasoning or mathematical logic as the basis for their epistemology (source of knowledge). They started with "self-evident truths" or postulates, from which they constructed a coherent and logical system of thought.

Rene Descartes (1596 – 1650) sought a basis for logic and thought he found it in man's ability to think. "I think; therefore, I am" was his most famous statement. That statement cannot be denied without thinking. Therefore, it must be an absolute truth that man can think. His proof depends upon logic alone.

Baruch Spinoza (1632 – 77) developed a rational pantheism in which he equated God and nature. He denied all free will and ended up with an impersonal, mechanical universe – a universe with no one there.

Gottfried Wilhelm Leibniz (1646 – 1716) worked on symbolic logic and calculus, and invented a calculating machine. He, too, had a mechanistic world-and-life view and thought of God as a hypothetical abstraction rather than persona.

Empiricists

Empiricists stressed inductive observation as the basis for their epistemology, in short, the scientific method. Their emphasis was on sensory experience.

John Locke (1632 – 1704) pioneered in the empiricist approach to knowledge and stressed the importance of environment in human development. He classified knowledge as 1) according to reason; 2) contrary to reason; and 3) above reason. Locke thought reason and revelation were both complementary and from God.

David Hume (1711 – 76) was a Scottish historian and philosopher who began by emphasizing the limitations of human reasoning and later became a dogmatic skeptic.

The people of the Enlightenment believed in absolutes; they were not relativists. They believed in absolute truth, absolute ethics, and absolute natural law. And they believed optimistically that these absolutes were discoverable by man's rationality. It wasn't long, of course, before one rationalist's "absolutes" clashed with another's.

The Enlightenment believed in a closed system of the universe in which the supernatural was not involved in human life. This was in sharp contrast to the traditional view of an open system in which God, angels, and devils were very much a part of human life on this earth.

The Philosophes

The Philosophes were popularizers of the Enlightenment, not professional philosophers. They were men and women "of letters," such as journalists and teachers. They frequented the salons, cafes, and discussion groups in France. They were cultured, refined, genteel intellectuals who had unbounded confidence in man's ability to improve society through sophistication and rational thought. They had a habit of criticizing everything in their path – including rationalism.

Francois-Marie Arouet (1694 – 1778) better known as Voltaire, was one of the most famous philosophes. He attended an upper-class Jesuit school in Paris and became well-known for his unusual wit and irreverence. His sharp tongue and "subversive" poetry led to an eleven-month imprisonment in the Bastille. Voltaire lived in England for several years and greatly admired the freedom in the relatively open English society. He accepted Deism and believed in a finite, limited God who he thought of as the Watchmaker of the universe. Characteristically, Voltaire relied on ridicule rather than reason to present his case.

Jean-Jacques Rousseau (1712 – 78) lived in Geneva until he was forced to flee to England because of what the government considered radical ideas. Rousseau thought of man in a simpler state of nature as "the noble savage" and sought to throw off the restraints of civilization. Rousseau saw autonomous freedom as the ultimate good. Later in life he decided that if a person did not want Rousseau's utopian ideas, he would be "forced to be free," an obvious contradiction in terms. Rousseau has been influential in western civilization for over two hundred years with his emphasis on freedom as a Bohemian ideal. His book on education, *Emile* (1762) is still popular, despite the fact that he left his five illegitimate children in an orphanage instead of putting his educational theories to work with his own children.

Chronology

The Enlightenment varied in emphasis from country to country; the French Enlightenment was not exactly the same as the English or German Enlightenment.

Distinctions can also be made chronologically in the development of Enlightenment thought. The end of the 17th and first half of the 18th century saw a reaction against "enthusiasm," or emotionalism and sought moderation and balance in a context of ordered freedom. From the mid-18th century the Enlightenment moved into a skeptical, almost iconoclastic phase where it was fashionable to deride and tear down. The last three decades of the 18th century were revolutionary, radical, and aggressively dogmatic in defense of various abstractions demanding a revolutionary commitment. "Love of mankind" made it one's duty to crush those who disagreed and thus impeded "progress." In short, the Enlightenment entered a utopian phase that became disastrous as it brought on the French Revolution.

The "Counter-Enlightenment"

The "Counter-Enlightenment" is a comprehensive term of diverse and even disparate groups who disagreed with the fundamental assumptions of the Enlightenment and pointed out its weaknesses. This was not a "movement," but merely a convenient category.

Theistic Opposition

German pietism, especially Count von Zinzendorf, (1700 – 60), leader of the Moravian Brethren, taught the need for a spiritual conversion and a religious experience. Methodism of the 18th century similarly taught the need for spiritual regeneration and a moral life that would demonstrate the reality of the conversion. Methodism was led by an Anglican minister, John Wesley, (1703 – 91). The Great Awakening in the English colonies in America in the 1730's and 1740's, led by Jonathan Edwards, had a similar result.

Roman Catholic Jansenism in France argued against the idea of an uninvolved or impersonal God. Hasidism in Eastern European Jewish communities, especially in the 1730's, stressed a joyous religious ferver in direct communion with God. Both of these were in sharp contrast to Deism, which at the same time gaining adherents in England.

Philosophic Reaction

Some philosophers questioned the fundamental assumptions of rationalist philosophy.

David Hume (1711 – 1776) for example, struck at faith in natural law as well as faith in religion. He insisted that "man can accept as true only those things for which he has the evidence of factual observation." (Then why accept Hume's statement as true?) Since the philosophes lacked indisputable evidence for their belief in the existence of natural law, Hume believed in living with a "total suspension of judgment." (But if one must be a dogmatic skeptic, then why not be skeptical about dogmatic skepticism?)

Immanuel Kant (1724 – 1794) separated science and morality into separate branches of knowledge. He said that science could describe the natural phenomena of the material world but could not provide a guide for morality. Kant's "categorical imperative" was an intuitive instinct, implanted by God in conscience. Both the ethical sense and aesthetic appreciation in human beings are beyond the knowledge of science. Reason is a function of the mind and has no content in and of itself.

BOURBON FRANCE

French Foreign Policy

France was the dominant European power from 1660 to 1713. Louis XIV, however, was unable to extend French boundaries to the Rhine River–one of his chief objectives.

From 1713 to 1789 no one European power dominated international politics. Instead, the concept of the Balance of Power prevailed. A readjustment of power was necessary in central and eastern Europe as a result of the decline of Sweden, Poland, and the Ottoman Empire. This period was characterized by a power struggle between France and England for colonial supremacy in India and in America.

France Under Louis XIV (1643 – 1715)

Louis XIV was vain, arrogant, and charming to the aristocratic ladies of his court. He was five feet five inches tall and wore shoes with high heels.

The king had great physical endurance for long hours of council meetings and endless ceremonies and entertainments. He seemed indifferent to heat and cold and survived a lifetime of abnormal eating.

Moreover, he aspired to be an absolute ruler with no one challenging his dictatorial powers.

The most significant challenge to royal absolutism in France in the 17th century was a series of three revolts (called *Frondes*, meaning "a child's slingshot") by some of the nobility and judges of the parlements or courts of Paris. Competition among the nobility, however, enabled the government to put down the revolts. All three of these occurred when Louis XIV was very young (ages 5 – 11) and made a lasting impression on him; he was determined that no revolt would be successful during his reign.

The king believed in absolute, unquestioned authority. Louis XIV deliberately got his chief ministers from the middle class in order to keep the aristocracy out of government. No members of the royal family or the high aristocracy were admitted to the daily council sessions at Versailles, where the king presided personally over deliberations of his ministers.

Council orders were transmitted to the provinces by intendants, who supervised all phases of local administration (especially courts, police, and the collection of taxes). Additionally, Louis XIV nullified the power of French institutions which might challenge his centralized bureaucracy.

Louis XIV never called the Estates-General. His intendants arrested the members of the three provincial estates who criticized royal policy; and the parlements were too intimidated by the lack of success of the *Frondes* to offer further resistance.

Control of the peasants, who numbered 95% of the French population, was accomplished by numerous means. Some peasants kept as little as 20% of their cash crops after paying the landlord, the government, and the Church. Peasants also were subject to the *corvee*, a month's forced labor on the roads. People not at work on the farm were conscripted into the French army or put into workhouses. Finally, rebels were hanged or forced to work as galley slaves.

Colbert, finance minister from 1661 to 1683, improved the economy and the condition of the royal treasury. He reduced the number of tax collectors; reduced local tolls in order to encourage domestic trade; improved France's transportation system with canals and a growing merchant marine; organized a group of French trading companies (the East India Company, the West India Company, the Levant Company, and the Company of the North); and paid bounties to ship builders to strengthen trade.

Palace of Versailles

Louis XIV moved his royal court from the Louvre in Paris to Versailles, twelve miles outside of Paris. The facade of his palace was a third of a mile long with vast gardens adorned with classical statuary, 1400 fountains, and 1200 orange trees.

In Paris, the court included six hundred people. At Versailles it grew to ten thousand noblemen, officials, and attendants. Sixty percent of the royal tax revenue was spent on Versailles and the upkeep of the court of Louis XIV.

The splendor of the court was in the beautiful gardens and Baroque architecture of the palace, in the luxurious furnishings of the apartments, and in the magnificent dress of men and women who went there. Often half of the income of nobles and their ladies was spent on clothing, furniture, and servants.

Extravagant amusements occupied the time of the aristocratic court: tournaments, hunts, tennis, billiards, boating parties, dinners, dances, ballets, operas, concerts, and theater. In order to celebrate the birth of his son in 1662, the king arranged a ball at the Palace of the Carrousel, which was attended by 15,000 people who danced under a thousand lights before massive mirrors.

Louis XIV's Policies Toward Christianity

The king considered himself the head of the French Catholic Church and claimed that the Pope had no temporal authority over the French Church. Louis XIV sided with the Jesuits against the Jansenists, or Catholics like Blaise Pascal who reaffirmed St. Augustine's doctrine of inherent depravity, i.e., that man is born by nature a sinner and salvation is only for the elect of God.

About a million French citizens were Protestant. Louis XIV attempted to eradicate Protestantism from France by demolishing Huguenot churches and schools, paying cash rewards to Protestants to convert to Catholicism, and by billeting soldiers in homes of those who refused to convert. In 1685 the king revoked the Edict of Nantes that had given many religious freedoms to Protestants at the time of Henry IV. The revocation took away civil rights from Protestants. Their children were required by law to be raised as Catholics. French Protestant clergymen were exiled or sent to the galleys. As many as 200,000 Huguenots fled from France – to England, Holland, and to English colonies in America. Protestantism did survive in France, but was greatly weakened.

France Under Louis XV (1715 – 74)

French people of all classes desired greater popular participation in government, rejecting royal absolutism. There was high resentment towards special privileges of the aristocracy. All nobles were exempt from certain taxes. Many were subsidized with regular pensions from the government. The highest offices of government were reserved for aristocrats. Promotions were based on political connections rather than merit. Life at Versailles was wasteful, extravagant, and frivolous.

There was no uniform code of laws, and a lack of justice in the French judicial system existed. The king had arbitrary powers of imprisonment. Government bureaucrats were often petty tyrants, many of them merely serving their own interests. The bureaucracy had become virtually a closed class within itself.

Vestiges of the feudal and manorial systems continued to upset the peasants, particularly when they were taxed excessively in comparison to other segments of society. The philosophes gave expression to these grievances and discontent grew.

Louis XV was only five years old when his great-grandfather died. Fifty-nine years later he too died, leaving many of the same problems he had inherited. Corruption and inequity in government were even more pronounced. Ominously, crowds lined the road to St. Denis, the burial place of French kings, and cursed the king's casket just as they had his predecessor.

France Under Louis XVI (1774–1792)

Louis XVI was the grandson of Louis XV. He married Marie Antoinette (1770), daughter of the Austrian Empress Maria Theresa.

Louis XVI was honest, conscientious, and sought genuine reforms, but he was indecisive and lacking in determination. He antagonized the aristocracy when he sought fiscal reforms.

One of his first acts was to restore to the French parlements their judicial powers. When he sought to impose new taxes on the under-taxed aristocracy, the parlements refused to register the royal decrees. In 1787 he granted toleration and civil rights to French Huguenots (Protestants).

In 1787 the king summoned the Assembly of the Notables, a group of 144 representatives of the nobility and higher clergy. At Versailles Louis XVI asked them to tax all lands, without regard to privilege of family; to establish provincial assemblies; to allow free trade in grain; and to abolish forced labor on the roads. The Notables refused to accept these reforms and demanded the replacement of certain of the king's ministers.

The climax of the crisis came in 1788 when the king was no longer able to achieve either fiscal reform or new loans. He could not even pay the salaries of government officials. By this time one-half of government revenues went to pay interest on the national debt (at 8%).

For the first time in 175 years the king called for a meeting of the Estates General (1789). When the Estates General formed itself into the National Assembly, the French Revolution was under way. Later in the radical phase of the revolution the National Convention voted 366 to 361 to execute the king, January 21, 1793.

SPAIN: HAPSBURG AND BOURBON

Spain in the Seventeenth Century

The Peace of Westphalia (1648) did not end the war between Spain and France; it continued for eleven more years. In the Treaty of the Pyrenees (1659), Spain ceded to France Artois in the Spanish Netherlands and territory in northern Spain. Marriage was arranged between Louis XIV, Bourbon king of France, and Maria Theresa, Hapsburg daughter of Philip IV, king of Spain. (Louis XIV's mother was the daughter of Philip III of Spain.)

The population of Spain in the 17th century declined as Spain continued expelling Moors from Spain, especially from Aragon and Valencia. In 1550 Spain had a population of 7.5 million; by 1660 it was about 5.5 million.

Formerly food-producing lands were deserted. In Castile sheep-raising took the place of food production. Food was imported from elsewhere in Europe. As production declined, inflation increased.

Work was looked upon as a necessary evil, to be avoided when possible. The upper classes preferred a life of cultured ease instead of developing and caring for their estates. Patents of nobility were purchased from the Crown, carrying with them many tax exemptions.

Capitalism was almost non-existent in Spain as savings and investment were viewed as beneath the dignity of the nobility. What industry there was in Spain – silk, woollens, and leatherwork – was declining instead of growing.

Catholic orthodoxy and aristocratic exclusiveness were high values in Spanish society. In 1660, the Spanish clergy numbered 200,000, an average of one for every thirty people.

The Spanish navy had ceased to exist by 1700; there were only eight ships left plus a few borrowed from the Genoese. Most of the soldiers in the Spanish army were foreigners.

Charles II (1665 - 1700)

Charles II, the last of the Spanish Hapsburg kings, was only four years old when his father, Philip IV, died. His mother, Marie Anne of Austria, controlled the throne as head of the council of regency. Afflicted with many diseases and of a weak constitution, the king was expected to die long before he did.

He intensely disliked the responsibilities of his office, and his timidity and lack of will power made him one of the worst rulers in Spanish history.

In 1680, he married Marie Louise of France and, on her death in 1689, he married Marie Anne of Bavaria. Since he had no child, Charles II's death in 1700 led to the War of the Spanish Succession.

Philip V (1700 – 1746)

The grandson of Louis XIV and the first Bourbon king of Spain was only seventeen years of age when he became king of Spain. The first dozen years of his reign were occupied with the War of the Spanish Succession which ended successfully for him. He modernized the Spanish army and brought it to a strength of 40,000 men.

Philip V centralized the Spanish government by using the intendant system of the French wherein the governors (or Intendants) of the provinces were under close supervision by the central government under the king. He abolished many pensions and government subsidies and restored fiscal health to the Spanish government.

Industry, agriculture, and ship-building were actively encouraged. The Spanish Navy was revived and the fleet was substantial by the end of his reign.

Philip V married the fourteen-year-old Marie Louise of Savoy, and when she died in 1714, he married Elizabeth Farnese of Parma. Philip V died during the War of the Austrian Succession and was succeeded by his son by Marie Louise, Ferdinand VI, who ruled for an uneventful thirteen years, 1746 – 1759.

Charles III (1759 – 1788)

Charles III had already had political experience as Duke of Parma and as King of the Two Sicilies. He was an able ruler and enacted many reforms during his long reign. Personally moral, pious, and hard-working, Charles III was one of the most popular of Spanish kings.

Charles helped to stimulate the economy by eliminating laws that restricted internal trade and by reducing tariffs. He encouraged new agricultural settlements and helped establish banks for farmers. He helped to create factories and gave them monopolies: woollens, tapestries, mirrors and glass, silks, and porcelain. Schools were established to teach the trades.

By the end of his reign the population of Spain had grown to 10.5 million.

Spain was a strongly Catholic country and Spanish intellectuals were not interested in the doctrines of the Enlightenment,repulsed by the irreligion of the philosophes. An ambassador wrote in 1789 that in Spain "one finds religion, love for the king, devotion to the law, moderation in the administration, scrupulous respect for the privileges of each province and the individual...."

AUSTRIAN HAPSBURGS AND CENTRAL EUROPE

History of the Hapsburgs

In 1273 Rudolph of Hapsburg was elected Holy Roman Emperor and gained permanent possession of Austria for the Hapsburg family. The Holy Roman Empire was still intact in the 18th century and consisted of 300 separate states, 51 free towns, and 1,500 free knights, each ruling a tiny state with an average of 300 subjects and an annual income of $500. The largest states of the Empire were the Hapsburg Monarchy, with a population of ten million inside the Empire and twelve million outside; Prussia, with a population of 5.5 million; Bavaria and Saxony, with a population of 2 million each; and Hanover, with a population of 900,000.

The Emperor also claimed authority over seventy-five small principalities.

The custom was to select the ruler of Austria as the Emperor because he alone had sufficient power to enforce Imperial decisions. (A brief exception was Charles VII of Bavaria.) After the War of the Spanish Succession (1701 – 13) and the Treaty of Utrecht (1713), the Spanish throne was occupied by a Bourbon, so Hapsburg power was concentrated in Austria. The Austrian Hapsburgs ruled the Empire: Naples, Sardinia, and Milan in Italy; the Austrian Netherlands (now Belgium); Hungary and Transylvania. Austria was not a national state; its lands included Germans, Hungarians, Czechs, Croats, Italians, Serbs, Rumanians, and others.

Government of the Austrian Empire

Since different parts of the Empire bore a different legal relationship to the Emperor, there was no single constitutional system or administration for all parts of the realm. The Emperor was duke of Austria, margrave of Styria, duke of Carinthia, Lord of Swabia, count of Tyrol, king of Bohemia, king of Hungary, Transylvania, Croatia, Slavonia and Dalmatia, besides his titles in Italy and the Austrian Netherlands.

The Hapsburg Empire had four chancelleries: the Austrian (with two chancellors); the Bohemian; the Hungarian; and the Translyvanian. There were also departments responsible for the affairs of Italy and the Austrian Netherlands.

In addition, the Central Government under the Emperor consisted of the Privy Council (Geheimer Rat) which discussed high policy; the Hofkammer, which made decisions regarding finance and trade; the Hofkriegsrat, which was the War Council; the Imperial Chancellery, which dealt with matters of Empire; and the Court Chancellery, which dealt with domestic matters.

Feudalism in the Hapsburg Empire

The lords of the manor had political as well as economic controls over the peasants. Peasants were under the judicial authority of the lord. They could not marry without the lord's consent. Their children could not work or serve an apprenticeship outside the estate. The peasant could not contract a loan or sell anything without the lord's consent. Peasants were obligated to the *corvée*, or compulsory labor, for as many as 100 days a year. Peasants were obliged to buy products supplied by the lord at the prices he set. There were tolls to pay, customs duties, duties on transactions, quit-rents and other taxes.

Music and Vienna

The most famous and popular of the arts in the Hapsburg Empire, and especially in Vienna, was music. Leopold I, a composer himself, was particularly significant as a patron of music. Royal concerts, ballets, and operas were part of the life of Vienna. Italians came to Austria, Bohemia, and Hungary to direct or improve their musical productions. The Slavs and Magyars excelled in singing and playing of instruments.

Adam Michna z Otradovic (1600 – 76) composed hymns based on Czech poetry and the famous St. Wenceslas Mass, honoring the national hero.

Emperor Leopold I (1658 – 1705)

Leopold I was the first cousin of King Louis XIV of France and also of King Charles II of Spain. He loved poetry, music, and was a patron of the arts. A devout Catholic, Leopold followed the advice of the Jesuits and sought to restrict severely his Protestant subjects. He employed German and Italian artists to build and decorate Baroque churches and palaces.

One of Leopold's most severe tests came with the Turkish invasion of Austria, and siege of Vienna itself, in 1683. The Turks were driven back by the Poles, Austrians, and Hungarians.

Emperor Leopold I was a key figure in the War of Spanish Succession.

Emperor Charles VI (1711 – 1740)

Following a brief reign by his older brother, Joseph I (1705 – 11), who died of smallpox at the age of thirty-three, Charles VI, son of Leopold I, came to the Austrian throne. Charles VI had a keen sense of duty and lived a conscientiously moral life. He was meticulous in his administration and personally involved in the details of governing.

Early in his reign he signed the Treaty of Szatmar with the Hungarians, recognizing their particular liberties and returning the Crown to St. Stephen. The Hungarian Chancellery was to be autonomous within the administration.

Maria Theresa (1740 – 1780)

Maria Theresa was not really the "Empress" although she was often referred to as such. First her husband and then her son was Emperor of the Holy Roman Empire. Technically she was "Queen of Bohemia and Hungary, Archduchess of Austria, ..." et. al.

Maria Theresa was a beautiful, courageous, high-minded, pious, and capable ruler. Her first reform was to increase the Austrian standing army from 30,000 to 108,000 by persuading the various estates to accept tax reforms and a tax increase. She gradually centralized the Empire and increased the power of the Austrian government.

Maria Theresa was a conservative Catholic, and considered the Church and the nobility to be the foundations of her state. She was concerned, however, with the freedom and well-being of her subjects and political realism was the hallmark of her reign. The two most important international events of her forty-year reign were the War of the Austrian Succession (1740 – 48) and the Seven Years' War (1756 – 63).

Joseph II (1765 – 1790)

Joseph II was co-regent with his mother for the last fifteen years of her reign. He sought to be an "enlightened despot" – with emphasis on despot. He wanted to govern decisively and forcefully, but rationally with the interests of his subjects in mind – at least as he envisioned them. He sought a full treasury, economy in government, and a strong military force. He sought to emulate the achievements and style of Frederick the Great of Prussia. His mother's adviser, Prince Anton von Kaunitz, provided a timely check on Joseph's ambitions. He wrote to the Emperor: "Despotic governments concern themselves with intimidation and punishment. But in monarchies [we must not forget] how much it is a joy worthy of a noble mind to govern free and thinking beings than to rule vile slaves."

Although the Emperor was a devout Catholic, he expanded the state schools of Austria and granted religious toleration to both Protestants and Jews. Joseph II died at the age of forty-nine, having suffered recent military defeats from the Turks and fearing both the growing power of Russia and revolts in the Austrian Netherlands.

PRUSSIA AND THE HOHENZOLLERNS

Brandenburg-Prussia in 1648

The Thirty Years' War had devastated Germany. Brandenburg had lost half its population through death, disease, and emigration.

Brandenburg was established by the Emperor Otto I in 950 A.D., and the ruler of Brandenburg was designated as an Elector of the Holy Roman Empire by Emperor Sigismund in 1417. By the time of the Thirty Years' War, despite its central location, Brandenburg was still an insignificant part of the Empire. By marriage, the House of Hohenzollern had also acquired widely-separated parts of the Empire. In the west, Hohenzollerns governed the duchy of Cleves and the counties of Mark and Ravensberg; in the east, they governed the duchy of East Prussia.

The Peace of Westphalia (1648) granted the Elector eastern Pomerania, three tiny bishoprics and the archbishopric of Magdeburg. Nothing in these possessions or any of the other disparate territories showed any promise of becoming a great power of Europe. Each province had its own estates, representing the towns and the nobility. They had little in common and no common administration. The terrain had no natural frontiers for defense and was not economically significant. Its population was sparse, its soil poor and sandy. It was cut off from the sea and was not on any of the trade routes of Europe.

Frederick William (1640 – 1688)

During his half-century reign the "Great Elector" established Prussia as a great power and laid the foundation for the future unification of Germany in the 19th century. He took the title "King of Prussia" since East Prussia lay outside the boundaries of the Holy Roman empire and thus was not in the jurisdiction of the Austrian Hapsburgs.

Frederick William was the nephew of King Gustavus Adolphus of Sweden and his wife was the granddaughter of William the Silent, hero of Dutch independence. He sought to emulate the government organization of the Swedes and the economic policies of the Dutch.

Frederick had been well-educated and spoke five languages. He was a strict Calvinist and settled 20,000 Huguenot refugees on his estates. He granted toleration, however, to both Catholics and Jews.

He encouraged industry and trade and brought in foreign craftsmen and Dutch farmers. In each province he established a local government, headed by a governor and chancellor, but with control from the central government in Berlin.

His most historically-significant innovation was the building of a strong standing army. He was able to do this only through heavy taxes, a rate of taxation twice as heavy as that of the French during the height of Louis XIV's power. But the Prussian nobility were not exempt from those heavy taxes, as were the French aristocracy.

The Elector sought to encourage industry and trade, but he was in danger of taxing it out of existence. New industries were started: woollens, cottons, linen, velvet, lace, silk, soap, paper, and iron products. One of his achievements was the Frederick William Canal through Berlin which linked the Elbe and Oder rivers and enabled canal traffic from Breslau and Hamburg to Berlin. He was the only Hohenzollern to be interested in overseas trade before Kaiser William II. But without ports and naval experience, the effort collapsed.

The central dynamic of Frederick William's life was his Calvinism, through which he became convinced of direct protection and guidance from God in all he did. He highly valued learning and founded the University of Pufendorf and the Berlin Library. He was greatly alarmed at the threat to Protestantism implied in Louis XIV's revocation of the Edict of Nantes in 1685 and joined the League of Augsburg in 1686.

Frederick I (1688 – 1713)

The Great Elector's son (i.e., Elector Frederick III and King Frederick I) was a weak and somewhat deformed man, but won the affection of his people as did no other Hohenzollern. He loved the splendor of the monarchy and elaborate ceremony. He built beautiful palaces and provided splendid uniforms of white satin edged with gold lace for his guards. Dinner was announced by twenty-four trumpeters. An orchestra played and the servants wore blue trimmed with gold lace.

Potsdam had been built by the Great Elector. Frederick I built a new palace in Berlin and Charlottenburg for his Queen, Sophie Charlotte, who joined her husband in the many philosophical and religious discussions common in the palace.

Frederick I founded the University of Halle in 1692, a center for two of the great concepts of the time, Pietism and Natural Law. The king welcomed as immigrants not only craftsmen, but also scholars such as Jacob Lenfant, historian of the Council of Trent, Isaac De Beausobre, translator of the New Testament, and Philip Speuer, a leading Pietist of his day. The Enlightenment philosopher Gottfried Wilhelm Leibnitz persuaded Frederick to found an academy of science.

Much of Frederick I's reign was spent at war. Prussia participated in the War of the League of Augsburg (1688 – 97) and the War of the Spanish Succession (1701 – 13). It did not gain territorially, but perpetuated the military tradition that was beginning. The costs of war were a heavy financial burden to the small state.

Frederick William I (1713 – 1740)

This king was quite different from his father. He cut the number of court officials drastically, not only for economy, but because he was impatient with ceremony.

He believed Prussia needed a strong standing army and a plentiful treasury and he proceeded to acquire both. Prussia's army grew from 45,000 to 80,000 during his reign, despite a population of only 2.5 million. Military expenditures consumed 80% of state revenues, compared with 60% in France and 50% in Austria. On the other hand, he only spent 2% of tax revenues to maintain his court, compared with 6% in Austria under Maria Theresa. Frederick built the fourth largest army in Europe, repaid all state debts, and left his successor a surplus of ten million thaler.

Prussia maintained a large standing army in order to avoid war, if possible. This policy was maintained during Frederick William's reign. The only time he went to war was when Charles XII of Sweden occupied Stalsund. Prussia immediately attacked and forced Sweden out of Stralsund. In 1720, Sweden agreed to the Prussian annexation of the port of Stettin and Pomeranian territory west of the river Oder.

Prussia continued close relations with Holland and with England. King George I of England was Frederick William's uncle and father-in-law. His mother was George I's sister and his wife was George's daughter.

Prussia developed the most efficient bureaucracy in Europe. In 1723 the king established a General Directory of four departments, each responsible for certain provinces. Taxes were high, but income from the royal estates (about one-third of the kingdom) largely paid for the army. The king made policy decisions and left it to the bureaucracy to work out the details.

Subordinate to the General Directory were the seventeen provincial chambers. Merit promotions rewarded efficiency and diligence. The civil bureaucracy as well as the military were based on the principle of absolute obedience and discipline.

For oversight, every provincial chamber included a special royal agent, or fiscal, to keep a close watch on how well the king's orders were carried out.. The king also required secret reports annually on all bureaucrats.

The whole Prussian bureaucracy consisted of only 14,000 poorly-paid civil servants (about 1/10th the proportionate number commonly found in 20th century European nations).

The king was a ceaseless worker and expected the same from those about him, including his son, the future Frederick the Great. The king entrusted his son's early education to his old governess, Mademoiselle de Rocoulles, a Huguenot refugee who taught Frederick to speak French better than German. The king regimented his son's education from 6:00 a.m. to 10:30 p.m. and the young boy learned all the fifty-four movements of the Prussian drill before he was five years old. The value that Frederick William placed on education is also demonstrated by the fact that he established a thousand schools for peasant children.

Frederick the Great (Frederick II: 1740 – 1786)

Frederick the Great inherited his throne at age 28. His father left him a prosperous economy, a full treasury, an income of seven million thalers, and an army of 80,000. Unlike his father, Frederick loved French literature, poetry, and music. He played the flute and wrote poetry all his life.

Frederick's philosophy of government soon became apparent. He wrote in 1740: "Machiavelli maintains that, in this wicked and degenerate world, it is certain ruin to be strictly honest. For my part, I affirm that, in order to be safe, it is necessary to be virtuous. Men are commonly neither wholly good nor wholly bad, but both good and bad ...." The king did not believe the state existed for the gratification of the ruler, but the ruler for the state: he must regard himself as "the first servant of the state". All his life, Frederick continued to ponder questions of religion, morality, and power. French literature dominated his reading.

In October 1740, the Emperor Charles VI died, and in December Frederick ordered a sudden attack on Silesia. Thus began twenty-three years of warfare where the Great Powers of Europe (France, Austria, and Russia) were aligned against Prussia. Their combined population was fifteen times that of Prussia. YetPrussia emerged a quarter century later with enlarged territories of rich land and nearly twice its former population, but at a cost of devastation. Prussia alone saw 180,000 killed and their entire society was seriously disrupted. Indeed, for a time, Frederick thought he would not survive "the ruin of the Fatherland." Instead, Prussia emerged as one of the Great Powers of Europe.

The remaining twenty-three years of the king's life were spent in re-building and reforming what he had very nearly destroyed. Frugality, discipline, and hard work, despite very high taxation, were the values stressed throughout the society. The king provided funds to rebuild towns and villages, used reserve grain for seed-planting, and requisitioned horses for farming. He suspended taxes in some areas for six months as an economic stimulant. He started many new industries. By 1773, 264 new factories had been built: sugar refineries, leather works, porcelain manufacturing, tobacco works, and so forth. The government drained marshes along the rivers and settled hundreds of families in colonizing former wastelands. He oversaw the reform of the judicial system in an attempt to produce a more equitable nation governed by law. His system was one of "constitutional absolutism."

In 1772, as part of the First Partition of Poland, Prussia acquired west Prussia thus linking most of its territories.

THE DUTCH REPUBLIC

Historical Background

The Netherlands (known today as Holland and Belgium) were governed by the Spanish Hapsburgs, but each of the seventeen provinces had its own special privileges and limited autonomy within the Spanish Empire.

During the Protestant Reformation of the 16th century, large numbers of Dutch were converted to Calvinism ("Reformed" Churches), especially in the North. Catholicism remained stronger in the South (now Belgium).

When Philip II, king of Spain, began demonstrating his determination to use the Spanish Inquisition to enforce laws against "heresy," the Netherlands began a revolt against Spain which continued intermittently for eighty years (1568 – 1648).

In 1578, the Duke of Parma restored many of the old privileges of self-government to the ten southern provinces and large numbers of Calvinists moved north. In 1581 the seven northern Dutch provinces, under the leadership of William the Silent, declared themselves independent of Spain. In 1588 the great Spanish Armada sent to attack both the English and the Dutch was partially destroyed by a storm and then defeated by the English seadogs.

In 1648 the Peace of Westphalia recognized the independence of the Republic of the United Provinces. This had already been conceded by Spain in the Treaty of Munster, January 20, 1648.

Government of the Netherlands

The Dutch republic consisted of the seven northern provinces of Zeeland, Utrecht, Holland, Gelderland, Overijssel, Groningen, and Friesland. Holland was the wealthiest and most powerful. Each province and each city was autonomous.

National problems were governed by the States General which consisted of delegates from the provinces which could act only on the instructions of the provincial assemblies. Each province had a Stadholder, or governor, who was under the authority and instructions of the assembly. In times of crisis the provinces would sometimes choose the same Stadholder, and he thereby became the national leader.

Dutch Economy

The 17th century was the Golden Age of the Dutch. Not only was it the Age of Rembrandt and other great Dutch painters, but the Netherlands was also the most prosperous part of Europe in the 17th century. It was also the freest. The Dutch did not have government controls and monopolies to impede their freedom of enterprise. As a result they became by far the greatest mercantile nation in Europe with the largest merchant marine in the world.

Medium-sized cities and ports such as Leyden, Haarlem, Gouda, Delft, and Utrecht (with populations from 20,000 to 40,000) were characteristic of the Netherlands. Amsterdam was the richest city in Europe with a population of 100,000. The quays and wharves of these Dutch cities were stocked with Baltic grain, English woollens, silks and spices from India, sugar from the Caribbean, salted herring, and coal.

The Dutch had almost no natural resources, but built their economy around the carrying of trade, mercantile businesses, and other service occupations. They were skilled in finishing raw materials. Coarse linens from Germany were bleached and finished into fine textiles. Furniture making, fine woollen goods, sugar refining, tobacco cutting, brewing, pottery, glass, printing, paper making, armament manufacturing, and shipbuilding were all crafts in which the Dutch excelled.

The Dutch taught accounting methods, provided banks and rational legal methods for settling disputes. Their low interest rate was a key to economic growth: 3%, half of the normal rate in England. The Dutch were discussed and written about all over Europe as champions of free enterprise and individual rights – in contrast to state absolutism, economic nationalism, mercantilism, and protective tariffs.

The Dutch East India Company and the Dutch West India Company were organized as cooperative ventures of private enterprise and the state. The various provinces contributed part of the capital for these ventures and the Companies were subject to the authority of the States General.

Dutch Art

The 17th century was the most significant in history for Dutch painting. Most of the Dutch painters came from the province of Holland. Rembrandt and Jan Steen were from Leyden; Cuyp came from Dordrecht; Van Goyen from the Hague; and Vermeer from Delft.

The artistic center of the Netherlands was Amsterdam where the Dutch school of painters was noted for their landscape and portrait painting, and especially for "genre painting" in which scenes of everyday life predominate. The Calvinist influence in Holland is reflected in their celebration, but not idealization, of God's Creation. The realistic portrait paintings show mankind as great and noble, but also flawed, or, as the Reformed Churches put it, "fallen creatures in a fallen world." Nevertheless, the flawed creation was still to be enjoyed and their pictures of Dutch life in the 17th century show it to be intensely joyful and satisfying in human relationships.

The Dutch painters were masters of light and shadow as were the later French Impressionists. They captured the subtlety and realism of an ordinary scene under the vast expanse of the sky; a storm at sea; or a rain shower "drifting across a distant landscape pursued by sunshine." It is an interesting comparison to contrast the equally-great Flemish contemporary school in the Spanish Netherlands strongly influenced by the counter-Reformation Baroque. Peter Paul Rubens from Antwerp is a good example.

Dutch Wars and Foreign Policy

The Peace of Westphalia (1648) ended eighty years of war between Spain and the Netherlands and resulted in independence for the Dutch Republic and continued Hapsburg rule of the Spanish Netherlands. After being freed from Spanish domination the Dutch were faced with a series of wars against England over trading rights and colonial competition. Then, Louis XIV's efforts to move into the Low Countries brought the Dutch into a drawn-out war with France.

The accession of William and Mary to the throne of England in 1688 brought an end to the warfare between the Dutch and English. In the War of the Spanish Succession, 1701 – 13, England and Holland fought against France and Spain.

ENGLAND, SCOTLAND AND IRELAND

The English Civil War (1642 – 1649)

One of the underlying issues in this conflict was the constitutional issue of the relationship between king and Parliament. (Could the king govern without the consent of Parliament or go against the wishes of Parliament?). In short, the question was whether England was to have a limited, constitutional monarchy or an absolute monarchy as in France and Prussia.

The theological issue focused on the form of church government England was to have – whether it would follow the established Church of England's hierarchical, episcopal form of church government, or acquire a presbyterian form?

The episcopal form meant that the king, the Archbishop of Canterbury, and the bishops of the church would determine policy, theology, and the form of worship and service. The presbyterian form of polity allowed for more freedom of conscience and dissent among church members. Each congregation would have a voice in the life of the church and a regional group of ministers, or, "presbytery," would attempt to insure "doctrinal purity."

The political implications for representative democracy were present in both issues. That is why most Presbyterians, Puritans, and Congregationalists sided with Parliament and most Anglicans and Catholics sided with the king.

Charles I (1625 – 1649)

Charles I inherited both the English and Scottish thrones at the death of his father, James I. He claimed a "divine right" theory of absolute authority for himself as king and sought to rule without Parliament. That rule also meant control of the Church of England.

The king demanded more money from Parliament. Parliament refused and began impeachment proceedings against the king's chief minister, the duke of Buckingham, who was later assassinated in 1628. Charles then levied a forced "loan" on many of the wealthier citizens of England and imprisoned seventy-six English gentlemen who refused to contribute. Sir Randolph Crew, Chief Justice of the King's Bench, was dismissed from office for refusing to declare those "loans" legal. Five of the imprisoned men applied for writs of *habeas corpus*, asking whether the refusal to lend money to the king was a legal cause for imprisonment. The court returned them to jail without comment.

By 1628 both houses of Parliament – Lords and Commons alike – united in opposition to the king.

The Petition of Right (1628)

The Parliament in effect bribed the king by granting him a tax grant in exchange for his agreement to the Petition of Right. It stipulated that no one should pay any tax, gift, loan, or contribution except as provided by Act of Parliament; no one should be imprisoned or detained without due process of law; all were to have the right to the writ of *habeas corpus*; there should be no forced billeting of soldiers in the homes of private citizens; and that martial law was not to be declared in England.

The Parliament of 1629

In the midst of a stormy debate over theology, taxes, and civil liberties, the king sought to force the adjournment of Parliament. But when he sent a message to the Speaker ordering him to adjourn, some of the more athletic members held him in his chair while the door of the House of Commons was locked to prevent the entry of other messengers from the king. (That famous date was March 2, 1629.) A number of resolutions passed. Innovations towards Catholicism or Arminianism were to be regarded as treason. Whoever advised any collection of taxes without consent of

Parliament would be guilty of treason. Whoever should pay a tax levied without the consent of Parliament would be considered a betrayer of liberty and guilty of treason.

A royal messenger was allowed to enter the Commons and declared the Commons adjourned and a week later Charles I dissolved Parliament – for eleven years, 1629 – 40. Puritan leaders and leaders of the opposition in the House of Commons were imprisoned by the king, some for several years.

Religious Persecution

The established Church of England was the only legal church under Charles I, a Catholic. Within the Church of England (i.e., Anglican Church), specific ministers might be more Catholic, Arminian Protestant, or Puritan (with both Calvinist and Lutheran emphases).

Conventicles were harshly suppressed. (Conventicles were secret meetings for worship in which the authorized Prayer Book was not used, but the Bible and the Psalter were.)

William Laud, Archbishop of Canterbury, sought to enforce the king's policies vigorously. Arminian clergymen were to be tolerated, but Puritan clergymen silenced. Criticism was brutally suppressed. No book or pamphlet could legally be printed or sold without a license. Puritans who wrote secret pamphlets were punished harshly: In 1630 Alexander Leighton was whipped, pilloried, and mutilated for printing *An Appeal to Parliament* in which he challenged episcopacy. Three others had their ears cut off; one was branded on the cheek with the letters, SL (Seditious Libeler). Several were executed.

National Covenant of Scotland (1638)

Dissatisfaction with royal absolutism reached a crisis in Scotland when representatives of the Scottish people met at Greyfriars Kirk in Edinburgh in 1638 to sign a national protest against the policies of King Charles, who was king of Scotland as well as king of England. The nobility and barons met and signed the National Covenanton one day and the burgesses and ministers, the next. The covenant affirmed the loyalty of the people to the Crown but declared that the king could not re-establish the authority of the episcopate over the church. (The Church of Scotland had a presbyterian form of church government since the Reformation of the sixteenth century under John Knox.)

King Charles foolishly declared everyone who signed the National Covenant a rebel and prepared to move an army into Scotland.

War in Scotland

King Charles called out the militia of the northern counties of England and ordered the English nobility to serve as officers at their own expense. A troop of the king's horses entered Scotland only to find their way blocked by a large Scots army. They returned south of the border without fighting.

Charles signed the Pacification of Berwick with the Scots in June, 1639, by which each side would disband its forces and a new General Assembly of the Church of Scotland and a Scottish Parliament would determine the future constitution of the government. The Church General Assembly confirmed the actions of its predecessor; the Scottish Parliament repealed laws in favor of episcopacy and increased its own powers; and the Scottish army remained in existence.

The Short Parliament

For the first time in eleven years the king convened the English Parliament to vote new taxes for the war with Scotland. Instead the Commons presented to the king a long list of grievances since 1629. These included violations of the rights of Parliament; of civil rights; of changes in church order and government; and of rights of property ownership. In anger the king again dissolved Parliament, which had met only from April 13 to May 5, 1640.

The Scots Invade

The Scots invaded the two northern counties of Northumberland and Durham unopposed. Charles called a Great Council of Lords such as had not met in England for over two hundred years. They arranged a treaty with the Scots to leave things as they were.

The Long Parliament

The king was cornered: he had no money, no army, and no popular support. He summoned the Parliament to meet in November 1640. The Commons immediately moved to impeach one of the king's principal ministers, Thomas Wentworth, Earl of Strafford.

Strafford's trial began in March 1641, and lasted three weeks without a verdict. He was accused of treason for subverting the fundamental laws of the realm with an arbitrary and tyrannical government. Treason was traditionally defined as an offense against the king, so the indictment read instead that he was guilty of "treason against the nation."

With mobs in the street and rumors of an army enroute to London to dissolve Parliament, a bare majority of an under-attended House of Lords passed a bill of attainder to execute the Earl. Agonizingly distraught, but fearing mob violence as well as Parliament itself, the king signed the bill and Strafford was executed. Archbishop William Laud was also arrested, and eventually tried and executed in 1645.

The House of Commons passed a series of laws to strengthen its position and to better protect civil and religious rights. The Triennial Act provided that no more than three years should pass between Parliaments. Another act provided that the current Parliament should not be dissolved without its own consent. Various hated laws, taxes, and institutions were abolished: the Star Chamber, the High Commission, power of the Privy Council to deal with property rights. Ship money, a form of tax, was abolished and tonnage duties were permitted only for a short time. The courts of common law were to remain supreme over the king's courts.

The Commons was ready to revoke the king's powerg over the Church of England, but there was disagreement over what form the state church would take: episcopal, presbyterian, or congregational. Puritans were in the majority.

Rebellion in Ireland and the Grand Remonstrance

Irish Catholics murdered thousands of their Protestant neighbors. The Commons immediately voted funds for a large army, but questions remained whether it was to be a parliamentary army or a royal army under the control of the king.

The Grand Remonstrance listed 204 clauses of grievances against the king and demanded that all officers and ministers of the state be approved by Parliament.

The English Civil War Begins

With mobs in the streets and gentlemen carrying swords to protect themselves, men began identifying themselves as Cavaliers, in favor of the king, or Roundheads, if they supported Parliament.

In one of his most foolish actions as king, Charles then ordered his Attorney General to prepare impeachment proceedings against five of the leading Puritans in the House of Commons. When the House refused to surrender their members to the custody of the king, Charles went in person to Parliament with four hundred soldiers to arrest the five members. While the five slipped away from Westminster to London, mobs turned out into the streets, including four thousand from Buckinghamshire who sought to defend their hero, Sir John Hotham.

The king withdrew to Hampton Court and sent the Queen to France for safety. In March 1642, Charles II went to York and the English Civil War began.

The Division of the Country

To some extent every locality was divided between supporters of the king and supporters of Parliament. Geographically, though, the north and west of England sided with the king, and the south and east, with Parliament. The Midlands was competitive between them.

Eighty great nobles sided with the king, thirty against him. The majority of the gentry supported the king, a large minority were for Parliament. The yeomen tended to side with the gentry of their areas; the peasants wanted to avoid the fighting.

A few London merchants were Royalists, but most businessmen in various towns sided with Parliament. London, which was strongly Presbyterian, supplied Parliament with many men and much money.

Parliament had two great advantages. The navy and merchant marine supported Parliament. They brought in munitions and revenue from customs as foreign trade continued. They hindered the coastal towns behind the king's lines. Parliament also had control of the wealthier and more strategic areas, including London, and were able to secure the three principal arsenals: London, Hull, and Portsmouth.

The King Attacks London

Charles put together a sizeable force with a strong cavalry and moved on London, winning several skirmishes. He entered Oxford but was beaten back from London. Oxford then became his headquarters for the rest of the war.

Oliver Cromwell

Oliver Cromwell, a gentleman farmer from Huntingdon, led the parliamentary troops to victory, first with his cavalry, which eventually numbered eleven hundred, and then as lieutenant general in command of the well-disciplined and well-trained New Model Army.

Early Stages of the War

The early part of the war went in favor of the king. Lincolnshire, Cornwall, and Devon were occupied by two of the king's armies in 1643. The Queen returned from France with reinforcements and supplies. The king planned a three-pronged assault on London, but was beaten back by the Earl of Essex. Charles sought allies among Irish Catholics and Parliament sought aid from Presbyterian Scotland.

In January 1644, a well-equipped Scottish army of 21,000 crossed into England, thereby greatly upsetting the military balance. The Duke of Newcastle, the king's general was forced into York and there besieged. Prince Rupert came to his rescue from the west, but precipitated the battle of Marston Moor in July 1644. Cromwell decisively defeated the king's cavalry in a royalist disaster. The north was now in Parliamentary hands.

The king was not beaten yet, however. James Graham, the Marquis of Montrose, raised troops for the king in the Scottish Highlands, much to the consternation of the Lowlands Scots.

Parliament reconstructed and improved its army, giving Oliver Cromwell the top command. In June 1645, Charles marched into enemy territory and was crushed by Cromwell's "Ironsides" at Naseby. The king was then a fugitive and surrendered himself to the Scots in May 1646.

Controversy Between Parliament and the Army

The majority of Parliament were Presbyterians, wanting to extend the Scottish National Covenant idea to England. Many soldiers, however, were Independents who believed in democracy in politics and congregational control of the church.

During the Civil War, under the authority of Parliament the Westminster Assembly convened to write a statement of faith for the Church of England that was Reformed or Presbyterian in content. Ministers and laymen from both England and Scotland participated for six years and wrote the *Westminster Confession of Faith*, still a vital part of Presbyterian theology.

When the war ended, Parliament ordered the army to disband without receiving the pay due them. The army refused to disband and in 1647 Parliament sought to disperse them by force. The plan was to bring the Scottish army into England and use it against the men who had won the war.

The army refused to obey Parliament and arrested the king when he was brought across the border. In August the army occupied London and some of their leaders wrote an "Agreement of the People" to be presented to the House of Commons. It called for a democratic republic with a written constitution and elections every two years, equal electoral districts and universal manhood suffrage, freedom of conscience, freedom from impressment, equality before the law, and no office of king or House of Lords.

The Death of the King

On the night of November 11, 1647, the king escaped from Hampton Court and went to the Isle of Wight. He had made a secret agreement with the Scots that he would establish Presbyterianism throughout England and Scotland if they would restore him to his throne.

The Second Civil War followed in 1648 but it consisted only of scattered local uprisings and the desertion of part of the English fleet.

The Scots invaded England but were defeated by Cromwell at Preston, Wigan, and Warrington in the northwest of England. After these victories the English army took control. London was again occupied. The army arrested 45 Presbyterian members of Parliament, excluded the rest and admitted only about 60 Independents, who acted as the "Rump Parliament."

The army then tried Charles Stuart, formerly king of England, and sentenced him to death for treason. They charged him with illegal deaths and with governing in a tyrannical way instead of by the constitutional system of limited power that he had inherited. The execution of the king particularly shocked the Scots because the English had specifically promised not to take the king's life when the Scots delivered him into English hands.

The Commonwealth (1649 – 1653)

After the execution of the king, Parliament abolished the office of king and the House of Lords. The new form of government was to be a Commonwealth, or Free State, governed by the representatives of the people in Parliament.

The entirety of the people, however, were not represented in Parliament. Many large areas of the country had no representatives in Parliament. The ninety Independents that controlled Parliament did not want elections.

The Commonwealth was in effect a continuation of the Long Parliament under a different name. Parliament was more powerful than ever because there was neither king nor House of Lords to act as a check.

The Commons appointed a Council of State and entrusted it with administrative power. Thirty-one of its forty-one members were also members of Parliament.

Opposition to the Commonwealth

Royalists and Presbyterians both opposed Parliament for its lack of broad representation and for regicide. The army was greatly dissatisfied that elections were not held, as one of the promises of the Civil War was popular representation.

The death of the king provoked a violent reaction abroad. In Russia the czar imprisoned English merchants. In Holland Royalist privateers were allowed to refit. An English ambassador at the Hague and another in Madrid were murdered by Royalists. France was openly hostile.

Surrounded by enemies, the Commonwealth became a military state with a standing army of 44,000. The army, with career soldiers, was probably the best in Europe, and the best paid. Forty warships were built in three years. The North American and West Indian colonies were forced to accept the government of the Commonwealth.

Ireland

In the summer of 1649 Cromwell landed in Dublin with a well-equipped army of 12,000. Despite a coalition of Protestant Royalists and Irish Catholics, the Irish did not put together an army to oppose him. Instead they relied on fortresses for safety.

Drogheda was the scene of the first massacre when Cromwell ordered the slaughter of the entire garrison of 2800. Another massacre took place at Wexford.

This campaign of terror induced many towns to surrender; by the end of 1649 the southern and eastern coast was in English hands. In 1650, Cromwell captured Kilkenny and left the rest of the conquest to others.

The lands of all Roman Catholics who had taken part in the war were confiscated and given in payment to Protestant soldiers and others. Two-thirds of the land in Ireland changed hands, controlled mostly by Protestant landlords.

Scotland

Scottish Presbyterians, offended by the Independents' control of the English Parliament and by the execution of the king, proclaimed Charles II as their king. Charles accepted the National Covenant and agreed to govern a Presbyterian realm.

On September 3, 1650, Cromwell defeated the Scots at Dunbar, near Edinburgh, and killed 3,000, taking 10,000 prisoner. The next year King Charles II led a Scots army into England, which was annihilated almost to the last man at Worcester. Charles was a fugitive for six weeks before escaping to France.

The Protectorate (1653 –1659)

When it became clear that Parliament intended to stay in office permanently without new elections, Cromwell took troops to Parliament and forced all members to leave, thus dissolving the Parliament.

Cromwell had no desire to rule either as king or military dictator. He called for new elections – but not under the old system, most office holders in the new system were chosen by Independent or Puritan churches.

Cromwell then agreed to serve as Lord Protector with a Council of State and a Parliament. The new government permitted religious liberty, except for Catholics and Anglicans.

England was not strongly opposed to military rule, particularly after Cromwell divided the country into twelve districts with a major general in charge of each.

Oliver Cromwell died on September 3, 1658. After Cromwell's death a new Parliament was elected under the old historic franchise.

The Restoration (1660 – 1688)

The new Parliament restored the monarchy, but the Puritan Revolution clearly showed that the English constitutional system required a limited monarchy, with the king as chief executive – but not as absolute ruler. Parliament in 1660 was in a far stronger position in its relationship to the king than it ever had been before.

Charles II (1660 – 1685)

Thirty years of age at the Restoration, the new king was dissolute, lazy, affable, intelligent, a liar, and a cunning deceiver. He loved the sea and the navy and was interested in science and trade. Because he had so little interest in religion, he was willing to be tolerant.

While still on the Continent, Charles II issued the Declaration of Breda in which he agreed to abide by Parliament's decisions on the postwar settlement.

The Convention Parliament (1660)

Parliament pardoned all those who fought in the Civil War except for fifty people listed by name. Of these, twelve were executed for "regicide."

Royalists whose lands had been confiscated by the Puritans were allowed to recover their lands through the courts, but those who had sold them should receive no compensation. That meant that both Roundheads and Cavaliers would be the land-owners of England.

To raise money for the government, Parliament granted the king income from customs duties and an excise on beer, ale, tea, and coffee. Feudalism was largely abolished.

The Clarendon Code

Of England's 9,000 parish churches, 2,000 were pastored by Presbyterian ministers 400 by Independents, and the rest by Anglicans. The Cavalier Parliament, elected early in 1661, sought to drive out all Puritans and exclude them from public and ecclesiastical life.

The Corporation Act of 1661 excluded from local government any one who refused to swear to the unlawfullness of resistance to the king and those who did not receive communion according to the pattern of the Church of England. The Act of Uniformity in 1662 issued a new Prayer Book and ordered ministers either to accept it or resign their positions and livelihood. 1,200 pastors refused and vacated their churches.

The Conventicle Act of 1664 and 1670 imposed harsh penalties on those who attended religious services which did not follow the forms of the Anglican Church. The

Five-Mile Act, 1665, prohibited ministers from coming within five miles of a parish from which they had been removed as pastor. A licensing act permitted the Archbishop of Canterbury and the bishop of London to control the press and the publishing of books.

The effect of all this was to divide England into two great groups – the Anglican Church and nonconformists. The church was purged of Puritans and regained its property. It levied tithes and controlled education at all levels. Nonconformists were excluded from the universities, from government, from many professions, and from membership in the House of Commons. Some, of course, became Anglicans outwardly but did not believe what they professed. Nonconformists became shopkeepers, artisans, small farmers, merchants, bankers, and manufacturers. Their diligence, thrift, and self-discipline brought prosperity. They were strengthened by the rise of Methodism in the 18th century.

Disasters for England

War with the Dutch cost enormously in ships and money. The bubonic plague hit London in 1665, killing 68,000. The Great Fire of London in 1666 destroyed 13,000 homes, 84 churches, and many public buildings, none covered by insurance.

Scotland's Independence

Scotland regained her independence at the restoration of Charles II in 1660. The Earl of Middleton was made the King's Commissioner in the Scottish Parliament and commander of the army in Scotland. Some of the Scottish Presbyterian ministers reminded the king of the National Covenant of 1638 and of his own covenant-oath in 1651, pledging that Scotland be governed according to Presbyterian polity and principles.

The king arrested the Marquis of Argyle, leader of the Covanenters and a Presbyterian He was charged with treason for his "compliance with Cromwell's government." Argyle and James Guthrie were both executed.

Charles II declared himself head of the Church of Scotland and decreed that the episcopal form of hierarchical church government would be used in Scotland.

In 1661 the Scottish Parliament declared that the National Covenant was no longer binding and prohibited anyone to renew any covenant or oath without royal permission.

Samuel Rutherford, influential author of *Lex Rex* and Principal of St. Mary's College, St. Andrews, was cited by the Privy Council for treason in 1661, but died before a trial could be held.

A dictatorship was established in Scotland to enforce episcopacy and rule by approved bishops. The government demanded absolute obedience and used illegal detention. Drastic fines were levied on hundreds of people suspected of being sympathetic to the Covenanters. Presbyterianism was outlawed and hundreds of ministers lost their positions.

By 1666 the covenanters finally took to arms against oppression and captured the commanding general at Dumfries.

Perhaps as many as 18,000 ordinary people died for the cause of religious liberty in the persecution that followed. Dragoons were sent to prevent people from meeting in the files and in "unlicensed" homes for the purpose of worshipping God and studying the Bible. Others were fined for not attending the parish church.

Archbishop James Sharp was assassinated by a group of over-zealous Covenanters on May 3, 1679. Covenanting leaders immediately repudiated the action, but it led to pitched battles between the king's troops and covenanters.

The last two years of Charles II reign in Scotland were known as The Killing Times because of the wholesale slaughter of hundreds who were shot down without trial if they refused to take the oath of objuration of the Covenant.

Charles II died on February 5, 1685, in his 56th year and received Roman Catholic absolution on his deathbed.

James II (1685 – 1688)

The new king, fifty-one years of age, was the brother of Charles II. He had served as Lord Admiral and commanded an English fleet against the Dutch.

James II began his reign in a strong position. The Whigs were weak and the Tories were in overwhelming strength in Parliament. They immediately voted the king an income from customs for life.

James II, a strong Roman Catholic, was determined to return England to Catholicism. He proceeded to appoint Catholics to many of the high positions in his government. In 1685, he created a court of Ecclesiastical Commission with power over the clergy and suspended the bishop of London from office. Three colleges at the University of Oxford were put under Roman Catholic Rule. (Oxford was an Anglican and Tory stronghold and so the king was jeopardizing his own supporters.)

In April 1687, King James issued a Declaration of Indulgence which declared both Catholics and nonconformists free to worship in public and to hold office. This was a bold move, but the nonconformists knew that the king's intent was to enable Catholics to eventually control the government. Instead of supporting the king, the nonconformists secured a promise from the Anglicans that they would eventually be given toleration.

The Glorious Revolution of 1688

The leaders of Parliament were not at all willing to sacrifice the constitutional gains of the English Civil War and return to an absolute monarchy. Two events in 1688 goaded them to action.

In May, James reissued the Declaration of Indulgence with the command that it be read on two successive Sundays in every parish church. Archbishop Bancroft and six bishops petitioned the king to withdraw his command. They printed and distributed their petition to the king. This was a technical violation of the law and the king ordered them prosecuted for publishing a seditious libel against his government. When a London jury reached a verdict of "not guilty," it was clear that the king did not have popular support.

On June 10, 1688, a son was born to the king and his queen, Mary of Modena. They had been married for fifteen years and their other children had died. As long as James was childless by his second wife, the throne would go to one of his Protestant daughters, Mary or Anne. The birth of a son, who would be raised Roman Catholic, changed the picture completely.

A group of Whig and Tory leaders, speaking for both houses of Parliament, invited William and Mary to assume the throne of England. William III was Stadtholder of Holland and son of Mary, the daughter of Charles I. Mary II was the daughter of James II by his first wife, Anne Hyde. They were both in the Stuart dynasty.

William was willing to assume the English throne only if he had popular support and only if accompanied by his own Dutch troops, despite the irritation their presence would cause in England.

The Dutch feared that King Louis XIV would attack Holland while their army was in England, but the French attacked the Palatinate instead and eliminated that fear. Louis XIV offered to James II the French fleet but James declined what would have been very little help. King Louis thought that William's invasion would result in a civil war which would neutralize both England and Holland, but he was mistaken. On November 5, 1688, William and his army landed at Torbay in Devon. King James offered many concessions, but it was too late. He advanced with his army to Salisbury, then returned to London, and finally fled to France.

William assumed temporary control of the government and summoned a free Parliament, which met in February 1689. Whigs and Tories met in a conciliatory spirit though party differences soon became evident. The Whigs wanted a declaration that the throne was vacant in order to break the royal succession and give the king a parliamentary title. The Tories declared that the king had abdicated so as to avoid admitting that they had deposed him. William and Mary were declared joint sovereigns, with the administration given to William.

The English Bill of Rights (1689) declared the following: 1) The king could not be a Roman Catholic; 2) A standing army in time of peace was illegal without Parliamentary approval; 3) Taxation was illegal without Parliamentary consent; 4) Excessive bail and cruel and unusual punishments were prohibited; 5) Right to trial by jury was guaranteed; and 6) Free elections to Parliament would be held.

The Toleration Act (1689) granted the right of public worship to Protestant nonconformists but did not permit them to hold office. The Act did not extend liberty to Catholics or Unitarians, but normally they were left alone.

The Trials for Treason Act (1696) stated that a person accused of treason should be shown the accusations against him and should have the advice of counsel. They should also not be convicted except upon the testimony of two independent witnesses.

Freedom of the press was permitted, but with very strict libel laws.

Control of finances was to be in the hands of Commons, including military appropriations. There would no longer be uncontrolled grants to the King.

The Act of Settlement in 1701 provided that should William or Anne die without children (Queen Mary had died in 1694) the throne should descend, not to the exiled Stuarts, but to Sophia, Electress Dowager of Hanover, a granddaughter of King James I, or to her Protestant heirs.

Judges were made independent of the Crown. Thus, England declared itself a limited monarchy and a Protestant nation.

Queen Anne (1702 – 1714)

Much of Queen Anne's reign was occupied with the War of the Spanish Succession (1702 – 13). The reign of Queen Anne is also called the Augustan Age of English elegance and wealth. Anne was a devout Anglican, a semi-invalid who ate too much and was too slow-witted to be an effective ruler. She had sixteen children, none of whom survived her.

The most important achievement of Queen Anne's reign was the Act of Union (1707), which united Scotland and England into one kingdom. The Scots gave up their Parliament and sent forty-five members to the English House of Commons and sixteen to the House of Lords. Presbyterianism was retained as the national church.

Eighteenth Century England

Following the Act of Settlement in 1701 and Queen Anne's death in 1714, the House of Hanover inherited the English throne in order to insure that a Protestant would rule the realm.

The Hanover dynasty was as follows: George I (1714 – 1727); George II (1727 – 60); George III (1760 – 1820); George IV (1820 – 30); William IV (1830 – 37); and Queen Victoria (1837 – 1901).

Because of the English Civil War, the Commonwealth, and the Glorious Revolution of 1688, the Hanovers were willing to rule as King-in-Parliament, which meant that to rule England, the king and his ministers had to have the support of a majority in Parliament. Sir Robert Walpole, who served forty-two years in the English government, created the office of Prime Minister, a vital link between king and Parliament. Other famous 18th century prime ministers were the Duke of Newcastle, George Grenville, William Pitt, the Elder (Earl of Chatham), Lord North, and William Pitt the Younger.

The loss of England's North American colonies in the American War for Independence (1775 – 83) was a major blow to the British Empire. Also during this period Ireland received very harsh treatment under British rule.

In March 1689, James II arrived in Dublin with 7,000 French troops and was joined by Irish Catholics seeking independence from England. Protestants fled to Londonderry which withstood a siege of 105 days. In June 1690, William landed in Ireland with an army of 36,000 and at the Battle of Boyne completely defeated James, who fled to France.

Repercussions in Ireland were harsh: no Catholic could hold office, sit in the Irish Parliament, or vote for its members. He could enter no learned profession except medicine. He was subject to discriminatory taxation. He could not purchase land or hold long leases.

The American War for Independence gave hope to the Irish that they might obtain autonomy or independence. British troops were withdrawn from Ireland to be sent to America and an Irish militia was formed.

The British did grant concessions to the Irish between 1778 and 1783. Roman Catholics could inherit property and hold long-term leases. The Irish Parliament was given its independence but continued to be controlled by Protestants. Executive officials continued to be appointed by the English Crown.

In 1800, the Irish Parliament was persuaded to vote itself out of existence in exchange for one hundred seats in the British House of Commons and thirty-two places in the House of Lords.

Scotland, at this time, was the scene of Jacobin efforts to restore the Stuarts to the throne.

In 1688 the Scots declared that James had "forfeited" the Scottish throne which they offered to William and Mary, with the understanding that Scotland would be Presbyterian. Some of the Highland clans, however, turned out in defense of James. They were defeated at the Battle of Killiecrankie in July 1689.

The settlement with William and Mary was marred by the brutal Glencoe Massacre of 1692, in which the Campbell clan slaughtered a large group of Macdonalds after giving them shelter and hospitality. In 1715, James II's son, then twenty-seven years old, raised an army of 10,000 Highlanders in a revolt. James Francis Edward Stuart, the "Old Pretender," was soundly defeated and fled to France. In 1745, James Francis Stuart's son, Charles Edward, the "Young Pretender," then in his mid-twenties, obtained two ships from the French and sought to incite an uprising in Scotland, winning lasting fame as "Bonnie Prince Charlie."

His spirit and ambition won him the backing of several Highland chiefs. He was a natural leader and his men respected him for enduring the hardships of the common soldier.

Charles was able to capture the city of Edinburgh, but not the fortified castle. Soon he was forced to retreat north to Inverness. At Culloden, in April 1746, he was completely defeated. The rebellion was followed with harsh English reprisals. There were many executions and parts of the Highlands were devastated. The Highlanders were disarmed and even the Highland kilt and tartan were forbidden.

SCANDINAVIA

Sweden in the Thirty Years' War

King Gustavus Adolphus drove the Imperial forces from Pomerania in 1630. Swedish troops occupied all of Bohemia, organized a new Protestant Union, and invaded Bavaria. Gustavus Adolphus was killed in 1632 in the Battle of Lutzen.

In the fall of 1634, Imperial forces decisively defeated the Swedish army at Nordlingen. The Treaty of Prague (1635) restored Catholic and Protestant lands to their status as of 1627.

Catholic France allied with Protestant Sweden against the Hapsburg Empire during the last phase of the war from 1635 – 1648. Sweden acquired western Pomerania as part of the Peace of Westphalia (1648), ending the Thirty Years' War.

Swedish Empire

The high point of Swedish power in the Baltics was in the 1650's. Population of the Swedish Empire including the German provinces was only three million, half of whom were Swedish.

Sweden was not a large or productive country. Maintaining a strong standing army proved to be too much of a strain on the economy. Sweden sought to control the trade of the Baltic Sea with its important naval stores, but even at the height of Swedish power only 10% of the ships in the Baltic trade were Swedish; 65% were Dutch.

Swedish provinces in the Baltic and in Germany were impossible to defend against strong continental powers such as Russia, Prussia, or Austria.

Political Situation

After the death of Gustavus Adolphus in 1632, the government was effectively controlled by an oligarchy of the nobility ruling in the name of the Vasa dynasty.

Christina, the daughter of Gustavus Adolphus, became queen at six years of age and ruled from 1632 to 1654. At age twenty-eight, she abdicated the throne to her cousin and devoted the rest of her life to the Catholic faith and to art.

Charles X Gustavus reigned from 1654 to 1660 during the First Northern War against Poland, Russia, and Denmark.

Poland ceded Livonia to Sweden by the Treaty of Olivia (1660). Denmark surrendered to Sweden the southern part of the Scandinavian Peninsula by the Treaty of Copenhagen (1660).

Charles XI (1660 – 1697) became king at age eleven. When he came of age, he spent the rest of his life attempting to regain powers lost to the Council. For this, he secured the aid of the Lower Estates of the Riksdag who in 1693 declared that Charles XI was "absolute sovereign King, responsible to no one on earth, but with power and might as his command to rule and govern the realm as a Christian monarch." This was in dramatic contrast to the centuries' long struggles in Holland and England to constitutionally limit their kings.

King Charles XII (1697 – 1718) came to the throne at age 15 and reigned for twenty-one years. He spent most of his life at war and was an outstanding military leader in the Great Northern War (1700 – 1721).

Denmark, Saxony, Poland, and Russia formed an alliance to destroy the Swedish Empire. In February 1700, Poland attacked Swedish Livonia and Denmark invaded Holstein. The Swedish navy defeated the Danes and attacked Copenhagen, forcing Denmark to make peace.

Charles then shifted his attention to Estonia and routed a Russian invasion in the Battle of Narva, inflicting heavy losses. Charles was then eighteen years of age.

The next several years were spent fighting in Poland, defeating both the Poles and the Russians. But in 1709, the Russians, outnumbering the Swedish forces two-to-one, defeated them. Peter the Great then took the Baltic provinces of Livonia and Estonia from Sweden.

Years of warfare, poor government, and high taxes finally led to Charles XII's alienation from his people. In 1718 he was killed by a stray bullet.

Eighteenth Century Sweden

The loss of the Empire meant a move to a more democratic, limited monarchy and the new freedom led to a sharp increase in peasant enterprises and independence. The Swedish economy prospered.

By 1756, parliament considered itself the sovereign Estates of the realm and many civil liberties were established. Principal decisions of government were made by the Riskdag (Parliament).

Under Gustavus III there was a temporary return to royal absolutism until he was assassinated in 1792.

Scandinavian Relations

Finland was part of the Swedish Empire in the seventeenth century and Norway was part of Denmark. In the early nineteenth century Sweden gave up Finland but acquired Norway as an autonomous part of a union of the two nations.

Denmark

Frederick III (1648 – 1670), established himself as absolute ruler.

Frederick IV (1699 – 1730) fought in the Northern War and achieved a rough parity in the Baltic with Sweden, but accepted Swedish control in the south of the Scandinavian Peninsula.

Christian VII experimented with both enlightened despotism and reforms that allowed more civil liberties and economic freedoms to the Danish people.

RUSSIA OF THE ROMANOVS

Ivan III (1442 – 1505)

Ivan III, "Ivan the Great," put an end in 1480 to Mongol domination over Russia. He married Sophie Paleologus (1472), the niece of the last emperor of Constantinople. (The Byzantine Empire was conquered by the Ottoman Turks in 1453). Ivan took the title of Caesar (i.e., Czar) as heir of the Eastern Roman Empire (i.e., Byzantine Empire). He encouraged the Eastern Orthodox Church and called Moscow the "Third Rome," many Greek scholars, craftsmen, architects, and artists were brought to Russia.

Ivan IV (1533 – 1584)

Ivan IV, "Ivan the Terrible," grandson of Ivan III, began westernizing Russia.

A contemporary of Queen Elizabeth, he welcomed both the English and the Dutch and opened new trade routes to Moscow and the Caspian Sea. English merchant adventurers opened Archangel on the White Sea and provided a link with the outer world free from Polish domination.

The "Time of Troubles" followed the death of Ivan IV in 1584 when the ruling Muscovite family died out. The Time of Troubles was a period of turmoil, famine, power struggles, and invasions from Poland.

The Romanov Dynasty

The Romanov dynasty ruled Russia from 1613 to 1917. Stability returned to Russia in 1613 when the Semski Sobor (estates general representing the Russian Orthodox Church, landed gentry, townspeople, and a few peasants) elected Michael Romanov as czar from 1613 to 1645.

Russia, with a standing army of 70,000, was involved in a series of unsuccessful wars with Poland, Sweden, and Turkey. In 1654, Russia annexed the Ukraine with its rich farmlands. The Ukranians were supposed to be granted full autonomy, but in the end were not.

It was under Michael Romanov that Russia continued its expansion into contiguous territory and created an enormous empire across Asia to the Pacific. Westernization, begun under Ivan IV, continued under Michael Romanov.

The Russian army was trained by westerners, mostly Scotsmen. Weapons were purchased from Sweden and Holland. Four Lutheran and Reformed Churches and a German school were established in Moscow. Western skills and technology, western clothes and customs became accepted in Russia. By the end of the 17th century, 20,000 Europeans lived in Russia, developing trade and manufacturing, practicing medicine, and smoking tobacco while Russians began trimming their beards and wearing western clothing.

Western books were translated into Russian. In 1649, three monks were appointed to translate the Bible for the first time into Russian. The Raskolniki (Old Believers) refused to accept any Western innovations or liturgy in the Russian Orthodox Church and were severely persecuted as a result. In twenty years, 20,000 of them were burned at the stake, but millions still called themselves Old Believers as late as 1917.

Peter the Great (1682 – 1725)

Peter was one of the most extraordinary people in Russian history. He was nearly seven feet tall with physical strength so great that he could bend a horse shoe with this bare hands. His restless energy kept him active doing things incessantly, perpetually at work building boats, extracting teeth, dissecting corpses, shoemaking, cooking, etching, writing dispatches and instructions sometimes for fourteen hours a day. He did not understand moderation and could be cruel and vicious. He often whipped his servants, killed people who angered him, and even tortured his son to death. When he received good news, he would sometimes dance around and sing at the top of his voice.

Peter was born in 1672, the son of Czar Alexis' second wife, Natalia. When Peter was only four years old, his father died and the oldest son Theodore ruled until 1682, when he also died without an heir. For seven years Peter and his older half-brother ruled with the older half-sister Sophia as regent. Discovering a plot by Sophia to kill him, Peter, in 1689, banished her to a monastery and began ruling in his own right with his mother Natalia as regent. When she died in 1694, Peter, at age 22, took over the administration of the Russian government.

The driving ambition of Peter the Great's life was to modernize Russia and he needed the West to accomplish that. At the same time he wanted to compete with the great powers of Europe on equal terms.

Peter visited western Europe in disguise in order to study the techniques and culture of the West. He worked as a carpenter in shipyards; attended gunnery school; and visited hospitals and factories. He sent back to Russia large numbers of European technicians and craftsmen to train Russians and to build factories, some of which were larger than any in the West. By the end of Peter's reign Russia produced more iron than England (though not more than Sweden or Germany).

Wars of Peter the Great

Peter built up the army through conscription and a 25-year term of enlistment. He gave flintlocks and bayonets to his troops instead of the old muskets and pikes. Artillery was improved and discipline enforced. By the end of his reign Russia had a standing army of 210,000 despite a population of only 13 million. Peter also developed the Russian Navy.

In 1696, Peter sailed his fleet of boats down the Don River and took Azov on the Black Sea from the Turks.

The Great Northern War (1700 – 1721)

In 1699 Peter allied with Poland and Denmark against Sweden.

Charles XII, the 18-year-old Swedish king, defeated the Russian army of 35,000, capturing its artillery and most of its senior officers.

The main Swedish effort, though, was against Poland but the Swedish war lasted for twenty years. In 1706, Sweden again defeated Russia at Grodno, but in 1709 Peter won at Poltava.

The Treaty of Nystad (1721) ended the war. Russia returned Finland. Livonia (Latvia) and Estonia became part of the Russian Empire. Russia now had possessions on the Baltic Sea and a "window on the West."

St. Petersburg

The building of this great city (now Leningrad) out of a wilderness and making it the capital as well as one of the two principal cities of Russia, was one of Peter's crowning achievements. Construction began in 1703, done by conscripted labor and supervised by the czar himself.

Peter sought to make St. Petersburg look like Amsterdam. It became a cosmopolitan, lively city with French theater and Italian opera. His palace imitated Versailles with its terraces, fountains, cascade, art gallery, and park. St. Petersburg was built mostly of stone and brick rather than from traditional Russian wood.

The czar ordered a specific number of noble families to move to St. Petersburg and build their houses according to Peter's plans. At Peter's death in 1725, St. Petersburg had a population of 75,000, the largest city in northern Europe.

Reforms Under Peter the Great

The czar ruled by decree (*ukase*). Government officials and nobles acted under government authority, but there was no representative body.

All land-owners owed life-time service to the state, either in the army, the civil service, or at court. In return for government service they received land and serfs to work their fields.

Conscription required each village to send recruits for the Russian army. By 1709, Russia manufactured most of its own weapons and had an effective artillery.

The Russian navy, mostly on the Baltic, grew to a fleet of 850 ships, but declined sharply after Peter's death.

Taxes were heavy on trade, sales, and rent. The government also levied a head tax on every male.

State-regulated monopolies brought income to the government, but stultified trade and economic growth and in the long-run were counter-productive economically. Half of the two hundred enterprises begun during Peter's reign were state-owned; the rest were heavily taxed.

Peter sought unsuccessfully to link the main rivers by canals. Thousands died in the effort but only one of his six great canals was completed: St. Petersburg was linked to the Volga by canal in 1732.

The budget of the Russian government at the end of Peter's reign was three times its size at the beginning, 75% of which was spent on the military. Peter also established naval, military, and artillery academies.

The Russian secret police ferreted out opposition and punished it as subversion.

The Swedish model was followed in organizing the central government. Russia was divided into twelve provinces with a governor in charge. This decentralized many of the functions previously performed by the national government.

Industrial serfdom mean that workers were brought and sold amongst the factories and invariably created inferior products.

Russia had a "conditional land tenure" system with the Czar as the theoretical owner of all land in a Russian-style feudal system where both nobility and serfs served the state.

When the Patriarch of the Russian Orthodox Church died in 1700, Peter abolished his authority and began treating the Church as a government department. He eventually gave governing authority to a Holy Synod.

18th Century Russian Czars After Peter the Great

Catharine I, who ruled from 1725 to 1727, was the second wife of Peter the Great.

Peter II (1727 – 30) the son of Alexis and grandson of Peter the Great, died at age 15.

Anna (1730 – 40) was dominated by German advisers. Under her rule the War of the Polish Succession (1733 – 35) gave Russia firmer control over Polish affairs. War against the Turks (1736 – 39) gave Azov to Russia once again. Russia agreed not to build a fleet on the Black Sea.

Ivan VI (1740 – 41) was overthrown by a military coup.

Elizabeth (1741 – 62) was the youngest daughter of Peter the Great. This was the Golden Age of the aristocracy as they freed themselves from some of the obligations imposed on them by earlier czars. Russia entered the Seven Years' War (1756 – 63) during Elizabeth's reign.

Peter III (1762) was deposed and killed in a military revolt.

Catharine II ("the Great"; 1762 – 96) continued the westernization process begun by Peter the Great. The three partitions of Poland, in 1772, 1793, and 1795 respectively, occurred under Catharine II's rule. Russia also annexed the Crimea and warred with Turkey during her reign.

ITALY AND THE PAPACY

The Papacy

For the first time in its long history the papacy was of secondary importance in European diplomacy. There were a number of factors contributing to the decline of the papacy:

1) The Protestant Reformation of the 16th century and the emergence of many Protestant kingdoms throughout Europe.

2) The emphasis on limited constitutional government adopted in the Protestant Reformation and accepted by many non-Protestants as well.

3) The relatively few sanctions available to the pope in an international atmosphere of realpolitik.

4) The beginnings of secularization of Europe through the growing influence of the Enlightenment.

5) The anti-clericalism associated with the Enlightenment spread a desire to reduce the power and economic holdings of the church in traditionally Catholic countries. Anti-clericalism reached a climax in the French Revolution.

6) The lack of papal leadership in countering the above. Most of the 17th and 18th century popes were more concerned about administering their own territories than with the wider political milieu.

Pope Innocent X (1644 – 55) protested against the Peace of Westphalia (1648) because it acknowledged the rights of Lutherans and Calvinists in Germany, but the diplomats at Westphalia paid him little attention.

Quiet obscurity characterized the next three popes, Alexander VIII (1655 – 67), Clement IX (1667 – 69), and Clement X (1670 – 76), though they did clash with King Louis XIV over the prerogatives of the Church versus the prerogatives of the Crown, particularly in the appointment of bishops.

Innocent XI (1676 – 89) was scrupulous in financial matters and worked actively against the Turkish invasion of Europe. He subsidized Poland's relief of Vienna in the great campaign against the Turks in 1683.

Clement XI (1700 – 21) sided with France in the War of the Spanish Succession and in the course of the war, the Papal States were invaded by Austria. Clement renewed the condemnation of Jansenism, which had made extraordinary progress in France. (Jansenism was an Augustinian Catholic reform movement akin to Protestant Calvinism in its theology.)

Benedict XIV (1740 – 58), much influenced by the Enlightenment, sought to salvage some of the Church's lost influence in absolute European states by compromising the state's influence in nationally-established Catholic churches.

Clement XIV (1769 – 74) ordered the Jesuit Society dissolved (July 21, 1773).

Pius VI (1775 – 99) felt the full force of French radical anti-clericalism, which finally led to the French invasion of the Papal States in 1796.

17th and 18th Century Italy

Italy in the 17th and 18th centuries remained merely a geographic expression divided into small kingdoms, most of which were under foreign domination. Unification of Italy into a national-state did not occur until the mid-nineteenth century.

In the 17th century Spain controlled most of the Italian peninsula. Spain owned Lombardy in the north and Naples, Sicily, and Sardinia, in the south. Lombardy (or

Milan) was the most valuable to Spain in the 17th century because of its strategic importance, linking Spain with Austria and with Flanders (through Franche Comt). It served as a barrier to French invasion of Italy. Naples and Sicily were not scenes of foreign invasion as was the north of Italy.

Independent Italian States

The Duchy of Tuscany had lost its earlier eminence in art and literature. The prosperous Republic of Genoa did not influence European affairs. The Republic of Venetia no longer challenged Turkey in the eastern Mediterranean.

Savoy

Savoy was the only state with a native Italian dynasty. In the early 16th century, Savoy was a battleground between the French and the Spanish.

Emmanuel Philibert, Duke of Savoy (1553 – 80), was rewarded by the Holy Roman Emperor with the restoration of the independence of Savoy. He built Savoy as a modern state.

Charles Emmanuel I (1580 – 1630), maintained his independence by playing off France diplomatically against Spain and vice versa. Neither country could permit the other to gain a foothold in strategic Savoy, so Savoy remained independent.

Victor Amadeus (1630 – 37), married Marie Christine, Louis XIII's sister, thus increasing French influence in Savoy. Charles Emmanuel II (1637 – 75) was similarly dominated by France.

Victor Amadeus II (1675 – 1731), championed the Protestant Vaudois against Louis XIV. He joined William of Orange and the League of Augsburg against France. France defeated Savoy and forced Savoy to change sides. Nevertheless, the Peace of Ryswick confirmed Savoy's independence and left Savoy the leading Italian state and an important entity in the balance of power.

In 1713 Victor Amadeus was awarded Sicily and in 1720 exchanged Sicily to Austria for the island of Sardinia. henceforth he was known as the King of Sardinia.

Charles Emmanuel III (1731 – 1773) joined France and Spain in the War of the Polish Succession in an unsuccessful attempt to drive Austria out of Italy. Savoy sided with Austria in the War of the Austrian Succession and received part of Milan as a reward.

The French Revolution and Napoleon's invasion of Austria completely changed the situation for Italy and in the 19th century Italian unification was achieved under a Sardinian king, Victor Emmanuel II.

THE OTTOMAN TURKISH EMPIRE IN EUROPE

Christian Europe versus Islamic Mediterranean

During the Middle Ages the Islamic Empire included Spain, North Africa, and the Middle East. Expansion of Islam into Europe was blocked by France in the West (and, after 1492, by Spain) and by the Byzantine Empire in the East. When Constantinople fell to the Ottoman Turks in 1453, Eastern Europe was open for Islamic expansion by force of arms.

Hungary and the Hapsburg Empire became the defenders of Europe. Under Suleiman the Magnificent (d. 1566) the Turks captured Belgrade and took over nearly half of Eastern Europe. Ottoman power extended from the Euphrates River to the Danube.

Turkish Decline in the 17th AND 18th Centuries

The Sultan headed an autocratic and absolutist political system, often controlled by intrigue, murder, and arbitrary capital punishment. Most Sultans were more preoccupied with their harem than with affairs of state.

Government finance was based more on spoils of war, tribute, and sale of offices than on a sound economy. The Turkish military and bureaucracy were dependent on the training and loyalty of Christian slaves, the famous Janissaries and officials of the Sultan's Household.

Mohammed IV (1648 – 1687)

His reign was characterized by the efficient rule of an Albanian dynasty of grand viziers, the Kiuprilis. Thirty thousand people were executed as the Sultan and grand vizier purged all opposition to their will.

In 1683, the Turks besieged Vienna with 200,000 men for six weeks, intending to take Vienna as they had Constantinople two centuries earlier. John Sobieski, the king of Poland, with 50,000 Polish troops, went to the relief of the city and of the Hapsburg Empire. The Turks massacred 30,000 Christian prisoners and were defeated in a terrible slaughter.

Mustapha II (1695 – 1703)

Austrian and Polish armies defeated the Turks again, killing 26,000 in battle and drowning 10,000. The Treaty of Karlowitz (1699) recognized Austrian conquests of Hungary and Transylvania. The Ottoman Empire never recovered its former power or aggressiveness.

Ahmed III (1703 – 1730)

In 1711, the Turks attacked the Russians and forced Peter the Great to surrender and restore the Black Sea part of Azov.

In 1716, Austria destroyed 20,000 men in forcing the Turks away from Belgrade, and overran Serbia. The Treaty of Passarowitz (1718) ceded the rest of Hungary and the great fortress of Belgrade to Austria. The Sultan abdicated in the face of a rebellion of the Janissaries.

Mahmud I (1730 – 1754)

Power was wielded by the chief eunuch in Mahmud's harem, Bashir, an Abyssinian slave who elevated and deposed sixteen grand viziers.

Austria and Russia coalesced to dismember the Turkish Empire. Russia regained Azov in 1737, but Austria was defeated and gave up Belgrade in 1739.

The Janissaries disintegrated as an effective military force when the Sultan began selling the rank of Janissary to anyone willing to pay for it.

Provincial governors also became more independent of the Sultan.

Abdul Hamid I (1774 – 1789)

In the Treaty of Kutchuk-Kainardji (1774) Catherine the Great forced the Turks to surrender the Crimea and to recognize Russia's right to protect Eastern Orthodox Christians in the Balkans.

Russia and Austria declared war on Turkey in 1788 and Austria re-captured Belgrade in 1789.

The Ottoman Empire was no longer an important power in Europe. Competition to take over parts of Eastern Europe, especially the Balkans, was called the "Eastern

Question" in European history and was a causal factor in starting World War I.

CULTURE OF THE BAROQUE AND ROCOCO

Age of the Baroque (1600 – 1750)

The baroque emphasized grandeur, spaciousness, unity, and the emotional impact of a work of art. The splendor of Versailles typifies the baroque in architecture: gigantic frescoes unified around the emotional impact of a single theme is baroque art; the glory of Bach's *Christmas Oratorio* expresses the baroque in music. Art reflects the world-and life-view (*Weltanschauung*– way of looking at the world) that is dominant in a given age. To better understand the 17th and 18th centuries, one needs to see the values, philosophy, and attitude of the age reflected in baroque art, architecture, and music. Although the baroque began in Catholic counter-reformation countries to teach in a concrete, emotional way, it soon spread to Protestant nations as well and some of the greatest baroque artists and composers were Protestant (e.g., Johann Sebastian Bach and George Frideric Handel).

Baroque Architecture

Michelangelo's work provided much of the initial inspiration for baroque architecture. A dynamic and unified treatment of all the elements of architecture combined in the baroque. Oval or elliptical plans were often used in baroque church design. Gianlorenzo Bernini (1598 – 1650) was perhaps the leading early baroque sculptor as well as an architect, and great painter. Bernini's most famous architectural achievement was the colonnade for the piazza in front of St. Peter's Basilica in Rome. Louis XIV brought Bernini to Paris to plan a design for the completion of the palace of the Louvre, but the final design selected was that of Claude Perrault (1613 – 1688).

Louis XIV's magnificent palace at Versailles was particularly the work of Louis LeVau (1612 – 70), and Jules Mansart. The geometric design of the palace included the gardens which excel in symmetry and balance. The many fountains are also typical of the baroque.

Baroque Art

Baroque art concentrated more on broad areas of light and shadow rather than on linear arrangements as in the High Renaissance. Color was an important element because it appealed to the senses and was more true to nature. The baroque was not as concerned with clarity of detail as with the overall dynamic effect. It was designed to give a spontaneous personal experience.

Leaders in baroque painting were Annibale Carracci (1560 – 1609) from Bologna and (Michelangelo Merisi) Caravaggio (1573 – 1610) from near Milan. They are known for the concrete realism of their subjects. Their work is forceful and dramatic with sharp contrasts of light and darkness (*chiaroscuro*).

The Flemish painter Peter Paul Rubens (1577 – 1640) is one of the most famous of baroque artists. He emphasized color and sensuality.

There existed, of course, other types of painting along with the baroque. An example was the school of Italian genre painters known as bamboccianti who painted street scenes of Roman peasant life on a small scale.

Rembrandt Van Rijn (1606 – 1669) the great Dutch painter, was so unique that he could not be considered typically baroque. Nicolas Poussin (1595 – 1665) also followed a different line of reasoning. His paintings were rationally organized to give with precision a total effect of harmony and balance; even his landscapes are orderly.

Baroque Music

A major underlying presupposition of baroque music was that the text should dominate the music rather than the music dominating the text, as was done formerly. The idea that music can depict the situation in the text and express the emotion and drama intended was a major innovation of the baroque period. Instead of writing lyrics appropriate to a musical composition, the lyrics or libretto came first and was determinative in the texture and structure of the composition. Dissonance was used freely to make the music conform to the emotion in the text. Devices of melody, rhythm, harmony, and texture all contribute to emotional effects.

The baroque was a conscious effort to express a wide range of ideas and feelings vividly in music. These were intensified by sharp contrasts in the music and a variety of moods experienced: anger, excitement, exaltation, grandeur, heroism, wonder, a contemplative mood, mystic exaltation.

Bach's "St. Matthew Passion" illustrates this with a frenzied effect of cruelty and chaos obtained by a double chorus of four voices singing, "Crucify him! Crucify Him!" The jubilant Easter Oratorio reflects the triumph of the Resurrection. Violins and violas maintain a steady progression of pizzicato chords to depict the gentle knocking of Christ in the cantata, "Behold I stand at the door and knock...."

The splendor and grandeur of baroque art and architecture was similarly expressed in baroque music. Giovannia Bargieli (1555 – 1612) pioneered this effect when he placed four groups of instruments and choirs, each complete in itself, in the galleries and balconies of St. Mark's Cathedral in Venice. The baroque followed his lead and Bargieli laid the foundation for the modern orchestra.

The concerto, involving interaction between a solo instrument and a full orchestra, was also an innovation of the baroque. Antonio Vivaldi (1678 – 1741) pioneered the concerto and standardized a cycle of three movements. The major-minor key system of tonality was also developed during the baroque period.

The baroque developed a new counterpoint, different from that of the Renaissance. There was still a blending of different melodic lines, but those melodies were subordinated to the harmonic scheme. Bach was particularly successful in balancing harmony and counterpoint and melody with polyphony. George Frideric Handel (1685 – 1759) was a master of baroque grandeur, especially in his dramatic oratorios. He brought to life in his music a poetic depth and his use of the chorus profoundly affected his audiences. Handel was like a painter who was at his best with gigantic frescoes that involved his audience in the whole uplifting experience.

Rococo

Rococo comes from a French word meaning shell or decorative scroll. It describes a tendency towards elegance, pleasantness, and even frivolity. It is in contrast to the impressive grandeur of the baroque. It has a similar decorativeness without the emotional grandeur of the baroque. It is simpler, but not plain. The effect was more sentimental than emotional.

The leader in the Rococo movement was France, and Francois Boucher (1703 – 1770) was one of the most famous French rococo painters. His paintings are elegant, delicate, innocent, and sensual all at the same time, as his paintings of Madame de Pompadour and Diana well illustrate.

Characteristics of the rococo can be found in the compositions of both Franz Josef Haydn (1732 – 1809) and Wolfgang Amadeus Mozart (1759 – 1791).

3 REVOLUTION AND THE NEW EUROPEAN ORDER (1789-1848)

THE FRENCH REVOLUTION I, 1789 – 1799

The shape of the modern world first became visible during ten years of upheaval in France, between the years 1789 and 1799. Radical ideas about society and government were developed during the 18th century in response to the success of the "scientific" and "intellectual" revolutions of the preceding two centuries. Armed with new scientific knowledge of the physical universe, as well as a new view of the human capacity to detect "truth," social critics assailed the existing modes of thought governing political, social, religious and economic life.

Thus, the modern world that came of age in the 18th century was characterized by rapid, revolutionary changes which paved the way for economic modernization and political centralization throughout Europe. The ideas and institutions created by the revolutionaries would be perpetuated and extended by Napoleon Bonaparte, who conquered and converted Europe.

IMPACT OF THE SCIENTIFIC REVOLUTION (C. 1500 – 1700)

The Scientific Revolution revolutionized human thinking about boththe physical universe and themselves. This new body of independent, scientific knowledge, based on measuring devices and new methods of observation and interpretation, suggested that humans would understand the operation of the physical world through use of their reason - aided by the modern scientific method of inquiry.

The "scientific method" involved identifying a problem or question, forming an hypothesis (unproven theory), making observations, conducting experiments, interpreting results with mathematics, and drawing conclusions.

Pioneers

Nicolaus Copernicus (1473 – 1543) rejected the geocentric (earth-centered) view of the universe and suggested a heliocentric (sun-centered) view. Thus began the tradition of modern scientific thinking.

Galileo Galilei (1564 – 1642) developed a powerful telescope and confirmed Copernicus' theories.

Tycho Brahe (1546 – 1642) is considered the greatest astronomer of the late 16th century. Having built one of the earliest modern observatories, he kept meticulous celestial observations.

Johannes Kepler (1571 – 1630) used Brahe's observations to prove that a mathematical order existed in the planetary system; he proved mathematically that the planets revolve around the sun.

Isaac Newton (1642 – 1727) discovered the laws of motion, gravity and inertia. By building on earlier discoveries he developed a systematic interpretation of the operation of the universe (Newtonian View of the Universe), wherein natural scientific laws all worked together to provide a clear and comprehensive explanation of the physical universe. After Newton, the scientific method was not solely a matter of theory or observation, but of both. Little wonder then that the poet Alexander Pope could write: "Nature and nature's laws lay hid in the night; God said, Let Newton be! and all was light."

Philosophical Trends

Empiricism (inductive method of reasoning) was advanced by Sir Francis Bacon (1561 – 1626), who believed knowledge was gained through systematic observation of the world and tested by experiment.

Rationalism (deductive method of reasoning) was advanced by René Descartes (1596 – 1650), who rejected the senses as a basis for knowledge and argued that reality could be known only by reasoning from self-evident axiomatic principles: "*Cogito ergo sum*" ("I think, therefore I am").

Consequences

The Scientific Revolution gave birth to the modern scientific community, whose goal was the expansion of knowledge based on modern scientific methods that rejected traditional knowledge.

It likewise convinced many persons that all the complexities of the universe, (including human relations), could be reduced to relatively simple mechanical laws such as those found in the physical universe.

INFLUENCE OF THE ENLIGHTENMENT (C. 1700 – 1800)

The Scientific Revolution gravely undermined the foundation on which the traditional social order of the 18th century rested, by producing a revolution in the world of ideas which seriously challenged the status quo. The enlightenment was a response to economic and political changes at work in European society. It heralded the coming of a new secular society.

The Philosophes: Agents of Change

The new learning was promoted by a relatively small number of thinkers called philosophes — not philosophers in a traditional sense, but rather, social activists for whom knowledge was something to be converted into reform. They were not always original thinkers, but moreso, popularizers of leading reformist thought. The philosophes believed their task was to do for human society what the scientists had done for the physical universe: apply reason to society for the purpose of human improvement, and in the process, discover the natural laws governing God, humans, and society.

While they came from virtually every country in Europe, most of the famous social activists were French. This was probably due to the fact that France was the center of this intellectual revolution.

Voltaire (1694 – 1778), considered the most brilliant and influential of the philosophes, argued for tolerance, reason, limited government and free speech.

Denis Diderot (1713 – 1784) served as editor of the *Encyclopedia*, the bible of the enlightenment period. This twenty-eight volume work was a compendium of all new learning; no self-respecting reformer would be found without a set.

Baron de Montesquieu (1689 – 1756) authored *The Spirit of the Laws* (1748), in which the separation of powers theory was found. Montesquieu believed such a separation would keep any individual, (including the king), or group, (including the nobles), from gaining total control of the government.

Jean Jacques Rousseau (1712 – 1778) wrote *The Social Contract* (1762) in an attempt to discover the origin of society and to propose that the composition of the ideal society was based on a new kind of social contract.

The dissemination of enlightenment thought was largely accomplished through philosophes touring Europe or writing and printing books and essays, the publication of the *Encyclopedia* (1751), and the discussions in the salons of the upper classes. The salons became the social setting for the exchange of ideas, and were usually presided over by prominent women.

Major Assumptions of the Enlightenment

Human progress was possible through change of one's environment; i.e., better people, better societies, better standard of living.

Humans were free to use reason to reform the evils of society.

Material improvement would lead to moral improvement.

Natural science and human reason would discover the meaning of life.

Laws governing human society would be discovered through application of the scientific method of inquiry.

Inhuman practices and institutions would be removed from society in a spirit of humanitarianism.

Human liberty would ensue, as individuals became free to choose what reason dictated, or required, as good.

Enlightenment Effect on Society

Changes or reform must be instituted when institutions cannot demonstrate a rational base of operation.

Religion. Deism or "natural religion" was inaugurated, which rejected traditional Christianity by promoting an impersonal God who does not interfere in the daily lives of the people. The continued discussion of the role of God led to a general skepticism associated with Pierre Bayle (1647 – 1706), a type of religious skepticism pronounced by David Hume (1711 – 1776), and a theory of atheism or materialism advocated by Baron Holbach (1723 – 1789).

Political Theory. John Locke (1632 – 1704) and Jean Jacques Rousseau (1712 – 1778) believed that people were capable of governing themselves, either through a political (Locke), or social (Rousseau), contract forming the basis of society. However, most philosophes opposed democracy, preferring a limited monarchy that shared power with the nobility.

Economic Theory. The assault on mercantilist economic theory was begun by the physiocrats in France, who proposed a "laissez-faire" (non-governmental interference) attitude toward land usage, which culminated in the theory of economic capitalism associated with Adam Smith (1723 – 1790) and his slogans of free trade, free enterprise and the law of supply and demand.

Attempting to break away from the strict control of education by the church and state, Jean Jacques Rousseau advanced the idea of progressive education, where children learn by doing and where self-expression is encouraged. This idea was carried forward by Johann Pestalozzi, Johann Basedow and Friedrich Frobel, and influenced a new view of childhood.

Psychological Theory. In the *Essay Concerning Human Understanding* (1690), John Locke offered the theory that all human knowledge was the result of sensory experience, without any preconceived notions. He believed that the mind at birth was a blank slate (tabula rasa) that registered the experience of the senses passively. According to Locke, since education was critical in determining human development, human progress was in the hands of society.

Gender Theory. The assertion of feminist rights evolved through the emergence of determined women who had been denied access to formal education, yet used their position in society to advance the cause of female emancipation. The enlightenment salons of Madame de Geoffren and Louise de Warens are an example of self-educated women taking their place alongside their male counterparts. One woman fortunate enough to receive education in science was Emilie du Chatelet, an aristocrat trained as a mathematician and physicist. Her scholarship resulted in the translation of Newton's work from Latin into French. The writing of Lady Mary Montagu and Mary Wollstonecraft promoted equal political and educational rights for women. Madame Marie Roland was an heroic figure throughout the early but critical periods of the French Revolution, as she attacked the evils of the Ancient Regime.

Era of "Enlightened Despotism"

Most philosophes believed that human progress and liberty would ensue as absolute rulers became "enlightened." The rulers would still be absolute, but use their power benevolently,as reason dictated. Their reforms were usually directed at increasing their power rather than the welfare of their subjects. Their creed was "Everything for the people, nothing by the people."

Most of the philosophes opposed democracy. According to Voltaire, the best form of government was a monarchy in which the rulers shared the ideas of the philosophes and respected the people's rights. Such an "enlightened" monarch would rule justly and introduce reforms. Voltaire's influence, as well as that of other philosophes, on Europe's monarchs produced the "enlightened despots" who nonetheless failed to bring about lasting political change. Some famous "despots" included Frederick "the Great" of Russia (1740 – 1786), Catherine "the Great" of Russia (1762 – 1796), and Joseph II of Austria (1765 – 1790).

Influence of the American Revolution

The American Revolution acted as a "shining beacon" to Europeans anxious for change, and helped prove that people could govern themselves without the help of monarchs and privileged classes.

France, the center of Enlightenment thought, was particularly vulnerable. Eighteenth-century ideas about the "Rights of Man" and the "Consent of the Governed" were discussed widely in French salons, as well as in the rest of Europe. French reformers believed that their nation was a perfect example of everything wrong with society. Philosophes and their admirers were galvanized into action.

Finally, the concept of revolution was validated as a legitimate means to procure social and political change, when it could not be effected through existing avenues. the The American Revolution, however, was not a radical revolution but a conservative movement: it preserved the existing social order and property rights, and led to a carefully thought-out constitutional system built on stability and continuity.

CAUSES OF THE FRENCH REVOLUTION

Cumulative Discontent with the Ancient Regime

The rising expectations of "enlightened" society were demonstrated in the increased criticism directed toward government inefficiency and corruption, and toward the privileged classes. The social stratification model failed to correspond to the realities of wealth and ability in French society. The clergy (First Estate) and nobility (Second Estate), representing only two percent of the total population of twenty-four million, were the privileged classes and were essentially tax exempt. The remainder of the population (Third Estate) consisted of the middle class, urban workers and the mass of peasants, who all bore the entire burden of taxation and the imposition of feudal obligations. As economic conditions worsened in the 18th century, the French state became poorer, and totally dependent on the poorest and most depressed sections of the economy for support, at the very time this tax base had become saturated.

The mode of absolute government practiced by the Bourbon dynasty was wed to the "Divine Right of Kings" philosophy. This in turn produced a government that was irresponsible and inefficient, with a tax system that was unjust and inequitable, and without any means of redress because of the absence of any meaningful representative assembly. The legal system was chaotic, with no uniform or codified laws.

The economic environment of the 18th century produced a major challenge to the state-controlled French economy (mercantilism), as businessmen and bankers assailed the restrictive features of this economic philosophy. With the growth of new industrial centers and the philosophic development of modern capitalist thought, the middle classes began to assert themselves, demanding that their economic power be made commensurate with political and social power – both of which were denied them. Within France, the estate system allowed the few to monopolize all economic benefits, while the many were "invisible." Thus, an inequitable and inefficient tax system haunted those least able to pay, while the mass of peasants had an additional burden – that of performing feudal obligations for the privileged classes, as well as the payment of outdated feudal taxes and fees.

The intellectual currents of the 18th century were responsible for creating a climate of opposition based on the political theories of John Locke, Jean Rousseau, Baron Montesquieu and other philosophes; the economic ideas of the French physiocrats and Adam Smith (the "Father of Modern Capitalism"); and the general reform-minded direction of the century.

Immediate Cause: Financial Mismanagement

The coming of revolution seemed a paradox in a nation that was one of the largest and richest nations in the world, with a population around twenty-four million and a capital city (Paris) which was considered the crossroads of Enlightenment civilization. Dissatisfaction with the way France was administered reached a critical stage during the reign of King Louis XVI (1774 – 1792).

The deepening public debt was of grave concern, and resulted from (1) the colonial wars with England, 1778 – 1783; (2) French participation in the American War of Independence; (3) maintaining large military and naval establishments; and (4) the extravagant costs of maintaining the Royal Court at Versailles. Unable to secure loans from leading banking houses in Europe (due to poor credit rating), France edged closer to bankruptcy.

Between 1730 and the 1780s, there was an inflationary spiral which increased prices dramatically, while wages failed to adjust accordingly. Government expenses continued to outstrip tax revenues. The "solution" to the debt problem was to either increase the rates of taxation or decree new taxes. The French tax system could not produce the amount of taxes needed to save the government from bankruptcy because of the corruption and inefficiency of the system. The legal system of "*Parlements*" (Courts), controlled by the nobility, blocked tax increases as well as new taxes in order to force the king to share power with the Second Estate.

As France slid into bankruptcy, Louis XVI summoned an Assembly of Notables (1787) in the mistaken hope they would either approve the king's new tax program, or consent to the removal of their exemption from the payment of taxes. They refused to agree to either proposal.

Estates General Summoned

Designed to represent the three estates of France, this ancient feudal body had only met twice, once at its creation in 1302 and again in 1614. When the French parlements insisted that any new taxes must be approved by this body, King Louis XVI reluctantly ordered it to assemble at Versailles by May, 1789. Each estate was expected to elect their own representatives. As a gesture to the size of the Third Estate, the king doubled the number of their representatives. However, the Parlement of Paris decreed that voting in the Estates General would follow "custom and tradition," i.e., by estate unit voting. Therefore the First and Second estates, with similar interests to protect, would control the historic meeting despite the increased size of the Third Estate.

Election fever swept over France for the very first time. The 1788 – 89 election campaign is sometimes considered the precursor of modern politics. Each estate was expected to compile a list of suggestions and complaints called "cahiers" and present them to the king. These lists of grievances emphasized the need for reform of government and civil equality. Campaigning focused on debate and the written word (pamphlets). The most influential writer was the Abbé Siéyès and his pamphlet, "What is the Third Estate?"; the answer was "everything."

The election campaign took place in the midst of the worst subsistence crisis in 18th century France, with widespread grain shortages, poor harvests, and inflated bread prices.

Finally, on May 5, 1789 the Estates General met and was immediately outraged over the voting method, i.e., voting by unit and not per capita. Each estate was ordered to meet and vote separately. The third estate refused and insisted on the entire assembly remaining together.

PHASES OF REVOLUTION

The National Assembly, 1789 – 1791

After a six-week deadlock over voting methods, the Third Estate declared itself the true National Assembly of France (June 17). They were immediately locked out of their meeting place by order of Louis XVI. Instead they assembled in an indoor tennis court, where they swore an oath never to disband until they had given France a constitution (Tennis Court Oath). The third estate had assumed sovereign power on behalf of the nation. Defections from the First and Second Estates then caused the king to recognize the National Assembly (June 27), after dissolving the Estates General. At the same time, Louis XVI ordered troops to surround Versailles.

The "Parisian" revolution began at this point. Angry because of food shortages, unemployment, high prices, and the fear of military repression, the workers and tradesmen began to arm themselves. On July 14 they stormed the ancient fortress of the Bastille in search of weapons. The fall of this hated symbol of royal power gave the revolution its baptism of blood. The king recalled his troops from Versailles. The spirit of rebellion spread to the French countryside, triggered by a wave of rumor and hysteria. A feeling of fear and desperation called "The Great Fear" took hold of the people. They attacked the manor houses, symbols of the upper class wealth, in an effort to destroy the legal records of their feudal obligations. The middle class responded to this lower class violence by forming the National Guard Militia to protect property rights. Hoping to put an end to further violence, the National Assembly voted to abolish feudalism in France and declare the equality of all classes (August 4). A virtual social revolution had taken place peacefully. The assembly then issued a constitutional blueprint, the "Declaration of the Rights of Man and Citizens" (August 26), a guarantee of due process of law and the sovereignty of the people. The National Assembly now proceeded to its twin functions of governing France on a day-to-day basis and writing a constitution.

Among the achievements of the National Assembly were the following:

1) *Secularization of Religion* — Church property was confiscated to pay off the national debt. The Civil Constitution of the Clergy (1790) created a national church with 83 bishops and a like number of dioceses. All clergy were to be democratically elected by the people and have their salaries paid by the state. The practical result was to polarize the nation over the question of religion.

2) *Governmental Reform* — To make the country easier to administer, the Assembly divided the country into 83 departments (replacing the old provincial boundary lines) governed by elected officials. With a new system of law courts, France now had a uniform administrative structure - 83 dioceses, departments and judicial districts.

3) *Constitutional Changes* — Despite a failed attempt by Louis XVI and his family to escape from France (June 20, 1791), to avoid having to approve the Constitution of 1791, the National Assembly completed what may have been its greatest task. They transformed France into a constitutional monarchy with a unicameral Legislative Assembly. Middle class control of the government was assured through an indirect method of voting and property qualifications.

The Legislative Assembly, 1791 – 1792

While the National Assembly had been rather homogeneous in its composition, the new government began to reflect the emergence of political factions in the revolution that were competing for power. The most important political clubs were republican groups, such as the Jacobins (radical urban) and Girondins (moderate rural), while the Sans-culottes (working-class extreme radical) were a separate faction with an economic agenda.

The focus of political activity during the ten-month life of the Legislative Assembly was the question of "war." Influenced by French nobles who had fled France beginning in 1789 (*Émigrés*), the two largest continental powers, Prussia and Austria, issued the Declaration of Pillnitz (August, 1791), declaring the restoration of French monarchy as their goal. With a sharply polarized nation, mounting political and economic chaos, and an unpopular monarch, republican sentiment gained strength, as war against all monarchs was promoted to solve domestic problems. Ideological fervor and anti-Austrian sentiment drove the Legislative Assembly to declare war on Austria (April, 1792). Unprepared, the French revolutionary forces proved no match for the Austrian military. The Jacobins blamed their defeat on Louis XVI, believing him to be part of a conspiracy with Prussia and Austria. Mobs reacted to the threat, made by the invading armies, to destroy Paris (Brunswick Manifesto) if any harm came to the royal family, by seizing power in Paris and imprisoning the king. The Legislative Assembly came under attack and obliged the radicals by suspending the 1791 Constitution, ordering new elections based on universal male suffrage, for the purpose of summoning a national convention to give France a republican form of government.

The National Convention, 1792 – 1795

Meeting for the first time in September, 1792, the Convention abolished monarchy and installed republicanism. Louis XVI was charged with treason, found guilty and executed on January 21, 1793. Later the same year, the queen, Marie Antoinette would meet the same fate.

By the spring of 1793 the new republic was in a state of crisis. England and Spain had joined Austria and Prussia in opposing the revolution. Food shortages and counter-revolution in western France threatened the radicals' grip on the revolution. A power struggle ensued between Girondins and Jacobins, until the Jacobins ousted their political enemy and installed an emergency government to deal with the external and internal challenges to the revolution. A Committee of Public Safety, directed by Maximilien Robespierre, responded to the food shortages and related economic problems by decreeing a planned economy (Law of the Maximum), which would also enable France to urge total war against its external enemies. Lazare Carnot, known as "The Organizer of Victory," was placed in charge of reorganizing the French army. The entire nation was conscripted into service (*Levée en masse*), as war was defined as a national mission.

The most notorious event of the French Revolution was the famous "Reign of Terror" (1793 – 1794), the government's campaign against its internal enemies and counterrevolutionaries. Revolutionary Tribunals were created to hear the cases of accused enemies brought to "justice" under a new Law of Suspects. Approximately 25,000 people throughout France lost their lives. Execution by guillotine became a spectator sport. A new political culture began to emerge, called the "Republic of Virtue." This was Robespierre's grand scheme to de-Christianize France and inculcate revolutionary virtue. The terror spiraled out of control, consuming leading Jacobin leaders (Danton, DesMoulins, and Hébert), until no one could feel secure in the shadow of Robespierre's dictatorship. On July 27, 1794 Robespierre was denounced in the Convention, arrested, and executed the next day, along with his close associate St. Just.

The fall of Robespierre was followed by a dramatic swing to the right called the Thermidorian Reaction (1794). Tired of terror and virtue alike, the moderate bourgeoisie politicians regained control of the National Convention. The Girondins were readmitted. A retreat from the excesses of revolution was begun. A new constitution was written in 1795, which set up a republican form of government. A new Legislative Assembly would choose a five-member executive, the Directory, from which the new regime was to take its name. Before its rule came to an end, the Convention removed all economic controls, which dealt a death blow to the Sans-culottes. Finally, the Convention decreed that, at least for the first two years of operation, the new government reserve two-thirds of the seats in the Legislative Assembly for themselves.

The Directory, 1795 – 1799

The Constitution of 1795 set the tone and style of government in France: voting and holding office was reserved to property owners. The middle class was in control. They wanted peace in order to gain more wealth, and to establish a society in which money and property would become the only requirements for prestige and power. These goals confronted opposition groups such as the aristocracy, who in October, 1795, attempted a royalist uprising. It might have succeeded were it not for the young Napoleon Bonaparte, who happened to be in Paris at the time and loyally helped the government put down the rebellion. The Sans-culottes repeatedly attacked the government and its economic philosophy but, leaderless and powerless, they were doomed to failure. Despite growing inflation and mass public dissatisfaction, the Directory government ignored a growing shift in public opinion. When elections in April, 1797 produced a triumph for the royalist right,the results were annulled and the Directory shed its last pretense of legitimacy.

Military success overshadowed the weak and corrupt Directory government.

French armies annexed the Austrian Netherlands, the left bank of the Rhine, Nice and Savoy. The Dutch republic was made a satellite state of France. The greatest military victories were won by Napoleon Bonaparte, who drove the Austrians out of northern Italy and forced them to sign the Treaty of Campo Formio (October, 1797) in return for which the Directory government agreed to Bonaparte's scheme to conquer Egypt and threaten English interests in the East.

The Directory government managed to hang on for two more years, thanks to the military successes. But a steady loss of support continued in the face of a government that was bankrupt, filled with corruption and unwilling to halt an inflationary spiral that was aggravating the already impoverished masses of French peasants. The spirit of revolution was being crushed in the land, and this fear gave rise to a conspiracy to save the Revolution and forestall a royalist return to power. Led by the famous revolutionary, the Abbé Siéyès, Napoleon Bonaparte was invited to join the conspirators, which he did upon returning from Egypt. On November 9, 1799, they ousted the Directory. The conspirators quickly promulgated a new constitution which established the Consulate Era.

European Reaction to the Events of 1789 – 1799

Liberals and radicals hailed the birth of liberty and freedom. Among those who explicitly defended the French Revolution were the German philosophers Immanuel Kant and Johann Fichte, the English scientist Joseph Priestly, and the American pamphleteer Tom Paine. Not all reaction was favorable. Conservatives predicted that societal anarchy would ensue everywhere if the French revolutionaries succeeded. Friedrich Von Gentz' and Edmund Burke's, 1790 "Reflections on the Revolution in France" remains to this day the classic statement of the conservative view of history. It was the romantic poet William Wordsworth who captured the sense of liberation and limitless hope inspired by the French Revolution:

"Bliss it was in that dawn to be alive
  But to be young was very heaven."

Results

The first ten years of revolution in France destroyed the old social system replaced it with a new one based on equality, ability and the law; guaranteed the triumph of capitalist society; gave birth to the notion of secular democracy; laid the foundations for the establishment of the modern nation-state; and gave the great mass of the human race what it had never had before except from religion: hope.

THE FRENCH REVOLUTION II: THE ERA OF NAPOLEON, 1799–1815

After the first ten years of revolution, the 1799 shift to a new group in power did not prepare anyone in France for the most dramatic changes that would distinguish this era from the changes of government of the past ten years. France was about to be mastered by a legendary "giant" and Europe overwhelmed by a mythical titan.

Background of Napoleon's Life

Napoleon was born of Italian descent on the island of Corsica, August 15, 1769 to a prominent Corsican family one year after France annexed the island. He pursued a military career while advocating Corsican independence. He associated with Jacobins and advanced rapidly in the army when vacancies were caused by the emigration of aristocratic officers. His first marriage was to Josephine de Beauharnais, who was divorced by Napoleon after a childless marriage. In 1810 Napoleon arranged a marriage of state with Marie Louise, daughter of the Austrian emperor. Their son was known as Napoleon II, "King of Rome."

Napoleon was a military genius whose specialty was artillery. He was also a charismatic leader with the nationalist's clarity of mind and the romantic's urge for action. Napoleon galvanized a dispirited, divided country into a unified and purposeful nation at the price of individual liberty.

Role in Directory Government, 1795 – 1799

In 1793 Napoleon was responsible for breaking the British siege of Toulon. Because of his loyalty to the revolution, he was made Commander of the Army of the Interior, after saving the new Directory government from being overthrown by a Parisian mob in 1795. He was selected to lead an army into Italy in the Campaign of 1796, against the First Coalition (1792 – 97), where he defeated the Austrians and Sardinians and imposed the Treaty of Campo Formio (1797) on Austria, effectively ending the First Coalition. England was thereby isolated.

The election results of 1797 forced the Directory government to abandon the wishes of the country and establish a dictatorship of those favorable to the revolution ("Post-Fructidorian Terror"). After defending the government, Napoleon launched his invasion of Egypt (1798), only to have his navy destroyed by England's Lord Nelson at the Battle of the Nile. Napoleon and the French army were isolated in North Africa.

Popular indignation against the Directory government, along with financial disorder and military losses, produced a crisis atmosphere in France. Fearing a return to monarchy, a group of conspirators headed by the Abbé Siéyès decided to save the revolution by overthrowing the Directory. Napoleon was invited to furnish the armed power, and his name, to the takeover (Coup d'État Brumaire, November 9, 1799).

Consulate Period, 1799 – 1804 (Enlightened Reform)

The new government was installed on December 25, 1799 with a constitution which concentrated supreme power in the hands of Napoleon.

Executive power was vested in three consuls, but the First Consul (Napoleon) behaved more as an enlightened despot than revolutionary statesman. His aim was to govern France by demanding obedience, rewarding ability and organizing everything in orderly hierarchical fashion.

Napoleon's domestic reforms and policies affected every aspect of society and had an enduring impact on French history. Among the features were the following:

1) strong central government and administrative unity;

2) religious unity (Concordat of 1801 with the Roman Catholic Church);

3) financial unity (Bank of France), emphasizing balanced budget and rigid economy in government;

4) economic reform to stimulate the economy, provide food at low prices, increase employment and allow peasants to keep the land they had secured during the revolution; and

5) educational reforms based on a system of public education under state control (University of France).

The Legal Unity provided the first clear and complete codification of French law (Code Napoleon), which made permanent many of the achievements of the French Revolution. It stipulated equality before the law, freedom of conscience, property rights, abolition of serfdom, and the secular character of the state. Its major regressive provisions denied women equal status with men, and denied true political liberty.

Thus, in the tradition of enlightened despotism, Napoleon repressed liberty, subverted republicanism and restored absolutism to France.

Empire Period, 1804 – 1814 (War and Defeat)

After being made Consul for Life (1801), Napoleon felt that only through an Empire could France retain its position and relate to other European states. On December 2, 1804, Napoleon crowned himself Emperor of France in Notre-Dame Cathedral.

Militarism and Empire Building

Beginning in 1805 Napoleon engaged in constant warfare that placed French troops in enemy capitals from Lisbon and Madrid to Berlin and Moscow, and temporarily gave Napoleon the largest empire since Roman times. Napoleon's Grand Empire consisted of an enlarged France and satellite kingdoms, as well as coerced allies.

The military campaigns of the Napoleonic Years included the War of the Second Coalition (1798–1801), the War of the Third Coalition (1805 – 1807), the Peninsular War (1808 – 1814), the "War of Liberation" (1809), the Russian Campaign (1812), the War of the Fourth Coalition (1813 – 1814), and the Hundred Days (March 20 – June 22, 1815)

French-ruled subject peoples viewed Napoleon as a tyrant who repressed and exploited them for France's glory and advantage. Enlightened reformers believed Napoleon had betrayed the ideals of the Revolution.

The downfall of Napoleon resulted from his inability to conquer England; economic distress caused by the Continental System (boycott of British goods); the Peninsular War with Spain; the German War of Liberation; and the Invasion of Russia.

The actual defeat of Napoleon was the result of the Fourth Coalition and the Battle of Leipzig ("Battle of Nations"). Napoleon was exiled to the island of Elba as a sovereign with an income from France.

After learning of allied disharmony at the Vienna peace talks, Napoleon left Elba and began the "Hundred Days" by seizing power from the restored French king, Louis XVIII.

Napoleon's gamble ended at Waterloo in June 1815. He was now exiled as a prisoner of war to the South Atlantic island of St. Helena, where he died in 1821.

Evaluation

The significance of the Napoleonic era lies in the fact that it produced the first egalitarian dictatorship of modern times. Although Napoleon ruled France for only fifteen years, his impact had lasting consequences on French and world history. He consolidated revolutionary institutions. He thoroughly centralized the French government. He made a lasting settlement with the Church. He also spread the positive achievements of the French Revolution to the rest of the world.

Napoleon also repressed liberty, subverted republicanism, oppressed conquered peoples, and caused terrible suffering.

The Napoleonic Legend, based on the personal memoirs of Napoleon, suggest an attempt by Napoleon to rewrite history by interpreting past events in a positive light.

THE POST-WAR SETTLEMENT: THE CONGRESS OF VIENNA, 1814 – 1815

The Congress of Vienna met in 1814 and 1815 to redraw the map of Europe after the Napoleonic era, and to provide some way of preserving the future peace of Europe. While Europe was spared a general war throughout the remainder of the 19th century, the failure of the statesmen who shaped the future in 1814 – 1815 to recognize the forces unleashed by the French Revolution, such as nationalism and liberalism only postponed the ultimate confrontation between two views of the world: change and accommodation, or maintaining the status quo.

The "Big Four"

The Vienna settlement was the work of the representatives of the four nations that had done the most to defeat Napoleon: England, Austria, Russia and Prussia.

Prince Klemens Von Metternich, who represented Austria, epitomized conservative reactionism. He resisted change, and was generally unfavorable to ideas of liberals and reformers because of the impact such forces would have on the multinational Hapsburg Empire.

Lord Castlereagh was England's representative. His principal objective was to achieve a balance of power on the continent by surrounding France with larger and stronger states.

Karl Von Hardenberg, as chancellor, represented Prussia. His goal was to recover Prussian territory lost to Napoleon in 1807 and gain additional territory in northern Germany (Saxony).

Czar Alexander I represented Russia. He was a mercurial figure who vacillated between liberal and reactionary views. The one specific "non-negotiable" goal he advanced was a "free" and "independent" Poland, with himself as its king.

While Perigord Talleyrand, the French Foreign Minister, was not initially included in the early deliberations, he became a mediator where the interests of Prussia and Russia clashed with those of England and Austria. He thereby brought France into the ranks of the principal powers.

The "Dancing Congress"

This European gathering was held amid much pageantry. Parties, balls, and banquets reminded the delegates what life had been like before 1789. This was intended to generate favorable "public opinion" and occupy the delegates, since they had little to do of any serious nature.

Principles of Settlement: Legitimacy, Compensation, Balance of Power

"Legitimacy" meant returning to power the ruling families deposed by more than two decades of revolutionary warfare. Bourbon rulers were restored in France, Spain and Naples. Dynasties were restored in Holland, Sardinia, Tuscany and Modena. Papal States were returned to the Pope.

"Compensation" meant territorially rewarding those states which had made considerable sacrifices to defeat Napoleon. England received far-flung naval bases (Malta, Ceylon, Cape of Good Hope). Austria recovered the Italian province of Lombardy and was awarded adjacent Venetia as well as Galicia (from Poland), and the Illyrian Provinces along the Adriatic. Russia was given most of Poland, with the Czar as King, as well as Finland and Bessarabia. Prussia was awarded the Rhineland, three-fifths of Saxony and part of Poland. Sweden was given Norway.

"Balance of Power" meant arranging the map of Europe so that never again could one state (like France) upset the international order and cause a general war.

Encirclement of France was achieved through the following: a strengthened Netherlands, by uniting Belgium (Austrian Netherlands) to Holland to form the Kingdom of the United Netherlands, a much larger state north of France; Prussia receiving Rhenish lands bordering on the eastern French frontier; Switzerland receiving a guarantee of perpetual neutrality; enhancing Austrian influence over the Germanies by creating the German Confederation (Bund) of thirty-nine states, with Austria designated as President of the Diet (Assembly) of the Confederation; and Sardinia having its former territory restored, with the addition of Genoa.

Enforcement Provisions (Concert of Europe)

Arrangements to guarantee the enforcement of the status quo as defined by the Vienna settlement now included two provisions. The "Holy Alliance" of Czar Alexander I of Russia, which was an idealistic and unpractical plan, existed only on paper. No one except Alexander took it seriously. The "Quadruple Alliance" of Russia, Prussia, Austria and England provided for concerted action to arrest any threat to the peace or balance of power.

England defined concerted action as the great powers meeting in "Congress" to solve each problem as it arose, so that no state would act unilaterally and independently of the other great powers. France was always believed to be the possible violator of the Vienna settlement.

Austria believed concerted action meant the great powers defending the status quo as established at Vienna against any change or threat to the system. Thus, liberal or nationalist agitation was unhealthy for the body politic.

Congress System

From 1815 to 1822, European international relations were controlled by the series of meetings held by the great powers to monitor and defend the status quo: the Congress of Aix-la-Chapelle (1818); the Congress of Troppau (1820); the Congress of Laibach (1821); and the Congress of Verona (1822).

The principle of collective security required unanimity among members of the Quadruple Alliance. The history of the Congress System points to the ultimate failure of this key provision in light of the serious challenges to the status quo after 1815

Evaluation

The Congress of Vienna has been criticized for ignoring the liberal and nationalist aspirations of so many peoples. Hindsight suggests the statesmen at Vienna may have been more successful in stabilizing the international system than we have been able to do in the 20th century. Not until the unification of Germany in 1870 – 71 was the balance of power upset; not until World War I in 1914 did Europe have another general war. But hindsight also instructs us that the leading statesmen at Vienna underestimated the new nationalism generated by the French Revolution, that they did not understand the change that citizen armies and national wars had effected among people in their attitude toward political problems. The men at Vienna in 1815 underestimated the growing liberalism of the age and failed to see that an industrial revolution was beginning to create a new alignment of social classes and to create new needs and issues.

THE INDUSTRIAL REVOLUTION

In the late 19th century the English historian Arnold Toynbee began to refer to the period since 1750 as "The Industrial Revolution." The term was intended to describe a time of transition when machines began to significantly displace human and animal power in methods of producing and distributing goods.

These changes began slowly, almost imperceptibly, gaining momentum with each decade, so that by the midpoint of the 19th century, industrialism had swept across Europe west to east, from England to eastern Europe. Few countries purposely avoided industrialization because of its promise of material improvement and national wealth.

The economic changes that constitute the "Industrial Revolution" have done more than any other movement in Western civilization to revolutionize Western life, by imparting to our cultures a uniqueness which never before, or perhaps since, has been matched or duplicated.

England Begins the Revolution in Energy and Industry

Essentially, the "Industrial Revolution" describes a process of economic change from an agricultural and commercial society into a modern industrial society. This was a gradual process, where economic, social and political changes nonetheless produced a veritable revolution, which Arnold Toynbee was the first to identify. He placed the origins of this remarkable transition in England.

Roots of the Industrial Revolution could be found in the following: 1) the Commercial Revolution (1500 – 1700), which spurred the great economic growth of Europe brought about by the Age of Discovery and Exploration, which in turn helped to solidify the economic doctrines of mercantilism; 2) the effect of the Scientific Revolution, which produced the first wave of mechanical inventions and technological advances; 3) the increase in population in Europe from 140 million people in 1750 to 266 million people by the mid-part of the 19th century (more producers, more consumers); and 4) the political and social revolutions of the 19th century, which began the rise to power of the "middle class", and provided leadership for the economic revolution.

England began the economic transformation by employing her unique assets:

1) a supply of cheap labor, as the result of the enclosure movement which created unemployment among the farmers (yeomen); those former agricultural laborers were now available for hire in the new industrial towns;

2) a good supply of coal and iron, both indispensable for the technological and energy development of the "revolution";

3) the availability of large supplies of capital from profitable commercial activity in the preceding centuries, ready to be invested in new enterprises;

4) a class of inventive people who possessed technological skill and whose independence and non-conformity allowed them to take risks;

5) as a colonial and maritime power, England had access to the raw materials needed for the development of many industries;

6) England had a government which was sympathetic to industrial development and well-established financial institutions ready to make loans available; and

7) after a long series of successful wars, England was undevastated and free to develop its new industries, which prospered because of the economic dislocations caused by the Napoleonic Wars.

Early Progress

The revolution occurred first in the cotton and metallurgical industries, because those industries lent themselves to mechanization.

A series of mechanical inventions beginning in 1733 and, lasting until 1793, would enable the cotton industry to mass- produce quality goods.

The need to replace wood as an energy source led to the use of coal, which increased coal mining and resulted ultimately in the invention of the steam engine and the locomotive as inventions which sought to solve practical problems.

The development of steam power allowed the cotton industry to expand and transformed the iron industry. The factory system, which had been created in response to the new energy sources and machinery, was perfected to increase the amount of manufactured goods.

A transportation revolution ensued, in order to distribute the productivity of machinery as well as deliver raw materials to the eager factories. This led to the growth of canal systems, the construction of hard-surfaced "macadam" roads, the commercial use of the steamboat demonstrated by Robert Fulton, and the railway locomotive made commercially successful by George Stephenson.

Subsequent revolution in agriculture made it possible for fewer people to feed humankind, thus freeing people to work in factories or in the many new fields of communications, distribution of goods, or services like teaching, medicine and entertainment.

Spread of Industrialization to Europe and the World

During the first fifty years of the 19th century, industrialism swept across Europe west to east, from England to eastern Europe. In its wake, all modes of life would be challenged and transformed.

The Challenges to the Spread of Industrialism

Continental economic growth had been retarded by the wars of the Napoleonic period.

Because England was so technically advanced, European countries found it difficult to compete. However, catching up to England was made easy by avoiding the costly mistakes of early British experiments and by using the power of strong central governments and banking systems to promote native industry. But on the continent there was no large labor supply in cities; iron and coal deposits were not as concentrated as in England.

Route of Industrialization

England was the undisputed economic and industrial leader until the mid-19th century. The industrialization of the continent occurred mostly in the latter half of the 19th century, and, in the southern and eastern regions, in the 20th century.

By 1830 industrialism had begun to spread from England to Belgium, France and other scattered areas of Europe. These successful industrial operations were due to the exportation from England of machines, management and capital. Germany was slower in following English methods until a tariff policy was established in 1834 (the *Zollverein*), which induced capital investment in German manufacturers.

Growth of Industrial Society

The undermining and eventual elimination of Western society's traditional social stratification model (i.e., clergy, nobility and the masses) would be the result of the Industrial Revolution.

The Bourgeoisie: The New Aristocracy

The middle class were the major contributors as well as the principal beneficiaries of early industrialism. They measured success in monetary terms and most tended to be indifferent to the human suffering of the new wage-earning class. The industrial bourgeoisie had two levels: 1) upper bourgeoisie, i.e., great bankers, merchants and industrialists who demanded free enterprise and high tariffs; and, 2) lower bourgeoisie, i.e., small industrialists, merchants and professional men who demanded stability and security from government.

The Factory Worker: The New Wage-Earning Class

The Industrial Revolution created a unique new category of people who were dependent on their job alone for income, a job from which they might be dismissed without cause. The factory worker had no land, no home, no source of income but his job. During the first century of the Industrial Revolution the factory worker was completely at the mercy of the law of supply and demand for labor.

Working in the factory meant more self-discipline and less personal freedom for workers. The system tended to depersonalize society and reduced workers to an impersonal status. The statistics with regard to wages, diet, and clothing suggest overall improvement for the workers, with some qualifications, since some industries were notoriously guilty of social injustices. Contemporary social critics complained that industrialism brought misery to the workers, while others claimed life was improving. Until 1850 workers as a whole did not share in the general wealth produced by the Industrial Revolution. Conditions would improve as the century wore on, as union action combined with general prosperity and a developing social conscience, to improve the working conditions, wages, and hours first of skilled labor, and later of unskilled labor.

Social Effects of Industrialization

The most important sociological result of industrialism was the urbanization of the world. The new factories acted as a magnet, pulling people away from their rural roots and beginning the most massive population transfer in history. Thus the birth of factory towns and cities that grew into large industrial centers.

The role of the city changed in the 19th century from governmental and cultural centers, to industrial centers with all the problems of urbanization.

Workers in cities became aware of their numbers and their common problems, so cities made the working class a powerful force by raising their consciousness and enabling them to unite for political action, to remedy their economic dissatisfaction.

It is in this urban setting that the century's great social and political dilemmas were framed: working class injustices, gender exploitation and standard-of-living issues.

Family structure and gender roles within the family were altered by the growth of industrialism. Families as an economic unit were no longer the chief unit of both production and consumption, but rather, consumption alone.

New wage economy meant that families were less closely bound together than in the past; the economic link was broken. Productive work was taken out of the home (cottage) and placed elsewhere. As factory wages for skilled adult males rose, women and children were separated from the workplace. A new pattern of family life emerged.

Gender-determined roles in the home and domestic life emerged slowly. Married women came to be associated with domestic duties ,while the male tended to be the sole wage earner.

Single women and widows had much work available, but that work commanded low wages and low skills and provided no way to protect themselves from exploitation.

Marriage as an institution in the wage economy began to change. Women were now expected to create a nurturing environment to which the family members returned after work. Married women worked outside the home only when family needs, illness or death of a spouse required them to do so.

Evaluation

The Industrial Revolution conquered and harnessed the forces of nature: water power, coal, oil, and electricity all provided power to replace human effort. The amount of wealth available for human consumption increased. Vast amounts of food, clothing and energy were produced and distributed to the workers of the world. Luxuries were made commonplace, life expectancy increased and leisure time was made more enjoyable.

But the workers would not begin to share in this dramatic increase in the standard of living until the second half of the 19th century, when all the evils associated with the factory system (low wages, poor working conditions, etc.) and early industrialism in general were corrected. In the first century of industrialism the wealth created went almost exclusively to the entrepreneur and the owner of capital—the middle class.

IMPACT OF THOUGHT SYSTEMS (ISMS) ON THE EUROPEAN WORLD

The mind set of Western civilization was being challenged in the first half of the 19th century by the appearance of numerous new thought systems. Not since the 18th century Enlightenment had humans sought to catalog, classify and categorize their thoughts and beliefs. Several of these systems of thought acted as change agents throughout the 19th century, while others would flow into the 20th century and continue to define the modern world.

Romanticism

Romanticism was a reaction against the rigid classicism, rationalism and deism of the 18th century. Strongest in application between 1800 and 1850, the romantic movement differed from country to country and from romanticist to romanticist. Because it emphasized change it was considered revolutionary in all aspects of life. It was an atmosphere in which events occurred and came to affect not only the way humans thought and expressed themselves, but also the way they lived socially and politically.

Characteristics

Romanticism appealed to emotion rather than to reason (i.e., truth and virtue can be found just as surely by the heart as by the head), and rejected classical emphasis on order and the observance of rules (i.e., let the imagination create new cultural forms and techniques).

It also rejected the enlightenment view of nature as a precise harmonious whole (i.e., viewed nature as alive, vital, changing and filled with the divine spirit), as well as the cold impersonal religion of Deism (i.e., viewed God as inspiring human nobility;

deplored decline of Christianity).

Romanticism further rejected the Enlightenment point of view of the past, which was counter-progressive to human history (i.e., viewed the world as an organism that was growing and changing with each nation's history unique), and expressed vital optimism about life and the future.

Romantics enriched European cultural life by encouraging personal freedom and flexibility. By emphasizing feeling, humanitarian movements were created to fight slavery, poverty and industrial evils.

Romantic Literature, Art, Music, and Philosophy

English romantics like Wordsworth and Coleridge epitomized the romantic movement, along with Burns, Byron, Shelley, Keats, Tennyson, Browning and Scott. The greatest German figures were Goethe, Schiller, Heine and Herder. French romantics were Hugo, Balzac, Dumas and Stendahl. The outstanding Russian exponents were Pushkin, Dostoevski and Turgenev. Among the greatest American figures were Longfellow, Cooper, Irving, Emerson, Poe, Whitman and Thoreau.

The leading romantic painters in popular taste were the Frenchmen Millet and David, the Englishmen Turner and Constable, and the Spaniard Goya. Gothic Revival Style marked the Romantic era in architecture.

Music did not change as dramatically as did literature. Classical forms were still observed, but new ideas and innovations were increasing. Beethoven was a crossover, while straight romantics would include Brahms, Schumann, Schubert, Berlioz, Chopin and Von Weber.

Romantic philosophy stimulated an interest in Idealism, the belief that reality consists of ideas, as opposed to materialism. This school of thought (Philosophical Idealism), founded by Plato, was developed through the writings of 1) Immanuel Kant whose work, *Critique of Pure Reason*, advances the theory that reality was two-fold — physical and spiritual. Reason can discover what is true in the physical, but not in the spiritual, world; 2) Johann Gottlieb Fichte, a disciple of Kant, and Friedrich Schelling, collaborator of Fichte; and, 3) Georg Wilhelm Hegel, the greatest exponent of this school of thought. Hegel believed that an impersonal God rules the universe and guides humans along a progressive evolutionary course by means of process called dialecticism; this is an historical process by which one thing is constantly reacting with its opposite (the thesis and antithesis), producing a result (synthesis), that automatically meets another opposite and continues the series of reactions. Hegel's philosophy exerted a great influence over Karl Marx who turned the Hegelian dialectic upside down to demonstrate that the ultimate meaning of reality was a material end, not a higher or spiritual end, as Hegel suggested.

Impact

Romanticism destroyed the clear simplicity and unity of thought which characterized the 18th century. There was no longer one philosophy which expressed all the aims and ideals of Western civilization. Romanticism provided a more complex, but truer, view of the real world.

Conservatism

Conservatism arose in reaction to liberalism and became a popular alternative for those who were frightened by the violence, terror and social disorder unleashed by the French Revolution. Early conservatism was allied to the restored monarchical governments of Austria, Russia, France and England. Support for conservatism came from the traditional ruling classes, as well as the peasants who still formed the majority of the population. Intellectual ammunition came from the pens of the Englishman Edmund Burke; the Frenchmen, Joseph de Maistre and Louis de Bonald; the Austrian Friedrich Gentz; and many of the early romantics. In essence, conservatives believed in order, society and the state; faith and tradition.

Characteristics

Conservatives viewed history as a continuum which no single generation can revoke.

Conservatives believed the basis of society was organic, not contractual. Society was not a machine with replaceable parts. Stability and longevity, not progress and change, mark a good society.

The only legitimate sources of political authority were God and history. The social contract theory was rejected because a contract cannot make authority legitimate.

Investing society with the theory of individualism ignored humans as social beings and undermined the concept of community, which was essential to life. Conservatives said self-interest does not lead to social harmony, but to social conflict.

Conservatives argued that measuring happiness and progress in material terms ignored humans as spiritual beings.

Conservatives rejected the philosophy of natural rights and believed that rights did not pertain to people everywhere, but were determined and allocated by a particular state.

With its exaggerated emphasis on reason and intellect, the conservatives denounced the philosophes and reformers for ignoring each human as an emotional being and for underestimating the complexity of human nature.

To conservatives, society was hierarchical, i.e., some humans were better able to rule and lead than those who were denied intelligence, education, wealth and birth.

Impact

Conservatism was basically "anti-" in its propositions. It never had a feasible program of its own. The object of their hatred was a liberal society which they claimed was antisocial and morally degrading. While their criticisms contained much justification, conservatives ignored the positive and promising features of liberal society. Conservative criticism did poke holes in liberal ideology, and pointed toward a new social tyranny, the aggressive middle class.

Liberalism

The theory of liberalism was the first major theory in the history of Western thought to teach that the individual is a self-sufficient being, whose freedom and well-being are the sole reasons for the existence of society. Liberalism was more closely connected to the spirit and outlook of the enlightenment than to any of the other "isms" of the early 19th century. While the general principles and attitudes associated with liberalism varied considerably from country to country, liberals tended to come from the middle class or bourgeoisie, and favored increased liberty for their class and indirectly, for the masses of people, as long as the latter did not in their turn ask for so much freedom that they endangered the security of the middle class. Liberalism was reformist and political rather than revolutionary in character.

Characteristics

Individuals are entitled to seek their freedom in the face of arbitrary or tyrannical restrictions imposed upon them.

Humans have certain natural rights and governments should protect them. These rights include the right to own property, freedom of speech, freedom from excessive punishment, freedom of worship, and freedom of assembly.

These rights are best guaranteed by a written constitution, with careful definition of the limits to which governmental actions may go. Examples include the American Declaration of Independence (1776) and the French Declaration of Rights of man (1789).

Another view of liberalism was presented by individuals who came to be known as the utilitarians. Their founder, Jeremy Bentham, held the pleasure-pain principle as the key idea – that humans are ordained to avoid pain and to seek pleasure.

Bentham equated pleasure with good and pain with evil. The goodness or badness of any act, individual or public, was found by balancing the pleasure against the pain it caused. Thus one came to test the utility of any proposed law or institution, i.e., "the greatest happiness of the greatest number."

Liberals advocated economic individualism (i.e., laissez-faire capitalism), heralded by Adam Smith in his 1776 economic masterpiece, *Wealth of Nations*. They regarded free enterprise as the most productive economy, and the one that allowed for the greatest measure of individual choice.

Economic inequality will exist and is acceptable, liberals held, because it does not detract from the individual's moral dignity, nor does it conflict with equality of opportunity and equality before the law.

Economic liberalism claimed to be based on the realities of a new industrial era. The "classical economists" (Thomas Malthus and David Ricardo) taught that there were inescapable forces at work – competition, the pressure of population growth, the iron law of wages, and the law of supply and demand – in accordance with which economic life must function. It was the duty of government to remove any obstacle to the smooth operation of these natural forces.

Internationally, liberals believed in the balance-of-power system and free trade because each track allowed individual nations the opportunity to determine its own course of action.

Liberals believed in the pluralistic society as long as it did not block progress. War and revolutionary change disrupt progress and enlarge the power of government.

Education was an indispensable prerequisite to individual responsibility and self-government.

Early 19th Century Advocates of Liberalism

In England, advocates included the political economists, the utilitarians and individuals like Thomas Robington Macaulay and John Stuart Mill; in France, Benjamin Constant, Victor Cousin, Jean Baptiste Say and Alexis de Tocqueville; in Germany, Wilhelm von Humboldt, Friedrich List, Karl von Rotteck and Karl Theodor Welcker.

Impact

Liberalism was involved in the various revolutionary movements of the early 19th century. It found concrete expression in over ten constitutions secured between 1815 and 1848 in states of the German Confederation. Its power was demonstrated in the reform measures that successive British governments adopted during these same decades. It affected German student organizations and permeated Prussian life.

Alexis de Toqueville spoke for many liberals when he warned against the masses' passion for equality, and their willingness to sacrifice political liberty in order to improve their material well-being. These fears were not without foundation. In the 20th century, the masses have sometimes shown themselves willing to trade freedom for authority, order, economic security and national power.

Nationalism

The regenerative force of liberal thought in early 19th century Europe was dramatically revealed in the explosive force of the power of nationalism. Raising the level of consciousness of people having a common language, a common soil, common traditions, a common history, a common culture and a shared human experience, to seek political unity around an identity of what or who constitutes the nation, was aroused and made militant during the turbulent French Revolutionary era.

Characteristics

Early nationalist sentiment was romantic, exuberant and cosmopolitan, as compared to the more intense, hate-filled nationalism of the latter half of the 19th century.

The breakdown of society's traditional loyalties to church, dynastic state and region began during the course of the 18th century. Impelled by the French Revolutionary dogma, new loyalties were fashioned — that people possessed the supreme power (sovereignty) of the nation and were, therefore, the true nation united by common language, culture, history, etc. Only then would people develop the sense of pride, tradition and common purpose which would come to characterize modern nationalism.

Nationalism, as loyalty to one's nation, did not originate in the early 19th century. Men and women have been fighting for, and living and dying for, their respective countries for hundreds of years. It wasn't until the early 19th century that this feeling and motivation changed into something far more intense and far more demanding than it had been. The focus of the loyalty changed from dynastic self-interest, to individual self-interest as part of a greater collective consciousness.

Impact

Nationalistic thinkers and writers examined the language, literature and folkways of their people, thereby stimulating nationalist feelings. Emphasizing the history and culture of the various European peoples tended to reinforce and glorify national sentiment.

Most early 19th century nationalist leaders adopted the ideas of the German philosopher-historian Johann Gottfried Herder (1744 – 1803), who is regarded as the father of modern nationalism.

Herder taught that every people is unique and possesses a distinct national character, or *Volksgeist*, which has evolved over many centuries. No one culture or people is superior to any other. All national groups are parts of that greater whole which is humanity.

Herder's doctrine of the indestructible *Volksgeist* led to a belief that every nation has the right to become a sovereign state encompassing all members of the same nationality. Since most Western states contained people of many different nationalities, and few states contained all the members of any one nationality, nationalism came to imply the overthrow of almost every existing government.

Evaluation

Because of its inherently revolutionary implications, nationalism was suppressed by the established authorities. Yet it flourished in Germany, where conservative and reactionary nationalists competed with a somewhat more liberal form of nationalism associated with intellectuals like Fichte, Hegel, Humboldt and Von Ranke. In Eastern Europe, conservative nationalists stressed the value of their own unique customs, culture and folkways, while Western European nationalists demanded liberal political reforms. The influence of the Italian Nationalist Mazzini and the Frenchman Michelet in stimulating nationalist feeling in the West was a key ingredient.

It should be noted that there was always a fundamental conflict between liberalism and nationalism. Liberals were rationalists who demanded objectivity in studying society and history, while nationalists relied on emotion and would do anything to exalt the nation, even subvert individual rights. By the late 19th century nationalism was promoting competition and warfare between peoples and threatening to douse liberal ideas of reason and freedom.

Socialism

With the chief beneficiaries of industrialism being the new middle class, the increasing misery of the working classes disturbed the conscience of concerned liberal thinkers (Bentham and Mill), who proposed a modification of the concept of laissez-faire economics. Other socially concerned thinkers, observing the injustices and inefficiencies of capitalistic society, began to define the social question in terms of human equality and the means to be followed in order to secure this goal. As cures for the social evils of industrialism were laid out in elaborate detail, the emerging dogma came to be called socialism.

Characteristics

Since biblical times humans have been concerned with the problem of social justice, but it was not until the 19th century that it possessed a broader intellectual base and a greater popular support than it had ever enjoyed in the past. The difficulty with the existing system, according to social critics of the day, was that it permitted wealth to be concentrated in the hands of a small group of persons and deprived the working classes of a just share in what was rightfully theirs. A social mechanism had to be developed so a just distribution of society's wealth could be attained. The result was a variety of approaches.

The Utopian Socialists (from *Utopia*, Saint Thomas More's book on a fictional ideal society) were the earliest writers to propose an equitable solution to improve the distribution of society's wealth. While they endorsed the productive capacity of industrialism, they denounced its mismanagement. Human society was to be organized as a community rather than a mixture of competing, selfish individuals. All the goods a person needed could be produced in one community.

Generally, the utopians advocated some kind of harmonious society, some form of model communities, social workshops or the like, where the ruthless qualities of an individualistic capitalism would disappear.

Utopian ideas were generally regarded as idealistic and visionary, with no practical application. With little popular support from either the political establishment or the working classes, the movement failed to produce any substantial solution to the social question. Leading Utopian thinkers included Henri de Saint-Simon (1760 – 1825), Charles Fourier (1772 – 1837), Robert Owen (1771 – 1858), and Louis Blanc (1811 – 1882).

The Anarchists rejected industrialism and the dominance of government. Auguste Blanqui (1805 – 1881) advocated terrorism as a means to end capitalism and the state.

Pierre Joseph Proudhon (1809 – 1865) attacked the principle of private property because it denied justice to the common people.

Christian Socialism began in England circa 1848. Believing that the evils of industrialism would be ended by following Christian principles, the advocates of this doctrine tried to bridge the gap between the anti-religious drift of socialism and the need for Christian social justice for workers. The best-known Christian Socialist was the novelist Charles Kingsley (1814 – 1875), whose writings exposed the social evils of industrialism.

"Scientific" Socialism, or Marxism, was the creation of Karl Marx (1818 – 1883), a German scholar who, with the help of Friedrich Engels (1820 – 1895), intended to replace utopian hopes and dreams with a brutal, militant blueprint for socialist working class success. The principal works of this revolutionary school of socialism were *The Communist Manifesto* and *Das Kapital (Capital)*.

The theory of Dialectical Materialism enabled Marx to explain the history of the world. By borrowing Hegel's dialectic, substituting materialism and realism in place of Hegel's idealism, and inverting the methodological process, Marx was able to justify his theoretical conclusions.

Marxism consisted of a number of key propositions: 1) The economic interpretation of history, i.e., all human history has been determined by economic factors (mainly who controls the means of production and distribution); 2) The class struggle, i.e., since the beginning of time there has been a class struggle between the rich and the poor or the exploiters and the exploited; 3) Theory of Surplus Value, i.e., the true value of a product was labor and, since the worker received a small portion of his just labor price, the difference was surplus value, "stolen" from him by the capitalist; 4) Socialism was inevitable, i.e., capitalism contained the seeds of its own destruction (overproduction, unemployment, etc.); the rich will grow richer and the poor will grow poorer until the gap between each class (proletariat and bourgeoisie) is so great that the working classes will rise up in revolution and overthrow the elite bourgeoisie to install a "dictatorship of the proletariat". As modern capitalism is dismantled, the creation of a classless society guided by the principle "From each according to his abilities, to each according to his needs," will take place.

Evaluation

Ideologies (isms) are interpretations of the world from a particular viewpoint. They are, or imply, programs of action, and thrive where belief in general standards and norms has broken down. The proliferation of so many thought systems, and movements based on them, after 1815, suggest that the basic division of society was between those who accepted the implications of the intellectual, economic, and political revolutions of the 18th and early 19th centuries, and those who did not. The polarization in ideology was the result.

EUROPE IN CRISIS, 1815 – 1833: REPRESSION, REFORM AND REVOLUTION

The Vienna peace settlement signaled the triumph of the political and social conservative order in Europe. The dangerous ideas (Liberalism and Nationalism) associated with the French Revolution and Napoleonic period had been "contained" by the territorial provisions of the 1815 agreement. The status quo had been once again defined. "Order" and "stability" was expected in the European state system.

Underestimating the power of ideas, the Conservative leadership after 1815 was, instead, faced with a dramatic confrontation between those who had been converted to the "new" ideas (which required political changes), and the traditional ruling classes, who were reluctant to make any accommodation with the believers in the "new" ideas. The result of such confrontation in most states was government-sponsored repression followed by revolution. Few states chose to respond to the call for liberal reform. Only nationalist impulses in Greece and Belgium were successful, for reasons which could hardly comfort liberals. The intellectual climate of Romanticism provided a volatile atmosphere in which these events unfolded.

Post-War Repression, 1815 – 1820

Initially, the great powers followed the lead of the Austrian statesman Prince Metternich (1773 – 1859) in suppressing any direct or indirect expression of liberal faith. Most leaders attempted to reinstitute conservative means of governmental control, in order to prevent reforms in the direction of greater participation by more people in government. The literate middle class, supported by urban workers, demanded reform and were willing to use violence to obtain it.

England

The Tory (Conservative) government that defeated Napoleon was in control of England. Facing serious economic problems that had produced large numbers of industrial unemployed, the conservatives tried to follow a reactionary policy.

The Corn Law of 1815 effectively halted the importation of cheaper foreign grains, aiding the Tory land-holding aristocracy, but increasing the cost of bread, and driving the poor and unemployed to protest and demand parliamentary reform.

The Coercion Acts of 1817 suspended "habeas corpus" for the first time in English history; provided for arbitrary arrest and punishment; and drastically curtailed freedom of the press and public mass meetings.

The "Peterloo Massacre" of 1819 occurred when several members of a large crowd, who were listening to reformers demand repeal of the Corn Laws and other liberal changes, were killed, with hundreds of others injured when police authorities broke up the meeting.

The Six Acts of Parliament in 1819, in response to the "Peterloo" episode, were a series of repressive measures which attempted to remove the instruments of agitation from the hands of radical leaders and to provide the authorities with new powers.

The Cato Street Conspiracy of 1820 took place when a group of extreme radicals plotted to blow up the entire British cabinet. It provided new support for repression by the Tories, as well as discrediting the movement for parliamentary reform.

By 1820 England was on the road to becoming a reactionary authoritative state, when numerous protests among younger Tories argued that such repressive legislation was not in the English tradition, and that the party itself might need to change its direction.

France

France emerged from the chaos of the long revolutionary period (1789 – 1815) as the most liberal large state on the continent. The period from 1815 – 1830 is always referred to as the Restoration era, signifying the return of the legitimate royal dynasty of France — the infamous Bourbon line.

Louis XVIII (reign 1814 – 1824) governed France as a Constitutional Monarch, by agreeing to observe the "Charter" or Constitution of the Restoration Period. This moderate document managed to limit royal power, grant legislative powers, protect civil rights, and uphold the Code Napoleon and other pre-restoration reforms.

Louis XVIII wished to unify the French populace, which was divided into those who accepted the Revolution and those who did not. The leader of those who did not was the Count of Artois (1757 – 1836), brother of the king and leader of the Ultra Royalists.

The 1815 "White Terror" saw royalist mobs murder thousands of former revolutionaries.

New elections in 1816 for the Chamber of Deputies resulted in the Ultras being rejected, in favor of a moderate royalist majority dependent on middle class support. The war indemnity was paid off, France was admitted to the Quadruple Alliance (1818), and liberal sentiment began to grow.

In February, 1820, the Duke of Berri, son of Artois and heir to the throne after his father, was murdered. Royalists charged that the left (Liberals) were responsible and that the king's policy of moderation had encouraged the left.

Louis XVIII began to move the government more and more to the right, as changes in the electoral laws narrowed the eligible voters to the most wealthy, and censorship was imposed. Liberals were being driven out of legal political life and into near-illegal activity. The triumph of reactionism came in 1823, when French troops were authorized by the Concert of Europe to crush the Spanish Revolution and restore another Bourbon ruler, Ferdinand VII.

Austria and the Germanys

Throughout the first half of the 19th century the Austrian Empire and the German Confederation were dominated by Prince Metternich, who epitomized conservative reactionism. To no other country or empire were the programs of liberalism and nationalism potentially more dangerous. Given the multi-ethnic composition of the Hapsburg empire, any recognition of the political rights and aspirations of any of the national groups would mean the probable dissolution of the empire.

It was Napoleon who reduced over 300 German states to 39, and the Congress of Vienna which preserved this arrangement under Austrian domination. The purpose of the German confederation (Bund) was to guarantee the independence of the member states, and by joint action, to preserve all German states from domestic disorder or revolution. Its organization of government was a Diet (assembly), presided over by Austria, as President.

The two largest states in the confederation were Austria and Prussia. Austria was ruled by the Hapsburg dynasty and, through Metternich's anti-liberal and nationalist pathology, held the line against any change in the status quo.

Prussia was ruled by the Hohenzollern dynasty, a very aggressive royal family when it came to expanding the borders of this northern German state, sometimes at the expense of other German rulers. For a short time after 1815 German liberals looked to Prussia as a leader of German liberalism, because of liberal reforms in government enacted after a humiliating defeat at the hands of Napoleon. These reforms were intended to improve the efficiency of government and were not the portent of a general trend. The Prussian government and its traditional ruling classes (Junkers) intended to follow the lead of Metternich in repressing all liberal-nationalist agitation.

Liberal-nationalist agitation was highly vocal and visible in and among German universities in the first half of the 19th century. Student organizations, such as the Burschenschaften, were openly promoting political arrangements that seemed radical and revolutionary at the time.

At the Wartbug Festival (1817), students burned various symbols of authority. Russian agent Kotzebue was assassinated in 1819 by Karl Sand, a student member of the

Burschenschaften.

The Carlsbad Diet (1819) was summoned by Metternich to end the seditious activity of German liberals and nationalists. The passage of a series of decrees effectively ended the activities of these change-agents. In fact, the movement was driven underground.

Russia

From 1801 to 1825 Czar Alexander I governed this traditional authoritarian state. A man of many moods, this Russian emperor thought he was called upon to lead Europe into a new age of benevolence and good will. After the Congress of Vienna, he became increasingly reactionary and a follower of Metternich.

Alexander I was torn between an intellectual attraction to the ideas of the Enlightenment and reform, and a very pragmatic adherence to traditional Russian autocracy (absolutism).

With the help of liberal adviser, Michael Speransky, plans were made for a reconstruction of the Russian government, due to the czar's admiration for Napoleon's administrative genius. This and other liberal policies alienated the nobility, and Speransky was dismissed.

Alexander I came to regard the Enlightenment, the French Revolution and Napoleon in biblical terms, seeing all three as anti-Christian. Turning to a new reactionary advisor, General Arakcheiev, repression became the order of the day. There could be no toleration of political opposition or criticism of the regime. The early years of possible liberal reform had given way to conservative repression.

REVOLUTIONS I (1820 – 1829)

Nationalism, liberalism and industrialism were all key factors in the outbreak of revolution during the first half of the 19th century. All three "isms" were opposed by the conservative groups of the population (royalists, clergy, landed aristocracy), who were rooted in the way of life before the French Revolution. Promoting the new forces of change was a younger generation, the heirs of the Enlightenment who believed in progress. Romanticism was the atmosphere against which these events were played out.

The International System: The Concert of Europe

At the 1815 Congress of Vienna, the enforcement provisions of the settlement were designed to guarantee stability and peace in the international arena. The Quadruple Alliance (Austria, Russia, Prussia, England) that had defeated Napoleon was to continue through a new spirit of cooperation and consultation that would be referred to as the "Concert of Europe." At the suggestion of Lord Castlereagh, England's Foreign Minister, foreign policy issues affecting the international order would be worked out in a series of meetings or Congresses, so that no one nation could act without the consent of the others. But under the leadership of Metternich, the Congress system became the means to preserve the political status quo of autocracy in Europe against all revolutionary ideas. The Congress system was short-lived because the continental powers could not always agree on cooperative action, and the English refused to support interference in the domestic affairs of nation-states. In the end, each nation became guided by its own best interests.

The Congress System of Conferences.

The Congress of Aix-la-Chapelle (1818) arranged for the withdrawal of the allied army of occupation from France, and the admission of France into the concert of Europe (Quintuple Alliance).

The Congress of Troppau (1820) was summoned by Metternich because of the outbreak of revolution in Spain. A policy statement (Protocol of Troppau),which would authorize armed intervention into any state that undergoes revolutionary change, was opposed by England.

The Congress of Laibach (1821) authorized Austrian troops to end the revolutionary changes in the Kingdom of the Two Sicilys, where revolutions had spread from Spain. No decision was made concerning Spain.

The Congress of Verona (1822) was called because of the continuing Spanish Revolution and the outbreak (1821) of revolution in Greece. When Russia, Prussia and Austria agreed to support French intervention in Spain, the new English Foreign Minister, George Canning (1770 – 1827), (Viscount Castlereagh had committed suicide), withdrew England from the Concert of Europe. Verona marked the effective end of the Congress system.

The Monroe Doctrine and the Concert of Europe

British fears that Metternich would attempt the restoration of Spain's colonies, then revolting in Latin America, prompted George Canning to suggest, and then support, the foreign policy statement of the United States of America known as the Monroe Doctrine (1823) ,which prohibited any further colonization and intervention by European powers in the Western Hemisphere.

England hoped to replace Spain in establishing her own trading monopoly with these former Spanish colonies. Throughout the 19th century British commercial interests dominated Latin America.

Latin America in Revolution

Inspired by the French Revolution and the Napoleonic period, the rise of Latin American nationalism between 1804 and 1824 would witness the end of three centuries of Spanish colonial rule and the emergence of new heroes such as Toussaint L'Ouverture, Jose San Martin, Bernardo O'Higgins, Simon Bolivar and Miguel Hidalgo.

The Revolutions of the 1820s

Spain (1820 – 1823). Beginning in January 1820, a mutiny of army troops under Colonel Rafael Riego began, in opposition to the persecution of liberals by the restored monarch, King Ferdinand VII. The Congress of Verona (1822) authorized a French army to invade Spain and crush the revolutionaries.

Italy (1820 – 1821). Incited to revolution by the activities of secret liberal-nationalist organizations ("carbonari"), liberals revolted in Naples in July 1820, protesting the absolute rule of Ferdinand I of the Kingdom of the Two Sicilys. The Congress of Laibach (1821) authorized Austria to invade and suppress the rebels. An attempted uprising (1821) in Piedmont was crushed by Austrian forces.

The Greek Revolt (1821 – 1830). The revolution which broke out in Greece in 1821, while primarily a nationalist uprising rather than a liberal revolution, was part of a larger problem known as "The Eastern Question." Greece was part of the Ottoman Empire, whose vast territories were gradually being recessed throughout the 18th and early 19th centuries. The weakness of the Ottoman Empire and the political and economic ramifications of this instability for the balance of power in Europe kept the major powers in a nervous state of tension.

Because of conflicting interests, the major powers were unable to respond in any harmonious fashion for several years. The revolt was a leading political question in Europe throughout the 1820s. Occurring in the Romantic era, the revolt touched the sensitivities of romantics in the West. A Greek appeal to Christian Europe did not move Prussia or Austria, but did fuse England, France and Russia into a united force that defeated a combined Turco-Egyptian naval force at Navarino Bay (1827). Greek independence was recognized through the Treaty of Adrianople (1829).

Russian intervention on the side of Greek revolutionaries was based on Russian national interest (i.e., any dimunition of Ottoman power increased Russian chances of further expansion into the Turkish empire).

Greek nationalism triumphed over the conservative Vienna settlement, and three of the five great powers had aided a movement that violated their agreement of 1815. The self-interests of the great powers demonstrated the growing power of nationalism in the international system.

The Decembrist Uprising in Russia (1825). The death of Alexander I on December 1, 1825 resulted in a crisis over the actual succession to the throne and, in turn ,produced the first significant uprising in Russian history. The expected succession of Constantine, older brother of Alexander I, who was believed somewhat more liberal than the late czar, did not materialize. Instead, the younger brother Nicholas, no liberal by any measure, prepared to assume the throne that Constantine had actually renounced.

Hoping to block Nicholas' succession, a group of moderately liberal junior military officers staged a demonstration in late December, 1825, in St. Petersburg, only to see it quickly dissipated by artillery attacks ordered by Czar Nicholas I.

The Decembrists were the first upper-class opponents of the autocratic Russian system of government, who called attention to the popular grievances among Russian society. The insurrection developed in Nicholas I a pathological dislike for liberal reformers.

A program called "Official Nationality,"with the slogan, "Autocracy, Orthodoxy and National Unity," was designed to lead Russia back to its historic roots. Through it, Nicholas I became Europe's most reactionary monarch.

Domestically, Russia became a police state with censorship and state-sponsored terrorism. There would be no representative assemblies, and education was not only limited, but university curricula were carefully monitored. A profound alienation of Russian intellectual life ensued.

In foreign affairs the same extreme conservatism was demonstrated. The Polish Revolution of 1830 – 31 was crushed, and Russian troops played a key role in stamping out Hungarian nationalism in the Hapsburg Empire, during the revolutionary uprisings of 1848 – 49. Russia's traditional desire for expansion in the direction of the Ottoman Empire, produced a confrontation between France and Russia over who was entitled to protect Christians and the Holy Places in the Near East. When the Sultan of Turkey awarded France the honor, Nicholas I was prepared to go to war against Turkey to uphold Russia's right to speak for Slavic Christians. The result was the Crimean War (1854 – 56), which Russia would lose. Nicholas I died (1855) during the course of fighting this war.

England Chooses Reform Over Revolution

The climax of repression in England was the Six Acts of Parliament (1819). Yet even as these laws were enacted, younger conservative politicians were questioning the wisdom of their party elders (Wellington, Castlereagh), and calling for moderation. During the 1820s, a new group of younger Tories would moderate their party's unbending conservatism.

Reform was promoted by George Canning and Robert Peel, in opposition to the reactionary policies of earlier Tory leaders. With the help of liberal Whig politicians, enough votes were found to put England on the road to liberal reform.

Canning inaugurated a liberal policy in foreign affairs, including abandonment of the Congress System. Robert Peel reformed prisons and the outdated criminal code, as well as established an efficient metropolitan police force ("Bobbies").

Mercantile and navigation acts were liberalized, enabling British colonies to trade with nations other than England.

The 1673 Test Act, which was a religious test used for barring non-Anglicans from participation in the government, was repealed. The Catholic Emancipation Act (1829) granted full civil rights to Roman Catholics. It was in defiance of the Test Act, which was prompted by the election of the Irish leader Daniel J. O'Connell to the British Parliament.

The momentum for liberal reform would continue into the 1830s, as Britain realized that accommodation with the new merchant and financial classes was in the spirit of English history. The acid test of liberal reform, however, would come to focus on the willingness of Parliament to repeal the Corn Laws and reform itself.

REVOLUTIONS II, 1830 – 1833

The Conservative grip on Europe following the turbulence of the 1820s was very quickly challenged, when revolution broke out in France in 1830. By then, the forces of liberalism and nationalism had become so strong that they constituted major threats to the security of many governments. In eastern Europe, nationalism was the greater danger, while in the West the demands of middle class liberals for various political reforms grew louder.

France: The July Revolution

The death of King Louis XVIII in 1824 brought his brother Charles, Count of Artois and leader of the Ultra Royalists, to the throne as Charles X, and set the stage for a return to the Old Regime or revolution.

Attempting to roll back the revolutionary gains, Charles X alienated the moderate forces on the right as well as the entire left. Continued violations of the Charter enabled French voters to register their displeasure in the elections of 1827 by giving the liberals a substantial gain in the Chamber of Deputies.

In 1829, when Charles X appointed a ministry led by the Prince of Polignac, who was the personification of reactionism in France, liberals considered this a declaration of war. Elections in 1830 produced a stunning victory for the liberals. Charles X responded by decreeing the Four Ordinances, which would have amounted to a royal *Coup d'État* if not stopped. The spark of revolt was set off by the radicals of Paris, with the workers and students raising barricades in the streets with the intention of establishing a republic. Charles X abdicated and fled France.

The Liberals in the Chamber of Deputies, under the leadership of Adolphe Thiers, preferred a constitutional monarchy without a Bourbon ruler. With the cooperation of Talleyrand and Lafayette, they agreed on Prince Louis Philippe, head of the Orleans family and cousin to Charles X.

France was now controlled by the bourgeoisie of upper-middle class bankers and businessmen. King Louis Philippe was "the Bourgeoisie King" who would tilt the government towards these interests. While the July Monarchy of Louis Philippe was politically more liberal than the restoration government, socially it proved to be quite conservative.

The news of the successful July Revolution in France served as a spark ("When France sneezes, the rest of Europe catches cold") to revolutionary uprisings throughout Europe.

The Belgian Independence Movement (1830 – 1831)

Since being merged with Holland in 1815, the upper classes of Belgium had never reconciled themselves to rule by a country with a different language, religion and economic life. Inspired by the news of the July Revolution in France, a revolt against Dutch rule broke out in Brussels, led by students and industrial workers. The Dutch army was defeated and forced to withdraw from Belgium by the threat of a Franco-British fleet. A national Congress wrote a liberal Belgian Constitution. In 1831, Leopold of Saxe-Coburg (1831 – 1865) became king of the Belgians. In 1839, the Great Powers declared the neutrality of Belgium.

Poland (1830 – 1831)

The new czar of Russia, Nicholas I (reign 1825 – 1855), had the first opportunity to demonstrate his extreme conservatism in foreign policy when a military insurrection broke out late in 1830, in Warsaw. This nationalist uprising challenged the historic Russian domination of Poland. The Russian garrison was driven out of Poland; the czar was deposed as king of Poland; and the independence of Poland was proclaimed by a revolutionary government.

Nicholas I ordered the Russian army to invade Poland; it ruthlessly proceeded to crush the nationalist rebellion. Poland became "a land of graves and crosses." The Organic Statute of 1832 declared Poland to be an integral part of the Russian empire.

Italy (1831 – 1832)

Outbreaks of liberal discontent occurred in northern Italy, centering on Modena, Parma, and the Papal States. The inspiration for Italian nationalists who spoke of a unification process was (1) Guiseppe Mazzini and his secret revolutionary society called Young Italy; and (2) the Carbonari, the secret nationalist societies, which advocated the use of force to achieve national unification. Still too disorganized, the Italian revolutionaries were easily crushed by Austrian troops under Metternich's enforcement of the Concert of Europe's philosophy. Still, the Italian Risorgimento (resurgence of the Italian spirit) was well under way.

Germany (1830 – 1833)

The Carlsbad Decrees of 1819 had effectively restricted freedom throughout Germany. At the news of France's July Revolution, German university students and professors led street demonstrations that forced temporary granting of constitutions in several minor states. These expressions of liberal sentiment and nationalistic desires for German unification were easily crushed by Metternich's domination of the German Confederation (Bund), and his influence over Prussia.

Great Britain: Reform Continues

The death of King George IV and the accession of King William IX in 1830 resulted in a general parliamentary election in which the oppositional political party, the Whigs, scored major gains with their platform calling for parliamentary reform. With the Tory party divided, the king asked the leader of the Whig party, Earl Grey (1764 – 1845) to form a government.

Immediately, a major reform bill was introduced, designed to increase the number of voters by fifty percent and to eliminate underpopulated electoral districts ("Rotten Boroughs") and replace them with representatives for the previously unrepresented manufacturing districts and cities.

After a national debate, new elections, and a threat from King William IV to alter the composition of the House of Lords, the Great Reform Bill of 1832 was enacted into law. While the Reform Bill did not resolve all political inequities in British political life, it marked a new beginning. Several more notable reforms would begin to redraw the sociological landscape of British life.

Evaluation

Neither the forces of revolution nor those of reaction, were able to maintain the upper hand between 1789 and 1848. Liberalism and nationalism, socialism and democracy were on the march, but the forces of conservatism and reaction were still strong enough to contain them. The polarization of Europe was becoming ever so clear: the liberal middle class West, which advocated constitutionalism and industrial progress; and the authoritarian East, which was committed to preserving the status quo. The confrontation would continue until one or the other side would win out decisively.

The Revolutions of 1848

The year 1848 is considered the watershed of the 19th century. The revolutionary disturbances of the first half of the 19th century reached a climax, in a new wave of revolutions that extended from Scandinavia to southern Italy, and from France to Central Europe. Only England and Russia avoided violent upheaval.

The issues were substantially the same as they had been in 1789. What was new in 1848 was that these demands were far more widespread and irrepressible than ever before. Whole classes and nations demanded to be fully included in society. The French Revolution of 1789 came at the end of a period ("Ancien Regime"), while the revolutions of 1848 signaled the beginning of a new age. Aggravated by a rapid growth in population and social disruption caused by industrialism and urbanization, a massive tide of discontent swept across the western world.

Generally speaking, the 1848 upheavals shared in common the strong influences of romanticism, nationalism, and liberalism, as well as a new factor of economic dislocation and instability throughout most of Europe. Some authorities believe that it was the absence of liberty that was most responsible for the uprisings.

Specifically, a number of similar conditions existed in several countries: 1) severe food shortages caused by poor harvests of grain and potatoes (e.g., Irish Potato Famine); 2) financial crises caused by a downturn in the commercial and industrial economy; 3) business failures; 4) widespread unemployment ; 5) a sense of frustration and discontent of urban artisan and working classes as wages diminished; 6) a system of poor relief which became overburdened; 7) living conditions which deteriorated in the cities, and; 7) the power of nationalism in the Germanys and Italys, as well as Eastern Europe, to inspire the overthrow of existing governments. Middle class predominance with the unregulated economy continued to drive these liberals to push for more reform of government and for civil liberty. They pursued this by enlisting the help of the working classes in putting more pressure on the government to change.

Republicanism: Victory in France and Defeat in Italy

In France, working class discontent and liberals' unhappiness with the corrupt regime of King Louis Philippe (reign 1830 – 1848) – especially his minister Guizot –

erupted in street riots in Paris on February 22 – 23, 1848. With the workers in control of Paris, King Louis Philippe abdicated on February 24, and a provisional government proclaimed the Second French Republic.

Heading the provisional government was the liberal Alphonse Lamartine (1790 – 1869), who favored a moderate republic and political democracy. Lamartine's bourgeoisie allies had little sympathy for the working poor, and did not intend to pursue a social revolution, as well.

The working class groups were united by their leader Louis Blanc (1811 – 1882), a socialist thinker who expected the provisional government to deal with the unemployed, and anticipated the power of the state being used to improve life and the conditions of labor. Pressed by the demands of Blanc and his followers, the provisional government established national workshops to provide work and relief for thousands of unemployed workers.

The "June Days" revolution was provoked when the government closed the national workshop. A general election in April resulted in a National Assembly, dominated by the moderate republicans and conservatives under Lamartine who regarded socialist ideas as threats to private property. The Parisian workers, feeling that their revolution had been nullified, took to the streets in revolution.

This new revolution (June 23 – 26) was unlike previous uprisings in France. It marked the inauguration of genuine class warfare; it was a revolt against poverty and a cry for the redistribution of property. It foreshadowed the great social revolutions of the 20th century. The revolt was extinguished after General Cavaignac was given dictatorial powers by the government. The June Days confirmed the political predominance of conservative property holders in French life.

The new Constitution of the Second French Republic provided for a unicameral legislative (with the National Assembly designating themselves as the first members), and executive power vested in a popularly-elected president of the Republic. When the election returns were counted the candidate of the government, General Cavaignac, was soundly defeated by a "dark horse" candidate, Prince Louis Napoleon Bonaparte (1808 – 1873), a nephew of the great emperor. On December 20, 1848, Louis Napoleon was installed as President of the republic.

It was clear the voters turned to the name of Bonaparte as a source of stability and greatness. They expected him to prevent any further working class disorder. However, the election of Louis Napoleon doomed the Second Republic. He was a Bonaparte, dedicated to his own fame and vanity, and not republican institutions. In December, 1852, Louis Napoleon became Emperor Napoleon III, and France retreated from republicanism again.

Italian nationalists and liberals wanted to end Hapsburg (Austrian), Bourbon (Naples and Sicily), and papal domination and unite these disparate areas into a unified liberal nation. A revolt by liberals in Sicily in January, 1848, was followed by the granting of liberal constitutions in Naples, Tuscany, Piedmont, and the Papal States. Milan and Venice expelled their Austrian rulers. In March, 1848, upon hearing the news of the revolution in Vienna, a fresh outburst of revolution from Austrian rule occurred in Lombardy and Venetia, with Sardinia-Piedmont declaring war on Austria. Simultaneously, Italian patriots attacked the Papal States, forcing the Pope, Pius IX, to flee to Naples for refuge.

The temporary nature of these initial successes was illustrated by the speed with which the conservative forces regained control. In the north, Austrian Field Marshal Radetsky swept aside all opposition, regaining Lombardy and Venetia and crushing Sardinia-Piedmont. In the Papal States, the establishment of the Roman Republic

(February 1849), under the leadership of Giuseppe Mazzini and the protection of Giuseppe Garibaldi, would fail when French troops took Rome in July, 1849, after a heroic defense by Garibaldi. Pope Pius IX returned to Rome cured of his liberal leanings. In the south and in Sicily the revolts were suppressed by the former rulers.

Within eighteen months the revolutions of 1848 had failed throughout Italy. Among the explanations for these failures were the failure of conservative, rural people to support the revolution; the divisions in aim and technique among the revolutionaries; the fear the radicals aroused among moderate groups of Italians, who would be needed to guarantee the success of any revolution; and the general lack of experience and administrative ability on the part of the revolutionists.

Nationalism Resisted in Austrian Empire

The Hapsburg Empire was vulnerable to revolutionary challenge. With its collection of subject nationalities (more non-Germans than Germans), the empire was stirred by an acute spirit of nationalism; its government was reactionary (liberal institutions were non-existent); and its social reliance on serfdom doomed the masses of people to a life without hope. As soon as news of the "February Days" in France reached the borders of the Austrian Empire, rebellions began. The long-suppressed opponents of the government believed the time had come to introduce liberal institutions into the empire.

Vienna

In March 1848, Hungarian criticism of Hapsburg imperial rule was initiated by Magyar nationalist leader, Louis Kossuth (1802 – 1894), who demanded Hungarian independence. Students and workers in Vienna rushed to the streets to demonstrate on behalf of a more liberal government. The army failed to restore order and Prince Metternich, the symbol of reaction, resigned and fled the country. Emperor Ferdinand I (reign 1835 – 1848) granted a moderately liberal constitution, but its short-comings dissatisfied more radical elements, and continual disorder prompted the emperor to flee from Vienna to Innsbruck, where he relied on his army commanders to restore order in the Empire. The Austrian imperial troops remained loyal to the Hapsburg crown. Prince Schwarzenberg was put in charge of restoring Hapsburg control.

A people's committee ruled Vienna, where a liberal assembly gathered to write a constitution. In Hungary and Bohemia, revolutionary outbreaks indicated ultimate success.

The inability of the revolutionary groups in Vienna to govern effectively made it easier for the Hapsburgs to lay siege to Vienna, in October 1848. The rebels surrendered, and Emperor Ferdinand abdicated in favor of his eighteen-year-old nephew, Francis Joseph (reign 1848 – 1916), who promptly restored royal absolutism.

The imperial government had been saved at Vienna through the loyalty of the army, and the lack of ruling capacity on the part of the revolutionaries. The only thing the revolutionaries could agree on was their hatred of the Hapsburg dynasty.

Bohemia

Nationalist feeling among the Czechs or Bohemians had been smoldering for centuries. They demanded a constitution and autonomy within the Hapsburg Empire.

A Pan-Slav Congress attempted to unite all Slavic peoples, but accomplished little, because divisions were more decisive among them than was unified opposition to Hapsburg control.

In June, 1848, Prague submitted to a military occupation, followed by a military dictatorship in July, after all revolutionary groups were crushed.

Hungary

The Kingdom of Hungary was a state of about twelve million under Hapsburg authority. Magyars or Hungarians, who represented about five million subjects of the emperor, enjoyed a privileged position in the empire. The remaining seven million Slavic and Rumanian natives were powerless.

In March, 1848, Nationalist leader Louis Kossuth took over direction of the movement, and tamed a more radical Hungarian rebellion; Hungarian autonomy was declared in April, but failed to win popular support for the revolution because of the tyrannical treatment of the Slavic minorities. Because the government in Vienna was distracted by revolutions everywhere in the empire in the summer and fall of 1848, Louis Kossuth had time to organize an army to fight for Hungarian independence.

War between Austria and Hungary was declared on October 3, 1848, and Hungarian armies drove to within sight of Vienna. But desperate resistance from Slavic minorities forced the Hungarians to withdraw. Hungary was invaded by an Austrian army from the West, in June, 1849, and a Russian army (Tsar Nicholas I of Russia offered assistance to new emperor Francis Joseph) from the north. Along with Serbian resistance in the south and Rumanian resistance in the east, the combined opposition proved too much for Louis Kossuth's Hungarian Republic (proclaimed in April 1849), which was defeated. Kossuth fled into exile, while thirteen of his guards were executed. Not until Austria was defeated by Prussia, in 1866, would Hungary be in a position again to demand governmental equality with the Austrians.

Italy

Charles Albert, King of Sardinia, having granted his people a constitution, and hoping to add the Hapsburgs' Italian holdings to his kingdom, declared war on Austria. Unfortunately, the Sardinian army was twice defeated in battle (Custozza and Novara) by the Austrian General, Radetsky.

King Charles Albert abdicated in favor of his son, Victor Emmanuel, who was destined to complete the unification of Italy in the second half of the 19th century.

The Revolutions of 1848 failed in Austria for several reasons. The subject nationalities sometimes hated each other more than they despised Austria. The Hapsburgs used the divisions between the ethnic groups as an effective weapon against each. The imperial army had remained loyal to its aristocratic commanders, who favored absolutism. There were too few industrial workers and an equally small number of middle class. The industrial workers could not exert any political power, and the middle class feared working-class radicalism and rallied to the government as defender of the status quo.

Liberalism Halted in the Germanies

The immediate effect of the 1848 Revolution in France was a series of liberal and nationalistic demonstrations in the German states (March, 1848), with the rulers promising liberal concessions. The liberals' demand for constitutional government was coupled with another demand: some kind of union or federation of the German states. While popular demonstrations by students, workers, and the middle class produced the promise of a liberal future,the permanent success or failure of these "promises" rested on Prussian reaction.

Prussia, The Frankfurt Parliament and German Unification

Under King Frederick William IV (reign 1848 – 1861), Prussia moved from revolution to reaction. After agreeing to liberalize the Prussian government following street rioting in Berlin, the king rejected the constitution written by a specially-called assembly. The liberal ministry resigned and was replaced by a conservative one. By the fall the king felt powerful enough to substitute his own constitution, which guaranteed royal control of the government, with a complicated three-class system of indirect voting that excluded all but landlords and wealthy bourgeoisie from office. This system prevailed in Prussia until 1918. Finally, the government ministry was responsible to the king and the military services swore loyalty to the king alone.

Self appointed liberal, romantic, and nationalist leaders called for elections to a constituent assembly, from all states belonging to the German Bund, for the purpose of unifying the German states. Meeting in May, 1848, the Frankfurt Parliament was composed of mostly intellectuals, professionals, lawyers, businessmen and middle class. After a year of deliberation over questions of (1) monarchy or republic; (2) federal union or centralized state; and (3) boundaries (i.e., only German-populated or mixed nationalities), the assembly produced a constitution.

The principal problem facing the Frankfurt Assembly was to obtain Prussian support. The smaller German states generally favored the Frankfurt Constitution, as did liberals throughout the large and middle-sized states. Austria made it clear that it was opposed to the work of the Assembly and would remain in favor of the present system.

The Assembly leaders made the decision to stake their demands for a united Germany on King Frederick William IV, of Prussia. They selected him as emperor in April, 1849, only to have him reject the offer because he was a divine-right monarch, not subject to popularly-elected assemblies. Without Prussia there could be no success, so the Frankfurt Parliament dissolved without achieving a single accomplishment.

The Prussian King Frederick William IV had his own plans for uniting Germany. Right after refusing a "crown from the gutter," he offered his own plan to the German princes, wherein Prussia would play a prominent role, along with Austria. When Austria demanded allegiance to the Bund, the Prussian king realized pushing his plan would involve him in a war with Austria and her allies (including Russia). In November, 1850, Prussia agreed to forego the idea of uniting the German states, at a meeting with Austria called the "Humiliation of Olmutz." Austrian domination of the German Bund was confirmed.

Great Britain and the Victorian Compromise

The Victorian Age (1837 – 1901) is associated with the long reign of Queen Victoria, who succeeded her uncle, King William IV at the age of eighteen and married her cousin, Prince Albert. The early years of her reign coincided with the continuation of liberal reform of the British government accomplished through an arrangement known as the "Victorian Compromise." The Compromise was a political alliance of the middle class and aristocracy to exclude the working class from political power. The middle class gained control of the House of Commons, the aristocracy controlled the government, army, and Church of England. The process of accommodation was working successfully.

Highlights of the "Compromise Era"

Parliamentary reforms continued after passage of the 1832 Reform Bill. Laws were enacted abolishing slavery throughout the Empire (1833). The Factory Act (1831) forbade the employment of children under the age of nine. The New Poor Law (1834) now required the needy who were able and unemployed to live in workhouses. The Municipal Reform Law (1835) gave control of the cities to the middle class. The last remnants of the mercantilistic age fell with the abolition of the Corn Laws (1846) and repeal of the old navigation acts (1849).

Working class protest arose in the wake of their belief that passage of the "Great Reform Bill" of 1832 would bring them prosperity. When workers found themselves no better off, they turned to collective action of a political nature. They linked the solution of their economic plight to a program of political reform known as Chartism, or the Chartist movement, from the charter of six points which they petitioned Parliament to adopt - universal male suffrage, secret ballot for voting, no property qualifications for members of Parliament, salaries for members of Parliament, annual elections for Parliament, and equal electoral districts.

During the age of Victorian Compromise these ideas were considered dangerously radical. Both the middle class and aristocracy vigorously opposed the working class political agenda. Chartism as a national movement failed. Its ranks were split between those who favored violence and those who advocated peaceful tactics. The return of prosperity, with steady wages and lower food prices, robbed the movement of momentum. Yet the chartist movement came to constitute the first large-scale, working class political movement that workers everywhere would eventually adopt if they were to improve their situation.

After 1846 England was more and more dominated by the middle class; this was one of the factors that enabled England to escape the revolutions which shook Europe in 1848. The ability of the English to make meaningful industrial reforms gave the working class hope that its goals could be achieved without violent social upheaval.

Evaluation

The revolutions of 1848 began with much promise, but they all ended in defeat for a number of reasons. They were spontaneous movements which lost their popular support as the people lost their enthusiasm. Initial successes by the revolutionaries were due less to their strength than to the hesitancy of governments to use their superior force. Once this hesitancy was overcome, the revolutions were smashed. They were essentially urban movements, and the conservative landowners and peasants tended, in time, to nullify the spontaneous actions of the urban classes. The middle class, who led the revolutions, came to fear the radicalism of their working class allies. While in favor of political reformation, the middle class drew the line at social engineering, much to the dismay of the laboring poor. Divisions among national groups, and the willingness of one nationality to deny rights to other nationalities, helped to destroy the revolutionary movements in central Europe.

However, the results of 1848 – 1849 were not entirely negative. Universal male suffrage was introduced in France; serfdom remained abolished in Austria and the German states; parliaments were established in Prussia and other German states, though dominated, to be sure, by princes and aristocrats; and Prussia and Sardinia-Piedmont emerged with new determination to succeed in their respective unification schemes.

The Revolutions of 1848 – 1849 brought to a close the era of liberal revolutions that had begun in France in 1789. Reformers and revolutionists alike learned a lesson from the failures of 1848. They learned that planning and organization is necessary; that rational argument and revolution would not always assure success. With 1848 the Age of Revolution sputtered out. The Age of Romanticism was about to give way to an Age of Realism.

EPILOGUE: THE VIEW FROM MID-19TH CENTURY EUROPE

A new age was about to follow the Revolutions of 1848-1849, as Otto von Bismarck, one of the dominant political figures of the second half of the 19th century, was quick to realize. If the mistake of these years was to believe that great decisions could be brought about by speeches and parliamentary majorities, the sequel would soon show that in an industrial era new techniques involving ruthless force were all too readily available. The period of *Realpolitik* — of realistic, iron-fisted politics and diplomacy — was about to happen.

By 1850 all humankind was positioned to become part of a single, worldwide, interacting whole. Based on military technology and industrial productivity, no part of the world could prevent Europeans from imposing their will.

The half century after 1850 would witness the political consolidation and economic expansion that paved the way for the brief global domination of Europe. The conservative monarchies of Sardinia-Piedmont and Prussia united Italy and Germany by military force, and gave birth to new power relationships on the continent. Externalizing their rivalries produced conflict overseas in a new age of imperialism, which saw Africa and Asia fall under the domination of the West.

Nationalism overtook liberalism as the dominant force in human affairs after 1850. Nationalists would be less romantic and more hardheaded. The good of the nation and not the individual became the new creed. The state would be deified.

After 1848 – 1849, the middle class ceased to be revolutionary. It became concerned with protecting its hard-earned political power and property rights against radical political and social movements. And the working classes also adopted new tactics and organizations. They turned to trade unions and political parties to achieve their political and social goals.

A great era of human progress was about to begin — material, political, scientific, industrial, social and cultural — shaping of the contours of the world.

4 REALISM AND MATERIALISM (1848-1914)

THE REVOLUTIONARY TRADITION

The era of reaction which had followed the collapse of the Napoleonic regime and the Congress of Vienna (1815) was followed by a wave of liberal and national agitation which was manifested in the Revolutions of 1820, 1825, and 1830.

The liberals, who tended to control the revolutionary agenda in Western Europe, desired constitutional government and the extension of individual freedoms – freedom of speech, press, and assembly. Liberal reforms and programs were advanced in the more economically advanced societies which had significant middle classes. In Central, Eastern, and Southern Europe, nationalism was the primary force for change. The advocates of nationalism sought to dismantle the traditional dynastic political controls which prohibited the formation of genuine nation-states. In addition to these factors, other reformers had succeeded in placing the need for social and economic improvement of the masses on the revolutionary platform; this was especially evident in France and England.

During the 1840s the movement toward revolutionary change was supported by four factors: 1) The failure of the existing regime to address the economic and social problems which accompanied the general economic collapse which occurred during the decade; 2) The regularity of significant food shortages in the major urban centers; 3) The increased popularity of the demands of the liberals and the nationalists; 4) The increasingly radical political, economic, and social proposals advanced by the Utopian Socialists (Charles Fourier, Robert Owen), the Anarchists (Pierre Proudhon), and the Chartists in England.

OUTBREAK AND DEVELOPMENT OF THE REVOLUTIONS OF 1848

France

The once liberal regime of King Louis Philippe (1830 – 1848) became increasingly conservative and oppressive under the leadership of Prime Minister Francois Guizot and the Chamber of Deputies. Guizot's opposition to reforms resulted in the further restriction of individual rights in general and the excessive use of censorship to silence critics of the regime.

The predominantly liberal opposition scheduled a banquet – which was a direct challenge to the regime – for the night of February 22, 1848. Guizot's government refused to sanction the banquet and, as a result, students and working class men took to the streets and violence erupted. In an effort to eliminate further difficulty, Louis Philippe dismissed Guizot; however, on the evening of February 23, 1848, a conflict between government troops and opponents of the regime occurred and over fifty people were killed. Reports of the "massacre" spread quickly and over a thousand barricades were erected. On February 24th, Louis Philippe attempted to develop a strategy which would permit him to remain in power; but, by the end of the day, he abdicated and fled to England.

A provisional government was established which represented the entire spectrum of opposition forces. The principal tasks of the provisional government were (1) to serve as an interim authority, and (2) to arrange for the elections to a National Constituent

Assembly. Among the representatives in the provisional government were Lamartine, a poet, and Louis Blanc, a socialist who was an advocate of National Workshops. During the spring of 1848 national workshops were established to resolve the problem of unemployment.

In April, French citizens voted for representatives to the National Constituent Assembly; the vote indicated that the nation supported the establishment of a republican government but that it was conservative in its economic and social philosophy. The Assembly convened in May and dissolved the national workshops; the result was the confrontation known as The June Days (June 23 – 27, 1848) during which French troops led by General Louis Eugene Cavaignac suppressed the radicals who wanted to maintain the workshops.

A new constitution was developed and accepted in October 1848. It established the Second French Republic which provided for a president and a single chamber assembly which would be elected on the basis of universal manhood suffrage; the president would serve a four-year term of office. The presidential election was held in December, 1848; Louis Napoleon, nephew of Napoleon I, easily defeated his rivals Cavaignac and Lamartine.

Prussia and the German States

News of the revolt in France resulted in rebellions in Prussia and other German states such as Baden, Bavaria, Hanover, and Saxony. The princes of the lesser states attempted to nullify the more strident demands of the revolutionaries by promising constitutions and appointing liberal ministers. However, King Frederick William IV of Prussia was adamant in his refusal to placate the revolutionaries; consequently, a violent revolution developed in Berlin.

On March 17, 1848, Frederick William IV relented and announced that a Prussian assembly (The Berlin Assembly) would be convened in April, 1848. A constitution would also be developed. Furthermore, he announced that internal reforms would be instituted, and that Prussia would assist in the development of a constitutional revitalization of the German Confederation.

The Frankfurt Assembly, which was a Pan-German assembly interested in the formulation of an integrated union of German states, convened in May 1848. During the next year, the group of liberals and nationalists developed a framework for a united Germany along the lines of the *Kleindeutsch* or Small Germany. This approach to German unification did not incorporate the Austrian Empire because of the great numbers of non-German peoples in that state; the advocates of the *Kleindeutsch* plan opposed the *Grossdeutsch* or Great Germany approach, which would have included Austria, because it violated the principle of national ethnic cohesion. In 1849, Frederick William IV received an offer to lead the new Germany. While interested in pursuing this opportunity, he declined because of the shift in the direction of the revolution; a reaction against the revolution had set in and most of the radical leaders fled the German states.

The Austrian Empire

Revolutionary activity broke out in Vienna on March 13, 1848. Within forty-eight hours, Prince Metternich, the symbol of reaction throughout Europe, resigned as Foreign Minister. Ferdinand I, the Austrian Emperor, acquiesced and granted concessions including a pledge to support the development of a constitution and the extension of individual liberties.

The nationalist ambitions of the Hungarians were advanced by Louis Kossuth. On

March 15, 1848, the Hungarian Diet declared a constitution which established a national assembly based on a limited franchise, specified individual freedoms, eliminated the remnants of the feudal order, and established an autonomous Hungary within the Austrian Empire. On March 31, 1848, the Austrian government accepted these substantive changes.

Czech nationalistic aspirations were manifested with the establishment of a Bohemian Diet in March. Its initial demands concerned universal manhood suffrage, guarantees of basic political and religious rights, and the parity of the Czech and German languages in education and government. On April 8th, Ferdinand I granted these concessions and rendered Bohemia an autonomous state. The further development of Czech nationalism was blurred by the emergency of the Pan-Slavic Congress (June 1848). The leaders of the Pan-Slavic Congress hoped to establish an autonomous government for Czechs, Slovaks, and other Slavs within the Austrian Empire.

The April Decree (April 11, 1848), which was issued by the Hapsburg government, pledged to eliminate the feudal services and duties which were still imposed on the peasants.

Italy

In the Italian peninsula, revolutionary activity broke out in Milan in March 1848 and was directed primarily by nationalists who were interested in expelling the Austrians from Lombardy and Venetia. King Charles Albert of Sardinia and Piedmont capitalized on the revolution by declaring war on Austria. In central Italy, Pope Pius IX expressed support for a unified Italian state. In the Kingdom of the Two Sicilies, an isolated revolt in Palermo, which occurred earlier than the rebellion in Paris, resulted in the granting of a liberal constitution by the reactionary King Ferdinand II.

Throughout Italy the revolution emphasized the cause of Italian nationalism and the re-emergence of Italian pride through the Risorgimento. There was no evidence that the revolution was seriously concerned with the economic and social problems which confronted the Italian peasants.

Austrian Field Marshal Josef Graf Radetzky von Radetz withdrew the Austrian forces to the Quadrilateral, a series of fortresses on the Adige and Mincia. There Radetzky regrouped, and in July 1848, launched a counter-offensive which resulted in the resounding defeat of the Italian forces under Charles Albert at Custozza (July 25, 1848). In 1849 Charles Albert undertook another military initiative but was defeated by Radetzky at Novara (March 23, 1849); Charles Albert abdicated in favor of his son, Victor Emmanuel II.

THE FAILURE OF THE REVOLUTIONS, 1848 – 1849

By the summer of 1848, the revolutionary effort had been spent and the earlier gains of the late winter and spring had been reversed or challenged in many countries. The June Days in France coincided with the dissolution of the Pan-Slavic Congress in Prague by General Alfred Windischgratz. By October, Windischgratz had suppressed the revolution in Vienna, and Radetzky's armies were moving successfully against the Italians. In the fall and winter (1848 – 1849) the revolutions were stifled in France, Prussia, Austria, Italy, and other states.

The failure of the Revolutions of 1848 was due to several major factors. The armed forces had remained loyal to the old leadership and demonstrated a willingness to assist in the suppression of the revolutions. In Western Europe, the revolutionaries were appeased by liberal political reforms. In most instances, the majority of citizens in the

West indicated that they were opposed to radical economic and social change.

In Central Europe, revolutions, which had been led by the middle class, did not express any interest in addressing social and economic problems. When the workers and students demanded social and economic revolution, the middle class became alienated from the revolution which they had led earlier; they desired only political change through the establishment of a constitutional process. This breach within the revolutionary camp was detected and exploited by the old regime.

In Eastern and Southern Europe, the nationalist revolutions lacked organization and, above all, the military capacity to resist the professional armies of the Austrian Empire.

By 1849 the revolutions had been suppressed or redirected. Only in France with the Second French Republic (1848 – 1852) and in Prussia (the Constitution of 1850) did some of the earlier gains endure.

REALPOLITIK AND THE TRIUMPH OF NATIONALISM

Cavour and the Unification of Italy

After the collapse of the revolutionary movements of 1848, the leadership of Italian nationalism was transferred to Sardinian leaders Victor Emmanuel II, Camillo de Cavour, and Giuseppe Garibaldi. They replaced the earlier leaders Giuseppe Mazzini of the Young Italy movement, Charles Albert, the once liberal Pius IX, and V. Gioberti and the Neo-Guelf movement, which a unified Italian state centered on the Papacy. The new leadership did not entertain romantic illusions about the process of transforming Sardinia into a new Italian Kingdom; they were practitioners of the politics of realism, *realpolitik.*

Cavour (1810 – 1861) was a Sardinian who served as editor of Il Risorgimento which was a newspaper that argued that Sardinia should be the basis of a new Italy. Between 1852 and 1861 Cavour served as Victor Emmanuel II's Prime Minister. In that capacity Cavour transformed Sardinian society through the implementation of a series of liberal reforms which were designed to modernize the Sardinian state and attract the support of liberal states such as Great Britain and France. Among Cavour's reforms were the following: 1) The Law on Convents and the Siccardi Law, which were directed at curtailing the influence of the Roman Catholic Church; 2) the reform of the judicial system; 3) the full implementation of the Statuto, the Sardinian constitution which was modeled on the liberal French constitution of 1830; and 4) support for economic development projects such as port and highway construction.

In 1855, under Cavour's direction, Sardinia joined Britain and France in the Crimean War against Russia. At the Paris Peace Conference (1856), Cavour addressed the delegates on the need to eliminate the foreign (Austrian) presence in the Italian peninsula and attracted the attention and sympathy of the French Emperor, Napoleon III.

Cavour and Napoleon III met at Plombiérès (July 20, 1859). The Plombières Agreement stated that in the event that Sardinia went to war with Austria, – presumably after being attacked or provoked – France would provide military assistance to Sardinia, and with victory, Sardinia would annex Lombardy, Venetia, Parma, Modena, and a part of the Papal states. Additionally, the remainder of Italy would be organized into an Italian Confederation under the direction of the Pope, France would receive Nice and Savoy, and the alliance would be finalized by a marriage between the two royal families. The Plombières Agreement was designed to bring about a war with Austria and to assist Sardinia in developing an expanded northern Italian kingdom.

The concept of an Italian confederation under the papacy was contributed by Napoleon III and demonstrates his lack of understanding about the nature of Italian political ambitions and values during this period.

After being provoked, the Austrians declared war on Sardinia in 1859. French forces intervened and the Austrians were defeated in the battles of Magenta (June 4) and Solferino (June 24). Napoleon III's support wavered for four reasons: 1) Prussia mobilized and expressed sympathy for Austria; 2) the outbreak of uncontrolled revolutions in several Northern Italian states; 3) the forcefulness of the new Austrian military efforts; and 4) the lack of public support in France for his involvement and the mounting criticism being advanced by the French Catholic Church, which opposed the war against Catholic Austria.

Napoleon III, without consulting Cavour, signed a secret peace (The Truce of Villafranca) on July 11, 1859. Sardinia received Lombardy but not Venetia; the other terms indicated that Sardinian influence would be restricted and that Austria would remain a power in Italian politics. The terms of Villafranca were clarified and finalized with the Treaty of Zurich (1859).

In 1860, Cavour arranged the annexation of Parma, Modena, Romagna, and Tuscany into Sardinia. These actions were recognized by the Treaty of Turin between Napoleon III and Victor Emmanuel II; Nice and Savoy were transferred to France. With these acquisitions, Cavour anticipated the need for a period of tranquility to incorporate these territories into Sardinia.

Giuseppe Garibaldi and his Red Shirts landed in Sicily (May 1860) and extended the nationalist activity to the south. Within three months, Sicily was taken and by September 7th, Garibaldi was in Naples and the Kingdom of the Two Sicilies had fallen under Sardinian influence. Cavour distrusted Garibaldi but Victor Emmanuel II encouraged him.

In February 1861, in Turin, Victor Emmanuel was declared King of Italy and presided over an Italian Parliament which represented the entire Italian peninsula with the exception of Venetia and the Patrimony of St. Peter (Rome). Cavour died in June 1861.

Venetia was incorporated into the Italian Kingdom in 1866 as a result of an alliance between Bismarck's Prussia and the Kingdom of Italy which preceded the German Civil War between Austria and Prussia. In return for opening a southern front against Austria, Prussia, upon its victory, arranged for Venetia to be transferred to Italy.

Bismarck was again instrumental in the acquisition of Rome into the Italian Kingdom in 1870. In 1870, the Franco-Prussian War broke out and the French garrison, which had been in Rome providing protection for the Pope, was withdrawn to serve on the front against Prussia. Italian troops seized Rome, and in 1871, as a result of a plebiscite, Rome became the capital of the Kingdom of Italy.

BISMARCK AND THE UNIFICATION OF GERMANY

During the period after 1815 Prussia emerged as an alternative to a Hapsburg-based Germany. During the early nineteenth century, Germany was politically decentralized and consisted of dozens of independent states. This multi-state situation had been in place for centuries and had been sanctioned by the Peace of Westphalia in 1648. Prussia had absorbed many of the smaller states during the eighteenth and early nineteenth centuries.

Otto von Bismarck (1810 – 1898) entered the diplomatic service of William I as the Revolutions of 1848 were being suppressed. By the early 1860s Bismarck had emerged as the principal adviser and minister to the King. Bismarck was an advocate of a Prussian-based (Hohenzollern) Germany. During the 1850s and 1860s Bismarck supported a series of military reforms which improved the Prussian army. In 1863 Bismarck joined the Russians in suppressing a Polish rebellion; this enterprise resulted in improved Russian-Prussian relations.

In 1863, the Schleswig-Holstein crisis broke. These provinces, which were occupied by Germans, were under the personal rule of Christian IX of Denmark. The Danish government advanced a new constitution which specified that Schleswig and Holstein would be annexed into Denmark. German reaction was predictable and Bismarck arranged for a joint Austro-Prussian military action. Denmark was defeated and agreed (Treaty of Vienna, 1864) to give up the provinces. Schleswig and Holstein were to be jointly administered by the victors, Austria and Prussia.

Questions of jurisdiction provided the rationale for estranged relations between Austria and Prussia. In 1865, a temporary settlement was reached in the Gastein Convention, which stated that Prussia would administer Schleswig and Austria would manage Holstein. During 1865 and 1866, Bismarck made diplomatic preparations for the forthcoming struggle with Austria. Italy, France, and Russia would not interfere, and Great Britain was not expected to involve itself in a Central European war.

The German Civil War (also known as The Seven Weeks' War) was devastating to Austria. The humiliating defeat at Koniggratz (July 4, 1866) demonstrated the ineptitude of the Austrian forces when confronted by the Prussian army led by General von Moltke. Within two months, Austria had to agree to the peace terms which were drawn up at Nikolsburg and finalized by the Peace of Prague (August 1866).

There were three principal terms. Austria would not be part of any new German state. The Kleindeutsch plan had prevailed over the Grossdeutsch plan. Venetia would be ceded to Italy. Austria would pay an indemnity to Prussia.

In the next year, 1867, the North German Confederation was established by Bismarck. It was designed to facilitate the movement toward a unified German state and included all the German states except Baden, Württemberg, Bavaria, and Saxony; the King of Prussia served as President of the Confederation.

In 1870, the deteriorating relations between France and Germany became critical over the Ems Dispatch. William I, while vacationing at Ems, was approached by representatives of the French government who requested a Prussian pledge not to interfere on the issue of the vacant Spanish throne. William I refused to give such a pledge and informed Bismarck of these developments through a telegram from Ems.

Bismarck exploited the situation by initiating a propaganda campaign against the French. Subsequently, France declared war and the Franco-Prussian War (1870–1871) commenced. Prussian victories at Sedan and Metz proved decisive; Napoleon III and his leading general, Marshal MacMahon, were captured. Paris continued to resist but fell to the Prussians in January 1871. The Treaty of Frankfurt (May, 1871) concluded the war and resulted in France ceding Alsace-Lorraine to Germany and a German occupation until an indemnity was paid.

The German Empire was proclaimed on January 18, 1871 with William I becoming the Emperor of Germany. Bismarck became the Imperial Chancellor. Bavaria, Baden, Württemberg, and Saxony were incorporated into the new Germany.

INTER-EUROPEAN RELATIONS, 1848 – 1878

Since the Napoleonic era the peace in Europe had been sustained because of the memories of the devastation and the disruption caused by the wars of the French

Revolution and Napoleonic Age; the primary structure that maintained the peace was the Concert System. The Concert of Europe was a rather loose and ill-defined understanding among the European nations that they would join together to resolve problems which threatened the status quo; it was believed that joint action would be undertaken to prohibit any drastic alteration in the European system or balance of power. The credibility of the Concert of Europe was undermined by the failure of the powers to cooperate during the revolution of 1848 and 1849. Between 1848 and 1878 the peace among the European powers was interrupted by the Crimean War (1854 – 56) and challenged by the crisis centered on the Russo-Turkish War of 1877 – 78.

THE CRIMEAN WAR

The origins of the Crimean War are to be found in the dispute between two differing groups of Christians (and their protectors) over privileges in the Holy Land. During the 19th century Palestine was part of the Ottoman Turkish Empire. In 1852, the Turks negotiated an agreement with the French to provide enclaves in the Holy Land to Roman Catholic religious orders; this arrangement appeared to jeopardize already existing agreements which provided access to Greek Orthodox religious orders. Czar Nicholas, unaware of the impact of his action, ordered Russian troops to occupy several Danubian principalities; his strategy was to withdraw from these areas once the Turks agreed to clarify and guarantee the rights of the Greek Orthodox orders. The role of Britain in this developing crisis was critical; Nicholas mistakenly was convinced that the British Prime Minister, Lord Aberdeen, would be sympathetic to the Russian policy. Aberdeen, who headed a coalition cabinet, sought to use the Concert of Europe system to settle the question. However, Lord Palmerston, the Home Secretary, supported the Turks; he was suspicious of Russian intervention in the region. Consequently, misunderstandings about Britain's policy developed. In October, 1853, the Turks demanded that the Russians withdraw from the occupied principalities; the Russians failed to respond and the Turks declared war. In February, 1854 Nicholas advanced a draft for a settlement of the Russo-Turkish War; it was rejected and Great Britain and France joined the Ottoman Turks and declared war on Russia.

With the exception of some naval encounters in the Gulf of Finland off the Aaland Islands, this war was conducted on the Crimean peninsula in the Black Sea. In September, 1854, over 50,000 British and French troops landed in the Crimea, determined to take the Russian port city of Sebastopol. While this war has been remembered for the work of Florence Nightengale and the "Charge of the Light Brigade," it was a conflict in which there were more casualties from disease and the weather than from combat. In December 1854, Austria, with great reluctance, became a co-signatory of the Four Points of Vienna which was a statement of British and French war aims. The Four Points specified that (1) Russia should renounce any claims to the occupied principalities, (2) the 1841 Straits Convention would be revised, (3) navigation in the mouth of the Danube River (on the Black Sea) should be internationalized, and (4) Russia should withdraw any claim to having a 'special' protective role for Greek Orthodox residents in the Ottoman Empire. In 1855, Piedmont joined Britain and France in the war. In March 1855 Czar Nicholas died and was succeeded by Alexander II who was opposed to continuing the war. In December 1855, the Austrians, under excessive pressure from the British, French, and Piedmontese, sent an ultimatum to Russia in which they threatened to renounce their neutrality. In response, Alexander II indicated that he would accept the Four Points.

Representatives of the belligerents convened in Paris between February and April 1856. The resulting Peace of Paris had the following major provisions. Russia had to acknowledge international commissions which were to regulate maritime traffic on the Danube, recognize Turkish control of the mouth of the Danube, renounce all claims to the Danubian Principalities of Moldavia and Wallachia (this later led to the establishment of Rumania), agree not to fortify the Aaland Islands, renounce its previously espoused position of protector of the Greek Orthodox residents of the Ottoman Empire, and return all occupied territories to the Ottoman Empire. The Straits Convention of 1841 was revised through the neutralization of the Black Sea. The Declaration of Paris specified the rules which would regulate commerce during periods of war. Lastly, the independence and integrity of the Ottoman Empire were recognized and guaranteed by the signatories.

THE EASTERN QUESTION TO THE CONGRESS OF BERLIN

Another challenge to the Concert of Europe developed in the 1870s with a seemingly endless number of Balkan crises. Once again, the conflict initially involved Russia and Ottoman Turks but it quickly became a conflict with Britain and Russia serving as the principal protagonists. British concerns over Russian ambitions in the Balkans reached a critical level in 1877 when Russia went to war with the Turks.

In 1876, the Turkish forces under the leadership of Osman Pasha soundly defeated the Serbian armies. Serbia requested assistance from the great powers and, as a consequence of the political pressures exercised by the great powers, the Turks agreed to participate in a conference in Constantinople; the meeting resulted in a draft agreement between the Serbs and the Turks. However, Britain quietly advised the Sultan, Abdul Hamid II, to scuttle the agreement, which he did. In June 1877 Russia dispatched forces across the Danube. During the next month, Osman Pasha took up a defensive position in Plevna. During the period of the siege, sympathy in the west shifted toward the Turks, and Britain and Austria became alarmed over the extent of Russian influence in the region. In March 1878, the Russians and the Turks signed the Peace of San Stephano; implementation of its provisions would have resulted in Russian hegemony in the Balkans and dramatically altered the balance of power in the eastern Mediterranean. Specifically it provided for the establishment of a large Bulgarian state which would be under Russian influence; the transfer of Dobrudja, Kars, Ardahan, Bayazid, and Batum to Russia; the expansion of Serbia and Montenegro; and the establishment of an autonomous Bosnia-Herzegovina which would be under Russian control.

Britain, under the leadership of Prime Minister Benjamin Disraeli, denounced the San Stephano Accord, dispatched a naval squadron to Turkish waters, and demanded that the San Stephano agreement be scrapped. The German Chancellor, Otto von Bismarck, intervened and offered his services as mediator.

The delegates of the major powers convened in June and July 1878 to negotiate a settlement. Prior to the meeting, Disraeli had concluded a series of secret arrangements with Austria, Russia and Turkey. The combined impact of these accommodations was to restrict Russian expansion in the region, reaffirm the independence of Turkey, and maintain British control of the Mediterranean. The specific terms of the Treaty of Berlin resulted in the following: 1) recognition of Rumania, Serbia and Montenegro as independent states; 2) the establishment of the autonomous principality of Bulgaria, 3) Austrian acquisition of Bosnia and Herzegovina; and 4) the transfer of Cyprus to Great Britain.

The Russians, who had won the war against Turkey and had imposed the harsh terms of the San Stephano Treaty, found that they left the conference with very little (Kars, Batum, etc.) for their effort. Although Disraeli was the primary agent of this anti-Russian settlement, the Russians blamed Bismarck for their dismal results. Their hostility toward Germany led Bismarck (1879) to embark upon a new system of alliances which transformed European diplomacy and rendered any additional efforts of the Concert of Europe futile.

CAPITALISM AND THE EMERGENCE OF THE NEW LEFT, 1848 – 1914

Economic Developments: The New Industrial Order

During the nineteenth century, Europe experienced the full impact of the Industrial Revolution. The new economic order not only altered the working lives of most Europeans, but also impacted on the very fiber of European culture. The shifts in demography were revolutionary; the process of urbanization was irreversible and the transformation of European values and lifestyle were dramatic. The Industrial Revolution resulted in improving aspects of the physical lives of a greater number of Europeans; at the same time, it led to a factory system with undesirable working and living conditions and the abuses of child labor. While the advantages of industrialism were evident, the disadvantages were more subtle; the industrial working class was more vulnerable than the agrarian peasants because of the fragile nature of the industrial economy. This new economy was based on a dependent system which involved (1) the availability of raw materials, (2) an adequate labor supply, and (3) a distribution system which successfully marketed the products; the distribution system was in itself dependent upon a satisfactory availability of money throughout the economic system. If any one of these requirements was impeded or absent, the industrial work force could be confronted with unemployment and poverty. The industrial system was based fundamentally in developing capitalism which itself was essentially grounded in an appreciation of material culture. The standard of living, neo-mercantilist attitudes towards national power, and the goal of accumulation of wealth were manifestations of this materialism.

As the century progresses, the inequities of the system became increasingly evident. Trade-unionism and socialist political parties emerged which attempted to address these problems and improve the lives of the working class. In most of these expressions of discontent, the influences of Utopian Socialism or Marxism were evident and can be detected readily. Socialism was steeped in economic materialism which had emerged in the eighteenth century and came to dominate the nineteenth and twentieth centuries. Economics was a component in the rise of scientism; by its very nature, it advanced the values of material culture.

Marx and Scientific Socialism

During the period from 1815 to 1848, Utopian Socialists, such as Robert Owen, Saint Simon, and Charles Fourier advocated the establishment of a political-economic system which was based on romantic concepts of the ideal society. The failure of the Revolutions of 1848 and 1849 discredited the Utopian Socialists, and the new "Scientific Socialism" advanced by Karl Marx (1818 – 1883) became the primary ideology of protest and revolution. Marx, a German philosopher, developed a communist philosophic system which was founded on the inherent goodness of man; this Rousseau-influenced position argued that men were basically good but had been corrupted by the artificial institutions (states, churches, etc.) from which they had evolved. Marx stated that the history of humanity was the history of class struggle and that the process of the struggle (the dialectic) would continue until a classless society was realized; the Marxian dialectic was driven by the dynamics of materialism. Further, he contended that the age of the bourgeois domination of the working class was the most severe and oppressive phase of the struggle. The proletariat, or the industrial working class, needed to be educated and led towards a violent revolution which would destroy the institutions which perpetuated the struggle and the suppression of the majority. After the revolution, the people would experience the dictatorship of the proletariat during which the Communist Party would provide leadership. Marx advanced these concepts in a series of tracts and books including *The Communist Manifesto* (1848), *Critique of Political Economy* (1859), and *Capital* (1863 – 64). In most instances, his arguments were put forth in scientific form; Marx accumulated extensive data and developed a persuasive rhetorical style. In the 1860s Marxism was being accepted by many reformers. Marx lived most of his adult life in London where he died in 1883.

The Anarchists

Anarchism emerged in the early 19th century as a consequence of the Industrial Revolution. Its early proponents, William Godwin (1756 – 1836) and Pierre Proudhon (1809 – 65) argued that anarchism, a situation where there would be no property or authority, would be attained through enlightened individualism. Proudhon, in *What is Property* (1840), stated that anarchism would be achieved through education and without violence. After the revolutions of 1848 and 1849, Michael Bakunin, a Russian, stated that violent, terrorist actions were necessary to move the people to revolt against their oppressors; anarchism has been associated with violence since Bakunin's time. A variation of anarchism, called syndicalism, was developed by Georges Sorel in France. Syndicalism, sometimes referred to as anarcho-syndicalism, involved direct economic actions in order to control industries. The strike and industrial sabotage were employed frequently by the syndicalists. Syndicalist influence was restricted to France, Spain (Confederacion Nacional del Trabajo, an organization of several syndicalist unions), and Italy (Filippo Corridoni and the young Benito Mussolini).

The Revisionist Movement

A reconsideration of Marxism commenced before Marx's death in 1883. In that year a group of British leftists organized themselves into the Fabian Society and declared that while they were sympathetic to Marxism – indeed, they considered themselves Marxists – they differed from the orthodoxy on two major points: (1) they did not accept the inevitability of revolution in order to bring about a socialist, i.e. communist society; democratic societies possessed the mechanisms which would lead to the gradual evolution of socialism; (2) the Fabians did not accept the Marxist interpretation of contemporary history; they contended the historical processes endured and were difficult to redirect and reform, while Marxists tended to accept the notion that world revolution was imminent. Sidney and Beatrice Webb, George Bernard Shaw, Keir Hardie, and several others joined in forming the Fabian Society. Later it would split over the Boer War but its members would serve in every Labor ministry.

In Germany the Social Democratic Party (SDP) had been established along the lines of Marxist orthodoxy. In the 1890s, Edward Bernstein (1850 – 1932), who was influenced by the Fabians, redirected the efforts and platform of the SDP toward the revisionist position. Within a few years, the SDP extended its credibility and support to acquire a dominant position in the Reichstag.

The French Socialist Jean Jaures (1859 – 1914) led his group to revisionism; their moderation led to increasing their seats in the Chamber of Deputies and in developing acceptance for their criticisms and proposals during the tumultuous years of the Dreyfus Affair.

While orthodox Marxists (Lenin) denounced the revisionist movement, the majority of socialists in 1914 were revisionists who were willing to use the democratic process to bring about their goals.

BRITAIN AND FRANCE

During the second half of the 19th century, Britain and France enjoyed considerable economic prosperity, experienced periods of jingoistic nationalism, and were confronted with demands for expanding democracy. Great Britain, under the leadership of Lord Palmerston, William Gladstone and Benjamin Disraeli, represented a dichotomy of values and political agendas. On one hand, Britain led Europe into an age of revitalized imperialism and almost unbridled capitalism; on the other hand, Gladstone and the Liberal Party advocated democratic reforms, an anti-imperialist stance, and a program to eliminate or restrict unacceptable working and social conditions. In France, the evolution of a more democratic political order was questioned by the collapse of the Second French Republic and the development of the Second Empire. However, in 1871, the Third Republic was established and the French moved closer to realizing democracy.

The Age of Palmerston

During the period from 1850 to 1865, Lord Palmerston was the dominant political power in Great Britain. Palmerston served in a range of positions including Foreign Secretary, Home Secretary, and Prime Minister. In foreign affairs Palmerston was preoccupied with colonial problems such as the Indian Muting of 1857, troubles in China, and British interests in the American Civil War; Palmerston tended to express little interest in domestic affairs. This period witnessed the realignment of political parties within British politico; the Tory Party was transformed into the Conservative Party under Disreali and the Whig Party became the Liberty Party with Gladstone serving as its new leader. It should be noted that John Bright, a manufacturer, anti-corn law advocate, and leader of the Manchester School, contributed significantly to the development of the Liberal Party. These changes in party organization involved more than appellations. The new structure more clearly represented distinct ideological positions on many substantive issues. The new political structure was facilitated by Palmerston's (the Whig) lack of interest in domestic issues and Lord Derby's (the Tory leader) indifference to political issues; he was preoccupied with his study of the classics and with horse racing.

Until the 1850s the British East India Company managed India for the British government. During this decade a new rifle, the Enfield, was introduced. The procedure for loading the Enfield required that the covering for the cartridges be removed by the teeth prior to inserting them in the rifle. Rumors circulated that the covering was a grease made from the fat of cows and swine; naturally, these rumors alarmed the Hindu and Muslim troops. Troops mutined in Calcutta in 1857 and within a few months over a third of India was in the hands of rebels and Europeans were being killed. A British led force of about 3,000 troops under Sir Hugh Rose suppressed the mutiny which lacked cohesion in its aims, organization, and leadership. By January 1858, Britain had re-established its control of India; the East India Company was dissolved and replaced by the direct authority of London.

During the 1850s and 1860s Palmerston sought to clarify British commercial access to China. In 1858, with the support of French troops, the British army took the Taka Forts on the Peiko River and, in 1860, captured Peking. As a result, China agreed to open Tientsin and other ports to the European powers.

The American Civil War (1861 – 65) curtailed the supply of unprocessed cotton to British mills. The British economy was affected adversely and significant unemployment and factory closings resulted. The American war also led to a discussion within Britain on the fundamental issues of liberty, slavery, and democracy. A crisis between Britain and the United States developed over the Trent Affair (1861) during which a British ship was boarded by American sailors. In the end, the British government and people supported the Union cause because of ideological considerations; even in the areas affected by the shortage of cotton, there was general support for the North.

Disraeli, Gladstone, and the Era of Democratic Reforms

In 1865 Palmerston died and during the next two decades significant domestic developments occured which expanded democracy in Great Britain. The dominant leaders of this period were William Gladstone (1809 – 1898) and Benjamin Disraeli (1804 – 1881). Gladstone, who was initially a Conservative, emerged as a severe critic of the Corn Laws and, as a budgetary expert, became Chancellor of the Exchequer under Palmerston. As the leader of the Liberal Party (to 1895), Gladstone supported Irish Home Rule, fiscal responsibility, free trade, and the extension of democratic principles. He was opposed to imperialism, the involvement of Britain in European affairs, and the further centralization of the British government. Disraeli argued for an aggressive foreign policy, the expansion of the British Empire, and, after opposing democratic reforms, the extension of the franchise.

After defeating Gladstone's effort to extend the vote in 1866, Disraeli advanced the Reform Bill of 1867. This bill, which expanded on the Reform Bill of 1832, was enacted and specified two reforms: 1) There would be a redistribution (similar to reapportionment) of seats which would provide a more equitable representation in the House of Commons; the industrial cities and boroughs gained seats at the expense of some depopulated areas in the north and west. 2) The right to vote was extended to include all adult male citizens of boroughs who paid £10 or more rent annually, and all adult male citizens of the counties who were £12 tenants or £5 leaseholders.

The consequence of this act was that almost all men over 21 years in age who resided in urban centers were granted the right to vote. In 1868, the newly extended electorate provided the Liberals with a victory and Gladstone commenced his first of four terms as Prime Minister.

Gladstone's first ministry (1868 – 1874) was characterized by a wave of domestic legislation which reflected the movement toward democracy. Among the measures which were enacted were five acts:

1) The Ballot Act (1872) which provided for the secret ballot; this act realized a major Chartist demand of the 1830s;

2) Civil Services Reform (1870) which introduced the system of competitive examination for government positions;

3) The Education Act (1870) which established a system of school districts throughout the country, and provided assistance in the organization of school boards,

and for the establishment of schools in poverty stricken regions; free elementary education in Britain would not be realized until 1891,

4) The Land Act (1870) was an attempt to resolve economic and social inequities in Ireland. However, it did not succeed in providing Irish tenants with reasonable safeguards against arbitrary eviction or the imposition of drastic increases in rent, and

5) The University Act (1870) eliminated the use of religious tests which provided a quota of seats in universities for members of the Anglican church.

Between 1874 and 1880 Disraeli served as Prime Minister, and while he was deeply concerned with foreign difficulties, he did succeed in developing the notion of Tory Democracy which was directed at domestic issues. Tory Democracy represented Disreali's views on how the Conservative Party would support necessary domestic action on behalf of the common good.

In 1875, through Disraeli's support, the following measures were passed: 1) Laws which lessened the regulation of trade unions; 2) Food and Drug Act which regulated the sale of these items; 3) Public Health Act which specified government requirements and standards for sanitation; 4) The Artisan's Dwelling Act.

While a few Conservatives, such as Lord Randolph Churchill, attempted to extend the progress of Tory Democracy and to incorporate it permamently within the Conservative program, most of the Conservative Party abandoned this approach after Disraeli's death in 1881.

During his remaining ministries (1880 – 85, 1886, and 1892 – 95), Gladstone was preoccupied with Ireland. However, a further extension of the franchise occurred in 1884 with the passage of the Representation of the People Act which granted the right to vote to adult males in the counties on the same basis as in the boroughs. In 1885 another redistribution of seats in the House of Commons was approved on the ratio of one seat for every 50,000 citizens.

The Second French Republic and the Second Empire

Louis Napoleon became the President of the Second French Republic in December 1848. It was evident that he was not committed to the Republic; in May 1849, elections for the Legislative Assembly clearly indicated that the people were not bound to its continuance either. In this election, the Conservatives and Monarchists scored significant gains; the republicans and radicals lost power in the Assembly. During the three year life of the Second Republic, Louis Napoleon demonstrated his skills as a gifted politican through the manipulation of the various factions in French politics. His deployment of troops in Italy to rescue and restore Pope Pius IX was condemned by the republicans, but strongly supported by the monarchists and moderates. As a consequence of the French military intervention, a French garrison under General Oudinot was stationed in Rome until the fall of 1870 when it was recalled during the Franco-Prussian War.

Louis Napoleon initiated a policy which minimized the importance of the Legislative Assembly, capitalized on the developing Napoleonic Legend, and courted the support of the army, the Catholic Church, and a range of conservative political groups. The Falloux Law returned control of education to the church. Further, Louis Napoleon was confronted with Article 45 of the constitution which stipulated that the president was limited to one four-year term; he had no intention of relinquishing power. With the assistance of a core of dedicated supporters, Louis Napoleon arranged for a coup d'etat on the night of December 1 – 2, 1851. The Second Republic fell and was soon replaced by the Second French Empire.

Louis Napoleon drafted a new constitution which resulted in a highly centralized government centered around himself. He was to have a ten year term, power to declare war, to lead the armed forces, to conduct foreign policy, and to initiate and pronounce all laws; the new Legislative Assembly would be under the control of the president. On December 2, 1852, he announced that he was Napoleon III, Emperor of the French.

The domestic history of the Second Empire is divided into two periods: 1851 to 1860, during which Napoleon III's control was direct and authoritarian, and 1860 to 1870, the decade of the Liberal Empire, during which the regime was liberalized through a series of reforms. During the Second Empire, living conditions in France generally improved. The government instituted agreements and actions which stimulated the movement toward free trade (Cobden-Chevalier Treaty of 1860), improved the efficiency of the French economic system (Credit Mobilier and the Credit Focier, both established in 1852), and conducted major public works programs in French cities with the assistance of such talented leaders as Baron Haussmann, the prefect of the Seine. Even though many artists and scholars (Victor Hugo, Jules Michelet, and Gustav Flaubert) were censored and, on occasion, prosecuted for their works, the artistic and scholarly achievements of the Second Empire were impressive. While Flaubert and Baudelaire, and in music, Jacques Offenbach, were most productive during these decades, younger artists, such as Renoir, Manet, and Cezanne began their careers and were influenced by the culture of the Second Empire. The progressive liberalization of the government during the 1860s resulted in extending the powers of the Legislative Assembly, restricting church control over secondary education, and permitting the development of trade unions. In large part, this liberalization was designed to divert criticism from Napoleon III's unsuccessful foreign policy. French involvement in Algeria, the Crimean War, the process of Italian unification, the establishment of colonial presences in Senegal, Somaliland, and Indo-China (Laos, Cambodia, and Viet Nam), and the ill-fated Mexican adventure (the short-lived rule of Maximilian), resulted in increased criticism of Napoleon III and his authority. The Second Empire collapsed after the capture of Napoleon III during the Franco-Prussian War (1870 – 71). After a regrettable Parisian experience with a communist type of government, the Third French Republic was established; it would survive until 1940.

IMPERIAL RUSSIA

The autocracy of Nicholas I's regime was not threatened by the revolutionary movements of 1848. The consequences of the European revolutionary experience of 1848 to 1849 reinforced the conservative ideology which was the basis of the Romanov regime. In 1848 and 1849, Russian troops suppressed disorganized Polish attempts to reassert Polish nationalism.

Russian involvement in the Crimean war met with defeat. France, Britain, and Piedmont emerged as the victors in this conflict; Russian ambitions in the eastern Mediterranean had been thwarted by a coalition of western European states. In 1855 Nicholas I died and was succeeded by Alexander II (1855 – 1881) who feared the forces of change and introduced reforms in order to remain in power.

Fearing the transformation of Russian society from below, Alexander II instituted a series of reforms which contributed to altering the nature of the social contract in Russia. With the regime in disarray after defeat in the Crimean War, Alexander II, in March 1856, indicated that Russian serfdom had to be eliminated. After several years of formulating the process for its elimination, Alexander II pronounced in 1861 that serfdom was abolished. Further, he issued the following reforms: 1) The serf (peasant) would no longer be dependent upon the lord; 2) all people were to have freedom of movement and were free to change their means of livelihood; and 3) the serf could enter into contracts and could own property.

In fact, the lives of most peasants were not affected by these reforms. Most peasants lived in local communes which regulated the lives of their members; thus, the requirements of commune life nullified the reforms of Alexander II. Another significant development was the creation of the *zemstvos*, which were assemblies which administered the local areas; through the *zemstvos* the Russian rural nobility retained control over local politics. Finally, Alexander II reformed the Russian judiciary system; the new judiciary was to be based upon such enlightened notions as jury trial, the abolition of arbitrary judicial processes, and the equality of all before the law. In fact, the only substantive change was the improvement in the efficiency of the Russian judiciary; however, the reforms did lead to expectations which were later realized.

The reforms of Alexander II did not resolve the problems of Russia. During the 1860s and 1870s criticism of the regime mounted. Moderates called for Russia to proceed along Western lines in a controlled manner in addressing political and economic problems; radicals argued that the overthrow of the system was the only recourse to the problems which confronted the Russian people. Quite naturally, Alexander II and other members of the power structure maintained that Russia would solve its own problems within the existing structure and without external intervention. The economic problems which plagued Russia were staggering. Under the three-field system which was utilized, one third of Russian agricultural land was not being used; the population was increasing dramatically but food protection was not keeping pace. Peasants were allowed to buy land and to live outside of the communes; however, even with the establishment of the Peasants Land Bank (1883), most peasants were unable to take advantage of this opportunity to become property owners. During years of great hardship, the government did intervene with emergency measures which temporarily reduced, deferred, or suspended taxes and/or payments.

While Russian agriculture appeared to have no direction, nor to have experienced any real growth during this period, Russian industry, particularly in textiles and metallurgy, did develop. Between 1870 and 1900, as the result of French loans, the Russian railroad network was expanded significantly. In large part, the expansion of Russian industry resulted from direct governmental intervention. In addition to constructing railroads, the government subsidized industrial development through a protective tariff and by awarding major contracts to emerging industries. From 1892 to 1903 Count S. Y. Witte served as Minister of Finance. As a result of his efforts to stimulate the economy, Russian industry prospered during most of the 1890s. During this same period the government consistently suppressed the development of organized labor. In 1899 a depression broke and the gains of the 1890s quickly were replaced by the increased unemployment and industrial shutdowns; this very difficult situation was aggravated by the outbreak of the Russo-Japanese war in 1904.

The last years of the reign of Alexander II witnessed increased political opposition which was manifested in demands for reforms from an ever more hostile group of intellectuals, the emergence of a Russian populist movement, and attempts to assassinate the czar. Some of the demands for extending reforms came from within the government from such dedicated and talented ministers as D. A. Miliutin, a Minister of War, who reorganized the Russian military system during the 1870s. However, reactionary ministers such as Count Dimitri Tolstoy, Minister of Education, did much to discredit any progressive policies emanating from the regime; Tolstoy repudiated academic freedom and advanced an anti-scientism bias. As the regime matured, greater importance was placed on traditional values. This attitude developed at the same time that nihilism, which rejected romantic illusions of the past in favor of a rugged realism, was being advanced by such writers as Ivan Turgenev in his *Fathers and Sons*.

The notion of the inevitability and desirability of a social and economic revolution was promoted through the Russian populist movement; originally, the populists were interested in an agrarian utopian order in which the lives of all peasants would be transformed into an idyllic state. The populists had no national base of support; government persecution of the populist resulted in the radicalization of the movement. In the late 1870s and early 1880s, leaders such as Andrei Zheleabov and Sophie Perovsky became obsessed with the need to assassinate Alexander II. In March, 1881, he was killed in St. Petersburg when his carriage was bombed; he was succeeded by Alexander III (1881 – 1894) who advocated a national policy based on "Orthodoxy, Autocracy, and Nationalism." Alexander III selected as his primary aides, conservatives such as Count Dimitri Tolstoy, now Minister of the Interior, Count Delianov, Minister of Education, and Constantine Pobedonostev, who headed the Russian Orthodox Church. Alexander III died in 1894 and was succeeded by the last of the Romanovs to hold power, Nicholas II (1894 – 1917). Nicholas II displayed his lack of intelligence, wit, and political acumen, and the absence of a firm will throughout his reign. From assertive ministers to his wife, Alexandra, to Rasputin, Nicholas tended to come under the influence of stronger personalities. The crisis confronting Imperial Russia required extraordinarily effective and cohesive leadership; with Nicholas II, the situation became more severe and, in the end, unacceptable.

The opposition to the Czarist government became more focused and thus, more threatening, with the emergence of the Russian Social Democrats and the Russian Social Revolutionaries; both groups were Marxist. Vladimir Ilyich Ulyanov, also known as Lenin, became the leader of the Bolsheviks, a splinter group of the Social Democrats. Until the impact of the 1899 depression and the horrors associated with the Russo-Japanese war were realized, groups advocating revolutions commanded little support. Even when the Revolution of 1905 occurred, the Marxist groups did not enjoy any political gains. By winter (1904 – 05), the accumulated consequences of inept management of the economy and in the prosecution of the Russo-Japanese War reached a critical stage. A group under the leadership of the radical priest Gapon marched on the Winter Palace in St. Petersburg (January 9, 1905) to submit a list of grievances to the czar; troops fired on the demonstrators and many casualties resulted on this "Bloody Sunday". In response to the massacre, a general strike was called; it was followed by a series of peasant revolts through the spring. During these same months, the Russian armed forces were being defeated by the Japanese and a lack of confidence in the regime became widespread. In June 1905, naval personnel on the battleship Potemkin mutinied while the ship was in Odessa. With this startling development, Nicholas II's government lost its nerve. In October 1905, Nicholas II issued the October Manifesto which called for the convocation of a Duma, or assembly of state, which would serve as an advisory body to the czar; extended civil liberties to include freedom of speech, assembly, and press; and announced that Nicholas II would reorganize his government.

The leading revolutionary forces differed in their responses to the manifesto. The Octobrists indicated that they were satisfied with the arrangements; the Constitutional Democrats, also known as the Cadets, demanded a more liberal representative system. The Duma convened in 1906 and, from its outset to the outbreak of the First World War, was paralyzed by its own internal factionalism which was exploited by the Czar's ministers. By 1907 Nicholas II's ministers had recovered the real power of government. Russia experienced a general though fragile economic recovery which was evident by 1909 and lasted until the war.

THE HAPSBURGS IN DECLINE: AUSTRIA-HUNGARY

After the disruptions of the Revolution of 1848 and 1849, the Austrian government had to address a series of major issues with which it found itself confronted: 1) The issue of German nationalism – the *Kleindeutsch* and the *Grossdeutsch*; 2) the problems associated with the rise of the national aspirations of the ethnic groups which resided in the Balkans; and 3) the management of an empire which was not integrated because of historic tradition and cultural diversification.

During the 1850s the Hapsburg leadership deferred any attempt to resolve these problems, and in doing so, lost the initiative. To the north, Bismarck was developing the Prussian army in anticipation for the struggle with Austria over the future of Germany; in the Balkans, the Hungarians and Czechs, while smarting from the setbacks of 1849, were agitating for national self-determination or, at the least, for a semi-autonomous state. In 1863 and 1864 Austria became involved with Prussia in a war with Denmark. This war was a prelude for the German Civil War of 1866 between Austria and Prussia; Prussia prevailed. The impact of these developments on the Austrian government necessitated a reappraisal of its national policies. Without doubt the most significant development resulting from this reappraisal was the Ausgleich or Compromise, which transformed Austria into the Austro-Hungarian Empire. The Hungarians would have their own assembly, cabinet, and administrative system, and would support and participate in the Imperial army and in the Imperial government. Not only did the Ausgleich assimilate the Hungarians and nullify them as a primary opposition group, it also led to a more efficient government.

During the period from 1867 to 1914, Austria-Hungary continued to experience difficulties with the subject nationalities and with adjusting to a new power structure in Central Europe in which Austria-Hungary was admittedly secondary to Germany. At the same time, it enjoyed a cultural revival in which its scholars (Sigmund Freud, Carl Menger, and Heinrich Friedjung), painters (Hans Makart and Adalvert Stiftor), dramatists (Hugo von Hofmannsthal), and writers (Stefan Zweig and Rilke) were renowned throughout the world.

THE BALKAN STATES AND THE DISINTEGRATION OF THE OTTOMAN EMPIRE

During the period from 1848 to 1914 the influence of the Ottoman Empire was eroded steadily because of its own internal structure and system, the ineptitude of its leaders, the lack of cohesion within the empire, the development of nationalist ambitions among many ethnic groups in the region, and the expansionist policies of Austria-Hungary and Russia in the Balkans, and of Great Britain in the eastern Mediterranean.

By 1914 Rumania, Serbia, Bulgaria, and Montenegro had been established as independent states, Austria had annexed Bosnia and Herzegovina, Britain held Cyprus, and Russia had extended its influence over the new Bulgaria.

ORIGINS, MOTIVES, AND IMPLICATIONS OF THE NEW IMPERIALISM, 1870-1914

During the first seven decades of the 19th century, the European powers did not pursue active imperial expansion. Internal European development preoccupied the powers; colonies were viewed as liabilities because of the direct costs associated with their administration. However, this attitude to extra-European activity began to change in the 1870s and, within the next twenty years, most of the European states were conducting aggressive imperial policies. This sharp departure from previous policy was caused by economic, political, and cultural factors. By the 1870s the European industrial economies had developed to a level where they required external markets to distribute the products which could not be absorbed within their domestic economies. Further, excess capital was available and foreign investment, while with some risk, appeared to offer the promise of high return. Finally, the need for additional sources of raw materials served as an economic rationale and stimulant for imperialism. In part, these economic considerations arose from the existing political forces of the era and, at the same time, motivated the contemporary political leadership to be sympathetic in their reappraisal of imperialism. Politicians were also influenced by the numerous missionary societies which sought government protection, if not support, in extending Christianity throughout the world; British and French missionary societies were vehement in their anti-slavery position. Further, European statesmen, cognizant of the emergence of a new distribution of power in Europe, were interested in asserting their national power overseas through the acquisition of strategic – and many not so strategic – colonies. Disraeli and Salisbury of England, Thiers and Ferry of France, and later Bismarck of Germany were influenced by yet another factor: the European cultural sentiments of the 1870s and 1880s. The writings of John Seeley, Anatole Leroy-Beaulieu and others suggested that the future status of the powers would be dependant upon the extent and significance of their imperial holdings; these thoughts were later amplified by the social and national Darwinists. Exploration and imperial policies were supported by the public throughout the era; national pride and economic opportunities were the factors upon which this popular support was based.

Unlike colonial policies of earlier centuries, the "New Imperialism" of the 1870s was comprehensive in scope and, as Benjamin Disraeli argued in 1872, a call to "greatness" where a nation was to fulfill its destiny. From Disraeli to Kipling to Churchill, there were few leaders who would differ sharply from this view. On the continent, the New Imperialism was opposed most vigorously by orthodox Marxists; even the revisionist groups such as the Social Democratic Party and, during the Boer War, the English Fabian Society, supported imperial policies.

The Scramble for Colonies

The focus of most of the European imperial activities during the late 19th century was Africa. Since the 1850s, Africa had commanded the attention of European explorers such as Richard Burton, Carl Peters, David Livingston, and many others, who were interested in charting the unknown interior of the continent, and, in particular, in locating the headwaters of the Nile. Initially, European interest in these activities was romantic; with John Hanning Speke's discovery of Lake Victoria (1858), Livingston's surveying of the Zambezi, and Stanley's work on the Congo River, Europeans became enraptured with the greatness and novelty of Africa south of the Sahara.

While Disraeli was involved in the intrigue which would result in the British acquisition of the Suez Canal (1875), Britain found itself becoming increasingly involved in establishing itself as an African power. During the 1870s and 1880s Britain was involved in a Zulu War and announced the annexation of the Transvaal, which the Boers regained after their great victory of Majuba Hill (1881) over the British. At about the same time, Belgium established its interest in the Congo; France, in addition to seizing Tunisia, extended its influence into French Equitorial Africa, which was the Ubangui River Basin; and Italy established small colonies in East Africa which would later be extended. During the 1880s Germany became interested in African acquisitions and acquired several African colonies including German East Africa, the Cameroons, Togoland, and German South West Africa. All of these imperial activities heightened tensions among the European powers. Consequently, the Berlin Conference (1884 – 85) was convened. The conference resulted in an agreement which specified the following: 1) The Congo would be under the control of Belgium through an International Association; 2) more liberal use of the Niger and Congo rivers; and 3) European powers could acquire African territory through first occupation and secondly notifying the other European states of their occupation and claim.

Between 1885 and 1914 the principal European states continued to enhance their positions in Africa. Without doubt, Britain was the most active and successful. From 1885 to 1890 Britain expanded its control over Nigeria, moved north from the Cape of Good Hope, and became further involved in East Africa. By this time Salisbury was the leader of the Conservative Party and, when in office, he fostered imperial expansion. Gladstone was still an anti-imperialist and the leader of the Liberal Party; he found the imperialist forces so formidable that he had to compromise his position on occasion when he was Prime Minister. During the 1880s an Islamic revolution under the Mahdi, an Islamic warrior, developed in the Sudan. In 1884 Gladstone sent General Charles Gordon to evacuate Khartoum; Gordon and the city's defenders were slaughtered by the Mahdi's forces in January, 1885. The British found themselves confronted with a continuing native insurrection in the Sudan which was not suppressed effectively until Kitchener's victory at Omdurman in 1898. The French were also quite active during this period; they unified Senegal, the Ivory Coast, and Guinea into French West Africa and extended it to Timbuktu, and moved up the Ubangui toward Lake Chad. While the British had difficulties in the Sudan, the French had to suppress a native insurrection in Madagascar which was prolonged to 1896.

The British movement north of the Cape of Good Hope resulted in a different type of struggle – one that involved Europeans fighting one another rather than a native African force. The Boers had a developed settlement in South Africa since the beginning of the nineteenth century. With the discovery of gold (1882) in the Transvaal, many English Cape settlers moved into the region. The Boers, under the leadership of Paul Kruger, restricted the political and economic rights of the British settlers and developed alternative railroads through Mozambique which would lessen the Boer dependency on the Cape colony. Relations between the British and Boers steadily deteriorated; in 1895, the Jameson Raid, an ill-conceived action not approved by Britain, failed to result in restoring the status of British citizens. The crisis mounted and, in 1899, the Boer War began; from 1899 to 1903, the British and Boers fought a war which was costly to both sides. Britain prevailed and by 1909, the Transvaal, Orange Free State, Natal, and the Cape of Good Hope were united into the Union of South Africa.

Another area of increased imperialist activity was the Pacific, where the islands appealed to many nations. In 1890, the American naval Captain Alfred Mahan published *The Influence of Sea Power Upon History*; in this book he argued that history demonstrated that those nations which controlled the seas prevailed. During the 1880s and 1890s naval ships required coaling stations. While Britain, the Netherlands, and France demonstrated that they were interested in Pacific islands, the most active states in this region during the last twenty years of the 19th century were Germany and the United States. Britain's Pacific interests were motivated primarily in sustaining its control of Australia. The French were interested in Tahiti; after a dispute with France over the Samoan Islands, the islands were split with France, Germany, and the United States. The United States acquired the Philippines in 1898; Germany gained part of New Guinea, and the Marshall, Caroline, and Mariana island chains. The European powers were also interested in the Asian mainland. In 1900, the Boxer Rebellion broke in Peking; it was a native reaction against Western influence in China. An international force was organized to break the siege of the Western legations. Most powers agreed with the American Open Door Policy which recognized the independence and integrity of China and provided economic access for all the powers. Rivalry over China (Manchuria) was a principal cause for the outbreak of the Russo-Japanese War in 1904.

THE AGE OF BISMARCK, 1871 – 1890

The Development of the German Empire

During the period from the establishment of the German Empire in January 1871 to his dismissal as Chancellor of Germany in March 1890, Otto von Bismarck dominated European diplomacy and established an integrated political and economic structure for the new German state. Bismarck established a statist system which was reactionary in political philosophy and based upon industrialism, militarism and innovative social legislation. German adaptation during the *Grundjahre* (the founding years of the new industrial order, 1870 – 1875) was staggering; remarkable increases in productivity and the expansion of industrialization took place during the first twenty years of the German Empire's history.

Until the mid-19th century, Germany consisted of numerous independent states which tended to be identified with regional rather than national concerns; to a large degree, this condition reflected the continuing impact of the Peace of Westphalia (1648). With the unification of Germany, a German state became a reality but the process of integration of regional economic, social, political, and cultural interests had not yet occurred. Bismarck, with the consent and approval of Wilhelm I, the German Emperor, developed a constitution for the new nation which provided for the following:

1) The Emperor would be the executor of state and, as such, establish the domestic and foreign policies; he was also the commander of the armed forces. The Chancellor (similar to Prime Minister) held office at the discretion of the Emperor.

2) A bicameral legislature was established. It consisted of the *Reichstag*; a lower body which represented the nation (the *Volk*); and the Bundesrat, an upper body which represented the various German states. During Bismarck's tenure the *Bundesrat* identified with reactionary conservative positions and served to check any populism which would be reflected in the Reichstag.

During the 1870s and 1880s Bismarck's domestic policies were directed at the establishment of a united strong German state which would be capable of defending itself from a French war of revenge which would be designed to restore Alsace-Lorraine to France. Laws were enacted which unified the monetary system, established an Imperial Bank and strengthened existing banks, developed universal German civil and criminal codes, and required compulsory military service. All of these measures contributed to the integration of the German state.

The German political system was multi-party. The most significant political parties of the era were (1) the Conservatives, which represented the Junkers of Prussia, (2) the Progressives, which unsuccessfully sought to extend democracy through continuing criticism of Bismarck's autocratic procedures; (3) the National Liberals, who represented the German middle class and identified with German nationalism and who provided support for Bismarck's policies; (4) the Center Party (also known as the Catholic Party), which approved Bismarck's policy of centralization and promoted the political concept of Particularism which advocated regional priorities, and (5) the Social Democratic Party (S.P.D.), a Marxist group, which advocated sweeping social legislation, the realization of genuine democracy, and the demilitarization of the German government. Bismarck was unsuccessful in stopping the influence of the Center Party through his anti-Catholic *Kulturkampf* (the May Laws) and in thwarting the growth of the Social Democrats.

In order to develop public support for the government and to minimize the threat from the left, Bismarck instituted a protective tariff, which maintained domestic production, and many social and economic laws which provided social security, regulated child labor, and improved working conditions for all Germans.

European Diplomacy

Bismarck's foreign policy was centered on the primary principle of maintaining the diplomatic isolation of France. After a few years of recovery from their defeat in the Franco-Prussian War, the French were regaining their confidence and publicly discussing the feasibility of a war of revenge to regain Alsace-Lorraine. In 1875, the War-In-Sight-Crisis occurred between the French and Germans. While war was avoided, the crisis clearly indicated the delicate state of the Franco-German relationship. In the crisis stemming from the Russo-Turkish War (1877 – 78), Bismarck tried to serve as the "Honest Broker" at the Congress of Berlin (see Chapter 5). Russia did not succeed at the conference and, incorrectly, blamed Bismarck for its failure. Early in the next year, a cholera epidemic affected Russian cattle herds and Germany placed an embargo on the importation of Russian beef. The Russians were outraged by the German action and launched an anti-German propaganda campaign in the Russian press. Bismarck, desiring to maintain the peace and a predictable diplomatic environment, concluded a secret defensive treaty with Austria-Hungary in 1879. The Dual Alliance was very significant because it was the first "hard" diplomatic alliance of the era. A "hard" alliance involved the specific commitment of military support; traditional or "soft" alliances involved pledges of neutrality or to hold military conversations in the event of a war. The Dual Alliance, which had a five year term and was renewable, directed that one signatory would assist the other in the event that one power was attacked by two or more states.

In 1881, another similar agreement, the Triple Alliance, was signed between Germany, Austria-Hungary, and Italy. In the 1880s, relations between Austria-Hungary and Russia became estranged over Balkan issues. Bismarck, fearing a war, intervened and, by 1887, had negotiated the secret Reinsurance Treaty with Russia. This was a "hard" defensive alliance with a three year term, renewable. Since these were "defensive" arrangements, Bismarck was confident that through German policy, the general European peace would be maintained and the security of Germany ensured through sustaining the diplomatic isolation of France. Bismarck also acted to neutralize the role of Great Britain in European affairs through the implementation of a policy which, in most but not all instances, was supportive of British interests.

In 1888 Wilhelm I died and was succeeded by his son Frederich III, who also died within a few months. Friedrich's son, Wilhelm II (1888 – 1918), came to power and soon found himself in conflict with Bismarck. Wilhelm II was intent upon administering the government personally and viewed Bismarck as an archaic personality. Early in 1890 two issues developed which led ultimately to Bismarck's dismissal. First, Bismarck had evolved a scheme for a fabricated attempted coup by the Social Democratic Party; his interest was to use this situation to create a national hysteria through which he could restrict the SPD through legal action. Secondly, Bismarck intended to renew the Reinsurance Treaty with Russia to maintain his policy of French diplomatic isolation. Wilhelm II opposed both of these plans; in March 1890, Bismarck, who had used the threat of resignation so skillfully in the past, suggested that he would resign if Wilhelm II would not approve of these actions. Wilhelm II accepted his resignation; in fact, Bismarck was dismissed. The diplomatic developments after 1890 (see Chapter 11) radically altered the alignment of power in Europe. The position of Chancellor of Germany was filled by a series of less talented statesmen including Count von Caprivi (1890 – 94), Prince Hohenlohe (1894 – 1900), Prince Bernhard von Bulow (1900 – 1909), and Chancellor Bethmann-Hollweg.

THE MOVEMENT TOWARD DEMOCRACY IN WESTERN EUROPE TO 1914

Great Britain

Even after the reform measures of 1867 and 1884 to 1885, the movement toward democratic reforms in Great Britain continued unabated. Unlike other European nations where the focus on democracy was limited to gaining the vote, British reform efforts were much more complex and sophisticated and involved social and economic reforms as well as continuing changes in the political process; participation in the system as well as representation were desired by many. During the 1880s and 1890s, new groups emerged which intended to extend the definition of democratic government to embrace new social and economic philosophies of the period. From women's suffrage and the condemnation of imperialism to the redistribution of wealth and the demise of nationalism, these groups represented a broad spectrum of radical and reform ideologies. Among the most significant was the Fabian Society (1883) which advanced a mode of revisionist Marxism and whose members included Sidney and Beatrice Webb, the Scottish politician Keir Hardie (who later led the Labor Party), George Bernard Shaw, H. G. Wells, the historian C. D. H. Cole, and the young Ramsay MacDonald, who became the first Labor Prime Minister. The Fabians argued for evolutionary political transformation which would result in full political democracy and economic socialism. In 1884, the Social Democratic Federation was formed by H. M. Hyndman. In 1893, Keir Hardie established the Independent Labor Party which rapidly became a vocal third party in British politics. The Labor Party attracted trade unionists, socialists, and those who thought that the Conservative and Liberal Parties had no genuine interest in the needs of the general public.

During the early years of the 20th century both the Conservatives and the Liberals advanced more aggressive social and economic programs. The Conservatives, through the efforts of Arthur James Balfour, promoted the Education Act of 1902 which they argued would provide enhanced educational opportunities for the working class. In fact, this act was criticized soundly for not providing what it claimed as its purpose. In 1905, the Liberals under Henry Campbell-Bannerman came to power. The government ministries were staffed by such talented leaders as Herbert Asquith, Sir Edward Grey, David Lloyd George, and Winston Churchill.

The most significant political reform of this long-lived Liberal government was the Parliament Act of 1911 which eliminated the powers of the House of Lords and resulted in the House of Commons becoming the unquestioned center of national power. All revenue bills approved by the House of Commons would automatically become law thirty days after being sent to the House of Lords. If the Lords voted favorably, the law would be enacted earlier. The Lords had no veto power.

Non-revenue bills which were opposed by the Lords would be enacted if passed by three consecutive sessions of Commons. It was not difficult to transform such measures into revenue bills.

Finally, the life-span of Parliament was reduced from seven to five years.

The British political climate during this period was rather volatile. Issues relating to trade unions, Ireland, and women's suffrage tended to factionalize British politics. The Liberal Party, which was in power from 1905 to the early 1920s, came to be institutionalized and in the process came to be identified as "the government." To many, the programs advanced by the Conservative and Labor parties provided the basis for debate and decision. The Liberal Party was withering because it lacked clarity of platform and encapsulated the unrealized domestic goals, the ambiguities of bureaucracy, and the horrors of war.

The most recurring and serious problem which Great Britain experienced during the period from 1890 to 1914 was the "Irish Question." Gladstone, in his final ministry, argued unsuccessfully for Irish Home Rule. In Ireland opposition to British rule and the abuses of British power was evident through the program of the National Land League, which was established in 1879 by Michael Davitt. This organization stimulated and coordinated Irish opposition to British and Irish landlords. The efforts of the National Land League resulted in support for Irish Home Rule. During the 1880s Charles Stewart Parnell led the Irish delegation to the House of Commons. Parnell, through the support of Gladstone, attained some gains for the Irish such as the Land Reform Act and the Arrears Act. In 1890 Parnell became involved in a divorce case and the scandal ruined his career; he died the next year. In 1893 Gladstone devised the Irish Home Rule bill which was passed by the House of Commons but rejected by the House of Lords. The Irish situation became more complicated when the Protestant counties of the north started to enjoy remarkable economic growth from the mid-1890s; they were adamant in their rejection of all measures of Irish Home Rule. In 1914, an Irish Home Rule Act was passed by both the Commons and the Lords but the Protestants refused to accept it; implementation was deferred until after the war.

The Third French Republic

In the fall of 1870, Napoleon III's Second Empire collapsed when it was defeated by the Prussian armies. Napoleon III and his principal aides were captured; later, he abdicated and fled to England. A National Assembly (1871 – 75) was created and Adolphe Thiers was recognized as its chief executive. At the same time, a more radical political entity, the Paris Commune (1870 – 71), came into existence and exercised extraordinary power during the siege of Paris. After the siege and the peace agreement with Prussia, the Paris Commune refused to recognize the authority of the National Assembly. Led by radical Marxists, anarchists, and republicans, the Paris Commune repudiated the conservative and monarchist leadership of the National Assembly; from March to May 1871, the Paris Commune fought a bloody struggle with the troops of the National Assembly. Thousands died and when Paris surrendered, there were thousands of executions – accepted estimates place the number of executions at 20,000 during the first week after Paris fell on May 28, 1871. It was within this historic framework that France began a program of recovery which led to the formulation of the Third French Republic in 1875. The National Assembly sought to (1) put the French political house in order, (2) establish a new constitutional government, (3) pay off an imposed indemnity and, in doing so, remove German troops from French territory, and (4) restore the honor and glory of France. In 1875 a Constitution was adopted which provided for a republican government with a president (with little power), a Senate, and a Chamber of Deputies, which was the center of political power. The politicians and factions which led France during the 1870s and 1880s had to address the dominant forces which served as the dynamic elements of French politics. These forces included the overwhelming influence of the French bourgeoisie (middle class), which was intent upon establishing and sustaining a French republican government; the mounting hostility between the Catholic Church and the French government (anti-clericalism was frequently manifested in the proceedings of the Chamber of Deputies); the unpredictability which accompanied multi-party politics; and, finally, the extreme nationalism which gripped France during these decades and which resulted in continuing calls for a war of revenge against Germany in order to regain Alsace-Lorraine.

During the early years of the Republic, Leon Gambetta (1838 – 1882) led the republicans. Beginning in the 1880s the Third French Republic was challenged by a series of crises which threatened the continuity of the Republic. The Boulanger Crisis (1887 – 1889), the Panama Scandal (1894), and the Dreyfus Affair (1894 – 1906) were serious domestic problems; in all of these developments, the challenge to republicanism came from the right. The sustenance of republicanism through this time of troubles came primarily from (1) the able leadership of the republican government, and (2) the continuing commitment of the bourgeoisie to republicanism. Since the founding of the Third Republic, monarchists and conservatives were interested in overthrowing the regime; however, until the appointment of General Georges Boulanger (1837 – 1891) as Minister of War in 1886, there was no one to lead the anti-republican cause. Boulanger won over the army by improving the basic conditions of military life. His public popularity was high in 1888 and his supporters urged him to conduct a coup; he delayed and by the spring of 1889, the republicans had mounted a case against Boulanger. He was directed to appear to respond to charges of conspiracy; Boulanger broke, fled to Belgium, and committed suicide in 1891. The Boulanger crisis resulted in renewed confidence in the republic; but what popular gains it made were unravelled in 1892 with the Panama Scandal. The French had been involved with the engineering and the raising of capital for the Panama Canal since the 1870s. Early in the 1890s the promoters of the project resorted to the bribery of government officials and of certain members of the press who had access to information which indicated that the work on the canal was not proceeding as had been announced. In 1892 the scandal broke and for months the public indicated that it thought that the entire French government was corrupt. However, by 1893, elections to the Chamber of Deputies resulted in the socialists making notable gains. The monarchists did not attract much public support.

Without a doubt, the most serious threat to the republic came through the Dreyfus Affair. In 1894 Captain Alfred Dreyfus was assigned to the French General Staff. A scandal broke when it was revealed that classified information had been provided to German spies. Dreyfus, a Jew, was charged, tried, and convicted. Later, it was determined that the actual spy was Commandant Marie Charles Esterhazy; however, he was acquitted in order to save the pride and reputation of the army. The monarchists used this incident to criticize republicanism; the republicans countered when Emile Zola took up Dreyfus's cause when he wrote an open letter entitled *J'accuse*, which condemned the General Staff's actions and pronounced Dreyfus's innocence. Leftists supported the Republic and, in 1906, the case was closed when Dreyfus was declared innocent and returned to the ranks. Rather than lead to the collapse of the republic, the Dreyfus Affair demonstrated the intensity of anti-Semitism in French society, the level of corruption in the French army, and the willingness of the Catholic Church and the monarchists to join in a conspiracy against an innocent man. The republicans launched an anti-clerical campaign which included the Association Act (1901) and the separation of church and state (1905).

From 1905 to 1914 the socialists under Jean Juares gained seats in the Chamber of Deputies. The Third French Republic endured the crises which confronted it and, in 1914, enjoyed the support of the vast majority of French citizens.

The Lesser States of Europe

In the Low Countries during the decades prior to 1914, there were differing approaches to extending democracy. An appreciation of democracy was evident in Belgium under the leadership of Leopold I (1865 – 1909) and Albert I (1909 – 1934); during their reigns the franchise was extended, social and economic reforms were introduced, and equity was the basis of the settlement between Flemish and French speaking Belgians. To the north, the Netherlands was slow to adopt democracy. By 1896, only 14% of the Dutch had the vote and it would not be until 1917 that universal manhood suffrage would be enacted.

Denmark experienced a struggle between the old guard represented by Christian IX (1863 – 1906), who opposed parliamentary government, and the Social Democrats who advocated democratic principles. The Danish Constitution of 1915 provided a basic democratic political system. Sweden, after a decade of debilitating debate, recognized the independence of Norway in 1905; Norway moved quickly toward democracy, granting women the vote in 1907. Sweden, under Gustavus V (1907 – 1950), pronounced a comprehensive democratic system in 1909.

In southern Europe, advocates of democracy did not meet with any substantive success prior to 1914. In Spain, Portugal, and Italy, the monarchist establishments were preoccupied with survival. While an occasional reform was promulgated, there was no intent to move toward full democracy.

EUROPEAN CULTURAL DEVELOPMENTS, 1848 – 1914

The great political and economic changes of this period were accompanied by cultural achievements which included the development of a literate citizenry and substantive innovations in science, literature, art, music and other areas of intellectual activity. In large part, these developments occurred as a reaction against the mechanistic sterility of the scientism and positivism of the age; however, some of the initial achievements, such as Darwin's theories of evolution and natural selection, resulted in extending the exaggerated claims of scientism. From Charles Darwin, Richard Wagner, Friedrich Nietzsche, and Sigmund Freud to Claude Monet, Richard Strauss, Igor Stravinsky, Oscar Wilde, Thomas Mann, and James Joyce, intelligent Europeans of the era pursued many differing, and at times opposing, approaches in their quest for truth and understanding. Many philosophers were critical of the movement toward democracy which they identified with mass culture and political ineptitude. Artists attempted to escape their plight through moving into symbolism with their pen or brush; there, they were free to express their fantasies of hope and despair.

Darwin, Wagner, Freud, and the Emergence of a New Tradition

In 1859, Charles Darwin's (1807 – 1882) *The Origins of the Species* was published; it argued the theory of evolution which had been discussed for more than a generation in Europe. Darwin's contributions to the advocacy of this theory were based (1) on the data which he provided to demonstrate the theory, and (2) in the formulation of a well structured and argued defense of the theory of natural selection (survival of the fittest). The reaction to *The Origins of the Species* was diverse, thorough, and enduring; some discussants were concerned with the implication of the theory on religion, while others were interested in applying aspects of the theory to the understanding of contemporary social problems. Within the Darwinian camp, factions emerged which supported or rejected one or more components of the theory. Samuel Butler and George Bernard Shaw accepted evolution but rejected natural selection; Thomas Huxley was Darwin's most consistent and loyal supporter. Herbert Spencer (1820 – 1903) developed a Social Darwinism which enjoyed extensive acceptance in both scholarly and general circles. One of the obvious consequences of Darwin's theory was that it necessitated a reevaluation of all of the issues relating to man's place in the cosmos. The doctrine of creation was challenged and thus the authenticity of prevailing religion was endangered.

In classical music, the erratic Richard Wagner (1813 – 1883) reflected the incongruities and the harshness of the new age. Wagner developed and imposed an aestheticism that had one fundamental element – it demanded absolute artistic integrity. Wagner shifted styles several times during his career; his *Ring* cycle was centered on German epics and advanced numerous fantasies about the history of the German people.

Sigmund Freud (1856 – 1939) established a new approach to understanding human behavior which was known as psychoanalysis. Freud accepted the impressionist interpretation that reality was not material; rather it was based on moods, concepts, and feelings which shift. In Vienna, Freud developed his concepts that the unconscious was shaped during the formative years, that sexuality was a dominant lifeforce, and that free will may not exist. Freud argued his theories in a formidable body of literature which included the *Origins of Psychoanalysis* and *Civilization and Its Discontents*. The establishment rejected his unorthodox views as threats to religion.

In science itself, new developments challenged the certainty and security of the old science. Max Planck's *Quantum Physics*, Albert Einstein's *Theory of Relativity*, and the impact of the Michelson-Morley Experiment (1887; regarding the measurement of speed; conducted in the United States) led to a new generation of scientists reexamining many of the assumptions of the past.

Impressionism and Symbolism: Forces of the New Art

The turbulence within European cultural life during the fifty years prior to the outbreak of the First World War can be seen most evidently in new attitudes which emerged in art and literature. Not only did the intellectuals find themselves looking for a new intellectual synthesis through which to offer new vision and hope, but they were also liberated from the limitations which had been imposed on their predecessors through a technological breakthrough. The development of photography resulted in artists no longer being required to produce actual representations. Painters were now free to pursue the dictates of their imaginations. Impressionism developed in France during the 1870s; Monet, Manet, Renoir, and others pioneered the new art. Impressionism soon gave way to Post-Impressionism and later Expressionism. At the turn of the century, more radical artistic forms such as Symbolism and Cubism enjoyed notoriety if not general acceptance.

Literature was transformed through the writings of such innovators as Oscar Wilde (*The Picture of Dorian Gray*), Thomas Mann (*Death in Venice*), and the young James Joyce (prior to 1914, *Portrait of the Artist as a Young Man* and *Dubliners*). These writers were interested in discussing the themes which had great personal value and meaning; Joyce will emerge as the most seminal stylist of the twentieth century.

INTERNATIONAL POLITICS AND THE COMING OF THE WAR, 1890 – 1914

During the generation prior to the outbreak of the First World War in the summer of 1914, conflicts and strained relations among the great powers increased in frequency and intensity. There can be no question that the primary factors which contributed to this situation were the heightened nationalism and the cultural materialism of the period.

The Polarization of Europe

In March 1890 Bismarck was dismissed as Chancellor of Germany by the immature, impetuous, and inexperienced Kaiser Wilhelm II. The particular issues which led to Bismarck's fall included the renewal of the Reinsurance Treaty (1887) with Russia and Bismarck's scheme to weaken the role of the Social Democratic Party (SPD) within German politics. With Bismarck's dismissal, the continuing dominance of the German agenda over European affairs was questionable. The intricate alliance system which Bismarck had constructed was directed at maintaining the diplomatic isolation of France.

Germany failed to renew the Reinsurance Treaty with Russia and consequently Russia looked elsewhere to eliminate its own perceived isolation. In 1891 secret negotiations were entered into by the French and Russians. By 1894 these deliberations resulted in the Dual Entente which was a comprehensive military alliance. This agreement was sustained through 1917 and allowed France to pursue a more assertive foreign policy. From the Russian perspective, the fears of isolation and of the development of an anti-Russian combination were abated. Within four years of Bismarck's dismissal, the essential imperative of German foreign policy in the late nineteenth century – the diplomatic isolation of France – was no longer a reality.

In 1895 a new Conservative government came to power in Great Britain. Led by Lord Salisbury, who served as Prime Minister and Foreign Secretary, this government included a wide range of talented statesmen including Joseph Chamberlain, John Morley, Lord Landsdowne, and the young Arthur James Balfour. The Salisbury government was interested in terminating the long-standing policy of "Splendid Isolationism" which had prevailed as Britain's response to European alliances. Salisbury came to argue that the new realities of world politics and economics deemed it advisable for Britain to ally itself with a major power. While coming under general European criticism for its role in the Boer War (1899 – 1902) in South Africa, British representatives approached Berlin in an attempt to develop an Anglo-German alliance. Germany declined the British advances because (1) the Germans were sympathetic to the Boers, (2) the Germans questioned the ability of the British army, (3) they believed that the British would never be able to reach an accommodation with the French or Russians, and (4) Wilhelm II was involved in a major naval building program – this effort would be jeopardized if the Germans were allied to the world's greatest naval power, Britain.

Consequently, Britain pursued diplomatic opportunities which resulted in the Anglo-Japanese Alliance (1902), the Entente Cordiale or Anglo-French Entente (1904), and the Anglo-Russian Entente (1907).

The Anglo-Japanese Alliance of 1902 resulted in the two powers agreeing to adopt a position of benevolent neutrality in the event that the other member state was involved in war. This arrangement was sustained through the First World War.

The Entente Cordiale (1904), which is also known as the Dual Entente or the Anglo-French Entente, was a settlement of long-standing colonial disputes between Britain and France over North African territories. It was agreed that northeast Africa (Egypt and the Anglo-Egyptian Sudan) would be a British sphere of influence and that northwest Africa (Morocco) would be a French sphere of influence. This was a colonial settlement, not a formal alliance; neither power pledged support in the event of war. However, the Entente Cordiale was of critical significance because it drew Britain into the French oriented diplomatic camp.

While Anglo-French relations improved during 1904 to 1905, the historically tense Anglo-Russian relationship was aggravated further through the Russo-Japanese War (1904 – 05). The Dogger Bank Incident resulted in a crisis between these powers when Russian naval ships fired on and sunk several British fishing boats in the North Sea. Britain, which earlier had adopted a sympathetic posture toward Japan, responded by deploying the Home Fleet and curtailing the activities of the Russian fleet. The crisis was resolved when Russia agreed to apologize for the incident and to pay compensation. In 1905 a Liberal government came to power in Britain, and Russia was absorbed in its own revolution which liberalized, at least temporarily, the autocratic regime. Negotiations between these powers were initiated and were facilitated by the French; in 1907 Britain and Russia reached a settlement on their outstanding colonial disputes. They agreed on three points:

1) Persia would be divided into three zones: a northern sector under Russian influence, a southern sector under British control, and a central zone which could be mutually exploited;

2) Afghanistan was recognized as a British sphere of influence;

3) Tibet was recognized as part of China and, as such, was to be free from foreign intervention.

By 1907 France, Britain, and Russia had formed a Triple Entente which effectively balanced the Triple Alliance. While Britain was not formally committed to an alliance system, Sir Edward Grey, British Foreign Minister from 1905, supported secret conversations between British and French military representatives. Thus, in terms of military power and economics, Germany became isolated by 1907.

The Rise of Militarism

During the period after 1890 Europeans began to view the use of military power as not only feasible but also as desirable to bring about a resolution to the increasingly hostile political conditions in Europe. The apparent inability of diplomats to develop lasting settlements supported the further development of this perception. The notion that a major European war was inevitable became acceptable to many.

Within the structure of the European states, militarists enjoyed increased credibility and support. The General Staffs became preoccupied with planning for the anticipated struggle and their plans affected national foreign policies. The Germans, under the influence of General Count Alfred von Schlieffen, developed the Schlieffen Plan by 1905. It was predicated on the assumption that Germany would have to conduct a two front war with France and Russia. It specified that France must be defeated quickly through the use of enveloping tactics which involved the use of German armies of about 1,500,000 men. After victory in the west, Germany would then look to the east to defeat the Russians, who would be slow to mobilize. The French developed the infamous Plan XVII, which was approved by Marshall Joseph Joffre. The French thought that the German attack would be concentrated in the region of Alsace-Lorraine and that the French forces should be massed in that area; the élan of the French soldiery would result in a victory.

The Arms Race

This wave of nationalistic militarism also manifested itself through a continuing arms race which resulted in several threats to the balance of power because of revolutionary technological developments. Field weapons such as mortars and cannons were improved sharply in range, accuracy, and firepower; the machine gun was perfected and produced in quantity. New weapons such as the submarine and airplanes were recognized as having the capacity to be strategic armaments.

In naval weaponry the rivalry between the British and the Germans over capital ships not only exacerbated the deteriorating relationship between the two powers, but also led to restrictions on the national domestic expenditures during peacetime in order to pay for the increasingly costly battleships and cruisers. In 1912, the British-sponsored Haldane Mission was sent to Berlin to negotiate an agreement; the Germans were suspicious and distrustful of the British and were not receptive to any proposal.

Imperialism as a Source of Conflict

During the late 19th century the economically motivated "New Imperialism" resulted in further aggravating the relations among the European powers. The struggle for increased world market share, the need for raw materials, and the availability of capital for overseas investment resulted in enhancing the rivalry among the European nations and, on several occasions, in causing crises to develop. The Fashoda Crisis (1898 –99), the Moroccan Crisis (1905 – 06), the Balkan Crisis (1908), and the Agadir Crisis (1911) demonstrated the impact of imperialism in heightening tensions among European states and in creating an environment in which conflict became more acceptable.

The Fashoda Crisis developed between France and Britain when the French, under the influence of Foreign Minister Theophile Delcasse, ordered Commandant Marchant and a small number of French troops to march across Africa and establish a French "presence" near the headwaters of the Nile. Marchant arrived in Fashoda (now Kodok) in 1898; Fashoda was located on the White Nile, south of Khartoum in the Anglo-Egyptian Sudan. A British army under General Herbert Kitchener, having defeated a native rebel army in the battle of Omdurman, advanced to Khartoum where he learned of the French force at Fashoda. Kitchener marched on Fashoda and a major crisis ensued for months. In the end, the French withdrew and recognized the position of the British in the Anglo-Egyptian Sudan; however, for several months there were serious consideration given to a major war over this colonial issue.

The Moroccan Crisis (1905 – 06) developed when Wilhelm II of Germany travelled to Tangier (March 1905) where he made a speech in support of the independence of Morocco; this position was at odds with that agreed to by the British and the French in the Entente Cordiale. Initially, the German position prevailed because of lack of organization within the Franco-Russian alliance; however, in 1906, at the Algerciras Conference, the German effort was thwarted and the French secured their position in Morocco. Russia, Britain, and even Italy, supported the French on every important issue. German diplomatic isolation—save for the Austrians—became increasingly evident.

The Balkan Crisis of 1908 involved an example of European imperialist rivalry within Europe. Since the Congress of Berlin in 1878, the Austro-Hungarian Empire had administered the Balkan territories of Bosnia and Herzegovina. Austrian influence in this area was opposed by Russia which considered the region as a natural area of Russian influence. Specifically, the Russians hoped to capitalize upon the collapse of the Ottoman Turkish Empire and to gain access to the Mediterranean Sea. In 1908 the decadent Ottoman Empire was experiencing domestic discord which attracted the attention of both the Austrians and the Russians. These two powers agreed that Austria would annex Bosnia and Herzegovina and that Russia would be granted access to the Straits and thus the Mediterranean. Great Britain intervened and demanded that there be no change in the status quo vis-a-vis the Straits. Russia backed down from a confrontation but Austria proceeded to annex Bosnia and Herzegovina. The annexation was condemned by the Pan-Slavists who looked to Russia for assistance; a crisis developed and it appeared that war between Austria and Russia was likely. However, the Russians disengaged from the crisis because of their lack of preparedness for a major struggle and because there were clear indications that Germany would support Austria. The Balkan Crisis was another example of the nature of European rivalries and the rather rapid recourse to sabre-rattling on the part of great powers. Further, it demonstrated that the fundamental regional problem—the developing nationalism among the diverse peoples of the Balkans—was not addressed.

The Agadir Crisis (1911) broke when France announced that its troops would be sent to several Moroccan towns to restore order. Germany, fearing French annexation of all of Morocco, responded by sending the Panther, a German naval ship, to Agadir. After exchanging threats for several weeks, the French and Germans agreed to recognize Morocco as a French protectorate and to transfer two sections of the French Congo to Germany.

An Assassination, and then a War

During the late 19th and early 20th centuries the Ottoman Empire was in a state of collapse. At the same time, Austria and Russia were interested in extending their influence in the region. Further, nationalism among the ethnic groups in the Balkans was rapidly developing. In addition to the Balkan Crisis of 1908 which was mentioned above, the region was involved in the Italian-Turkish War (1911) and the Inter-Balkan Wars of 1912 and 1913.

On June 28, 1914, Archduke Franz Ferdinand, heir to the Austro-Hungarian throne, and his wife were assassinated while on a state visit to Sarajevo, the capital of Bosnia. Their assassin was a radical Serb, Gavrilo Princip, who opposed Franz Ferdinand's plan to integrate the Slavs more fully into the government. The assassination resulted in a crisis between Austria-Hungary and Serbia, and would be the trigger for a series of events that in just two months would envelop Europe in war.

CONCLUSION

Between 1848 and 1914 Europeans experienced revolutionary changes in their culture. These alterations were based on a new sense of reality, and values in which materialism and the notion of human progress were manifested in the pragmatism of the era. Nationalism, science and technology, and the rapid expansion of the population were primary factors which contributed to these changes and to the further expansion of European culture throughout the world. The growth in the European standard of living was uneven. Western Europe developed most comprehensively, Central Europe—especially German urban centers—witnessed remarkable growth during the last decades of the period; and Southern and Eastern Europe lagged behind and, by 1914, the standard of living had not dramatically improved from that of the earlier century. Reaction to these changes varied from the development of Marxism, anarchism, and trade unionism in response to the adverse consequences of capitalism and industrialism, to the emergence of Impressionism, Expressionism, and Symbolism in reaction to the perceived intellectual sterility of mechanistic positivism. Nineteenth century Europe, which was identified with hope, progress, and rationality, gave way to the uncertainty, violence, and irrationality of the twentieth century. Politically, economically, and culturally, Europe between 1848 and 1914 continued the process of accelerated change which had been initiated in the previous century with revolutionary developments in production, and in the fundamental concepts about the relationships of man and the state and of man and the economy.

5 WORLD WAR I AND EUROPE IN CRISIS (1914-1935)

THE ORIGINS OF WORLD WAR I

In August 1914, most of the world's major powers became engaged in a conflict that most people welcomed romantically and believed would last only a few months. Instead, a war of global dimensions evolved that saw the clash of outdated military values with modern technological warfare. A war that most welcomed and that no one seemed to be able to win lasted over four years and resulted in 12 million deaths.

The origins of World War I can be traced to numerous root causes, beginning as far back as the creation of modern Germany in 1871. Achieved through a series of wars, the emergence of this new German state destroyed Europe's traditional balance-of-power, and forced its diplomatic and military planners back to their drawing boards to rethink their collective strategies to maintain proper military and diplomatic balance. In the period between 1871 and 1914, a number of developments took place that heightened tensions between the major powers.

Balance of Power and Europe's Alliance System

One of the major themes in 19th-century Europe's diplomatic arena was an effort by the major powers to organize their international relationships in such a way as to keep any single or collective group of nations from gaining a dominant diplomatic or military advantage on the Continent.

From 1871 to 1890, this balance was maintained through the network of alliances created by the German Chancellor, Otto von Bismarck, and centered on his *Dreikaiserbund* (League of the Three Emperors), which isolated France, and the Dual (Germany, Austria) and Triple (Germany, Austria, Italy) Alliances. Bismarck's fall in 1890 resulted in new policies that saw Germany move closer to Austria, while England and France (Entente Cordiale, 1904), and later Russia (Triple Entente, 1907), drew closer.

Arms Buildup and Imperialism

Germany's dramatic defeat of France in 1870–71 coupled with Kaiser Wilhelm II's decision in 1890 to build up a navy comparable to that of Great Britain created a reactive arms race that haunted Europe. This, blended with European efforts to carve out colonial empires in Africa and Asia—plus a new spirit of nationalism and the growing romanticization of war—helped create an unstable international environment in the years before the outbreak of the World War.

IMMEDIATE CAUSE OF WORLD WAR I

The Balkan Crisis

The Balkans (*balkan* is Turkish for "mountain"), a region which today embraces the former Yugoslavia, Albania, Greece, Bulgaria, and Rumania, was notably unstable. Part of the rapidly decaying Ottoman (Turkish) Empire, it saw two main forces at work: ethnic nationalism among a number of small groups who lived there and intense rivalry between Austria-Hungary and Russia over spheres of influence. Existing friction between Austria and Serbia heated up all the more after Austria annexed Bosnia and Herzegovina in 1908. In 1912, with Russia's blessing, the Balkan League (Serbia, Montenegro, Greece, and Bulgaria) went to war with Turkey. Serbia, which sought a port on the Adriatic, was rebuffed when Austria-Hungary and Italy backed the creation of an independent Albania. Russia, meanwhile, grew increasingly protective of its southern Slavic cousins, supporting Serbia's and Montenegro's claims to Albanian lands. Just weeks after the outbreak of World War I, the new Albanian state collapsed.

THE OUTBREAK OF THE WORLD WAR

Assassination and Reprisals

On June 28, 1914, the Archduke Franz Ferdinand (1863–1914), heir to the Austrian throne, was assassinated by Gavrilo Princip, a young Serbian nationalist. Princip was working for the Serbian Army Intelligence in Sarajevo, then the capital of Bosnia. Austria's rulers felt the murder provided them with an opportunity to move against Serbia and end anti-Austrian unrest in the Balkans. Austria consulted with the German government on July 6 and received a "blank check" to take whatever steps were necessary to punish Serbia. Serbia stood accused of harboring radical anti-Austrian groups like the "Black Hand." On July 23, 1914, the Austrian government presented Serbia with a 10-point ultimatum that required Serbia to suppress and punish all forms of anti-Austrian sentiment there. On July 25, 1914, three hours after mobilizing its army, Serbia accepted most of Austria's terms; it asked only that Austria's demand to participate in Serbian judicial proceedings against anti-Austrian agitators—a demand that Serbia described as unprecedented in relations between sovereign states—be adjudicated by the International Tribunal at The Hague.

The Conflict Expands

Austria immediately broke off official relations with Serbia and mobilized its army. Meanwhile, between July 18–24, Russia let the Austrians and the Germans know that it intended fully to back Serbia in the dispute. France, Russia's ally, voiced support of Russia's moves. Last-ditch attempts by Britain and Germany to mediate the dispute and avoid a general European war failed. On July 28, 1914, Austria went to war against Serbia, and began to bombard Belgrade the following day. At the same time, Russia gradually prepared for war against Austria and Germany, declaring full mobilization on July 30.

Germany and the Schlieffen Plan

German military strategy, based in part on the plan of the Chief of the General Staff, Count Alfred von Schlieffen, viewed Russian mobilization as an act of war. The Schlieffen Plan was based on a two-front war with Russia and France. It was predicated on a swift, decisive blow against France while maintaining a defensive position against slowly mobilizing Russia, which would be dealt with after France. Attacking France required the Germans to march through neutral Belgium, which would later bring England into the war as a protector of Belgian neutrality.

War Begins

Germany demanded that Russia demobilize in 12 hours, and appealed to its ambassador in Berlin. Russia's offer to negotiate the matter was rejected, and Germany declared war on Russia on August 1, 1914. Germany asked France its intentions and Paris replied that it would respond according to its own interests. On August 3, Germany declared war on France. Berlin asked Belgium for permission to send its troops through Belgian territory to attack France, which Belgium refused. On August 4, England, which agreed in 1839 to protect Belgian neutrality, declared war on Germany; Belgium followed suit. Between 1914 and 1915, the alliance of the Central Powers (Germany, Austria-Hungary, Bulgaria, and Turkey) faced the Allied Powers of England, France, Russia, Japan, and in 1917, the United States. A number of smaller countries were also part of the Allied coalition.

THE WAR IN 1914

The Western Front

After entering Belgium, the Germans attacked France on five fronts in an effort to encircle Paris rapidly. France was defeated in the Battle of the Frontier (August 14 – 24) in Lorraine, the Ardennes, and in the Charleroi-Mons area. However, the unexpected Russian attack in East Prussia and Galicia from August 17 to 20 forced Germany to transfer important forces eastward to halt the Russian drive.

To halt a further German advance, the French army, aided by Belgian and English forces, counterattacked. In the Battle of the Marne (September 5 – 9), they stopped the German drive and forced small retreats. Mutual outflanking maneuvers by France and Germany created a battle front that would determine the demarcation of the Western Front for the next 4 years. It ran, in uneven fashion, from the North Sea to Belgium and from northern France to Switzerland.

The Eastern Front

Russian forces under Pavel Rennenkampf and Aleksandr Samsonov, invaded East Prussia and Galicia in mid-August. With only 9 of 87 divisions in the east, the German defense faltered. Generals Paul von Hindenburg and Erich Ludendorff, aided by two corps from the Western Front, were sent on August 23 to revive the Eighth Army in East Prussia.

In the Battles of Tannenberg (August 25 – 31) and Mazurian Lakes (September 6 – 15), the Russian 2nd Army, under Samsonov, met the German Eighth Army. Suffering from poor communications and Rennenkampf's refusal to send the 1st Army to aid him, Samsonov surrendered with 90,000 troops and committed suicide. Moving northward, the German 8th Army now confronted Rennenkampf's 1st Army. After an unsuccessful initial encounter against the Germans, Rennenkampf rapidly retreated, suffering significant losses.

Nikolai Ivanov's Southwest Army group enjoyed some successes against Austro-Hungarian forces in Galicia and southern Poland throughout August. By the end of 1914, they were poised to strike deeper into the area.

The Germans retreated after their assault against Warsaw in late September. Hindenburg's attack on Lodz ten days after he was appointed Commander-in-Chief of the Eastern Front (Nov. 1) was a more more successful venture; by the end of 1914 this important textile center was in German hands.

THE WAR IN 1915

The Western Front

With Germany concentrating on the East, France and England launched a series of small attacks throughout the year that resulted in a few gains and extremely heavy casualties. Wooed by both sides, Italy joined the Allies and declared war on the Central Powers on May 23 after signing the secret Treaty of London (April 26). This treaty gave Italy Austrian provinces in the north and some Turkish territory. Italian attacks against Austria in the Isonzo area towards Trieste were unsuccessful because of difficult terrain, and failed to lessen pressure on the Russians in the East.

The Eastern Front

On January 23, 1915, Austro-German forces began a coordinated offensive in East Russia and in the Carpathians. The two-pronged German assault in the north was stopped on February 27, while Austrian efforts to relieve their besieged defensive network at Przemysl failed when it fell into Russian hands on March 22. In early March, Russian forces under Nikolai Ivanov drove deeper into the Carpathians with inadequate material support.

German forces, strengthened by troops from the Western Front under August von Mackensen, began a move on May 2 to strike at the heart of the Russian Front. They used the greatest artillery concentration of the war at that time as part of their strategy. In June, Mackensen shifted his assault towards Lublin and Brest-Litovsk, while the German XII, X and Niemen armies moved toward Kovno in the Baltic. By August 1915, much of Russian Poland was in German hands.

In an effort to provide direct access to the Turks defending Gallipoli, Germany and Austria invaded Serbia in the early fall, aided by their new ally, Bulgaria. On October 7, the defeated Serbian army retreated to Corfu. Belated Allied efforts to ship troops from Gallipoli to help Bulgaria failed.

Command Changes

Allied frustration resulted in the appointment of Marshal Joseph Joffre as French Commander-in-Chief, and Field Marshal Douglas Haig as British Commander in December 1915.

The Eastern Mediterranean

Turkey entered the war on the Central Power side on October 28, 1914, which prevented the shipment of Anglo-French aid to Russians through the Straits.

The Western stalemate caused Allied strategists to look to the eastern Mediterranean for a way to break the military deadlock. Winston Churchill, Britain's First Lord of the Admiralty, devised a plan to seize the Straits of the Dardanelles to open lines to Russia, take Constantinople, and isolate Turkey. These unsuccessful efforts occured between February 19 and March 18, 1915.

On April 25, Allied forces invaded Gallipoli Peninsula in a different attempt to capture the Straits. Turkish troops offered strong resistance, and forced the Allies (after suffering 252,000 casualties) to begin a three week evacuation that began on December 20, 1915.

The Middle East, 1914 – 1916

In an effort to protect its petroleum interests in the Persian Gulf, an Anglo-Indian force took Al Basrals (Basra) in Southern Iraq in November 1915. The following year, British forces moved north and took Al Kut (Kut al Irnara) from Turkey on September 28. To counter failures on the Western Front, British forces now tried to take Baghdad, but were stopped by the Turks at Ctesiphon on November 22. Turkish forces besieged Al Kut on December 8, and captured it on April 29, 1916. Two-thirds of the 10,000 captured British POW's died of Turkish mistreatment.

THE WAR IN 1916

The Western Front

In order to break the stalemate on the Western Front and drain French forces in the effort, the Germans decided to attack the French fortress town of Verdun.

The Battle for Verdun lasted from February 21 to December 18, 1916. From February until June, German forces, aided by closely coordinated heavy artillery barrages, assaulted the forts around Verdun. The Germans suffered 281,000 casualties while the French, under Marshal Henri Petain, lost 315,000 while successfully defending their position.

To take pressure off the French, an Anglo-French force mounted three attacks on the Germans to the left of Verdun in July, September and November. After the Battle of the Somme (July 1 – November 18), German pressure was reduced, but at great loss. Anglo-French casualties totaled 600,000.

The Eastern Front

Initially, the Allies had hoped for a general coordinated attack on all fronts against the Central Powers. Now efforts centered on relieving pressure at Verdun and on the Italians at Trentino.

Orchestrated by Aleksei Brusilov, The Brusilov Offensive (June 4 – September 20) envisoned a series of unexpected attacks along a lengthy front to confuse the enemy. By late August, he had advanced into Galicia and the Carpathians. The number of enemy troops dead, wounded or captured numbered 1.5 million. Russian losses numbered 500,000.

Rumania entered the war on the Allied side as a result of Russian successes and the secret Treaty of Bucharest (August 17). This treaty specified that Rumania would get Translyvania, Bukovina, the Banat and part of the Hungarian Plain if the Allies won. The ensuing Rumanian thrust into Translyvania was pushed back, and on December 6, a German-Bulgarian army occupied Bucharest as well as the bulk of Rumania.

Central Powers Propose Peace Talks

The death of Austrian Emperor Franz Joseph on November 21 prompted his successor, Charles I, to discuss the prospect of peace terms with his allies. On December 12, the four Central Powers, strengthened by the fall of Bucharest, offered four separate peace proposals based on their recent military achievements. The Allies rejected them on December 30 out of a belief that they were insincere.

War on the High Seas, 1914 – 1916

Britain's naval strategy in the first year of the war was tototally disrupt German shipping world-wide with the aid of the French and the Japanese. Germany sought ways to defend itself and weaken Allied naval strength. By the end of 1914, Allied fleets had gained control of the high seas, which caused Germany to lose control of its colonial empire.

Germany's failure in 1914 to weaken British naval strength prompted German naval leaders to begin to use the submarine as an offensive weapon to weaken the British. On February 4, Germany announced a war zone around the British Isles, and advised neutral powers to sail there at their own risk. On May 7, 1915 a German submarine sank a British passenger vessel, the Lusitania because it was secretly carrying arms. There were 1201 casualties, including 139 Americans.

The United States protested the sinking as a violation of the Declaration of London (1909). After four months of negotiations, Germany agreed not to sink any passenger vessels without warning, and to help all passengers and crew to life boats. Germany shifted its U-boat activity to the Mediterranean.

The main naval battle of World War I was the Battle of Jutland/Skagerrak (May – June 1916). This confrontation pitted 28 British dreadnoughts and 9 cruisers against 16 German dreadnoughts and 5 cruisers. In the end, the battle was a draw, with England losing 14 ships and Germany 11. It forced the German High Sea Fleet not to venture out of port for the rest of the war. Instead, they concentrated on use of the U-boat.

New Military Technology

Germany, Russia, and Great Britain all had submarines, though the Germans used their U-boats most effectively. Designed principally for coastal protection, they increasingly used them to reduce British naval superiority through tactical and psychological means.

By the spring of 1915, British war planners finally awoke to the fact that the machine gun had become the mistress of defensive trench warfare. In a search for a weapon to counter trench defenses, the British developed tanks as an armored "land ship," and first used them on September 15, 1916, in the battle of the Somme. Their value was not immediately realized because there were too few of them to be effective, and interest in them waned. Renewed interest came in 1917.

Airplanes were initially used for observation purposes in the early months of the war. As their numbers grew, mid-air struggles using pistols and rifles took place, until the Germans devised a synchronized propeller and machine gun on its Fokker aircraft in May 1915. The Allies responded with similar equipment and new squadron tactics during the early days of the Verdun campaign in February 1916, and briefly gained control of the skies. They also began to use their aircraft for bombing raids against Zeppelin bases in Germany. Air supremacy shifted to the Germans in 1917.

During the first year of the war, the Germans began to use Zeppelin airships to bomb civilian targets in England. Though their significance was neutralized with the development of the explosive shell in 1916, Zeppelins played an important role as a psychological weapon in the first two years of the war.

In the constant search for methods to counter trench warfare, the Germans and the Allied forces experimented with various forms of internationally outlawed gas. On October 27, 1914, the Germans tried a nose/eye irritant gas at Neuve-Chapelle, and by the spring of 1915 had developed an asphyxiating lachaymatory chlorine gas at the battle of Spres. The British countered with a similar chemical at the battles of Champagne and Loos that fall. Military strategists initially had little faith in gas since its use depended heavily on wind conditions, which could change the direction of the gas at any moment. However, as they desperately struggled to find ways to break the deadlock on the Western Front, they devised tactics and protection methods that enabled them to integrate the use of gas into their strategy.

THE RUSSIAN REVOLUTIONS OF 1917

Two events that would have a dramatic impact on the war and the world were the February and October Revolutions in 1917. The former toppled the Romanov Dynasty and spawned that country's brief flirtation with democracy under the temporary Provisional Government. It collapsed later that year as a result of the October Revolution, which brought Lenin and his Bolshevik faction to power.

Plagued for centuries by a backward autocratic government and a rural serf economy, Russia seemed on the verge of dramatic change after Czar Alexander II (1855 – 1881) freed the serfs in 1861. Emancipation, however, coupled with other important government and social reforms, created chaos nationwide and helped stimulate a new class of violent revolutionaries bent on destroying the Tsarist system. Terrorists murdered Alexander II, which prompted the country's last two rulers, Alexander III (1881 – 1894) and Nicholas II (1894 – 1917) to turn the clock backward politically.

The Russo-Japanese War and the 1905 Revolution

In February 1904, war broke out between Russia and Japan over spheres-of-influence in Korea and Manchuria. Russia's inability to support adequately its military forces in Asia, coupled with growing battlefield losses, prompted a nationwide revolution after police fired on peaceful demonstrators in January 1905. A groundswell of strikes and demonstrations swept the country and neutralized the government, which was on the verge of collapse. Nicholas II survived because he agreed in his October Manifesto (October 30, 1905) to create a constitution, share power with a legislature (Duma), and grant civil rights. This decree defused the crisis and enabled the government to survive and rebuild its political base.

Era of Reaction and Reforms, 1906 – 1912

Once the czar diminished the threat to his throne, and felt more comfortable, he issued the Fundamental Laws (May 6, 1906), which severely limited the power of the Duma. Regardless, over the next eleven years, four growingly conservative Dumas met, and provided a tradition of constitutional governments for the country. This, blended with the emergence of workers' and soldiers' Soviets (councils), and political parties (Kadets, Constitutional Democrats; Octobrists), created an atmosphere of challenge and change for Russia. To counter this mood, the czar appointed Peter Stolypin as Prime Minister (1906 – 1911) to initiate mollifying reforms for the peasants and develop a private agricultural system throughout the country. These efforts, and an industrial boom, influenced Russia's economic potential for the better.

Rasputin and Upheaval, 1912 – 1914

The death of Stolypin in 1911, coupled with a governmental system incapable of dealing with new labor unrest associated with industrial development, brought to the fore a semi-illiterate holy man, Gregorii Rasputin. He seemed to possess powers to save the czar's hemophiliac son, Alexei, and obtained tremendous influence over the royal family.

RUSSIA AT WAR: THE HOME FRONT, 1914 – 1917

Russia's entrance into the World War was met with broad public acceptance and support. Serious problems, however, plagued the government, the military, and the economy that threatened to undermine a military effort that most expected would win the war in a matter of months.

The Military

The draft increased Russia's armed forces from 1,350,000 to 6,500,000 during the war, though the government was only able to equip fully a small percentage of these troops. In addition, the country's military leaders differed on whether to concentrate their efforts on the Austrians or the Germans. While in the field, commanders were handicapped by inadequate communication and maps. As a result, German drives in the spring and summer of 1915 saw Russian spirit collapse as defensive efforts proved ineffective. However, by the end of that year, High Command personnel changes, aided by new industrial output, enabled the Russians to briefly turn the tide of battle.

The Civilian Economy

At first, Russian agricultural production proved adequate for the war's needs, but in time, because of growing labor shortages, production of foodstuffs fell by one-third.

The military only received about one-half of their grain requests because of the collapse of the transportation system. Regardless, by 1917, the country still had enough food for its military and civilian population. Skilled labor shortages, the loss of Poland, and inadequate government planning kept industry from producing the material necessary to supply the military. Consequently, despite a trade surplus in 1914, Russia encumbered a trade deficit of 2.5 billion rubles by 1917 from its Allies.

The Government and the Bureaucracy

As the country's problems mounted, the czar responded by assuming direct command of his army on the front in September 1915, leaving the government in the hands of his wife, Alexandra, and Rasputin. Those in government who appeared critical of the czar's policies were dismissed, and in time the country lost its most effective leaders. The Duma, which was forced to assume more and more leadership responsibilities, formed the Progressive Bloc, a coalition mainly of Kadets and Octobrists, in an effort to try to force the czar to appoint more competent officials. The Czar's refusal to accept this group's proposals led to increasing criticism of his policies. In November 1916, distant relatives of the czar and a Duma member secretly murdered Rasputin.

THE FEBRUARY REVOLUTION

The February Revolution, so named because the Russian calendar at the time was 13 days behind that of the West, was a spontaneous series of events that forced the collapse of the Romanov Dynasty.

Riots and Strikes

Growing discontent with the government's handling of the war saw a new wave of civilian unrest engulf the country. Estimates are that 1,140 such occurrences swept Russia in January and February, which prompted officials to send extra troops into Petrograd (old St. Petersburg) to protect the royal family. Particularly troublesome were food riots. Military and police units ordered to move against the mobs either remained at their posts or joined them.

The Duma

Though ordered by the czar not to meet until April, Duma leaders began to demand dramatic solutions to the country's problems. Its President, M. V. Rodzianko, was in constant consultation with the czar about the growing crisis. On March 12, he informed Nicholas II that civil war had broken out, and that he needed to create a new cabinet responsible to the legislature. Though dissolved on March 11, the Duma met in special session on March 13 and created a Provisional Committee of Elders to deal with the unrest. After two days of discussions, it decided that the czar must give up his throne, and on March 15, 1917, Rodzianko and A. I. Guchkov, leader of the Octobrist Party, convinced the czar to abdicate. He agreed and turned the throne over to his brother, the Grand Duke Michael, who gave it up the following day.

THE PROVISIONAL GOVERNMENT IN POWER (MARCH – NOVEMBER, 1917)

From March through November 1917, a temporary Provisional Government ruled Russia. It tried to move the country towards democracy and keep Russia in the war as a loyal western ally.

Leadership

The principle figures in the new government were Prince George Lvov, a Kadet Party and *zemstvo* leader, who served as Prime Minister and Minister of the Interior; Paul Miliukov, head of the Kadet Party, Foreign Minister; A.I. Guchkov, an Octobrist leader, Minister of War; and Alexander Kerensky, a conservative Socialist Revolutionary and Vice-Chairman of the Petrograd Soviet, Minister of Justice.

Problems

The Provisional Government was made up of middle class and intellectual leaders, and had little contact or sympathy with the problems or concerns of the workers or peasants. Its leaders, particularly Miliukov, felt the government had to remain a loyal ally and stay in the war to maintain its international credibility. Despite pressure to redistribute land, Lvov's government felt that it did not have the authority to deal with this complex issue. Instead, it left the problem to a future Constituent Assembly that would convene within a year. The Provisional Government did, however, implement a number of far-reaching reforms, including full political and religious freedom, election of local officials, an eight hour working day, and legal and judicial changes.

THE PETROGRAD SOVIET

On the eve of Nicholas II's abdication, a "shadow government," the Petrograd Soviet, was formed from among the capital's workers, and took control of the city administration. Briefly, it shared the Tauride Palace with the Provisional Government.

Creation

On March 13, delegates were elected to a Soviet of Worker's Deputies, later renamed the Soviet of Workers and Soldiers Deputies. It was made up of 1,300 representatives, and grew to 3,000 the following week with the addition of military delegates. Because of its size, the Petrograd Soviet created an Executive Committee headed by N.S. Chkeidze, a Menshevik, to make its most important decisions.

Policies

In response to an unsuccessful request to the Provisional Government to absolve soldiers from potentially treasonous actions during the March Revolution, the Petrograd Soviet issued Order No. I (March 14) that granted them amnesty and stated that officers were to be elected by their units. It later issued Order No. II for units throughout the country. These decrees, hesitatingly approved later by the Provisional Government, caused a significant collapse of discipline in the armed forces.

LENIN RETURNS TO RUSSIA

Vladimir Ilyich Ulyanov (Lenin) (1870 – 1924) became involved in revolutionary activity after the execution of his brother for an assassination plot against Alexander III. A committed Marxist, he split with the Menshevik wing of the Russian Social Democratic Party and formed his "Bolshevik" (majority) faction in 1903. Lenin felt the party should be led by a committed elite. He spent much of the period between 1905 and 1917 in exile, and was surprised by the February Revolution. However, with the aid of the Germans, he and some followers were placed in a sealed train and transported from Switzerland via Stockholm to Russia.

The April Theses

On April 16, Lenin arrived at Petrograd's Finland Station and went into hiding. The next day, he proposed his April Theses to the city's Bolshevik leaders, who rejected them. Lenin felt that the Bolsheviks should oppose the Provisional Government and support the theme "All Power to the Soviets." The Soviets, he concluded, should control the government while the war should become a revolution against capitalism, with all soldiers on both sides joining the struggle. In addition, he wanted the country's land, factories, and banks to be nationalized, and the Bolshevik Party should begin to call itself the Communist Party.

THE FIRST COALITION

Paul Miliukov's decision on May 1 to insure the Allies that his country would not sign a separate agreement with Germany and continue to fight until a "decisive victory" was won, caused public demonstrations that forced his resignation and the Lvov government to disavow his note. The Soviet now permitted its members to join the Provisional Government, a new one, known as the First Coalition, and was formed under Prince Lvov that included nine non-socialists and six socialist representatives. Some of its more prominent members were: Alexander Kerensky, who now became Minister of War and the Navy; Victor Chernov, a leading Socialist Revolutionary, now Minister of Agriculture; M. I. Tereshchenko, previously Finance Minister, as Foreign Minister; and H. Tsereteli, the Menshevik leader and head of the Petrograd Soviet, as Minister of Posts and Telegraph. In many instances, the Coalition's new socialist members felt more loyal to the Petrograd Soviet than to the government itself.

THE JULY CRISES

Because of Allied pressure, the Provisional Government decided to mount an offensive on the Eastern Front to counter French military failures and mutinies on the Western Front.

The July Offensive

Kerensky, determined to revive the Russian army, toured the front to rally his forces, and created special "shock" battalions to lead them into battle. On July 1, Russian forces attacked the Austrians in the Lvov area of Galicia and initially scored some successes, though within 12 days the Russian advance was halted, and a week later, Austro-German troops began to push the Russians back. Their retreat turned into a panic and desertions became rampant. The Provisional Government restored the death penalty on July 25 to stop this rupture in discipline, though it did little to stop the army's collapse.

The Second Coalition

In the midst of the July Offensive, the First Coalition collapsed. On July 16, four Kadet members resigned because of the Coalition's decision to grant the Ukraine quasi-federal status, while several days later, Prince Lvov stepped down as Prime Minister over the land question and efforts to strengthen Soviet influence in the Cabinet. Alexander Kerensky became Prime Minister, and twice made cabinet changes between July 25 and August 6. On August 22, he announced that elections for the Constituent Assembly would be on November 25, and that it would open on December 11.

The July Days

Prompted by the failures of the July offensive and the resignation of Kadet ministers from the Cabinet, military units and workers mounted a spontaneous protest against the Provisional Government on July 16. After hesitating, the Bolsheviks agreed to lead the demonstrations, which saw over 500,000 march on the Tauride Palace, demanding that the Petrograd Soviet seize power. The Soviet leaders refused, and on July 18 troops loyal to the Provisional Government put the demonstrations down. Afterwards, the government claimed that Bolshevik leaders were German agents, and tried to arrest them. Many top Bolsheviks went underground or fled abroad.

THE SECOND COALITION AND THE KORNILOV AFFAIR

In an effort to rebuild support for his government, Kerensky decided to call a meeting of delegates representing numerous organizations from throughout the country in late August. The rifts that developed there led to the Kornilov Crisis several weeks later.

The Moscow State Conference (August 26 – 28)

In an effort to find an alternative base of support for the Petrograd Soviet before elections to the Constituent Assembly, Kerensky convened the Moscow State Conference on August 26.

Over 2,000 delegates, representing the Duma, the military, the Soviets, the professions and other groups, met in Moscow. The Bolsheviks opposed the meeting and responded with a general strike.

The conference accentuated the growing difference between Kerensky and the conservatives, who looked to the government's Commander-in-Chief, General Lavr Kornilov, as a leader. Kornilov represented elements who decried the collapse of military discipline and left the Moscow Conference convinced that Kerensky did not have the ability to restore order and stability to the nation and the military.

The Kornilov Affair

The mutual suspicion between Kerensky and Kornilov resulted in a series of indirect, unofficial negotiations between the two that ended in Kornilov's dismissal on September 9. Kornilov responded by ordering his Cossack and "Savage" divisions to march to Petrograd to stop a Bolshevik coup. The Petrograd Soviet rallied to save the revolution, and freed the Bolsheviks from prison to help with defense preparations. Kornilov's coup collapsed, and he surrendered on September 14. Kerensky now became Supreme Commander-in-Chief.

The Third Coalition

On September 14, Kerensky restructured his government as a temporary Directory of Five, and declared Russia a Republic. Thirteen days later, he convened a large gathering of 1,200 representatives from throughout the country to rebuild his power base. From it emerged a Third Coalition government on October 8, that consisted of Socialist Revolutionaries, Mensheviks, Kadets, and ministers without ties to any faction. The conference also decided to establish a Council of the Russian Republic or preparliament with 555 delegates that would open on October 20. The Bolsheviks and other leftists opposed these efforts, which weakened Kerensky's efforts.

THE BOLSHEVIK OCTOBER REVOLUTION

The Kornilov affair and Kerensky's failure to rebuild support for the Provisional Government convinced the Bolshevik's two leaders, Lenin and Leon Trotsky, that now was the time for them to attempt to seize power.

Lenin's Decision to Seize Power

After learning that the II All-Russian Congress of Soviets of Workers and Soldiers Deputies would open on November 7, Lenin began to think of a simultaneous seizure of power, since he was convinced that while the Bolsheviks could dominate that II Soviet Congress, they would not be able to do the same with the Constituent Assembly that was to open later. On October 23 – 24, he returned from Finland to meet with the Party's Central Committee to plan the coup. Though he met with strong resistance, the Committee agreed to create a Political Bureau (Politburo) to oversee the revolution.

Trotsky and the Military Revolutionary Committee

Leon Trotsky, head of the Petrograd Soviet and its Military Revolutionary Committee, convinced troops in Petrograd to support Bolshevik moves. While Trotsky gained control of important strategic points around the city, Kerensky, well-informed of Lenin's plans, finally decided on November 6 to move against the plotters.

The Coup of November 6 – 7

In response, Lenin and Trotsky ordered their supporters to seize the city's transportation and communication centers. The Winter Palace was captured later that evening, along with most of Kerensky's government.

The II Congress of Soviets

The II Congress opened at 11 p.m. on November 7, with Lev Kamenev, a member of Lenin's Politburo, as its head. Over half (390) of the 650 delegates were Bolshevik supporters, and its newly selected 22 member Presidium had 14 Bolsheviks on it. Soon after the II Congress opened, many of the moderate socialists walked out in opposition to Lenin's coup, leaving the Bolsheviks and the Left Socialist Revolutionaries in control of the gathering. Lenin now used the rump Congress as the vehicle to announce his regime.

At the Congress, it was announced that the government's new Cabinet, officially called the Council of People's Commissars (Sovnarkom), and responsible to a Central Executive Committee, would include Lenin as Chairman or head of government, Trotsky as Foreign Commissar, and Josef Stalin as Commissar of Nationalities. The Central Executive Committee of 101 (later 110) delegates would be the government's temporary legislature. The II Congress also issued two decrees on peace and land. The first called for immediate peace without any consideration of indemnities or annexations, while the second adopted the Socialist Revolutionary land program that abolished private ownership of land and decreed that a peasant could only have as much land as he could farm. Village councils would oversee distribution.

THE CONSTITUENT ASSEMBLY

The Constituent Assembly, long promised by the Provisional Government as the country's first legally elected legislature, presented serious problems for Lenin, since he knew the Bolsheviks could not win a majority of seats in it. Regardless, Lenin allowed elections for it to be held on November 25 under universal suffrage. Over 41,000,000 Russians voted. The SR's got 58% of the vote, the Bolsheviks 25%, the Kadets and other parties, 17%. The Assembly was to open on January 18, 1918, though for the next seven weeks, the Bolsheviks did everything possible to discredit the election results. When it convened on January 18 in the Tauride Palace, the building was surrounded by Red Guards and others. The Assembly voted down Bolshevik proposals and elected Victor Chernov, a Socialist Revolutionary, as president. The Bolsheviks walked out. After it adopted laws on land and peace, and declared the country a democratic federal republic, it was adjourned until the next day. When the delegates later returned to the Tauride Palace, they found it surrounded by troops, who announced that the Constituent Assembly was dissolved.

WORLD WAR I: THE FINAL PHASE, 1917 – 1918

In early 1917, the new French commander, General Robert Nivelle, altered the earlier policy of attrition against the Germans, and began to plan distracting Somme attacks with a major assault against the Germans at Champagne. These plans caused friction with Field Marshal Douglas Haig, who had a different strategy and resented serving under Nivelle.

The French Offensive

The Champagne offensive began near Reims on April 16. By May 9, it failed at the second Battle of the Aisne. As a result, a series of mutinies broke out in the French army (May 3 – 20) that forced the replacement of Nivelle for Marshal Henri Petain, who restored order.

The British Offensive

To shore up the failing French battle effort, General Haig began a series of attacks in Flanders on June 7 that resulted in the capture of Messines Ridge the following day. Against French wishes, Haig began a new series of unsuccessful assaults (Third Battle of Ypres from July 31 to November 4) that were designed to capture the Flemish port cities of Ostend and Zeebrugge. These attempts ultimately failed. He did succeed in capturing the Passchendaele Ridge and seriously damaged the strength of the German 4th Army, though his own troops suffered heavy loses.

The Italian Front and the Battle of Caporetto

In response to increased Italian attacks against Austro-Hungary in the Isonzo area in August and September 1917, the German High Command decided to strengthen Central Power resistance with troops from the Eastern Front to defeat the Italians. Consequently, on October 24, a Central Power campaign began at Caporetto, which resulted in an Italian retreat through November 12 and the capture of 250,000 Italians. The loss convinced the Allies to form a Supreme War Council at Versailles to enhance Allied cooperation.

The Tank Battle of Cambrai

From November 20 to December 3, the largest tank battle of the war took place at Cambrai involving 400 British tanks. After breaking through the German Hindenburg Line, a German counter offensive on November 30 pushed the British back.

THE MIDDLE AND NEAR EAST, 1917

Mesopotamia

The British revived their Mesopotamian campaign in 1917 and retook Al Kut on February 23. They captured Baghdad on March 11.

Palestine

British forces in Palestine unsuccessfully attacked Gaza on March 26 – 27, and reassaulted it with the same consequences on April 17 – 19. In the third offensive against Gaza from October 31 to November 7, Turkish forces retreated, which opened the way for a British attack on Jerusalem. While Col. T.E. Lawrence worked to stir Arab passions against the Turks, General Sir Edmund Allenby took Jerusalem on December 9 – 11.

THE U.S. ENTERS THE WAR

American Neutrality

Woodrow Wilson, the American President, issued a declaration of neutrality four days after war broke out in 1914, and offered to work to settle differences between both sides.

The U.S. and Freedom of the Seas

As the war expanded into the Atlantic, Allied efforts to stifle Central Power trade and the German use of the submarine created problems for the United States. In October 1914, President Wilson asked both sides to abide by the Declaration of London (1909) which laid out rules of actions and rights for neutrals and belligerents in war. Germany and its allies agreed to accept its terms because of their inferior naval strength, while the Allied powers refused.

Germany and Submarine Warfare

Throughout the latter part of 1915 and 1916, the U.S. was able to restrict most German submarine activity in the Atlantic because Berlin wanted to avoid any crisis that might bring America into the war. However, the failure of peace initiatives at the end of that year convinced German leaders, who felt their submarine fleet was now capable of a successful full blockade of England, to reinstitute unlimited submarine warfare in the Atlantic on January 31, 1917. Though they knew this policy would probably bring the U.S. into the war, they felt they could defeat Great Britain well before the U.S. could significantly alter its course.

The Zimmerman Telegram

On March 2, British intelligence published the Zimmerman Telegram, a note from the German Foreign Minister to his ambassador in Mexico that ordered him to seek an alliance with that country that would allow Mexico to seize the American Southwest if the U.S. entered the war. The message, which was revealed several days after a number of Americans died on the *Laconia* from a U-boat attack, helped – along with the creation of a democratic Provisional Government in Russia – convince the president and American public opinion that it was now time to enter the war. The United States did enteredthe war on April 6, 1917.

RUSSIA LEAVES THE WAR

One of the cornerstones of Bolshevik propaganda throughout 1917 was a promise to end the war after they had seized power. Once in control, Soviet authorities issued a decree that called for immediate peace "with no indemnities or annexations" at the II Congress of Soviets on November 8, 1917.

The Armistice at Brest-Litovsk

As order collapsed among Russian units along the Eastern Front, the Soviet government began to explore cease fire talks with the Central Powers. Leon Trotsky, the Commissar of Foreign Affairs, offered general negotiations to all sides, and signed an initial armistice as a prelude to peace discussions with Germany at Brest-Litovsk on December 5, 1917.

Trotsky and Initial Peace Negotiations with Germany

Trotsky, who replaced Adolf Joffe as principal delegate soon after talks began, felt he could utter a few revolutionary phrases and close up shop. He was shocked by German demands for Poland, Lithuania and Kurland when negotiations opened on December 22, 1917. This prompted him to return to Moscow for consultations with the Bolshevik leadership.

Soviet Differences Over Peace Terms

Three different perspectives emerged over the German peace terms among the Soviet leadership. One group, led by Nikokai Bukharin, wanted the conflict to continue as a revolutionary war designed to spread Bolshevism. Lenin, however, felt the country needed peace for his government to survive. Western revolution would take place later. Trotsky wanted a policy of no war and no peace.

At a Bolshevik meeting on January 21, 1918, the Soviet leadership barely selected Bukharin's proposal, while the Central Committee overrode this decision on January 24 in favor of Trotsky's proposal.

Negotiations Resume at Brest-Litovsk

Trotsky returned to the peace talks and tried to stall them with his no war, no peace theme. He left Brest-Litovsk on February 10, and eight days later, the Germans responded with broad attacks all across the Eastern Front that met with little Soviet opposition.

The Soviet Response and the Treaty of Brest-Litovsk

On the day the German offensive began, Lenin barely convinced Party leaders to accept Germany's earlier offer. Berlin responded with harsher ones, which the Soviets grudgingly accepted, and were integrated into the Treaty of Brest-Litovsk of March 3, 1918. According to its terms, in return for peace, Soviet Russia lost its Baltic provinces, the Ukraine, Finland, Byelorussia, and part of Transcaucasia. The area lost totalled 1,300,000 square miles and included 62 million people.

THE ALLIED BREAKTHROUGH

By the end of 1917, the Allied war effort seemed in disarray. The French and Italian governments had changed hands in an effort to revive war spirits, while an Anglo-French force arrived to stop the Central advance after Caporetto. To strengthen Allied resolves, the United States declared war on Austro-Hungary on December 6, 1917, while the Allies developed new mining policies to handicap German U-boat movements.

The American Presence: Naval and Economic Support

The United States, which had originally hoped that it could simply supply the Allies with naval and economic support, made its naval presence known immediately and helped Great Britain mount an extremely effective blockade of Germany and, through a convoy system, strengthened the shipment of goods across the Atlantic.

Despite the difficulties of building a military system from scratch, the United States was slowly able to transform its peacetime army of 219,665 men and officers into a force of 2 million. An initial token group, the American Expeditionary Force under General John J. Pershing, arrived in France on June 25, 1917, while by the end of April 1918, 300,000 Americans a month were placed as complete divisions alongside British and French units.

The German Offensive of 1918

Emboldened by their victory over Russia, the German High Command decided to launch an all-out offensive against the Allies in France to win the war.

Strengthened by forces from the Russian front, Erich Ludendorff, the Germans' principal war planner, intended to drive his divisions, which outnumbered the Allies 69 to 33, between the British and the French, and push the former to the Channel.

Beginning on March 21, 1918, Ludendorff mounted four major attacks on the Allied forces in France: Somme (March 21 – April 4), Lys (April 9 – 29), Aisne (May 27 – June 6), and Champagne-Marne (July 15 – 17). The success of the assaults so concerned the Allies that they appointed the French Chief of Staff, Ferdinand Foch, Generalissimo of Allied Forces on April 14. In the third attack on Aisne, the Germans came within 37 miles of Paris. However, the increasing appearance of fresh, though untried American forces, combined with irreplaceable German manpower losses, began to turn the war against the Germans. Four days after the decisive German crossing of the Marne, Foch counterattacked and began to plan for an offensive against the Germans.

The Allied Offensive of 1918

Stirred by the successes on the Marne, the Allies began their offensive against the Germans at Amiens on August 8, 1918. Ludendorff, who called this Germany's "dark day," soon began to think of ways to end the fighting. By September 3, the Germans retreated to the Hindenburg Line. On September 26, Foch began his final offensive, and took the Hindenburg Line the following day. Two days later, Ludendorff advised his government to seek a peace settlement. Over the next month, the French took St. Quetin (October 1), while the British occupied Cambrai, Le Cateau, and Ostend.

On September 14, Allied forces attacked in the Salonika area of Macedonia and forced Bulgaria to sue for peace on September 29.

On September 19, General Allenby began an attack on Turkish forces at Megiddo in Palestine and quickly defeated them. In a rapid collapse of Turkish resistance, the British took Damascus, Aleppo, and finally forced Turkey from the war at the end of October.

On October 24, the Italians began an assault against Austria-Hungary at Vitto Veneto and forced Vienna to sign armistice terms on November 3.

THE ARMISTICE WITH GERMANY

Several days after Ludendorff advised his government to seek peace, Prince Max of Baden assumed the German Chancellorship. On October 4, he asked President Wilson for an armistice, based on the American President's "Fourteen Points" of January 8, 1918. The Allies hesitatingly agreed to support the President's terms, with qualifications, which were given to the Germans on November 5. On November 11 at 11:00 a.m., the war ended on the Western Front.

THE COLLAPSE OF THE GERMAN MONARCHY AND THE CREATION OF THE GERMAN REPUBLIC

The dramatic collapse of German military fortunes had seriously undercut the credibility of the Kaiser, Wilhelm II, and strengthened the hand of the country's politicians. Stimulated by the growing threat of revolution after the German naval rebellion in Kiel on October 28, that had spread to the army, efforts were made to try to get the Kaiser to abdicate in hopes that this would enable Germany to receive better terms from the Allies. The Kaiser fled to army headquarters in Belgium, while on November 9 the Chancellorship was transferred to Friederich Ebert after his fellow socialist leader, Phillip Scheidemann, announced the creation of a German Republic on the same day.

THE PARIS PEACE CONFERENCE OF 1919 – 1920

To a very great extent, the direction and thrust of the discussions at the Paris Peace Conference were determined by the destructive nature of the war itself and the political responsibilities, ideals, and personalities of the principle architects of the settlements at Paris: President Woodrow Wilson of the United States, Prime Minister Lloyd George of Great Britain, Prime Minister/Minister of War Georges Clemenceau of France, and Prime Minister Vittorio Orlando of Italy.

As politicians, they reflected the general mood of victorious Europe's population, who wanted the principal Central Powers, Germany and Austria-Hungary, punished severely for this inhuman calamity. Total losses are not accurately known. Consequently, high and low estimates are given in some categories:

1) France: 1,500,000/1,363,000 dead and 4,797,800/4,660,800 wounded.

2) British Empire: 1,000,000/908,000 dead and 2,282,235/2,190,235 wounded.

3) Italy: 500,000/460,000 dead and 1,737,000/1,697,000 wounded.

4) United States: 116,708/100,000 dead and 104,000/87,292 wounded.

5) Russia: 1,700,000 dead and 7,450,000 wounded.

6) Germany: 2,000,000/1,774,000 dead and 5,368,558/5,142,588 wounded.

7) Austria-Hungary: 1,250,000/1,200,000 dead and 5,820,000/5,770,000 wounded.

WOODROW WILSON AND THE FOURTEEN POINTS

Not handicapped by significant financial or territorial concerns, Wilson idealistically promoted his Fourteen Points that he issued on January 8, 1918 – particularly the last, which dealt with a League of Nations – as the basis of the armistice and the peace settlement. They included 1) Open Covenants of Peace; 2) Freedom of the Seas; 3) Removal of Trade Barriers; 4) Arms Reduction; 5) Settlement of Colonial Claims; 6) Evacuation of Russia; 7) Restoration of Belgium; 8) Return of Alsace-Lorraine to France; 9) Adjustment of Italy's Borders along Ethnic Lines; 10) Autonomy for the Peoples of Austria-Hungary; 11) Evacuation and Restoration of the Balkans; 12) Autonomy for the Non-Turkish Parts of the Turkish Empire; 13) Independent Poland with an Outlet to the Sea; and 14) a League of Nations.

SECRET ALLIED AGREEMENTS CONCLUDED DURING WORLD WAR I

Throughout the war, the Allied powers had concluded a number of secret agreements designed to encourage countries to join their side or as compensation for war efforts. In March 1915, England and France had promised Russia Constantinople, the Straits, and the bordering areas as long as they were openly accessible. In April of the following year, England and France had promised one another, respectively, spheres in Mesopotamia and Palestine, as well as Syria, Adana, Cilia, and southern Kurdistan. The Sykes-Picot Treaty in May 1916 better defined both countries' Arabian spheres. Russia was to have similar rights in Armenia, portions of Kurdistan, and northeastern Anatolia. The Allies gave Italy and Rumania significant territories to encourage them in their war effort in April 1915 and August 1916, while the English promised to support Japan's desire for Germany's Asian possessions. France and Russia agreed to promote one another's claims at a future peace conference, while Arab independence and creation of a Jewish homeland were also promised to others.

PRELIMINARY DISCUSSIONS

The sudden, unexpected end of the war, combined with the growing threat of communist revolution throughout Europe created an unsettling atmosphere at the conference. As a result of the Bolshevik victory in Russia, delegates from the United States, England, France, Italy, and later Japan, hurriedly began informal peace discussions on January 12, 1919. In time, this group was transformed into a Council of Ten, consisting of two representatives from each of these countries. This body conducted most of the significant talks in Paris until March 24, 1919, when the "Big Four" of Wilson (U.S.), Clemenceau (France), Lloyd-George (England), and Orlando (Italy) took over the discussions. Initially, the Allied Powers had hoped for a negotiated settlement with the defeated powers, which necessitated hard terms that would be negotiated down. However, the delays caused by uncertainty over direction at the beginning of the conference, Wilson's insistence that the League of Nations be included in the settlement, and fear of European-wide revolution resulted in a hastily prepared, dictated peace settlement.

France and the Rhineland Conflict

Once talks began among the Big Four, France insisted on the return of Alsace-Lorraine from Germany and the creation of an independent buffer state along the Rhine to protect it from Germany. The United States and Great Britain opposed these claims because they felt it could lead to future Franco-German friction. In return for an Allied guarantee of France's security against Germany, France got the Saar coal mines, and the demilitarization of the Rhine, with portions occupied by the Allies for fifteen years.

German Disarmament

Lloyd-George and Wilson saw German arms reductions as a prelude to a European-wide plan after the conference. They also opposed the draft, though agreed with the French about the need for a small German army.

Reparations

Each of the major powers had differing views on how much compensation Germany should pay for war indebtedness. At British insistence, civilian losses were added to the normal military ones. The "War Guilt" clause, Article 231, was included to justify heavy reparations, while the actual determination of the amount was left to a Reparations Commission.

THE TREATY OF VERSAILLES

The Treaty of Versailles, which was only between Germany and the Allied powers, had fifteen major sections, and almost 450 articles. Any country that ratified it, in turn accepted these terms as well as the League of Nations' Covenant in the first article: 1) Covenant of the League of Nations; 2) Boundaries of Germany; 3) Other Territories of Germany; 4) Germany's Overseas Boundaries and Rights; 5) Germany's Military and Naval Restrictions; 6) Prisoners of War; 7) War Guilt; 8) Reparations; 9) Costs of the War; 10) Customs Agreement and Other Covenants; 11) Aerial Navigation; 12) Freedom of Movement on Europe's Waterways; 13) Labor Organizations; 14) Guarantees; and 15) Mandates for German Colonies and Other General Provisions.

Most Significant Clauses

The treaty's war guilt statements were the justification for its harsh penalties. The former German king, Wilhelm II, was accused of crimes against "international morality and the sanctity of treaties," while Germany took responsibility for itself and for its allies for all losses suffered by the Allied Powers and their supporters as a result of German and Central Power aggression.

Germany had to return Alsace and Lorraine to France and Eupen-Malmedy to Belgium. France got Germany's Saar coal mines as reparations, while the Saar Basin was to be occupied by the major powers for 15 years, after which a plebiscite would decide its ultimate fate. Poland got a number of German provinces and Danzig, now a free city, as its outlet to the sea. Additionally, Germany lost all of its colonies in Asia and Africa.

The German Army was limited to 100,000 men and officers with 12 year enlistments for the former and 25 for the latter. The General Staff was also abolished. The Navy lost its submarines and most offensive naval forces, and was limited to 15,000 men and officers with the same enlistment periods as the army. Aircraft and blimps were outlawed. A Reparations Commission was created to determine Germany's war debt to the Allies, which it figured in 1921 to be $31.4 billion, to be paid over an extended period of time. In the meantime, Germany was to begin immediate payments in goods and raw materials.

German Hesitance to Sign the Treaty

The Allies presented the treaty to the Germans on May 7, 1919, but Foreign Minister Count Brockdorff-Rantzau refused to sign it, precipitating a crisis on both sides. The Germans stated that its terms were too much for the German people, and that it violated the spirit of Wilson's Fourteen Points. After some minor changes were made, the Germans were told to sign the document or face an Allied advance into Germany. The treaty was signed on June 28, 1919, at Versailles.

TREATIES WITH GERMANY'S ALLIES

After the conclusion of the Treaty of Versailles, responsibility for concluding treaties with the other Central Powers fell on the shoulders of the Council of Foreign Ministers and later, the Conference of Ambassadors.

The Treaty of St. Germain (September 10, 1919)

The Allied treaty with Austria legitimized the breakup of the Austrian Empire in the latter days of the war and saw Austrian territory ceded to Italy and the new states of Czechoslovakia, Poland, and Yugoslavia. The agreement included military restrictions and debt payments.

Treaty of Neuilly (November 27, 1919)

Bulgaria lost territory to Yugoslavia and Greece and also had clauses on military limitations and reparations.

Treaty of Trianon (June 4, 1920)

The agreement with Hungary was delayed because of the communist revolution there in 1919 and Rumania's brief occupation of Budapest. Hungary lost two-thirds of its prewar territory in the agreement to Rumania, Yugoslavia, and Czechoslovakia, and became an almost purely Magyar nation. Reparations and military reduction terms were also in the accord.

Treaty of Sevres (August 10, 1920)

Turkey lost most of its non-Turkish territory, principally in the Middle and Near East, and saw the Straits and the surrounding area internationalized and demilitarized. The Turkish revolution of Mustafa Kemal Pasha ultimately saw its terms neutralized, and renegotiated, as the Treaty of Lausanne (July 24, 1923) with Turkey gaining territory in Anatolia, Smyrna, and Thrace.

PROBLEMS OF ALLIED UNITY: JAPAN, ITALY, AND THE U.S.

During and after the meetings in Paris that resulted in the Treaty of Versailles, disputes arose among the Allies that caused friction among them later.

Japan

During the treaty talks, Japan asked for Germany's Shantung Province in China, its Pacific colonies, and a statement on racial equality in the League Covenant. Japan got what it essentially wanted on the first two requests, despite protests from China on Shantung. However, Japan's request for a racial equality clause met strong opposition from the United States and some members of the British Commonwealth, who feared the impact of the statement on immigration. The proposal was denied, principally at the instigation of President Wilson.

Italy

The Italians came to Paris expecting full realization of the secret Treaty of London (1915), plus more. When Orlando proved stubborn on this matter, Wilson appealed directly to the Italian people regarding the issue on April 23, which prompted the Italian delegation to leave the conference temporarily. Italy got the Tyrol, as well as Istria and some Adriatic islands in the Treaty of Rapallo (December 12, 1920). Dalmatia, however, went to Yugoslavia, while Fiume was seized by the Italian patriot/poet Sabhiele D'Annunzio, on September 12, 1919. After a 14-month occupation he departed, leaving its destiny to Italy and Yugoslavia. The Treaty of Rome (January 27, 1924) divided the city between the two, with Italy getting the lion's share of the area.

The United States

Although public and political sentiment was initially in favor of the treaty and its League provisions, Wilson's failure to include Senate representatives in the negotiating, and fear of Presidential usurpation of Congressional war powers created suspicions between Republicans and the President. These suspicions, coupled with concern over the obligations of the United States in future European affairs (particularly those cited in Article X – which would, according to its opponents, give the United States no freedom of choice in deciding whether or not to intervene in world crises) prompted the Senate to reject it twice in 1919 and 1920, though by only seven votes on the latter occasion. The United States concluded a separate peace with Germany in 1921 and never joined the League, though it was active in some of its corollary organizations.

POLITICAL DEVELOPMENTS IN POST-WAR EUROPE, 1918 – 1929

England, 1918 – 1922

Like most other European powers that emerged from the First World War, England had a set of problems unique to its status as a nation absolutely dependent on trade and commerce for its economic well-being.

With the war at an end, the Coalition government of David Lloyd George held the first parliamentary elections since 1910. Known as the "Coupon" or "Khaki" elections, the question of victory, the nature of the settlement with Germany, and the Prime Minister himself were the election's burning issues. Before it took place, the Representation of the Peoples Act granted women over 30 the right to vote. Lloyd George and his Conservative Coalition won a landslide victory (478 seats) while his opponents gained only 87.

Afterwards, England enjoyed an economic boom fueled by government policies and economic production based on pre-war conditions. Unfortunately, government retrenchment, blended with tax increases and over production, resulted in a severe recession by the end of 1921. It began in 1920 with almost 700,000 unemployed by the end of that year and jumped to 2 million within months. Until the Depression, unemployment averaged 12% annually. This resulted in the passage of the Unemployment Insurance Acts (1920, 1922) for workers, and the construction of 200,000 subsidized housing units.

Triggered by the Easter Rebellion of 1916, the extremist Sinn Fein faction gained prominence in Ireland. In 1918, three quarters of its members elected to the British

Parliament instead declared Irish independence in Dublin. This prompted a civil war between the Irish Republican Army and the Black and Tan, England's special occupation forces there. The Lloyd George government responded with a Home Rule division of Ireland with two legislatures, which only the northern six counties accepted. In October 1921, London created the Irish Free State, from which Ulster withdrew, as a part of the British Commonwealth.

Politics, 1922 – 1924

These problems caused the Conservatives to withdraw from Lloyd George's coalition. Andrew Bonar-Law replaced him as head of a new Conservative government, though ill health forced him to resign in 1923, followed briefly by Stanley Baldwin. Continued unemployment and labor problems, coupled with a decline to adopt more protectionistic trade policies resulted in a significant doctrine in support for the Conservatives in the elections of November 1923. Baldwin resigned, followed in office by Ramsey MacDonald, head of the Labour Party. His minority government only lasted nine months, and fell principally because of his efforts to establish formal ties with Russia.

England and Stanley Baldwin, 1924 – 1929

Baldwin entered his second Prime Ministership with a solid electoral victory (411 Seats) and strong Conservative Party backing. The year 1925 marked a turn in the economic crisis, with an increase in prices and wages. The country's return to the gold standard, which made the pound worth too much, affected British trade. In May 1926, a general strike in support of miners who feared a dramatic drop in their already low wages swept the country. Baldwin refused to concede to the miners' demands, broke the strike, and in 1927 sponsored the Trade Unions Act, which outlawed such labor action. On the other hand, the government passed a number of pieces of social legislation that further allowed support for housing construction and expanded pensions through its Widows', Orphans', and Old Age Pensions Act (1925). It also passed new legislation in 1928 that gave women the same voting privileges as men. In foreign affairs, Baldwin cancelled the 1924 commercial agreement with the Soviet Union, and, as a result of Soviet espionage activities, broke formal ties with the USSR in 1927.

FRANCE

The human losses in the war deeply affected France because of a population growth slowdown that had begun in the mid-19th century. Robbed of the flower of its youth, the Third Republic reflected in its political life and foreign policy a country ruled by an aging leadership that sought comfort in its rich past.

The Bloc National, 1919 – 1924

The election of November 1919 represented a momentary shift rightward with the moderate-conservatives winning almost two-thirds of the seats in the Chamber of Deputies. The new government, headed by Premier Alexandre Millerand, was a coalition known as the Bloc National. Aristide Briand replaced Millerand in January 1921, but was removed a year later because of lack of firmness on the German reparations question and was succeeded by Raymond Poincare.

France had borrowed heavily during the war and spent great sums afterwards to rebuild its devastated economy. Unfortunately, it relied on German reparations to fund many of these costs. Problems with these repayments created a financial crisis that saw the French public debt increase accompanied by a steady decline in the value of the franc.

Growing Franco-German differences over Germany's willingness to meet its debt payments created friction between both countries and toppled the government of August Briand. In December 1922, Poincare declared Germany in default on its reparations payments. In January, France and Belgium occupied the Ruhr. Efforts to obtain payments in kind via Franco-Belgium operation of the Ruhr's mines and factories failed because of passive resistance by German workers in the area. The Ruhr's occupiers gained little more financially in payments than they had through normal means, and found the cost of occupation expensive. Consequently, the French government had to raise taxes 20% to cover the cost of the occupation.

The Cartel des Gauches, 1924 – 1926

Poincare's Ruhr occupation policy had divided French voters, while tax increases helped defeat the Bloc National in the May 1924 elections, though it did gain 51% of the popular vote. A Radical/Socialist coalition, the Cartel des Gauches, had majority control of the Chamber. It selected Edouard Herriot, a Radical leader, as Premier, while Millerand continued as President, and Aristide Briand as Foreign Minister. Millerand's interference in policy questions forced his removal on June 10, 1924, with his successor, Gaston Doumergne serving as President until 1931.

France's ailing economy was plagued by a declining franc and inflation. Herriot's efforts to raise direct taxes, force higher levies on the rich, and lower interest rates on government bonds met with radical opposition, which sought indirect tax increases and cuts in government expenditures. Herriot was removed from office on April 10, 1925, and replaced by Paul Painleve, who served for eight months.

Briand, who dominated French foreign affairs until 1932, pursued a policy of reconciliation with Germany and better relations with Europe's other pariah, the USSR. France granted diplomatic recognition to Soviet Russia in 1924, though relations quickly worsened because of the difficulty in getting the tsarist debt question resolved and the Soviets' use of their Paris embassy for espionage activities.

The Union Nationale, 1926 – 1928

The most crucial domestic problem faced by the Carte des Gauches was the declining franc, which by 1926 was only worth one-tenth of its prewar value. Its fall caused a political crisis so severe that the country had six cabinets over a nine month period. Consequently, on July 15, 1926, Briand resigned his premiership, succeeded by Poincare, who formed a Union National cabinet that had six former premiers in it. This coalition was backed by the Radicals as well as Conservatives and centrist parties in the legislature. To resolve the franc problem, the Chamber granted Poincare special authority. Over the next two years, he dramatically raised taxes and was able to get capital that had been taken out of the country reinvested in government bonds or other areas of the economy. By 1928, the franc had risen to 20% of its prewar value, and Poincare was considered a financial miracle worker. Unfortunately, the political and psychological scars left by the crisis would haunt France for two more decades.

WEIMAR GERMANY, 1918 – 1929

The dramatic collapse of the German war effort in the second half of 1918 ultimately created a political crisis that forced the abdication of the King and the creation of a German Republic on November 9.

Provisional Government

From the outset, the Provisional Government, formed of a coalition of Majority and Independent Socialists, was beset by divisions from within and threats of revolution throughout Germany. The first Chancellor was Friedrich Ebert, the Majority Socialist leader. On November 22, state leaders agreed to support a temporary government until elections could be held for a nationally elected legislature, which would draw up a constitution for the new republic.

Elections for the new National Constituent Assembly, which was to be based on proportional representation, gave no party a clear majority. A coalition of the Majority Socialists, the Catholic Center Party, and the German Democratic Party (DDP) dominated the new assembly. On February 11, 1919, the assembly met in the historic town of Weimar and selected Friedrich Ebert President of Germany. Two days later, Phillip Scheidermann formed the first Weimar Cabinet and became its first Chancellor.

On August 11, 1919, a new constitution was promulgated, which provided for a bicameral legislature. The upper chamber, the Reichsrat, represented the Federal states, while the lower house, the Reichstag, with 647 delegates elected by universal suffrage, supplied the country's Chancellor and Cabinet. A President was also to be elected separately for a 7-year term. As a result of Article 48 of the Constitution, he could rule through emergency decree, though the Reichstag could take this authority from him.

Problems of the Weimar Republic, 1919 – 1920

The new government faced a number of serious domestic problems that severely challenged or undercut its authority. Its forced acceptance of the hated Friedensdiktat ("the dictated peace") seriously undermined its prestige, while the unsuccessful, though violent Communist Spartikist Rebellion (January 5 – 11, 1919) in Berlin created a climate of instability. This was followed three months later by the brief communist takeover of Bavaria, and the rightist Kapp Putsch (March 13 – 17, 1920) in the capital the following year.

The territorial, manpower, and economic losses suffered during and after the war, coupled with a $30.4 billion reparations debt, had a severe impact on the German economy and society, and severely handicapped the new government's efforts to establish a stable governing environment.

In an effort of good faith based on hopes of future reparation payment reductions, Germany borrowed heavily and made payments in kind to fulfill its early debt obligations. The result was a spiral of inflation later promoted by the Weimar government to underline Allied insensitivity to Germany's plight, that saw the mark go from 8.4 to the dollar in 1919 to 7,000 marks to the dollar by December 1922. After the Allied Reparations Commission declared Germany in default on its debt, the French and the Belgians occupied the Ruhr on January 11, 1923.

Chancellor Wilhelm Cuno encouraged the Ruhr's Germans passively to resist the occupation, and printed worthless marks which dropped from 40,000 to the dollar in January 1923 to 4.2 trillion to the dollar eleven months later. The occupation ended on September 26, and helped prompt stronger Allied sympathy to Germany's payment difficulties, though the inflationary spiral had severe economic, social, and political consequences.

Weimar Politics, 1919 – 1923

Germany's economic and social difficulties deeply affected its infant democracy. From February 1919 to August 1923, the country had six Chancellors.

In the aftermath of the Kapp Putsch, conservative demands for new elections resulted in a June defeat for the ruling coalition that saw the Democrats (DDP) lose seats to the German National People's Party (DVP) headed by Gustav Stresemann, and the Majority Socialists lose seats to the more reactionary Independent socialists. Conservative Germans blamed the Weimar Coalition for the hated Versailles "Diktat" with its war guilt and reparations terms, while leftist voters felt the government had forgotten its social and revolutionary ideals.

Growing right-wing discontent with the Weimar Government resulted in the assassination of the gifted head of the Catholic Center Party, Matthias Erzberger, on August 29, 1921, and the murder of Foreign Minister Walter Rathenau on June 24, 1922. These were two of the most serious of over 350 political murders in Germany since the end of the war.

The Policies of Gustav Stresemann

The dominant figure in German politics from 1923 to 1929 was Gustav Stresemann, the founder and leader of the DVP. Though he served as Chancellor from August 12 to November 23, 1923, his prominence derives from his role as Foreign Minister from November 1923 until his death on October 3, 1929. He received the Nobel Peace Prize for his diplomatic efforts in 1926.

As Chancellor, Stressmann's felt that the only road to recovery and treaty revision lay in adherence to the Versailles settlement and positive relations with France and its allies. Consequently, on September 26, he ended passive resistance in the Ruhr and began to search for a solution to Germany's reparations payment problem with France. To restore faith in the currency, the government introduced a new one, the Rentenmark, on November 20, 1923, that was equal to 1 billion old marks, and was backed by the mortgage value of Germany's farm and industrial land.

In an effort to come up with a more reasonable debt payment plan for Germany, the Western Allies developed the Dawes Plan that accepted the need for Germany to pay its war debts and blended England's desire for balance with France's needs for repayment assurances. According to its terms, Germany was to begin small payments of a quarter of a billion dollars annually for four years, to be increased if its economy improved. In return, the Allies agreed to help revitalize Germany's ailing economy with a $200 million American loan and withdrawal from the Ruhr.

The crowning achievement in Stresemann's efforts to restore Germany to normal status in the European community was the Locarno Pact, December 1, 1925.

Weimar Politics, 1924 – 1928

Reichstag elections were held twice in 1924. The May 4 contest reflected a backlash against the country's economic difficulties, and saw the Communists win 3,700,000 votes and the Nazis almost 2 million, at the expense of the moderate parties. The December 7 elections were something of a vote on the Dawes Plan and economic revival, and saw the Nazis and the Communists lose almost a million votes apiece.

Following the death of President Ebert on February 28, 1925, two ballots were held for a new President, since none of the candidates won a majority on the first vote. On the second ballot on April 26, the Reichsblock, a coalition of Conservative parties, was able to get its candidate elected. War hero Paul von Hindenburg was narrowly elected against a Centrist coalition and the communists, who had a much smaller showing. Hindenburg, who some conservatives hoped would turn the clock back, vowed to uphold Weimar's Constitution.

The elections of May 20, 1928, saw the Social Democrats get almost one-third of the popular vote which, blended with other moderate groups, created a stable moderate majority in the Reichstag, which chose Hermann Muller as Chancellor. The Nazis, who held 14 Reichstag seats at the end of 1924, lost one, while Communist strength increased.

ITALY

Like other countries that had fought in the World War, Italy had suffered greatly and gained little. Its economy, very weak even before the war broke out, relied heavily upon small family agriculture which contributed 40% of the country's GNP in 1920. Consequently, many of the social, political, and economic problems that plagued the country after the war could not be blamed solely on the conflict itself.

Italian Politics, 1918 – 1919

As a result of growing discontent over the country's troubled economy, the Italian public looked to the parties that offered the most reasonable solutions. Strengthened by universal suffrage, and new proportional representation in Parliament, the Socialists doubled the number of seats to 156 in the Chamber of Deputies in the elections of November 16, 1919. The new Catholic People's Party gained 99 positions. The former party had little faith in the current state, and longed for its downfall, while the latter mixed conservative religious ideals with a desire for political moderation. Most importantly, no strong majority coalition emerged in this or the Parliament elected in May 1921 that was able to deal effectively with the country's numerous problems.

Government of Giovanni Giolitti, 1920 – 1921

From June 9, 1920 until June 26, 1921, Italy's Premier was Giovanni Giolitti, a gifted musician and pre-war figure who had dominated Italian politics between 1901 and 1914. His tactics, to resolve Italy's international conflicts and stay aloof of its domestic conflicts, exacerbated the country's problems. The Socialists took advantage of this atmosphere and promoted a series of strikes and other labor unrest in August and September 1920 that became violent and divided the country and the Socialist movement. Giolitti let the strikes run their course, and worked successfully to lower the government's deficit by 50%.

Benito Mussolini and Italian Fascism

Benito Mussolini, named by his Socialist blacksmith father after the Mexican revolutionary, Benito Juarez, was born in 1883. After a brief teaching stint, he went to Switzerland to avoid military service but returned and became active in Socialist politics. In 1912, he became editor of the Party's newspaper, *Avanti.* Several months after the outbreak of the World War, he broke with the party over involvement in the war, and began to espouse nationalistic ideas that became the nucleus of his fascist movement. He then opened his own newspaper, *Popolo d'Italia* (The People of Italy) to voice his ideas. Mussolini was drafted into military service in 1915, and was badly wounded two years later. After recuperating, he returned to his newspaper, where he blended his feelings about socialism and nationalism with an instinct for violence.

Italy's post-war conflict with its allies at the Paris Peace conference over fulfillment of the terms of the 1915 Treaty of London and the additional request for Fiume played into Mussolini's hands. Mussolini supported the D'Annunzio coup there.

Mussolini, capitalizing on the sympathy of unfulfilled war veterans, disaffected nationalists, and those fearful of communism, formed the Fascio di combattmento (Union of Combat) in Milan on March 23, 1919. Initially, Mussolini's movement had few followers, and it did badly in the November 1919 elections. However, Socialist strikes and unrest enabled him to convince Italians that he alone could bring stability and prosperity to their troubled country.

Fascism's most significant growth came in the midst of the Socialist unrest in 1920. Strengthened by large contributions from wealthy industralists, Mussolini's black-suited Squadristi attacked Socialists, communists, and ultimately, the government itself. Mussolini's followers won 35 seats in the legislative elections in May 1921, which also toppled the Giolitti cabinet.

The center of Fascist strength was in the streets of northern Italy, which Mussolini's followers, through violence, came to control. Mussolini now transformed his movement into the Fascist Party, dropped his socialist views, and began to emphasize the predominance of Italian nationalism.

The resignation of the Bonomi Cabinet on February 9, 1922, underlined the government's inability to maintain stability. In the meantime, the Fascists seized control of Bologna in May, and Milan in August. In response, Socialist leaders called for a nationwide strike on August 1, 1922, which Fascist street violence stopped in 24 hours. On October 24, 1922, Mussolini told followers that if he was not given power, he would "March on Rome." Three days later, Fascists began to seize control of other cities, while 26,000 began to move towards the capital. The government responded with a declaration of martial law, which the king, Victor Emmanuel III, refused to approve. On October 29, the king asked Mussolini to form a new government as Premier of Italy.

Mussolini's Consolidation of Power

Using tactics similar to those of D'Annunzio to seize Fiume earlier, Mussolini built a government made up of a number of sympathetic parties.

Mussolini formed a coalition cabinet that included all major parties except the Communists and the Socialists. After he assured the Chamber of Deputies that his government intended to respect personal liberties but with "dignity and firmness...," it approved his government in a 306 to 116 vote. Nine days later, the Chamber granted him quasi-dictatorial powers for a year.

To enhance his political control of the government, one of Mussolini's assistants, Giacomo Acerbo, successfully introduced a bill to the Chamber on July 21, 1923 (later approved by the Senate) that stated that the party that got the largest number of votes in a national election with a minimum of 25% of the votes cast would control two-thirds of the seats in the Chamber. Mussolini also began to remove non-Fascists from his Cabinet, the Civil Service, and other organs of government. The king kept his throne though Mussolini now became Head of State.

In violence-marred elections on April 6, 1924, the Fascists gained 60% of the popular vote and two-thirds of the Chamber's seats. In response to Fascist campaign tactics, Giacomo Matteotti, a Socialist Chamber member, attacked the Fascists for their misdeeds on May 30. Several days later, Fascist supporters kidnapped and murdered him, provoking his supporters, unwisely, to walk out of the Chamber in protest. Momentarily, Italy was stunned, and Mussolini was vulnerable. The opposition asked the king to dismiss Mussolini, but he refused.

Consolidation of the Dictatorship

On January 3, 1925 Mussolini accepted responsibility for events of the past year. He warned that this instability, caused by his opponents, would be quickly resolved. What followed was a new reign of terror that arrested opponents, closed newspapers, and eliminated basic civil liberties for Italians. On December 24, 1925, the legislature's powers were greatly limited, while those of Mussolini were increased as the new Head of State. Throughout 1926, Mussolini intensified his control over the country with legislation that outlawed strikes and created the syndicalist corporate system. A failed assassination attempt prompted the "Law for the Defense of the State" of November 25, 1926, that created a Special Court to deal with political crimes and introduced the death penalty for threats against the king, his family or the Head of State.

The Fascist Party

In December 1922, Mussolini created a Grand Council of Fascism made up of the Party's principle leaders. In 1928, the Grand Council became the most important organ of government in Italy. The structure of the Fascist Party did not reach final form until November 12, 1932. It was defined as a "civil militia" with the *Duce* (Mussolini) as its head. Its day-to-day affairs were run by the National Directorate headed by a Secretary, with two Vice Secretaries, an Administrative Secretary, and six other members. The Secretary of the National Directorate belonged to the Grand Council. The Party's Provincial Secretaries, appointed by Mussolini, oversaw local Party organizations, the *Fasci di Combattimento*. There were also separate Fascist youth organizations such as the *Piccole Italiane* (under 12) and the *Giovane Italiane* (over 12) for girls; the *Balilla* (8 – 14), the *Avanguardisti* (14 – 18), and the *Giovani Fascisti* (18 – 21) for boys. After 1927, only those who had been members of the *Balilla* and the *Avanguardisti* could be Party members.

The Syndicalist-Corporate System

In an effort to institutionalize his theories about relations between labor and management, Mussolini began to adopt some of the syndicalist theories of his followers. What emerged was a legal superstructure of labor-employer syndicates followed later by a series of government coordinated corporations to oversee the economy.

On April 3, 1926, the Rocco Labor Law created syndicates or organizations for all workers and employers in Italy. It also outlawed strikes and walkouts. Later altered, it created nine syndicate corporations: four for workers and four for employers in each of the major segments of the economy and a ninth for professionals and artists.

On July 1, 1926, Corporations were created to coordinate activities between the worker-employer syndicates, while later that year a Ministry of Corporations came into existence. On February 5, 1934, a Law on Corporations created 22 such bodies that oversaw every facet of the economy, coordinated management-labor relations, and economic production and shipment in every segment of the economy. Each Corporation was overseen by a Minister or other important government or Party official, who sat on the National Council of Corporations that was headed by Mussolini.

Foreign Policy

Some have called the first decade of Mussolini's reign the "time of good behavior." This was more because of his deep involvement in domestic affairs than his creative desire for foreign stability. This, plus the nation's wish for post-war peace and stability saw Italy participate in all of the international developments in the 1920's aimed at securing normalcy in relations with its neighbors.

Because Italy did not receive its desired portions of Dalmatia at the Paris Peace Conference, Italian Nationalist Gabriele D'Annunzio seized Fiume on the Adriatic in the fall of 1919. D'Annunzio's daring gesture as well as his deep sense of Italian national pride deeply affected Mussolini. However, in the atmosphere of detente prevalent in

Europe at the time, he agreed to settle the dispute with Yugoslavia in a treaty on January 27, 1924, which ceded most of the port to Italy, and the surrounding area to Yugoslavia.

In the fall of 1923, Mussolini used the assassination of Italian officials, who were working to resolve a Greek-Albanian border dispute, to seize the island of Corfu. Within a month, however, the British and the French convinced him to return the island for an indemnity.

SOVIET RUSSIA

Soon after the Bolshevik seizure of power, opposition forces began to gather throughout Russia that sought to challenge Soviet authority or use the occasion to breakup the Russian Empire.

Origins of the Russian Civil War, 1918

After Brest-Litovsk, Lenin's government agreed to ship part of a large group of Czech POW's through Vladivostok to the Western Front. On May 14, 1918, a brawl took place between these units and Hungarian POW's at Chelyabinsk in the Urals that led to a Czech rebellion against Soviet authorities and the seizure of the Urals area and eastern Siberia by late summer.

In the spring of 1918, Russia's old war allies had begun to land forces in Russia at major shipping points such as Murmansk, Archangel, and Vladivostok to protect supplies they had sent the Provisional Government. The Czech rebellion stirred the Allied leaders meeting at Paris to upgrade their efforts in Russia to aid the Czechs and other Communist opponents in a limited, and hopefully, non-combative manner. They began to land limited military contingents at the above ports, at Baku and in Odessa to support a victor that would revive the Eastern Front, and to a lesser degree, counterbalance Lenin's threatening communist movement.

Opposition to the Soviet takeover had begun immediately after Lenin's seizure of Petrograd. General M.V. Alexeev had formed a Volunteer Army, whose command was shared and later taken over by General Anton Denikin, who fled to the Don area in early 1918. Another center of White resistance was created first by Socialist Revolutionaries at Omsk, followed later by a government there under Admiral Alexander Kolchak, who was backed by Czech forces and would declare himself Supreme Commander of White forces in the Civil War. In time, most of the major White Commanders would recognize Kolchak's authority. General Eugune Miller created a White opposition outpost at Archangel, and General Nicholas Yudenich another in Estonia.

To meet these threats, Lenin appointed Leon Trotsky as Commissar of War on March 13, 1918, with orders to build a Red Army. By the end of the year, using partial conscription, the new Soviet forces began to retake some of the areas earlier captured by the Whites.

The Russian Civil War, 1919 – 1920

The White forces, constantly weakened by lack of unified command and strategy, enjoyed their greatest successes in 1919, when Deniken, operating from the south, took Kharkov and later Odessa and Kiev. On the other hand, Yudenich was driven from Petrograd, while Deniken lost Kharkov and Kiev. Kolchak had been defeated earlier, and Omsk was taken by November.

By early 1920, White fortunes had begun to collapse. On January 4, Kolchak abdicated in favor of Denikin, and was turned over by his Czech protectors to the Soviets who executed him on February 7. In the meantime, Denikin's capital, Rostov, was taken by the Red Army and his command was taken over later by General Peter Wrangel, whose forces were beaten that fall. Both armies were evacuated from the Crimea.

The Polish-Soviet War, 1920

The new Polish state under Marshal Joszef Pilsudski sought to take advantage of the Civil War in Russia to retake territory lost to Russia during the Polish Partitions in the late 18th century. Polish forces invaded the Ukraine on April 25, and took Kiev two weeks later. A Soviet counteroffensive reached Warsaw by mid-August, but was stopped by the Poles. Both sides concluded an armistice on October 12 and signed the Treaty of Riga on March 12, 1921 that placed Poland's border east of the Curzon Line.

Domestic Policy and Upheaval, 1918 – 1921

In order to provide more food to Russia's cities, the Soviet government implemented a "War Communism" program that centered around forced grain seizures and class war between "Kulaks" (ill-defined middle class peasants) and others. All major industry was also nationalized. These policies triggered rebellions against the seizures that saw the amount of land under cultivation and the total grain produced drop between 1918 – 1921.

The Civil War and War Communism had brought economic disaster and social upheaval throughout the country. On March 1, 1921, as the Soviet leadership met to decide on policies to guide the country in peace, a naval rebellion broke out at the Kronstadt naval base. The Soviet leadership sent Trotsky to put down the rebellion, which he did brutally by March 18.

The New Economic Policy, 1921 – 1927

The Kronstadt rebellion strengthened Lenin's resolve to initiate new policies approved at the X Party Congress that would end grain seizures and stimulate agricultural production. Termed the New Economic Policy (NEP), the government maintained control over the "Commanding Heights" of the economy (foreign trade, transportation, and heavy industry) while opening other sectors to limited capitalist development. It required the peasants to pay the government a fixed acreage tax, and allowed them to sell the surplus for profit. Once the government had resolved the inconsistencies in agricultural and industrial output and pricing, the NEP began to near 1913 production levels. The country remained dominated by small farms and peasant communes. Industrial production also improved, though it was handicapped by outdated technology and equipment which would hinder further output or expansion beyond 1913 levels.

The Death of Lenin and the Rise of Josef Stalin

Vladimir Ilyich Lenin, the founder of the Soviet State, suffered a serious stroke on May 26, 1922 and a second in December of that year. As he faced possible forced retirement or death, he composed a secret "testament" that surveyed the strengths and weaknesses of his possible successor, Stalin, who he feared would abuse power. Unfortunately, his third stroke prevented him from removing Stalin from his position as General Secretary. Lenin died on January 21, 1924.

Josef Visarionovich Dzugashvili (Stalin)(1879 – 1953) was born in the Georgian village of Gori. He became involved in Lenin's Bolshevik movement in his 20's and became Lenin's expert on minorities. Intimidated by the Party's intellectuals, he took over numerous, and in some cases, seemingly unimportant Party organizations after the Revolution and transformed them into important bases of power. Among them were

Politburo (Political Bureau), which ran the country; the Orgburo (Organizational Bureau), which Stalin headed, and which appointed people to positions in groups that implemented Politiburo decisions; the Inspectorate (Rabkrin, Commissariat of the Workers' and Peasants' Inspectorate), also under Stalin's control, which tried to eliminate Party corruption; and the Secretariat, which worked with all Party organs and set the Politburo's agenda. Stalin served as the Party's General Secretary after 1921.

Leon Trotsky

Lev Davidovich Bronstein (Trotsky) (1879 – 1940) was a Jewish intellectual active in Menshevik revolutionary work, particularly in the 1905 Revolution. He joined Lenin's movement in 1917, and soon became his right-hand man. He was Chairman of the Petrograd Soviet, headed the early Brest-Litovsk negotiating team, served as Foreign Commissar, and was father of the Red Army. A brilliant organizer and theorist, Trotsky was also brusque and, some felt, overbearing.

The Struggle for Power, 1924 – 1925

The death of Lenin in 1924 intensified a struggle for control of the Party between Stalin and Trotsky and their respective supporters. Initially, the struggle, which began in 1923, appeared to be betweenthree men. Kamenev, head of the Moscow Soviet, Zinoviev, Party chief in Petrograd and head of the Comintern, and Trotsky. The former two, allied with Stalin, presented a formidable opposition group to Trotsky.

Initially, the struggle centered around Trotsky's accusation that the trio was drifting away from Lenin's commitment to the revolution and "bureaucratizing" the Party. Trotsky believed in the theory of "permanent revolution" that blended an ongoing commitment to world revolution and building socialism with the development of a heavy industrial base in Russia.

Stalin responded with the concept of "Socialism in One Country," that committed the country to building up its socialist base regardless of the status of world revolution.

In the fall of 1924, Trotsky attacked Zinoviev and Kamenev for the drift away from open discussion in the Party and for not supporting Lenin's initial scheme to seize power in November 1917. As a result, Trotsky was removed as Commissar of War on January 16, 1925, while two months later the Party accepted "Socialism in One Country" as its official governing doctrine.

The Struggle for Power, 1925 – 1927

Zinoviev and Kamenev, who agreed with the principles of "Permanent Revolution," began to fear Stalin and soon found themselves allied against him and his new Rightist supporters, Nikolai Bukharin, Alexis Rykov, Chairman of the Council of People's Commisars (Cabinet), and Mikhail Tomsky, head of the trade unions.

The XIV Party Congress rebuffed Kamenev and Zinoviev, and accepted Bukharin's economic policies. It demoted Kamenev to candidate status on the Politburo, while adding a number of Stalin's supporters to that body as well as the Central Committee. Afterwards, Kamenev and Zinoviev joined Trotsky in their dispute with Stalin. As a result, Trotsky and Kamenev lost their seats on the Politburo, while Zinoviev was removed as head of the Comintern.

In early 1927, Trotsky and his followers accused Stalin and the Right of a "Thermidorian Reaction," Menshevism, and further criticized recent foreign policy failures in England and China. Trotsky and Zinoviev lost their positions on the Central Committee, which prompted them to participate in anti-Rightist street demonstrations on November 7, 1927. Both were then thrown out of the Party, followed by their supporters. Trotsky was forced into external exile in Central Asia, while Zinoviev and Kamenev, humiliated and defeated, begged successfully to be allowed to return to the fold.

At the XV Party Congress, Stalin indicated that the Party would now begin gradually to collectivize the country's predominantly small-farm agricultural system. His shocked Rightist allies, now outnumbered by Stalinists on the Politburo, sought an uncomfortable alliance with the defeated Left. Over the next two years, the major old Rightist allies of Stalin, Bukharin, Rykov, and Tomsky, lost their Politburo seats and other Party positions, and ultimately, their Party membership. Brief exile followed in some cases.

Soviet Constitutional Development

Soviet Russia adopted two constitutions in 1918 and 1924. The first reflected the ideals of the state's founders and created the Russian Soviet Federative Socialist Republic (RSFSR) as the country's central administrative unit. An All-Russian Congress of Soviets was the government's legislative authority, while a large Central Executive Committee (CEC), aided by a cabinet or Council of People's Commissars (Sovnarkom) wielded executive power. The Communist Party was not mentioned in the 1918 constitution or in the 1924 constitution. The 1924 document was similar to the earlier one, but also reflected the changes brought about by the creation of the Union of Soviet Socialist Republics (USSR) two years earlier. The CEC was divided into a Council of the Union and a Council of Nationalities, while a new Supreme Court and Procurator was added to the governmental structure. A similar political division was duplicated on lower administrative levels throughout the country. The new constitution also created a Supreme Court and a Procurator responsible to the CEC.

Foreign Policy, 1918 – 1929

Soviet efforts after the October Revolution to openly foment revolution throughout Europe and Asia, its refusal to pay Tsarist debts, and international outrage over the murder of the royal family in 1919 isolated the country. However, adoption of the NEP required more integration with the outside world to rebuild the broken economy.

Russia and Germany, Europe's post-World War I pariahs, drew closer out of necessity. By the early 1920's, Russia was receiving German technological help in weapons development while the Soviets helped train German pilots and others illegally. On April 16, 1922, Soviet Russia and Germany agreed to cancel their respective war debts and to establish formal diplomatic relations.

By 1921, the British concluded a trade accord with the Soviet government and in 1924 extended formal diplomatic recognition to the USSR. Strong public reaction to this move, coupled with the publication of the "Zinoviev Letter" of unknown origin helped topple the pro-Soviet MacDonald government, because the letter encouraged subversion of the British government. Relations were formally severed in 1927 because of Communist support of a British coal mine strike, discovery of spies in a Soviet trade delegation, and Soviet claims that it hoped to use China as a means of hurting England.

The Soviets worked to consolidate their sphere-of-influence acquired earlier in Mongolia, and helped engineer the creation of an independent, though strongly pro-Soviet, People's Republic of Mongolia in 1924.

In China, in an effort to protect traditional Asian strategic interests and take advantage of the chaotic "war lord" atmosphere in China, the Soviets helped found a young Chinese Communist Party (CCP) in 1921. However, when it became apparent that Sun Yat-sen's revolutionary Kuomintang (KMT) was more mature than the infant

CCP, the Soviets encouraged an alliance between its Party and this movement. Sun's successor, Chiang Kai-shek, was deeply suspicious of the Communists and made their destruction part of his effort militarily to unite China.

Founded in 1919, the Soviet-controlled Comintern (Third International or Communist International) sought to coordinate the revolutionary activities of communist parties abroad, though it often conflicted with Soviet diplomatic interests. It became an effectively organized body by 1924, and was completely Stalinized by 1928.

EUROPE IN CRISIS: DEPRESSION AND DICTATORSHIP, 1929 – 1935

England: Ramsay MacDonald and the Depression, 1929 – 1931

Required by law to hold elections in 1929, the May 30 contest saw the Conservatives drop to 260 seats, Labour rise to 287, and the Liberals 59. Ramsay MacDonald formed a minority Labour government that would last until 1931. The most serious problem facing the country was the Depression, which caused unemployment to reach 1,700,000 by 1930 and over 3 million, or 25% of the labor force, by 1932. To meet growing budget deficits caused by heavy subsidies to the unemployed, a special government commission recommended budget cuts and tax increases. Cabinet and labor union opposition helped reduce the total for the cuts (from 78 million to 22 million), but this could not help restore confidence in the government, which fell on August 24, 1931.

The "National Government," 1931 – 1935

The following day, King George VI helped convince MacDonald to return to office as head of a National Coalition cabinet made up of 4 Conservatives, 4 Laborites, and 2 Liberals. The Labour Party refused to recognize the new government and ejected MacDonald and Snowden from the Party. MacDonald's coalition swept the November 1931 general elections winning 554 of 615 seats.

The British government abandoned the gold standard on September 21, 1931, and adopted a series of high tariffs on imports. Unemployment peaked at 3 million in 1932 and dropped to 2 million two years later.

In 1931, the British government implemented the Statute of Westminster, which created the British Commonwealth of Nations, granted its members political equality, and freedom to reject any act passed by Parliament that related to a Dominion state.

The Election of 1935

MacDonald resigned his position in June 1935 because of ill health, and was succeeded by Stanley Baldwin, whose conservative coalition won 428 seats in new elections in November.

France Under Andre Tardieu, 1929 – 1932

On July 27, 1929, Poincare resigned as Premier because of ill health. Over the next three years, the dominant figure in French politics was Andre Tardieu, who headed or played a role in Moderate cabinets.

Tardieu tried to initiate political changes along American or British lines to create a stable two party system that would help France deal with the world economic crisis. He convinced the Laval government and the Chamber to accept electing its members by a plurality vote, though the Senate rejected it. In 1930, the government passed France's most important social welfare legislation, the National Workingmen's Insurance Law. It provided various forms of financial aid for illness, retirement, and death.

The Depression did not hit France until late 1931, and it took it four years to begin to recover from it. At first, however, the country seemed immune to the Depression and the economy boomed. Its manufacturing indices reached a peak in 1929, but began gradually to slide through 1932. The economy recovered the following year, and dropped again through 1935.

Return of the Cartel des Gauches, 1932 – 1934

The defeat of the Moderates and the return of the leftists in the elections of May 1, 1932, reflected growing concern over the economy and failed efforts of the government to respond to the country's problems.

France remained plagued by differences over economic reform between the Radicals and the Socialists. The latter advocated nationalization of major factories, expanded social reforms, and public works programs for the unemployed, while the Radicals sought a reduction in government spending. This instability was also reflected in the fact that there were six Cabinets between June 1932 and February 1934.

The government's inability to deal with the country's economic and political problems saw the emergence of a number of radical groups from across the political spectrum. Some of the more prominent were the Fascist Francistes, the Solidarite Francaise, the "Cagoulards" (Comite Secret d'Action Revoluntionnaire), the Parti Populaire Francaise (PPF) and the Jeunesses Patriotes. Not as radical, though still on the right were the Croix de Feu and the Action Francaise. At the other extreme was the French Communist Party.

The growing influence of these groups exploded on February 6, 1934, around a scandal involving a con-man with government connections, Serge Stavisky. After his suicide on the eve of his arrest in December 1933, the scandal and his reported involvement with high government officials stimulated a growing crescendo of criticism that culminated in riots between rightist and leftist factions that resulted in 15 dead and 1,500 to 1,600 injured. The demonstrations and riots, viewed by some as a rightist effort to seize power, brought about the collapse of the Daladier government. He was immediately succeeded by ex-President Gaston Doumergue, who put together a coalition cabinet dominated by Moderates as well as Radicals and Rightists. It contained six former premiers and Marshal Petain.

Struggle for Stability, 1934 – 1935

The accession of Gaston Doumergue (who had been President from 1924 to 1931) with his "National Union" cabinet, stabilized the public crisis. The new Premier (influenced by Tardieu) used radio to try to convince the public of the need to increase the power of the President, (Albert Lebrum; 1932 – 1940), and to enable the Premier to dissolve the legislature. Discontent with Doumergue's tactics resulted in resignations from his Cabinet and its fall in November 1934.

Between November 1934 and June 1935, France had two more governments under Pierre-Etienne Flandin and F. Bouisson. The situation somewhat stabilized with the selection of Pierre Laval as Premier, who served from June 1935 through January 1936. Laval's controversial policies, strengthened by the ability to pass laws without legislative approval, were to deflate the economy, cut government expenditures, and remain on the gold standard. Laval's government fell in early 1936.

GERMANY

The Young Plan

One of the last accomplishments of Stresemann before his death on October 3 was the Young Plan, an altered reparations proposal that required Germany to make yearly payments for 59 years that varied from 1.6 to 2.4 billion Reichsmarks. In return, the Allies removed all foreign controls on Germany's economy and agreed to leave the Rhineland the following year. Efforts by the conservative extremists to stop Reichstag adoption of the Young Plan failed miserably, while a national referendum on the reactionary bill suffered the same fate.

Germany and the Depression

The Depression had a dramatic effect on the German economy and politics. German exports, which had peaked at 13.5 billion marks in 1929, fell to 12 billion marks in 1930, and to 5.7 billion marks two years later. Imports suffered the same fate, going from 14 billion marks in 1928 to 4.7 billion marks in 1932. The country's national income dropped 20% during this period, while unemployment rose from 1,320,000 in 1929 to 6 million by January 1932. This meant that 43% of the German work force were without jobs (compared to one-quarter of the work force in the U.S.).

The Rise of Adolf Hitler and Nazism.

The history of Nazism is deeply intertwined with that of its leader, Adolf Hitler.

Adolf Hitler was born on April 20, 1889, in the Austrian village of Braunau-am-Inn. A frustrated artist, he moved to Vienna where he unsuccessfully tried to become a student in the Vienna Academy of Fine Arts. He then became an itinerant artist, living in hovels, until the advent of the World War, which he welcomed. His four years at the front were the most meaningful of his life up to that time, and he emerged a decorated corporal with a mission now to go into politics to restore his country's bruised honor.

In 1919, Hitler joined the German Workers Party (DAP), which he soon took over and renamed the National Socialist German Workers Party (NAZI). In 1920, the Party adopted a 25-point program that included treaty revision, anti-Semitism, economic, and other social changes. They also created a defense cadre of the Sturmabteilung (SA), "Storm Troopers," or "brown shirts," which was to help the party seize power. Some of the more significant early Nazi leaders were Ernst Röhm, who helped build up the SA; Dietrich Eckart, first head of the Party paper, the *Volkischer Beobachter*; Alfred Rosenberg, who replaced Eckart as editor of *Volkischer Beobachter* and became the Party's chief ideologist; Hermann Göering, World War I flying ace, who took over the SA in 1922; and Rudolf Hess, who became Hitler's secretary.

The Beer Hall Putsch, 1923

In the midst of the country's severe economic crisis in 1923, the Party, which now had 55,000 members, tried to seize power, first by a march on Berlin, and then, when this seemed impossible, on Munich. The march was stopped by police, and Hitler and his supporters were arrested. Their trial, which Hitler used to voice Nazi ideals, gained him a national reputation. Though sentenced to five years imprisonment, he was released after eight months. While incarcerated, he dictated *Mein Kampf* to Rudolf Hess.

The Nazi Movement, 1924 – 1929

Hitler's failed coup and imprisonment convinced him to seek power through legitimate political channels, which would require transforming the Nazi Party. To do this, he reasserted singular control over the movement from 1924 to 1926. Party districts were set up throughout Germany, overseen by *Gaulieters* personally appointed by Hitler.

They were subdivided into Kreise (districts), and then Ortsgruppen (local chapters). A court system, the *Uschla*, oversaw the Party structure. The Party grew from 27,000 in 1925 to 108,000 in 1929. A number of new leaders emerged at this time, including Joseph Goebbels, who became Party Chief in Berlin and later Hitler's propaganda chief, and Heinrich Himmler, who became head of Hitler's private body guard, the SS (*Schutzstaffel*), in 1929.

Weimar Politics, 1930 – 1933

Germany's economic woes and the government's seeming inability to deal with them, underlined the weaknesses of the country's political system and provided the Nazis with new opportunities.

In March 17, 1930, the alliance of Social Democratic, DVP and other parties collapsed over who should shoulder unemployment benefit costs. A new coalition, under Heinrich Breunig, tried to promote a policy of government economic retrenchment, and deflation, which the Reichstag rejected. Consequently, President Hindenburg invoked Article 48 of the Constitution, which enabled him to order the implementation of Breunig's program. The Reichstag overrode the decree, which forced the government's fall and new elections:

Reichstag Elections of September 14, 1930

The September 14 elections surprised everyone. The Nazis saw their 1928 vote jump from 800,000 to 6.5 million (18.3% of the vote), which gave them 107 Reichstag seats, second only to the Social Democrats, who fell from 152 to 143 seats. Bruenig, however, continued to serve as Chancellor of a weak coalition with the support of Hindenburg and rule by presidential decree. His policies failed to resolve the country's growing economic dilemmas.

Presidential Elections of 1932

Hindenburg's seven year presidential term expired in 1932, and he was convinced to run for reelection to stop Hitler from becoming President in the first ballot of March 13. Hitler got only 30% of the vote (11.3 million) to Hindenburg's 49.45% (18.6 million). Since German law required the new president to have a majority of the votes, a runoff was held on April 10 between Hindenburg, Hitler, and the Communist candidate, Thalmann. Hindenburg received 19.3 million votes (53%), Hitler 13.4 million (37%), and Thalmann 2.2 million votes.

The von Papen Chancellorship

On June 1, Bruenig was replaced by Franz von Papen, who formed a government made up of aristocratic conservatives and others that he and Hindenburg hoped would keep Hitler from power. He held new elections on July 31 that saw the Nazis win 230 Reichstag seats with 37% of the vote (13.7 million), and the Communists 89 seats. Offered the Vice Chancellorship and an opportunity to join a coalition government, Hitler refused. Von Papen, paralyzed politically, ruled by presidential decree. Von Papen dissolved the Reichstag on September 12, and held new elections on November 6. The Nazis only got 30% of the vote and 196 Reichstag seats, while the Communists made substantial gains (120 seats from 89). Von Papen resigned in favor of Kurt von Schleicher, one of the president's closest advisers, as the new Chancellor.

Hitler Becomes Chancellor

Von Papen joined with Hitler to undermine Schleicher, and convinced Hindenburg to appoint Hitler as Chancellor and head of a new coalition cabinet with 3 seats for the Nazis.

Hitler dissolved the Reichstag and called for new elections on March 5. Using Presidential decree powers, he initiated a violent anti-communist campaign that included the lifting of certain press and civil freedoms. On February 27, the Reichstag burned which enabled Hitler to get Hindenburg to issue the "Ordinances for the Protection of the German State and Nation," that removed all civil and press liberties as part of a "revolution" against Communism. In the Reichstag elections of March 5, the Nazis only got 43.9% of the vote and 288 Reichstag seats but, through an alliance with the Nationalists, got majority control of the legislature.

Hitler now intensified his campaign against his political and other opponents, placing many of them in newly opened concentration camps. He also convinced Hindenburg to issue the Enabling Act on March 21 that allowed his Cabinet to pass laws and treaties without legislative backing for 4 years. The Reichstag gave him its full legal approval two days later, since many felt it was the only way legally to maintain some influence over his government.

Once Hitler had full legislative power, he began a policy of *Gleichschaltung* (coordination) to bring all independent organizations and agencies throughout Germany under his control. All political parties were outlawed or forced to dissolve, and on July 14, 1933, the Nazi Party became the only legal party in Germany. In addition, German state authority was reduced and placed under Nazi-appointed *Stattholder* (governors), while the Party throughout Germany was divided into *Gaue* (districts) under a Nazi-selected *Gauleiter*. In addition, non-Aryans and Nazi opponents were removed from the civil service, the court system, and higher education. On May 2, 1933, the government declared strikes illegal, abolished labor unions, and later forced all workers to join the German Labor Front (DAF) under Robert Ley. In 1934 the Reichsrat was abolished and a special People's Court was created to handle cases of treason. Finally, the secret police or GESTAPO (*Geheime Staatspolizei*) was created on April 24, 1933 under Göering to deal with opponents and operate concentration camps. The Party had its own security branch, the SD (*Sicherheitsdienst*) under Reinhard Heydrich.

Hitler Consolidates Power

A growing conflict over the direction of the Nazi "revolution" and the power of the SA *vis a vis* the SS and the German army had been brewing since Hitler took power. Ernst Röhm, head of the SA, wanted his forces to become the nucleus of a new German army headed by himself, while the military, Hitler, and the SS sought ways to contain his growing arrogance and independence. The solution was the violent Röhm purge on the night of June 30, 1934 ("The Night of the Long Knives"), coordinated by the GESTAPO and the SS, that resulted in the arrest and murder of Röhm plus 84 SA leaders, as well as scores of other opponents that Hitler decided to eliminate under the cloud of his purge.

The final barrier to Hitler's full consolidation of power in Germany was overcome with the death of Hindenburg on August 2, 1934. Hitler now combined the offices of President and Chancellor, and required all civil servants and workers to take a personal oath to him as the "Führer of the German Reich and people."

Religion and Anti-Semitism

A state Protestant church of "German Christians" under a Bishop of the Reich, Ludwig Muller, was created in 1934. An underground opposition "Confessing Church" was formed under Martin Niemoller that suffered from severe persecution. On July 8, 1933, the government signed a concordat with the Vatican that promised to allow traditional Catholic rights to continue in Germany. Unfortunately, the Nazis severely restricted Catholic religious practice, which created growing friction with the Vatican.

From the inception of the Nazi state in 1933, anti-Semitism was a constant theme and practice in all *Gleichschaltung* and nazification efforts. Illegal intimidation and harassment of Jews was coupled with rigid enforcement of civil service regulations that forbade employment of non-Aryans. This first wave of anti-Semitic activity culminated with the passage of the Nuremburg Laws of September 15, 1935, that deprived Jews of German citizenship and outlawed sexual or marital relations between Jews and other Germans, thus effectively isolating them from the mainstream of German society.

International Affairs

Hitler's international policies were closely linked to his rebuilding efforts to give him a strong economic and military base for an active, aggressive, independent foreign policy. On October 14, 1933, Hitler had his delegates walk out of the Disarmament Conference because he felt the Allied powers had reneged on an earlier promise to grant Germany arms equality. The Reich simultaneously quit the League of Nations. On January 26, 1934, Germany signed a non-aggression pact with Poland, which ended Germany's traditional anti-Polish foreign policy and broke France's encirclement of Germany via the Little Entente. This was followed by the Saarland's overwhelming decision to return to Germany. The culmination of Hitler's foreign policy moves, though, came with his March 15, 1935, announcement that Germany would no longer be bound by the military restrictions of the Treaty of Versailles, that it had already created an air force (Luftwaffe), and that the Reich would institute a draft to create an army of 500,000 men. Allied opposition to this move was compromised by England's decision to conclude a naval pact with Hitler on June 18, 1935, that restricted German naval tonnage (excluding submarines) to 35% of that for England.

ITALY

Fascist Economic Reforms

Increased economic well-being and growth were the promised results of Mussolini's restructuring of the economic system, while the general goals of the regime were to increase production through more efficient methods and land reclamation, with less dependency upon outside resources.

Efforts to increase the land under cultivation through reclamation projects were handicapped by Mussolini's emphasis on model propaganda projects, though the government had reclaimed 12 million acres by 1938. In fact, the small farmer suffered under these policies, because of Mussolini's quiet support of the larger landowner. In 1930, for example, 87.3% of the population controlled 13.2% of the land. The large farm owners, who made up only 0.5% of the population, controlled 41.9% of the land, while the mid-level farmer, who made up 12.2% of the population, controlled 44.9% of the countryside. Regardless, grain products did increase from 4,479 metric tons in 1924 to 8,184 metric tons in 1938, which enabled the government to cut grain imports by 75%. On the other hand, land needed to produce other agricultural products was used to increase wheat and grain output.

To aid firms affected by the Depression, the government created the I.R.I. (*Instituto per la ricostruzione industriale*) which helped most big companies while smaller unsuccessful ones failed. The result was that the vast majority of Italy's major industry came under some form of government oversight. Italian production figures are unimpressive during this period, with increases for industrial production rising between 1928 and 1935. Steel output dropped, while pig-iron, oil products, and electrical output enjoyed moderate increases in the 1930's.

The overall impact of Mussolini's economic programs saw the country's national income rise 15% from 1925 to 1935, with only a 10% per capita increase during this period. The value of exports dropped from 44,370 million lira in 1925 to 21,750 in 1938 because of the decision in 1927 to peg the lira to an artificially high exchange rate.

Church and State

Until Mussolini's accession to power, the pope had considered himself a prisoner in the Vatican. In 1926, Mussolini's government began talks to resolve this issue, which resulted in the Lateran Accords of February 11, 1929. Italy recognized the Vatican as an independent state, with the pope as its head, while the papacy recognized Italian independence. Catholicism was made the official state religion of Italy, and religious teaching was required in all secondary schools. Church marriages were now fully legal, while the state could veto papal appointments of bishops. In addition, the clergy would declare loyalty to the Italian state. Additionally, the government agreed to pay the Church a financial settlement of 1.75 billion lira for the seizure of Church territory in 1860 – 1870.

A conflict soon broke out over youth education and in May 1931 Mussolini dissolved the Catholic Action's youth groups. The pope responded with an encyclical, *Non abbianio bisogno*, which defended these groups, and criticized the Fascist deification of the state. Mussolini agreed later that year to allow Catholic Action to resume limited youth work.

Foreign Policy

The appointment of Adolph Hitler as Chancellor of Germany in early 1933 provided Mussolini with his most important thrust of diplomatic action since he came to power, while it underlined the currency of fascism as a ruling ideology and strengthened his claim to revision of the 1919 Paris Peace accords.

Since the late 1920's, Mussolini began to support German claims for revision of the Treaty of Versailles to strengthen ties with that country and to counter-balance France, a nation he strongly disliked. These goals were current in his Four Power Pact proposal of March 1933 that envisioned a concert of powers – England, France, Italy, and Germany – that included arms parity for the Reich. French opposition to arms equality and treaty revision, plus concerns that the new consortium would replace the League of Nations, saw an extremely weakened agreement signed in June that was ultimately accepted only by Italy and Germany.

In an effort to counter the significance of France's Little Entente with Czechoslovakia, Yugoslavia, and Rumania, Mussolini concluded the Rome Protocols with Austria and Hungary on March 17, 1934 which created a protective bond of friendship between the three countries.

The first test of the new alliance between Italy and Austria came in July 1934, when German-directed Nazis tried to seize control of the Austrian government. Mussolini, opposed to any German Anschluss with Austria, mobilized Italian forces along the northern Renner Pass as a warning to Hitler. The coup collapsed from lack of direct

German aid.

In response to Hitler's announcement of German rearmament in violation of the Treaty of Versailles on March 16, 1935, France, England, and Italy met at Stresa in northern Italy on April 11 – 14, and concluded agreements that pledged joint military collaboration if Germany moved against Austria or along the Rhine. The three states criticized Germany's recent decision to remilitarize and appealed to the Council of the League of Nations on the matter.

Ethiopia (Abyssinia) became an area of strong Italian interest in the 1880's. The coastal region was slowly brought under Italian control until the Italian defeat at Ethiopian hands at Adowa in 1894. In 1906, the country's autonomy was recognized and in 1923 it joined the League of Nations. Mussolini, driven by a strong patriotic desire to avenge the humiliation at Adowa and to create an empire to thwart domestic concerns over the country's economic problems, searched for the proper moment to seize the country. Acquisition of Ethiopia would enable him to join Italy's two colonies of Eritrea and Somalia, which could become a new area of Italian colonization.

Mussolini, who had been preparing for war with Ethiopia since 1932, established a military base at Wal Wal in Ethiopian territory. Beginning in December 1934, a series of minor conflicts took place between the two countries, which gave Mussolini an excuse to plan for the full takeover of the country in the near future.

Mussolini refused to accept arbitration over Ethiopia, and used Europe's growing concern over Hitler's moves there to cover his own secret designs in Ethiopia. On October 2, 1935, Italy invaded Ethiopia, while the League of Nations, which had received four appeals from Ethiopia since January about Italian territorial transgressions, finally voted to adopt economic sanctions against Mussolini. Unfortunately, the League failed to stop shipments of oil to Italy and continued to allow it to use the Suez Canal. On May 9, 1936, Italy formally annexed the country and joined it to Somalia and Eritrea, which now became known as Italian East Africa.

SOVIET RUSSIA

The period from 1929 to 1935 was a time of tremendous upheaval for the USSR as Stalin tried to initiate major programs of collectivization of agriculture and massive industrial development.

Collectivization of Soviet Agriculture

At the end of 1927, Stalin, concerned over problems of grain supply, ordered the gradual consolidation of the country's 25 million small farms, on which 80% of the population lived, into state-run collective farms.

According to the First Five Year Plan's goals (1928 – 1932), agricultural output was to rise 150% over five years, and 20% of the country's private farms transformed into collectives.

In an effort to link agricultural efficiency with heavy industrial development, Stalin decided by the end of 1929 to rapidly collectivize the country's entire agriculture system. Because of earlier resistance from peasants between 1927 and 1929, Stalin ordered war against the kulak or "middle class" peasant class. Some sources claim that as many as 5 million ill-defined kulaks were internally deported during this period.

The above, combined with forced grain seizures, triggered massive, bloody resistance in the country-side. Though half of the nation's peasants were forced onto collectives during this period, they destroyed a great deal of Russia's livestock in the process. In the spring of 1930, Stalin called a momentary halt to the process, which prompted many peasants to leave the state farms.

Over the next seven years, the entire Soviet system was collectivized, and all peasants forced onto state farms. The two major types of farms were the *sovkhoz*, where peasants were paid for their labor; and the *kovkhoz*, or collective farm, where the peasants gave the government a percentage of their crops and kept the surplus. The three types of *kovkhozs* were the Artel, the most common, where the peasant had a small garden plot; the *toz*, where he owned his tools and animals; and the *commune*, where the state owned everything. One of the most important components of the collective and the state farm system was the Machine Tractor Station (MTS) which controlled the tractors and farm equipment for various government run farms.

Direct and indirect deaths from Stalin's collectivization efforts totaled 14.5 million. Grain production levels did not reach 1928 levels until 1935. It did, though, break the back of rural peasant independence and created a totalitarian network of control throughout the countryside. It also undercut his own base of political support within the Party.

Industrialization

Stalin, concerned that Russia would fall irreparably behind the West industrially, hoped to achieve industrial parity with the West in a decade. At this time, Russia was barely on par with Italy in pig-iron and steel production. To stimulate workers, labor unions lost their autonomy and workers, including impressed peasants, were forced to work at locations and under conditions determined by the state. A special "Turnover" tax was placed on all goods throughout the country to help pay for industrialization.

The industrialization goals of the First Five Year Plan, supported hopefully by a flourishing agricultural system, were to increase total industrial production by 236%, heavy industry by 330%, coal, 200%, electrical output, 400%, and pig-iron production, 300%. Workers were to increase their efforts over 100%. Efficiency was also a hallmark of this program, and production costs were to drop by over a third, and prices by a quarter.

In most instances, the Plan's unrealistic goals were hard to meet. Regardless, steel production doubled, though it fell short of the Plan's goals, as did oil and hard coal output. Total industrial production, however, did barely surpass the Plan's expectations.

The Second Five Year Plan (1933 – 1937) was adopted by the XVII Party Congress in early 1934. Its economic and production targets were less severe than the first Plan, and thus more was achieved. The model for workers was Alexis Stakhanov, a coal miner who met 1400% of his quota in the fall of 1935. A Stakhanovite movement arose to stimulate workers to greater efforts. By the end of the Second Plan, Soviet Russia had emerged as a leading world industrial power, though at great costs. It gave up quality for quantity, and created tremendous social and economic discord that still affects the USSR. The tactics used by Stalin to institute his economic reforms formed the nucleus of his totalitarian system, while reaction to them within the Party led to the Purges.

Party Politics and the Origin of the Purges

The tremendous upheaval caused by forced collectivization, blended with the remnants of the Rightist conflict with Stalin, prompted the Soviet leader to initiate one of the country's periodic purges of the Party. Approved by the top leadership, suspected opponents were driven from Party ranks while Zinoviev and Kamenev were briefly exiled to Siberia. Continued uncertainty over the best policies to follow after the initiation of the Second Five Year Plan ended with the murder at the end of 1934 of

Sergei Kirov, Stalin's supposed heir, and Leningrad party chief. Though the reasons for Kirov's murder are still unclear, his more liberal tendencies, plus his growing popularity, made him a threat to the Soviet leader. In the spring of 1935, the recently renamed and organized secret police, the NKVD, oversaw the beginnings of a new, violent Purge that eradicated 70% of the 1934 Central Committee, and a large percentage of the upper military ranks. Stalin sent between 8 and 9 million to camps and prisons, and caused untold deaths before the Purges ended in 1938.

Foreign Policy, 1929 – 1935

The period from 1929 to 1933 saw the USSR retreat inward as the bulk of its energies were put into domestic economic growth. Regardless, Stalin remained sensitive to growing aggression and ideological threats abroad such as the Japanese invasion of Manchuria in 1931 and Hitler's appointment as Chancellor. As a result, Russia left its cocoon in 1934, joined the League of Nations, and became an advocate of "collective security" while the Comintern adopted Popular Front tactics, allying with other parties against fascism, to strengthen the USSR's international posture. Diplomatically, in addition to League membership, the Soviet Union completed a military pact with France.

INTERNATIONAL DEVELOPMENTS, 1918 – 1935

The League of Nations

Efforts to create some international body to arbitrate international conflicts gained credence with the creation of a Permanent Court of International Justice to handle such matters at the First Hague Conference (1899). At a similar meeting eight years later, concern was expressed over Europe's growing arms race, though no country was willing to give the Permanent Court adequate authority to serve as a legitimate arbitrator. Leon Bourgeois, a French statesman, however, pushed for some sort of strong international peacekeeping body, but no major efforts towards this goal were initiated until 1915, when pro-League of Nations organizations arose in the United States and Great Britain. Support for such a body grew as the war lengthened, and creation of such an organization became the cornerstone of President Woodrow Wilson's post-war policy, enunciated in his "Fourteen Points" speech before Congress on January 8, 1918. His last point called for an international chamber of states to guarantee national autonomy and independence. At the Paris Peace Conference, the major Allied leaders created a Commission for the League to draft its constitution, while the covenant of the League was placed in the Treaty of Versailles.

The Preamble of the League's Covenant

This statement defined the League's purposes, which were to work for international friendship, peace, and security. To attain this, its members agreed to avoid war, maintain peaceful relations with other countries, and honor international law and accords.

The Organization of the League of Nations

Headquartered in Geneva, the League came into existence as the result of an Allied resolution announcing their intentions on January 25, 1919, and the signing of the Treaty of Versailles on June 28, 1919.

The 26 article Covenant determined terms of membership and withdrawal (two-thirds vote to join and two years notice to resign) and means to amend the Covenant (unanimous vote of Council with majority approval from Assembly).

The League's Council originally consisted of five permanent members (France, Italy, England, Japan, and the U.S.), though the U.S. seat was left vacant because the U.S. Senate refused to ratify the Treaty of Versailles. Germany filled the vacancy in 1926. It also had four 1-year rotating seats (increased to 6 in 1922, and raised to 9 seats in 1926). The Council, with each member having one vote, could discuss any matter that threatened international stability, and could recommend action to member states. It also had the right, according to Article 8 of the League Covenant, to seek ways to reduce arms strength, while Articles 10 through 17 gave it the authority to search for means to stop war. It could recommend through a unanimous vote ways to stop aggression, and could suggest economic sanctions and other tactics to enforce its decisions, though its military ability to enforce its decisions was vague. It met four times a year from 1923 to 1929, and then three times annually afterwards.

The League's legislative body had similar debating and discussion authority, though it had no legislative powers. It initially had 43 members, which rose to 49 by the mid-1930's, though six others, including Italy, Germany, and Japan, withdrew their membership during the same period. The USSR, which joined in 1934, was expelled six years later.

The League's judicial responsibilities were handled by the "World Court" that was located at The Hague in The Netherlands. Created in 1921 and opened the following year, it would consider and advise on any case from any nation or the League, acting as an arbiter to prevent international conflict. The court's decisions were not binding: it relied on voluntary submission to its decisions. It initially had eleven judges (later 15) selected for five year terms by the League.

The day-to-day affairs of the League were administered by the General Secretary (Sir Eric Drummond to 1933; J. Avenol afterwards) and his bureaucracy, the Secretariat, which was composed of an international collection of League civil servants.

Lesser known functions of the League dealt with the efforts of its International Labor Organization (I.L.O.) which tried to find ways to reduce labor-management and class tensions; and the Mandates Commission, which oversaw territories taken from the Central Powers and were administered – as a prelude to independence – under mandate from League members. In addition, the League tried to provide medical, economic, and social welfare aid to depressed parts of the world.

THE WASHINGTON CONFERENCE, 1921 – 1922

The first post-war effort to deal with problems of disarmament was the Washington Conference (November 1921 – February 1922). Its participants, which included the major powers in Europe and Asia plus the meeting's sponsor, the United States, discussed a number of problems that resulted in three separate agreements:

The Washington Naval Treaty (Five Power Treaty)

France, Italy, England, the United States, and Japan agreed to halt battleship construction for ten years, while limiting or reducing capital shipping levels to 525,000 tons for the U.S. and England, 315,000 tons for Japan, and 175,000 tons for Italy and France.

The Four Power Treaty

The United States, England, France, and Japan agreed not to seek further Pacific expansion or increased naval strength there and to respect the Pacific holdings of the other signatory powers.

The Nine Power Treaty

To grant China some sense of autonomy not offered at the Paris Peace Conference, an agreement was signed by Japan (after Japan's agreement to return Kiachow to China), the Netherlands, Portugal, Belgium, Italy, France, England, the U.S., and China, , guaranteed China's independence and territorial autonomy.

THE DRAFT TREATY OF MUTUAL ASSISTANCE (1923)

In the ongoing search for ways to encourage continuing disarmament talks and provide security, particularly for France, which continued to worry about future threats from Germany, the League of Nations had set up a Temporary Mixed Commission (TMC) of specialists to study disarmament. The TMC submitted a Draft Treaty of Mutual Assistance to the League Assembly in September 1923 that would enable the Council to determine the guilty nation in the event of a war, and to intervene on the side of the victim. France, Italy, and Japan were the only major states to support the approved treaty. All other important countries rejected it because they were concerned about its regional limitations, its protection for only those that disarmed, and the League's role in such actions, particularly in defining aggression.

THE GENEVA PROTOCOL (1924)

The failure of many important nations to accept the Draft Treaty prompted the British and the French to search for a different solution to the problem of protection for those that disarmed. The result was the Protocol for the Pacific Settlement of International Disputes, or the Geneva Protocol, that stated that the nation that refused to submit to arbitration by the World Court, the League Council, or special arbitrators, would be termed the aggressor. The agreement was tied to a further disarmament conference and a network of regional security pacts. Approved by the Assembly in October 1924, France and its Little Entente allies backed it quickly. England, however, backed by Commonwealth members, disapproved because of the broad commitments involved, which sank any prospect of final approval of the Protocol.

THE LOCARNO PACT (1925)

Failure of the European powers to create some type of international system to prevent aggression was followed by regional efforts prompted by Germany's visionary Foreign Minister, Gustav Stresemann, who in early 1925 approached England and France about an accord whereby Germany would accept its western borders in return for early Allied withdrawal from the demilitarized Rhine area. Stresemann also wanted League membership for his country. While England responded with guarded regional interest, France hesitated. Six months after consultation with its eastern allies, Paris countered with a proposal that would include similar provisions for Germany's eastern borders, secured by a mutual assistance pact between Italy, Great Britain, and France. These countries, along with Belgium, Czechoslovakia, and Poland, met for two months in Locarno, Switzerland, and concluded a number of separate agreements.

Treaty of Mutual Guarantees (Rhineland Pact)

Signed on October 16, 1925, by England, France, Italy, Germany and Belgium, they guaranteed Germany's western boundaries and accepted the Versailles settlement's demilitarized zones. Italy and Great Britain agreed militarily to defend these lines if flagrantly violated.

Arbitration Settlements

In the same spirit, Germany signed arbitration dispute accords that mirrored the Geneva Protocol with France, Belgium, Poland, and Czechoslovakia, and required acceptance of League-determined settlements.

Eastern Accords

Since Germany would only agree to arbitration and not finalize its eastern border, France separately signed guarantees with Poland and Czechoslovakia to defend their frontiers.

Germany Joins the League

The Locarno Pact went into force when Germany joined the League on September 10, 1926, acquiring, after some dispute, the U.S.'s permanent seat on the Council. France and Belgium began to withdraw from the Rhineland, though they left a token force there until 1930.

THE PACT OF PARIS (KELLOGG-BRIAND PACT)

The Locarno Pact heralded a new period in European relations known as the "Era of Locarno" that marked the end of post-war conflict and the beginning of a more normal period of diplomatic friendship and cooperation. It reached its peak, idealistically, with the Franco-American effort in 1928 to seek an international statement to outlaw war. The seed for this new proposal arose on the eve of the tenth anniversary of the American entrance into the World War, and centered around interest in a mutual statement outlawing war as a theme in national policy. In December 1927, Frank Kellogg, the American Secretary of State, proposed that this policy be offered to all nations in the form of a treaty. On August 27, 1928, fifteen countries, including the U.S., Germany, France, Italy and Japan, signed this accord with some minor limitations, which renounced war as a means of solving differences and as a tool of national policy. Within five years, 50 other countries signed the agreement. Unfortunately, without something more than idealism to back it up, the Kellogg-Briand Pact had little practical meaning.

THE WANING SEARCH FOR DISARMAMENT

The Depression did not diminish the desire for disarmament. In fact, it added a new series of problems and concerns that made the search more difficult, and with growing threats of aggression in Asia and Europe, these effortss were destryed.

London Naval Disarmament Treaty

In March 1930, Great Britain and the United States sought to expand the naval limitation terms of the Five Power Treaty of 1922. France and Italy could not agree on terms, while the U.S., England, and Japan accepted mild reductions in cruiser and destroyer strength.

World Disarmament Conference

The starting point for implementation of the 1924 Geneva Protocol was a disarmament conference, which, though envisioned for 1925, did not convene until February 5, 1932. Attended by 60 countries including the USSR and the United States, initial discussions centered around a French proposal that wanted a protective monitoring system and required arbitration before considering disarmament. On the other hand, the U.S. asked for one-third reduction of current treaty shipping strength. Germany countered with demands for arms parity before disarmament. Though this was a front for more complex issues, the Germans left the conference when rebuffed in September 1932, only to be lured back later by a Five Power statement that agreed, in spirit, to Germany's demand. Hitler's accession to power on January 30, 1933, halted any further consideration of this point, which prompted Germany's withdrawal from the conference and the League. This, and France's continued insistence on pre-disarmament security guarantees, neutralized conference efforts, and it closed in failure in June 1934.

LEAGUE AND ALLIED RESPONSE TO AGGRESSION

By 1931, international attention increasingly turned to growing acts or threats of aggression in Europe and Asia, and transformed Europe from a world that hoped for eternal peace to a Continent searching desperately for ways to contain growing aggression.

The League's Lytton Report and Manchuria

On September 19, 1931, the Japanese Kwantung Army, acting independently of the government in Tokyo, began the gradual conquest of Manchuria after fabricating an incident at Mukden to justify their actions. Ultimately, they created a puppet state, Manchukuo, under the last Chinese emperor, Henry Pu Yi. China's League protest resulted in the creation of an investigatory commission under the Earl of Lytton, that criticized Japan's actions and recommended a negotiated settlement that would have allowed Japan to retain most of its conquest. Japan responded by resigning from the League on January 24, 1933.

The Stresa Front

Hitler's announcement on March 15, 1935, of Germany's decisions to rearm and to introduce conscription in violation of the Treaty of Versailles prompted the leaders of England, France, and Italy to meet in Stresa, Italy (April 11 – 14) to discuss a response. They condemned Germany's actions, underlined their commitment to the Locarno Pact, and re-affirmed the support they collectively gave for Austria's independence in early 1934. Prompted by these actions, the League Council also rebuked Germany, and created an investigatory committee to search for economic means to punish the Reich. Great Britain's decision, however, to protect separately its naval strength vis a vis a German buildup in the Anglo-German Naval Treaty of June 18, 1935, effectively compromised the significance of the Stresa Front.

Italy and Ethiopia

By the end of 1934, Italy had begun to create a number of incidents in Ethiopia as a prelude to complete absorption of that country. The Emperor of Ethiopia, Haile Sellasie, appealed directly to the League on the matter in January 1935. Franco-British efforts to mediate the crisis failed, while Ethiopia continued to look to the League to contain Italian aggression. Mussolini was convinced that he could act with impunity when he realizedthat the League was reluctant to do more than make verbal objections to the Italian actions. Consequently, on October 3, 1935, Italy invaded Ethiopia, which prompted the League to declare the former country the aggressor. Ineffective economic sanctions followed on October 19. Independent Anglo-French efforts to halt separately Italian aggression by granting Mussolini most of Ethiopia (with economic predominance) failed in December because of a strong public outcry over the terms. Italy completed its conquest in early May 1935, and annexed Ethiopia on May 9.

6 WORLD WAR II TO THE DEMISE OF COMMUNISM (1935-1996)

THE AUTHORITARIAN STATES

The Soviet Union (U.S.S.R.) and Stalin

The Bolsheviks under Lenin and Trotsky came to power in the revolution of 1917. In a power struggle following the death of Lenin (1924), Josef Stalin won control of the Communist Party and Soviet Government from his rival, Leon Trotsky, who was eventually sent into exile. In 1928 Stalin began to build "socialism in one country." The first and second five-year plans resulted in a degree of centralized control over the nation and its economy unparalleled in history.

The 1936 Constitution was a recognition of the success of socialism. It gave the people civil rights, such as freedom of speech, customary in democracies. In addition it guaranteed a right to work, rest, leisure, and economic security. In fact, these rights were largely ignored by Stalin's government, or they existed only within the limits set by the ruling Communist Party of which Stalin was General Secretary.

Stalin's absolute dictatorship and inability to tolerate any opposition or dissent was revealed to the world by the Great Purge Trials (1936–1938). In 1936, 16 old Bolsheviks—including Gregory Zinoviev (first head of the Communist International) and Lev Kamenev—were placed on trial, publicly confessed to charges of plotting with foreign powers, and were executed. In 1937 Marshal Michael Tukhachevski and a group of the highest-ranking generals were accused of plotting with the Germans and Japanese, and executed after a secret court martial. Other purges and trials followed, including the 1938 trial of Nicolai Bukharin, Alexei Rykov, and other prominent Bolsheviks charged with Trotskyite plots and wanting to restore capitalism.

These events tended to discredit Russia as a reliable factor in international affairs. By the late 1930s the U.S.S.R. presented two images to the world: one a regime of absolute dictatorship and repression exemplified by the Great Purges and the other of undeniable economic progress during a period of world depression. Industrial production increased an average of 14% per annum in the 1930s, and Russia went from 15th to third in production of electricity. The Bolshevik model was, however, one of progress imposed from above at great cost to those below. These impressions help explain the reluctance of British and French leaders throughout the 1930s to rely on the Soviet Union when they had to deal with acts of aggression by Hitler and Mussolini.

Events in Nazi Germany

The Nazi state (Third Reich) was a brutal dictatorship established with Hitler's appointment as Chancellor in 1933. By 1936 Hitler had destroyed the government of the Weimar Republic (established in 1919 at the end of the First World War), suppressed all political parties except the Nazi Party, and consolidated the government of Germany under his control as Fuhrer (leader). Mass organizations such as the Nazi Labor Front and the Hitler Youth were established. The Nazis instituted propaganda campaigns and a regime of terror against political opponents and Jews (who were made scapegoats for Germany's problems). Germany was a police state by 1936. In 1938 the Nazis used the assassination of a German diplomat by a Jewish youth as the excuse for extensive pogroms, or massacres. Scores were murdered and much Jewish property was destroyed or damaged by gangs of Nazi hoodlums. Persecution of the Jews increased in intensity, culminating in the horrors of the war-time concentration camps and the mass murder of millions.

Final control over the armed forces and the foreign office was achieved by Hitler in 1937–1938. He moved against Blomberg (the Minister of War) and Fritsch (the commander-in-chief of the army), taking advantage of the scandals in which they were involved (in the case of Fritsch the accusations were false). Hitler made himself Minister of War and established the High Command of the Armed Forces under his personal representative, General Keitel. At the same time Joachim von Ribbentrop was made Minister of Foreign Affairs, giving the Nazis complete control over the German Foreign Office.

Nevertheless the Nazi regime enjoyed success in part, at least, because it was able to reduce unemployment from 6,000,000 in 1932 to 164,000 by 1938 through so-called four-year plans aimed at rearming Germany and making its economy self-sufficient and free of dependence on any foreign power. The improving economic condition of many, together with Hitler's successes in foreign affairs, gave him a substantial hold over the German people.

By the beginning of World War II Germany had been transformed into a disciplined war machine with all dissent stifled and ready to follow the *Führer* wherever he might lead.

Fascist Italy: The Corporate State

Mussolini's Fascist dictatorship in Italy began with the "March on Rome" in 1922. In the early 1930s Italy suffered from severe economic depression intensified by lack of raw materials and an unfavorable trade balance. In 1935 Mussolini embarked upon the conquest of Ethiopia, and despite condemnation by the League of Nations and unfavorable reactions among the powers, completed the conquest and formally annexed Ethiopia May 9, 1936.

The pattern of Mussolini's dictatorship was that of the "Corporate State." Political parties and electoral districts were abolished. Workers and employers alike were organized into corporations according to the nature of their business. Twenty-two such corporations were established, presided over by a minister of corporations. The corporations and the government (with the balance heavily favoring the employers and the government) generally determined wages, hours, conditions of work, prices, and industrial polices. The structure was completed in 1938 with the abolition of the Chamber of Deputies in the Parliament and its replacement by a Chamber of Fasces and Corporations representing the Fascist Party and the corporations.

Fascism provided a certain excitement and superficial grandeur but no solution to Italy's economic problems. Italian labor was kept under strict control. No strikes were allowed and by 1939 real wages were below those of 1922. Emphasis on foreign adventures and propaganda concerning a new Roman Empire were used to maintain a regime of force and brutality.

Other Authoritarian Regimes

The democratic hopes of those who established independent states in eastern and central Europe following World War I remained unfulfilled in the 1930s. Authoritarian monarchies — military regimes or governments on the fascist model — were established everywhere: Poland by 1939 was under a military regime established by Admiral Horthy, Greece by General Metaxas. Yugoslavia, Rumania, and Bulgaria were ruled by authoritarian monarchies. In Spain General Franco established a fascist dictatorship after the Civil War (1936 – 1939). In Austria the clerical-fascist regime of Kurt Schuschnigg ruled until the *Anschluss* (annexation by Germany) in 1938 and in

Portugal Salazar ruled as dictator.

THE DEMOCRACIES

Great Britain

In Great Britain the Labor Party emerged as the second party in British politics along with the Conservatives. The first Labor government under Ramsey MacDonald governed from January to November, 1924. A second MacDonald cabinet was formed in 1931 but resigned in August because of financial crisis and disagreement over remedies. A national coalition government under Ramsey MacDonald governed from October 1931 to June 1935 when Stanley Baldwin formed a Conservative cabinet. Baldwin was succeeded by Neville Chamberlain (1937 – 1940) whose government dealt with the problem of German and Italian aggression by a policy of appeasement.

France: The Popular Front

In France a coalition of Radical Socialists, Socialists, and Communists campaigned in 1936 on a pledge to save the country from fascism and solve problems of the depression by instituting economic reforms. The Popular Front government, under Socialist Leon Blum, lasted just over a year. Much reform legislation was enacted, including a 40-hour work week, vacations with pay, collective bargaining, compulsory arbitration of labor disputes, support for agricultural prices, reorganization of the Bank of France, and nationalization of armaments and aircraft industries. Blum was attacked by conservatives and fascists as a radical and a Jew. ("Better Hitler than Leon Blum.") The Popular Front government was defeated by the Senate which refused to vote the government emergency financial powers. Eduard Daladier then formed a conservative government which began to devote its attention to foreign affairs, collaborating with Chamberlain in the appeasement policy. Democracy was preserved from the fascist attacks of the early 1930s, but the Popular Front was not as successful in making permanent changes as might have been hoped, and it was a demoralized and dispirited France that had to meet the German attack on Poland in 1939.

Other Democratic States

Czechoslovakia was the one state of Eastern Europe that maintained a democratic, parliamentary regime. It came under heavy attack from Nazi Germany following the annexation of Austria and was ultimately deserted by its allies, France and Britain, whose leaders forced Czech compliance with the terms of the Munich Agreement of 1938. Switzerland maintained a precarious neutrality throughout the 1930s and World War II with the help of the League of Nations, which freed Switzerland of any obligation to support even sanctions against an aggressor. Sweden also maintained its democratic existence by a firm policy of neutrality. Denmark and Norway were seized by the Germans early in 1940 and remained under German control during World War II. All of the Scandinavian countries were models of liberal democratic government.

CULTURE IN THE LATE 1930S: ENGAGEMENT

The 20th century generally has been one in which there has been a feeling of fragmentation and uncertainty in European thought and the arts. Much of this was due to the discoveries of Freud and Einstein: one emphasizing that much of human behavior is irrational and the other undermining in his theories of relativity the long-held certainties of Newtonian science. The Dutch historian Johan Huizinga noted in 1936 "almost all things which once seemed sacred and immutable have now become unsettled. ... The sense of living in the midst of a violent crisis of civilization, threatening complete collapse, has spread far and wide." (Huizinga, *In the Shadow of Tomorrow*, London, 1936). Intellectuals came increasingly to see the world as an irrational place in which old values and truths had little relevance. Some intellectuals became "engaged" in resistance to fascism and Nazism. Some like Arthur Koestler flirted with communism but broke with Stalin after the Great Purges. Koestler's *Darkness at Noon* (1941) is an attempt to understand the events surrounding those trials. German intellectuals such as Ernst Cassirer and Erich Fromm escaped Nazi Germany and worked in exile. Cassirer, in his *The Myth of the State* (1946), noted that the Nazis manufactured myths of race, leader, party, etc., that disoriented reason and intellect. Fromm published *Escape from Freedom* in 1941 which maintained that modern man had escaped *to* freedom from the orderly, structured world of medieval society but was now trying to escape *from* this freedom and looking for security once again. The artist Picasso expressed his hatred of fascism by his painting of Guernica, a Spanish town subjected to aerial bombardment by the German air force as it intervened in the Spanish Civil War.

Existentialism is the philosophy that best exemplified European feelings in the era of the World Wars. Three 19th-century figures greatly influenced this movement: Kierkegaard, Dostoevski, and Nietzsche. Martin Heidegger (though he rejected the term), Karl Jaspers, Jean-Paul Sartre, and Simone de Beauvoir are four noted figures in 20th-century existentialism, which sought to come to grip with life's central experiences and the trauma of war, death, and evil.

INTERNATIONAL RELATIONS:THE ROAD TO WAR

Several factors need to be understood concerning the events leading to World War II. First, there has been little debate over causes: Germany, Italy, Japan, and the U.S.S.R. were not satisfied with the peace settlement of 1919. They used force to achieve change, from the Japanese invasion of Manchuria in 1931 to the outbreak of war in 1939 over Poland. Hitler, bit by bit, dismantled the Versailles Treaty in central and eastern Europe. Responsibility has also been placed to some degree on Britain and France and even the United States for following a policy of appeasement which it was hoped would satisfy Hitler's demands.

Secondly, Britain and France as well as other democratic states were influenced in their policy by a profound pacifism based on their experience with the loss of life and devastation in World War I and by a dislike of the Stalinist regime in Russia.

Thirdly, while the U.S.S.R. was a revisionist power, it was profoundly distrustful of Germany, Italy, and Japan. The threat to their interests led the Soviet leaders to pursue a policy of collective security through the League of Nations (which they joined in 1934). Only after evidence of Anglo-French weakness did Stalin in 1939 enter an agreement with Hitler. This event, like the Great Purges, only heightened suspicion of Soviet motives and was later to become the subject of debate and recrimination in the Cold War that followed World War II.

Finally, Neville Chamberlain's policy of appeasement was not based on any liking for Hitler, whom he considered "half-crazed," but on a genuine desire to remove causes of discontent inherent in the Versailles settlement and thus create conditions where peace could be maintained. His error lay in his belief that Hitler was open to reason, preferred peace to war, and would respect agreements.

THE COURSE OF EVENTS

Using a Franco-Soviet agreement of the preceding year as an excuse, Hitler, on March 7, 1936, repudiated the Locarno agreements and reoccupied the Rhineland (an area demilitarized by the Versailles Treaty). Neither France (which possessed military superiority at the time) nor Britain was willing to oppose these moves.

The Spanish Civil War (1936 – 1939) is usually seen as a rehearsal for World War II because of outside intervention. The government of the Spanish Republic (established in 1931) caused resentment among conservatives by its programs, including land reform and anti-clerical legislation aimed at the Catholic Church. Labor discontent led to disturbances in industrial Barcelona and the surrounding province of Catalonia. Following an election victory by a popular front of republican and radical parties, right-wing generals in July began a military insurrection. Francisco Franco, stationed at the time in Spanish Morocco, emerged as the leader of this revolt which became a devastating civil war lasting nearly three years.

The democracies, including the United States, followed a course of neutrality, refusing to aid the Spanish government or to become involved. Nazi Germany, Italy and the U.S.S.R. did intervene despite non-intervention agreements negotiated by Britain and France. German air force units were sent to aid the fascist forces of Franco and participated in bombardments of Madrid, Barcelona, and Guernica (the latter incident being the inspiration for Picasso's famous painting which became an anti-fascist symbol known far beyond the world of art). Italy sent troops, tanks, and other materiel. The U.S.S.R. sent advisers and recruited soldiers from among anti-fascists in the United States and other countries to fight in the international brigades with the republican forces. Spain became a battlefield for fascist and anti-fascist forces with Franco winning by 1939 in what was seen as a serious defeat for anti-fascist forces everywhere.

The Spanish Civil War was a factor in bringing together Mussolini and Hitler in a Rome-Berlin Axis. Already Germany and Japan had signed the Anti-Comintern Pact in 1936. Ostensibly directed against international communism, this was the basis for a diplomatic alliance between those countries, and Italy soon adhered to this agreement, becoming Germany's ally in World War II.

Italy, in addition to its involvement in Spain, in 1935 launched a war to conquer the African kingdom of Ethiopia. The democracies chose not to intervene in this case, either, despite Emperor Haile Selassie's plea to the League of Nations. By 1936 the conquest was complete.

In 1937 there was Nazi-inspired agitation in the Baltic port of Danzig, a city basically German to its population, but which had been made a free city under the terms of the Versailles Treaty.

In 1938 Hitler renewed his campaign against Austria which he had unsuccessfully tried to subvert in 1934. Pressure was put on the Austrian Chancellor Schuschnig to make concessions to Hitler, and when this did not work, German troops annexed Austria (the *Anschluss*). Again Britain and France took no effective action, and about six million Austrians were added to Germany.

Hitler turned next to Czechoslovakia. Three million persons of German origin lived in the Sudetenland, a borderland between Germany and Czechoslovakia given to Czechoslovakia in order to provide it with a more defensible boundary. These ethnic Germans (and other minorities of Poles, Ruthenians, and Hungarians) agitated against the democratic government (the only one in eastern Europe in 1938) despite its enlightened minority policy. Hitler used the Sudeten Nazi Party to deliberately provoke a crisis by making demands for a degree of independence unacceptable to the Czech authorities. He then claimed to interfere as the protector of a persecuted minority. In May 1938 rumors of invasion led to warnings from Britain and France followed by assurances from Hitler. Nevertheless in the fall the crisis came to a head with renewed demands from Hitler. Chamberlain twice flew to Germany in person to get German terms. The second time, Hitler's increased demands led to mobilization and other measures towards war. At the last minute a four-power conference was held in Munich with Hitler, Mussolini, Chamberlain and Daladier in attendance. At Munich, Hitler's terms were accepted in the Munich Agreement. Neither Czechoslovakia nor the U.S.S.R. was in attendance. Britain and France, despite the French alliance with Czechoslovakia, put pressure on the Czech government to force it to comply with German demands. Hitler signed a treaty agreeing to this settlement as the limit of his ambitions. At the same time the Poles seized control of Teschen, and Hungary (with the support of Italy and Germany and over the protests of the British and French) seized 7,500 square miles of Slovakia. By the concessions forced on her at Munich, Czechoslovakia lost the frontier defenses and was totally unprotected against any further German encroachments.

In March 1939 Hitler annexed most of the rump Czech state while Hungary conquered Ruthenia. At almost the same time Germany annexed Memel from Lithuania. In April Mussolini, taking advantage of distractions created by Germany, landed an army in Albania and seized that Balkan state in a campaign lasting about one week.

Disillusioned by these continued aggressions, Britain and France made military preparations. Guarantees were given to Poland, Rumania, and Greece. The two democracies also opened negotiations with the U.S.S.R. for an arrangement to obtain that country's aid against further German aggression. Hitler, with Poland next on his timetable, also began a cautious rapproachement with the U.S.S.R. Probably Russian suspicion that the Western powers wanted the U.S.S.R. to bear the brunt of any German attack led Stalin to respond to Hitler's overtures. Negotiations which began very quietly in the spring of 1939 were continued with increasing urgency as summer approached and with it, the time of Hitler's planned attack on Poland. On August 23, 1939, the world was stunned by the announcement of a Nazi-Soviet treaty of friendship. A secret protocol provided that in the event of a "territorial rearrangement" in eastern Europe the two powers would divide Poland. In addition Russia would have the Baltic states (Latvia, Lithuania, and Estonia) and Bessarabia (lost to Rumania in 1918) as part of her sphere. Stalin agreed to remain neutral in any German war with Britain or France.

World War II began with the German invasion of Poland on September 1, 1939, followed by British and French declarations of war against Germany on September 3.

WORLD WAR II

The Polish Campaign and the "Phony War"

The German attack (known as the "blitzkrieg" or "lightning war") overwhelmed the poorly equipped Polish army which could not resist German tanks and airplanes. The outcome was clear after the first few days of fighting, and organized resistance ceased within a month.

In accordance with the secret provisions of the Nazi-Soviet Treaty of August 1939, Russia and Germany shared the Polish spoils. On September 17 the Russian armies attacked the Poles from the east. They met the Germans two days later. Stalin's share of Poland extended approximately to the Curzon Line (a line originally proposed in 1919 and named for the British foreign minister, Lord Curzon, and which was never implemented). Russia also made demands on Finland. Later, in June 1940, while Germany was attacking France, Stalin occupied the Baltic states of Latvia, Lithuania, and Estonia.

Nazi Germany formally annexed the port of Danzig and the Polish Corridor and some territory along the western Polish border. Central Poland was turned into a German protectorate called the Government-General.

Following the successful completion of the Polish campaign, the war settled into a period of inaction on the part of both Germans and the British and French known as the "phony war" or "sitzkrieg." The British and French prepared for a German attack on France and Belgium such as that at the beginning of World War I but failed to take any offensive action. Some peace-feelers were extended by the Germans but met with no success. At sea, a campaign began between the British navy and German submarines which began to prey on Allied shipping. The British were also concerned with finding a way to prevent vital Swedish iron ore from reaching Germany by a route which led over northern Norway and then by ship down the Norwegian coast to German Baltic ports. Any effective blockade would have involved violation of Norwegian territorial waters, however, and this the Chamberlain government was reluctant to do.

The "Winter War" Between Russia and Finland

The only military action of any consequence during the winter of 1939 – 1940 resulted from Russian demands made on Finland, especially for territory adjacent to Leningrad (then only 20 miles from the border). Finnish refusal led to a Russian attack in November 1939. The Finns resisted with considerable vigor, receiving some supplies from Sweden, Britain and France, but eventually by March had to give in to the superior Russian forces. Finland was forced to cede the Karelian Isthmus, Viipuri, and a naval base at Hangoe. Britain and France prepared forces to aid the Finns but by the time they were ready to act the Finns had been defeated.

The German Attack on Denmark and Norway

The period of inactivity in the war in the west came suddenly to an end. On April 8, 1940, the British and French finally announced their intent to mine Norwegian coastal waters to blockade German ships transporting Swedish iron ore. On April 9, as the Norwegians were about to protest this action, the Germans struck. Denmark and Norway were simultaneously attacked. Denmark was quickly occupied. In Norway, German forces landed by air at strategic points with the main forces coming by sea. The British and French responded by sending naval and military forces to Narvik and Trondheim in an effort to assist the Norwegians and to capture some bases before the Germans could overrun the entire country. They were too slow and showed little initiative, and within a few weeks the forces were withdrawn, taking the Norwegian government with them into exile in London.

The Battle of France

On May 10 the main German offensive was launched against France. Belgium and the Netherlands were simultaneously attacked. According to plan, British and French forces advanced to aid the Belgians. At this point the Germans departed from the World War I strategy by launching a surprise armored attack through Luxembourg and the Ardennes Forest (considered by the British and French to be impassable for tanks). As these forces moved towards the Channel coast they divided the Allied armies leaving the Belgians, British Expeditionary Force, and some French forces virtually encircled. The Dutch could offer no real resistance and collapsed in four days after the May 13

German bombing of Rotterdam — one of the first raids intended to terrorize civilians. Queen Wilhemina and her government fled to London. The Belgians, who had made little effort to coordinate plans with the British and French, surrendered May 25th, leaving the British and French in serious danger from the Germans who were advancing to the Channel coast; however, Hitler concentrated on occupying Paris. This provided just enough time for the British to effect an emergency evacuation of some 230,000 of their own men as well as about 120,000 French from the port of Dunkirk and the adjacent coast. This remarkable evacuation saved the lives of the soldiers, but all supplies and equipment were lost including vehicles, tanks, and artillery — a very severe blow to the British Army.

Churchill Becomes British Prime Minister

Even before the offensive against France, on May 7 and 8 an attack was launched in the House of Commons on Prime Minister Chamberlain, prompted by the bungling of the Norwegian campaign but which extended to the whole conduct of the war to that point. Chamberlain, a man of peace who had never properly mobilized the British war effort or developed an effective plan of action, fell from power. A government was formed under Winston Churchill, whose warnings of the German danger and the need for British rearmament all during the 1930s made him Chamberlain's logical successor. The opposition Labor Party agreed to join in a coalition with Clement Attlee becoming deputy prime minister. Several other Laborites followed his lead by accepting cabinet posts. This gave Britain a government which eventually led the nation to final victory but which could do little in 1940 to prevent the defeat of France.

France Makes Peace

Paris fell to the Germans in mid-June. In this crisis Paul Reynaud succeeded Eduard Daladier as premier but was unable to deal with the defeatism of some of his cabinet. On June 16th Reynaud resigned in favor of a government headed by aged Marshal Petain, one of the heroes of World War I. The Petain government quickly made peace with Hitler, who added to French humiliation by dictating the terms of the armistice to the French at Compiegne in the same railroad car used by Marshal Foch when he gave terms to the Germans at the end of the First World War. The complete collapse of France in so short a time came as a tremendous shock to the British as well as to Americans. The failure was not due to treachery or cowardice but to poor morale, a defensive "Maginot" mentality, and a failure on the part of French leaders to think in modern terms or to understand as did the Germans the nature of modern mechanized warfare.

Mussolini chose the moment of French defeat to attack France, declaring war on both France and Britain on June 10th. He gained little by this action, and Hitler largely ignored the Italian dictator in making peace with France.

Hitler's forces remained in occupation of the northern part of France, including Paris. He allowed the French to keep their fleet and overseas territories probably in the hope of making them reliable allies. Petain and his chief minister Pierre Laval established their capital at Vichy and followed a policy of collaboration with their former enemies. A few Frenchmen, however, joined the Free French movement started in London by the then relatively unknown General Charles de Gaulle.

FROM THE FRENCH DEFEAT TO THE INVASION OF RUSSIA

Germany's "New Order" in Europe

By mid-summer 1940, Germany, together with its Italian ally, dominated most of western and central Europe. Germany began with no real plans for a long war, but continued resistance by the British made necessary the belated mobilization of German resources. Hitler's policy included exploiting those areas conquered by Germany. Collaborators were used to establish governments subservient to German policy. These received the name "Quislings" after the Norwegian traitor Vidkun Quisling, who was made premier of Norway during the German occupation. Germany began the policy of forcibly transporting large numbers of conquered Europeans to work in German war industries. Jews especially were forced into slave labor for the German war effort, and increasingly large numbers were rounded up and sent to concentration camps where they were systematically murdered as the Nazis carried out Hitler's "final solution" of genocide against European Jewry. Although much was known about this during the war, the full horror of these atrocities was not revealed until Allied troops entered Germany in 1945.

The Battle of Britain

With the fall of France, Britain remained the only power of consequence at war with the Axis. Hitler began preparations for invading Britain (Operation "Sea Lion"). Air control over the Channel was vital if an invasion force were to be transported safely to the English Coast. The German Air Force (Luftwaffe) under Herman Göring began its air offensive against the British in the summer of 1940. The British, however, had used the year between Munich and the outbreak of war to good advantage, increasing their production of aircraft to 600 per month, almost equal to German production. The Spitfire and Hurricane fighters which were the Royal Air Force's mainstay were designed and produced somewhat later than similar German planes and proved superior. The British had also developed the first radar just in time to be used to give early warning of German attacks. British intelligence was also effective in deciphering German military communications and in providing ways to interfere with the navigational devices used by the German bombers. The Germans concentrated first on British air defenses, then on ports and shipping, and finally in early September they began the attack on London. The Battle of Britain was eventually a defeat for the Germans, who were unable to gain decisive superiority over the British, although they inflicted great damage on both British air defenses and major cities such as London. Despite the damage and loss of life British morale remained high and necessary war production continued. German losses determined that bombing alone could not defeat Britain. Operation "Sea Lion" was postponed October 12th and never seriously taken up again, although the British did not know this and had to continue for some time to give priority to their coastal and air defenses.

Involvement of the United States

The Churchill government worked actively to gain help from the United States, and their efforts obtained a sympathetic response from President Franklin Roosevelt, although in his efforts to enact "measures short of war" to aid Britain he had to deal with strong isolationist sentiment in the United States exemplified by the America First movement. Wendell Willkie, his Republican opponent in the 1940 presidential election, took an identical international position. As early as November 1939 neutrality legislation was amended to lift the ban on the sale of arms to belligerents. Late in 1940, when a crisis developed with respect to protection for British shipping, Roosevelt negotiated an agreement by which Congress was persuaded to transfer to the British 50 World War I destroyers in return for naval bases on British possessions in the Western Hemisphere. In 1941, when British assets in the U.S. had been depleted, the U.S.

president and Congress enacted the Lend-Lease Program to provide resources for continued purchases of weapons and supplies by the British. Later the program was extended to supply Russia and other powers which became involved in the struggle against the Axis. The U.S. also introduced its first peacetime draft and began a tremendous program of military expansion. Bases were obtained in Greenland and Iceland, and American warships began to convoy Allied shipping as far as Iceland. The U.S. was already waging an "undeclared war" against Germany months before the Pearl Harbor attack led to formal American involvement.

Germany Turns East

During the winter of 1940 – 1941, having given up Operation "Sea Lion," Hitler began to shift his forces to the east for an invasion of Russia (Operation "Barbarossa"). The alliance of August 1939 was never harmonious, and German fears were aroused by Russia's annexation of the three Baltic states in June 1940, by the attack on Finland, and by Russian seizure of the province of Bessarabia from Rumania. Russian expansion towards the Balkans dismayed the Germans, who hoped for more influence there themselves. In addition, Hitler's ally Mussolini had, on October 28, 1940, begun an ill-advised invasion of Greece from bases in Albania which the Italians had seized earlier. Within a few weeks the Greeks repulsed the Italians and drove them back into Albania.

The Balkan Campaign

These events prompted Hitler to make demands early in 1941 on Rumania, Bulgaria, and Hungary which led these powers to become German allies accepting occupation by German forces. Yugoslavia resisted and the Germans attacked on April 6th, occupying the state despite considerable resistance. They then advanced to the aid of the Italians in their attack on Greece. Greece was quickly overrun despite aid from the British forces in the Middle East. The Greek government took refuge on Crete some sixty miles off the Greek coast, but that island was also captured from its British garrison. On May 20th German parachute troops and airborne forces established footholds at key points on the island. The defenders were unable to repel the Germans and at the end of May Crete was evacuated by the British, with the Greek government also going into exile in London.

Barbarossa — The Attack on Russia

The German invasion of Russia began June 22, 1941. The invasion force of three million included Finnish, Rumanian, Hungarian, and Italian contingents along with the Germans and advanced on a broad front of about 2,000 miles. In this first season of fighting the Germans seized White Russia and most of the Ukraine, advancing to the Crimean Peninsula in the south. They surrounded the city of Leningrad (although they never managed to actually capture it). Advanced German units came within about 25 miles of Moscow. Government offices were evacuated. In November the enemy actually entered the suburbs, but then the long supply lines, early winter, and Russian resistance (strong despite heavy losses) brought the invasion to a halt. During the winter a Russian counterattack pushed the Germans back from Moscow and saved the capital. Then on December 7th the United States was brought into the war by the surprise Japanese attack on the U.S. naval base at Pearl Harbor, and the entire balance of power in this conflict would ultimately change.

The Far Eastern Crisis

With the coming of the Great Depression and severe economic difficulties,

Japanese militarists gained more and more influence over the civilian government which was unable to control its armed forces — especially the Kwantung army which garrisoned the Japanese-controlled railroad lines in the Chinese province of Manchuria. Believing a policy of expansion and empire-building on the Asian mainland would help solve Japan's difficulties and bring ultimate prosperity, the officers of the Kwangtung army engineered an explosion on one of the railroad lines. On September 18, 1931, using this as an excuse, the Japanese occupied all of Manchuria. On July 7, 1937, a full-scale Sino-Japanese war began with a clash between Japanese and Chinese at the Marco Polo Bridge in Peking (now Beijing). An indication of ultimate Japanese aims came on November 3, 1938, when Prince Konoye's government issued a statement on "A New Order in East Asia." This statement envisaged the integration of Japan, Manchuria (now the puppet state of Manchukuo), and China into one "Greater East Asia Co-Prosperity Sphere" under Japanese leadership. In July 1940 the Konoye government was re-formed with General Hideki Tojo (Japan's principal leader in World War I) as minister of war. Japan's policy of friendship with Nazi Germany and Fascist Italy was consolidated with the signing of a formal alliance in September 1940. The war in Europe gave Japan further opportunities for expansion. Concessions were obtained from the Vichy government in French Indochina and Japanese bases were established there.

All of these events led to worsening relations between Japan and the two states in a position to oppose her expansion — the Soviet Union and the United States. Despite border clashes with the Russians, Japan avoided any conflict with that state, and Stalin wanted no war with Japan after he became fully occupied with the German invasion. The United States viewed Japanese activities with increasing disfavor, especially the brutal war against China. A trade treaty was not renewed and exports of scrap metals, oil, etc., necessary to the Japanese war effort, were embargoed by the American government. By 1941 a crisis developed, and although the American government did not know the details at the time, in Japan decisions had already been made that would finally lead to the attack on American naval forces moved to Hawaii as a deterrent to further Japanese expansion. There has been much controversy surrounding the Japanese surprise attack on the Pearl Harbor naval base on December 7, 1941. Here it is sufficient to say that the United States forces were caught off guard and suffered a disastrous defeat which fortunately was not as complete as the Japanese planned. It did, however, put the United States on the defensive for a year or more. In a few weeks Japanese forces were able to occupy strategically important islands (including the Philippines and Dutch East Indies) as well as territory on the Asian mainland (Malaya, with the British naval base at Singapore, and all of Burma to the border of India).

The Japanese attack brought the United States not only into war in the Pacific but also resulted in German and Italian declarations of war which meant the total involvement of the United States in World War II.

The "Turning of the Tide"

The basic strategy for winning the war had been evolved well before Pearl Harbor. Pre-war American strategic planning (the so-called Rainbow plans) provided for several possibilities, always keeping in mind the defense of the Western Hemisphere as the major goal. During 1940 and 1941, as it became more and more apparent that the United States would become involved as an ally first of Britain and then the Soviet Union, plans changed accordingly. A two-front war became increasingly likely, and U.S. strategists decided — with British concurrence — that priority should be given to the war in Europe (a "Germany first" policy), because the danger to both Britain and the U.S.S.R. seemed more immediate than the threat from Japan. As it turned out, the

United States mobilized such great resources that sufficient forces were available to go over to the offensive in the Pacific at the same time European theater requirements were being met and the war against Japan ended only a few weeks after the German surrender.

American involvement in the war was ultimately decisive, for it meant that the greatest industrial power of that time was now arrayed against the Axis powers. The United States became, as President Roosevelt put it, "the arsenal of democracy." American aid was crucial to the immense effort of the Soviet Union. Despite almost unanimous expert opinion that the Russians would collapse under German attack, Roosevelt had his personal assistant Harry Hopkins visit Russia and assess the situation, and based on Hopkins' recommendations Lend-Lease aid was extended to Russia. By 1943 supplies and equipment were reaching Russia in very considerable quantities. Routes were found through the Persian Gulf and overland and also through the Russian Arctic port of Murmansk. The latter route was exceedingly dangerous because of the proximity of German forces based in Norway and on one or two occasions, losses were so great that convoys had to be temporarily suspended until their defenses could be improved. Nevertheless in this modern war where the supply and equipment of vast forces over great distances was a major factor, American industrial strength was decisive.

The Second German Offensive in Russia: Stalingrad

Despite losses that included their richest farm land, one-half of their industry and millions of the population, the Russians not only stopped the Germans and their allies just short of Moscow, but in a winter offensive drove the center German army group back some 80 miles from the capital. Nevertheless, with Hitler in personal control, the German forces launched a second offensive in the summer of 1942. This attack concentrated on the southern part of the front, aiming at the Caucasus and vital oil fields around the Caspian Sea. At Stalingrad on the Volga River the Germans were stopped. There were weeks of bitter fighting in the streets of the city itself. With the onset of winter, Hitler refused to allow the strategic retreat urged by his generals. As a result the Russian forces crossed the river north and south of the city and surrounded 22 German divisions. On January 31, 1943, following the failure of relief efforts, the German commander Paulus surrendered the remnants of his army. From then on the Russians were, with only few exceptions, always on the offensive.

The North African Campaigns

After entering the war in 1940, the Italians invaded British-held Egypt from Libya. In December 1940 the British General Wavell launched a surprise attack. The Italian forces were driven back about 500 miles and 130,000 were captured. Then Hitler intervened, sending General Erwin Rommel with a small German force (the Afrika Korps) to reinforce the Italians. Rommel took command and exploiting the weakness of the British following the dispatch of forces to aid the Greeks, launched a counter-offensive which put his forces on the border of Egypt. Then Rommel in turn had to give up his reserves for the Russian campaign. He managed to recover from a second British attack, however, and by mid-1942 had driven to El Alamein, only 70 miles from Alexandria.

A change in the British high command now placed General Harold Alexander in charge of Middle Eastern forces with General Bernard Montgomery in immediate command of the British Eighth Army. After thorough preparations Montgomery attacked at El Alamein, breaking Rommel's lines and starting a British advance which was not stopped until the armies reached the border of Tunisia.

Meanwhile the British and American leaders, realizing that the forces at their disposal in 1942 would not be sufficient to invade France and start the drive on Germany itself (which was their ultimate goal), decided that they could launch a second offensive in North Africa (Operation "Torch") which would clear the enemy from the entire coast and make the Mediterranean once again safe for Allied shipping. To avoid fighting the French forces which garrisoned the main landing areas (at Casablanca, Oran and Algiers), the Allied command under the American General Dwight Eisenhower, made an agreement with the French commander Admiral Darlan. Darlan did, indeed, assist the Allies to a degree, but there was a loud public outcry in Britain and the U.S. at this alliance with a person who condoned fascism. Darlan was assassinated in December, leading to a struggle for leadership among the French in North Africa, de Gaulle's Free French, the French Resistance and other factions. Roosevelt and Churchill publicly supported senior French officer General Henri Giraud, who had just escaped from imprisonment by the Germans, against the independent and imperious de Gaulle, who was especially disliked by Roosevelt and was not kept informed of the North African operation or allowed to participate. De Gaulle proved his political as well as military talent by completely outmaneuvering Giraud and within a year he was the undisputed leader of all the French elements.

The landings resulted in little conflict with the French and indeed the French forces soon joined the war against the Axis. The Germans and Italians were a different matter, however. Hitler quickly sent German forces under General von Arnim to occupy Tunisia before the Anglo-American forces could get there from their landing points. It was only a matter of time, however, before these forces, together with those commanded by Rommel, were forced into northern Tunisia and forced to surrender. American forces, unused to combat, suffered some reverses at the Battle of the Kasserine Pass, but gained valuable experience. The final victory came in May 1943, about the same time as the Russian victory at Stalingrad.

Winning the Battle of the Atlantic

Another important though less spectacular turning point came in the long, drawn-out battle against German submarines in the North Atlantic. Relatively safe shipping routes across the North Atlantic to Britain were essential to the survival of Britain and absolutely necessary if a force was to be assembled to invade France and strike at Germany proper. At times early in the war the Germans sank ships at a higher rate than the two Allies could replace them, but gradually they began to develop effective countermeasures. New types of aircraft, small aircraft carriers, more numerous and better-equipped escort vessels, new radar and sonar (for underwater detection), extremely efficient radio direction finding, decipherment of German signals plus the building of more ships (including the mass-produced "Liberty Ship" freighter), turned the balance against the Germans despite their development of improved submarines. Again the tide of battle turned by early 1943 and the Atlantic became increasingly dangerous for German submarines .

A Turning Point

Success in these three campaigns — Stalingrad, North Africa, and the Battle of the Atlantic — gave new hope to the Allied cause and made certain that eventually victory would be won. Together with the beginning of an offensive in late 1942 in the Solomon Islands against the Japanese, they made 1943 the turning point of the war.

Allied Victory

At their conference at Casablanca in January 1943 Roosevelt and Churchill developed detailed strategy for the further conduct of the war. The decision to clear the Mediterranean was confirmed, and Sicily was to be invaded to help achieve this purpose. This led almost inevitably to Italy proper. Historians differ as to the significance of the Casablanca decisions. The Italian campaign did knock Italy out of the war and cause Hitler to send forces to Italy that might otherwise have opposed the 1944 landing in Normandy, and it did bring about the downfall of Mussolini and Italian surrender. It also ensured, by using up limited resources such as landing craft, that no second front in France could be opened in 1943 — a fact most unpalatable to Stalin, whose Russian armies were fighting desperately against the bulk of the German army and air force. Also the drawing off of forces from Italy to ensure a successful landing in France made it extremely difficult to achieve decisive victory in Italy and meant a long drawn-out and costly campaign there against skillful and stubborn resistance by the Germans under Marshal Kesselring. Rome was not captured by the Allied forces until June 4, 1944. With a new Italian government now supporting the Allied cause, Italian resistance movements in Northern Italy became a major force in helping to liberate that area from the Germans.

The Second Front in Normandy

At the Teheran Conference, held in November 1943 and attended by all three major Allied leaders (Stalin had previously declined to leave Russia), the final decision reached by Roosevelt and Churchill some six months earlier to invade France in May 1944 was communicated to the Russians. Stalin promised to open a simultaneous Russian offensive.

Despite the claims of General George Marshall and General Sir Alan Brooke (the American and British chiefs of staff, respectively) Roosevelt and Churchill decided on General Dwight Eisenhower, their North African commander, to be supreme commander of the coming invasion. Planning had already been carried for some time under the British General Frederick Morgan when Eisenhower arrived in London to establish Supreme Headquarters Allied Expeditionary Forces (SHAEF) and to weld together an international staff to command the invasion. He proved extremely adept at getting soldiers of several nations to work together harmoniously. British Air Marshal Tedder was his deputy supreme commander and Montgomery initially commanded the ground forces. Included in the invasion army were American, British, Canadian, Polish, and French contingents.

The Normandy invasion (Operation "Overlord") was the largest amphibious operation in history and was preceded by the most elaborate preparations and an enormous buildup of men and supplies. Plans included an air offensive with a force of 10,000 aircraft of all types, a large naval contingent and pre-invasion naval bombardment of the very strong German defenses, a transport force of some 4,000 ships, artificial harbors to receive supplies after the initial landings, and several divisions of airborne troops to be landed behind enemy coastal defenses the night preceding the sea-borne invasion. The landings actually took place beginning June 6, 1944. The first day, 130,000 men were successfully landed. Strong German resistance hemmed in the Allied forces for about a month. Then the Allies, now numbering about 1,000,000, managed a spectacular breakthrough. By the end of 1944 all of France had been seized. A second invasion force landed on the Mediterranean coast in August, freed southern France, and linked up with Eisenhower's forces. By the end of 1944 the Allied armies stood on the borders of Germany ready to invade from both east and west.

The Eastern Front: Poland

Russian successes brought their forces to the border of Poland by July 1944. Russian relations with the Polish government in exile in London, however, had by that time been broken off after the Poles had voiced their suspicions that the Russians and not the Germans might have caused the mass executions of a large number of Polish officers in the Katyn Forest early in the war.

Stalin's armies crossed into Poland July 23, 1944, and three days later the Russian dictator officially recognized a group of Polish Communists (the so-called Lublin Committee) as the government of Poland. As the Russian armies drew near the eastern suburbs of Warsaw, the London Poles (who controlled a large and well-organized resistance movement in Warsaw and who hoped to improve their position by a military effort) on August 1st launched their underground army in an attack on the German garrison. Stalin's forces waited outside the city while the Germans brought in reinforcements and slowly wiped out the Polish underground army in several weeks of heavy street fighting. The offensive then resumed and the city was liberated by the Red Army, but the local influence of the London Poles was now virtually nil. Needless to say, this incident aroused considerable suspicion concerning Stalin's motives and led both Churchill and Roosevelt to begin to think through the political implications of their alliance with Stalin.

Greece, Yugoslavia, and the Balkans

By late summer of 1944 the German position in the Balkans began to collapse. The Red Army crossed the border into Rumania leading King Michael II to seize the opportunity to take his country out of its alliance with Germany and to open the way to the advancing Russians. German troops were forced to make a hasty retreat. At this point Bulgaria saw the light and changed sides. The German forces in Greece, threatened with being cut off, withdrew in October with British forces moving in to take their place. The British hoped to bring about the return of the Greek government in exile from London.

From October 9 – 18, Winston Churchill visited Moscow to try to work out a political arrangement regarding the Balkans and Eastern Europe. (Roosevelt was busy with his campaign for election to a fourth term.) In Moscow Churchill worked out the famous agreement which he describes in his book on World War II. Dealing from a position of weakness, he simply wrote out some figures on a sheet of paper: Russia to have the preponderance of influence in certain countries like Bulgaria and Rumania, Britain to have the major say in Greece, and a fifty-fifty division in Yugoslavia and Hungary. Stalin indicated his agreement. The Americans refused to have anything to do with this "spheres of influence" arrangement.

In Greece Stalin maintained a hands-off policy when the British used military force to impose a settlement there. The Communist-led Greek resistance refused to agree to the return of the Greek government in exile. Fighting between the factions broke out. In December Churchill went to Athens to deal personally with the situation. British forces suppressed the Communist revolt and a regency was established under the Archbishop of Athens to end the political dispute. The British task was much simplified by the fact that Russia gave no support to the Greek Communists but treated Greece as a British sphere of influence.

The German Resistance and the 1944 Attempt to Assassinate Hitler

It was obvious even before the Normandy invasion that Germany was losing the war. Some German officers and civilians had formed a resistance movement. As long as Hitler's policy was successful it had little chance of overthrowing the German dictator. Four years of aerial bombardment, however, had reduced German cities to rubble by early 1944 and virtually destroyed the *Luftwaffe*. The Russians were on the offensive and many German officials did not like to think, after what had happened in Russia, what the Russian armies might do if they reached German soil. Hitler was in direct control of German forces and disregarded professional advice which might have provided a better, less costly defense. Knowing the war was lost after the success of the Normandy invasion, the Resistance plotted to assassinate Hitler. The leaders were retired General Ludwig Beck, Carl Goerdeler (former Mayor of Leipzig), and Count Claus Shenck von Stauffenberg — a much-decorated young staff officer who undertook the dangerous task of actually planting the bomb in Hitler's headquarters on July 20, 1944. Hitler miraculously survived the explosion and launched a reign of terror in reprisal which resulted in imprisonment, torture, and death for anyone even suspected of a connection with the plot. His survival ensured that the war would be fought out on German soil to the bitter end.

Final Questions of Strategy

In General Eisenhower's headquarters there was some dispute over the best way to invade Germany and end the war. Because of the long and rapid drive across France, supplies were insufficient for an immediate broad advance into Germany. Montgomery argued that his forces in the north should be given priority and allowed to push ahead into the North German Plain as the quickest way to end the war. Eisenhower's final decision to reject this and advance on a broad front took into account his fear that some German forces might retreat into mountain areas in southern Germany and in these easily defensible positions, prolong the war.

Before any final attack could be made, however, the Germans launched an offensive of their own beginning December 16. Hitler gathered his last reserves and sent them to attack the Allies in the Ardennes forest region with the goal of breaking through between the Allied forces and driving to the Channel coast. The offensive became known as the Battle of the Bulge. Bad weather for some days made impossible the effective use of Allied air power. The Allied lines held, however, and by the end of the first week of January 1945 the German offensive had been broken and the lines restored. Whether it had any value is open to argument. In Yugoslavia it certainly worked, and Tito (the Communist resistance leader) emerged as head of government and managed to maintain a position of independence not achieved by any other East European country.

The End of the War in Europe

In early spring of 1945 the Allied armies crossed the Rhine. The Americans used a railway bridge at Remagen which they captured just before the Germans had time to destroy it. As the Americans and British and other Allied forces advanced into Germany the Russians attacked from the east. While the Russian armies were fighting their way into Berlin, Hitler committed suicide in the ruins of the bunker where he had spent the last days of the war. Power was handed over to a government headed by Admiral Karl Doenitz. On May 7th, General Alfred Jodl, acting for the German government, made the final unconditional surrender at General Eisenhower's headquarters near Reims.

The Yalta and Potsdam Conferences

The future treatment of Germany, and Europe generally, was determined by decisions of the "Big Three" (Churchill, Stalin, and Roosevelt). There were two summit meetings attended by all three leaders. Even before the first of these was held at Teheran, Churchill and Roosevelt had met at Casablanca and laid down a basic policy of demanding the unconditional surrender of their enemies. Stalin was agreeable to this.

The first of the major conference convened at Teheran November 28, 1943, and lasted until December 1st. Here the two Western allies told Stalin of the May 1944 date for the planned invasion of Normandy. In turn Stalin confirmed a pledge made earlier that Russia would enter the war against Japan after the war with Germany was concluded. Political questions were barely touched upon. Poland and other topics were raised but not dealt with. Roosevelt reflected the views of his military leaders who were concerned with the quickest ending to the war. Hence he was willing to postpone political decisions on the Balkans and Eastern Europe and concentrate on a second front in France and the shortest road to Berlin. This was agreeable to Stalin since any postponement would only better his position by allowing time for the Red Army to take control of the areas in question. Churchill seems to have had in mind political questions far more than his American colleague (hence his October 1944 visit to Moscow and "spheres of influence" agreement with Stalin referred to above), but as the American participation in the war grew in magnitude, British influence declined, and he had to defer to the wishes of the Americans. It was not softness on communism, as charged by some critics of wartime diplomacy, but rather a desire for a quick military decision, that prompted Roosevelt to cooperate as he did with Stalin despite the fears of Churchill.

The Yalta Conference was the second attended personally by Stalin, Churchill and Roosevelt. It lasted from the 4th to the 11th of February 1945. A plan to divide Germany into zones of occupation, which had been devised in 1943 by a committee under British Deputy Prime Minister Clement Attlee, was formally accepted with the addition of a fourth zone taken from the British and American zones for the French to occupy. Berlin, which lay within the Russian Zone, was divided into four zones of occupation also. Access to Berlin by the Western powers was not as clearly worked out as it should have been.

Such lack of precision was characteristic of other parts of the Yalta agreements as well, leading to future disputes and recriminations between the Western powers and the Russians. Stalin suggested a figure of $20 billion in reparations to be taken from German heavy industry and other assets, and Roosevelt and Churchill agreed this might be a goal but felt it might have to be modified later depending on conditions in Germany. A Declaration on Liberated Europe promised to assist liberated nations in solving problems through elections and by "democratic" means.

In Poland, Churchill and Roosevelt had to allow Stalin to do what he pleased. An eastern frontier was established, corresponding roughly to the old Curzon Line drawn after World War I. Poland, in turn, was allowed to occupy territory in the west up to the line of the Oder and Neisse rivers. These boundaries were not, however, agreed upon as permanent boundaries but might be negotiated later when a peace treaty could be made with Germany. In fact they became permanent when relations between the wartime allies broke down and the Cold War began.

It was agreed that the nucleus of the post-war Polish government would be Stalin's Lublin Committee. The only concession was an agreement to add a number of "democratic leaders" (London Poles), but these, as it turned out, were powerless to affect the course of events and prevent an eventual total takeover of Polish government by the Communists.

In the Far East, in return for his agreement to enter the war against Japan after Germany's defeat, Stalin was promised the southern part of Sakhalin Island, the Kurile

Islands, a lease on the naval base at Port Arthur, a pre-eminent position in control of the commercial port of Dairen, and the use of Manchurian railroads.

There has been much dispute over these concessions and whether they were really necessary. Looking back it is easy to see that Japan was close to defeat, with American and Allied forces near enough to commence a destructive aerial bombardment of Japanese cities and to blockade the main islands. At that time, considering how tenaciously the Japanese had resisted in the various Pacific island campaigns, it was believed that the war might last a considerable time. An invasion of the main islands of Japan was being planned by the American command with estimates of considerable casualties. Any help from the Russians which might pin down the considerable Japanese forces in Manchuria was believed to be extremely desirable. No one could be sure of the secret atomic bomb — which was nearing completion in American laboratories but which [illegible] less tried in actual combat.

T[illegible] place at Potsdam outside Berlin after t[illegible] Pacific war was still going on. The confe[illegible] Churchill, and the new American Presid[illegible] died suddenly, shortly after the concl[illegible] conference was in session, the results of the British [illegible] was defeated, his place taken by his wartim[illegible] Clement Attlee. The meeting confir[illegible] y. A Potsdam Declaration, aimed at Japa[illegible] hinted at the consequences that would [illegible] the conference, American leaders receiv[illegible] atomic bomb in the New Mexico desert, [illegible] that such a destructive weapon might [illegible]

The A[illegible]

De[illegible] theoretical possibility following the first splittin[illegible] Fritz Hahn at the Kaiser Wilhelm Institu[illegible] quickly and both the British and Ameri[illegible] t develop a weapon based on this princip[illegible] atomic bomb first. In Britain a researc[illegible] valuable work had been done by the tim[illegible] United States entered the war. At that point the decision was made to concentrate the work in the United States with its vastly greater resources of power and industrial capacity. The Manhattan Engineering District under Major General Leslie Groves was established to manage the immense research, development, and production effort needed to develop an atomic weapon. By early 1945 it appeared that a weapon would soon be available for testing, and in July the successful test was completed.

President Truman established a committee of prominent scientists and leaders to determine how best to utilize the bomb. They advised the president that they could not devise any practical way of demonstrating the bomb. If it was to be used it had to be dropped on Japan, and President Truman then made the decision to do this. On August 6, 1945, the bomb was dropped by a single plane on Hiroshima and an entire city disappeared with the instantaneous loss of 70,000 lives. In time many other persons died from radiation poisoning and other effects. Since no surrender was received, a second bomb was dropped on Nagasaki, obliterating that city. Even the most fanatical of the Japanese leaders saw what was happening and surrender came quickly. The only departure from unconditional surrender was to allow the Japanese to retain their emperor (Hirohito), but only with the proviso that he would be subject in every respect to the orders of the occupation commander. The formal surrender took place September 2, 1945, in Tokyo Bay on the deck of the battleship *Missouri*, and the occupation of Japan began under the immediate control of the American commander General Douglas MacArthur.

EUROPE AFTER WORLD WAR II: 1945 TO 1953

General Nature of the Peace Settlement

After World War II there was no clear-cut settlement in treaty form as there was after World War I with the Versailles Treaty and other treaties which formed the Paris Peace Settlement of 1919. What planning there was had been done at the series of major wartime conferences between the leaders of Great Britain, the United States, and the Soviet Union. Then, in the years immediately following the German surrender, a series of de facto arrangements were made, shaped by the course of events during the occupation of Germany and the opening years of the so-called Cold War which followed the breakdown of the wartime alliance between the Western powers (Britain, France, and the U.S.) and the Soviet Union.

The Atlantic Charter

Anglo-American ideas about what the postwar world should be like were expressed by Roosevelt and Churchill at their meeting off the coast of Newfoundland in August 1941 in the form of an "Atlantic Charter." This was a general statement of goals: restoration of the sovereignty and self-government of nations conquered by Hitler, free access to world trade and resources, cooperation to improve living standards and economic security, and a peace that would ensure freedom from fear and want and stop the use of force and aggression as instruments of national policy.

Postwar Planning During World War II

At the Casablanca Conference the policy of requiring unconditional surrender by the Axis powers was announced. This ensured that at the end of the war all responsibility for government of the defeated nations would fall on the victors, and they would have a free hand in rebuilding government in those countries. No real planning was done in detail before the time arrived to meet this responsibility. It was done for the most part as the need actually arose.

At Teheran, the Big Three did discuss in a general way the occupation and demilitarization of Germany. They also laid the foundation for a post-war organization — the United Nations Organization — which like the earlier League of Nations was supposed to help regulate international relations and keep the peace and ensure friendly cooperation between the nations of the world.

One possible postwar plan for Germany was initially accepted by Roosevelt and Churchill in September 1944 and then quietly discarded when its impracticality became apparent to all. This was the Morgenthau Plan, named after U.S. Secretary of the Treasury Henry Morgenthau, Jr., who was instrumental in proposing it. This harsh scheme would have largely destroyed Germany as an industrial power and returned it to an agricultural/pastoral economy. Both British and Americans came quickly to realize that Germany could not return to the 18th century before the Industrial Revolution. They also realized that the resources of German heavy industry would be necessary to the recovery and vitality of the rest of Europe. This episode did point up the importance of a healthy German economy to Europe as a whole, and Allied recognition of this.

At the Yalta Conference early in 1945, the Big Three agreed on a number of matters, at least tentatively. The eastern boundary of Poland was set approximately at the old Curzon Line which had been proposed at the end of World War I to run as closely as possible along ethnic lines separating Poles and Russians. Poland was to occupy formerly German territory in the West including the old Polish Corridor, Danzig (Gdansk), and territory up to the Oder and Neisse rivers. Germany was to be disarmed and divided into four zones of occupation: Russian, British, and American, and a zone for France taken from what had been originally agreed to be British and American territory. The principle of German reparations was established but no firm figure was set. Half of the reparations were to go to the Soviet Union.

At Yalta, agreement was also reached with regard to a government for Poland. The Communist Lublin Committee established by Stalin was to be the nucleus of a provisional government with the addition of representatives of other "democratic" elements (*i.e.*, the London Polish Government recognized by Britain and the U.S.). A verbal agreement for the "earliest possible establishment through free elections of governments responsive to the will of the people" cost Stalin little, and there proved to be no way in any event for the other powers to ensure the integrity of such elections if held. The Declaration on Liberated Europe, with its promise of rights of self-determination, provided a false sense of agreement.

The territorial arrangements with regard to Poland and the eastern boundary of Germany, agreed to provisionally at Yalta, were confirmed at Potsdam in July following the German surrender. Although the arrangements were to be provisional pending a formal peace treaty with Germany, they became permanent when no agreement could be reached among the wartime allies on a German treaty.

At Potsdam, agreement was also reached to sign peace treaties as soon as possible with former German allies. A Council of Foreign Ministers was established to draft the treaties. Several meetings were held in 1946 and 1947 and treaties were signed with Italy, Rumania, Hungary, Bulgaria, and Finland. These states paid reparations and agreed to some territorial readjustments as a price for peace. No agreement could be reached on Japan or Germany. In 1951 the Western powers led by the U.S. concluded a treaty with Japan without Russian participation. The latter made their own treaty in 1956. A final meeting of the Council of Foreign Ministers broke up in 1947 over Germany, and no peace treaty was ever signed with that country. The division of Germany for purposes of occupation and military government became permanent with the three Western zones joining and eventually becoming the Federal Republic of Germany and the Russian zone becoming the German Democratic Republic.

Arrangements for the United Nations Organization were confirmed at the Yalta Conference: the large powers would predominate in a Security Council where they would have permanent seats together with several other powers elected from time to time from among the other members of the U.N.O. Consent of all the permanent members was necessary for any action to be taken by the Security Council (thus giving the large powers a veto). The General Assembly was to include all members.

EASTERN EUROPE: 1945 – 1953

The Soviet Union

The ability of the Soviet Union to withstand the terrific pressure of the German invasion and to recover, drive back, and destroy the bulk of the German invaders indicated its great inherent strength. Despite these victories, the Russian government faced tremendous immediate problems. Much of European Russia had been devastated and about 25 million people made homeless. Recovery was achieved using the same drastic, dictatorial methods used by the Communists during the 1930s. Stalin's dictatorship became more firmly entrenched than ever. Any potential opposition was purged. In March 1946 a fourth five-year plan was adopted by the Supreme Soviet intended to increase industrial output to a level 50% higher than before the war. Industrial equipment was collected from areas occupied by the Red Army. In 1947 the state planning commission announced that while goals had not been met in 1946, the yearly goal for 1947 had been surpassed. A bad harvest and food shortage in 1946 had been relieved by a good harvest in 1947, and in December 1947, the government announced the end of food rationing. At the same time a drastic currency devaluation was put through which brought immediate hardship to many people but strengthened the Soviet economy in the long run. As a result of these and other forceful and energetic measures, the Soviet Union was able within a few years to make good most of the wartime damage and to surpass pre-war levels of production. While this was being done at home Stalin pursued an aggressive foreign policy and established a series of Soviet satellite states in Eastern Europe.

The Communization of Eastern Europe

The fate of Eastern Europe (including Poland, Hungary, Rumania, Bulgaria, Czechoslovakia, and the Russian zone of Germany) from 1945 on was determined by the presence of Russian armies in that area. Stalin undoubtedly wanted a group of friendly nations on his western border from which invasion had come twice during his lifetime. The Russian Communists were also determined to support the advance of a communist system similar to that developed in Russia into the countries of Eastern Europe. The presence of the Red Army allowed Russia to do this just as the presence of American forces in Japan determined the postwar course of that nation.

Communization of Eastern Europe and the establishment of regimes in the satellite areas of the Soviet Union occurred in stages over a three year period following the end of the war. The timetable of events varied in each country. Coalitions with other parties existed first, with the Communists forming a front with socialist and peasant parties. Initial measures were taken to punish those who had collaborated with the Nazis during the wartime occupation, on measures such as land reform. Eventually all opposition parties were ousted and in each case the government became one totally dominated by the local Communist party.

Poland: A Test Case

As agreed at Yalta, the Lublin Committee was expanded into a provisional government by the inclusion of Stanislas Mikolajczyk and other leaders from the London Polish government in exile. Communists occupied ministries controlling police, internal affairs, and the military, ensuring that power eventually remained in their control. The Polish Workers (Communist) Party knew it had very little backing among the Polish people who were strongly Catholic and anti-Russian, and they maintained tight control over them from the beginning. Elections agreed to at Yalta were finally held in 1947, but under conditions that made the victory of the Communists inevitable. Mikolajczyk, frustrated in his efforts to influence the government, resigned, went into opposition, and then finally fled the country later in 1947.

Hungary

Toward the end of the war, with German control weakened by defeats at the hands of the Russians, the Hungarian government changed hands and a new regime concluded an armistice on January 20, 1945. Hungary then changed sides and joined the United Nations in the war against Germany. In November 1945 a general election gave victory to the anti-Communist Smallholders Party, whose leader, Zoltan Tildy, formed a coalition government. The government found itself in increasing economic difficulties, and by 1947 the Communists — with Soviet support — began a purge and takeover of the government. In February 1947 Bela Kovacs, secretary general of the Smallholders Party, was arrested and charged with plotting against the Soviet occupation forces. A general election held in August gave the Communists a majority. In January 1948 the Communists engineered a fusion of Communists and Social Democrats into a United Workers Party in which the Communists were dominant. Although the Smallholders Party still held some seats in the cabinet, effective power was in the hands of deputy premier Matyas Rakosi (Communist). A new constitution was promulgated August 7, 1949. The Communist regime was now firmly established and began a program of nationalization of industry followed by a five-year plan of development on the Russian model.

The refusal of the Roman Catholic Church in Hungary to make concessions to the government led to the arrest and trial of Josef Cardinal Mindszenty, who was sentenced in February 1949 to life imprisonment. Other bishops continued their opposition to the government for about two years before they finally took an oath of allegiance to the people's republic in July 1951.

Bulgaria

Postwar developments in Bulgaria were decisively influenced by the Red Army which invaded the country in 1944. The Soviet-sponsored government established in September contained only a few Communists, but they occupied key positions of power. Bulgaria formally capitulated on October 28, 1944, and remained under occupation by the Red Army. An election held in November 1945 gave overwhelming support to a Communist-controlled coalition called the Fatherland Front. In 1946 the Communists made a sweeping purge of the government, executing or removing some 1,500 high-ranking officials of the old regime and many more lesser government officials. A referendum in September formally rejected any restoration of the pre-war monarchy, and later that same month Bulgaria was declared a people's republic.

With considerable government interference, a constituent assembly was elected with a Communist majority. Veteran Communist Georgi Dimitrov returned from Moscow to become premier in February 1947. In that year a Bulgarian Peace Treaty was signed at Paris requiring Bulgaria to pay indemnities and limiting the size of its armed forces. During 1947 the government began a program of nationalization by taking over banks and industries. In December, Soviet forces ended their occupation, leaving behind a firmly entrenched Communist regime which signed a treaty of friendship with the Soviet Union the following year.

Rumania

During the war, Rumania, was governed by a pro-fascist regime which allied the country with the Axis. With Russian armies invading the country, King Michael dismissed the government and accepted armistice terms from the United Nations. The Russians occupied the capital of Bucharest in August 1944. As in other areas of Eastern Europe, a coalition government was first formed with Communists participating along with other parties, but from the beginning the Communists held the real power. In November 1945 a general election took place preceded by a campaign of government violence against opposition parties. During 1947 the leaders of opposition parties such as the National Peasant Party were arrested and sentenced to prison for espionage and treason and their parties dissolved. At the end of the year, King Michael abdicated under Communist pressure. Following elections in 1948, a new constitution was adopted patterned after the Russian model. Relations with Western powers became virtually nil because of accusations of espionage made against Western diplomats. By the end of 1949 Rumania had become completely Communist and a satellite of the Soviet Union.

East Germany

In the Russian zone in Eastern Germany a Soviet satellite state was also established. During the Nazi period, a number of German Communists fled to Moscow. When the Red Army invaded Germany, these exiles returned under the leadership of Wilhelm Pieck and Otto Grotewohl. As relations broke down between the four occupying powers, the Soviet authorities gradually created a Communist state in their zone. Elections in May 1948 resulted in a constituent assembly with a two-thirds majority of Communists. By the end of the month a draft constitution had been approved. On October 7, 1948, a German Democratic Republic was established. Pieck became president and Grotewohl head of a predominantly Communist cabinet. The Soviet military regime was replaced by a Soviet Control Commission. In June 1950 an agreement with Poland granted formal recognition of the Oder-Neisse Line as the boundary between the two states. Economic progress was unsatisfactory for most of the population, and on June 16 – 17, 1953, riots occurred in East Berlin which were suppressed by Soviet forces using tanks. In East Germany a program of economic reform was announced which eventually brought some improvement.

Special Cases

Czechoslovakia is an example of a country whose government tried to remain relatively free and democratic, while at the same time attempted to reach agreement with the Soviet Union that would provide the basis for peaceful coexistence with Russia after the war. The government in exile in London under President Eduard Benes maintained good relations with Moscow during the war. In April 1945 Benes appointed a national front government which was a genuine coalition of parties. The government moved to Prague May 10, 1945. A sweeping purge of those who had collaborated with the Germans was carried out. In addition, on August 3 all those ethnic Germans living in the Sudetenland and elsewhere in the country were deprived of their citizenship and eventually expelled. The period from October 1945 to June 1946 was devoted to choosing a national assembly and establishing a permanent government. Elections held in May 1946 gave the Communists 114 of 300 assembly seats and the Communist Klement Gottwald formed a coalition cabinet. Benes was unanimously re-elected president of the republic. On July 7, 1947, the Czech government decided to accept Marshall Plan aid and to participate in the carrying-out of the plan. At this point Soviet pressure caused the Czech government to break off this policy and withdraw.

The period of genuine coalition government lasted about three years in Czechoslovakia. But here as elsewhere in Eastern Europe, the Communists seized total control of the government, eliminating other political elements. The Communist coup was carried out February 26, 1948. The Communist Party had prepared by infiltrating members into government services and trade unions. With Russian support they then put pressure on President Benes to agree to a cabinet under Klement Gottwald which would be primarily Communist. On March 10 a major obstacle to communization was removed when Foreign Minister Jan Masaryk (son of Thomas Masaryk, founder of the Czech Republic) was killed in a fall from his office window which the authorities reported as suicide. A far-reaching purge in the next several months transformed a democratic Czechoslovakia into a "people's democracy" with a single party government. On May 9 a constituent assembly adopted a new constitution. National elections, in which only a single list of candidates (Communist) appeared on the ballot, confirmed the Communist victory. President Benes resigned June 7 because of ill health and died shortly after on September 3. On June 14, Klement Gottwald became the new president and on January 1, 1949, a Soviet-style five year plan of industrial development began with the aim of making the country independent of the West.

In June 1949 a campaign began against the Roman Catholic Church which as elsewhere in Eastern Europe proved to be a source of opposition to the Communist program. The government formed its own Catholic Action Committee to take control of the local church from Archbishop Joseph Beran and the Catholic hierarchy. On October 14 the government assumed full control of all Catholic affairs. The Catholic clergy were required to swear a loyalty oath to the Communist state.

Czech politics followed a course of increasingly repressive measures paralleling that of Stalin during his last years in the Soviet Union. In 1950 a series of purges were carried out against enemies of the government, including some of its own members who were accused of anti-Soviet, pro-Western activities. Beginning in April, the Czech military was completely reorganized on Soviet lines. In March 1951 further purges were carried out to remove "Titoist" elements (a reference to the Yugoslav Communist leader whose independent policy had earned him the enmity of Stalin). Reports of economic difficulties, including a severe shortage of coal and the failure of a program to collectivize farming, were made public by the government in 1952. Simultaneously, a mass treason trial opened in November. At the trial, Rudolph Slansky, former Czech Communist Party Secretary General, pleaded guilty to treason, espionage, and sabotage.

In Yugoslavia, Marshal Tito and his Communist partisan movement emerged from the war in a strong position because of their effective campaign against the German occupation. Tito was able to establish a Communist government despite considerable pressure from Stalin, and pursue a course independent of the Soviet Union unique among the countries of Eastern Europe.

Elections held November 11, 1945 gave victory to Tito's Communist-dominated National Front. A few days later the Yugoslav monarchy was abolished and the country declared to be the Federal People's Republic of Yugoslavia. A new constitution was adopted January 31, 1946. The new regime was recognized by the Western powers despite its Communist nature and pro-Soviet inclination. Enemies of the new regime were dealt with severely. General Drazha Mihailovich, leader of an anti-Tito wartime resistance movement, was captured, tried, and executed July 17. Archbishop Stepinac, the Catholic leader of Croatia, was arrested on charges of collaborating with the Germans and sentenced to 17 years imprisonment at hard labor.

In 1947 Yugoslavia appeared to follow the lead of the other East European states when it concluded treaties of friendship and alliance with a number of these states and became a founding member of the Communist Information Agency (Cominform) — an organization created to take the place of the old Communist International which had been abolished by Stalin in 1943 as a gesture of goodwill to his wartime allies. In April 1948, Tito announced the start of a five-year plan of development. Tito followed a policy independent of the wishes of Stalin, causing the Russian dictator to try to exert pressure on Yugoslavia and finally to recall Russian advisors and break off relations. On June 28, 1948, the Cominform formally expelled Yugoslavia.

Tito retained the support of his own party, however, when he denied Cominform charges against him at a Congress of the Yugoslavian Communist Party and received a vote of confidence. The dispute continued in 1949 when the satellites of Eastern Europe breaking off economic relations with Yugoslavia. In September the Soviet Union denounced its Treaty of Friendship with Tito's regime. Tito's position was shown to be secure, however, when elections in March 1950 gave overwhelming victory to his People's Front candidates. Tito followed a policy of informal rapprochement with the West. He announced his opposition to Chinese intervention in the Korean War; established diplomatic relations with Greece, and withdrew support from the Communist guerrillas waging war against the government. Tito also made overtures to Italy to repair relations with that country. In November 1951 Tito even went so far as to make an agreement with the United States for the latter to supply equipment, materiel, and services to the Yugoslavian army. In July 1952 the United States agreed to supply tanks, artillery, and jet aircraft to the Yugoslavs despite the fact that Tito — while retaining independence of Stalin — remained staunchly Communist in his government of Yugoslavia.

WESTERN EUROPE: 1945-1953

Italy

In Italy, following the end of hostilities with Germany, the leaders of the Resistance in the north ousted Premier Ivan Bonomi and placed one of their own top leaders, Ferruccio Parri, in power. Parri was the leader of a faction — the Party of Action — which was socialist in its program. Although he was a man of great moral stature, he was a poor administrator and did not appeal to the public. He was left politically isolated when the Socialist leader Pietro Nenni made an alliance with the Communists. Meanwhile, more conservative forces had been gathering strength, and in November 1945, Parri was forced to resign.

The monarchy which had governed Italy since the time of unification in the mid-19th century was now discarded in favor of a republic. On May 9, 1946, King Victor Emmanuel III, compromised by his association with Mussolini's Fascist regime, resigned in favor of his son, who became King Umberto II. His reign was short-lived, for a referendum in June 1946 established a republic. In simultaneous elections for a constituent assembly, three parties predominated: the Social Democrats with 115 members, the Communists with 104, and the Christian Democrats with 207. Under the new regime Enrico de Nicola was chosen president and Alcide de Gasperi formed a new coalition cabinet.

The Christian Democrats and their leader Alcide de Gasperi dominated Italian politics for the next several years. On February 10, 1947, a peace treaty was signed at Paris. Italy paid $350 million in reparations and suffered some minor losses of territory. Trieste, which was in dispute between Italy and Yugoslavia, became a free territory. De Gasperi's government followed a policy of cooperation with the West and kept Italy non-Communist. In April 1948 in the first elections under the new constitution, the Christian Democrats won an absolute majority of seats in the Italian parliament. The issue of communism remained very much alive, and there was considerable Communist-inspired unrest, especially after an attempt was made on the life of the Communist leader Palmiro Togliatti. The Marshall Plan helped stabilize the situation in Italy. In 1948, Italy received $601 million in aid vital to the Italian economy. On April 4, 1949, Italy signed the North Atlantic Treaty and became a member of NATO, firmly allied to the West. The de Gasperi era came to an end in 1953. He won a narrow electoral victory as the head of a coalition in June and resigned July 28 after a vote of no confidence. He died a year later, August 19, 1954.

France

In the last two years of the war, France recovered sufficiently under the leadership of General Charles de Gaulle to begin playing a significant military and political role once again. In July 1944 the United States recognized de Gaulle's Committee of National Liberation as the de facto government of those areas liberated from the German occupation. As the war ended, this provisional government put through a purge of collaborators, including Marshal Petain and Pierre Laval, who had headed the Vichy regime during the war.

In October 1945 elections for a constituent assembly showed the strength of left-wing forces: Communists, 152; Socialists, 151; and the Popular Republican Movement (MRP), 138. De Gaulle, after a period in which he tried to work with the more radical forces, finally resigned in January 1947 and went into retirement. In May 1946 a popular referendum rejected the proposed constitution. In June a new assembly was elected, dominated by the MRP with the Communists second and the Socialists third. A revised constitution was adopted in October establishing a Fourth Republic, very much like the Third, with a weak executive dominated by a strong legislature. This situation resulted in cabinet instability with a series of governments over the next several years. Communist agitation and obstructionism combined with economic difficulties created an increasingly wide split between Communist and non-Communist members of the cabinet which resulted in the exclusion of five Communist members in May 1947.

Meanwhile General de Gaulle had assumed control of a nationwide *Rassemblement du Peuple Français* (RPF) intended to unify non-Communist elements and reform the system of government. For a time the RPF grew in strength at both the local and national level although de Gaulle himself remained out of office. Then, with the lessening of the Communist danger and improvements in the economy, moderates began to oppose what they perceived to be de Gaulle's authoritarian tendencies. By 1953 the RPF had faded from the scene, and de Gaulle returned to retirement.

Economically, France became a welfare state. De Gaulle, during his provisional government, inaugurated this welfare state to associate the working classes with a new spirit of national unity and to deprive the Communists of their propaganda advantage. During the year and a half following de Gaulle's retirement, the three parties (Socialist, Communist and MRP) which dominated politics during that period agreed on a program building on reforms begun during the Popular Front of the 1930s. This program, which included nationalization of coal mines, banking, insurance, gas and electricity as well as allowances for dependent children, was the beginning of a comprehensive system of social security legislation which eventually came to cover more than 50% of the French people.

These changes were accepted by all subsequent regimes as a fait accompli. Although excessively bureaucratic and regulatory, the welfare state did provide a cushion of security for the French population during the period of inflation and economic hardship in the immediate postwar years prior to the advent of the Marshall Plan. The establishment of a national planning office under Jean Monnet was a significant achievement which provided the French government with a framework for guiding economic development which Italy and West Germany lacked. This was important in directing French resources effectively when production began to rise during the prosperous years of the 1950s.

In foreign affairs France played a role in the occupation of Germany. In addition, the Fourth Republic was faced with two major problems abroad when it attempted to assert its authority over Indochina and Algeria. The Indochina situation resulted in a long and costly war against nationalists and Communists under Ho Chi Minh. French involvement ended with the Geneva accords of 1954 and French withdrawal. The Algerian struggle reached a crisis in 1958 which resulted in the return to power of General de Gaulle and the creation of a new Fifth Republic.

Germany

In May 1945, when Germany surrendered unconditionally, the country lay in ruins and faced a tremendous job of recovering economically and politically from the tragic consequences of the Hitler era. About three-quarters of city houses had been gutted by air raids, industry was in a shambles, and the country was divided into zones of occupation ruled by foreign military governors. Economic chaos was the rule, currency was virtually worthless, food was in short supply, and the black market flourished for those who could afford to buy in it. By the Potsdam agreements Germany had lost about one-quarter of its pre-war territory. In addition, some 12 million expelled people of German origin driven from their homes in countries like Poland and Czechoslovakia had to be fed, housed and clothed along with the indigenous population.

Demilitarization, denazification, and democratization were the initial goals of the occupation forces. All four wartime allies agreed on the trial of leading Nazis for a variety of war crimes and "crimes against humanity." An International Military Tribunal was established at Nuremburg to try 22 major war criminals and lesser courts tried many others. The four prosecuting powers gathered massive evidence of the crimes of the Hitler era from captured German archives, interviews, etc., and introduced it into evidence. Most of the defendants were executed, although a few like Rudolf Hess were given life imprisonment. At the time and later, questions were raised concerning the proceedings. Some charges such as the waging of aggressive war and genocide were new to jurisprudence. There was also the question of whether this was not simply "victors' justice." Also, one of the prosecuting powers was the Soviet Union which many felt was guilty of some of the same crimes charged against the Nazi defendants.

The denazification program met with indifferent success. It started out as an effort to investigate everyone who had any connection to the Nazi Party. This included so many that the proceedings became bogged down. It became apparent after a time that not all could be investigated because of the sheer magnitude of the task. Some important Nazi officials were found and punished. Often it was easier to prosecute those less involved, and some important offenders escaped. There was quiet sabotage and a conspiracy of silence by a cynical population. Eventually wider amnesties were granted. The process never officially ended but simply faded away.

The re- establishment of German government in the Western zones met with more success. As relations between the three Western powers and the Soviets gradually broke down in Germany, East and West became separate states. In the West the British and American zones were fused into one in 1946, with the French joining in 1948. Political parties were gradually re-established. First local government was once again run by Germans under close supervision, then gradually more independence was accorded to the Germans to govern themselves at the higher state level. Political parties were authorized by the end of 1945. In January 1946 elections for local offices in the American zone the Christian Democrats were first and the Social Democrats second. Elections in the British and French zones brought the same results.

During 1947 there were two meetings of the Council of Foreign Ministers to work out a peace treaty for Germany. Both failed and the occupying powers began to go their own way in their own zones — the Russians to create a Communist satellite state in East Germany and the British, Americans, and French to create a West German Federal Republic.

In February 1948 a bi-zonal charter granted further powers of government to the Germans in the American and British zones. During 1948 the Allied Control Council (comprised of the military commanders in the four zones) broke down. The Russian delegate walked out of the Council after charging that the three Western powers were undermining four-power cooperation in Germany. Later that year the Russians and East Germans, in an effort to force the Western powers out of their zones in Berlin, began a blockade of the city which was located within the Russian zone. The response was an allied airlift to supply the city, and eventually after some months the blockade was called off.

Meanwhile reconstruction in western Germany proceeded. On June 1, 1948, a six-power agreement of the three Western powers and Belgium, the Netherlands, and Luxembourg was reached, calling for international control of the Ruhr industrial area, German representation in the European Recovery Program (Marshall Plan), and the drafting of a federal constitution for a western Germany.

In April 1949 the three Western powers agreed on an Occupation Statute for Western Germany which gave the Germans considerable autonomy at the national level while reserving wide powers of intervention to the occupying powers. In May a parliamentary council representing the state governments adopted a Basic Law for a Federal Republic of Germany with its capital at Bonn. Elections in August gave the Christian Democrats a slight lead over the Social Democrats, and the next month Konrad Adenauer (Christian Democrat) became Chancellor of the new West German government. Theodore Heuss (Free Democrat) was elected president. For the next 14 years Adenauer (who was 73 at the start) and the Christian Democrats remained in power.

West Germany regained complete independence and sovereignty within a short period of time. As a result of the Korean War (which started in 1950) and fear of Soviet aggression in Europe, the process moved rapidly. West German rearmament was felt by the Western powers to be necessary to the defense of Western Europe. West Germany became firmly allied with the West and eventually with the military organization within NATO.

It should be noted that West German economic recovery had made it the strongest industrial power of Western Europe. Wartime damage to German industry was less than appeared on the surface, and despite early taking of industrial assets as reparations, recovery was rapid once the Marshall Plan came into being. Even the expellees from the east were an asset as they provided extra labor — sometimes skilled. A program of industrial expansion with careful planning and investments, aided by the willingness of the population to accept relatively modest living standards and to work hard, paid dividends. There was little labor strife and for several years no need to provide for military expenditures. By 1950 industrial production surpassed prewar production. All of this made West Germany a great potential asset in the defense of Western Europe.

The possibility of West German rearmament aroused strong protests from the Soviet Union and opposition within West Germany itself from the Social Democrats. Nevertheless, in March 1954 President Heuss signed a constitutional amendment allowing German rearmament. By the end of the year Germany and France had worked out their disagreements over the Saar, and France joined the other Western powers in agreeing to German membership in the Western alliance. On May 5, 1955, West Germany gained sovereign status and joined NATO four days later, and the division of

Germany into two separate states was complete.

Postwar Great Britain

During the war, Great Britain mobilized its resources and more thoroughly and efficiently allocated man power than the Germans. The whole population was affected. Rationing of food and other necessities created hardships which had been shared equally by rich and poor alike. There was little black market activity. During the war the standard of living for the poor had actually risen. No reversal of this equality of sacrifice and opportunity was possible. A program of restoring the balance of trade, directing investment of resources to insure efficiency, and a vast new outlay for social services was agreed on by the parties even before the war ended. As early as 1942 a report known for its author, Sir William Beveridge, proposed "full employment in a free society" and social security "from the cradle to the grave."

As the war ended in May 1945, elections were held that returned a Labor government under Clement Attlee in July. The new government enacted an extensive program increasing unemployment insurance and providing insurance for old age and various contingencies. A comprehensive medical and health service for the entire population was established. Educational facilities were extended, and new planned housing projects built. Efforts were made to rehabilitate depressed areas.

In addition, Labor nationalized the Bank of England, the coal mines, transportation, iron and steel, and utilities (including electricity, gas, and communications). The Conservatives accepted much of this program but centered criticism on Labor's program of nationalizing the "commanding heights" of the economy — especially the iron and steel industry.

In order to complete this extensive series of reforms before its mandate expired in five years, Labor enacted a Parliament bill that reduced the power of the House of Lords to delay legislation from three years to one year. Inheritance and income taxes were sharply increased to pay for the new measures.

Labor found its majority reduced to seven from 148 in the 1950 elections. No further important reform legislation was passed in view of the very slim margin of voting power. In another election, in 1951 a Conservative majority was returned, and Winston Churchill became prime minister again. The new regime immediately reversed the nationalization of iron and steel. Other measures survived, however, especially the universal health care program which proved to be one of the most popular parts of the Labor achievement. The welfare state was permanently established in Britain through the activities of the Labor government. In April 1955 Churchill resigned for reasons of age and health and turned over the prime minister's office to Anthony Eden.

THE MARSHALL PLAN

European recovery from the effects of the war was slow for the first two or three years after 1945. Economic difficulty made for weakness in the face of Communism which, with Russian support, had taken over in Eastern Europe and threatened to take over in Western Europe as well if something was not done. In 1947 in a commencement address at Harvard University, George C. Marshall, the wartime army chief of staff who was now secretary of state under President Truman, proposed an aid program for Western European countries and others if they desired to join. This would revitalize the economies of the European nations and strengthen them to better resist Communism. The European Recovery Program (Marshall Plan) which began the next year showed substantial results in all the Western European countries that took part. By 1950 France and Italy were well above their 1938 levels of production, although population increases of about 10% ate up some of the gains. In Great Britain, Marshall Plan aid was of considerable importance. The most remarkable gains, however, were in West Germany. By early 1949, less than a year after the currency reform in the Western zones, West German production was about 85% of 1936 levels. The country soon experienced gains so great as to constitute what many called an "economic miracle." In Western Europe during the first two years of the Marshall Plan about $8 billion of American aid is estimated to have resulted in an overall expansion of some $30 billion annual output of goods and services.

THE MOVEMENT TOWARD WEST EUROPEAN ECONOMIC UNITY

In May 1951 French Foreign Minister Robert Schuman came forward with the Schuman Plan for a European Coal and Steel Community. This called for a pooling of resources in heavy industry and the elimination of tariffs throughout Western Europe (including France, West Germany, Italy, Belgium, the Netherlands, and Luxembourg). By April 1951 a treaty was signed incorporating the proposals of the Schuman Plan and creating the community from which other steps toward European unity grew (Common Market, General Agreement on Trade and Tariffs, etc.). The five-year period of implementation gave vested interests in each country time to adjust to new conditions.

THE COLD WAR

The question of Poland initiated the breakdown of the wartime alliance between the United States and Britain on the one hand and the U.S.S.R. on the other even before the war ended. It became plain that Stalin intended to install the Communists of the Lublin Committee as a Polish government. All of Eastern Europe was made Communist within two or three years from the end of the war in 1945. There were to be common policies for the whole of Germany, and there was no plan in the beginning to divide the country. However, seemingly irreconcilable differences between the Communist Soviet Union and the Western democracies were present from the beginning of the occupation — differences going back to the revolution in Russia in 1917 which embittered and complicated international relations through the 1920s and 1930s.

World War II was an exception to the rule of general hostility between capitalism and communism. It turned out, however, to be an alliance of expediency only. It therefore broke down when the common enemy was no longer a threat. More fundamental differences came to the fore again and made cooperation difficult if not impossible. In addition, given Stalin's fears and suspicious nature, one should not be surprised at the beginnings of a period of occasional limited conflict and tension short of outright military conflict known as the Cold War. Early in 1946, in a notable speech at Westminster College in Fulton, Missouri, Winston Churchill gave voice to the feelings of many when he announced that "from Stettin in the Baltic to Trieste on the Adriatic, an Iron Curtain has descended across the Continent."

CONFLICT IN GERMANY

After German surrender, the British and American armies withdrew from areas of

Germany and Eastern Europe to within the zones of occupation agreed to in the spring of 1945. A Control Council of allied military governors was created to establish common policies for Germany, but almost immediately there were difficulties with the Russians — a situation made no easier by the fact that there were additional differences between Britain, France, and the U.S. In the Eastern zone the Russians made it plain they intended to Communize the area in the same manner as in Eastern Europe. Early in 1946 they forced through a unification of the Social Democratic party and the Communists in which the Socialists, although originally much stronger, lost any separate identity or ability to influence policy.

The Russians followed their own economic policy, too. Reparations were a cause of recrimination. Figures of $20 billion had been mentioned but not formally agreed to at the wartime conferences with half to go to the Soviet Union. The Western powers had no intention, however, of allowing exports of supplies and equipment from their zones to proceed to a point where they would be forced to import goods just to keep their populations alive and at a minimal standard of living. Eventually the Americans and British halted any further deliveries from their zones to the Russians.

In their own zone the Russians not only dismantled factories and shipped industrial equipment to the Soviet Union but also took reparations from current production, which was specifically forbidden in the Potsdam agreements. The Soviets operated their zone as a single economic entity, violating the agreement that Germany was to be treated as a single unit for purposes of trade. They failed to furnish information and statistical returns for their zone. The Western powers were moved to respond. In May 1946 General Lucius Clay, American military governor, suspended reparations deliveries to the Russian zone in retaliation for Russian intransigence on the Control Council. In December 1946 in a speech at Stuttgart, Secretary of State James Byrnes announced the fusion of the American and British zones into an entity called Bizonia which the French later joined. The Western powers also raised the permitted level of German production and began to move from treating the Germans as conquered enemies to preparing them for a future role as allies of the West.

Breakdown of the Council of Foreign Ministers

Meanwhile, the Council of Foreign Ministers charged with drafting a peace treaty with Germany failed to reach agreement. The Council's last meeting was held November 25 to December 15, 1947, after which it adjourned never to meet again. It had limited successes in arranging treaties with minor states but completely failed to reach any compromise that would unite Germany. Likewise the Allied Control Council broke down. The last meeting was held in March 1948 when the Russian representative, Marshal Sokolovsky, walked out in protest over an Anglo-American invitation to the French to join their zone of Bizonia.

In the same year, Russia and its East German ally precipitated a great crisis in the form of a blockade of the Western sectors of Berlin, which led to the Berlin airlift. Russian action was prompted by a currency reform in the Western zones, but more broadly was aimed at forcing the Western powers to desist from their plan to establish a federal government which would eventually become independent.

THE CONTAINMENT POLICY

There were other areas of Western-Soviet disagreement. Iran, which had been occupied during the war to provide a route for transport of Lend-Lease supplies to Russia, was to be evacuated after the end of hostilities. From 1945 until 1947 Russian forces remained in the north and gave aid to a separatist movement seeking independence from the rest of Iran. Russia also put pressure on Turkey for control of the vital straits from the Black Sea to the Mediterranean — an area long contested by the great powers. In the Far East, the Soviets, although prevented by the American occupation from playing any important role in postwar Japan, did create a Communist regime in North Korea. They had occupied the northern part of the Korean peninsula in the days immediately preceding the Japanese surrender, and they later resisted efforts by the United Nations Organization to reunite the area with South Korea. In addition, the activities of the Chinese Communists (behind which the United States tended to see the machinations of the Soviet Union) and the outbreak of civil war with the Nationalist government under Chiang Kai-shek, did nothing to improve relations.

By 1947 the American government adopted a policy of "containment" to deal with this problem of Soviet Communist expansion. The Truman administration was strongly influenced by the reports of diplomat George Kennan, whose position as counselor at the embassy in Moscow gave him a chance to express his opinion of Russian intentions and how to deal with them. Kennan also wrote in 1947, under the pseudonym of "X", a widely read article entitled "The Sources of Soviet Conduct," published in the influential journal *Foreign Affairs*, in which he suggested a patient but firm, long-term policy of resisting Soviet expansionism. When General George C. Marshall was made secretary of state by President Truman in 1947, he established a Policy-Planning Staff in the State Department and made Kennan the first head.

The Truman Doctrine and aid to Greece

The Truman administration and its successors translated containment into a policy of military alliances, foreign aid, and American bases abroad to ring and contain the Soviet Union militarily, as well as a policy of resisting Communist-inspired wars of "liberation" in unstable areas of the world. The new policy was applied in Greece. In February 1947 the British government made known to Washington that it could no longer give aid to Turkey or to the royalist government installed in Greece by Britain in 1944 – 1945. The Greek government was experiencing attacks from Communist-led guerillas. On March 12 President Truman spoke to Congress. His message was a clear warning to the Soviet Union. The U.S., he announced, "would support free peoples who are resisting subjugation by armed minorities or by outside pressure." The president asked for $400 million to aid Turkey and Greece. Congress complied, and the aid thus proved effective in Greece.

The Berlin Blockade

Another great crisis, already alluded to, was the blockade of the three Western zones of Berlin — Stalin's answer to the merging of the American and British zones, the currency reform instituted in Western Germany, and his fear that a separate and independent West German state was being created. With the help of Communist East German "People's Police," barriers were raised to any traffic over land from the West to Berlin. President Truman responded with a massive airlift and also by stationing bombers in Britain capable of carrying nuclear weapons. The next year, with the failure of their efforts to drive the Western powers from Berlin, the Russians allowed land traffic to proceed once more. The creation of a West German state could only be countered by the creation of independent Communist East Germany. Neither side pushed the affair to extremes because of the fear of all-out war and the disastrous consequences for all.

The Chinese Civil War and the Establishment of the People's Republic of China

During World War II the United States followed a policy of trying to bring about cooperation in the war against the Japanese between the Nationalist Government of Chiang Kai-shek and the Communists under Mao Tse-tung. The war ended with the Nationalist government recognized as the legitimate government, but the Communists had a strong position at Yenan in north China and a military force which had proved effective behind enemy lines and was therefore in a good position to compete with the government forces for control of former Japanese-occupied territory. With American help the Nationalists succeeded in garrisoning the cities of Manchuria and other occupied areas, but the Communists controlled much of the surrounding territory. They were able to get additional weapons and supplies from the surrendering Japanese.

The Marshall Mission

The uneasy truce which prevailed during the war almost immediately broke down. The Truman administration sent a diplomatic mission under General George C. Marshall (wartime army chief of staff) to mediate the conflict. Marshall was able to arrange a temporary truce, but even his considerable skill as a mediator proved inadequate to keep the truce from breaking down again into full-scale civil war.

Aid to the Nationalists: the Wedemeyer Mission

Despite the shortcomings of Chiang Kai-shek's regime, and in the atmosphere of the Cold War, the United States believed that it had to aid the Nationalists to prevent a Communist takeover. A mission was sent under General Albert Wedemeyer, supplies and equipment were provided, and loans made to support the Chinese currency and alleviate inflation. All this was to no avail as the Communist forces defeated the Nationalist armies in a series of battles and eventually drove them from the mainland to the island of Taiwan (Formosa). In October 1949, even before the campaign was finally completed, the Communists established the Chinese People's Republic with the capital once again at Peking (Beijing). The Chinese Communist victory was seen at the time by the American government and by many others in the West as a disaster in the Cold War and a defeat for containment.

THE KOREAN WAR

In 1945 the U.S.S.R. declared war on Japan after the dropping of the atomic bomb. During that brief period, Russian armies invaded Manchuria and occupied the northern part of Korea to approximately the 38th parallel. American forces occupied the southern part of Korea at the same time they occupied Japan itself. Agreements were made to divide Korea for administrative purposes along the 38th parallel, and Korea was split into two states: a Communist People's Republic of Korea in the North and a U.N.-backed Republic of South Korea below the 38th parallel. Efforts to unify the country through elections failed. South Korea was allowed to have only a small army equipped with no heavy weapons because of fears that President Syngman Rhee might use such an army to attack the North in his own effort to unify the country. A North Korean Army was created, however, which was supplied with some heavy weapons, such as tanks, by the Russians. By early in 1950 it appeared that the United States, which had withdrawn all its forces to Japan, would not defend South Korea, and the North Koreans were encouraged to launch an invasion and make all Korea Communist.

NSC-68

In the United States the Truman administration had been conducting a general review of the situation created by the Cold War in Europe and elsewhere. The conclusions reached were stated in a secret National Security Council study called NSC-68 which was completed in April 1950. The thesis was that the Soviet Union was an aggressor bent on overrunning Europe and Asia. To counter this, the United States should proceed to develop a thermonuclear (hydrogen) bomb. It should also obtain bases from which it could be delivered against the Soviet Union. United States troops, the document said, should reinforce NATO. Despite obvious reluctance on the part of Europeans who had suffered from German depredations during the war, West Germany should be rearmed. A considerable buildup of American armed forces was proposed with corresponding increases in the military budget. The sudden beginning of the Korean War in June 1950 only confirmed the need for a military program which otherwise might have been difficult to sell to Congress. The U.S. had already in 1947 created a separate Air Force and unified the three services under an overall Department of Defense. Congress also authorized the creation of the Central Intelligence Agency which began to function in the Cold War as not only a collector of intelligence but more and more as a clandestine arm of the government: carrying out secret, often illegal, operations abroad justified as being necessary to combat the clandestine operations of the Soviet Union and its satellites.

The North Korean Invasion

In June 1950 as the North Korean invasion of South Korea got underway, the United States decided on a policy of intervention. Taking advantage of a temporary absence of the Russian delegates, the United States was able to propose intervention and to get U.N. support. Before the war was over, 17 Western or Western-oriented countries had sent contingents to Korea. The South Korean forces, and U.S. forces sent from Japan, supplied most of the U.N. army. General Douglas MacArthur, commander of the occupation forces in Japan, was made overall U.N. commander. After initial defeats and withdrawals, MacArthur carried out an amphibious landing by the newly formed Tenth Corps at Inchon near the South Korean capital of Seoul. This force and the main Eighth Army driving north managed to surround and in a few weeks virtually destroy the invading army.

The Decision to Cross the 38th Parallel

By early fall of 1950 the U.N. forces were back to the 38th parallel and the question arose whether to stop there or continue north and reunify the whole of Korea. Despite warnings against this from the Chinese Communists sent through India, the decision was made to continue north. Some forces had actually reached the Manchurian border when in November the Chinese Communists entered the battle, creating what MacArthur called a new war. Initially surprised by the Chinese attack the U.N. forces were driven back below the 38th parallel again. The commander of the Eighth Army, General Walton Walker, was killed at this time, but under a new commander, General Matthew Ridgway, the army recovered, recaptured Seoul and reached a line approximately at the 38th parallel once again.

During this period of Chinese intervention the Truman administration had been increasingly in conflict with General MacArthur over what should be United States policy. Washington feared that widening the war to China proper might cause intervention by the Russians. In April 1951, after repeated warnings, President Truman relieved MacArthur of his command.

Instead of expanding the war, long and difficult negotiations were begun for an armistice. Eventually, in July 1953 an agreement was signed which still remains in force. No formal peace treaty was ever made, and the Korean War concluded with the situation essentially as it was before the North Korean invasion began. The Korean War prevented the United States from recognizing or establishing formal relations with the Chinese Communist regime (as Great Britain and other European nations had quickly done) until the time of the Nixon administration in the early 1970s.

STRENGTHENING OF NATO

One result of the Korean War was the strengthening of the NATO alliance begun in 1949. A mood approaching panic set in after the North Korean invasion began. The U.S. expressed its fear that NATO would be too weak to resist a possible Russian attack which might come while American forces were engaged in the Far East. The U.S. insisted on a policy of rearming West Germany. Eventually Western European nations accepted West German rearmament but only after agreement to make German forces part of a European defense under NATO control. This policy of military buildup changed the emphasis of foreign aid under the Marshall Plan. In the first two years the aid was primarily economic with few strings attached. Later it became increasingly military aid.

LOSS OF EUROPEAN OVERSEAS EMPIRES

World War II created disruptions that resulted in irresistible pressures for independence in areas overseas against the rule of European powers weakened by that struggle. British, Dutch, French, Portuguese, and Belgian empires in Asia and Africa virtually disappeared in the space of about 15 years following the war. In some instances withdrawal was accomplished by a relatively peaceful transfer of power (as with the British withdrawal from India in 1947), but in other cases the colonial power resisted separation and long, bitter military conflicts resulted. In every case independence created internal problems with which new governments had to struggle, often with violence ensuing and often with foreign intervention.

BRITISH OVERSEAS WITHDRAWAL

Palestine, Israel, and the Arab-Israeli Conflict

Britain received a mandate from the League of Nations following World War I to govern Palestine. Britain had earlier indicated in the Balfour Declaration of November 2, 1917, that it favored the creation of a Jewish "national home" in Palestine. The British position there was complicated by their involvement in the creation of Arab states such as Saudi Arabia and Transjordan, which were adamantly opposed to any Jewish state in Palestine.

Creation of Israel

Following World War II there was a considerable migration of Jews who had survived the Nazi Holocaust to Palestine to join Jews who had settled there earlier. Conflicts broke out with the Arabs. The British occupying forces tried to suppress the violence and to negotiate a settlement between the factions. In 1948, after negotiations failed to achieve agreement, the British, feeling they could no longer support the cost of occupation, announced their withdrawal. Zionist leaders then proclaimed the independent state of Israel and took up arms to fight the armies of Egypt, Syria, and other Arab states which invaded the Jewish-held area. The new Israeli state quickly proved its technological and military superiority by defeating the invaders. Over 500,000 Arabs were displaced from their homes in establishing Israel. Efforts to permanently relocate them failed, and they became a factor in the continued violence in the Middle East.

The Jews of Israel created a modern parliamentary state on the European model with an economy and technology superior to their Arab neighbors. The new state was thought by many Arabs to be simply another manifestation of European imperialism made worse by religious antagonisms.

Further Arab-Israeli Wars

Several further Arab-Israeli wars have served to keep the Middle East in turmoil. In 1956 the Israelis chose the opportunity created by the ill-fated Anglo-French attempt to retake the Suez Canal to launch their own attack on Egypt. Public opinion eventually forced the withdrawal of the British and French, and although the Israelis had achieved military successes, they found themselves barred from use of the Canal by Egypt, which was now in control.

In 1967 the Egyptians closed the Gulf of Aqaba to Israeli shipping, and this together with continued exclusion from the Suez Canal prompted Israel to launch a six-day war against Egypt (and Syria and Jordan, which were allied with Egypt). The Arab forces were badly defeated, and the Israelis occupied additional territory including the Jordanian sector of the city of Jerusalem. An additional million Arabs came under Israeli rule as a result of this campaign.

The Palestine Liberation Organization

Although defeated, the Arabs refused to sign any treaty or to come to terms with Israel. Palestinian refugees living in camps in states bordering Israel created grave problems. A Palestine Liberation Organization (PLO) was formed to fight for the establishment of an Arab Palestinian state on territory taken from Israel on the west bank of the Jordan River. The PLO resorted to terrorist tactics both against Israel and other states in support of their cause.

In October 1973 the Egyptians and Syrians launched an attack on Israel known as the Yom Kippur War. With some difficulty the attacks were repulsed. A settlement was mediated by American Secretary of State Henry Kissinger. The situation has remained unstable, however, with both sides resorting to border raids and other forms of violence short of full-scale war.

The Egyptian Revolution

The British exercised control over Egypt from the end of the 19th century and declared it a British protectorate in December 1914. In 1922 Egypt became nominally independent, and in 1936 an Anglo-Egyptian treaty provided for British forces to withdraw to the Suez Canal Zone where they might keep 10,000 troops. Britain could expand the force in time of war. During World War II the presence of British forces in Egypt, which was the British headquarters in the Middle East, resulted in fighting on Egyptian territory despite efforts by Egypt to remain neutral.

The government under King Farouk did little to alleviate the overriding problem of poverty after the war. In 1952 a group of army officers, including Gamal Abdel Nasser and Anwar Sadat, plotted against the government, and on July 23 the king was overthrown. For a short time the plotters ruled through a figurehead — General

Muhammad Naguib; a Revolutionary Command Council held the real power. Colonel Nasser, the outstanding figure of the group, replaced Naguib as premier in April 1954. A treaty with Britain later that year resulted in the withdrawal of all British troops from the Canal Zone.

The Suez Canal Crisis

Nasser made several agreements in 1955 and 1956 with Communist-bloc nations, establishing trade relations and obtaining weapons. The United States and Britain then withdrew offers of aid in building the Aswan Dam on the Nile River. Nasser in turn nationalized the Suez Canal shortly after the British garrison there had been withdrawn. A crisis ensued when Israeli forces suddenly invaded Egypt. Britain and France, ignoring U.N. attempts to mediate, gave an ultimatum to Israel and Egypt to cease fighting and withdraw from the Canal Zone. When this failed the two powers began a bombardment and invaded the area. Pressure from both the United States and the Soviet Union caused Britain, and then France and Israel to cease fire. A U.N. force was then formed to police the Canal Zone and the cease fire. Eventually foreign forces were withdrawn from Egypt, except that the Israelis remained in possession of the Gaza Strip.

India and Pakistan

British rule in India, the largest and most populous of the colonial areas ruled by Europeans, came to an end in 1947 with a relatively peaceful transfer of power. Pressure for self-government had grown in the 1930s, and the British had granted a constitution, a legislature, trained an Indian civil service, and made other concessions to Indian nationalism. During World War II Britain promised dominion status to India after the war. This did not satisfy the Indian Congress Party, whose leaders wanted full and immediate independence. Complications ensued when Muslim leaders, representing some 100 million Muslims, did not want to live in a state dominated by Hindus and the Congress Party and insisted on a state of their own.

Partition

The British decided to partition the subcontinent into two separate dominions which quickly became independent republics: India — predominantly Hindu with 350 million population, and Pakistan — predominantly Muslim with 75 million population. About 40 million Muslims remained within Indian borders. Independence resulted in bloody rioting between the religious factions, mass expulsions, and the emigration of millions of people. Perhaps a million people lost their lives before the rioting eventually died out. The territory of Kashmir remained in dispute but finally was joined to India in 1975.

India

India under Jawaharlal Nehru and the Congress Party became a parliamentary democracy. Nehru died in 1964. His daughter, Indira Gandhi, became prime minister from 1966 on. The country made economic progress, but gains were largely negated by a population increase to 600 million from 350 million. In 1975 Indira Gandhi was found guilty of electoral fraud. She resorted to force to keep herself in power. When elections were permitted in 1977 she was ousted by the opposition. Eventually her son, Rajiv Ghandi, became prime minister.

Pakistan

Pakistan retained the trappings of democracy with a written constitution and parliamentary form of government, but became in reality a military dictatorship. Gains in population outpaced economic growth as in India. In addition the country was divided into East and West Pakistan separated by 1,000 miles of Indian territory. The two areas had the same religion but different traditions, resulting in a quarrel that led East Pakistan in 1971 to declare itself the independent state of Bangladesh. The Pakistan government in Karachi sent military forces to the east to regain control and bloody fighting ensued. India then intervened militarily, and after defeating the Pakistani army, forced the recognition of an independent Bangladesh.

Malaya, Burma, and Ceylon

Malaya, Burma, and Ceylon were other parts of the British Asian empire that received their independence as did India and Pakistan. All three became members of the British Commonwealth with ties to Great Britain. The Commonwealth, which also includes some former British colonies in Africa, became a significant political grouping associated on an entirely voluntary basis. Malaya suffered nine years of internal strife which delayed independence to 1957 when the Federation of Malaya was created.

THE FRENCH IN INDOCHINA AND ALGERIA

Indochina

Following World War II the French returned to Indochina and attempted to restore their rule there. The opposition nationalist movement was led by the veteran Communist Ho Chi Minh. War broke out between the nationalists and the French forces. Despite materiel aid from the U.S., the French were unable to maintain their position in the north of Vietnam. In 1954 their army was surrounded at Dienbienphu and forced to surrender. This military disaster prompted a change of government in France.

The 1954 Geneva Conference: French Withdrawal

This new government under Premier Pierre Mendes-France negotiated French withdrawal at a conference held at Geneva, Switzerland in 1954. Cambodia and Laos became independent and Vietnam was partitioned at the 17th parallel. The North, with its capital at Hanoi, became a Communist state under Ho Chi Minh. The South remained non-Communist. Under the Geneva Accords, elections were to be held in the South to determine the fate of that area. However, the United States chose to intervene and support the regime of Ngo Dinh Diem, and elections were never held. Eventually a second Vietnamese war resulted with the United States playing the role earlier played by France.

Algeria

Following World War II there was nationalist agitation in Algeria, Tunisia, and Morocco. The French government granted independence to Tunisia and Morocco, but Algeria was considered to be different. It was legally part of metropolitan France. Government there was heavily weighted in favor of the French minority (about 10% of the total population), and the Arab majority had few rights. In 1954 a large-scale revolt of Arab nationalists broke out. The French government began a campaign of suppression lasting over seven years and involving as many as 500,000 troops. Military casualties totaled at least 100,000 Arabs and 10,000 French killed with thousands more civilian casualties. The savage campaign led to torture and other atrocities on both sides.

Army Revolt and Return of General de Gaulle

Egypt and other Arab states gave aid to the Algerian Liberation Front. Algerian terrorists spread the violence as far as Paris itself. The government of the Fourth Republic faced a military and financial burden with no clear end in sight. French Army officers in Algeria and European settlers were adamant, against any concessions, and eventually, under the leadership of General Jacques Massu (in Algeria) and General Raoul Salan (army chief of staff), created a committee of public safety and seized control of government in Algeria. The rebellion threatened to spread to France itself. It led to the downfall of the Fourth Republic and the return to power of General de Gaulle, who established the Fifth Republic with himself as a strong president.

Algerian Independence

De Gaulle moved step by step towards a policy first of autonomy and then independence for Algeria. In a referendum, on January 8, 1961, the French people approved of eventual Algerian self-determination. The army leaders then rebelled, forming a terrorist secret army (the OAS) to oppose de Gaulle's policy with bombings and assassinations. De Gaulle prevailed in the struggle, and in July 1962 French rule ended in Algeria. General Salan (OAS leader) was arrested, tried, and sentenced to life imprisonment. There was a mass exodus of Europeans from Algeria, but most Frenchmen were grateful to de Gaulle for ending the long Algerian conflict.

THE DUTCH AND INDONESIA

During World War II the Japanese conquered the Dutch East Indies. At the end of the war they recognized the independence of the area as Indonesia. When the Dutch attempted to return, four years of bloody fighting ensued against the nationalist forces of Achmed Sukarno. In 1949 the Dutch recognized Indonesian independence but with some ties still with The Netherlands. In 1954 the Indonesians dissolved all ties totally. Sukarno's regime became one of increasing dictatorship thinly disguised by terms like "guided democracy." The constitution was set aside, parliament suspended, and Sukarno became president for life. In 1966 Sukarno was overthrown and replaced by a more stable administration under General Suharto which made more economic and social progress.

THE COLD WAR AFTER THE DEATH OF STALIN

Following Stalin's death, Russian leaders — while maintaining an atmosphere first of tension and then of relaxation in international affairs — appeared more willing than Stalin to be conciliatory and to consider peaceful coexistence among the major competing economic and political systems.

Eisenhower and the 1955 Geneva Summit

In the U.S. the atmosphere also changed with the election of President Dwight Eisenhower; and despite the belligerent rhetoric of Secretary of State John Foster Dulles, conciliatory gestures were not always automatically considered appeasement of the Communists. In 1955 a summit conference of Eisenhower, the British and French leaders, and Khrushchev met at Geneva in an atmosphere more cordial than any since World War II. The "spirit of Geneva" did not last long, however.

The U-2 Incident and Breakup of the Paris Conference, 1960

The United States Central Intelligence Agency developed a high-flying reconnaissance aircraft known as the U-2. Under Eisenhower it was used to make secret flights over the Soviet Union in order to take aerial photographs. At first the Russians were unable to shoot the airplane down, but in 1960 a flight was shot down well inside the Soviet Union. The plane's pilot, Francis Gary Powers, was captured alive. At first the Eisenhower administration denied Russian charges of spying, but then when Khrushchev produced the pilot and remains of the aircraft, they admitted what had happened and accepted responsibility. A summit conference was due to convene shortly in Paris, and an indignant Khrushchev used the occasion to condemn Eisenhower and then break up the meeting.

Kennedy and Khrushchev: The Bay of Pigs Incident

John Kennedy replaced Eisenhower as president of the United States in 1960. He proved to be a "hard liner" in relations with the Soviet Union and a strong opponent of Communism. He inherited the American dispute with Cuban leader Fidel Castro, who had ousted the U.S.-backed, right-wing dictator Fulgencio Battista in January 1959. Castro had dealt with the problem of economic dependency on the U.S. by nationalizing many economic assets — sugar mills, oil refineries, banks — that were American owned. The U.S. retaliated with economic sanctions, and Castro established ties with the Soviet Union, which agreed to buy Cuban sugar and provide goods denied by the U.S. Eisenhower and the CIA then prepared a plan to overthrow Castro using Cuban exiles as an invasion force. Kennedy carried out this plan which resulted in a fiasco at the Bay of Pigs. The Cubans landed, the population did not rise to join them, and the small force was quickly overwhelmed.

Khrushchev and Berlin

After the Berlin Blockade of 1948–1949 Berlin became a symbol of freedom — an oasis of Western influence in the heart of East Germany. Thinking it best to keep Germany divided, Khrushchev tried to exert pressure on the Western powers through Berlin to recognize permanent division of Germany into two states. Late in 1958 he threatened to make unilateral changes in the status of Berlin, but backed down in 1959. In June 1961, following the U-2 incident and breakup of the Paris summit, Khrushchev presented an ultimatum to President Kennedy, threatening to sign a peace treaty with East Germany and then give the new state control over access to Berlin. Shortly after, the East German border was closed and a wall was built through Berlin separating the Russian and Western sectors and preventing any unauthorized travel or communication between them. Despite pressure to take a strong stand, Kennedy simply moved an additional 1,500 American troops to Berlin while accepting the wall rather than risk war.

The Cuban Missile Crisis

In an attempt to protect the Castro regime and to project its power to the borders of the U.S., Khrushchev initiated a policy of installing Russian missiles in Cuba. Aerial reconnaissance revealed this to the American government in October 1962. A 13-day crisis followed. President Kennedy established a "quarantine" of Cuba using the American Navy. (The term quarantine was used because a blockade is an act of war under traditional international law.) Eventually Russian ships, carrying the missiles and nuclear warheads to complete the installation, turned back rather than risk possible war. Khrushchev did obtain an American pledge not to invade Cuba and a commitment to remove American missiles from Turkey, but he had been publicly humiliated. For this and because of the failure of his domestic agricultural development program, his colleagues forced him to retire in 1964.

THE VIETNAM WAR

Before 1954 the conflict in Vietnam involved French armies against the Communist-led nationalist movement. By the 1954 Geneva Accords France withdrew its forces, Vietnam was divided at the 17th parallel, the Communists under Ho Chi Minh held the North, and the South became the Republic of Vietnam with an anti-Communist regime. Elections to unite the country were never held. Instead the United States began to play an ever larger role in South Vietnam, believing that if South Vietnam fell all Southeast Asia would fall like a row of dominos. First Eisenhower, then Kennedy, then Johnson believed this and reacted accordingly, and America's role increased until after 1964 the U.S. was engaged in a full-scale second Vietnam War with the hope of establishing an anti-Communist regime that could "win the hearts and minds of the people" and provide an effective barrier to further Communist expansion. China and the Soviet Union were involved in supporting North Vietnam and the liberation movement mainly by sending supplies and equipment of various kinds. Most NATO countries gave only lukewarm, if any, support to the American war in Vietnam. Eventually public opinion at home brought an end to America's most unpopular war, and Western Europe could breath more easily.

THE CHANGING BALANCE OF POWER

De Gaulle as the Leader of an Independent Europe

After his return to power in France in 1958, General de Gaulle endeavored to make France a leader in European affairs with himself as spokesman for a Europe that he hoped would be a counter to the "dual hegemony" of the U.S. and U.S.S.R. His policies at times were anti-British or anti-American. He vetoed British entry into the Common Market, developed an independent French nuclear force, and tried to bridge the gap between and East and West Europe. Despite his prestige as the last great wartime leader, he did not have great success. Nevertheless Western Europe came into its own as a factor in international affairs.

Detente

The policy of rapprochement interrupted by the Cuban Missile Crisis resumed. Despite the continuing war in Vietnam, Soviet and American leaders exchanged visits. From 1969 on, under President Nixon and National Security Adviser Henry Kissinger, the policy of better relations became known as detente. Negotiations on strategic arms resulted in the SALT I treaty signed during President Nixon's 1972 visit to Moscow. In this spirit of detente, trade between Western Europe and the Soviet Union increased several times. The Soviet Union, faced with agricultural problems, began to purchase large amounts of American grain. In 1975 agreements were reached at Helsinki in Finland between 35 nations for peaceful cooperation. All agreed to accept boundaries in Europe established following World War II, including the Oder-Neisse Line between the German Democratic Republic and Poland.

Nuclear Weapons and the Arms Race

Nuclear weapons were a growing concern in the U.S., the Soviet Union, and other countries—especially those of Western Europe. The enormous destructive power of these weapons had been first revealed when atomic bombs were dropped by the U.S. on Hiroshima and Nagasaki in August 1945. Initial debates on control of nuclear weapons were held in the United Nations at a time when the United States had a monopoly on the atomic bomb. The Soviet Union finally insisted by 1948 that the banning of atomic weapons was of primary importance. No agreement could be reached on inspection procedures, however.

Soon after this the Russians exploded their first atomic bomb. During 1949 and 1950, wars were taking place in Korea, Malaya, and Indochina, and rearmament was the dominant policy, with both the U.S. and the U.S.S.R. starting programs to develop more effective nuclear weapons. These included the hydrogen bomb whose awesome power had to be measured in terms of megatons of conventional explosive.

The war in Korea and the rearmament of West Germany within NATO prevented any serious disarmament negotiations. Europe was divided into separate armed camps: NATO, and the Warsaw Pact led by the Soviet Union. In the next several years the world moved into the age of rocketry, nuclear-powered submarines, and other military products of so-called "high technology." Russia tested its first bomb in 1949. By 1952 the British had tested an atomic bomb. The U.S. successfully developed and tested a thermonuclear weapon (H-bomb) in 1952. In 1953 the Russians exploded a similar weapon. In 1961 the Soviet Union exploded a 60-megaton H-bomb. The French joined the nuclear powers in February 1960. They tested an H-bomb in August 1968. China also became a nuclear power, exploding its first nuclear device in 1964. It fired its first rocket with a nuclear warhead in October 1966 and tested an H-bomb in June 1967. Even Israel and India built reactors with the potential for producing weapons.

The International Arms Trade and Military Expenditures

In the years following World War II, the U.S., the U.S.S.R., and many other countries maintained large standing military establishments—conventional as well as nuclear. An international trade in weapons and military supplies flourished in the 1960s and after with the U.S. and U.S.S.R. as the chief sources of supply. Between 1960 and 1975 the world's annual military expenditures nearly doubled. The U.S. and U.S.S.R accounted for about 60%. In less affluent Afro-Asian nations, spending on weapons expanded and helped contribute to political instability and mistrust. Before World War II, military expenditures are estimated to have been less than 1% of the total world gross national product. In 1983 the figure had risen to 6%.

Agreements on Nuclear Weapons

The radiation and fallout from the various testing programs created a fear that the atmosphere would be poisoned, damage of a genetic nature might be done to plants and animals, and unborn generations of humans might be endangered in ways which were only beginning to be understood. These years prompted the U.S., Britain, and the Soviet Union to sign in April 1963 a treaty to ban nuclear testing in the atmosphere, under water, and in outer space. France and China did not join but went on to develop weapons of their own. The proliferation of nuclear weapons prompted the U.S. and U.S.S.R. also to sign a non-proliferation treaty to which 62 nations subscribed. Among the exceptions were France, China, and West Germany. Following the Cuban Missile Crisis, a direct communications link between Washington and Moscow called the "hot line" was established in order to avoid misunderstandings that might trigger nuclear war. In 1976, in a period of relatively relaxed relations, the two superpowers agreed to limit underground testing to explosions no more than eight times the power of the Hiroshima bomb (the equivalent of 20,000 tons of conventional explosives). Finally, for the first time, in the late 1980s the Russians and the U.S. agreed to limited on-site inspection by outsiders of their tests as well as monitoring of the agreements.

The Space Race and its Implications

A large step was taken toward space exploration during World War II with the development of the German V-2 rocket. German rocket experts were recruited by both the U.S. and U.S.S.R. after World War II. In 1957 the Russians launched the first unmanned satellite to orbit the earth. For a time, they pulled ahead of the U.S. in development of rocket boosters able to put sizable payloads into space. The Russians achieved another first when they put a manned spacecraft into orbit.

Under President Kennedy space exploration was given priority and a goal set of putting a man on the moon by the end of the decade. The U.S. soon caught up with the Russians in the development of large rockets and achieved its goal of sending men to the moon in 1969.

Both nations deployed experimental space stations and unmanned probes of the planets. Many satellites for communication—and some for military purposes such as espionage by aerial photography—were launched in the period after 1960. Some cooperation was achieved when U.S. and Soviet astronauts orbited simultaneously and brought their ships together in outer space. Russia launched space probes to the vicinity of Venus and Mars. Then the U.S. succeeded in landing instruments on the surface of Mars which sent back photographs and other data. Some critics complained of the enormous cost of these activities and of the neglect of problems here on Earth, but others saw future benefits for all resulting.

The military of the U.S. and U.S.S.R. (and other nations to a lesser degree) took advantage of developments in space exploration, rocketry, and related sciences to develop self-propelled missiles of all sizes, including intercontinental ballistic missiles which could carry nuclear warheads across the continents in a matter of minutes. In neither country was an effective anti-missile defense developed; instead, each relied on a policy of deterrence. If the other side knew that its enemy had a missile force capable of surviving any initial attack and returning the attack against the original aggressor then no one would start a nuclear war because of the certainty that they, too, would be destroyed—the theory known as MAD, or mutually assured destruction.

The Reagan Strategic Defense Initiative

To date no sure defense against nuclear attack exists. Extensive civil defense programs are reported to exist in the former Soviet Union, Switzerland, and China which are designed to protect the populace in the event of nuclear attack. It is doubtful if these would prove very effective. Evacuation of civilians from cities that would be targets takes time—more time than would be available.

The alternative was to use missiles to destroy incoming missiles. The U.S. had a program of this sort in the 1950s and 1960s but gave it up in the SALT I agreements. The SALT I agreements also contained an Anti-Ballistic Missile Treaty limiting the use of ABMs. Many experts felt at the time that such a system with its complicated radar and computers simply could not be made effective against incoming missiles. Another development that threatened to overwhelm any conceivable defense was the multiple independently targeted re-entry vehicle—a missile with several warheads, each of which could be aimed independently at a separate target as the missile approached its destination.

The idea of a ballistic missile defense system surfaced again in the U.S. during the presidency of Ronald Reagan. This "Strategic Defense Initiative" quickly became known among its detractors as "Star Wars" (after a popular science fiction movie). The new proposal would rely on platforms in outer space from which particle beams, lasers, and other advanced devices would destroy incoming missiles.

Experts disagreed over the time required to develop and deploy SDI—assuming it could be built. In addition, there was wide disagreement over the vulnerability of such a system to enemy countermeasures In the late 1980s the U.S. Congress had started by funding research for such a system, but the ultimate outcome was uncertain. Reaction in the Soviet Union was predictably negative, and many in the West felt it would simply lead the Soviets to escalate the arms raise once again and invest heavily in weapons to defeat the system.

A NEW ERA BEGINS

Russia after Stalin

Joseph Stalin died in March 1953. His career had been one of undoubted achievements but at tremendous cost. Within Russia, Stalin established a dictatorship unparalleled in history. His ruthlessness and paranoid suspicions grew worse towards the end of his life. Postwar economic reconstruction was accompanied by ideological intolerance and a regime of terror and persecution accompanied by overtones of anti-Semitism. There were indications of a new series of purges coming when Stalin died.

A so-called "troika" consisting of Georgi Malenkov (Chairman of the Council of Ministers), Lavrenti Beria (Stalin's chief of police), and Vyacheslav Molotov (foreign minister) took over government. A power struggle took phce in which the first event was the secret trial and execution of Beria. Eventually a little-known party functionary, Nikita Khrushchev, became Communist Party General Secretary in 1954. Malenkov and Molotov were demoted to lesser positions and eventually disappeared from public view.

Khrushchev's Secret Speech and the Anti-Stalin Campaign

Khrushchev in 1956 delivered a "secret speech" to the 20th Congress of the Communist Party of the Soviet Union. It soon became public knowledge that he had accused Stalin of wholesale "violations of socialist legality" and of creating a "cult of personality." This signified the victory of Khrushchev's policy of relaxing the regime of terror and oppression of the Stalin years. The period became known as "The Thaw" after the title of a novel by Ilya Ehrenburg.

Change occurred in foreign affairs also. Khrushchev visited Belgrade and reestablished relations with Tito, admitting that there was more than one road to socialism. He also visited the United States, met with President Eisenhower, and toured the country. Later, relations became more tense after the U-2 spy plane incident. Khrushchev's policy generally was one where a period of relaxation would be followed by a period of pressure, threats, and tension.

Following the loss of face sustained by Russia as a result of the Cuban Missile Crisis and the failure of Khrushchev's domestic agricultural polices, he was forced out of the party leadership and lived in retirement in Moscow until his death in 1971.

Khrushchev's Successors: Brezhnev, Andropov, and Gorbachev

After Khrushchev's ouster, the leadership in the Central Committee divided power, making Leonid Brezhnev party secretary and Aleksei Kosygin chairman of the council of ministers, or premier. Brezhnev's party position ensured his dominance by the 1970s. In 1977 he presided over the adoption of a new constitution that altered the structure of the regime very little. The same year he was elected president by the Supreme Soviet.

Stalin's successors rehabilitated many of Stalin's victims. They also permitted somewhat greater freedom in literary and artistic matters and even allowed some political criticism. Controls were maintained, however, and sometimes were tightened. Anti-Semitism was also still present, and Soviet Jews were long denied permission to emigrate to Israel. American pressure may have helped to relax this policy in the 1970s when about 150,000 Jews were allowed to leave Russia. Other evidences of continued tight control were the 1974 arrest for treason and forcible deportation of the writer Alexander Solzhenitsyn and the arrest and internal exile for many years of the physicist Andrei Sakharov, who was an outspoken critic of the regime and its violations of human rights.

Brezhnev occupied the top position of power until his death in 1982. He was briefly succeeded by Yuri Andropov (a former secret police chief) and then by Mikhail Gorbachev, who carried out a further relaxation of the internal regime. Gorbachev pushed disarmament and detente in foreign relations, and attempted a wide range of internal reforms known as *perestroika* ("restructuring").

CHANGE IN EASTERN EUROPE

Poland

Khrushchev's speech denouncing Stalin was followed almost immediately by revolts in Poland and Hungary, apparently encouraged by what was happening in Russia. In Poland Wladyslaw Gomulka, previously discredited and imprisoned for "nationalist deviationism," emerged to take over the government. Khrushchev and the Russians decided to tolerate Gomulka, who had wide support. His regime proceeded to halt collectivization of agriculture and curb the use of political terror.

The Solidarity Movement

In the 1980s the trade union movement known as Solidarity and its leader, Lech Walesa, emerged as a political force, organizing mass protests in 1980–1981 and maintaining almost continuous pressure on the government headed by General Wojciech Jaruzelski. Despite government efforts to maintain strong central control and suppress the opposition, the strength of the movement was such that the ruling Communists were forced to recognize the opposition and make concessions.

Hungary

In Hungary in 1956 rioting against the Communist regime broke out and brought Imre Nagy to power. Nagy's policies went too far for the Russians, and Khrushchev intervened forcibly, sending in Russian troops and tanks to replace Nagy with a regime subservient to Moscow under Janos Kadar. The outbreak of the Suez Canal crisis at this time distracted the Western powers from events in Hungary. Despite the immediate political outcome in Hungary, a more flexible economic policy was allowed in Eastern Europe. Collectivization was slowed and a somewhat less restrictive atmosphere resulted even in Hungary.

Intervention in Czechoslovakia, 1968: The Brezhnev Doctrine

Early in 1968 Alexander Dubcek became leader of the Czechoslovakian Communist Party and began a process of liberalization which went further than any other East European country had gone at that time. Kremlin leaders were nervous and in May Premier Aleksei Kosygin went to Czechoslovakia and brought back a reassuring report. However, a manifesto entitled "Two Thousand Words" (issued by Czech intellectuals and calling for even faster reform) and the publication of a draft of rule changes for the Czech Communist Party (allowing an unprecedented range of freedom within the party itself) apparently convinced the Russians to use military force. On August 23 they (together with East Germany, Hungary, Poland, and Bulgaria) sent in troops and established a military occupation. Censorship was reintroduced and changes forced on the country, designed to crush any revolutionary tendency and prevent any democratization. In April 1969 Dubcek was forced out of power and a new regime established under Gustav Husak more compliant with Soviet wishes. Nevertheless, a few changes remained such as the federalization of the country to give equality to the Slovaks.

Continued Change in Eastern Europe

Despite the political limits imposed by the Soviet Union on their East European satellites, economic developments took place during the 1970s and 1980s which eventually led to further liberalization and change in Eastern European countries. The U.S.S.R., short of capital for development, could not supply the needs of East European states, and these began to turn to Western banks. With increasing economic ties and more East-West trade the political situation changed. The Czechs, despite the 1968 intervention, voiced criticism of Soviet missiles on their territory. The Bulgarian government called for making East Europe a nuclear-free zone.

In Rumania, too, change occurred when the government insisted with some success on greater independence in foreign affairs. The Rumanians also resisted Soviet pressure for closer economic ties and greater dependence on the Soviet Union.

CHANGE IN WESTERN EUROPE

NATO and the Common Market

The military pact called the North Atlantic Treaty Organization was originally established in 1948 and strengthened during the early 1950s as a result of the Korean War. It combined armed forces of the U.S., Canada, Portugal, Norway, Iceland, Denmark, Italy, Britain, France, and the Benelux countries (Belgium, the Netherlands, and Luxembourg). Greece and Turkey soon joined. West Germany became a member in 1956 and Spain joined in 1982. It has mainly been an alliance to contain Communism and to protect Western Europe from any threat of Russian attack or subversion.

In addition to NATO, institutions to promote economic unity have been established in the last three decades. Six members (West Germany, France, Italy, and the Benelux countries) formed the European Steel and Coal Community in 1951. Economic collaboration progressed favorably, and in March 1957, inspired chiefly by Belgian Foreign Minister Paul Henri Spaak, two treaties were signed in Rome creating a European Atomic Energy Commission (Euratom) and a European Economic Community (the Common Market)—which eventually absorbed Euratom. The EEC was to be a customs union creating a free market area with a common external tariff with other nations. Toward the outside world the EEC acted as a single bargaining agent for its members in commercial transactions, and it reached a number of agreements with other European and Third World states.

In 1973 the original six were joined by three new members—Britain, Ireland, and Denmark. The name was changed to "European Community." In 1979 there were three more applicants—Spain, Portugal, and Greece. These latter states were less well off and created problems of cheap labor, agricultural products, etc., which delayed their reception as members until 1986. On December 10 and 11, 1991, in the two Treaties of Maastricht (a provincial capital in southeastern Netherlands), the EC members committed to moving toward a new common market—entailing a political and economic union of the 12 nations—that ultimately would have a common currency. The EC today is the world's largest single trading area, with one-fifth of global trade.

Great Britain Since 1951

After the postwar Labor government under Clement Attlee had achieved its major reforms, transforming Britain into a welfare state, it was succeeded by Conservative governments from 1951 to 1964 under Winston Churchill, Anthony Eden, and finally Harold Macmillan. During this period the Conservatives restored truck transportation and iron and steel to private control, introduced some fees into the national health insurance program, and favored private over public development of housing projects. They did not, however, fundamentally alter the social security and health insurance program initiated by Labor, but accepted the welfare state.

Labor returned to power under Harold Wilson from 1964 to 1970. Public housing and slum clearance were again emphasized, the educational system was democratized, free medical services were restored, and social security pensions were increased. A Conservative regime under Edward Heath governed from 1970 to 1974, only to be ousted by Labor once again. Harold Wilson served as Labor prime minister from 1974 to 1976 when he retired to be succeeded by James Callahan. In 1979 the Conservatives returned under the leadership of the first woman prime minister in British history, Margaret Thatcher, whose success in a male-dominated political situation earned her the name "the Iron Lady."

Britain's major postwar problems have been economic. Some $40 billion in foreign investments were liquidated to pay for the British war effort. Thus, investment income was lost after the war, making necessary a considerable expansion of exports to pay for needed imports. There was difficulty in competing for foreign markets. Labor was low in productivity and Britain was outstripped by both West Germany and Japan. Demands for austerity and sacrifice from labor unions to control inflationary pressures resulted in a nationwide coal strike and prolonged work stoppage in 1972. Inflationary pressure increased with the Arab oil embargo and the drastic increase in oil prices during the winter of 1973–1974.

After 1974 Labor changed its policies and sought to cut public expenditures, use public funds for private investment, and limit wage increases. Priority was given to industrial expansion in several key industries with the most promise of growth. Labor for the first time in decades favored the private sector. The pound sterling was devalued from about $4 in 1945 to $1.60 in 1976 to provide more favorable trade conditions. British industry continued to be plagued by poor management and frequent strikes. Imports and pressures for higher wages and welfare benefits continued to fuel inflation.

Relations with Northern Ireland proved a burden to successive British governments. The 1922 settlement had left Northern Ireland as a self-governing part of the United Kingdom. Of 1.5 million inhabitants, one-third were Roman Catholic and two-thirds were Protestant. Catholics claimed they were discriminated against and pressed for annexation by the Republic of Ireland. Activity by the Irish Republican Army brought retaliation by Protestant extremists. From 1969 on, there was considerable violence, causing the British to bring in troops to maintain order. Over 1,500 were killed in the next several years in sporadic outbreaks of violence. Britain could find no solution satisfactory to both sides and the violence continued.

Separatist pressure of a far less violent kind was prevalent in Wales and Scotland. In 1976 Welsh and Scottish regional assemblies were established with jurisdiction over housing, health, education, and other areas of local concern. Budgets, however, remained under the control of London. The Scots were especially motivated to seek change because of the discovery of North Sea oil deposits, much of which lay in Scottish territorial waters.

Under Prime Minister Thatcher in the 1980s the British economy improved somewhat. London regained some of its former power as a financial center. Southern England was prosperous, but the industrial midlands remained in the doldrums with continued widespread unemployment and poverty. In recent years an influx of people from former colonies in Asia, Africa, and the West Indies has caused some racial tensions.

Prime Minister Thatcher has been a partisan of free enterprise. She fought inflation with austerity and let economic problems spur British employers and unions to change for greater efficiency. She received a boost in popularity when Britain fought a brief war with Argentina over the Falkland islands and emerged victorious. She stressed close ties with the Republican administration of Ronald Reagan in the U.S. Her popularity remained undiminished whereas the Labor opposition has been plagued by internal strife. Both the old Liberal party and the new Social Democratic party made gains at the expense of Labor, but neither gained any significant power. A Conservative victory in 1987 elections made Thatcher the longest-serving prime minister in modern British history.

France Under the Fifth Republic

The Fourth Republic established in the wake of World War II suffered from the weaknesses of the Third: a strong legislature and a weak executive leading to competition between factions and instability in government together with problems in trying to maintain French rule in Indochina and Algeria. In June 1958 the Assembly made General de Gaulle premier with six months emergency powers to deal with Algeria and problems posed by a rebellious army.

Under de Gaulle a new constitution was drafted and approved establishing the Fifth Republic with a much strengthened executive in the form of a president with power to dissolve the legislature and call for elections, to submit important questions to popular referendum, and if necessary to assume emergency powers. De Gaulle used all these powers in his eleven years as president.

De Gaulle eventually settled the Algerian problem by granting independence in July 1962. Elsewhere in foreign policy de Gaulle's tenure as first president of the Fifth Republic was marked by an attempt to make France an independent force in world affairs. He saw the struggle as one between powers, not ideologies. France became the world's fourth atomic power in 1960 and developed its own nuclear striking force. De Gaulle refused to follow the lead of either Britain or the U.S. At one time he advocated that Quebec free itself from Canada and at another sided with the Arabs against Israel. Many came to view his foreign policy as quixotic.

In domestic politics de Gaulle strengthened the power of the president by often using the referendum and bypassing the Assembly, as when he secured passage of a constitutional amendment providing for future direct popular election of the president. De Gaulle was re-elected in 1965, but people became restless with what amounted to a republican monarch. Labor became restive over inflation and housing while students objected to expenditures on nuclear forces rather than education. In May 1968 student grievances over conditions in the universities caused hundreds of thousands to revolt. They were soon joined by some 10 million workers who paralyzed the economy. De Gaulle survived by promising educational reform and wage increases. New elections were held June 1968, and de Gaulle was returned to power. Promised reforms were begun, but in April 1969 the president suffered a defeat on a constitutional amendment which he had set up as a vote of confidence. He therefore resigned and died about a year later.

De Gaulle's immediate successors were Georges Pompidou (1969–1974) and Valery Giscard d'Estaing (1974–1981). Both provided France with firm but not particularly radical leadership, and continued to follow an independent foreign policy without De Gaulle's more flamboyant touches.

In 1981 François Mitterand succeeded Giscard d'Estaing. He inherited an economy with troubles. Earlier during the 1970s France had prospered and become the third largest producer of aerospace technology next to the U.S. and the U.S.S.R. Believing prosperity would continue, Giscard d'Estaing's government did not invest sufficiently and allowed wages and social services to increase at high rates. During his first year Mitterand tried to revitalize economic growth, granted wage hikes, reduced the work week, expanded paid vacations, and nationalized 11 large private companies and banks. The aim was to stimulate the economy by expanding worker purchasing power and confiscating the profits of large corporations for public investment. Loans were made abroad to finance this program. When results were poor, these foreign investors were reluctant to grant more credit. Mitterand then reversed his policy and began to cut taxes and social expenditures. By 1984 this had brought down inflation but increased unemployment. The French public generally denounced big government but nevertheless wanted government benefits and services.

Germany After Adenauer: Erhard as Chancellor

The Christian Democrats remained in power after West German independence for two main reasons: (1) prosperity which by the mid-1950s was reaching all classes of Germans, and (2) the unique personality of Chancellor Konrad Adenauer, who kept the country firmly allied with NATO and the West. Christian Democratic victories in 1953 and 1957 showed the public's approval of the laissez-faire policy of Adenauer's economics minister, Ludwig Erhard. Adenauer's long tenure made him the key figure, lessened the importance of parliament, and resulted in much government bureaucracy. Adenauer claimed to want the reunification of Germany, but he insisted on free elections which the Communists of East Germany could not accept, and thus effectively blocked any negotiated solution to the unification problem. Adenauer's last electoral victory was in September 1961. The next year or two the aged Chancellor spent trying to remain in office despite party feeling that he should retire.

In April 1963 the Christian Democrats finally named Erhard to succeed Adenauer. Erhard had quite a different style—treating ministers and department heads as colleagues and equals. There was more of a collegial atmosphere but less drive and vigor, especially in foreign affairs.

By 1966 the Christian Democrats decided on a change. In November 1966 they formed a so-called "great coalition" with the Social Democrats under Willy Brandt. Kurt

Georg Kiesinger became chancellor, and Brandt the Socialist took over as foreign minister. Brandt announced his intention to work step by step for better relations with East Germany, but found that in a coalition of two very dissimilar parties he could make no substantial progress.

In domestic affairs, pressure for change in the German universities led to outbreaks of student violence just before the similar outbreaks among students in France. Early in 1969 Gustav Heinemann (SD) was elected president. An active campaign won the Socialists a gain the Bundestag elections which occurred later in 1969. The Socialists were pined by the Free Democrats and obtained the majority necessary to make Willy Brandt chancellor in October 1969.

Brandt, the former mayor of West Berlin, was Germany's first Socialist chancellor in almost 40 years. In foreign affairs he opened the way for British entry into the Common Market. The German mark was revalued at a higher rate, emphasizing German's true economic strength. Brandt was now able also to move for improved relations with the East (the policy of *Ostpolitik*). He offered improved economic relations to Poland and the U.S.S.R, and in return those states labeled his approach "positive." In the summer of 1970 he negotiated a treaty with the U.S.S.R. in which both parties renounced the use of force in European affairs. Later that year an agreement was made with Poland recognizing the Oder-Neisse line as the legal border between Poland and Germany. Relations improved also with East Germany. Walter Ulbricht retired from government in 1971, and the next year Brandt signed a treaty with East Germany to normalize relations and improve communications. Both states entered the United Nations. The question of whether division was permanent was bypassed.

Elections in November 1972 gave Brandt's coalition a clear victory and a 50-seat majority in the parliament. But there were problems for the chancellor, who had concentrated too much on foreign affairs. Brandt seemed to many too tolerant of disorders among university students. There was criticism also of his sometimes over emotional approach to foreign policy, as in relations with Israel. The discovery of a spy in his immediate office was an excuse for replacing him. Brandt put up little resistance, and Helmut Schmidt (SD) became chancellor in the spring of 1974.

Problems with the economy and the environment brought an end to Schmidt's chancellorship and the rule of the Socialists in 1982. An organization called the Greens, which was a loosely organized coalition of environmentalists alienated from society, detracted from Socialist power. In 1982 the German voters turned to the more conservative Christian Democrats again, and Helmut Kohl became chancellor. The economy continued strong on the whole and the new leadership followed a policy of using German influence to reduce U.S.-U.S.S.R. confrontation and tension.

Italy

Italian politics was plagued with problems caused by lack of common interests among different areas. The Christian Democrats, who were closely allied with the Roman Catholic Church, dominated the national scene. Their organization, though plagued by corruption, did provide some unity to Italian politics by supplying the prime ministers for numerous coalitions.

Italy advanced economically. In the period 1958–1962 the nation moved into the top 10 industrial powers. Natural gas and some oil was discovered in the north and the Po valley area especially benefited.

Unfortunately, business efficiency found no parallel in the government or civil service. Italy suffered from terrorism, kidnappings, and assassinations on the part of extreme radical groups such as the Red Brigades. These agitators hoped to create conditions favorable to the overthrow of the democratic constitution. The most notorious terrorist act was the assassination in 1978 of Aldo Moro, a respected Christian Democratic leader.

In 1983 the Christian Democrats received only about one-third of the popular vote and as a result of this weakness, Bettino Craxi (Socialist) became prime minister at the head of an uneasy coalition which lasted four years—the longest single government in postwar Italian history. After Craxi's resignation, no strong leader emerged.

Spain and Portugal

In the Iberian Peninsula two similar events have been the most important of the postwar era. In Portugal, Europe's longest right-wing dictatorship came to an end in September 1968 when a stroke incapacitated Antonio Salazar, who died two years later. A former collaborator, Marcelo Caetano, became prime minister, and an era of change began. Censorship was relaxed and some freedom was given to political parties.

In 1974 General Antonio de Spinola published his views on the long struggle of Portugal to hold on to its African colonies. This event sparked even more change. Caetano dismissed the general, whose popularity grew nevertheless. In April 1974 the Getano regime was overthrown and a "junta of national salvation" took over, headed by General Spinola. The general proved too conservative and cautious for younger officers, and he was unable to work with the strong forces of the Communist and Socialist parties, which had emerged from secrecy with the collapse of the dictatorship. Spinola retired and went into exile. Portugal went through a succession of governments. Its African colonies of Mozambique and Angola were finally granted independence in 1975. Portugal joined the Common Market in 1986.

In Spain, dictatorship was also brought to an end. Franco, who had been ruler of a fascist regime since the end of the Civil War in 1939, held on until he was close to 70. He then designated the Bourbon prince, Juan Carlos, to be his successor. In 1975 Franco relinquished power and died three weeks later. Juan Carlos proved a popular and able leader and over the next several years took the country from dictatorship to constitutional monarchy. Basque and Catalan separatist movements, which had caused trouble for so long, were appeased by the granting of local autonomy. Spain entered the Common Market in 1986, at the same time as Portugal.

END OF THE COLD WAR AND COLLAPSE OF COMMUNISM

U.S.S.R.: Reforms Lead to Change, 1987–1991

By 1985, when Mikhail Gorbachev became leader of the Soviet Union, that country faced severe economic difficulties. Pollution of rivers, increasing incidence of health problems, a rise in infant mortality in several regions, a decline in industrial production, over-centralization of planning and control, poor worker morale, and the burden of the arms race—all led to pressure for political and economic change. Confidence in central planning and leadership was further undermined and considerable fear generated throughout Europe and abroad by the disaster at the atomic power plant at Chernobyl (which is near Kiev). The reactor's explosion exposed more than 600,000 people to high doses of radiation, according to Leonid Toptunov, a former Soviet scientist.

Gorbachev introduced reforms that had widespread and often unanticipated consequences. Some freedom was allowed for private enterprise, and decentralization of control over industry and agriculture began. Censorship of the media was relaxed and press conferences were held. Gorbachev sought favor with the cultural and scientific elite by bringing back Andrei Sakharov, the noted physicist and dissident, from internal exile. The government also allowed the hitherto proscribed works of Alexander Solzhenitsyn to be openly published. In the area of foreign affairs, a new U.S.-U.S.S.R. agreement on intermediate-range ballistic missiles was reached in 1987.

The most radical of Gorbachev's reforms was to separate the Communist Party from the Soviet government. Between 1988 and 1991 a multi-party democracy with a parliament was introduced, and the Communist Party's monopoly of political life ended. Interest groups became free to organize as political parties, support candidates for office, and solicit votes. A new constitution was adopted in 1988. The new parliament, consisting of a Congress of People's Deputies and a Supreme Soviet, was elected and took office in 1989. In 1990 Gorbachev was elected President.

An unexpected result of Gorbachev's policies of *perestroika* (restructuring) and *glasnost* (openness) was the revival of separatist movements in Eastern Europe and within the multi-national Soviet Union itself. Both Lithuania and Georgia voted for independence from the U.S.S.R.

The Revolution of 1991

In 1991, conservatives and hard-liners attempted a coup d'état against Gorbachev. The revolt was overcome thanks to the determined stand taken by Boris Yeltsin, who headed popular resistance. Although Gorbachev remained in office for a few months more, the real power passed to Yeltsin, and in December—with the dissolution of the U.S.S.R.—Gorbachev resigned and Yeltsin took his place.

Changes Since 1991 Under Yeltsin

The old Soviet Union broke apart once the controls were removed. The Baltic provinces (Latvia, Lithuania, and Estonia) opted for independence, as did the Ukraine and other provinces of the union dominated for so long by the huge Russian Republic. A loose confederation known as the Commonwealth of Independent States emerged, containing 11 of the former Soviet republics. Four— Latvia, Lithuania, Estonia, and Georgia—refused to join.

Economic difficulties associated with the transition to a free economy, the mishandled repression of the Chechnya independence movement, and the forceful dispersal of Yeltsin's parliamentary opponents in 1993 gave ammunition to Yeltsin's opponents. In the 1996 elections, Yeltsin retained office as President despite reports of poor health. Following reelection Yeltsin underwent successful heart surgery, but his health problems and continuing political difficulties made his future as Russia's leader uncertain.

REVOLUTION IN EASTERN EUROPE

Poland

The Solidarity labor movement, led by Lech Walesa (who received the Nobel peace prize in 1983), gained power as the Communist government of General Wojciech Jaruzelski failed to master Poland's economic problems. Power passed to the Polish Parliament, and in the elections held in June 1989, Solidarity won an overwhelming majority. A movement began to transform the state-run economy into one based on market forces. Lech Walesa became President of Poland. By 1993-94, however, economic problems resulted in a Communist majority and a change of administration, but there was no return to the old Communist dictatorship. In 1993, Poland experienced 4% economic growth and appeared to be making a successful transition from a centrally planned to a market economy.

Hungary

Communist leader Janos Kadar was forced out of power in 1987. By March 1990, Hungary had formed a multi-party system and had held free elections that resulted in an overwhelming repudiation of the Communists. As in Poland, the problems of the next four years led to the return of a Communist Social Democratic majority that promised to maintain economic reforms and work for greater social justice.

Czechoslovakia

Communism also met with defeat in Czechoslovakia. Popular demonstrations in Prague in November 1989 resulted in a new government led by the playwright-dissident Václav Havel, who was confirmed in the office of President in elections held in June 1990. Bitter national rivalry caused the nation, created at the end of the first World War, to split into the Czech and Slovak republics on January 1, 1993. Since then, the Czech Republic has experienced relative prosperity, compared with high unemployment and other problems in the Slovak Republic.

The Reunification of Germany

In East Germany, Erich Honecker's government was overthrown in October 1989, and in November the Berlin Wall was breached and removed. In elections held in March 1990, proponents of German reunification won overwhelmingly, and by October, East and West Germany were once again reunited as one country, with its capital at Berlin. By 1995, significant progress had been made in overcoming the problems associated with reunification and a faltering East German economy.

WESTERN EUROPE

Great Britain

The Conservative (or Tory) Party retained power but under changed leadership. Margaret Thatcher, the first woman Prime Minister, differed with her party over Britain's participation in the European Economic Community (the Common Market) and the projected introduction of a common currency. Having lost the support of the Conservatives in Parliament, Thatcher resigned and was replaced by Chancellor of the Exchequer John Major. Under Major's leadership, the Conservatives have had to deal with slow economic growth, unemployment, and racial tensions caused by resentment over the influx of persons from the Commonwealth. In addition, there remains the chronic problem of Northern Ireland, with its Protestant-Roman Catholic animosities; this has been made more difficult by the Irish Republican Army, which has resorted to terrorism and violence to attain unity with Ireland proper. In 1995–96, retired United States Senator George Mitchell assisted in negotiations. So far, no solution has been reached.

France

Socialist President François Mitterand's policies of nationalization and decentralization of the governmental apparatus, put in place by Napoleon almost 200 years earlier, were slowed by conservative resistance to basic change. Slow industrial growth, inflation, and unemployment remained problems. Mitterand lost his Socialist majority in Parliament in 1986, but regained it in 1988. His regime favored close cooperation with the United States and a policy of moderation in domestic affairs. An ailing Mitterand retired at the end of his term in 1995 and died in January 1996.

Italy

By the 1990s, Italian industry and the economy generally had advanced to a point where Italy was a leading center in high-technology industry, fashion, design, and banking. These advances, however, were concentrated around the cities of the north. Southern Italy continued to have problems associated with economic backwardness and poverty.

Political instability has been the mark of Italian politics ever since the end of World War II. Corruption within a system dominated by the Christian Democrats resulted in criminal trials in the 1990s that sent a number of high government officials to prison. In 1993, the electoral system for the Senate of the Italian Parliament was changed from proportional representation to a system that gave power to the party with the majority of votes. The 1994 elections for Parliament brought to power the charismatic, conservative Silvio Berlusconi and his Forzia Italia ("Let's go Italy") movement.

EUROPE'S CHANGING ROLE IN INTERNATIONAL RELATIONS

New Role for NATO?

NATO, which had originated as a Western alliance against the Soviet Union, lost its reason for being with the collapse of the Soviet Union and revolution in Eastern Europe. In his 1996 re-election campaign speeches, U.S. President Bill Clinton suggested that NATO be expanded to include Eastern Europe and that it provide a collective guarantee against any aggression by one power against another. In another area, NATO provided a vehicle for occasional armed intervention in the Balkans in the Bosnian conflict.

Europe and the United Nations

The United Nations continued to play a limited but significant role in world affairs. It served as a vehicle for intervention in disputes between the Arab nations and Israel, in the Sudan, and, more recently, in the Balkans. It has provided humanitarian aid, mediated disputes, and maintained international military units to police peace agreements. In a number of less well-known instances such as telecommunications, international aviation, relief of distress among children, and support of international work in education, the arts, and science, the United Nations and its constituent organizations have played a crucial role.

The Balkan Crisis (Yugoslavia and Its Successor States)

Marshall Tito managed to hold together a nation of six republics with numerous rival ethnic groups, despite difficulties with the economy and in relations with Stalin and the Soviet Union. Even after Tito's death in 1980, the system continued to function for a number of years. But with the turmoil in Eastern Europe and the collapse of the Soviet Union, Yugoslav unity ended in 1991 and various factions took up arms against each other that summer. Slovenes and Croats broke away from Serbian control, and Bosnia and Herzegovina declared independence by the end of the year. Armed conflict broke out between Serbs, Croats, Bosnian Muslims, and other factions and interest groups.

The United Nations sent Cyrus Vance (U.S. Secretary of State under President Carter) and Lord David Owen (a former British Foreign Secretary) to mediate the dispute, but several truces and agreements that had been arranged all broke down. The European states, including Russia, all deplored the strife in the former Yugoslavia. On several occasions NATO intervened with air strikes and economic sanctions against the Serbs, but no agreement could be reached on military action sufficient to force an end to the conflict. In 1995 Richard Holbrooke of the United States negotiated a peace agreement, and in 1996 a multi-national force (which included United States troops for the first time) was sent in to police the agreement and maintain peace.

Europe, the Gulf War, and the Arab-Israeli Peace Movement

In August 1990, in a campaign which met little resistance and lasted only a few days, the army of Saddam Hussein, dictator of Iraq, seized control of its neighbor, Kuwait. The European powers and the United States—seeing a threat to their oil supplies—organized under the leadership of President George Bush. Through the United Nations, they called on Iraq to withdraw, and when this did not occur, an international army led by the United States was mobilized on the border between Kuwait and Saudi Arabia. Even Yeltsin's Russia gave political and economic support. Air strikes against Iraq began in January 1991. When these failed to bring about Iraqi withdrawal from Kuwait, a ground attack by the allied armies, under the command of American General Norman Schwarzkopf, was launched. Iraqi resistance collapsed and in just over four days, the allies had freed Kuwait and driven the Iraqi army back to the Euphrates River. At this point President Bush called a halt to hostilities, and Iraq was forced to give up any claim to Kuwait and to make peace on United Nations terms. Saddam Hussein remained in power, however, and continued to cause difficulties for the United States and its European allies.

The greatest source of instability in the Middle East since World War II has been the continuing conflict between the state of Israel (created by Jews in Palestine in 1948 after British withdrawal) and its Arab neighbors. In 1964, the Palestine Liberation Organization, led by Yassir Arafat, was formed among Arab refugees who had been expelled from their ancestral homes by the Israelis. Its stated goal was the destruction of Israel. By the 1990s, however, possibilities for peace seemed good. By then both Egypt and Jordan had signed peace treaties with Israel. After 50 years of intermittent warfare, the Arab-Israeli struggle was taken to the bargaining table despite resistance from both Arab and Israeli hard-liners. The Palestine Liberation Organization was extended recognition by Israel. In 1993, using the good offices of President Clinton, Prime Minister Itzhak Rabin and PLO leader Arafat concluded agreements for limited self-government for Palestinians in Israel. Despite the assassination of Prime Minister Rabin in 1995 and the election in the spring of 1996 of a more conservative Prime Minister, Benjamin Netanyahu, some progress continued to be made toward a general peace settlement between the Arabs and Israelis.

CULTURAL AND SOCIAL DEVELOPMENTS SINCE WWII

Science and Technology

Advances in science and technology have caused considerable change in the period since World War II. In 1900 there were about 15,000 trained scientists engaged in research and teaching—most in Europe. In the postwar years the figure reached

500,000; in addition to Central and Western Europe, the Soviet Union, the United States, and Japan were heavily involved in scientific research and development of technologies that applied scientific advances to everyday life.

Much of the early work on such devices as rockets, the jet aircraft engine, radar, and the computer was done in England and Germany during and immediately after World War II. The English mathematician Alan Turing was influential in wartime cryptographic work in which machines were developed to discover, by high-speed computation, the random settings of German cipher machines. Significant research on computers was done in places such as the University of Manchester following the war; in the last three decades, however, the lead in computers has been taken by the United States and Japan.

Rapid change occurred in medicine with the development of sulfa drugs, penicillin, cortisone, and antibiotics to cure formerly crippling infections. Vaccines were developed for poliomyelitis (1955) and other diseases. Remarkable developments in surgery included transplantation of vital organs. Research in genetics led to genetic engineering, in which scientists actually learned to create new and different living organisms. Some of this work was done in Europe, but more than ever before the balance was shifting to other areas, including the United States, Russia, and Japan.

In astronomy and space science, Western Europe was unable to match the vast resources of the super powers, but has nevertheless made significant advances. France became a leader in aerospace technology. England became a pioneer in radio astronomy with the work of Sir Bernard Lovell, using the great radio telescope at Jodrell Bank.

After World War II, European countries made extensive use of nuclear reactors for production of electric power. West Germany had the largest nuclear power program in Europe into the late 1970s, but after 1975 built only one more plant because of increasing costs. In Russia, nuclear power stations in recent years have cost up to twice as much as coal-fired plants. With Britain's discovery and exploitation of oil from under the North Sea, the economics of power changed considerably. France maintained its commitment to nuclear power and expected to obtain one-half or more of its power from that source by the year 2000.

The disastrous accident at the reactor at Chernobyl in the Ukraine in April 1986 caused many Europeans to rethink the whole matter of nuclear reactors and public safety. By the late 1980s, given the increasing concern about nuclear accidents and the disposal of radioactive wastes, nuclear power no longer seemed to hold the promise it had in the wake of World War II.

Two technological developments of the highest importance for everyday life were television and the computer. In 1980 there were 33 television sets for every 100 West Germans and 29 for every 100 persons in France. Not the least disturbing thing about television for Europeans was the influx of programs from the U.S.: some 20% of British television and 50% of French television was imported by the 1980s, mainly from the U.S. The ability of television to bring far-away events into the ordinary living room meant an ever-increasing use of the medium to influence politics and other important areas of life in ways just beginning to be studied and understood. The computer has developed from large devices available only for limited use to small personal machines widely available to many people. Its influence on everyday living has been at least as great as that of television.

Religion

In postwar Europe the ecumenical movement among the various branches of the Christian Church has been a notable development. The Second Vatican Council of

1963 supported ecumenicism and called for greater toleration among Christians. Most branches of the Christian Church continued to support traditional beliefs which has meant a continuation of conflict with the teachings of modern science and such philosophies as Marxism. The Roman Catholic Church, in particular, has been outspoken in opposition to nuclear weapons.

Literature and Art

Important work in literature and art has been done in all of the European countries since World War II. Even in Russia, despite censorship, such writers as Pasternak and Solzhenitsyn produced important works that were published abroad, although not in Russia until the political changes of the 1990s. The English writer George Orwell achieved fame for his frightening portrayal of a future totalitarian society in the novel *1984* (published in 1949). Writers such as Frantz Fanon in *The Wretched of the Earth* (published in French in 1961) and Jean-Paul Sartre in his *Critique of Dialectical Reason* condemned colonialism and called attention to the enormous discrepancies between the wealth of Europe and the United States and the underdeveloped nations of the so-called third world.

German writers of the older generation, such as Carl Zuckmayer and Bertholt Brecht, as well as younger writers like Wolfgang Borchert, Günter Grass, and the Swiss Heinrich Böll, produced notable works. Zuckmayer's play, *The Devil's General*, although written in the United States at the end of World War II, gave a remarkable picture of wartime Germany. Grass's novel *The Tin Drum* (1959), also set in Nazi Germany, became a best-seller that was translated into English and other languages.

Censorship in the Soviet Union under Stalin and his successors failed to stifle creativity and criticism. Boris Pasternak's *Doctor Zhivago* was an epic covering the period before, during, and after the 1917 Revolution. Its author, however, was not allowed to leave Russia to accept the Nobel Prize for literature. Alexander Solzhenitsyn's novel *One Day in the Life of Ivan Denisovich* won critical acclaim. A later work, *The Gulag Archipelago*, was a detailed description and indictment of the whole apparatus of forced labor camps run by the secret police during the Stalin era. The author was arrested for treason and forced into exile in 1974.

In film, the work of the Swedish director Ingmar Bergman (*The Seventh Seal*, *Wild Strawberries*) and the Italians Roberto Rosselini (*Open City*) and Vittorio de Sica (*Bicycle Thief*) attracted attention and critical acclaim. In art the greatest figure was Pablo Picasso, who began work before the first World War and whose productivity in many styles lasted until his death in 1973.

Social and Economic Trends

The high level of economic achievement in Europe and other developed areas by the 1990s did not prevent concern over a variety of issues. Among the most notable were the status of women and the environment. Switzerland was the last advanced Western nation to accord women the right to vote, in 1989. Elsewhere in Europe and Great Britain, women attained legal and political rights at different times. Still, they remained subject to wage and job discrimination.

As a result of scientific research and the activities of environmental groups, the world's leaders became cognizant of potentially severe problems affecting the global environment. Although a United Nations Conference on the Human Environment held in Stockholm in 1972 failed to achieve serious agreements, it did give a lot of publicity to the problems that modern industrialization and increased population have created.

In the 1990s, as Europe, the U.S., and Japan vie for power in the global economy, it remains to be seen if the trend toward European unity—both political and economic—will allow Europe to regain some of its leadership in world affairs.

THE ADVANCED PLACEMENT EXAMINATION IN

European History

TEST 1

THE ADVANCED PLACEMENT EXAMINATION IN

European History

TEST 1

1. Ⓐ Ⓑ Ⓒ Ⓓ Ⓔ
2. Ⓐ Ⓑ Ⓒ Ⓓ Ⓔ
3. Ⓐ Ⓑ Ⓒ Ⓓ Ⓔ
4. Ⓐ Ⓑ Ⓒ Ⓓ Ⓔ
5. Ⓐ Ⓑ Ⓒ Ⓓ Ⓔ
6. Ⓐ Ⓑ Ⓒ Ⓓ Ⓔ
7. Ⓐ Ⓑ Ⓒ Ⓓ Ⓔ
8. Ⓐ Ⓑ Ⓒ Ⓓ Ⓔ
9. Ⓐ Ⓑ Ⓒ Ⓓ Ⓔ
10. Ⓐ Ⓑ Ⓒ Ⓓ Ⓔ
11. Ⓐ Ⓑ Ⓒ Ⓓ Ⓔ
12. Ⓐ Ⓑ Ⓒ Ⓓ Ⓔ
13. Ⓐ Ⓑ Ⓒ Ⓓ Ⓔ
14. Ⓐ Ⓑ Ⓒ Ⓓ Ⓔ
15. Ⓐ Ⓑ Ⓒ Ⓓ Ⓔ
16. Ⓐ Ⓑ Ⓒ Ⓓ Ⓔ
17. Ⓐ Ⓑ Ⓒ Ⓓ Ⓔ
18. Ⓐ Ⓑ Ⓒ Ⓓ Ⓔ
19. Ⓐ Ⓑ Ⓒ Ⓓ Ⓔ
20. Ⓐ Ⓑ Ⓒ Ⓓ Ⓔ
21. Ⓐ Ⓑ Ⓒ Ⓓ Ⓔ
22. Ⓐ Ⓑ Ⓒ Ⓓ Ⓔ
23. Ⓐ Ⓑ Ⓒ Ⓓ Ⓔ
24. Ⓐ Ⓑ Ⓒ Ⓓ Ⓔ
25. Ⓐ Ⓑ Ⓒ Ⓓ Ⓔ
26. Ⓐ Ⓑ Ⓒ Ⓓ Ⓔ
27. Ⓐ Ⓑ Ⓒ Ⓓ Ⓔ
28. Ⓐ Ⓑ Ⓒ Ⓓ Ⓔ
29. Ⓐ Ⓑ Ⓒ Ⓓ Ⓔ
30. Ⓐ Ⓑ Ⓒ Ⓓ Ⓔ
31. Ⓐ Ⓑ Ⓒ Ⓓ Ⓔ
32. Ⓐ Ⓑ Ⓒ Ⓓ Ⓔ
33. Ⓐ Ⓑ Ⓒ Ⓓ Ⓔ
34. Ⓐ Ⓑ Ⓒ Ⓓ Ⓔ
35. Ⓐ Ⓑ Ⓒ Ⓓ Ⓔ
36. Ⓐ Ⓑ Ⓒ Ⓓ Ⓔ
37. Ⓐ Ⓑ Ⓒ Ⓓ Ⓔ
38. Ⓐ Ⓑ Ⓒ Ⓓ Ⓔ
39. Ⓐ Ⓑ Ⓒ Ⓓ Ⓔ
40. Ⓐ Ⓑ Ⓒ Ⓓ Ⓔ
41. Ⓐ Ⓑ Ⓒ Ⓓ Ⓔ
42. Ⓐ Ⓑ Ⓒ Ⓓ Ⓔ
43. Ⓐ Ⓑ Ⓒ Ⓓ Ⓔ
44. Ⓐ Ⓑ Ⓒ Ⓓ Ⓔ
45. Ⓐ Ⓑ Ⓒ Ⓓ Ⓔ
46. Ⓐ Ⓑ Ⓒ Ⓓ Ⓔ
47. Ⓐ Ⓑ Ⓒ Ⓓ Ⓔ
48. Ⓐ Ⓑ Ⓒ Ⓓ Ⓔ
49. Ⓐ Ⓑ Ⓒ Ⓓ Ⓔ
50. Ⓐ Ⓑ Ⓒ Ⓓ Ⓔ
51. Ⓐ Ⓑ Ⓒ Ⓓ Ⓔ
52. Ⓐ Ⓑ Ⓒ Ⓓ Ⓔ
53. Ⓐ Ⓑ Ⓒ Ⓓ Ⓔ
54. Ⓐ Ⓑ Ⓒ Ⓓ Ⓔ
55. Ⓐ Ⓑ Ⓒ Ⓓ Ⓔ
56. Ⓐ Ⓑ Ⓒ Ⓓ Ⓔ
57. Ⓐ Ⓑ Ⓒ Ⓓ Ⓔ
58. Ⓐ Ⓑ Ⓒ Ⓓ Ⓔ
59. Ⓐ Ⓑ Ⓒ Ⓓ Ⓔ
60. Ⓐ Ⓑ Ⓒ Ⓓ Ⓔ
61. Ⓐ Ⓑ Ⓒ Ⓓ Ⓔ
62. Ⓐ Ⓑ Ⓒ Ⓓ Ⓔ
63. Ⓐ Ⓑ Ⓒ Ⓓ Ⓔ
64. Ⓐ Ⓑ Ⓒ Ⓓ Ⓔ
65. Ⓐ Ⓑ Ⓒ Ⓓ Ⓔ
66. Ⓐ Ⓑ Ⓒ Ⓓ Ⓔ
67. Ⓐ Ⓑ Ⓒ Ⓓ Ⓔ
68. Ⓐ Ⓑ Ⓒ Ⓓ Ⓔ
69. Ⓐ Ⓑ Ⓒ Ⓓ Ⓔ
70. Ⓐ Ⓑ Ⓒ Ⓓ Ⓔ
71. Ⓐ Ⓑ Ⓒ Ⓓ Ⓔ
72. Ⓐ Ⓑ Ⓒ Ⓓ Ⓔ
73. Ⓐ Ⓑ Ⓒ Ⓓ Ⓔ
74. Ⓐ Ⓑ Ⓒ Ⓓ Ⓔ
75. Ⓐ Ⓑ Ⓒ Ⓓ Ⓔ
76. Ⓐ Ⓑ Ⓒ Ⓓ Ⓔ
77. Ⓐ Ⓑ Ⓒ Ⓓ Ⓔ
78. Ⓐ Ⓑ Ⓒ Ⓓ Ⓔ
79. Ⓐ Ⓑ Ⓒ Ⓓ Ⓔ
80. Ⓐ Ⓑ Ⓒ Ⓓ Ⓔ

European History

TEST 1 – Section I

TIME: 55 Minutes
80 Questions

DIRECTIONS: Each of the questions or incomplete statements below is followed by five suggested answers or completions. Select the one that is best in each case.

1. Henry VIII's principal assistant in enhancing monarchial controls during the 1530s was
   (A) Thomas Cranmer.
   (B) Thomas More.
   (C) Thomas Wolsey.
   (D) William Cecil.
   (E) Thomas Cromwell.

2. The Colloquy of Marburg in 1529
   (A) was an attempt by the Catholic Church to develop a strategy to combat the Protestant movement.
   (B) was a meeting which declared Luther to be an outlaw throughout the Holy Roman Empire.
   (C) was a debate between Luther and Zwingli which resulted in a formal split within Protestantism.
   (D) was an attempt by Charles V to reconcile Luther to the Catholic Church.
   (E) resulted in the fall of Thomas Wolsey as Chancellor of England.

3. English Puritanism developed during the reign of Elizabeth I
   (A) in reaction to the failure of the Elizabethan Religious Settlement to implement the reforms of the Council of Trent.
   (B) because of Elizabeth I's intention to extend Protestant sentiment throughout the realm.
   (C) because of the dissatisfaction with the scope and breath of the Elizabethan Religious Settlement among the Marian Exiles and others who were influenced by Calvinist views.
   (D) as a direct reaction to the Jesuit Mission led by Edmund Campion.

(E) to maintain the hierarchical and ceremonial aspects of the previous era.

4. The Petition of Right (1628–29)

(A) was an attempt by James I to secure additional tax revenues through the Parliament.

(B) resulted in Parliament voting to execute the Duke of Buckingham.

(C) was directed at addressing a range of Parliamentary grievances before approving new sources of revenue which were requested by Charles I.

(D) denounced the left-wing religious policies of Charles I's government.

(E) was approved by the Addled Parliament.

5. René Descartes maintained or has been credited with all of the following EXCEPT

(A) first publication of the discovery of coordinate or analytical geometry.

(B) developing the science of optics through the laws of refraction of light.

(C) established as his famous philosophic starting place: "cogito ergo sum" — I think therefore I am.

(D) the concept of God was unnecessary in his concept of the universe.

(E) Cartesian Dualism was the link between the physical and spiritual worlds.

6. The Instrument of Government (1653)

(A) recognized the demands of the leaders of the Fronde.

(B) was a plan devised by John Locke for the government of the Carolina policy.

(C) specified that Charles I was to be executed.

(D) recognized Scotland and Ireland as free and independent nations.

(E) established the Protectorate and resulted in Cromwell's designation as Lord Protector.

7. Henry IV provided French Huguenots with the right to practice their religion through the

(A) Edict of Potsdam.

(B) Edict of Fontainebleau.

(C) Edict of Nantes.

(D) agreement with the Papacy.

(E) Peace of Amiens.

8. During the second half of the 17th century the power of Brandenburg-Prussia was enhanced primarily through the efforts of

(A) Elector Frederick III.
(B) King Frederick I.
(C) Elector Frederick William.
(D) Leopold.
(E) Bismarck.

9. Which of the following thinkers identified most closely with the following statement "renounce notions, and begin to form an acquaintance with things"?

(A) Galileo
(B) Bacon
(C) Descartes
(D) Spinoza
(E) Boyle

10. For several decades during the late 17th century Austria fought on two fronts against which two countries?

(A) Italy and Prussia
(B) England and Russia
(C) France and the Ottoman Empire
(D) Prussia and the Ottoman Empire
(E) France and Italy

11. The Peace of Utrecht

(A) resulted in the political and economic collapse of France.
(B) elevated England to the greatest power in the world.
(C) terminated the Wars of the Age of Louis XIV and restored peace to Europe.
(D) transferred Canada to England.
(E) resulted in the unification of Germany.

12. The Siccardi Law and the Law on Convents were two devices which Cavour utilized to

(A) restrict the influence of the Catholic Church in Piedmont.
(B) attract the support of Bismarck in an alliance directed against France.
(C) pave the way for the entrance of Piedmont into the Crimean War.
(D) enhance his personal relationship with King Victor Emmanuel II.
(E) demonstrate his opposition to the *Syllabus of Errors.*

13. The Reform Bills of 1832, 1867, and 1884–85 in Great Britain resulted in

(A) eliminating child labor abuses in the textile industry.
(B) eliminating the power of the House of Lords.
(C) alleviating the most drastic problems confronting the Irish.
(D) extending the franchise and redistributing the seats in Parliament.
(E) giving the vote to all adults over 21.

14. The Dual Alliance of 1879 may be described as all of the following EXCEPT
    (A) a defensive pact between Germany and Austria.
    (B) from the German perspective, it was directed at the diplomatic isolation of France.
    (C) from the Austrian perspective, it was directed at Italian encroachment in the Balkans.
    (D) it was renewed through the First World War.
    (E) it addressed German concerns over growing anti-German sentiment in Russia.

15. During the era of the French Revolution, the Thermidorean Reaction
    (A) initiated the Reign of Terror.
    (B) resulted in the dissolution of the National Assembly.
    (C) terminated the Reign of Terror and led to the execution of Robespierre.
    (D) was the direct cause of the rise of Napoleon.
    (E) witnessed the execution of Louis XVI and Marie Antoinette.

16. Which of the following intellectuals did not participate in the Enlightenment?
    (A) Edward Gibbon
    (B) David Hume
    (C) Benjamin Franklin
    (D) Leopold von Ranke
    (E) Adam Smith

17. The era of the Napoleonic Wars was concluded by the
    (A) Peace of Utrecht.
    (B) Congress of Berlin.
    (C) Peace of Westphalia.
    (D) Congress of Vienna.
    (E) Peace of Paris.

18. The Decembrist Revolution of 1825 occurred in
    (A) Prussia.
    (B) France.
    (C) Austria.
    (D) Russia.
    (E) Spain.

19. Charles Fourier, Robert Owen, and Claude Saint-Simon can best be described as
    (A) anarchists.
    (B) Marxists.

(C) advocates of capitalism. (D) pre-Marxist socialists.

(E) revisionists.

20. The July Revolution in France resulted in the
    (A) development of democracy in France.
    (B) installation of Louis Philippe as king.
    (C) presidency of Louis Napoleon.
    (D) establishment of a republican form of government.
    (E) the withdrawal of Prussian troops.

21. The map shown here indicates the locations of European revolutions during what year?
    (A) 1820
    (B) 1830
    (C) 1848
    (D) 1919
    (E) 1825

22. The Frankfurt Assembly was
    (A) a Pan-German assembly interested in the formulation of an integrated union of German states.
    (B) Bismarck's instrument to bring about a Prussian-dominated Germany.
    (C) a group of German representatives who were concerned primarily with local economic issues.
    (D) an Austrian effort to obstruct Bismarck's plan for German unification.
    (E) a group dedicated to the *Grossdeutsch* plan.

23. The failure of the Revolutions of 1848 may be attributed to all the following factors EXCEPT

    (A) the continuing loyalty of the armed forces to the old leadership.

    (B) the intelligence and cunning of the old leadership in manipulating the revolutionary forces.

    (C) the lack of effective organization among the nationalist revolutionaries in Eastern and Southern Europe.

    (D) the failure of the liberal revolutionaries in Central Europe to address serious social and economic issues.

    (E) the acceptance of political reforms by the liberal revolutionaries in the West at the expense of social and economic considerations.

24. The industrial economy of the 19th century was based upon all of the following EXCEPT

    (A) the availability of raw materials.

    (B) an adequate labor supply.

    (C) the availability of capital.

    (D) a distribution system to market finished products.

    (E) an equitable distribution of profits among all those who were involved in production.

25. Which author advanced the argument that anarchism would be achieved through education and without violence in *What Is Property?*

    (A) William Godwin

    (B) Michael Bakunin

    (C) Georges Sorel

    (D) Pierre Proudhon

    (E) Charles Fourier

26. The Revisionist Marxist movement

    (A) failed to gain a following during the late 19th century.

    (B) supported the Marxist concept of revolution but differed with numerous other Marxist prescriptions.

    (C) encompassed the Fabian Society, the Social Democratic Party in Germany, and the French Socialist movement led by Jean Jaures.

    (D) was the base upon which Lenin developed his support for the deployment of Communism in Russia.

    (E) never attracted much support except in such Asian societies as China and Vietnam.

27. The New Economic Plan (NEP) was

(A) Lenin's plan to revitalize the Russian economy after the Russian Civil War.

(B) a scheme developed by Trotsky to enhance his control over the Communist Party organization through economic concessions.

(C) Gorbachev's 1989 plan for the restructuring of the Russian economy.

(D) Nicholas II's last attempt to recover political support through economic concessions.

(E) the name given to Stalin's first economic plan which emphasized collective farming and improvements in heavy industry.

28. The Congress of Berlin resulted in all of the following EXCEPT

(A) the recognition of Rumania, Serbia, and Montenegro as independent states.

(B) the realization of Russian war aims in its conflict with the Ottoman Empire.

(C) the transfer of Cyprus from the Ottoman Empire to Great Britain.

(D) the establishment of the autonomous principality of Bulgaria.

(E) Austrian acquisition of Bosnia and Herzegovina.

29. In *Emile* Rousseau

(A) advanced his views on the Social Contract.

(B) called for a "natural" education free of the artificial encumbrances imposed by institutions such as the church.

(C) denounced Voltaire for his pedantic and unproductive lifestyle.

(D) identified with Montesquieu's sympathy for the English constitutional monarchy as a model for a future French government.

(E) advanced his case for atheism.

30. Czar Alexander II of Russia (1855–1881)

(A) established the *zemstvos,* which were assemblies that allowed the Russian rural nobility to maintain control over local politics.

(B) liberated the Russian serfs, thereby improving the political, social, and economic well-being of all Russians.

(C) made a half-hearted effort to reform the Russian judicial system.

(D) reformed the Russian military and curtailed its abuses of the civilian population.

(E) was motivated to reform Russian society not out of fear but because of his genuine desire to improve the condition of all of his people.

31. The Fashoda Crisis

    (A) was a colonial dispute in West Africa between England and France.

    (B) led to the Berlin Convention to settle the problems associated with the "Scramble" for Africa.

    (C) demonstrated that relatively insignificant colonial disputes could bring the great powers to the threshold of general war.

    (D) was concluded when Kitchener's forces defeated the French Force led by Commandant Marchand.

    (E) was caused by the French Foreign Minister, Georges Clemenceau, to divert French public opinion from the Dreyfus Affair.

32. The failure of Wilhelm II's government to continue the Reinsurance Treaty with Russia

    (A) led the Russians to adopt a position of "Splendid Isolationism."

    (B) eventually led to the isolation of Germany.

    (C) resulted in the Austrian-Russian Entente of 1894.

    (D) caused the Russians to undertake a massive naval building program.

    (E) led the Russians to support the establishment of Poland as a buffer state.

33. The Russian Revolution of 1905

    (A) resulted in the abdication of the Czar.

    (B) was immediately suppressed by Nicholas II.

    (C) led to the issuing of the October Manifesto which introduced democratic government to Russia.

    (D) was the primary cause for the defeat of Russia in the Russo-Japanese War.

    (E) led Nicholas II to issue the October Manifesto which called for an advisory assembly (the Duma) to be formed.

34. The Anglo-Russian Entente of 1907

    (A) was a defensive alliance associated with France.

    (B) was a trade agreement which led to improved Anglo-Russian relations.

    (C) was a settlement of colonial disputes involving Persia, Afghanistan, and Tibet.

    (D) is also referred to as the Entente Cordiale.

    (E) was a disarmament agreement involving capital ships.

35. Oscar Wilde's *Portrait of Dorian Gray* and Thomas Mann's *Death in Venice*

    (A) are examples of the romantic literature which dominated the literary scene at the turn of the 20th century.

    (B) embodied a new symbolist direction in literature which addressed themes which were ignored previously.

    (C) emphasized a new sense of realism in literature.

    (D) were representative of a literary movement known as expressionism.

    (E) were not well received by the intellectuals of the era.

36. All of the following statements concerning the Third French Republic are accurate EXCEPT

    (A) the Dreyfus Affair, Panama Scandal, and Boulanger Crisis were serious threats to its continuance.

    (B) the Third French Republic was established in the midst of French defeat in the Franco-Prussian War.

    (C) it was threatened upon its creation by the Paris Commune.

    (D) it established a Constitution in 1875 which provided for a republican form of government.

    (E) it supported an extension of the position of the Catholic Church in French society.

37. The Berlin Conference of 1884–85

    (A) specified that Britain would have control over the Niger and Congo rivers.

    (B) established the principle that an imperial claim had to be supported by occupation and notification to the European powers.

    (C) specified that the Congo would be under Portuguese control.

    (D) supported the dream of Cecil Rhodes for a Cape-to-Cairo railroad under British control.

    (E) established Italian authority in Libya.

38. Bismarck's *Kulturkampf*

    (A) consisted of a series of measures which were intended to eliminate the impact of Marxism in German politics.

    (B) were anti-Catholic laws directed at curtailing the influence of the Center Party.

    (C) was his diplomatic strategy to maintain the diplomatic isolation of France.

(D) were intended to disrupt the progress of the Social Democratic Party.

(E) was denounced by Pope Pius X.

39. The Parliament Act of 1911 included all of the following provisions EXCEPT that the

(A) life-span of Parliament was reduced from seven to five years.

(B) revenue bills approved by the House of Commons automatically became law after being sent to the House of Lords.

(C) House of Lords had no veto power over revenue bills.

(D) House of Lords could effectively veto non-revenue bills.

(E) House of Lords could only delay enactment of non-revenue bills.

40. Who established the Independent Labour Party in 1893?

(A) Sidney and Beatrice Webb

(B) George Bernard Shaw

(C) Keir Hardie

(D) H. G. Wells

(E) H. M. Hyndman

41. The Haldane Mission was a British effort to

(A) curtail the naval arms race with Germany.

(B) eliminate colonial disputes with France.

(C) involve the United States in the war against Germany.

(D) reestablish British interests in the eastern Mediterranean.

(E) coordinate its policies with the Low Countries.

42. All of the following inventions were made after 1830 and expanded the scope of the Industrial Revolution EXCEPT

(A) Ericsson's screw propeller.

(B) Faraday's discovery of electromagnetic induction.

(C) Daguerre's invention of photography.

(D) Goodyear's rubber vulcanization.

(E) John Kay's "flying shuttle."

43. The expansion of the "division of labor" and of "mass production" through the development of standard parts and manufacturing processes were stimulated by

(A) the institution of bank credit.

(B) the factory system.

(C) competition.

(D) economic imperialism.

(E) local political rivalry.

44. Thomas Malthus, David Ricardo, Nassau Senior, and James Mill have been identified as

(A) positivists.

(B) romantic idealists.

(C) classical economists.

(D) utilitarians.

(E) utopian socialists.

45. Who was the dominant personality at the Congress of Vienna?

(A) Metternich

(B) Bismarck

(C) Alexander I

(D) Talleyrand

(E) Wellington

46. In 1829 the Ottoman Turks were forced to accept the Treaty of Adrianople which

(A) recognized the independence of Bulgaria.

(B) recognized the independence of Greece.

(C) granted Christians access to the Holy Places in Palestine.

(D) permitted Russia to have access to the Mediterranean.

(E) recognized the independence of Serbia.

47. In 1919 the Weimar Republic was challenged by the Communists or Spartacists led by

(A) Ebert.

(B) Scheidemann.

(C) Liebknecht and Luxemburg.

(D) Michaelis.

(E) Erzberger.

48. The League of Nations was successful in resolving all of the following disputes EXCEPT the

(A) Albanian boundary dispute.

(B) Greek-Bulgarian border violation dispute.

(C) Aaland Islands dispute.

(D) Mosul boundary dispute.

(E) Danzig Crisis.

49. The Treaty of Brest-Litovsk
    (A) concluded hostilities between Great Britain and Turkey.
    (B) ended the war between the allies and Hungary.
    (C) concluded hostilities between the allies and Bulgaria.
    (D) was a humiliating agreement which the Russians signed with Germany.
    (E) concluded the war between the allies and the Ottoman Empire.

50. The Locarno Treaty (1925) was a major diplomatic achievement by
    (A) Leon Trotsky.
    (B) Gustav Stresemann.
    (C) Charles Evans Hughes.
    (D) Benito Mussolini.
    (E) Ramsay MacDonald.

51. As a result of the Easter Rebellion, Eamon DeValera and Arthur Griffith experienced growing support for
    (A) the Irish Republican Army.
    (B) Irish Home Rule.
    (C) their Sinn Fein Movement.
    (D) The Public Safety Act.
    (E) maintaining the British army in Ireland.

52. The Spanish Constitution of 1931
    (A) was an attempt to establish a democratic and secular republic.
    (B) reinforced the monarchy of Alfonso XIII.
    (C) installed Franco as President for life.
    (D) supported the positions of the Church and landowners in Spanish society.
    (E) resulted in the direct intervention of Mussolini's fascist Italy.

53. The Washington and London Naval Conferences
    (A) declared war to be illegal.
    (B) denounced Japanese aggression in China.
    (C) attempted to restrict specific categories of naval weaponry.
    (D) were international efforts designated to end the Chinese Civil War.
    (E) were limited to topics which affected Southeast Asia.

54. The chart which follows indicates that
    (A) nations with large populations were better able to respond to the impact of the Depression than nations with smaller populations.

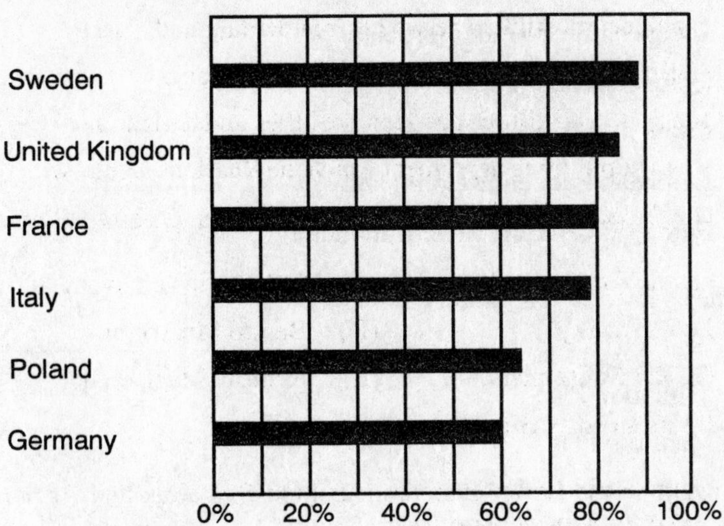

(B) advanced industrial societies had lower rates of unemployment during this period.

(C) the post-war economies in Central and Eastern Europe were fragile and subject to rapid deterioration during an economic collapse.

(D) Sweden and the United Kingdom had the strongest economic systems in the world.

(E) nations with small populations were better able to respond to the impact of the Depression than nations with larger populations.

55. The aftermath of the Suez Crisis of 1956 resulted in the fall of

(A) Charles de Gaulle as President of France.

(B) Nasser as President of Egypt.

(C) John Foster Dulles as Secretary of State.

(D) Anthony Eden as British Prime Minister.

(E) Pierre Laval as French Premier.

56. The "Fascintern" was a pact

(A) directed at subverting the interests of Britain and France.

(B) between Germany, Italy, and Japan designed to coordinate the development of fascism throughout the world and the defeat of communism.

(C) between Germany and Italy directed at the Soviet Union.

(D) between Germany and Russia during the summer 1939.

(E) whose members stressed the racial superiority of Germans.

57. The Treaty of Rome (1957) established which of the following?

(A) European Free Trade Association

(B) Colombo Plan

(C) Council of Europe

(D) European Economic Community

(E) European Coal and Steel Community

58. The map shows which military deployment?

(A) Plan XVII

(B) Schlieffen Plan

(C) Manstein Plan

(D) German troops during the Franco-Prussian War

(E) Ludendorff's Spring offensive

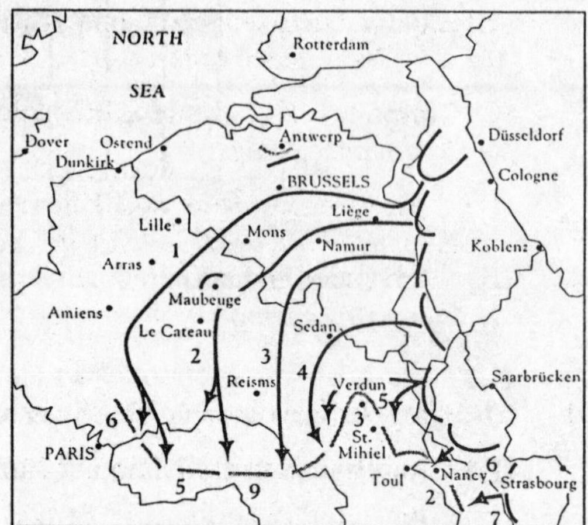

59. What does the following cartoon refer to?

(A) The continuing cooperation between Hitler and Stalin during the 1930s
(B) The contradictions inherent in the Russo-German Non-Aggression Pact
(C) The delight shared by Stalin and Hitler
(D) The defeat of Czechoslovakia
(E) The defeat of Finland

60. The Vienna Summit
(A) between Kennedy and Khrushchev was disrupted because of the U-2 spy plane crisis.
(B) between Eisenhower and Khrushchev was disrupted because of the U-2 spy plane crisis.
(C) between Nixon and Khrushchev was disrupted because of the U-2 spy plane crisis.
(D) between Kennedy and Khrushchev was focused on nuclear test ban negotiations and the war in Laos; it was followed in the next year by the Cuban missile crisis.
(E) led to the establishment of NATO.

61. The Glorious Revolution of 1688–89 resulted in all of the following EXCEPT
(A) the flight and abdication of James II.
(B) the passage of the Bill of Rights.
(C) the elevation of William III and Mary as the monarchs.
(D) specification that all future monarchs must be members of the Church of England.
(E) an agreement that in the event of no heirs, the Hanover house would succeed the Stuarts.

62. In *Hard Times* Charles Dickens depicted an English community which
(A) was enjoying the fruits of an industrialized-based progress.
(B) was preoccupied with religious constraints.
(C) was characterized by difficult personal, class, and environmental adjustments caused by the industrial order.
(D) prevailed through its repudiation of the Industrial Revolution.
(E) emphasized British nationalism.

63. The text of Denis Diderot's *Encyclopedia* was centered primarily on
(A) theology.
(B) technology.
(C) history.
(D) philosophy.
(E) poetry.

64. Arnold Toynbee's *A Study of History* and Oswald Spengler's *Decline of the West* advanced a form of history which is described as

(A) narrative.
(B) scientific.
(C) cyclical.
(D) static.
(E) economic determinism.

65. In the following poem, the Hungarian-Swiss Tzara provides a sample of which 20th century literary movement?

"The aeroplane weaves telegraph wires
and the fountain sings the same song,
...
At the rendez-vous of the coachmen the aperitif is orange
but the locomotive mechanics have blue eyes.
The lady has lost her smile in the woods."

(A) Symbolism
(B) Expressionism
(C) Deconstructionism
(D) Dadaism
(E) Idealism

66. Which of the following European intellectuals is not identified with existentialism?

(A) Jean-Paul Sartre
(B) Martin Heidegger
(C) Karl Jaspers
(D) Jacques Maritain
(E) Albert Camus

67. The driving force behind Hegel's dialectic was

(A) nationalism.
(B) racial superiority.
(C) universal reason.
(D) materialism.
(E) religious values.

68. The response of the Catholic Church to the Reformation was delayed because

(A) the Papacy feared the remnants of the Conciliar Movement within the church itself.
(B) Rome wanted to coordinate its policy with secular Catholic leaders.
(C) church leaders thought that the opposition would self-destruct.
(D) the situation did not appear to be that serious from the Roman perspective.
(E) the Church did not possess the monetary resources which were required to confront Protestantism.

69. Since 1950 the Soviet Union has suppressed movements toward more liberal governments in all of the following European countries EXCEPT

(A) East Germany.
(B) Poland.
(C) Czechoslovakia.
(D) Yugoslavia.
(E) Hungary.

70. Who was the first individual to serve as Prime Minister of Great Britain?

(A) William Pitt
(B) William Gladstone
(C) Lord Palmerston
(D) Lord North
(E) Robert Walpole

71. Friedrich Nietzsche advanced his philosophy in which works?

(A) *Thus Spake Zarathustra* and *The Will to Power*
(B) *The Golden Bough* and *The Wild Duck*
(C) *The Return of the Native* and *Jude the Obscure*
(D) *Civilization and Its Discontents* and *The Riddle of the Universe*
(E) *The Descent of Man* and *The Weavers*

72. In this painting, entitled "The Eternal City," by the American painter Peter Blume (1937),

(A) fascist Italy is dominated by the personality of Mussolini.
(B) fascism in Italy appears to have improved the general condition of the people.
(C) Mussolini emerges as a benevolent dictator who was genuinely concerned with the condition of the people.

(D) presents a sympathetic rendering of the impact of fascism on Italian life and institutions.

(E) recounts the March on Rome in 1922.

73. "Men are born, and always continue free and equal in respect of their rights. Civil distinctions, therefore, can be founded only on public utility." In 1789 these statements were part of

(A) the Bill of Rights.

(B) the Constitution of the Year III.

(C) the Declaration of the Rights of Man and the Citizen.

(D) Quesnay's statement on Physiocrat philosophy.

(E) *What Is the Third Estate?* by Abbé Siéyès.

74. During the "June Days" in Paris (1848)

(A) conservative monarchists were overwhelmed by the mob.

(B) the forces led by Louis Blanc prevailed.

(C) the army suppressed the radical revolutionary element.

(D) Louis Napoleon came to power.

(E) Lamartine was recognized as the primary leader of the revolution movement.

75. Who led the fight to repeal the Corn Laws (1846)?

(A) William Gladstone

(B) Lord Melbourne

(C) Benjamin Disraeli

(D) Lord Palmerston

(E) Robert Peel

76. In an effort to conduct a successful economic war against Britain, Napoleon created the

(A) Bank of France.

(B) Confederation of the Rhine.

(C) Continental System.

(D) Napoleonic Code.

(E) Kingdom of the Two Sicilies.

77. The 1909 budget proposed by Lloyd George advocated

(A) progressive income and inheritance taxes.

(B) an end to all property taxes.

(C) drastic reductions in funding for domestic programs.

(D) drastic reductions in expenditures for weaponry.

(E) a redistribution of excessive tax revenues.

78. In this painting, "Guernica" (1937) by Pablo Picasso, the artist rendered his interpretation of

(A) the chaos caused by the Versailles Peace Conference.

(B) Hitler's invasion of Poland.

(C) the impact of the aerial bombardment of a Spanish town by the German Condor Legion during the Spanish Civil War.

(D) the effect of the depression on French society.

(E) the fall of France.

79. What actions by Iraq led to the Persian Gulf War?

(A) Iraq attacked Israel.

(B) Iraq continued to persecute the Kurds.

(C) Iraq invaded Kuwait and seized control.

(D) Iraq refused to sell oil to the United States.

(E) Iraq refused to release American hostages.

80. Who replaced Margaret Thatcher as Prime Minister of Great Britain?

(A) John Major

(B) George Mitchell

(C) Clement Atlee

(D) Edward Heath

(E) Robert Owen

European History

TEST 1 – Section II

TIME: Reading Period – 15 minutes
Writing Time for all three essays – 115 minutes

DIRECTIONS: Read over both the Document-Based Essay question in Part A and the choices in Part B during the Reading Period, and use the time to organize answers. All students must answer Part A (the Document-Based Essay Question); and choose TWO questions from Part B to answer.

PART A – DOCUMENT-BASED ESSAY

This question is designed to test your ability to work with historical documents. As you analyze each document, *take into account its source and the point of view of the author.* Write an essay on the following topic that integrates your analysis of the documents. You may refer to historical facts and developments not mentioned in the documents.

Analyze the scope of William Hogarth's criticism of 18th century English society.

Historical Background: William Hogarth (1725–1763) has been recognized as one of England's greatest artists. Hogarth was interested in everyday English life; he wrote "I had rather see the portrait of a dog I know than all the allegories you can show me." Hogarth "felt that art should do more than entertain; it should 'improve the mind' and be 'of public utility.'"

Document 1
"Inhabitants of the Moon"

Some of the Principal Inhabitants of ye MOON, as they Were Perfectly Discover'd by a Telescope brought to ye Greatest Perfection since ye last Eclipse; Exactly Engraved from the Objects, whereby ye Curious may Guess at their Religion, Manners, &c.

Price Six Pence

Document 2
"Chairing the Members"

Document 3
"Gin Lane"

Document 4
"Beer Street"

The initial inscription reads:

Beer, happy Produce of our Isle
    Can sinewy Strength impart,
And wearied with Fatigue and Toil
    Can chear each manly Heart

Document 5
"John Wilkes, Esquire"

PART B – ESSAY QUESTIONS

1. The nature and motivation for warfare in Europe has altered many times during the modern era. Describe, compare, and analyze the motivation for the Wars of Louis XIV and Napoleon.

2. Describe and analyze the causes for the rise of fascism in Germany and Italy.

3. The Stuarts have been held at least partially accountable for the decline of monarchical power in Great Britain. Describe and analyze the justification for such a position.

4. Discuss and analyze the ideological legacy of the French Revolution of 1789.

5. At the Versailles Peace Conference Germany was forced to recognize its responsibility for the First World War. Discuss and analyze the causes which led to the outbreak of the war.

6. Assess the extent to which the overseas empires impacted upon European economic and political life from 1870 to 1914.

THE ADVANCED PLACEMENT EXAMINATION IN

European History

TEST 1 – ANSWERS

1.	**(E)**	21.	**(C)**	41.	**(A)**	61.	**(E)**
2.	**(C)**	22.	**(A)**	42.	**(E)**	62.	**(C)**
3.	**(C)**	23.	**(B)**	43.	**(B)**	63.	**(B)**
4.	**(C)**	24.	**(E)**	44.	**(C)**	64.	**(C)**
5.	**(D)**	25.	**(D)**	45.	**(A)**	65.	**(D)**
6.	**(E)**	26.	**(C)**	46.	**(B)**	66.	**(D)**
7.	**(C)**	27.	**(A)**	47.	**(C)**	67.	**(C)**
8.	**(C)**	28.	**(B)**	48.	**(E)**	68.	**(A)**
9.	**(B)**	29.	**(B)**	49.	**(D)**	69.	**(D)**
10.	**(C)**	30.	**(A)**	50.	**(B)**	70.	**(E)**
11.	**(C)**	31.	**(C)**	51.	**(C)**	71.	**(A)**
12.	**(A)**	32.	**(B)**	52.	**(A)**	72.	**(A)**
13.	**(D)**	33.	**(E)**	53.	**(C)**	73.	**(C)**
14.	**(C)**	34.	**(C)**	54.	**(C)**	74.	**(C)**
15.	**(C)**	35.	**(B)**	55.	**(D)**	75.	**(E)**
16.	**(D)**	36.	**(E)**	56.	**(B)**	76.	**(C)**
17.	**(D)**	37.	**(B)**	57.	**(D)**	77.	**(A)**
18.	**(D)**	38.	**(B)**	58.	**(B)**	78.	**(C)**
19.	**(D)**	39.	**(D)**	59.	**(B)**	79.	**(C)**
20.	**(B)**	40.	**(C)**	60.	**(D)**	80.	**(A)**

Detailed Explanations of Answers

TEST 1

1. **(E)** Thomas Cromwell assisted in the reorganization of the government which enhanced Henry VIII's power during the 1530s. Thomas Cranmer served as the Archbishop of Canterbury; Thomas More was out of favor and was executed for treason concerning Henry VIII's marriage to Anne Boleyn. William Cecil was an aid to Elizabeth I at the end of the 16th century.

2. **(C)** At the Colloquy of Marburg in 1529 Luther and Zwingli failed to concur on such issues as the nature of the Eucharist and the concept of predestination; this resulted in fragmenting Protestantism. (A) was incorrect because the Catholic strategy was centered on the establishment of new religious orders and the decrees and reforms of the Council of Trent. Luther was declared an outlaw by Charles V at the Diet of Worms in 1521. Charles V's attempts to reconcile Luther with the Church were confined to a series of debates which occurred prior to 1521. Thomas Wolsey's fall from power as Henry VIII's principal advisor was not related to the Colloquy of Marburg; it stemmed from the divorce crisis.

3. **(C)** English Puritanism developed during the reign of Elizabeth I because of the dissatisfaction with the scope and breath of the Elizabethan Religious Settlement among the Marian Exiles and others who were influenced by Calvinist views. Obviously, (A) is incorrect because the Council of Trent advanced Catholic doctrines; Elizabeth I was interested in consolidating not extending (B) Protestantism in England; the Jesuit Mission (D) occurred in 1580 and was not related to Puritanism; Puritanism (E) opposed the earlier Catholic forms of worship.

4. **(C)** The Petition of Right addressed perceived constitutional abuses related to the proceedings of the Court of the Star Chamber, a ship's tax, and the quartering of British troops in private dwellings; upon its acceptance by Charles I, additional sources of revenue were provided to alleviate the financial crisis caused by unsuccessful wars against Spain and France. (A) is incorrect because it refers to James I who died in 1625; (B) is false because Parliament did not vote Buckingham's execution — he was murdered in 1628; (D) Charles I's religious policies cannot be labelled left-wing — indeed they were right-of-center and resulted in the charge that Charles I was sympathetic to Catholicism; (E) the

Addled Parliament convened in 1614 and was not connected with the Petition of Right.

5. **(D)** Descartes argued that the reality of God was essential to his concept of the universe. Obviously, Descartes did discover coordinate or analytical geometry, develop the science of optics, used "cogito ergo sum" as his starting place, and contended that his dualism was the link between the physical and spiritual worlds.

6. **(E)** The Instrument of Government of 1653 replaced the Rump Parliament with the Protectorate as the government for the Commonwealth; Cromwell became the Lord Protector and served until his death in 1658. (A) is incorrect because the Fronde was an uprising of French nobility and was unrelated to the Instrument of Government. John Locke's (B) plan for the government of the Carolina Colony was developed during the 1660s and was known as the Framework of Government. (C) Charles I had been executed in 1649 upon the vote of Parliament. Scotland and Ireland (D) were not recognized as free and independent nations during this century.

7. **(C)** The Edict of Nantes of 1598 was issued by Henry IV and allowed the French Huguenots to practice their religion and maintain schools. The Edict of Fontainebleau (B) was issued by Louis XIV in 1685 and revoked the Edict of Nantes. The Edict of Potsdam (A) was decreed by Elector Frederick William of Brandenburg-Prussia in 1686; it invited French Protestants who were fleeing France to settle in Brandenburg-Prussia. The Papacy (D) opposed the Edict of Nantes and all other agreements which tolerated Protestant groups in Catholic countries. The Peace of Amiens (E) was a treaty during the early 19th century.

8. **(C)** Elector Frederick William of Brandenburg-Prussia (1640–88). Elector Frederick III (A) and King Frederick I (B) were the same person; he was the son of Elector Frederick William and did little to enhance the position of his nation. Leopold (D) was the Holy Roman Emperor during the late 17th and early 18th centuries. Bismarck (E) was Chancellor of the German Empire (1871–90).

9. **(B)** Francis Bacon advanced his empiricism during early 17th century. (A) While Galileo accomplished much in the development of science, he did not provide substantive contributions to the philosophy of science. Descartes' *Discourse on Method* (1637) approaches science from a more deductive mathematically-oriented approach; Baruch Spinoza's (D) contributions occurred later and were in mathematics and ethics. In addition to formulating Boyle's Law (concerning gas and temperature), Robert Boyle (E) was a chemist who did much to discredit alchemy during the second half of the 17th century.

10. **(C)** France and the Ottoman Empire. Austria was attacked twice during the period from 1660 to 1685 by the Ottoman Turks and was confronted during

the same time by wars with France. (B) is incorrect because Italy did not exist as a political ally of Austria in the wars against France. (C) is incorrect because England was allied with Austria and Russia was undergoing political crises which were not stabilized until Peter the Great seized power and reformed the government. (D) is incorrect because of Austria's alliance with Prussia and (E) is incorrect because Italy did not exist as a nation-state.

11. **(C)** The Peace of Utrecht terminated the wars of the Age of Louis XIV, restoring peace to Europe. (A) and (B) are incorrect because France, though defeated, was still the most powerful nation in Europe. (D) is incorrect because Canada was not transferred to England until the Treaty of Paris in 1763. (E) is incorrect because the Peace of Utrecht was unrelated to the unification of Germany which occurred in 1871.

12. **(A)** The Siccardi Law and the Law on Convents were two devices which Cavour utilized to (A) restrict the influence of the Catholic Church in Piedmont. They curbed the number of religious orders and limited the number of holy days in Piedmont; these laws were received sympathetically by Liberals but condemned by Conservatives. (B) is incorrect because Bismarck in 1855 did not possess the influence nor entertain interest in pursuing a Prussia-Piedmont alliance directed against France. (C) is incorrect because Cavour's decision to join Britain and France in the Crimean War against Russia was not connected to these two domestic laws. (D) Cavour enjoyed the support of Victor Emmanuel II and did not initiate these laws for personal political gain. (E) Pope Pius IX's *Syllabus of Errors* was published in 1864 — many years after these enactments and after Cavour's death.

13. **(D)** The Reform Bills of 1832, 1867, and 1884-85 in Great Britain were significant milestones in the development of democracy in Great Britain and resulted in (D) extending the franchise and redistributing the seats in Parliament. In addition to extending the vote to most men over the age of 21. These measures redistributed the seats in Parliament; this action eliminated many "rotten boroughs" and provided the industrialized cities of the Midlands with Parliamentary representation. Efforts to eliminate child labor abuses were embodied in a series of enactments including the Factory Act of 1833. The influence of the House of Lords was not curtailed until the passage of the Parliament Bill of 1911. The myriad of political, economic, and social ills which confronted the Irish were not resolved in the 19th century. In 1918 all men over 21 and women over 30 were given the right to vote; women over 21 were enfranchised in 1928.

14. **(C)** From the Austrian perspective, the Dual Alliance was directed at Russian — not Italian — encroachment in the Balkans. The Dual Alliance (1879) was a defensive pact between Austria and Germany which was renewed through the First World War, and addressed German concerns over the diplomatic isolation of France and growing anti-German sentiment.

15. **(C)** The Thermidorean Reaction of July 1794 (C) terminated the Reign of Terror and led to the execution of Robespierre. The Reign of Terror was initiated by the June Days of 1793 when the radical Jacobins overthrew the Girondins; the National Assembly was dissolved in 1791 when the Legislative Assembly was formed; Napoleon did not come to power until the *coup d'état* of Brumaire in 1799; Louis XVI and Marie Antoinette were executed by vote of the Convention prior to the seizure of that institution by the radical Jacobins.

16. **(D)** Leopold von Ranke, the 19th century German historian, was not a contributor to the Enlightenment. Englishman Edward Gibbon (*The Decline and Fall of the Roman Empire*) and Scots David Hume (*History of England* and many works in philosophy) and Adam Smith (*Wealth of Nations*) were contributors. Benjamin Franklin, a major force in the American revolution, was a multi-faceted genius of the Enlightenment.

17. **(D)** The Congress of Vienna concluded the wars of the Napoleonic era. The Peace of Utrecht (1713) concluded the War of the Spanish Succession; the Congress of Berlin (1878) terminated the Russo-Turkish War of 1877–78; The Peace of Westphalia closed the Thirty Years' War; and the Peace of Paris (1856) ended the Crimean War.

18. **(D)** The Decembrist Revolution of 1825 occurred in Russia. Prussia, France, Austria, and Spain did not experience any revolutions during 1825; when most of Europe underwent revolution in 1848, Russia and Great Britain did not experience any such activity.

19. **(D)** Charles Fourier, Robert Dawn, and Claude Saint-Simon can best be described as pre-Marxist socialists; some authorities identify them as Utopian Socialists. Anarchism was introduced by Pierre Proudhon in *What is Property?*; Marx and Engels developed Scientific Socialism, or Marxism; and the term *revisionists* is applied to Marxists who differ with one or more of the basic Marxian notions. All of these individuals and groups were opposed to capitalism.

20. **(B)** Louis Philippe was installed as King of France as a result of the liberal July Revolution of 1830. While Louis Philippe and his advisors were "liberal" at the beginning of the reign, they were not democrats (A) and became increasingly conservative. The July Revolution established a constitutional monarchy, not a republic (D). Louis Napoleon was elected President of France in 1848 (C). The withdrawal of Prussian troops (E) was not related to the July Revolution.

21. **(C)** The map indicates the revolutions which occupied Europe during 1848. The revolutions of 1820 (A), 1825 (E), and 1830 (D) were not as significant nor as widespread as the revolutions of 1848. In 1919 revolutions (usually attempts by Marxists) occurred in Berlin and several other cities in central and eastern Europe.

22. **(A)** The Frankfurt Assembly was a Pan-German assembly interested in the formulation of an integrated union of German states; the representatives were interested in the *Kleindeutsch* (Small Germany) not the (E) *Grossdeutsch* (Big Germany). Bismarck (B) was not in power during the history of the Frankfurt Assembly (1849–50); the primary interest of the delegates (C) was political not economic unification. The Austrians (D) had little influence in the Frankfurt Assembly.

23. **(B)** The failure of the Revolutions of 1848 cannot be attributed to the intelligence and cunning of the old leadership in manipulating the revolutionary forces. Indeed, the old guard proved to be rather inept and did not indicate any inspired leadership when the revolutions broke; there was a sense of inevitably concerning the revolutions which led to despair and initial compliance with the revolutionary demands. It was only after the revolutionary leaders made a series of errors (A) (C) (D) and (E) that the old regime found itself able to restore itself to power.

24. **(E)** The industrial economy of the 19th century was not based upon an equitable distribution of profits among all those who were involved in production. Marxists and other critics of capitalism condemned the creed of capitalists and the abhorrent conditions of the industrial proletariat. Raw materials, a constant labor supply, capital, and an expanding marketplace were critical elements in the development of the industrial economy.

25. **(D)** Pierre Proudhon (D) advanced a justification for anarchism in *What is Property?* in which he asserted that change could be realized through education and non-violence. William Godwin's (A) *Enquiry Concerning Social Justice* argued for a utopia based upon the perfectibility of all individuals. Michael Bakunin (B) was an anarchist who attacked Marx and his philosophy. Georges Sorel (C) founded an anarchist variation known as Syndicalism. Charles Fourier (E) was a Utopian Socialist.

26. **(C)** The Revisionist Marxist movement encompassed the Fabian Society (Sidney and Beatrice Webb, George Bernard Shaw, Keir Hardie, et al.), the Social Democratic Party (Eduard Berstein), and the French socialist movement led by Jean Jaures. Revisionist Marxism gained a significant following (A) during the late 19th century; it opposed the Marxist imperative of revolution; Lenin was an orthodox Marxist and opposed (D) the revisionists; most Asian Marxists did not identify with the revisionist movement.

27. **(A)** The New Economic Plan (NEP) was Lenin's plan (1921) to revitalize the Russian economy after the Russian Civil War. It was not (B) a scheme by Trotsky to control the Communist Party, nor (D) Nicholas II's last attempt to recover political support through economic concessions. Obviously, it was not (C) Gorbachev's 1989 plan for the restructuring of the Russian economy although there are valid points of comparison between the 1921 and 1989 schemes.

Stalin's first economic plan (E) was known as the first Five-Year Plan; it resulted in a long-term commitment to collectivization and the expansion of Russian heavy industry.

28. **(B)** The Congress of Berlin (1878) did not result in the realization of Russian war aims in its conflict with the Ottoman Empire. The Russians wanted to establish a large Bulgarian state, gain access to the Mediterranean Sea, and extend their control in the Black Sea and eastern Balkan areas. A small, autonomous principality of Bulgaria (D) was established; Rumania, Serbia, and Montenegro were recognized as independent states (A); Cyprus (C) was transferred to Great Britain; and Austria acquired Bosnia and Herzegovina (E).

29. **(B)** In *Emile* Rousseau (B) called for a "natural" education free of the artificial encumbrances imposed by institutions such as the church. His view on the social contract (A) was advanced separately; Rousseau did not (C) denounce Voltaire for his pedantic and unproductive lifestyle; nor did Rousseau in *Emile* identify with (D) Montesquieu's sympathy for the English Constitutional monarchy. Since the concept of God was essential in Rousseau's thought, he did not advance his case for atheism (E).

30. **(A)** Czar Alexander II of Russia (1855–1881) (A) established the *zemstvos* which were assemblies that allowed the Russian rural nobility to maintain control over local politics. Alexander II's Emancipation of the Serfs (1861) did not (B) improve the political, social, and economic well-being of the Russian serfs. However, Alexander II did (C) make substantive improvements in the Russian judiciary; he did not (D) reform the Russian military. Alexander II was motivated (E) by fear of the masses, not out of any genuine desire to improve the condition of the Russian people.

31. **(C)** The Fashoda Crisis (1898–99) between Great Britain and France demonstrated that relatively colonial disputes could bring the great powers to the threshold of a general war. Fashoda was in East Africa not (A) West Africa; the Berlin Convention was held during 1884–85, more than a decade prior to the crisis; no major military engagement (D) occurred during the Fashoda crisis. Delcasse (E) was the French leader during the Fashoda affair.

32. **(B)** The failure of Wilhelm II's government to continue the Reinsurance Treaty with Russia eventually led to the isolation of Germany. Russia was not interested in any (A) isolationist or non-aligned position; the German action contributed to the formation of the (C) Franco-Russian Entente or Dual Entente of 1894 — Austria was allied with Germany. Russia was opposed to (E) an independent Poland because such a development would result in a loss of territory; while the Russian navy expanded slightly during this period, the Russian economy was not able to (D) support a massive naval building program.

33. **(E)** The Russian Revolution of 1905 led Nicholas II to issue the October Manifesto which called for an advisory assembly (the Duma) to be formed. It did not (A) result in the abdication of the Czar (he would resign in March, 1917), nor was it (B) suppressed by Nicholas II. The October Manifesto was not (C) democratic in nature; the Revolution of 1905 occurred (E) after Russian forces were being defeated in the Russo-Japanese war. The death in the war was a factor which stimulated the revolution.

34. **(C)** The Anglo-Russian Entente of 1907 was a settlement of colonial disputes involving Persia, Afghanistan, and Tibet; Persia was divided into three zones, Afghanistan was recognized as a British sphere of influence, and Tibet was recognized as part of China. No defensive (A) alliance between Britain, France, and Russia was signed prior to 1914; the Anglo-Russian Entente was not a reciprocal trade agreement (B) nor did it involve naval disarmament (E). (D) The Entente Cordiale refers to the Anglo-French agreement of 1904.

35. **(B)** Oscar Wilde's *Portrait of Dorian Gray* and Thomas Mann's *Death in Venice* embodied a new symbolists' direction in literature which addressed themes which were ignored previously; these themes include fantasies relating to the perpetual "youth" in exchange for the soul, and homosexuality. These works and others of this vintage could not be (A) construed as examples of romantic literature in the literary tradition of romanticism nor can they be categorized as examples of the (C) new sense of realism in literature or examples (D) of any expressionist literary movement. Both of these works were applauded by intellectuals at the time of their publication.

36. **(E)** The Third French Republic did not support an extension of the Catholic Church in French society. Quite to the contrary, the policies of the Third French Republic tended to restrict the influence of the Catholic Church; on occasion, the policies can be described accurately as anti-clerical. The (A) Dreyfus Affair, Panama Scandal, and Boulanger Crisis were serious threats to the continuance of the Third French Republic which had been established (B) in the midst of the French defeat in the Franco-Prussian War (1870–71). During the spring, 1871, the Paris Commune (C) threatened the new republic but the Commune collapsed. In 1875 (D) a constitution was adopted which formalized the establishment of the Third French Republic.

37. **(B)** The Berlin Conference of 1884–85 established the principle that an imperial claim had to be supported by occupation and notification to the European powers. The Berlin Conference, which was directed at curtailing the growth of Britain's Empire, did not (A) specify that Britain would have control over the Niger and Congo rivers, nor did it support (D) the dream of Cecil Rhodes for a Cape-to-Cairo railroad under British control. Further, the conference did not (C) specify that the Congo would be under Portuguese control; it turned the Congo over to Belgium. Italy obtained Libya during the first decade of the 20th century.

38. **(B)** Bismarck's *Kulturkampf* were anti-Catholic laws directed at curtailing the influence of the Center Party. While Bismarck opposed the popularization of Marxist principles (A) through the Social Democratic Party (D), he utilized other devices to restrict that party's growth and influence. The *Kulturkampf* had nothing to do with the centerpiece of Bismarck's foreign policy — (C) maintaining the diplomatic isolation of France. While the Papacy condemned the *Kulturkampf*, it was not led by Pope Pius X who became the Pontiff during the early 20th century.

39. **(D)** The Parliament Act of 1911 did not permit the House of Lords to effectively veto non-revenue bills. In addition to a brief delay in the event of a veto by the House of Lords, the House of Commons could redraft the measure and transform it into a revenue bill immediately. The Act did (A) reduce the life span of a Parliament from seven to five years; obviously, the House of Lords (C) has no veto power over revenue bills.

40. **(C)** The Independent Labour Party was established in 1893 by Keir Hardie, a Scottish socialist member of Parliament. Sidney and Beatrice Webb (A) and George Bernard Shaw (B) were socialists and founders of the Fabian Society. H. G. Wells (D) and H. J. Hyndman (E) were other left-wing political spokesmen during the late 19th century.

41. **(A)** The Haldane Mission was a British effort (1912) to curtail the naval arms race with Germany. It had no relation to a (B) colonial dispute with France, (C) involving the United States in the war against Germany, (D) reestablishing British interests in the Eastern Mediterranean, or (E) coordinating British policies with the Low Countries.

42. **(E)** John Kay's "flying shuttle" was made during the 18th century. Ericsson's screw propeller (A), Faraday's discovery of electromagnetic induction (B), Daguerre's invention of photography (C), and Goodyear's rubber vulcanization process (D) all appeared after 1830.

43. **(B)** The expansion of the "division of labor" and of "mass production" through the development of standard parts and manufacturing processes were stimulated by (B) the factory system. While the (A) institution of bank credit and (B) competition were important elements in the development of capitalism, they did not stimulate the "division of labor" or "mass production." (D) Economic imperialism will be a byproduct of the system; (E) local political rivalry — although different than in the past — was not directly related to this development.

44. **(C)** Thomas Maltus, David Ricardo, Nassau Senior, and James Mill have been identified as classical economists. None of these individuals could be described as (E) utopian socialists, (A) positivists, or (B) romantic idealists; James Mill was associated with the (D) utilitarians.

45. **(A)** The dominant personality at the Congress of Vienna was Metternich. Alexander I (C), Talleyrand (D), and Wellington (E) attended the Congress but none of them could be considered as dominant. (B) Bismarck was an essential statesman a half century after the close of the Congress of Vienna.

46. **(B)** In 1829 the Ottoman Turks were forced to accept the Treaty of Adrianople which (B) recognized the independence of Greece. Bulgarian independence (A) would not be recognized until the Congress of Berlin in 1878. Serbian independence (E) was not recognized fully until the 1880s. The (C) Christian right of access to the Holy Places in Palestine was a factor in the origins of the Crimean War (1854), and Russian access to the Mediterranean was a constant item on the agenda of East Mediterranean affairs until it was realized in 1967.

47. **(C)** In 1919 the Weimar Republic was challenged by the Communists or Spartacists led by (C) Karl Liebknecht and Rosa Luxemburg. (A) Ebert, (B) Scheidemann, (D) Michaelis, and (E) Erzberger were all involved — some critically — with the emergence and development of the Weimar Republic.

48. **(E)** The League of Nations succeeded in resolving the Albanian boundary dispute between Greece, Italy, and Yugoslavia in 1921, the (B) Greek-Bulgarian dispute of 1926, the (C) Aaland Islands dispute between Sweden and Finland in 1931, and the (D) Mosul Boundary dispute between Great Britain and Turkey in 1926. However, the League of Nations had no success in resolving the Danzig Crisis (E) between Germany and Poland (supported by Britain and France) in 1939.

49. **(D)** The Treaty of Brest-Litovsk (March, 1918) was (D) a humiliating agreement which the Russians signed with Germany. The Treaty of Neuilly (C) concluded hostilities between the allies and Bulgaria; the Treaty of Trianon (B) ended the war between the allies and Hungary; the Treaty of Sèvres (E) ended the war between the allies and the Ottoman Empire. There was no formal separate treaty concluding hostilities between Great Britain and Turkey.

50. **(B)** The Locarno Treaty (1925) was a major diplomatic achievement by Gustav Stressmann, the German Foreign Minister. Leon Trotsky (A) was being ousted from power by Stalin and forced to flee the Soviet Union; (C) Charles Evan Hughes was the American Secretary of State at this time — in 1924, Hughes was instrumental in the development of the Dawes Plan; (D) Benito Mussolini was in power and his government was involved in the Locarno negotiations; and (E) Ramsay MacDonald was the leader of the Labour Party in Great Britain.

51. **(C)** As a result of the Easter Rebellion, Eamon DeValera and Arthur Griffith experienced growing support for their Sinn Fein Movement. They were not directly involved with (A) the Irish Republican Army, or the old (B) Irish

Home Rule movement; they opposed (D) the Public Safety Act and (E) maintaining the British army in Ireland.

52. **(A)** The Spanish Constitution of 1931 was an attempt to establish a democratic and secular republic. King Alfonso XIII, (B) fled the country; Franco (C) would not seize power until his victory in the Spanish Civil War in 1939; the 1931 Constitution undermined (D) the positions of the Church and the landowners in Spanish society. Mussolini's Italy (E) would not be involved until the outbreak of the Spanish Civil War in 1936.

53. **(C)** The Washington (1921–22) and London (1930) Naval Conferences attempted to restrict specific categories of naval weaponry. The Kellog-Briand Pact (1927) declared (A) war to be illegal; the Japanese aggression in China (B) began in 1931 after the London Naval Conference; the Chinese Civil War (D) did not begin until 1927 — long after the close of the Washington Conference; and, while Southeast Asia (E) was a major item on the agenda of these conferences, the limitations on naval weaponry cannot be construed as a regional issue.

54. **(C)** The chart indicates that the post-war economics in Central and Eastern Europe were fragile and subject to rapid deterioration during an economic collapse.

55. **(D)** The aftermath of the Suez Crisis of 1956 resulted in the fall of Anthony Eden as British Prime Minister. Eden had succeeded Churchill in 1955 but his tenure as Prime Minister was cut short by his support of an interventionist action in Egypt; the United States condemned the joint British-French-Israeli action. Charles deGaulle (A) became President of the Fourth French Republic in 1958; Gamel Abdel Nasser remained as President of Egypt until his death in 1970; John Foster Dulles held the position as the American Secretary of State until his death in 1959; Pierre Laval was a leader of the Third French Republic and the Vichy Regime — he was executed as a collaborator after the Second World War.

56. **(B)** The "Fascintern" was a pact between Germany, Italy, and Japan designed to coordinate the development of fascism throughout the world and the defeat of communism. While one may argue that the Fascintern was intent upon (A) subverting the interests of Britain and France, these countries were not specified. It was obviously not (D) an agreement between Germany and Russia (not to be confused with the Russian-German Nonaggression Pact of 1939), nor did the pact specify the racial superiority of Germans (E) — neither the Italians nor the Japanese were inclined to accept such a provision. (C) is incorrect because Japan was omitted.

57. **(D)** The Treaty of Rome (1957) established the European Economic Community. The European Free Trade Association (A), the Colombo Plan (B), the Council of Europe (C), and the European Coal and Steel Community (E)

were all significant events in the recovery of Europe after the Second World War. The European Economic Community will expand to include most of the western European nations.

58. **(B)** The map indicates the Schlieffen Plan, which was developed in 1905 and deployed in August 1914 upon the outbreak of the First World War. Plan XVII (A) was the French plan which was based on the assumption that the Germans would attack in eastern France; the French hoped to seize Alsace and Lorraine. The Manstein Plan (C) was the German military strategy devised by General Erich von Manstein that led to the collapse of France during May-June 1940. The map surely does not indicate the movement of German troops during the Franco-Prussian war in 1870–71, nor Ludendorff's Spring Offensive in 1918.

59. **(B)** The "Rendezvous" (1939) by British cartoonist David Lou referred to the contradiction inherent in the Russo-German Nonaggression Pact. It does not refer to (D) Czechoslovakia, (E) Finland, or (C) any delight shared by Stalin and Hitler, both of whom suspected each other's motives.

60. **(D)** The Vienna Summit (1961) between Kennedy and Khrushchev was focused on nuclear test ban negotiations and the war in Laos; it was followed in the next year by the Cuban missile crisis. Many analysts make a direct connection between the Vienna Summit and the Cuban missile crisis because Khrushchev departed from the meeting convinced that Kennedy was weak and that his presidency provided opportunities for Soviet expansion. (A), (B), and (C) are incorrect because the U-2 plane crisis broke up the Paris Summit between Eisenhower and Khrushchev. (E) NATO was established in 1949.

61. **(E)** The Glorious Revolution of 1688–89 did not result in an agreement that in the event of no heirs, the Hanover house would succeed the Stuarts. Such an arrangement was specified in the Act of Succession of 1701, a year before William III's death and the succession of Queen Anne. She survived all her children. Upon her death in 1714, George I became the first Hanoverian King of England.

62. **(C)** In *Hard Times*, Charles Dickens depicted an English community that (C) was characterized by difficult personal, class, and environmental adjustments caused by the industrial order. Certainly, Dickens' portrait of English industrial life during the 1850s did not indicate that (A) the people were enjoying the fruits of industrial-driven progress, that the people of Coketown were (B) preoccupied with religious constraints, that this society (D) repudiated the industrial order, nor a society that (E) emphasized British nationalism.

63. **(B)** The text of Denis Diderot's *Encyclopedia* was centered primarily on (B) technology. While history (C) and philosophy (D) were important elements, technological innovations and science were emphasized in this profusely illustrated work. Theology (A) and poetry (E) were not given much attention.

64. **(C)** Arnold Toynbee's *A Study of History* and Oswald Spengler's *Decline of the West* advanced a form of history which is described as (C) cyclical. Both Toynbee and Spengler approached history from the perspective of human institutions being organisms — born, develop, mature, grow old, and die.

65. **(D)** In the poem, the Hungarian-Swiss Tzara provides a sample of a 20th century literary movement known as Dadaism. This post-World War I literary episode was a reaction against the order which led to the war and its horrors; Dadaism, which was short-lived, contributed to the emergence of surrealism. Symbolism (A) was the appellation given to the wider literary movement and which was addressed in Edmund Wilson's *Axel's Castle*. Expressionism (B) and (E) idealism are terms which relate to many facets of art — both literary and other. Deconstructionism (C) is a term which applies to post-1950 literary values and criticism.

66. **(D)** All of the listed European intellectuals identified with existentialism except Jacques Maritain. Maritain, a Christian humanist, advanced a persuasive Neo-Thomism in a broad range of studies including *Man and the State.* Sartre (A), Heidegger (B), Jaspers (C), and Camus (E) were leading proponents of varying forms of existentialism.

67. **(C)** The driving force behind Hegel's dialectic was universal reason — the Hegelian God. Marx will identify materialism (D) as the key historical force. Hegel's philosophy has been used, and manipulated, by those who identify with (A) nationalism, (B) racial superiority, and, to a much lesser extent, (E) religious values.

68. **(A)** The response of the Catholic Church to the Reformation was delayed because the Papacy feared the remnants of the Conciliar Movement with the church itself. The Conciliar Movement, which was clearly evident at the Council of Constance (1414) and later at the Councils of Basel and Florence, was a tradition in the Roman Catholic Church which asserted that authority within the church resided in the assembly of bishops; it was a challenge to the concept of Petrine Supremacy and the authority of the Papacy. Rome (B) had little interest in coordinating its policy with secular leaders, although the early support of Charles V and Henry VIII was well received. By the 1530s most intelligent Church leaders did not (C) think that Protestantism would self-destruct or that (D) the situation was not a serious crisis. The monetary situation of the Church (E) was not relevant to taking a position against Protestantism.

69. **(D)** Since 1950 the Soviet Union has suppressed movements toward more liberal governments in East Germany (A), Poland (B), Czechoslovakia (C) and Hungary (E) but not Yugoslavia (D). Marshall Tito's Yugoslavia developed a position of independence from the Soviet Union during the 1950s; its approach to Communism was more innovative and resulted in a more fluid economic

system. The Soviet Union's suppression of liberalism in East Germany and Poland (1953), Hungary (1956), and Czechoslovakia (1968) was violent and followed by the installation of pro-Soviet regimes.

70. **(E)** The first individual who served as Prime Minister of Great Britain was Robert Walpole who initiated the Cabinet system of government between 1721 and 1740; an absence of monarchial leadership on the part of George I and George II resulted in the need for a new entity to provide executive leadership. William Pitt (A) and Lord North (D) led governments during the 18th century; Palmerston (C) and Gladstone (B) were prominent Prime Ministers during the second half of the 19th century.

71. **(A)** Friedrich Nietzsche advanced his philosophy in such works as (A) *Thus Spake Zarathustra* and *The Will to Power*. (B) *The Golden Bough* was written by Sir James Frazer, an English anthropologist, and *The Wild Duck* was a play by Henrik Ibsen. (C) *The Return of the Native* and *Jude the Obscure* were by Thomas Hardy. (D) *Civilization and Its Discontents* was by Sigmund Freud and *The Riddle of the Universe* was by the biologist, Heinrich Haeckel. (E) *The Descent of Man* was by Charles Darwin and *The Weavers* was by Gerhard Hauptmann.

72. **(A)** In the painting "The Eternal City," the American painter Peter Blume portrays a (A) fascist Italy which is dominated by the personality of Mussolini. Obviously, the painting does not depict (B) how fascism in Italy improved the general condition of the people, (C) Mussolini as a benevolent dictator, (D) a sympathetic rendering of the impact of fascism on Italian life and institutions, nor does it (E) recount the March on Rome in 1922.

73. **(C)** "Men are born, and always continue free and equal in respect of their rights. Civil distinctions, therefore, can be found only on public utility." In 1789 these statements were part of (C) the Declaration of the Rights of Man and the Citizen which was passed by the National Assembly in France. The English Bill of Rights (1689) was a consequence of the Glorious Revolution which resulted in William and Mary coming to power. The Constitution of the Year III (1795) established the Directory in France; it was a government which was advised by experts or intellectuals. In *What Is the Third Estate*? (1788) Abbé Siéyès maintained that the Third Estate of the Estates-General was in fact a "National Assembly" and representative of the national sovereign power.

74. **(C)** During the "June Days" in Paris (1848) the (C) army suppressed the radical revolutionary element. The workers who had identified with or had been supported by the National Workshop Program (Louis Blanc) were opposed to the conservative policies of the new elect Assembly; they revolted and were suppressed by military units which were loyal to the government. Obviously, this situation indicates that (A) and (B) were incorrect responses. (D) Louis Napoleon

did not come to power until the subsequent elections for the presidency of the Second French Republic. (E) Lamartine was a poet and republican leader who enjoyed support during the Winter and Spring of 1848; thereafter, Lamartine's influence declined.

75. **(E)** The repeal of the Corn Laws (1846) in England was led by (E) Robert Peel who was the Prime Minister during the 1840s. While William Gladstone (A), Benjamin Disraeli (C), and Lord Palmerston (D) were prominent political leaders, they did not determine the decision on the Corn Laws' repeal. The repeal of these measures alleviated the burden on the general population by removing restrictions which raised the price of grain. Lord Melbourne (B) was Prime Minister during the 1830s.

76. **(C)** In an effort to conduct a successful economic war against Britain, Napoleon created the (C) Continental System. Its primary goal was the economic isolation of Britain through the closing of European markets for British goods. Earlier, Napoleon established (A) the Bank of France to consolidate the French national economy; the (D) Napoleonic Code was a codification and reform of French law. The (B) Confederation of the Rhine was supported by Napoleon and was intended to decentralize German states. The (E) Kingdom of the Two Sicilies appeared earlier.

77. **(A)** The 1909 budget proposed by Lloyd George advocated (A) progressive income and inheritance taxes. This liberal budget was designed to tax those who could afford it — the wealthy class, and to raise revenues for defense and domestic social programs. (B) Property taxes did not cease nor were there drastic reductions in funding for (C) domestic programs or (D) weapons. Obviously, the 1909 budget did not specify a (E) redistribution of excessive tax revenues.

78. **(C)** In this painting entitled "Guernica" (1937), Pablo Picasso portrayed (C) the impact of the aerial bombardment of a Spanish town by the German Condor Legion during the Spanish Civil War. Both German and Italian military "volunteers" assisted Franco's fascist forces in the struggle against the republicans.

79. **(C)** Iraq invaded Kuwait, controlling the entire country. Kuwait is a major supplier of oil to the United States and Western Europe. (D) is incorrect because Iraq did not attempt to boycott sales of oil to the U.S. or any other country, though the invasion of Kuwait destabilized a region that is among the chief suppliers of oil to the world. Iraq did threaten Israel (A) and launched Scud missiles into Israel, but this happened after the war had begun. Though Iraq did at the time and later continued to persecute the Kurdish minority (B), this was not the reason for the invasion of the multinational coalition. Iraq released Americans (E) in its territory before the war began.

80. **(A)** John Major replaced "the Iron Lady" as Great Britain's Prime Minister. George Mitchell (B) is a former United States Senator whom President Clinton dispatched on a mission to Northern Ireland to find avenues for reconciliation between Roman Catholics and Protestants. Clement Atlee (C) served as British Prime Minister from 1945-1951, granting independence to India, Pakistan, Burma, and Ceylon, and giving up British control over Egypt and Palestine. Edward Heath (D) was British Prime Minister from 1970-1974. Choice (E), Robert Owen (1771-1858), was a Welsh social reformer.

Sample Answer to Document-Based Question

Eighteenth century English urban life has been viewed as violent and on occasion, almost out of control. William Hogarth was perhaps the most significant social critic of the century; rather than direct his artistic interest and talent to the common portrait paintings of the period or replicating the neo-classicism which was popular on the continent at that time, Hogarth addressed serious social issues in a format which appealed to a larger audience.

In "Chairing the Members" Hogarth criticized the method of 'electing' members of Parliament during the mid-eighteenth century. The procedure led to corruption and abuse and resulted in reforms during the next century. Hogarth was concerned — indeed, he was outraged — by the detachment of the British establishment from the problems which plagued the general populace. In "Inhabitants of the Moon" Hogarth accused the establishment — the monarchy, the church, and the courts — of corruption and exploitation. In "Gin Lane" and "Beer Street" Hogarth condemned the massive consumption of cheap gin and urged people to drink beer; the gin business was riddled with corruption and resulted in excessive profits for the gin brokers and those who financed its production. In "John Wilkes, Esquire" Hogarth found an advocate for political reform; Wilkes was elected repeatedly to the House of Commons but ultimately was tried for his radical views.

Hogarth's social criticisms did not resolve the ills of 18th century but they enhanced awareness of the problems. Later, with reformers such as Bentham, Mill, and Wilberforce, reforms would be implemented which eliminated many of these abuses.

Sample Answers to Essay Questions

1. For more than 50 years (1660–1715) the policies of Louis XIV dominated European history. Through the War of Devolution, the Dutch War, the War of the League of Augsburg, and the War of the Spanish Succession, Louis XIV attempted to establish personal control over Western and Central Europe. To Louis XIV war was a means to demonstrate his greatness and to acquire a significant place in history. While Napoleon entertained similar personal notions and a vision of the greatness of France, the Napoleonic wars differed from those of Louis XIV because there was an ideological consideration — the revolution — which motivated the French to support his policies. Further, the Napoleonic wars involved a proportionately higher number of "citizens" than did the military enterprises of Louis XIV.

During the last four decades of the 17th century Louis XIV's France enjoyed a position of hegemony over European affairs. The War of Devolution, which was related to property claims in small towns in the Spanish Netherlands, resulted in the establishment of an alliance, anchored with Great Britain and the

Netherlands, against France. The British and the Dutch feared that unless Louis XIV was contained that he would establish such an overwhelming base of power that he would alter the balance of power and eliminate the sovereignty of many nations by destroying the European equilibrium. In the Dutch War, the War of the League of Augsburg, and the War of the Spanish Succession, the European powers responded to French aggression through the establishment of coalitions. The success of the coalitions maintained the balance of power and, in the end, not only thwarted Louis XIV's aspirations but also demonstrated that France was basically isolated. States as diverse as Britain, Austria, the Netherlands and Prussia joined to preserve their independence. At the Peace of Utrecht in 1713–14 France was still recognized as the greatest European power; however, France did not achieve its goals and was in fact defeated in the War of the Spanish Succession and had to make concessions to the coalition victors.

The Napoleonic Wars (1799–1815) constituted a more serious threat to the European political structure than did the wars of Louis XIV. Napoleon carried with him the liberal ideology and reforms of the French Revolution; the French revolutionary tradition was viewed as more dangerous than the might of the French armies. Upon achieving victory, Napoleon not only would establish French control over the defeated state or region; but he would also introduce political and economic reforms which threatened the basis of the old order's power. Legal reforms in Spain, economic reforms in the German states, and other similar developments rendered the Napoleonic Wars much more complex than earlier struggles. The other nations of Europe responded to French power and the revolution through resurrecting the coalition concept which had prevailed against Louis XIV. From the outbreak of resistance in Spain in 1808 to the defeat in Russia (1812–13) and the devastation of French defeat at Waterloo in June, 1815, the coalition against Napoleon succeeded in suppressing this second French attempt to alter the European political system.

In the wars of Louis XIV many of the coalition members were motivated by dynastic considerations; Britain and the Netherlands were clearly motivated by national values. During the Napoleonic period, the coalition was generally motivated by nationalism, although dynastic priorities were not absent. In Central and Southern Europe nationalism prevailed over the revolutionary tradition; however, in spite of efforts to suppress this tradition, it would reappear in the Revolutions of 1820, 1830, and 1848.

2. While the development and support of fascism in Germany and Italy had many parallel or similar experiences, the causes for the rise of fascism in each of these nations was unique.

When Adolph Hitler became the German Chancellor in January, 1933, the fascist movement achieved a victory which only a few years before was considered well beyond its reach. Beginning in 1919 the Nazi Party adopted the fascist corporate approach to government, which viewed the state as a entity in its own right; the state was more important than the individuals who resided in it. German fascism was romantic, militaristic, highly nationalistic, and espoused a racist totalitarianism which was fundamentally anti-democratic. During the 1920s

Hitler and his Nazi Party were considered radical dissidents who never would come to power; the Weimar Republic continued to enjoy the support of the German people until the impact of the Depression which began to devastate the German economy in 1930. The fascist success in Germany can be attributed to (1) the continuing economic and social crisis caused by the Depression, (2) the inability of the Weimar Republic to advance a credible policy to alleviate the widespread distress, (3) the organization of the Nazi Party, (4) the continuing humiliation from defeat in the war, and (5) the charisma of Adolph Hitler. Through Hitler's direction the Nazis gained a significant base of strength in the German *Reichstag* from which he was able to demand a place in the new Hindenberg government in 1933. Once in power Hitler moved quickly to consolidate his position; he passed the Enabling Act which gave him dictatorial powers and purged Germany of his political enemies.

The rise of fascism in Italy via Benito Mussolini can be attributed to a number a number of factors, including (1) the failure to obtain the expected gains for Italy's involvement and sacrifices during the First World War, (2) the post-war economic collapse, (3) "1919ism" — the fear of Bolshevism, (4) the ineptitude of the centrist Italian parties in handling the political and economic crisis which gripped Italy after the war, and (5) the opportunistic Mussolini. During the war Italians had entertained thoughts that they would acquire colonies and great power status as a result of their involvement with the allies; at the Versailles Conference and in the subsequent treaty it was evident that these goals were not realized. At the same time Britain and the United States ceased making loans after the armistice; this action resulted in a financial crisis in Italy which was aggravated by the rapid demobilization of the Italian army, high unemployment, and inflation. "1919ism" was the Italian Red Scare, the fear that the economic crisis would provide the Bolsheviks with an opportunity to initiate a revolution; this anxiety resulted in polarizing Italian society with the wealthy classes identifying with order and the preservation of their own interests. During the chaotic period from 1918 to 1922, the Italian political system proved unable to resolve the crisis; Italian political parties were not able to overcome their own party factionalism and sustain a durable coalition government. Into this void of leadership stepped Mussolini, a flamboyant and egocentric demagogue who promised to reestablish order and a sense of national pride to Italy. Mussolini's seizure of power — the March on Rome (1922) — was not opposed.

3. When James I assumed the throne upon the death of Elizabeth I in 1603, the monarchy in Britain was a strong executive position which was restricted by the English constitutional concept of the "King in Parliament." By the time that Queen Anne — the last Stuart — died in 1714, the alignment of English domestic political power had shifted. While there were many factors which led to this alteration, the Stuart monarchs contributed to this erosion of monarchical power through inept leadership and policies which did not consider the English historical tradition nor the forces which were current during the 17th century.

James I (1603–25) alienated Parliament by asserting his support for royal absoluticism and the "Divine Right of Kings." During his reign, James convened few Parliaments and those which were held were confrontational — the Addled Parliament of 1614 is a good example. Further, James I did not address the continuing religious crisis which centered on Puritanism; the Hampton Court Conference reinforced the Anglican status quo and led to a loss of support for James among the Puritans. James I's personal life did not enhance his public reputation; his purported bisexuality, his awkward physical appearance, and his Scots accent rendered him "unkingly" to many. Charles I (1625–49) succeeded his father and found himself involved with unsuccessful and costly foreign enterprises in Spain and France; in 1628, the King's favorite, the Duke of Buckingham, was assassinated and Charles I was forced to convene a Parliament for funds to pay his debts caused by the foreign wars. Parliament forced Charles to sign the Petition of Rights which was an statement of grievances; Charles pledged not to improperly collect the ships' tax, not to abuse the use of martial law as it related to the public billeting of troops, and to respect the writ of habeas corpus. After Parliament provided the funds, Charles I decided to rule without a Parliament — from 1629 to 1640 no Parliament sat. During this period Charles I and his aid, Archbishop William Laud, attempted to suppress Puritanism throughout the country. In 1637 Charles I and Laud extended this policy in Scotland; the Scottish reaction led to war and reluctantly, in the spring of 1640, Charles I summoned what became known as the Short Parliament — it lasted for only three weeks. The suppressed Parliamentary and Puritan forces demanded that Charles I meet their demands before they would grant funds to raise an army; Charles I dissolved the Short Parliament. With the Scottish problem becoming more acute, Charles summoned the "Long" Parliament in the fall of 1640 — it sat for years. Between 1640 and 1660 English politics were in a state of flux; the English Civil War, the execution of Charles I, the establishment of the Commonwealth and the Protectorate, and the Restoration of the Stuarts in the person of Charles II transpired during those decades. The Parliament was strengthened and the monarchy weakened as a result of these development. The monarchy which was restored in 1660 was a modified and restricted executive force.

In 1688 and 1689 another constitutional crisis gripped the nation. James II, a Catholic, had a male heir and baptized the child a Catholic. Faced with the likelihood of having a series of Catholic monarchs over a Protestant nation, Tory and Whig politicians in Parliament arranged for William and Mary to replace James II who later fled the nation. This Glorious Revolution was formalized with the Bill of Rights in April 1689 which stipulated that the Parliament, through its control of finances, was the dominant force in English politics. The monarch was still very significant and exercised considerable power; however, the power enjoyed by the great Tudor monarchs, Henry VIII and Elizabeth I, would not be seen again.

4. Any attempt to reflect upon the ideological legacy of the French Revolution of 1789 must be preceded by a brief review of the intellectual forces which impacted on the revolution and the ideology which was manifested during the revolution. The revolution which broke in France in 1789 and continued for the next decade was ideologically motivated by the political and philosophic con-

cepts which were advanced during the Enlightenment — the Age of Reason. While many varying sentiments emerged during the 18th century, there was a common ideological basis: 18th century intellectuals were interested in developing a rationally based human society which was free from the assumptions of the past and which would advanced human progress. One of the best sources on this topic is Keith M. Baker's *Inventing the French Revolution*.

During the revolution itself, there was a great debate over how to realize these goals. This debate, which continued long after the revolutions were suppressed, was one of the major ideological legacies of the French Revolution — an open and public dialogue on issues of concern. It anticipated an environment which fostered intellectual activity; the anti-intellectualism of the past would be replaced. During the 19th century attempts were made to curtail the freedom of speech through varying forms of censorship; the July Ordinances and the later actions of Francois Guizot in the 1840s were examples of this censorship. Freedom of speech or debate was the underlying component of the radical philosophic tradition which emerged from the French Revolution. Another major factor which endured was the revision of the notion of humanity which developed during the revolutionary period. The thoughts of Rousseau, Montesquieu, and others and the historic experience of the revolution influenced Marx, Proudhon, and John Stuart Mill in the 19th century as well as Sartre, Freud, and others in the 20th century as they attempted to develop an understanding of humanity and the individual. The notion of the role and rights of "the people" were altered; the last vestiges of the medieval order were struggling to survive. Related to the changing concept of "the people," was a broadening of the idea of the "nation." Further no longer would man be viewed primarily in a religious context; humankind was to be examined and measured within a political, economic, or social context.

Finally, any consideration of the ideological legacy must include comments on the "cult of progress." While J. B. Bury and others have considered this issue, the impact of the "concept of progress" as a consequence of the French Revolution must be revised continually. Further, the interrelationship of "progress" with other developments such as racism, democracy, and totalitarianism. The French Revolution of 1789 initiated a global revolutionary tradition which was not limited to France or Europe.

5. While Germany was forced to agree with the infamous War Guilt clause (Article 231) of the Versailles Treaty, the outbreak of the First World War involved many diverse factors which renders any assignment of specific national guilt a rather futile undertaking. The immediate circumstances which led to the outbreak of the war were focused on the diplomatic crisis of the summer of 1914; the Austrians, with German support, reacted to the assassination of Archduke Franz Ferdinand by directing an ultimatum at Serbia, which was supported by Russia. The alliance systems were deployed and the war was underway by early August.

The causes which led to this situation were (l) the polarization of Europe into two armed camps, (2) imperialism, and (3) militarism and the arms race. Since Bismarck's dismissal in 1890 the European diplomatic situation had become more complex; by 1907, it was clear that two separate and opposing groups of nations existed. In 1890 Germany failed to renew the Reinsurance Treaty with Russia; within four years, the Russians entered into the Dual Entente with France which terminated the key element in Bismarck's foreign policy, the diplomatic isolation of France. During the late 1890s Germany rebuffed British overtures for an alliance; this rejection resulted in the British entering into the Anglo-Japanese alliance (1902), the Anglo-French Entente (or Entente Cordiale) (1904), and the Anglo-Russian Entente (1907). While these arrangements did not obligate Britain to any direct military action in the event of war, they did affiliate Britain with the French oriented diplomatic system. This affiliation was evident during the Algerciras Conference in 1906. Germany and Austria-Hungary were isolated.

Imperialistic rivalries contributed to a increasingly hostile environment among the European powers. From the Fashoda Crisis of 1898–99 to the First and Second Moroccan Crises and the continuing Balkan conflicts, the European powers found themselves in conflict with one another — frequently over areas that were unrelated to their national security or interests. This conflicting environment was exacerbated by the growing influence of the military within European governments. A sense of the "inevitably" of war led the great powers to develop war plans such as the German Schlieffen (1905) and the French Plan XVII (1912). These developments implied that a military resolution to a crisis was acceptable; there was dissatifaction with the "indecisive" nature of diplomatic settlements. Further aggravating this militarism was the impact of technology on weaponry. During the two decades immediately prior to the outbreak of the war, improvements and innovations in weapons were revolutionary. The development of new classes of capital ships with enhanced ranges and armament, the revolution in artillery, and innovations in field weapons such as the machine gun and in the quality of repeating rifles resulted in an arms race which directed funds away from domestic needs.

In the summer of 1914 the mediation efforts which had worked on previous occasions failed and Europe stumbled into a war for which it had longed prepared. While Germany must be faulted for William II's "Blank Cheque" to the Austrians, most of the major powers were responsible for contributing to an situation in which a general war was acceptable. The causes for this war and, in many incidents, most wars are to be found in the mentality of the age which permits nations to adopt confrontational policies and procedures.

6. From Disraeli's call for a "New Imperialism" in the early 1870s to 1914, the European powers participated in the most reckless and active era of colonial expansion. Bolstered by economic need, aspects of social Darwinism, and the zealousness of militant Christianity and European nationalism, the European powers participated in the "Scramble for Africa," for a position in China, and for Pacific islands. Considerable resources were expended in the acquisition and maintenance of these colonial empires; the conseqences of imperialism resulted in national and domestic political rivalries and mixed economic results.

From the perspective of the impact of imperialism on the relations between nation-states, one can divide this era into two chronological periods: before and after the Berlin Convention of 1884–85. This meeting established the principle that any claim to a territory had to be supported by occupation and notification to the other European powers of the claim; this was intended to regulate colonial claims and to limit the expansion of the British Empire. Throughout the entire era, imperialism resulted in conflicts between the European powers; the Afghan wars, the Fashoda crisis, the Venezulean dispute, the Boer War, the First and Second Moroccan Crises, and the Libyan crisis illustrate the extent and frequency of these conflicts. Further, imperialism emerged as a domestic political issue in Britain, France, Germany, Italy, and Belgium. In England, Disraeli and his Conservative Party supported imperial expansion and involved the nation in a series of colonial wars including the Ashanti and Zulu wars. Disraeli's Liberal rival was William Gladstone, an espoused anti-imperalist. Gladstone found that it was extremely difficult to maintain his anti-imperialist position during his four tenures as Prime Minister; this was due to international and national political factors. Thus, Gladstone found himself despatching General Charles Gordon to the Sudan and then sending an expeditionary force to rescue Gordon. Within England the Fabian Society was consistently anti-imperialist until the Boer War when the Fabians were factionalized over British involvement in South Africa. In Germany and France liberal and socialist political parties opposed the imperialist policies advanced by the rightist and conservative governments and parties.

European economic life was stimulated by the increased trade which resulted from imperialism and the establishment of colonies. Not only did the European powers acquire new sources of raw materials, but also — and more importantly in most instances — they acquired new markets where they could distribute their finished goods. Domestic industries which provided transport or products associated with transport and new settlements profited from the expansion. At the same time, imperial activities diverted capital away from domestic investments and programs; some contend that the Western European economies possessed excess capital during this period which could not be absorbed by the domestic economies. Another negative economic factor was the continuing costs associated with the administration and defense of colonies; this involved human as well as financial resources. It appears that the immediate economic impact was positive but that the long-term result was negative. It should also be noted that the economic gains during the early decades of this period resulted in deferring consideration of domestic economic problems which affected the working classes.

THE ADVANCED PLACEMENT EXAMINATION IN

European History

TEST 2

THE ADVANCED PLACEMENT EXAMINATION IN

European History

TEST 2

1. Ⓐ Ⓑ Ⓒ Ⓓ Ⓔ
2. Ⓐ Ⓑ Ⓒ Ⓓ Ⓔ
3. Ⓐ Ⓑ Ⓒ Ⓓ Ⓔ
4. Ⓐ Ⓑ Ⓒ Ⓓ Ⓔ
5. Ⓐ Ⓑ Ⓒ Ⓓ Ⓔ
6. Ⓐ Ⓑ Ⓒ Ⓓ Ⓔ
7. Ⓐ Ⓑ Ⓒ Ⓓ Ⓔ
8. Ⓐ Ⓑ Ⓒ Ⓓ Ⓔ
9. Ⓐ Ⓑ Ⓒ Ⓓ Ⓔ
10. Ⓐ Ⓑ Ⓒ Ⓓ Ⓔ
11. Ⓐ Ⓑ Ⓒ Ⓓ Ⓔ
12. Ⓐ Ⓑ Ⓒ Ⓓ Ⓔ
13. Ⓐ Ⓑ Ⓒ Ⓓ Ⓔ
14. Ⓐ Ⓑ Ⓒ Ⓓ Ⓔ
15. Ⓐ Ⓑ Ⓒ Ⓓ Ⓔ
16. Ⓐ Ⓑ Ⓒ Ⓓ Ⓔ
17. Ⓐ Ⓑ Ⓒ Ⓓ Ⓔ
18. Ⓐ Ⓑ Ⓒ Ⓓ Ⓔ
19. Ⓐ Ⓑ Ⓒ Ⓓ Ⓔ
20. Ⓐ Ⓑ Ⓒ Ⓓ Ⓔ
21. Ⓐ Ⓑ Ⓒ Ⓓ Ⓔ
22. Ⓐ Ⓑ Ⓒ Ⓓ Ⓔ
23. Ⓐ Ⓑ Ⓒ Ⓓ Ⓔ
24. Ⓐ Ⓑ Ⓒ Ⓓ Ⓔ
25. Ⓐ Ⓑ Ⓒ Ⓓ Ⓔ
26. Ⓐ Ⓑ Ⓒ Ⓓ Ⓔ
27. Ⓐ Ⓑ Ⓒ Ⓓ Ⓔ
28. Ⓐ Ⓑ Ⓒ Ⓓ Ⓔ
29. Ⓐ Ⓑ Ⓒ Ⓓ Ⓔ
30. Ⓐ Ⓑ Ⓒ Ⓓ Ⓔ
31. Ⓐ Ⓑ Ⓒ Ⓓ Ⓔ
32. Ⓐ Ⓑ Ⓒ Ⓓ Ⓔ
33. Ⓐ Ⓑ Ⓒ Ⓓ Ⓔ
34. Ⓐ Ⓑ Ⓒ Ⓓ Ⓔ
35. Ⓐ Ⓑ Ⓒ Ⓓ Ⓔ
36. Ⓐ Ⓑ Ⓒ Ⓓ Ⓔ
37. Ⓐ Ⓑ Ⓒ Ⓓ Ⓔ
38. Ⓐ Ⓑ Ⓒ Ⓓ Ⓔ
39. Ⓐ Ⓑ Ⓒ Ⓓ Ⓔ
40. Ⓐ Ⓑ Ⓒ Ⓓ Ⓔ
41. Ⓐ Ⓑ Ⓒ Ⓓ Ⓔ
42. Ⓐ Ⓑ Ⓒ Ⓓ Ⓔ
43. Ⓐ Ⓑ Ⓒ Ⓓ Ⓔ
44. Ⓐ Ⓑ Ⓒ Ⓓ Ⓔ
45. Ⓐ Ⓑ Ⓒ Ⓓ Ⓔ
46. Ⓐ Ⓑ Ⓒ Ⓓ Ⓔ
47. Ⓐ Ⓑ Ⓒ Ⓓ Ⓔ
48. Ⓐ Ⓑ Ⓒ Ⓓ Ⓔ
49. Ⓐ Ⓑ Ⓒ Ⓓ Ⓔ
50. Ⓐ Ⓑ Ⓒ Ⓓ Ⓔ
51. Ⓐ Ⓑ Ⓒ Ⓓ Ⓔ
52. Ⓐ Ⓑ Ⓒ Ⓓ Ⓔ
53. Ⓐ Ⓑ Ⓒ Ⓓ Ⓔ
54. Ⓐ Ⓑ Ⓒ Ⓓ Ⓔ
55. Ⓐ Ⓑ Ⓒ Ⓓ Ⓔ
56. Ⓐ Ⓑ Ⓒ Ⓓ Ⓔ
57. Ⓐ Ⓑ Ⓒ Ⓓ Ⓔ
58. Ⓐ Ⓑ Ⓒ Ⓓ Ⓔ
59. Ⓐ Ⓑ Ⓒ Ⓓ Ⓔ
60. Ⓐ Ⓑ Ⓒ Ⓓ Ⓔ
61. Ⓐ Ⓑ Ⓒ Ⓓ Ⓔ
62. Ⓐ Ⓑ Ⓒ Ⓓ Ⓔ
63. Ⓐ Ⓑ Ⓒ Ⓓ Ⓔ
64. Ⓐ Ⓑ Ⓒ Ⓓ Ⓔ
65. Ⓐ Ⓑ Ⓒ Ⓓ Ⓔ
66. Ⓐ Ⓑ Ⓒ Ⓓ Ⓔ
67. Ⓐ Ⓑ Ⓒ Ⓓ Ⓔ
68. Ⓐ Ⓑ Ⓒ Ⓓ Ⓔ
69. Ⓐ Ⓑ Ⓒ Ⓓ Ⓔ
70. Ⓐ Ⓑ Ⓒ Ⓓ Ⓔ
71. Ⓐ Ⓑ Ⓒ Ⓓ Ⓔ
72. Ⓐ Ⓑ Ⓒ Ⓓ Ⓔ
73. Ⓐ Ⓑ Ⓒ Ⓓ Ⓔ
74. Ⓐ Ⓑ Ⓒ Ⓓ Ⓔ
75. Ⓐ Ⓑ Ⓒ Ⓓ Ⓔ
76. Ⓐ Ⓑ Ⓒ Ⓓ Ⓔ
77. Ⓐ Ⓑ Ⓒ Ⓓ Ⓔ
78. Ⓐ Ⓑ Ⓒ Ⓓ Ⓔ
79. Ⓐ Ⓑ Ⓒ Ⓓ Ⓔ
80. Ⓐ Ⓑ Ⓒ Ⓓ Ⓔ

European History

TEST 2 – Section I

TIME: 55 Minutes
80 Questions

DIRECTIONS: Each of the questions or incomplete statements below is followed by five suggested answers or completions. Select the one that is best in each case.

1. Renaissance Humanism was a threat to the Church because it

   (A) espoused atheism.

   (B) denounced scholasticism.

   (C) denounced neo-Platonism.

   (D) emphasized a return to the original sources of Christianity.

   (E) advanced an amoral philosophy.

2. *Defense of the Seven Sacraments* was a tract

   (A) written by Thomas More in which the Church is attacked because of its sacramental theology.

   (B) written by Zwingli which argued that the Eucharist was a symbolic reenactment of the Last Supper.

   (C) in which Luther called upon the German nobility to accept responsibility for cleansing Christianity of the abuses which had developed within the Church.

   (D) written by Henry VIII in which the Roman Catholic Church's position on sacramental theology was supported.

   (E) in which Thomas Cranmer argued that the Edwardian Prayer Book was justified by the sacraments.

3. Erasmus of Rotterdam was the author of

(A) *The Praise of Folly.*
(B) *The Birth of Venus.*
(C) *Utopia.*
(D) *The Prince.*
(E) *Don Quixote.*

4. The Henrician reaffirmation of Catholic theology was made in the

(A) Ten Articles of Faith.
(B) Six Articles of Faith.
(C) Forty-two Articles of Faith.
(D) Act of Supremacy.
(E) Act of Uniformity.

5. The Peace of Augsburg

(A) recognized that Lutheranism was the true interpretation of Christianity.
(B) recognized the principle that the religion of the leader would determine the religion of the people.
(C) denounced the Papacy and Charles V.
(D) resulted in the recognition of Lutheranism, Calvinism, and Catholicism.
(E) authored the seizure of all Church property in German states.

6. The Catholic Counter-Reformation included all of the following EXCEPT

(A) the *Index of Prohibited Books.*
(B) the Council of Trent.
(C) a more assertive Papacy.
(D) the establishment of new religious orders.
(E) a willingness to negotiate non-doctrinal issues with reformers.

7. Where did the Saint Bartholomew's Day Massacre occur?

(A) France
(B) England

(C) Spain (D) The Netherlands

(E) The Holy Roman Empire

8. The Price Revolution of the 16th century was caused by

(A) the establishment of monopolies.

(B) the importation of silver and gold into the European economy.

(C) a shortage of labor.

(D) the wars of religion caused by the Reformation.

(E) an unfavorable balance of trade.

9. The Peace of Westphalia (1648)

(A) transferred Louisiana from France to Britain.

(B) recognized the independence of the Netherlands.

(C) recognized the unity of the German Empire.

(D) was a triumph of the Hapsburg polity to unity.

(E) recognized the primacy of Russia in the Baltic.

10. Sir Isaac Newton's intellectual synthesis was advanced in

(A) *Principia.* (D) *Three Laws of Planetary Motion.*

(B) *Discourse on Method.* (E) *The Prince.*

(C) *Novum Organum.*

11. Richelieu served as "Prime Minister" to

(A) Louis XII. (D) Louis XIII.

(B) Henry IV. (E) Francis I.

(C) Louis XIV.

12. In the Edict of Fontainebleau, Louis XIV

(A) abrogated the Edict of Nantes.

(B) abrogated the Edict of Potsdam.

(C) announced his divorce from Catherine de Medici.

(D) denounced Cardinal Mazarin.

(E) initiated the War of the Spanish Succession.

13. In order to seize the Russian throne, Peter the Great had to overthrow his sister

(A) Theodora.

(B) Natalia.

(C) Sophia.

(D) Catherine.

(E) Elizabeth.

14. Peter the Great's principal foreign policy achievement was

(A) the acquisition of ports on the Black Sea.

(B) the acquisition of ports on the Baltic Sea.

(C) the Russian gains in the three partitions of Poland.

(D) the defensive alliance with England.

(E) the defeat of France in the Great Northern War.

Unemployment
(Numbers in thousands & percentage of appropriate work force)

	Germany		**Great Britain**	
1930	3,076	15.3	1,917	14.6
1932	5,575	30.1	2,745	22.5
1934	2,718	14.9	2,159	17.7
1936	2,151	11.6	1,755	14.3
1938	429	2.1	1,191	13.3

15. The chart above indicates

(A) that Germany and Great Britain recovered from the Depression at about the same level and rate.

(B) that Hitler's Germany reduced unemployment at a remarkable rate during the period from 1936 and 1938.

(C) that Britain was complacent about its double-digit unemployment during the 1930s.

(D) that the German economic system was superior to that of Great Britain.

(E) none of the above.

16. A moderate proposal which called on France to adopt a political system similar to Great Britain was an element espoused by Montesquieu in

(A) *The Social Contract.*

(B) *The Spirit of the Laws.*

(C) *The Encyclopedia.*

(D) *The Declaration of the Rights of Man and the Citizen.*

(E) *Two Treatises on Civil Government.*

17. Which of the following chronological sequences on the French Revolution is correct?

(A) Directory, Consulate, Legislative Assembly

(B) Legislative Assembly, Convention, Directory

(C) Convention, Consulate, Directory

(D) National Assembly, Convention, Directory

(E) Consulate, Empire, Directory

18. Thomas Hobbes' political philosophy can be most clearly identified with the thought of which of the following?

(A) Rousseau

(B) Voltaire

(C) Quesnay

(D) Montesquieu

(E) Robespierre

19. Who was the most important enlightened political ruler of the 18th century?

(A) Catherine the Great

(B) Louis XV

(C) Maria Theresa

(D) Frederick the Great

(E) Joseph II

20. The reaction to the Peterloo Massacre was characteristic of the conservative policies advanced by the British government under

(A) George Canning.
(B) Robert Peel.
(C) Lord Melbourne.
(D) Lord Liverpool.
(E) Horatio Hunt.

21. The Factory Act of 1833

(A) established the five-day work week in Britain.
(B) eliminated child labor in the mining of coal and iron.
(C) required employers to provide comprehensive medical coverage for all employees.
(D) alleviated some of the abuses of child labor in the textile industry.
(E) specified that pregnant women could not work in environmentally unsafe conditions.

22. The Anglo-French Entente (also known as the Entente Cordiale)

(A) was a defensive treaty directed at containing German expansion in Europe.
(B) was a defensive treaty directed at containing German expansion overseas.
(C) resolved Anglo-French colonial disputes in Egypt and Morocco.
(D) was a 19th century agreement which ended the diplomatic isolation of Britain.
(E) was an agreement to finance the building of the Trans-Siberian railroad.

23. Who was the most prominent British advocate for the abolition of slavery during the early 19th century?

(A) William Pitt the Younger
(B) the Duke of Wellington
(C) William Wilberforce
(D) William Wordsworth
(E) William Blake

24. English Utilitarianism was identified with the phrase

    (A) all power to the people.

    (B) from each according to his labor, to each according to his need.

    (C) universal reason.

    (D) the greatest good for the greatest number.

    (E) collectivistic nationalism.

25. An economic philosophy identified with "bullionism" and the need to maintain a favorable balance of trade was

    (A) Utopian Socialism.

    (B) Marxism.

    (C) Capitalism.

    (D) Syndicalism.

    (E) Mercantilism.

26. Which British Prime Minister was associated closely with the Irish Home Rule bill?

    (A) Benjamin Disraeli

    (B) William Gladstone

    (C) Lord Salisbury

    (D) Joseph Chamberlain

    (E) Robert Peel

27. The Balfour Declaration (1917)

    (A) denounced the use of chemicals by the Germans on the Western Front.

    (B) was a pledge of British support for the future.

    (C) was a mediation effort to resolve the Anglo-Irish crisis.

    (D) was an attempt to persuade the United States to abandon its neutrality.

    (E) repudiated the notion of war aims involving territory and compensation.

28. The Boulanger Crisis

    (A) was a left-wing attempt engineered by Leon Gambetta to overthrow the Third French Republic.

(B) involved a financial scandal associated with raising funds to build the Panama Canal.

(C) was caused by a right-wing scheme to overthrow the Third French Republic and install General Georges Boulanger as the political leader.

(D) broke when the Dreyfus scandal became known to the French press.

(E) resulted in the monarchists gaining a majority in the Chamber of Deputies.

29. All of the following were plots against Elizabeth I EXCEPT

(A) the Babington Plot.

(B) the Throckmorton Plot.

(C) the Ridolfi Plot.

(D) the Rising of the Northern Earls.

(E) the Wisbech Stirs.

30. The map below indicates the partition of Africa in what year?

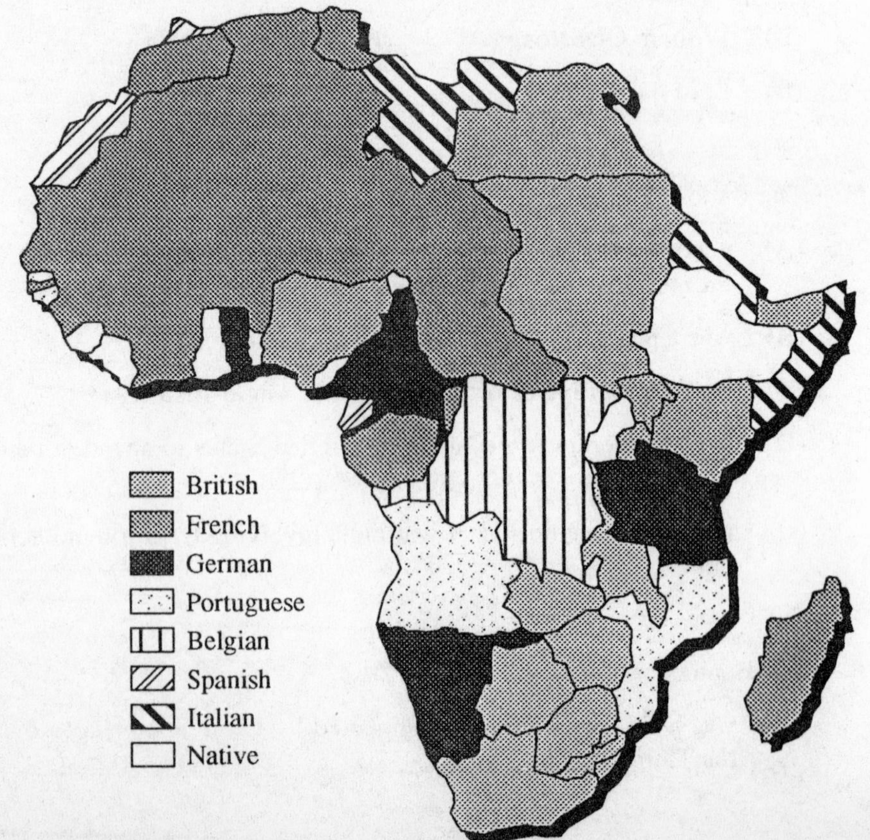

(A) 1815
(B) 1914
(C) 1870
(D) 1960
(E) 1848

31. The French essayist Montaigne was representative of which intellectual movement?

(A) Enlightenment
(B) Baroque
(C) Positivism
(D) Utopian Socialism
(E) Symbolism

32. The Hundred Days was

(A) the label given to the reactionary period which followed the Manchester riots in Britain.

(B) an unsuccessful attempt by Napoleon to restore himself as a credible European leader.

(C) the worst phase of the Reign of Terror.

(D) a period which witnessed British defeats in Africa and the Low Countries.

(E) the reactionary phase of the Revolutions of 1848.

33. Jeremy Bentham, James Mill and John Stuart Mill were

(A) Positivists.
(B) Romantic Idealists.
(C) Utilitarians.
(D) Utopian Socialists.
(E) early advocates of Marxism.

34. The Russian blockade of Berlin in 1948–49 was a reaction to

(A) the unification of the British, French, and American zones into West Germany.

(B) the Truman Doctrine.

(C) the Marshall Plan.

(D) the formation of NATO.

(E) the Chinese revolution.

35. The Revolutions of 1848 reflected the interest of all of the following EXCEPT

(A) the Liberals.
(B) the Utopians.
(C) the Nationalists.
(D) the middle class.
(E) the Marxists.

36. In the "April Theses" Lenin

(A) challenged the policies of the Provisional Government.
(B) outlined a plan for a Russian class war after the Revolution of 1905.
(C) denounced the revisionist elements within socialism.
(D) called for continuing the war against Germany.
(E) designated Kerensky as his successor.

37. Mazzini's Roman Republic was

(A) instrumental in the unification of Italy in 1870.
(B) was suppressed by the armies of Charles Albert.
(C) was suppressed by units of the French army.
(D) was suppressed by the Swiss Guard.
(E) approved in Cavour's plan for a unified Italy.

38. The Schleswig-Holstein question was a contentious issue between

(A) Prussia and Sweden.
(B) Austria and Prussia.
(C) Prussia and Russia.
(D) Prussia and the Netherlands.
(E) Prussia and Great Britain.

39. Who was the leader of the Hungarians during the Revolutions of 1848?

(A) Windischgratz
(B) Louis Kossuth
(C) Metternich
(D) Radetsky
(E) Castlereagh

40. The Dogger Bank Incident resulted in a diplomatic crisis between which two countries?

(A) Great Britain and France

(B) France and Germany

(C) Great Britain and Russia

(D) Russia and France

(E) Belgium and France

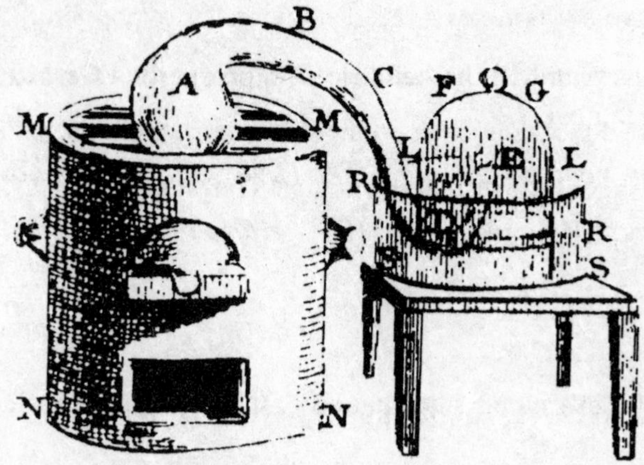

41. The above drawing represents

(A) the "Leyden Jar."

(B) the Stephen Gray experiment which demonstrated that electricity could be conducted by means of threads.

(C) the "Phlogiston" theory.

(D) Lavoisier's Apparatus for the Decomposition of Air.

(E) Franklin's device for the processing of alcohol.

42. "1919ism" identifies the

(A) economic crisis after the First World War.

(B) the post-war euphoria.

(C) hysteria known as the Red Scare.

(D) triumphs of fascism in Italy.

(E) horrors associated with the Russian Civil War.

43. The Dawes Plan

(A) was an international proposal to outlaw war.

(B) was a reparations plan designed to eliminate the friction which led to the Ruhr Crisis.

(C) was denounced by Gustav Stresemann.

(D) was a permanent reparations settlement which survived until the 1930s.

(E) resulted in the dismemberment of Czechoslovakia.

44. Thomas Mann described the collapse of a prosperous German commercial family in which novel?

(A) *Death in Venice*

(B) *The Magic Mountain*

(C) *Buddenbrooks*

(D) *Lady Chatterley's Lover*

(E) *Mario and the Magician*

45. Arthur Koestler examined the situation of the victims of the Stalinist purges in

(A) *Revolt of the Masses.*

(B) *The Myth of the State.*

(C) *Darkness at Noon.*

(D) *Escape from Freedom.*

(E) *The Treason of the Intellectuals.*

46. The rise of fascism in Germany can be attributed to all of the following EXCEPT

(A) the failure of the Weimar Republic to address the crisis caused by the Depression.

(B) the effective organization of the Nazi Party.

(C) the charisma of Adolph Hitler.

(D) the lingering humiliation of defeat in the First World War.

(E) the policies of Gustav Stresemann.

47. The sketch shown below is of

(A) Richard Arkwright's water frame.

(B) the spinning jenny which was invented by James Hargreaves.

(C) Eli Whitney's cotton gin.

(D) James Watt's silk-making machine.

(E) Franklin's paper-making machine.

48. In *A Study of History* a religious-based philosophy of history is advanced by

(A) Oswald Spengler.

(B) William McNeill.

(C) Arnold Toynbee.

(D) T. S. Eliot.

(E) Christopher Dawson.

49. In order "To overcome nothingness ... individuals must define life for themselves and celebrate it fully, instinctively, heroically." This statement reflected the philosophy of which of the following?

(A) Ernst Cassirer

(B) Jacques Maritain

(C) Fredrich Nietzsche

(D) Paul Tillich

(E) Karl Barth

50. In 1968, who led Czechoslovakia's "Prague Spring" — an attempt to develop "socialism with a human face"?

(A) Havel
(B) Marshall Tito
(C) Erich Honecker
(D) Lech Walesa
(E) Alexander Dubcek

51. In 1834 German states (excluding Austria) agreed to eliminate tariffs between the states through a customs union known as the

(A) *Furstenstaat.*
(B) The Confederation of the Rhine.
(C) The Frankfurt Assembly.
(D) *Zollverein.*
(E) Hanseatic League.

52. "Do you not hear them repeating unceasingly that all that is above them is incapable and unworthy of governing them; that the present distribution of good throughout the world is unjust; that property rests on a foundation which is not an equitable foundation? ... I believe that we are at this moment sleeping on a volcano.'' Alexis de Tocqueville made these remarks to

(A) the American Senate in 1838.
(B) the Chamber of Deputies in 1848.
(C) the court of Charles X in 1830.
(D) the new leaders of the Third French Republic in 1871.
(E) none of the above.

53. In *English Constitution* (1867) an argument was advanced which contended that the British Cabinet system of government was superior to the American constitutional system. Who wrote this book?

(A) Walter Bagehot
(B) Robert Southey
(C) Thomas Carlyle
(D) John Henry Newman
(E) John Ruskin

54. A late Renaissance reformer who maintained that "the Hermetic philosophy, with its mystical approach to God and nature, held the key to true wisdom," was

(A) Descartes.
(B) Montaigne.
(C) Francis Bacon.
(D) Giordano Bruno.
(E) Newton.

55. The maps below indicate changes in the western border of Russia between what years?

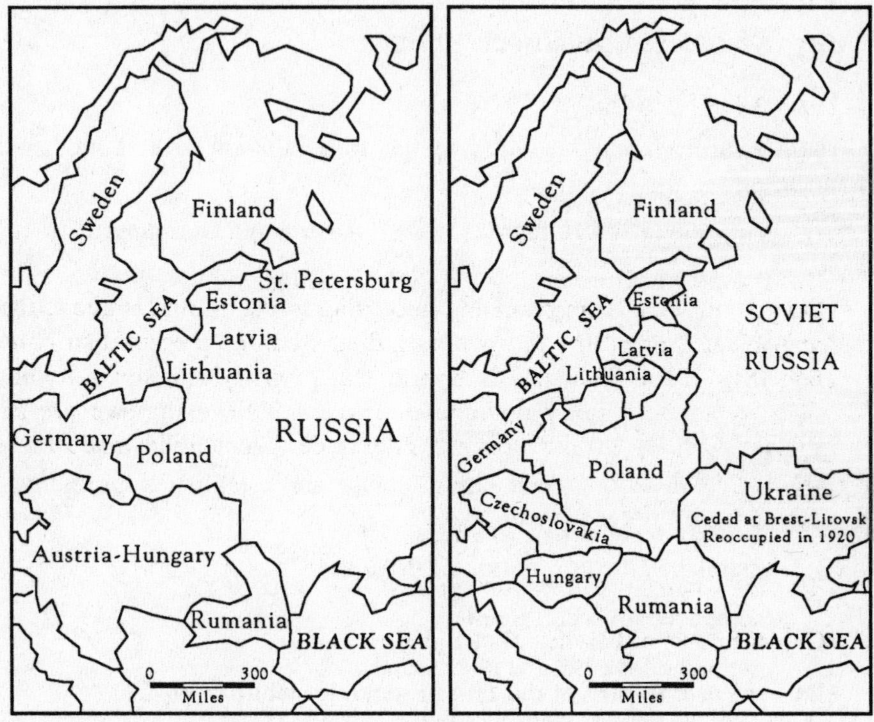

(A) 1815 and 1921
(B) 1848 and 1945
(C) 1914 and 1921
(D) 1914 and 1950
(E) 1725 and 1920

56. Britain established direct authority over India after the suppression of the

(A) Opium Wars.
(B) Boxer Rebellion.
(C) Sepoy Mutiny.
(D) assassination of Gandhi.
(E) Warren Hastings affair.

57. Which of the following African societies was not under European rule by 1914?

(A) The Congo
(B) South Africa
(C) Nigeria
(D) Angola
(E) Ethiopia

58. The British policy of "Splendid Isolationism" was terminated with the

(A) Anglo-French Entente.
(B) Anglo-Russian Entente.
(C) Anglo-Japanese Alliance.
(D) Second Moroccan Crisis.
(E) Boer War.

59. The Versailles Treaty resulted in the formation of several new nations including

(A) Yugoslavia and Hungary.
(B) Poland and Greece.
(C) Poland and Italy.
(D) Austria and Germany.
(E) Austria and Italy.

60. Article 231 of the Versailles Treaty

(A) is known as the "War Guilt" clause and established Germany's responsibility for the war.
(B) established the new nation of Poland.
(C) denounced all secret treaties.
(D) established the League of Nations.
(E) resulted in the decentralization of Germany.

61. After 1945 the policies of the Soviet Union resulted in all of the following EXCEPT

(A) the continuing development of Soviet military power.
(B) a slow demobilization from a war economy.
(C) consistency in the exercise of power by the Communist Party.
(D) a general improvement in the standard of living.
(E) extensive influence in the United Nations during the years immediately following the Second World War.

62. The pessimism which permeated the works of intellectuals between the First and Second World Wars was evident in works by all of the following EXCEPT

(A) T. S. Eliot.
(B) William Butler Yeats.
(C) Johan Huizinga.
(D) Carl Gustav Jung.
(E) Herbert Spencer.

63. In bringing about a centralized Italy, who was Cavour's most significant non-Italian ally?

(A) Bismarck
(B) Napoleon III
(C) Palmerston
(D) Franz Joseph
(E) Queen Victoria

64. Syndicalism was a manifestastion of anarchism which was founded by

(A) Kropotkin.
(B) Sorel.
(C) Bakunin.
(D) Sidney Webb.
(E) Mazzini.

65. The achievements of the Jacobins included all of the following EXCEPT

(A) abolition of slavery.
(B) the franchise given to all adult males.
(C) adoption of the metric system.
(D) decreeing the law of the maximum — fixed prices on essentials and raised wages.
(E) distribution of all land among the peasants.

66. The British working class demonstrated unity during the

(A) demonstrations by anarchists prior to the First World War.
(B) movements towards female suffrage.
(C) General Strike of 1926.

(D) post-World War I recession.

(E) depression which occurred after the Napoleonic Wars.

67. During the late 1930s efforts to perpetuate the Third French Republic were centered in the Popular Front which was under the leadership of

(A) Pierre Laval.
(B) Léon Blum.
(C) Philippe Pétain.
(D) Marcel Deat.
(E) Marc Bloch.

68. In 1938 the Austrian Republic was incorporated formally into the Third Reich through the

(A) Nuremburg Laws.
(B) military conquest.
(C) *Anschluss.*
(D) Munich accord.
(E) occupation of the Rhineland.

69. Karl Marx believed in all of the following EXCEPT

(A) the importance of the role of the Communist Party.
(B) the dialectic view of history.
(C) materialism was the driving force of history.
(D) the importance of gaining power through legal means.
(E) that private property was a primary cause of economic, social, and political distress.

70. The definitive "Whig" interpretation of British history was advanced in the 19th century by

(A) David Hume.
(B) Edward Gibbon.
(C) Thomas Babington Macaulay.
(D) John Stuart Mill.
(E) Jeremy Bentham.

71. The following map indicates the thesis advanced by H. Mackinder in 1904 that

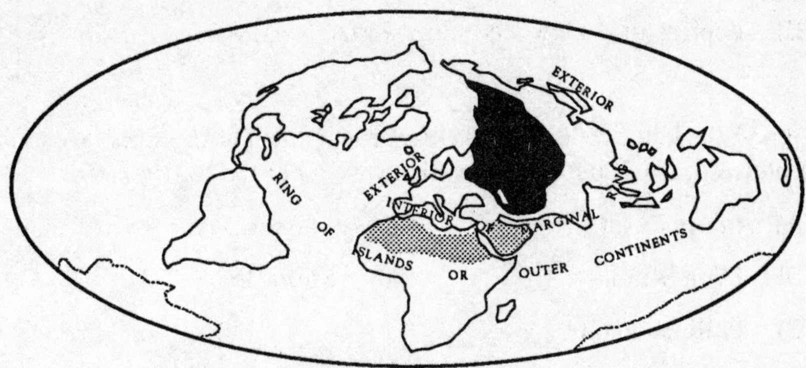

(A) the continental part of Eurasia forms the world heartland and constitutes a potential threat for sea powers.

(B) only a combined Anglo-American-Russian alliance could prevent German world domination.

(C) the theory advanced by Alfred Mahan in *The Influence of Sea Power Upon History* was correct.

(D) sea powers must dominate land powers through containment.

(E) the Southern Hemisphere is as significant as the Northern Hemisphere.

72. German isolation was evident at the

(A) Portsmouth Conference.

(B) Algerciras Conference.

(C) Berlin Convention.

(D) Congress of Berlin.

(E) World Peace Conference.

73. The map shown on the following page indicates

(A) the political boundaries in the Near East in 1960.

(B) the political boundaries in the Near East during the Presidency of Gamel Nasser in Egypt.

(C) the partition of the Ottoman Empire after the First World War.

(D) The scope of the European colonial holdings in the Near East after 1945.

(E) the status of the Ottoman Empire after the Congress of Berlin.

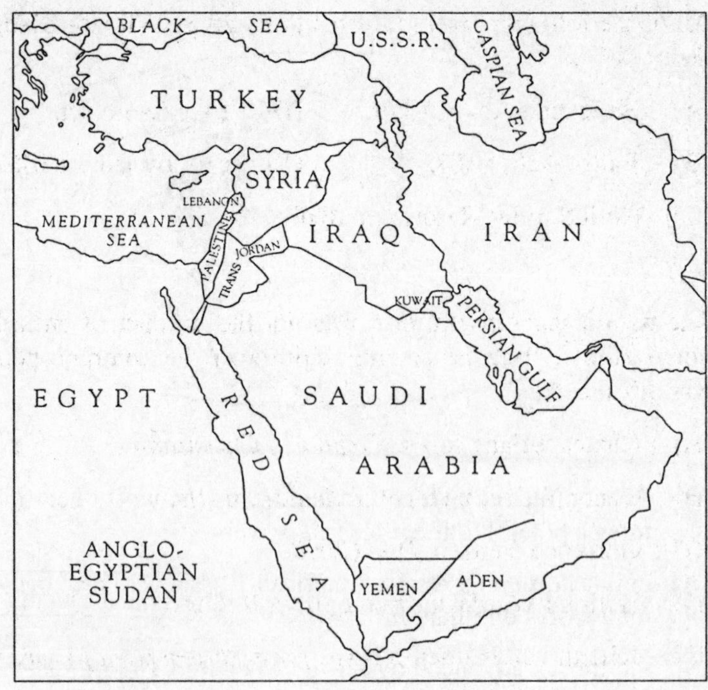

74. The *Marriage of Figaro, Don Giovanni*, and *The Magic Flute* were operas by

(A) Franz Joseph Haydn.
(B) Wolfgang Amadeus Mozart.
(C) Johann Sebastian Bach.
(D) George Frederick Handel.
(E) Henry Purcell.

75. The drawing shown here by Karl Arnold appeared in *Simplicissimus* (July, 1924) and was entitled *Neue Typen: Der Rassemensch —New Types: The Racial Man* or *The Man of Breeding*). It was a critical comment on

(A) the Prussian Junkers who condemned the Versailles Treaty.
(B) the anti-Semites who supported Hitler and the emerging Nazi Party.
(C) German capitalism.
(D) German social decadence.
(E) the ineptitude of the Social Democratic Party.

76. All of the following were reforms initiated by William Gladstone EXCEPT the

(A) Education Act of 1870.
(B) Ballot Act of 1872.
(C) Civil Service Reform of 1870.
(D) Irish Land Act.
(E) Reform Bill of 1867.

77. The notion that "civilization was not the product of an artificial, international elite ... but the genuine culture of the common people, the *Volk*" was advanced by

(A) Chateaubriand in *The Genius of Christianity*
(B) Georg Wilhelm Hegel in *Reason in History*
(C) Giuseppe Verdi in *Don Carlo*
(D) William Wordsworth in *Lyrical Ballads*
(E) Johann von Herder in *Ideas for a Philosophy of Human History*

78. Enclosures were required

(A) to reinforce the concept of private property.
(B) to eliminate continuing boundary disputes.
(C) to permit scientific farming.
(D) to assist in accurate property tax collections.
(E) to permit the newly rich to acquire property.

79. What were the three Soviet Baltic provinces that broke away from the U.S.S.R. in 1991?

(A) Ukraine, Lithuania, Estonia
(B) Latvia, Lithuania, Estonia
(C) Poland, Czechoslovakia, Hungary
(D) Lithuania, Chechnya, Georgia
(E) Serbia, Bosnia, Croatia

80. Who led the Polish Solidarity movement?

(A) Lech Valesa

(B) Wojciech Jaruzelski

(C) Boris Yeltsin

(D) Pope John Paul II

(E) Janos Kadar

European History

TEST 2 – Section II

TIME: Reading Period – 15 minutes
Writing Time for all three essays – 115 minutes

DIRECTIONS: Read over both the Document-Based Essay question in Part A and the choices in Part B during the Reading Period, and use the time to organize answers. All students must answer Part A (the Document-Based Essay Question); and choose TWO questions from Part B to answer.

PART A – DOCUMENT-BASED ESSAY

This question is designed to test your ability to work with historical documents. As you analyze each document, *take into account its source and the point of view of the author.* Write an essay on the following topic that integrates your analysis of the documents. You may refer to historical facts and developments not mentioned in the documents.

Analyze the rivalry between Benjamin Disraeli and William Gladstone which dominated English politics from the late 1860s to 1880.

Historical Background: During the late 1860s the political rivalry between the Conservative Benjamin Disraeli and the Liberal Gladstone blossomed and continued until Disraeli's death in 1881. This period witnessed the extension of the franchise, a wide range of domestic legislation, and a debate on imperialism.

Document 1
"Hoity-Toity"

Document 2
Letter from Queen Victoria to William Gladstone — May 6, 1870

...The circumstances respecting the Bill to give women the same position as men with respect to Parliamentary franchise gives her an opportunity to observe that she had for some time past wished to call Mr. Gladstone's attention to the mad & utterly demoralizing movement of the present day to place women in the same position as to professions — as *men*;—& amongst others, in the *Medical Line* ....

The Queen is a women herself—& knows what an anomaly her *own* position is:—but that can be reconciled with reason & propriety tho' it is a terribly difficult & trying one. But to tear away all the barriers w^{h} surround a woman, & to propose that they sh^{ld} study with *men*—things w^{h} c^{ld} not be named before them—certainly not *in a mixed* audience—w^{hd} be to introduce a total disregard of what must be considered as belonging to the rules & principles of morality.

The Queen feels so strongly upon his dangerous & unchristian & unnatural *cry* & movement of "women's rights,"—in w^{h} she knows Mr. Gladstone *agrees*; (as he sent her that excellent Pamphlet by a Lady) that she is most anxious that Mr. Gladstone & others sh^{ld} take some steps to check this alarming danger & to make whatever use they can of her name.

She sends the letters w^{h} speak for themselves.

Let woman be what God intended; a helpmate for a man—but with totally different duties & vocations.

Document 3
"The Conservative Programme"

Document 4
"The Colossus of the World"

Document 5
"On the Dizzy Brink"

Document 6
"A Bad Example"

PART B – ESSAY QUESTIONS

1. Using the Glorious Revolution of 1688, the French Revolution of 1789, and the Russian Revolution of 1917, discuss and analyze the nature and scope of the revolutionary tradition in modern Europe.

2. Describe and analyze the impact of the Counter-Reformation on European history.

3. Describe and analyze the characteristics of fascism.

4. Describe and compare the origins and proposals of the utopian socialists, the marxists, the anarchists, and the revisionists during the 19th century.

5. Describe and analyze the development of democracy in Great Britain during the 19th and 20th centuries.

6. Describe and compare the unification of Germany and Italy during the 19th century.

THE ADVANCED PLACEMENT EXAMINATION IN

European History

TEST 2 – ANSWERS

1.	(D)	21.	(D)	41.	(D)	61.	(E)
2.	(D)	22.	(C)	42.	(C)	62.	(E)
3.	(A)	23.	(C)	43.	(B)	63.	(B)
4.	(B)	24.	(D)	44.	(C)	64.	(B)
5.	(B)	25.	(E)	45.	(C)	65.	(E)
6.	(E)	26.	(B)	46.	(E)	66.	(C)
7.	(A)	27.	(B)	47.	(B)	67.	(B)
8.	(B)	28.	(C)	48.	(C)	68.	(C)
9.	(B)	29.	(E)	49.	(C)	69.	(D)
10.	(A)	30.	(B)	50.	(E)	70.	(C)
11.	(D)	31.	(B)	51.	(D)	71.	(A)
12.	(A)	32.	(B)	52.	(B)	72.	(B)
13.	(C)	33.	(C)	53.	(A)	73.	(C)
14.	(B)	34.	(A)	54.	(D)	74.	(B)
15.	(B)	35.	(E)	55.	(C)	75.	(B)
16.	(B)	36.	(A)	56.	(C)	76.	(E)
17.	(B)	37.	(C)	57.	(E)	77.	(E)
18.	(B)	38.	(B)	58.	(C)	78.	(C)
19.	(D)	39.	(B)	59.	(A)	79.	(B)
20.	(D)	40.	(C)	60.	(A)	80.	(A)

Detailed Explanations of Answers

TEST 2

1. **(D)** Renaissance Humanism was a threat to the Church because it (D) emphasized a return to the original sources of Christianity — the Bible and the writings of the Fathers of Church. In that light, the humanists tended to ignore or denounce the proceedings of Church councils and pontiffs during the Middle Ages. While many Renaissance humanists denounced scholasticism, there was no inherent opposition to it and many retained support of the late Medieval philosophy. Renaissance humanism did not espouse atheism nor did it advance an amoral philosophy; it tended to advance a neo-Platonism through the writings of such individuals as Pico Della Mirandola and Marsiglio.

2. **(D)** The *Defense of the Seven Sacraments* was a tract (D) written by Henry VIII in which the Roman Catholic Church's position on sacramental theology was supported. This 1521 publication repudiated Luther's views on the sacraments which were advanced in pamphlets during the preceding year. While some earlier authorities have asserted that the real author of the tract was Thomas More (A), contemporary scholarship has affirmed that, while More no doubt provided assistance, authorship should be attributed to Henry VIII. Zwingli (B) did maintain that the Eucharist was a symbolic reenactment of the Last Supper but he did not write this tract. Obviously, Luther (C), to whom it was directed, and Cranmer (E), who came to prominence during the next decade, were not the authors.

3. **(A)** Erasmus of Rotterdam was the author of (A) *The Praise of Folly* which was a criticism of the ambitions of the clergy. *The Birth of Venus* (B) was not a literary work. Thomas More was the author of *Utopia* (C); Niccolo Machiavelli wrote (D) *The Prince*; and Cervantes was the author of *Don Quixote.*

4. **(B)** The Henrican reaffirmation of the Catholic Theology was made in the (B) Six Articles of Faith of 1539. In response to mounting criticism and the vague (A) Ten Articles of Faith (1536) and the dissolution of the monasteries, Henry VIII retreated from the movement toward Protestantism. The (D) Act of Supremacy and (E) Act of Uniformity were passed by the Reformation Parliament to decree and enforce Henry VIII's authority over the Church in England.

The Forty-Two Articles of Faith (E) was a statement of Protestant doctrines developed by Thomas Cranmer during the early 1550s.

5. **(B)** The Peace of Augsburg (1555) (B) recognized the principle that the religion of the leader would determine the religion of the people; it was a major victory for Lutheranism and a defeat of the Hapsburg aspirations to effectively control the Holy Roman Empire. Lutheranism (A) was not recognized as the true interpretation of Christianity nor did it (E) authorize the seizure of all Church property in German states. Calvinism (D) was not recognized until the Peace of Westphalia in 1648; (C) Charles V and the Papacy were negotiators in formulating the Peace of Augsburg.

6. **(E)** The Catholic Counter-Reformation did not include (E) a willingness to negotiate non-doctrinal issues with reformers; indeed, the Catholic Church considered all confrontational issues to be doctrinal. The Council of Trent (B) was convened in three sessions from 1545 to 1564 and reaffirmed traditional Catholic doctrines; new religious orders (D) such as the Jesuits and Oratorians appeared; the papacy (C) became more assertive as can be seen in the issuing of the *Index of Prohibited Books* in 1558-59.

7. **(A)** The St. Batholomew's Day Massacre occurred in 1572 in (A) France; it was the work of Queen Catherine De Medici and involved the execution of thousands of French Huguenots during the subsequent months. Obviously, this event did not transpire in (B) England, (C) Spain, (D) the Netherlands, or (E) the Holy Roman Empire.

8. **(B)** The Price Revolution of the 16th century was caused by (B) the importation of silver and gold into the European economy; the influx of specie from Latin America resulted in eliminating the scarcity of money — the result was a general fourfold increase in prices. The establishment of monopolies (A) and the maintenance of a favorable balance of trade (E) were important elements in 17th century mercantilism. While there were occasional labor shortages (C) and the wars of religion (D) did not disrupt economic activities, these developments did not have any substantive impact on the price revolution.

9. **(B)** The Peace of Westphalia (1648) (B) recognized the independence of the Netherlands and Switzerland. Louisiana (A) was not transferred to Britain; Sweden not Russia (E) was recognized as the primary power in the Baltic; and the Hapsburg plan (D) and (C) for a unified central Europe was destroyed.

10. **(A)** Sir Isaac Newton's intellectual synthesis was advanced in (A) *Principia* in 1687; he established scientism as a credible alternative to preceding intellectual approaches and methods. *Discourse on Method* (B) was written by René Descartes in 1637; *Novum Organum* (C) was a work by Francis Bacon which addressed the issue of empiricism; Kepler developed the Three Laws of Planetary Motion (D); and *The Prince* was written by Machiavelli.

11. **(D)** Richelieu served as "Prime Minister" to (D) Louis XIII. For over two decades during the turbulence of the Thirty Years' War and the LaRochelle crisis with the Huguenots, Cardinal Richelieu administered France for Louis XIII. Henry IV (B) was Louis XIII's father; Louis XIV (C) was his son. Louis XII (A) and Francis I (E) were earlier French monarchs.

12. **(A)** In the Edict of Fontainebleau (1685), Louis XIV (A) abrogated the Edict of Nantes of 1598 in which Henry IV had to extend some religious liberties to French Protestants. Fontainebleau directed that all Frenchmen would conform to Catholicism. The Edict of Potsdam (1686) (B) was issued by Elector Frederick William of Brandenburg-Prussia; it invited French Protestants to migrate to Brandenburg. (E) The War of the Spanish Succession commenced in 1702; the Fontainebleau decree was not related to (C) Catherine De Medici or (D) Cardinal Mazarin.

13. **(C)** In order to seize the Russian throne, Peter the Great had to overthrow (1689) his sister (C) Sophia. His mother, (B) served as regent until 1694 when Peter took over the government. Catherine (D) and Elizabeth (E) were Russian leaders in the 18th century. (A) Theodora was not a Romanov ruler.

14. **(B)** Peter the Great's principal foreign policy achievement was (B) the acquisition of ports on the Baltic Sea. Peter's victory over Sweden (E) in the Great Northern War — Peace of Nystadt, 1721 — provided Russia with direct access to the Baltic and then to the Atlantic. His efforts to acquire ports on the Black Sea (A) were not realized; later Catherine the Great would expand in this area at the expense of the Ottoman Turks. The partitions of Poland (C) occurred after Peter's death; Russia did not enter into any alliance with England (D) during this period.

15. **(B)** This chart indicates (B) that Hitler's Germany reduced unemployment at a remarkable rate during the period from 1936 to 1938; the fascist economic controls facilitated this development. (A), (C), (D) are incorrect; the German economy was not "superior" to Britain's nor was Britain content with excessive unemployment — while there is much to criticize about the manner in which the Labour and Conservative parties handled economic recovery, one must remember that free economies are naturally more difficult to direct than state controlled economic systems.

16. **(B)** A moderate proposal which called on France to adopt a political system similar to that of Great Britain was an element espoused by Montesquieu in (B) *The Spirit of the Laws. The Social Contract* (A) was written by Jean Jacques Rousseau; *The Encyclopedia* (C) was by Denis Diderot; *The Declaration of the Rights of Man and the Citizen* (D) was produced by the National Assembly in August, 1789; and John Locke wrote *Two Treatises on Civil Government*.

17. **(B)** The correct chronological sequence is (B) Legislative Assembly

(1791–92), Convention (1792–95), and Directory (1795–99). The National Assembly existed from 1789 to 1791; the Consulate from 1799 to 1804; and the Empire from 1804 to 1814.

18. **(B)** Thomas Hobbes' political philosophy can be most clearly identified with the thought of (B) Voltaire. Voltaire maintained that Enlightened Despotism would be the best form of government for France; this position concurs with the Hobessian view that people need to be governed, not government by the people; (C) Quesnay's program was similar though not as directly related. (A) Rousseau, (D) Montesquieu, and (E) Robespierre entertained political theories which were more revolutionary in the context of sovereign power and the exercise of that power.

19. **(D)** The most prominent enlightened political ruler of the 18th century was (D) Frederick the Great of Prussia. He had a genuine interest in enlightened government and introduced a wide range of reforms. Catherine the Great (A) of Russia considered herself enlightened but her barbarism did not support that claim. Louis XV (C) and Maria Theresa (C) were opposed to the thought of the enlightenment; Maria Theresa's son, Joseph II (E), introduced some reforms but became a reactionary after the outbreak of the French Revolution.

20. **(D)** The reaction to the Peterloo Massacre was characteristic of the conservative policies advanced by the British government under (D) Lord Liverpool. While George Canning (A) and Robert Peel (B) were involved in the government, they were not very influential at this time. Melbourne (C) became Prime Minister during the 1830s; Horatio Hunt (E) was the radical who spoke to the crowd at St. Peter's Field, Manchester, prior to the riot.

21. **(D)** The Factory Act of 1833 (D) alleviated some of the abuses of child labor in the textile industry. The five-day work week (A) did not become a reality until the 20th century; reforms in the use of children in mining and heavy industry (B) were not implemented until later in the 19th century; employers were never required (C) to provide comprehensive medical coverage for all employees; this measure made no provision for the special treatment of (E) pregnant women.

22. **(C)** The Anglo-French Entente (also known as the Entente Cordiale) (C) resolved Anglo-French colonial disputes in Egypt and Morocco; northeast Africa (Egypt and the Sudan) was recognized as a British sphere of influence, northwest Africa (Morocco and Algeria) was recognized as a French sphere of influence. This arrangement was not (A) directed at German expansion in Europe or (B) overseas; it was signed in 1904 and therefore was not (D) a 19th century agreement; the Trans-Siberian railroad had been funded by French loans during the 1880s and 1890s, it was not mentioned in this agreement.

23. **(C)** The most prominent British advocate for the abolition of slavery

during the early 19th century was (C) William Wilberforce. While Wordsworth (D) and Blake (E) were sympathetic to abolitionism, they were not in the forefront of opposition to slavery. William Pitt the Younger (A) and Wellington (B) were preoccupied with the Napoleonic Wars.

24. **(D)** English Utilitarianism was identified with the phrase (D) "the greatest good for the greatest number." Jeremy Bentham, James Mill, and John Stuart Mill were prominent Utilitarians. "All power to the people" and "From each according to his labor, to each according to his need" (B) were elements in Lenin's rhetoric. "Universal reason" (C) is identified with Georg Wilhelm Hegel; and "collectivistic nationalism" is associated with Johann Fichte.

25. **(E)** Mercantilism was an economic philosophy identified with "bullionism" and the need to maintain a favorable balance of trade. Utopian Socialism (A) was an early 19th century philosophy which emphasized the need for a more equitable distribution of wealth; (B) Marxism and (D) Syndicalism were leftist approaches to economics and politics. (C) Capitalism was the developing condition in which mercantilism operated.

26. **(B)** The British Prime Minister who was associated closely with Irish Home Rule was (B) William Gladstone. Gladstone maintained through his four ministries that one of his principal tasks was "to pacify Ireland." Robert Peel's (E) career was over before the Irish crisis broke during the second half of the 19th century. Benjamin Disraeli (A), Lord Salisbury (B), and Joseph Chamberlain (D) were not particularly interested or sympathetic to the Irish.

27. **(B)** The Balfour Declaration (1917) (B) was a pledge of British support for the future establishment of a Jewish state. It was not related to (A) the German use of chemicals, (C) the Anglo-Irish crisis stemming from the Easter Rebellion, (D) American neutrality, or (E) war aims.

28. **(C)** The Boulanger Crisis (C) was caused by a right-wing scheme to overthrow the Third French Republic and install General Georges Boulanger as the political leader; it was supported by monarchists and other rightist enemies of the republic. It was not (A) a left-wing scheme, nor was it related to the (B) Panama Canal or (D) the Dreyfus Affair. When the crisis failed, the monarchists did not (E) gain a majority of seats in the Chamber of Deputies.

29. **(E)** While the (A) Babington Plot, (B) the Throckmorton Plot, (C) the Ridolfi Plot, and (D) the Rising of the Northern Earls were attempts to overthrow Elizabeth I, the Wisbech Stirs of the late 1590s was a controversy among Catholics over control of the outlawed English Catholic Church.

30. **(B)** The map indicates the partition of Africa in (B) 1914 after most of the European powers had participated in establishing colonial empires.

31. **(B)** The French essayist Montaigne was representative of an intellectual movement known as (B) Baroque which was an intellectual quest for a new synthesis; it was caused by the chaos of the Reformation/Counter-Reformation era. The Enlightenment (A) developed in the 18th century and constituted an elaboration on the new scientific snythesis which emerged during the 17th century. (C) Positivism, (D) Utopian Socialism, and (E) Symbolism were 19th century intellectual movements.

32. **(B)** The Hundred Days (1815) was (B) an unsuccessful attempt by Napoleon to restore himself as a credible European leader. The Hundred Days concluded in June, 1815 at the Battle of Waterloo when Wellington's army defeated Napoleon. Obviously, the Hundred Days did not relate to (A) the reactionary period in Britain following the Manchester riots, (C) the Reign of Terror, (D) British defeats in Africa and the Low Countries, or (E) the collapse of the Revolutions of 1848.

33. **(C)** Jeremy Bentham, James Mill and John Stuart Mill were (C) Utilitarians who argued the case "the greatest good for the greatest number." Auguste Comte established (A) Positivism; Fichte and Hegel were German Romantic Idealists (B); Robert Owen and Charles Fourier were Utopian Socialists (D); and the only early advocates of Marxism (E) were Karl Marx and Friedrich Engels.

34. **(A)** The Russian blockade of Berlin in 1948–49 was a reaction to (A) the unification of the British, French, and American zones into West Germany. While the (B) Truman Doctrine was directed at preventing communist victories in Greece and Turkey, and the Marshall Plan (C) was designed to assist in accelerating the economic recovery of Europe, they were not the direct causes of the blockade. NATO (D) was formed after the blockade began and the Chinese Communist (E) victory did not occur until October 1949.

35. **(E)** Marxist interests were not reflected during the Revolutions of 1848 because Marxism was still in the process of development; while the *Communist Manifesto* was written at this time, it was not distributed widely and had no impact on the revolution. *Das Kapital* was not completed until the 1860s. The Liberal (A) desire for constitutional government, the radical economic alternatives of the Utopian Socialists (B), the nationalists (C) call for self-determination, and the enfranchisement of the middle class (D) were all evident during the revolutions of 1848.

36. **(A)** In the "April Theses" (1917) Lenin (A) challenged the policies of the Provisional Government; Lenin was opposed (D) to continuing the war against Germany. (B) is incorrect because the "April Theses" were not related to the 1905 revolution; Lenin denounced the revisionists in *What Is to Be Done?* in 1902; he did not support Kerensky (E) as his successor — Kerensky had fled to Western Europe.

37. **(C)** Giuseppi Mazzini's (1805-1872) idealistic Young Italy movement was originally supported by both Pope Pius IX and Charles Albert, the king of Sardinia. But the failure of the Revolutions of 1848 and the Roman Republic (of which Mazzini was one of the leaders) convinced the pope to abandon his support. The pope's control over the Papal States was restored through intervention by the French Army, which suppressed Mazzini's government.

Mazzini's actions had no positive effects of the later unification of Italy in 1870 (A); Charles Albert himself was defeated by an Austrian army following the pope's denunciation of the 1848 liberal movements (B); the Swiss Guard played no real role in the Roman Republic's suppression (D); and Camillo Benso di Cavour's (1810-1861) pragmatic understanding of the political forces at work during the period contrasted sharply with Mazzini's idealism.

38. **(B)** The Schleswig-Holstein question was a contentious issue between (B) Austria and Prussia during the 1860s; it was a contributing factor to the outbreak of the German Civil War (1866) between these powers. Bismarck manipulated the crisis to create a favorable situation for Prussia. Neither Sweden (A), Russia (C), the Netherlands (D), nor Great Britain (E) were involved critically with the Schleswig-Holstein issue.

39. **(B)** The leader of the Hungarians during the Revolutions of 1848 was (B) Louis Kossuth who advanced the nationalist aspirations of the Hungarian people and identified with liberal constitutional reforms. Windischgratz (A) dissolved the Pan-Slavic Congress in Prague in June, 1848; Metternich (C) was the conservative Austrian Foreign Minister who was removed during the early weeks of the 1848 revolution in Vienna. (D) Radetsky defeated the army of Charles Albert of Piedmont and thus thwarted aspirations for Italian unification in 1848. (E) Castlereagh was the British Foreign Secretary during the Congress of Vienna in 1815.

40. **(C)** The Dogger Bank Incident resulted in a diplomatic crisis (1904) between (C) Great Britain and Russia. Russian naval units in the North Sea attacked British fishing boats — mistaking them for Japanese ships. Britain, which adopted a position of benevolent neutrality to Japan at the outbreak of the Russo-Japanese war due to its obligations under the Anglo-Japanese treaty of 1902, threatened to go to war with Russia. Russia apologized for the incident and paid compensation to the victims. France (A), Germany (B), and Belgium (E) were not involved in the incident.

41. **(D)** The drawing represents (D) Lavoisier's Apparatus for the Decomposition of Air. The Leyden Jar (A) was a means of storing electricity and was used by Benjamin Franklin (E) in his kite experiment. While Stephen Gray did make contributions to the science of electricity (B) and the erroneous Phlogiston theory (C) was toppled during this period, they were not related to the illustration.

42. **(C)** "1919ism" identifies the (C) hysteria known as the Red Scare; there

was widespread concern the Bolsheviks would take over many of the European governments after the First World War. This concern was aggravated by the economic (A) consequences of the post-war era and the turbulence in Central, Southern, and Eastern European politics. The Russian Civil War did not conclude until 1921 (E); Mussolini did not come to power in Italy until 1922 (D).

43. **(B)** The Dawes Plan (B) of 1924 was a reparations plan designed to eliminate the friction which led to the Ruhr Crisis. The Kellogg-Briand Pact (1927) was (A) an international proposal to outlaw war. Stresemann (C) supported the Dawes Plan to gain the withdrawal of French and Belgian troops from the Ruhr Valley. The Dawes Plan was not permanent (D); in 1929, it was replaced by the Young Plan. The Munich agreement of 1938 (E) resulted in the dismemberment of Czechoslovakia.

44. **(C)** Thomas Mann described the collapse of a prosperous German commercial family in (C) *Buddenbrooks* which was published in 1901. Mann also wrote *Death in Venice* (A), *The Magic Fountain* (B), and *Mario the Magician* (E); *Lady Chatterley's Lover* was written by D. H. Lawrence (D).

45. **(C)** Arthur Koestler examined the situation of the victims of the Stalinist purges in (C) *Darkness at Noon* which was published in 1941. Through the central character, Rubashov, Koestler described the plight of the Old Bolsheviks. *The Revolt of the Masses* (1930) (A) was written by José Ortega y Gasset. *The Myth of the State* (1946) was the last work by Ernst Cassier; *Escape from Freedom* (1941) was written by Erick Fromm; and *The Treason of the Intellectuals* (1927) was by Julien Benda, a French critic.

46. **(E)** The rise of fascism in Germany (1933) cannot be attributed to the policies of Gustav Stresemann who died in 1929. Stresemann was one of the few able leaders to emerge during the Weimar Republic; he did much to restore German prestige and establish stability in Central Europe. The (A) failure of the Weimar Republic to address the crisis caused by the Depression, the (B) effective organization of the Nazi Party, the (C) charisma of Adolph Hitler, and (D) lingering humiliation of defeat in the First World War were factors which contributed to the rise of fascism in Germany.

47. **(B)** The sketch is of the spinning jenny which was invented by James Hargreaves.

48. **(C)** In *A Study of History* a religious based philosophy of history was advanced by (C) Arnold Toynbee. William McNeill (B) wrote *The Rise of the West*; Oswald Spengler (A) wrote *The Decline of the West;* T. S. Eliot (D) and Christopher Dawson (E) were influenced significantly by religion and religious values.

49. **(C)** In order "To overcome nothingness. ... individuals must define life for themselves and celebrate it fully, instinctively, heroically." This statement reflected the philosophy of (C) Fredrich Nietzsche. Ernst Cassier was a German philosopher who wrote *The Myth of the State*; he defended rationalism and interpreted Nazism as the triumph of "mythical thinking." (B) Jacques Maritain was a French philospher who advanced Neo-Thomism is works such as *Man and the State.* Paul Tillich (D) and Karl Barth (E) developed Protestant-based philosophies.

50. **(E)** In 1968 Czechoslovakia's "Prague Spring' — an attempt to develop "socialism with a human face" was led by (E) Alexander Dubcek. Havel (A) is a dissident Czech playwrite who later became President of Czechoslovakia. (B) Marshall Tito was the post-war leader of Yugoslavia; (C) Erick Honecker was the leader of East Germany during the 1970s and 1980s; and Lech Walesa (D) is the Polish labor and political reformer.

51. **(D)** In 1834 German states (excluding Austria) agreed to eliminate tariffs between the states through a customs union known as the (D) *Zollverein.* The *Furstenstaat* (A) was a term which indicated the "state of the prices," the decentralized German political condition established by the Peace of Westphalia in 1648. The Confederation of the Rhine (B) was organized by Napoleon as a means of administering German states and maintaining the decentralized German political situation. The Frankfurt Assembly (C) emerged in 1848 as part of the revolutionary movement; it was interested in a unified Germany. The Hanseatic League (E) was a medieval organization of German and other North Sea and Baltic governments.

52. **(B)** In January, 1848 — only weeks prior to the outbreak of the February revolution in Paris — Alexis de Tocqueville addressed (B) the Chamber of Deputies with the remarks quoted in the question. In this statement de Tocqueville addressed the concerns of French liberalism during 1848 — the need to open the political system to the people and the urgency of the economic crisis caused by a maldistribution of wealth. De Tocqueville did not (A) address the United States Senate in 1838, (C) the court of Charles X in 1830, or (D) the new leaders of the Third French Republic in 1871.

53. **(A)** In *English Constitution* (1867) an argument was advanced which contended that the British Cabinet system of government was superior to the American constitutional system; this book was written by (A) Walter Bagehot. Robert Southey (B) (1774–1843) was an historian who wrote biographies of Nelson and Wesley. Thomas Carlyle (C) (1795–1881) wrote a wide range of historical works including *The French Revolution, Oliver Cromwell's Letters and Speeches*, and *History of Frederick the Great.* John Henry Newman (D) (1801–1890) was a prominent Catholic leader and author of several books including *Apologia pro Vita Sua* and *The Idea of a University.* John Ruskin (E) (1819–1900) was a critic of art and architecture.

54. **(D)** Giordano Bruno (D) (1548–1600) was a late Renaissance reformer who maintained that "the Hermetic philosophy, with its mystical approach to God and nature held the key to true wisdom." Descartes (A), who argued for the necessity of God, looked for an order in the cosmos which could be understood by mathematics. Montaigne (B) was a Baroque philosopher and essayist. Francis Bacon (C) asserted that the empirical method was the only approach to understanding nature. Sir Isaac Newton published *Principia* in 1687 and advanced a new intellectual synthesis which is the basis of scientism.

55. **(C)** The maps indicate changes in the western border of Russia between (C) 1914 an 1921. These changes were associated with developments and decisions which were caused by the First World War, the Russian Revolution, and the rise of nationalism in eastern Europe — the creation of Poland and other new nation states.

56. **(C)** Britain established direct authority over India after the suppression of the (C) Sepoy Mutiny of 1857. This mutiny, which was caused directly by a violation with Islamic practices, had its roots in the manner in which the East India Company had administered the colony. The (A) Opium Wars (1840s) involved Britain in a series of minor conflicts with Asian princes over the distribution of opium. The Boxer Rebellion (1899–1900) was an anti-foreign outburst against foreign influence in China; it resulted in the siege of the foreign legations in Beijing and the use of a multi-national force to raise the siege. The assassination of Gandhi in January 1948 occurred after Britain had withdrawn from India; India had become a free nation and held dominion status in the British Commonwealth of Nations. The Warren Hastings Affair (E) was a scandal which involved British management of India during the late 18th century.

57. **(E)** By 1914 only (E) Ethiopia of the nations listed was independent of foreign rule. The Congo (A) was under Belgian authority; South Africa (B) and Nigeria (C) were part of the British Empire; and (D) Angola was administered by Portugal.

58. **(C)** The British policy of "Splendid Isolationism" was terminated with the (C) Anglo-Japanese Alliance of 1902; it specified that each nation would adopt a position of benevolent neutrality in the event that the other was attacked by another state. This agreement which was maintained through the First World War preceded the (A) Anglo-French Entente (1904), the (B) Anglo-Russian Entente (1907), and the (D) Second Moroccan Crisis (1911). The Boer War (D) preceded the Anglo-Japanese accord.

59. **(A)** The Versailles Treaty resulted in the formation of several new nations including (A) Yugoslavia and Hungary; Yugoslavia was a new kingdom which was based on an expanding Serbia; Hungary came from the Austro-Hungarian Empire which was dissolved. (B) and (C) are incorrect because while Poland was a new state in 1919, both Italy and Greece had existed previously.

(D) and (E) are incorrect because Germany and Italy both existed earlier; Austria was a new nation which emerged from the Austro-Hungarian Empire.

60. **(A)** Article 231 of the Versailles Treaty (A) is known as the "War Guilt" clause and established Germany's responsibility for the war; the case for reparations was based on the assignment and the acceptance of guilt. While (B) the establishment of Poland, (C) the denounciation of secret diplomacy, and (D) the establishment of the League of Nations were provided for in other clauses of the treaty, the Versailles agreement did not (E) result in the decentralization of Germany.

61. **(E)** After 1945 the policies of the Soviet Union resulted in (A) the continuing development of Soviet military power, (B) a slow demobilization from a war economy, (C) consistency in the exercise of power by the Communist Party, and (D) a general improvement in the standard of living. The Soviet Union did NOT (E) enjoy extensive influence in the United Nations during the years immediately following the Second World War; the American influence at the United Nations was sustained through the 1960s when the Soviets did gain considerable influence in the international assembly, especially among the new developing nations of the Third World.

62. **(E)** The pessimism which permeated the works of intellectuals between the First and Second World Wars was evident in the works of (A) T. S. Eliot ("The Waste Land," 1922), (B) William Butler Yeats ("The Second Coming," 1919), (C) Johan Huizinga (*In the Shadow of Tomorrow*, 1936), and (D) Carl Gustav Jung (*Modern Man in Search of a Soul*, 1933). The correct response is (E) Herbert Spencer, the social Darwinist and advocate of progress of the 19th century.

63. **(B)** Cavour's most significant non-Italian ally in bringing about a centralized Italy was (B) Napoleon III, Emperor of the French. Napoleon III was influenced by Cavour's remarks at the Paris meeting which closed the Crimean War and in 1858 and 1859 became an ally of Piedmont; consequently, Piedmont seized Lombardy from Austria. Bismarck (A) assisted Italy in gaining Venetia in 1866 but Cavour was dead by that time. Neither the British Prime Minister Lord Palmerston (C), Queen Victoria (E), nor the Austrian Emperor Franz Joseph (D) provided substantive support to Cavour or to the cause of Italian unification.

64. **(B)** Syndicalism was a manifestation of anarchism which was founded by (B) Georges Sorel, a French radical. Syndicalism, which was based on control of trade unions and dissident political groups, gained some success in France, Spain and Italy. (A) Prince Peter Kropotkin and (C) Michael Bakunin were Russian anarchists who espoused a comprehensive anarchist philosophy and strategy. Sidney Webb (D) was a founder of the Fabian Society, a revisionist, and a member of the London Municipal government during the 20th century. (E) Mazzini advanced a liberal nationalism which influenced pre-1848 groups — Young Italy, Young Germany, and the Pan-Slavic movements.

65. **(E)** Among the achievements (some of which were short-lived) of the Jacobins were (A) the abolishment of slavery, (B) giving the franchise to all adult males, (C) adaption of the metric system, and (D) decreeing the law of the maximum which fixed prices on essentials and raised wages. The Jacobins did not succeed in the (E) distribution of all land among the peasants.

66. **(C)** The British working class demonstrated unity during the (C) General Strike of 1926. This labor action was initiated as a dispute in the coal industry and it quickly became a demonstration of the dissatisfaction of the laboring class. Such working class unity was not discernible in (A) demonstrations by anarchists prior to the First World War, (B) during the movement towards female suffrage, the (D) post-World War I recession, or even during the devastating (E) depression which occurred after the Napoleonic Wars.

67. **(B)** During the late 1930s efforts to perpetuate the Third French Republic were centered in the Popular Front which was under the leadership of (B) Léon Blum. Pierre Laval (A) and Philippe Pétain (C) did not have confidence in the republic and were moving to the right. Marc Bloch (E) was an historian who contributed to the establishment of the *Annales* school. Marcel Deat (D) was a French "Neo-Socialist" — a fascist.

68. **(C)** In 1938 the Austrian Republic was incorporated formally into the Third Reich through the (C) *Anschluss*. This action realized the hopes of the advocates of the *Grossdeutsch* plan for a greater Germany. The (A) Nuremburg Laws were the racial laws passed by Hitler regime during the mid-1930s. While German troops occupied Austria, there was no (B) military conquest. The Munich accord took place in September, 1938 and involved the future of Czechoslovakia. The (E) occupation of the Rhineland occurred earlier; it was Hitler's first violation of the Versailles Treaty.

69. **(D)** Karl Marx believed in (A) the importance of the role of the Communist Party in leading the revolution and educating the people, (B) the dialectic view of history, (C) materialism as the driving force of history, and (E) that private property was a primary cause of economic, social, and political distress. Marx did NOT believe in (D) the importance of gaining power through legal means; indeed, to gain power in such a manner would corrupt the new government because it did not abolish all vestiges of the old regime — a comprehensive and total revolution was needed.

70. **(C)** The definitive "Whig" interpretation of British history was advanced in the 19th century by (C) Thomas Babington Macaulay. Macaulay argued that the rise of Parliament and the corresponding decrease of monarchial power was the central, continuing, and positive theme of British political history. David Hume (A) *Constitutional History of England* and Edward Gibbon (B) *Decline and Fall of the Roman Empire* were English historians of the 18th century. (E) Jeremy Bentham established English Utilitarianism and (D) John Stuart Mill *On*

Civil Government and *On Liberty*, while identified as a Utilitarian, was a multifaceted political philosopher and reformer of the 19th century.

71. **(A)** The map indicates the thesis advanced by H. Mackinder in 1904 that (A) the continental part of Eurasia forms the world's heartland and constitutes a potential threat for sea powers. Mackinder and other geopoliticians influenced many policy makers during this period; later, during the 1930s, Mackinder will abandon this thesis because of technology and economic trends. (D) A consequence of Mackinder's thesis may have been that sea powers must dominate land powers through containment; such a conclusion would have been supported by (C) the American strategist Alfred Mahan who wrote *The Influence of Sea Power Upon History*. Obviously, Mackinder did not contend that (B) only a combined Anglo-American-Russian alliance could prevent German world domination or that (E) the Southern Hemisphere is as significant as the Northern Hemisphere.

72. **(B)** German isolation was evident at the (B) Algerciras Conference in 1906. At this Spanish conference, which was called to resolve the First Moroccan Crisis, Germany found itself opposed by France, Russia, and Great Britain as well as by a number of lesser powers; only Austria-Hungary supported the German position. The (A) Portsmouth Conference resolved the Russo-Japanese war; the (C) Berlin Convention (1884–85) established principles for the colonization of Africa and settled the issue of the Congo; the (D) Congress of Berlin (1878) terminated the Russo-Turkish War of 1877–78; and the (E) World Peace Conference(s) were non-confrontational meetings prior to the First World War.

73. **(C)** The map indicates the partition of the Ottoman Empire after the First World War. The further emergence of new nations from colonies and the independence of Israel in 1948 render (A), (B), and (D) incorrect. The Congress of Berlin (E) occurred in 1878 and did not result in any substantive changes in the boundaries of the Near East except for Britain obtaining the island of Cyprus.

74. **(B)** *The Marriage of Figaro, Don Giovanni*, and *The Magic Flute* were operas by (B) Wolfgang Amadeus Mozart. Franz Joseph Haydn (A), Johann Sebastian Bach (C), and George Frederick Handel (D) were major 18th century composers; Henry Purcell (E) was the great English Baroque composer of the 17th century.

75. **(B)** The drawing, *Neue Typen: Der Rassemensch* by Karl Arnold (July 1924) was a critical commentary on (B) the anti-Semites who supported Hitler and the emerging Nazi Party. Obviously, (A), (C), (D), and (E) are incorrect responses.

76. **(E)** While William Gladstone initiated (A) the Education Act of 1870, the (B) Ballot Act of 1872, the (C) Civil Service Reform of 1870, and (D) the Irish Land Act of 1870, he was not responsible for (E) the Reform Bill of 1867. That measure was enacted under the leadership of Gladstone's Conservative rival, Benjamin Disraeli.

77. **(E)** The notion that "civilization was not the product of an artificial, international elite ... but of some genuine culture of the common people, the *Volk*" was advanced by (E) Johann von Herder in *Ideas for a Philosophy of Human History.* Herder influenced Fichte, Hegel (B), and other German nationalists and intellectuals. William Wordsworth's (D) *Lyrical Ballads* did not advance such a direct political and national theme; the conservative (A) Chateaubriand emphasized the role of Divine intervention and the human response to religion in *The Genius of Christianity.* Such sentiments are not reflected in Verdi's *Don Carlo.*

78. **(C)** Enclosures were required (C) to permit scientific farming. Other devices were available to (A) reinforce the concept of private property, (B) eliminate continuing boundary disputes, and (D) assist in accurate property tax collections. (E) Permission for newly rich to acquire property was not a consideration.

79. **(B)** Latvia, Lithuania, and Estonia were the three Baltic provinces that broke away from the Soviet Union in 1991. Ukraine broke away from the Soviet Union about the same time as Latvia, Lithuania, and Estonia, but it is not a Baltic state (A). Poland, Czechoslovakia, and Hungary (C) were never part of the Soviet Union. As of 1996, Chechnya was fighting a war to gain independence from Russia. Georgia broke away from the Soviet Union about the same time as other states, but it is not a Baltic state (D). Serbia, Bosnia, and Croatia (E) were formed with the break-up of Yugoslavia, not the Soviet Union.

80. **(A)** The leader of Poland's Solidarity movement was Lech Walesa, who would go on to be elected Poland's president. Jaruzelski (B) was Poland's last Communist leader; Yeltsin (C) became the Russian president in 1991, and Kadar (E) was the Hungarian Premier between 1956 and 1958 and again between 1961 and 1965. Pope John Paul II (D) is the current head of the Roman Catholic Church.

Sample Answer to Document-Based Question

Between the passage of the Reform Bill of 1867 and the death of Benjamin Disraeli, Disraeli and William Gladstone were the leaders of the Conservative and Liberal parties respectively. They were classic rivals who attacked one another on every possible occasion and who appeared to prosper as a result of the antagonism. During the early 1870s Gladstone initiated a series of reforms which included the Education Act of 1870, the Ballot Act of 1872, and reforms of the military and municipal governments. Disraeli characteristically denounced the reforms as absurd or for not going far enough in resolving a particular problem. In 1872 Disraeli in his famous "Crystal Palace Speech" introduced the concept of the New Imperialism; Disraeli advocated British imperialism and Gladstone emerged as the staunch anti-imperialist.

Punch magazine capitalized on this personal rivalry during the 1870s in scores of cartoons. In its cartoons *Punch* sought to attack those people and institutions which took themselves too seriously; no topic or issue — except the person of Queen Victoria — was immune from ridicule. In "Hoity-Toity!!!" the lingering issue of the Alabama claims crisis with the United States was held up for scorn. In the second document, the letter from Victoria to Gladstone, the Queen advances the argument of her class in her opposition to extending the vote to women and in providing women with an equal opportunity in the professions. In "The Conservative Programme" *Punch* attacked Disraeli for being evasive in describing the domestic policies and programs of the Conservative Party. This criticism was targeted at Disraeli because of the absence of specific Conservative programs; this was especially noticeable when compared to the apparantly endless list of Gladstone's proposals which was ridiculed in "The Colossus of Words" in 1879. Disraeli daring was the subject of "On the Dizzy Brink" when the Conservative leader appeared politically vulnerable in 1878. Within a few months Disraeli nullified his critics when he emerged as the victor at the Congress of Berlin (June-July, 1878) which settled the Russo-Turkish War of 1877–78. The final cartoon "A Bad Example" was critical of both Disraeli and Gladstone for their personal attacks on one another. In spite of their antagonism, Britain was well served by its two most distinguished prime ministers of the second half of the 19th century.

Sample Answers to Essay Questions

1. The concept of "revolution" and "the revolutionary tradition" cannot be defined uniformly within the context of modern European history except in the most general terms. The notion of "revolution" was transformed from the political, Glorious Revolution of 1688 in Great Britain, to the mostly, but not exclusive, politicial French Revolution of 1789, and to the political, economic, and social Russian Revoltion of 1917. The revolutionary tradition in modern

European history has been extended or broadened since the 17th century to include most aspects of human activity; however, even in the revolutions in Eastern Europe in 1989, the orientation was basically political. The notion that political change will serve to correct problems — many of which are economic and social rather than political in nature — has been sustained for 300 years.

The Glorious Revolution of 1688 resulted in the installation of William and Mary and, in April 1689, the enactment of the Bill of Rights. This measure established the primacy of Parliament in controlling the revenues of the government; the monarch was still influencial but was clearly limited in power. This "revolution" was basically non-violent; it was a revolution which was conducted by consensus within the aristocracy. The Glorious Revolution was political — constitutional — in scope and intent; economic and social issues were considered only in the light of the political settlement. The French Revolution of 1789 (which includes the subsequent developments of the next decade) was much more complex. To most of the participants the revolution was political; but there were some (the Jacobins) who were intent upon extending the revolution to all aspects of French and European culture. Redistribution of land, eliminating the power of the church, and the adoption of a new calendar were some of the more radical aspects of this movement. The concept of "Citizen" which emerged was based on democratic and egalitarian notions which were not evident during the Glorious Revolution; during the hundred years between the these two revolutions, two major developments occurred which affected the scope and definition of the revolution: namely, the Enlightenment and the Industrial Revolution. During the following century (the 19th century) the Industrial Revolution continued to develop and democracy emerged in western Europe. The Communist Russian Revolution of 1917, while still fundamentally political in process was cultural in intent; it attempted to remedy the abuses which afflicted humanity by establishing a new order which was based on justice and equality through a state of classlessness. The Russian Revolution, after a turbulent civil war, commanded the support of the Russian people through the party for the next 70 years.

2. The Counter-Reformation or the Catholic Reformation was the reaction of the Roman Catholic Church to the Reformation. It was composed of several distinct developments which had varying impacts on European history; however, the general impact of the Counter-Reformation was negative because the Church identified with the old order and adopted a defensive ideological position which solidified doctrines and the precepts of the Church. This was anti-intellectual and resulted in the Church being identified as a remnant of the medieval order rather than as an active power in the shaping of modern European society.

The Roman Church was slow to react to the Lutheran Reformation because of the fear that the conciliar movement within the church would reassert itself. The conciliar movement, which maintained that ultimate power in the church resided in the bishops meeting in council — not the Papacy, was evident during the 15th century at the Councils of Constance, Florence, and Basel. During the 1520s and 1530s, other than decrees of excommunication and the like, the response of the church was limited to the establishment of new religious orders.

Among these orders were the Theatines, the Oratorians, and the Jesuits; they were intended to create a new, more positive image of the Catholic clergy and generally stressed the pastoral needs of the people. The Jesuits were founded by Ignatius Loyola, a retired Spanish miltary officer; this order would serve the interests of the Papacy and regain the people and territory which had been lost because of Protestantism. Reinforced by pledges of loyalty and by a deteriorating position, Rome convened the Council of Trent in 1545; this Council would meet in three sessions from 1545 to 1564 and constitute the most important component of the Counter-Reformation. Traditional church doctrines on the sacraments and an elite ordained priesthood were reaffirmed; the Council of Trent formalized the split within Christendom — doctrinal determinations rendered any compromise with Protestant leaders impossible. During 1558–59 the Papacy decreed that it established the *Index of Prohibited Books* (1559–1967) which listed works which were contrary to church teaching; Catholics, under pain of sin, were directed to refrain from these books. During the late 16th century and for the next two centuries, the Roman church relied on the Inquisition to enforce its doctrines and to defend the Church's interests.

The anti-intellectual and reactionary characteristics of the Counter-Reformation continued to dominate Catholic thought and policy until the 20th century. Pope Pius IX denounced most aspects of modern culture in *Syllabus of Errors* in 1864; at the First Vatican Council (1870–71) the doctrine of papal infallibility was adopted. During the first decade of the 20th century Pope Pius X denounced "modernism." Within the context of European history, the Counter-Reformation was equated frequently with authoritarianism and the medieval order.

3. The characteristics of fascism include (1) the corporate view of society, (2) nationalism, (3) romanticism, (4) totalitarianism, (5) militarism, and (6) racism. The ideology of fascism developed during the late 19th and early 20th centuries as a reaction to the perceived failure of democratic governments to address the mounting social and economic problems of the period. Fascism was opposed to individualism and to the Marxist view of history and Communism. In many ways, fascism was ideologically connected to German romantic idealism and other conservative philosophies of the early 19th century.

In the fascist model the state's (nation, *volk*) interests have primacy over individual desires and rights; there are no individual rights which are "sacred" that must be respected. The state is an organic corporate entity which must be sustained by the labors of the people; individuals are assets as long as they are making a positive contribution to the historic progress of the state. National pride and patriotism are more than demonstrations of civic responsibility, they are essential virtues in this ideology which is based on romanticism. Rather than emphasizing the value of reason and rational processes, fascists were more interested in a society based on faith, intuition, and deep conviction. The fascist implementation of these sentiments rendered their approach fundamentally anti-intellectual; they maintained deep-rooted suspicion of all intellectuals. Another characteristic of fascism was totalitarianism; the fascist revolution would by necessity be comprehensive and affect every aspect of human activity. For the sake of the whole, each individual must comply with the regulations which were established and implemented by an authoritarian elite which had been provided with legitimate and unquestionably valid historic insight and knowledge. Since the state was an organism, it had to demonstrate regularly through military action that it was growing and strong; a nation that was preoccupied with peace-at-any-cost was decadent and invited attack by younger, more virile nations. Fascism was also characterised by racism. While many historians, such as Hannah Arendt (*The Origins of Totalitarianism*) have argued successfully that racism was interwoven with the totalitarianism of the modern age, it is extremely important to note that racism was an integral component of fascism. Fascist societies in Germany, Italy, Spain, Japan, Brazil, Argentina, and elsewhere advanced racist positions which were based on hatred and which were anti-intellectual and untenable; nonetheless the ideology of racism was one of the most visible and pernicious characteristics of fascism.

Fascism was an assault on freedom, on the value of the individual, on rationality, and on democracy. It was an anti-modernist force which was reactionary and which was rendered more dangerous than the dictatorships of the past because of technology and the manipulation of mass culture.

4. During the 19th century several political and economic alternatives to capitalism were developed in response to the negative consequences of the Industrial Revolution, the lingering sentiments associated with the French Revolution, and the absence of participatory governments.

The Utopian Socialists emerged early in the 19th century under the leadership of Charles Fourier, Robert Owen, and Claude Saint-Simon. They were interested in alleviating the distress associated with the industrial revolution and unregulated urban life in general. They maintained that employers who provided for the economic and social well-being of their employees would be rewarded through increased productivity. Further, community-held businesses would prosper because all participants had a stake in the success of the effort. The Utopian Socialists had a rather naive understanding of history and the forces which were current during their own time — they underestimated the depth of human greed and they failed to appreciate that many Europeans did not entertain any sense of "economic" responsibility to their employees. Several attempts at establishing utopian communities were undertaken by Robert Owen; several achieved initial success and survived for several decades.

The tactics and the philosophy of the utopian socialists were discredited by the failure of the revolutions of 1848. Marxism, or scientific socialism, emerged as a "realistic" alternative to utopian socialism. In many works such as *The Communist Manifesto, Critique of Political Economy*, and *Das Capital* Karl Marx argued that one must understand that history was in fact a struggle — the dialectic — in which "the people" had been suppressed; material culture or economics was the driving force of Marx's dialectic. The future progress of humanity demanded that a violent revolution occur in which all aspects of *bourgeoisie* culture would be destroyed — churches, governmental institutions, capitalism, etc. After a period known as "the dictatorship of the proletariat" (led by the Communist Party), the people would overthrow the party and enter into a "classless society." The Marxist philosophy attracted the support of many intellectuals and reformers during the second half of the 19th century. While most accepted his conceptual arguments, many Marxists departed from Marx on the necessity of revolution. These "evolutionists", or revisionists, contended that revolution was not required when the people could elect a marxist government to implement the revolutionary reforms. Among the revisionists were Sidney and Beatrice Webb, Keir Hardie, and George Bernard Shaw (who were all involved in the formation of the Fabian Society in Great Britain), Edward Berstein who led the Social Democratic Party (SDP) in Germany, and the French socialist Jean Jaures. The revisionist approach was denounced by Lenin in *What is to be Done?* (1902).

Anarchism was a political philosophy which was originated by the French radical Pierre Proudhon who wrote *What Is Property*? immediately prior to the revolutions of 1848. Proudhon and the Russian anarchists Michael Bakunin and Prince Peter Kropotkin envisioned a simple society along Jacobin lines; individuals would live in harmony and equality after the artifical structures (religion, nations, etc.) had been eliminated. The people would rise in general revolution after their oppressors. Unlike the Marxists who were literate-oriented, the anarchists placed their hopes with the common uneducated people. Anarchism attracted considerable support, especially in Southern Europe.

5. The process of the democratization of British politics during the 19th and 20th centuries was as much a reaction to changing economic and social conditions as it was to a commitment to the "concept of democracy." The Industrial Revolution led to expanding the urban population and increased literacy; these factors in turn led to a political awareness which had to be directed through political reforms.

In 1832, under the leadership of Earl Grey, the first of several measures was enacted which began the process of extending the franchise. The Reform Bill of 1832 added freemen who paid 10 shillings rent per year to the electoral rolls; further, it redistributed Parliamentary seats by eliminating so-called "rotten boroughs" which were over-represented, and by creating new seats for the industrial communities of the Midlands. In the 1860s both the Conservatives and the Liberals recognized the need to extend the process further; in 1867, under Prime Minister Benjamin Disraeli, the Reform Bill of 1867 gave the vote to almost all males living in urban centers; it also redistributed Parliamentary seats. The Reform Bills of 1884–85, during Gladstone's ministry, resulted in giving the vote to all men and in redistribution of seats based on population shifts. The movement for female suffrage emerged during the second half of the 19th century and was led by dedicated women such as Sylvia and Christabel Pankhurst. Their efforts and those of many others did not result in female suffrage until after the First World War; in the initial measure women over the age of 30 were given the same voting rights as men who were 21 years old, in 1928, the Flapper Act resulted in reducing the age for women to 21.

Another important measure in the process of democratization was the Parliament Act of 1911. This measure removed the effective veto power of the House of Lords and recognized that the nation was represented in the House of Commons. As a result of the Parliament Act the House of Commons had complete control over all revenue measures; the House of Lords could delay the enactment of non-revenue measures for three weeks. If a non-revenue measure was significant, it could be redrafted as a revenue statue and enacted immediately.

The process of extending democracy in Great Britain was relatively peaceful. While demonstrations and an occasional riot occurred, there was no general insurrection as was the case on the continent during the same period.

6. The unification movements in Germany and Italy paralleled one another during the period from 1850 to 1870. Both efforts were based on expanding an existing state; both involved domestic adjustments and international conflicts; and both movements capitalized upon national sentiments which had been expressed during the revolutions of 1848. The architect of German unification was the Prussian Otto von Bismarck; Italian unification was supported by Camillio Cavour, Napoleon III, Giuseppe Garibaldi, and King Victor Emmanuel II.

During the revolutions of 1848 many German statesmen and intellectuals had anticipated that Prussia would be the nucleus of a new Germany. While that goal was not realized at that time, Prussia emerged in the 1850s and 1860s as an aggressive state which was interested in consolidating its position in north central Europe. Under the leadership of William I and Bismarck Prussia introduced a constititutional government in 1850, domestic political and legal reforms during the 1850s, and expanded its army. During the early 1860s Prussia was allied with Austria in a brief war (1863) with Denmark over the provinces of Schleswig and Holstein; as a result of the Danish defeat the provinces came under the joint administration of the victors. In turn, this led to a situation which Bismarck exploited in his preparations for the showdown with Austria. With guarantees of Italian participation on a southern front and of French neutrality, Bismarck fabricated a crisis to which the Austrians responded by declaring war. The German Civil War of 1866 resulted in the humiliating defeat of Austria. Bismarck did not exact any territory from Austria; it was evident that Prussia was the preeminent power in Central Europe. In 1867 Bismarck established the North German Confederation as a means of transforming Prussia influence into a German State. During the summer 1870 a diplomatic crisis developed between France and Prussia over the "Ems Despatch." Arguing that William I had been insulted by French diplomats in discussions relating to the Spanish succession, Bismarck created a crisis which led to a French declaration of war. The Franco-Prussian War of 1870–71 resulted in the defeat of France, the surrender of Napoleon III, the end of the Second French Empire, Prussian occupation of much of France, and, in January 1871, the establishment of the German Empire.

In 1848 Italian unification was supported by King Charles Albert of Sardinia-Piedmont. After initial successes, his forces were defeated by the Austrians. In Rome Mazzini's ill-fated Roman Republic was overthrown by French troops and an increasingly conservative Pope Piux IX was restored to power.

During the 1850s Camillio Cavour, who served as Prime Minister to Victor Emmanuel II, emerged as the leader of an expanded Sardinian state, which it was anticipated would result in a unified Italy. Cavour attracted the support of European liberals through a range of social, constitutional, and economic reforms; Sardinia was a participant with Britain and France in the Crimean War against Russia. In 1856 at the Paris Peace Conference, Cavour spoke on the need to establish an Italy which was governed by Italians — a direct attack on the continuing Austrian control of Lombardy and Venetia. His remarks were received sympathetically by Napoleon III, the French Emperor who had been raised in Italy. In 1858 Cavour and Napoleon III signed the secret Plombières Agreement which pledged French support in driving the Austrians from the two provinces if the Austrians declared war. Cavour construed a crisis and the Austrians obliged by declaring war (1859). As a result of this brief war, Sardinia obtained Lombardy but Austria retained Venetia. Cavour died shortly thereafter. In 1860 Garibaldi and an army of 1,000 men landed in Sicily and within three months seized control of the Kingdom of the Two Sicilies. This new acquisition was incorporated into a Sardinian-dominated Italian Confederation. In 1866 the Italians acquired Venetia in return for their participation in the German Civil War. Italian unification was realized in the fall of 1870 when Italian forces, capitalizing on the withdrawal of the French garrison (Franco-Prussian War), seized Rome — the Patrimony of St. Peter.

THE ADVANCED PLACEMENT EXAMINATION IN

European History

TEST 3

THE ADVANCED PLACEMENT EXAMINATION IN

European History

TEST 3

1. Ⓐ Ⓑ Ⓒ Ⓓ Ⓔ
2. Ⓐ Ⓑ Ⓒ Ⓓ Ⓔ
3. Ⓐ Ⓑ Ⓒ Ⓓ Ⓔ
4. Ⓐ Ⓑ Ⓒ Ⓓ Ⓔ
5. Ⓐ Ⓑ Ⓒ Ⓓ Ⓔ
6. Ⓐ Ⓑ Ⓒ Ⓓ Ⓔ
7. Ⓐ Ⓑ Ⓒ Ⓓ Ⓔ
8. Ⓐ Ⓑ Ⓒ Ⓓ Ⓔ
9. Ⓐ Ⓑ Ⓒ Ⓓ Ⓔ
10. Ⓐ Ⓑ Ⓒ Ⓓ Ⓔ
11. Ⓐ Ⓑ Ⓒ Ⓓ Ⓔ
12. Ⓐ Ⓑ Ⓒ Ⓓ Ⓔ
13. Ⓐ Ⓑ Ⓒ Ⓓ Ⓔ
14. Ⓐ Ⓑ Ⓒ Ⓓ Ⓔ
15. Ⓐ Ⓑ Ⓒ Ⓓ Ⓔ
16. Ⓐ Ⓑ Ⓒ Ⓓ Ⓔ
17. Ⓐ Ⓑ Ⓒ Ⓓ Ⓔ
18. Ⓐ Ⓑ Ⓒ Ⓓ Ⓔ
19. Ⓐ Ⓑ Ⓒ Ⓓ Ⓔ
20. Ⓐ Ⓑ Ⓒ Ⓓ Ⓔ
21. Ⓐ Ⓑ Ⓒ Ⓓ Ⓔ
22. Ⓐ Ⓑ Ⓒ Ⓓ Ⓔ
23. Ⓐ Ⓑ Ⓒ Ⓓ Ⓔ
24. Ⓐ Ⓑ Ⓒ Ⓓ Ⓔ
25. Ⓐ Ⓑ Ⓒ Ⓓ Ⓔ
26. Ⓐ Ⓑ Ⓒ Ⓓ Ⓔ
27. Ⓐ Ⓑ Ⓒ Ⓓ Ⓔ
28. Ⓐ Ⓑ Ⓒ Ⓓ Ⓔ
29. Ⓐ Ⓑ Ⓒ Ⓓ Ⓔ
30. Ⓐ Ⓑ Ⓒ Ⓓ Ⓔ
31. Ⓐ Ⓑ Ⓒ Ⓓ Ⓔ
32. Ⓐ Ⓑ Ⓒ Ⓓ Ⓔ
33. Ⓐ Ⓑ Ⓒ Ⓓ Ⓔ
34. Ⓐ Ⓑ Ⓒ Ⓓ Ⓔ
35. Ⓐ Ⓑ Ⓒ Ⓓ Ⓔ
36. Ⓐ Ⓑ Ⓒ Ⓓ Ⓔ
37. Ⓐ Ⓑ Ⓒ Ⓓ Ⓔ
38. Ⓐ Ⓑ Ⓒ Ⓓ Ⓔ
39. Ⓐ Ⓑ Ⓒ Ⓓ Ⓔ
40. Ⓐ Ⓑ Ⓒ Ⓓ Ⓔ
41. Ⓐ Ⓑ Ⓒ Ⓓ Ⓔ
42. Ⓐ Ⓑ Ⓒ Ⓓ Ⓔ
43. Ⓐ Ⓑ Ⓒ Ⓓ Ⓔ
44. Ⓐ Ⓑ Ⓒ Ⓓ Ⓔ
45. Ⓐ Ⓑ Ⓒ Ⓓ Ⓔ
46. Ⓐ Ⓑ Ⓒ Ⓓ Ⓔ
47. Ⓐ Ⓑ Ⓒ Ⓓ Ⓔ
48. Ⓐ Ⓑ Ⓒ Ⓓ Ⓔ
49. Ⓐ Ⓑ Ⓒ Ⓓ Ⓔ
50. Ⓐ Ⓑ Ⓒ Ⓓ Ⓔ
51. Ⓐ Ⓑ Ⓒ Ⓓ Ⓔ
52. Ⓐ Ⓑ Ⓒ Ⓓ Ⓔ
53. Ⓐ Ⓑ Ⓒ Ⓓ Ⓔ
54. Ⓐ Ⓑ Ⓒ Ⓓ Ⓔ
55. Ⓐ Ⓑ Ⓒ Ⓓ Ⓔ
56. Ⓐ Ⓑ Ⓒ Ⓓ Ⓔ
57. Ⓐ Ⓑ Ⓒ Ⓓ Ⓔ
58. Ⓐ Ⓑ Ⓒ Ⓓ Ⓔ
59. Ⓐ Ⓑ Ⓒ Ⓓ Ⓔ
60. Ⓐ Ⓑ Ⓒ Ⓓ Ⓔ
61. Ⓐ Ⓑ Ⓒ Ⓓ Ⓔ
62. Ⓐ Ⓑ Ⓒ Ⓓ Ⓔ
63. Ⓐ Ⓑ Ⓒ Ⓓ Ⓔ
64. Ⓐ Ⓑ Ⓒ Ⓓ Ⓔ
65. Ⓐ Ⓑ Ⓒ Ⓓ Ⓔ
66. Ⓐ Ⓑ Ⓒ Ⓓ Ⓔ
67. Ⓐ Ⓑ Ⓒ Ⓓ Ⓔ
68. Ⓐ Ⓑ Ⓒ Ⓓ Ⓔ
69. Ⓐ Ⓑ Ⓒ Ⓓ Ⓔ
70. Ⓐ Ⓑ Ⓒ Ⓓ Ⓔ
71. Ⓐ Ⓑ Ⓒ Ⓓ Ⓔ
72. Ⓐ Ⓑ Ⓒ Ⓓ Ⓔ
73. Ⓐ Ⓑ Ⓒ Ⓓ Ⓔ
74. Ⓐ Ⓑ Ⓒ Ⓓ Ⓔ
75. Ⓐ Ⓑ Ⓒ Ⓓ Ⓔ
76. Ⓐ Ⓑ Ⓒ Ⓓ Ⓔ
77. Ⓐ Ⓑ Ⓒ Ⓓ Ⓔ
78. Ⓐ Ⓑ Ⓒ Ⓓ Ⓔ
79. Ⓐ Ⓑ Ⓒ Ⓓ Ⓔ
80. Ⓐ Ⓑ Ⓒ Ⓓ Ⓔ

European History

TEST 3 – Section I

TIME: 55 Minutes
80 Questions

DIRECTIONS: Each of the questions or incomplete statements below is followed by five suggested answers or completions. Select the one that is best in each case.

1. "...there is no place for industry...no arts; no letters; no society; and which is the worst of all, continual fear, and danger of violent death; and the life of man, solitary, poor, nasty, brutish, and short." This quotation from Thomas Hobbes' *Leviathan* (1651) described the concept known as

   (A) natural rights.
   (B) state of nature.
   (C) social contract.
   (D) reason of state (raison d'état).
   (E) nationalism.

2. Which one of the following would most likely oppose *laissez-faire* policies in 19th century Europe?

   (A) Factory owner
   (B) Liberal
   (C) Free trader
   (D) Socialist
   (E) Middle-class businessman

3. The painting above by François Dubois, an eyewitness, describes the massacre on St. Bartholomew's Day of 1572 of

(A) Dutch nobility.
(B) German peasants.
(C) French Calvinists.
(D) Spanish Catholics.
(E) English merchants.

4. Which one of the following was a characteristic of the peace settlements at the end of World War I?

(A) Division of Germany into two parts
(B) Expansion of the territory of the Ottoman Empire
(C) The emergence of the Soviet Union as a significant part of the European diplomatic system
(D) The long-term stationing of American troops in Europe
(E) Germany was required to pay reparations

5. All of the following are characteristics of Renaissance humanism EXCEPT

(A) sanctity of the Latin texts of scriptures.
(B) belief that ancient Latin and Greek writers were inferior to later authors.

(C) rejection of Christian principles.

(D) it functioned as a primary cause of the Reformation.

(E) accomplished scholarship in ancient languages.

6. The October Manifesto of Tsar Nicholas II promised all of the following EXCEPT

(A) a Duma.

(B) political reforms.

(C) a Russian parliament.

(D) a fair, democratic voting system.

(E) full civil liberties.

7. Ferdinand and Isabella's policies of Spanish nationalism led to the expulsion, from Spain, of large numbers of Spanish

(A) Protestants.

(B) Catholics.

(C) Jews.

(D) Calvinists.

(E) monks.

8. During the Thirty Years' War, the Lutheran movement was saved from extinction by the military intervention of which foreign monarch?

(A) French king, Philip the Fair

(B) English king, Henry VIII

(C) Swedish king, Gustavus Adolphus

(D) Austrian Emperor, Charles V

(E) Spanish king, Philip II

9. All of the following were significant economic trends in Germany during the 1920s EXCEPT

(A) large amounts of money leaving the country to pay reparations.

(B) periods of high inflation.

(C) a very stable currency (the mark).

(D) periods of high unemployment.

(E) the German government placed large amounts of paper money in circulation.

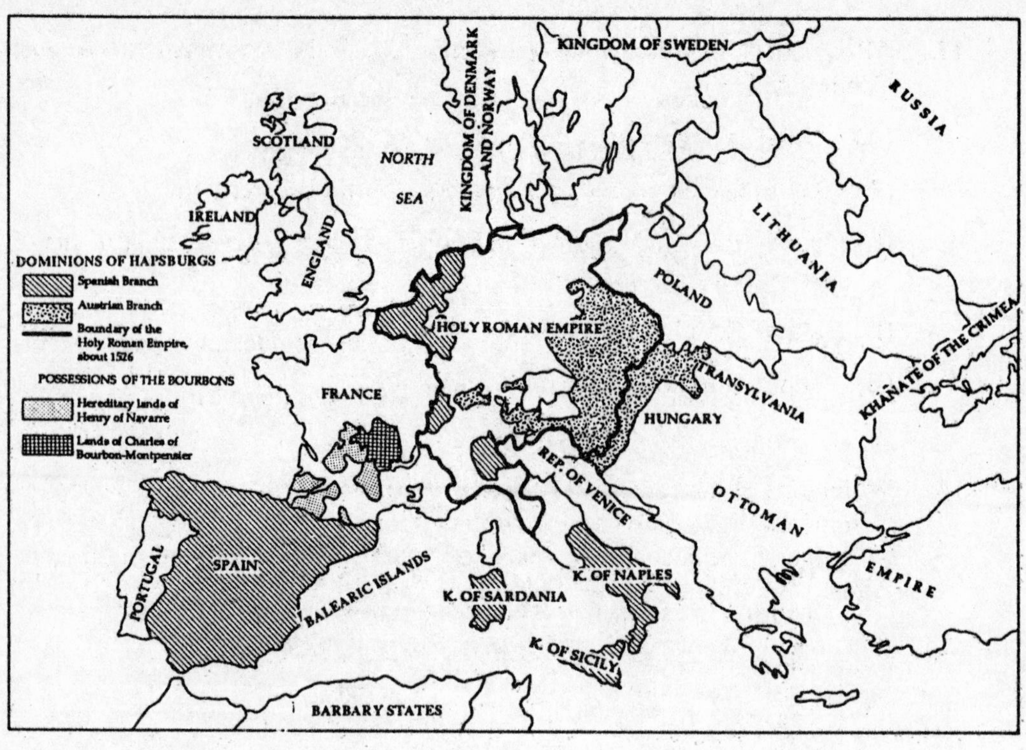

10. The map above depicts Europe around

(A) 1800. (D) 1950.

(B) 1500. (E) 1900.

(C) 1700.

11. Which European nation failed to establish an African colony when its expeditionary force was overwhelmingly defeated by a native force at Adowa, Ethiopia in 1896?

(A) Italy. (D) Britain.

(B) Belgium. (E) Austria

(C) Portugal.

12. "Sturm und Drang" was a significant period in the career of

(A) Rousseau. (D) Stendahl.

(B) Goethe. (E) Kant.

(C) Mill.

13. All of the following were characteristics of the Positivism of August Comte EXCEPT

    (A) belief in a three-stage view of history.

    (B) belief that all knowledge must be scientifically verified.

    (C) achievement of Progress and Order through a government of major scientists and philosophers.

    (D) a new Religion of Science.

    (E) admiration for science and technology.

14. Which one of the following best characterizes the relationship between the Commercial Revolution and the Italian Renaissance?

    (A) The Commercial Revolution caused Europeans to concentrate on their own continent, to the exclusion of the rest of the world.

    (B) The Commercial Revolution was a result of the Italian Renaissance.

    (C) The new merchant class of the Commercial Revolution was more interested in the secular world and less interested in religion.

    (D) There is no connection.

    (E) The Commercial Revolution enriched Italian farmers.

15. "Imperialism emerged as a development and direct continuation of the fundamental properties of capitalism....imperialism is the monopoly stage of capitalism."

    The writer quoted above would most likely accept which of the following statements as true?

    (A) Imperialism was caused by European advances in science and technology.

    (B) A desire for national prestige drove Europeans into a race to gain colonies.

    (C) Imperialism was a natural and predictable result of the growth of capitalism.

    (D) A country with an advanced capitalistic system might become the "colony" of another country.

    (E) Imperialism fed the egos of the smaller, less powerful nations of Europe.

16. "Intendants" were

(A) secret letters of arrest.

(B) courts where secret trials were held.

(C) censors employed by Louis XIV.

(D) secret emissaries of the pope.

(E) regional government agents in France.

17. The early 20th century pacifist and winner of the Nobel Peace Prize for her book *Lay Down Your Arms* (1889) was

(A) Tirpitz.

(B) Luxemberg.

(C) von Suttner.

(D) von Bethmann-Hollweg.

(E) Cosima Wagner.

18. When the heir to the Austrian throne was assassinated in August, 1914, and the Russian government responded to the ensuing crisis by mobilizing its troops, Germany followed its obligations under the Triple Alliance and declared war on Russia. Which of the following countries did Germany invade first?

(A) Russia

(B) Austria-Hungary

(C) France

(D) Britain

(E) Italy

19. According to the graph shown on the following page, which one of the following statements is true?

(A) Industrial production had a greater impact than agricultural production in Britain in 1800.

(B) Agricultural production had a greater impact than industrial production in Germany in 1900.

(C) Agriculture became less significant in Britain and Germany by 1900.

(D) Britain produced fewer industrial products than Germany.

(E) During the period shown, industrial production was an insignificant part of the British economy.

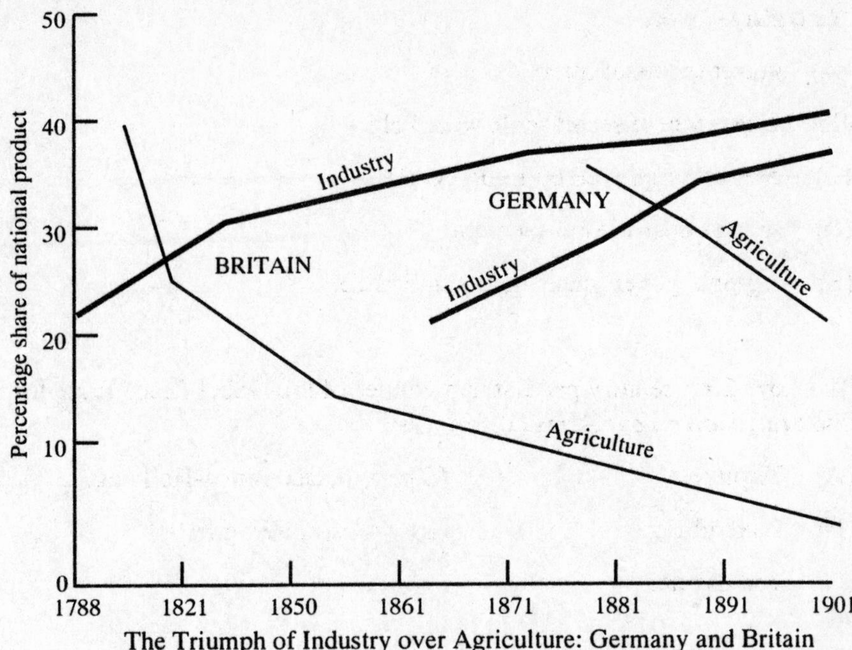

The Triumph of Industry over Agriculture: Germany and Britain

20. During the Reformation, Anabaptism drew its membership mostly from the ranks of the

(A) nobility.
(B) middle class.
(C) peasants.
(D) businessmen.
(E) Army officers.

21. All of the following were part of the Counter-Reformation EXCEPT

(A) the Index.
(B) the Augsburg Confession.
(C) the Inquisition.
(D) the Council of Trent.
(E) the Society of Jesus.

22. This drawing below by Isaac Newton illustrates his experiments with

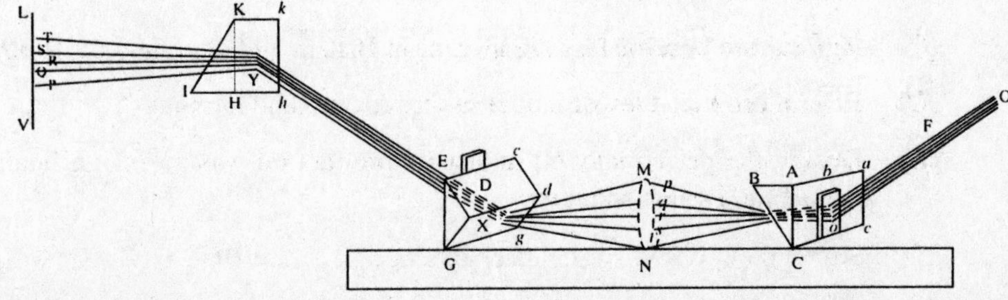

(A) fluids. (D) gravity.

(B) energy. (E) gases.

(C) light.

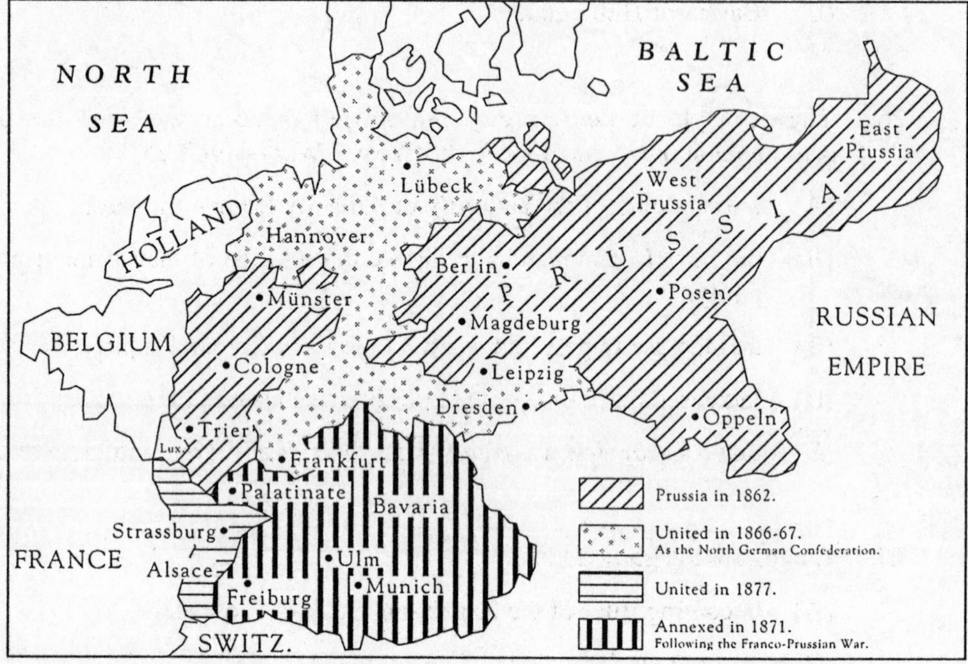

23. According to the map above, Prussia

(A) held territory in both eastern and western Germany before 1870.

(B) assumed control of Alsace-Lorraine after 1866.

(C) annexed Bavaria to Prussia in 1866.

(D) was able to unite all of Germany in 1866.

(E) occupied more territory than the Austrian Empire.

24. Which of the following forms of government would most likely win the approval of a *politique*?

(A) Secular government in which religion plays no role

(B) Theocracy

(C) Parliamentary government

(D) Huguenot government

(E) Government based on the ideas of Pope Innocent III

25. The first Swiss leader of the movement which became Calvinism was

(A) Calvin.
(B) Zwingli.
(C) Balthasar Hubmeier.
(D) Menno Simons.
(E) Cranmer.

26. The principle of *cuius regio, eius religio*—incorporated into the peace settlement at the close of the Thirty Years' War—signified

(A) a weakening of the authority of the Holy Roman Emperor.
(B) the power of monarchs to dictate the religion of their state or principality.
(C) an increase in papal authority in the Holy Roman Empire.
(D) increased authority for the nobility in religious controversies.
(E) that religion was a private matter to be decided by each individual.

27. Lorenzo Valla gained fame for

(A) becoming ruler of the Renaissance city of Florence.
(B) proving the Donation of Constantine a fraud.
(C) his inventions.
(D) challenging the authority of Voltaire.
(E) helping to unify Italy.

28. The "Commenda" was a commercial contract involving a merchant and

(A) a serf.
(B) bankers.
(C) an artisan.
(D) merchant-adventurers.
(E) his local monarch.

29. The "Weber thesis" attempted to explain the connections between the rise of Calvinism and the rise of

(A) absolute monarchies.
(B) capitalism.
(C) the nation-state.
(D) Anglicanism.
(E) Lutheranism.

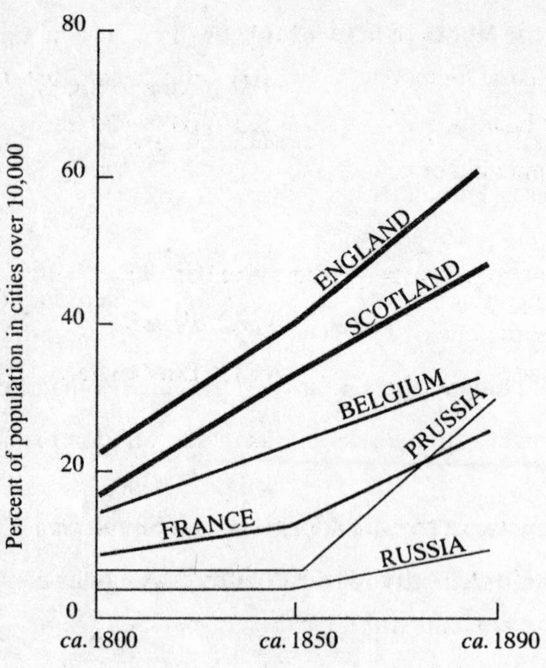

The Urbanization of Europe

30. According to the graph above, which was the most urbanized part of Europe in the 19th century?

(A) Eastern Europe
(B) Prussia
(C) France
(D) Central Europe
(E) The British Isles

31. The Fronde were directed primarily against

(A) the power of French landlords.
(B) the authority of the absolute monarchy.
(C) the influence of the nobility.
(D) the wealth of the church.
(E) the poverty of the peasants.

32. "Anxiety, or the idea of anxiety, permeates modern thought in all its aspects. You find it almost everywhere you look: in Freudian psychology, in the philosophy of existentialism, in poetry and the novel, in the language of religion...and...of course, in contemporary political movements."

This passage is an example of writing in

(A) intellectual history.
(B) social history.
(C) economic history.
(D) diplomatic history.
(E) political history.

33. "The greatest good for the greatest number" was a belief of

(A) Marx.
(B) Bentham.
(C) Mill.
(D) Freud.
(E) DeMaistre.

34. All of the following are true about the Nazi-Soviet pact of 1939 EXCEPT

(A) it was also known as the Molotov-Ribbentrop Pact.
(B) it was a nonaggression pact.
(C) it was signed shortly before the beginning of World War II.
(D) it protected the sovereignty of Poland.
(E) it was an agreement between governments which were thought to be ideological enemies.

35. Prussia's acquisition of the Rhineland area of Germany at the Congress of Vienna proved to be a significant development because

(A) the Rhineland became a buffer zone between Germany and France.
(B) most German industry developed in the area.
(C) it proved to be a very fertile agricultural area.
(D) in military terms, it was the easiest part of Germany to defend.
(E) it was welcomed by France.

36. A long-term trend which was a basic cause of World War I was

(A) the decline of the Ottoman Empire.
(B) the rise of Poland.
(C) Italian interest in the Balkans.
(D) Russian refusal to become involved in the Balkans.
(E) a decline in nationalist sentiment in Europe.

37. The Wars of the Roses advanced the cause of absolutism in England by

(A) strengthening the English economy.

(B) weakening the older nobility.

(C) weakening the power of the church.

(D) increasing the number of nobility in the realm.

(E) stimulating English exploration of North America.

38. The English author of *Utopia* (1516) was

(A) More.

(B) Tyndale.

(C) Molière.

(D) Cromwell.

(E) Spenser.

39. Henry VIII of England was awarded the title of "Defender of the Faith" by the pope for his

(A) appointment of Thomas Cranmer as Archbishop of Canterbury.

(B) criticisms of Lutheranism.

(C) wars against Charles V.

(D) participation in the Crusades.

(E) financial support of the papacy.

40. Elizabeth I of England attempted to quiet religious controversies in her realm through a compromise creed of faith known as the

(A) Act of the Six Articles.

(B) Test Act.

(C) Thirty-Nine Articles.

(D) Toleration Decree.

(E) League of Augsburg.

41. Which of the following was most influential in the spread of Protestantism in 16th century Europe?

(A) The universities

(B) The Holy Roman Emperors

(C) The printing press

(D) Lectures

(E) Monarchical authority

42. Which one of the following *philosophes* opposed Voltaire's concept of Enlightened Despotism?

(A) Condorcet
(B) Montesquieu
(C) Diderot
(D) d'Holbach
(E) Helvetius

43. The first German attempt at democracy was known as the

(A) First German Republic.
(B) Second Empire.
(C) Third Reich.
(D) Weimar Republic.
(E) Bismarckian empire.

44. A group which reacted to the Industrial Revolution by smashing machinery was known as the

(A) Utopian Socialists.
(B) Levellers.
(C) Luddites.
(D) Chartists.
(E) Union of Welfare.

45. According to the map below, which of the following was not part of Napoleon's "Grand Empire"?

EXTENT OF NAPOLEONIC POWER, 1812

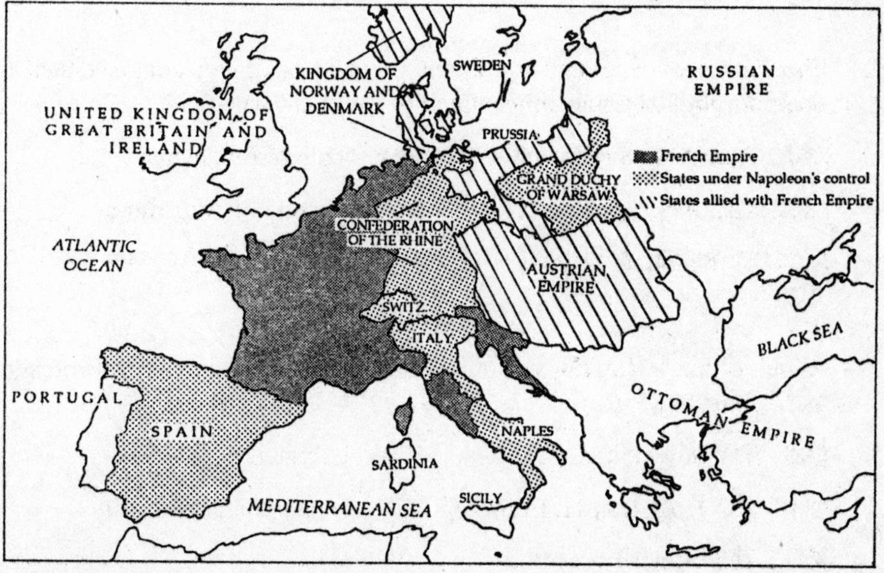

(A) Most of Germany
(B) Spain
(C) Austria
(D) The Netherlands
(E) France

46. The term "Utopian Socialism" was coined by

(A) Fourier.
(B) Marx.
(C) Guizot.
(D) Renan.
(E) Lenin.

47. The novel *Sybil* (1845), which surprised many readers by expressing sympathy for the working class in the 19th century, was written by

(A) George Sand.
(B) Disraeli.
(C) Wordsworth.
(D) Gladstone.
(E) Clemenceau.

48. The primary problem of France when Charles DeGaulle became president of the nation during the 1950s was

(A) to increase French participation in the North Atlantic Treaty Organization (NATO).
(B) to settle the Algerian problem.
(C) the recovery from the devastation of World War II.
(D) to end the occupation of France by German forces.
(E) the deficit budgets of the French government.

49. The "Humiliation of Olmuetz" was the result of an Austrian and Prussian dispute over

(A) Poland.
(B) territory.
(C) reparations.
(D) the Zollverein.
(E) the border between the two countries.

50. "Existence precedes essence" was coined in the 20th century by

(A) Nietzsche.
(B) Kierkegaard.
(C) Gasset.
(D) Benda.
(E) Sartre.

51. The Vienna Circle is generally associated with the movement known as

(A) Existentialism.
(B) Logical Positivism.
(C) Marxism-Leninism.
(D) Structuralism.
(E) Impressionism.

52. The "stream of consciousness" as a method of narrative fiction was developed by

(A) W. B. Yeats.
(B) Virginia Woolf.
(C) Henrik Ibsen.
(D) Samuel Beckett.
(E) Bertolt Brecht.

53. The "Sick Man of Europe," which British and French foreign policy sought to preserve in the 19th century, was

(A) the Russian Empire.
(B) Poland.
(C) Switzerland.
(D) the Ottoman Empire.
(E) the Austrian Empire.

54. Which of the following was partitioned and annexed by three powerful neighbors in the late 18th century?

(A) Italy
(B) Poland
(C) Finland
(D) Sweden
(E) Spain

55. Which one of the following was true about the European middle class in the 19th century?

(A) Its political influence decreased throughout the century

(B) It was most sizable in Russia

(C) It called for government aid to business

(D) It held great wealth in the form of land

(E) It espoused liberalism

56. The Defenestration of Prague was a cause of which war?

(A) War of the Spanish Succession

(B) Hundred Years' War

(C) War of Jenkins Ear

(D) Thirty Years' War

(E) War of Austrian Succession

57. "Paris is worth a Mass" was said by

(A) Henry VIII.

(B) Louis XVIII.

(C) Louis XIV.

(D) Henry IV.

(E) Louis Philippe.

58. Which of the following is a reasonable conclusion from the graph shown here?

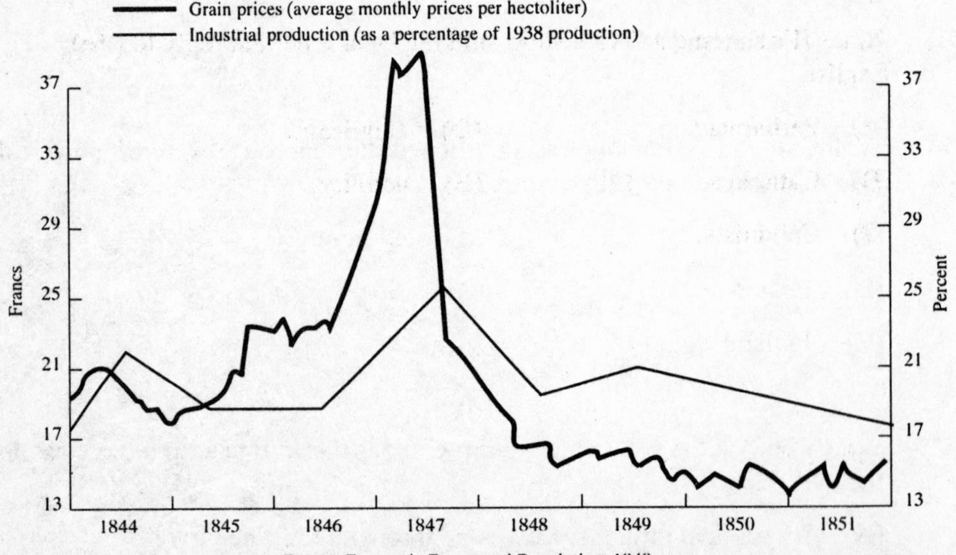

France: Economic Forces and Revolution, 1848

(A) There was no connection between grain prices and industrial production.

(B) High grain prices were a factor in the revolution of 1848 in France.

(C) Industrial production and grain prices sometimes declined in tandem.

(D) High industrial production caused grain prices to rise.

(E) Declining industrial production caused grain prices to fall.

59. "We Italians then owe to the Church of Rome and to her priests for our having become irreligious and bad; but we owe her still a greater debt... that the Church has kept and still keeps our country divided."
This passage expresses the opinion of

(A) Luther.
(B) Calvin.
(C) Pope Boniface VIII.
(D) Machiavelli.
(E) Dante Alighieri.

60. Hohenzollern authority in ruling Prussia depended on the cooperation and support of the

(A) bankers.
(B) Junkers.
(C) courts.
(D) constitution.
(E) intellectuals.

61. James II's statement "No bishop, no king" was a defiant reply to (the) English

(A) Parliament.
(B) Catholics.
(C) Calvinists.
(D) Anglicans.
(E) nobility.

62. This Soviet poster of 1930 was an attack on

    (A) militarism.

    (B) war.

    (C) religion.

    (D) capitalism.

    (E) pacifism.

63. The most powerful ruler of the time of the Reformation — who held the title of Holy Roman Emperor, King of Spain, and Emperor of Austria—was

    (A) Maria Theresa.

    (B) Charles V.

    (C) Philip the Fair.

    (D) Henry VIII.

    (E) William the Silent.

64. Which social group was the major beneficiary of the Corn Laws in early 19th century Britain?

    (A) Nobility

    (B) Middle class

    (C) Businessmen

    (D) Small farmers

    (E) Industrialists

65. Which novel satirized obsolete standards of feudalism and chivalry?

    (A) *Tom Jones*

    (B) *Candide*

    (C) *Don Quixote*

    (D) *Emile*

    (E) *War and Peace*

66. "Mother died today...or maybe yesterday. I can't be sure." These are the first words of a 20th century novel by

(A) Joyce.
(B) Grass.
(C) Camus.
(D) Sartre.
(E) Malraux.

67. Which of the following best characterizes the attitude of 19th century Russian Slavophils?

(A) All Slavs should be united under a single government.
(B) All western influences should be rejected.
(C) Westernization should not be allowed to destroy the distinctive aspects of Slavic culture.
(D) Russia should have no role in the leadership of the Slavic nations.
(E) Russia should become completely westernized.

68. During the first half of the 19th century, which of the following tended to hold down population growth in Ireland?

(A) Bloody Sunday
(B) The Peterloo Massacre
(C) The Potato Blight
(D) The Home Rule issue
(E) Industrialization

69. All of the following were characteristics of Russia when Peter the Great assumed the throne EXCEPT

(A) a weak nobility.
(B) a split in the Russian Orthodox church.
(C) lack of access to the Baltic and Black Seas.
(D) limited contact with the rest of Europe.
(E) an economy based on agriculture.

70. Which of the following best characterizes the Zimmerman telegram of World War I?

(A) It led to a German invasion of Belgium.
(B) It became a cause of the Franco-Prussian war of 1870.

(C) It suggested that Mexico help the German government.

(D) It was a German ultimatum to Poland.

(E) It was a major reason for Britain's entry into the war.

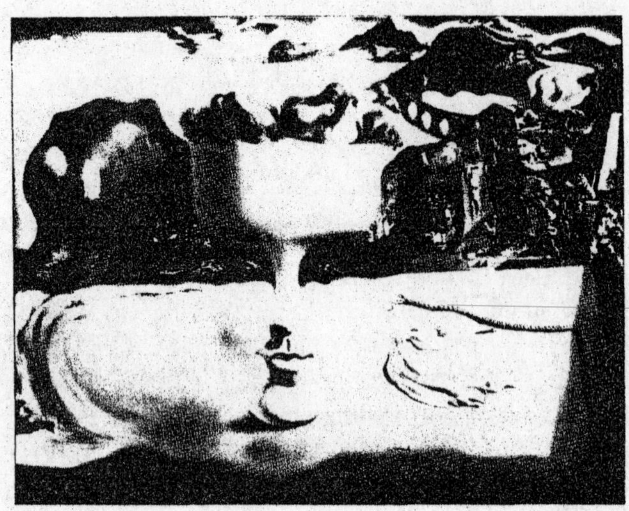

71. The painting above, by Salvador Dali, illustrates the 20th century style of painting known as

(A) Dadaism.
(B) the Fauvres.
(C) cubism.
(D) surrealism.
(E) impressionism.

72. The principle that "form follows function" was a basic tenet of the 20th century school of architecture known as

(A) the Oxford Movement.
(B) the Bauhaus school.
(C) the Bloomsbury circle.
(D) the Jacobins.
(E) neo-Romanticism.

73. All of the following are preconditions for the Industrial Revolution EXCEPT

(A) an adequate road system.

(B) a failing agricultural system.

(C) adequate raw materials.

(D) a spirit of entrepreneurship.

(E) a source of financing to build factories.

74. Which one of the following statements best characterizes the Babylonian Captivity?

(A) The Jewish people were forced to live in Babylon as slaves.

(B) The papacy was dominated by the French monarchy.

(C) Martin Luther was kidnapped by sympathetic noblemen.

(D) Galileo was forced to bow to church authority.

(E) Papal lands were annexed by the new government of a united Italy in 1870.

75. Keynesianism (the economic doctrines of the 20th century British economist John Maynard Keynes) teaches that during times of economic downturns governments should

(A) practice austerity.

(B) increase taxes.

(C) create budget deficits.

(D) institute wage and price controls.

(E) nationalize major industries.

76. The establishment of French absolutism was primarily the work of royal ministers such as Richelieu and

(A) Mazarin.

(B) Colbert.

(C) Walpole.

(D) Montesquieu.

(E) LaMettre.

77. The agreement that provided for increased European economic unity is known as the

(A) Treaty of Versailles.

(B) Maastricht Treaties.

(C) Geneva Accords.

(D) Potsdam Treaty.

(E) Treaty of Paris.

78. Which of the following best characterizes Burke's *Reflections on the Revolution in France*?

(A) It condemned the French Revolution as a source of radical ideas used in the American Revolution.

(B) It praised the French Revolution as a sincere attempt to spread liberty and promote equality.

(C) It condemned the violence and anarchy of the French Revolution.

(D) It praised the French Revolution and condemned the American Revolution.

(E) It condemned all revolutions.

79. A 19th century novel which asserted the superiority of science to traditional ways of thinking was

(A) *Les Misérables* by Hugo.

(B) *Crime and Punishment* by Dostoyevsky.

(C) *Degeneration* by Nordau.

(D) *Frankenstein* by Shelley.

(E) *Fathers and Sons* by Turgenev.

80. Which was the last advanced Western nation to grant women the right to vote, in 1989?

(A) Sweden

(B) France

(C) Spain

(D) Switzerland

(E) Ireland

European History

TEST 3 – Section II

TIME: Reading Period – 15 minutes
Writing Time for all three essays – 115 minutes

DIRECTIONS: Read over both the Document-Based Essay question in Part A and the choices in Part B during the Reading Period, and use the time to organize answers. All students must answer Part A (the Document-Based Essay Question); and choose TWO questions from Part B to answer.

PART A – DOCUMENT-BASED ESSAY

This question is designed to test your ability to work with historical documents. As you analyze each document, take into account the source and the point of view of the author. Write an essay on the following topic that integrates your analysis of the documents. You may refer to historical facts and developments not mentioned in the documents.

Analyze the nature and causes of the Great Fear in the French Revolution of 1789, and assess the validity of the following statement about the Great Fear.

"The Great Fear can be explained by the economic, social, and political circumstances prevailing in France in 1789...(it) gathered the peasants together; allowed them to achieve the full realization of their strength and reinforced the attack already launched against (feudalism)...it played its part in preparations for the (revolution) and on these grounds alone must count as one of the most important episodes in the history of the French nation."

—Georges Lefebvre, *The Great Fear of 1789*

Historical Background: The Great Fear began in the Spring of 1789, when peasants throughout the rural areas of France armed themselves in response to rumors of aristocratic plots and roving bands of brigands. Peasants mistakenly attacked other peasants; much of the violence was directed against local noblemen. The violence and anarchy of the Great Fear gained the attention of both royal ministers and the National Convention of the revolution. Both groups moved to release the peasants from their remaining obligations under feudalism.

Document 1
Background of the French Revolution

FRENCH POPULATION IN 1789
TOTAL: from 22,000,000 to 25,000,000

First Estate	Clergy	100,000 to 130,000
Second Estate	Nobility	400,000 or fewer
Third Estate	*Upper Bourgeoisie *Bourgeoisie Urban Proletariat	5,250,000, more or less*
	Peasantry	16,250,000 to 21,500,000

* All bourgeois did not live in cities and towns. Many–especially doctors, lawyers and *rentiers* (those living on income from investments)–lived in the country or in small villages. Total *urban* population was surely less than 4,000,000 and perhaps as low as 2,000,000.

Document 2

"The first cause is the small yield of this year's harvest which in some districts did not even produce the quantities of a normal year...Second, the rains and inundations of 1787, the hail and drought of 1788...Third, the usury...the closing of granaries by landed proprietors...Fourth, private sales from the granaries...Fifth, the lack of supplies at the market place..."

—Report to the Paris parliament on the increases in grain prices, December, 1788.

Document 3

"The backwardness of France is beyond credibility. From Strasburg hither, I have not been able see a newspaper...well dressed people are now talking of the news of two or three weeks past, and plainly by their discourses know nothing of what has been passing. The whole town of Besançon has not been able to afford me the *Journal de Paris*, nor of any other paper that gives certain of the transactions of the states; yet it is the capital of a province, large as half a dozen English counties, and containing 25,000 souls...No one paper has been established in Paris for circulation in the provinces..."

—Arthur Young, English tourist, July 17, 1789.

Document 4

"...information in France (is not so) diffusive as I imagined. Of the active citizens...nearly half, particularly in the country, can neither write nor read."

—William Taylor, English tourist, June, 1790.

Document 5

" ...(to the south of Romily) rumors said that brigands had appeared in the canton; they had been seen going into the woods. The tocsin was sounded and three thousand men gathered to hunt down these alleged brigands...but the brigands were only a herd of cows."

—From a report in the *Journal de Troyes*, a newspaper, July 28, 1789.

Document 6

(Jacques Turgot, one of the finance ministers of King Louis XVI, made a concerted attempt to institute administrative and economic reforms during his brief tenure. Some of the reforms abolished the last feudal obligations of the peasants, including the corvée, which required the peasants to provide free labor for public works or other tasks as directed by the nobility.)

"We have noted with pain that...works have been executed, for the most part, by means of the corvées required of our subjects...while they have been paid no wages for the time they are so employed...The weight of this obligation does not fall, nor can it ever fall, anywhere else than upon the poorest part of our subjects, upon those who have no property other than their hands and their industry, upon the peasants, the farmers. The landowners, almost all of whom are...exempt, contribute but very little."

—From a decree of Turgot abolishing the corvée, 1776.

Document 7

"The high price of corn has occasioned many insurrections in some of the provincial towns, and particularly at Rheims and Vendôme: at St. Quentin a barge laden with 2,000 sacks of the above-mentioned commodity belonging to the very rich individual of the place, who was accused in the neighboring villages of having made his fortune by entirely engrossing the article, was seized upon by the populace and the whole of the cargo was thrown into the river."

—Lord Dorset to Lord Carmarthen, British nobility, March 19, 1789.

Document 8

"In the early Spring of 1789...the Duc d'Orléans was very popular in Paris. The previous year he had sold many paintings from the fine collection in his palace, and it was generally believed that the eight millions raised by the sale had been devoted to relieving the suffering of the people during the hard winter which had just ended. In contrast, whether rightly or wrongly, there was no mention of any charitable gifts from the royal princes or from the king and queen...Nor did the king ever show himself. Hidden away at Versailles or hunting in the nearby forests, he suspected nothing, foresaw nothing, and believed nothing he was told."

—*Escape from Terror: the Journal of Madame de la Tour du Pin* (ed. and trans. Felice Harcourt, Folio Society, 1979),p. 79.

Document 9

"One hundred and fifty chateaux...have already burned. What should I say about the atrocities, the murders committed against the noblemen? A nobleman who was paralyzed, and left on a funeral pile...They burned the feet of another so that he would give up his title-deeds."

—Marquis de Ferrières, French nobleman, deputy of the Estates-General, Memoirs, July 1789.

Document 10

"The National Convention, after hearing the report of its committee on public safety, decreed that all persons who spread false news or cite terror in the provinces, arouse the citizens, or cause disturbances and trouble, shall be brought before the extraordinary tribunal and punished as counter-revolutionary...It was not necessary that there should be uprisings and disturbances; only news that might lead to these."

—Durand deMaillane, historian, from his *History of the National Convention* (1820).

(The National Convention subsequently abolished all feudal obligations.)

Cartoon of a French peasant supporting representatives of the nobility and clergy, while the peasant's grain is eaten by doves and rabbits which were reserved by law for the sport of the nobility.

PART B – ESSAY QUESTIONS

1. Assess and analyze the extent to which the English Civil War and Glorious Revolution of 1688 advanced the cause of constitutionalism in England in the 17th century.

2. Describe and assess the role of the British policy of "splendid isolation" in balance-of-power diplomacy in 19th century Europe.

3. Describe and compare the political beliefs of the 18th century French *philosophes* Voltaire and Montesquieu.

4. Describe and analyze the effects of the Industrial Revolution on European society in the 19th century.

5. Assess and analyze the extent to which the peace settlements in Europe at the end of World War I became causes of World War II.

6. Describe and compare the major doctrines of the three prominent groups of the Protestant Reformation—Lutheranism, Calvinism, and Anabaptism.

THE ADVANCED PLACEMENT EXAMINATION IN

European History

TEST 3 – ANSWERS

1.	(B)	21.	(B)	41.	(C)	61.	(C)
2.	(D)	22.	(C)	42.	(B)	62.	(C)
3.	(C)	23.	(A)	43.	(D)	63.	(B)
4.	(A)	24.	(A)	44.	(C)	64.	(A)
5.	(E)	25.	(B)	45.	(C)	65.	(C)
6.	(D)	26.	(B)	46.	(B)	66.	(C)
7.	(C)	27.	(B)	47.	(B)	67.	(C)
8.	(C)	28.	(D)	48.	(B)	68.	(C)
9.	(C)	29.	(B)	49.	(D)	69.	(A)
10.	(B)	30.	(E)	50.	(E)	70.	(C)
11.	(A)	31.	(B)	51.	(B)	71.	(D)
12.	(B)	32.	(A)	52.	(B)	72.	(B)
13.	(D)	33.	(B)	53.	(D)	73.	(B)
14.	(C)	34.	(D)	54.	(B)	74.	(B)
15.	(C)	35.	(B)	55.	(E)	75.	(C)
16.	(E)	36.	(A)	56.	(D)	76.	(A)
17.	(C)	37.	(B)	57.	(D)	77.	(B)
18.	(C)	38.	(A)	58.	(C)	78.	(C)
19.	(C)	39.	(B)	59.	(D)	79.	(E)
20.	(C)	40.	(C)	60.	(B)	80.	(D)

Detailed Explanations of Answers

TEST 3

1. **(B)** Although "quotation" questions may ask the name of the author or the book title, this question requests more than factual recall. It requires an ability to recognize the main idea of the passage—to read the quotation and understand its philosophic implications. Knowledge of the terminology of 17th century writers is also helpful. Hobbes' *Leviathan* described early human society (the "state of nature") as an anarchic "war of all against all." For self-protection, citizens agreed among themselves to form the first government, an agreement termed by Hobbes the "social contract." It is especially important to read the quotation carefully, since two of the answers (B) and (C) are from the *Leviathan*; you may be misled into choosing (C) because you have studied the *Leviathan* in a class and the "social contract" sounds familiar. If the correct answer is not apparent after a second reading of the quotation, it may at least be possible to eliminate the other two answers. The concept of natural rights, incorporated into the French Declaration of the Rights of Man and the Bill of Rights to the United States Constitution, was summarized by John Locke as the idea that human beings are born "free, equal, and independent." "Reason of state" was the justification used by French statesmen such as Cardinal Richelieu to defend measures to create a centralized absolute monarchy in France. Answer (E), nationalism, is not only incorrect but also irrelevant to this question.

2. **(D)** *Laissez-faire* (from the French *laissez-nous faire*, leave us alone), described the economic outlook of 19th century liberals, many of whom were businessmen or industrialists who sought an end to government regulation of business. Proponents of *laissez-faire* envisioned an era of free economic activity in Europe without tariff barriers ("free trade"). Thus factory owners, liberals, and free traders" were all supporters of *laissez-faire*. Not so 19th-century socialists, who saw *laissez-faire* as an obstacle to even minimal measures to help the working class, such as government safety inspections of factories. This question tests both your knowledge and your analytical skills. It requires that you draw inferences or conclusions from the information given. It also requires an understanding of terminology (liberals, free traders and middle-class businessmen), as well as an ability to analyze the implications of *laissez-faire* for groups such as factory owners and socialists. If you realize that at least two of the answers are virtually

the same (for example, liberals and free traders), these answers may be eliminated. Since only (A) and (D) are left as possible answers, the chances of a successful guess have increased to 50%. Because only .25 point is subtracted for incorrect answers, guessing is recommended when one, and especially two, of the answers may be eliminated.

3. **(C)** The St. Bartholomew's Day Massacre in Paris of French Calvinists, often termed "Huguenots", led to a civil war in France (the War of the Three Henries) and the first Bourbon monarch (Henry IV). When dealing with questions based on illustrations (paintings or drawings), it is important to look for explicit details or other information in the question and in the illustration itself, since it is usually not possible to arrive at a correct answer by eliminating answers. The clues in this case are in the question rather than in the painting. If the primary clue is not sufficient ("St. Bartholomew's Day"), there is a secondary clue in the obviously-French name of the painter. Do not be misled by the use of the term "French Calvinists" instead of the name "Huguenots", which is the term usually used by textbook writers; the use of the term "French Calvinists" is another detail testing your knowledge and understanding of European history.

4. **(A)** At first glance this question appears to test only the memorization of facts, but another look will show that it also requires understanding of the diplomatic situation in Europe around 1920. The correct answer may require some thought, since there was no political division of Germany into two governments, as happened at the end of World War II. The "division of Germany into two parts" refers to the "Polish Corridor", created by the peacemakers in order to give Poland an "outlet to the sea." The "Polish Corridor", a strip of fomerly-German land ceded to Poland in order to provide access to the port city of Danzig, isolated eastern Prussia from the remainder of Germany. It may be possible to arrive at the correct answer by analyzing the other four answers and eliminating them; each is untrue. The end of World War I brought the final collapse of the Ottoman Empire and its reduction to the borders of modern Turkey. The newly Communist government of Russia, which came to power in 1917, was ostracized by the other great powers when the war ended. Answer (D) may be tempting because the United States left large numbers of troops in Europe after World War II. This question refers to World War I, however. The United States withdrew from Europe both militarily and diplomatically after that war, preferring to return to "normalcy." Under the terms of the Treaty of Versailles, Germany was required to pay reparations.

5. **(E)** This question is partly knowledge-based, but it also requires an understanding of the principles of Christian Humanism and an ability to analyze what ideas they would disapprove (A) and (C) and approve (E). Renaissance Humanism, also known as Christian Humanism, combined studies of ancient languages with a zeal to make the Scriptures available in the local languages. Virtually all Christian Humanists translated portions of the Scriptures into European languages, using the Latin text which was the sole version available during the

Middle Ages. Very few Christian Humanists were connected with the Reformation; the most famous of them, Erasmus of Rotterdam, criticized laxness within the Catholic church but refused to join with the Protestant reformers.

6. **(D)** Although the tsar's manifesto succeeded in calming and ending the Revolution of 1905, the document's promises of reforms contained a loophole: no mention was made of election procedures for the promised Duma, or parliament. When Nicholas II called the Duma into session after the revolution of 1905, he instituted voting procedures which gave considerably heavier representation to the wealthy and to districts around Moscow, which were considered the most loyal to the government.

7. **(C)** While this question calls for fact retention, it also requires an ability to analyze the implications of their policies—unless the answer is apparent upon first reading. The first monarchs of a united Spain, Ferdinand and Isabella achieved that unity by gaining control of the remaining Muslim sections of southern Spain. In an effort to promote cultural unity and establish a national identity, they defined Spanish nationalism in terms of their understanding of orthodox Catholicism. Those not fitting their definition of orthodoxy were condemned as disloyal or subversive. Two particular groups, Jews and Muslims who had converted to Christianity but retained Muslim customs or dress, were forced into exile by Spanish authorities.

8. **(C)** The diversity of monarchs listed in the answers should indicate that guessing is a possiblity. Two were devout Catholics (D) and (E), while a third (A) predates the Reformation by almost 200 years. During the Thirty Years' War, when Catholic forces from southern Germany and Austria were close to pushing Lutheran forces into the Baltic sea, the Lutheran convert Gustavus Adolphus intervened in Germany, saving the Lutheran cause. Adolphus was himself killed during a key battle.

9. **(C)** Answers (B) and (C) are opposites; high inflation almost always affects the value of a country's currency. If you recognize this conflict, it will become apparent that one of these two answers is the correct answer. If necessary, it is worthwhile guessing, since your odds are 50% and only .25 point is deducted for an incorrect guess.

10. **(B)** On the map several areas of Europe are depicted with dark shading. These areas are the lands controlled by the Hapsburgs in the 16th century. Answer (C) is incorrect, since Spain was lost by the Hapsburgs in the 1600s. A further clue: the large size of the Ottoman Empire, covering the entire Balkan peninsula, precludes any answer after about 1870.

11. **(A)** The mention of Ethiopia may bring Italy to mind. If not, a possible guess is indicated if you are able to remember Mussolini's invasion of Ethiopia during the 1930s. The sole European nation to have its plans to establish an

African colony in the late 19th century blocked by a native African force, Italy for some time regarded the incident a national humiliation. The incident was one of several reasons the Italian dictator Mussolini gave for his successful military takeover of Ethiopia in 1935.

12. **(B)** Knowledge-based questions such as this are not usually susceptible to successful guessing, since the other answers cannot be eliminated unless you know as least two or three of them well. As a young man, the German poet Goethe anticipated elements of Romanticism, and his youthful writings, such as *The Sorrows of the Young Werther* (1774), exhibited some Romantic characteristics. This period is often termed his "Sturm und Drang" (storm and stress) period.

13. **(D)** Comte, an early 19th century writer, based his system of Positivism on the belief that history was entering a third, scientifically-oriented stage. In this new era, only statements that might be scientifically verified were to be considered knowledge. A committee of scientists and philosophers would govern, creating "Progress and Order." Religion would be considered outdated.

14. **(C)** Here two different developments (the Commercial Revolution and Italian Renaissance) are tied, and you are asked to explain the connection. The correct answer requires memory retention, understanding of terminology, and an ability to analyze the social and economic connections between the two developments. The Commercial Revolution describes the expansion of trade and the establishment of a broad system of joint-stock companies and banks in pre-Renaissance Italy. The new merchants of the Commercial Revolution held few ties to the earlier Middle Ages. They established new towns in Italy, such as Florence; they preferred "worldly" reading material on topics such as etiquette and politics; and for some time their new towns held no cathedrals or even smaller churches. In effect, the Commercial Revolution created a new, secular middle class which financed much of the artistic and literary work of the Italian Renaissance. The other answers are either incorrect or irrelevant.

15. **(C)** Although knowledge of terminology is a great help, in this question careful reading and analyzing of the implication of statements is essential. This quotation, from Vladimir Lenin, father of the Soviet Revolution of 1917, is part of his argument that capitalism held internal contradictions which would lead to its self-destruction; a major contradiction was the uncontrolled race for colonies. [Source: Lenin, *Imperialism: The Highest Stage of Capitalism* (New York: International Publishers, 1934)]

16. **(E)** In their work to strengthen the French absolute monarchs, royal ministers Cardinals Mazarin and Richelieu placed government agents, or intendants, in areas throughout France, where they acted as both the "king's ears" and as collectors of revenue. The move established a "royal presence" in major areas of the country. Answers (A) (*lettres de cachet*) and (B) were other steps taken to strengthen absolutism in France.

17. **(C)** The first woman to be awarded the Nobel peace Prize, Bertha von Suttner, an Austrian, gained wide attention for her book, which contributed to the founding of Peace Societies in Austria and Germany. Admiral Tirpitz represented the opposite pole; he masterminded Germany's plans, beginning in the 1890s, to create a German navy to rival the British navy. Rosa Luxemberg, a German Marxist, was killed during a failed revolutionary attempt in Germany in 1919. Theobald von Bethmann-Hollweg was the chancellor of Germany during the early stages of World War I. Cosima Wagner was the influential wife of composer Richard Wagner.

18. **(C)** This question deals with a complex situation at the start of the war. It requires analytical thinking, an understanding of a complex chain of events, and some knowledge of terminology (although the key term—"Schlieffen Plan"—does not appear in the question). Answer (A) may be eliminated, since such an obvious answer is unlikely to be the correct one on an advanced test. During frequent renewals of the Triple Alliance during the late 19th century, Germany was consistently pushed by Austria to make increasingly specific and secret promises of aid to Austria in the event of war. According to one German promise, a Russian mobilization was to lead to a German declaration of war. German military planners, however, were worried about a two-front war, to both the east (Russia) and west (France). A commission working under the German Count Alfred von Schlieffen produced the famous Schlieffen Plan, which required that Germany immediately invade the weaker country of the two in overwhelming numbers, with the goal of quickly defeating the weaker country. The writers of the Schlieffen Plan assumed the weaker nation was France.

19. **(C)** Of the first three answers, the only one that is a correct interpretation of the graph is (C). Answer (D) may or may not be true, but the graph (which indicates percentage shares of national product) does not provide the kind of information required to decide.

20. **(C)** This question is a thorough test of your knowledge of the Reformation, since it asks about the social basis of a Protestant group. Some answers may be eliminated, if you already know the social bases of Calvinism and Lutheranism. Each of the three major Protestant groups—Lutheran, Calvinist, and Anabaptist—relied in major ways on particular social elements. Although Lutheranism drew support from a broad social spectrum, Luther himself was forced to rely on sympathetic members of the nobility of the Holy Roman Empire in order to defend Lutheranism against the Holy Roman Emperor. Calvinism held special appeal for the new middle class, particularly business elements. Anabaptism drew most of its membership from the peasantry in western Germany and the Low Countries.

21. **(B)** If the "Augsburg Confession" is not recognized at first glance, attempt to eliminate the other answers. All of the other terms are part of the Counter-Reformation. Once again, terminology is important. Pope Paul III called

the Council of Trent into session in 1545 as a means of revitalizing and reforming parts of the church. The Council approved restrictions on the reading material of ordinary Catholics (the Index), commissions to investigate the spread of Protestantism (which is what the Inquisition was originally designed to do), and a new group to combat the spread of Protestant ideas (the Society of Jesus, or Jesuits). The Augsburg Confession was a compromise confession of faith written by Luther's friend Philip Melanchthon in a vain attempt to reconcile Protestant and Catholic princes in the Holy Roman Empire.

22. **(C)** In answering this question, study the drawing carefully. The prism-shaped objects are indeed prisms, splitting light entering from the right into a spectrum, recombining it, and splitting it again. Answer (D) may attract those who do not study the drawing, since Newton formulated laws of gravity and motion; carefully looking at the drawing should allow you to avoid this mistake.

23. **(A)** As shown by the variously marked areas of the map, Prussia was able to unite most of northern Germany in 1867 and combine it with Prussian land in both eastern and western Germany. Answers (B), (C), (D) and (E) will be ruled out by a careful study of the map.

24. **(A)** The *politiques*, who emerged from the French civil war of religion (the War of the Three Henries) as the leading political group in France, argued that government should be based purely on political principles. Religion in politics was seen an an obstacle to good government. Answers (B) (government by religious leaders), (D), and (E) might be eliminated, since they represent an opposite viewpoint. A *politique* might accept answer (D), but parliamentary government developed only later in France was irrelevant to the central concerns of the *politiques*.

25. **(B)** The wording of the question ("first Swiss leader") indicates that the easy answer—Calvin—must be incorrect. If the correct answer is unknown, it may be possible to eliminate answer (D), who was the best-known Anabaptist leader. Answer (C) is a lesser-known Anabaptist and (E) is the name of the Archbishop of Canterbury who helped Henry VIII create the Church of England. Before the French lawyer John Calvin assumed the leadership of the movement which would bear his name, Calvinism was known as "Zwinglism." It leader, Ulrich Zwingli, created a religious community in Switzerland before his death in a battle with Swiss Catholic armies.

26. **(B)** Questions such as this underline the importance of not only understanding terminlogy but also its implications. Short of knowing Latin, a reasonable approach to this question would be to identify which answers were not results of the Thirty Years' War. The Thirty Years' War ended with a compromise settlement which allowed local monarchs or princes in the Holy Roman Empire to dictate the religious denomination of their area. Dissenters among their subjects were expected to convert or to move to another territory.

27. **(B)** In this case, it is not enough to be able to name a Christian Humanist or explain the ideas of the Christian Humanist. This question tests the depth of your knowlege about Christian Humanism and the Renaissance. Even if you can identify Valla, the correct answer also requires that you know a particular term ("Donation of Constantine"). The Donation was a document which canon (church) lawyers used against Holy Roman emperors who challenged papal authority. Ostensibly a signed document in which the Roman emperor Constantine acknowledged papal superiority in both the religious and temporal (nonchurch) realms, the Donation was proved a fraud by Valla on the basis of Latin usage not appropriate for its date and for references to historical events which occurred at a later date.

28. **(D)** Italian economic success during the Renaissance was partly the result of ingenious devices which Italian merchants created to lessen the risks involved in long-distance travel and trade on the treacherous and frequently stormy Mediterranean sea. The commenda freed the merchant himself from dangerous journeys; it was a contract between the merchant who furnished goods for sale and a "merchant-adventurer" who agreed to take the goods to distant locations and return with the proceeds. The merchant-adventurer was generally paid one-third of the resulting profits. If the term "commenda" is unknown the clue "Italian Renaissance" may lead to the realization that answer (A) is unlikely. If you are unable to eliminate more answers, however, guessing may not prove profitable.

29. **(B)** Answering this question requires more than terminolgy, since it also asks for an understanding of the implications of the Weber thesis. Note, however, that some answers appear unlikely. Answers (A) and (C) were in development before the rise of Calvinism. Anglicanism should seem an unlikely choice, since it was restricted to only one part of Europe and was a result of the political and personal desires of King Henry VIII. Weber, an early 20th century German sociologist, theorized that a mutually helpful relationship existed between Calvinism and capitalism because they both were based on common virtues such as industriousness, thrift, etc. Answer (E) is simply incorrect.

30. **(E)** This question requires that you not only interpret the graph correctly but also use your knowledge of history and geography. The two most urbanized areas (England and Scotland) are major parts of the British Isles.

31. **(B)** Beginning with terminology ("identify the Fronde"), this question asks for an analysis of the purpose of these periodic revolts by the nobility of France. A phenomenon of largely the 16th and 17th centuries, they were regarded as threats to royal authority by monarchical ministers Mazarin and Richelieu, who suppressed them ruthlessly. Most ended when Louis XIV involved the most powerful members of the nobility in sterile and useless ceremonial lives at his palace of Versailles.

32. **(A)** Intellectual historians study the role of ideas and intellectuals in his-

tory. Do not let the quotation intimidate you; read the quotation and note what kind of subject matter is involved. For a careful reader, the answer is not difficult.

33. **(B)** Jeremy Bentham, who used this slogan to describe his philosophy of Utilitarianism, believed that one of the unsettled tasks remaining from the Enlightenment was the creation of a new, nonreligious system of morality that would be socially beneficial. His "moral calculus" sought to create a system of morality and laws that would reward the obedient with pleasure and criminals with painful emotions. Note that answer (A) is an attempt to mislead you; it seems a plausible answer, but is not the correct one. DeMaistre was an early 19th century French conservative writer and a Romantic.

34. **(D)** When the Soviet dictator Joseph Stalin changed policies and decided to seek accommodation with Hitler's Germany in 1939, a Nazi-Soviet nonaggression pact was negotiated by foreign ministers Ribbentrop and Molotov. It contained a secret provision providing for invasion of Poland by both countries and partition of Poland between them. This question demands a detailed knowledge of the pact, even if the answer is to be arrived at by elimination. If you are able to eliminate two or three of the answers, guessing is indicated.

35. **(B)** Relinquished by Austria because its distance from Vienna had made it difficult to defend against Napoleon Bonaparte, the Rhineland was awarded by the Congress of Vienna to Prussia, which had sought territorial rewards for its role in defeating the French emperor. After 1850, the Rhineland, with its supplies of coal and iron ore and its location along the Rhine river, became the major industrial area of Germany. This questions asks for the significance and implications of a geographical change. One possible way to arrive at the correct answer is to try to recall other incidents involving the Rhineland in German history. If you can remember that the French invaded the area in 1923 to take control of industrial centers there, you may realize that answer (B) must be correct.

36. **(A)** Although the war began as a result of the assassination of the heir to the Austrian throne and an ensuing dispute between Austria and Serbia, the background to these events was the steady decline of the Ottoman Empire, which at one time had controlled most of the Balkan peninsula. The resulting power vacuum allowed Austrian expansion into the Balkans, a development which created friction with new nations in the peninsula such as Serbia. Questions such as these test your breadth of knowledge and your analytical skills. Textbooks frequently designate the causes of the First World War as being trends such as secret alliances or yellow journalism; background events such as the decline of the Ottoman Empire are generally implicit.

37. **(B)** The English Wars of the Roses (named for the flowers appearing on rival family crests) of the late 15th century exhausted and impoverished much of the English nobility, allowing the family which emerged victorious in the wars,

the Tudors, to create a more powerful monarchy. The Tudors created new nobility by rewarding loyal followers with titles and land, thus making much of the nobility a service class dependent on the monarch's good will and generosity. In this question the emphasis is upon your understanding of terminology (absolutism) and the impact of historical events: what were the results of the Wars of the Roses? In approaching the question, consider which of the answers would have increased monarchical authority; all of the other answers are either irrelevant or would have weakened the monarchy.

38. **(A)** More's *Utopia* was not the first imaginary society of the future—Plato wrote about an equally famous utopia—but it gained much attenton with its portrait of an ideal society where wars were avoided by bribes or assassinations, where a council of families ruled instead of a monarch, and where religious disputes were avoided by requiring only three simple, uncontroversial religious beliefs of all citizens. If the answer is not known at first, consider that the question contains a clue: the author is English. Answer (C) (a French playwright) may be eliminated. Cromwell was a famous Puritan leader, and Tyndale an English Biblical scholar. Spenser was an English poet of the Elizabethan era.

39. **(B)** One of the ironies of history was that Henry, who would split the Church of England from the Roman Catholic church because of the pope's refusal to sanction a "divorce" from Henry's first wife, had earlier written a leaflet severely criticizing Luther's doctrines. The title, awarded by a grateful pope, is still used by British monarchs. A key phrase in the question is "awarded by the pope", suggesting that Henry had been of service to the Church. Charles V was a devout Catholic, and the pope would not have pleased by attacks on Charles' authority. Cranmer leaned toward Protestantism. The Crusades occurred several centuries before Henry's reign. Answer (E) is irrelevant and, after Henry's break with the papacy, untrue.

40. **(C)** By the time of Elizabeth's reign, the Church of England created by her father Henry VIII was torn between high church (leaning toward Catholic forms of worship) and low church (leaning toward Protestant forms) members as well as early Calvinists. Her ministers persuaded Parliament that religious peace might be restored by the Thirty-Nine Articles, a broad creed of faith. The Act of the Six Articles was a law requested by Elizabeth's father, Henry VIII, retaining six of the Roman Catholic sacraments in the new Church of England. Test Acts and Toleration decrees were royal and parliamentary documents dealing with the issue of religious qualifications for government office holders. The War of the League of Augsburg was one of the many wars of Louis XIV of France.

41. **(C)** Movable type printing came into use shortly before the Reformation, and it made possible the production of cheap leaflets, and Biblical translations on a large scale. The question asks you to make a judgment—the "most influential." Answer (B) may be eliminated quickly. The military power of Charles V, Holy Roman Emperor during the Reformation, was an obstacle to the spread of Protestantism.

42. **(B)** The *philosophes* were the leading writers of the French Enlightenment of the 1700s. Voltaire turned to the idea of Enlightened Despotism because he was personally and intellectually opposed to rule by the nobility in France. The alternative to rule by the nobility, he reasoned, was rule by a monarch educated in the advanced outlook of the *philosophes*. Montesquieu, one of the few *philosophes* from the noble class, argued in his *Spirit of Laws* (1748) that power needed to be limited in government. His solution, a separation of powers between different elements of the government, was in reality a scheme to increase the power of the noblility at the expense of the monarch. The same idea emerged, with a different meaning, in the United States Constitution.

43. **(D)** The Weimar Republic (1920-1933), created by three parties in the German Reichstag in the wake of World War I, was never fully accepted by most Germans who saw it as weak and an expedient measure to seek better peace terms from the American president Woodrow Wilson and his European allies. The Republic was ended by Adolf Hitler, who was legally appointed chancellor of the Republic in January, 1933. Hitler called his government the Third Reich ("Reich" meaning "empire"). Although basic fact retention may be of help here, the question also tests your understanding of the significance of the Weimar Republic. Answer (B) may be eliminated (a democracy is unlikely to be called an "empire"). Answers (C) and (E) may be eliminated as well, if you realize that "Reich" means "empire," or that the "Third Reich" was the title of Hitler's German government.

44. **(C)** The Luddites, a largely British phenomenon, were workers who believed that early machines threatened their livelihood. Mobs of Luddites invaded factories and newspaper offices, attempting to vandalize the offending machines. The Levellers appeared in 17th century England; most sought an egalitarian society. Utopian Socialists were early 19th century thinkers who attempted to devise plans to mitigate the social evils of the Industrial Revolution. Chartism, a 19th century movement, circulated mass petitions in attempt to convince the British parliament to expand the right to vote. The Union of Warfare, led by army officers, attempted to overthrow the Russian tsarist government in the Decembrist Revolt of 1825. Note that this question attempts to test how precise your knowledge is by listing two names that sound similar (Luddites and Levellers); Levellers may even sound like a more plausible name for people who destroyed machinery.

45. **(C)** Of the areas mentioned, only Austria is part of the dotted area ("allied with Napoleon"). A straightforward exercise in map reading, this question illustrates the importance of careful reading: the word "not" is the key part of the question.

46. **(B)** Karl Marx presented his own socialism as "scientific," based on a grasp of the scientific laws of economics and history. He ridiculed earlier socialists who had sought to help the working class by rolling back the Industrial

Revolution, generally through Utopian communities or through government sponsored workshops. Fourier was an example. Guizot was a leading French politician in the reign of Louis Philippe (1830-1848). Renan was a 19th century French linguist, historian, and writer on early Christianity. Although he was a Marxist, Lenin did not coin the term "Utopian Socialism."

47. **(B)** Disraeli's *Sybil* symbolized his social concerns and his desire to modernize the British Conservative party, which he led. Disraeli sought to move the party away from its exclusive reliance on the British nobility, broadening its platform to attract the middle and working classes. George Sand (pseudonym of Baroness Dudevant) was a novelist. William Wordsworth was a prominent British Romantic poet. Gladstone, leader of the opposition Liberal party, was Disraeli's great political rival in the years 1866-1881. Clemenceau was the leader of France during World War I.

48. **(B)** DeGaulle, a World War II hero, came to power as a result of a crisis caused by independence riots in Algeria, where a native population pushed for independence while a sizable French population clamored for continued ties with France. After granting Algerian independence, DeGaulle steered France on an independent course in Europe, insisting on the withdrawal of NATO bases from the country while continuing to cooperate with NATO.

49. **(D)** After the Congress of Vienna (1814-1815), which reduced the number of states and independent cities in Germany to 39, Prussia and Austria both aspired to unite the country under their leadership. In 1834, Prussia formed the Zollverein, a tariff-free union, with several of the German states. It aggressively moved to expand the Zollverein throughout Germany. Fearing a backdoor unification under Prussian leadership, Austria threatened war. During a meeting between diplomats of the two countries at Olmuetz, Prussia backed down. If these facts are not known, there is probably no way to arrive at a successful guess for a question such as this.

50. **(E)** Sartre, one of the most prominent of the French existentialists, coined the phrase which gave the movement its name. Benda and Gasset may be eliminated; the first was the author of a book (*The Betrayal of the Intellectuals*) which argued that intellectuals had lost objectivity by becoming too involved in world affairs; the latter was notable for his warnings during the 1920s and 1930s that democracy signified a levelling of culture to mass tastes. Nietzsche and Kierkegaard may be tempting answers, since both are forerunners of Existentialism, but they lived during the 19th, and not the 20th, century.

51. **(B)** The Vienna Circle, which denotes a loosely organized group of individuals in 1920s and 1930s Vienna, sought to redefine philosophy to make it more precise and more useful to the natural sciences. The result, often termed "logical positivism" or "linguistic analysis," was formulated by individuals such as Ludwig Wittgenstein and Rudolf Carnap. It had nothing to do with Marxism

or Existentialism. Structuralism, intially a part of lingustic studies, has spread into many fields in the 20th century; in language studies, it describes the belief that many languages share common structures because language is based on common traits in the human mind. Impressionism describes a school of artists in the second half of the 19th century.

52. **(B)** Although many 20th century writers experimented with the stream of consciousness method—in which a story is told from an uniterrupted flow of one individual's thoughts and conscious experiences—the writer who used the method almost exclusively was Virgina Woolf. Perceptive test takers may note that she is the only novelist in the group of names. Yeats was a poet. Beckett, Ibsen, and Brecht were playwrights.

53. **(D)** Fearing a general European war if the Ottoman Empire collapsed and neighboring European states bickered over the division of the spoils, both Britain and France sought to protect the Empire. The two nations were the instigators of the Crimean War in the 1850s, regarding an invasion of southern Russia as the only way to halt Russian pressure on the Ottoman Empire. If the answer is not clear on first reading, some may be eliminated (Poland, which did not exist as an independent nation in the 19th century, and Switzerland, which has not been part of the European diplomatic system). A clue is furnished by the mention of Britain and France, since the correct answer has to be an area where they shared a common interest or concern.

54. **(B)** While this question mentions the lesser-known countries of Finland and Sweden, which you may not be able to eliminate since their history is not general knowledge, at least some of the answers may be eliminated. Part of northern Italy was held in the 19th century by a powerful neighbor (the Austrian Empire), but it was not divided among its neighbors. If you realize that there was no partition of Spain, the correct answer may be arrived at by guesswork and elimination.

55. **(E)** A question which requires both fact retention and analysis, this question must contain four untrue statements and one true one. The impact of the middle class grew throughout the century (thus answer (A) is untrue), and its size was greatly expanded by the Industrial Revolution (thus answer (B) is untrue). Its *laissez-faire* ideology was the opposite of answer (C) and, as a product of the Industrial Revolution, it did not hold its wealth in the form of large amounts of land, as the old nobility did.

56. **(D)** This fact-based question contains a major clue (the Defenestration of Prague) which refers to an incident in which a group of young men were pushed out of a window at Prague in the early 17th century. If that term is not known, it may be possible to use knowledge of the other wars to eliminate them. The War of the Spanish Succession won for Louis XIV of France the right to put a branch of his Bourbon family on the throne of Spain. The Hundred Years' War ended

English control over much of France. The War of Jenkins Ear involved England and Spain in a war over trading rights in the Caribbean in the 1700s. In the War of the Austrian Succession, Frederick the Great challenged Maria Theresa's right to the Austrian throne. The location of the "Defenestration" (in central Europe) may make it possible to eliminate answers (A), (B), and (C).

57. **(D)** All but answer (A) are French monarchs; the correct answer is the furthest back in history and, possibly, the least known. A Huguenot, Henry of Navarre, agreed to help end France's major religious war (the War of the Three Henries in the 16th century) by becoming both a Catholic and monarch (Henry IV). (The quotation signifies his commitment to national interests). If at least two answers are eliminated (say, the English king Henry VIII and Louis Philippe, a 19th century French monarch), it is worthwhile guessing, since only .25 point is deducted for an incorrect answer.

58. **(C)** From the information given in the graph, the only statement that is reasonable is (C) (from late 1847 to 1851). The other statements may or may not be true, but the graph does not give sufficient information to test them.

59. **(D)** A careful reading and understanding of the passage is essential. Because this passage is critical of papal involvement in politics, it is possible to eliminate answer (C). Answer (A) may sound tempting but, once again, the "obvious" answer is incorrect; Luther was German, and not Italian. Of the remaining answers, it may be possible to arrive at answer (D) because you have previously read Machiavelli and know of his strong criticisms of papal involvement in Italian politics.

60. **(B)** This question relies on not only knowledge but also understanding of the social system in Prussia—the German state which united all of Germany in 1870. The Prussian Junkers, whose income came largely from huge landed estates in eastern Prussia, provided the major civil servants and army leadership for the Hohenzollerns (the Prussian ruling family); they were found in prominent German positions as late as World War II. Prussia had no constitution until 1850. Answer (C) might be partially correct, since the Junkers often were judge and jury on their own landed estates and filled significant Judicial posts, but it is not the best answer. In the 19th century, middle class German businessmen and bankers saw the Junkers as political rivals, since the Junkers pushed for tariff and tax policies which favored agriculture over industry.

61. **(C)** At the Hampton Court conference of 1610, James II issued this response to English Calvinists who wanted to eliminate the system of bishops (which they saw as obstacles to Calvinist-oriented reforms in the Church of England).

62. **(C)** Although a large cannon barrel looms large in the poster, below it is a cross and a man in clerical garments. Not only are answers (A) and (B) the

same—indicating that they should be eliminated—but the purpose of the cannon barrel appears to be to accuse religion of hypocrisy (of sanctioning war while preaching love and peace). Answer (D) is for those who do not study the poster carefully; it seems plausible but is not the correct answer.

63. **(B)** The Hapsburg family, with Austria as its base, also held the crown of Spain until that throne was gained by the French Bourbons in the War of the Spanish Succession (1701-1714). Their power and wealth allowed them to place many of their sons in the position of Holy Roman Emperor. Charles V's powerful base allowed him to block Henry VIII's "divorce" from his first wife, Catherine of Aragon, an aunt of Charles; it also made him the leader of military efforts to exterminate early Protestantism. Since Philip the Fair was a French king, Henry VIII was an English monarch and William the Silent was a leader in the Dutch struggle for independence from Spain during the 16th and early 17th centuries, they may be eliminated.

64. **(A)** This question draws on knowledge-based analytical skills, requiring both a knowledge of the Corn Laws and an ability to analyze their social impact. Passed by the British Parliament during the Napoleonic Wars, when goods were frequently in short supply, the Corn Laws applied to grain grown within Britain. In times when the supply of grain was low, the tariff on foreign grain increased dramatically. The laws guaranteed that the owners of farms and farm lands, mainly the nobility, would make a fortune during times of food shortage. Businessmen and industrialists objected to the laws because they restricted foreign trade, since other countries could not sell their agricultural products to Britain in order to buy British factory-made goods. Thus answers (B) through (E) are incorrect.

65. **(C)** Miguel Cervantes' *Don Quixote* is the story of a errant and aged Spanish knight whose semihumorous misadventuries are parodies of medleval standards of chivalry. Tom Jones is an 18th century novel describing the adventures of a young Englishman. *Candide* is a satirical story by the 18th century French *philosophe* Voltaire. *Emile*, by the late 18th century French political and social writer Rousseau, details his criticisms of the education of children in his time. *War and Peace*, by the Russian writer Tolstoy, describes aristocratic life in Russia during the Napoleonic Wars.

66. **(C)** Camus' portrait of an alienated, emotionally uninvolved "hero" emerged at the beginning of his novel *The Stranger*, probably the most popular novel associated with the Existentialist movement (although Camus rejected the label Existentialist). Although knowledge of the other authors may be of some help, this question is almost entirely based upon fact rentention. Andre Malraux was a 20th century French writer and public official.

67. **(C)** This question illustrates the importance of knowing the exact meaning of terminology. The Slavophiles did not reject western influences for Russia, but

many wanted to retain the distinctiveness of Russian culture. Thus (B) and (E) are incorrect. Answers (A) and (D) refer to the movement named Pan Slavism, which was a different movement from Slavophilism. Pan Slavists wanted to unite all Slavs (which includes most of the people of eastern Europe) under a single nation, generally Russia. But not all Slavophiies espoused Pan Slavism, or vice versa.

68. **(C)** The question calls for analytical abilities, since the correct answer is usually not described in textbooks as a means of population control. To arrive at the correct answer, you must analyze the probable effects of the Potato Blight, a disease which destroyed much of the major food crop of Ireland during the 1830s and 1840s. Of the remaining answers, one (A) occurred in Russia in the early 20th century. In the Peterloo Massacre (B), an army unit charged into a crowd of citizens demonstrating for expansion in the number of people who could vote in Great Britain in 1819. "Home Rule" (D) does apply to Ireland, but was the name of the political issue, debated in the British parliament in the late 19th century, of whether to grant Ireland limited self-government. (E) is simply incorrect.

69. **(A)** By the time Peter ascended the throne, the power of the boyars, the original Russian nobility, had been weakened by previous tsars such as Ivan IV ("the Terrible"), but they still wielded considerable influence. The other statements are all true. The Russian church had been split in the 1600s by liturgical disputes; Russia did not win access to either sea until the reign of Peter, who opened the way to the Baltic; and Russian contact with the west had been of a limited nature.

70. **(C)** The question offers a vital clue—that the Zimmerman telegram was sent during World War I. It may be easy to confuse it with the "Ems telegram" or the "Ems Dispatch" that the German chancellor Otto von Bismarck cleverly edited in 1870, thus causing France to declare war on Prussia. The Zimmerman telegram, sent from the German foreign office to the government of Mexico, suggested that Mexico take military or other actions to divert the United States from becoming militarily involved in Europe. In the event of a German victory in the war, Mexico might be rewarded by regaining California, Texas, and other parts of the United States which were originally Mexican territory. Answer (E) is incorrect; Britain entered the war mainly because of the German army invasion of France by marching through neutral Belgium.

71. **(D)** It is likely that a question about art will appear on the test. Occasionally only the painting itself will be a clue to the correct answer, although in this case the name of the artist is also given and points the way to surrealism, which many of Dali's paintings typified. Surrealism, popular during the 1920s and 1930s in Europe, often produced bizarre, dream-like images of great emotional power. If you cannot eliminate one or two of the answers, it may be best to pass this question by. The Fauvres ("wild beasts") emerged during the 1890s, producing paintings of strong color and intensity, sometimes based on African or Cen-

tral American art. Dadaism has been described as "antiart" protesting the meaninglessness of World War I. Cubist art often tried to portray articles as if seen from several points of view simultaneously. Impressionism was a 19th century movement.

72. **(B)** The Bauhaus school, which flourished in 1920s Germany and was brought to the United States by German emigrees during the 1930s, reacted against the opulence of the earlier Victorian age. The skyline of many large American cities demonstrates the continuing influence of this school. Of the other answers, the Oxford Movement was a "high church" movement in the 19th century Anglican church. The Bloomsbury circle was a literary group in 1920s Britain. The Jacobins were the leaders of France during the "Reign of Terror" of the French Revolution of 1789. Neo-Romanticism in architecture tends to favor a less austere and more ornamental style than the Bauhaus school.

73. **(B)** Britain, the first nation into the Industrial Revolution, held the advantages of coal and iron ore deposits, a good road system, and a nobility which was willing to underwrite the risky venture of opening factories ("entrepreneurship"). You may be able to eliminate these answers. If not, you may arrive at answer (B) by a process of analysis. The Agricultural Revolution, which increased farm yields but placed many small farmers out of work, created a large labor supply for the factories. Plus, financing for many early factories came from a nobility which owned most of the land and depended, at least initially, on farm income.

74. **(B)** The closest to a "trick" question you may encounter, this item deals with a topic which appears on achievement tests with some frequency, perhaps because answer (A) may appear very tempting. During the early 14th century, Pope Boniface VIII was kidnapped by henchmen of King Philip the Fair of France. The following century—-when the popes were forced to live at Avignon, France under domination of the French monarchy—was termed "the Babylonian captivity" by papal defenders who compared it to the Jewish people's experience. You should not be tempted to select (A), because this is, after all, a test in European history. The remaining answers are true events, but are moot or irrelevant for this question.

75. **(C)** For this fact question, you must not only know the facts about Keynes but also understand the logic of his economic system. Without this understanding, your chances of selecting the correct answer are slight, since the correct answer may appear to be the least likely. Keynes asserted that governments should spend more money during economic crises—even to the point of running deficits—in order to "prime the pump" of the economy.

76. **(A)** Another fact-based question, this one assumes that you already are able to identify Richelieu; the question tests the depth of your knowledge of political history. Mazarin followed Richelieu as chief royal minister in France and continued his policies. Of the remaining answers, Walpole was the first

British prime minister; Colbert was a finance minister in France; Montesquieu and LaMettre were 18th century French *philosophes*.

77. **(B)** The Maastricht Treaties marked the agreement in 1991 among members of the European Community to begin measured steps toward an economic and political union that would ultimately have its own currency.

78. **(C)** When somewhat complicated answers appear, as in this case, it is important to read the answers carefully, since the misreading of one word (such as "not") may cause you to pick an incorrect answer. Like many Englishmen, Burke was sympathetic with the French Revolution's aims during its early stages but later, when he wrote the book, he was appalled at the violence of the revolution. Since the American Revolution occurred before the French Revolution, answer (A) is not possible. Answer (D) gives Burke's opinion in reverse.

79. **(E)** *Fathers and Sons* is probably not one of the better known books of the century, and there may even be a temptation to choose *Frankenstein* (a book which suggests that there may be evil in human tinkering with nature). The best clue to the correct answer is the title *Fathers and Sons*, a title which suggests generational conflict. The other answers simply do not fit the description in the question. Hugo's book was a novel of social justice. Dostoyevsky's work was a psychological novel, and *Degeneration* was an alarmist warning that human evolution might proceed backwards.

80. **(D)** Switzerland became the last advanced Western nation to grant women the right to vote, in 1989. Other nations in the West granted women this right at various other times.

Sample Answer to Document-Based Question

In the myriad of events which shaped the French Revolution of 1789, much attention has been given to occurrences in the capital city of Paris, where mobs in the streets weakened a royal government already under attack from an increasingly restive middle class. Less attention has been given to the reactions of the French peasants, or small farmers, whose grievances and concerns emerged during a period of anarchy and violence called the Great Fear.

The restiveness of the French peasants had been aggravated by both natural and political events. Three years of substandard harvests had contributed to economic misery in the rural areas of France. As grain prices rose, the peasants complained about the burden of their remaining feudal obligations. These included the corvée, the necessity of providing free labor for public works projects or other tasks as assigned by the local nobility.

It was not surprising that peasant grievances were initially directed against the nobility they saw as contributing to their misery. Rumors of aristocratic plots swept the countryside, including rumors of food horders among a greedy nobility. Some of the first violence of 1789 was in the rural areas, where peasants took control of local granaries and attacked members of the nobility.

The situation appeared to worsen because of lack of accurate information. An English observer noted the lack of rural newspapers. Word of mouth became the source of information. The most common rumor was that bands of brigands were operating in the area. Responding to such rumors, organized groups of armed peasants sometimes attacked other groups of peasants by mistake. In one case, the band of brigands turned out to be a herd of cows.

At the very least, such sporadic violence demonstrated the decline of the old regime: the decline of royal control in the rural areas of France. There were signs that peasant unhappiness was increasingly directed against the monarchy itself. It was noted that, although some noblemen contributed their personal funds to buy food for the peasants, the king made no appearance in the countryside, nor did he comment on events. The king remained a distant figure, hunting wildlife that the peasants were forbidden to hunt.

Although the leaders of the revolution in Paris were from the middle class, the Great Fear obviously had considerable impact. When King Louis XVI called the Estates General into session in 1789, the Third Estate—consisting of a middle class minority and an overwhelming peasant majority—emerged as the dominant group in France. When the Third Estate was transformed into a National Convention, the Convention became so alarmed by the Great Fear that it made rumormongering a criminal offense. Later, the Convention acknowledged one of the major concerns of the peasants by abolishing the remaining feudal obligations in France.

While the peasants were less educated and sophisticated than the middle class politicians who led France during the revolution, they clearly had an impact on events. The Great Fear united the peasants and made them aware of their own power.

In their own disorganized way, the peasants had made the end of feudalism one of the great achievements of the Revolution.

This essay l) uses documents in a careful way, even quoting some indirectly; 2) has a clear introduction and conclusion; 3) centers each paragraph around a single theme or idea; 4) cites specific examples; 5) includes "outside" information; and 6) clearly addresses itself to the topic. All but point l) are also demonstrated in the following essays as well.)

Sample Answers to Essay Questions

1. Other Europeans sometimes regarded the English as a country of madmen during the 17th century, when the English overthrew two monarchs, even executing one. Yet the English Civil War and the Glorious Revolution of 1688 were singular constitutional events, pushing England ahead of the rest of Europe in terms of political development.

Both events transferred some elements of royal power to the English Parliament, which had existed since the 13th century; In the years since, the relationships between kings and Parliament had not always been smooth. The Tudor monarchs of the 16th century had handled Parliament with skill, using a mixture of compromise, guile, bribes, and cleverness to maintain royal authority. Their successors, the Stuarts, proved less successful in dealing with Parliament. Parliament tried to outlaw Roman Catholic advisers to James I by passing a Test Act, which required that high civil servants be members of the Church of England. When James tried to nullify the Test Act with his own Toleration Decree, Parliament cut his funding. Like other Stuart monarchs, James relied on subsidies from foreign monarchs.

Charles I continued the Test Act-Toleration Decree cycle. He also tried to combat the growing Calvinist (Puritan) presence in the Church of England. Many Puritans became Anglicans when Elizabeth I instituted the Thirty-Nine Articles, a broad creed of faith designed to quiet religious controversy within the Church of England. When Civil War broke out in 1641, the king was confronted with two armies: the army of Parliament and the army of the Puritans.

Charles' defeat and execution at the end of the war did not directly advance constitutionalism, since the following years of Puritan rule were neither successful nor favorable to the growth of parliamentary power. Oliver Cromwell personally ruled for a time as Lord High Protector. Upon his death, parliament chose to restore the monarchy by inviting Charles II to rule.

While Charles II avoided reopening old wounds, his successor, James II returned to the cycle of Test Acts and Toleration decrees. The resulting Glorious Revolution saw James flee the country and Parliament once again placed in a position to select a new monarch. Their choices—James' daughter Mary and her Dutch husband—conceded considerable amounts of royal power to parliament. For example, they agreed to a Bill of Rights banning royal interference in court proceedings and guaranteeing freedom from arbitrary arrests. The events of 1688 finally established the sovereignty of Parliament.

The political violence and chaos of the 17th century brought changes to

England that France would undergo a century later. The unwritten English constitution had been considerably revised, and Parliament had become a sovereign, significant presence in the English political system.

2. During the century between the Congress of Vienna and World War I, balance-of-power diplomacy helped Europe to avoid a continent-wide war. The primary reason for the success of this diplomacy was the British policy of "splendid isolation", meaning no permanent alliances and freedom to join with other nations temporarily to block expansionist or threatening moves by other European states. Britain came to "splendid isolation" through circumstances rather than design. At the Congress of Vienna, the British representative Castlereagh stood apart from the other diplomats on the issue of restoring all monarchs removed from their thrones by Napoleon Bonaparte. Castlereagh feared such actions would lead to future revolutions and instability on the European continent. When the great powers sent French troops to suppress a Spanish revolt of 1820, Castlereagh responded by withdrawing Britain from membership in the Quadruple Alliance formed at Vienna. For the rest of the century, other British diplomats proudly followed the policy of "splendid isolation", accepting Castlereagh's view that the continental powers were not to be trusted.

One of the first results was a British suggestion to the United States government, proposing that the two countries issue a joint declaration that the time had passed for European nations to establish colonies in North or South America. The United States declined—memories of the American Revolution and War of 1812 were strong—but the American President James Monroe later issued essentially the same declaration. Only one major attempt was made by a European power during the century to establish a colony in North America, an unsuccessful Austrian attempt to make a colony of Mexico during the United States Civil War. The real "enforcer" of the Monroe Doctrine, however, was the British navy, whose presence astride the Atlantic ocean was the most significant deterrent to foreign adventurers by continental powers.

Throughout the 19th century, British foreign policy worked to limit expansionist plans by the other great powers. A common target was Russia. British policy sought to block Russian designs in Afghanistan; the same applied to Persia, where Britain had its own colonial interests. Objecting to Russian "bullying" of the Ottoman Empire on the issue of Russian Orthodox monasteries in the Empire, Britain and France sent troops to southern Russia in the Crimean War. When a Russo-Turkish war of 1877 ended with a treaty which the British prime minister Disraeli regarded as too favorable for Russia, he led the other European powers in successfully demanding revisions more favorable to the Ottoman Empire.

After 1870, the rise of new European nations, plus British difficulties in the Age of Imperialism, led the British government to seek allies. The appearance of a powerful and united Germany in the center of Europe was one reason, although the German chancellor Bismarck played the role of "honest broker"' in continental disputes. Yet his successor as leader of Germany, Emperor William II, alarmed the British government by his plans to construct a German navy rivaling the British fleet.

During the Boer War in South Africa, British military actions were widely criticized in Europe, and Britain had no allies to speak up in its defense.

The end of "splendid isolation" came in 1902, when Britain cautiously allied itself with non-European Japan. From 1904 through 1907, Britain became a member of the Triple Entente with France and Russia, one of the two major alliances of World War I.

The driving force in balance of power diplomacy in 19th century Europe, "splendid isolation" helped maintain the 100-year European peace of 1815-1914, when Europe became, for a time, the dominant economic and military force in the world.

3. Although the French *philosophes* of the 18th century shared a common outlook on many issues, they often differed on the practical steps to achieve their goals. Such was the case with Voltaire and Montesquieu, two of the best-known writers on the political issues of the period.

Although he was educated in Jesuit schools, Voltaire became a determined opponent of both religious influence in French politics and the political power of the French nobility. Voltaire's hatred of the nobility was partly personal, the result of a court case where he was found guilty of slandering a nobleman and went into self-imposed exile in England for a time. More importantly, Voltaire regarded the nobility as the greatest obstacle to changes and reforms sought by many of the *philosophes*.

As a privileged class, the nobility would, Voltaire believed, always oppose the social and political reforms which the *philosophes* thought would create a better environment for nurturing future generations. These included the establishment of a new, simplified religion (Deism), which Voltaire expected the nobility to oppose because most high clergy were from the ranks of the aristocracy.

Voltaire placed his hopes for achieving such reforms in the French monarchy, which he saw as the only alternative to rule by the nobility. Educated in the ideas and outlook of the *philosophes*, monarchs would become Enlightened Despots who would force reforms upon their subjects in a "revolution from above."

Montesquieu approached politics from an entirely different perspective. A member of the French nobility, Montesquieu shared the other *philosophes'* quest to find objective, semiscientific methods to improve their society. His major work, the *Spirit of Laws*, sought to define the factors which explained why the French government was so different from other governments, such as the government of Turkey.

Montesquieu regarded the growth of the absolute monarchy in France as a sign of decline. He particularly objected to the king's attempts to restrict the authority of the *parlements*, the French courts traditionally controlled by the nobility. Opposing Enlightened Despotism, Montesquieu instead wrote of the importance of maintaining a separation of powers in government. The idea was applicable outside of France—it appeared in the United States Constitution—but within France it signified a way to nullify royal authority.

Starting from similar principles, Voltaire and Montesquieu produced very different political solutions for France, solutions which would be made moot by the French Revolution of 1789. Their writings demonstrate the wide range of diverse ideas produced by the French Enlightenment.

4. By the end of the 19th century, the Industrial Revolution had helped to make Europe the dominant economic and military power in the world. It also, however, had created major social problems as European countries became increasingly urbanized, a large but vulnerable working class emerged, and a burgeoning and increasingly affluent middle class demanded its share of political power.

Although the Industrial Revolution stretched from the mid-1700s, when Britain entered the industrial age, until the early 20th century, when industrialization emerged in Russia, the sufferings of the working class became obvious as early as the 1830s. Early factories were only marginally profitable, and they paid subsistence wages, required long hours of work, and frequently shut down for several months because managers had miscalculated demands for their products. Until Britain began regulating working hours in the 1830s, men might work up to 15 or 16 hours a day, women 12 to 14, and children 10. A British parliamentary commission discovered in the early 1830s that children who worked in mines frequently had one leg that grew shorter than another, because the children carried burlap sacks of coal generally on the same side of their body.

The middle class—whose occupations included the financing of the factories (banks), the management of the factories, or selling factory products—generally showed little concern for the working class. It is often observed that the middle class showed little social conscience, preferring to promote its own political agenda of gaining the right to vote for middle class males and increasing the authority of parliaments or legislatures. In Britain, the self-proclaimed "Workshop of the World" in the 19th century, the middle-class liberals also envisioned a "free-trade" world, where manufactured goods would be sold throughout the world without tariff barriers.

As new factories led to the rise of new cities and the rapid growth of existing urban centers, there was also growth in social problems such as illegitimacy and prostitution. The famous "Victorian Code" of the century, with its stern code of sexual conduct, was probably an attempt to both combat and cover up such problems.

Since middle class liberals preferred to ignore the problems of the working classes, movements to help the working class grew up outside the umbrella of liberalism. Movements to help the workers were labeled socialism. In the first half of the century, most socialists were Utopian Socialists, who preferred to return Europe to pre-industrialist days. Some, such as Charles Fourier, preferred to establish communities where factories were unnecessary. Karl Marx rejected Utopian Socialism because he saw the Industrial Revolution as a great industrial advance; the problem, as he saw it, was the ownership of the factories and the small percentage of profits going to the workers.

Industrialization came first to western European countries (Britain and France), proceeded to central Europe (Germany and Italy), and emerged last in the easternmost nation of Russia. Some of the nations where the Industrial Revolution occurred later appeared to have special problems in adjusting to industrialization. In Germany, the Junker class, a noble class whose wealth was based on large-scale farming in eastern Germany, forced the middle class to share power with it until nearly World War II. In Russia, writers named the Slavophiles saw industrialization as a western influence that threatened to destroy the uniquely Russian traits of the country. In fact the communist revolution of 1917 marked the triumph of the opposite school, the westerners.

While the Industrial Revolution made Europe for a time the preeminent continent in the world, it also was the cause of much social suffering, class division, and cultural confusion.

5. Described by wartime propaganda as the "war to end all wars," World War I was followed by peace settlements which promoted bitterness and disillusionment in Europe. In this way, the settlements may have themselves become causes of World War II.

Three treaties ended the war—the Treaty of Versailles with Germany and the Treaties of St. Germain and Neuilly with Austria and the Ottoman Empire. The Treaty of Versailles was criticized within Germany as the "imposed treaty," so called because it was not the treaty promised when Germany asked for a cease fire in November of 1918. Germany had been promised a negotiated treaty, but the Treaty of Versailles, written by Germany's enemies, had been forced upon Germany with the choice of signing the treaty or resuming hostilities.

Already embittered by a continuing British naval blockade of Germany in 1919, after the war ended—which, rightly or wrongly, was blamed by many Germans as the cause of starvation in the country—Germans were especially unhappy with some parts of the treaty. The German army was limited to 100,0000 men; training was prohibited in tanks and planes; and Germany was required to pay an unspecified amount of reparations. To many Germans it appeared their nation was being blamed for starting the war and for all destruction resulting from the war.

The Treaty of Versailles opened the way for politicians such as Adolf Hitler, who argued that Britain and France were not to be trusted and their democracies were not to be emulated. Although Hitler's National Socialist party was never able to garner more than 34% of the vote, he probably spoke for many Germans when he dismissed the German government formed after the war, the Weimar Republic, as an expedient and weak government formed in hopes of gaining easier peace terms from Woodrow Wilson and his allies.

In order to convince many Germans that military force was necessary to roll back the hated treaty, Hitler also could point to two other parts of the peace settlements. Germany had lost much of mineral-rich Silesia to the recreated Poland, even though the majority of Silesians had chosen, in a referendum, to remain with Germany. Hitler also exploited the issue of the "Polish Corridor," a strip of formerly-German land awarded to Poland in order to give the Poles an outlet to the sea.

The treaties with Austria and the Ottoman Empire allowed the victorious allies to create a series of new nations in eastern Europe. The new nations were not particularly stable, struggling with internal divisions and bickering with their neighbors over borders and territory. In his book *Mein Kampf*, Hitler, an Austrian, looked at these areas as a natural direction for future German expansion.

Disillusionment over the peace settlement was not restricted to Germany. Britain and France had been promised a collective security agreement with the United States by Woodrow Wilson. When the United States, instead, withdrew from the European diplomatic system after the war, both European nations struggled to find new ways to make themselves secure. By the 1930s, many British citizens and some French citizens had come to believe that the Treaty of Versailles had been too harsh. The result, unfortunately, was a tendency to view Hitler as a mere statesman with valid grievances who needed to be "appeased."

It would be inaccurate to say the treaties at the end of World War I became the major causes of World War II. The major causes lay in the personality and ideas of Adolf Hitler. By helping Hitler's rise to power, and by failing to establish a stable diplomatic system to block him, the treaties were, however, a factor.

6. United on a major principle—the preeminence of Scriptures over theological or papal authority—the three Protestant groups of the Reformation differed in significant ways on the implications of the Scriptures.

The two major doctrines of Martin Luther became part of most Protestant theology, although not necessarily by the names that Luther used. Like most Protestants of the Reformation, Luther found the New Testament letters of St. Paul a source of inspiration. St. Paul's statement that "the just shall live by faith" led to Luther's doctrine of "justification by faith". Arguing (somewhat erroneously) that Roman Catholic doctrines held that "good works" could compensate for sins, Luther taught that human sin was too great to be balanced out by good deeds. In his doctrine of "justification by faith," the emphasis was upon God's grace and upon salvation given in return for individual faith.

Luther's portrayal of individuals alone before God's judgment, penitent and seeking salvation, led to his other doctrine which became widely accepted within Protestantism: the priesthood of the believer. Rejecting priests as unnecessary intermediaries, most Protestants viewed their ministers as having no special status except as pastors to a congregation.

Calvinism was distinctive for its doctrine of Predestination. The doctrine of Predestination had been considered and rejected by St. Augustine, and few other groups in Protestantism gave it much attention. John Calvin made it a central theme in his *Institutes of the Christian Religion*. Popular Calvinism added the idea that God would not allow the "elect of God" to suffer in this life; "success" became the sign of salvation. For some, success in business became a mark of salvation.

Anabaptism, which largely drew its membership from the peasantry, tended to hold that belief should be based on the Scriptures alone. Although Anabaptist beliefs tended to vary from congregation to congregation, and from town to town, Anabaptists were generally less educated than other Protestants and regarded with suspicion any ideas or doctrines not clearly articulated in the Scriptures.

One area of major difference between the three Protestant groups of the Reformation was in their attitudes toward the Eucharist, or communion. Luther believed that Christ was present during communion, but he tended to reject the Catholic belief that Christ was present in the elements of communion, the bread and wine. Calvinists and Anabaptists were likely to regard Communion as a memorial service, without the physical presence of Christ.

In sum, while the three major groups of the Protestant Reformation drew different lessons from Scripture, they found agreement in their outlooks on the role of the churches and the relationship of sinners to God.

THE ADVANCED PLACEMENT EXAMINATION IN

European History

TEST 4

Test 4 is also on CD-ROM in our special interactive AP European History TEST*ware*®. It is highly recommended that you first take this exam on computer. You will then have the additional study features and benefits of enforced timed conditions, individual diagnostic analysis, and instant scoring. See page vi for guidance on how to get the most out of our AP European History book and software.

THE ADVANCED PLACEMENT EXAMINATION IN

European History

TEST 4

1. Ⓐ Ⓑ Ⓒ Ⓓ Ⓔ	26. Ⓐ Ⓑ Ⓒ Ⓓ Ⓔ	56. Ⓐ Ⓑ Ⓒ Ⓓ Ⓔ
2. Ⓐ Ⓑ Ⓒ Ⓓ Ⓔ	27. Ⓐ Ⓑ Ⓒ Ⓓ Ⓔ	57. Ⓐ Ⓑ Ⓒ Ⓓ Ⓔ
3. Ⓐ Ⓑ Ⓒ Ⓓ Ⓔ	28. Ⓐ Ⓑ Ⓒ Ⓓ Ⓔ	58. Ⓐ Ⓑ Ⓒ Ⓓ Ⓔ
4. Ⓐ Ⓑ Ⓒ Ⓓ Ⓔ	29. Ⓐ Ⓑ Ⓒ Ⓓ Ⓔ	59. Ⓐ Ⓑ Ⓒ Ⓓ Ⓔ
5. Ⓐ Ⓑ Ⓒ Ⓓ Ⓔ	30. Ⓐ Ⓑ Ⓒ Ⓓ Ⓔ	60. Ⓐ Ⓑ Ⓒ Ⓓ Ⓔ
6. Ⓐ Ⓑ Ⓒ Ⓓ Ⓔ	31. Ⓐ Ⓑ Ⓒ Ⓓ Ⓔ	61. Ⓐ Ⓑ Ⓒ Ⓓ Ⓔ
7. Ⓐ Ⓑ Ⓒ Ⓓ Ⓔ	32. Ⓐ Ⓑ Ⓒ Ⓓ Ⓔ	62. Ⓐ Ⓑ Ⓒ Ⓓ Ⓔ
8. Ⓐ Ⓑ Ⓒ Ⓓ Ⓔ	33. Ⓐ Ⓑ Ⓒ Ⓓ Ⓔ	63. Ⓐ Ⓑ Ⓒ Ⓓ Ⓔ
9. Ⓐ Ⓑ Ⓒ Ⓓ Ⓔ	34. Ⓐ Ⓑ Ⓒ Ⓓ Ⓔ	64. Ⓐ Ⓑ Ⓒ Ⓓ Ⓔ
10. Ⓐ Ⓑ Ⓒ Ⓓ Ⓔ	35. Ⓐ Ⓑ Ⓒ Ⓓ Ⓔ	65. Ⓐ Ⓑ Ⓒ Ⓓ Ⓔ
11. Ⓐ Ⓑ Ⓒ Ⓓ Ⓔ	36. Ⓐ Ⓑ Ⓒ Ⓓ Ⓔ	66. Ⓐ Ⓑ Ⓒ Ⓓ Ⓔ
12. Ⓐ Ⓑ Ⓒ Ⓓ Ⓔ	37. Ⓐ Ⓑ Ⓒ Ⓓ Ⓔ	67. Ⓐ Ⓑ Ⓒ Ⓓ Ⓔ
13. Ⓐ Ⓑ Ⓒ Ⓓ Ⓔ	38. Ⓐ Ⓑ Ⓒ Ⓓ Ⓔ	68. Ⓐ Ⓑ Ⓒ Ⓓ Ⓔ
14. Ⓐ Ⓑ Ⓒ Ⓓ Ⓔ	39. Ⓐ Ⓑ Ⓒ Ⓓ Ⓔ	69. Ⓐ Ⓑ Ⓒ Ⓓ Ⓔ
15. Ⓐ Ⓑ Ⓒ Ⓓ Ⓔ	40. Ⓐ Ⓑ Ⓒ Ⓓ Ⓔ	70. Ⓐ Ⓑ Ⓒ Ⓓ Ⓔ
16. Ⓐ Ⓑ Ⓒ Ⓓ Ⓔ	41. Ⓐ Ⓑ Ⓒ Ⓓ Ⓔ	71. Ⓐ Ⓑ Ⓒ Ⓓ Ⓔ
17. Ⓐ Ⓑ Ⓒ Ⓓ Ⓔ	42. Ⓐ Ⓑ Ⓒ Ⓓ Ⓔ	72. Ⓐ Ⓑ Ⓒ Ⓓ Ⓔ
18. Ⓐ Ⓑ Ⓒ Ⓓ Ⓔ	43. Ⓐ Ⓑ Ⓒ Ⓓ Ⓔ	73. Ⓐ Ⓑ Ⓒ Ⓓ Ⓔ
19. Ⓐ Ⓑ Ⓒ Ⓓ Ⓔ	44. Ⓐ Ⓑ Ⓒ Ⓓ Ⓔ	74. Ⓐ Ⓑ Ⓒ Ⓓ Ⓔ
20. Ⓐ Ⓑ Ⓒ Ⓓ Ⓔ	45. Ⓐ Ⓑ Ⓒ Ⓓ Ⓔ	75. Ⓐ Ⓑ Ⓒ Ⓓ Ⓔ
21. Ⓐ Ⓑ Ⓒ Ⓓ Ⓔ	46. Ⓐ Ⓑ Ⓒ Ⓓ Ⓔ	76. Ⓐ Ⓑ Ⓒ Ⓓ Ⓔ
22. Ⓐ Ⓑ Ⓒ Ⓓ Ⓔ	47. Ⓐ Ⓑ Ⓒ Ⓓ Ⓔ	77. Ⓐ Ⓑ Ⓒ Ⓓ Ⓔ
23. Ⓐ Ⓑ Ⓒ Ⓓ Ⓔ	48. Ⓐ Ⓑ Ⓒ Ⓓ Ⓔ	78. Ⓐ Ⓑ Ⓒ Ⓓ Ⓔ
24. Ⓐ Ⓑ Ⓒ Ⓓ Ⓔ	49. Ⓐ Ⓑ Ⓒ Ⓓ Ⓔ	79. Ⓐ Ⓑ Ⓒ Ⓓ Ⓔ
25. Ⓐ Ⓑ Ⓒ Ⓓ Ⓔ	50. Ⓐ Ⓑ Ⓒ Ⓓ Ⓔ	80. Ⓐ Ⓑ Ⓒ Ⓓ Ⓔ
	51. Ⓐ Ⓑ Ⓒ Ⓓ Ⓔ	
	52. Ⓐ Ⓑ Ⓒ Ⓓ Ⓔ	
	53. Ⓐ Ⓑ Ⓒ Ⓓ Ⓔ	
	54. Ⓐ Ⓑ Ⓒ Ⓓ Ⓔ	
	55. Ⓐ Ⓑ Ⓒ Ⓓ Ⓔ	

European History

TEST 4 – Section I

TIME: 55 Minutes
80 Questions

DIRECTIONS: Each of the questions or incomplete statements below is followed by five suggested answers or completions. Select the one that is best in each case.

1. All of the following statements are true about the 18th century French philosopher Voltaire EXCEPT

   (A) he admired the British political system.

   (B) he was an atheist.

   (C) he believed that religious considerations had biased the French judicial system.

   (D) he favored Enlightened Despotism.

   (E) he wrote a novel as a reply to the German philosopher Leibniz.

2. Which one of the following statements best characterizes the Russian *strelski*?

   (A) They comprised an elite military group, with great influence in Russian politics.

   (B) As intellectuals, they were an important group at court.

   (C) They were the leaders of the Decembrist revolt of 1825.

   (D) As church leaders, they contributed to the myth of Holy Russia.

   (E) They were foreigners who chose to live in Russia.

3. The Abbé Sièyés exerted a major influence on the French Revolution through his book

   (A) *Essay on Human Understanding.*

(B) *What Is to Be Done?*

(C) *The Progress of the Human Mind.*

(D) *The Third Estate.*

(E) None of the above

4. With papal encouragement, Spain in 1494 agreed to recognize that one other nation had valid claims to parts of South and Central America. Which nation was it?

(A) Great Britain

(B) Portugal

(C) Austria

(D) Italy

(E) France

5. A major result of Pride's Purge (1648) was to

(A) rid Parliament of opposition to Puritanism.

(B) give Oliver Cromwell virtual control of Parliament.

(C) ban all Puritans from Parliament.

(D) add to the number of Puritans in high office.

(E) create a Republic.

6. All of the following statements about the Edict of Nantes are true EXCEPT

(A) it banned Huguenot military forces and fortresses.

(B) it promoted religious toleration.

(C) it guaranteed freedom of worship for French Calvinists.

(D) it followed a major civil war in France.

(E) it was revoked by Louis XIV.

7. Which one of the following statements best characterizes the differences between John Locke's "state of nature" and Rousseau's "state of nature"?

(A) Locke called for reform; Rousseau was satisfied with the status quo.

(B) Rousseau's "state of nature" did not have political connotations.

(C) Rousseau's "state of nature" was one of economic equality.

(D) Locke's "state of nature" ended with a "social contract," while Rousseau's did not.

(E) Locke's "state of nature" was a violent and dangerous society.

8. All of the following were achieved during the Prussian Era of Reform, 1806-1821, EXCEPT

(A) improvements in the number and quality of Prussian soldiers.

(B) the abolition of serfdom.

(C) the end of the Junker monopoly on landholding.

(D) universal manhood suffrage.

(E) reform of the state bureaucracy.

9. Which one of the following statements best explains the political and military decline of Poland by the late 18th century?

(A) A lack of a parliamentary system

(B) The liberum veto

(C) The impact of religious wars in Poland

(D) The selection of any Polish monarchs from the ranks of the nobility

(E) The strength of the Polish monarchy

10. During the Third French Republic, 1875-1945, which one of the following describes a famous political crisis centered around the accusations of treason against a French military officer?

(A) The Irish Question

(B) The Panama Canal Scandal

(C) The Zabern Affair

(D) The Dreyfus Affair

(E) The "Daily Telegraph Affair"

11. The Risorgimento was the name of

(A) the emergence of a prosperous Europe from the ashes of World War II.

(B) the movement to unify Italy.

(C) the high cultural achievements of the Italian Renaissance.

(D) Napoleonic rule in Italy.

(E) the movement to unify Germany.

12. The cause of the Crimean War included British and French objections to

(A) Russian foreign policy toward the Ottoman Empire.

(B) Austrian foreign policy in the Balkans.

(C) the aggressive foreign policy of the Ottoman Empire.

(D) Austrian occupation of northern Italy.

(E) the foreign policy of Bismarck.

13. Robert Walpole was notable for

(A) being the first English prime minister.

(B) his work to perfect the steam engine.

(C) his leadership of the British trade union movement.

(D) his work as a physicist.

(E) his novels.

14. In the post-World War II period, which one of the following Soviet writers was not allowed to travel to Stockholm to receive his Nobel prize for literature?

(A) Shostakovitch

(B) Pasternak

(C) Beria

(D) Brezhnev

(E) Prokofiev

15. All of the following statements about Eastern Europe from 1945 to 1960 are true EXCEPT

(A) all Eastern Europe nations were subservient to the Soviet government.

(B) Eastern European nations rejected the Marshall Plan.

(C) there was a revolt in Hungary.

(D) there was a revolt in East Germany.

(E) almost all of the nations of Eastern Europe were militarily allied with the Soviet Union.

16. Which one of the following was a major reason for the failure of attempts to unite Germany and Austria in 1934?

(A) The German government rejected the plan.

(B) Austria threatened war if the plan was implemented.

(C) Mussolini was opposed to the merger.

(D) Britain and France opposed the merger.

(E) Hitler opposed uniting the two countries.

17. Among the issues advocated by the Action Française of Charles Maurras was

(A) opposition to monarchies.

(B) anti-Semitism.

(C) a smaller French army.

(D) loyalty to the Third French Republic.

(E) parliamentary government.

18. The following map depicts the late 18th century partitions of

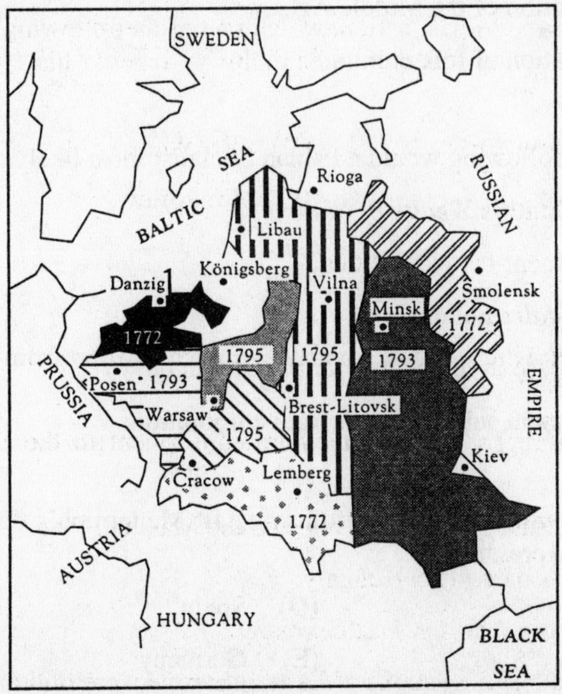

(A) Hungary.
(B) Austria.
(C) Poland.
(D) Russia.
(E) France.

19. The Locarno treaties of the mid-1920s committed

(A) Britain and France to defend Poland.
(B) the Soviet Union to respect the borders of its Eastern European neighbors.
(C) the League of Nations to intervene in the Soviet Union.
(D) Germany to make changes in its borders only by peaceful means.
(E) the United States to protect the borders of France.

20. All of the following are characteristics of the Romantic movement EXCEPT

(A) focus on emotion or intuition over reason.
(B) rejection of the study of history as useless.
(C) admiration for the Enlightenment.
(D) glorification of the Middle Ages.
(E) glorification of folk culture.

21. Which of the following would a Fabian Socialist most likely approve?

(A) Adam Smith's *Wealth of Nations*
(B) Government-owned utilities
(C) *Laissez-faire* policies
(D) An increase in the budget for the British navy
(E) Government subsidies to private corporations

22. Before 1870, which one of the following fit Metternich's description of a "geographic expression"?

(A) France
(B) Britain
(C) Russia
(D) Spain
(E) Germany

23. In 1820, freedom of the press and student activities were suppressed throughout Germany as part of the

(A) Charter of 1814.
(B) Declaration of the Rights of Man.
(C) Holy Alliance.
(D) Carlsbad Decrees.
(E) Schlieffen Plan.

24. The "King's Friends" was used by King George III to

(A) finance Hessian soldiers in the American Revolution.
(B) attempt to control Parliament.
(C) prevent revolutions in Britain.
(D) weaken royal authority.
(E) finance early British factories.

25. "By pursuing his own interest (every individual) frequently promotes that of society more effectively than when he really intends to promote it. I have never known much good done by those who affected to trade for the public good."

This passage expresses the opinion of

(A) Thomas Malthus in *Essay on Population.*
(B) Adam Smith in *Wealth of Nations.*
(C) Karl Marx in *Das Kapital.*
(D) Charles Darwin in *Origin of Species.*
(E) Jane Austen in *Pride and Prejudice.*

26. The First Estate in the Estates-General was

(A) the nobility.
(B) the middle class.
(C) the peasants.
(D) the clergy.
(E) the factory owners.

27. Which of the following was a result of the Civil Constitution of the Clergy?

    (A) The clergy were given a privileged position in the Estates-General.

    (B) The church was made a department of the French state.

    (C) The clergy were condemned to execution during the Reign of Terror.

    (D) The office of bishop was abolished.

    (E) The church was made completely independent from the state.

28. Which one of the following is a description of the Charter of 1814?

    (A) A grant of land

    (B) A constitution

    (C) An anti-parliamentary tirade

    (D) A proclamation of religious freedom

    (E) A proclamation establishing a national bank in France

29. Locke's *Two Treatises on Civil Government* approved of revolution provided that

    (A) the revolution was not violent.

    (B) the government has violated property rights.

    (C) the poor are oppressed.

    (D) the government has not held elections.

    (E) the government is a monarchy.

30. The Clarendon Code, enforced in England from 1661 through 1665,

    (A) attempted to reestablish Puritan rule in England.

    (B) was approved by the new monarch, Charles II.

    (C) excluded Catholics and Presbyterians from high office.

    (D) required English colonies to trade only with the mother country.

    (E) was a document favoring religious toleration.

31. The "idols" of Francis Bacon, as explained in his *Novum Organum*, were

(A) strict standards of scientific accuracy.

(B) impediments to clear scientific thinking.

(C) religious objects.

(D) famous scientists.

(E) political objectives.

Part of the text in the illustration reads
"So soon as a coin in coffer rings,
The soul into heaven springs."

32. The individual depicted on the horse in the picture above is

(A) Calvin.

(B) Tetzel.

(C) Boniface VIII.

(D) Luther.

(E) Henry VIII.

33. In transforming the Roman Catholic church in his realm into the Church of England, Henry VIII

    (A) ended the Catholic sacraments.

    (B) disbanded the monasteries.

    (C) brought Protestant influences into the church.

    (D) radically altered the religious doctrines of the church.

    (E) strengthened the authority of the pope over English churches.

34. In the final stages of the Thirty Years' War, Cardinal Richelieu of France sent aid to

    (A) the Catholic Austrian Hapsburgs.

    (B) the Protestant monarchs of the Dutch Republic and Sweden.

    (C) the Catholic Spanish Hapsburgs.

    (D) Russia.

    (E) Prussia.

35. Which slogan best describes the proclaimed policy of the Soviet Union during the late 1950s and early 1960s toward the capitalist nations of the world?

    (A) "V for Victory"

    (B) "The Third Force"

    (C) "Peaceful Coexistence"

    (D) "Peace, Land, and Bread"

    (E) "Peace in Our Time"

36. Which one of the following was NOT part of the early years of the Cold War?

    (A) Berlin blockade

    (B) Atomic monopoly by the United States

    (C) Soviet occupation of Eastern Europe

    (D) Rearmament of Germany

    (E) A Communist government was established in Poland.

37. The author of the *Decline of the West* (1918) was

(A) Mann.
(B) Spengler.
(C) Joyce.
(D) Proust.
(E) Beckett.

38. Stalin's policy of "Socialism in One Country" required the Soviet Union to avoid

(A) industrialization.
(B) factories.
(C) a large working class.
(D) wars.
(E) government-controlled economy.

39. According to the ideas of Karl Marx, the LAST of the major European powers to have a proletarian revolution was supposed to be

(A) Britain.
(B) Italy.
(C) France.
(D) Germany.
(E) Russia.

40. The "gap theory" was used by the German politician Bismarck to end the

(A) Corn Law Crisis.
(B) Army Bill Crisis.
(C) Revolution of 1848.
(D) Crimean War.
(E) Boulanger Crisis.

41. Which of the following was most closely associated with the Reign of Terror during the French Revolution of 1789?

(A) Danton
(B) The Jacobins
(C) The Duke of Brunswick
(D) Lafayette
(E) Clemenceau

42. "I dissent from those who are unwilling that the sacred Scriptures should be read by the unlearned and translated into the vulgar tongue, as though Christ had taught such subtleties that they can scarcely be understood even by a few theologians...."

This passage expresses the opinion of

(A) Ignatius Loyola.
(B) Machiavelli.
(C) Galileo Galilei.
(D) Erasmus of Rotterdam.
(E) Robert Boyle.

43. The Enclosure movement of the 17th and 18th centuries

(A) attempted to reunite all Christians in one church.
(B) sought to group factories closely together for maximum efficiency.
(C) fenced in public land for private use.
(D) sought to ban trade with nations outside of Europe.
(E) sought to ban emigration from Europe to North America.

44. Although he was a Roman Catholic, which one of the following individuals was most like Calvin in his efforts to reform the church and society?

(A) Savonarola
(B) Ignatius Loyola
(C) Thomas More
(D) Lavoissier
(E) Charles V

45. During the 16th and 17th centuries, all of the following represented challenges to royal authority EXCEPT

(A) the parliaments.
(B) New Model Army.
(C) the palace of Versailles.
(D) Puritans.
(E) the Roundheads.

46. The emblem shown above was that of

(A) Frederick the Great.
(B) Peter the Great.
(C) Louis XIV.
(D) Charles XII.
(E) Philip II.

47. In terms of political and military power, the major losers from the rise of Peter the Great's Russia were

(A) Portugal and the Dutch Republic.
(B) Sweden and Poland.
(C) Austria and Prussia.
(D) Italy and Spain.
(E) Britain and France.

48. The Royal Society of London, founded in 1662, was one of the first

(A) societies dedicated to geographic exploration.
(B) groups to stage Shakespearean plays.
(C) literary clubs.
(D) scientific societies.
(E) political clubs.

49. Before he became president of Czechoslovakia, Václav Havel was known as a dissident and a

(A) shipyard worker.
(B) filmmaker.
(C) playwright.
(D) soldier.
(E) poet.

50. "Écrasez l'infame," Voltaire's slogan of "crush the infamous thing," called for the suppression of

(A) the church.
(B) immorality.
(C) the French monarchy.
(D) censorship.
(E) French universities.

51. Rousseau's concept of the ideal government was centered on

(A) the general will.
(B) a strengthened monarchy.
(C) a theocracy.
(D) abolition of the government.
(E) a strengthened army.

52. Which of the following issues made the most important contribution to the defeat of Italy's Christian Democratic party?

(A) Poverty throughout the country
(B) Chronic food shortages
(C) Political corruption and instability
(D) Religious conservatives in the party alienated many Italians
(E) Italy's support of the United States during the Persian Gulf War

53. "Behold, an immense people united in a single person; behold this holy power, paternal, and absolute; behold the secret cause which governs the whole body of the state, contained in a single head; you see the image of God in the king, and you have the idea of royal majesty..."

This passage by the French bishop Bossuet illustrates the concept of

(A) sovereignty.

(B) absolutism.

(C) divine right.

(D) papal authority.

(E) parliamentary government.

54. The Pugachev rebellion was a threat to the power of

(A) Frederick the Great.

(B) Mussolini.

(C) Catherine the Great.

(D) Peter the Great.

(E) Louis XIV.

55. Which of the following best characterizes the Table of Ranks of Peter the Great of Russia?

(A) It separated the Russian population into distinct classes.

(B) It set educational and performance levels for civil servants.

(C) It required the nobility to serve in the Russian army.

(D) It legalized serfdom.

(E) It established a Russian parliament.

56. In the "Diplomatic Revolution" of 1756

(A) Prussia became an ally of Britain.

(B) Austria became an ally of Britain.

(C) France fought Austria.

(D) the Holy Roman Empire was abolished.

(E) the Austrian government was overthrown by a popular revolt.

57. A primary factor in the influence of the *sans-culottes* in the French Revolution of 1789 was

(A) their admiration for the monarchy.

(B) their large military forces.

(C) their alliance with the Jacobins.

(D) their lack of concern for economic issues.

(E) their contempt for the middle class.

58. The British Chartist movement of the 19th century drew much of its support from the

(A) nobility.

(B) middle class.

(C) small farmers.

(D) workers.

(E) factory owners.

59. During the revolutions of 1848, attempts to unite Germany under the leadership of the Prussian monarch were made by

(A) the royal ministers of Prussia.

(B) a national parliament at Frankfurt.

(C) the Prussian king.

(D) the king's relatives.

(E) the Prussian army.

60. *"We don't want to fight,*
But, by jingo, if we do,
We've got the ships,
We've got the men,
We've got the money too."

This saying, popular with British crowds reacting to tense British-Russian relations in 1877, gave rise to the term

(A) chauvinism.
(B) rule Britannia.
(C) Workshop of the World.
(D) jingoism.
(E) Fortress of Democracy.

61. Italy was unified in 1870 under the leadership of the Italian state of

(A) Sicily.
(B) Piedmont.
(C) Corsica.
(D) Venetia.
(E) Tuscany.

62. During the Persian Gulf War, what action did Russia take?

(A) Russia supported Iraq by selling arms.
(B) Russia supported Iraq with troops and weapons.
(C) Russia supported Iraq diplomatically, but not materially.
(D) Russia supported the international army led by the United States.
(E) Russia remained neutral.

63. "After reports of the renunciation by the Hereditary Prince of Hohenzollern had been officially transmitted...to the Imperial Government of France, the French Ambassador presented to His Majesty the King...the demand...that His Majesty the King would obligate himself for all future time never again to give his approval to the candidacy of the Hohenzollerns should it be renewed."

This passage is from the text of

(A) the Fourteen Points.
(B) the Treaty of Versailles.
(C) the Ems Telegram.
(D) the British Constitution.
(E) the Congress of Berlin.

64. The Paris Commune, established at the close of the Franco-Prussian war of 1870, was suppressed by

(A) the Prussian army.
(B) the French army.
(C) the Russian army.
(D) the Spanish army.
(E) the British army.

65. All of the following were characteristics of the Second Industrial Revolution EXCEPT

(A) emergence of major steel industries.
(B) large growth of the textile industry.
(C) emergence of the German chemical industry.
(D) application of electricity to industrial production.
(E) the widespread use of oil.

66. In World War II, the Battle of Britain was fought largely as a

(A) naval battle.
(B) land battle.
(C) air battle.
(D) diplomatic battle.
(E) submarine battle.

67. The map on the following page illustrates the

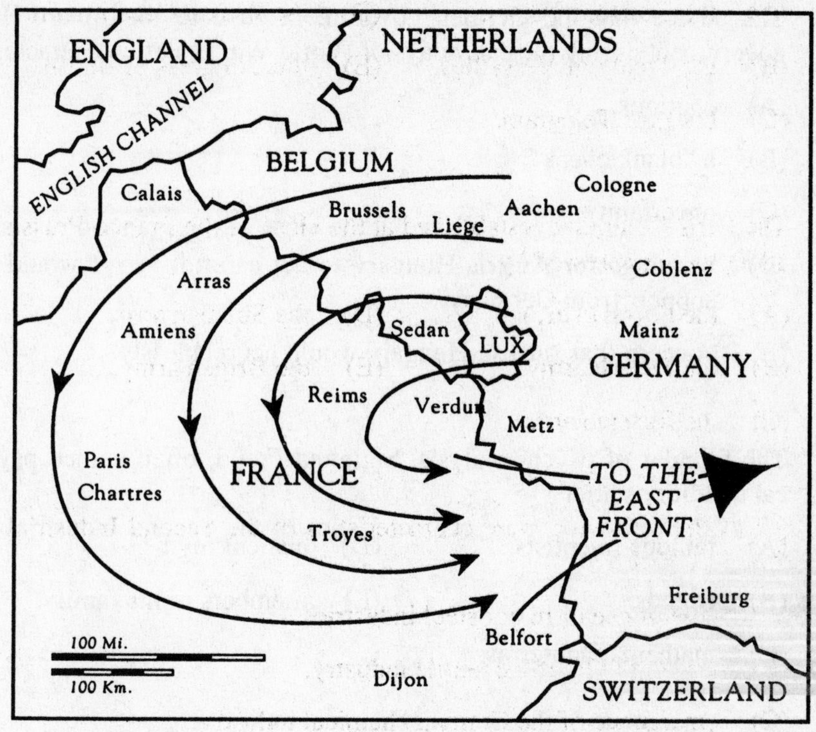

(A) Maginot Line.

(B) Schlieffen Plan.

(C) German invasion of France in 1940.

(D) "soft underbelly of Europe."

(E) French defenses in World War I.

68. The earliest form of Communism in the Soviet Union was called

(A) Marxist-Leninism.

(B) Socialism in One Country.

(C) Let a Thousand Flowers Bloom.

(D) War Communism.

(E) Strength through Unity.

69. The term "iron curtain," used to describe Soviet-dominated areas of Eastern Europe, was coined in the late 1940s by

(A) Churchill.

(B) de Gaulle.

(C) Adenauer.

(D) Khrushchev.

(E) Stalin.

70. The advice that the German government gave to the Austro-Hungarian government during the early days of World War I is often characterized as

    (A) cautious.

    (B) a "blank check."

    (C) uncertainty.

    (D) warnings for Austria-Hungary to act carefully so it would not lose support from Germany.

    (E) concern that Austria-Hungary would act recklessly.

71. The founder of psychoanalysis, Sigmund Freud, often named psychological conditions after

    (A) famous scientists.

    (B) friends.

    (C) mathematical terms.

    (D) ancient myths.

    (E) members of his family.

THE CHANGE IN NATIONAL POPULATIONS AT THE TURN OF THE CENTURY (POPULATION IN MILLIONS)

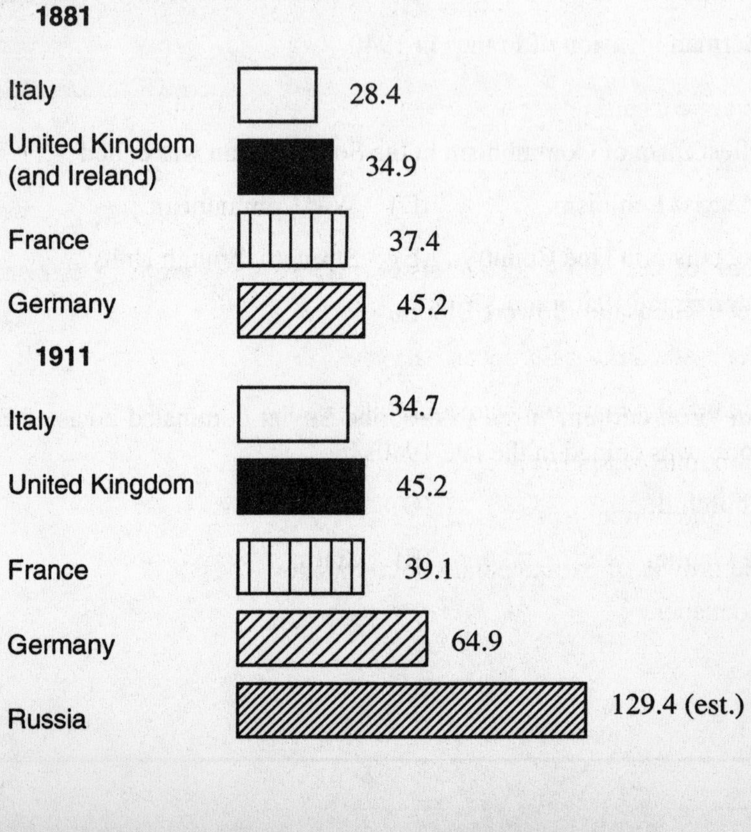

1881

Italy 28.4

United Kingdom (and Ireland) 34.9

France 37.4

Germany 45.2

1911

Italy 34.7

United Kingdom 45.2

France 39.1

Germany 64.9

Russia 129.4 (est.)

72. All the following statements are reasonable conclusions about the graph shown on the previous page EXCEPT

(A) the United Kingdom gained more people than France.

(B) the United Kingdom gained more people than Italy.

(C) in percentage terms, Russia experienced the greatest population growth.

(D) Germany gained more people than France.

(E) much of Europe was experiencing a population growth.

73. Which of the following describes an important trend in Britain during the Depression of the 1930s?

(A) Interest rates rose rapidly.

(B) Unemployment remained high.

(C) Property values rose.

(D) National industrial production was at an all-time high.

(E) Military spending increased rapidly.

74. The United Nations was originally envisioned in a document known as the

(A) Truman Doctrine.

(B) Atlantic Charter.

(C) Molotov Plan.

(D) Brussels Pact.

(E) Treaty of Rapallo.

75. Which one of the following factors stimulated the growth of fascism in Europe during the 1920s and 1930s?

(A) Free trade among European nations

(B) The development of cheaper armaments

(C) Economic prosperity

(D) Fear of communism

(E) The growth of parliamentary governments

76. The Nuremberg trials were

(A) mass purges in the Soviet Union.

(B) trials of war criminals.

(C) the trials which placed Hitler in prison as a young man.

(D) trials of manufacturers who were war profiteers in World War I.

(E) trials of German army officers who conspired to kill Hitler during World War II.

77. A primary element in National Socialist ("Nazi") ideology was the belief in

(A) the equality of all Germans.

(B) democratic elections.

(C) the need for *Lebensraum.*

(D) the need to restrain nationalist feelings.

(E) peaceful cooperation among nations to prevent war.

78. Which of the following best characterizes the beliefs of St. Simon (1760-1825)?

(A) Admiration for industrialization

(B) Fear of modern trends

(C) Admiration for religion

(D) Rejection of the usefulness of science

(E) Concern that Europe was in decline

79. *"Nature and nature's law lay hid in night,*
God said, 'Let Newton be,' and all was light."

This passage, which is from a poem praising science and Newton, was written by

(A) Tennyson.

(B) Yeats.

(C) Pope.

(D) Wordsworth.

(E) Zola.

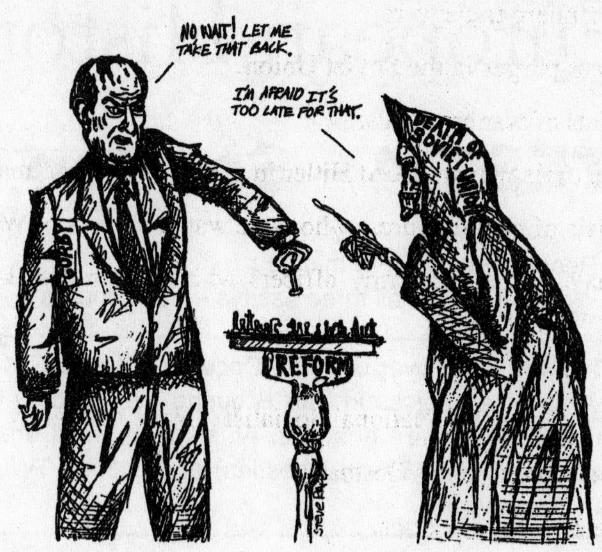

Steve Raper

80. The political cartoonist is most strongly making the point that

(A) Gorbachev never really favored either *glasnost* or *perestroika*.

(B) Gorbachev's reforms were implemented too slowly to be effective.

(C) Gorbachev believed that the Russian Republic would be better off economically and militarily by leaving the Soviet Union.

(D) once implemented, reform measures proved difficult for the CPSU to control.

(E) the attempted August 1991 coup pushed Gorbachev into moves with which he was not comfortable.

European History

TEST 4 – Section II

TIME: Reading Period – 15 minutes
Writing Time for all three essays – 115 minutes

DIRECTIONS: Read over both the Document-Based Essay question in Part A and the choices in Part B during the Reading Period, and use the time to organize answers. All students must answer Part A (the Document-Based Essay Question) and choose TWO questions from Part B to answer.

PART A – DOCUMENT-BASED ESSAY

This question is designed to test your ability to work with historical documents. As you analyze each document, take into account the source and the point of view of the author. Write an essay on the following topic that integrates your analysis of the documents. You may refer to historical facts and developments not mentioned in the documents.

Analyze the nature of the Peterloo Massacre of 1819, and assess the validity of the following statement about the event.

"Peterloo...proved to be a watershed. A nice, neat little massacre occurring within a quarter of an hour. No long drawn-out horror to numb the sensibilities. Not too many casualties, but sufficiently occasioned, with sabres slashing, children screaming, and horses trampling, to shock....(it) galvanized the middle-class Radicals, prodded the Whigs, and stiffened the Government into action."
—Joyce Marlow, *The Peterloo Massacre*

Historical Background: The Peterloo Massacre occurred during a time of turmoil and tension in Great Britain. The Napoleonic Wars had ended just four years before. Food prices were rising, and some blamed the Corn Laws, which the Tories had passed through parliament during the Napoleonic Wars. By imposing large tariffs on foreign grain during times of shortage, the Corn Laws were designed to increase food prices and benefit the nobility financially. Only the very wealthy—almost all nobility—voted for the elected house of Parliament, the House of Commons. Middle-class orators who were demanding the expansion of the electorate cited the Corn Laws as an example of the evils of the nobility's monopoly of Parliament. As new industrial cities arose, orators also complained about the "rotten boroughs" (election districts which were over-represented in Parliament because their population had declined). In 1819, one of the middle-class orators promoting expansion of the electorate, Henry Hunt, called for a rally to be held at St. Peter's Field in the relatively new, industrial city of Manchester. Despite its rapid growth, Manchester did not have a representative in Parliament. Local authorities, fearing violence, sent local militia and an army cavalry unit into the crowd. In the ensuing panic, a number of people in the crowd were killed and many injured. This event was later dubbed the "Peterloo Massacre."

Document 1

Contemporary drawing of the Peterloo Massacre.

Document 2

"(They should) take the liberty to recommend to those poor fellows, the language of whose petition breathed throughout every line a feeling of despondency and forlorn hope...to seek a redress of their manifold grievance...He advised them to give up all ideas of leaving the country...to join with the great body of people who...had embarked in a firm and constitutional way to reform the House of Commons, and never were either to the right or left until Annual Parliaments, Universal Suffrage, and Election by Ballot shall be established in the land."

—J. T. Saxton, radical reform leader, to the distressed weavers of Manchester in June 1819.

Document 3

"...we are unsound in the vitals...,that's the seat of the mischief—the Constitution's become rotten at the core—Corruption's at the very helm of the state; it sits and rules in the very House of Commons; this is the source, the true and the only one of all our sufferings—what the remedy, then? Why, reform—a radical and complete constitutional reform; we want nothing but this...to mend our markets and give every poor man plenty of work and good wages for doing it."

—From a letter to the *Manchester Mercury* in August 1819.

Document 4

"'We are very well as we are,' says the hereditary Lord, who squanders away his 30,000 British pounds a year in every species of debauchery and dissipation...'We are very well as we are,' say the Representatives and Aristocratical Proprietors of Rotten Boroughs. But what say seven millions of persons in this country who are totally *unrepresented?* What say the liberal minded—the independent—the friends of freedom—and the friends of thought?"

—From an article in the *Manchester Gazette,* December 16, 1818.

Document 5

"You will meet on Monday next, friends, and by your *steady, firm, and temperate* deporting, you will convince all your enemies, that you feel you have an *important* and *imperious public duty* to perform. Our Enemies will seek every opportunity to...excite a riot, that they may have a pretence for Spilling our Blood....Come, then, friends, to the meeting with no other Weapon but that of a self approving conscience; determine not to suffer yourself to be irritated or excited, by any means whatsoever, to cause any breach of the public peace."

—Statement by Hunt, announcing the rally at St. Peter's Field.

Document 6

(Local authorities stationed themselves in buildings near the rally to observe the crowd; after the rally had begun, they ordered the local militia (the Yeomanry) and an army cavalry unit, both of which were waiting in nearby streets, to move into the crowd to maintain order.)

"At first (the movement of the Manchester Yeomanry) was not rapid, and there was some show of an attempt to follow their officer in regular succession, five or six abreast; but they soon increased their speed...they had long been insulted with taunts of cowardice, (and) continued their course, seemed to vie with each other which should be first...As the cavalry approached the dense mass of people they used their utmost efforts to escape; but so closely were they pressed in opposite directions by the soldiers, the special constables,... and their own immense numbers, that immediate escape was impossible...On the arrival (of the troops)...a scene of dreadful confusion ensued."

—Account of the Rev. Edward Stanley, an eyewitness.

Document 7

LIST OF THE DEAD AT "PETERLOO"

Thomas Ashworth. Sabred and trampled.
John Ashton. Sabred and trampled on by the crowd.
Thomas Buckley. Sabred and trampled.
James Crompton. Trampled on by the cavalry.
William Fildes. Two years old. Ridden over by the cavalry.
Sarah Jones. No cause given.
John Lees. Sabred.
Arthur O'Neill. Inwardly crushed.
Martha Partington. Thrown into a cellar and killed.
John Rhodes. Died several weeks later.
Joseph Ashworth. Shot.
William Bradshaw. No cause given.
William Dawson. Sabred and crushed.
Edmund Dawson. Died of sabre wounds.

—From a list compiled from many sources by a modern historian.

Document 8

"The inscriptions upon the flag are "Parliaments Annual, Suffrage Universal." I cannot say that I see anything wrong in either of these. 'Unity Strength.' 'Liberty and Fraternity.' Now are these...calculated to produce dissatisfaction and contempt and hatred to His Majesty's Government?

—Justice Bayler, defense attorney, at the trial of Hunt, describing banners at the St. Peter's Field rally.

Document 9

"The results of yesterday will bring down the name of Hunt and his accomplices...With a fractious perverseness...they have set open defiance upon the timely warning of the magistrates...and daringly invited the attendance of a mass of people which may be computed at near 100,000....Yesterday's proceedings showed that the Revolutionary attempts of this base Junto was no longer to be tolerated."

—From one of the first newspaper accounts of the massacre, in the *Manchester Mercury,* August 17, 1819.

Document 10

(The Peterloo Massacre was regarded as a civil insurrection by the Tories in Parliament, who used their majority to force through Parliament a series of laws restricting basic liberties, the Six Acts. The rival Whigs opposed the Six Acts and tended to see the incident as evidence of popular discontent and proof of the need for electoral reform.)

"He felt himself bound to recommend to the House, if it wished to avoid civil dissension, if it wished to avoid the greatest of all evils, the shedding of English blood by English hands, to examine fairly and freely into the state of representation…."

—From a speech by a Whig member of Parliament, December 1819.

Document 11

"For many months, we had suffered the terrors of siege, having enemies within as well as without; and when we went to bed at night, we knew not, but that our town would be in flames before morning….Who shall complain of Peterloo, when the *organized terrors of months of slavery and fear* had driven us to make a desperate stand for all, which Britons can value."

—A Tory speaker defending the authorities' handling of the crowd.

Document 12

"…it must be admitted that taxation is ponderous, and that the middle class are like enough to fall into the state of the lower, and the lower into a state of starvation. But what can Reform, or any other nostrum of political agitation do here? We are suffering the effects of the late war and bad harvests, and must wait patiently until the tide turns. It is absurd to attribute such calamities to borough-mongering and the Bourbons."

—Lord Gatliffe to Lord Farington, June 5, 1819 (The Bourbons were the French ruling family).

Document 13

"The policy which is meant to suppress or fetter discussion is...doubtful; for the best vent for passion…is the freedom of using angry words."

—A Whig comment on the Six Acts, from an article in the *London Times.*

Document 14

(Among those expressing disapproval of the Six Acts was the young Tory Robert Peel, later to be prime minister of England. During the 1820s, Peel and other "reform" Tories would convince Parliament to approve legal and other reforms.)

"Do you not think that the tone of England…is more liberal…than the policy of the government? Do you not think there is more a feeling, becoming daily more general…in favor of some undefined change in the role of governing the country…?"

—Robert Peel, Letter of 1819.

Document 15

(The Tories controlled Parliament until 1831. During an election in 1829, the Duke of Wellington, campaigning for the Tories, was greeted by signs bearing the words "Remember Peterloo." By the time of major national elections in 1831, the Whigs had committed themselves to expanding the electorate. When they won, they passed legislation giving the suffrage to half of the adult middle-class males, beginning a process that continued throughout the century.)

"Peterloo was Tory justice, and is what they would repeat should they ever come to power again."

—From a Liberal party pamphlet directed against the Conservative party (formerly called the Tories) in the election of 1874.

PART B – ESSAY QUESTIONS

1. Describe and compare the policies of mercantilism and *laissez-faire.*

2. Describe and analyze why the debate over a sun-centered versus earth-centered solar system was the primary controversy of the Scientific Revolution.

3. Assess and analyze how problems in the World War II alliance of the United States, Great Britain, and the Soviet Union helped lead to the Cold War.

4. "The French Enlightenment" was a fountainhead of humanitarian and libertarian principles; it articulated grievances and sought alternatives. The German Enlightenment was more abstract and less practical."

   Analyze and assess the validity of this statement, citing specific individuals.

5. Describe and assess the importance of primogeniture in creating a distinctive social structure in Great Britain, as compared to continental European nations such as France.

6. Louis XIV (reigned 1643-1715) was France's most famous absolute monarch, while Napoleon III (reigned 1851-1870), a nephew of Napoleon Bonaparte, became emperor of France in an army-direct coup d'état and ruled in conjunction with a two-house legislature.

   Starting with the portraits shown on the following page, analyze similarities and differences in the nature and style of these two monarchies.

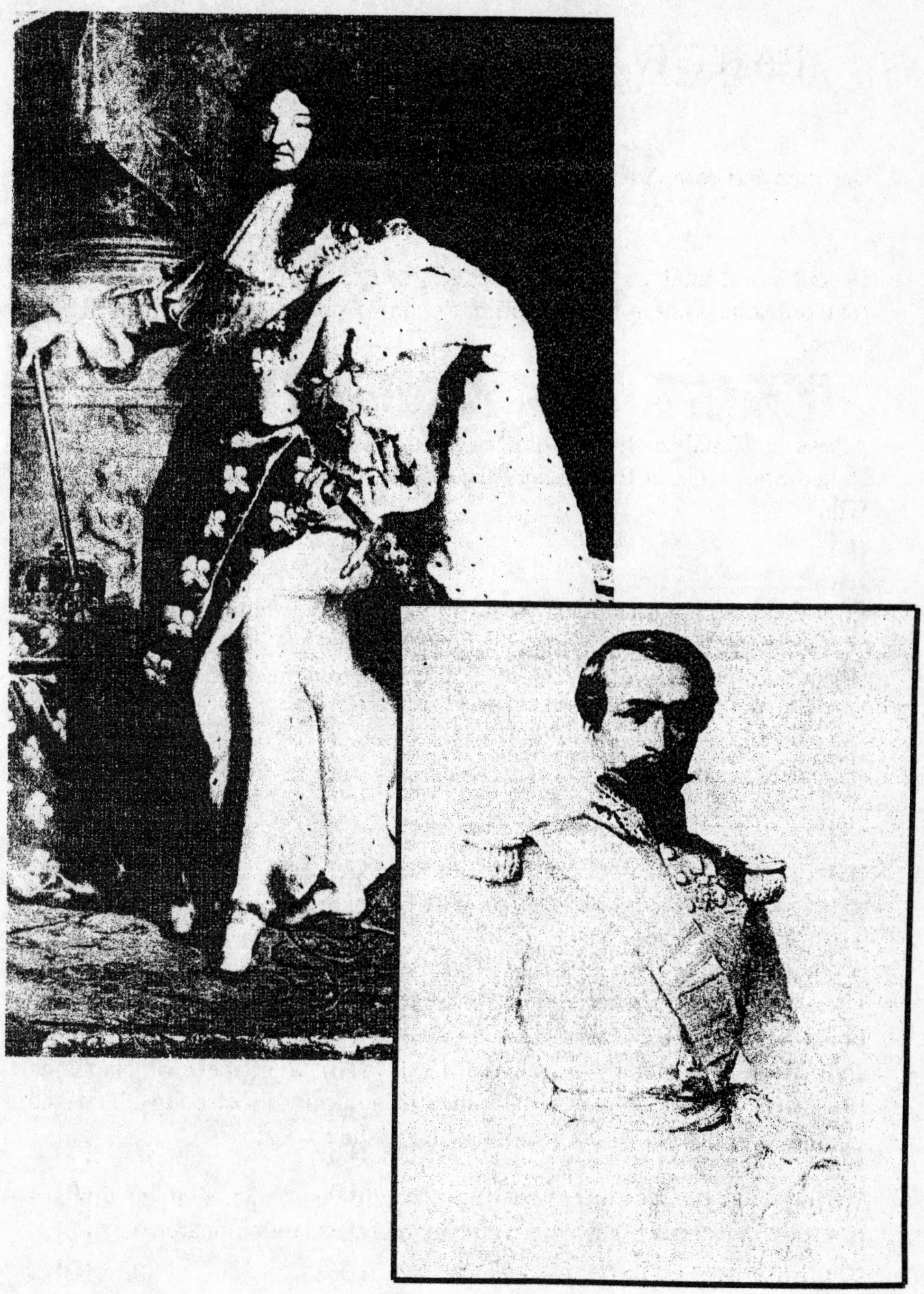

THE ADVANCED PLACEMENT EXAMINATION IN

European History

TEST 4 – ANSWERS

1. **(B)**
2. **(A)**
3. **(D)**
4. **(B)**
5. **(B)**
6. **(A)**
7. **(C)**
8. **(D)**
9. **(B)**
10. **(D)**
11. **(B)**
12. **(A)**
13. **(A)**
14. **(B)**
15. **(A)**
16. **(C)**
17. **(B)**
18. **(C)**
19. **(D)**
20. **(C)**
21. **(B)**
22. **(E)**
23. **(D)**
24. **(B)**
25. **(B)**
26. **(D)**
27. **(B)**
28. **(B)**
29. **(B)**
30. **(C)**
31. **(B)**
32. **(B)**
33. **(B)**
34. **(B)**
35. **(C)**
36. **(D)**
37. **(B)**
38. **(D)**
39. **(E)**
40. **(B)**
41. **(B)**
42. **(D)**
43. **(C)**
44. **(A)**
45. **(C)**
46. **(C)**
47. **(B)**
48. **(D)**
49. **(C)**
50. **(A)**
51. **(A)**
52. **(C)**
53. **(C)**
54. **(C)**
55. **(B)**
56. **(A)**
57. **(C)**
58. **(D)**
59. **(B)**
60. **(D)**
61. **(B)**
62. **(D)**
63. **(C)**
64. **(B)**
65. **(B)**
66. **(C)**
67. **(B)**
68. **(D)**
69. **(A)**
70. **(B)**
71. **(D)**
72. **(C)**
73. **(B)**
74. **(B)**
75. **(D)**
76. **(B)**
77. **(C)**
78. **(A)**
79. **(C)**
80. **(D)**

Detailed Explanations of Answers

TEST 4

1. **(B)** "Exclusion" questions, which ask you to identify the single answer which does not fit with the others, may be approached in two different ways. One approach is to identify the single answer that is false; the other is to eliminate all true answers. Although he criticized Christianity as "superstition" and believed that religious bias caused French Huguenots to be unjustly convicted of crimes, Voltaire retained God in his philosophy. His version of religion, Deism, envisioned God as a creator of the universe; a minimal number of simple religious beliefs were to be part of Deism, in order to avoid constant theological arguments. The remaining answers are true: Voltaire favored the reform of French society from "above" by the monarch (Enlightened Despotism); during a brief stay in England, he wrote a book praising the English political system; and he wrote his cynical and skeptical book *Candide* as a reply to the German philosopher Leibniz, who insisted that this is the best of all possible worlds.

2. **(A)** The *strelski*, or Moscow guards, created and toppled tsars; the nobility sought their favor. Peter the Great destroyed the *strelski* after a revolt in 1698. With some knowledge of Russian history, one or two of the other answers may be eliminated. Answer (C) is not likely, since the date of the Decembrist revolt places it much too late in Russian history.

3. **(D)** Sièyés' *The Third Estate* sought to use a military coup d'état to create a strong, but unelected, executive. The book suggested goals that Napoleon Bonaparte later accomplished. *What Is to Be Done?* was the title of Vladimir Lenin's book detailing the path to proletarian revolution in Russia. In his *Essay on Human Understanding*, John Locke argued that human personality is formed entirely by the environment, rather than by innate or preconceived ideas. *The Progress of the Human Mind*, by the philosopher Condorcet, argued that human perfectibility was possible and that "nature has set no limits to our hopes."

4. **(B)** Portuguese navigators played a role in the explorations of the New World. If this fact is not known, there are other possible approaches. Consider clues that you may already know: Portuguese is the language of Brazil, the

largest nation in South America. Some elimination may also be done: (D) is obviously incorrect, since there was no united Italy until 1870.

5. **(B)** Pride's Purge, named for the colonel who carried it out, occurred after the English Civil War of the 1640s, which was won by a faction of the Puritans (the Congregationalists) under Oliver Cromwell. All opponents of Cromwell were removed from Parliament, including Puritans who belonged to the other faction, the Presbyterians. Only about 50 supporters of Cromwell were left in Parliament. The remaining answers are untrue or simply not applicable.

6. **(A)** Here is another example of an "exclusion" question. The Edict of Nantes was issued by Henry IV, France's first Bourbon monarch, after France's major religious war. A Huguenot, Henry became monarch by promising to convert to Roman Catholicism. The war left France exhausted, and convinced many that religious issues should be kept strictly separate from political issues. Thus there was support for the Edict, which guaranteed the Huguenots freedom of worship and the right to have their own fortresses in the countryside. Louis XIV, the most powerful of the French monarchs and a devout Catholic, later revoked the Edict, asserting that the right of Huguenots to have their own fortresses was a violation of his royal sovereignty.

7. **(C)** Locke envisioned the "state of nature" as a time of relative peace and harmony. The "social contract," by which the first government was established, was necessary only because certain tasks, such as road building, might be done only collectively. Rousseau also used the term "social contract," but his "state of nature" was a time of economic equality; insisting that "property is theft," Rousseau argued that economic inequality began when human beings began to place value on objects that might be hoarded, such as gold or precious stones (unlike food, which was perishable).

8. **(D)** Although the first three answers plus answer (E) were achieved during the Era of Reform—including abolition of much of the power of the Junkers, the nobility which owned the large farm estates in eastern Prussia—the monarchy did not institute universal manhood suffrage (all adult males being allowed to vote) until 1850. Even then, the votes of the wealthy "counted" for much more than the middle class or the poor.

9. **(B)** A major cause was the failure of the Polish parliament, the Diet, to function effectively. The liberum veto, which allowed any member to force adjournment by objecting to the topic under discussion, made the Diet ineffective. The other answers are either not applicable or untrue. Poland had no religious wars. The Polish nobility, deeply split among themselves, often selected foreigners as monarchs rather than pick someone from their own ranks. Thus answer (E) is also incorrect; Poland had more problems with weak monarchs than with overly assertive monarchs.

10. **(D)** The first 30 years of the Third French Republic were tumultuous, as Monarchists bitterly tried to gain control of the Republic. When doubts began to surface over the guilt of Alfred Dreyfus, a military intelligence officer convicted by a Royalist-controlled court martial of passing military secrets to Germany, the rival Republicans were able to use the issue to destroy Royalist credibility in France. As for the other answers, the Irish Question signified British debates over pacifying unhappy Ireland in the 19th century, when all of Ireland was part of Britain. The Zabern Affair described the shooting of demonstrators in the Alsace-Lorraine section of Germany by a German army unit in 1913. The Panama Canal scandal was another attempt of Royalists to turn public opinion to their side; it concerned financial scandals in a failed French project to build the canal. In the "Daily Telegraph Affair," the German Emperor William II was embarrassed by a controversy over the publication of comments which he made to a British newspaper reporter.

11. **(B)** The Risorgimento, or "resurgence," began early in the 19th century with Italians such as Mazzini, who sought a unified and liberal Italy, with a parliament elected by universal suffrage. Note that answer (E) requires you not only to know that the term Risorgimento refers to national unification but also to identify the correct country.

12. **(A)** The war began when Britain and France objected to what they saw as Russian bullying of the Ottoman Empire in a dispute over monasteries in the Holy Land. Austria tried to stay neutral for much of the war; during the 19th century, the weakening Ottoman Empire tended to avoid aggressive foreign policies. Answer (E) is incorrect because Bismarck did not come to power until nearly a decade after the Crimean War.

13. **(A)** Since the first two Hanoverian monarchs of the 1700s had little interest in government, Parliament increasingly assumed royal powers. Although he did not have the actual title of "prime minister," Walpole in fact assumed that role by first, representing the largest faction in Parliament and second, taking the responsibility to explain the monarch's point of view in parliamentary debates.

14. **(B)** Pasternak was forbidden to receive the prize personally after the publication of his novel *Dr. Zhivago,* which included critical comments about the 1917 communist revolution. Shostakovitch and Prokofiev were Soviet composers; Beria a head of the KGB, the secret police; and Brezhnev a ruler of the Soviet Union during the late 1960s and 1970s.

15. **(A)** Under the leadership of Marshall Tito, a communist and World War II hero, Yugoslavia refused to follow Soviet directives after World War II. This "exclusion" question may also be answered by identifying the remaining answers as true. Eastern European nations were forbidden by the Soviet government to participate in the Marshall Plan. A revolt in East Germany in 1953 was suppressed by the country's government, and a Hungarian revolt of 1956 was put

down by the Soviet army. Almost all Eastern European nations were militarily allied with the Soviet Union through the Warsaw Pact.

16. **(C)** Although Britain and France were not in favor of the attempts, their opposition had little impact on Hitler's attempts to unite Germany with the country that was his birthplace, Austria. The significant opposition came from Mussolini, who worried that the Italian minority in Austria would be mistreated by a racially-minded Nazi government. The two countries were united in 1938 when Hitler and Mussolini reached a private understanding. Note the importance of the date ("1934") in the question.

17. **(B)** Nurtured during the early years of the Third French Republic, when Royalists in France bitterly tried to gain control over the state, the Action Française advocated an authoritarian government with a strengthened military. The organization, a pre-fascist movement, also advocated anti-Semitism.

18. **(C)** The major clues are the date (which tests historical knowledge) and the geography of the map (which tests your knowledge of geography in history). Note that the word "Poland" does not appear on the map. Of the incorrect answers, all but France also appear on the map, and there may be a tendency to select one of them.

19. **(D)** A series of two-nation treaties, the Locarno treaties included a German-French understanding in which Germany accepted its post-World War I borders. The treaties cleared the way for German membership in the League of Nations. Despite promises made by the American President Woodrow Wilson, the United States withdrew from the European diplomatic system after the war.

20. **(C)** In general, the Romantics regarded the Enlightenment as an era which worshipped cold, mechanical Reason and failed to appreciate the variety and spontaneity of human experiences. While the Enlightenment philosophers thought history might furnish lessons for morality and government, the Romantics emphasized history as an emotional experience. The Middle Ages were particularly admired, to the point that replicas of castles and "new" ruins of buildings were constructed during the Romantic era. In contrast to the cosmopolitan atmosphere of the French Enlightenment, many Romantics championed the worth of individual nations and cultures.

21. **(B)** The Fabian Socialists were a largely British movement which attracted the support of notables such as George Bernard Shaw and H. G. Wells. Led by Sydney and Beatrice Webb, they called for increasing the public ownership of private industry, even to the point of state ownership. Such changes, they insisted, were to come peacefully.

22. **(E)** Until 1866-1870, Germany was divided into a multitude of states that

at one point totaled more than 300. Because most of the other European states, unlike Germany, had developed strong national monarchies, many of them had been unified much earlier.

23. **(D)** Prussia and Austria, the two largest German states, combined in 1820 to issue the Carlsbad Decrees, which established a system of press censors and university inspectors. The goal was to suppress liberal movements. The other answers are not applicable. The Charter of 1814 was France's second constitution. It was issued by Louis XVIII, the first monarch after the Napoleonic period, in hopes of guaranteeing his acceptance by the French people. The Holy Alliance was formed at the Congress of Vienna and required the great powers to conduct their diplomacy according to the principles of Jesus Christ. The Declaration of the Rights of Man was issued during the French Revolution of 1789. The Schlieffen Plan was a German military plan, implemented in World War I, for an invasion of France.

24. **(B)** After his predecessors, the first two Hanoverian monarchs of the 1700s, virtually ignored Parliament, George III was a more serious monarch. Parliament, which had assumed much of the king's powers during the period of weakened monarchs, resisted. The formation of such a faction of supporters in Parliament, the "king's friends," was intended to give the throne a group of dedicated spokesmen and admirers within the parliamentary system.

25. **(B)** Smith's book, which appeared in 1776, opposed mercantilism and predicted that the greatest prosperity would be reached when individuals were free to pursue their own selfish interests without government interference or regulation.

26. **(D)** A product of the Middle Ages, the Estates-General reflected the society of that time. The clergy were preeminent, the nobility were the Second Estate, and the Third Estate comprised the remainder of the population (the peasants and middle class). Factory owners, non-existent in the Middle Ages, were present in the Estates-General only as part of the Third Estate.

27. **(B)** Passed by the National Assembly during the French Revolution, the Civil Constitution of the Clergy reflected the anticlericalism of many revolutionaries. It denied papal power to appoint bishops or other clergy, substituting popular election instead, and made them salaried officials of the state. While some clergy perished in the Reign of Terror, there was no direct connection between these events and the Civil Constitution. Note that answer (E) flatly contradicts answer (B), suggesting that one of these two is the correct answer.

28. **(B)** The Charter was the first constitution issued by a monarch. It created a two-house legislature that helped govern the country, in different forms, throughout the century. As mentioned in the explanation for Question No. 23, the monarch, Louis XVIII, issued the document to insure popular acceptance of his rule.

29. **(B)** Locke approved of a revolution carried through by the educated and propertied, provided that the monarch has violated property rights. In the case of James II, ousted in the Glorious Revolution of 1688, Locke believed that his government had extracted "forced loans" from prominent citizens in order to underwrite government expenses. American forefathers copied the phrase "life, liberty, and the pursuit of happiness" from Locke, although in Locke's words it was originally "life, liberty, and the right to property."

30. **(C)** Directed against Charles II, the monarch who restored the Stuart monarchy after the period of Puritan rule in England, the Code was passed by Parliament in an attempt to deny Charles the right to appoint close Catholic friends as his advisers.

31. **(B)** Bacon's book asserted that scientists ideally should be clear-minded thinkers, untouched by religious or political biases or philosophical preconceptions. He listed a series of biases or preconceptions which might be obstacles to scientific work, terming them "idols." Answer (C) is too obvious an answer to consider seriously.

32. **(B)** The picture depicts the sale of indulgences in early 1500s Germany by the Dominican monk Tetzel. The incident angered Luther and set him on the path which led to the Reformation. The wording of the question may mislead you by causing you to examine the picture for major clues. This approach is not likely to be helpful. The real clues are in the "jingle," which you may even remember from a history course. If you do, the question then asks for something more: the name of the monk who sold indulgences in Luther's part of Germany.

33. **(B)** Henry's break with the papacy was personal, centered around his desire to "divorce" his first wife because she had not produced a male heir to the throne. The sole change Henry desired was a transfer in the major authority of the church from the pope to himself (thus answer (E) is incorrect). He retained six of the church's sacraments with the Act of the Six Articles and resolutely opposed Protestant influences, keeping a close eye on his Archbishop of Canterbury, who favored Protestantism. In order to persuade many of the nobility to accept his changes, Henry dissolved the Roman Catholic monasteries and distributed their wealth among influential noblemen.

34. **(B)** During Europe's final religious war, and one of its most destructive—rivalling the damage to Germany at the end of World War II—the Hapsburgs sought to destroy Protestantism in Europe and advance Hapsburg interests. Operating on the principle of raisons d'état ("reasons of state"), Richelieu, although a Catholic Cardinal, decided that his country's best interests lay in weakening the rival Hapsburgs. He chose to do so by sending aid to Protestant forces, at least until he believed it necessary for France to intervene in the war directly.

35. **(C)** Khrushchev, ruler of the Soviet Union after the death of Stalin, proclaimed the superiority of the Soviet system and predicted a continued competition with capitalism, but he added that the struggle would be peaceful. Answer (A) was a World War II slogan of the Allies fighting Germany and Italy. Answer (B) was the slogan during the 1960s of the French president Charles DeGaulle, who predicted increasing European independence from the "superpowers" of the United States and the Soviet Union. Answer (D) was one of Lenin's slogans in pre-revolutionary Russia. "Peace in Our Time" was the prediction made by the British Prime Minister Chamberlain in 1938 following the Munich conference over the fate of Czechoslovakia.

36. **(D)** One possible approach to this "exclusion" question is to try to identify which answer was not true of the post World War II period. Germany, divided into non-Communist and Communist states, was not allowed to have an army until non-Communist West Germany joined the North Atlantic Treaty Organization in 1955 and Communist East Germany joined the corresponding Warsaw Pact. An alternate approach is to determine that answers (A) through (C), plus answer (E), were true of the postwar period, leaving (D) as the correct answer by elimination.

37. **(B)** Spengler portrayed history as a series of cycles in which civilizations rose and decayed. His assertions that Western culture was nearing the end of its cycle found a large audience after World War I among embittered Germans who spoke of building a new, nondemocratic and, in some cases, a racist, civilization. While this question appears to require exact knowledge of the book involved, the key to the question is the types of writers represented. Only Spengler was an expository writer; all of the others were literary writers. Thomas Mann was Germany's most famous novelist in the years between World War I and World War II. Joyce's *Ulysses* (1921) has been termed the most influential English novel of the century. Proust pioneered the "stream of consciousness" method of writing in his autobiographical *Remembrance of Things Past* (1913-1927). Beckett, an Irish playwright, became famous for plays such as *Waiting for Godot* (1953).

38. **(D)** Although at first glance this appears to be a knowledge-based question, it actually requires an ability to analyze your knowledge and to understand the implications of Stalin's policy. "Socialism in One Country," primarily a plan to industrialize Russia through five-year plans, required husbanding all national resources for domestic use; attempts to aid foreign communist parties and attempts to foment revolution in other European nations were to be abandoned. The policy, however, also required avoiding wars or foreign alliances which might lead to war.

39. **(E)** A test of the thoroughness of your knowledge of Marx' ideas and your ability to analyze the implications of your knowledge, this question focuses on the fact that Marx believed revolution to be a logical outcome of the growth of

capitalism. The most industrialized nations would have the first large proletarian classes, and thus also have the first revolutions. Nations which had not yet begun to industrialize would have revolutions last; Marx, in fact, ridiculed the large peasant class in Russia, which he believed would be innately opposed to major change.

40. **(B)** The question asks for knowledge of terminology ("gap theory") but adds a major clue ("Bismarck"). Since the country in which the Army Bill Crisis occurred is not identified, you must know that term as well. Bismarck was brought to power in Prussia by the crisis, which was a stalemate between the Prussian king and his legislature over reforms of the Prussian army. Bismarck solved the stalemate by insisting that the Prussian constitution contained a "gap": there was no mention of what was to be done if such a logjam developed. Since the king had granted the constitution, Bismarck insisted that the monarch might ignore the liberals in the legislature and follow his own judgment. Answer (E) (the name of a political crisis in France during the 1880s) is designed to tempt those who know that the "gap theory" solved a crisis but are not certain of the name of the crisis.

41. **(B)** The answer is a choice between (A) and (B). (C) (the name of a brother of King Louis XVI), (D) (a member of the French nobility sympathetic to the revolution), and (E) (the head of the French government during World War I) are irrelevant. Danton was, in fact, a politician who was a victim of the Reign of Terror and of the dominant political faction of the time, the Jacobins.

42. **(D)** A test of your historical knowledge and ability to apply it, this question cites a quotation that illustrates the Christian Humanists' interest in translating the Bible from Latin into the local languages of Europe. The only Christian Humanist listed in the answers is Erasmus. Loyola was founder of the Society of Jesus, or Jesuits; Machiavelli was a political writer during the Italian Renaissance; Galileo was a scientist during the Scientific Revolution; and Robert Boyle was one of the first prominent European physicists and chemists.

43. **(C)** During the 1600s and early 1700s, when prices for wool rose significantly, the nobility sought grazing land for large herds of sheep. In Western Europe, and especially in England, public lands and small farms were fenced in ("enclosed") to create large grazing territories. Answers (A) and (D) attempt to sound plausible for those who do not know the Enclosure Movement. Answer (B) may be tempting for those with only a slight knowledge of the movement since, in England, the Enclosure Acts threw peasants out of work and thus created a source of cheap labor for the early factories.

44. **(A)** In late 15th century Florence, the monk Savonarola decried worldly influences in church and society, insisting that while the church itself could not be corrupt, the leaders of the church might be corrupted. His efforts to enforce repentance and ban sinful influences are reminiscent of Calvin's Geneva.

45. **(C)** In this case, the problem is to identify the opposition or challenges to royal authority—and then to identify the single answer which represents the opposite, a development or event which strengthened absolutism. Four of the five answer choices may be eliminated because they attempted to weaken monarchies—the parliaments (French courts controlled by the nobility, and frequent platforms for opposing royal power); the New Model Army (the name for the army of Oliver Cromwell, the victor over Charles I in the English Civil War); the Puritans themselves, major opponents of Charles in that war; and the Roundheads, the term used to describe the military opposition to Charles. Only Louis XIV's palace of Versailles, where many of the French nobility lived and became involved in useless ceremonial lives, helped strengthen absolutism. Note that this question mixes events in two countries (France and England), requiring you to use "comparative history."

46. **(C)** The emblem of Louis XIV in front of the sun, with the sun's rays visible around his head, symbolizes his title of "the Sun King." The remaining answers—the 18th century Prussian monarch Frederick, the late 16th and 17th century rulers Peter of Russia and Charles of Sweden, and the 16th century Spanish monarch Philip II are not applicable.

47. **(B)** Peter's reforms, and his creation of a Russian navy based on the Baltic Sea, challenged the power of Sweden, which saw Peter's construction of a new capital city in northeastern Russia as a direct challenge. By Peter's reign, Poland had already declined considerably from the late 1400s when a union of Poland and Lithuania had stretched from the Baltic Sea almost to the Black Sea.

48. **(D)** The wars of religion in Europe had the ironic effect of stimulating interest in science, which some Europeans argued was less emotional and less likely to lead to warfare. The 17th century saw the establishment of scientific societies in most European nations.

49. **(C)** The correct answer is (C). Havel worked as a playwright.

50. **(A)** An example of a question which requests knowledge of a particular kind of terminology—slogans—this question asks for your understanding of Voltaire's outlook and the major target of his writings. If enough is known about Voltaire, some answers may be eliminated; since Voltaire favored (and helped coin the name) Enlightened Despotism, answer (C), for example, is not correct. Answer (D) sounds plausible, but is not the correct answer.

51. **(A)** Rousseau's political ideas remain the subject of much debate, but it is clear that he believed that political problems might be solved through the "general will," an amorphous idea which his interpreters have variously described as a democratic majority or government by a fascist oligarchy. Answer (B) summarizes Voltaire's position; (C) a theocracy, which means rule by church elites, would have been rejected by virtually all leading French thinkers of Rousseau's

day.

52. **(C)** The correct answer is (C). Political corruption and instability were the central causes of the downfall of the Christian Democrats in the 1990s. Corruption landed a number of them in jail, and the party had never been able to maintain a stable ruling coalition in the Italian Parliament for the duration of the entire post-war period. Though the economic status of southern Italy lagged that of the prosperous North, poverty (A) was not widespread in Italy; food shortages (B) were not a problem for Italy; the Christian Democrats, despite their name, were a centrist and largely secular political party (D), and Italy did indeed support the U.S. during the Persian Gulf War (E), a fact unrelated to the fortunes of the Christian Democrats.

53. **(C)** This question demands both knowledge of terminology and careful reading skills. Answers (A) through (C) are so closely related that a second reading of the passage is recommended in order to distinguish between them. Although the passage deals with sovereignty and may be used to defend an absolute monarch, the last part of the passage ("You see the image of God in the king...") makes clear that the writer is using "divine right" to justify monarchies. "Divine right of kings" was the name given to arguments that monarchs held their throne by divine authority: God had seen that they were born into the royal family, God had safeguarded them to adulthood, and God had preserved their health. Another side of the argument was that revolution was contrary to God's will. Answer (D) is an attempt to test those who see the word "God" in the passage but otherwise do not read it carefully.

54. **(C)** Claiming to be Catherine the Great's dead husband, Emelyan Pugachev led a large peasant rebellion from 1773 through 1775, nearly toppling Catherine, who had gained the throne by arranging for the murder of her husband. The central, or eastern-European sounding, name of "Pugachev" is a clue that answer (B) is probably incorrect.

55. **(B)** The Table of Ranks set educational and training standards for Russian high civil servants, almost all of whom were nobility; promotion was also based on the same criteria. It was part of Peter's attempt to supplement the old boyar nobility with a new, service-based nobility beholden to the tsar.

56. **(A)** In 1756, Britain, which for some time had been allied with Austria, signed an alliance with Austria's great rival, Prussia. That event led to a new French-Austrian alliance the same year.

57. **(C)** A mixed, largely middle class group which included shopkeepers and artisans, the *sans-culottes* (meaning "those without kneebreeches," a reference to their refusal to wear the fine clothes of the upper classes) hated the food shortages and rising food prices of the early stages of the revolution. Their discontent focussed on the social inequalities in France; in the National Assembly, their

representatives joined with the Jacobins to create a bare, one-vote majority favoring the execution of King Louis XVI.

58. **(D)** Convinced that liberalism spoke for the middle class, many workers joined the Chartist movement, which during the 1830s and 1840s presented several mass petitions to Parliament demanding the abolition of property qualifications for voting, secret ballots, universal suffrage, and payment for members of Parliament.

59. **(B)** Although Prussia would later unite Germany through wars, the Prussian king rejected the crown of united Germany when it was offered by a national assembly, the Frankfurt Parliament, during the revolution of 1848. The reason he gave was that he refused to accept the crown from the hands of revolutionaries. A careful look at the answers will show that answer (B) is distinctively different from the other three, indicating that it is either the correct answer or a ploy to tempt those who know nothing about the topic. Answer (E) is a plausible-sounding, but incorrect, answer.

60. **(D)** Jingoism, taken from the word "jingo" in the second line of the saying, came to mean emotional, mindless nationalism. The other answers are attempts to create plausible alternatives. For example, British citizens proudly boasted in the 19th century that their nation, the most highly industrialized in the world at the time, was the "Workshop of the World."

61. **(B)** Camillo Cavour, the diplomat who planned most of the steps of Italian unification, was royal minister for the kingdom of Piedmont in northwest Italy. The role of Prussia in unifying Germany is much better known, but Piedmont basically played the role of Prussia in Italy and Cavour played the role of Bismarck. Sicily was part of a southern Italian monarchical state until Italy was unified. Corsica is a Mediterranean island south of France. Venetia, in northeast Italy, was largely held by Austria from 1815 to 1867. The region of Tuscany, in northwest Italy, played a lesser role in unification than did Piedmont.

62. **(D)** The correct choice is (D). Russia backed the international force led by the United States. Since this army was mobilized against Iraq because of Saddam Hussein's invasion of Kuwait, any choice indicating Russian neutrality or support for Iraq would, by inference, have to be dismissed.

63. **(C)** The Ems Telegram was a carefully edited version of a telegram which the Prussian king sent to Bismarck in 1870. The Spanish throne was vacant, and a young member of the Prussian ruling family (the Hohenzollerns) had been asked to become the new monarch of Spain. The French Emperor Napoleon III vigorously opposed this arrangement, seeing it as an attempt to encircle France with German monarchs. Rather than risk war, the Prussian king withdrew the "Hohenzollern candidacy" to the Spanish throne. When Napoleon III ordered the French ambassador to obtain the king's promise that the situation would not

recur, the king reported this conversation to Bismarck through a telegram. In order to anger France and cause Napoleon III to declare war, Bismarck edited the telegram—overemphasizing the insulting nature of the French ambassador's demand—and released it to the press. The Fourteen Points of Woodrow Wilson, summarizing American war aims in World War I, and the Treaty of Versailles, the main treaty to end World War I, are later in history. Answer (D) should not be tempting; the British constitution is unwritten. During the Congress of Berlin of 1878 (a diplomatic conference), the great powers of Europe successfully pressured Russia to soften a harsh treaty it had forced on the Ottoman Empire.

64. **(B)** Answer (A) appears too obvious, and it is. When the French government, which had moved to the city of Bordeaux, signed a peace agreement with Prussia in 1871, the city of Paris, which was under siege by Prussia, refused to accept the surrender. A separate government in Paris, the Commune, spoke of nationalizing banks in order to finance continued resistance to the German invaders. French troops loyal to the government suppressed the Commune, but the event left a trauma among much of the French middle class, which feared that radicalism was growing in France.

65. **(B)** The term "Second Industrial Revolution" describes an economic shift in the second half of the 19th century when steel, electricity, oil, and chemicals became important parts of industrialization, supplementing the steam, iron, and textiles which had been central to the First Industrial Revolution. The one item in the answers that belongs to the First, rather than the Second, Industrial Revolution is textiles.

66. **(C)** The Battle of Britain was the name given to the period in 1940 and 1941 when German planes ceaselessly bombed England, beginning with the bombing of air bases and expanding to day-and-night bombing of the city of London. Most of the German Luftwaffe, or air force, was lost in the battle; some historians believe the outcome prevented a German invasion attempt.

67. **(B)** The Schlieffen Plan, a German army contingency plan first formulated in the 1870s, called for a quick defeat of France in the event of a future European war. The plan was a solution to the German generals' nightmare of a future two-front war; after a French surrender, the German army would be prepared to fight Russia. The words "to the east front" show that this map does not describe events in World War II, since the German invasion of France in that war preceded their invasion of Russia. The Maginot Line describes a series of fortifications the French built along their border with Germany during the 1920s. Answer (D) was the name of Winston Churchill's belief that Germany was vulnerable to invasion through Southern Europe.

68. **(D)** Believing that the Russian revolution of 1917 had prepared Russia for full Marxism, the country's new leader, Lenin, attempted to create a society which would be as close to an ideal Marxist society as possible. War Communism (1918-1921), so called because Russia was in the midst of a civil war between Marxists and monarchists, attempted to eliminate management from factories and place the farmers on a basic salary. The system was replaced with a more capitalistic one (the New Economic Policy) in 1921, partly because War Communism contained no incentives to encourage farmers and workers to increase their production.

69. **(A)** Invited to deliver a speech at a small Missouri college, Churchill predicted a long era of ideological struggle between the Soviet Union and the "free world." Answer (D) may be eliminated immediately; Khrushchev was ruler of the Soviet Union during the late 1950s and early 1960s, following some 25 years of Stalin's rule. Adenauer was the head of the West German government during the 1950s.

70. **(B)** In urging Austria-Hungary to deal with Serbia quickly while public sympathy still lay with Austria (which had lost its heir to the throne in an assassination), Germany failed to exercise any kind of restraint on Austro-Hungarian actions. Some historians have characterized Germany's advice as a "blank check" which implied that Germany would support whatever actions Austria-Hungary took.

71. **(D)** Freud thought that many of the problems he analyzed in human behavior had already been portrayed in ancient Greek myths and plays. An example was the "Oedipus complex," named after a tragic play about a man who unknowingly murders his father and marries his mother.

72. **(C)** Answer (C) is not a reasonable conclusion because the graph indicates growth in actual numbers ("population in millions") rather than percentages. The percentage of growth for Russia cannot be calculated since the graph does not give the numerical population of Russia at the start of the period (1881).

73. **(B)** As late as 1937, Britain still had 1.5 million persons unemployed. The other answers are all untrue. Property values, production, and interest rates fell, and depression-time Britian was ill-prepared to cope with the rise of Hitler's Germany.

74. **(B)** The product of a meeting off the coast of Newfoundland in 1941 between British prime minister Churchill and the American President Roosevelt, the Atlantic Charter listed joint war aims in World War II, including the goal of a United Nations. The Truman Doctrine was a pledge to "contain" Communism by the American president of the same name. The Molotov Plan was a Soviet counterpart to the Marshall Plan of economic aid to postwar Europe. The Brussels Pact laid the groundwork for the NATO alliance after World War II. The Treaty

of Rapallo, signed during the 1920s, established diplomatic ties between Weimar Germany and the new communist government of Russia.

75. **(D)** Fascist leaders often portrayed themselves as the only alternative to the spread of communism across Europe. The Depression helped bring fascist leaders such as Hitler to power and also caused European nations to enact protectionist policies, leading to a marked decline in trade in Europe. Fascism tended to gain support in nations without a tradition of successful parliamentary government.

76. **(B)** At the end of World War II, former Nazi leaders were placed on public trial in Nuremberg as war criminals guilty of crimes against humanity. The other answers are irrelevant [(A) and (C)] or untrue (there were no major European trials of alleged "war profiteers" at the end of World War I); or simply incorrect (the trials of army officers who conspired against Hitler were not named the "Nuremburg trials)."

77. **(C)** Answers (A), (B), (D), and (E) are the opposite of Nazi beliefs. A common theme in Nazi speeches and writings was the need to capture additional living space (*Lebensraum*) for the German people.

78. **(A)** A forerunner of August Comte, the founder of the philosophy of Positivism, St. Simon believed that industrialization, aided by science, would bring a wondrous new age to Europe. Despite the religious sound of his name, Answer (C) is incorrect.

79. **(C)** Pope, an 18th century writer, is an example of popular fascination with Newton's work and with the emergence of science in particular. Answer (A) may be eliminated since Tennyson, a 19th century poet, used his poems to express doubts about the lack of humane values in science and nature.

80. **(D)** The correct answer is (D). By 1990, Gorbachev attempted to slow down some aspects of *glasnost* and *perestroika.* However, the influence of the media and more moderate elements of the CPSU continued to push for reform. As Gorbachev was increasingly viewed as "politically irrelevant" following the August 1991 coup attempt, he signed the dissolution agreement for the Soviet Union on December 25, 1991, and resigned political office.

Sample Answer to Document-Based Question

Although it was not a large "massacre" by modern standards, the Peterloo Massacre of 1819 proved to be a significant event in British political history, leading to repressive legislation, dividing Tories from Whigs, helping convert the Whigs to the cause of electoral reform, and remaining a political issue for years to come.

Some facts are undisputed; others will probably never be resolved. The Napoleonic Wars left suffering in their wake and exacerbated social problems in Britain. During the wars, the British nobility, who controlled Parliament, had passed the Corn Laws, which were designed to enrich the nobility in time of food shortage. Although great shortages had not yet developed, this example of the use of Parliament for the economic ends of the nobility disturbed many in the British middle class.

The middle class also was excluded from Parliament. Voting was open—and oral—and restricted to a small number of the wealthy, almost all nobility. The years immediately after 1815 saw the rise of a number of public speakers who demanded the expansion of the suffrage—the right to vote—to encompass the middle class. Some went further, demanding annual parliaments or voting rights for all adult males. Among the latter group was Henry Hunt, a so-called "radical reformer."

Hunt and his colleagues planned a protest meeting on a farm field—St. Peter's Field outside of the industrial city of Manchester. The selection of Manchester was deliberate. Like many new industrial cities, Manchester was growing rapidly, but it lacked representation in Parliament. On the other hand, many older and formerly prosperous cities, such as the port city of Dover, had fallen on hard times and lost population. Yet Dover had representation in Parliament. Cities such as Dover, with undeserved representation, were termed "rotten boroughs."

Exactly what happened remains a matter of dispute. Hunt had issued a proclamation to the public before the rally, urging a peaceful demonstration and implying that conservative forces might try to provoke the crowd into violence. There appears to be no evidence that the crowd was violent; but the local authorities, fearful of a crowd estimated at 100,000, sent the local militia (the Manchester Yeomanry) into the crowd. They were followed by an army calvary unit. What followed next is unclear; some say that the soldiers were provoked, and others that they were out of control. People were trampled and slashed with sabres. The number of dead was small—by a modern historian's account, about 14. But the injuries of the dead appear to confirm that they were killed by a the militia or army, rather than trampled by an unruly crowd. Almost all of the dead were "sabred."

Conservatives in Britain, particularly the Tories, saw the Peterloo incident as a popular riot, a possible forerunner of a revolution like the recent French experience. Radical reformers saw brutality by the authorities against peaceful protesters. They were eventually joined in that view by many Whigs. Some Tories such as Robert Peel, later a famous Tory reformer, seemed to agree that the incident had been handled poorly by local authorities. The Whig-Tory split widened when the Tories, who controlled Parliament, passed the Six Acts, a series of repressive laws which suppressed civil liberties.

The course of repression did not serve the Tories well, During the 1820s, reformers such as Peel tried an alternative approach—recognizing that such incidents indicated popular unrest about injustices in the British system. Peel convinced Parliament to reform the British legal and police system during the 1820s.

The Peterloo incident may have helped make expansion of the electorate a key concern of the Whigs. During the late 1820s, when the Tory Duke of Wellington campaigned, he was met by signs that read "Remember Peterloo." When the Whigs won election in 1831—with their name changed to the Liberal Party—they pledged to expand the right to vote. Only half of the male members of the middle class was given the right to vote by the Whigs, but it was a start of a process which continued throughout the century. The Peterloo issue was alive as late as the 1870s, when a Liberal party pamphlet reminded voters of "Tory Justice."

A seemingly minor political incident became a seminal and festering issue in British politics, focussing the attention of the Whigs on electoral reform and providing them with a continuing political issue against the Tories or Conservatives.

Sample Answers to Essay Questions

1. Mercantilism, an economic policy developed during the age of absolute monarchies, and *laissez-faire,* preeminent during the era of industrialization and the rise of the middle class, were virtually completely opposite economic policies. Yet each was popular during its own time, largely for reasons connected with the political and economic conditions of the eras.

In many ways, mercantilism, popular during the late 17th and 18th centuries, represented an attempt to extend the powers of absolutism to trade and colonies. Assuming that resources were strictly limited and that European nations would engage in a prolonged struggle to control those resources, the ministers of European monarchs attempted to tie the economies of their colonies closely to that of the mother nation. Colonies were to function as both a market for the mother country's products and also as a source of raw materials.

Mercantilist policies seldom functioned as hoped, as illustrated by the case of Britain, which had begun to gather an extensive colonial empire. North American industries frequently wanted to produce their own versions of products made in Britain, but royal ministers promoted legislation to prevent such colonial competition. Raw materials were also, at times, available more cheaply from other nations than from Britain's own colonies.

The problems involved in mercantilism were obvious by the time Adam Smith published his *Wealth of Nations* in 1776. Smith argued for an era of economic freedom, where individuals might pursue their own economic self-interest without government regulation or limitation. The result, he believed, would be economic expansions that would create new resources. His book coincided with the early stages of the Industrial Revolution, and Britain, far ahead of the rest of Europe in industrialization by the early 1800s, liked the idea of a tariff-free Europe, an era of "free trade."

The middle class, growing rapidly in size as industrialization proceeded, also liked the *laissez-faire* idea of keeping government separate from business. Building on the ideas of Thomas Malthus, who argued that the food supply increased much more slowly than the population, the Scottish economist Ricardo produced the iron law of wages: wages to the working class might not be increased in real terms. Wage hikes would only produce inflation—and no real improvement for the workers.

Ricardo's work seemed to demonstrate that natural economic law kept the working class in dire straits, and not economic exploitation. His work probably soothed the consciences of any middle-class business people who feared government regulation of factories. Yet it illustrated a basic contradiction in *laissez-faire* ideas: Smith argued that resources were not finite but might be expanded by free economic activity, while Ricardo argued that there was only a limited amount of wealth.

2. Starting from the basic premise that the old, Earth-centered view of the solar system had become too complicated, scientists during the Scientific Revolution gradually moved to the Copernican version of a sun-centered solar system. In the process, the Copernican system challenged church authority, helped the newer inductive reasoning triumph over the deductive reasoning of the Middle Ages, and became a testing ground for the emergence of scientific methods.

During the Middle Ages, the earth-centered view had met the requirements of Scholasticism, the medieval system of deductive logic and knowledge which emphasized reliance on church authorities. Where church authorities had not written on a problem, an outside—even pagan—author might be approved. The earth-centered system of the second-century Greek-Egyptian astronomer Ptolemy was given church approval partly because it seemed to conform to Scriptures—where the sun was described as moving backward—but also because it illustrated the supreme medieval irony: human beings were sinful and wretched but also important enough to be at the center of not only the solar system but the entire universe.

In the 16th century, the Polish astronomer Copernicus pointed to the increasing complexity of the Ptolemaic system as a reason to consider alternatives. As a high official in the Catholic church, Copernicus merely suggested alternative hypotheses. His work, however, began a process in which facts gained through observation were assembled into alternative theories; "induction" replaced deduction.

When the Italian Galileo used his observations with a telescope to support the Copernican system, he fell victim to church discipline in a famous trial. His work on inertia, however, and upon the speed of falling bodies, however, led to research by others. The Central European astronomer Kepler added to the Copernican trend by producing three laws of planetary motion which favored the Copernican view. Devoutly religious, however, Kepler believed that he was functioning, not as a critic of religion, but as a prophet discovering the mysteries of God's creation.

The work of Newton illustrated the importance of mathematics for scientific work, producing another scientific "principle" to oppose church authority. Newton's work on gravity virtually confirmed the Copernican system, which could not be proved by methods involving observations and experiments. Gravity, for Newton, was a property of all matter and was strongest in the largest bodies. His work implied that the most massive object in the solar system, the sun, would have to be at the center of the system. Newton arrived at his answers through mathematics, but others saw the virtues of inductive thinking revealed in the triumph of the Copernican view. While writers like Descartes praised deduction, Francis Bacon insisted that the new scientific method of induction would solve all of the of riddles of nature in perhaps a century.

The Copernican controversy became central to the Scientific Revolution because it combined so many elements in the emergence of science—the replacement of deductive reasoning (to some degree) by induction, the emergence of the scientific method as an "authority" in itself, and calls for the freedom of scientists to pursue their work without theological restrictions. Few other developments in the Scientific Revolution were quite so broad and far-reaching.

3. Thrust into World War II by the actions of fascist Germany and Japan, the three major or non-fascist powers—the United States, Britain, and the Soviet Union—discovered during the course of the war that the sole point of total agreement among them was their opposition to the totalitarian governments they were fighting.

Some historians have referred to the alliance as the "Accidental Alliance," the alliance created, not by a common outlook of its members, but by the events of the war. Britain had been brought into the war by the German attack on Poland; the Soviet Union had entered because Hitler, wanting to impress on Britain how isolated it was, had sent German troops into the Soviet Union; and the United States had entered the war because of an attack by Japan, Germany's ally, on an American naval installation in Hawaii.

While the United States and Britain shared a common language and similar forms of government, the Soviet Union had little in common with its allies. Relations between the Soviet Union and British government had been particularly cool. During the 1930s, when the aggressive diplomacy of Hitler had been met with general British-French acquiescence, Stalin appeared to believe that this "appeasement" was a deliberately anti-Soviet policy. Documentary evidence is lacking—Stalin's archives are not available to historians of either east or west—

but Stalin appeared to believe that the British hoped to use Hitler, an avowed anti-Communist, to rid the world of Communism. Stalins' suspicions may have deepened when a Soviet observer who attended the Munich conference of 1938 was rebuffed by Britain and France when he suggested a collective security agreement against Germany. Possibly this rebuff explains the Soviet government's decision to sign a nonaggression pact with Germany in 1939, shortly before the German invasion of Poland. But the pact contained a provision for a de facto partition of Poland between Germany and the Soviet Union. In effect, Stalin cleared the way for the start of World War II. The British government, which went to war to defend the sovereignty of Poland, did not forget Stalin's role in the events of 1939. The British prime minister Winston Churchill was especially suspicious of his Soviet ally, particularly when the Soviet Union announced formation of a Polish communist government in exile to replace the civilian government which had fled to London.

Representing a country that had remained distant from prewar European diplomacy, the American President Roosevelt took a more tolerant view of Stalin, whom he termed "Uncle Joe." Roosevelt worked with Churchill to solve a problem which arose when the two leaders decided to delay a landing in France until landings and victories were assured in North Africa and Italy. Stalin had been demanding a "second front" in France to relieve pressure on Soviet troops. In an attempt to assure Stalin that no separate peace would be signed with Hitler—that a German victory in the Soviet Union would not end the struggle—both men issued a proclamation that their nations would not leave the war until unconditional surrender by Germany. Despite the conciliatory offer, Stalin refused to declare war against Japan. In fact, the Soviet Union would declare war against Japan only three days before the war ended, and only after two atomic bombs had been dropped on Japanese cities.

By the time of the Normandy landings in mid 1944, German troops were retreating from the territory of the Soviet Union. Stalin appeared to believe that victory over Germany had been achieved almost entirely by his troops; the landing of his allies in France might be a mopping up operation. Stalin's ambitions in Eastern Europe loomed large. When the Soviet army approached Warsaw, the Polish underground revolted against the German rulers of the city. The Soviet advance halted just long enough for the Germans to eliminate this politically active group of Poles.

The conferences at Yalta and Potsdam at the end of the war have been criticized for ceding Eastern Europe to Stalin, but they largely recognized what had already happened to that area, which was occupied by Soviet troops. For the British—who had gone to war to preserve Poland—the loss of that nation was particularly bitter. A Winston Churchill speech in 1946 coined the term "iron curtain" and pointed to the major issue of the Cold War: the Soviet domination of Eastern European nations which had enjoyed a brief period of self-determination between 1919 and 1939.

The total reasons for Soviet occupation of Eastern Europe are probably mixed and complex. Fear of a resurgent Germany, desire for a buffer zone against a future German invasion, use of opportunities to spread Communist revolutions—it is difficult to sort out which played the major role. It is clear, however, that the tensions and suspicions among the antifascist allies of World War II laid no basis for their cooperation in the post-war world. Instead, they appeared to guarantee division between the two sides once World War II had ended.

4. Although the Enlightenment is often portrayed as a single historical period, there were actually three Enlightenments—English (late 1600s), French (1700s), and German (second half of 1700s). Each was a response to the particular conditions prevailing in those nations; not surprisingly, each produced somewhat different solutions.

All three tended to agree on basic tenets. All three favored Reason—the common ability of human beings to interpret nature logically and to find common, logical solutions to their problems. All three tended to reject intolerance, unjustified biases, and dogmatic religion. There was also a shared admiration of natural science, not surprising considering that the Scientific Revolution had occurred in the previous two centuries.

The French Enlightenment was a very cosmopolitan period, focussed on issues which the philosophes believed to be of concern to all mankind. A major reason was because the philosophes, most of whom lived in Paris, were of several nationalities. Baron d'Holbach, champion of materialism, was German; Beccaria, who argued that the purpose of the law was not to impress God's will but to bring the greatest happiness of greatest number, was Italian. It is said that the first appearance of the word "humanity" was in the French language during this period.

Nevertheless, purely French conditions had a significant influence. Voltaire's call for a secular French society, and his condemnation of Christianity as superstition and prejudice, reflected the traditional intolerance shown to religious minorities in France by the state. French Huguenots, who had gained freedom of worship and the right to bear arms by the Edict of Nantes, lost these when Louis XIV revoked the edict in 1685. Voltaire himself deplored the the French army's destruction of the Huguenot city of Port Royal. The most famous court case in which he became involved, the Calas case, concerned a Huguenot father found guilty of murdering a son who, it was said, desired to convert to the Roman Catholicism of his fiancée.

In order to achieve a secular society, the philosophes became reformers, proposing specific social arrangements or solutions. *Candide* showed Voltaire's reformist bent, since it was written in angry reaction to the German philosopher Leibniz' statement that this is the best of all possible worlds. Voltaire did not reject religion entirely; he kept God as a Creator in his own Deism, in which there were to be no complicated doctrines to nurture theological arguments. God the creator sounded suspiciously like Newton's portrait of God as the "clockwinder" of the universe.

The same faith in secular reform drove Diderot to publish his famous

Encyclopedia; led Voltaire and others to believe that Enlightened Despots might reform their countries in a "revolution from above"; and caused Rousseau, who in some ways was a philosophe and in some ways was not, to seek citizen participation in government through his idea of the "general will."

None of the philosophes were scientists, but it was clear that they envisioned a universe and society governed by immutable and rational laws. While it would be difficult to tie the philosophes directly to the French Revolution, it appears they made criticisms of the French government and society respectable in their country.

Conditions in Germany were quite different. Germany was, according to a famous saying, a "geographic expression" which contained more than 300 states, many with their own petty monarch. The major religious war in Germany had ended in 1648 with arrangements which allowed each monarch to dictate the official religious denomination of his area. While the French absolute monarchs of the 1700s imposed censorship in an almost half-hearted way, German petty monarchs included religious authority in their sovereignty. The German middle class, smaller in numbers than the French middle class, did not challenge monarchical power the way the French had. Observers commented about the subservience of the German burgher; the spirit of reform was lacking.

The two major German figures of the Enlightenment, Leibniz and Kant, admired natural science, but their attitudes toward it were quite different from the French philosophes'. Leibniz tended to be interested in rationalism, and he, along with Newton and the French mathematician Descartes, is given credit for the discovery of calculus. Yet Leibniz rejected Newton's theory of gravity and was unimpressed with the experimental work that led to that theory or that seemed to confirm that theory.

Kant also was interested in Reason, but his emphasis was on the ability of the mind, through Reason, to shape reality. Kant had been appalled at the work of the Scottish philosopher Hume, who seemed to challenge the validity of science by demonstrating that "cause and effect" was always assumed in science but could not be proven. Kant sought to demonstrate that the mind operated in such a way that "cause and effect" was always perceived; while "cause and effect" might not be proven, the mind operated in a regular and consistent ways, according to its own internal laws. His *Critique of Pure Reason* was an attempt to rescue science from philosophical skepticism. It also attempted to lay the basis for a new, nonreligious morality; the "categorical imperative" was a moral rule that was logically self-evident.

Monarchical authority intervened when Kant, in his subsequent book, *Critique of Practical Reason*, speculated that while the existence of God might not be proven, belief in God was a practical necessity. After the appearance of the book, he was commanded by the Prussian monarch to halt his commentaries on religious matters. Perhaps this incident is one reason why Kant, when writing of the ideal state, wrote in terms of abstractions rather than specifics, and entirely avoided reform proposals.

More likely, the German Enlightenment, and Kant, reflected the domination of German monarchs over matters of free thought and religion, as well as the deferential attitude of the German middle class toward monarchs and nobility. Kant's ideal state was a state which met certain abstract philosophic criteria, rather than a state which was judged on the basis of specific, practical results, such as prosperity or free speech.

The future direction of German thought was evident in two traits seen in Kant: (1) his "inwardness," or emphasis on the internal workings of the mind, and (2) his attempts to define the ideal government on theoretical rather than practical grounds. Beginning with German Idealism in the early 19th century, German thinkers were often accused of being much more abstract than French or British counterparts, of emphasizing internal freedom over external rights, and of justifying the status quo more than challenging it. That trend appeared to be clear as early as the German Enlightenment.

Despite their shared belief in similar qualities such as Reason, the German and French Enlightenments were quite different periods. The French Enlightenment sought to strengthen humanitarian impulses such as toleration and to encourage free thought and criticism. Such traits were lacking in the German Enlightenment, which spoke of the "ideal" than the "real."

5. Although the practice of primogeniture was no longer legally required in Great Britain after the Renaissance, it was continued by many noble families as a matter of tradition. In this way it exerted a significant impact on British society and politics.

Primogeniture required that upon the death of a nobleman, the title and land passed only to one child—the eldest son, or to his male heir if he was not alive. If the eldest son was not living and had left no heir, the title and landed estate went to the next eldest son. The remaining noble children might inherit wealth, but not the title or the landed estate of the family.

At first glance it might be assumed that the system would guarantee the continuation of feudalism, since it derived from the medieval system of overlords, who often passed their positions down through families. It did result, in Britain, in the preservation of the landed estates and the wealth of noble families. Significantly, however, it created a distinctively British class, the gentry, the titleless sons and daughters of the nobility. The gentry might often have great wealth—they might inherit wealth other than the estate. For those who found their own success in business, their wealth might conceivably be greater than that of the family member who inherited the title and the estate.

The gentry class proved to have a distinctive impact on Britain. Because they were less tied to family tradition than the major family heir, they felt less loyalty to the monarch and were more likely to act independently of the throne. In the English Civil War of the 1640s, the gentry were prominent in the armies opposing Charles I; many were found in the Puritan forces. The existence of the gentry may also explain the greater openness of the British nobility to the world, as compared to continental nobility. One reason why Britain entered the Industrial Revolution before other European nations was because of the willingness of some noblemen to finance the first factories. It is likely that the British nobility became more involved in business through their relatives, the gentry. In fact, the British nobility was much less isolated from the remaining elements of their society than their continental cousins. The famous Victorian Compromise—by which middle class and nobility in 19th century Britain shared political power and preserved a role for the nobility in the political system—was a probable result of primogeniture.

While primogeniture was used on the continent, its implementation was much less systematic than in Britain. Only one other nation, Hungary, developed a gentry. As a result, the nobility in countries like France were as a group less prosperous. By the time of the French Revolution of 1789, landed estates had been divided between so many children and grandchildren in France that many noble families were in real financial distress. The French peasants of 1789 were not the only Frenchmen in financial straits.

Without a gentry class of relatives to serve as windows to the outside world, the continental nobility tended to stay more isolated from new financial and economic developments. French noblemen were likely to be isolated from business, regarding real labor as being degrading and unworthy—except in the case of hobbies like rose gardening. Isolated from society in a way their English counterparts were not, the French nobility found it more difficult to comprehend, and compromise with, the middle class and its demands for constitutional government. French conservatives like Chateaubriand and DeMaistre saw in past ages the only forms of society that God approved, whereas the English conservative Burke insisted only that change be measured and not rashly done.

Although it was an archaic and rapidly-disappearing tradition, primogeniture—by giving Britain special advantages in the era of constitutionalism and industrialization—was a major reason why Britain, more than any other European state in the 19th century, represented the nation of social and political reform.

6. Although paintings and drawings of monarchs are often enigmatic—since it is not always clear whether they reveal the artist's real assessment of the subject or are intended as propaganda—illustrations such as these are often useful and revealing.

The painting of Louis XIV, France's "Sun King," portrays a great and noble figure who embodied the "glory" he sought for France. Louis' lavish, almost sumptuous lifestyle at his palace of Versailles is evident in the curtains and in Louis' own robes, which bear the *fleur de lis,* or lily, symbolic of Bourbon monarchs. There is a touch of vanity in the stilted and somewhat delicate pose. The overall impression is worshipful, a suitable approach for a monarch who convinced much of the French upper nobility that it was a special honor to live with him at Versailles.

The sword is a curious touch. Perhaps it signifies his status as an absolute monarch who wielded powers of life and death over his subjects. It may also signify the iron hand of a monarch whose ministers created a highly centralized government by using measures such as imprisonment without formal arrest or court proceedings.

The sword may also be an attempt to indicate the strong will and energy of a monarch who carried out numerous wars to advance French interests in Europe. If so, if makes Louis appear to be a more active military man than he actually was, since he left the conduct of wars to his generals and engineers.

Two elements often associated with Louis are missing from the portrait. First, there are no emblems of his self-promoted role as "Sun King." Second, although the portrait appears to show strength and determination, there is no sign of the religiously intolerant monach who ruthlessly suppressed Jansenism in France and forced most Huguenots into exile with his revocation of the Edict of Nantes.

The illustration of Napoleon III is a marked contrast to that of the "sun king." The portrait is both austere and vague. The one definite impression is that he was a military leader, but this is probably a touch of propaganda. Napoleon III exploited the name of his famous uncle, but he himself lacked a military reputation. In 1859, during an invasion of Italy, Napoleon III was so sickened by a tour of a battlefield that, within days, he withdrew his forces from Italy. His lack of a strong military record, plus his ineptness as a young Romantic revolutionary, led to rumors that he was not truly a Bonaparte—that his mother and father had been separated for 10 months before his birth.

The vagueness and austerity of the picture reflects Napoleon III's style of rule. Unlike Napoleon Bonaparte, Napoleon III did not hold unchallenged power. He had relied on the support of the army to reach the throne; his empire included a two-house legislature. In many ways he was like the "bourgeois king," Louis Philippe (reigned 1830-1848), who attempted to rule in a style befitting the rapidly rising middle class. Napoleon III believed that government existed in order to guarantee prosperity for its citizens, and the middle and working classes did benefit from rising incomes during his reign. His appearance in the illustration as a conscientious, hard-working monarch is reminiscent of the image cultivated by another monarch associated with the middle class, Queen Victoria.

The austerity of the portrait is a bit surprising, however, for a man whose wife, Eugenie, was the fashionsetter for her time. Napoleon III also desired to be remembered in history for his rebuilding and beautification of central Paris. Of course, the rebuilding was also motivated by practical considerations. The new broad avenues made it very difficult for revolutionaries to build barricades, and the new circular plazas facilitated the movement of artillery by the French army in an emergency.

The lack of detail in the portrait is also appropriate for an emperor who could play the role of political cameleon and who, in 1860, found it necessary to alter his style of rule. During the 1850s, when he played the role of an authoritarian monarch who allowed the legislature to discuss only the matters he had approved, elections for the legislature gradually began turning against the Emperor's stable of parties. From 1860 through 1870, he was the "Liberal Emperor," attempting to retain his popularity by removing restrictions on the legislature and the press.

Unlike Louis XIV, Napoleon III was never really an absolute monarch. His portrait attempts not to overwhelm the viewer but to impress the viewer with his competence. The differences between the two portraits reflect the wide gaps between their reigns. The contrast is between a serenely confident monarch and a monarch who was attempting, very late in European history, to ignore the tides of history and the trends toward constitutional and parliamentary government in Europe.

THE ADVANCED PLACEMENT EXAMINATION IN

European History

TEST 5

Test 5 is also on CD-ROM in our special interactive AP European History TEST*ware*®. It is highly recommended that you first take this exam on computer. You will then have the additional study features and benefits of enforced timed conditions, individual diagnostic analysis, and instant scoring. See page vi for guidance on how to get the most out of our AP European History book and software.

THE ADVANCED PLACEMENT EXAMINATION IN

European History

TEST 5

1. Ⓐ Ⓑ Ⓒ Ⓓ Ⓔ	26. Ⓐ Ⓑ Ⓒ Ⓓ Ⓔ	56. Ⓐ Ⓑ Ⓒ Ⓓ Ⓔ
2. Ⓐ Ⓑ Ⓒ Ⓓ Ⓔ	27. Ⓐ Ⓑ Ⓒ Ⓓ Ⓔ	57. Ⓐ Ⓑ Ⓒ Ⓓ Ⓔ
3. Ⓐ Ⓑ Ⓒ Ⓓ Ⓔ	28. Ⓐ Ⓑ Ⓒ Ⓓ Ⓔ	58. Ⓐ Ⓑ Ⓒ Ⓓ Ⓔ
4. Ⓐ Ⓑ Ⓒ Ⓓ Ⓔ	29. Ⓐ Ⓑ Ⓒ Ⓓ Ⓔ	59. Ⓐ Ⓑ Ⓒ Ⓓ Ⓔ
5. Ⓐ Ⓑ Ⓒ Ⓓ Ⓔ	30. Ⓐ Ⓑ Ⓒ Ⓓ Ⓔ	60. Ⓐ Ⓑ Ⓒ Ⓓ Ⓔ
6. Ⓐ Ⓑ Ⓒ Ⓓ Ⓔ	31. Ⓐ Ⓑ Ⓒ Ⓓ Ⓔ	61. Ⓐ Ⓑ Ⓒ Ⓓ Ⓔ
7. Ⓐ Ⓑ Ⓒ Ⓓ Ⓔ	32. Ⓐ Ⓑ Ⓒ Ⓓ Ⓔ	62. Ⓐ Ⓑ Ⓒ Ⓓ Ⓔ
8. Ⓐ Ⓑ Ⓒ Ⓓ Ⓔ	33. Ⓐ Ⓑ Ⓒ Ⓓ Ⓔ	63. Ⓐ Ⓑ Ⓒ Ⓓ Ⓔ
9. Ⓐ Ⓑ Ⓒ Ⓓ Ⓔ	34. Ⓐ Ⓑ Ⓒ Ⓓ Ⓔ	64. Ⓐ Ⓑ Ⓒ Ⓓ Ⓔ
10. Ⓐ Ⓑ Ⓒ Ⓓ Ⓔ	35. Ⓐ Ⓑ Ⓒ Ⓓ Ⓔ	65. Ⓐ Ⓑ Ⓒ Ⓓ Ⓔ
11. Ⓐ Ⓑ Ⓒ Ⓓ Ⓔ	36. Ⓐ Ⓑ Ⓒ Ⓓ Ⓔ	66. Ⓐ Ⓑ Ⓒ Ⓓ Ⓔ
12. Ⓐ Ⓑ Ⓒ Ⓓ Ⓔ	37. Ⓐ Ⓑ Ⓒ Ⓓ Ⓔ	67. Ⓐ Ⓑ Ⓒ Ⓓ Ⓔ
13. Ⓐ Ⓑ Ⓒ Ⓓ Ⓔ	38. Ⓐ Ⓑ Ⓒ Ⓓ Ⓔ	68. Ⓐ Ⓑ Ⓒ Ⓓ Ⓔ
14. Ⓐ Ⓑ Ⓒ Ⓓ Ⓔ	39. Ⓐ Ⓑ Ⓒ Ⓓ Ⓔ	69. Ⓐ Ⓑ Ⓒ Ⓓ Ⓔ
15. Ⓐ Ⓑ Ⓒ Ⓓ Ⓔ	40. Ⓐ Ⓑ Ⓒ Ⓓ Ⓔ	70. Ⓐ Ⓑ Ⓒ Ⓓ Ⓔ
16. Ⓐ Ⓑ Ⓒ Ⓓ Ⓔ	41. Ⓐ Ⓑ Ⓒ Ⓓ Ⓔ	71. Ⓐ Ⓑ Ⓒ Ⓓ Ⓔ
17. Ⓐ Ⓑ Ⓒ Ⓓ Ⓔ	42. Ⓐ Ⓑ Ⓒ Ⓓ Ⓔ	72. Ⓐ Ⓑ Ⓒ Ⓓ Ⓔ
18. Ⓐ Ⓑ Ⓒ Ⓓ Ⓔ	43. Ⓐ Ⓑ Ⓒ Ⓓ Ⓔ	73. Ⓐ Ⓑ Ⓒ Ⓓ Ⓔ
19. Ⓐ Ⓑ Ⓒ Ⓓ Ⓔ	44. Ⓐ Ⓑ Ⓒ Ⓓ Ⓔ	74. Ⓐ Ⓑ Ⓒ Ⓓ Ⓔ
20. Ⓐ Ⓑ Ⓒ Ⓓ Ⓔ	45. Ⓐ Ⓑ Ⓒ Ⓓ Ⓔ	75. Ⓐ Ⓑ Ⓒ Ⓓ Ⓔ
21. Ⓐ Ⓑ Ⓒ Ⓓ Ⓔ	46. Ⓐ Ⓑ Ⓒ Ⓓ Ⓔ	76. Ⓐ Ⓑ Ⓒ Ⓓ Ⓔ
22. Ⓐ Ⓑ Ⓒ Ⓓ Ⓔ	47. Ⓐ Ⓑ Ⓒ Ⓓ Ⓔ	77. Ⓐ Ⓑ Ⓒ Ⓓ Ⓔ
23. Ⓐ Ⓑ Ⓒ Ⓓ Ⓔ	48. Ⓐ Ⓑ Ⓒ Ⓓ Ⓔ	78. Ⓐ Ⓑ Ⓒ Ⓓ Ⓔ
24. Ⓐ Ⓑ Ⓒ Ⓓ Ⓔ	49. Ⓐ Ⓑ Ⓒ Ⓓ Ⓔ	79. Ⓐ Ⓑ Ⓒ Ⓓ Ⓔ
25. Ⓐ Ⓑ Ⓒ Ⓓ Ⓔ	50. Ⓐ Ⓑ Ⓒ Ⓓ Ⓔ	80. Ⓐ Ⓑ Ⓒ Ⓓ Ⓔ
	51. Ⓐ Ⓑ Ⓒ Ⓓ Ⓔ	
	52. Ⓐ Ⓑ Ⓒ Ⓓ Ⓔ	
	53. Ⓐ Ⓑ Ⓒ Ⓓ Ⓔ	
	54. Ⓐ Ⓑ Ⓒ Ⓓ Ⓔ	
	55. Ⓐ Ⓑ Ⓒ Ⓓ Ⓔ	

European History

TEST 5 – Section I

TIME: 55 Minutes
80 Questions

DIRECTIONS: Each of the questions or incomplete statements below is followed by five suggested answers or completions. Select the one that is best in each case.

1. "…I have heard him say, that after his Booke of the *Circulation of the Blood* came out, that he fell mightily in his Practice, and that it was believed by the Vulgar that he was crack-brained."

   This excerpt, taken from an account by John Aubrey, describes

   (A) Paracelsus.
   (B) Galvani.
   (C) Lorenzo Valla.
   (D) William Harvey.
   (E) Francis Bacon.

2. The phrase "Cogito ergo sum" ("I think, therefore I am"), reflecting the process of logical deduction, is associated with

   (A) Hugo Grotius.
   (B) Jean Bodin.
   (C) Galileo.
   (D) Joseph Dalton Hooker.
   (E) René Descartes.

3. Known as the "Prince of the Humanists," in such works as *In Praise of Folly* he criticized the clergy and abuses that he saw in the Christian Church. His given name was

   (A) Petrarch.
   (B) Desiderius Erasmus.
   (C) Agricola.
   (D) Pico della Mirandola.
   (E) Pierre d'Ailly.

4. The 16th century religious wars that had plagued France were largely ended with the

   (A) accession of Louis XI.

   (B) Edict of Nantes.

   (C) Massacre of St. Bartholomew's Day.

   (D) Treaty of Cateau-Cambresis.

   (E) resolution of the Hapsburg-Bourbon conflict by the Peace of Augsburg.

5. The German sociologist Max Weber advanced the thesis that a significant result of the Protestant Reformation was that

   (A) Protestantism, particularly Calvinism, fostered capitalism.

   (B) Luther's strong support of the German peasant class weakened his appeal in southern Germany.

   (C) a close alliance evolved between Luther and the leaders of the Anabaptist movement.

   (D) it greatly enhanced Europe's overseas exploration.

   (E) Protestant opposition to usury hampered the growth of industry in Germany.

6. Had Pope Alexander VI's Treaty of Tordisillas been observed

   (A) England would have remained Catholic.

   (B) the Dutch would have traded the Cape Colony for Brazil.

   (C) Spain and Portugal would have dominated the overseas world.

   (D) England would have received the Ohio Valley in exchange for French holdings in the Caribbean.

   (E) Switzerland would have remained under the control of the Hapsburgs of Austria.

7. The Portuguese explorer Vasco da Gama was the first European to

   (A) circumnavigate the globe.

   (B) reach the southernmost tip of Africa.

   (C) reach Japan and trade with the people of that land.

(D) touch upon the coast of Brazil.

(E) find an all-water route to India.

8. "All are not created on equal terms, but some are preordained to eternal life, others to eternal damnation; and, accordingly, as each has been created for one or the other of these ends, we say that he has been predestined to life or death..."

   This statement reflects an essential view of

   (A) Thomas Hobbes.
   (B) John Calvin.
   (C) Martin Luther.
   (D) the Council of Trent.
   (E) Ulrich Zwingli.

9. "The state of the monarchy is the supremest thing upon the earth; for kings are not only God's lieutenants upon earth, and sit upon God's throne, but even by God himself they are called gods…"

   This concept of the status of monarchy would best reflect the view of

   (A) Frederick the Great.
   (B) John Locke.
   (C) James I Stuart.
   (D) William III of England.
   (E) Joseph II of Austria.

10. During the French Revolution the most powerful member of the Committee of Public Safety was

   (A) Maximilien de Robespierre.
   (B) Georges Danton.
   (C) Napoleon Bonaparte.
   (D) Gracchus Babeuf.
   (E) the Marquis de Lafayette.

11. The principle of territoriality (the right of the legitimate ruler to determine the faith of his subjects) was embodied in the

   (A) Edict of Nantes.
   (B) Peace of Augsburg.
   (C) Six Articles of Henry VIII.
   (D) *Spiritual Exercises* of Ignatius Loyola.
   (E) doctrinal pronouncements of the Council of Trent.

12. A *philosophe* of 18th century France would

(A) strongly advocate the nationalistic aspirations of the monarchy.

(B) ridicule the idea of progress.

(C) support the political theories earlier advocated by Thomas Hobbes.

(D) oppose religious intolerance and superstition.

(E) reject the mechanistic view of the world advanced by earlier scientists.

13. The "Great Fear" that swept through the French countryside in 1789 had its origin in

(A) the movement of the armies of Prussia and Austria on Paris.

(B) that the leaders of the "Reign of Terror" in Paris were preparing to extend it to all of France.

(C) that brigands were attacking villages and burning crops.

(D) that the execution of the French king would lead England to declare war on France.

(E) that the overthrow of the Jacobins would result in a restoration of the monarchy.

14. Come forth into the light of things,
Let Nature be your teacher…
Enough of Science and of Art
Close up those barren leaves
Come forth, and bring with you a heart
That watches and receives

Such a view would most likely be expressed by a

(A) deist.

(B) follower of Rousseau.

(C) physiocrat.

(D) disciple of Diderot.

(E) philosophe.

15. The thesis that "population, when unchecked, increases in a geometrical ratio...subsistence only arithmetically, was advanced in the *Essay on Population* by

(A) Saint-Simon.

(B) Thomas Malthus

(C) Jeremy Bentham. (D) Henri Bergson.

(E) Herbert Spenser.

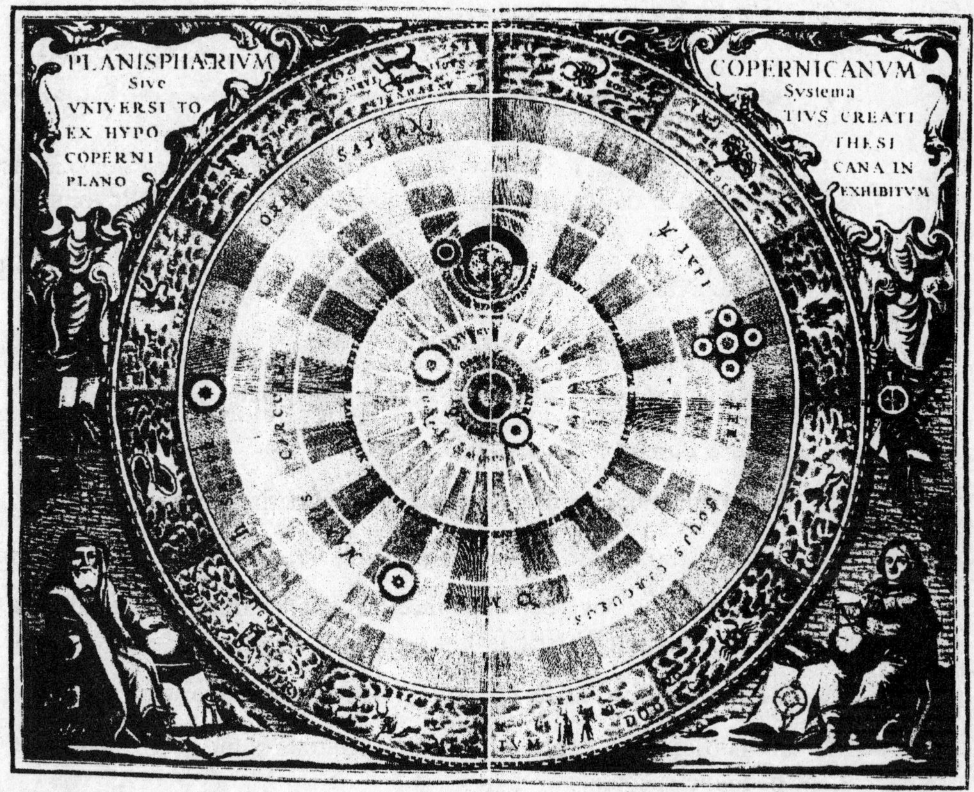

16. The illustration above, an early depiction of Copernicus's concept of the universe, indicates that he was in error

    (A) in that he still retained the medieval concept of placing heaven at the outermost reaches of the universe.

    (B) by retaining Ptolemy's geocentric theory.

    (C) by adhering to the view that the orbits of the planets are circular.

    (D) in that he failed to take into consideration the advances which had been made by Kepler.

    (E) by rejecting the heliocentric theory.

17. "If votes are taken by order, five million citizens will not be able to decide anything for the general interest, because it will not please a couple of hundred thousand privileged individuals. The will of a single individual will veto and destroy the will of more than a hundred people".

This complaint, voiced on the eve of the meeting of the Estates General in 1789, was expressed by

(A) Abbe Siéyès.

(B) Jacques Necker.

(C) Anne Robert Turgot.

(D) the Marquis of Pombal.

(E) a leader of the *emigrés* faction.

18. As a consequence of the English "Glorious" or "Bloodless" Revolution of 1688–89,

(A) the Hanoverian dynasty came to the throne.

(B) Oliver Cromwell was overthrown.

(C) Anglicanism was proclaimed the faith of the state.

(D) Charles I Stuart was executed.

(E) the principle of constitutional monarchy was firmly established.

19. All of the following have been advanced as explanations for the coming of the French Revolution EXCEPT

(A) the desire of the middle class for a greater voice in government.

(B) an inefficient and corrupt government aroused the anger of a mass of the French people.

(C) the nobility of France sought to enhance their power.

(D) a majority of the French populace desired to replace the monarchy with a republic.

(E) the activities of the philosophes had weakened faith in traditional values and institutions.

20. "Man is born free; and everywhere he is in chains...How did this change come about? I do not know. What can make it legitimate? That question I think I can answer."

These words began the famous work, treating the nature of the social contract, by

(A) Edmund Burke.

(B) Jean Jacques Rousseau.

(C) John Locke.

(D) Ferdinand de Lesseps.

(E) Denis Diderot.

21. Following the execution of King Charles I Stuart, England was governed by

(A) William and Mary.

(B) Mary Tudor.

(C) the Lord Protector Oliver Cromwell.

(D) the "Old Pretender."

(E) his son Charles II.

22. All of the following statements about Cardinal Richelieu are true EXCEPT that he

(A) sought to weaken the power of the nobility.

(B) waged war on the French Protestants.

(C) deprived the Huguenots of their religious rights.

(D) supported the German Protestants in their struggle with the Hapsburgs.

(E) supported Gustavus Adolphus in his military operations in Germany.

23. "Whereas you…in the year 1615 were denounced to this Holy Office for holding as true the false doctrine taught by many, that the sun is the center of the world and immovable, and that the earth moves, and also with a diurnal motion…."

This was the charge brought against

(A) Nicholas Copernicus.

(B) Johannes Kepler.

(C) Galilei Galileo.

(D) Tycho Brahe.

(E) Anton van Leeuwenhoek.

24. According to the mercantilist theory, colonies

(A) should receive their independence as soon as they were economically self-sufficient.

(B) were a military burden to the mother country.

(C) should be encouraged to develop their own industry.

(D) were strongest if allowed to trade freely with other countries.

(E) should serve as markets and sources of raw materials for their mother country.

25. "I believe in the equality of man; and I believe that religious duties consist in doing justice, loving mercy, and endeavoring to make all our fellow creatures happy...All national institutions of churches, whether Jewish, Christian, or Turkish, appear to me no other than human inventions, set up to terrify and enslave mankind, and monopolize power and profit."

This view would best reflect the attitudes of a

(A) Quietist.
(B) Deist.
(C) Hutterite.
(D) Jensenite.
(E) follower of Michael Servetus.

26. Martin Luther believed that the problem of personal sin had its solution in

(A) good works.
(B) acceptance of the doctrine of predestination.
(C) justification by faith.
(D) an inner awakening to the spirit of God.
(E) adherence to the teachings of the Church councils.

27. In 1995-1996, retired United States Senator George Mitchell assisted in negotiations between

(A) Great Britain and the Irish Republican Army.
(B) Israel and the Palestine Liberation Organization.
(C) Serbia and Bosnia.
(D) East and West Germany.
(E) Slovakia and the Czech Republic.

28. Peter the Great's purpose in building the city of St. Petersburg was

(A) to escape the influence of Mongol forces in Moscow.

(B) the establishment within Russia of a region free of serfdom.

(C) to throw off the powerful pressures of the monks of the Greek Orthodox Church.

(D) to hasten the Westernization of Russia.

(E) to create a defensive barrier against the aggression of the Poles.

29. A major figure in the Age of Exploration, Prince Henry the Navigator of Portugal sponsored

(A) the exploration of the west coast of Africa.

(B) the establishment of colonies in Brazil.

(C) Hernando Cortez's conquest of the Maya.

(D) the creation of an important trading post in Goa.

(E) the earliest efforts to discover a Northwest Passage.

30. The Thirty Years' War

(A) began when the Bohemians attempted to place a Catholic on the throne.

(B) served to promote German unity.

(C) did not involve France.

(D) resulted in the expulsion of the Ottoman Turks from the Balkans.

(E) saw Danish troops fighting on the side of the German Protestants.

31. "The prince is to the nation he governs what the head is to the man; it is his duty to see, think, and act for the whole community, that he may procure it every advantage of which it is capable. He must be active, possess integrity, and collect his whole powers, that he may be able to run the career he has commenced."

This concept of the obligations of the ruler would best reflect the views of

(A) Peter the Great.
(B) James I Stuart.
(C) Frederick the Great.
(D) Louis XIV.
(E) Bishop Bossuet.

32. The War of the Roses was a dynastic conflict between the house of York and that of the

(A) Hanoverians.
(B) Lancastrians.
(C) Windsors.
(D) Stuarts.
(E) Plantangenets.

33. Kepler's contribution to the Scientific Revolution was his

(A) presentation of sound mathematical proof supporting Ptolemy's geocentric theory.
(B) demonstration that the planets move at a constant speed.
(C) demonstration that the surface of the moon was not smooth.
(D) proving mathematically that the orbits of the planets are elliptical.
(E) demonstration of the errors in the astronomical measurements of Tycho Brahe.

34. "That the pretended power of suspending the laws, or for execution of laws, by regal authority, without the consent of Parliament is illegal.... That the raising or keeping of a standing army within the kingdom in the name of peace, unless it be with the consent of Parliament, is against the law."

The first English monarch to accept and rule in accordance with these decrees was

(A) George I.
(B) William III.
(C) Queen Anne.
(D) Charles II.
(E) Henry VIII.

35. The Protestant Reformation

(A) represented a rejection of many aspects of primitive Christianity.

(B) weakened nationalistic feelings.

(C) tended to strengthen the power of secular rulers.

(D) resulted in the first Christian missionaries seeking converts in the Far East.

(E) served to weaken the hold of spiritual beliefs on the minds of Europeans.

36. In his *An Essay Concerning Human Understanding*, John Locke held that human knowledge was derived from

(A) heredity and faith.

(B) conscience and emotions.

(C) intuition and moral law.

(D) environment and reason.

(E) divine inspiration and innate perception.

37. All of the following are correctly matched EXCEPT

(A) Pizarro—conquest of the empire of the Incas.

(B) Coronado—early exploration of the American Southwest.

(C) Balboa—exploration of the Mississippi Valley.

(D) Cortez—conquest of the Aztecs.

(E) Bartholomeu Diaz—reaches the southernmost tip of Africa.

38. The map-graph on the following page indicates that the greatest advance in the speed of travel between A.D. 1500 and 1700

(A) resulted from the development of roads through the passes of the Alps.

(B) brought Venice into closer contact with the capital of the Byzantine Empire.

(C) was within the Italian peninsula.

(D) was in overland travel to Eastern Europe.

(E) was in areas accessible by sea.

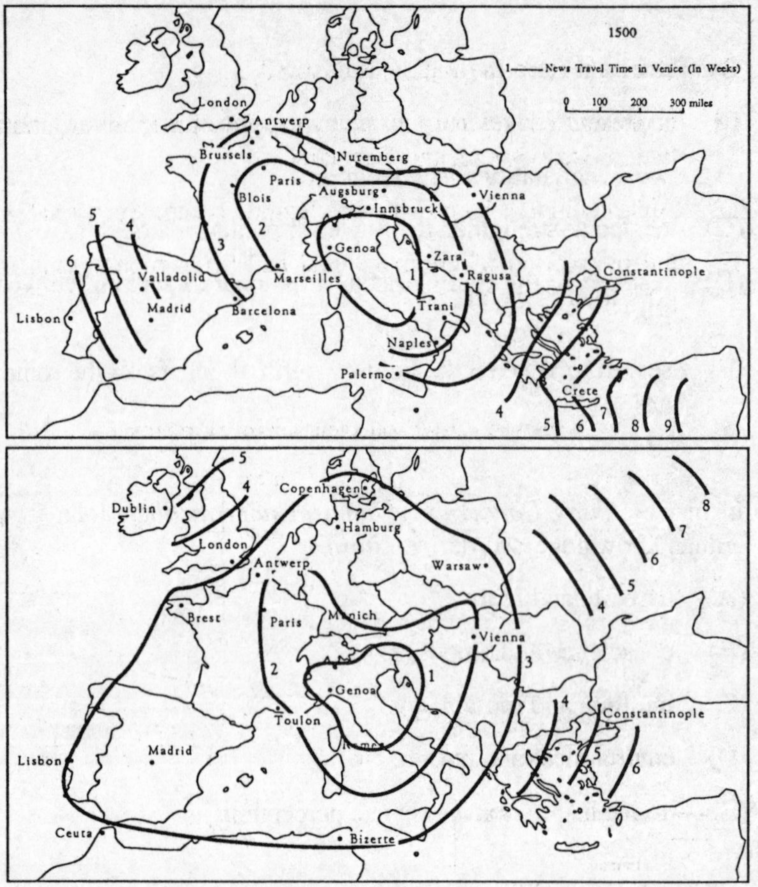

39. "The only way to erect such a common power as may be able to defend them from the invasion of foreigners and the injuries of one another, and thereby secure them in such sort as that by their own industry and by the fruits of the earth they may nourish themselves and live contentedly, is to confer all their power and strength upon one man, or upon one assembly of men, that they may reduce all their wills by plurality of voices unto one will…"

This theory of government reflected the view of

(A) John Locke.
(B) Jean Bodin.
(C) John Napier.
(D) Baron de Montesquieu.
(E) Thomas Hobbes.

40. A conclusion which might be drawn from the graphs shown on the following page is that

(A) Russia on the eve of the First World War, had still failed to develop her industrial base.

(B) France was on the decline industrially.

(C) economic factors may have entered into the mounting antagonism between Great Britain and Germany.

(D) Austrian industrial growth was lagging behind even small Belgium.

(E) the unification of Germany had had little impact upon the industrial growth of that country.

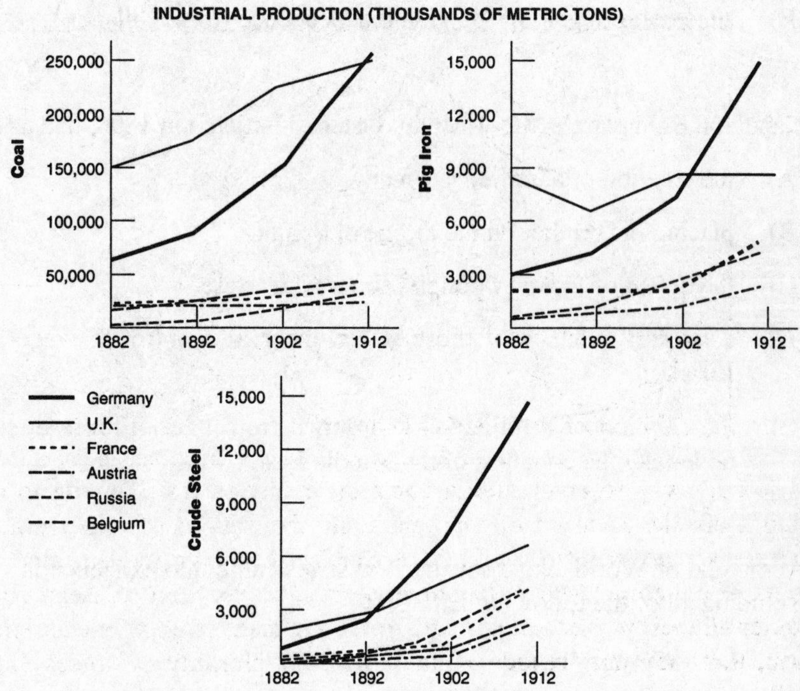

41. In the wake of the failure of the Beer Hall Putsch, Hitler determined that

(A) it would be necessary to recruit officers from the regular army.

(B) he had to eliminate the paramilitary groups around him who frightened the conservative, middle class of Germany.

(C) Bavaria was not a suitable region in which to build his political power.

(D) the way to achieve political power was not through force but through the democratic elections and party politics.

(E) it was necessary to form an alliance with the Social Democratic Party.

42. The Decembrist Revolution of 1825 was

(A) an effort of liberal Russian army officers to introduce governmental reforms.

(B) the initial attempt of Italian nationalists to bring about the unification of that land.

(C) an early example of the growing Pan-Slavic movement in the Balkans.

(D) a movement on the part of the Norwegians to win independence from Denmark.

(E) successful in gaining Belgian independence from Holland.

43. Napoleon Bonaparte's "Continental System," initiated in 1806, had as its goal

(A) the creation of a unified Germany.

(B) placing his brother on the throne of Spain.

(C) the defeat of Britain through economic warfare.

(D) a military alliance of those states under his control to wage war on Russia.

(E) the creation of a military force drawn from many European states to undertake the conquest of the Middle East.

44. At the end of World War I several new states came into existence in Europe, including all of the following EXCEPT

(A) Czechoslovakia.

(B) Yugoslavia.

(C) Estonia.

(D) Finland.

(E) Albania.

45. The defacing of the political poster, as seen in the illustration on the following page, was a prelude to

(A) the failed Nazi attempt to overthrow the Weimar Republic in 1923.

(B) the Munich Conference.

(C) the Nazi annexation of Austria in 1938.

(D) Hitler's occupation of the Rhineland.

(E) the seizure of Danzig.

46. A concept of Bolshevism, advanced by Lenin, but NOT to be found in the writings of Marx is

(A) that the industrial class, exploited by the bourgeoisie, will rise in rebellion and overthrow their oppressors.

(B) that there is a need for an elite cadre to control the "dictatorship of the proletariat," giving impetus and direction to the revolution.

(C) that control of society throughout the ages has rested in the hands of those who control the tools of production.

(D) the concept of economic determinism.

(E) the view that the existing governments, mere tools of the dominant economic class, would not sincerely act on behalf of the working class.

47. All of the following were factors contributing to the rise of Hitler to power EXCEPT

    (A) German anger over what was viewed as the unfair terms of the Treaty of Versailles.

    (B) the failure of the Weimar Republic to solve the economic problems confronting the nation.

    (C) the struggle between the Social Democrats and Communists.

    (D) mounting German fears of a remilitarized France.

    (E) the political machinations of von Papen.

48. Lenin's New Economic Policy (NEP), introduced in 1921, was designed to

    (A) bring about the rapid industrialization of the Soviet Union.

    (B) restore limited economic freedom.

    (C) collectivize Russian agriculture through the establishment of communes.

    (D) set five-year goals.

    (E) speed up the process of nationalization of industry.

49. The German philosopher Friedrich Nietzsche saw Western civilization as

    (A) placing too much stress upon rational thinking.

    (B) requiring a reorientation based upon Christian morality.

    (C) weakened because not enough emphasis was placed on social morality.

    (D) requiring that greater stress be placed upon political democracy.

    (E) placing too much emphasis on elitist elements in society.

50. The Treaty of Nanking (1842) ended a conflict between Great Britain and Manchu China which had its origin in

    (A) British concern over Russian penetration of Korea.

    (B) opium smuggled into China from British India.

    (C) the activities of Chinese pirates in the South China Sea.

    (D) Chinese expulsion of British diplomats from Peking.

    (E) the attacks of Chinese on Christian missionaries and Chinese converts.

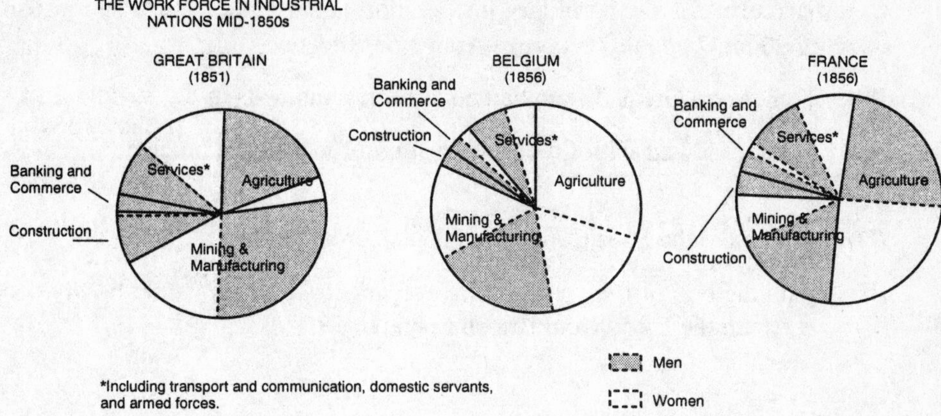

51. On the basis of the charts above, it is clear that for the countries represented, in the mid-19th century

   (A) women were still largely excluded from the labor force in industrialized states.

   (B) in Great Britain the role of women in agriculture was on the decline.

   (C) construction remained solely a male occupation.

   (D) in France and Belgium mining and manufacturing were increasing steadily.

   (E) women had yet to participate in banking and commercial activities in Great Britain.

52. The Sudeten question which led to the calling of the Munich Conference of 1938 centered on

   (A) Hitler's introduction of German troops into the demilitarized Rhineland.

   (B) ethnic Germans in the western regions of Czechoslovakia.

   (C) territory disputed between Germany and Poland.

   (D) the free city of Danzig.

   (E) the unification of Germany and Austria.

53. The Balfour Declaration, issued during World War I, stated that

    (A) in return for their military cooperation against the Turks, the British and French would recognize Arab independence.

    (B) France and Great Britain had no territorial interests in the Middle East.

    (C) Britain viewed with favor the creation of a Jewish homeland in Palestine.

    (D) Egypt and the Suez Canal were British protectorates.

    (E) with the end of the conflict former Turkish holdings would be divided between the French and British as mandates.

54. Following the abdication of Czar Nicholas II in February of 1917, political power in revolutionary Russia passed into the hands of

    (A) Vladimir Lenin.
    (B) Leon Trotsky.
    (C) Alexander Kerensky.
    (D) Joseph Stalin.
    (E) Admiral Kolchak.

55. The immediate spark igniting World War I was the

    (A) invasion of Belgium by the German army.

    (B) assassination of Archduke Francis Ferdinand.

    (C) Austrian annexation of Bosnia-Herzegovina.

    (D) announcement of Italy's decision to ally with France.

    (E) joint Russo-Serbian attack on Austria.

56. A major consequence of the Sepoy or Indian Mutiny was that

    (A) Great Britain annexed all of India.

    (B) the East India Company was dissolved and its authority assumed by the British government.

    (C) the Thugges of the country were severely repressed.

    (D) native Indians were no longer permitted to serve in the military.

    (E) Indians were not allowed to hold positions in the Indian Civil Service.

57. As a consequence of the Russo-Japanese War,

(A) Russia was forced to sell Alaska to the United States.

(B) Russia and Japan divided Korea.

(C) Japan annexed Manchuria.

(D) China was forced to cede her Maritime Provinces, including Vladivostok, to Russia.

(E) Russia abandoned her interests in Manchuria.

58. As a result of the Crimean War, Russia

(A) gained control of the Black Sea.

(B) was confronted with a revolution.

(C) saw the introduction of a number of important reforms.

(D) tightened control over the serfs.

(E) introduced a national Duma, or parliament.

59. Social Darwinism provided theoretical support for all of the following EXCEPT

(A) economic individualism.

(B) militarism.

(C) the growth of big industry.

(D) cosmopolitanism.

(E) imperialism.

60. Viewing history and the evolution of civilizations in biological terms, he believed that the West had entered a stage of decline. He was

(A) Oswald Spengler.

(B) Sidney Webb.

(C) Karl Peters.

(D) Leander Jameson.

(E) Vincenzo Lombardi.

GERMAN ELECTIONS TO THE WEIMAR ASSEMBLY AND REICHSTAG, 1919-1933
(Number of seats obtained by the major parties, arranged with the Left at the top, the Right at the bottom)

	Jan. 1919	June 1920	May 1924	Dec. 1924	May 1928	Sept. 1930	July 1932	Nov. 1932	Mar. 1933
Communists	—a	2	62	45	54	77	89	100	81
Independent Socialists	22	81	—b						
Social Democrats	163	112	100	131	152	143	133	121	125
Democrats	74	45	28	32	25	14	4	2	5
Center	71	68	65	69	61	68	75	70	74
People's party	22	62	44	51	45	30	7	11	2
Nationalists	42	66	96	103	78	41	40	51	52
Nazis			38	20	12	107	230	196	288

a—The Communist party boycotted the elections to the Weimar constituent assembly.

b—In these and succeeding elections the Independent Socialists had merged with the Social Democrats.

61. The chart above indicates that

(A) the Nazi Party benefited the most politically from the Great Depression.

(B) a coalition of the moderates in 1933 could have halted Hitler's gaining control of the German state.

(C) in the 1920s the major threat to the Social Democrats' power came from the Center.

(D) the French-Belgian occupation of the Ruhr resulted in loss of support for the Communists.

(E) the economic recovery the Weimar Republic experienced in the mid-1920s substantially helped the Nazis win support.

62. The threat of a communist revolution in Germany in the days following the end of World War I was seen in the

(A) the activities of the Frei Korps.

(B) efforts of the socialist leaders of the Weimar Republic.

(C) Spartacist movement.

(D) Munich Beer Hall Putsch of 1923.

(E) actions of Bela Kun.

63. In his philosophical view there existed beneath the conscious intellect a "will," a force that is the real conduct of human behavior. He was

(A) Arthur Schopenhauer.
(B) Max Weber.
(C) Emile Durkheim.
(D) Samuel Smiles.
(E) Herbert Spenser.

64. What was the original purpose of NATO?

(A) To provide a peaceful resolution in the Balkans
(B) To provide an army to enforce United Nations decisions
(C) To protect Europe from Soviet aggression
(D) To work to protect human rights throughout the world
(E) To protect Israel from Arab aggression

65. A significant difference between the problem created for the Austro-Hungarian empire by Czech nationalism and that of the Serbs was that

(A) the Serbs were more politically advanced than the Czechs.
(B) a majority of the Serbs were willing to accept autonomy within the Dual Monarchy, while the Czechs sought complete independence.
(C) the Czechs could look to Germany for support.
(D) an independent Serbian state existed to encourage their ethnic kinsmen within the Dual Monarchy.
(E) a majority of Czechs were concerned with their cultural rights rather than independence.

66. In the course of World War I Britain was faced with a serious rebellion on the part of her subjects in

(A) the Union of South Africa.
(B) India.
(C) Ireland.
(D) Palestine.
(E) Cyprus.

67. Attacking the society of his day for its conformity and subjugation to what he deemed a Christian "slave" morality, he longed for the strong individuals who could overthrow current values and through disciplined struggle and sacrifice achieve their "wholeness."

(A) Karl Barth
(B) Friedrich Nietzche
(C) Jean-Paul Sartre
(D) Soren Kierkegaard
(E) Paul Tillich

68. Werner Heisenberg's contribution to 20th century science was

(A) the development of the "Big Bang" theory regarding the origin of the universe.

(B) the theory of plate techtonics and continental drift.

(C) to raise serious questions regarding the ability of the scientist to know, in fact, the way things actually are.

(D) the discovery of the oldest known *homonic* at that time, at a site in East Africa.

(E) the invention of the radio telescope.

69. In the works of Arthur de Gobineau and Houston Stuart Chamberlain were concepts which contributed significantly to the

(A) development of existentialism.

(B) doctrines of the National Socialist Workers Party.

(C) economic doctrines of Neo-Mercantilism.

(D) policy of appeasement pursued by France and Great Britain in the 1930s.

(E) Dadaist movement.

70. 1. Open covenants openly arrived at…diplomacy shall proceed always frankly and in the public view.

2. Absolute freedom of navigation...alike in peace and war.

3. Adequate guarantees...that national armaments will be reduced to the lowest point consistent with domestic safety.

The statements above constitute a portion of those found in the

(A) Atlantic Charter.
(B) Treaty of Versailles.
(C) Fourteen Points of Woodrow Wilson.
(D) McMahon Letters.
(E) Kellogg-Briand Pact.

71. In 1958, Charles de Gaulle came to power in France in the midst of a crisis provoked by

(A) the popular debate as to the policy to be pursued in the conduct of conflict in Indo-China.
(B) widespread riots on the part of French university students.
(C) the issue of French membership in NATO.
(D) controversy over the struggle being waged against Algerian nationalists.
(E) the question of French membership in the Common Market.

72. The philosopher José Ortega y Gasset, reflecting the mood of pessimism which was prevalent among many intellectuals following World War I, argued that

(A) Western civilization was destined to give way to that of Asia.
(B) modern technology, particularly that in the military area, would lead to the annihilation of European society.
(C) the only solution to the problems confronting European society was submission to totalitarian rule.
(D) the greatest threat to the highest achievements of Western civilization was to be found in the rise of the masses.
(E) the cultural dominance that was held by Europe had passed into the hands of the people of the New World.

73. In France of the 1930s, the activities of organizations such as the *Croix de Feu* and *Action Française* served as evidence of the

(A) threat to government stability from the political left.

(B) increasing tendency toward isolationism on the part of the French people.

(C) strong popular support in France for the Republican cause in Spain.

(D) existence in France of a strong fascist element.

(E) widespread popular backing for the Popular Front of Leon Blum.

74. "Aside from the demoralizing effect on the world at large, and the possibilities of disturbances as a result of the desperation of the people concerned... it is logical that the United States should do whatever it is able to do to assist in the return of normal economic health in the world, and without which there can be no political stability and no assured peace."

These sentiments, expressed in the course of a speech given on June 5, 1947, reflected the program subsequently established by

(A) Winston Churchill.

(B) George C. Marshall.

(C) Dwight D. Eisenhower.

(D) Franklin D. Roosevelt.

(E) John Foster Dulles.

75. A major scientific breakthrough came in the 1950s with the work of James D. Watson and Francis H. C. Crick in

(A) the area of artificial intelligence.

(B) the field of biological inheritance and DNA molecules.

(C) viral infections.

(D) the nature and origin of Black Holes.

(E) discovery of holes in the Earth's ozone layer and the danger of global warming.

76. The decision of the French, British, and Israelis to launch an invasion of Egypt in 1956 was the result of the

(A) formation of the United Arab Republic as a prelude to a coordinated attack on Israel.

(B) Egyptian announcement that they would permit the Soviet navy to use the naval facilities of the port of Alexandria.

(C) Russia's announcement that it would assist Egypt in the construction of the Aswan Dam in return for military bases.

(D) plans of Nasser to nationalize the Suez Canal.

(E) Egyptian support of the communist rebels of North Yemen.

77. What accident caused Europeans to rethink expansion of nuclear power?

(A) Three Mile Island

(B) Chernobyl

(C) The atomic bombing of Nagasaki and Hiroshima

(D) Bhopal

(E) North Korea

78. The Brezhnev Doctrine held that

(A) Russia had an obligation to aid Communist revolutions anywhere in the world.

(B) each country had the right to pursue its own road to communism.

(C) the development of the agricultural section of the Russian economy should take precedence over heavy industry.

(D) Communist countries had the right to intervene in the internal affairs of other Communist countries.

(E) Jewish dissidents in the Soviet Union would henceforth be permitted to leave the country.

79. The Korean War began when

(A) Communist China sent troops across the Yalu River into North Korea.

(B) General Douglas MacArthur was named head of the United Nations forces in Korea.

(C) the Communist Peoples Democratic Republic of North Korea invaded South Korea.

(D) United States forces were sent into South Korea to crush a Communist insurrection supported by the Soviet Union.

(E) the Republic of Korea invaded North Korea.

80. In 1956, Soviet troops brutally crushed a movement to democracy in

(A) Yugoslavia.

(B) Poland.

(C) Afghanistan.

(D) Czechoslovakia.

(E) Hungary.

European History

TEST 5 – Section II

TIME: Reading Period – 15 minutes
Writing Time for all three essays – 115 minutes

DIRECTIONS: Read over both the Document-Based Essay question in Part A and the choices in Part B during the Reading Period, and use the time to organize answers. All students must answer Part A (the Document-Based Essay Question), and choose TWO questions from Part B to answer.

PART A – DOCUMENT-BASED ESSAY

This question is designed to test your ability to work with historical documents. As you analyze each document, take into account the source and the point of view of the author. Write an essay on the following topic that integrates your analysis of the documents. You may refer to historical facts and developments not mentioned in the documents.

The view expressed by the author of Document 1 has long influenced historians of Imperialism, accepted by many, and subjected to modification or rejection by others. Utilizing the documents presented here, evaluate its validity or possible weaknesses.

Document 1

Analysis of the actual course of modern Imperialism has laid bare the combination of economic and political forces which fashions it. The forces are traced to the sources in the selfish interests of certain industrial, financial, and professional classes seeking private advantages out of a policy of imperial expansion.

—J. A. Hobson, anti-imperialist economist, *Imperialism, A Study*, 1902

Document 2

"Our connection with them [the Malay States] is due to the simple fact that seventy years ago the British government was invited, pushed, and persuaded into helping the rulers of certain states to introduce order into their disorderly, penniless, and distracted households by sending trained British civil servants to advise the rulers in the art of administration and to organize a system of government which would secure justice, freedom, safety for all, with the benefits of what is known as civilization."

–Frank Swettenham, British Colonial Official, circa 1869

Document 3

"No one acquainted with the actual state of society in the West Indies...can doubt that, if they were left, unaided by us, to settle amongst themselves in whose hands power should be placed, a fearful war of colour would probably soon break out,...and civilization would be thrown back for centuries."

–Lord Grey, Head, British Colonial Office, 1853

Document 4

"Everyone will admit...the value of that commerce which penetrates to every part of the globe; and many of these colonies give harbours and security to that trade, which are most useful in times of peace, but are absolutely necessary in time of war."

–Lord John Russell, British Prime Minister, 1850

Document 5

"If persons, knowing the risks they run, owing to the disturbed state of these countries, choose to hazard their lives and properties for sake of large profits which accompany successful trading, they must not expect the British Government to be answerable if their speculation proves unsuccessful."

–Governor, Straits Settlements, circa 1860

Document 6

"Let us endeavour to strike our roots into the soil by the gradual introduction and establishment of our own principles and opinions; of our laws, institutions, and manners; above all, as the source of every other improvement, of our religion, and consequently of our morals."

–William Wilberforce, British Statesman/Humanitarian, circa 1825

Document 7

"The position of Russia in Central Asia is that of all civilized states which are brought into contact with half-savage nomad populations possessing no fixed social organization."

"In such cases, the more civilized state is forced in the interest of the security of its frontier, and commercial relations, to exercise a certain ascendancy over her turbulent and undesirable neighbors. Raids and acts of pillage must be put down. To do this, the tribes of the frontier must be reduced to a state of submission. This result once attained, these tribes take to more peaceful habits, but are in turn exposed to the attacks of the more distant tribes against whom the State is bound to protect them."

–Prince Gorchakov, Russian Foreign Minister, 1864

Document 8

Onward Christian Soldiers, on to heathen lands,
Prayer-books in your pockets, rifles in your hands
Take the glorious tidings where trade can be done:
Spread the peaceful gospel—with a Maxim gun.

–Henri Labouchère, Anti-Imperialist Editor, *Pioneers' Hymn*, 1893

Document 9

"Throughout the Century of Peace...man's mind had become open to the truth, had become sensible to the diversity of species, had become conscious of Nature's law of development...The stern logic of facts proclaimed the Negro and Chinaman below the level of the Caucasian, and incapacitated from advance towards his intellectual standard. To the development of the White Man, the Black Man and the Yellow must ever remain inferior, and as the former raised itself higher and yet higher, so did those latter seem to sink out of humanity and appear nearer and nearer to the brutes."

–W. D. Hay, Social Darwinist author, *Three Hundred Years Hence*, 1881

Document 10

"At this time, as you know, a warship cannot carry more than fourteen days worth of coal, no matter how perfectly it is organized, and a ship which is out of coal is a derelict on the surface of the sea, abandoned to the first person who comes along. Thus the necessity of having on the oceans provisions stations, shelters, ports for defense and revictualizing. And it is for this that we needed Tunisia, for this that we needed Saigon, and the Mekong Delta, for this that we need Madagascar, that we are at Diego-Suarez and Vohemar and will never leave them. Gentlemen, in Europe as it is today...a policy of peaceful seclusion or abstention is simply the highway to decadence."

–Jules Ferry, French Imperialist, speech to French National Assembly, 1883

Document 11
Population (in millions)

	Great Britain	Russia	France	Germany	Italy
1796		29			
1800	10-9			24-5	18-1
1801			27-3		
1830	16-5			29-6	
1831			31-9		
1850	20-9			35-4	23
1851			35-8		
1858		67			
1870	26-2			40-9	26-6
1871			36-1		
1897		129			
1900	37			56-4	32-4
1901			39		
1910	40-8				
1911			39-2		34-8
1914		142		67-8	
1921	42		39-2		38-4

Document 12

"We stand on nationalism in our belief that the unfolding of economic and political power by the German nation abroad is the prerequisite for all far-reaching social reforms at home."

–Manifesto of the *Nationalsozialer Verein*, 1897

Document 13

THE NEW AFRICAN MISSION.

Rev. Mr. Fun ...."THIS, DEARLY BELOVED BROTHER, IS OUR CIVILISATION. A TEMPTING PICTURE, IT IS NOT?"

Document 14

"Nations may be roughly divided between the living and the dying...For one reason or another—from the necessities of politics or under the pretence of philanthropy—the living nations will gradually encroach on the territory of the dying, and the seeds and the causes of conflict among civilized nations will speedily appear."

–Lord Salisbury, British Minister, 1898

Document 15

"...No doubt there will remain people like the aged savage who in his old age went back to his savage tribe and said that he had 'tried civilization for forty years, and it was not worth the trouble,' but we not take account of the mistaken ideas of unfit men and beaten races."

–Walter Bagehot, *Physics and Politics*, 1869

Document 16

"Early in November [1897] several Ministers, including myself, received a memorandum drawn up by Count Muraviov. It pointed out that the occupation of Kiao-Chow by the Germans offered a favourable occasion for us to seize one of the Chinese ports, notably Port Arthur...He pointed out that these ports had an enormous strategical importance."

–Count Witte, Russian Finance Minister, *Memoirs*

Document 17

Take up the White Man's burden—
Send forth the best ye breed—
Go bind your sons to exile—
To serve your captives' need;
To wait in heavy harness,
On fluttered folk and wild—
Your new-caught, sullen peoples,
Half-devil and half-child.

–Rudyard Kipling, Imperialist poet, 1893

Document 18

"An Empire such as ours requires as its first condition an Imperial Race—a race vigorous and industrious and intrepid. Health of mind and body exalt a nation in the competition of the universe. The survival of the fittest is an absolute truth in the conditions of the modern world."

–Lord Rosebery, former British Prime Minister, *The Times*, 1900

Document 19

"In order to save the 40,000,000 inhabitants of the United Kingdom from a bloody civil war, we colonial statesmen must acquire new lands to settle the surplus population, to provide new markets for the goods produced by them in the factories and mines. The Empire, as I have always said, is a bread and butter question. If you want to avoid civil war, you must become imperialists."

–Cecil Rhodes, South African Statesman and Apostle of Imperialism, 1895

PART B – ESSAY QUESTIONS

1. In the course of the17th century "absolutistic" regimes spread, with varied degrees of success, across much of Continental Europe. Why? What were the conditions and forces at work to make this form of government desirable—or at least seem desirable?

2. Discuss the complaints and aspirations of the various social classes in France on the eve of the French Revolution.

3. The peoples of Europe, convinced that their nations' causes were just, entered World War I in August of 1914 enthusiastically, in the belief that victory would be theirs by Christmas. What went wrong? Why did they, civilian and military alike, have such a mistaken concept of the nature of modern warfare? What changes had taken place in previous decades to so dramatically alter the nature of warfare?

4. At the outset of the Age of Exploration and Discovery it was the nations of the Iberian Peninsula—Portugal and Spain—that led the way. Why? What particular circumstances, advantages, motives, favored these states taking the lead?

5. Karl Marx made a number of assertions regarding how the governments would respond to the industrialization of society and expanding capitalism. Discuss the basic theses upon which he predicated these assertions and the specific nature of these assertions. Having done this, discuss Marx's record as a "prophet," indicating the extent to which his predictions proved valid.

6. The late 19th and early 20th centuries saw the long-held concept of the fundamental rationality of man come under attack: there were those who perceived man as being driven by forces other than those of a conscious (i.e., rational) nature. Discuss the reasons for this intellectual, yet anti-rational movement, and indicate some of its leading spokesmen.

THE ADVANCED PLACEMENT EXAMINATION IN

European History

TEST 5 – ANSWERS

1.	**(D)**	21.	**(C)**	41.	**(D)**	61.	**(A)**
2.	**(E)**	22.	**(C)**	42.	**(A)**	62.	**(C)**
3.	**(B)**	23.	**(C)**	43.	**(C)**	63.	**(A)**
4.	**(B)**	24.	**(E)**	44.	**(E)**	64.	**(C)**
5.	**(A)**	25.	**(B)**	45.	**(C)**	65.	**(D)**
6.	**(C)**	26.	**(C)**	46.	**(B)**	66.	**(C)**
7.	**(E)**	27.	**(A)**	47.	**(D)**	67.	**(B)**
8.	**(B)**	28.	**(D)**	48.	**(B)**	68.	**(C)**
9.	**(C)**	29.	**(A)**	49.	**(A)**	69.	**(B)**
10.	**(A)**	30.	**(E)**	50.	**(B)**	70.	**(C)**
11.	**(B)**	31.	**(C)**	51.	**(E)**	71.	**(D)**
12.	**(D)**	32.	**(B)**	52.	**(B)**	72.	**(D)**
13.	**(C)**	33.	**(D)**	53.	**(C)**	73.	**(D)**
14.	**(B)**	34.	**(B)**	54.	**(C)**	74.	**(B)**
15.	**(B)**	35.	**(C)**	55.	**(B)**	75.	**(B)**
16.	**(C)**	36.	**(D)**	56.	**(B)**	76.	**(D)**
17.	**(A)**	37.	**(C)**	57.	**(E)**	77.	**(B)**
18.	**(E)**	38.	**(E)**	58.	**(C)**	78.	**(D)**
19.	**(D)**	39.	**(E)**	59.	**(D)**	79.	**(C)**
20.	**(B)**	40.	**(C)**	60.	**(A)**	80.	**(E)**

Detailed Explanations of Answers

TEST 5

1. **(D)** William Harvey, an English physician and experimentalist, advanced the view in 1628 that the blood circulated and the heart acted as a pump. Paracelsus was a 16th century physician who attacked the long accepted theories of "humors" as a source of disease (A). Lorenzo Valla, a Renaissance humanist, demonstrated that the "Donation of Constantine" was a forgery (C). Galvani was an 18th century anatomist and experimenter with electricity (B). Francis Bacon (1561–1626) was an ardent advocate of the inductive approach to scientific research (E).

2. **(E)** René Descartes was a 17th century French geometer and mathematician and a proponent of deductive reasoning. Hugo Grotius was a Dutch legal theorist in the area of international law (A). Jean Bodin was a 16th century French *politique* and advocate of religious toleration (B). Galileo was a famed Renaissance physicist and astronomer (C). Joseph Dalton Hooker was a 19th century British botanist (D).

3. **(B)** Desiderius Erasmus, a Dutch humanist of the Northern Renaissance, was a strong critic of abuses within the Church, but was not a supporter of the Reformation launched by Luther, who had been influenced by him. Petrarch was a leading literary figure in the early Renaissance in Italy (A). Agricola was a 16th century scientist in the field of mining technology (C). Mirandola was a Renaissance humanist (D). Pierre d'Ailly, bishop of Cambrei and Puy and Chancellor of the University of Paris, was a leading figure in the Conciliar Movement of the 14th and 15th centuries (E).

4. **(B)** Enacted by King Henry IV, the Edict of Nantes granted limited religious and political autonomy to the Huguenots. Louis XI came to the throne following the Hundred Years' War in the 15th century (A). The St. Bartholomew's Day Massacre was an incident, inaugurating the bloodiest phases of the Religious Wars (C). The Treaty of Cateau-Cambresis (1559) ended the Hapsburg-Valois conflict (D).The Peace of Augsburg was a settlement between German Protestants and Catholics in the Reformation (E).

5. **(A)** A 19th century German sociologist, Weber advanced the theory of the "Protestant work ethic" and its significance in the emergence of capitalism. Luther supported neither the south German peasants (B), who demonstrated "revolutionary" tendencies in the early days of the Reformation nor the Anabaptists (C): indeed, he called for their extermination. The Reformation, if anything, deterred Protestant involvement in overseas exploration (D), a movement Catholic Portugal and Spain had already inaugurated. The Protestants took a more lenient view towards usury than did the medieval church (E).

6. **(C)** The treaty (1494) established a line of demarcation, with Portugal to have all lands to the east of it, and Spain all those to the west. England had nothing to do with the treaty, nor did she or other nations pay any heed to it (A). The Dutch did not gain control of the Cape region of South Africa until the 17th century (B), while the Ohio Valley was not to be penetrated for several centuries (D). The treaty had nothing to do with the Swiss, who by the end of the 15th century had largely gained their independence from the Hapsburgs (E).

7. **(E)** Vasco da Gama reached the port of Calicut on the Malabar coast of India in 1497. Bartholomeu Dias reached the tip of Africa in 1488 (B), while Magellan of Spain was the first to circumnavigate the globe (A) (actually it was his captain, del Cano, as Magellan was slain in the Philippines). Portuguese seamen reached Japan in 1530 (C), while Cabral landed in Brazil (D) in 1500 (although there is slight evidence that other Portuguese explorers landed there earlier).

8. **(B)** This statement is an example of the doctrine of "Double Predestination," a core element in Calvin's teachings. Thomas Hobbes (A) was a political writer in 17th century England and the author of the *Leviathan*. While the doctrine of predestination had long been a concept in Christianity, neither Luther (C), the Catholic Council of Trent (D), nor Zwingli (E) placed the great emphasis on it seen in Calvin's works.

9. **(C)** This statement reflects the doctrine of the "Divine Right of Monarchy," a theory held by the early Stuart monarchs of England. Neither Frederick the Great (A) nor Joseph II of Austria (E), both "Enlightened Despots," would have written or spoken in such terms, while William III of England (D), king by selection of the Parliament, would also have been hesitant to claim such power. John Locke (B), an outspoken exponent of "constitutional monarchy," would have rejected such an idea out-of-hand.

10. **(A)** One of the "Twelve who Ruled" on the Committee of Public Safety, Robespierre was its most articulate spokesman. None of the other men was ever a member of the committee: Lafayette (E), a moderate aristocrat, fled France before it came to power; Babeuf (D), a "communist" revolutionary, was executed by the Directory, while Napoleon (C) did not rise to prominence in France until

after its fall. Danton (B), a leading figure in the early days of the revolution, fell victim to the "Terror" inaugurated by the Committee.

11. **(B)** The Peace of Augsburg was a religious accord reached among the German princes in 1155. The Edict of Nantes (1595) ended the religious wars in France (A). The Six Articles (1534) defined heretical acts in the eyes of the Anglican Church (C). The *Spiritual Exercises* (D) was a manual written by the founder of the Jesuits. The Council of Trent (1545–64) was a part of the Catholic Counter-Reformation (E).

12. **(D)** The *philosophes* of the Age of Reason strongly opposed religious intolerance and what they viewed as irrational superstition of religious beliefs. Cosmopolitan in outlook and generally anti-monarchial (A), they were convinced of mankind's ability to progress (B), and were strongly under the influence of earlier scientists and their concept of the universe (E).

13. **(C)** Rumors had spread among the peasants that the monarch and aristocracy intended to crush them through the use of brigands. Prussia and Austria were not at war with France in 1789 (A), nor had the king been executed (D), nor the Jacobin "Terror" begun (B).

14. **(B)** The poem reflects a romantic view, questioning the merits of science and extolling nature and the emotions. The other answers refer to men or movements which were strongly influenced by reason and science and had little regard for the "sentiments of the heart."

15. **(B)** Thomas Malthus was an 18th century forerunner in the field of human demography. Saint-Simon (A) was a prominent utopian socialist of the early 19th century, Bentham (C) the founder of Utilitarianism. Bergson (D) was a social philosopher of the late 19th century, the advocate of the *élan vital*, and Spenser (E) was an ardent Social Darwinist.

16. **(C)** The fact that the orbits were elliptical was determined by Kepler after the death of Copernicus. Copernicus's theory rejected both the medieval (A) and Ptolemaic (B) concept of the universe while advancing the heliocentric theory (E). Kepler's work (D) was conducted after the death of Copernicus.

17. **(A)** The quotation is from his pamphlet "What is the Third Estate?", a strong argument against the Estates General voting "by the order." Necker (B) and Turgot (C) had passed from the political scene by 1789, while Pombal (D) was a Portuguese statesmen. The *emigrés* or aristocrats generally favored voting by the order (E).

18. **(E)** The new monarchs, William and Mary, were required to accept the "Bill of Rights" and, in essence, the ultimate authority of Parliament. The

Hanoverian dynasty (A) only assumed the throne on the death of Queen Anne (1714), while Cromwell (B) died a natural death nearly three decades prior to 1688. Anglicanism was proclaimed the religion of England in the reign of Henry VIII in the early 16th century (C).

19. **(D)** The *cahiers* or list of grievances of 1789 indicated that a majority of the French people wanted the monarchy reformed, not abolished. All of the other complaints or demands have been advanced as probable factors in the coming of the Revolution.

20. **(B)** These are the opening words of Rousseau's *Social Contract*. Locke (C) was an earlier English statesman, political theorist, and scientist, while Burke (A) was an English politician and the author of *Reflections on the Revolution in France*. Diderot (E) was a philosophe of the Age of Reason and the editor of the monumental *Encyclopedie*. De Lesseps (D) was the architect and builder of the Suez Canal.

21. **(C)** Cromwell governed as a virtual military dictator following the execution of Charles I. Tudor (B) reigned in the mid-16th century, while William and Mary came to the throne in 1688 (A). The "Old Pretender," the son of the banished James II, never reigned (D). Charles II, son of Charles I, came to the throne in 1661 following the death of Cromwell (E).

22. **(C)** While waging war on the French Protestants (Huguenots) and depriving them of certain political and military privileges, he did not deny their religious rights. His major goal was the enhancement of the power of the crown, which meant weakening the influence of the aristocracy and that of the Hapsburgs through aid to the German Protestants and King Gustavus Adolphus in the Thirty Years' War.

23. **(C)** This is a passage from the notes of the Inquisition trial of Galileo for advancing his astronomical views. Copernicus (A), Kepler (B), and Brahe (D), all astronomers, were dead by 1615, while the Dutchman Leeuwenhoek (E) was the first man to use the microscope to observe microorganisms.

24. **(E)** The utilization of colonies as "feeders" of raw materials to the mother country, and closed markets to the finished products of the mother country, was a standard concept of the mercantile system. There was no desire to see colonies gain their independence (A) in the mercantile system, to develop their own industry (C), nor to be permitted to trade with other countries (D), both or all of which would serve as competition to the mother country. Colonies, as in the case of the American holdings of England, were customarily expected to defend themselves (B).

25. **(B)** The words, those of Thomas Paine, reflect a deistic, almost agnostic,

religious outlook. All other groups, regardless of their sectarian views, would hold a more traditional view of religion and, specifically, of Christianity.

26. **(C)** Justification by faith constituted the central pillar of the Lutheran faith. All other concepts noted were either rejected by Luther or viewed as of secondary importance.

27. **(A)** The correct answer is (A). Former United States Senator Mitchell went to assist in negotiations between the British and the Irish Republican Army at the request of U.S. President Bill Clinton, who himself was cheered by large crowds when he travelled to strife-torn Northern Ireland in 1996 to champion the cause of peace between Roman Catholics and Protestants.

28. **(D)** He specifically spoke of the city as his "window to the West," the avenue through which Western trade and technology would flow into Russia. When Peter came to the Russian throne, the power of the Mongols had already been broken (A) and he was to weaken that of the Orthodox Church (C) through means not related to the establishment of St. Petersburg. Poland was on a marked path of decline (E) and he tightened the controls on the serfs (B) rather than loosening them.

29. **(A)** In the first half of the 15th century his seamen explored the west coast of Africa as far south as the Cape Verde Islands. Brazil (B) was first discovered by the Portuguese seamen in 1500, four decades after Prince Henry's death, while Goa (D), in India, was also established by the Portuguese some time after his passing. Cortez, in the service of Spain, conquered the Aztecs (C), not the Mayas, and Portugal's explorations were directed southward, not to the northwest (E).

30. **(E)** The Danes briefly entered the conflict to support the German Protestants and, if possible, acquire territory. The roots of the war were to be found in the attempt of the Bohemians to place Frederick II of the Palatinate, a Calvinist, on the throne (A). Rather than promoting German unity (B), the struggle resulted in continued division. France throughout the conflict supported the German Protestants and their allies (E). The war did not involve the Ottomans, who were driven from the Balkans only in the 19th century (D).

31. **(C)** The role of the prince is seen as a "career," not a God-given right: this was the concept held by the Enlightened Despots, of whom Frederick the Great, whose words these are, was a prime example. All of the other monarchs and individuals noted were strong advocates of the concept of "divine right" monarchy.

32. **(B)** The Lancastrians triumphed in the person of Henry VII, a Tudor in 1485. The Hanoverians (A) and Windsors (C), actually the same dynasty (its German name was changed in World War I), came to the throne with the death of Queen Anne in 1713, the Stuarts (D) on the death of Elizabeth I in 1603, while the Plantangenets (E) were a medieval dynasty.

33. **(D)** By abandoning Copernicus's concept of circular orbits, Kepler demonstrated the validity of the former's heliocentric theory. He proved the error of Ptolemy's theory (A) and demonstrated that the speed of the planets in their orbits varies in relation to their distance from the sun (B). It was Galileo who, using a telescope, saw for the first time the rough surface of the moon (C). Kepler utilized many of the measurements of Brahe, his former employer (E).

34. **(B)** The words are from the English Bill of Rights, accepted by King William before he came to the throne in 1688. George I (A) and Anne (C), coming to the throne after the enactment of the Bill of Rights, accepted it, while Charles II (D) and Henry VIII (E) reigned earlier (and probably would have rejected it).

35. **(C)** Religious conformity increasingly became a means by which the power of the prince was enhanced. Protestants tended strongly to look to the primitive Christian Church and community for what they saw as correct guidance (A). Nationalistic feelings were an integral aspect of the Reformation (B), while the religious enthusiasm of Europeans assumed near-fanatic proportions (E). The practice of sending missionaries to the Eastern lands can be seen almost from the time of the crucifixion (D).

36. **(D)** Man's mind, a "blank tablet" at birth, gained knowledge only through sensory perception and reflection on the knowledge so acquired. Locke rejected any sources of knowledge other than the information he gained through his sensory contacts with the world about him and his integration of that knowledge through his powers of reasoning.

37. **(C)** Balboa was the first European to gaze on the waters of the Pacific. All other matches are correct.

38. **(E)** The seaports of Ceuta, Lisbon, Brest, London, and Copenhagen, formerly six or more days of travel from Venice, have been brought within three days of travel time. Travel times to all of the other regions, primarily overland, have remained virtually unaltered.

39. **(E)** The concept, that of "absolutism," was supported by Hobbes in his work the *Leviathan*. John Locke (A), in his *Two Treatises on Civil Government*, clearly rejected such a concept. Bodin (B) and Montesquieu (D), French political theorists of the 16th and 18th centuries respectively, would also have rejected

such a concept of absolutism. Napier (C) was a scientist, the deviser of logarithms.

40. **(C)** By 1902 Germany had surpassed Great Britain, in some cases markedly, in basic industrial production, a fact that created increasing tension between the two states. Russia (A), if not one of the major industrial powers of Europe, had established a base. France (B), if not as productive as Germany or England, was increasing its production, as was Austria (D). Clearly German unification in 1871 led to an explosion in her industrial growth (E).

41. **(D)** It was to be through the electoral process that the Nazis gained power. Hitler gained the somewhat qualified support of the aristocratic officer corps only after attaining power (A). His first paramilitary backing, the SA or "Storm Troopers," were broken by Hitler only in 1935 (B). He continued to work out of Bavaria until the early 1930s (C), while he was always in opposition to the SD Party (E).

42. **(A)** The revolutionaries were a small group of young Russian army officers who had been stationed in post-revolutionary France. The Italian unification movement (B) only resorted to open revolt in the 1840s; the Pan-Slavic movement (C) also emerged later than 1825. In 1825 Norway was a part of Sweden (D), and the Belgians gained their independence from Holland in 1832 (E).

43. **(C)** It was designed to exclude England from all trade with the Continent. Joseph Bonaparte was placed on the Spanish throne in 1809 (B). France had little desire to see a unified Germany (A), although the "Redaction of 1803" did reduce the number of German states to 39. He was allied with Russia in 1806 (D), going to war with her only in 1812. After his earlier activities in Egypt, he undertook no further military operations in that region (E).

44. **(E)** Albania came into existence in the 19th century. Estonia (C) and Finland (B) came into existence in the wake of the Russian Revolution, Czechoslovakia (A) with the breakup of the Austro-Hungarian Empire, and Yugoslavia (B) with the unification of various Slavic states.

45. **(C)** Dr. Dollfuss, the individual portrayed on the defaced poster, was chancellor of Austria. He was murdered by Austrian Nazis in 1933, five years before the *Anchluss*, or German annexation of Austria. Hitler's target in 1923 was basically the Bavarian government, not the Weimar Republic (A). The Munich Conference (B) was the prelude to the seizure of the Sudetenland and eventually all of Czechoslovakia. The German military occupied the demilitarized Rhineland in 1935 (D), while Danzig (E) was seized in the opening days of World War II.

46. **(B)** The idea that an elite cadre was necessary to give leadership to the

anticipated revolution was that of V. I. Lenin. For Marx, such a revolution was inevitable as the condition of the working class grew intolerable (A). Since, in Marx's view, the "capitalist class," controlling the "modes" or tools of production, dominated society (C), including government (E), they would not permit the state to aid the working class. "Economic Determinism" (D) is a concept at the core of Marxism.

47. **(D)** France, having constructed the Maginot Line, was inclined to assume a defensive stand in the 1930s. German bitterness of the Treaty, the "Diktat," was deep (A), while the economic failures of the Weimar Republic (B), together with its association with the "Diktat," hurt it in the eyes of the Germans. As the Communist influence arose at the expense of the SDs, many Germans felt the Nazis represented the only alternative (C). Von Papen (E) aided Hitler in gaining the office of chancellor in the belief that he could "control" him.

48. **(B)** Introduced in the face of falling production and popular discontent, the NEP allowed greater economic freedom in the hope of increasing production. The First Five-Year plan (D), linked to the collectivization of agriculture (C) and the effort to expand industry greatly (A), was introduced in the late 1920s by Stalin. The NEP represented a "step back" from nationalization of industry (E).

49. **(A)** He placed great emphasis on man utilizing his inner "will," an intuitive, irrational force. Highly contemptuous of Christian "slave mentality," (B) contemporary moral standards (C), and democracy (D), he called for an elite "superman" who depended on his "will" to lead society (E).

50. **(B)** The war it ended was the "First Opium War," begun when Chinese officials sought to halt the importation of opium. The Russian threat (A) had not yet emerged at the time of the war, while British officials (D) had not yet been permitted to enter Peking. Attacks on Christian missionaries (E) only came later in the 19th century. Piracy was as much a problem for the Chinese as it was for the British (C).

51. **(E)** The pie chart for Great Britain indicates women had not yet broken into the ranks of banking and commerce. In each of the three charts women are seen to represent a factor in all areas except banking and commerce in England.

52. **(B)** Hitler demanded that the large ethnic German population in the Sudentenland be united with Germany. The unification of Germany and Austria (the *Anschluss*) had already occurred (E), as had the occupation of the Rhineland (A). Danzig (D) became the center of a territorial dispute between Germany and Poland in 1939 (C).

53. **(C)** Issued in 1917, it recognized the Zionist aspirations to establish a homeland in the Holy Land. Recognition of the Arab desire for independence (A)

came in the so-called McMahon Letters. The French and British did have territorial interests in the Near East (B), as indicated by the secret Skyes-Picot Treaty (E). Egypt and the Canal (D) were already under British control before the war.

54. **(C)** While Prince Lvov briefly headed the Provisional Government that sought to control Russia following the February Revolution, the figure most closely associated with that failed government was Kerensky. While Lenin (A), together with Trotsky (B) and Stalin (D), were active in this period, they came to real power only with the revolution of October 1917. Kolchak (E) was a leader of one of the anti-Bolshevik White Russian armies.

55. **(B)** The assassination of the archduke and his wife in Sarajevo on June 28, 1914 led to an Austrian ultimatum to Serbia which, in turn, resulted in the outbreak of hostilities. The German invasion of Belgium (A) after the war had started led to England's entry into the conflict. Bosnia-Herzegovina had been annexed earlier (C). Italy joined France (D) in 1915. The Russian and Serbian armies attacked only after the war had broken out (E).

56. **(B)** The British East India Company, which had earlier lost its trade monopoly, was dissolved and replaced by the authority of the British government in those areas it had controlled. The British never formerly annexed all of India (A), many regions remaining under the nominal control of local princes. The cult of Thugge (C) had been eliminated earlier. Indians constituted the bulk of the Indian Army (D) and served in the civil service (E), though not in higher positions.

57. **(E)** With her defeat in the war, Russian interests in the Far East were abandoned for the time being. The Japanese did not annex Manchuria (C) until 1931, while in 1910 they annexed all of Korea (B). Russia had sold Alaska (A) earlier and also acquired the Maritime Provinces (D) from China at an earlier date.

58. **(C)** Alexander II began a series of reforms, including the emancipation of the serfs. Russia had acquired access to the Black Sea earlier (A), in the reign of Catherine the Great, while a Duma (E) was established in 1905. There was no revolution in the years immediately following the Crimean War (B), the first occurring in 1905.

59. **(D)** Social Darwinism tended to be highly nationalistic rather than cosmopolitan. With utilization of the concept of "survival of the fittest" derived from Darwin's theories, all of the other activities mentioned could be justified.

60. **(A)** Oswald Spengler was the German author of *The Decline of the West*, a pessimistic view of the future of Western civilization. Sidney Webb (B) was a British socialist while Karl Peters (C) and Leander Jameson (D) were imperialists in Africa. "Vincenzo" Lombardi (E) is better known as the late Vince Lombardi, noted coach of the Green Bay Packers professional football team.

61. **(A)** The elections of 1928, prior to the onset of the Depression, saw the Nazis as the smallest party of those represented on the chart; by 1933, they were the largest. A union of all the parties represented on the chart for March 1933 would still not have outvoted the Nazis (B). The major threat to the SDs in the 1920s came either from the Independent Socialists, the Nationalists, or the Nazis (C). The French-Belgian occupation of the Ruhr (D), occurring in 1923, boosted the Communist representation in the Assembly notably, while the Weimar Republic's subsequent economic recovery (E) hurt the Nazis.

62. **(C)** The Spartacists, led by Rosa Luxemberg, seized control of Berlin for a week in January 1918, hoping to inaugurate the communist revolution in Germany. They were crushed by Frei Korps units. The Frei Korps (A), composed of ex-German soldiers, were largely politically conservative or reactionary. The socialists (B), who gained control of the Weimar Republic from the outset, were anti-communists. The Beer Hall Putsch (D), led by Hitler, was rabidly anti-communist. Bela Kun (E), a communist, was active in Hungary, not Germany.

63. **(A)** A German philosopher of the early 19th century, Schopenhauer believed man was driven by the "will," an inner, irrational and creative force. Weber (B) and Durkheim (C) were sociologists of the late 19th century, Spenser (E) a strong advocate of Social Darwinism, as was Smiles (D).

64. **(C)** NATO, the North Atlantic Treaty Organization, was founded in 1949 to protect Europe from Soviet aggression. Following the collapse of the Soviet Union, U.S. President Clinton suggested that NATO provide a collective guarantee against any aggression by one power against another. Though NATO, among other international groups, has sought a solution to the Balkan crisis (A), this was not its founding purpose. Choice (B) is not the best answer because while NATO countries have supplied troops for U.N. missions, such activity is not part of NATO's charter. Choice (D) is incorrect because although NATO members have generally supported human rights, they have usually considered preventing expansion of Soviet influence their primary objective. Finally, NATO nations' support of Israel (E) has been inconsistent, and never part of NATO's overall objective.

65. **(D)** Serbia was extremely active in stirring up the nationalistic feelings of Serbs living within Austrian territory, an activity that contributed greatly to the coming of World War I. The Czechs were, in fact, more advanced politically than the Serbs (A). Both wanted independence (B) and (E). Germany, as a close ally of the Austrians, was not inclined to support the Slavic Czechs (C).

66. **(C)** The Sinn Fein, the nationalist party in Ireland, broke out in open revolt at Easter of 1916. It was crushed. All of the other regions remained loyal during the war.

67. **(B)** The future hope of mankind, Nietzche believed, lies with the strong-

willed individual who would be guided by his inner, "creative" will. Barth (A), Tillich (E), and Kierkegaard (D) were theologians, while Sartre (C) was a post-World War I exponent of existentialism.

68. **(C)** Heisenberg's "uncertainty principle" stated that no fixed model of the atoms of a given element was possible, only an approximation. The "Big Bang" theory (A) is the result of the work of a number of astronomers, among the earliest of whom were Lemaitre and Gamow, while the same is true of the geological theory of plate tectonics (B)—the German Alfred Lothar Wegener being among the earliest to conceive of Continental drift. Claims as to who has discovered the oldest homonid (D) are contested between several anthropologists. Richard Leakey is among the leading claimants. The first major radio telescope was constructed under the supervision of Sir Bernard Lovell (E).

69. **(B)** Both men, one a Frenchman, the other English, were ardent racists, believing firmly in the superiority of the German "race." Existentialism (A) as a philosophy developed largely after their deaths, as did the Dadaist art movement (E). They wrote little or nothing in the area of economics (C), and they died prior to 1930.

70. **(C)** These are three of the "Fourteen Points" of Woodrow Wilson which he tried to make the basis of the treaty ending World War I. The Atlantic Charter (A) was an agreement stating the vision of the post-war world signed by Churchill and Roosevelt. The Treaty of Versailles (B), ending World War I, did not incorporate any of the Fourteen Points. The McMahon Letters (D) related to Anglo-Arab relations during the First World War, while the Kellogg-Briand Pact (E) was an international agreement of the 1920s.

71. **(D)** De Gaulle came to power in the midst of the bitter conflict between the French and Algerian nationalists. By the time de Gaulle came to power, the French had withdrawn from Indo-China (A), the other questions arose subsequent to his assuming power.

72. **(D)** He envisioned that society was sinking to a level of mediocrity as the vision of mass education set in. The other issues did not greatly concern him or did not reflect the central thrust of his argument.

73. **(D)** These political factions were ardently reactionary and to a degree pro-Nazi. Far to the right, they were opposed to Leon Blum (E), and the leftist Republicans of Spain were inclined to look to Nazi Germany as an ally. They never achieved political power.

74. **(B)** The speech, made by Secretary of State George C. Marshall, marked the inauguration of the idea of the Marshall Plan designed to bring about the economic rehabilitation of Europe following World War II. It was firmly sup-

ported by the other statesmen noted, save Roosevelt, who had died in 1945.

75. **(B)** The men were joint discoverers of the so-called Double Helix. The other scientific discoveries were not associated with Watson and Crick.

76. **(D)** Israel invaded Egypt after Nasser attempted to nationalize the Suez Canal. The invasion was a failure, largely due to the pressure put on the invaders by the United States and the United Nations. The other diplomatic activities on the part of Egypt, while occurring, were not related to the invasion.

77. **(B)** The explosion at the Chernobyl nuclear power plant near Kiev caused Europeans to rethink expansion of nuclear power: One former Soviet scientist, Leonid Toptunov, has reported that more than 600,000 people received high doses of radiation—and their names have been entered in a medical register for the rest of their lives—because of the 1986 accident. Three Mile Island (A), in Middletown, Pa., was the site of a nuclear power plant accident in 1979 that resulted in the release of small amounts of radioactive gases through the plant's venting system and the formation of a hydrogen gas bubble in the reactor's containment vessel. The atomic bombing of Nagasaki and Hiroshima (C), Japan, was carried out by the United States at the end of World War II. In 1984, Bhopal (D), India, was the site of a massive chemical plant explosion and poisonous gas leak.

78. **(D)** This right of intervention was clearly seen in the invasion of Czechoslovakia by the Warsaw Pact States. The idea of assisting communist revolutions around the world (A) has been asserted from an early period, while the idea of communist states having the right to pursue their own path (B), such as Yugoslavia or China, did not set well with most Soviet leaders. Even today, the rights of dissident Jews to emigrate is not wholly free (E).

79. **(C)** The North Koreans launched a surprise attack on the South Koreans. The Chinese entry into the war (A) came only when it had been underway for many months, as did the naming of MacArthur (B) to head the United Nations' forces, which came into the struggle only after it had broken out (D).

80. **(E)** All of these states except Yugoslavia have been invaded by Soviet troops, but in 1956 it was Hungary's turn.

Sample Answer to Document-Based Question

J. A. Hobson, an economist and publicist with a brilliant mind, had a great impact both in his own day and subsequent decades upon the study of Imperialism and its roots. Among those he influenced were V. I. Lenin, who drew upon him heavily for his work *Imperialism, the Highest Stage of Capitalism*, the major Marxian discussion of the subject. However, in his own day and, to a greater extent, in recent years, scholars have raised questions regarding his conclusions. There are to be seen in these documents a number of the assertions, attitudes, and claims held by prominent statesmen and intellectuals of the Age of Imperialism which seem, if not to wholly discredit Hobson's views, to raise questions as to whether they alone can account for the colonial expansion of Europe in the 19th century.

In Document 2 there is seen the assertion by an English official familiar with the colonial scene that the impetus for the penetration of a region did not always come from the European governments themselves: rather, there were native elements within countries or regions that welcomed foreigners. In this case, according to the English official, princes of the Malaysian regions found it desirable to draw upon British expertise in organizing their relatively primitive governments along more efficient lines. It is possible to demonstrate that there were in many other areas of Africa and Asia native elements who found contact with Europeans advantageous. Thus in many lands merchants, seeking to expand their own trade, found in the Europeans a ready market. Document 5 also indicates that it was not always the home government, in this case England, which pushed or even supported the economic penetration of the backward regions: if merchants wished to trade in areas of instability they did so at their own risk and should expect no assistance from their own governments. Admittedly, both documents pre-date the great Age of Imperialism, an age in which, in the wake of intensified economic competition among the major states of Europe, gunboat diplomacy became more common.

Much has been written about the White Man's Burden as a factor in European Imperialism. This concept, eulogized in Kipling's poems (Document 17) held it was a virtual obligation of Westerners, possessing a superior civilization, to bring the benefits of that civilization—or at least those aspects of it that they could absorb—to the backward peoples of Asia and Africa. This moralistic view was early seen in the writings of William Wilberforce, a statesman and humanitarian who had demonstrated his real concern for mankind in his ardent struggle to end slavery in all English holdings and, indeed, worldwide. Certainly many of those Europeans who were involved in the colonial regions of the globe were sincere in their efforts to improve the welfare of their subjects. The activities of the British in India in seeking to eradicate suttee (i.e., widow burning), the cult of thuggee, and to improve food production and health services provides evidence of this. It could be argued, however, that this paternalistic attitude, if beneficent, still maintained the colonial peoples as subjects. Once established in a colony, it was possible to argue, not without some justification, that the continued presence of the civilizing influence of the Europeans was necessary to prevent the natives from falling back into a state of anarchy and near-barbarism (Document 3). Clearly there were those who, opposed to imperialism, questioned this humanitarianism as nothing more than a cloak to conceal more selfish motives. Thus Documents 8 and 13 portray the missionary as little more than the vanguard of a nation's political and economic interests.

It is clear that as the 19th century advanced, this paternalistic attitude for man took a less humane twist as the impact of Social Darwinism was felt. Now, rather than a humanitarian duty, the subjugation of backward peoples was seen as a natural part of the struggle for the survival of the fittest (Documents 9, 14, 15, and 18) in which the needs of the weak need not be taken into consideration. There is evident, too, a strong element of racism, for the white race is destined to triumph over the inferior black and yellow races. In Document 14, there is the suggestion that the struggle in the colonial sphere is also becoming one in which the Western states themselves are in a mounting and, in Social Darwinistic terms, natural struggle in which the stronger, living nations will overcome the weaker, dying Western states.

Clearly it was not always solely or even primarily economic advantages that the colonial powers sought in imposing their rule on the peoples of Asia and Africa. Bases for strategic purposes were often a goal (Documents 4, 10, 16). As the maritime and naval expansion of Europe took place, this became all the more true. While it might be argued that such harbors and fortified sites were utilized to enhance and expand a nation's economic interests, it is also true that they served as protection against potential threats from other European powers. British expansion into the inhospitable and costly Northwest Territories was due more to a perceived threat from Russia to India than from visions of economic gain. Clearly, a Russian foreign minister found it logical to justify his country's expansion into central Asia on the basis of the threat presented by the semi-civilized peoples of that region.

Documents 11, 12, and 19 provide evidence of yet two more explanations which have been advanced to explain, if not justify, Europe's imperialistic surge. Document 11 indicates that Eastern Europe, in the course of the 19th century, experienced a large growth in its population. To the leaders of many of these countries this growth seemed to demand that a safety valve be found for the surplus population. To many the solution lay in the establishment of overseas colonies. This argument was seen in the claims of Cecil Rhodes, virtually the personification of Imperialism (Document 19) and in the claims of many German advocates of colonial expansion that *Lebensraum* (living space) represented a logical solution to their expanding population. Documents 12 and 19 provide yet a second motive for the acquisition of colonies: they were necessary for the economic vitality of the mother country, not solely to provide profits for Hobson's "certain industrial, financial, and professional classes," but, rather, for the working class of the nation in general. It would, in the view of the *Nationalsozialer Verein* Manifesto, contribute to social reform in Germany, while Rhodes, more dramatically, argued that it was the only alternative to civil war in England.

To argue that Hobson was wrong in arguing for the significance of economic factors in the 19th century surge of European Imperialism would be in error, for it is obvious that many of the documents presented here do take note of the role of that factor, even though it might not be the central idea discussed. It would be correct however, as many scholars have done, to insist that to explain a major movement in history such as Imperialism on the basis of mono-causation is in error. Any such movement is the consequence of the interaction of numerous forces. Even where one force such as economics may be of paramount importance, it can and often is multi-faceted: profits derived from the colonial world certainly benefited certain of the capitalist elements in the state: but such prosperity could also serve the interests of the masses and make them no less eager for colonial expansion. Nor is it possible to contend that there were no Imperialists who were not motivated by truly humanitarian sentiments rather than solely visions of profit, or a statesman who was not concerned with the defense of his country rather than financial gain for privileged elements in his nation. Great historical movements are too complex to have simple, singular explanations.

Sample Answers to Essay Questions

1. The efforts of European princes to bring the affairs of their states more firmly under their control had their origins both in internal elements which constituted, or were seen as constituting disruptive forces threatening their realm's stability and strength and, at the same time, changes in the nature of relations between states.

Internally, many states were, in the wake of the Reformation, confronted with the pressure of religious groups which, although in the minority, were extremely militant in their desire to gain recognition of their particular form of Christianity. France in the mid-16th century had been torn apart by conflicts which, in part, had their origins in the bitter conflict between Calvinist Huguenots and the predominant Catholic population. In the 16th and 17th centuries too, England and Germany endured, to varying degrees, bitter struggles having their roots at least in part in the clash of Catholic and Protestant sects. The answer to many princes was uniformity, the imposition on the state's population of one faith, that of the prince. The dissenters' choices were generally limited—accept the state religion, suffer persecution, or flee. Although Cardinal Richelieu, unable to tolerate the special political and military privileges the Huguenots received as a result of the Edict of Nantes, crushed them on the battlefield, he did not deprive them of their religious rights. Such an act of toleration, however, was relatively rare for the age: King Louis XIV, in persecuting the Huguenots for their religious beliefs, was far closer to the norm. Even the recognized church was sometimes seen as a potential threat: such was the case in France, where the feared loyalty of Catholic ecclesiasts to Rome led to French monarchs seeking to bring their churchmen more firmly under their control in the form of the Gallican Church.

Religious groups were not the only elements in the states of Europe that were seen as threats to stability. The aristocracy of Europe had emerged from the medieval period possessing many privileges and rights which acted as significant obstacles to the exercise of princely power. Jealous of their privileged position, they were determined to retain and, provided the opportunity, to expand it. They were willing to endanger the security of their country in order to do so, as was demonstrated both in the course of the French Religious Wars and, in the mid-17th century, the Fronde, a revolt on the part of aristocratic elements aimed at curtailing the trend toward centralization initiated by Richelieu and Mazarin.

Nor were religious and aristocratic groups the only potentially disruptive elements in society, for in many states there were other virtually autonomous elements enjoying rights which exempted them from the complete control of the state. Such was the case with the Comuneros, an urban bourgeois movement crushed by Charles V, a Hapsburg in 1523.

In addition to the instability generated by various internal forces, changes in the nature of relations between states served to enhance the presumed need for concentrating power in the hands of a central administration, controlled by the prince. Competition become more intense and, for at least a few states, had assumed a "global" nature. If a nation was to survive, much less thrive, it had to be able to defend itself and, if the opportunity presented itself, to take advantage of its neighbors. Such ability was to a large extent dependent on the existence of a strong military establishment. As armies grew larger—Louis XIV maintained a standing army of 400,000—the costs entailed in maintaining them, together with the expense of extensive fortifications, arsenals, supply depots, transportation facilities, and administrative support systems necessary to sustain them increased steadily. This, in turn, demanded more effective control of the state's revenues and, equally important, increasing those revenues as much as possible. The fiscal affairs of the state consequently entailed the expansion and centralization of the necessary organs of state. Moreover, in an age of expanding commercial activities, the economic well-being of the state was seen as requiring close state involvement in every facet of its economic activity. Mercantilism, the economic side of absolutism, was oriented toward strengthening the economic vitality of the state at the expense of one's enemies or possible enemies.

These various threats, internal and external, to the state's well-being led many to conclude that the only solution was to vest ultimate and absolute power in the hands of the prince, one whose concern would be for the welfare of the entire nation, not simply one class or element. Such was the argument advanced by Thomas Hobbes in his *Leviathan*, where he argued that the alternative to placing sovereignty in the hands of one man was, in essence, anarchy. Such was the power Louis XIV envisioned when he proclaimed "I am the state."

2. When one initially contemplates the classes of pre-Revolutionary France there is a tendency to think of the "Three Estates" and to envision each as a monolithic unit, with the attitudes and aspirations of its individual members in

general accord. This was, in fact, not the case. As the Estates General met in the summer of 1789, sharp divisions within each of the estates developed which placed elements of each in disagreement.

The "First Estate," the clergy, is an excellent example of this discord. Constituting one percent of the population, the church held one-third of the land. It was from these, and from the annual tithe imposed upon the annual production of land tilled by laymen, that it derived its major revenues, a yearly income perhaps one-half that of the monarchy. Rather than paying a tax upon this great wealth, the church gave only a "free gift," an insignificant amount in relation to its revenue. Not all clergy enjoyed equal wealth, however, and, far from being a unified group, they were actually splintered into several factions. The primary division was the great prelates—archbishops, bishops, and abbots—and the urban and village priests. Drawn overwhelmingly, if not solely, from the aristocracy, interests of the upper clergies were linked to that class and with the protection of their own privileged position. While there were undoubtedly those who took their ecclesiastical duties seriously, many were content to relegate their duties to subordinates and enjoy the pleasures of Paris or Versailles. The urban and villages curés, in contrast, were drawn from the bourgeoisie. Laboring for their flocks, they were increasingly angered at the lifestyle of the higher clergy and the many abuses they saw. While a majority of the village priests remained committed to the doctrines of the church, many urban priests, having fallen under the influence of the *philosophes* were questioning those doctrines.

The "Second Estate," the aristocracy, was also split into several factions. The Nobles of the Sword, hereditary aristocrats, enjoyed virtual exemption from taxes and held a monopoly on army commissions and high ecclesiastical posts. They desired to retain and expand their privileged status and to extend their political influence. The Nobles of the Robe were aristocrats who had acquired their title through purchase. Generally wealthier than the Nobles of the Sword and holding key government posts, they were among the most ardent defenders of the monarchy and, like their hereditary counterparts, envisioned extending their control over the throne and reenforcing their status. Not all aristocrats were wealthy, for the *hobereaux*, the "little falcons," were little better off than the average peasant. Possessing feudal and manorial rights which permitted them to impose levies on the peasantry, they did so with increasing vigor, to the growing hatred of the peasants.

The "Third Estate," constituting ninety-eight percent of the population, presented the greatest diversity of aspirations and complaints. While the wealthy bourgeoisie, men involved in commerce or the professions, might envision one day entering the ranks of the aristocracy, they, like all bourgeoisie, found the social arrogance of the aristocracy abhorrent. It was among them, and among the middle class, that the criticisms of the *Ancien Régime* and the calls for reform raised by the *philosophes* took hold. The wealth and arrogance of the higher clergy and the aristocrats, the regime's ineffective foreign policy, the presumed corruption of the administration, the inequity of the tax system, the mercantilist and guild systems, even the basic concepts of Christianity were attacked and calls for reform made by them. Well-educated, articulate, and well aware of their significant contribution to the economic life of France, above all they wanted a greater voice in the political life of the country.

The peasantry of France were, on the whole, better off than those elsewhere, serfdom having virtually disappeared in the country. Their complaints, however, were many. A severe land shortage led them to covet the lands of the church and aristocracy. There was anger over an unequal and onerous tax system, with its income, land, and poll taxes and the despised *gabelle* or salt tax, the burden of which fell particularly heavily upon them. Hated even more was the imposition of manorial and feudal levies. While a majority of the peasantry remained loyal to the church and their village priests, they, too, held the higher clergy in contempt. Even those peasants who held land were constantly confronted with the threat of disaster in the face of droughts, while their incomes in the best of times hardly kept up with the rising inflation; for those who had no land, poverty was a constant companion.

For the lower classes in the cities, a group that had not found a collective voice, the complaints were many: low wages, high unemployment, social degradation, and hunger, to name but a few.

The *cahiers*, or list of grievances, drawn up on the eve of the Revolution expressed the wishes of many in society, and particularly the middle class: personal freedom for all citizens, freedom of expression, an end to a harsh and unequal system of justice, a greater voice in the affairs of government. They called for reform of the monarchy, not its overthrow—that would only come later.

3. Europe, in the summer of 1914, had seen but three major international conflicts in the century since the defeat of Napoleon Bonaparte. These conflicts, the Austro-Prussian, Franco-Prussian, and Crimean Wars had been relatively clean wars—relatively short and characterized more by the glamour of battle—cavalry charges and colorful uniforms—rather than bloodshed. Even the costly futility of the "Charge of the Light Brigade" was surrounded with jingoistic glory rather than the reality of the carnage it represented. Beyond this, the peoples of the major powers knew only of conflicts waged in the remote Balkans or the colonial regions of the world by professional soldiers or backward peoples. Few people, including the professional military, seemed to perceive that the nature of warfare had seen any changes since 1850, changes resulting from the industrialization of Europe, advances in transportation and military technology, the massive mobilization of the manpower of Europe, and the enhanced ability of governments to utilize propaganda to martial the minds and energy of the masses to a cause.

The Industrial Revolution had seen a tremendous increase in the manufacturing capabilities of Europe. This increase was seen not only in consumer goods but in the weapons of war. A true arms race had engulfed the nations of the Continent in the second half of the 19th century as arms, munitions, ever-larger guns and ships rolled off the assembly line. These were readily available to any nation possessing the financial resources to acquire them and believing, rightly or wrongly, that it required them to defend their honor. Moreover, not only were arms in greater supply than ever before, they were of a greater destructive nature than any previously used by man.

Not only were the arms present in abundance, the same was true of the men to use them. Following the Franco-Prussian War many states, emulating the obviously efficient Prussian military system, adopted national military service: the consequence was that by 1914 these states had millions of men under arms or in reserve ready to take up arms.

Beyond the mere presence of millions of men prepared to take up arms, there had come into existence a mind-set which seemed to both justify and indeed glorify war. Drawing upon the doctrines of Social Darwinism, there were those who argued that the battlefield was the ultimate proving ground upon which the merit of men and of their culture was tested: the strong survived, the weak perished. Further, as the people of Europe became more literate and as newspapers—as a consequence of the technological advances such as the rotary press, the linotype, and cheap paper from wood pulp—sprang up in ever increasing numbers, governments were not slow in using them for propaganda purposes. Through the press it was possible to inculcate in the peoples' minds the idea that their nation's cause was always correct. Nationalism, assuming the role of a secular religion, dictated that one must be prepared to fight and, if necessary, die, for the Motherland.

It was with this fanaticism that Germans, Frenchmen, Austrians, Russians, and others, after several decades of international tension, joyously marched to war in August of 1914, determined to defeat the foe in a "short little conflict." The realities of modern warfare quickly became clear: above all was the fact that the defensive tactics and tools of war had negated the possibility of a rapid and successful offensive war. Even a momentary breakthrough of the enemies' lines was rapidly closed as reserve troops could be quickly moved up via railroads to close the breach. As the western front settled down to trench warfare, the machine gun, barbed wire, endless barrages of heavy artillery, and poison gas demonstrated that sheer courage or even manpower could not bring victory: it was a lesson that cost millions of lives. On the eastern front, the Russian fate demonstrated the inadequacy of numbers if a nation lacked the industrial base to support them. Nor were the civilians spared, for even if they were not in the line of march of the armies engaged in battle, they could be made to suffer through blockades of food supplies as the submarines roved the seas or zeppelins or bombers struck from above.

The result was that, rather than the "quick little war" all of the combatants had anticipated, Europe waged a horrible struggle for four years—years which cost ten million and more lives, both military and civilian, billions of dollars in property, and four empires. Victory, if it could be called that, came in the end not, as the result of military triumph on the battlefield, but through attrition.

4. Initially Portugal, and soon after, Spain, took the lead in overseas exploration in the 14th century, exploration which culminated in the discovery of both an all-water route to the Far East and the New World. Both states enjoyed several advantages arising from their geographical and political circumstances as well as scientific and technological advances achieved by them. To these factors must be added that of strong motivational forces which had their origins in economic and spiritual factors.

Clearly, their geographical location, particularly that of Portugal, provided easy access to the Atlantic and provided greater familiarity with its waters. Geography played a role in that both Iberian states, distant from Venice,which held a virtual monopoly on trade with the Near East, paid a heavy price for items of both a luxury nature and those essentials which were obtained from the Near East and regions further east. In addition to the economic motive, the peoples of Portugal and Spain were driven by an extremely strong one of an ideological nature, that of the spirit of the crusader. For centuries they had been involved in an ongoing crusade against the Moslems for control of their countries. It was only in 1492 that the Spanish, with the fall of the Moslem stronghold of Grenada, had reclaimed their land. This prolonged struggle had several consequences. On one hand it tended to weld the Christians of the two states into a more unified force under their respective monarchs. No less important, it instilled in them the mentality of the crusader: exploration and discovery was, for them, also a mission of faith, an opportunity to hunt down the Moslem—or any non-Christian they might encounter—and convert or destroy them.

Long before the voyages of Vasco da Gama of Portugal, or Spain's Columbus, penetration of the Atlantic had begun. In 1270 the Portuguese seaman Malocello reached the Canaries, while in 1290 the Genoese Dorio and Vivaldo set out to explore the west coast of Africa, a voyage from which they never returned. Knowledge of these earlier activities, together with spiritual, economic, and scientific motives, were clearly united in the person of Prince Henry the Navigator, the third son of King John I of Portugal. A crusader himself, early in the 15th century he established a base at Sagres in southern Portugal, a primitive research and development laboratory: for nearly forty years he dedicated himself to the dual mission of taking the conflict to the Moslems and, closely linked to that mission, exploration of the west coast of Africa. To facilitate this venture he assembled an array of experts in the area of marine science and technology: chart-makers, sea captains, shipbuilders, and instrument makers, men predominantly from Venice and Genoa, but also from Scandinavia—almost certainly drawing upon the knowledge of men of that region regarding the long existing colonies established by Norsemen in Iceland and Greenland and perhaps even the brief effort to establish a colony on the mainland of North America—and Germany, as well as Jewish scholars, Arabs from North Africa, and native tribesmen from West Africa. Under Prince Henry's leadership these men assembled a pool of knowledge regarding the waters about Africa, and began to construct superior navigation instruments and a better type of sea-going vessel, the caraval. Most important, Prince Henry regularly dispatched his sea captains to penetrate the waters of the Atlantic. In 1418 the Madeira Islands and in 1427 the Azores were discovered. His seamen also began to gradually make their way down the west coast of Africa: in 1433 Cape Bojador was reached and, in 1445, Cape Verde. These discoveries resulted in the establishment of a brisk trade with the region. Before his death in 1460 his seamen had sailed as far as the Senegal and Gambia rivers and discovered the Cape Verde Islands. Portuguese exploration continued after his death and, by 1488, Bartolomeu Dias reached the Cape of Good Hope at the southernmost tip of Africa. Nine years later Vasco da Gama sailed to Calicut on the Malabar Coast of India and, by 1513, Portuguese merchant seamen were penetrating the Spice Islands of the East Indies and had reached Canton in China. By this time, of course, the voyage of Columbus for Spain had revealed a "New World" to the West. There is some evidence, by no means conclusive, that seamen sailing for Portugal, sailed to Greenland and perhaps Newfoundland as early as the 1470s, and perhaps to Brazil by that time or even earlier.

The advantages of location and motive were not the only ones enjoyed by the peoples of the Iberian Peninsula. They were early unified states and, as such, able to throw more firmly the support of the government behind the effort to explore, as seen in the activities of Prince Henry, and Queen Isabella of Spain's support of Columbus. In sharp contrast, the other main regions of Western Europe were involved in either internal conflict or wars among themselves. The Hundred Years' War raged between France and England until 1453, after which France was occupied first, with rebuilding its strength, and then conflicts in Italy and internal religious strife throughout much of the 16th century. Meanwhile, England was first plunged into the War of the Roses and then had problems related to its own Reformation. Germany and Italy, lacking unity and frequently involved in wars and the interference of the more powerful states, were in no position to exploit the opportunities that had been revealed by the Portuguese and Spanish, while Holland, England and France could do so gradually. By that time Spain and Portugal had established vast overseas empires.

5. At the heart of Marx's concept of history was the theory of economic determinism: it was the economic structure of a given society and, more important, who controls the means of production that determined its religious, artistic, and political orientation: its superstructure—its intellectual, cultural, and political concepts—were designed to serve and protect the interests of those who controlled the all-important economic substructure. History, he contended, had passed through several phases which had seen society based primarily upon slave labor and then upon the labor of serfs. History, he argued, was the unveiling of "class struggle," the struggle between those who controlled the means of production and those whose labor they exploited. In his day, he held, in a number of states as well—at least in those which had become industrialized—that society's economic foundation was built upon industrial "wage slaves" who were increasingly controlled and exploited by the capitalist class.

In this industrial society, he maintained, it was inconceivable that governments would act on behalf of the working class, for governments were simply a derivative of the economic foundation and under the thumb of that segment of society which controlled that base—in this case the capitalist. Clearly, he held, for the capitalist class to permit governments to act in the interests of the workers, and thus against their own, was inconceivable. The condition of the wage slave, already wretched, would grow worse as the capitalist class, seeking to maintain and enhance their own profits in an increasingly competitive world, would steadily exploit the workers more and more. Further, the ranks of the middle class would be steadily thinned as, losing in the struggle to obtain a share of the ever-diminishing profits available, they were themselves driven down to the status of wage slaves. When the conditions of the working class became intolerable, they would rise in a great, violent revolution, overthrowing the capitalist class, and take into their own hands possession of the modes of production (i.e., the machines and tools of industry). At this point in time a one class society or, in Marx's terms, a classless society would come into existence and, as there was no longer a ruling class requiring coercion, the state would also cease to exist: mankind would enter a golden age characterized only by material abundance and the elimination of crime, greed, and war.

Marx's vision of the future appealed to many, worker and intellectual alike, and as it gained dedicated followers, terrified the middle and upper classes and the governments of most nations. Yet it became clear that the historical developments which Marx held to be inevitable were not occurring. Governments—or at least significant elements within them—did begin to intervene on the behalf of the working class. In England this was due to a number of different factors. The development of a two-party system, each party competing for votes, saw a gradual extension of the franchise to an ever larger percentage of the population. Beginning in 1832, fifteen years before publication of *The Communist Manifesto* and thirty-five years before *Das Kapital*, this trend was applied to the middle class and by the early 1900s virtually every adult male had the right to vote. No less important, the working class, forming political parties, gained an increasing voice in Parliament, thus allowing pressure for the enactment of pro-labor legislature. Long before this, however, numerous laws were passed which served to ease the admittedly wretched conditions of the working classes in the early stages of the Industrial Revolution. Whether these reforms stemmed from truly humanitarian motives, elements within the "ruling class," or from clashes of interest among that class—as between the landowners and industrialists—the state did intervene. In Germany, Bismarck, concerned over the perceived threat of socialism, created the first state socialism from above. While state intervention came slowly and often begrudgingly, it did come and, moreover, the condition of the working class in much of western Europe gradually improved while the ranks of the middle class, rather than thinning, expanded.

In the face of the seeming failure of Marx's predictions as to the fate of the industrial-capitalistic states, Marxists and others sought an explanation. The most ardently argued was that through the exploitation of colonial peoples—imperialism—capitalism gained exorbitant profits, some of which were allowed to sift down to the working class, easing their condition and temporarily, but only temporarily, delaying the inevitable workers' revolution. The merits of this argument are still debated by Marxists and non-Marxists alike. Perhaps the most obvious failure of Marx's prophecies was the fact that when the workers' revolution did occur, it was in a state with little industrial development and that the state, far from withering away, became stronger, indeed, totalitarian, with a clear ruling class—the Communist elite.

6. From the Scientific Revolution of the 16th and 17th centuries onward, European society had witnessed the steady expansion of man's knowledge of the physical world about him and, through the technological application of this knowledge, of his material world. While there had been those, such as the romantics of the early 19th century, who had questioned the true worth of reason as against the sentiments found in the heart and expressed alarm over the dehumanization of the individual, science and technology continued to advance even more rapidly and, in so doing altered the face of much of Western Europe and, at the same time, brought marked changes in the social structure and intellectual atmosphere of that region. These advances, bringing increasing creature comfort and economic betterment, an economic betterment that even encompassed increasing numbers of the working classes, seemed to reinforce the vision of the 18th century *philosophes* in the unending progress to be achieved through the application of reason and the tools of science.

As the 19th century drew to a close there were those who, if not questioning the achievements of science and technology in the past, or doubting that in the future they would continue to expand man's knowledge and benefit him and society materially, challenged what they saw as an extension of science into areas outside its proper sphere—areas related to human activities. Not unlike the romantics, they opposed what they saw as the virtual deification of science and reason and the deterministic, mechanistic concept of the universe—and man—the scientist seemed to be erecting. The impact of industrialization, urbanization, and capitalism were also seen as but a few of the elements of the age which were serving to subordinate the individual in the morass of the masses of industrial society, and to remove the human element from culture. The era of the *fin de si`ecle* saw those who sought to point out this peril and, in some cases, provide alternatives.

Friedrich Nietzche held that the masses possessed a "herd mentality," were ensnared by Christianity, (a "slave religion"), traditional morality, and bourgeois materialism, and were unable to break free of the decadent cultural malaise of mediocrity of the age. A basic cause of this decadence, he maintained, was the excessive development of the rational faculty at the expense of a creativity which he felt came only from the spontaneity of intuition or "will," a malady he traced back to Socrates and Plato. The hope for the future, he felt, rested in those superior individuals who, drawing upon an "inner will to power," an inner, primitive life force, could free himself of the bonds of slave morality and reason and release a fundamental, inner creativity.

A similar vision of an inner, non-rational, intuitive life force was to be seen in the *élan vital* of Henri Bergson, a vital impetus which he perceived as a non-mechanistic explanation for mankind's evolution in the past and the true hope for future progress. Samuel Butler, seeing science as having evolved into a virtual religion dominated by priest-like scientists, spoke of free will, spontaneity, and cunning—in a force having its origin not in man's consciousness or reason but in an inner spiritual subconscious level of man's mind, as the truly creative force advancing civilization.

This perception of man being driven by irrational, animal forces, having their roots in its subconscious being, appeared to receive scientific support in the work of Darwin, with his emphasis upon man's primitive, animal origins. Even more so, Sigmund Freud, in arguing that man's consciousness—rationality as traditionally understood—was hardly more than veneer concealing a subconscious world of repressed sexuality and neuroses of which he had little or no knowledge or control, reinforced the vision of man's fundamental irrationality.

Science itself was advancing theories which tended to disturb the stable, orderly Newtonian "world machine" which for nearly two centuries had constituted a basic cornerstone in man's vision of the universe. The work of Einstein, Planck, and Heisenberg served to alter, if not destroy, the perception of absolutes which man had come to believe existed on the basis of classical Newtonian physics: space, time, motion, and matter became less certain in the mind of man, as did science's ability to ever find absolute solutions in all spheres of knowledge.

The doubts raised regarding the true merit of reason as a beneficial guide for civilization and, indeed, whether man was in fact, truly rational, gave rise to new literary and artistic schools which sought to penetrate and reveal the subconscious, inner reality of the human spirit. It contributed, too, although it was not the sole source, to the new totalitarian political concepts, as seen in the Nazi utilization of their grossly distorted version of Nietzche's superman.

THE ADVANCED PLACEMENT EXAMINATION IN

European History

TEST 6

Test 6 is also on CD-ROM in our special interactive AP European History TEST*ware*®. It is highly recommended that you first take this exam on computer. You will then have the additional study features and benefits of enforced timed conditions, individual diagnostic analysis, and instant scoring. See page vi for guidance on how to get the most out of our AP European History book and software.

THE ADVANCED PLACEMENT EXAMINATION IN

European History

TEST 6

1. Ⓐ Ⓑ Ⓒ Ⓓ Ⓔ	26. Ⓐ Ⓑ Ⓒ Ⓓ Ⓔ	56. Ⓐ Ⓑ Ⓒ Ⓓ Ⓔ
2. Ⓐ Ⓑ Ⓒ Ⓓ Ⓔ	27. Ⓐ Ⓑ Ⓒ Ⓓ Ⓔ	57. Ⓐ Ⓑ Ⓒ Ⓓ Ⓔ
3. Ⓐ Ⓑ Ⓒ Ⓓ Ⓔ	28. Ⓐ Ⓑ Ⓒ Ⓓ Ⓔ	58. Ⓐ Ⓑ Ⓒ Ⓓ Ⓔ
4. Ⓐ Ⓑ Ⓒ Ⓓ Ⓔ	29. Ⓐ Ⓑ Ⓒ Ⓓ Ⓔ	59. Ⓐ Ⓑ Ⓒ Ⓓ Ⓔ
5. Ⓐ Ⓑ Ⓒ Ⓓ Ⓔ	30. Ⓐ Ⓑ Ⓒ Ⓓ Ⓔ	60. Ⓐ Ⓑ Ⓒ Ⓓ Ⓔ
6. Ⓐ Ⓑ Ⓒ Ⓓ Ⓔ	31. Ⓐ Ⓑ Ⓒ Ⓓ Ⓔ	61. Ⓐ Ⓑ Ⓒ Ⓓ Ⓔ
7. Ⓐ Ⓑ Ⓒ Ⓓ Ⓔ	32. Ⓐ Ⓑ Ⓒ Ⓓ Ⓔ	62. Ⓐ Ⓑ Ⓒ Ⓓ Ⓔ
8. Ⓐ Ⓑ Ⓒ Ⓓ Ⓔ	33. Ⓐ Ⓑ Ⓒ Ⓓ Ⓔ	63. Ⓐ Ⓑ Ⓒ Ⓓ Ⓔ
9. Ⓐ Ⓑ Ⓒ Ⓓ Ⓔ	34. Ⓐ Ⓑ Ⓒ Ⓓ Ⓔ	64. Ⓐ Ⓑ Ⓒ Ⓓ Ⓔ
10. Ⓐ Ⓑ Ⓒ Ⓓ Ⓔ	35. Ⓐ Ⓑ Ⓒ Ⓓ Ⓔ	65. Ⓐ Ⓑ Ⓒ Ⓓ Ⓔ
11. Ⓐ Ⓑ Ⓒ Ⓓ Ⓔ	36. Ⓐ Ⓑ Ⓒ Ⓓ Ⓔ	66. Ⓐ Ⓑ Ⓒ Ⓓ Ⓔ
12. Ⓐ Ⓑ Ⓒ Ⓓ Ⓔ	37. Ⓐ Ⓑ Ⓒ Ⓓ Ⓔ	67. Ⓐ Ⓑ Ⓒ Ⓓ Ⓔ
13. Ⓐ Ⓑ Ⓒ Ⓓ Ⓔ	38. Ⓐ Ⓑ Ⓒ Ⓓ Ⓔ	68. Ⓐ Ⓑ Ⓒ Ⓓ Ⓔ
14. Ⓐ Ⓑ Ⓒ Ⓓ Ⓔ	39. Ⓐ Ⓑ Ⓒ Ⓓ Ⓔ	69. Ⓐ Ⓑ Ⓒ Ⓓ Ⓔ
15. Ⓐ Ⓑ Ⓒ Ⓓ Ⓔ	40. Ⓐ Ⓑ Ⓒ Ⓓ Ⓔ	70. Ⓐ Ⓑ Ⓒ Ⓓ Ⓔ
16. Ⓐ Ⓑ Ⓒ Ⓓ Ⓔ	41. Ⓐ Ⓑ Ⓒ Ⓓ Ⓔ	71. Ⓐ Ⓑ Ⓒ Ⓓ Ⓔ
17. Ⓐ Ⓑ Ⓒ Ⓓ Ⓔ	42. Ⓐ Ⓑ Ⓒ Ⓓ Ⓔ	72. Ⓐ Ⓑ Ⓒ Ⓓ Ⓔ
18. Ⓐ Ⓑ Ⓒ Ⓓ Ⓔ	43. Ⓐ Ⓑ Ⓒ Ⓓ Ⓔ	73. Ⓐ Ⓑ Ⓒ Ⓓ Ⓔ
19. Ⓐ Ⓑ Ⓒ Ⓓ Ⓔ	44. Ⓐ Ⓑ Ⓒ Ⓓ Ⓔ	74. Ⓐ Ⓑ Ⓒ Ⓓ Ⓔ
20. Ⓐ Ⓑ Ⓒ Ⓓ Ⓔ	45. Ⓐ Ⓑ Ⓒ Ⓓ Ⓔ	75. Ⓐ Ⓑ Ⓒ Ⓓ Ⓔ
21. Ⓐ Ⓑ Ⓒ Ⓓ Ⓔ	46. Ⓐ Ⓑ Ⓒ Ⓓ Ⓔ	76. Ⓐ Ⓑ Ⓒ Ⓓ Ⓔ
22. Ⓐ Ⓑ Ⓒ Ⓓ Ⓔ	47. Ⓐ Ⓑ Ⓒ Ⓓ Ⓔ	77. Ⓐ Ⓑ Ⓒ Ⓓ Ⓔ
23. Ⓐ Ⓑ Ⓒ Ⓓ Ⓔ	48. Ⓐ Ⓑ Ⓒ Ⓓ Ⓔ	78. Ⓐ Ⓑ Ⓒ Ⓓ Ⓔ
24. Ⓐ Ⓑ Ⓒ Ⓓ Ⓔ	49. Ⓐ Ⓑ Ⓒ Ⓓ Ⓔ	79. Ⓐ Ⓑ Ⓒ Ⓓ Ⓔ
25. Ⓐ Ⓑ Ⓒ Ⓓ Ⓔ	50. Ⓐ Ⓑ Ⓒ Ⓓ Ⓔ	80. Ⓐ Ⓑ Ⓒ Ⓓ Ⓔ
	51. Ⓐ Ⓑ Ⓒ Ⓓ Ⓔ	
	52. Ⓐ Ⓑ Ⓒ Ⓓ Ⓔ	
	53. Ⓐ Ⓑ Ⓒ Ⓓ Ⓔ	
	54. Ⓐ Ⓑ Ⓒ Ⓓ Ⓔ	
	55. Ⓐ Ⓑ Ⓒ Ⓓ Ⓔ	

European History

TEST 6 – Section I

TIME: 55 Minutes
80 Questions

DIRECTIONS: Each of the questions or incomplete statements below is followed by five suggested answers or completions. Select the one that is best in each case.

1. The Northern Renaissance differed from the Renaissance in Italy in that

   (A) it lacked the strong financial foundation provided by the city-states of Italy.

   (B) while attaining triumphs in the architectural area, it did not demonstrate the artistic glory seen in the south.

   (C) it placed a greater emphasis upon religious piety.

   (D) it drew more heavily on the Byzantine tradition via contacts with the Russian Orthodox Church.

   (E) it reflected more strongly the influence of contacts with the civilizations of the New World.

2. "…It is, then, much safer to be feared than to be loved …for touching human nature, we may say in general that men are untruthful, unconstant, dissemblers, they avoid dangers and are covetous of gain. While you do them good, they are wholly yours… but when (danger) approaches, they revolt."

   Such was the lesson taught to rulers by

   (A) Lorenzo Valla.

   (B) Machiavelli.

   (C) Montaigne.

   (D) Hugo Grotius.

   (E) Johan Huizinga.

3. The monarch who, by invading Italy in the 1490s, upset the balance of power in that region was

   (A) Charles V Hapsburg.
   (B) Henry VII of England.
   (C) Charles VIII of France.
   (D) Ferdinand of Spain.
   (E) Suleiman the Magnificent.

4. As a consequence of the English War of the Roses

   (A) English territorial holdings in France were lost.
   (B) Anglicanism was proclaimed the state religion.
   (C) the Tudor dynasty came to the throne.
   (D) monasticism in England was abolished.
   (E) the kingdoms of England and Scotland were unified.

5. The specific abuse that Luther addressed in his "Ninety-Five Theses" was

   (A) simony.
   (B) the sale of indulgences.
   (C) clerical marriage.
   (D) lay investiture.
   (E) recognition of secular authority.

6. All of the following were factors in the success of Luther's religious movement EXCEPT

   (A) the printing press.
   (B) German nationalism.
   (C) his alliance with German princes.
   (D) widespread concern in Germany over the political intentions of the Hapsburg emperor.
   (E) his support of the new concepts of the universe resulting from the ideas of Copernicus and other scientists.

7. The basic idea of mercantilism was

(A) to acquire colonies.

(B) the promotion of social welfare through increased economic activity.

(C) to gain access to raw materials.

(D) the maintenance of a favorable balance of trade in order to increase the country's holdings in gold and silver.

(E) pursuit of a policy of *laissez faire* to maintain an equitable balance of trade.

8. Perhaps the most significant reason for the weakness of New France in comparison with the British holdings in North America was that

(A) the Indian tribes tended to be much more favorably inclined to the British.

(B) the population of England was much larger, permitting more settlers to migrate to its New World colonies.

(C) the French government maintained a highly restrictive immigration policy.

(D) French explorers failed to penetrate the interior and construct forts.

(E) the ardent missionary activities of French missionaries alienated the Indians.

9. Under the domestic system in England

(A) shipbuilding was made a state monopoly.

(B) spinning and weaving of yarn and cloth was done in the workers' homes.

(C) factory workers were prohibited from joining unions.

(D) farmers expanded the use of crop rotation and fertilization.

(E) the immigration of foreign workers was expanded to take advantage of the skills of French textile workers.

10. The *Asiento*, granted to the English in the Peace of Utrecht, gave them

(A) possession of Gibraltar.

(B) the exclusive right to sell African slaves in the Spanish colonies of the New World.

(C) permission to trade freely in the Spanish islands of the Caribbean.

(D) the French island of Guadaloupe.

(E) the territory of Florida.

11. The map of France above, showing the boundaries of the local governments together with that country's immediate neighbors, would have been familiar to which of the monarchs listed below?

(A) Louis XIV
(B) Louis Philippe
(C) Napoleon Bonaparte
(D) Louis Napoleon III
(E) Henry IV

12. Holding that man's life in a "state of nature" was "solitary, poor, nasty, brutish, and short, strong," absolutistic government (to bring order out of chaos) was advocated by

(A) Thomas Hobbes.
(B) John Milton.
(C) William Blackstone.
(D) Baron d'Holbach.
(E) Jacques Bossuet.

13. All of the following states were militarily involved in the Thirty Years' War EXCEPT

(A) Sweden.
(B) Austria.
(C) France.
(D) Denmark.
(E) England.

14. As a consequence of the Great Northern War, Peter the Great

(A) replaced his insane half-brother Feodor as czar of Russia.
(B) drove the Turks from the northern shores of the Black Sea.
(C) extended Russian holdings into central Siberia.
(D) gave Russia a "window to the West" on the Baltic Sea.
(E) destroyed the political influence of the *streltsy* and Old Believers religious sect.

15. One of the main failures of the Peace of Augsburg (1555) was

(A) it left Italy disunited and a prey of the great powers.
(B) it did not provide for recognition of the Calvinists.
(C) by recognizing the rights of the Anabaptist, it introduced a radical religious faction into Germany.
(D) it allowed France too many special privileges in Germany.
(E) the powers of the emperor were not clarified.

16. The theory of the separation of powers was most clearly enunciated in the works of

(A) Voltaire.
(B) Montesquieu.

(C) Jean Jacques Rousseau. (D) John Locke.

(E) Thomas Hobbes.

17. While "Puritanism" encompassed a number of religious groups, its core was based upon the doctrines of

(A) Martin Luther. (D) John Huss.

(B) Jacob Hutter. (E) Michael Servetus.

(C) Zwingli and Calvin.

18. The second enclosure movement, occurring in England in the 18th century, was designed to

(A) stimulate the growth of industrialization.

(B) strengthen the mining industry.

(C) replenish the forests of the country.

(D) increase and consolidate crop lands.

(E) expand lands available for sheep-raising.

19. The map below indicates that

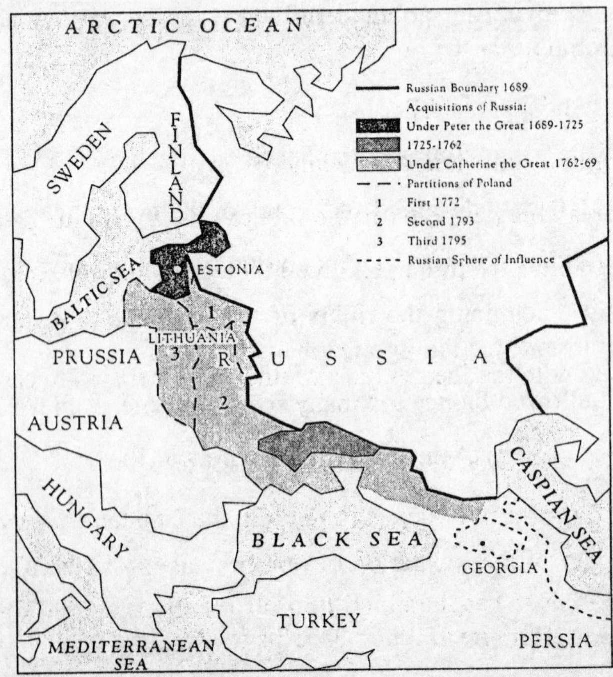

(A) prior to the reign of Peter the Great, Russia was completely shut off from access to the open seas.

(B) prior to 1800, the greatest acquisition of territory occurred during the reign of Catherine the Great.

(C) during the reign of Peter the Great, Russia gained access to the waters of the Mediterranean Sea.

(D) Peter the Great's expansion in the south was limited to the establishment of ports on the Black Sea.

(E) the partitions of Poland saw Russia gain the greatest share of the spoils.

20. A vocal element in the French Revolution, the *sans-culottes* were

(A) impoverished peasants.

(B) the urban and village priests.

(C) the urban working class.

(D) nobles forced to flee to the safety of the German states.

(E) opponents of the Civil Constitution of the Clergy.

21. Those members of the Estates General who took the famous Tennis Court Oath swore to

(A) overthrow Louis XVI.

(B) establish a republic.

(C) draft a constitution for France.

(D) break the ties between the French church and the papacy.

(E) establish the principle of complete religious toleration in France.

22. Obsessed with the idea of his sinfulness, Luther finally came to the conclusion that

(A) salvation was to be found in good works.

(B) it was by faith, and faith alone, that humans can be justified in the sight of God.

(C) as Christ had humbled himself on the cross, so man must humble himself in life to attain benefits in afterlife.

(D) the sacraments of Baptism and the Eucharist were instruments essential to obtaining God's grace.

(E) without absolute adherence to the guidance provided by the clergy, man had no hope of salvation.

23. Which of the following statements is FALSE? Scientific research conducted in the 17th and 18th centuries

(A) assumed an international scope as governments supported scientific inquiry, hoping new discoveries would have immediate and practical application.

(B) laid firm foundations in physics, chemistry and medicine as independent and rapidly expanding disciplines.

(C) was centered primarily in the major universities, which were richly endowed by merchants and entrepreneurs.

(D) was stimulated by the belief that the comprehension of and harnessing of the laws of nature would benefit mankind.

(E) received the encouragement of rulers who saw the practical value of discoveries to the mercantilistic policies of their states.

24. The Thirty Years' War was brought to an end by the

(A) Battle of White Mountain.
(D) Edict of Restitution.
(B) Treaty of Tilsit.
(E) Treaty of Westphalia.
(C) death of Gustavus Adolphus.

25. The battle waged between Generals Wolfe and Montcalm on the Plains of Abraham determined

(A) that the Stuart dynasty would never again rule England.

(B) the fate of France's North American empire.

(C) that Austria had lost control of Silesia to the Prussians.

(D) the ultimate victor in the War of the Spanish Succession.

(E) whether France or Great Britain would have paramount influence in India.

26. All of the following statements are in accord with the theories of the Deists EXCEPT

    (A) absolute standards of good and evil do not exist: good simply results in pleasure, evil in pain.

    (B) God does not respond to individual petitions to intervene with the laws of nature on their behalf.

    (C) God should be perceived as the prime mover, the source of the laws of nature which are comprehensible to the mind of man.

    (D) the concept of divine predestination is in opposition to the human dignity reason bestows upon the individual.

    (E) the individual possesses the freedom and rational ability to determine what is good and evil and to choose between them.

27. Ecumenicism, which has characterized the Catholic Church since the Second Vatican Council in 1963, is best described as

    (A) a call for dogmatic adherence to church teachings.

    (B) increasing evangelic activity.

    (C) tolerance among Christians.

    (D) constituting missionary work.

    (E) encouraging less church involvement in politics.

28. An important source of labor for the new factories of an industrialized England was the

    (A) consequence of the abolition of serfdom.

    (B) importation of slaves.

    (C) influx of new immigrants.

    (D) workers left unemployed as a result of the second enclosure movement.

    (E) indentured laborers.

29. The Portuguese gained control of Brazil as a colony as a consequence of

    (A) the need for it as a base on the route to India.

    (B) the Treaty of Tordesillas.

    (C) the fact that the Spanish mistakenly believed it to be of no value.

    (D) Spain ceding it to Portugal in return for the Philippine Islands.

    (E) the Treaty of Utrecht.

30. The English Navigation Acts were designed to

    (A) restrict the number of vessels constructed to prevent overbuilding.

    (B) establish regulations for safer travel.

    (C) ensure that vessels carried sufficient insurance to safeguard investors.

    (D) weaken Dutch trade and encourage that of England.

    (E) permit English ships to violate the monopolistic practices of the Spanish.

31. Which of the following statements about the mid-18th century is most accurate?

    (A) The British controlled the trade in all of India.

    (B) The Chinese had begun to realize the technological advantages enjoyed by the West.

    (C) The Moslems had begun to enjoy a political renaissance.

    (D) The English had begun to break into the monopoly that the Spanish had previously enjoyed in Japan.

    (E) West African rulers prevented European control of the slave trade in Africa.

32. Russian national development was thwarted for two centuries by

(A) disunity among the various branches of the Russian people.

(B) the subjection to the Ottoman Turks.

(C) the Golden Horde.

(D) the excessive influence of the Russian Orthodox Church.

(E) the domination of the Teutonic Knights.

33. The Royal Society of London is most logically associated with

(A) the Scientific Revolution.

(B) James II Stuart of England.

(C) efforts to bring the Christian faith to the natives of Africa.

(D) financing the establishment of colonial settlements in British North America.

(E) supporting commercial activities in the Far East.

34. "It appears then that wages are subject to a rise or fall from two causes: First, the supply and demand of labourers. Secondly, the price of the commodities on which the wages of labour are expanded...With a population pressing against the means of subsistence, the only remedies are either a reduction of people or a more rapid accumulation of capital."

These words are best associated with

(A) Jeremy Bentham.

(B) David Ricardo.

(C) Robert Owen.

(D) Robert Peel.

(E) David Hume.

35. The Levellers were

(A) anti-industrial woolen weavers deprived of their jobs by mechanization.

(B) radical religious revolutionaries of the 17th century who sought social and political reform.

(C) landowners in 19th century England opposed to the imposition of duties on imported grain.

(D) followers of Gracchus Babeuf.

(E) the armed supporters of Oliver Cromwell.

36. Historical research indicates that the long-term consequence of the Industrial Revolution for the working class was to

(A) reduce their standard of living by removing them from their agricultural roots.

(B) increase the length of their workday.

(C) reduce the financial contribution of women to the family income.

(D) increase their standard of living.

(E) leave their standard of living at about the same level, but deprive them of the advantages provided by rural life.

37. Catherine the Great

(A) introduced reforms easing the burden on the serfs.

(B) inaugurated the Slavophile movement.

(C) annexed the Maritime Provinces of Manchu China.

(D) extended Russia's territorial holdings at the expense of the Crimean Tatar.

(E) reduced the power of the nobility.

38. All of the following were causes of Gorbachev's reform of the Soviet Union EXCEPT

    (A) Environmental problems

    (B) Increasing health problems among Soviet citizens

    (C) Decline in industrial production

    (D) Increasing oil prices

    (E) Over-centralization of the economy

39. Edmund Burke

    (A) believed that revolutionary change would benefit all people.

    (B) strongly advocated the use of military force to crush the American Revolution.

    (C) proposed uprooting political institutions that were not as useful as they had been in the past.

    (D) advocated evolution rather than revolution.

    (E) in 1783 wrote his *Reflections* on the American Revolution.

40. The most dominant figure at the Congress of Vienna was

    (A) Talleyrand.

    (B) Metternich.

    (C) Viscount Castlereagh.

    (D) Czar Alexander II.

    (E) Baron von Stein.

41. The most serious error made by the statesmen assembled at the Congress of Vienna was

    (A) initiating a conflict with the Ottoman Turks.

    (B) restoring Louis XVIII to the throne of France.

    (C) ignoring the nationalistic and democratic sentiments alive in Europe.

(D) ceding Denmark to Norway.

(E) imposing the Carlsbad Decrees on Prussia.

42. Czar Alexander II undertook all of the following reforms EXCEPT

(A) emancipation of the serfs.

(B) establishment of a national Duma or Parliament.

(C) relaxation of press censorship.

(D) the creation of local *zemstovos* or provincial assemblies.

(E) expansion of educational opportunities.

43. A common element among the revolutionary movements that swept through Europe in 1848 was

(A) unity of purpose among middle-class liberals and urban workers.

(B) rejection of ethnic rivalry in the name of nationalistic aspirations.

(C) coordinated and timely action on the part of experienced leaders.

(D) initial success as a result of the hesitation of governmental leaders to use their superior forces.

(E) no fear of the intervention of external, foreign forces.

44. The reign of Napoleon III ended when he

(A) was forced to resign as a consequence of his Mexican fiasco.

(B) was driven from France in the wake of the violence of the Paris Commune of 1871.

(C) was assassinated in 1870.

(D) surrendered to Prussian troops at Sedan.

(E) allowed the British to gain control of the Suez Canal.

45. In 1902, in response to what it viewed as threats to its colonial interests, Great Britain entered into a defensive alliance with

(A) Italy.
(B) Russia.
(C) Japan.
(D) France.
(E) Germany.

46. All of the following statements about the outset of World War I are true EXCEPT

(A) the idea of conflict was enthusiastically received by the general public in all lands.

(B) few, including military men, anticipated the nature of the war that erupted.

(C) socialist politicians in every country opposed their governments' decision to enter the war.

(D) each side was convinced its cause was just.

(E) the Austrian effort was hampered by ethnic disunity.

47. The political cartoon illustrated below, appearing in a French newspaper of 1902, suggests

(A) Japan's military aggression in China was a threat to Western economic interests.

(B) China was a target of Russian imperialism.

(C) Japan was running a great risk challenging Russian power in the Far East.

(D) Russia was planning to invade Japan.

(E) an alliance between Japan and Russia would threaten French interests in China.

48. World War I saw the use of all the following weapons of war EXCEPT

(A) machine guns.
(B) flame throwers.
(C) poison gas.
(D) incendiary bombs.
(E) tanks.

49. A powerful pacificistic work, the horrendous nature of warfare in the First World War was depicted in a famous novel by

(A) Günter Grass.
(B) John Steinbeck.
(C) D.H. Lawrence.
(D) Arthur Koestler.
(E) Erich Maria Remarque.

50. Which of the following statements about totalitarianism is FALSE?

(A) It frequently had a cult leader as head of state.
(B) It demanded absolute commitment to its ideology.
(C) It had no connections with 19th century ideologies.
(D) Extreme nationalism was a primary element of its ideology.
(E) Its political structure was monolithic, one party alone being tolerated.

51. War "as an instrument of national policy" was renounced by those nations that signed the

(A) Locarno Treaties.
(B) Kellogg-Briand Pact.
(C) Versailles Peace Treaty.
(D) Lytton Commission Report.
(E) Treaty of Rapallo.

52. The Truman Doctrine was designed to

(A) assist in the economic reconstruction of post-World War II Japan.

(B) assist with military advisors and aid any country threatened by communism.

(C) prevent a conflict between Greece and Turkey as a consequence of their dispute over Cyprus.

(D) supply and maintain direct contact with Berlin during the blockade of that city by the Russians from June 1948 to May 1949.

(E) seek a peaceful solution to the conflict between India and Pakistan over Kashmir.

53. The Mau Mau were

(A) fanatical anti-Zionist followers of the Grand Mufti of Jerusalem.

(B) Basque separatists using terrorist tactics against the post-Franco government of Spain.

(C) a terrorist government fighting the British in Kenya.

(D) followers of the Congolese radical Patrice Lamumba.

(E) early opponents of the policy of apartheid in South Africa.

54. All of the following nations have had a woman as head of state since World War II EXCEPT

(A) India.

(B) England.

(C) France.

(D) Pakistan.

(E) Israel.

55. All of the following statements regarding Great Britain's economic status following World War I are true EXCEPT that

(A) many of her overseas investments had been liquidated.

(B) her industrial plant was growing antiquated.

(C) as a result of immigration, she experienced a labor shortage.

(D) there was a sharp rise in the cost of living.

(E) the United States, Canada, and Germany were strong industrial rivals.

56. The late former President François Mitterand of France was a member of what political party?

    (A) Conservative

    (B) Labor

    (C) Communist

    (D) Socialist

    (E) Christian Democratic

57. "Take up the White Man's burden
    Send forth the best you breed
    Go bind your sons to exile
    To serve your captives' need"

    Thus wrote the poet laureate of imperialism,

    (A) Cecil Rhodes.

    (B) Rudyard Kipling.

    (C) Leander Jameson.

    (D) W.B. Yeats.

    (E) Thomas Arnold.

58. The French fought bitterly against the Algerian rebels because

    (A) having lost their Indo-Chinese holdings, de Gaulle was determined they would not lose Algeria.

    (B) Algeria was a significant source of oil for France.

    (C) the French viewed Algeria as an integral part of France.

    (D) the French feared the existence of a communist state so close to their country.

    (E) there were no significant anti-imperialist feelings in France.

59. The mandate system established following World War I
    (A) was only applied to former German colonies.
    (B) served to weaken European imperialism since all mandates were promised their independence in ten years.
    (C) involved only France and Great Britain.
    (D) quickly was the source of unrest in the Near East.
    (E) was not accepted by the League of Nations.

60. In the years of its existence only one country was expelled from the League of Nations. This country was
    (A) Japan, as a consequence of its aggression against China.
    (B) Nazi Germany, in the wake of its attack on Austria.
    (C) the Soviet Union, following its invasion of Finland.
    (D) Italy, for its assault on Ethiopia.
    (E) the regime of Francisco Franco, as a result of his brutal crushing of the Spanish Republicans.

61. Europeans demonstrated a greater interest in Africa's interior after 1850 as a result of
    (A) the fact that it was no longer possible to obtain sufficient slaves in the coastal regions.
    (B) medical advances which made it easier for them to live there.
    (C) growing concern over the expanding influence of the Moslems in central Africa.
    (D) the opportunities for economic territorial gain in Asia were fading.
    (E) the successful independence movements in Latin America had closed off its markets to Europe.

62. ARTICLE III
It being obviously necessary and desirable, that British subjects should have some port whereat they may careen and refit their Ships, when required, and keep stores for that purpose, His Majesty the Emperor of China cedes to Her Majesty the Queen of Great Britain, etc., the Island of Hongkong, to be possessed in perpetuity by her Britannic Majesty...

The statement above is derived from the treaty ending the

(A) Boxer Rebellion.
(B) Sepoy Rebellion.
(C) Russo-Japanese War.
(D) First Opium War.
(E) Tai-ping Rebellion.

63. In the early 1930s Stalin altered the Soviet Union's foreign policy

(A) when he sought closer ties with Nazi Germany.
(B) by increasing the revolutionary activities of the Comintern worldwide.
(C) by drawing Russia into isolation.
(D) through seeking closer cooperation with the western democracies.
(E) by withdrawing from the League of Nations.

64. By the close of the 19th century virtually all of Africa had been cut up into colonial holdings by the great powers of Europe, there remaining few independent nations. Those few states which retained their independence are designated on the map on the following page by which marking?

(A) 1
(B) 2
(C) 3
(D) 4
(E) 5

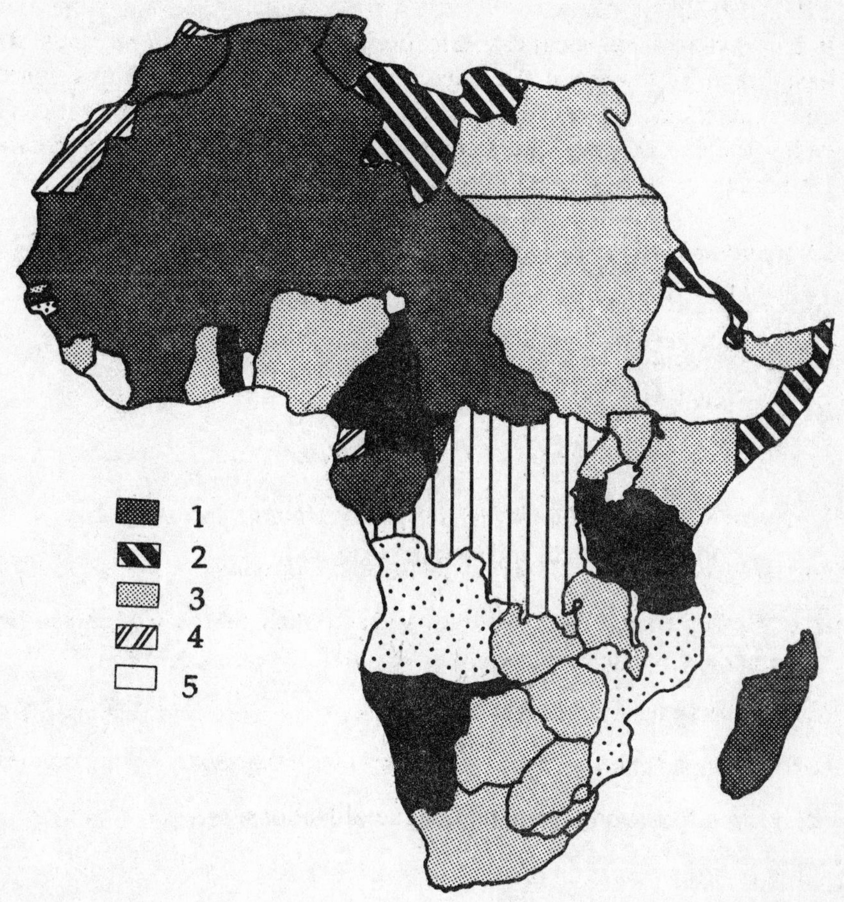

65. "I say to the House as I said to Ministers who have joined this government, 'I have nothing to offer but blood, toil, sweat, and tears.' We have before us an ordeal of the most grievous kind. We have before us many, many months of struggle and suffering."

So spoke

(A) Otto von Bismarck
(B) Georges Clemenceau
(C) Winston Churchill
(D) Sir Edward Grey
(E) Franklin D. Roosevelt

66. Wladyslaw Gomulka, Alexander Dubcek, and Marshal Tito all had in common the fact that they

(A) stood in opposition to de-Stalinization.

(B) abandoned socialism.

(C) saw their countries occupied by Soviet troops under the Brezhnev Doctrine.

(D) came into confrontation with the Soviet Union.

(E) supported Mao Tze-tung in his conflict with Stalin.

67. Since the end of the Second World War, separatist movements have led to violence in

(A) Northern Ireland, Spain, and Yugoslavia.

(B) Spain, Greece, and Holland.

(C) Northern Ireland, Holland, and Portugal.

(D) Greece, Yugoslavia, and Spain.

(E) Portugal, Greece, and Northern Ireland.

68. The name of Auschwitz will always stand as a reminder of the

(A) betrayal of the Czechs to Hitler by the French and British in 1939.

(B) "Final Solution."

(C) rapid defeat of French military forces by the Nazis in 1940.

(D) Nazi annexation of Austria in 1938.

(E) courageous, if futile, Warsaw uprising of 1945.

69. Economic aid from the United States for the reconstruction of Europe following World War II was announced in 1947 by

(A) Adlai Stevenson.

(B) George Kennen.

(C) George C. Marshall.

(D) Dwight D. Eisenhower.

(E) John Foster Dulles.

70. Which of the following is closely associated with the name of Lech Walesa?

(A) *Glasnost*

(B) The Red Brigade

(C) Solidarity

(D) Soviet dissidents

(E) The Hungarian Uprising of 1956

71. The Soviet desire to reduce the level of international tensions during the Khrushchev era stemmed from his

(A) conviction that Stalin had wholly misunderstood the intentions of the United States.

(B) desire to create in the West a false sense of security in preparation for the "final, inevitable triumph" of international communism.

(C) belief that the forces of Western capitalism were too strong to overcome.

(D) desire to move the Soviet Union away from the basic doctrines of Marxism-Leninism toward true "democratic socialism."

(E) need to strengthen his position within the Soviet Union and avert the disintegration of the Communist bloc in Eastern Europe.

72. The fact that the Nationalist Socialists were able to gain sufficient electoral support in the early 1930s to come to power was due, in part, to the anger generated by the Treaty of Versailles and the

(A) Communist efforts to seize power by force.

(B) triumph of Mussolini in Italy.

(C) achievements of Gustav Stresemann.

(D) inflation of the 1920s and depression of the early 1930s.

(E) ardent support they received from the much-revered President Hindenburg.

73. The Green Party in West Germany is closely associated with

(A) the interests of the country's influential agricultural bloc.

(B) the resurgence of Neo-Nazism.

(C) a strong environmentalist element in German society.

(D) the leading elements seeking the reunification of East and West Germany.

(E) a revived Pan-Germanic movement.

74. The Franco-Algerian conflict resulted in

(A) a confrontation between the United States and the Soviet Union.

(B) the intervention of NATO as a "peace keeping" force.

(C) France being compelled to withdraw her military from French Indo-China.

(D) the fall of the Fourth French Republic.

(E) reaffirmation of French political control over the region.

75. Which of the following books may be said to have been the most influential expression of post-World War II European pessimism?

(A) *Red and Black*

(B) *The Decline of the West*

(C) *Arms and the Man*

(D) *Foundations of the Nineteenth Century*

(E) *1984*

76. Factors which have contributed to the rapid rise in world population in recent decades include all of the following EXCEPT

(A) a reversal in the traditional balance between births and deaths.

(B) medical advances eliminating or reducing earlier great plagues.

(C) the absence of any truly effective contraceptives.

(D) opposition of Third World leaders to either sterilization or birth control devices on the basis of the view these are actually a subtle form of Western genocide.

(E) marked declines in infant mortality.

77. A significant feature in the capitalist global economy in recent decades has been

(A) the increasingly low rate of profits.

(B) the transfer of jobs from the Third World nations to the countries of the First World.

(C) the rise of multi-national corporations.

(D) an inability to produce sufficient consumer goods to meet the ever mounting demand.

(E) a resistance of the advanced nations to supply the much needed capital to those countries designated as "backward."

78. The most significant stimulus to colonial revolt against the West was

(A) the voluntary decision of the Dutch to abandon their holdings in the Indonesian area following World War II.

(B) Great Britain's abandonment of its colonial holdings in favor of the creation of the Commonwealth of Nations in the 1930s.

(C) the military defeat of Western powers by a non-Western country in World War II.

(D) the decision of the French to abandon her colonies in 1945.

(E) the example of Hitler standing up to Great Britain and France.

79. The Baltic states have demanded independence from the Soviet Union on the basis that

(A) they were illegally annexed by Stalin in 1939.

(B) the Russians had not withdrawn their troops from those countries at the end of World War II as they had pledged to at the Yalta Conference.

(C) they have no historical link with Russia.

(D) they are ethnically distinct from the Slavic Russians.

(E) they wish reunification with the now unified Germany.

80. The theory of history advanced by Marx appealed to many of the working class largely because

(A) the *Communist Manifesto* held out the vision of the unity of the working class worldwide.

(B) it placed heavy emphasis upon the bonds of nationalistic sentiment so close to the hearts of the working class.

(C) it held out the vision of a near-utopian society for the proletariat in the wake of the inevitable revolutionary process.

(D) it provided the vision of a revolutionary-minded leadership in the form of the communist cadre.

(E) its vision of the alliance of the working and middle class gave promise of ultimate triumph over the capitalist class.

European History

TEST 6 – Section II

TIME: Reading Period – 15 minutes
Writing Time for all three essays – 115 minutes

DIRECTIONS: Read over both the Document-Based Essay question in Part A and the choices in Part B during the Reading Period, and use the time to organize answers. All students must answer Part A (the Document-Based Essay Question); and choose TWO questions from Part B to answer.

PART A – DOCUMENT-BASED ESSAY

This question is designed to test your ability to work with historical documents. As you analyze each document, take into account the source and the point of view of the author. Write an essay on the following topic that integrates historical facts and developments not mentioned in the documents.

The last four centuries, centuries which saw the evolution of the national State in its modern form, have produced almost endless debates as to the rights and obligations of the individual citizen in relation to the State and the nature of the State itself. On the basis of the concepts advanced in the documents present here, discuss the diverse and changing views related to the citizen and the State which they reveal.

Document 1

The Great Leviathan or State, Frontispiece to *Leviathan* by Thomas Hobbes, 1651

Document 2

"The state of monarchy is the supremest thing upon earth; for kings are not only God's lieutenants upon earth, and sit upon God's throne, but even by God Himself they are called gods...they may make and unmake their subjects, they have power of raising and casting down, of life and of death, judges over all their subjects and in all causes and yet accountable to none but God only."

—James I of England, Speech before Parliament, 1609

Document 3

"Princes are gods and participate somehow in divine independence...There is only God who may judge over their judgements and their persons...The prince may correct himself when he knows that he has done evil, but against his authority there is no remedy other than his own authority...The prince as prince is not regarded as an individual; he is a public personage...Let God withdraw His hand, and the world will fall into nothing; let authority cease in the realm, and all will be in confusion."

—Jacques-Bénigne Bossuet, circa 1660

Document 4

"The only way to erect such a common power, as may be able to defend them [the people] from the invasion of foreigners, and the injuries of one another, and thereby to secure them in such sort, as that by their own industry, and by the fruits of the earth, they may nourish themselves and live contentedly; is to confer all their power and strength upon one man, or upon one assembly of men...there can happen no breach of covenant on the part of the sovereign; and consequently none of his subjects, by any pretence of forfeiture, can be freed from his subjection..."

—Excerpt from *Leviathan* by Thomas Hobbes, 1651

Document 5

"A man, as has been proved, cannot subject himself to the arbitrary power of another; and having, in the state of Nature, no arbitrary power over the life, liberty, or possession of another, but only so much as the law of Nature gave him for the preservation of himself and the rest of mankind, this is all he doth, or can give up to the commonwealth, and by it to the legislative power, so that the legislative can have no more than this. Their power in the utmost bounds of it is limited to the public good of society. It is a power that hath no other end but preservation, and therefore can never have a right to destroy, enslave, or designedly to impoverish the subjects..."

—John Locke, *Two Treatises on Civil Government*, 1690

Document 6

"Government cannot be good, if it does not have sole power...There cannot be two powers in one state...It is a great fortune for the prince and for the state when there are many philosophers to impress their teachings on the minds of men...The philosophers have no special interest, and are able to speak only in favor of reason and the public interest...The happiest thing that can happen to men, is for the prince to be a philosopher...He furthers the development of reason."

—Voltaire, "The Voice of the Sage and of the People," 1750

Document 7

"[The prince] ought often to recollect he himself is but a man, like the least of his subjects. He is only the first servant of the state, who is obliged to act with probity and prudence; and to remain as totally disinterested as if were each moment liable to render an account of his administrations to his fellow citizens."

—Frederick II, King of Prussia, "Duties of a Prince," 1781

Document 8

"To the end, therefore, that the social compact should not prove an empty form, it tacitly includes this engagement, which only can enforce the rest, *viz.* that whosoever refuses to pay obedience to the general will, shall be liable to it by the force of the whole body...It is agreed that what an individual alienates of his power, his possession, or his liberty, by the social compact, is only such parts of them whose use is of importance to the community; but it must be confessed also, that the sovereign is the only proper judge of this importance."

—J. J. Rousseau, *Social Contract*, 1762

Document 9

"[The liberties of Englishmen constitute an] entailed inheritance derived to us from our forefathers, and to be transmitted to our posterity as an estate specially belonging to people of this kingdom...A partnership in all art, a partnership in every virtue, and in all perfection. As the ends of such a partnership cannot be obtained in many generations, it becomes a partnership not only between those who are living, but between those who are living and those who are to be born."

—Edmund Burke, *Reflections on the Revolution in France*, 1790

Document 10

"Love your country. Your country is the land where your parents sleep, where is spoken that language in which the chosen of your heart blushing whispered the first word of love; it is the home that God has given you, that by striving to perfect yourselves therein, you may prepare to ascend to Him. It is your name, your glory, your sign among the people. Give it your thoughts, your counsels, your blood. Raise it up, great and beautiful as it was foretold by our great men."

—Giuseppe Mazzini, circa 1840

Document 11

"The citizen body is sovereign in the sense that no individual, no faction, no association can arrogate to itself a sovereignty not delegated to it by the people. But, there is a part of human life which necessarily remains individual and independent, and has the right to stand outside all social control. Where the independent life of the individual begins, the jurisdiction of the sovereignty ends. Rousseau failed to see this elementary truth, and the result of his error is that the *control social*, so often invoked in favor of liberty, is the most formidable ally of all despotisms."

—D. Constant, *Cours de politique constitutionnelle*, 1839

Document 12

"The sole end for which mankind is warranted, individually or collectively, in interfering with the liberty of action of any of their numbers, is self-protection...the only purpose for which power can be rightfully exercised over any member of a civilized community, against his will, is to prevent harm to others. His own good, either physical or moral, is not sufficient warrant. He cannot rightfully be compelled to do or forebear because it will be better for him to do so, because it will make him happier, because, in the opinion of others, to do so would be wise, or even true...No society in which these liberties are not, on the whole, respected, is free. The only freedom which deserves the name, is that of pursuing our own good in our own way, so long as we do not attempt to deprive others of theirs, or impeding their efforts to obtain it."

—John Stuart Mill, *On Liberty*

Document 13

"The State is in the first instance power, that it may maintain itself; it is not the totality of the people itself, as Hegel assumed in his deification of the State—the people is not altogether amalgamated with it; but the State protects and embraces the life of the people, regulating it externally in all directions. On principle it does not ask how the people is disposed; it demands obedience: its laws must be kept, whether willingly or unwillingly...When the State can no longer carry out what it wills, it perishes in anarchy...History wears thoroughly masculine features; it is not for sentimental natures or for women. Only brave nations have a secure existence, a future, a development; weak and cowardly nations go to the wall, and rightly so."

—Heinrich von Treitschke, *Lectures on Politics*, circa 1880

Document 14

"It is that in all places people of the same race, the same language, the same religion, and the same customs regard each other as brothers and work for independence and self-government, and organize a more perfect government to work for the public welfare and to oppose the infringement of other races."

—Liang Ch'i-ch'ao, "The Renovation of the People," 1902

Document 15

"What is the significance of this revolution? Its significance is, in the first place, that we shall have a soviet government, without the participation of bourgeoisie of any kind. The oppressed masses will of themselves form a government. The old state machinery will be smashed into bits and in its place will be created a new machinery of government by the soviet organizations. From now on there is a new page in the history of Russia, and the present, third Russian revolution shall in its final result lead to the victory of Socialism."

—V.I. Lenin, Petrograd, November 1917

Document 16

"The State is only a means towards an end. Its highest aim is the care and maintenance of those primeval racial elements which create the beauty and dignity of a higher civilization...The dead mechanism [of the old State] must be replaced by a living organism based on the herd instinct, which appears when all are of one blood...One must never forget it: the majority can never replace the leader. It [the majority] is not only stupid but cowardly. You cannot get the wise man out of a hundred fools, and a heroic decision cannot come out of a hundred cowards."

—Adolf Hitler, *Mein Kampf*, 1924

PART B – ESSAY QUESTIONS

1. "The Crimean War, 1852–1856, was one of the silliest wars ever fought; yet its consequences were extraordinarily important for Russia and for Europe as a whole..."
—William H. McNeill, *A History of the World Community*

   Discuss, briefly, the origins of this "silly war" and, having done so, indicate the "extraordinarily important" consequences of it on Russia and Europe.

2. The Reformation inaugurated by Martin Luther was primarily a religious protest. At the same time it unleashed or soon gave rise to a number of other diverse protests and calls for change in areas which, while related to social, political, and economic issues rather than spiritual matters, were advanced by religious groups. Discuss, giving specific examples of the various protests or calls for change.

3. Historians frequently speak of the "Old Imperialism," that of the period between roughly 1500 and 1750, and the "New Imperialism" of the late 19th and early 20th centuries. Compare and contrast these, indicating differences and similarities that may have existed and the reasons for changes which might have occurred.

4. The Scientific Revolution of the 16th and 17th centuries was more than simply an advance in man's understanding of the physical world. It marked the inauguration of revolutions in man's perception of and relations with that world, with society, and with his fellow man: it was, in essence, a social, cultural, intellectual, and political revolution. Discuss.

5. A question which has long intrigued historians is that of the "hero"—the "great man" in history. Is history shaped by the "strong man," the dynamic individual, or are such individuals simply a product of their times—the consequence of the political, social, cultural, etc., conditions of the age? With this question in mind, assess the rise of Adolf Hitler to dominance in Germany. Was his ascent to power inevitable, or simply a consequence of the times?

6. The Agricultural and Industrial Revolutions of the 18th and early 19th centuries dramatically altered the economic base of English society. They also brought marked changes in its social and political structure and its demographic face. Discuss, giving specific examples of the changes wrought.

THE ADVANCED PLACEMENT EXAMINATION IN

European History

TEST 6 – ANSWERS

1.	**(C)**	21.	**(C)**	41.	**(C)**	61.	**(B)**
2.	**(B)**	22.	**(B)**	42.	**(B)**	62.	**(D)**
3.	**(C)**	23.	**(C)**	43.	**(D)**	63.	**(D)**
4.	**(C)**	24.	**(E)**	44.	**(D)**	64.	**(E)**
5.	**(B)**	25.	**(B)**	45.	**(C)**	65.	**(C)**
6.	**(E)**	26.	**(A)**	46.	**(C)**	66.	**(D)**
7.	**(D)**	27.	**(C)**	47.	**(C)**	67.	**(A)**
8.	**(C)**	28.	**(D)**	48.	**(D)**	68.	**(B)**
9.	**(B)**	29.	**(B)**	49.	**(E)**	69.	**(C)**
10.	**(B)**	30.	**(D)**	50.	**(C)**	70.	**(C)**
11.	**(C)**	31.	**(E)**	51.	**(B)**	71.	**(E)**
12.	**(A)**	32.	**(C)**	52.	**(B)**	72.	**(D)**
13.	**(E)**	33.	**(A)**	53.	**(C)**	73.	**(C)**
14.	**(D)**	34.	**(B)**	54.	**(C)**	74.	**(D)**
15.	**(B)**	35.	**(B)**	55.	**(C)**	75.	**(B)**
16.	**(B)**	36.	**(D)**	56.	**(D)**	76.	**(C)**
17.	**(C)**	37.	**(D)**	57.	**(B)**	77.	**(C)**
18.	**(D)**	38.	**(D)**	58.	**(C)**	78.	**(C)**
19.	**(B)**	39.	**(D)**	59.	**(D)**	79.	**(A)**
20.	**(C)**	40.	**(B)**	60.	**(C)**	80.	**(C)**

Detailed Explanations of Answers

TEST 6

1. **(C)** The piety of the Northern Renaissance was reflected in the writings of the Christian humanists such as Erasmus and Thomas à Kempis and the religious art of Dürer. Like the Southern or Italian Renaissance, the Renaissance in the north had a strong financial basis (A), that of the wealth of the commercial enterprises of southern Germany, the Flemish region, and the Hansa cities. Both its architectural (B) and artistic achievements were significant. There was little Byzantine influence (D), nor was there any indication of New World influences (E).

2. **(B)** Author of, among other works, *The Prince*, a realistic, albeit cynical look at the manner in which the ruler should govern his Renaissance state, Lorenzo Valla (A) was a humanist scholar of the Italian Renaissance who demonstrated that the "Donation of Constantine" was a forgery; Montaigne was a significant French humanist and philosopher of the late 16th century (C); while Grotius (D) was a Dutch legal theorist who wrote on international law, particularly as it related to warfare. Huizinga (E) was a modern historian of the early modern period.

3. **(C)** In 1494, at the invitation of the duke of Milan, Charles invaded Italy, initiating a conflict with the Hapsburgs which was to last 65 years. Charles V Hapsburg (A) did not come to the imperial throne until 1519, while Henry VII of England (B) was occupied with domestic problems. Suleiman (E) was not involved in Italy while Ferdinand (D), having dynastic interests in Italy, initially opposed the French invasion.

4. **(C)** The Tudor dynasty was established in the person of Henry VII. England lost its holdings in France (A) at the end of the Hundred Years' War in 1453, while Anglicanism (B) was proclaimed the religion of England during the reign of Henry VIII and the monastic establishments were abolished (D) during the same reign. England and Scotland were unified (E) only in the first decade of the 18th century.

5. **(B)** The activities of the Dominican Tetzel and his unbridled commercialism in the sale of indulgences prompted Luther to act. The other issues noted, while at various times severe problems within the church, were not of immediate concern to Luther when he posted the "Ninety-Five Theses."

6. **(E)** Copernicuss views were only published *after* Luther's death. All of the other factors mentioned were significant in contributing to the ultimate success of the religious protest inaugurated by Luther in the German area.

7. **(D)** Mercantilism might be envisioned as economic warfare in which one nation sought to gain an advantage over another through the acquisition of wealth in terms of precious metal. Items (A), (B), and (C), while facets of mercantilism, were secondary and contributory to the main goal of the acquisition of wealth. *Laissez faire* economics (E) were diametrically in opposition to the fundamental principles of mercantilism.

8. **(C)** France applied very rigid religious and political restrictions on those permitted to migrate to the New World. The Indians, in contact with the French and British, overwhelmingly supported the French (A). France's population was larger than that of England (B). The French explorers and merchants penetrated the interior to a much greater extent than the English (D) and their missionaries were generally more successful in their relations with the Indians (E).

9. **(B)** Raw wool was distributed to the workers, frequently peasants, who spun and wove it in their own homes. The domestic system was not related to ship construction (A) which was not under any circumstances a state monopoly. The true factory had not yet appeared in the textile industry, though when it did unions (C) were long prohibited. It was not related to agricultural practices (D) and had little or no relation to the admission of foreign workers (E).

10. **(B)** The Royal African Company of Great Britain received the right to provide slaves for a period of thirty years. Gibraltar was ceded to England in the Treaty of Utrecht (A). Spain did not grant Britain a free hand to trade in her Caribbean holdings (C), nor were Guadaloupe (D) or Florida (E) involved in the Treaty of Utrecht.

11. **(C)** As the map demonstrates that France has been divided into over eighty "departments," it could not represent France prior to the Revolution, since that division was one of the achievements of the National Assembly. Nor could it represent France after 1806, for the Holy Roman Empire, which came to an end in that year, is shown as still existing.

12. **(A)** The phrase is from Hobbes' major work, *The Leviathan*. John Milton (B), an English poet and Cromwell's secretary, was the author of *Paradise Lost*; Blackstone was a leading English legalist (C); d'Holbach was a French

philosophe (D); and Bossuet was an advisor of King Louis XIV and an ardent defender of the theory of divine right monarchy (E).

13. **(E)** Sweden, France, Austria, and Denmark were all involved militarily in the conflict. England, involved in the struggle between the Stuarts and Puritans, remained aloof.

14. **(D)** Defeating Sweden in the conflict, Peter gained control of extensive areas of the southern shores of the Baltic Sea and built the city of St. Petersburg. Peter's half-brother (A) was Alexis. Although he sought to gain access to the Black Sea, Peter failed to defeat the Turks (B), an achievement later of Catherine the Great. The push across the vastness of Siberia (C) had been carried out earlier, while the defeat of the *streltsy* (palace guards) and Old Believers (E) was unrelated to the Great Northern War.

15. **(B)** The Peace of Augsburg related only to those of the Catholic and Lutheran faiths. The Peace of Augsburg did not touch upon either Italy (A) or France (D), while no mention was made of the Anabaptists (C), a sect persecuted by all major religions. The powers of the emperor *were* clearly defined (E).

16. **(B)** In his *Spirit of the Laws* he divided the functions of government into the executive, judicial, and legislative bodies. The other men all wrote on the subject of government, their views ranging from favoritism of absolutistic government (Hobbes) to democracy (Rousseau), but none focused specifically on the issue of separation of power as did Montesquieu.

17. **(C)** Calvin's religious beliefs, giving rise to such sects as the Calvinists, Puritans, and Presbyterians, drew upon the foundation in Geneva laid by Zwingli. Luther (A) rejected a number of the doctrines of "Puritanism," particularly that of predestination. Hutter (B) was an Anabaptist, while Huss (D) and Servetus (E) were pre-Reformation religious reformers.

18. **(D)** By forcing smaller peasants from the land, hitherto open fields were consolidated into larger, more efficiently operated farms. Indirectly, through the creation of a large labor pool, the enclosure movement contributed to industrialization (A) and as a result of that, the increased need for coal, iron, and other metals (B), but this was not the primary objective, nor was reforestation (C). The *first* enclosure movement of an earlier period was designed to benefit the raising of sheep (E).

19. **(B)** Catherine's military victories at the expense of the Crimean Tatars, together with the extensive territories gained at the expense of the Poles in three partitions of their country, achieved a significant expansion of her country's holdings. Russian access to ports on the Mediterranean remained markedly limited by Turkish control of the Dardanelles well into the 20th century (C). Prior to

Peter the Great, direct assess to open waters in European Russia was limited to Archangel on the White Sea (Arctic Ocean). While Peter the Great attempted to expand toward the Black Sea, he was unsuccessful (D). On the basis of the information provided on the map, it is impossible to determine the extent of Russia's share of the partition.

20. **(C)** *Sans-culottes*–without the breeches"–associated with the clothing of the upper classes and aristocracy. Opponents of the Civil Constitution of the Clergy (E), which included many peasants (A) and priests (B), were simply viewed as counter-revolutionaries, while those nobles who fled the violence of the revolution for safety in the German region (D) were designated as emigres.

21. **(C)** Proclaiming themselves a national assembly, they swore not to disband until they had established a constitution for the country. The other objectives noted only came as the revolution gained momentum.

22. **(B)** For Luther, ultimate salvation rested in the individual's faith in the promise of salvation given by Christ. Good works (A) were of secondary importance to Luther, while Baptism and the Eucharist (D), perceived of as being of importance, were also secondary to faith, as was humility (C). Luther placed emphasis upon the guidance of the Bible, not that of the clergy (E), which could conceivably err.

23. **(C)** The universities, tending to be dominated by the church, did not provide the proper atmosphere for scientific research. All of the other statements regarding the role of and attitude toward scientific investigation are valid.

24. **(E)** Negotiated over a period of five years, the treaty was finally signed on October 24, 1648. The Treaty of Tilsit (B), involving France, Prussia, and Russia, was signed during the Napoleonic Wars. Gustavus (C) was killed during the course of the Thirty Years' War, but it continued on for several years. The Battle of White Mountain (A) occurred at the outset of the conflict. The Edict of Restitution (D), relating to the restoration of ecclesiastical estates, was signed in 1629.

25. **(B)** Fought on the outskirts of Quebec, Canada, in 1759, the battle led to the annexation of virtually all French holdings in North America by the British in the Treaty of Paris in 1763. The defeat of the Stuarts in the Battle of Culloden, April 16, 1746, basically ended their efforts to reclaim the English throne (A). In the course of the Seven Years' War, Austria did, in fact, lose Silesia to Prussia, but in a struggle distinct from that between Britain and France (C). The War of the Spanish Succession (D) occurred a half century earlier. The struggle for India (E), waged between Clive and Dupleix, was decided at the Battle of Plassey.

26. **(A)** The Deists, if having reservations about the doctrines of the estab-

lished religions, did believe that there existed basic standards of what was right and wrong. Perceiving God as the prime creator and mover (C), they believed that, having established the natural laws by which man should act (D), did not intervene in his everyday life (B). Man, possessing reason, should learn to live in conformity (E) with those natural laws.

27. **(C)** Ecumenicism, one of several important reforms of the Roman Catholic Church of the Second Vatican Council, is a call for toleration among Catholics as well as cooperation among Christian denominations. While choices (B), increasing evangelic activity, and (D), missionary work, might seem plausible, there is no direct link with ecumenicism. Preaching dogma (A) runs counter to this idea, and choice (E), less church involvement in politics, again unconnected to ecumenicism, is a statement that's also belied by the Roman Catholic Church's outspoken opposition to nuclear weaponry, among other issues.

28. **(D)** The second enclosure movement, seeking the consolidation of small farm holdings for efficiency, saw many peasants driven from the land, thus creating a significant labor pool. Serfdom (A) had basically disappeared from England many decades earlier. Slavery (B) was disappearing as an institution from England, while neither immigration (C) nor indentured labor (E) represented a significant source of labor.

29. **(B)** The Treaty, enacted by Pope Alexander VI in 1494, divided the world between the Spanish and Portuguese. At the request of the Portuguese the original line drawn down the Atlantic Ocean was moved westward, thus including a section of Brazil. Since this occurred prior to the official discovery of Brazil, it has been theorized that the Portuguese already knew of its existence. It was not on the Portuguese route to the East (A). The Spanish were not aware of its existence when the Portuguese claimed it (C) and (D). The Treaty of Utrecht (E) ended the War of the Spanish Succession several centuries later.

30. **(D)** The Navigation Acts were fundamentally laws designed to strengthen England's economy and foreign trade. They were initially designed to weaken that of Holland, in the mid-17th century the most powerful mercantile state in Europe. While designed to enhance England's trade, they did not legalize infringing upon Spain's monopolistic trade system—infringement which, in fact, had long been undertaken by English merchants.

31. **(E)** While Europeans, particularly England, were in a dominant position in the transportation of slaves to the New World and elsewhere, within Africa itself, native rulers, together with Moslem slave traders, held control. While having obtained a paramount position in India by the mid-18th century, she did not control all of India (A), many regions remaining under the rule of local princes. The Chinese (B) were very slow in perceiving technological advantages enjoyed by the West, becoming aware of them only well into the 19th century. Japan had isolated herself from virtually all Western trade from the early 17th century (D),

while the Moslem world (C) was in political decline.

32. **(C)** The Mongols, conquering much of Russia in the mid-13th century, dominated much of that land as the Golden Horde well into the 14th century when, at the Battle of Kulikovo in 1380, Dmitri Donskoi turned the tide against the Tatars. The Ottoman Turks (B) long remained a threat and obstacle to Russian expansion, but in the southern regions. The Russian Orthodox religion (D) served as a strong unifying force among the Russians (A). The Teutonic Knights (E) were defeated by Alexander Nevski in 1242.

33. **(A)** Founded during the reign of Charles II Stuart (B), the Royal Society was dedicated to scientific investigation. The Royal Society was not involved directly in religious (C), colonial (D), or economic activities (E).

34. **(B)** The words are derived from Ricardo's writings on the so-called "Iron Law of Wages." Jeremy Bentham (A) was the founder of the Utilitarian school of social philosophy; Robert Peel was an important English politician and reformer of the early 19th century (D); David Hume was an English *philosophe* of the 18th century (E), while Robert Owen was an English utopian socialist (C).

35. **(B)** Among other reforms they sought were the vote for virtually every male adult and parliamentary elections every year. The Luddites, opposing mechanization which they saw as threatening their livelihood, sought to destroy machines (A). English landowners (C) generally approved of duties to protect their agricultural interests. Babeuf (D), a proto-Communist of revolutionary France, had a handful of followers known as the Society of Equals. The Levellers were opponents of Cromwell (E).

36. **(D)** While it was a gradual improvement, studies have shown that an improvement in the conditions of the working class in European industrial societies did take place. The standard of living in agrarian society, it has been shown, was not necessarily superior to that of the industrial worker (A). While hours were perhaps increased initially, laws gradually cut the hours of labor (B). Women's financial contribution (C) tended to increase as their numbers in the labor force mounted.

37. **(D)** Through her military activities, Catherine added extensively to Russian territory in the Crimean and Black Sea areas. While imposing ever greater restrictions on the serfs (A), she enhanced the privileges of the nobles (E). The Slavophile movement (B), like the expansion of Russia to Vladivostok (C), was a later development in Russian history.

38. **(D)** By the 1980s, the political, economic, and enviromental climate of the Sovet Union was precarious. Oil prices actually remained fairly stable during the period leading up to Gorbachev's reforms. The totalitarian regimes that preceded Gorbachev (A) had allowed environmental problems to proliferate, one consequence of which was increasing health problems for Soviet citizens (B). Declin-

ing industrial production made it difficult for the Soviet Union to compete with the West in developing arms and providing its citizens with a level of industrial output to which Western Europeans and Americans had become accustomed (C). This was due in part to an over-centralized economy (E) that provided no incentives for factory managers and industrial entities to become more efficient.

39. **(D)** In his *Reflections on the Revolution in France* he spoke out for evolutionary, not revolutionary, change. Opposed to the radical changes taking place in France (A), he saw the American Revolution (E) as the result of a natural, evolutionary process and held that the colonials should be allowed to go free without a struggle (B). Institutions (C) such as the French monarchy, if not attuned to the times, should be reformed, not simply destroyed.

40. **(B)** Metternich of Austria was to be the dominant statesman of continental Europe for 33 years, the so-called "Coachman of Europe." The other statesmen noted, while present at Vienna, played roles secondary to that of Metternich, in whose shadow they stood.

41. **(C)** Much of the 19th century was to see revolutionary violence stemming from nationalistic and liberal aspirations thwarted by the decisions made at Vienna. The decisions reached at Vienna did not touch upon the Ottomans (A). Louis (B), overall, did not prove a bad king. Norway was ceded to Sweden at Vienna (D), while the Carlsbad Decrees (E) were passed several years after the Congress of Vienna (1819).

42. **(B)** The Duma was established in Russia only in 1905 by Czar Nicholas II. All of the other reforms noted were part of the program of Alexander II.

43. **(D)** The Austrians in Italy and their own country were slow to react to the revolutionary violence in its initial stages, as were the Prussian and French rulers. Class conflict (A), ethnic rivalries (B), and lack of strong unity among the revolutionary elements (C) tended to characterize the revolutionary movements. Fear of external intervention (E), as occurred in Hungary, where Russian troops intervened, was not uncommon.

44. **(D)** In the defeat of his country in the course of the Franco-Prussian War, he surrendered with a large part of the French army at Sedan and, abdicating, fled the country. He survived the failure of his imperialist policy in Mexico (A) and fled the country prior to the outbreak of the Paris Commune (B). The British gained control of the Suez Canal (E) in 1882, after Napoleon III's fall.

45. **(C)** The Anglo-Japanese Alliance of 1902 was, from the British point of view, designed primarily to protect India against a perceived Russian threat. England's alliance with Russia (B) and France (D) came in response to the Dual Alliance (Germany (E) and Austria), while she formed an alliance with Italy (A) only in the course of World War I (1915).

46. **(C)** Socialists, except for the most radical, generally strongly supported the national interests of their own countries during the conflict. All of the other statements are true.

47. **(C)** The cartoon depicts the kimono-clad Japanese as walking a tight-wire (or in this case a wobbly bamboo pole) clearly arousing the ire of the Russian bear. There are no indications in the cartoon of the nature of the risk Japan was running or of any outside power being involved in the affair.

48. **(D)** Incendiary bombs were introduced in the course of World War II. All of the other weapons were utilized in World War I.

49. **(E)** *All Quiet on the Western Front* is recognized as one of the great anti-war novels of the 20th century. Steinbeck (B), Koestler (D), and Grass (A), novelists of the Depression and World War II eras, did not treat the first World War with the intensity of Remarque, although Grass did deal with World War II. Lawrence (D) dealt more with human relations and sexuality.

50. **(C)** The ultra-nationalistic, elitist, and racial theories, to name a few elements of the fascist movement, all had strong roots in diverse 19th century ideologies. The cult leader (A) (i.e., Der Fuehrer, Il Duce, etc.), the monolithic party (E) ultra-nationalism (D), and the demand for absolute loyalty (B), were all elements of the fascist movement.

51. **(B)** An international accord of the Locarno Era, it was signed by a score of nations in 1928 with the overly optimistic idea of "outlawing warfare." The Locarno Treaties (A) were a series of international accords signed in 1925, including a guarantee of Germany's western borders and a mutual defense accord between France, Poland, and Czechoslovakia. The Treaty of Versailles (C) ended World War I between Germany and the Allies. There were two Treaties of Rapallo (E), one in 1920 between Italy and Yugoslavia which made Fiume a free state and ceded Zara to Italy, the second in 1922 between Germany and the Soviet Union cancelling the former's reparation payments. The Lytton Commission Report (D) dealt with Japanese aggression in Manchuria in 1931.

52. **(B)** The Truman Doctrine was introduced primarily as a result of the perceived threat of communist supported insurgents seeking to overthrow the established Greek government. It had nothing to do with the economic rebuilding of Japan (A), the conflict over the Kashmir region (E) or the subsequent conflict between Turks and Greeks on the island of Cyprus (C). The supplying of Berlin (D) was essentially a matter of food, not a military crisis.

53. **(C)** The Mau Mau—terrorists to some, freedom fighters to others—fought to end English control of Kenya. The Grand Mufti (A), having widespread support among the Arabs, was the founder of the Moslem Brotherhood. The other movements referred to were, and in some cases continue to be, internal struggles for greater freedom or complete independence.

54. **(C)** France has not had in the modern era a woman who served either as premiere or president, the two principal executive offices. All of the other nations have at one time or another had a woman as their chief executive officer: India—Nehru; England—Thatcher; Pakistan—Buto; Israel—Meir.

55. **(C)** With the discharge of tens of thousands of soldiers and the general industrial slump that occurred in the years following the end of the war, Great Britain's problem was one of severe unemployment, not a labor shortage. All of the other statements regarding Great Britain's economic situation are true.

56. **(D)** Mitterand, who died in 1996, was a Socialist. France's Conservative Party is headed by Jacques Chirac (A). While France has a Communist Party, it has not been very significant in French politics since the end of the 1980s (C). Labor (B) and Christian Democratic (E) are party names associated with other countries.

57. **(B)** The excerpt is from the poem "The White Man's Burden" by Kipling, one of the great apostles of English imperialism. Cecil Rhodes (A) was a South African gold and diamond magnate, statesman, and a great practitioner of imperialism, while Jameson (C) was his agent in his efforts to gain control of the Transvaal from the Boers. Yeats (D) was a British poet, Arnold (E) a literary critic.

58. **(C)** Algeria, long the home of many thousands of French from metropolitan France, was recognized as a department of metropolitan France, hence viewed as an integral part of that nation.

59. **(D)** The Arabs, formerly under Ottoman domination, felt they had been deprived of the independence promised them when they were placed under mandates. Also, the struggle between Zionist and Arab claims in Palestine quickly erupted. Ottoman lands (A) as well as German were taken. The term of the mandate holdings varied (B). Japan, South Africa, and the United States also received mandates (C). The mandates were technically under the supervision of the League (E).

60. **(C)** The Soviet Union was the only nation to be expelled from the League, this for her "Winter War" with Finland. Germany, Japan, and Italy walked out of the League, while Franco did not represent the legal Spanish government.

61. **(B)** Long viewed as a graveyard of Europeans, medical advances—particularly the introduction of quinine—reduced the peril of disease greatly. By the mid-19th century the demand for slaves was diminishing greatly as Britain waged a struggle for the abolition of slavery (A). Islam (C), as a religion, had long been present in parts of central Africa, but did represent a particular incentive to European imperialism. Both Asia (D) and Latin America (E) continued to provide ample opportunities for European economic and territorial imperialism.

62. **(D)** The excerpt is from the Treaty of Nanking (1842) ending the First Opium War and seeing the island of Hong Kong ceded to England. The Tai-ping Rebellion (E) was an internal rebellion in China in the mid-19th century, while the Sepoy Rebellion (B) occurred in India at approximately the same time. The Russo-Japanese War (C) and the Boxer Rebellion (A) took place in the first decade of the 20th century and neither directly involves Great Britain or touched upon control of Hong Kong.

63. **(D)** Frightened by the rise of an aggressive Japan and Germany, Stalin sought closer relations with anti-fascist (A) governments in the West. Stalin's actions represented an attempt to break with the isolation of Russia (C) which had previously existed. To win favor with the West, the Comintern was dissolved (B). Formerly not a member of the League of Nations, the Soviet Union was admitted to that organization in 1934 (E).

64. **(E)** Liberia and Abyssinia were the only independent nations in Africa in 1900. 1, British; 2, Italian; 3, Belgian; 4, Spanish.

65. **(C)** The excerpt is from a speech made by Winston Churchill in the days immediately following the evacuation of British military forces from Dunkirk. Otto von Bismarck (A), the "Iron Chancellor," was the chancellor of Prussia in the second half of the 19th century, Clemenceau was the premiere of France during the First World War (B), Sir Edward Grey was England's foreign minister during that conflict (D), while Roosevelt was the president of the United States (E) from 1934 to 1945.

66. **(D)** Gomulka (Poland) Dubcek (Czechoslovakia), and Tito (Yugoslavia) all came into confrontation with the Soviet Union. None were great supporters of Stalinism (A), though none rejected socialism (B). Yugoslavia, unlike the other two countries, never experienced occupation by Soviet troops (C) nor were they supporters of Mao of China (E).

67. **(A)** Northern Ireland has been the scene of a blood struggle on the part of those Irish Catholics who wish unification with the Republic of Ireland, while the Basques in Spain and Croats of Yugoslavia have also carried on terrorists activities directed at separatism. Greece, Portugal, and Holland have experienced no such movements.

68. **(B)** Auschwitz was one of the most notorious of the Nazi death camps where the murder of tens of thousands of Jews and others was carried out by the Nazis. The Munich Conference is associated with the sell-out of Czechoslovakia (A); the *Anschluss* was the annexation of Austria (D). No specific, one-word terms are associated with either the French (C) or Polish (E) defeats.

69. **(C)** Marshall, Secretary of State in 1947, enunciated the so-called

Marshall Plan. Stevenson (A), governor of Illinois, was a presidential candidate on the Democratic slate in 1952; he was defeated by Eisenhower. Kennen (B) was an important official with the State Department; Eisenhower (D) was supreme commander of the Western Allied forces in the invasion of Europe in World War II and twice president of the United States, and Dulles (E) was Secretary of State under Eisenhower.

70. **(C)** Walesa founded and went on to lead the Solidarity movement in Poland and was later elected his nation's president. *Glasnost* (A) is the term applied to the reform movement led by Gorbachev in the Soviet Union; the Red Brigade (B) is a radical leftist terrorist group active in Western Europe. Imre Nagy (E) is associated with the failed efforts of the Hungarians to pursue a course of domestic policy independent of the Soviet Union in 1956, while no one individual stands out as the leader of the Soviet dissidents (D).

71. **(E)** Strains were already beginning to show on the domestic scene of the Soviet Union, particularly in the area of consumer goods, as they were in terms of the Soviet's relations with her satellite states. Khrushchev, although he initiated the de-Stalinization campaign, had no doubts, at least openly expressed, regarding the superiority of the Soviet system or the certainty of the Marxist-Leninist theory of history.

72. **(D)** Germany was severely hit by the Depression and many of the middle and upper class, fearing Communism, turned to Hitler seemingly as the only alternative. The Communists, like Hitler, sought power through the ballot box (A). Mussolini's rise to power (B), occurring a decade earlier, had little or no effect on the situation in Germany. Stresemann (C), who had pulled Germany to her feet after the disastrous depression of 1923, had actually set back Hitler's political aspirations. President Hindenburg (E) loathed Hitler.

73. **(C)** The Green Party has led a strong environmentalist drive in West Germany, holding that the extensive, and unchecked, industrialization of the country was destroying the atmosphere and landscape. Neither Neo-Nazi (B) nor Pan-Germanic (E), the Green Party's attitude toward German reunification (D) or agricultural (A) policies do not represent its primary goals.

74. **(D)** Amid tremendous agitation generated by those who either favored maintaining a firm hold on Algeria or those who opposed doing so, the Fourth French Republic fell and Charles de Gaulle came to power. Neither the Soviet Union, the United States (A) nor NATO (B) became involved in the conflict; and France, which had already withdrawn from Indo-China (C) when the Algerian struggle erupted, was in the end forced to recognize the independence of that region.

75. **(B)** The author of the work, Oswald Spengler, was convinced that Western

civilization had reached its zenith and was entering a stage of rapid decline. G.B. Shaw's *Arms and Man* (C), Stendahl's *Red and Black* (A), and H.S. Chamberlain's *Foundations of the Nineteenth Century* (D, were all written prior to the First World War. Orwell's *1984* (E) deals with a futuristic totalitarian state.

76. **(C)** Numerous contraceptive devices have been developed in the years since the end of World War II and have been available to a significant portion of the world's population. All of the other factors mentioned have contributed significantly to the ballooning global population.

77. **(C)** The world of high finance and commercial and industrial activity has tended to become dominated by the great international corporations. None of the other statements regarding post-World War II are valid.

78. **(C)** The victories won by the Japanese in the early days of World War II, bringing as they did the humiliation of colonial peoples' former Western masters together with the establishment of puppet—but native—governments, was an extremely significant factor in the rise of anti-colonialism. The Dutch fought ardently to prevent Indonesian independence (A) in the early days of the struggle, while the creation of the Commonwealth of Nations came more as a response to anti-colonialism than a cause for it (B). The French (D) were very hesitant to give up their colonies, as seen in Indo-China, and the struggle between Hitler and the Allies (E) was simply seen by Asian and Africans as a case of Europeans killing Europeans for world domination.

79. **(A)** The Baltic peoples long maintained—and the Soviets under Gorbachev have conceded—that they were illegally annexed in 1939 by Stalin. The Soviets did not withdraw their troops (B), but they had given no such promise to do so at Yalta. The Baltic peoples, at least the Estonians and Latvians, were under Russian domination from the time of Peter the Great to 1919 (C), when they gained their independence in the wake of the Russian Revolution. They are ethnically different, although each of the Baltic states has a sizeable number of ethnic Russians living in them (D). They have no desire to be under German control (E).

80. **(C)** "Come the Revolution," Marx held out the vision of the rise of a classless "workers' paradise." While the idea of the unity of the workers of the world (A) was a facet of Marx's doctrines, it was seen as merely a step in the desired end of a workers' paradise. Marx opposed nationalism (B), which he thought weakened the true goals of the ultimate revolution. He did not speak of an elite leadership (D) (this was Lenin's idea) and he did not perceive of an alliance (E) between the working and middle classes, seeing them as actually enemies.

Sample Answer to Document-Based Question

The major states of Western Europe had, in the course of the 16th century, begun to assume a more modern form. As competition among the nations both intensified and increasingly became of a global nature, the need for both internal unity and strength against potential foreign foes increased. Yet, emerging from the medieval period, there remained in the states numerous domestic forces that hampered the development of truly centralized administrations, strong administrations which were essential if the state was to survive and thrive. Feudal aristocracies jealous of the privileged position, a peasant class whose concept of political loyalty frequently did not extend beyond the local village or, at best, their own province, and deep divisions along religious lines were but a few of these divisive elements.

Lacking anything but the vaguest perception of the modern idea of nationalism, it was the princes who became—and deliberately made of themselves—the focal point of the state, the symbol about which the people of the state were expected to rally and to whom they were to give their unswerving obedience. This was the age of the absolute monarch and the divine right monarch. Documents 1 through 4 present both visual and written portraits of, and justification for, such rulers. As is seen in the illustration from Hobbes's *Leviathan*, the monarch is conceived of as embodying in his person all of his subjects. James I Stuart of England, one of the most ardent exponents of "divine-right" rule, saw the monarchs' unchallengeable status as being derived from God: princes were indeed, in his eyes, no less than gods on earth. Whether he actually believed this or, fearing that a state lacking a supreme, unquestioned sovereign power would fall into a state of confusion as held by Bishop Bossuet, simply sought to wrap his rule in a cloak of divinity is difficult to determine. Certainly King Louis XIV of France, tutored by Bossuet, was convinced that an aura of the divine shrouded his reign. James's vision of his status did not, in fact, go unchallenged, for in England, unlike France, there existed a strong middle-class element and a parliamentarian tradition to stand in opposition, one so strong that it eventually brought his son Charles I to the execution block. It was as a consequence of the Puritan Revolution that Hobbes, horrified by what he perceived as anarchy, argued for the need to vest absolute power in the hands of one man or body of men: his argument was based not on any concept of the ruler possessing a mandate from God but, rather, the belief that the only alternative was the confusion Bossuet had prophesied.

Locke (Document 5), like Hobbes, admitted man, if completely unchecked by authority, could be a threat to the welfare of others. But while recognizing the need for authority, unlike Hobbes he did not believe that men, in forming a covenant with a sovereign power, surrendered completely all their rights and freedoms, rights which, in the course of the "Glorious Revolution" of 1688, an event in which Locke was intimately involved, the English embodied in their Bill of Rights. That revolution established the fact that England's monarch, far from being a divine or absolute ruler, was a constitutional monarch and that ultimate power rested in the hands of parliament and the representatives of the people—or in 1688 at least that small segment of the people who actually had a political voice.

While Louis XIV, the "Sun King," who had proclaimed "I am the State," had been extremely successful in surrounding himself with the trappings of majesty, by the time of his death in 1715 the "Age of Absolutism" had given way to the "Age of Reason." Reflecting the achievements of the men of the Scientific Revolution, emphasis was placed on reason as seen in Voltaire's (Document 6) call for a prince who "furthers the development of reason"—an "Enlightened Despot" who sought to rule according to "reason" and the "laws of nature." Such a monarch was Frederick II (Document 7) who, denying any divinity, claimed only to be the "first servant of the state." It was still absolutism, but in a new dress.

By the mid-18th century a new concept of the state was emerging in the more developed nations of Europe—that the state was not the prince, but the totality of the individuals who composed it. This is seen in Rousseau's *Social Contract*, where his "General Will" is conceived of as being, in essence, the consensus view as to what was in the best interests of the whole community: sovereignty is found in the people, not the prince or assembly.

The French Revolution and Napoleonic era served to reinforce this concept of the State being, in fact, the people. Indeed, it went further: the "State" or Nation came to possess an existence of its own—it was seen as a living organism that was more than the total of all its parts (i.e., its citizens). The conservative Burke (Document 9) saw the English "Nation" as a legacy of that land's long history, one the living had to nurture and pass on to future generations.This concept was greatly amplified in the course of the 19th century as various peoples of Europe struggled to free themselves of foreign masters or to extend their liberties against reactionary regimes. In the mind of Mazzini (Document 10), the Romantic Italian, his country became his "mother" and "father," a parent to whom he owed everything and for whom he was prepared to sacrifice everything. Increasingly the concept of the State as an entity having a life of its own came to be associated with a common language, a common heritage, a common race. Such a vision of the State was transmitted beyond Europe, as seen in the words of Liang Ch'i-ch'ao, subsequently a founder of the Communist Party of China.

The second half of the 19th century saw other ideological concepts which influenced the vision of the State and the citizens relations to it. Social Darwinism, placing emphasis on the idea of "survival of the fittest," gave rise to the idea of the State in constant competition—warfare declared or undeclared—with its rivals. For Treitschke (Document 13), a Prussian historian, the State is seemingly perceived of as an army, its citizens little more than soldiers in the ranks who must obey. This vision of the ever-aggessive state, combined with an emphasis upon the unity—and superiority—of a particular race (*Volk*), and yet another ideological spin-off of Social Darwinism, elitism, combined to produce a concept of the State which plagued the first half of the 20th century, the Fascist, or Totalitarian, regime. This concept was succinctly stated in Hitler's *Mein Kampf* (Document 16), where the deification of the State as a "living organism," the exaltation of the "leader" as the personification of that State, and the ultimate contempt for the individual citizen, stupid and cowardly, is clearly set forth. Absolutism had returned in a terrifying form.

There were, of course, other views of the nature of the state and of its relations to the individual. Both Constant (Document 11) and, even more so, Mill (Document 12) argued that the authority of the State is limited and that the individual always retains certain rights which cannot be alienated: the State exists for the protection of the citizen, but it cannot infringe upon his liberties as long as those do not threaten others.

Lenin (Document 15) represented a different concept of the State, one also having its roots in 19th century ideology, that of Marxism. In theory what was envisioned was a classless State or, indeed, *no state*, for a State existed only as a tool of class oppression and, in a classless society would not be necessary. What emerged from the Russian Revolution was, of course, quite different than the theory—a totalitarian State in which an elite, the Communist Party member and a cult leader, Stalin, dominated a subservient citizenry—totalitarianism in a different guise.

Sample Answers to Essay Questions

1. The conflict, sparked by a relatively absurd conflict between Russia and France over the protection of Christian holy sites in Jerusalem, had its real roots in the "Eastern Question." Great Britain and France, having commercial, military, and political interests in the eastern Mediterranean and Near East, were opposed to any Russian encroachment upon the Turkish Straits or Turkish territory in that region. When a war broke out between Russia and Turkey, both Great Britain and France, fearing Russian intentions, quickly came to the Turks' support. The conflict itself, characterized by military ineptitude on all sides—ineptitude personified by the gallant but senseless "charge of the Light Brigade"—and the humanitarian activities of Florence Nightingale, ended in the defeat of Russia.

For Russia, defeat brought more than defeat on the battlefield. It brought clearly to the fore the backwardness of the Russian economic, social, and political structure. In the aftermath of the war the new Czar, Alexander II, inaugurated a series of reforms, including the emancipation of the serfs, introduction of *zemstvos* or provincial parliaments, and the extension and liberalization of the educational system. While these reforms did not go far enough, particularly in regard to the emancipation of the serfs, and were subsequently further hamstrung by Alexander's successors and conservative elements in Russian society, they were reflective of the severe domestic problems confronting Russia, problems that grew in subsequent decades. On the international scene, defeat in the war had served to block Russia's territorial ambitions in the Near East and Balkans temporarily: as a consequence, these were directed towards the Far East, where in the 1860s they annexed the Maritime Provinces, regions claimed by Manchu China, and southward towards Afghanistan. This expansion in the Asian area gave rise to increasing tensions with Great Britain and, eventually, the emerging Japan.

The Austro-Hungarian Empire, while not directly involved in the war, pursued a policy that was to have marked repercussions for it and, indeed, for all of Europe. In 1849, in accordance with the principles of the "Concert of Europe," Russia had come to the military assistance of Austria when it was confronted with a Hungarian uprising. When the Crimean War erupted, Russia looked to Austria for assistance, if only of a diplomatic nature, only to find her pursuing a policy of "neutrality." When, a decade later, Austria found itself faced with the threat presented by Otto von Bismarck's efforts to unify Germany under the leadership of Prussia, Russia, angered at Austria's "ingratitude" offered no help to her former ally: the "Concert of Europe" had been broken. Bismarck, on the other hand, while pursuing a policy of "friendly neutrality," secretly assisted Russia, thus reinforcing cordial relations to be utilized when the moment arrived.

The circumstances surrounding the Crimean War presented Austria with still another danger. Piedmont-Sardinia's Prime Minister Cavour, while having no real interest in the conflict, brought his country into the war on the side of Great Britain and France. Envisioning the unification of Italy, he realized that this would mean a war with Austria, a war his country could not win without the support of a powerful ally. France, whose ruler was Napoleon III, a man already sympathetic to the idea of Italian unification, was the logical choice. Permitted to plead his cause at the peace conference held in Paris, he was able to win Napoleon's promise of military support in Piedmont's inevitable war with Austria. Austria, isolated, fell victim to the unification ambitions of both Bismarck and Cavour and, with the eventual unification of Germany and Italy, the map—and history—of Europe were dramatically changed.

Britain, while a victor in the war, came away with a bitter taste, convinced of the wisdom of returning to a policy of "splendid isolation," seeking to avoid involvement in the affairs of the Continent. Time was to suggest this policy was a serious error, coming as it did on the eve of the unification of Germany and Italy and the beginning of the formation of a series of alliances which were to contribute significantly to the outbreak of World War I.

The Crimean War, albeit a "silly war" fought on the periphery of the Continent, clearly had major consequences which extended far beyond the battlefield or the specific terms ending it, consequences which were to markedly alter the subsequent course of European history.

2. Decades before Luther posted his Ninety-Five Theses, religious unrest had been smouldering throughout Europe, unrest occasionally erupting in revolt as seen in the movements of Wycliffe in England and John Hus in Bohemia. In these spiritual movements, nationalistic sentiments were also involved. This was particularly evident in England, where Wycliffe began to translate the Bible into English and called for the King of England, not the Pope, to be recognized head of the English church. Clearly Wycliffe's ideas, aside from doctrinal convictions,

reflected a nationalistic spirit arising from England's involvement in the Hundred Years' War and a conviction that the Avignon papacy was a mere tool of the French. Wycliffe's movement also revealed another protest, this of a social nature. The Lollards, his followers, came largely from the lower class. Hungering for land, unhappy with the failings of the church and jealous of its wealth, suffering from the impact of the Black Death and the war, their anger was directed as much against the feudal and manorial system, the great landowners, and a regime which imposed hated dues and taxes upon them and sought to keep them in a socially subservient position as it was against doctrinal concepts. The Peasants' Revolt of 1381, numbering among its leaders the Lollard priest John Bull, was an overt display of this social unrest.

These and other protests and calls for change emerged even more clearly following Luther's revolt. He early translated the Bible into German, a national language. In his *Address to the Christian Nobility of the German Nation*—a nation that in fact did not exist—he made a frankly patriotic appeal to his countrymen to reject the authority of the papacy and argued that, as the church could not reform itself, the secular authorities must do so. Depending heavily upon the German princes for support, he early established the close relationship that would long exist between the Lutheran Church and the state. Nor was this alliance of state and church limited to Lutheran regions. In England, Henry VIII's "Reformation," motivated on his part more by "reasons of state" than those of a religious nature, created a national religion, Anglicanism, adherence to which was demanded as a sign of loyalty to king and state. This trend to national religions was not limited to Protestant states, for French monarchs worked to create a "Gallican Church," Catholic but controlled by the throne rather than the papacy. The unity of Christendom was giving way to national religions. Neither the Germans nor the Czechs, however, were to benefit from this trend.

Luther emphasized the Bible as the ultimate source of truth. Many took his words to heart: the problems such pursuits of truth presented quickly became evident, for the Scriptures and the picture they painted of the primitive Christian community lent themselves to diverse and at times revolutionary social, economic, and political interpretations. As early as the 1520s, peasants of southwestern Germany, suffering under the pressure of customary rents and services imposed upon them by their lords in a decaying feudal and manorial system, argued that they could find no Scriptural justification for their burdens. Many revolted in 1524, seeking to throw off the hated obligations. While they found some support from religious leaders such as Zwingli, Luther was now in close alliance with the princes of Protestant Germany, and turned violently on them.

The "Anabaptists," a term of derision applied to sects holding a broad spectrum of beliefs but having in common the practice of adult baptism, were seen by more conservative Protestants and Catholics alike as a danger to the social order. Communal ownership of property, including wives, the imminent return of Christ, anarchism, and withdrawal from the affairs of the secular state were among the ideas certain sects adhered to. In 1525 in Münster, Thomas

Munzer, once an associate of Luther, established a communistic theocratic society, only to be crushed before the end of the year. More radical were the Melchorites who, under the leadership of John of Leiden, gained control over the ordinary workers and craft guilds in Münster and established their "heavenly Jerusalem." Burning all books except the Bible, abolishing private property, introducing polygamy, they lived in an atmosphere of abandon and chaos—although probably not as much as their critics maintained—awaiting the coming of the Messiah. The Protestants and Catholics allied to crush them brutally. The more moderate Anabaptists, viewing themselves as a Christian community which, while recognizing the authority of the state, sought to live as an entity apart from the state, were long cruelly persecuted by Lutherans, Calvinists, and Catholics. Interestingly, the Anabaptists were among the earliest to advocate yet another "revolutionary" idea—religious toleration.

The revolutionary calls for changes in the social, economic, and political spheres on the part of the religious groups did not end with the close of the 16th century, nor were they confined to the German area. Seventeenth century England saw such movements as the Levellers,who called for the vote for all adult males and the yearly parliamentary elections, Fifth Monarchy Men, and the communist Diggers.

3. While the term "imperialism" dates only from the 1880s, the objectives it implied are as old as history, to be seen when the first state sought to politically, economically, or culturally dominate another. The appearance of the term, however, indicated that the earlier goals, and the motives behind them, had been formulated into a more cohesive concept.

The "Old Imperialism" saw Europeans explore many corners of the globe and, where possible, colonize extensively. As with the subsequent "New Imperialism," the forces which led the Europeans to do so were varied. Much emphasis has been placed by scholars since the time of Marx upon the economic factors that drove Europeans to expand their influence in the colonial regions after *circa* 1871. Yet economic factors were not lacking in the earlier period. Certainly the vision of "El Dorados" to match the vast treasures of the Aztecs and Incas long led men to explore uncharted lands. In addition to the dream of vast hoards of gold, silver, and precious stones that drove the earlier explorers, the spices, jewels, cottons, silk, and porcelains of India, China, and the East Indies, together with the slaves of Africa, provided an economic stimulus to the European merchants and the countries they represented. The nations of the age of the "New Imperialism" saw their colonies as sources of raw materials and as markets for their finished products: the same was no less true of the earlier period, particularly in relation to their holdings in the New World.

Yet another reason advanced for the imperialistic surge of Europe in the late 19th century has been the missionary zeal of many Europeans: yet the earlier "God" of the cry of "God, Gold, and Glory" symbolized the ardent, even fanatical drive on the part of explorers to spread their faith, whether by sword or teaching. Nor was the quest for "glory" on the part of men such as Cortez,

Pizarro and others wholly lacking from men such as Cecil Rhodes or Henry M. Stanley.

Any study seeking to compare the "Old Imperialism" with the "New" will disclose other factors broadly parallel. The European states of the late 19th century enjoyed, as a consequence of the Industrial Revolution and a strong scientific and technological orientation, marked advantages, particularly in the military area: the gunboat and machine gun came to be symbols of European imperialism. But four centuries earlier the Portuguese, Spanish, and those who followed them also enjoyed the advantage of superior ships and firepower. The acquisition of colonies for strategic purposes or to deter the expansion of rival European powers was also characteristic of imperialism in the two periods, as was the pursuit of economic policies of mercantilism or "Neo-Mercantilism."

If there are many broad parallels between the Old Imperialism and the New, are there any differences? Three stand out. In the 1500s the Spanish encountered great civilizations in the New World: these, however, were not able to resist European firepower, discipline, and disease. In North America the natives, at best, could offer only temporary resistance. The result was that the lands of the New World were largely open to European exploitation and colonization. The situation in Asia and Africa was markedly different, for such dynasties as the Moghuls of India, Mings and Manchus of China, and Togukawa of Japan were able to control the handful of Europeans who came to their ports, while the adverse health conditions of sub-Saharan Africa deterred penetration of the interior. Nor did pre-industrial Europe have any items for sale really desired by those lands. As a result, European merchants went as supplicants, content to purchase the items so desired in the West. After the mid-19th century this situation altered dramatically. On one hand the Asian dynasties were undergoing internal decay, a situation the Westerners quickly exploited. Too, the rise of native elements in these regions who saw advantages in cooperating with the Europeans provided another wedge the latter could exploit. In Africa, medical advances permitted the Europeans to penetrate and exploit the interior.

In the economic sphere, the Industrial Revolution and second Commercial Revolution had also altered the picture dramatically. There was now extensive surplus capital to be invested for high profits in overseas areas. As these investments mounted, it was only natural that there was a desire on the part of the investors that their governments "protect" their interests, even if this necessitated military intervention or outright annexation. As the industrial plants of Europe demanded more and more raw materials, governments sought spheres of influence where these could be guaranteed: such spheres for the sale of the finished products of the plants were also sought. The consequence of these forces was that by 1900 virtually every nation and people of Africa and Asia was either governed directly or under the strong influence of a Western power.

In the era of the Old Imperialism the inevitable clashes of interest between the European powers in the colonial regions had often resulted in war. In the later period, while tensions remained, diplomacy often resolved before war erupted.

4. There developed in the millennium before 1500 a concept of the universe and of man's place in it providing an ordered, hierarchical structure, preordained by the Creator. In this universe every object, animate or inanimate, knew its place: to upset this balance was in the eyes of the Church, since it had been established by God, a sin. This "Medieval Synthesis," reaching its culmination in the 11th and 12th centuries, was an amalgam of the scientific ideas of Aristotle, Ptolemy, and Galen, the "authorities" of Antiquity, and the doctrines of the Church. At the heart of this synthesis was its conception of the cosmos. At the center of the universe was the earth, motionless, changing, and corruptible. It was surrounded by nine crystalline spheres with which the sun, moon, planets, and stars were associated. Moving in perfect circular orbits, this heavenly realm was one of perfection and incorruptibility. Beyond the ninth sphere was the empyrean, the region of the blessed spirits.

Even before the 16th century questions were being raised regarding the validity of the medieval synthesis. Professors at Oxford, Padua, and Paris began to apply mathematical reasoning to problems of physics and astronomy, raising questions regarding the theories of Aristotle and Ptolemy, while the study of anatomy by Renaissance artists served to undermine the authority of Galen; humanists, in their studies of antiquity, discovered Greek philosophers who held theories in opposition to Aristotle and Ptolemy. The consequence of this doubting and questioning became clear in the 16th century with the publication of Vesalius' *On the Structure of the Human Body* and Copernicus' *On the Revolution of Heavenly Bodies*. Vesalius, while not rejecting wholly the authority of Galen, demonstrated the value of information gained through dissection. Copernicus' work, although advanced only as a theory, struck a sharper blow at a fundamental tenet of the Medieval Synthesis. Aware of ancient theories that the sun was the center of the universe and that the earth moved about it, he utilized mathematics to demonstrate that the universe constructed on these concepts presented a simpler, more logical explanation for the movements of the heavenly bodies than Ptolemy's complex system of epicycles. While Copernicus did not reject Ptolemy's ideas entirely, retaining the concept of the circular orbits of heavenly bodies and a finite sphere of fixed stars, he had sharply challenged authority.

In the decades that followed, Francis Bacon emphasized the need for inductive reasoning and empirical research while René Descartes reenforced the essential role of mathematical analysis and theory in scientific investigation. Others, using these new tools, steadily increased man's pool of knowledge: Gilbert in magnetism, Harvey in the circulation of blood,desedd Torricelli with vacuums, while others were expanding man's mathematical tools—Descartes with analytical geometry, Newton and Leibniz with calculus. Contributing to the advance of science was the beginning of an alliance of the artisan with the skills to construct superior equipment and the scientist who used them, an alliance that proved fruitful.

The 17th century, the "Century of Genius," saw a seemingly unbroken chain of discoveries which totally altered man's conception of the universe, the forces behind it, and man's place in it. Kepler, substituting elliptical orbits for Ptolemy's perfect circles, corrected Copernicus' error and validated the heliocentric theory. Galileo, using the newly invented telescope, revealed the moon was not a perfect globe and that the sun was not changeless, that the earth moved, and hinted that the earth and heavens were subject to the same forces and laws. Newton, drawing on Kepler's astronomy, Galileo's physics, his own mathematical skills and inductive reasoning, removed the distinctions between celestial and earthly physics: the "Medieval Synthesis" had been destroyed, replaced by the "World Machine" of Newton.

Man, in a sense, had been displaced from the center of the universe by Copernicus, Kepler, and Galileo: his mind, if not his physical being, had been restored to that position by the accomplishments of Descartes, Newton, and other scientists. They had demonstrated that, through the application of the proper tools—inductive reasoning, empiricism, and mathematics—the secrets of the universe could be unveiled. In doing so, they had also challenged and severely weakened the "Authorities," those of antiquity and of the Church. But the achievements of these scientists had provided man with a new vision, that of an ordered universe governed by "natural" laws, and new "authorities"—science, the scientific method, and his own reason. Intellectuals of Western Europe, deeply impressed with the achievements of the scientists, were convinced that through the proper application of these tools not only could the mysteries of the physical world be solved, but those of society itself. The 18th century, the "Age of Reason," saw men, the *philosophes*, seek to find solutions to the social, economic, and political problems they perceived to exist. Imbued with a spirit of optimism, they believed it possible to discover, through reason, the natural laws which governed society and man's relations with man. They, like the scientists, were prepared to challenge authority, whether that of the monarch, the church, or the established traditions of the day. That their conception of what was wrong in society was frequently based upon personal or class convictions did not deter their conviction that reason would lead to the reconstruction of society in accord with the laws of nature.

5. Any discussion of Hitler's rise to power must take into consideration numerous factors pre-dating his emergence as an historical figure or over which he had no control. These, rather than being shaped by Hitler, served to shape him.

Certainly the most significant of these was Germany's defeat in World War I. That conflict was a devastating experience for all participants, its cost in destroyed lives and property immense. The same was also true in terms of the psychological impact of the struggle, the spirits of the victors and vanquished alike being shattered. For the Germans this was particularly true, for their propaganda had convinced them they were actually winning the war. When defeat came, many could not believe that their military establishment, long of paramount importance in German society, had been beaten. Quickly the myth arose that the army had been "stabbed in the back" by Jews, socialists, and other "traitors," a myth which the military and others propagated and Hitler subsequently exploited. The Treaty of Versailles, imposing on Germany what most of its citizens believed a harsh, extremely unjust, and humiliating burden, served to enhance their bitterness. The fact that politicians of the Weimar Republic, the successor to the German Empire, had signed the hated treaty or, in the minds of the Germans, the "Diktat," brought down on that government the hatred of many, an enmity which contributed to its ultimate fall.

In the immediate aftermath of the war, Europe, and the defeated nations in particular, were in social turmoil. Bolshevism's vision of an impending "World Revolution" terrified the middle and upper classes. The activities of the Spartacists and Kurt Eisner in Germany, as well as those of Bela Kun in Hungary, made the threat seem very real. While these movements failed, the specter of a "Red Revolution" remained strong in the minds of many. It was a fear contributing to Mussolini's rise to power in Italy a decade before Hitler became chancellor.

Another factor which, while aiding Hitler attain power, was beyond his control, were the economic problems confronting Germany and, indeed, the entire world in the inter-war years. In 1923 Germany suffered, as a result of the Franco-Belgian occupation of the Ruhr, a depression of monumental proportions. The savings of the middle class were virtually destroyed and political upheaval threatened from both the Left and the Right. It is not strange that it was at this time that Hitler, now head of the Nazi Party, tried unsuccessfully to overthrow the Bavarian government, the first step in the envisioned takeover of all Germany.

Certainly the strongest evidence that Hitler's rise to power was not inevitable or wholly within his control is seen in the fact that after 1923, as economic stability was restored to Germany and she re-entered the "family of nations," his following diminished greatly, reduced to only the hard-core cadre.

The crucial event in his rise was unquestionably the "Great Depression" of 1929, a development which, again, he could not control but which he could exploit. As unemployment spread across Germany, the Communists again became active. The Social Democrats, who controlled the Weimar Republic, could not find solutions to the plight of the people. The Nazis, now seeking power legally, increased their strength in the both national Reichstag and state governments. In January 1933, although winning only a simple majority in the elections, Hitler was named chancellor in a coalition government. A year later virtually all political opposition had been eliminated.

The despair and anger over the World War I settlement, the fear of Bolshevism, the economic crises, were factors which, while assisting Hitler in his quest for power, he could not control. Even the fanatical ideology he espoused—the anti-Semitism, the Aryan supremacy, the ardent nationalism, the vision of "*Lebensraum*"—were derived from ideas long present in Germany and Austria.

To what extent was his ultimate triumph the result of his own "will to power"? His political genius lay in his ability to read the minds of the German people, their fears, animosities, and aspirations, and to hold out to them the vision of fulfillment of their dream of restoring Germany, a Germany cleansed of impure and undesirable elements, to the status of a world power. A charismatic speaker understanding his audience, he held out to all segments of society—

workers, farmers, students, middle and upper classes, the military, industrialists alike—the promises they wanted to hear. While many Germans had marked reservations regarding the Nazis, alarmed by their brutality and fanaticism, it seemed to them that, in light of the failure of the Social Democrats, their alternatives were limited to the Nazis or the Communists, the latter a choice unacceptable to a majority of the German people. Some believed they could control Hitler, others that the responsibility of office would temper his extremism: they quickly learned they were wrong.

6. The Agricultural and Industrial Revolutions dramatically altered the economic structure of England and changed forever the physical face of the country as it shifted from a land dominated by small, peasant operated farms to one where large industrial cities and big, capitalist-oriented agricultural establishments dotted the countryside. Many other changes, even more significant if not so visible, also took place in the ideological, social, and political structure and outlook of English society.

The Agricultural Revolution and the Enclosure Movement had seen many peasants forced from the land. Some found employment as tenant farmers or agricultural laborers. Others, moving into the blossoming industrial cities, constituted the basis of the expanding industrial working class. The new urban, industrial centers of England tended to be in Wales, the Midlands, and the north, this as a result of the location of ore and coal deposits. This population expansion was enhanced by the fact that from the early 1600s England, like many regions of the world, experienced a steady increase in its birthrate and, perhaps more significant, a lowering mortality rate and increased longevity. Previously these regions had been underpopulated and, more significant, had little or no representation in Parliament. By contrast, the south and southeast of England, in earlier days the agricultural heartland of England, dominated Parliament. Even though the population was shifting away from the south, political power long remained in the hands of the landowners and commercial class of that region who, through their control of "rotten" and "pocket" boroughs, were in a position to manipulate large segments of the House of Commons in their own interests. The powerful House of Lords also represented the older, vested interests. In the decades before the French Revolution, tensions were mounting as the new industrial middle and upper class demanded they receive more equitable representation. While their demands were pushed into the background by that conflict, with its end they came to the fore once again, now assuming a more threatening nature, as seen in the "Peterloo Massacre" (1819) and the abortive Cato Street Conspiracy of 1820. Following a period of repressive efforts on the part of conservative elements in the government to repress the calls for reforms, after 1822 more liberal elements began to introduce reforms, including weakening the protective mercantile system, a reform desired by manufacturers, revising antiquated criminal laws, and repealing the Combination Acts which prohibited the formation of unions. These reforms were capped by the Third Reform Bill of 1832: this abolished more than fifty "rotten" and "pocket" boroughs, redistributing the seats in Parliament to areas previously without representation, and the extension of the vote to a larger segment of the middle class, including those in the industrial sphere. In the decades that followed, although political change came gradually, *it did come*. This was due, in part, to the competition between the two major parties for the vote, a factor that led to an increasing extension of the franchise to a larger segment of the male population (women would have to wait until the 1920s to obtain the vote). Another factor was the increasing political activism of the middle and lower classes. The working class, initially lacking political cohesion, began to become more articulate and, through the formation of political parties, gain a voice in the chambers of Parliament. By 1911, virtually every male in Great Britain had gained the right to vote, the secret ballot had been introduced, and the powers of the House of Lords, normally a reactionary body, had been dramatically curtailed. Parliament had assumed a very "modern appearance."

The changes which were taking place in the political structure of England were mirrored in and influenced by changes in the social structure of the country. Those who were in the fore of the industrialization of England came, in many cases, from a different social strata than the aristocratical, landowning and commercial elements which had dominated Parliament since the "Glorious Revolution" of 1688. Thus many were members of the "dissenting churches," such as the Quakers and Methodists, rather than the "established" or Anglican Church. Many traced their roots back to the artisan or, in the 19th century, even working, class. As such, they tended to be viewed as outsiders or *nouveau riche* by the dominant element in society. However, as their economic role in society became more and more important and, eventually, dominant, they gradually gained social as well as political acceptance. Social mobility being greater in Great Britain than it was in many nations of the Continent, marriage between the industrial capitalists and the old families became increasingly common. They were becoming, politically and socially, part of the Establishment.

If the gradually enhanced status of the middle and upper class of England's industrial society was taking place, the same was true of those who, at the outset of the Industrial Revolution, had constituted the lower strata, the working class enduring wretched working conditions in the factories, miserable pay, and generally intolerable living conditions. Gradually, albeit very gradually, working conditions improved through the enactment of various labor regulations. Their incomes began to rise, permitting many to enter the ranks of the middle class. Increasingly their voice in the political arena became louder.

Clearly by the advent of the 20th century the Agricultural and Industrial Revolutions had brought into being a "new" England, its face changed physically, socially, and politically.

THE ADVANCED PLACEMENT EXAMINATION IN

European History

ANSWER SHEETS

Section II

Use the following pages on which to write your essays. If you need more space than is provided here use your own standard ruled paper on which to complete additional pages.

INSTALLING REA's TEST*ware*®

System Requirements

14-inch monitor or larger, CD-ROM Drive

Macintosh: Any Macintosh with a 68020 or higher processor or Power Macintosh, 4 MB of RAM minimum, System 7.1 or later. At least 5 MB of hard-disk space available.

Windows: Any PC with 4 MB of RAM minimum, Windows 3.1x, Windows 95 or 98. At least 5 MB of hard-disk space available.

MACINTOSH INSTALLATION

1. Insert the AP European History TEST*ware*® CD-ROM into the CD-ROM drive.
2. Double-click on the REA AP European History Installer icon. The installer will automatically place the program containing the AP European History TEST*ware*® into a folder entitled "REA AP European History." If the name and location are suitable, click the Install button. If you want to change this, type over the existing information, and then click Install.
3. Start the AP European History TEST*ware*® application by double-clicking on its icon.

WINDOWS INSTALLATION

1. Insert the AP European History TEST*ware*® CD-ROM into the CD-ROM drive.
2. From the Start Menu, choose the Run command. When the Run dialog box appears, type d:\setup (where D is the letter of your CD-ROM drive) at the prompt and click OK.
3. The installation process will begin. The standard (typical or compact) installation will install the AP European History TEST*ware*®. A dialog box proposing the directory "REA_AP European History" will appear. If the name and location are suitable, click OK. If you wish to specify a different name or location, type it in and click OK.
4. Start the AP European History TEST*ware*® application by double-clicking on its icon.

TECHNICAL SUPPORT

REA TEST*ware*® is backed by customer and technical support. For questions about **installation or operation of your software**, contact us at:

Research & Education Association
Phone: (732) 819-8880 (9 a.m. to 5 p.m. ET, Monday–Friday)
Fax: (732) 819-8808
Website: http://www.rea.com
E-mail: info@rea.com

USING YOUR INTERACTIVE TEST*ware*®

REA's AP European History TEST*ware*® is **EASY** to **LEARN AND USE.** To achieve maximum benefits, we recommend that you take a few minutes to go through the on-screen tutorial on your computer. The "screen buttons" are also explained here to familiarize you with the program.

Program Help and Test Directions

To get help at any time during the test, choose the **Program Help** button, which reviews basic functions of the program. The **Test Directions** button allows you to review the specific exam directions during any part of the test.

Stop Test

At any time during the test or when you are finished taking the test, click on the **Stop** button. The program will advance you to the next screen.

Once you leave this test, without suspending the exam, you will not be able to return to this test.

GO TO NEXT TEST | SUSPEND EXAM | RETURN TO WHERE I WAS

This screen allows you to go to the next test section, suspend or quit the entire test, or return to the last question accessed prior to clicking the **Stop** button.

Arrow Buttons

When an answer is selected, click on the **Right Arrow** button or press the **Return** key to proceed to the next question.

Mark Questions

If you are unsure about an answer to a particular question, the program allows you to mark it for later review. Flag the question by clicking on the **Mark** button.

Table of Contents

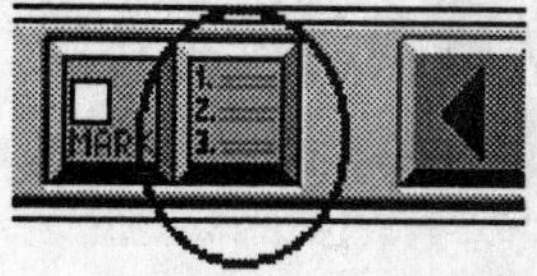

To review all marked questions, review answer choices, or skip to any question within a test section, click on the **Table of Contents** button.

Results

Review and analyze your performance on the test by clicking on the **Results** button.

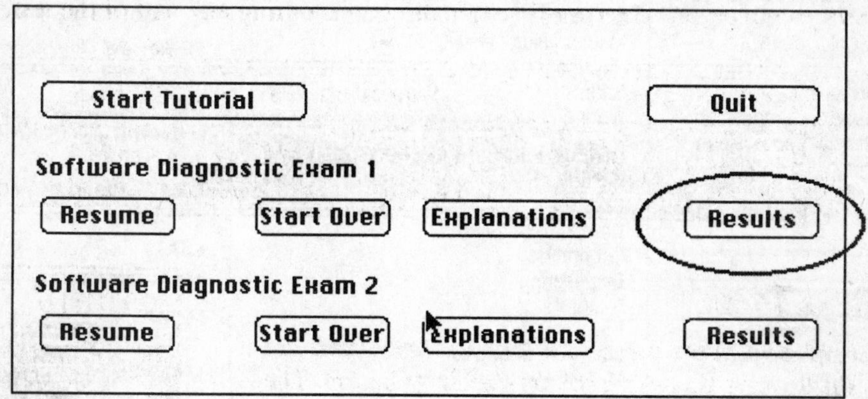

Explanations

In Explanations mode, click on the **Explanation** button to display the detailed explanation for any test item. To help you button up your studies, every explanation refers you to the relevant section of the book's topical review.

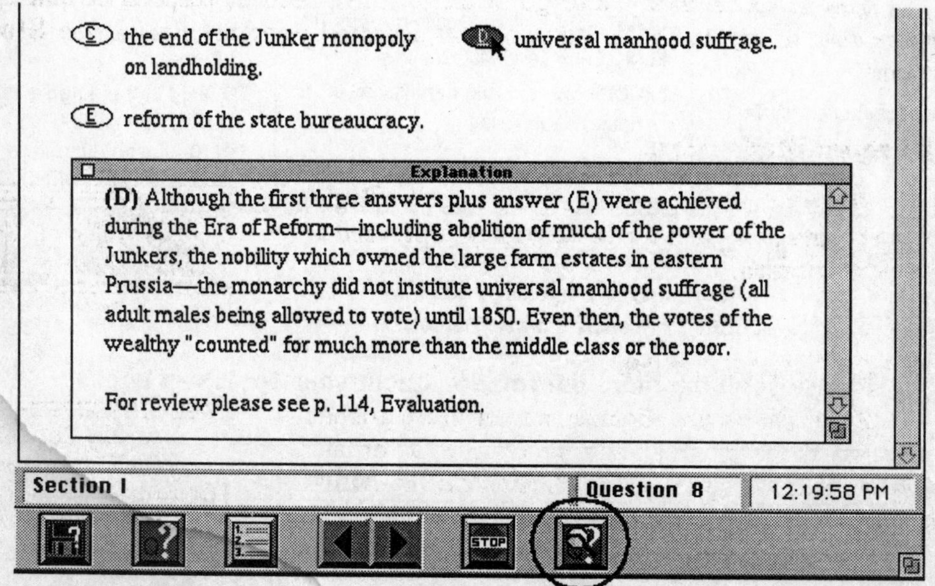

(more on next page)

REA's Test Prep Books Are The Best!

(a sample of the <u>hundreds of letters</u> REA receives each year)

“ Great way to get a 5! The review — comprehensive. The tests — awesome. [Your *AP European History* test prep] is the only book I know of that offers full-length AP-like tests. ”

Student, New York, NY

“ Your book is a wonderful preparation for the AP [European History exam]. ”

Student, Valley Stream, NY

“ Your book was such a better value and was so much more complete than anything your competition has produced (and I have them all!). ”

Teacher, Virginia Beach, VA

“ I did well because of your wonderful prep books... I just wanted to thank you for helping me prepare for these tests. ”

Student, San Diego, CA

“ Your book was responsible for my success on the exam, which helped me get into the college of my choice... I will look for REA the next time I need help. ”

Student, Chesterfield, MO

“ I recently got the *French SAT II* Exam book from REA. I congratulate you on first-rate French practice tests. ”

Instructor, Los Angeles, CA

(more on previous page)